MW01156649

EARTH'S CATASTROPHIC PAST

GEOLOGY, CREATION & THE FLOOD

VOLUME 1

EARTH'S CATASTROPHIC PAST

GEOLOGY, CREATION & THE FLOOD

VOLUME 1

ANDREW A. SNELLING

INSTITUTE
for CREATION
RESEARCH

Dallas, Texas
www.icr.org

EARTH'S CATASTROPHIC PAST
GEOLOGY, CREATION & THE FLOOD
VOLUME 1

by Andrew A. Snelling

First printing: December 2009
Second printing: February 2011

Copyright © 2009 by Andrew A. Snelling

All rights reserved. No portion of this book may be used in any form without written permission of the publisher, with the exception of brief excerpts in articles and reviews.

Published by Institute for Creation Research
P. O. Box 59029, Dallas, TX 75229
www.icr.org

ISBN: 978-0-932766-94-6
Library of Congress Catalog Number: 2009922120

Please visit our website for other books and resources: www.icr.org.

Printed in the United States of America.

CONTENTS

VOLUME 1. THE GENESIS RECORD OF CREATION AND THE FLOOD DEFENDED

Section V. The Modern Geological Synthesis

FOREWORD

Three great worldwide events are mentioned in the first eleven chapters of Genesis, which contain the history of early earth. The first is the creation of all things, in a completed, fully-functioning, "very good" state, as related in Genesis chapter one. All of nature was in harmony, with no death, disease, or carnivorous activity among living things, and no tectonic or meteorological disturbances in the earth itself. This harmony was disrupted when creation rebelled against the Creator, disobeying His commands. The curse of Genesis three impacted every thing and every system in creation. Indeed, the entire creation groans under the penalty of this rebellion. Finally, the rebellion culminated in a great convulsion of nature in Genesis six through nine, a massive flood that judged the planet. Not only was this a watery cataclysm, but a tectonic wrenching of the once peaceful environment.

Where could one go and not see evidence of creation? If God created it all, all things would bear His fingerprints. If He created it all, every rock, every life form, every system we study must give evidence of this recent creation. We observe intricate details in living things and rightly give Him credit for His creative majesty. At every level we look, we see a transcendence of design, far beyond the reach of mere chance. We see the flagella of bacteria, we see the interdependence of organs, the balance of ecology, fine-tuned interaction between stellar bodies. "All things were created by him, and for him" (Colossians 1:16). Nothing we could ever observe could be fully and correctly explained without creation. Our object of study might be far removed from the original creation, but all things ultimately derive from what transpired in Genesis one and two.

Likewise, where could we go in this universe and not see evidence of His universal judgment of sin? We read in Genesis three that due to Adam's rejection of God's authority, the plants were cursed, and the animals also, the serpent more than the rest (Genesis 3:18, 14). Furthermore the physical realm was cursed, as we see in Genesis 3:17. All of this had been placed under Adam's dominion, and his failure passed to all his domain. Finally, Adam and Eve tasted God's justice, as pronounced in Genesis 3:15-19. Indeed, "the wages of sin is death" (Romans 6:23), death in every aspect of creation. All we observe participated in the curse, or descended from that which did so participate.

The final great worldwide cataclysm was the great Flood of Noah's day. Described in no uncertain terms as global in extent, it covered the world. Certainly not a tranquil flood, it conquered the entire surface of the world, destroying all evidence of civilization, altering all ocean and atmospheric currents, eroding rock, depositing sediments, uplifting mountains, burying remains of plants and animals, etc. Nothing survived and nothing escaped its devastation, except those preserved on the Ark and some water-dwelling organisms. Where could we venture on planet earth and not encounter a flooded terrain? All things would bear the signature of death and destruction of this great Flood, whereby the world that then was, perished (2 Peter 3:6).

So now as we do our scientific study of earth's history, we find three curtains drawn, hindering a clear view. We can see the faded remnant of a once-perfect creation, marred by sin. To be sure, many aspects are still quite stunning, but how much are we unable to see? When we gaze upon creation's grandeur, we wonder how much more it must have been, for its ruination to look like this.

Our experience is only in the present; we cannot imagine a world where our bodies don't wear out. We observe the effects of sin everywhere, as we see everything grow old and wear down. How tightly the universal "watch" must have been wound, for it to have run down for so long and still be working. How could a distorted cosmos run so smoothly?

The most recent "curtain" is that of the great Flood. Can our eyes or even our minds truly understand? The entire world has been so twisted. Can we put it back together even in thought experiments? The world before the one we experience must have been so different. Even with a great deal of care and knowledge, can it be reconstructed? Certainly "the present is not the key to the past."

But still we must try, doing our best work. God is honored and pleased as we attempt to "think His thoughts after Him." The Christian's faith is strengthened as sight is clearer. God's Word more fully unfolds as problems are solved. The skeptic is challenged to consider a better worldview as he sees it make sense.

Dr. Andrew Snelling has done his best work on this volume elucidating *Earth's Catastrophic Past*. A man of deep scholarship and much faith, God prepared him for this job. He stands on the shoulders of giants, who stood against the tide in years past, and erects an even firmer structure. Modeled loosely after the groundbreaking and God-honoring book *The Genesis Flood*, it adds insights gained from decades of work by numerous individuals.

He starts from a position of biblical inerrancy, and delves deeply into geology. Early chapters weave a careful scriptural case for the Flood's catastrophic nature and global extent. He answers questions many people have about that Flood and the Ark of Noah. From that firm foundation, he ventures into the world of geology.

Intervening years have witnessed a revolution in geology, largely due to the impact of *The Genesis Flood*. After being stifled for two hundred years of staid uniformitarianism, many earth science professionals have turned to dynamic catastrophic processes to explain the earth, thus there are many new ideas and much new data to include. Our minds have been expanded by witnessing numerous local catastrophes, and they help us comprehend the unseen global cataclysm. We stand on the verge of an even greater restructuring of geologic thought, and this treatise will certainly play a part.

But there are more weighty things to consider than geology, things of even longer durations and more significance, and this book can help us comprehend them. The creation will be made new as the curse is repealed, and it will forever fulfill the Creator's intent. Best of all, we are offered a home in it. For too long, geologic interpretations have been used to doubt and disbelieve, and with treatment, we have a better understanding than ever. I pray God will honor this book in the way He did its forerunner, and that He will be pleased.

Dr. John D. Morris
President, Institute for Creation Research

PREFACE

Any project of this magnitude has to have had a history behind it. And this project certainly does! Many people have provided help and encouragement along the way.

As a young Christian, I became interested in geology at nine years of age. It wasn't long before I struggled with the issue of how to relate the geology I was reading in the textbooks with what I was reading about in God's Word concerning creation and the Flood. During my teenage years, my parents obtained for me and I read *The Genesis Flood* by Drs. John Whitcomb and Henry Morris. That book convinced me that God's Word provides the only reliable basis for understanding geology. This was the foundation for my calling into full-time creation ministry after I had completed my university training and gained professional experience working in the mining industry. I am indebted, like so many others, to Dr. Whitcomb and Dr. Morris for this landmark book that stood unashamedly on the authority of God's Word. Many lives have been changed for eternity as a result of that book. They need to be continually acknowledged for the foundation they laid for the modern creation science movement.

After I worked with Ken Ham in creation ministry in Australia for several years, Ken and his family were released by the Australian ministry to work with the Institute for Creation Research, founded by Dr. Henry Morris in 1970. As part of his duties at ICR, Ken participated in tours to the Grand Canyon, led by ICR's geologist Dr. Steve Austin. Ken realized that I might benefit from a visit to ICR and a trip to the Grand Canyon, at least if only to "broaden my horizons" and increase my geological knowledge. So he "twisted the arm" of Dr. Steve Austin.

Thus I first came to visit ICR in 1990, where I met all their scientists, and participated in a Grand Canyon tour. The following year I was invited back to their next Grand Canyon tour, "graduating" from the bus trip to one of the hiking groups. I was graciously received by ICR and its scientists, and greatly benefited from the interaction with them and with other scientists ICR had invited to be involved in their Grand Canyon tours. As a result, I was invited to join a research group looking into how a model of catastrophic plate tectonics could provide the framework for understanding geology within the context of the Genesis Flood. The insights provided by Drs. Steve Austin, John Baumgardner, Kurt Wise, Russ Humphreys, and Larry Vardiman were extremely stimulating and beneficial to my growing understanding of how the geological evidence can be fully reconciled with the clear teaching of God's Word. My friendship with them all, and with Dr. John Morris, grew.

For some years Dr. Henry Morris had evidently been keen for an updated and revised version of his landmark book with Dr. John Whitcomb, *The Genesis Flood,* to be written. However, he did not feel able to accomplish that task, preferring to see a younger person (or persons) with up-to-date geological knowledge tackle the project. To my surprise, during one of my visits to ICR en route to the Grand Canyon, Dr. Morris drew me aside and asked me if I would be willing to take up this needed assignment. Needless to say, I felt honored and overawed. I was also somewhat embarrassed, as I am to this day. After all, my good friend, colleague, and mentor, Dr. Steve Austin, should have been the one to write this book! I freely acknowledge that I have learnt so much from Steve, and this book has greatly benefited from his carefully researched work and publications.

Back in Australia, I tried to find the time to make a start on this daunting book project. However, it wasn't until God opened the door in 1998 for me to work for ICR that this task began in earnest. My good friend Dr. John Morris graciously invited me to join the staff at the Institute for Creation Research, with one of my main duties being to work on this book project. It also meant I could spend more time alongside Steve Austin, both on Grand Canyon trips and in teaching for ICR's Graduate School. In preparing to teach eager graduate students, I needed to review the latest geological textbooks on a number of subjects that were highly relevant to the task of writing about how geology, understood in the light of God's Word, fits the biblical framework of earth history.

By this time ICR had called together a group of scientists to research the issue of radioisotopes and the age of the earth. Headed by ICR's Dr. Larry Vardiman, this RATE research group consisted of Drs. Steve Austin, John Baumgardner, Russ Humphreys, Don DeYoung, and Gene Chaffin, and later included Dr. Steven Boyd. That eight-year research effort, of which I was privileged to be a part, yielded results that would become an important part of this book. I am indebted to these scientists for their friendship and their work. During this time, progress in writing the book was sporadic, but I was spurred on by my friends Dr. John Morris and Dr. Larry Vardiman, and by Dr. Henry Morris, of course.

So this book has finally come to fruition, after more than a decade of effort interspersed with other duties. It was a great relief to finally submit the completed manuscript to Drs. John Morris and Henry Morris III for ICR to publish. Our only regret is that Dr. Henry Morris is not here to see the final product, the realization of his dream. It would nevertheless be my prayer that this book fulfills his wishes and successfully builds on the foundation he faithfully laid.

Many people have contributed to this book and they must be acknowledged. Indeed, this book would never have been written if I had not had the benefit of the encouragement and support of so many, as well as their prodigious, robust research. Thus I acknowledge the work of Drs. Steve Austin, John Baumgardner, Kurt Wise, Russ Humphreys, and Larry Vardiman, and that of Mike Oard and John Woodmorappe. Mark Armitage has been a tireless helper, supporting and collaborating with me in my own research effort. I would also acknowledge the careful work done by Adventist scientists and colleagues Drs. Ariel Roth, Art Chadwick, Leonard Brand, Elaine Kennedy, and Harold Coffin. Their outstanding research has proven very beneficial. Of course, I apologize if I have forgotten anyone else who should be given an honorable mention here, as there are many others whose work I have interacted with along the way.

There are also many who have encouraged, supported, and helped me with this project. In particular, Drs. John Morris, Larry Vardiman, John Baumgardner, and Kurt Wise have faithfully kept me on task and assisted in various ways. On practical matters, I would like to thank Lawrence Ford and his team at ICR for their work on turning my manuscript into this book. I know that Drs. John Morris and John Baumgardner very helpfully reviewed the manuscript. Dr. John Morris is thanked for writing the Foreword. However, any remaining blemishes in this book remain my responsibility. In terms of practical support, though, I must acknowledge my personal assistant of more than 20 years, Laurel Hemmings. As she has done with so many other projects, she typed the manuscript, corrected it many times, and drafted the diagrams. Without her faithful and tireless help, the final book would not have been possible.

My family has always stood behind and with me, through all the highs and lows in such an enormous project as this, as well as with my wholehearted participation in creation ministry over more than 25 years. My three (now adult) children, Philip, Peter, and Rachel, have had to cope with an often absent father—on many ministry and research trips, and during many hours locked away in my office. Yet we have still had many memorable family times together. It is a constant source of overwhelming joy that they are walking with the Lord and now fulfilling His callings on their lives. However, it is my loving wife, Kym, who has faithfully and tirelessly worked, supported, and coped with me for more than 33 years, following with me the Lord's leading. She has believed in me through all the trials, raised a family, and endured all the highs and lows we have had to go through together. She has truly been God's "helpmeet."

Finally, without God's sovereign grace in my life, calling me to Himself, I would not have been equipped and sent by Him into the creation ministry. It is all His work with this marred piece of clay. All praise must go to Him—Father, Son, and Holy Spirit—as our Creator. Furthermore, because God the Son, Jesus Christ, willingly laid down His life for me, no sacrifice I can make could ever be large enough to repay the debt I owe Him. And without the light of God's Word, both His written Word and the Word incarnate, Jesus Christ, we would all be in darkness and unable to understand who we are and the world in which we live.

Without God's grace, mercy, and salvation, we would not have an eternal hope of living for eternity with Him. As I dedicate this book to Him, it would be my prayer that He might somehow use the book to draw many other people from darkness into the glorious light of His kingdom. All praise and glory be to our triune Creator God!

Dr. Andrew A. Snelling
Director of Research, Answers in Genesis

INTRODUCTION

Why Take Genesis Seriously?

The first eleven chapters of the Bible have been relegated by many professing Christians today to the category of myths or stories, not real history. These stories are said to *contain* spiritual truth, but they cannot be taken seriously as records of real people and real events.

The sad reality is that while many sincere Christians who thoroughly believe the Bible and attend conservative, evangelical churches would dismiss the above statements as false, they do not know what their pastors believe about the historicity of Genesis. And what about those seminary professors charged with training pastors-to-be? Is it safe to assume that these men believe in the following truths?

1. God created everything in six literal 24-hour days.
2. Adam and Eve were real people.
3. God cursed a perfect world as a judgment for Adam and Eve's sin.
4. Noah constructed an Ark by which two of every kind of air-breathing, land-dwelling animal were saved along with Noah's family from a global, mountain-covering flood.
5. The confusion of languages at the Tower of Babel produced the people and language groups that are found around the world today.

To the shock of Bible-believing churchgoers, an alarming number of Christian leaders and teachers instead believe that God "created" through evolutionary processes (with or without His direct input) over millions and even billions of years, that Adam and Eve are the names of a human pair who descended from a hominid population and into whom God placed the human spirit, and that there has never been a global flood in human history, suggesting that the account of Noah and the Ark is just a story adapted from a Babylonian myth about some terrifying local flood in the Mesopotamian region.

How did we arrive at such a sad state of affairs? While there have always been those who have held dissenting interpretations, mainstream Christian orthodoxy regarded the opening chapters of Genesis as just as real and reliable as the rest of the Bible until 150 to 200 years ago. Even during the early decades of the twentieth century, most devout churchgoers would have been labeled as Bible-believing and conservative, if not evangelical. So what has happened to bring about such a radical shift in Christian belief about the early history of the universe, the earth, and man?

Any analysis of intellectual movements within and without the church would quickly conclude that this downgrading of the early chapters of Genesis has coincided with the rise of uniformitarian philosophy as the cornerstone of modern geology and of the theory of evolution as the core of modern biology. Technological advances in the wake of spectacular scientific discoveries have brought about better living conditions and health standards, along with higher levels of education at all strata of society, not just in the Christianized West. In the last half of the twentieth century, the incredible development of television, computers, and satellites that orbit the earth has produced an explosion in mass communication of knowledge and technology, catapulting the world into a global society. There seems no end to what man can achieve!

In this apparent utopia, supposedly built because of man's knowledge and the technology that has been spawned by it, scientists and technologists became highly respected. Their views were popularized amongst the masses, so that millions of years of geological ages and the evolution of all life forms including man have been taught and accepted as established facts. The widespread availability of public and private education, staffed by several generations of teachers who in their youth imbibed uniformitarianism and evolution as scientific fact, has been the dominant force in this indoctrination.

Christians have not been immune from this almost universal indoctrination, and like the proverbial frog slowly boiling in the pot of water on a stove, most have been blithely ignorant of the process that has gradually changed their thinking and thus their whole approach to the Bible. Consequently, an increasing number of Christian churches throughout the world reject the early chapters of Genesis as reliable history, resulting in all manner of compromise intended to force geological ages and organic evolution into the Scriptures. While there are those who have resisted this trend, many Christians have shelved this apparent conflict between the Bible and science (so-called) as being divisive, too difficult to resolve, and/or totally irrelevant to the Gospel at the heart of the Christian faith.

Genesis as Reliable History

Yet the conflict over whether the early chapters of Genesis should be taken seriously as reliable history still rages in the church. There are those who have not capitulated to the teaching of a multi-billion-year-old earth and the evolution of all life, as facts. What makes this conflict sharper and more intense is that in the ranks of those Christians who have not compromised are many scientists with doctoral degrees. These scientists have been through the modern education system, sat under professors of the uniformitarian and evolutionary worldview, and yet remained unwavering in their commitment to Genesis as literal history. Some that began with a uniformitarian/evolutionary worldview later rejected it after being challenged by the scientific evidence supporting the Scriptures in opposition to a multi-billion-year earth and organic evolution, and/or by a spiritual conversion and personal transformation brought about by yielding to the Creator God of the Bible and the claims of Jesus Christ.

During the last 150 to 200 years, many have sought to remain faithful to the Bible as the Word of God, accepting Genesis as reliable history. There were even organizations and groups that formed as rallying points for the faithful few who wanted to take a public stand and try to stem the tide sweeping into the church and society as a whole. However, it was the publication of the book *The Genesis Flood: The Biblical Record and Its Scientific Implications* by theologian Dr. John C. Whitcomb and hydraulic engineer Dr. Henry M. Morris in 1961 that catalyzed the young-earth creationist cause in a major way.

The Evolution Protest Movement (now the Creation Science Movement) in Great Britain, with a long history already, received a boost from the widespread circulation of that book. It was also the impetus for the formation in 1963 of the Creation Research Society, which now boasts a membership of over 600 individuals with graduate degrees in science. The Bible-Science Association (now Creation Moments, Inc.) was formed soon afterwards in 1964.

The Institute for Creation Research began in 1970 as a division of Christian Heritage College in San Diego, but moved to its own facilities in April 1972. Unlike previously formed creationist groups and organizations, the Institute for Creation Research employed scientists with Ph.D.s to work full-time in creation research, writing, and teaching. This proved to be a catalyst for many new creationist books and publications covering the relevant issues in the full gamut of scientific disciplines. The circulation of these books and publications began to impact churches and Christians not only in North America, but around the world. Other creationist groups and organizations were subsequently formed in the following years so that today there are creationist groups and organizations in all corners of the globe.

So why would hundreds, indeed thousands, of highly-trained scientists not only believe Genesis to be reliable history, but base their scientific research on the details and implications of that history? Their acceptance of the Bible in its entirety as a record of the true history of the world stems first and foremost from their Christian convictions.

Of course, the Bible never claims to be a textbook on history or science, but it does claim more than 3,000 times to be a direct communication from the God who tells us that in the beginning He created the heaven and the earth, prepared a home for man, and then created man, all in six days. If God is who He claims to be, then He has always existed and has all knowledge and power. He is perfect, so He never makes mistakes. He is pure and honest, so He never tells lies. Therefore, if the Bible is the Word of God, then it must be truthful in its entirety, even when it touches upon matters of history and science. Otherwise, this Creator God is a liar and not who He claims to be. The very character of God requires the first eleven chapters of Genesis to be a trustworthy record of real history.

The essential elements of this framework for earth history recorded in the first eleven chapters of Genesis are:

1. God created the heaven and the earth and everything in them in six literal days of approximately 24 hours duration.
2. There was a definite sequence of creative acts by God during those six days:
    a. Day 1—the heaven and earth were created in darkness with the earth covered completely by water, and then light was created so that night was followed by daylight to complete the first cycle of a normal day.
    b. Day 2—separation and elevation of some of the water on the earth's surface with an expanse placed between the waters.
    c. Day 3—the formation of dry land as distinct from the ocean and the covering of the land with plants.
    d. Day 4—the creation of the sun, moon, and stars.
    e. Day 5—the creation of all sea creatures and flying animals, including whales and birds.
    f. Day 6—the creation of land animals and "creeping things," followed by the creation of Adam, his placement in the Garden of Eden and naming of the animals there, and finally the creation of Eve from Adam's side.
3. The temptation of Adam and Eve and their subsequent disobeying of God's instructions, resulting in God pronouncing the Curse of physical death and suffering upon man, the animals, and the earth, and the banishment of Adam and Eve from the Garden of Eden.
4. The growth of the human population into a pre-Flood civilization with all manner of technology that included the building of cities, metal tools, and musical instruments.
5. Because of the increasing wickedness of the pre-Flood civilization, Noah was instructed by God to build the Ark (an ocean-going wooden ship). When it was ready, two of every kind of air-breathing, land-dwelling animal were sent to go onboard the Ark with Noah and his family to escape the global, mountain-covering Flood that God was about to unleash upon the earth.
6. The Flood was upon the earth for over a year, covering even the highest mountains and destroying all the air-breathing, land-dwelling life from the face of the earth.
7. The emergence of Noah, his family, and all the animals from the Ark,

after which they rapidly increased in numbers, being commanded by God to spread out to inhabit the revegetated earth.

8. Instead of spreading out across the revegetated earth as they had been commanded, the growing post-Flood human family again rebelled against God by remaining in one place, the plain of Shinar. They built a city and a tower in defiance of God, which resulted in God's intervention to confuse the people's languages, after which they dispersed, forming the many different language and people groups. The city was therefore named Babel.

9. Since Genesis carefully records the genealogies and lifespans of Adam and his descendants, it can be calculated that human history covers a period of only 6,000 to 7,000 years. Yet, as already noted, the earth was made six days before Adam, at the beginning of Day 1, so the earth itself also can only be 6,000 to 7,000 years old.

The subsequent pages of Genesis recount the early history of the nation of Israel, beginning with God's selection of Abraham as the progenitor of this new nation. Few conservative Christian scholars would deny the historicity of these later chapters in Genesis. Yet many would regard the language used in the creation account as a form of ancient Hebrew poetry, even though in reality the genre throughout the first eleven chapters of Genesis is no different to that used in the remainder of the book.

So why are some scholars skeptical? Certainly not because of style and language, which are precisely the same as in other biblical accounts of historical events. No, the conflict occurs with supposedly established scientific facts that insist on a multi-billion-year-old earth and organic evolution. A choice has to be made between Scripture, which is authored by God, and modern science, which is authored by men.

Just how were these early chapters of Genesis recorded at the time they happened? Archaeologists tell us that writing was not invented until about the time of Abraham. Most liberal Christian scholars insist that the book of Genesis was written much later in Jewish history, perhaps as late as the post-Babylonian exile, derived from old traditions and stories distorted by the many years of oral transmission from generation to generation. But such claims overlook the testimony of the early chapters of Genesis, where we are told that in the pre-Flood world, people built cities, had tools of brass and iron, and made musical instruments. This denotes quite an advanced civilization.

For instance, in order to have metal tools, there must have been mines and smelters. In Genesis 5, at the end of Adam's life, the record of his genealogy ends with the expression "this is the book of the generations of Adam." There is no reason to suppose that Adam and his descendants were not able to write and keep records, remembering that in the Garden of Eden, on the sixth day of creation, Adam had named all the animals before Eve was created from his side, thus demonstrating his intellectual capacity.

Moses, the traditionally recognized author of Genesis, simply had to compile the book of Genesis from the records kept by Adam and his descendants. Of course, Adam wasn't present when God created the world, but God was, and the text emphasizes a number of times that "God saw what He had made." Thus, Genesis reads as an eyewitness account, which is the hallmark of a reliable record of real history.

In any case, if the Creator God of the Bible is who He says He is, then not only is He capable of accurately telling us about the early history of the universe, the earth, and man, but He is capable of having the details truthfully recorded, faithfully copied, and transmitted down through successive generations.

Jesus Regarded Genesis as Real History

The eyewitness account of the life and deeds of Jesus Christ recorded by His disciple John begins by declaring of Jesus, "All things were made by him, and without him was not any thing made that was made" (John 1:3). When the disciple Peter declared that Jesus was "the Christ, the Son of the living God" (Matthew 16:16), Jesus did not rebuke him for blasphemy or for being mistaken, but instead praised him for his confession and acknowledged that God ("my Father which is in Heaven") had revealed this truth to him. Furthermore, Jesus claimed, "I and my Father are one" (John 10:30). And Jesus also claimed, "I am the way, the truth, and the life" (John 14:6). If Jesus was telling lies when He made these claims and approved of others for making incorrect claims about Him, then He is not "the truth."

That He was neither a liar nor a deceiver, but was in fact who He said He was, is substantiated by the undeniable fact of history that He rose from the dead as He said He would. As a resurrected man with flesh and bones (Luke 24:39), Jesus was seen many times by many witnesses, including 500 people on one occasion, and history records the resolute witness of millions of people who have been prepared to die if necessary for their Christian faith. Why would anyone die for a delusion or a lie? Those who have carefully examined and weighed the evidence have always come to the conclusion that Jesus did rise from the dead, and that therefore He was Who He claimed to be—Jesus Christ, the Son of God, and the Creator Himself.

So if Jesus was (and is) both the Creator God and a perfect man, then His pronouncements are always and absolutely trustworthy. Therefore, it is significant that Jesus confirmed that Moses was the author of the book of Genesis by endorsing the Jewish subdivision of the Old Testament Scriptures: "These are the words which I spake unto you, while I was yet with you, that all things must be fulfilled, which were written in the law of Moses, and in the prophets, and in the psalms, concerning me" (Luke 24:44). Furthermore, it is recorded in the Gospels that Jesus referred directly to details in each of the first seven chapters of Genesis a total of fifteen times, as well as making an allusion to a detail recorded in Genesis 9.

For example, Jesus referred to Genesis 1:26-27 when He said in Mark 10:6, "But from the beginning of the creation God made them male and female." In the very next verse, Jesus quoted directly from Genesis 2:24 when He said, "For this cause shall a man leave his father and mother, and cleave to his wife; and they twain shall be one flesh; so then they are no more twain, but one flesh." The same comments by Jesus are also recorded in Matthew 19:4-6. It should be noted that Jesus confirmed the details of Genesis 1 when He said that man was created male and female "from the beginning of the creation," not after millions of years of evolution. Five times Jesus refers to Noah and/or the destructive global Flood of Genesis 6-7 in Matthew 24:37-39 and Luke 17:26-27. One is forced to conclude that Jesus regarded Genesis as real history, and if He, as the Creator, was actually a witness to the events of Genesis 1-11, then we have absolutely no alternative but to likewise regard these opening chapters of the Bible as reliable literal history.

The Apostle Peter's Prophecy

In the closing chapter of his final letter (2 Peter 3), the apostle Peter prophesied that there would be scoffers in the last days choosing to be willingly ignorant of the fact that by His command, God created the heaven and the earth, with dry land separated from water on the earth's surface, and that God later destroyed everything on the surface of the earth that He had made by a global watery cataclysm. Two things should be kept in mind here. First, Peter had, of course, spent three full years traveling in the company of Jesus Christ Himself, during which time He listened to all that He had to say and was able to ask questions for any clarification. Then Peter was a witness to Jesus' death and the physical bodily resurrection, which unmistakably confirmed Jesus' divine credentials. It is also recorded (Acts 2) that Peter and the other disciples of Jesus received extraordinary ability and authority when they received the gift of God's Holy Spirit with outward physical manifestations. Thus, the books of the New Testament that bear his name not only come from his pen, but have the stamp of the authority of God Himself upon them and upon what they tell us, including this prophecy.

Second, this prophecy of Peter was among the last words he wrote to all his fellow Christians before he died, and he emphasized the utmost importance of this prophecy in his preamble to it (2 Peter 3:1-3). He stated that he was writing this second letter in order to stir their minds to remember all that the prophets had spoken about, and all that the apostles had told them about the words and deeds of Jesus Christ. But then in verse 3, he used the words "knowing this first," or as sometimes translated, "first of all." This obviously denotes something of utmost importance that Peter wanted them to remember above everything else he had told them. In other words, Peter placed first priority on this prophecy, which is about those who would reject the account of creation and the global Flood in Genesis 1-11 as real history.

What is quite remarkable is the explanation Peter gave as to why these scoffers would choose to reject the clear testimony of God Himself, that He created the heavens and the earth and sent a global, mountain-covering Flood, and also reject the physical evidence that these events left behind. Peter told us (2 Peter 3:4) that the hallmark of these scoffers will be their philosophy that "all things continue as they were from the beginning of the creation." This expression that things continue as they always have from the beginning is an apt description of the philosophy of uniformitarianism, introduced first by James Hutton in 1795 and popularized by Charles Lyell in the 1830s. They argued that the "the present is the key to the past." Thus, we can study the geological processes shaping the earth today and then extrapolate those processes and their rates back in time to explain how the rock strata of the earth's crust, the continents, and mountains were formed and came to be the way they are.

It was on the basis of this philosophy and the principles embodied in it that the testimony of Genesis 1-11 came to be rejected, because the evidence for creation and the global Flood were seemingly explained in terms of millions and billions of years of slow and gradual geological processes. These ideas became the foundation for modern geology. The millions and billions of years provided the timescale necessary for the acceptance of the theory of organic evolution to explain the development of all life on the earth, instead of accepting that God had created it all.

While some aspects of uniformitarianism promoted by Lyell have been rejected or modified today, it is still true that modern geologists rely upon present-day processes, including gradual continental drift (or plate tectonics), to explain how the geological record and the continents themselves came to be as they are today. Because modern geology seemingly has an alternative explanation for the geological evidence, Lyell, his followers, and today's geologists have almost universally rejected the opening chapters of Genesis as reliable literal history, thereby influencing Christian scholars to explain Genesis 1-11 as myths or exaggerated stories based on oral traditions of a vague memory of a devastating local flood in Mesopotamia that came to the Jews from their Babylonian ancestors.

However, the fact that Peter wrote such an accurate description of these scoffers more than 1,700 years before this prophecy was fulfilled puts an unquestionable stamp of authority upon this prophecy. We therefore cannot ignore the testimony of the apostle Peter in this powerful fulfilled prophecy. Peter believed that the opening chapters of Genesis were real history, and he predicted what we see today—the rejection of special creation by God and the rejection of the global Flood as an explanation of the earth's geology, even with overwhelming scientific evidence. This rejection is not just by unbelievers, but also by those who claim to be Christians.

The Reliability of the Whole Bible Depends on Genesis as History

It almost seems self-evident that if the reliability of the first eleven chapters of Genesis as real history is rejected, then the trustworthiness of other parts of the Bible is called into question. Indeed, it is impossible to reject the historicity and divine authority of the book of Genesis without undermining and, in effect, repudiating the authority of the entire Bible. If Genesis is not true, then neither are the testimonies of those prophets and apostles who believed it was true. In the Old Testament, for example, Adam is mentioned by name in Deuteronomy, Job, and 1 Chronicles, while Noah is mentioned in 1 Chronicles, Isaiah, and Ezekiel. We have already noted in detail the apostle Peter's testimony to Genesis, but it is significant that the first eleven chapters of Genesis, which have been the object of the greatest attacks of skepticism and unbelief, have in fact had the greatest influence on the New Testament. There are at least 100 quotations or direct references to Genesis 1-11 in the New Testament. Furthermore, every one of those eleven chapters is alluded to somewhere in the New Testament, and every one of the New Testament authors refers somewhere in his writings to Genesis 1-11.

Finally, in not one of these many instances where the Old or New Testament refers to Genesis is there the slightest suggestion or evidence that the writers regarded the events or the people as myths or allegories. To the contrary, they viewed these first eleven chapters of Genesis as absolutely historical, true, and authoritative. To underscore this, on at least six different occasions Jesus Christ Himself, as we have already seen, quoted from or made specific reference to something or someone in each of the first seven chapters of Genesis.

It can be argued that the first eleven chapters of the book of Genesis are probably the most important passages ever written. If these chapters were somehow totally expunged from the Bible, then the rest of the Bible would be incomprehensible. It would be like a building without any foundations. Genesis 1-11 gives vital information concerning the origin of so many things (and therefore their meaning) which otherwise we would never know about. The word *genesis* means "beginnings" or "origin," and so it is that Genesis 1-11 records for us God's provision of the only true and reliable account of origins, including the origin of the universe, the solar system, the earth, the atmosphere and the oceans, of order and complexity, life, man, marriage, evil, language, government, culture, nations, and religion, not to mention the origin of rocks and fossils. Thus, Genesis 1-11 is of such foundational importance to all history that without it there is no true meaning to, or understanding of, ourselves and all aspects of the world around us.

What we believe about our origin will inevitably determine our beliefs concerning our purpose and our destiny. Any naturalistic concept of our beginnings gives us no more meaning than any other form of life or object in the universe, and so provides only a naturalistic program for the future without hope of there being anything more than what we see around us. On the other hand, an origin at the hands of an all-powerful, pure, and loving God guarantees a divine purpose in history and meaning to our existence, a future in the hands of a caring God who made us and has made provision for us and our future. Since those details progressively unfold throughout the rest of the Bible, if Genesis 1-11 is not literal history, then the reliability of the whole Bible is undermined. By not taking Genesis seriously, many Christians have in fact undermined the rest of the Bible they claim to believe and follow. They are also in danger of unwittingly accusing Jesus Christ of being a false witness, deceived, or a deceiver, and making His claims about being the Son of God blasphemy.

The Pivotal Importance of the Flood

The creation account in Genesis 1 is undoubtedly the most profound chapter in Genesis, and indeed the whole Bible, with its description of the ultimate origin of all reality around us. However, the global Flood in Noah's day is of pivotal importance in understanding the present geology of the earth. This is mirrored by the fact that the account of the Flood and its aftermath are allocated almost four chapters (Genesis 6-9), compared to the two chapters for the creation account (Genesis 1-2). Furthermore, more than any other branch of science, geology has been most affected by the philosophy of uniformitarianism. This philosophy has provided the millions and billions of years timescale that is the underpinning for the theory of evolution in biology, so that together, uniformitarianism and evolution have brought about the rejection of Genesis 1-11 as reliable history, even by Christians. It is no wonder that the apostle Peter was led by the Holy Spirit to single out the scoffers who would come rejecting the Genesis account of creation and the Flood as real history. God has left in the rocks, fossils, and living world evidence that unmistakably testifies to the trustworthiness of the Genesis record.

Therefore, our purpose in this book is to focus on the global Flood as described in Genesis, and with the scientific evidence that has convinced many today, including Christian geologists, that Genesis must be taken seriously as literal history. It is quite logical to expect that if God is who He says He is and has told us the truth in Genesis 1-11 about the early history of the earth and man, then the evidence we can observe and study in the world today should be totally consistent with what we read in the opening chapters of God's Word. Again, this is not to suggest that the Bible is a textbook of science and history, but because it is God's Word, even details of science and history must be correct. Neither is it suggested that the Bible can be proved from scientific and other evidence. To the contrary, science cannot directly observe what happened in the past, so all we can do is infer from the evidence we observe in the present. Thus, we are only entitled to conclude that the evidence we observe today is consistent with what has been faithfully recorded for us by God in Genesis 1-11.

To achieve our stated objective, we first need to re-examine the biblical record and the details it gives that argue for the Flood being global and mountain-covering (Section I). Then we need to deal with the non-geological arguments that are often used to discount the Genesis account of the Flood as literal history (Section II), plus the arguments over Noah, the Ark, and the animals (Section III). It is important also to study the compromises with uniformitarian geology that have been made in attempted harmonizations with the Scriptures, and to discredit the feasibility of these. At the same time, it is both crucial and encouraging to know that there have always been scientifically well-qualified Christians—the equal of their peers—who have firmly stood their ground in defense of a literal Genesis. So often the appeal is made to the majority in determining whether a scientific matter has validity or not, but truth will always be truth, regardless of the majority vote, and a minority will always be significant when defending God's Word. With such matters dealt with, the next task is to build the framework for a biblical geology (Section IV).

In dealing with the scientific evidence, we first need to understand the essential "ingredients of the modern geological synthesis" (Section V). Then, the question to ask is this: If the biblical account of creation and the Flood is true, then what evidence should we look for? Asking the right question will mean that the evidence is seen from a new perspective. The description of the Flood in the biblical record implies catastrophism and utter devastation, and therefore we would expect the field data of the geological record to be in harmony with such an assessment, which is what we will examine in detail in Section VI.

Because Genesis 1-11 is a record of the true history of the earth, we also need to explore the framework it provides for understanding geology from a truly biblical perspective, as well as examining the supportive evidence (Section VII). However, the biggest obstacles to be dealt with are the perceived scientific problems with a biblical geology, including the radioactive dating methods (Section VIII) and other techniques in modern geochronology (Section IX), and geological puzzles engendered by the claimed evidence that certain types of rocks, geological processes, coal beds, oil, mineral deposits, and more can only be explained by uniformitarianism's gradualism (Section X). In all instances, the perceived problems are countered by scientific evidence itself.

Finally, the adequacy of the biblical framework of earth history is emphasized in the concluding challenges, making it relevant to Christians in our 21st-century world. It is sincerely hoped that by the end of this study, readers will have their faith restored in Genesis as real, literal history, and be convinced that the scientific evidence, correctly discerned and applied, is indeed consistent with God's record of our origins and history found in Genesis 1-11.

Section I

The Biblical Record
of the Global Genesis Flood

1

MOSES COMPILED GENESIS

The account of the Flood in Genesis 6-9 has been "one of the showpieces of literary criticism,"[1] that liberal scholarship claims is a composite of two or more traditions committed to writing more than a thousand years after the events occurred. That such views continued to be expounded even a century after they reached their zenith is preposterous, since these higher critical views were soundly refuted as early as 1895 by Princeton scholar William Henry Green.[2] More recent studies have independently argued for the literary integrity of Genesis 6-9,[3] making continued assertions that these chapters can be dissected into two parallel accounts totally untenable.

The authorship of Genesis is, of course, closely tied to that of the rest of the Pentateuch, the first five books of the Old Testament, and there is abundant support for it being authored and/or compiled by Moses. The Pentateuch itself claims that important parts were written by Moses (for example, Exodus 24:4, 7; Deuteronomy 31:9, 24-26). Internal evidence also shows that the Pentateuch was written by an eyewitness who, for example, was obviously familiar with Egypt and Egyptian customs, names, words, and geography, as evidenced in those parts of the Pentateuch that were set in Egypt or refer to it. Furthermore, the claims in the Pentateuch for authorship by Moses are supported in the rest of the Old Testament and by the statements by Jesus Christ in the Gospels.

As early as Joshua's day, the law of Moses was in written form (Joshua 1:7-8; 8:32,

---

1   B. Kidner, 1967, *Genesis: An Introduction and Commentary,* The Tyndale Old Testament Commentaries, Leicester, UK: InterVarsity Press, 97-100.

2   W. H. Green, 1979, *The Unity of the Book of Genesis*, Grand Rapids, MI: Baker Book House (originally published by Charles Scribner's Sons, 1895).

3   A number of studies are listed by G. J. Wenham, 1987, *Word Biblical Commentary, Volume 1, Genesis 1-15*, Waco, TX: Word Books. They are: B. W. Anderson, 1978, From Analysis to Synthesis: The Interpretation of Genesis 1-11, *Journal of Biblical Literature,* 97: 23-39; G. J. Wenham, 1978, The Coherence of the Flood Narrative, *Vetus Testamentum,* 28: 336-348; R. E. Longacre, 1979, The Discourse Structure of the Flood Narrative, *Journal of the American Academy of Religion,* 47 (supplement): 89-133; I. M. Kikawada and A. Quinn, 1985, *Before Abraham Was: The Unity of Genesis 1-11,* Nashville, TN: Abingdon Press; G. Larsson, 1985, The Documentary Hypothesis and the Chronological Structure of the OT, *Zeitschrift für die Alttestamentliche Wissenschaft,* 97: 316-333; and G. A. Rendsburg, 1986, *The Redaction of Genesis*, Winona Lake, IN: Eisenbrauns.

34; 22:8), and similar references are found in later books of the Old Testament (e.g., 1 Kings 2:3; 2 Chronicles 23:18; 34:14; Ezra 3:2; 6:18; Nehemiah 8:1-8; Daniel 9:11, 13). Jesus on numerous occasions spoke of the law of Moses, sometimes of the "book of Moses" (Mark 12:26), twice of "Moses and the prophets" (Luke 16:29, 31) or Moses, the prophets, and the Psalms (Luke 24:44), obviously ensuring it was understood that he regarded Moses as the author of the first part of the Old Testament on a par with its other major sections.

The early church, the church of later centuries, and the Jews almost unanimously accepted that Moses authored Genesis and the other books of the Pentateuch. It wasn't until the rise of "higher criticism" at the end of the 19th century that this view was questioned. The position that Moses was the author and/or compiler of Genesis is too strongly supported to be dismissed by liberal rationalism.

Of course, the claim that Moses authored the book of Genesis in particular does not assume that Moses wrote without the use of sources. Abraham came from a very sophisticated background in Ur, where all sorts of records were meticulously kept. Joseph rose to a place of leadership in a very literate society. Noah and his sons obviously had the technological ability and background to be able to build the Ark in such enormous proportions under divine guidance that there can be little doubt Noah and his family were able to keep written records. As early as Genesis 4 in the record of Adam and his descendants, we read about Cain and others building a city (v. 17), musical instruments (v. 21), and craftsmen in brass and iron (v. 22), all of which imply a civilization able to quarry, mine, and smelt rock to acquire metals in order to make tools, musical instruments, and build cities. Such a civilization is more than able to keep written records.

Furthermore, the recurring phrase "these are the generations of …," which occurs in eleven places through the book of Genesis, appears to give a clue that family records may have been kept by successive patriarchs. Wiseman[4] has interpreted this recurring phrase or refrain as a colophon, an identifying phrase at the end of a cuneiform clay tablet, which could be translated "these are the historical origins of…." In other words, the phrase always marks the conclusion of a section, rounding off the archives presumably written or kept through the years by the signatory, for example, Adam (Genesis 5:6) and Noah (Genesis 6:9), resulting in a growing series of clay tablets with the family history then entrusted to successive heads of the family.

However, occasionally this phrase, translated from the word *tôlʻdôt*, has been viewed as a heading of a section.[5] Indeed, Leupold translated the *tôlʻdôt* as the phrase "this is the story of," because as a heading it summarizes the ensuing

---

4   P. J. Wiseman, 1936, *New Discoveries in Babylonia About Genesis*, London: Marshall, Morgan and Scott.

5   H. C. Leupold, 1980, Exposition of Genesis, vol. 1, Grand Rapids, MI: Baker Book House (originally published by The Wartburg Press, 1942). See F. Kiel and F. Delitzsch, 1949, *Biblical Commentary on the Old Testament: The Pentateuch*, trans. James Martin, Grand Rapids, MI: Eerdmans.

discussion, combining narrative and genealogy to trace the development of the subject from a starting point to an end.

Alan Ross concluded that the colophon view of Wiseman cannot be accepted because the evidence from cuneiform is unconvincing.[6] On the cuneiform tablets, the colophons are titles that are repetitions of the tablet's first line and not a description of the contents. Ross argues that as a concluding statement for sections of the book of Genesis, the colophon interpretation is unworkable. Indeed, Ross points out that elsewhere in the Bible, outside of Genesis, the *tôl^edôt* does not refer to what preceded it, but in every place it occurs it can and often must refer to what follows (e.g., Ruth 4:18; Numbers 3:1). Ross thus maintains that the *tôl^edôt* heading announces the historical development from the ancestor (or beginning point) and could be paraphrased in translation as "this is what became of ...," or "this is where it started from" (with reference to the following subject). Thus, Ross argues that each section is a narrative depicting what became of someone, the Flood account being in the *tôl^edôt* of Noah (Genesis 6:9 – 9:29).

Nevertheless, the biblical evidence strongly favors the Wiseman interpretation of these colophons. The first such colophon in Genesis 2:4 clearly refers back to the Genesis 1 account of creation, and *not* the details in Genesis 2-4. Similarly, the Genesis 5:1 colophon refers back to the life of Adam. The view of Ross, on the other hand, negates the eyewitness nature of these clay tablet records, which in turn undermines them as literal, written historical accounts.

This *tôl^edôt* structure, then, is the very fabric around which the whole of Genesis was constructed, confirming its unity under the authorship of Moses directed by the Holy Spirit. This understanding of the significance of the *tôl^edôt* provides a hint that Moses may well have utilized previously existing written documents when compiling Genesis.

Thus, the conviction here is that the opening chapters of Genesis, including the Flood account, are an integral part of Genesis, which is equally the infallible Word of God, verbally inspired in the original autographs, that is, men of God such as Moses wrote under the direction of the Holy Spirit (2 Peter 1:21). As a reliable record of the early history of the earth, the details provided in Genesis must be our starting point in investigating the geographical extent of the Flood.

Surprising as it may be to some, not all conservative Christian scholars, past and present, believe that Genesis teaches a universal or global flood.[7] Baxter states:

---

6   A. P. Ross, 1996, *Creation and Blessing: A Guide to the Study and Exposition of Genesis,* Grand Rapids, MI: Baker Book House.

7   For example, J. S. Baxter, 1960, *Explore the Book: A Basic and Broadly Interpretive Course of Bible Study from Genesis to Revelation,* Grand Rapids, MI: Zondervan Publishing House; H. N. Ross, 1998, *The Genesis Question: Scientific Advances and the Accuracy of Genesis,* Colorado Springs, CO: NavPress.

Was the Flood in Noah's day universal? As to the *fact* of the Flood, the testimony of universal tradition and of 20th-century archaeology have put that finally beyond doubt: but was the Flood *universal?* ... let us clearly understand that it is not vital to the inspiration of the Scriptures to maintain that the Noachian Flood was universal.

It is indeed vital, and all the biblical arguments in favor of the Flood's universal extent should be carefully elaborated. Without exception, the commentators and scholars who maintain that the Flood was not global have drawn their arguments and evidence from science, particularly geology, forgetting that like any other human activity, science uses human wisdom to interpret the observational data and build models of, for example, what the earth was like in the past.

Rather than starting with fallible human opinion, it is crucial that we examine the question of the extent of the Flood from the wisdom and knowledge of God as provided by the Holy Spirit in the opening pages of Genesis.

2

THE DURATION OF THE FLOOD

One of the distinctive features of the Flood account in Genesis is the fullness and precision of the dates given—a precision described by Wenham as "astonishing."[1] The only other place in Scripture with similar precision is in Ezekiel, where his prophecies are clearly dated. Thus, these dates in Genesis 6–9 should attract our immediate attention as being significant. Indeed, we are given the date when the Flood began (Genesis 7:11) and the date when the Flood ended and Noah disembarked from the Ark (Genesis 8:14), making the Flood exactly one year and eleven days in duration. This equates to 371 days, if it is assumed that the calendar being referred to functioned on the basis of twelve 30-day months in a 360-day year. That this is indeed the case can readily be established from a careful study of the chronological data in the biblical text (see Table 1). For the Flood to continue for more than a year is astounding, to say the least, but it is totally consistent with the Flood's global extent. On the other hand, a year-long flood is hard to reconcile with the view widely held today that it was only local, confined to the Mesopotamian region. So while there may be differences of opinion as to other details concerning the Flood, there should be no dispute as to the Flood's duration.

Forty Days of Rain

The Flood began seven days after Noah, his family, and the animals entered the Ark, and we are told in Genesis 7:11-12 that as "the fountains of the great deep" were broken up, the "windows of heaven were opened" and it rained for forty days and nights continuously and torrentially. Devastating local floods are known from recorded history to have resulted from several days of intense rain that then tapers off. However, the biblical account clearly indicates that the intense rain cascaded down continuously for forty days and forty nights, two days short of six weeks. While we can only imagine the devastation resulting from the "floodgates of heaven" (literally) opening and the water pouring down upon the earth for that length of time, it is hard to conceive from this description that the Flood was only local. With that much water falling down upon the earth and spreading out, there is no doubt that Scripture is describing a global flood. Of course, we

---

1   Wenham, 1987, 179.

are told that water also came from within the earth—from "the fountains of the great deep"—so the amount of water involved is only compounded to the point where nothing short of a universal flood of global extent is consistent with the biblical description.

Table 1. The chronology of the Flood*.

Period	Days
There were forty days during which the rain fell	40
Throughout another 110 days the waters continued to rise, making 150 days in all for their "prevailing" (7:24)	110
The waters occupied 74 days in their "going and decreasing" (AV margin). This was from the 17th day of the seventh month to the 1st of the tenth month (8:5). There being 30 days to a month, the figures in days are 13 plus 30 plus 30 plus 1	74
Forty days elapsed before Noah sent out the raven (8:6–7)	40
Seven days elapsed before Noah sent out the dove for the first time (8:8). This period is necessary for reaching the total and is given by implication from the phrase "other seven days" (8:10)	7
Seven days passed before sending out the dove for the second time (8:10)	7
Seven days more passed before the third sending of the dove (8:12)	7
Up to this point 285 days are accounted for, but the next episode is dated the 1st of the first month in the 601st year. From the date in 7:11 to this point in 8:13 is a period of 314 days; therefore an interval of 29 days elapses	29
From the removal of the covering of the Ark to the very end of the experience was a further 57 days (8:14)	57
TOTAL	371

* This table appears in E. F. Kevan's Commentary on Genesis in Davidson, 1953, 84–85. As is pointed out in the discussion here, the Flood probably reached its maximum depth after the first forty days, instead of rising throughout the 150 days as Kevan indicates.

150 Days of "Prevailing"

The popular perception is that the Flood only lasted for forty days because that was the length of time it rained so intensely. However, the biblical account states three times that the waters "prevailed" (Genesis 7:18, 19, 24), the word "prevailed" in the original Hebrew conveying the meaning "were overwhelmingly mighty."[2] We are also told that "the waters increased," "the waters prevailed, and were increased greatly," "the waters prevailed exceedingly," and "the waters prevailed" (Genesis 7:17, 18, 19, 24) for 150 days. Thus, the forty days and forty nights of continual intense rain was only the beginning of this 150-day period. In fact, we are told in Genesis 8:1-2 that it was only after this 150-day period that the fountains of the

---

2   H. M. Morris, 1995, *The Defenders Study Bible,* Grand Rapids, MI: World Publishing, 23.

deep and the windows of heaven were stopped so that the rain was "restrained." The fact that this prevailing is repeated four times in the space of eight verses is meant to emphasize what was happening. No local flood continues rising for 150 days. If this were a description of the rivers in the Mesopotamian valley region overflowing, then it is completely misleading and exaggerated, to say the least.

Leupold suggested that the Flood attained its maximum depth after the first forty days of intense rainfall and continued to maintain that level for the additional 110 days of this 150-day "prevailing" period.[3] This conclusion was also favored by Whitcomb and Morris,[4] who emphasized that in Genesis 7:4, 12 we are twice told that the rain was upon the earth forty days and forty nights, and then in Genesis 7:17 we are also told that "the Flood was [or better, 'was coming'[5]] forty days upon the earth." They maintain that most of the water which came through the "windows of heaven" fell in the intense rainfall of that first period of forty days and that although the "windows of heaven" were not stopped for another 110 days, the rainfall during that period may have contributed only to the maintaining of the Flood waters at their maximum height.

However, it seems just as reasonable to regard the description in Genesis 7:17-20 as implying that the waters continued to rise continually during the entire "prevailing" period of 150 days. In sequence, the account records that "the waters increased" (v. 17), "and the waters prevailed, and were increased greatly upon the earth" (v. 18), "and the waters prevailed exceedingly upon the earth" (v. 19) and "the mountains were covered" (v. 20). Leupold translates these expressions as "the waters grew mighty and mounted greatly over the earth" (v. 18), and "the waters grew extremely mighty upon the earth" (v. 19).[6] Thus, the waters were still increasing on the earth's surface and therefore rising.

It needs to be remembered that "the fountains of the great deep" were also open for this 150-day "prevailing" period, and that it is possible that just as much, if not more, water came out onto the earth's surface through these fountains as the water that fell as rain through the "floodgates of heaven." If this indeed was the case, then it is even harder to escape from the inevitable conclusion. If the Flood waters were rising continually over the space of five long months (five 30-day months = 150 days), then because water will always spread out and seek a uniform level, the Flood was of such magnitude with the quantities of water involved that the extent had to be universal and global.

---

3   Leupold, 1942, 300, 306.

4   J. C. Whitcomb and H. M. Morris, 1961, *The Genesis Flood: The Biblical Record and Its Scientific Implications,* Philadelphia, PA: Presbyterian and Reformed Publishing Company, 4.

5   H. M. Morris, 1976, *The Genesis Record: A Scientific and Devotional Commentary on the Book of Beginnings,* Grand Rapids, MI: Baker Book House, 199.

6   Leupold, 1942, 300.

221 Days of "Assuaging" and "Abating"

The turning point during the Flood year occurred when "God remembered Noah" (Genesis 8:1), after which "God made a wind to pass over the earth, and the waters assuaged [literally, calmed or soothed]." This happened at the end of the 150 days of the waters "prevailing." From this point, the record tells us it took 221 days for the Flood waters to completely abate [literally, diminish, become less in amount] and for the surface of the ground to dry out sufficiently for Noah, his family, and the animals to disembark the Ark.

In reality, these time periods need to be carefully understood, for it is all too easy to miss the implications. Indeed, it is staggering to envisage that the Flood was so overwhelming, far-reaching, and gigantic as to have covered all the high mountains of the earth's pre-Flood topography within a period of probably only six weeks, with the waters then continuing to increase and prevail over those mountains for an additional sixteen weeks, during which the face of the earth was a shoreless ocean! However, if the biblical description of a global flood which covered even the tops of the mountains for sixteen consecutive weeks (110 days) is hard to reconcile with the somewhat inadequate local flood concept, then how much harder to reconcile is the fact that an additional 31 weeks (221 days, or more than seven months) were required for the Flood waters to subside sufficiently for Noah to disembark safely in "the mountains of Ararat."

During this period of 221 days, when the Flood waters were abating and the new land surface was drying out, there are a number of stages elaborated in the biblical narrative that are sometimes easily confused.[7] In addition to the Flood waters abating after 150 days (five months) when the fountains of the deep and the windows of heaven were stopped, we read in Genesis 8:4 that the Ark also came to rest "upon the mountains of Ararat." There is then a 74-day period (see Table 1) in which "the waters decreased continually" (Genesis 8:5), and at the end of that period we read that the tops of the mountains were visible. In other words, during that 74-day period, the continual rapid decrease in the water level exposed the tops of the mountains surrounding where the Ark had come to rest.

---

7   H. N. Ross, 1998, 147, 148, is clearly confused or has deliberately ignored the clear chronological details in Genesis 7-8 when he refers to the Flood waters receding over an 11-month period. He has obviously arrived at this figure because he only regards the waters as rising during the 40 days of rainfall (p. 148), 11 months (330 days) being the balance of the duration of the Flood event after 40 days are subtracted from the total 371 days. However, as has already been emphasized, the scriptural record clearly states that the Flood waters prevailed [literally, were overwhelmingly mighty] upon the earth for 150 days (Genesis 7:24) before the waters "assuaged" (Genesis 8:1), the fountains of the deep and the windows of heaven stopped, and the rain restrained (Genesis 8:2), and the waters returned from off the earth continually (Genesis 8:3). In fact, Genesis 8:3 specifically states that after the end of the 150 days, the waters were abated. There is really no excuse for misreading the biblical text and as a result publicly misleading his readers, but then his erroneous calculations from his incorrect reading of the Scriptures are seemingly more supportive of his local flood concept than the true biblical figures for the duration of the rising and prevailing of the Flood waters.

But Noah waited another forty days before he opened the window of the Ark in order to send out the raven.

Custance misunderstands these details. He suggests that in the 74 days from the grounding of the Ark on the mountains of Ararat until the tops of the mountains were seen, the water level had only dropped between 25 and 30 feet (a little more than the presumed draught of 15 cubits for the Ark), so that dry land became visible only at the end of those 74 days.[8] In support of this contention, he maintains that the raven was released during this 74-day period and wandered to and fro without finding a landing place because the dry land had not yet appeared. Custance then uses this misreading of the biblical text to arrive at a rate for the decreasing water level of 25 feet in 74 days, or about four inches per day, which of course is admirably consistent with his insistence that the Flood was only local.

However, Custance is wrong, because the chronology for this period of the abating waters, as outlined in Table 1, is very clear from the progression of verses in Genesis 8. In any case, it must be emphasized that at the end of the 74-day period, after the grounding of the Ark on the mountains of Ararat, we are specifically told that it was not merely the top of the high mountain on which the Ark rested that was seen, but "the tops of the mountains." In other words, the Flood waters must have subsided hundreds of feet in order for various mountain peaks of different altitudes to be seen by then. Nor are the Scriptures teaching that the tops of the mountains were still submerged on the last day of the ninth month (day 73 after the Ark came to rest), and then suddenly emerged on the first day of the tenth month (day 74).

Furthermore, Noah did not subsequently send out the raven to determine whether any mountain peaks had emerged, as Custance assumes, but to gain information about the nature of those exposed areas. The raven's failure to return to the Ark did not mean it hadn't achieved the purpose Noah had intended. On the contrary, it was a good sign, because being a hardy bird it would have survived on carrion even though the exposed ground of the mountain tops was still inhospitable to other creatures. The total impossibility of Custance's scenario is that if the raven was released forty days after the grounding of the Ark, within the 74-day period, then the dove would have been released three times in successive seven-day periods, and returned after having plucked the fresh olive leaf, more than two weeks before the tops of the mountains were exposed on day 74! We do well to follow the clear chronology outlined in the biblical narrative, allowing the Scriptures to speak for themselves, rather than force them to bolster a local flood interpretation.

The order in the stages for the abating of the Flood waters as given in Genesis 8, then, is as follows:

---

8   A. C. Custance, 1979, The extent of the Flood, in *The Flood: Local or Global?*, vol. IX: The Doorway Papers, Grand Rapids, MI: Zondervan, 22-24.

- After the waters had "prevailed upon the earth" for 150 days, the waters began to "assuage" [literally, calm].

- The Ark rested upon the mountains of Ararat the same day that the waters began to assuage, for the seventeenth day of the seventh month was exactly 150 days after the Flood began.

- The waters continued to abate and subside, so that by the first day of the tenth month (74 days later), the tops of various lower mountains could be seen. In this 74-day period after the Ark grounded on perhaps the highest peak of the mountains of Ararat, more and more of the lower peaks emerged, so that doubtless during much of the ninth month the tops of the various mountains were seen. Nevertheless, it is also true that on the first day of the tenth month "were the tops of the mountains seen," Moses under the direction of the Holy Spirit choosing that particular date to mark the end of this stage in the abating of the waters. This whole process would suggest a drop in water levels of thousands of feet at a rate of perhaps 15 or 20 feet per day, at least during this initial 74-day stage of the assuaging period.

- The Flood level continued to fall for forty more days, so that Noah no longer feared the Flood would return and hence sent the raven out to investigate conditions outside the Ark on the exposed mountain tops.

As Whitcomb and Morris have already established,[9] instead of constituting an objection to the global extent of the Flood, this rate of decline of the water level, in stark contrast to Custance's spurious calculations, thus becomes a strong argument in its favor. If nothing else but the tops of the mountains could be seen after the waters had been subsiding for 74 days, then we are left with no other alternative than to conclude that the waters of the Flood must have covered the whole earth.

The details of the flights of the dove as recorded in Genesis 8:8-12 are also instructive. Noah first sent out the dove seven days after the raven had flown off and not returned, as suggested by the phrase "yet other seven days" (v. 10). Even though the mountainsides were now well and truly exposed, Noah again wanted to find out more about the ground conditions, so he sent out the dove, which as a cleaner bird would only be satisfied if it found a clean and dry resting place. The first time the dove was sent out, no such resting place was found and it returned. Seven days later when the dove was sent out a second time, it returned that evening with an olive leaf in its mouth. This was plucked from what was no doubt the budding of a piece of olive tree debris that had floated on the Flood

---

9   Whitcomb and Morris, 1961, 7.

waters, but now was partly buried in the newly exposed ground surface and had thus been regenerated during the seven days since the dove's previous flight. When the dove did not return after being sent out again seven days later, Noah knew that the Flood waters had abated sufficiently for the dove to find a clean and dry resting place with food for its needs.

These details also add to the complete picture as recorded in the Scriptures of definite stages in this abating of the waters period, and in the drying out of the ground. The speed at which the ground became hospitable for the dove so soon after the raven had gone also adds to the picture of rapidly falling water levels and rapidly regenerating vegetation. Such revegetation would have been accomplished asexually from the sprigs, or from floating seeds, that had survived from what had been a flood of global extent. Even the progression in Genesis 8:11, 13, 14 in the descriptions from "the waters were abated from off the earth" to "the waters were dried up from off the earth," "the face of the ground was dry" and "the earth dried," signifies the final drying out stages of the Flood waters were in a progression, which included another 86 days after the dove failed to return. This period of almost three months again emphasizes that this was no ordinary local flood which, if the details of local floods in recorded history are anything to go by, would have taken a lot less time for the ground to have dried out and the vegetation to be re-established.

Thus, the duration of the Flood in its assuaging, abating, and drying out, as well as in its prevailing, compels us to think of this event as a global and universal cataclysm, and not merely some localized catastrophe.

3

THE DEPTH OF THE FLOOD

One of the most important statements in the biblical narrative that argues for a universal flood is found in Genesis 7:19-20:

> And the waters prevailed exceedingly upon the earth; and all the high hills, that were under the whole heaven, were covered. Fifteen cubits upward did the waters prevail; and the mountains were covered.

The extent of the actions of the rising Flood waters so forthrightly expressed makes the tremendous implications of the biblical narrative at this point readily evident to any reader. Even if only one high mountain had been covered with water, to say nothing of *all* the mountains, the Flood would have been absolutely universal, simply because water must seek its own level and it does so very quickly!

Leupold makes the following comments about these crucial statements in the biblical narrative:

> A measure of the waters is now made by comparison with the only available standard for such waters—the mountains. They are said to have been "covered." Not a few merely but "all the high mountains under all the heavens." One of these expressions alone would almost necessitate the impression that the author intends to convey the idea of the absolute universality of the Flood, e.g., "all the high mountains." Yet since "all" is sometimes used in a relative sense, the writer removed all possible ambiguity by adding the phrase "under all the heavens." A double "all" (*kol*) cannot allow for so relative a sense. It almost constitutes a Hebrew superlative. So we believe that the text disposes of the question of the universality of the Flood."[1]

Leupold then deals with the potential objection of those who maintain the Flood was limited in extent, perhaps only as far as mankind may have populated the earth's surface at that time, and who would thus insist that *kol* can be used in a relative sense, as it is in other passages such as Genesis 41:57; Exodus 9:25; 10:15;

---

1   Leupold, 1942, 301.

Deuteronomy 2:25; 1 Kings 10:24. However, he insists that such an argument is inadequate because these verses use a single *kol*, whereas here in Genesis 7:19 a double *kol* is used to give the double emphasis which cannot be interpreted as only relative.

The phrase "15 cubits upward did the waters prevail" does not mean that the Flood was only 15 cubits (22 feet) deep, for the phrase is qualified by the one which immediately follows: "And the mountains were covered."[2] Nor does this phrase necessarily mean that the mountains were covered to a depth of only 15 cubits, because this would require that all the pre-Flood mountains had exactly the same altitude.

The true meaning of this depth of water is very clear when we refer back to Genesis 6:15, where we are told that the height of the Ark was 30 cubits. Most commentators agree that the "15 cubits" in Genesis 7:20 must therefore refer to the draft of the Ark, which must have sunk into the water to a depth of 15 cubits (just one-half of its total height) when fully laden. This information adds further support to the depth of water argument for a global flood because it tells us that the Flood waters "prevailed" over the tops of the highest mountains to a depth of *at least* 15 cubits (22 feet). Quite obviously, if the Flood had not covered the mountains by at least such a depth, then the Ark could not have floated over them during the five months (150 days) in which the waters "prevailed" across the face of the earth.

However, those who actively propound the local flood view do not take issue with this clear statement in the biblical narrative of the waters prevailing 15 cubits over the mountains. Rather, the "sticking point" for them is whether Genesis is here really suggesting that present-day Mt. Ararat, with an altitude of about 17,000 feet, and beyond that Mt. Everest in the Himalayas, with an altitude of over 29,000 feet, were covered by the Flood waters. Two difficulties raised are the tremendous mass and weight of water even three miles, let alone six miles, deep (Keil[3], Baxter[4]) and the inability of our planet from internal and external sources to be able to supply the required quantity of water for such a global inundation (Ross[5]).

These objections are, of course, based on the assumption that both Mt. Ararat and Mt. Everest were in existence prior to the Flood, which in turn is based on the view that since the biblical Flood occurred approximately 4,500 years ago—in contrast to the 4.5-billion-year geological timescale for the earth—it was thus

2   Whitcomb and Morris, 1961, 2.

3   C. F. Keil, 1875, *Biblical Commentary on the Old Testament (Genesis)*, Edinburgh: T. and T. Clark, cited in Leupold, 1942, 302-301.

4   Baxter, 1960, 41.

5   H. N. Ross, 1998, 147-148.

insignificant geologically. Ross, for example, follows in the footsteps of many other commentators by insisting that the Flood was limited to the Mesopotamian Valley, the presumed "world" of Noah's day (more on this later). Thus, Ross insists that the Hebrew words used in Genesis 7:19 can be interpreted as the waters falling upon, or running over, hills or hill country, and that Noah on the upper deck of the Ark, floating on water 200 or 300 feet deep in the middle of the vast Mesopotamian Plain, would not have been able to see any hills or mountains due to his view being limited by the earth's curvature "atmospheric conditions, and aging eyes, and other factors."[6] Such views and interpretations do "violence" both to the Hebrew text of the biblical narrative and to the obvious scientific implications of these early chapters of Genesis.

First, Wenham says of Genesis 7:18-19 that "the waters do not merely multiply greatly; they triumph," as in the victory in a military battle.[7] He further comments:

> [N]ote the repetition of the key words, and the way the remark "the waters triumphed and multiplied greatly" in v. 18 is heightened here to "the waters triumphed exceedingly [greatly greatly]." Just how deep the water was is indicated by the high mountains being submerged.

Then Cassuto says of Genesis 7:24:

> [T]he paragraph closes, with an awe-inspiring picture of the mighty waters covering the entire earth. We see water everywhere, as though the world had reverted to its primeval state at the dawn of Creation, when the waters of the deep submerged everything. Nothing remained of the teeming life that had burst forth upon the earth.[8]

Second, it is an inescapable conclusion that as a result of the Flood "all flesh died that moved upon the earth" (Genesis 7:21), "all in whose nostrils was the breath of life...died" (v. 22), and "every living substance was destroyed which was upon the face of the ground...and they were destroyed from the earth" so that "Noah only remained alive, and they that were with him in the ark" (v. 23). Echoing Cassuto's comments, these statements imply destruction from off the face of the earth of all life that God had created in Genesis 1, so we need not be surprised at the scientific evidence for such destruction in the vast thicknesses of water-transported sediments now found as rock layers containing countless billions of fossils.

---

6   H. N. Ross, 1998, 145-146.

7   Wenham, 1987, 182-183.

8   U. Cassuto, 1964, *A Commentary on the Book of Genesis 1-11*, vol. 2, trans. I. Abrahams, Jerusalem: Magnes Press, 97.

In this context, it is important to note that Mt. Ararat is a volcanic mountain whose lavas cover fossil-bearing sedimentary rocks. Obviously, if these fossil-bearing sedimentary rocks beneath Mt. Ararat are a product of the Genesis Flood, then Mt. Ararat was not there prior to the Flood. Similarly, marine-fossil-bearing layers near the summit of Mt. Everest would likewise have been a product of the Flood, so that Mt. Everest, and thus all the Himalayas which are also geologically "recent" mountains, would not have been there prior to the Flood. Thus, the Flood waters did not have to be 3-6 miles deep to carry the Ark over Mt. Ararat and Mt. Everest. This understanding negates the claimed problems of the weight of such a depth of water and the ability of sources in and around the earth to supply that quantity of water.

Furthermore, beneath the floor of the Mesopotamian Valley are fossil-bearing sedimentary rocks also, so that the Mesopotamian Valley also wasn't there prior to the Flood. As will be demonstrated below, the picture the Scriptures give, both here in Genesis and elsewhere, is that the earth's total surface was changed as a result of the Flood, including its geology and geography. Thus, whatever the height of the pre-Flood mountains, the Genesis narrative insists that all the mountains were covered to a depth of at least 22 feet (15 cubits). Furthermore, from simple observation of the behavior of water, if the Flood waters were deep enough to cover the high mountains in one region to a depth of more than 22 feet for up to five months (150 days), then it is obvious that the waters must necessarily spread themselves out over the entire earth's surface. Thus, to maintain this depth for such a length of time, the Flood waters would have had to reach a similar depth everywhere else on the planet.[9] Therefore, all of these arguments put together can only lead an honest reader of the Scriptures to the overwhelming conclusion that the depth of the Flood waters as described must imply that the Flood was of universal and global extent.

---

9   Leupold, 1942, 302, and J. C. Whitcomb, 1988, *The World That Perished,* revised ed., Grand Rapids, MI: Baker Book House, 47.

4

GEOLOGICAL DETAILS OF THE FLOOD

Because of the apparent success of modern geology, with its uniformitarian–evolutionary synthesis based on the multi-million-year geological timescale, many Christians and Christian scholars have accepted that synthesis and timescale without objections. Attempts are made to reconcile the Scriptures with it, but as a result they usually compromise the Scriptures and argue for a local flood of minimal effect. Thus, so many arguments against the Flood being of global extent have been based upon supposed geological objections, and yet the scriptural narrative of the Flood does provide us with some very important geological details.

Indeed, the first recorded event of the Flood is that "the same day were all the fountains of the great deep broken up" (Genesis 7:11). According to Brown, Driver, and Briggs, the Hebrew word *t^hôm* translated "deep" in this verse has the primary meanings of 1) "deep, of subterranean waters," 2) "sea," and 3) "primeval ocean, deep."[1] Most other commentators agree.[2] Leupold refers to the "great deep" as being subterranean water,[3] while Wenham suggests that there was "a great subterranean ocean."[4] Thus, there seems little doubt that the phrase *t^hôm rabbâh* ("great deep") refers back to the *t^hôm* of Genesis 1:2 and to the oceanic depths and possible underground reservoirs of the pre-Flood world.

Whitcomb and Morris thus suggest that the ocean basins were presumably fractured and uplifted sufficiently to pour waters over the continents, in conjunction with the torrential rain which fell through the "windows of heaven."[5] Kidner suggests that there was a vast upheaval of the sea-bed,[6] while Vos translates the expression as "the springs of the great deep were cleft asunder," often interpreted

---

1   F. Brown, S. R. Driver and C. H. Briggs, 1906, *A Hebrew and English Lexicon of the Old Testament*, Boston, New York and Chicago: Houghton, Mifflin and Company, 1062.

2   For example, L. Koehler and W. Baumgartner, 1953, *Lexicon in Veteris Testamenti Libros*, vol. II, Grand Rapids, MI: Eerdmans Publishing Company, 1019, give the first two meanings of *t^hôm* as (1) the primeval ocean, and (2) the subterranean water.

3   Leupold, 1942, 295.

4   Wenham, 1987, 181.

5   Whitcomb and Morris, 1961, 9.

6   Kidner, 1967, 91.

as some convulsion of the earth's crust releasing stores of subterranean waters.[7] Wenham likewise notes that the expanded explicit description of the Flood's arrival—"all the springs of the great deep burst open"—suggests "water gushing forth uncontrollably from wells and springs which draw from a great subterranean ocean."[8] However, Vos maintains that geologists have thus far been unable to find evidence of such subterranean reserves, or of any general and cataclysmic alteration of the earth's crust that may have eliminated such reservoirs by the collapse of geological structures above them. But such a conclusion needs to be qualified because of the abundant evidence in the earth's crust of upheavals that have distorted, folded, and heated the rocks.

So, it is conceivable that such a cataclysmic upheaval could indeed have eliminated pre-Flood reservoirs, which may have presumably collapsed once the waters they contained burst forth. This fits the description in the biblical narrative of being "broken up" (Genesis 7:11). In support of these pre-Flood subterranean reservoirs, Morris refers back to the description in Genesis 2:10-14 of the river system that flowed out of the Garden of Eden.[9] We are told that this river system began as one stream that divided into four rivers. The implication is that they were fed from controlled fountains or springs in the Garden where water must have emerged from deep-seated sources in the earth's crust. Morris suggests that such subterranean reservoirs may have been all interconnected, so that the entire complex constituted one "great deep."

Whitcomb and Morris maintain that the close connection that exists between Genesis 7:11 and 1:2-10 should be evident to those who study the text with care. They cite Delitzsch, who comments:

> [I]t was by a co-operation of subterranean and celestial forces, which broke through the restraints placed upon the waters on the second and third days of creation, that the Deluge was brought to pass.[10]

So impressed by the geological implications of the description in the biblical narrative, Lange wrote this of the Flood:

> [T]he earth-crisis, on which it was conditioned, must have been universal. With the opening of the fountains of the deep stands the opening of the windows of heaven in polar contrast…as an earth-crisis, the Flood was probably universal.[11]

---

7   H. F. Vos, 1982, *Everyman's Bible Commentary: Genesis,* Chicago, IL: Moody Press, 40.

8   Wenham, 1987, 181.

9   Morris, 1976, 194-195.

10   F. Delitzsch, 1899, *A New Commentary on Genesis,* trans. S. Taylor, New York: Scribner and Welford, 267.

11   J. P. Lange, ed., *A Commentary on the Holy Scriptures: Genesis,* Grand Rapids, MI: Zondervan Publishing

Leupold suggests that the chief source of the Flood waters was the rain from above, whereas the fountains of the great deep were only the auxiliary source, even though they are mentioned first in the narrative.[12] However, he concedes that tremendous geological possibilities lie behind the vast upheavals on every hand that would have been involved in the breaking open of the fountains of the great deep, the vastness of these eruptions being in proportion to the actual depth of the Flood.

On the other hand, Morris maintains that the breaking up (literally, "cleaving open") of the fountains of the great deep being mentioned first was evidently the initial action that in turn triggered the opening of the "windows of heaven."[13] It is conceivable that as a result of the build-up of pressure in the subterranean reservoirs due to the earth's internal heat, the conduits all developed uncontrollable fractures on the same day. Once the first "fountain" cracked open, the water surging through would immediately weaken adjacent conduits, resulting in a rapid worldwide chain reaction developing to cleave open all the fountains of the great deep right around the globe.

However, as noted by Whitcomb and Morris, it is a most significant fact that these geological upheavals were not confined to a single day. In fact, the scriptural record states that this breaking up of "the fountains of the great deep" continued for a period of *five months*, because it was not until after the 150 days had passed that "the fountains also of the deep…were stopped" (Genesis 8:2). Such vast geological upheavals on the ocean floor breaking up the earth's crust and water flowing out from these underground reservoirs continuously for such a prolonged period simply cannot be reconciled with the view that the Flood was merely a local inundation in the Mesopotamian Valley. Instead, these geological details provided by the biblical narrative give overwhelming support to the concept of a geographically universal flood.

More recently, Baumgardner (references later) has suggested that the cleaving open of the fountains of the great deep is an amazingly accurate description of what must have occurred along narrow zones many tens of thousands of miles in length, where sections of the pre-Flood ocean floor were pulling apart rapidly during the Flood. These narrow V-shaped gashes in the ocean bottom would have been filled by spectacular supersonic steam jets that entrained vast amounts of ocean water and like fountains rose high into the stratosphere. The steam formed as water at the bottom of these channels came in contact with molten rock gushing from below to fill the gaps between the rapidly spreading slabs of ocean floor. These features of the Flood cataclysm will be discussed in more detail later.

House, 296.

12   Leupold, 1942, 295-296.

13   Morris, 1976, 196-197.

5

THE SIZE OF THE ARK

In Genesis 6:15, we are told that Noah was commanded to build the Ark according to the following specifications: "The length of the ark shall be three hundred cubits, the breadth of it fifty cubits, and the height of it thirty cubits." To understand these dimensions in terms of modern units, the first question to be considered is the length of a cubit as used here in the Scriptures. The cubit was, all are agreed, measured from a man's elbow to the tip of his fingers, but there were some variations in the lengths of the standard cubits that were used by people in the early post-Flood world. For example, the Babylonians had a "royal" cubit of about 19.8 inches, the Egyptians had a longer and a shorter cubit of about 20.65 inches and 17.6 respectively, while the Hebrews apparently had a long cubit of 20.4 inches and a common cubit of about 17.5 inches.[1]

Most commentators adopt without question the Hebrews' common cubit, which is virtually identical to the Egyptian shorter cubit. This would logically make sense with Moses, a Hebrew with an Egyptian upbringing, writing in the first instance to Hebrews. However, most commentators simplify the calculations by adopting a rounded figure of 18 inches or 45 centimeters for the cubit. When all these considerations are taken into account, a conservative estimate for the dimensions of the Ark would be 450 feet (approximately 135 meters) long, 75 feet (22.5 meters) wide, and 45 feet (13.5 meters) high. Since the Ark had three decks (Genesis 6:16), it had a total deck area of approximately 98,800 square feet (approximately 9,100 square meters), which is equivalent to slightly more than the area of twenty standard basketball courts. The total volume of the Ark would also have been approximately 1.45 million cubic feet (approximately 41,000 cubic meters), which is approximately equal to the volumetric capacity of 540 standard livestock cars used on modern U.S. railroads.[2] The displacement tonnage of the Ark, defined as the weight of seawater displaced by the volume of the ship when submerged to its design draft, assumed to be 15 cubits (half its height) because Genesis 7:20 refers to the Flood waters prevailing higher than 15 cubits over the mountains so that the Ark cleared them, would have been almost

---

1   Whitcomb and Morris, 1961, 10.

2   Morris, 1976, 181 gave a similar estimate. However, a different estimate is given in this volume on page 135.

20,700 tons (more than 21,000 tonnes). The gross tonnage of the Ark, which is a measurement of cubic space rather than weight—one ton in this case being equivalent to 100 cubic feet of usable storage space—would have been about 14,500 tons (approximately 14,730 tonnes), which would place it well within the category of large metal oceangoing ships today.

Against the tide of scholarly opinion, Custance questioned whether the dimensions of the Ark could have been so huge and suggested, without evidence, that the cubit in Noah's day may have been much shorter than 18 inches. He also questioned the magnitude of the building task:

> I think anyone who tries to visualize the construction of a vessel 450 feet long by four men would realise that the size of the timbers alone for a "building" 45 feet high (analogous to a 4-storey apartment building) would seem by their sheer massiveness to be beyond the powers of four men to handle. With all the means later at their disposal, subsequent builders for 4,000 long years constructed seaworthy vessels that seldom seemed to have exceeded 150 to 200 feet at the most....it was not until 1884 apparently that a vessel, the Eturia, a Cunard liner, was built with a length exceeding that of the Ark. It would have to be a very solidly constructed ship for its decks to carry such a load as two elephants, for example, weighing four to five tons apiece.[3]

While silent on the subject, nothing in the Scriptures would suggest that Noah and his three sons had to construct the Ark on their own, so it is not unreasonable to expect that Noah could have had the help of hired men. Furthermore, the references in Genesis 4:17, 21, 22 to the technological abilities in the pre-Flood civilization to build cities, to make musical instruments, and to make metal tools, which therefore required the mining and smelting of metal ores, imply that Noah and his sons could have personally had the necessary technical skills to have directed the construction of the Ark with such huge dimensions. Of course, we need to also remember that the "blueprint" for the Ark was given to Noah by divine instruction (Genesis 6:14-16).

Confirmation of the God-given design of the Ark can be seen in its seaworthiness and tested ability to be able to withstand the rigors of stormy seas and raging Flood waters for the five months of the "prevailing" stage until the waters were calmed by the wind that God sent (Genesis 8:1). It must be remembered that the dimensions of the Ark were not necessarily that of a ship with a sleek hull designed for cruising at speed through the water, but were apparently the dimensions of a gigantic flat-bottom barge with maximum carrying capacity. It is reported that as early as 1609-1621, a Dutchman, Peter Janssen, built a two-fifths scale model of the Ark and experimented with it to demonstrate its seaworthiness and high storage

---

3   Custance, 1979, 37.

capacity.[4] In fact, Danish barges called *Fleuten* were evidently modeled after the Ark and proved to be very seaworthy and almost impossible to capsize.[5] Indeed, the length to width ratio of 6:1 is very similar to that of modern oceangoing ships designed for speed, whereas the Ark was only meant to float, yet this ratio is important from the point of view of stability, of pitching and of rolling.[6]

Morris undertook a study of the stability of the Ark and found it could be shown hydrodynamically that a gigantic box of such dimensions would be exceedingly stable, almost impossible to capsize even in a sea of gigantic waves. In fact, the Ark could be tilted through any angle up to just short of 90° and it would immediately thereafter right itself again.[7] So, it would have to be turned completely vertical before it could be tipped over. Furthermore, it would tend to align itself parallel with the direction of major wave advance, and thus be subject to minimum pitching most of the time.[8] He concluded:

> [I]ts relatively great length (six times its width) would tend to keep it from being subjected to wave forces of equal magnitude through its whole length, since wave fields tend to occur in broken and varying patterns, rather than in a series of long uniform crest-trough sequences, and this would be particularly true in the chaotic hydrodynamic phenomena of the Flood. Any vortex action to which it might occasionally be subjected would also tend to be resisted and broken up by its large length-width ratio. The ark would, in fact, tend to be lined up by the spectrum of hydrodynamic forces in currents in such direction that its long axis would be parallel to the predominate direction of wave and current movement. Thus it would act as a semi-streamlined body, and the net drag forces would usually be minimal. In every way, therefore, the ark as designed was highly stable, admirably suited for its purpose of riding out the storms of the year of the great Flood.[9]

In a more recent study, model tests were performed using one-fiftieth scaled models of three possible hull forms for the Ark in a large towing tank at the Korea Research Institute of Ships and Engineering, Taejon, South Korea, with a wave generating system in order to validate a theoretical analysis of the seaworthiness of the Ark.[10] It was found that the center of gravity is the most important parameter

---

4   Leupold, 1942, 272, and Wenham, 1987, 173.

5   B. Ramm, 1964, *The Christian View of Science and Scripture,* Exeter, U.K.: The Paternoster Press, 157.

6   F. A. Filby, 1970, *The Flood Reconsidered: A Review of Evidences of Geology, Archaeology, Ancient Literature and the Bible,* London: Pickering and Inglis Limited, 93.

7   H. M. Morris, 1971, The Ark of Noah, *Creation Research Society Quarterly,* 8(2): 142-144.

8   Morris, 1976, 181.

9   Morris, 1971, 143-144.

10   S. W. Hong et al, 1994, Safety investigation of Noah's Ark in a seaway, *Creation Ex Nihilo Technical Journal,* 8(1): 26-36.

that determines the safety of a ship, and that the behavior of a ship at sea depends mainly on the wave height, wave direction, and ship speed. However, because the Ark was designed to just drift, the effect of speed would be negligible. Twelve other hull forms were analyzed and tested along with the Ark's hull form, and when the American Bureau of Shipping's rule for safety classification was applied to all these hull forms, it was found that the Ark was thirteen times more stable than the standard for safety required by the ABS rule. According to all criteria, the net result was that the Ark had superior safety compared to the other hull forms tested. Furthermore, the study found that the Ark could have withstood waves more than 30 meters (approximately 100 feet) high, so it was concluded that the Ark as a drifting ship had a reasonable length-width-depth ratio for the safety of the hull, crew, and cargo in the high winds and waves imposed on it by the Genesis Flood.

The spatial dimensions of the Ark therefore constitute a remarkable testimony to the internal consistency and objective rationality of the biblical Flood account. The sheer massiveness of the Ark certainly staggers the imagination, but the evidence of its divine design is witnessed by its optimum dimensions for stability and safety to ride out the raging storms and massive waves that undoubtedly occurred during the Flood, according to the implications of the description given of the Flood in the Scriptures. Furthermore, the very point of the argument here is that for Noah to have built a vessel of such magnitude simply for the purpose of escaping a local flood is inconceivable. Indeed, the very size and credibility of the Ark should effectively eliminate the local flood view from serious consideration among those who take the book of Genesis at face value.

6

THE NEED FOR THE ARK

The incredible dimensions of the Ark, the enormous effort involved to build it, and the Ark's seaworthiness also provide another logical argument that has seemingly escaped the notice of those who maintain that the Flood was only local. Put simply, not only would an ark of such gigantic proportions have been unnecessary for a flood of only local extent, but there would have been no need for an ark at all!

The whole procedure of constructing such a vessel, involving over 100 years of planning and toiling, simply to escape a local flood, can hardly be described as anything but utter foolishness and unnecessary.[1] How much more sensible it would have been for God merely to have warned Noah of the coming destruction, and to have told him to move to an area that would not have been affected by the Flood, even as Lot was led out of Sodom before the fire fell from heaven. Furthermore, the great numbers of animals of all kinds, and certainly the birds, could easily have also moved away from the area to be flooded, rather than having to be stored and tended for a year in the Ark. The biblical account borders on the ridiculous if the Flood was only confined to some section of the Near East. It is simply not possible to harmonize the scriptural details with the concept of a local flood.

However, in spite of the irresistible force of this argument for a global flood, many conservative biblical scholars continue to promote the concept of a local flood, yet discuss the design, dimensions, capacity, and purpose of the Ark with little apparent appreciation of the obvious inconsistency of such a study. One would think that the biblical description of the dimensions of the Ark would be ignored by such scholars, whose view of the Flood would bring into serious question the need for an ark, to say nothing of an ark of such enormous dimensions.

One of the few to face the implications of this particular argument, by trying to present an alternative, is Custance, who has suggested that the Ark was simply an object lesson for the benefit of the pre-Flood people:

---

1   Whitcomb and Morris, 1961, 11.

It would require real energy and faith to follow Noah's example and build other arks, but it would have required neither of these to pack up a few things and migrate. There is nothing that Noah could have done to stop them except by disappearing secretly. Such a departure could hardly act as a kind of warning that the deliberate construction of the Ark must have done. And the inspiration for this undertaking was given to Noah by leaving him in ignorance of the exact limits of the Flood. He was assured that all mankind would be destroyed, and he probably supposed that the Flood would therefore be universal. This supposition may have been essential for him.[2]

However, as Whitcomb and Morris have already pointed out,[3] how can one read the Flood account of Genesis 6-9 with close attention and then arrive at the conclusion that the Ark was built merely to warn the ungodly, and not mainly to save the occupants of the Ark from death by drowning? And how can we exonerate God from the charge of deception if we say that He led Noah to believe that the Flood would be global, in order to encourage him to work on the Ark, when He knew all the time that it would not be global?

Similarly, Ross accepts the enormity of the Ark's dimensions and defends the ability of Noah to build the Ark, even accepting the likelihood that Noah may have employed many more people than just his family members to assist in the construction project. However, while he admits that God could have instructed Noah to pack up and depart to a region far away where Noah and those with him would be out of harm's way, Ross insists that the purpose for the Ark was so that Noah, as a prophet and God's spokesperson, could use the scaffolding around the Ark as his preaching platform:

> The efforts of a middle-aged (or slightly older) man, a distinguished patriarch, to build an enormous vessel in the middle of a desert plain that receives scant rainfall certainly would have commanded attention. Noah's persistent devotion to this immensely challenging project for 100 years would have heightened the drama. As crowds gathered to jeer, not cheer, Noah patiently preached. He warned his listeners of impending doom if they failed to repent. He freely offered passage to anyone who would heed his warning and call upon God for mercy. Perhaps one reason for the enormous size of the ship was to demonstrate the sincerity of this offer.

> [H]e could have built the ark much faster if he had spent less time preaching, but the magnitude of the impending disaster compelled him

2   Custance, 1979, 34.

3   Whitcomb and Morris, 1961, 12.

to give more than ample warning to his contemporaries.[4]

Again, these statements distort what is specifically stated in the text of Genesis, that the Ark was built primarily to save Noah, his family, and the animals that went aboard it. Likewise, Ross promotes a geographically limited flood ("though universal with respect to people and their animals"), Noah and the world's people at that time supposedly being confined only to the desert plain of Mesopotamia, which of course wrongly assumes that pre-Flood geography was virtually identical to our own.

With respect to the animals in the Ark, Custance takes the view that they were only the domesticated varieties of use to man:

> There is much evidence to show that the domestication of animals was first undertaken somewhere in this general area [Mesopotamia]. Assuming that such species as had been domesticated in the centuries between Adam and Noah were confined to the areas settled by man and had not spread beyond this, any flow which destroyed man would also wipe out these animals. The process of domestication would then have to be begun all over again and probably under far less ideal conditions....It is almost certain that such domesticated animals could not have migrated alone.... For this reason, if for no other, some animals at least would have to be taken on board—but these were probably of the domesticated varieties.[5]

In his approach to the same issue, Ross examines the Hebrew words used for the animals to be taken on board the Ark and concludes:

> All these words refer to birds and mammals, though some can be used a little more broadly. We see a high correlation between this list and the list of soulish animals God created on the fifth and sixth creation days, animals that held significance in the preparation of earth for humankind. Clearly, the survival of these creatures would be important to the restoration and survival of human society after the Flood. Nothing in the Genesis text compels us to conclude that Noah's passengers included anything other than birds and mammals.[6]

However, Ross subsequently narrows his guidelines even further to just "every bird and mammal species living in the region where human beings lived."[7] But where does the Genesis record suggest that Noah was to take into the Ark only domesticated animals, or only birds and mammals, living in the region where

4   H.N. Ross, 1998, 160.

5   Custance, 1979, 35-36.

6   H. N. Ross, 1998, 163.

7   H. N. Ross, 1998, 164.

man lived?

We are clearly and repeatedly told that the purpose of the Flood was to destroy "both man, and beast, and the creeping thing, and the fowls of the air" (Genesis 6:7), and "to destroy all flesh, wherein is the breath of life, from under heaven" (Genesis 6:17, also Genesis 6:12-13, 19-21; 7:2-4, 8, 14-16; 8:1, 17-19; 9:8-17). Furthermore, this was accomplished when "all flesh died that moved upon the earth, both of fowl, and of cattle, and of beast, and of every creeping thing that creepeth upon the earth, and every man: All in whose nostrils was the breath of life, of all that was in the dry land, died. And every living substance was destroyed which was upon the face of the ground, both man, and cattle, and the creeping things, and the fowl of the heaven; and they were destroyed from the earth" (Genesis 7:21-23). These are exactly the same descriptive terms used in Genesis 1 to describe the various kinds of land animals which God created. If only domesticated animals or just birds and mammals from the Mesopotamian region were to be taken into the Ark, are we to assume that only domesticated animals or just birds and mammals in the Mesopotamian region were created by God back in Genesis 1? The fact is that no clearer terms could have been employed by Moses under the direction of the Holy Spirit than those which he did employ to express the idea of *the totality of air-breathing, land-dwelling animals in the world.*

Once this point is conceded, all controversy as to the geographical extent of the Flood ends, because no one could possibly maintain that all land animals were confined to the Mesopotamian region in days of Noah!

> The fact that every living creature was to be destroyed would indicate that the whole earth was subject to the Flood (Genesis 7:4). Probably the animals had scattered over much of the earth; a universal flood would have been needed to destroy them....Certainly all the main groups of animals were represented on the Ark.[8]

Francis Schaeffer adamantly maintained:

> Another difficulty arises if the Flood is not universal, and I don't see how anyone can quite get around this factor. If a Flood occurs in a limited area, a lot of animals can be drowned but not all of them. There is no way you can eliminate them all unless they are all in a sealed canyon. When a forest fire or flood comes, the animals take off.[9]

Those biblical scholars who promote the view that the Flood was only local usually do so for scientific and archaeological reasons, trying to find the physical evidence

---

8   J. P. Free, 1956, *Archaeology and Bible History,* fifth ed. revised, Wheaton, IL: Scripture Press, 42.

9   F. A. Schaeffer, 1972, *Genesis in Space and Time: The Flow of Biblical History,* London: Hodder and Stoughton, 134.

in the vicinity of Mesopotamia in recent surficial geological deposits, because they accept without question the geological and archaeological dating that places the advent of man on the earth's surface hundreds of millions of years after the arrival of animals and billions of years after the formation of the earth itself. Thus, Kidner[10] and Youngblood[11] believe the Flood was confined to the Mesopotamian region, and thus the inundation of the earth was complete in the relative sense of Mesopotamia, supposedly the confines of world of mankind. However, while Kidner ignores the question of why the Ark would be needed at all if the Flood were only local, Youngblood sees no problem with Noah building a huge ark to escape a local flood. He comments on the purpose of the Ark:

> [The Ark was] more than simply a ship in which to ride out a flood. It was just as much a part of Noah's witness to his friends and neighbours as were his actual words. It served as a graphic warning to them that they could choose either to heed or ignore. Migration by Noah and his family [to escape the local flood] would not have had nearly the same powerful effect.[12]

However, if such an ark was really not needed, how can the reader of the Genesis account avoid the impression of unreality, absurdity, and even dishonesty in the whole Ark-building project? Significantly, however, some very recent biblical commentators such as Wenham,[13] Hamilton,[14] and Ross[15] focus almost exclusively on the text, showing far more concern with questions of textual interpretation rather than dealing with questions raised by the scientific and archaeological considerations. But they consistently avoid discussing the need for the Ark, perhaps because the inescapable conclusion from the text is that the Flood had to be global and geographically universal. Their silence is indicative of their discomfort in promoting the local flood view, because they know the text doesn't support that position, yet they likewise know that to promote a geographically universal, global flood would place them embarrassingly out of step with their scientific colleagues.

On the other hand, philosophers of science such as Ratzsch,[16] and scientists such as Johnson,[17] likewise avoid the question of why an ark of such enormous

10   Kidner, 1967, 94-96.

11   R. F. Youngblood, 1980, *How It All Began,* Ventura, CA: Regal Books.

12   Youngblood, 1980, 132.

13   Wenham, 1987.

14   V. P. Hamilton, 1990, *A New International Commentary on the Old Testament: The Book of Genesis Chapters 1-17,* Grand Rapids, MI: Eerdmans Publishing Company.

15   A. P. Ross, 1996.

16   D. Ratzsch, 1996, *The Battle of Beginnings: Why Neither Side is Winning the Creation-Evolution Debate,* Downers Grove, IL: InterVarsity Press.

17   M. R. Johnson, 1988, *Genesis, Geology and Catastrophism: A Critique of Creationist Science and Biblical*

dimensions needed to be built. They prefer instead to focus on the apparent scientific difficulties of the biblical Flood account, thus relegating Genesis to "dramatized history" or a "theological drama" designed to teach us about the holiness of God, His judgment against sin as an inevitable consequence, and the grace of God who personally acts to rescue His people from a corrupt and sinful world.[18]

However, one who is prepared to discuss the need for an ark is Morton.[19] He originally believed the Scriptures taught a global flood, but then growing doubts, due to the apparent conflict of the geological evidence with the biblical account of the Flood, resulted in a crisis of faith and a shift to promoting a local flood which occurred after billions of years of geological history. In answer to his own question, "But if there was a local flood, why wouldn't God simply have Noah and his sons climb the hills surrounding the Mediterranean?" Morton suggests two possible reasons:

> First, Noah and his sons could not preach to the people if they were gone. Presumably there was still enough room on his boat for a few late converts. Unfortunately there were none. After all, in a land such as the Mediterranean Basin, where rain had probably not been observed, who is going to believe a crazy old coot who claimed the land was going to be flooded? Secondly, as we will see, unless Noah was a long way from the basin (e.g., hundreds of kilometers), he would be just as likely to die as those who were at the bottom.[20]

Furthermore, Morton quotes Custance in order to support the contention that the Ark was not really that large after all, perhaps being "significantly smaller than is assumed by Whitcomb and Morris."[21] Yet as we have already seen, the dimensions for the Ark suggested by Whitcomb and Morris from the description given in the biblical account is almost universally supported by all Bible commentators and scholars, even those such as Kidner who support the local flood view.

So, the necessity of an ark to save air-breathing, land-dwelling creatures through the Flood is devastating to any compromise position with regard to the extent of the Flood. Even if only a small portion of the earth escaped the Flood, there would have been no need for an ark at all. The fact that Noah was commanded to build an ark "to the saving of his house" (Hebrews 11:7), and was commanded to bring in two of every kind of air-breathing, land-dwelling animal "to keep seed

---

Literalism, Exeter, UK: The Paternoster Press.

18   Johnson, 1988, 134.

19   G. R. Morton, 1995, *Foundation, Fall and Flood: A Harmonization of Genesis and Science*, Dallas, TX: D.M.D. Publishing Company.

20   Morton, 1995, 135.

21   Morton, 1995, 136.

alive upon the face of all the earth" (Genesis 7:3), proves conclusively that the Flood was geographically universal in scope. The only acceptable solution is to take the Scriptures for what they say—the Flood covered the entire globe.

7

THE TESTIMONY OF THE APOSTLE PETER

Outside of the book of Genesis itself, one of the most important biblical passages dealing with the magnitude of the Flood is 2 Peter 3:3-7.

> Knowing this first, that there shall come in the last days scoffers, walking after their own lusts, and saying, Where is the promise of his coming? For since the fathers fell asleep, all things continue as they were from the beginning of the creation. For this they willingly are ignorant of, that by the word of God the heavens were of old, and the earth standing out of the water and in the water: Whereby the world that then was, being overflowed with water, perished: But the heavens and the earth, which are now, by the same word are kept in store, reserved unto fire against the day of judgment and perdition of ungodly men.

In this passage from his second and last letter to the church, the apostle Peter, under the guidance of the Holy Spirit, writes of a day, yet future from his standpoint, when people would no longer think seriously of, or even believe in, Christ's Second Coming as a cataclysmic, universal intervention by God into the course of world affairs. The reason for this haughty skeptical attitude is a blind adherence to the doctrine of total uniformitarianism, a doctrine that maintains that natural laws and processes have in the past always continued as they do today, never having been interrupted by direct intervention of God in a total destruction of human civilization. We would thus be told by these skeptics that because such destruction by God's intervention has never been the case in past history, then there should be no cause to fear that it will ever occur in the future!

To answer these scoffers of the end-time, the apostle Peter pointed to two events in the past that cannot be explained on the basis of uniformitarianism, the belief that natural processes are all that have operated through time to produce all that is around us on the earth and in the heavens above us. The first of these two events was the creation of the world: "by the word of God the heavens were of old, and the earth"; and the second event was the Flood: "the world [*kosmos*] that then was, being overflowed with water, perished [*apoleto*]."

However, it is the second of these two events, the Flood, which served as the basis of Peter's comparison with the Second Coming of the Lord Jesus Christ and the final destruction of the world (cf. 2 Peter 3:7, 10 with Revelation 20:11-21:8). Just as "the world that then was" was destroyed by *water*, so "the heavens and the earth, which are now," protected as they are by God's eternal promise from another watery cataclysm (Genesis 9:11-19), nevertheless "by the same word are kept in store, reserved unto *fire* against the day of judgment and perdition of ungodly men."

The implications of this passage should be carefully examined with respect to the geographical extent of the Flood. In speaking of the events of the second and third days of creation (2 Peter 3:5), Peter used the terms "the heavens were of old, and the earth" in a sense that is obviously universal. By the same token, no one can deny that Peter also used terms "the heavens and the earth, which are now" (2 Peter 3:7) in the strictly universal sense. Otherwise, Peter would be speaking of the creation and final destruction of only a part of the earth!

The one event that the apostle Peter sets forth as having brought about a transformation, not only of the earth but also of the very *heavens*, was the Flood! It was the Flood that constituted the line of demarcation between "the heavens… of old" and "the heavens…which are now" in the Apostle Peter's thinking. It was the Flood that utilized the vast quantities of water out of which, and amidst which, the ancient earth had been "compacted" (the literal meaning of "the earth standing out of the water and in the water" in 2 Peter 3:5), to bring about the utter destruction of the *kosmos* "that then was." It was the Flood to which Peter also appealed as his final and incontrovertible answer to those who would choose to remain in willful ignorance of the fact that God had *at one time* in the past demonstrated His holy wrath and omnipotence by subjecting "all things" to an overwhelming, cosmic catastrophe that was on an absolute par with the final day of judgment, in which God will yet consume the earth with fire and will cause the very elements to dissolve with fervent heat (2 Peter 3:10).

If the Flood was limited to only the Mesopotamian region, it is difficult to see how Peter's appeal to the Flood would have any value as a contradiction to the doctrine of uniformitarianism, which assumes that "all things" have *never* yet been upset by a supernatural and universal cataclysm. Nor is it easy to excuse the apostle Peter of gross exaggeration and inaccuracy when he depicted the Flood in such cosmic terms and in such an absolutely universal context, if the Flood was in fact only a local inundation.

Unger emphasizes the crucial significance of Peter's statements in determining the magnitude and affects of the Flood:

> That the antediluvian era, described by Peter as "the world that then was," was obviously different climatically and geologically from the "heavens" and "the earth…that are now" (2 Peter 3:7), is clearly implied in the

Apostle's stern warning to naturalistic skeptics who mock at the idea of Christ's supernatural Second Advent on the ground that "all things continue as they were from the beginning of the creation" (2 Peter 3:4). Against the false naturalistic theory of uniformity, the Apostle urges the truth of supernatural catastrophism as evidenced by the Noahic Flood.[1]

It is instructive, therefore, that Kidner, a prominent advocate of the local flood theory, should comment:

> [W]e should be careful to read the [Flood] account whole-heartedly in its own terms, which depict a *total* judgment on the ungodly world already set before us in Genesis—not an event of debatable dimensions in a world we may try to reconstruct. The whole living scene is blotted out, and the New Testament makes us learn from it the greater judgment that awaits not only our entire globe but the universe itself (2 Peter 3:5-7).[2]

If "the New Testament makes us learn" from the Genesis Flood account that the coming judgment will involve "not only our entire globe but the universe itself," one must ask how this lesson can be learned from a flood that was only local in extent?

Similarly, the well-respected conservative scholar Michael Green questions whether Peter means to suggest that the whole earth was destroyed by the Flood, but then comments:

> The present heavens and earth would then be contrasted with the previous ones. It is just conceivable that our author believed that the whole universe had been renewed since the Flood...does Peter teach that the whole world will be destroyed by fire? There is no *a priori* reason why he should not.
>
> [A]nd so here, while we may not exclude the possibility that Peter is envisaging fiery destruction of the whole universe (by no means incredible to a generation which lives after Hiroshima), all that he actually says is

---

1   M. F. Unger, 1956, *Archaeology and the Old Testament,* third ed., Grand Rapids, MI: Zondervan Publishing House, 62. There are some writers who have applied 2 Peter 3:6 ("the world that then was, being overflowed with water, perished") to Genesis 1:2 instead of to Genesis 6-9—for example, J. S. Baxter, 1960, *Explore the Book,* Grand Rapids, MI: Zondervan Publishing House, 42. However, such an application is impossible for three reasons: (1) Genesis 1:2 does not speak of a world perishing by being overflowed with water, whereas four entire chapters of Genesis are devoted to a description of the Flood which fits the apostle Peter's description perfectly; (2) 2 Peter 3:5 describes the earth's condition during the second and third days of the Creation Week (Genesis 1:6-10), and the catastrophe of 2 Peter 3:6 obviously follows this; and (3) Peter has already referred to the Flood twice before in his two letters (1 Peter 3:20; 2 Peter 2:5), and therefore the context would demand that 2 Peter 3:6 refer to the same Flood. Baxter does not offer any proof for his interpretation, and the vast majority of commentators agree that Peter is referring to the Flood.

2   Kidner, 1967, 95.

that the heavens and the earth are kept in store for fire in anticipation of the judgment of ungodly men....The parallel between flood and fire is emphasized by the use of the same root in each case for "perished" (verse 6) and *perdition*.[3]

However, Lloyd-Jones did not hesitate to preach that, just as the coming destruction of the earth by fire would be global, the Flood was also global:

> Peter's argument on the facts is this. As God destroyed the old world, so God will destroy the present world....In exactly the same way the ancient world was there in apparent eternal stability, and God commanded the Flood. And the waters came down from the heavens and rose up out of the earth and the ancient world was destroyed....The world seems very stable, it seems fixed and immovable; but we must remember that the God who made and controls it and the entire cosmos is this Almighty God Who can bring things into being out of nothing, and destroy them in a moment, the God Who can handle the world and play with constellations as if they were but atoms. It is this Almighty God Who has reserved this world for punishment. As He has made it once and destroyed it, so with the same word He can destroy it again."[4]

After presenting support for the local flood interpretation of Genesis 6-9, Youngblood stated:

> The Apostle Peter, however, seems to assume that the Flood and its devastation were universal and total, except for Noah and his family.[5]

One would think that the statements of the apostle Peter should settle the matter of how the Genesis account must be understood. Elsewhere, Youngblood argues that Peter's use of the term *kosmos* (2 Peter 3:6) allows for a local flood,[6] but he admits that the immediate context (verses 5 and 7) "speak of the heavens and the earth in a clearly universal sense." This, it would surely seem, should indeed settle the matter.

Schaeffer also could not escape the clear implications from the testimony of the apostle Peter that the Flood was universal, that is, global in extent:

> In 2 Peter 3:3-7 the Flood is again paralleled to the Second Coming of

3   M. Green, 1968, *The Second Epistle General of Peter and the General Epistle of Jude: An Introduction and Commentary*, Tyndale Testament Commentaries, London: InterVarsity Press, 131-133.

4   D. M. Lloyd-Jones, 1983, *Expository Sermons on 2 Peter*, Edinburgh: The Banner of Truth Trust, 173-174.

5   R. F. Youngblood, 1985, *In the NIV Study Bible*, edited by K. Barker, Grand Rapids, MI: Zondervan Bible Publishers, 15.

6   Youngblood, 1980, 133.

Christ. Prior to the time when Jesus is to come, there will be scoffers who will say, "Where is the promise of His coming? For since the fathers fell asleep, all things continue as they were from the beginning of the creation." To paraphrase this in 20th-century language: "Where is the promise of His coming? There has been an absolute uniformity of natural causes in the closed system. Why are you talking about something catastrophic? It has always been like this, and we say it's going to keep on being like this." Peter explains this reaction: "For this they willingly are ignorant of, that by the word of God the heavens were of old, and the earth standing out of the water and in the water: whereby the world that then was, being overflowed with water, perished: but the heavens and the earth, which are now, by the same word are kept in store, reserved unto fire against the day of judgment and perdition of ungodly men." Thus past historical events in the time of Noah are paralleled with coming historical events. But there is a further note here—a note of universality. If the judgement at the Second Coming of Christ is taken to be universal, isn't the judgement by water at the time of Noah also universal? Christians who love the Scripture have discussed at length whether the Flood was universal or not. I believe it was…rather, the argument for universality rests on other factors, including the parallel between the Second Coming of Christ and the Flood as it is given in the New Testament passages we have just considered. The tone of the language that is used in Genesis suggests this as well. It seems to have a totality about it, the same kind of thrust as Genesis 1—a thrust conveying universality. For instance, in Genesis 7:23 we read, "And every living thing was destroyed [blotted out] that was upon the face of the ground, both man, and cattle, and the creeping things, and birds of the heavens; and they were destroyed [blotted out] from the earth: and Noah only was left, and they that were with him in the Ark." That sounds universal.[7]

Thus, in conclusion, the third chapter of 2 Peter provides powerful New Testament support for the geographical universality of the Flood. Anything less than a catastrophe of such proportions would upset the entire force of the apostle Peter's argument and would give much encouragement to those who teach what he so solemnly condemned.

---

7   Schaeffer, 1972, 132-133.

8

The Testimony of the Lord Jesus Christ

It would almost seem as though our Lord made a special point of choosing His illustrations and warnings from those portions of the Old Testament He knew would become objects of unbelieving scorn and ridicule by scoffers throughout future centuries. For example, in Matthew 19:4-6, He referred to the creation of Adam and Eve in the Garden of Eden; in Luke 17:29, to the destruction of Sodom by fire and brimstone from heaven; in Luke 17:32, to the transformation of Lot's wife into a pillar of salt; in Matthew 12:40, to the experience of Jonah in the whale's belly for three days and three nights; and in Luke 11:32, to the repentance of the Ninevites at the preaching of Jonah. Furthermore, in addition to all of these, the Lord Jesus Christ made special reference to Noah and the Flood in Luke 17:26-30, where we read in context:

> And as it was in the days of Noe, so shall it be also in the days of the Son of man. They did eat, they drank, they married wives, they were given in marriage, unto the day that Noah entered into the ark, and the flood came, and destroyed them all. Likewise also as it was in the days of Lot; they did eat, they drank, they sold, they planted, they builded; but the same day that Lot went out of Sodom it rained fire and brimstone from heaven, and destroyed them all. Even thus shall it be in the day when the Son of man is revealed. (cf. Matthew 24:39)

Of course, it is always very important to note the context of any statement in the Scriptures, and in this instance the context into which our Lord places the Flood destruction. It is placed alongside the destruction of Sodom and the destruction of the ungodly at the time of Christ's Second Coming, both events being compared with the Flood. Thus, first of all it is clear that our Lord regarded the Flood as just as much a literal and historical event as the destruction of Sodom in the days of Abraham and his nephew Lot in Genesis 19. Second, this context into which our Lord places the Flood destruction is of tremendous significance in helping us to determine what He was teaching with respect to the extent of the Flood, which is evident in the way He uses the word "all" in reference to those who were destroyed by the Flood.

The logic of the argument is as follows: the force of Christ's warning to the ungodly concerning the doom which awaits them at the time of His Second Coming, by reminding them of the destruction of the Sodomites, would be *immeasurably weakened* if we knew that *some* of the Sodomites had somehow escaped. This would offer hope to the ungodly that some of *them* might escape the wrath of God in that coming day of judgment when the Son of Man is revealed. However, we have absolutely no reason to think that any Sodomite escaped the destruction when the fire fell from heaven.

In exactly the same manner, Christ's warning to future generations, on the basis of what happened to the ungodly in the days of Noah, would have been pointless if part of the human race had somehow escaped the judgment of the Flood waters. In fact, the only characterization which our Lord made of those who perished in the Flood was that they ate, drank, married, and were given in marriage. Thus, those who argue that people living in other parts of the world in Noah's day may not have been as wicked as those who lived in the local area affected by the Flood should note well that our Lord's characterization did not involve degrees of ungodliness, but rather the utter absence of that positive godliness which was essential to salvation.

Therefore, Christ's use of the word "all" in Luke 17:27 must be understood in the absolute sense, for otherwise the analogies would collapse and the warnings would lose their force. A heavy burden of proof rests upon those, such as Ramm, who would maintain that only part of the human race was destroyed in the Flood,[1] in view of the clear statements of the Lord Jesus Christ.

Matthew 24:35-42 is a parallel passage in which the Lord Jesus Christ again compares His Second Coming with the destruction of the Flood. The emphasis and certainty that Jesus placed on the words of His own pronouncements should be noted in verse 35 ("Heaven and earth shall pass away, but my words shall not pass away"), so we do well to heed how the Lord Jesus viewed the extent of the Flood. Schaeffer comments:

> More striking yet is the parallel which Jesus drew between His own future space-time coming and the Flood in the past. Jesus emphasizes that His future Second Coming is a historic event, "but of the day and hour knoweth no man, no, not the angels of heaven, but my Father only. But as the days of Noah were, so shall also the coming of the Son of Man be" (Matthew 24:36-37). The word translated *coming* used throughout the New Testament in relation to Christ's Second Coming means *presence*. It is "a being alongside of," that is, there is coming a future time when Jesus will be present on the earth—historically, space-time present in the same way as He was on earth when He spoke these words. Jesus continues, "For as in the days before the Flood they were eating and drinking, marrying

---

and giving in marriage, until the day that Noah entered into the Ark, and knew not until the Flood came, and took them all away; so shall also the coming [here again *presence*] of the Son of Man be. Then shall two be in the field; the one shall be taken, and the other left. Two women shall be grinding at the mill; the one shall be taken, and the other left" (vv. 38-41). The parallel is interesting even in detail, for it takes up the normality of life on the earth before the Flood came and parallels it with the normality of life just before Jesus comes. Just as life was going along in an unbroken line and the Flood came, so life will be going on in an unbroken line and the first step in the Second Coming of Christ will occur.[2]

While Schaeffer is emphasizing that Noah's Flood is a historic event, his quoting of Jesus' words in this passage were to emphasize that Jesus was making a very specific comparison between the extent of the effect of His Second Coming with the extent of the effect of the Flood. That the Lord Jesus regarded the Flood as geographically global should be noted in verse 39, but also in the following verses where He warns that at the instant in time when He comes again it will be in the middle of the day in some places where men are working in the field, and early in the morning in other places where women will be grinding at the mill. In Luke 17:34, He adds that at the same moment in time when He comes there will be men in bed, it being night where they are living. It is only physically possible for it to be night, early morning, and the middle of day in different places all at the same moment in time if the Lord Jesus is referring to people living all around the globe. Thus, if the Flood came and took all people away in the same manner as His Second Coming will, when people are living, working, and sleeping all at the same moment but in different time zones all around the globe, then He was clearly teaching that the Flood was geographically universal and of global extent. We cannot escape the force of the absolutely reliable testimony of our Lord to the global extent of the Flood.

---

2   Schaeffer, 1972, 131.

9

The Total Destruction of a Widely-Distributed Human Race—All Mankind Perished

It should already be clear from the testimony of the Lord Jesus, which we have just noted, that the Flood was geographically global in extent, and therefore totally destroyed a widely-distributed human race, just as people involved in different pursuits around the globe will in the same instant at His Second Coming be likewise judged. This argument for a universal flood is thus based upon the biblical testimony of the total destruction of the human race outside of the Ark. Yet to be conclusive in demonstrating that the Flood was geographically global, this argument logically involves two sub-arguments:

1. That the Bible teaches all mankind perished in the Flood, and
2. That the human race had spread far beyond the area closest to where the Garden of Eden was, perhaps even all around the earth, by the time of the Flood.

There are four major reasons for believing that the Scriptures teach a total destruction of the pre-Flood human population, and three major reasons for believing that people had become widely distributed across the face of the earth by the time of the Flood.

All Mankind Perished

Even though there has been controversy about the Flood over the last 200 years, there has usually been little question among conservative Christian scholars as to the total destruction of the human race by the Flood. In 1845, it could be said without fear of contradiction:

> Among the Christian philosophers who dispute on this arena, there is a perfect agreement on the most important point, viz., that by the Flood, the *whole* population of the world was destroyed. With the Mosaic narrative before them, no other opinion could be entertained.[1]

---

1   C. Burton, 1845, *Lectures on the Deluge and the World After the Flood*, London: Hamilton, Adams and Co., 21.

Sadly, the same situation does not prevail today. Although there is a general unanimity of opinion amongst most evangelical scholars, there are exceptions, and therefore it is necessary to give the four biblical reasons that allow us to be adamant that the Bible unequivocally teaches a total destruction of the human race by the Flood.

1.   The moral purpose of the Flood.

The Flood must have destroyed the entire human population outside of the Ark because the Scriptures clearly state that the purpose of the Flood was to wipe out a sinful and degenerate humanity, and this purpose could not have been accomplished by destroying only those people living in a localized area, such as Mesopotamia. The most important relevant passages of Scripture are Genesis 6:5-7 and 11-13:

> And GOD saw that the wickedness of man was great in the earth, and that every imagination of the thoughts of his heart was only evil continually. And it repented the LORD that he had made man on the earth, and it grieved him at his heart. And the LORD said, I will destroy man whom I have created from the face of the earth; both man, and beast, and the creeping thing, and the fowls of the air; for it repenteth me that I have made them. (6:5-7)

> The earth also was corrupt before God, and the earth was filled with violence. And God looked upon the earth, and, behold, it was corrupt; for all flesh had corrupted his way upon the earth. And God said unto Noah, The end of all flesh is come before me; for the earth is filled with violence through them; and, behold, I will destroy them with the earth. (6:11-13)

The constant, almost monotonous repetition of phrases depicting the utter depravity of pre-Flood humanity can only make us astonished and dismayed. Every statement seems calculated to impress upon us the idea of *universal sin*; not just the exceptional sins of one group of people living in one region, nor even of specific times or occasions, but rather the sin of an entire age and an entire human population that had utterly corrupted its way upon the earth and was now ripe for the judgment of a Holy God:

> The appalling condition of things is summed up in a few terrible words, words which bellow and burn: *wickedness, evil imagination, corruption,* and *violence*; and these things were *great, widespread,* "in the earth," *continuous,* "only evil continually," *open* and *daring,* "before God," *replete,* "filled," and *universal,* "all flesh."

[T]his is an astounding event! After over 1,600 years of human history the race was so utterly corrupt morally that it was not fit to live; and of all mankind only four men and four women were spared, because they did not go with the great sin drift."[2]

Hamilton comments:

What God saw was both the extensiveness of sin and the intensiveness of sin. Geographically, the problem is an infested earth. Note that in 6:5-13, the *earth* (*hâ'âres*) is mentioned eight times. The description has all the appearances of a universal condition rather than a local one....the situation is further aggravated because such depravity controls not only man's actions, but also his thoughts...finally, this verse informs that this kind of malaise is a chronic condition, not just a spasmodic lapse. It is important to observe that right at the beginning there is a clear-cut moral motivation behind sending the Flood.[3]

In the light of these facts, it is unmistakably self-evident that God's clearly stated purpose of destroying "man whom I have created," because of his hopeless depravity and therefore in order to start afresh with Noah, could not have been accomplished by destroying only part of the human population and allowing the rest of Adam's descendents to continue in their sinful ways.

2.   The exceptional case of Noah.

The fact that all mankind, rather than just a part of the human population living at that time, was destroyed in the Flood is emphasized in the Scriptures by the repeated statements that Noah and his family were the *only* ones who escaped the judgment of the Flood waters. The relevant passages in Genesis read as follows:

But Noah found favor in the eyes of the LORD....Noah was a just man and perfect in his generations, and Noah walked with God (6:8-9).

[E]very thing that is in the earth shall die. But with thee will I establish my covenant; and thou shalt come into the ark, thou, and thy sons, and thy wife, and thy sons' wives with thee (6:17-18)....And the LORD said unto Noah, Come thou and all thy house into the ark; for thee have I seen righteous before me in this generation (7:1).

[A]nd they were destroyed from the earth: and Noah only remained alive, and they that were with him in the ark. And the waters prevailed upon the earth an hundred and fifty days. And God remembered Noah (7:23, 24; 8:1).

2   W. G. Scroggie, 1953, *The Unfolding Drama of Redemption*, vol. I, London: Pickering and Inglis, 74, 77.

3   Hamilton, 1990, 273.

Furthermore, to remove any lingering doubt as to whether or not Noah's family constituted the *sole* survivors of the Flood, there are two emphatic statements by the apostle Peter on this matter:

> [T]he long suffering of God waited in the days of Noah, while the ark was a preparing, wherein few, that is, eight souls were saved by water (1 Peter 3:20).

> And [God] spared not the old world [*kosmos*], but saved Noah the eighth person, a preacher of righteousness, bringing in the flood upon the world [*kosmos*] of the ungodly (2 Peter 2:5).

It is patently obvious from these passages that Noah was spared because of his righteous character, and that by the same reasoning, the Flood came to destroy others because they were unrighteous. If in fact only some of the people outside of the Ark were destroyed by the Flood, then we must conclude one of two things:

1. There were people outside of the Ark who were as righteous as Noah and thus were permitted by God to escape the Flood waters also; or
2. Having a righteous character was not the only factor that determined who was to escape the Flood.

Of these two alternatives, the first is quite inconceivable, because the exceptional and unique righteousness of Noah is emphasized repeatedly throughout the entire Bible (Genesis 5:29; 6:8, 9, 18; 7:1; 9:1; Ezekiel 14:14, 20; Hebrews 11:7; 2 Peter 2:5). The abysmal, universal wickedness of the pre-Flood people is attested to by an impressive array of scriptural testimony (Genesis 6:1-6, 11-13; Luke 17:26-27; 1 Peter 3:20; 2 Peter 2:5; Jude 14-15). To deny this is simply to deny the Word of God.

However, the second alternative is equally untenable, because the Scriptures give no hint anywhere that men were destroyed for any other reason than for their ungodliness. If any ungodly people actually did escape the Flood waters, then they must have done so by virtue of the fact that they did not happen to live in that particular area where the Flood came (assuming that the Flood was local), or else they were stronger or more ingenious than other sinners and thus, in one way or another, managed to escape the onrushing Flood waters. But if this were the case, then those who died in the waters did so only because they were unfortunate enough to be living in the wrong place or because they were not sufficiently strong or clever, and not simply because they were ungodly!

However, can such reasoning be tolerated by, and fitted into, a sane and sensible interpretation of the biblical doctrine of the Flood? Scholars may disagree on how the Scriptures should be interpreted, or even on whether the biblical record is to be accepted as authentic, trustworthy and credible. But if mature, trained scholars can examine the scriptural account of the Flood, in both the Old and New Testaments, and still conclude that the Bible *does not really intend to teach* that the Flood was sent to destroy *all ungodly men*, then the discipline of biblical interpretation degenerates into an unscientific, subjective game of words.

Consequently, both of the above-mentioned alternatives must be rejected without hesitation. The Scriptures *do* teach that the Flood destroyed all mankind outside of the Ark, because none outside of the Ark were godly and the Flood was sent by God to destroy the ungodly.

3. The testimony of the Lord Jesus Christ.

The Lord Jesus Christ stated that the Flood destroyed *all* men except Noah's family, just as the fire destroyed *all* Sodomites except Lot's family (Luke 17:26-30). Similarly, in Matthew 24:35-42, the Lord Jesus Christ compares the extent of His Second Coming with the extent of the judgment on the total human population at the time of the Flood. As already noted earlier, there can be no escape from the thrust of the absolute sense in which Jesus Christ used the word "all." If the Flood did not destroy all people outside of the Ark, then the Lord Jesus Christ could be accused of misleading comments designed to deceive, and thus He could hardly claim to be "the truth" (John 14:6).

4. God's covenant with Noah after the Flood.

One of the most difficult problems to be faced by those who deny that the Flood was anthropologically universal is the covenant which God made with Noah after the Flood had ended. If the Flood had destroyed only a part of the human race, then those who had escaped the Flood waters would not have been included in the covenant of the rainbow. God three times repeated the promise never to wipe out "everything living" and "all flesh" again by a flood (Genesis 8:21; 9:11, 15). This makes it totally impossible to accept the view that only part of the human race was destroyed by the Flood. Otherwise, only toward the descendants of Noah would the birds, beasts, and fishes show fear and dread (Genesis 9:2); they only would be prohibited from eating flesh with blood (Genesis 9:3-4); and they only would have the authority to take life (Genesis 9:5-6).

If God's covenant with Noah means anything at all, then it must be a covenant with the entire human race. On the other hand, if it is insisted that the terms used here are to be understood in a limited sense, then we have to conclude that God has broken His promise repeatedly because millions have perished in vast, destructive local floods in many parts of the earth since God made this promise. The same argument is decisive against the view that the Flood was only geographically local though anthropologically universal, because God promised not only to spare all of mankind from another flood, but "everything living" and also *the earth itself* (Genesis 8:21; 9:11; Isaiah 54:9). The Scriptures repeatedly state that God made this covenant of the rainbow with Noah and his sons (Genesis 9:1-17), so therefore the whole of mankind has descended from Noah's family and the Flood destroyed the entire pre-Flood human population. Schultz concluded:

> Had any part of the human race survived the Flood outside of Noah and his family they would not have been included in the covenant God made here. The implication seems to be that all mankind descended from Noah so that the covenant with its bow in the cloud as a reminder would be for all mankind.[4]

Similarly, Davis Young, Geology Professor at Calvin College and a vocal proponent of interpreting Scripture consistent with conventional long-ages geology, has had to admit:

> The biblical data tend to support the idea that the flood was essentially global in nature, although it is worthy of consideration that the story was written from the point of view of an individual experiencing the flood. The arguments for a local flood seem to be rendered rather weak in the light of God's promise never again to cut off all flesh or destroy the earth with a flood (Genesis 9:11), a promise that seems to have universal implications.

> ...[T]he flood was a cataclysmic *judgment* upon a wicked human race whose every imagination of the thoughts of the heart was only evil continually; moreover, the flood was a *means of gracious deliverance and salvation* for Noah and his family, who found grace in God's eyes.[5]

---

4   S. S. Schulz, 1955, The Unity of the Race: Genesis 1-11, *Journal of the American Scientific Affiliation VII*, 52.

5   D. A. Young, 1977, *Creation and the Flood: An Alternative to Flood Geology and Theistic Evolution*, Grand Rapids, MI: Baker Book House, 172-173.

10

THE TOTAL DESTRUCTION OF A WIDELY-DISTRIBUTED HUMAN RACE—THE HUMAN RACE HAD SPREAD AROUND THE EARTH

Those who acknowledge the tremendous weight of biblical testimony concerning the total destruction of the human race outside of the Ark, and yet who are still unwilling to admit that the Flood was geographically universal, usually maintain that mankind had not spread beyond the limits of the Mesopotamian region during the period from Adam to Noah. However, such a position cannot be successfully defended for at least three reasons.

Longevity and Population Growth

The remarkable longevity and fecundity of pre-Flood mankind strongly imply a rapid increase of population during the *minimum* of 1,656 years which elapsed between Adam and the Flood. Even a cursory examination of Genesis 5 reveals some rather startling statistics.

In that chapter, we read that Adam lived 930 years, Seth 912, Enosh 905, Kenan 910, Mahalalel 895, Jared 962, Enoch 365 (he did not die, being translated into God's presence), Methuselah 969, Lamech 777, and Noah 950. The average of these ages, omitting Enoch, is 912 years. In stark contrast, after the Flood we read in Genesis 11 that Shem lived for only 600 years, Arphaxad 438, Salah 433, Eber 464, Peleg 239, Reu 239, Serug 430, Nahor 148, and Terah (the father of Abraham) 205 years. Several generations later, we read in Genesis 50:26 that Joseph died at 110 years, the declining lifespans continuing with David living only 70 years (2 Samuel 5:4-5; 1 Kings 2:11).

These details are plotted on a graph in Figure 1 (page 441), along with the ages of the patriarchs at maturity, which in this instance has been defined as a patriarch's age when his first son was born. Adam, of course, is an exception, as is Enoch, who did not die. It is quite obvious upon viewing this graph that something extremely significant happened at the time of the Flood, because the lifespans of the patriarchs began immediately to decline drastically in what appears to be close to an exponential decay curve. Of course, this also assumes that Genesis 5 and

11 are complete genealogies with no generations missing, and that the ages given for the patriarchs are literal and not exaggerations. Sadly, there are some biblical scholars who insist that the numbers given in Genesis 5 and 11 are not literally true but instead follow some discernable pattern that has theological significance,[1] or represent folklore with parallels to the Sumerian king lists.[2]

However, Kidner admits that "reinterpretations of the longevity of these men are less than happy....as far as we can tell, then, the life-spans are intended literally."[3] Furthermore, any supposed relationships with the Sumerian king lists have largely been abandoned, with the most complete refutation that of Hasel.[4] Also, the best summary refuting all the arguments raised against these being literal long ages for the patriarchs is provided by Borland.[5] Wenham has summed up the situation:

> Much ingenuity has been devoted to these problems but without conspicuous success. It is often suggested that the years of Genesis 5 may have been much shorter than ours, perhaps equivalent to a month or two. But the Flood story makes it quite clear that the years of Genesis were about 360 days.
>
> ...Another suggestion (W. H. Green, *BSAC* [1890] 285-303) is that the genealogy is not intended to be complete, that generations have been omitted, and therefore it should not be used for chronological purposes. However, the Hebrew gives no hint that there were large gaps between father and son in this genealogy. 4:25 makes it clear that Seth was Adam and Eve's third son. At the other end of the genealogy, Lamek [i.e., Lamech] comments on Noah's birth, and Ham, Shem and Japet [Japheth] were contemporaries of their father. It therefore requires special pleading to postulate long gaps elsewhere in the genealogy. Attempts to explain the great ages of the patriarchs by reference to ancient Near Eastern parallels are also disappointing.[6]

There is thus no alternative but to take these genealogies and the long ages of the patriarchs as literal history.

---

1   D. L. Christensen, Did People Live to be Hundreds of Years Old before the Flood? No, in *The Genesis Debate: Persistent Questions about Noah and the Flood*, 1990, ed. R.F. Youngblood, Grand Rapids, MI: Baker Book House, chapter 8, 166-183.

2   U. Cassuto, 1961, A Commentary on the Book of Genesis, Jerusalem: Magnes Press; J. Walton, 1981, The Antediluvian Section of the Sumerian King List in Genesis 5, Biblical Archaeologist, 44: 207-208.

3   Kidner, 1967, 83.

4   G. F. Hasel, 1978, The Genealogies of Genesis 5 and 11 and Their Alleged Babylonian Background, *Andrews University Seminary Studies*, 16: 361-374.

5   J. A. Borland, 1990, Did People Live to be Hundreds of Years Old Before the Flood? Yes, in *The Genesis Debate: Persistent Questions About Creation and the Flood*, ed. R.F. Youngblood, Grand Rapids, MI: Baker Book House, chapter 8, 166-183.

6   Wenham, 1987, 133.

The fact, then, is that something extremely significant happened to man at the time of the Flood to cause this drastic decline in the ages of the post-Flood patriarchs. Of course, the Flood was a global cataclysm which engulfed the whole earth, so it is possible that environmental factors which affect the aging process in man could have drastically changed as a consequence. Thus, it is unclear what the scientific explanation is, but we do know of some dozen major factors which affect human lifespans. These include:

1. radiation from radioisotopes (uranium, thorium, radium, potassium) in rocks and soils
2. cosmic radiation
3. biochemically "programmed" cell death (apoptosis)
4. accumulated genetic mutations (genetic load)
5. disease
6. inadequate nutrition
7. chemical carcinogens
8. ultraviolet radiation
9. solar x-ray radiation
10. inadequate exercise
11. metabolic rate
12. stress

Looking at this list, it is not hard to see that some of these factors could have been radically different prior to the Flood, thus enabling the patriarchs to live such long ages, whereas with the cataclysmic upheavals of the Flood there could have been sufficient changes which then had an increasing affect in the post-Flood world leading to the drastic decline in human lifespans. From a medical point of view, therefore, such long human lifespans are conceivable given our knowledge of the factors controlling the aging process. However, the fact that the death of our cells seems to be biochemically "programmed" does suggest that our Creator could have foreordained human lifespans pre-programmed, and then later could have readjusted that programming. In any case, it is clear that there are possible physical explanations for the pre-Flood human longevity and for its decline after the Flood, which will be discussed again later in the context of the possible scientific details of the Flood. However, it has been important thus far to recognize the reality of these literal human lifespans because significant consequences follow with respect to the world population before the Flood.

The details elaborated upon in Genesis 5 clearly imply that the pre-Flood patriarchs had large families. Although in most cases only one son is named in each family (which was obviously for the purpose of tracing the line of descent from Adam to Noah), we are also told that each "begat sons and daughters" in addition to the primary son, so each family must have thus had at *least* five children, and probably many more. Furthermore, the ages of the fathers at the births of each of the *named* sons ranged from 65 years (in the case of Mahalalel and Enoch) to 500 years (in the exceptional case of Noah). This observation also adds credence to the biblical record of the longevity of the patriarchs, because after the Flood when lifespans drastically declined, the ages of the patriarchs at the births of their named sons likewise declined proportionally, except for some notable exceptions (see Figure 1). Consequently, the Scriptures imply that before the Flood:

1. Men typically lived for hundreds of years.
2. Their procreative powers persisted over hundreds of years also.
3. Thus, through the combined affects of long lives and large families, mankind was rapidly "filling the earth" (Genesis 6:1, 11), just as God had commanded (Genesis 1:28).

Taking all factors into consideration, it is entirely reasonable to estimate that each family had six children and each new generation required ninety years on average. This assumes the first family (Adam and Eve) had six children, the three families that could be established from these had six children each, and the nine families resulting from these each had six children, and so on. In all probability, each family had far more than six children, but this figure will allow for those who did not marry, who died prematurely, etc. If we allow a generation span to be ninety years on average, which seems far higher than was probably the case, then there would have been eighteen generations in the 1,656 years from Adam to the Flood.

Whitcomb and Morris provide a simple calculation.[7] The total number of people in the nth generation can be calculated on this basis as equal to $2(3)^n$. Thus, at the end of the first generation (n = 1), the number in the family would have been $2(3)$, or 6. At the end of two generations, it would have been $2(3)^2$, or 18. Repeating the calculations through the sequence of generations, at the end of seventeen generations, the number would have been 258 million, and at the end of eighteen generations, it would have been 774 million! If at the time of the Flood only one previous generation was still living, then the total population of the earth would have then been over one billion! Of course, these calculations are extremely conservative and only assume the truth of the biblical record. Morris stated, "If we use rates appropriate in the present world…over 3 billion people could easily have been on the earth at the time of Noah."[8]

Such rates of population increase are hardly unreasonable given the current world population "explosion." The present world population is more than seven billion. The three billion mark was estimated to have been passed in 1962, and so at the present rate of growth of approximately two percent per year, the world population doubled in less than forty years. Of course, earlier population increases are believed to have been lower due to the effects of war, disease, and starvation, but

---

7   Whitcomb and Morris, 1961, 26.

8   H. M. Morris, 1984, *The Biblical Basis of Modern Science*, Grand Rapids, MI: Baker Book House, 421.

on the other hand, without birth control measures families were often larger than they are today. Nevertheless, Morris has calculated, using standard population growth models, that the present world population could have been produced in the 4,300-4,500 years estimated since the Flood from Noah and his three sons at a growth rate of only 0.5 percent per year, which is a quarter of the present growth rate.[9]

All of these calculations, therefore, show that it is entirely feasible to suggest that by the time of the Flood there could have been a population between one and three billion people inhabiting the earth. The very fact that the pre-Flood patriarchs lived to such great ages would indicate that famine and disease were not serious problems that would have significantly restrained a rapid population increase in the pre-Flood period. In the early centuries especially, there would have been every reason to have as many children as possible, and thus multiplication would have been very rapid. In any case, the whole purpose of these calculations and this estimate is to show that a population of one to three billion people could hardly have been confined to one particular area, such as the Mesopotamian Valley suggested by local flood advocates. Instead, for all practical purposes, such a large number of people would have of necessity spread far and wide to have literally "filled the earth" as described in the Scriptures. Indeed, an estimated population of one billion people would be equivalent to the estimated population of the earth in 1850, the earliest date for which there is any really accurate estimate of world population, and the entire earth could certainly have been described at that time as having been "filled." Such would have been the case even more so when the world population is estimated to have been three billion in about 1962. Thus, the extensive distribution of the pre-Flood population necessitated by the rapid population increase to one to three billion people by the time of the Flood would have required the Flood waters to be global in extent in order to destroy all of mankind not on the Ark.

The Prevalence of Violence

Early in the controversy over the geographical extent of the Flood, the most common arguments for a limited pre-Flood population, as set forth by Smith,[10] Hitchcock,[11] and Miller,[12] were that the extreme sinfulness of mankind then made rapid population growth impossible, and that the patriarchs did not beget children until late in life, with only a few children being mentioned even then. However, the Scriptures clearly say that "the *earth*" itself was "*filled*" with

9   Morris, 1984, 425-426.

10   J. P. Smith, 1854, *The Relation Between the Holy Scriptures and some parts of Geological Science,* 5th ed., London: Henry G. Bohn, 269-270.

11   E. Hitchcock, 1852, *The Religion of Geology and its connected Sciences,* Boston: Phillips, Sampson and Co., 132.

12   H. Miller, 1875, *The Testimony of the Rocks,* New York: Robert Carter and Brothers, 316-319.

"violence" (Genesis 6:11, 13). In other words, the very text that has been put forward in support of the population being limited because of rampant violence is actually upon closer examination even more effective in arguing for the universal distribution of the pre-Flood human population. Furthermore, if we were to make a valid analogy with post-Flood history, then we would prove beyond any doubt that extreme sinfulness, strife, and violence in human society are factors that force the scattering, rather than the centralizing, of groups of people. The history of the Indian tribes in the Americas and of the Gothic and Germanic tribes in Europe clearly illustrates this fact. Also, nations that today boast the world's highest birth rates, such as India and Indonesia, are not necessarily the most righteous!

The related argument against a large pre-Flood population has been that children were not born until the patriarchs were well advanced in years, and that even then few children are named in the genealogies of Genesis. For example, Noah lived 500 years before his first son was born, and then only three sons are named. However, such an argument is refuted by the following considerations:

1. Noah must have been the exception to the rule, because with *every other patriarch* the phrase "begat sons and daughters" is used.
2. Noah did not have any children until he was 500 years old (which cannot be proved), then he was also the exception, because all the other patriarchs had children when they were less than 200 years old, and most of them (if we include Adam) when they were less than 130 years old.
3. The fact that Noah was 500 years old when his three sons were born is important, because it proves that the patriarchs were capable of begetting children for hundreds of years.
4. It is possible that the sons named in Genesis 5 were *not* the firstborn sons in each case, because we know that Adam had sons and daughters (Cain, Abel, and Cain's wife, at the very least) long before we read in Genesis 5:3, "and Adam lived an hundred and thirty years and begat a son in his own likeness, after his image; and called his name Seth."
5. God's command to Adam and his descendants was to "be fruitful, and multiply, and replenish [fill] the earth" (Genesis 1:28), and this command was obeyed "when men began to multiply on the face of the earth" (Genesis 6:1).

Sauer has commented:

> Already in the time of Cain, apparently in his advanced age, a city could be built (probably at first simply an established colony), Genesis 4:17. This is the less astonishing, since the life-energy of the youthful race must at the beginning have been very powerful. Also, with the long lives of the parents, the number of children must have been much greater than later on; and, for the same reason, many generations must have lived alongside of each other at the same time. With an average of only six children per

family, by the time Cain was only 400 years old he would have had far more than 100,000 descendants.[13]

Keil suggested that one explanation for the amazing longevity of the pre-Flood patriarchs was "that the after-effects of the condition of man in paradise would not be immediately exhausted," and that "this longevity, moreover, necessarily contributed greatly to the increase of the human race."[14] To this may be added the comments by Sutcliffe:

> In view of the insistence shown by the sacred writer on the multiplication of the race by the repeated declaration that each of the patriarchs begat "sons and daughters," and that he allows so much time between Adam and the Flood (MT 1656 years, Samaritan text 1307, LXX 2256), it is hardly to be assumed that he thought all men could still be living in one region. In fact, the text indicates the contrary, for God not only gave the command to increase and multiply, but also to "fill the earth," 1:28.[15]

Some have argued for a limited geographical distribution of only a relatively small pre-Flood human population, because the preaching of Noah had to be within the hearing of all people alive at that time. For example, Custance has commented that:

> If people were living at that time in Europe and the Far East and, which is worse, in the New World, it is exceedingly doubtful whether they could ever have heard his [Noah's] message. The very method by which God forewarned men implies the situation in which the population of the world was still fairly well congregated.[16]

However, nowhere in Scripture are we told that the preaching of Noah was within the hearing of all the people living in his day. The apostle Peter says that Noah was "a preacher of righteousness" (2 Peter 2:5), and the author of Hebrews tells us that Noah by faith "prepared an ark to the saving of his house; by the which he condemned the world" (Hebrews 11:7). But this is not equivalent to saying that Noah preached directly to all the people alive in his day.

While it is true that multitudes of people may have heard Noah's impassioned warnings directly, Noah's condemnation of the world undoubtedly was due to the stark contrast between his godly and believing life with the utterly corrupt lives of

---

13   E. Sauer, 1964, *The Dawn of World Redemption*, trans. G.H. Lang, Exeter, U.K.: Paternoster Press, 67.

14   C. F. Keil, 1951, *Biblical Commentary on the Old Testament*, vol. I, trans. J. Martin, vol. I, Grand Rapids, MI: Eerdmans Publishing Company, 123-124.

15   E. F. Sutcliffe, 1953, *Genesis, A Catholic Commentary on Holy Scripture*, New York: Thomas Nelson and Sons, 190.

16   Custance, 1979, 34-35. Ramm, 1964, 163, attempts to use the same argument to prove that the Flood was anthropologically local, affecting only a small part of the human race.

all others in his time, as Genesis 6:9 tells us that "Noah was a just man and perfect in his generations, and Noah walked with God." Only to him could God say: "Come thou and all thy house into the ark, for thee have I seen righteous before me in this generation" (Genesis 7:1). The fact that no other person of that time had Noah's faith and righteousness brought condemnation upon the world. Faith that produced *obedience* (Genesis 6:22), even to the point of building the Ark, was the only kind of faith that could bring deliverance from the judgment of the Flood. No one else of Noah's day had that kind of faith which produced complete obedience, so therefore the world was condemned. Similarly, only relatively few people in the world ever saw the Lord Jesus Christ during His earthly ministry, but it is nevertheless true that "the world knew him not" (John 1:10), and "this is the condemnation, that light is come into the world, and men loved darkness rather than light, because their deeds were evil" (John 3:19).

However, even if the fact that Noah's Ark-building faith "condemned the world" is meant to imply that everyone in the world heard the warnings of Noah about the coming Flood judgment, it would by no means follow that all mankind at that time had to be confined to one small region of the earth. During the 120-year period of grace "when once the longsuffering of God waited in the days of Noah, while the ark was a preparing" (Genesis 6:3; 1 Peter 3:20), the news of Noah's remarkable activities and alarming warnings could easily have spread throughout the entire earth. After all, with a population of between one and three billion people in Noah's day all speaking the same language, and with the technology capable of building cities and an oceangoing boat like the Ark with metal tools, it is to be expected the news of Noah's words and his sensational Ark-building enterprise could easily have spread to a globally-scattered population in the time available.

Thus, in summary, it is easy to understand how the earth could have been filled with people by the time of the Flood when we realize the enormous extent of pre-Flood human longevity and fecundity, plus God's command to "fill the earth" (Genesis 1:28), *and* that by the time of Noah the earth is described as being "filled with violence" (Genesis 6:11). The characteristics of patriarchal family life and the wickedness of pre-Flood mankind are both recorded in the Scriptures as indicative of an enormous, widely-scattered, pre-Flood human population which was condemned because of Noah's righteousness, not because he preached to them all.

Human Fossil Evidence

Because all local flood advocates accept the uniformitarian geological timescale for the earth's rocks, most of the earth's history had occurred by the time Noah and his contemporaries were living in what they regard as the Mesopotamian Valley. Depending then on when they date the Flood as occurring will determine how they accommodate the evidence of human fossil remains in widely scattered areas of the earth. There is, of course, considerable debate over the demarcation line between which ancient fossils are genuinely human and which are not, but it is nevertheless apparent that of those fossil remains which all agree are genuinely human, most are found hundreds, and even thousands, of kilometers from the Mesopotamian Valley.

This leaves local flood advocates with a number of dilemmas. If they insist the Flood was both geographically local and anthropologically universal, then they are forced to maintain one of two possibilities:

1. All these genuine human fossils have to be post-Flood, and thus the Flood pre-dates them.
2. Some of the genuine human fossils are pre-Flood and of people who died before the Flood, but when the Flood itself came, all existing humans for some reason had moved into the Mesopotamian Valley.

Local flood advocates largely base their stance on a conviction that radioisotope and radiocarbon dates are correct and that true humans have existed for 150,000 to 250,000 years. This implies that if all these genuine human remains are post-Flood, then the date for the Flood is so early that the advent of civilization after the Flood (generally understood to be only about 5,000-10,000 years ago according to radiocarbon dates) would be so far removed time-wise from the Flood itself that the resulting chronology could not be reconciled either with the scriptural record or with the secular view of history. On the other hand, if the Flood was more recent, after the dawn of civilization but still anthropologically universal, then those pre-Flood human populations logically could not have continued to live in those distant regions where more ancient human fossils are found, but must somehow have migrated back into Mesopotamian Valley so that all of them could then be drowned in a limited flood confined to the Mesopotamian Valley. Yet the fossil evidence does not allow this latter option. There were Indians, for example, living in North and South America across the interval that civilization arose in the Near East. There is no evidence whatever they migrated to the Mesopotamian Valley at any point during the past 10,000 years according to the radiocarbon timescale.

It would therefore seem that in this confusing maze of options, for local flood advocates to accept both the uniformitarian geological timescale and the secular interpretation of history, yet remain as faithful as possible to the Scriptures, they must date the Flood as fairly recent, not long before the dawn of civilization in the Mesopotamian Valley, but must logically conclude that those genuine human remains which are far older in secular terms and are found in regions far distant to the Mesopotamian Valley therefore must pre-date the Flood. That is, to be consistent they must conclude that the Flood was not only geographically local, but anthropologically local also, which is the view taken by both Ramm and Custance.

However, to maintain this view, advocates must reject the clear teaching of the Scriptures that God sent the Flood to destroy *all* of mankind, whose every intent of the thoughts of their hearts was only evil continually, resulting in the earth being overwhelmed with violence. Moreover, the evidence of genuine human fossil remains in widely scattered areas of the earth makes it even more difficult to maintain that men did not migrate beyond the Mesopotamian Valley before the time of the Flood. Once having done so, men would not have needed to spread very far before *some* would have occupied higher ground, which thus required a flood of considerable depth, and logically, of global extent to destroy them.

On the other hand, if the uniformitarian geological timescale is rejected, and the Flood was a global cataclysm that engulfed the whole earth and reshaped its surface, then the genuine human fossils found in widely scattered areas across the earth's surface logically must be the remains of post-Flood people who migrated from the Mesopotamian region after the Flood. Although the Mesopotamian Valley is the area Noah and his descendants settled after the Flood, it is important to realize that this geographic feature did not even exist in its present form prior to the Flood. The earth's surface was radically transformed during the Flood by large-scale tectonic processes that tore continents apart, covered continental surfaces with sediments eroded and transported by the Flood waters, and created new mountain ranges (more of this later). Thus, the paleontological evidence of human remains is consistent with a recent global Flood, once the uniformitarian geological timescale is abandoned.

Obviously, the evidence from paleontology presents some extremely embarrassing problems for those who believe that the Flood was local and that all the pre-Flood people were destroyed by the Flood because they were confined to the region of Mesopotamia. People would have not needed to have spread very far from the Mesopotamian Valley before some at least would have occupied higher ground, which in turn requires a flood of considerable depth, which then also implies global extent. This has led many to conclude that the Flood must also have been anthropologically local. But as we have seen, this flies in the face of the repeated statements in Scripture that God intended to use the Flood as a judgment on a wicked human race that had filled the earth with violence. Of course, it would only take the finding of one genuine pre-Flood human fossil in some region remote from Mesopotamia to put beyond doubt the global extent of the Flood. Nevertheless, we ultimately do not need that evidence when the Scriptures are so clear and decisive in their description of a year-long, mountain-covering Flood, which we are told in Genesis 6:13 was designed not only to judge pre-Flood mankind, but to destroy the earth with them.

11

Summary and Conclusion

The geographical universality of the Flood as a mountain-covering, globe-engulfing event has been established from *eight major biblical arguments*:

1. The scriptural record of the Flood clearly states that the Flood waters rose and prevailed upon the earth, covering all the mountains under the whole heaven for a period of five months, and that an additional seven months were then required for the waters to subside sufficiently for Noah and his family to disembark from the Ark in the mountains of Ararat.

2. The Bible says that the waters of the Flood covered the highest mountains to a depth at least sufficient for the Ark to float over them.

3. The expression "fountains of the great deep were broken up" is clearly indicative of vast geological disturbances during the Flood, which are totally incompatible with the concept of a local flood, especially when these geological disturbances are said to have continued for five months.

4. The construction of the Ark with a capacity of at least 41,000 cubic meters just for the purpose of carrying eight people and a few animals through a local flood is utterly inconceivable.

5. If the Flood was only geographically limited, then there would have been no need for an ark at all, for there would have been plenty of time for Noah's family to escape from the danger area, as would be the case also for the birds and animals.

6. The apostle Peter's use of the Flood as a basis for refuting uniformitarian skeptics in the last days, as well as using the Flood as a forewarning of the judgment by fire to come at the "day of the Lord," would have been absolutely pointless if the Flood had merely been of local extent, especially when the cosmic setting into which Peter placed the Flood cataclysm (2 Peter 3:3-7) is considered.

7. The Lord Jesus Christ unhesitatingly compared the human conditions and what happened at the Flood with human conditions and what will happen at the time of his Second Coming, which would mean that if the Flood was not global, then Jesus' Second Coming will likewise not be global, and thus Jesus was misleading and/or not telling us the truth, which of course is absolutely inconceivable given who the Lord Jesus Christ is as the Creator Himself.

8. The human race had to have been widely distributed at the time of the Flood, and therefore could not have been destroyed by a local flood.

There are four biblical reasons for the necessity of the total destruction of pre-Flood humanity by the Flood:

1. Because the stated purpose of the Flood was the punishment of sinful mankind, such a purpose could not have been accomplished if only part of pre-Flood humanity had been so judged.
2. The purpose of the Flood to destroy all of mankind is conclusively underlined by the repeated statements in Genesis, 1 Peter, and 2 Peter that *only* Noah and his family were spared.
3. The Lord Jesus Christ clearly stated that all men were destroyed by the Flood (Luke 17:26-30).
4. God's covenant with Noah after the Flood becomes totally meaningless if only part of the human population in Noah's day had been destroyed by the Flood.

Additionally, three reasons were given for believing that the pre-Flood human population could not have been confined to today's Mesopotamian Valley at the time of the Flood:

1. The longevity and fecundity of the pre-Flood patriarchs would have resulted in a very rapid population growth, so that even if there were only 1,656 years between Adam and the Flood, the population in Noah's day could have been between one and three billion people.
2. The Genesis account describes the earth as being "filled" with violence, an inevitable result due to the prevalence of strife and violence, encouraging the people to separate and thus become widely distributed rather than being confined to a single locality.
3. The evidence of genuine human fossils in widely scattered parts of the world makes it very difficult for local flood advocates to insist that men did not migrate beyond the Mesopotamian region before the time of the Flood and still be faithful to the details of the scriptural account.

If these basic arguments are carefully weighed by Bible-believing Christians, then they should prove to be sufficiently powerful and compelling to convincingly settle the long-debated question of the geographical extent of the Flood. Of course, this does not discount the perceived serious scientific difficulties that a universal flood entails, but such matters will be examined in the pages to follow. However, it is insisted that no problem, be it scientific or philosophical, can be of sufficient magnitude to offset the combined force of these eight biblical arguments for the Genesis Flood in the days of Noah being geographically universal.

Section II

NON-GEOLOGICAL ARGUMENTS USED AGAINST THE GLOBAL GENESIS FLOOD

12

INTRODUCTION

In the preceding section clear and compelling arguments were presented to demonstrate that the Genesis Flood was global both geographically and anthropologically. The evidence points to the fact that the entire human population outside of the Ark perished in the Flood, which therefore engulfed the entire globe.

However, while conservative Christian scholars in the past were practically unanimous in their adherence to this view, recently there has been an increasing tendency among them, on supposedly scientific grounds, to accept the view that the flood simply could not have destroyed the entire human race except for Noah's family. This departure from the traditionally-held view of a geographically and anthropologically global Flood based on the Scriptures arose from the perceived reliability of the prevailing interpretation of geological evidence, which has, in turn, led many evangelical Christian scholars to err further and deny that the entire human race was involved in the Flood, which of course results in a complete capitulation to non-Christian thinkers who scoff at the entire biblical account of the Flood.

Most objections voiced by conservative Christian scholars for a geographically global flood are related directly to the modern interpretation of geological data. These arguments will be considered in great detail in subsequent sections. However, there are a number of major objections that are not strictly geological in nature, so it is the goal of this and the following chapters to examine these objections, beginning with arguments used against an anthropologically universal Flood. After all, if it could be shown on scientific grounds that the Flood did not destroy the entire human race in the days of Noah, then efforts to defend a geographically universal Flood would be pointless.

In the controversial volume *The Christian View of Science and Scripture*, published in 1954, the Baptist scholar Bernard Ramm challenged the evangelical world to relinquish its "hyperorthodox" attitude toward uniformitarian science and surrender the notion that the Flood was universal in either a geographical or anthropological sense.[1] Other evangelical scholars have since looked with favor upon this view, so that it is increasingly prevalent today. Thus, for example, Davis Young, former Professor of Geology at Calvin College, Grand Rapids, Michigan, has written:

> The development of new techniques for dating archeological materials, especially the radiocarbon method, has given us a much more detailed understanding of the structure of human and animal history during the past few tens of thousands of years. Archeology and paleontology are sufficiently constrained by well-documented chronological data to have established beyond a reasonable doubt that there is no known physical or paleontological evidence for a global flood. It is manifestly clear that mammoths and their contemporaries did not die in such a catastrophe, and, if we accept the Biblical testimony that human beings had mastered the arts of agriculture and metalworking prior to the flood, it is also clear that the mammoths died out long before the flood could have occurred in any case. In addition, the fossil record of North American caves provides another compelling line of evidence against the concept of worldwide animal migration to the ark.
>
> Archeology has firmly demonstrated that the civilization described in Genesis 4 was in place by at least 6000 BC, thus constraining the Biblical deluge to a date more recent than that, and evidence associated with the Gilgamesh epic seems to imply that the Biblical deluge would have to have occurred closer to 3000 BC. Archeological evidence rules out the occurrence of a widespread deluge ten or twenty thousand years ago. Most of those who support the notion that a deluge occurred at that more distant date are seeking to establish the viability of an event that, even if confined to the Near East, could have destroyed the whole human race. But archeological investigations have established the presence of human beings in the Americas, Australia, and southeastern Asia long before the advent of the sort of Near Eastern civilization described in the Bible and thus long before the Biblical deluge could have taken place. In the light of the wealth of mutually supportive evidence from a variety of disciplines and sources, it is simply no longer tenable to insist that a deluge drowned every human on the face of the globe except Noah's family.[2]

It is therefore imperative that we first examine the arguments that are so forcefully used to dismiss the biblical arguments for a geographically universal Flood.

Before doing so, however, it is vital to grasp what a profoundly crucial role modern

---

1   B. Ramm, 1971, *The Christian View of Science and Scripture*, 5th ed., Exeter, U.K.: The Paternoster Press.

2   D. A. Young, 1995, *The Biblical Flood: A Case Study of the Church's Response to Extrabiblical Evidence*, Grand Rapids, MI: William B. Eerdmans Publishing Company, and Carlisle, U.K.: The Paternoster Press, 241-242.

dating methods play in the interpretation of the observations. Davis Young's arguments, just quoted, depend critically on the general validity of radiocarbon dating. So an essential issue to address is whether radiocarbon dates are generally accurate to within a small margin of error, or whether there might be a plausible reason they might be systematically incorrect by as much as tens of thousands of years. Radiocarbon dating, like the geological sciences in general, makes the fundamental assumption that uniformitarianism is a valid interpretative principle. Uniformitarianism is the conviction that extrapolating the present state of affairs in the physical world backward in time is a reliable means for reconstructing the past (in simpler terms, "the present is the key to the past"). This approach can fail in dramatic ways if there have been, in reality, major discontinuities in the world's physical history, such as the global cataclysm described in Genesis 6-8.

In the case of radiocarbon dating, the assumption is made that the atmospheric C-14 level has been similar to that of today as far back in time as the method can measure, which in terms of uniformitarian assumptions is about 40,000 years. But what if there really was a world-destroying Flood only about 5,000 years ago? How might that affect the interpretation of the C-14 levels measured in dead plants and animals? This will be addressed in detail in a later chapter. But the short answer is that radiocarbon dates of items more than about 4,000 years old are affected dramatically, causing organisms which lived during the decades and centuries immediately after the Flood to have very low C-14 levels and to date many thousands, in some cases tens of thousands, of years older than they actually are.

Christian scholars today generally have not availed themselves of this information, so they blithely assume the secular uniformitarian interpretation is unassailable and trustworthy. This has led to all sorts of needless compromises relative to the plain meaning of the biblical record. Let us now examine some of the consequences of assuming standard radiocarbon dates are correct.

13

THE GENESIS FLOOD STORY DERIVED FROM THE BABYLONIAN FLOOD MYTH

The Babylonian flood story—the Gilgamesh Epic—is referred to by Young as a credible ancient document which can stand beside the Scriptures in describing the Genesis Flood and when it occurred. Ramm had earlier referred to parallels between the Babylonian and biblical Flood accounts:

> If the evidence is certain that the American Indian was in America around 8,000 BC to 10,000 BC, then a universal Flood or a destruction of man, must be before that time, and due to Genesis and Babylonian parallels there is hardly an evangelical scholar who wishes to put the flood as early as 8,000 BC to 10,000 BC.[1]

Thus, the first argument against the doctrine that all men outside of the Ark were destroyed by the Flood rests upon a question of relative chronology drawn, in part, from parallels between the Babylonian and biblical Flood accounts. While neither Ramm nor Young explicitly imply that the Genesis Flood story was derived from the Babylonian flood account, other conservative Christian scholars have been more forthright in expressing the view that the writer (or writers) of Genesis derived details of the Flood story from the previously-written Babylonian account. For example, Wenham has stated:

> Our purpose in comparing the Mesopotamian accounts of the flood with Genesis is exegetical. Comparison should shed light not only on the Biblical writer's method, but on his theological purpose in relating the flood story. Again problems arise, however, since it is difficult to be sure what version of the flood story the writer of Genesis knew. Is he simply repeating, more or less unchanged, an earlier version of the flood story? Is he taking an earlier account of the flood story, somewhat different from any of the existing versions, and giving it a theological interpretation of his own? Does he actually know something like the Mesopotamian versions, and is he self-consciously rewriting them to express Hebrew theology instead of Babylonian mythology?[2]

---

1   Ramm, 1971, 234.

2   Wenham, 1987, 162-163.

Such comments place emphasis on a human writer as the source of the Genesis text rather than acknowledging that the Genesis Flood account was penned under divine guidance and in dependence upon the Holy Spirit providing direct divine revelation. Echoing Wenham's postulated presence of a literary structure in the Flood account,[3] Johnson takes the human authorship of the Genesis Flood account derived from the Babylonian flood story a step further away from divinely-guided authorship as the conservative, evangelical position when he wrote:

> The presence of a distinctive literary structure is added evidence that we are dealing with either "dramatized history"—assuming that some extraordinary historical event does in fact lie behind the traditions—or else a "theological drama" in which an ancient story circulating widely in the Near East was transformed by the Israelites into a didactic instrument furthering their own religious objectives. In its new guise it took a stand against the polytheistic ideas of Israel's neighbours, while at the same time teaching certain basic truths about Yahweh and the human race.... Adoption of a basically non-literal interpretative approach, coupled with a recognition that it is not the function of Scripture to teach scientific and historical facts as such, need not lead to any significant diminution of the religious instruction received from Genesis 1-11.[4]

A thorough examination of the significance of any parallels between the Babylonian and biblical Flood accounts is needed to reaffirm the pre-eminent reasonableness of the divinely-inspired biblical account of the Genesis Flood as a real, globe-encircling, historical event.

Excavators at Nineveh in the early 1850s discovered in the library of Ashurbanipal twelve clay tablets which contain the now-famous Gilgamesh Epic. However, it wasn't until 1872 that George Smith in the British Museum came across a small fragment of a tablet on which he was able to decipher from the cuneiform script the words, "The mountain of Nisir stopped the ship. I sent forth a dove, and it left. The dove went and turned, and a resting place it did not find and it returned." Smith immediately recognized that these words resembled part of the biblical account of the Flood and immediately began to search for other fragments of the story. In time, he found other parts of this account and other copies. He put these together (still with many gaps) and published the details in 1873. The Babylonian flood account was found to be written on Tablet XI of the 12-tablet Gilgamesh Epic.

Semitic scholars generally agreed that the date of the composition of the Gilgamesh Epic, at least in its 12-tablet Akkadian poetic form, was approximately 1800-1600

---

3   G. J. Wenham, 1978, The Coherence of the Flood Narrative, *Vetus Testamentum*, 28: 336-348.

4   Johnson, 1988, 133-134.

BC. Tigay[5] has claimed that the Flood story of Tablet XI of the Epic was not in the earliest Old Babylonian fragments and thus was probably a later addition. He has asserted that the much older Atrahasis Epic provided the source for the flood narrative of the Gilgamesh Epic, as the evidence points to the flood narrative having existed in independent written form long before it was incorporated into the completed Gilgamesh Epic. Tigay has even suggested the story was inspired by a specific flood in southern Mesopotamia around 2900 BC, the written accounts of it dating back to the Old Babylonian period and the Sumerian deluge story.

Thus, the Semitic Babylonians, who produced the amazing Gilgamesh Epic, may have borrowed many elements of their flood narrative from the Sumerians whose culture they adopted. As mentioned, the Sumerians also had a legend about the Flood that was discovered on a fragment of clay tablet at Nippur dated as around 2100 BC. Because the Babylonian flood account contains closer parallels to the biblical account, it could be assumed either that the Sumerians had more than one version and the Babylonians copied the most accurate one, or that the Babylonians received their flood tradition directly from their Amorite ancestors, who apparently had closer ties with Abraham's ancestors than did the Sumerians.

It is indeed astonishing that there are so many areas of general agreement between the biblical and Babylonian flood accounts. Wenham[6] has identified that both accounts:

1. State that the Flood was divinely planned for the destruction of mankind.
2. Agree that the impending catastrophe was divinely revealed and a warning given to the hero of the Flood.
3. Assert that the hero of the Flood was divinely commanded to build an ark to preserve life.
4. Tell of the obedience of the hero of the Flood.
5. Tell of the Divine command to enter the Ark.
6. Tell of the entry into the Ark.
7. Mention the closing of the Ark door.
8. Give a description of the Flood.
9. Detail the destruction of life by the Flood.
10. Tell of the end of the rain and the abating of the Flood waters.
11. State that the Ark grounded on a mountain.
12. Mention that the hero of the Flood opens the window of the Ark.
13. Tell of the sending forth of birds at certain intervals and their reconnaissance to ascertain the decrease of the waters.
14. Tell of the disembarkation from the Ark.
15. Describe the acts of worship and the sacrifices made by the hero after his deliverance.

---

5   J. Tigay, 1982, *The Evolution of the Gilgamesh Epic*, Philadelphia, PA: University of Pennsylvania Press.

6   Wenham, 1978, 346-347; Wenham, 1987, 163-164.

16. Mention the divine smelling of the hero's sacrifices.
17. Elude to the bestowment of special blessings upon the hero after the Flood disaster.

Additionally, Unger[7] had pointed out other similarities where both accounts:

18. Connect the Flood with defection in the human race.
19. Tell of the deliverance of the hero of the Flood and his family.
20. Indicate the physical causes of the Flood.
21. Specify the duration of the Flood.
22. Name the landing place of the Ark.

It is, of course, hard to believe that all these similarities are purely coincidental, and so it is not hard to postulate some sort of relationship between these two accounts. Of course, those scholars who insist the main Mesopotamian versions considerably antedate the commitment to writing of the Genesis account thus maintain that the latter was in some way derived from the former. However, such a position denies the ability of Noah and his family to have accurately kept written records, and denies the ability of the Creator Himself to divinely protect the accuracy of the Genesis account written well before the Mesopotamian clay tablet records.

Furthermore, it must be recognized that there are so many important *differences in detail* between the two accounts. The biblical Flood account is far more rational and consistent than the Babylonian. Thus, it is clearly unacceptable and impossible to assume that Genesis in any way depends upon the Gilgamesh Epic as a source.

Heidel[8] is one of many scholars who have carefully analyzed a number of these differences, among which are the following:

1. *The authors of the Flood.* Genesis records that the one and only true God, the Creator, creates the Flood because of the moral depravity of mankind. In the Babylonian account, the Flood is sent because of the rashness of Enlil, and in opposition to the will of the other gods, Enlil's reason being that mankind was multiplying too much and making too much noise.
2. *The announcement of the Flood.* Genesis records that God Himself instructs Noah to build an Ark and warns that mankind has 120 years to repent. In the Babylonian account, the Flood is kept a secret by the gods, but Utnapishtim (the Babylonian Noah) is given a hint of the coming disaster by the god Ea or Enki without the knowledge of Enlil.

---

7   Unger, 1956, 55-65.

8   A. Heidel, 1949, The Gilgamesh Epic and Old Testament Parallels, 2nd ed., Chicago: University of Chicago Press, 224-258.

3. *The Ark and its occupants.* Genesis records that the Ark is 300 cubits by 50 cubits by 30 cubits with three decks and carries eight people, two of each unclean animal, and seven of the clean, plus food. In the Babylonian account, the Ark is 120 x 120 x 120 cubits with nine decks and carries all of Utnapishtim's family and relations, the boatmen, all the craftsmen (or learned men), "the seed of all living creatures," and all his gold and silver.

4. *Causes and duration of the Flood.* Genesis records that the Flood is caused by the breaking up of the fountains of the "great deep" and opening of the "windows of heaven," and these conditions continue for 150 days, followed by an additional 221 days during which the waters abate. In the Babylonian account, rain is the only cause mentioned and it ceases after only six days. After an unspecified number of days, Utnapishtim and the others leave the Ark.

5. *The release of birds.* Genesis records that a raven is sent out first and then a dove three times at intervals of seven days. In the Babylonian account, a dove is sent out first, then a swallow, and finally a raven, at unspecified intervals. The Babylonian story does not mention the olive leaf.

6. *The sacrifice and blessings.* Genesis records that God graciously receives Noah's sacrifice of burnt offerings, gives him and his family power to multiply and fill the earth, emphasizes the sanctity of human life, and promises not to destroy the earth again by a flood, with the rainbow given as a covenant sign. In the Babylonian account, hungry gods "gathered like flies over the sacrificer" because they had been deprived of sacrifices for so long. A quarrel then occurs between the gods Enlil and Ea, and Enlil finally blessed Utnapishtim and his wife after being rebuked by Ea for his rashness in bringing the Flood. Utnapishtim and his wife are rewarded by being made gods and are taken to the realm of the gods.

The greatest contrast is the gross polytheism and confusion of details in the Babylonian account. The pettiness of the Babylonian gods' motives and their capricious nature creates uncertainty about the future as far as mankind is concerned. Their weakness is demonstrated also, for when the storm arrived they were unable to control it—they were frightened and "cowered like dogs." In contrast, Genesis records God's absolute control of the Flood, so that when He caused a wind to pass over the earth, the waters receded.

Since the book of Genesis contains God's inspired record of the Flood, which is therefore a sober, believable, and trustworthy account, the Babylonians had to have received their version of the Flood account via oral transmission, notorious for accumulating discrepancies and changes. On one hand, the remarkable similarities between the two accounts make it extremely unlikely that the Babylonians received their flood account from a tradition that was transmitted orally over a long period of time. This would seem to limit the timespan from the dispersion of nations from Babel to about 3000 BC, when writing is said to have been invented. At that point, the account could have been written down for future inclusion in the eleventh tablet of the Gilgamesh Epic.

On the other hand, if it is assumed the Indians had been inhabiting North America continually since around 10,000 BC, which suggests that the dispersion from Babel was earlier and the Flood earlier still, then at least 7,000 years of oral transmission of the Flood account would have been needed. Over such a lengthy period of time, the distortion of details would surely have eradicated most of the similarities between the biblical and Babylonian accounts.

It should be immediately apparent that the insertion of at least 7,000 years between Babel and Abraham around the time of the Sumerians creates more problems than it solves. There are a number of reasons for believing the post-Flood genealogy in Genesis 11 constitutes a tight chronology, that is, with very few if any gaps or apparent discrepancies. First, in terms of biblical chronology it would seem rather incongruous in the history of redemption for there to be a period of about 2,000 years for the history of Israel to the coming of Christ, and then to insist that the period from Noah to Abraham spanned at least 7,000 years. Second, the timespan between the Flood and Babel is comparatively short, yet contains six generations (at least half) of the post-Flood patriarchs, given that the judgment at the Tower of Babel occurred during the life of Peleg. So, the remaining four generations from Babel to Abraham cannot be stretched to cover any extended timespan beyond a comparable timespan between the Flood and Babel. Related to that, it is absurd to space Reu, Serug, and Nahor, linking Peleg and Abraham's father, Terah, over thousands of years, especially in view of the fact that various Mesopotamian towns are named after them.

Furthermore, it is difficult to harmonize the early chapters of Genesis with a period of universal illiteracy spanning 7,000 years or more between the judgment of Babel and the rise of Near Eastern civilizations in the third millenium BC. To the contrary, the Scriptures clearly imply that written records were made and kept by at least a portion of the human race during the entire period from Adam to Abraham. With respect to the pre-Flood period, even Ramm admits:

> In the fourth and fifth chapters of Genesis we have lists of names, ages of people, towns, agriculture, metallurgy, and music. This implies the ability to write, to count, to build, to farm, to smelt, and to compose. Further, this is done by the immediate descendants of Adam.[9]

Thus, if it is granted that the Scriptures imply men could read and write before the Flood, is it not reasonable to assume that Noah and his sons could have provided an accurate eyewitness written account of the Flood for post-Flood humanity? Furthermore, it logically follows then that a large number of their descendants would likewise have possessed the ability to read and write, even at the time of the

---

9   Ramm, 1971, 228.

judgment at Babel, even if that were several centuries after the Flood. This seems to be indicated by the unity of their speech (Genesis 11:1), the unity of their purpose in defying God's direct commands to fill the earth (Genesis 11:3-4; cf. Genesis 1:28; 9:1), and above all, the magnitude of their building project at Babel ("Let us build us a city and a tower, whose top may reach unto heaven," Genesis 11:4), which presupposes a knowledge of mathematics and engineering.

Furthermore, it is clear that literacy and written records did not vanish from the earth even after the judgment of Babel, because the Bible provides us with a list of patriarchs and their ages, not only for the pre-Flood and the pre-Babel periods, but also for the post-Babel period down to Abraham. Even if there were gaps in the genealogical record and we do not have a complete list of the human links in this portion of the Messianic line, the fact that we have the names of the patriarchs Peleg, Reu, Serug, Nahor and Terah, together with their ages at the birth of their first sons and their total lifespans, indicates that a genealogical record was kept somehow and by some means throughout the entire post-Flood period.[10]

Thus, the early chapters of Genesis imply that there was at least a small pocket of civilization in the Near East linking the civilization of Babel with that of the Sumerians and Babylonians (Genesis 10:6-14). The memory of the "golden age" which preceded the confusion of languages and the scattering of people at Babel must have lingered afterward in the minds of men, providing fertile seed for the rise of a new civilization in the third millennium BC, even as the so-called "dark ages" which followed the fall of Rome were merely a transition to the even higher cultural achievements of the Renaissance period.

Under these circumstances, it is very difficult to conceive of as much as 4,000 or 5,000 years or more intervening between the judgment of Babel and the time of Abraham. After all, if writing were known in any part of the Near East during those thousands of years, then it is strange that the earliest form of writing known consists of pictographs dating (that is, according to conventional dating methods) no earlier than the middle of the fourth millennium BC. It would be more consistent with the biblical evidence to suppose that the Amorites (and possibly the Sumerians) received their superior account of the Flood from the direct ancestors of Abraham who had kept the written records intact since the time of Babel. Therefore, even though the Sumerians undoubtedly invented their own form of script independently, the Flood account (and obviously the accounts of the creation and the Fall) would have been kept pure for many generations after Babel in written records that have long since disappeared.

---

10   It is conceivable, of course, that God could have supernaturally sustained a pure oral tradition of the details of Genesis 1-11 within the line of post-Babel patriarchs if He so choose; or that He may have revealed all these details to Moses directly, apart from any oral or written sources. Neither hypothesis would clear the way for an unlimited stretching of the post-Flood period, however. It is important to remember that whatever may have been the sources employed by Moses in the composition of Genesis— whether written records, oral traditions, or direct revelation—verbal inspiration guarantees its absolute authority and infallibility (Matthew 5:18; Luke 24:25-27; John 5:46; 10:35).

In conclusion, the parallels between the Babylonian and biblical Flood accounts indicate a common source, but the numerous distinct differences, and the grotesqueness and untenable distortions of the Babylonian account, indicate that it was derived by oral transmission from the biblical account in Genesis. Nevertheless, the large number of parallels between the two accounts indicates that the Flood itself (and the judgment of Babel) could not have occurred before 10,000 BC, as suggested by Ramm, while the suggestion by Young of a 3000 BC date for the Flood is reasonably consistent with the chronology provided by the genealogy in Genesis 11. Thus, these conclusions are certainly valid, not only because of the problem of accounting for the remarkable Babylonian flood tradition as the end product of millenniums of purely oral transmission, but even more importantly because of the impossibility of fitting the biblical picture of post-Flood civilization and the line of post-Babel patriarchs into such a chronological framework. Genesis 11 simply cannot be stretched to cover a period of 8,000 to 10,000 years.

14

No Global Flood in Recent Geological and Human History

According to Young, as quoted above, modern age determination methods in archaeology and paleontology have established that no global flood has occurred in recent geological and human history. He thus infers that because many lines of evidence point to the biblical Flood occurring prior, but close, to 3000 BC, this flood must have been only local. Or, in terms of the problem posed by Ramm, if the Flood did not occur earlier than 10,000 BC, then are we to conclude that North America and the American Indians were not affected by the Flood? Absolutely not! Both Ramm and Young, in keeping with secular scholars, have mistakenly put their faith in modern scientific dating methods to determine the chronological framework for early man and for the geological strata. It can be demonstrated that these dating methods are seriously unreliable for artifacts and fossil material older than about 4,000 years. Therefore, we do not have to accept that the direct ancestors of the American Indians were living in North America around 10,000 BC.

Young has also stated this objection more clearly with the following comment:

> No physical evidence exists of a catastrophe that obliterated human beings in North America during the last 12,000 years. Nor is there clear evidence for a later wave of immigrants who might have arrived after such a catastrophe. In other words, archeology indicates that humans have been in North America for at least 12,000 years and that no flood wiped them out during that time. Those who claim that the flood was anthropologically universal thus have to assume that it occurred more than 12,000 years ago—but that conflicts with the conclusion based on biblical references for prediluvian agriculture and metalworking that the flood could not have occurred more than 10,000 years ago.[1]

Obviously such statements concerning the American Indians are contradicted by the testimony of God's Word (e.g., 2 Peter 3:3-7). The biblical framework

---

1   D. A. Young, 1995, 234.

implies that the American Indians migrated to the North American continent following the confusion of tongues at Babel, after the Flood sometime in the third millennium BC. The reason Young and other scholars have not found physical or paleontological evidence for a global Flood in the recent geological record is because they have assumed that age determination methods such as radiocarbon are completely reliable. They are therefore looking in the wrong portion of the record!

The radiocarbon dating method rests upon doubtful presuppositions and therefore needs to be applied with great caution, particularly in the light of many contradictory results that severely question the integrity and reliability of the method. For example, it is well known from numerous incidents that radiocarbon "dates" can often be in conflict with dates derived from archeological and other evidence:

> C14 dating was being discussed at a symposium on the pre-history of the Nile Valley. A famous American colleague, Professor Brew, briefly summarized a common attitude among archeologists towards it, as follows:

> "If a C14 date supports our theories, we put it in the main text. If it does not entirely contradict them, we put it in a foot-note. And if it is completely 'out of date,' we just drop it."[2]

The entire question of all age determination methods and their presuppositions will be discussed at much greater length in a later chapter. In any case, it needs to be stated at this point that the radiocarbon method cannot be applied to periods in the remote past, because the biblical doctrine of a global Flood implies a non-uniformitarian history of the earth's atmosphere, and thus of cosmic-ray activity and radiocarbon concentrations.

Thus, when one abandons the spurious chronology these flawed dating methods have spawned and embraces the chronological structure provided by God's inerrant Word under the direction of His Spirit, the evidence for the global Flood in the days of Noah around 3000 BC becomes glaringly obvious, as will be discussed later.

---

2   T. Säve-Söderbergh and I. U. Olsson, 1969, C14 dating an Egyptian chronology, in *Radiocarbon Variations and Absolute Chronology*, ed. I. U. Olsson, Stockholm: Almqvist and Wiksel, and New York: Wiley Interscience, 35.

15

ALL MANKIND NOT DESCENDED
FROM NOAH'S FAMILY

Another argument often used to discredit the view from both biblical and scientific viewpoints is that the Flood was anthropologically universal. It is presented by Ramm in the following way:

> The derivation of all races from Noah is only possible if one accepts a universal flood or a flood as universal as man. It is pious fiction to believe that Noah had a black son, a brown son and a white son....As far as can be determined the early chapters of Genesis center around the stream of humanity (part of the Caucasoid race) which produced the Semitic family of nations of which the Hebrews were a member. The sons of Noah were all Caucasian as far as can be determined, and so were all of their descendants. The Table of Nations gives no hint of any Negroid or Mongoloid peoples....Suffice it to say that the effort to derive the races of the entire world from Noah's sons of the Table of Nations is not necessary from a biblical standpoint, nor possible from an anthropological one.[1]

Young has expressed the same argument more succinctly, but just as adamantly:

> Other distinct human racial groupings pose similar if not more intractable problems for proponents of an anthropologically universal flood. Archeological and anthropological evidence indicates that the Australian aboriginals have been isolated on Australia for the past 30,000 to 40,000 years, for instance. And in addition to the issue of geographical isolation and continuity of such populations, their genetic uniqueness clearly establishes the point that they could not all have descended from the three sons of Noah at any point in recent human history.[2]

In dealing with this argument, it first needs to be analyzed in its component parts:

---

1   Ramm, 1971, 233-234.

2   Young, 1995, 234-235.

1. Noah could not have had a black son, a brown son, and a white son.
2. The Table of Nations in Genesis 10 speaks only of Caucasian peoples.
3. It is not necessary to derive all nations from Noah's family from a biblical standpoint.
4. It is impossible to do so from an anthropological standpoint.

A fifth component part, particularly from Young's expression of this argument, is that all mankind could not have been descended from Noah's family because scientific "dating" methods place people groups such as the North American Indians and the Australian Aboriginals in the countries where they now reside thousands of years before the biblical Flood. Furthermore, because there is no evidence that these peoples were affected by a global flood, then it has been alleged that the biblical Flood could not have been anthropologically global. However, as will be discussed in detail later, these age determination methods fail to account for the global Flood cataclysm in their assumptions, and therefore yield dramatically incorrect ages. Thus, once the dates for the settlement of these people groups in their respective lands are corrected, there is no impediment to their migration having in fact taken place in the post-Flood, post-Babel dispersion, which means that the ancestors of these people groups, like everyone else alive today, were affected by the anthropologically global Flood described in Genesis.

The Sons of Noah

The first component of the argument—that Noah could not have had a black son, a brown son, and a white son—is spurious because no advocate of an anthropologically universal Flood has promoted this absurd hypothesis that Noah's three sons and their wives were racially distinct. While not expressing this component of the argument in that absurd way, Young nevertheless refers to the "genetic uniqueness" of people groups such as the North American Indians and the Australian Aboriginals as precluding their descent from Noah's three sons. However, such comments ignore what is known from human and population genetic studies. Even as early as the 1950s, a simple response to this argument could be made with these very helpful comments:

> We need not adopt the view that has sometimes been expressed that the three sons were black, yellow and white. If they were so, what were their wives? Rather we would say that in these six people were all the genes which have separated out into the modern races.... Shem may have had the genes for kinky hair and yellow skin, Ham for white skin and Mongoloid eyes, etc. But the genes we would have to say were all there whether in evidence in the body characteristics or not.[3]

Ongoing research has confirmed these comments. After explaining how human

---

3   R. Laird Harris, 1955, Racial dispersion, *Journal of the American Scientific Affiliation*, 7(3): 52.

genetics works with respect to such racial characteristics as skin color and eye shape, Ham et al state:

> Noah and his family were probably mid-brown, with genes for both dark and light skin, because a medium skin colour (dark enough to protect against skin cancer, yet light enough to allow vitamin D production) would be the most suitable in the world before the Flood.[4]

The same authors argue also that a mixture of genes for all the other different racial characteristics were present in Noah's family and in their immediate post-Flood descendants:

> After the Flood, for the centuries until Babel there was only one language and only one culture group. Thus, there were no barriers to marriage within this group. This would tend to keep the skin colour of the population away from the extremes. Very dark and very light skin would appear, of course, but people tending in either direction would be free to marry someone less dark or less light than themselves, ensuring that the average colour stayed roughly the same. The same would be true of other characteristics, not just skin colour. Under these sorts of circumstances, distinct racial lines will never emerge.[5]

The Table of Nations

The second part of this argument against a flood that destroyed all mankind, namely, that the Table of Nations in Genesis 10 speaks only of Caucasian peoples, is at best merely an argument from silence. In fact, Genesis 10 only speaks of nations, families, and languages, and the Scriptures teach that God has "made of one blood all nations of men" (Acts 17:26).[6] Thus, it is rash indeed to insist that the ancestors of the Negroid and Mongoloid peoples are not included in the Table of Nations in Genesis 10, and that the "genetic uniqueness" of the North American Indians, Australian Aboriginals, and other people groups preclude their descent from Noah's family and descendants at Babel.

---

4   K. Ham, A. A. Snelling and C. Wieland, 1990, How did all the different races arise (from Noah's family)?, in *The Answers Book: detailed answers to 12 of the most commonly asked questions on creation/evolution*, Brisbane, Australia: Creation Science Foundation, 146.

5   Ham et al, 1990, 146.

6   Harris (1955) points out that race is a physical term that has been defined as an "assembly of genetic lines represented in a population," and that in ancient racial studies based upon literary sources, men were more often described according to language and culture than according to physical characteristics (p. 52). Ham et al (1990) also point out that the Scriptures only distinguish people by tribal or national groupings, and not by skin color or physical appearances. However, because there are different groups of people who have certain features (e.g., skin color) in common, for convenience we often refer to these groups as races even though they are all part of the one biological species *Homo sapiens* that can freely interbreed and produce fertile offspring because the biological differences are not very great at all (p. 132).

That all today's people groups could have arisen from the heterogeneous genetic mixture of features in the population at Babel, which consisted of all Noah's descendants, can be easily demonstrated:

> To obtain such separate lines, you would need to break a large breeding group into smaller groups and keep them separate, that is, not interbreeding any more. This is exactly what happened at Babel. Once separate languages were imposed, there were instantaneous barriers. Not only would people tend not to marry someone they couldn't understand, but entire groups which spoke the same language would have difficulty relating to and trusting those which did not. They would tend to move away or be forced away from each other, into different environments. This, of course, is what God intended. It is unlikely that each small group would carry the same broad range of skin colours as the original, larger group. So one group might have more dark genes, on average, while another might have more light genes. The same thing would happen to other characteristics: nose shape, eye shape, etc. And since they would interbreed only within their own language group, this tendency would no longer be averaged out as before.[7]

Stephen Jay Gould, formerly of Harvard University, has also commented:

> We all shared a common origin, and therefore a common genetics and morphology, as a single ancestral population....Differences have accumulated as populations separated and diversified. ...Tiny populations, in particular, can undergo marked increases in rate, primarily by random forces of genetic drift....The Tower of Babel may emerge as a strikingly accurate metaphor. We probably did once speak the same language, and we did diversify into incomprehension as we spread over the face of the earth.[8]

Most scientists today insist that man evolved in and from Africa, and therefore was originally a Negroid.[9] However, this notion is totally rejected here, because it is maintained that most of the fossils claimed to be man's ancestors by evolutionary scientists are merely extinct apes, and that the fossil data can be satisfactorily explained in terms of post-Flood and post-Babel migrations from the Middle East of apes and humans respectively (the different timeframes notwithstanding).[10]

---

7   Ham et al, 1990, 146-147.

8   S. J. Gould, 1989, Grimm's greatest tale, Natural History, 98(2): 22, 27-28. Gould was commenting on a paper by L. L. Cavalli-Sfoza, A. Piazza, Menozzi and J. Mountain, 1988, Reconstruction of human evolution: bringing together genetic, archeological, and linguistic data, *Proceedings of the National Academy of Sciences*, USA, 85: 6002-6006.

9   For example, Gould, 1989, 21, 25.

10   A number of researchers have attempted a reinterpretation of paleoanthropological and archaeological data within a strict biblical framework. These include A. J. M. Osgood, 1986, A better model for the

According to Genesis 10, descendants of all three sons of Noah were living in western Asia after the Tower of Babel. Therefore, it is impossible to say from which son or sons the Negroid and Mongoloid peoples have descended.[11] Nevertheless, there are at least a number of possibilities suggested by the Genesis 10 Table of Nations.

Furthermore, the geographical extent of the descriptions in Genesis 10 does not leave one with the impression that only the people in the Mesopotamian Valley were affected by the Flood. The sons of Japheth are depicted as moving into various parts of Europe, including Tarshish (probably Spain), and some of Ham's descendants settled in northern and eastern Africa (Cush, Misraim, and Put). Are we to suppose, then, on the basis of the theory that Noah's descendants were only "Caucasian," that all of Europe, northern Africa, and the Near East were completely lacking any human populations until the "Caucasian" descendants of Noah moved into those areas? If that were the case, then the inhabitants of those areas would have to have been wiped out by the Flood. But that leaves the problem of explaining how the Flood could have covered such a vast area of the globe without at the same time covering the whole earth. On the other hand, to say that people were already living in all of those regions when the descendants of Noah were scattered abroad after the judgment of the Tower of Babel contradicts the clear statement in the scriptural record that "of them was the whole earth overspread" (Genesis 9:19; cf. Genesis 10:5, 32; 11:1, 9).[12]

The Bible and Racial Distribution

The third component of this argument that all mankind did not descend from Noah's family—in order to discredit the anthropologically universal Flood view— is that the effort to derive the races of the entire world from Noah's sons in the Table of Nations is not necessary from a biblical standpoint. However, this most definitely begs the question, because it has already been shown in the preceding

---

Stone Age, *Ex Nihilo Technical Journal,* 2: 88-102; A. J. M. Osgood, 1988, A better model for the Stone Age - Part 2, *Ex Nihilo Technical Journal,* 3: 73-95; G. Beasley, 1990, Pre-Flood giantism: a key to the interpretation of fossil hominids and hominoids, *Ex Nihilo Technical Journal,* 4: 5-53; W. R. Cooper, 1990, The early history of man: part 2, the Table of Nations, *Ex Nihilo Technical Journal,* 4: 65-90.

11 It is worth noting that Cush (Ham's son), at least, must have had descendants with very dark skins: "Can the Ethiopian [Cushite] change his skin, or the leopard his spots?" (Jeremiah 13:23; cf. Numbers 12:1; Jeremiah 38:7; Amos 9:7; Acts 8:27). As already demonstrated, racial differences would have occurred very quickly after the judgment of the Tower of Babel because of the sudden dispersion and isolation of families and nations.

12 While Ramm traced only the Caucasian languages back to Babel (Ramm, 1971, 236), W. S. LaSor (Does the Bible teach a universal Flood? *Eternity,* volume XI (10), 1960) took an even more extreme view by suggesting that the dispersion of people in Genesis 10 took place before the judgment of Babel and that this judgment involved only the Semites (descendants of Shem). Such a view fails to take into account the Old Testament characteristic of chronological overlapping (for example, Genesis 1 and 2; 4 and 5; 5:6-12 and 7:13-17; etc.); or the necessity of interpreting the term "earth" in Genesis 11:1, 4, 9 in the light of Genesis 10:32; or the incongruity of having the Scriptures explain the origin of Semitic tongues without explaining the origin of Japthetic and Hamitic tongues (Genesis 10:5, 20); or the fact that Babel became a Hamitic rather than a Semitic city (Genesis 10:10).

chapters that:

1. The very purpose of the Flood would have been frustrated if only a part of sinful humanity had been destroyed.
2. Many passages in the Old and New Testaments emphasize that *only* Noah and his family were spared.
3. The Lord Jesus Christ clearly stated that *all* men were destroyed except those in the Ark.
4. The Covenant of the Rainbow would have been utterly meaningless if only a part of the human race was involved.

If these biblical arguments are cogent, then it *is* necessary to derive all the people groups of the world from Noah's sons, from a biblical standpoint.

16

ANTHROPOLOGY AND RACIAL DISPERSION

The fourth component of the argument against the descent of all mankind from Noah's family requires more detailed consideration, because it appeals to anthropology for proof that the present distribution of humanity could not have been accomplished since the Flood. Alternately, according to the view espoused by Young, anthropology provides proof that at least some people groups were settled well before the Flood in the areas where they now still live, according to scientific age determination methods. Since there is no evidence that the Flood affected those people groups, then the Flood was only local anthropologically. Quite clearly, if such proofs could be adduced from anthropology, they would indeed present a serious problem for the view that the Flood was both geographically and anthropologically global. However, where is such proof? Once again, Ramm argues from silence, not supporting his statements with positive evidence, while Young relies on the assumed reliability of age determination methods such as radiocarbon.

Recent Migration from Asia

Does anthropological evidence actually prove a very gradual distribution of modern people groups during hundreds of thousands of years? Not at all.

Most anthropologists now agree that the Australian Aborigines probably represent the earliest migration of peoples from southeast Asia, yet that migration is generally estimated to have begun around 40,000 years ago,[1] based on radiocarbon dating (which has already been shown to be fraught with uncertainties) of bones at former inhabited sites in Australia. It is interesting to note also that the Australian Aborigines appear similar to tribal groups in southern India and the Celebes,[2] and that they have always practiced circumcision[3] (first instituted by God with

---

1   J. Isaacs, 1987, *Australian Dreaming: 40,000 Years of Aboriginal History,* Sydney, Australia: Lansdowne Press, 11; and J. Flood, 1987, *Archaeology of the Dreamtime,* Sydney, Australia: Lansdowne Press, 31-37.

2   Wandjuk Marika, Foreword, in Isaacs, 1987, 5. It should be emphasized here that since it is possible to link the Australian Aborigines to a tribal group in southern India, and then before that the colonization of India by post-Babel people from Mesopotamia (see Osgood, 1988), a complete chain of migration connects the Australian Aborigines back to Babel.

3   Flood, 1987, 242.

Abraham and his descendants). Other migration waves from southeast Asia followed that of the Australian Aborigines—to China about 20,000 years ago, then on to North America across the Bering land-bridge about 15,000 years ago, and further southwards into South America 12,000 years ago.[4] The Polynesians are believed to have migrated from southeast Asia as late as 3,000 years ago.

With respect to the Negroes, before scientists began in the last decade or so to insist that man evolved in and from Africa and was therefore a Negroid, anthropologists such as William Howells considered Negroes to have migrated from southern Asia into Africa in comparatively recent times.[5] If, as it is insisted here, most of the fossils claimed to be man's ancestors are merely extinct apes, and the fossil data can be satisfactorily explained in terms of post-Flood and post-Babel migrations from the Middle East of apes and humans respectively, then the Negroes did not originate in Africa, but descended from language groups who migrated there post-Babel in comparatively recent times, just as anthropologists used to infer from the available data.

In discussing the problem of the original distribution of Negroes and Negritoes, Howells stated:

> They are doubtless "newer" races than the Australian, because they are specialized, particularly in hair....Their final outward spread, however, would have been recent, because the Negritoes would have needed true boats to arrive in the Andamans or the Philippines. The Negroes would have made their Asiatic exit still later, with a higher (Neolithic) culture, and probably also with boats. A relatively recent arrival of Negroes in Africa should not shock anthropologists... And there are no archaeological signs of pre-Neolithic people in the Congo at all, and it might have been empty when the Negritoes and the Negroes came.[6]

After emphasizing the "stupendous growth of the last 10,000 years" and "the recent spread of man," Howells, states:

> If we look, first of all, for that part of the world which was the hothouse of the races, we can make only one choice. All the visible footsteps lead away from Asia.[7]

4　　C. G. Turner, 1989, Teeth and prehistory in Asia, *Scientific American,* 260(2): 70-77.

5　　W. Howells, 1947, *Mankind So Far,* New York: Doubleday and Co., 299.

6　　Howells, 1947, 299.

7　　Howells, 1947, 295. Similar testimony has been given by William A. Smalley: "The Scriptural record is of the spread of peoples from their origin in the approximate center of the great Europe-Asia-Africa land mass. The biblical picture is so close to the best anthropological reconstructions of the original dispersion and divergences of races that it is used as the allegorical picture of scientific findings by Dr. Ruth Benedict and Miss Gene Weltfish in their population booklets combating race prejudice, and is basic in their map." (W. A. Smalley, 1950, A Christian View of Anthropology, *Modern Science and Christian*

In view of all this vast dispersion of people groups from Asia, particularly during the past 12,000-20,000 years (on the basis of time-reckonings commonly employed by evolutionary anthropologists), what becomes of Ramm's assertion that the derivation of modern races from Noah's sons is impossible from an anthropological standpoint? Furthermore, once the results of age determinations by methods such as radiocarbon are discarded as unreliable beyond 4,000 years ago, then the justification for the claims of both Ramm and Young is nullified, and the anthropological evidence remains consistent with the derivation of today's people groups from Noah's family and the present distribution of humanity in the time since the judgment at the Tower of Babel, as recorded in the Scriptures.

Universal Flood Traditions

An even more interesting line of evidence than that of ethnic diversification and human migration is to be found in universal Flood traditions. Hundreds of such traditions have been found in every part of the world, and common to most of them is the recollection of a great flood that once covered the earth and destroyed all but a tiny remnant of the human race. Some estimates go as high as more than 80,000 Flood accounts in some seventy languages describing a cataclysmic deluge, more than 80 percent of them mentioning a large vessel that saved the human race from extinction.[8] Many of the documented Flood accounts, even those which have been found among the North American Indians, tell of the building of a great boat which saved human and animal seed from total destruction by the Flood, and which finally landed upon a mountain.

LaHaye and Morris list more than 200 documented Flood traditions grouped by global distribution in continents and regional areas.[9] Based on the availability of sufficient data for appropriate analysis, it was nonetheless found that in these more than 200 Flood traditions, 88 percent involved a favored family, in 70 percent this family's survival was due to a boat, and in 95 percent a flood catastrophe was exclusively responsible for the destruction of mankind. Furthermore, and of crucial importance, 95 percent of these Flood traditions speak of the Flood being global, which is quite remarkable given the limited geographical locations of many of the tribal groups who have these Flood traditions, and their limited knowledge of the world and its geography and people. Because of the importance of these Flood traditions from nearly every nation under heaven, lengthy discussions of them are usually found in large Bible reference works.[10]

Faith, 2nd ed., Wheaton, IL: Van Kampen Press, 116.)

8   Ross, 1998, 167.

9   T. F. LaHaye and J. D. Morris, 1976, *The Ark on Ararat,* Nashville, TN: Thomas Nelson Inc. Publishers, and San Diego, CA: Creation-Life Publishers, 233-236.

10   Sir James George Frazer, 1919, *Folk-Lore in the Old Testament,* vol. I, London: Macmillan and Co. Ltd., 104-361, describes over 100 Flood traditions from Europe, Asia, Australia, the East Indies, Melanesia, Micronesia, Polynesia, South America, Central America, North America, and East Africa. Frazer acknowledges his main source to be the large work by German geographer and anthropologist Richard

It is to be expected, of course, that non-Christian scholars would not acknowledge such traditions as constituting confirmation of the historicity of the Genesis account, because they have assigned that portion of the Bible (among others) to the realm of myth and legend.

The astonishing manner in which modern scholarship has misinterpreted the true significance of the Gilgamesh Epic is a vivid example of this anti-supernaturalistic bias. Conservative Christian scholars have in the past almost unanimously considered the eleventh tablet of that epic, which contains the Babylonian flood account, to be one of the most remarkable confirmations of Genesis ever discovered in ancient literature. As has already been noted, in spite of the polytheistic elements, the Babylonian account contains amazing parallels to the Genesis account, even in matters of detail. The Genesis Flood account, being free from any of the corrupting elements which abound in the Babylonian version, is undoubtedly based upon written records that were kept pure and accurate down through the centuries by the providence of God. Sir William Dawson wrote more than a century ago:

> I have long thought that the narrative in Genesis 7 and 8 can be understood only on the supposition that it is a contemporary journal or log of an eye-witness incorporated by the author of Genesis in his work. The dates of the rising and fall of the water, the note of soundings over the hill-tops when the maximum was attained, and many other details as well as the whole tone of the narrative, seem to require this supposition.[11]

In all the other Flood traditions, including the Babylonian account, there are elements introduced into the story that could *not* have been witnessed by the survivors. Any embellishments are entirely missing in the scriptural account, which reads as an eyewitness record.

However, instead of admitting that the Babylonian is a highly corrupted cognate of the pure Genesis account, critical scholarship has directly perverted the true relationship of these records by making Genesis a corruption of the Gilgamesh Epic:

Andree, 1891, *Die Flutsagen*, Ethnologist Betrachtet, Brunswick, Germany: Viehweg und Sohn. An interesting chart representing the principal ideas of the biblical account of the Flood in the non-biblical traditions is found in Byron C. Nelson, 1968, *The Deluge Story in Stone*, Minneapolis, MO: Augsburg Publishing House and Bethany Fellowship Inc., 169. Nelson's book contains two appendices (pp. 165-190) on details of these Flood traditions, as does Alfred M. Rehwinkel, 1951, *The Flood (in the Light of the Bible, Geology and Archaeology)*, St Louis, MO: Concordia Publishing House, 127-152. Furthermore, Arthur C. Custance lists many of these Flood traditions and discusses the significances of their details in one of his Doorway Papers, largely reproduced in A. C. Custance, 1972, Flood Traditions of the World, *A Symposium on Creation IV*, D. W. Patten, ed., Grand Rapids, MI: Baker Book House, 9-44; and A. C. Custance, 1979, Flood Traditions of the World, *The Flood: Local or Global?*, Vol. IX: The Doorway Papers, part II, Grand Rapids, MI: Zondervan Publishing House, 65-106.

11   J. W. Dawson, 1980, *The Story of the Earth and Man*, 6th ed., London: Hodder and Stoughton, 290 (as quoted by Custance, 1972, 21 and 1979, 79).

By the investigations of George Smith among the Assyrian tablets of the British Museum, in 1872, and by his discoveries just afterwards in Assyria, it was put beyond a reasonable doubt that a great mass of accounts in Genesis are simply adaptations of earlier and especially of Chaldean myths and legends....the Hebrew account of the Deluge, to which for ages theologians had obliged all geological research to conform, was quietly relegated, even by the most eminent Christian scholars, to the realm of myth and legend.[12]

The extraordinary circular reasoning that can follow from such a false premise, combined with the tunnel vision of an anti-supernaturalistic bias, can be seen in the following statement:

Formerly under the influence of the biblical tradition, enquirers were disposed to identify legends of the great Flood, wherever found, with the familiar Noachian deluge, and to suppose that in them we had more or less corrupt and apocryphal versions of that great catastrophe, of which the only true and authentic record is preserved in the book of Genesis. Such a view can hardly be maintained any longer. Even when we have allowed for the numerous corruptions and changes of all kinds which oral tradition necessarily suffers in passing from generation to generation and from land to land through countless ages, we shall still find it difficult to recognize in the diverse, often quaint, childish or grotesque stories of a great Flood, the human copies of a single divine original. And the difficulty has been greatly increased since modern research has proved the supposed divine original in Genesis to be not an original at all, but a comparatively late copy, of a much older Babylonian or rather Sumerian version. No Christian apologist is likely to treat the Babylonian story, with its strongly polytheistic colouring, as a primitive revelation of God to man; and if the theory of inspiration is inapplicable to the original, it can hardly be invoked to account for the copy.[13]

In this most extraordinary statement, it is first of all assumed—without proof—that the biblical account is borrowed from the Babylonian or Sumerian account. Having "established" that, it follows logically that the biblical account, being a borrowed one, could not possibly be an inspired account since it is borrowed from a grossly polytheistic original! Having therefore demonstrated that it cannot possibly be inspired, it follows quite logically that it could never be treated as the lone inspired original of which all the other native traditions are human copies. According to the quoted writer, he has thus "proved" his case! Obviously, it never occurred to the writer because of his "one-eyed" bias that at one time the actual log

---

12   A. D. White, 1955, *A History of the Warfare of Science with Theology and Christendom*, New York: George Brazillier, 237-238.

13   Frazer, 1919, 334.

book which Noah wrote may have been preserved intact and kept as an heirloom within the family of Shem, who therefore had the true account from which Mesopotamian civilization several centuries later derived their own particular scripts, made copies, and took liberties which the Hebrew people would not have taken with the original records that under divine guidance were to become part of the Scriptures.

Custance has quite rightly observed that one strong indication that the biblical account *is* older lies in the fact that in the cuneiform accounts more sophisticated terms are used in reference to the vessel itself. It is called a ship, not an ark, and it is spoken of as sailing, whereas Genesis merely says that "the ark went."[14] Furthermore, in the Babylonian and Sumerian flood accounts, the vessel boasted a "steering-man" (that is, a helmsman). Obviously, those committed to an evolutionary worldview would be reluctant to derive the story of a barge without sails or a helm out of a story of a ship with sails and rudder, since this is to derive the less sophisticated out of the more sophisticated. Yet that is exactly what scholars have capitulated to when they espouse this view that the Genesis Flood account in the inspired Word of God was derived from the grotesque pagan Babylonian and Sumerian accounts.

Unfortunately, the situation has remained largely unchanged during the years which have passed since White and Frazer wrote their comments, and as Unger has pointed out, the idea that the Hebrews borrowed their Flood story from the Babylonians "is the most widely accepted explanation at the present."[15]

More than five decades later that assessment is still correct. However, whereas practically all evangelical scholars would have united their voices five decades ago in denunciation of this bland and uncritical prejudice on the part of liberal and secular scholarship,[16] today more and more evangelical scholars and leaders have compromised, quietly going "soft" on the early chapters of Genesis and relegating them to myth and legend, or simply regarding them as irrelevant.[17]

---

14   Custance, 1972, 24-25 and 1979, 82.

15   Unger, 1956, 69.

16   Ramm comments: "It is typical of radical critics to play up the similarity of anything biblical with the Babylonian, and to omit the profound differences or gloss over them" (Ramm, 1964, 69).

17   For a survey of the positions held by many current evangelical scholars in their writings, see Young, 1995, chapter 18, 277-299. An example of the not-so-subtle compromise among evangelical scholars are these comments by Wenham: "But to affirm that Genesis 2-3 is 'a factual report' is not to say it is history, at least history in the normal meaning of the term....Less question-begging is the view that Genesis 2-3, because it is dealing with events before written records began, could at best be described as pre-history. But whether even this term is an apt description of the nature of the material in these chapters is a matter of debate. In discussing the parallel Near-East material, Jacobsen has coined the term 'mytho-historical,' in that Atrahasis and the Sumerian flood story are relating stories about the gods and men sequentially and in terms of cause and effect. The same is true of Genesis, though as often observed, the more obviously mythical features have been eliminated, so if 'mytho-historical' is not considered an apt description, perhaps 'proto-historical' story or tale would be preferable" (Wenham, 1987, 54). Note Wenham's adoption of the secular evolutionary viewpoint that the pre-Flood patriarchs could not write

Thus, if such scholars have failed to hide what really amount to their anti-biblical prejudices in the relatively simple case of the derivation of the distorted Babylonian account from the sober Genesis Flood account, what confidence can we place in their dogmatic assertions that the vast multitude of flood traditions throughout the world offer no evidence whatever of an original flood of the magnitude described in the book of Genesis?

One excuse which anthropologists have often used for denying the significance of universal Flood traditions in connection with the biblical Flood account is that other traditions, obviously fictitious, have been found among primitive peoples in widely separated areas, having several elements in common. For example, Kroeber has described the so-called magic flight legend as follows:

> There is one folklore plot with a distribution that leaves little doubt as to its diffusion from a single source. This is the incident known as the magic flight or the obstacle pursuit. It recounts how the hero, when pursued, throws behind him successively a whetstone, a comb, and a vessel of oil or other liquid. The stone turns into a mountain or a precipice, the comb into a forest or a thicket, the liquid into a lake or a river. Each of these obstacles impedes the pursuer and contributes to the hero's final escape.[18]

Since this legend was told by many primitive peoples from Europe across Asia to North America, it has been used by anthropologists as an example of how the Flood legend spread from a common center from tribe to tribe around the world, without the people themselves necessarily having carried the story with them as they migrated to their present areas of distribution.

However, while the possibility must be readily granted of explaining universal Flood legends on the principle of *diffusion*, it is insisted that it is equally possible, from an anthropological standpoint, to explain them on the principle of *tradition*:

> Whatever may be the truth—universal or local Flood—memory of the Flood transmitted from generation to generation as a tradition or from people to people by diffusion—the problems are there and the data are anthropological. Anthropology cannot do much to orient the prehistory of man in relation to the Flood until the geological flood questions are settled, or until a lead presents itself, but the questions and data are anthropological from there on."[19]

---

or record history, which view is clearly repudiated by the details preserved in the divine record of Genesis 4-5 of the pre-Flood civilization.

18   A. L. Kroeber, 1948, *Anthropology*, New York: Harcourt, Brace and Co., 544.

19   Smalley, 1950, 189.

Therefore, anthropology has no right to decide one way or the other concerning *the true significance of these Flood legends*. All it can do is describe them and give some cautious tentative explanations, which are unavoidably colored by the presuppositions of the one who makes them. Even Kroeber admits as much in his introduction to the chapter which contains his discussion of the Flood legends:

> A considerable part of the endeavors of anthropology consists of a groping into these dimly lit realms, of collecting shreds of evidence and partial orientations, and of construing them into the best probability attainable....This chapter accordingly reviews a number of problems to which only partial or probable answers can be given—reviews them as a sample of the type of approach that anthropology mobilizes in avowedly inferential situations.[20]

Such a profession of humility and scientific objectivity is to be commended when investigators grope "in avowedly inferential situations." But the same spirit of impartiality and objectivity is completely lacking in Kroeber's discussion of the Flood legends in relation to Genesis:

> Flood myths are told by probably the majority of human nations. Formerly this wide distribution was thought to prove the actuality of the biblical Flood, or to be evidence of the descent of all mankind from a single nation that had once experienced it. Refutation is hardly necessary.[21]

Statements like this, however, are quite misleading, because conservative Christian scholars do not look upon the Flood traditions as constituting *proof* of the Genesis Flood. Instead, they look upon these traditions as providing important *circumstantial evidence* that the Flood was at least anthropologically universal. Such evidence, while perhaps inconclusive in itself, is nevertheless significant when it is combined with the overwhelming biblical evidence for such a catastrophe early in human history, and so it has been legitimately used by Christians through the centuries as corroboration for the book of Genesis. In other words, if there actually was a Flood that destroyed mankind, as the Bible teaches, then universal Flood traditions would be exactly what we would *expect* to find. Some tribal groups would perpetuate the story of the Ark, the favored family, the landing on a mountain, and the sending forth of the birds, whereas others would remember only the Flood itself and the purpose for which it was sent, and still others would have retained only the barest outline of events connected with that most stupendous crisis in human history.

However, the real question is this: What would non-Christian anthropologists say about the Genesis Flood account if there were *no* legends or traditions anywhere

---

20   Kroeber, 1948, 538-539.

21   Kroeber, 1948, 545.

in the world of such a flood? Would they not use this very lack of circumstantial evidence as a weighty objection to the veracity of the biblical account? MacRae put his finger on the heart of the matter when he wrote:

> If a universal flood occurred centuries after the creation, it would be natural to expect that all humanity would recall many of its details for a long time, even though some points would tend to become quite garbled, as people more and more forgot the cause and purpose of the catastrophe.[22]

In discussing the evidence of Flood traditions, Ramm fails to delineate the issues clearly. He quite clearly, like so many other Christian scholars, realizes the strengths of these traditions as circumstantial evidence for an anthropologically global flood, so he focuses his attack upon those who would use such traditions as evidence for a geographically global Flood:

> We must carefully distinguish between what is certainly related to the biblical accounts; what is probably related; what is conscious or unconscious assimilation of flood data as related by missionaries and merged into local flood stories; and what are purely local affairs having no connection at all with the Bible....The data are not such that from a wide spread of flood legends a *universal* flood may be properly inferred.[23]

Of course, this is sidestepping the main issue, and Ramm is thus guilty of minimizing the amazing similarities of detail among these Flood traditions by suggesting that a large number of them may have arisen out of "purely local affairs" or from the preaching of missionaries! It is scientifically absurd to place the Flood traditions in such a light. Bright has discussed this "local inundations" view and confessed that "it is difficult to believe that so remarkable a coincidence of outline as exists between so many of these widely separated accounts can be accounted for in this way."[24]

It hardly seems necessary to refute the notion that *missionaries* were responsible for the spread of Flood legends in any appreciable way.[25] Nelson refutes this theory

---

22   A. A. MacRae, 1950, The relation of archaeology to the Bible, *Modern Science and Christian Faith*, 2nd ed., Wheaton, IL: Van Kampen Press, 234.

23   Ramm, 1964, 164-165 (italics are his). This is part of Ramm's refutation of a geographically universal Flood.

24   J. Bright, 1942, Has archaeology found evidence of the Flood?, *The Biblical Archeologist*, V(4): 56, 58-59. Similarly, Dods observed that "local flood happenings at various times in different countries could not give birth to the minute coincidences found in these traditions, such as the number of persons saved, and the sending out of birds." W. Robertson Nicoll, ed., 1890, *The Expositor's Bible*, vol. I, the Book of Genesis, 4th ed., London: Hodder and Stoughton, 55.

25   Frazer doubted whether "a single genuinely native tradition of a great flood has been recorded" in all of Africa. After describing in detail two remarkable flood traditions discovered by German scholars in East Africa, he summarily dismisses them because "the stories are plainly mere variations of the biblical

with three logical observations:

1. There are no universal legends of other great miracles recorded in the Bible, such as the crossing of the Red Sea.
2. If missionaries were responsible for Flood traditions, it is difficult to explain the many important differences of emphasis and detail in these traditions.
3. The vast majority of Flood traditions have been gathered and recorded, not by Christian missionaries, but by secular anthropologists who had no interest in verifying the Genesis account:

    The Flood legends…were collected by men whose chief interests were anthropological. They had no interest in establishing the truth of the biblical account, and they were concerned to secure native traditions, not traditions given to the natives by missionaries.…[they] were students of the native races and nothing more.[26]

To these arguments it can be added that Christian missionaries have never in the past reached all these remote tribes, and even if they had, they would have preached the Gospel instead of concentrating all their teaching on the Genesis Flood.

---

narrative, which has penetrated through the savages through Christian or possibly Mohammedan influence." Frazer, 1919, 329-332. One can only marvel at the naivety of such a statement!

26   Nelson, 1968, 167-168.

17

UNIVERSAL TERMS: USED IN A LIMITED SENSE?

The argument most frequently used by Christian scholars—even present-day evangelical Christian leaders—against the global Flood view is one that purports to find its support in the Bible itself. It is the claim that universal terms, such as "all" and "every," need not always be understood in a strictly literal sense.[1]

For example, when we read in Genesis 41:57 that "all countries came into Egypt to buy grain," we are not to interpret this as meaning that people from North America and Australia came to Egypt for grain. Thus, it is argued, by comparison, that the statement of Genesis 7:19, "*all* the high hills [mountains, in some translations], that were under the *whole* heaven, were covered," may be interpreted as *some* high mountains under *part* of the heavens.

Most Universal Terms Are to Be Interpreted Literally

However, in spite of the seeming logic of this argument, which has been used and reused among evangelical scholars and Christian leaders, there are several important considerations that render it untenable. After all, not even the most fervent local flood advocates would deny that there are many places in the Bible where the words "all" and "every" *must* be understood in the literal sense. For example, note the wording of Matthew 28:18-20:

> And Jesus came and spake unto them, saying, All power is given unto me in heaven and in earth. Go ye therefore, and teach *all* nations...Teaching them to observe *all* things whatsoever I have commanded you."

Are we at liberty to substitute the words "much" and "many" for the word "all" in this passage, just because there are some passages in the Bible that infer universal

---

1   The evangelical Christian scholars who promote this argument include H. N. Ross, 1998, 142-143; R. Forster and P. Marston, 1989, *Reason and Faith: Do Modern Science and Christian Faith Really Conflict?*, Eastbourne, Sussex, U.K.: Monarch Publications Ltd, 235-239; G. R. Morton, 1995, 134-135; D. C. Boardman, 1990, Did Noah's Flood cover the entire world?, in *The Genesis Debate*, R. F. Youngblood, ed., 223-227; A. C. Custance, 1979, An examination of the record itself, in *The Flood: Local or Global?*, 15-22; F. A. Filby, 1970, 81-84; and Ramm, 1964, 164.

terms in a limited sense? Obviously not! There are *many* passages, indeed the great majority of passages in the Bible, where the universal terms employed must be interpreted literally. In fact, the Bible contains many such statements which lose their meaning with a limited usage interpretation. Thus, as Ramm admits, "there are cases where all means all, and every means every, *but the context tells us where this is intended.*"[2]

The Context Determines the Meaning

This leads to the second observation, namely, that it is the immediate and general *context* in which such terms are used that determines the sense in which they are to be understood. It is this fact which provides one of the greatest arguments for interpreting *literally* the universal terms of Genesis 6-9. Kalisch, a leading Hebrew scholar of the nineteenth century, strongly opposed those who tried to tone down the universal terms of the Genesis Flood account:

> They have thereby violated all the rules of a sound philology. They have disregarded the spirit of the language, and disregarded the dictates of common sense. It is impossible to read the narrative of our chapter [Genesis 7] without being irresistibly impressed that the *whole* earth was destined for destruction. This is so evident throughout the whole of the description, that it is unnecessary to adduce single instances....In our case *the universality does not lie in the words merely, but in the tenor of the whole narrative.*[3]

Thus, the analogy with Genesis 41:57 utterly breaks down, because *the constant repetition of universal terms* throughout the four chapters of Genesis 6-9 show conclusively that the question of the magnitude and geographical extent of the Flood was not a merely incidental one in the mind of the Holy Spirit-directed writer, but was rather one of primary importance to the entire Flood narrative. In fact, so frequent is the use of universal terms, and so powerful are the points of comparison ("high hills" and "whole heaven"), that it is impossible to imagine what more could have been said to express the concept of a *universal* Flood![4]

---

2   Ramm, 1964, 164 (emphasis mine).

3   M. M. Kalisch, 1858, *Historical and Critical Commentary on the Old Testament*, London: Longman, Brown, Green, et al., 209-210 (emphasis mine). According to one historian, Kalisch's commentaries on the Old Testament "at the time of publication "are the best commentaries on the respective books in the English language and are not yet wholly superseded, having a special value as the work of a learned Jew." S. M. Jackson, ed., *The New Schaff-Herzog Encyclopædia of Religious Knowledge*, 1950, vol. VI, Grand Rapids, MI: Baker Book House, 293.

4   The very nature of the Hebrew language accentuates the importance of context for the full understanding of terms. Thus, *ha-'ares* (the earth) in Genesis 7:19 must be understood to mean the entire globe because the following words speak of "all the high hills [mountains] under the whole heaven." Heidel, 1949 (250) concludes that the biblical account "plainly asserts the universality of the Deluge." James Barr, then Oriel Professor of the Interpretation of Holy Scripture at Oxford University, England, and a renowned Hebrew scholar, is on record as saying, in a letter to David C. C. Watson dated April 23, 1984: "...so far as I know, there is no Professor of Hebrew or Old Testament at any world-class

The book of Genesis is clearly divided into two main sections:

1. Chapters 1-11 deal with *universal* origins (the material universe, the plant and animal kingdoms, humans, sin, redemption, and the nations of the earth).
2. Chapters 12-50, on the other hand, concentrate on the *particular* origin of the Hebrew nation and its tribes, mentioning other nations only in so far as they came in contact with Israel.[5]

The realization of this fact sheds important light on the question of the magnitude of the Flood. Furthermore, the biblical account of the Flood catastrophe occupies *three and a half chapters* in the midst of these eleven chapters on universal origins, while only *two chapters* are devoted to the creation of all things!

From a purely literary and historical perspective, therefore, we are perfectly justified in coming to the account of the Flood in Genesis 6-9 with the expectation of reading about *a catastrophe of global proportions*. And if we are thus willing to approach the scriptural narrative of the Flood with a mind conditioned by the perspective which the Word of God itself supplies for us, unencumbered with uniformitarian presuppositions, we will not be surprised to discover that the number of Hebrew superlatives used to describe the magnitude of the Flood is entirely proportional to the amount of space allotted to it in the first eleven chapters of Genesis.

Most advocates of the local flood view would maintain that "the Deluge was universal *in so far as the area and observation and information of the narrator extended*."[6] But even if we were to assume, for the sake of argument, that the mountain ranges of the world were as high before the Flood as they are now (as most local flood advocates would either claim or simply assume[7]), then what are we to say of the idea that Noah's "observation and information" about geography was limited to the Mesopotamian Valley? Even if Noah were a man of only average intelligence, he could have learned a great deal about his own continent

---

university who does not believe that the writer(s) of Genesis 1-11 intended to convey to their readers the ideas that…Noah's Flood was understood to be world-wide and extinguish all human and animal life except for those in the ark. Or to put it negatively, the apologetic arguments which suppose…the flood to be a merely local Mesopotamian flood are not taken seriously by any such Professors, as far as I know."

5   W. H. Griffith Thomas, 1946, *Genesis: A Devotional Commentary*, Grand Rapids, MI: Eerdmans, 18-19.

6   Ramm, 1964, 163 (italics his).

7   It is a total misrepresentation of Flood geology to claim or assume that the pre-Flood mountain ranges were as high as those today. Indeed, today's mountain ranges were formed by the Flood. For example, there are ammonite fossils in limestone layers near the top of Mt. Everest, indicating that the rocks making up the Himalayas were deposited during the Flood, and the Himalayas were uplifted as a result of the catastrophic plate tectonics during the Flood (discussed in chapter 87). Although we don't know exactly how high the pre-Flood mountain ranges were, they were not the same as today's mountain ranges, and probably not as high. In any case, the scriptural account clearly says that "all the high hills, that were under the whole heaven were covered… and the mountains were covered" (Genesis 7:19-20).

of Asia (where the world's highest mountains are found today) during the six centuries that he lived before the Flood came. And assuming again, for the sake of argument, that Genesis 6-9 depicts the Flood from Noah's standpoint and not from God's,[8] could he have been so ignorant of the topography of southwestern Asia as to think that the Flood covered "all the high mountains that were under the whole heaven" when, as a matter of fact, it covered only a few foothills?[9]

Some have tried to shield Noah from the accusation of childish ignorance by asserting that "the terms employed were the rather natural expression of a man overwhelmed by the devastation of his own community and countryside,"[10] or that the terrific downpour of rain prevented him from making clear distinctions between mountains and foothills, and that therefore "the entire record must be interpreted phenomenally."[11] But to say that the record must be interpreted "phenomenally" is only a polite way of saying that Noah *thought* the high mountains were covered, when actually they were not. Whether such impressions were due to his ignorance of how high the mountains in the Near East really were, or to his inability to evaluate the situation properly because of adverse weather conditions or being overwhelmed by the devastation, makes little difference. Such an interpretation must be rejected without qualification, because it does to the entire Flood narrative exactly what the local creation theory of John Pye Smith (1839, 1854)[12] did to the creation account. Concerning this theory, even Ramm protests:

> The weakness of the theory is that it essentially cheapens Genesis 1. The majestic language, the chaste and factual terminology, and the celestial-

---

8   Actually, there is nothing in this entire passage of Scripture to indicate that Noah is recording his personal impressions of the Flood. Instead, it is all seen from God's viewpoint. *God* looks down upon mankind and sees that it is corrupt; *God* chooses Noah and commands him to build the Ark; *God* calls him into the Ark and shuts the door; *God* remembers Noah and the animals and gradually brings the Flood to an end; and *God* commands them to leave the Ark and gives them His special covenant. In fact, Noah does not speak a single word in the entire passage, until the very end of chapter 9, when *God* puts into his mouth the remarkable prophecy concerning his three sons.

9   To illustrate the extent to which some scholars have gone in this direction, a paper read by Lt. Col. F. A. Molony before the Victoria Institute in London in 1936 is quoted: "Now the part of the great Mesopotamian Plain which lies below the 500' contour is as large as England without Wales. Hence it is probable that *Noah and his sons never saw a mountain in their lives*…15 cubits is only about 23 feet, so it would seem that the word we translate 'mountains' would be better rendered mounds, probably raised by human labour…the chronicler knew that the artificial mounds were very seldom more than 15 cubits high. He saw that they were all covered, so he wrote '15 cubits upward did the waters prevail; and the mountains were covered.' " The Noachian Deluge and its probable connection with Lake Van, 1936, *Journal of the Transaction of the Victoria Institute*, LXVIII: 44, 51-52, emphasis mine. Molony went on to explain that the Flood was caused by a sudden emptying of Lake Van (in eastern Turkey) into the Mesopotamian Valley. Lifting the Ark above the artificial mounds, the lake water threatened to sweep it out into the Persian Gulf. But in order to avoid such a fate, Noah "may have rigged jury masts and sails, and anchored when the wind was northerly." Comment hardly seems necessary!

10   Custance, 1979, 22.

11   Ramm, 1964, 163.

12   John Pye Smith, *The Relation Between the Holy Scriptures and some parts of Geological Science*, 1854.

terrestrial scope of the passage lose so much of their import and force if restricted to a small patch of the earth. Rather than having six majestic acts of creation of the world and all its life, we have a small scale remodeling job.[13]

However, the "limited observation and information" theory and the "phenomenal" theory do the very same thing to the "majestic language, the chaste and factual terminology, and the celestial-terrestrial scope" of the Flood account. They cheapen and reduce it to a small-scale disaster. Yet evangelical scholars today still appeal to John Pye Smith's arguments to support a local flood view. For example, Forster and Marston write:

To be faithful to Scripture, however, we still need to ask two important questions:

1. What did the actual words mean to the writer, i.e., to what concepts in his mind did they relate?
2. In what way is the language being used, e.g., as literal, sarcasm, hyperbole, etc.?

On [question] 1 the point of departure for interpreting any biblical passage must be to try to understand what the writer intended by the language he used. To do this, one needs first to understand the concepts in the mind of the writer. Some have suggested that the Genesis writer believed in some kind of primitive cosmology, but we know of no evidence that this was so. On the other hand, there is no indication that the Genesis writer had a concept of a spherical planet Earth. The Hebrew *eretz*, which is translated "earth" in Genesis 1:1 and various verses in Genesis 6, does not mean "planet earth" as we now think of it. That we may choose to read this into, say, Genesis 1:1, this is a modern re-interpretation. The writer simply meant "earth" as distinct from the heavens or as distinct from the sea (Genesis 1:10). No particular cosmology, either primitive or modern, was implied.

It is, in fact, unlikely that any early Old Testament writer had in mind a globe when he used the word *eretz*. Elsewhere the word is actually more commonly translated "land" (1476 times) or "country" (140 times) or "ground" (96 times). Thus to translate, for example, "the whole *eretz*" as "the whole earth" is really misleading to the modern reader, for he or she thinks of "earth" in terms of "globe." To translate it "the whole land" would much better convey the kind of concept in the mind of the writer.[14]

---

13   Ramm, 1964, 132.

14   Forster and Marston, 1989, 235-236.

To put it bluntly, it is irrelevant what concepts either Noah or Moses might have had in mind, or Adam for that matter, when the words of Genesis 1-11 were recorded in writing, since the ultimate author is God Himself, who moved the human writers to record what He wanted by the Holy Spirit. Thus, the only perspective which is relevant concerning the meaning of the words used, including *eretz*, is that of God Himself, who well understood that He was referring to a spherical planet earth in Genesis 1:1. To reduce the text of the Scriptures here in Genesis 1-11 to the level of what modern scholars perceive was the "primitive" cosmology of the human pen-men is an affront to the divine authorship, and has the hallmark of the modern secular viewpoint of the evolution of man from primitive to civilized and modern. It matters not how many times elsewhere in the Old Testament the word *eretz* is translated "land," "country," or "ground," because it is the context which determines how this word should be translated. As has already been emphasized, the context of Genesis 1-11 is a global perspective.

Forster and Marston draw extensively from the work of Filby, yet even he admits:

> But in Hebrew the word *ERETZ* by no means always, or even usually, meant the entire planet. Its primary meaning was "earth" in our sense of "ground" i.e., solid-rocky-stony or clayey material, and it is only by an extension of its meaning that it comes to mean the "entire planet." The study of a Hebrew concordance will prove this and show that the meaning must be determined by the context. In such verses as Genesis 1:1 "God created the heaven and the earth," Genesis 2:1 "The heavens and the earth were finished," Genesis 14:22 "The Most High God, possessor (probably, Creator) of heaven and earth," the context shows that beyond any doubt the entire planet is intended.[15]

Yet Filby insists that *eretz* in Genesis 6-9 still should only be translated as "all the land" as Noah knew it, in spite of the context which, as has already been noted, was written entirely from God's viewpoint—obviously that of the entire spherical planet earth. Filby also goes on to deny that the expression "everywhere under the heavens" in Genesis 7:19 should be interpreted in an absolutely universal sense, because he maintains there are other passages where it is not so used.[16] For example, it must be used in a limited sense in Deuteronomy 2:25 ("the peoples everywhere under the heavens") because Moses went on to limit it to "the peoples...who...hear the report of you." In a parallel passage in Deuteronomy 11:25, Moses further limited this expression to mean "all the land on which you set foot."

However, this is precisely the point which has already been emphasized. When

---

15   Filby, 1970, 82.

16   Filby, 1970, 83.

the context limits the meaning of universal terms, they must *not* be understood in the absolutely universal sense. On the other hand, when the context does not limit the meaning of such terms, they *almost certainly* are to be understood in the absolute sense. When the context *demands* a worldwide scope, as has been demonstrated to be the case in Genesis 6-9, a refusal to accept this fact simply indicates an attitude of unbelief at this point.

Boardman[17] and Morton[18] both repeat the claims made by Custance[19] about the translation of the word *eretz*. Custance also tries to argue for *eretz* to be translated "land" rather than "earth" by counting the occurrences of each translation so as to demonstrate that the matter should be decided by which translation of the word occurs most often. He also proceeds to quote numerous examples in both the Old and New Testaments where the context favors a localized understanding of the universal terms used in Scripture, which is invariably based on the context. When he applies the context to Genesis 1:1-2, he admits that there *eretz* does mean "earth in the broader sense," but when it comes to the context of Genesis 6-9, he insists, "It is surely not intended by the writer that the whole earth was in view." Yet as shown earlier, the context does demand a global perspective, so Custance's choice of translation for the word *eretz* is, as with so many other local flood advocates, purely a matter of personal choice to bolster his viewpoint that the Flood account is written from the perspective of Noah, rather than submitting to the authorship of the Holy Spirit, who fully expressed God's perspective on this judgment which He sent.

Morton, however, attempts an additional argument. Quoting Genesis 6:13, he suggests everyone knows that the people were destroyed by the Flood, but if the term *eretz* is meant in a global, planet-wise sense, then God did not destroy the earth as a whole, only the land where Noah and the people lived. However, that God did in fact destroy the earth is precisely what will shortly be argued and graphically demonstrated from the point of view of the total geological renovation of the whole of planet earth during the Flood.

After discussing the ambiguity of such terms as "earth" (*eretz*) and "ground" (*adamah*), Archer concludes:

> The phrase "under the whole heaven" in Genesis 7:19 may not be so easily disposed of. It is doubtful whether anywhere else in the Hebrew Scriptures this expression "the whole heaven" can be interpreted to include a mere geographical region. For this reason most careful exegetes, like Franz Delitzsch in the last century and most recently H. C. Leupold, have not conceded the exegetical possibility of interpreting Genesis 7 as

---

17   Boardman, 1990, 224-226.

18   Morton, 1995, 134-135.

19   Custance, 1979, 15-22.

describing a merely local flood.[20]

20   G. L. Archer, Jr, 1974, *A Survey of Old Testament Introduction*, revised ed., Chicago, IL: Moody Press, 204-205.

18

UNIVERSAL TERMS ARE LITERAL IN GENESIS 6-9 BECAUSE OF THE PHYSICAL PHENOMENA

Yet another compelling reason for interpreting the universal terms of Genesis 6-9 literally is that the physical phenomena described in those chapters are inconceivable if the Flood had been confined to only one section of the earth. While it would be entirely possible for a seven-year famine to have gripped the Near East without at the same time affecting Australia and the Americas (Genesis 41:53-57), it would *not* have been possible for water to cover even *one* high mountain in the Near East without inundating Australia and the Americas too!

Respected Hebrew scholar, Samuel R. Driver, one-time Professor of Hebrew at Oxford University and co-author with F. Brown and C. A. Briggs of *A Hebrew and English Lexicon of the Old Testament*, insisted in his commentary on Genesis that the local flood theory "does not satisfy the terms of the narrative of Genesis" and says:

> It is manifest that a flood which would submerge Egypt as well as Babylonia must have risen to at least 2,000 feet (the height of the elevated country between them), *and have thus been in fact a universal one*...a flood, on the other hand, which did less than this *is not what the biblical writers describe*, and would not have accomplished what is represented as having been the entire *raison d'etre* of the Flood, the destruction of all mankind.[1]

Past advocates of the local flood theory felt the force of such reasoning, and many

---

1   S. R. Driver, 1904, *The Book of Genesis*, London: Methuen and Co., 101. A similar conclusion was argued by John Skinner, *A Critical and Exegetical Commentary on Genesis*, vol. I of the *International Critical Commentary*, 165. Driver, Skinner, and Kalisch (previously quoted) were of the old liberal school of theology. Such scholars did not believe that there ever was a Flood of such magnitude, an Ark of such dimensions, or a patriarch named Noah who was 600 years old. In fact, they did not really accept the historicity of the book of Genesis at all. However, they had little patience for those who professed to accept the historicity of Genesis and yet did not hesitate to take the plain statements of the text and mold them into conformity because of their own scientific presuppositions. Many modern evangelical scholars, who claim to be Bible-believing, continue to do this, instead of humbly recognizing that science is a fallible human activity which should submit to the clear, unambiguous statements recorded by God Himself in Genesis 1-11 under the direction of the Holy Spirit.

of them, perhaps in desperation, resorted to Hugh Miller's bizarre hypothesis that the Near East sank as far as the Flood waters rose, in order that the Flood might cover the mountains of Ararat and still not be universal! Miller calculated that if the Near East had suddenly began to sink at a rate of 400 feet a day, reaching a depth of over 16,000 feet in forty days, the ocean waters could have poured into the resulting basin, covering the mountains that were in it.[2] Jamieson perpetuated this fantastic theory in the *Jamieson, Fausset and Brown Commentary*,[3] and Ramm seems to have been influenced by it too (he quotes Jamieson at length), although he is careful to omit any reference to the rate at which the Near East must have been lowered to make it into a "natural saucer."[4]

Delitzsch, on the other hand, defended the local flood view by assuming that the waters could have covered mountains in one region without at the same time flowing into other regions:

> The waters could, just where the extermination of the numerous population who have fled to the mountains was to be effected, *stand at such a height, without reaching a similar height elsewhere or uniformly covering the whole earth.*[5]

It is hard not to assume that Delitzsch here must have been appealing to the supernatural power of God, as an invisible wall, to hold the Flood within the Near East! However, if he was appealing to the laws of physics, hydrology, and hydrostatics, he committed a serious scientific blunder, because such a condition, continuing throughout an entire year, would contradict all laws of water action known to those scientific disciplines.[6] Pieters, another past advocate of the limited Flood view, frankly admits the problems that this view entails:

---

2   Hugh Miller, 1857, *The Testimony of the Rocks*, New York: Gould and Lincoln, 358-359. This book proved to be immensely popular during the last half of the 19th century when the local flood view was so much in vogue.

3   R. Jamieson, 1948, *Critical and Experimental Commentary*, vol. I, Grand Rapids, MI: Eerdmans, 100.

4   Ramm, 1964, 162-163. He claims that "some sort of geological phenomenon...caused the ocean waters to creep up the Mesopotamian Valley. The waters carried the ark up to the Ararat Range...by the reversal of the geological phenomenon, the water is drained back from the valley." After quoting Jamieson's statement "the Caspian Sea...and the Sea of Aral occupy the lowest part of a vast space, whose whole extent is not less than 100,000 square miles, hollowed out, as it were, in the central region of the great continent, and no doubt formerly the bed of the ocean," Ramm asserts that "into this natural saucer the ocean waters poured," and "from this natural *saucer* the waters were drained."

5   Delitzsch, 1899, 270 (emphasis mine).

6   It is of interest to note that his co-worker, C. F. Keil, was strongly opposed to the local flood concept: "A flood which rose 15 cubits above the top of Ararat could not remain partial, if it only continued a few days, to say nothing of the fact that the water was rising 40 days, and remained at the highest elevation for 150 days. To speak of such a flood as partial is absurd. Even if it broke out at only one spot, it would spread over the earth from one end to the other, and reach everywhere to the same elevation. However impossible, therefore, scientific men may declare it to be for them to conceive of a universal flood of such height and duration in accordance with known laws of nature, this inability on their part does not justify anyone in questioning the possibility of such an event being produced by the omnipotence of God." Keil, 1951, 146.

If the relative elevation of the continents above the sea level was as at present, and if the "mountains of Ararat" mentioned as the resting place of the ark are the table land now known by that name, the flood must have been universal or nearly so; for that region is now nearly 5,000 feet above sea level, and an inundation sufficient to cover it would cover the whole world, with the exception of the highest mountain ranges. But it is not at all certain that the levels have not changed."[7]

You would think that as a result of these clearly admitted difficulties with the local flood view among well-qualified scholars in days past, and with the clear presentation of these difficulties and the powerful defense from Scripture of the Flood being global by Whitcomb and Morris in their book, *The Genesis Flood,* that evangelical leaders and Bible-believing scholars today would unanimously believe and preach that God's record unambiguously speaks in universal terms of a global catastrophic flood. However, sadly, many today continue to promote the local flood view and chide those who have remained faithful to God's Word teaching a global flood, even when those being chided are well-qualified in scientific disciplines relevant to researching and propounding the scientific evidences that are consistent with the Flood being global. Furthermore, many of these evangelical leaders and scholars who claim to be Bible-believing still use the same old arguments and refer to the same liberal scholars of yesteryear that were soundly refuted in a scholarly manner by Whitcomb and Morris. It is hard not to conclude that those who hold to the local flood view do so with almost complete disregard for the Scriptures in order to conform to the contemporary, monolithic, uniformitarian-evolutionary viewpoint of the secular scientific establishment.

For example, Forster and Marston specifically cite the books of Hugh Miller and John Pye Smith as providing clear and detailed arguments "for interpreting the Bible to mean a local flood" and refer to British and American geologists who provided "strong lines of argument, linguistic and geological," their "valid interpretation" receiving support from Hebrew commentator Delitzsch. Forster and Marston chide Whitcomb and Morris for disregarding "the actual language and intent of the writer" of Genesis, and for backing up their position by appealing to science! Yet it is Forster and Marston who have disregarded the divine authorship of the clearly stated global perspective in Genesis, and who appeal to the outdated and outrageous geological hypotheses of Hugh Miller and John Pye Smith to support a local flood view which even Delitzsch, as we have seen, admits needs the waters of the Flood to somehow be held back at a height to cover the mountains in the

---

7   A. Pieters, 1947, *Notes on Genesis,* Grand Rapids, MI: Eerdmans, 119. Perowne, another past advocate of a limited flood, was also embarrassed by the same problem: "On reading this narrative it is difficult, it must be confessed, to reconcile the language employed with the hypothesis of a partial deluge....The real difficulty lies in the connecting of this statement [7:19] with the district in which Noah is supposed to have lived, and the assertion that the waters prevailed fifteen cubits upward." J. J. S. Perowne, 1896, "Noah," *Dr William Smith's Dictionary of the Bible,* vol. III, ed. H.B. Hackett and B. Abbot, Boston: Houghton, Mifflin and Co., 2181-2182.

region where Noah was so as not to escape and uniformly cover the whole earth! Forster and Marston conclude:

> We believe, therefore, that the Bible implies there was an individual Noah, and a physical Flood throughout all the land. It leaves open to modern re-interpretation whether or not that "land" implied the whole globe, though the actual language would intend on the whole to imply not.[8]

Upon what basis has such "modern re-interpretation" been made? Clearly, if biblical scholars and theologians the equal of today's down through the centuries have been almost unanimous that God intended us to understand from the language of Genesis that it was a global flood, then it must be geological science that has governed the "modern re-interpretation" of Forster and Marston, which is borne out by their appeal to geologists for clear and detailed arguments for a local flood. Thus, it is ultimately not what God's Word says which decides this issue for local flood advocates. Rather, it is what modern uniformitarian geology teaches which has shaped their treatment of God's Word. So, if Forster and Marston, like Ramm, accept the conclusions of modern uniformitarian geology and appeal to Hugh Miller's bizarre hypothesis that the Near East suddenly began to sink at a rate of 400 feet a day for forty days, then where are the modern geologists with the evidence of such a geological phenomenon supposedly having occurred about 5000 to 6000 BC? Not until evangelical leaders and Christian scholars show a willingness to break completely with uniformitarian geology will they begin to understand the full significance of the Genesis Flood and see that the geological evidence is in fact consistent with the divine perspective in Genesis of a fully global flood.

Morton takes this compromise with modern uniformitarian geology further by shifting Noah and the human population of his time into a dry, desolate, and empty Mediterranean basin, with the waters of the Atlantic Ocean held back by a natural dam across the Straits of Gibraltar.[9] Thus, Noah's Flood occurred when that dam catastrophically failed and the waters of the Atlantic Ocean came pouring into the Mediterranean basin, filling it up to make it the Mediterranean Sea we have today. The Ark in which Noah and the animals escaped from this flood was washed onto the shore of the northeast African coastline, up the Nile River basin! This happened 5.5 million years ago, and Noah was the ancestor of the *Homo erectus* population that eventually evolved and moved out of the Africa.[10] Sadly, not even modern uniformitarian geologists agree with this scenario, the latest speculation being that Noah's Flood was actually a catastrophic flooding of the Black Sea when water from the Mediterranean Sea burst through a land ridge across the

---

8 Forster and Marston, 1989, 241-242.

9 Morton, 1995, 136-138.

10 Morton, 1995, 141-145.

Bosphorus.[11] Thus, compromising with the shifting fallible human opinions of uniformitarian geology leads to a local flood view in which the clear wording of Holy Scripture must then be re-interpreted. Perhaps the famous agnostic, T. H. Huxley, was not far from the truth when he said:

> If we are to listen to many expositors of no mean authority, we must believe that what seems to be clearly defined in Genesis—as if very great pains had been taken that there should be no possibility of mistake—is not the meaning of the text at all....A person who is not a Hebrew scholar can only stand aside and admire the marvelous flexibility of a language which admits of such diverse interpretations.[12]

Ultimately, the local-Flood proponents depend on the presumed "limited observation and information" of Noah and the presumed Bible writers of the Flood account to maintain their viewpoint, but this reduces the historical statements of Scripture to the level of mere fallible human opinion. The worldview of Bible writers, we are told, must be understood from the standpoint of their "cultural environment," which is a sophisticated way of saying that their statements are not always dependable. In discussing this and other subtle methods of undermining the clear statements of Scripture, Payne has commented:

> In recent conservatively-oriented publications, the principles of *usus loquendi*, normativeness, and progressive revelation seem to have shifted in function from that of an x-ray for exposing the meaning of Scripture to that of a cloak for avoiding it. In reference, for example, to the extent of the Flood, Bernard Ramm has concluded that when interpreted "phenomenally" and according to the cultural use of the narrator, the Deluge need be understood as covering only part of the earth's surface as lay within the observation of the man who recorded it. But that the principle of *usus loquendi* is not the real basis for this interpretation is shown by Ramm's own summarization, as follows:
>
> 1. The Flood is local, though spoken of in universal terms, and so the destruction of man is local though spoken of in universal terms.
> 2. The account, in other words, conveys the thought of a universal catastrophe; but rational induction discountenances the possibility of a world-wide flood. It is, therefore, left to the rule of hermeneutics to gloss over the unacceptable words.[13]

---

11 W. Ryan and W. Pitman, 1998, *Noah's Flood: The Scientific Discoveries about the Event that Changed History,* New York: Simon and Schuster.

12 Quoted in O. T. Allis, 1951, *God Spake by Moses,* Philadelphia: The Presbyterian and Reformed Publishing Co., 158. Allis was firmly convinced that the book of Genesis teaches a geographically universal Flood, as stated clearly in his book (p. 24).

13 J. B. Payne, 1960, Hermeneutics as a cloak for the denial of Scripture, *Journal of the Evangelical Theological Society,* 3(4): 94.

Yet twenty years after these words were penned, Ramm's thinking was still being perpetuated by Youngblood:

> The biblical flood narrative, with its carefully recorded chronological notations and other details, reads like a log book kept by Noah himself. If so, the "high mountains" were mountains that he knew of or had heard of or could see, the low-lying eminences of Shinar or Babylon (see 11:2) rather than the lofty peaks of the Zagros or Caucasus ranges, or—even less likely the Himalayas. Height, after all, is a relative matter.[14]

Thus, because conservative theologians continue to compromise with uniformitarian geology and perpetuate this deficient view of the Scriptures, as does Boardman,[15] men such as Morton[16] and Ross[17] simply accept the local flood view as somehow proven from Scripture, which in turn allows them to remain comfortable with the secular uniformitarian and evolutionary paradigm.

However, it is concluded here that the argument based upon a limited usage of universal terms must be rejected. It does not do justice to the context of the Flood narrative, it fails to cope with the physical phenomena described in those chapters, and it has encouraged Christian thinkers to take utterly unwarranted liberties with the text of Scripture. Our primary responsibility as honest exegetes of God's Word must not be to find ways to manipulate and mold the text of the biblical narratives into the framework of contemporary scientific theories. Instead, our concern must be to discover exactly what God has said in the Scriptures concerning the past history of the earth, being fully aware of the fact that our contemporary scientists, laboring under the handicap of non-biblical philosophical presuppositions (such as materialism, naturalism, organic evolution, and geological uniformitarianism), are thus in no position to give us an accurate reconstruction of the early history of the earth and of its inhabitants. Likewise, any theologian, biblical scholar, conservative evangelical, or Bible-believing scientist who has used these non-biblical philosophical presuppositions in his study of the Genesis Flood account has invariably sought to reduce the use of universal terms in the biblical text to be only describing a local flood or, worse still, simply a story, with or without any historical basis.

---

14 Youngblood, 1980, 126. Noah must have been an abysmally ignorant man to live for 600 years and still know nothing of real mountains! For a careful analysis of the universal terms used in the Flood narrative of Genesis 6-9, see G. F. Hasel, 1975, The biblical view of the extent of the Flood, *Origins*, 2(2): 77-95.

15 Boardman, 1990, 210-229.

16 Morton, 1995, 134-138.

17 H. N. Ross, 1998, 141-157.

19

Summary and Conclusions

The basic arguments against an anthropologically universal Flood really come down to this: the Flood was too recent to allow for the present population of the world, in its racial types and geographical distribution, to have descended from Noah's family. Thus, evangelical scholars who maintain that the Flood was only local argue that on the basis of the claims that all mankind could not have descended from Noah's family, and that there is no global flood recorded in recent geological and human history, the Genesis Flood story being derived from the Babylonian flood myth. In answer to these assertions, it has been shown:

1. *Negatively*, that there is no way of proving scientifically that the present distribution of mankind occurred at a date prior to that which the Bible suggests for the Flood, and
2. *Positively*, that the relatively recent global distribution of all people groups from the Mesopotamian region, together with the circumstantial evidence provided by universal Flood traditions, is consistent with an anthropologically universal Flood and not with the concept of an anthropologically local flood.

Furthermore, while the parallels between the Babylonian and biblical Flood accounts indicate a common source, the numerous distinct differences and the grotesqueness and untenable distortions of the Babylonian account indicate that it was derived by oral transmission from the true account in Genesis. Thus, it must be concluded that arguments against a flood that destroyed all of mankind in the days of Noah are inadequate, being sustained by neither science nor Scripture.

Three other most commonly used non-geological arguments against a geographically universal flood have also been discussed in this section. The first of these was the argument based upon the limited use of universal terms. In responding to this argument, three cogent reasons have been given for maintaining a literal interpretation of the universal terms employed in Genesis 6-9:

1. In most cases the Bible uses such terms in a literal sense.
2. The context of Genesis 6-9, including the tenor of the entire Flood narrative,

demands a literal interpretation of the universal terms.
3. The physical phenomena described in these chapters would be meaningless if the universal terms were not taken in the literal sense.

Section III

Noah, the Ark, and the Animals

20

GATHERING THE ANIMALS TO THE ARK

Another familiar group of objections to the reality of a global flood pertains to the perceived problems of how the animals were brought into the Ark and then cared for during the 371 days of the Flood. Christians holding the local flood view do so because they consider it an impossibility for Noah to have gathered from around the world two of every kind of land-dwelling, air-breathing animal and then cared for them in the Ark for a whole year. Consequently, they insist that Noah only had to collect a few domesticated animals from within the Mesopotamian region, which would then have been much more easily cared for on the Ark. They assert that even if Noah could have collected such a vast number of animals, the Ark could not possibly have contained them, nor could they have been properly cared for by eight persons on the Ark for an entire year.

Sadly, such skepticism toward God's Word has also encouraged secular scholars and rationalist skeptics to lampoon and ridicule the biblical account of Noah and the animals on the Ark, often using caricatures that hold God and His Word up to derision, thus embarrassing many Christians into conceding that the Genesis Flood account is merely a quaint story that may not even be true history. Such compromises and concessions have not only intimidated Christians, but have reduced God's Word to antiquated irrelevancy in the eyes of many unbelievers, causing them ultimately to ignore God's offer of reconciliation. However, the clearly expressed details in Scripture concerning what literally occurred to Noah, the animals, and the Ark can be more than satisfactorily defended in a rigorous manner to convince any honest inquirer.

Since 1840, when John Pye Smith first set forth these objections,[1] those who promote the local flood view have seemingly tried to outdo one another in their efforts to depict the supposed absurdities in the biblical account. For example, Jamieson wrote in 1870:

> On the hypothesis, therefore, of a universal flood, we must imagine motley groups of beasts, birds, and reptiles, directing their way from the

1   John Pye Smith, 1854, 145.

most distant and opposite quarters to the spot where Noah had prepared his ark—natives of the polar regions and the torrid zones preparing to sojourn in a temperate country, the climate of which was unsuited alike to Arctic and equatorial animals. What time must have been consumed! what privations must have been undergone for want of appropriate food! what difficulties must have been encountered! what extremes of climate must have been endured by the natives of Europe, America, Australia, Asia, Africa, and the numerous islands of the sea! They could not have performed their journeys unless they had been miraculously preserved.[2]

Twenty years later, Dods added to this caricature of Genesis by suggesting that the animals of Australia,

> visited by some presentiment of what was to happen many months after, selected specimens of their number, and that these specimens...crossed thousands of miles of sea...singled out Noah by some inscrutable instinct, and surrendered themselves to his keeping.[3]

However, by this time several important fallacies had become apparent in the arguments that Dods and others were proposing to refute the universal Flood view. For example, it was recognized that there was definite danger involved in removing every supernatural element from the Genesis Flood and explaining everything on a purely naturalistic basis. Thus, one defender of a local flood who clearly saw this danger wrote in 1896, rebuking Dods:

> That doubtless is the way Dr. Dods would set about it..."get the animals to select specimens of their number," though the learned divine does not condescend to tell us whether it would be by ballot or by show of hands. However, the Supreme Being is not necessarily confined to Dr. Dods' methods. Even if the Deluge were universal, the difficulties enumerated would not prove insuperable to the Almighty....Such writing ignores the supernatural character of the episode, endeavors to explain it on naturalistic principles, and thereby comes very near holding up to ridicule Him who is God blessed forevermore.[4]

In the century since, local flood proponents have simply reverted to highlighting the supposed difficulties with naturalistic explanations of animal migration to the Ark, and it has been evangelical scientists who have been at the forefront of defending a local flood. Thus, to make the Flood account more palatable to the minds of Christians heavily influenced by secular education and rationalistic

---

2   R. Jamieson, 1948, 99.

3   M. Dods, 1890, *The Book of Genesis*, vol. I of *The Expositor's Bible*, ed. W.R. Nicoll, fourth ed., London: Hodder and Stoughton, 55.

4   J. C. Jones, 1897, *Primeval Revelation: Studies in Genesis I-VIII*, New York: American Tract Society, 356.

thinking, these scientists have opted to limit the animals Noah needed to take on board the Ark to just domesticated varieties. For example, Filby wrote:

> Kangaroos would have had to come a long way from Australia, and as far to return—but if Australia was not part of "the whole land" known to Noah there was no need for the kangaroo to come. The giraffe would have required a special stall to enable him to stretch his neck—but if central Africa was not part of the world Noah knew, no problem arises. The mastodon of South America must have made a long journey to reach Sumeria and the giant panda from China would have required a special stock of bamboo shoots for his year's food—but it seems that the Bible does not really require mastodons and giant pandas on the ark. Dogmatism is obviously out of place when we really do not know the answers, but it is far more reasonable to suppose that Noah collected—maybe tamed—oxen, sheep, goats, horses, asses, camels, relatives of the deer, animals of the cat, dog, beaver, fox, pig, mole, rat and rabbit tribes, and many birds.[5]

Similarly, Custance wrote:

> It is almost certain that domesticated animals could not have migrated alone. ...domesticated sheep, cattle, pigs, fowl, goats, perhaps camels, and possibly asses—to mention only the more common ones—might not have fared too well in a natural environment still quite outside man's control. For this reason, if for no other, some animals at least would have to be taken on board—but these were probably of the domesticated varieties.... it is quite obvious that some territories are determined by temperature—the Arctic regions or deserts, for example. Consequently it is difficult to conceive how creatures accustomed to these very well-defined climatic conditions could pass through great stretches of country with entirely different environmental conditions as they made their way to the ark. Yet this would be necessary if the Flood was world-wide. Desert lizards from central America, polar bears from the Arctic, kangaroos from Australia, and giraffes from Africa would all have to make their way over thousands of miles of unfamiliar territory, and in one case by sea, to Asia Minor, where the environmental conditions might very well be "unsuitable" for any of them. Multiply this circumstance to cover thousands of creatures who are so small that the journey could only be completed by a tenth or even the twentieth generation descending from those who began it, and one gets a fair idea of the miraculous supervision required to assemble a crew sufficient to preserve every species from a global Flood.[6]

---

5 Filby, 1970, 85.

6 Custance, 1979, 36, 40-41.

Subsequently, Morton revels in exaggerations in order to cast doubts on the biblical account of migration to the Ark:

> The snails could not do it. The average speed that a snail travels is 8 centimeters per minute. Assuming that the snail must use two-thirds of its time for feeding (not an unreasonable assumption) then while it is migrating to the ark, it must spend two-thirds of its time traveling up and down trees. Thirty percent of terrestrial snails scrape algae off of tree trunks. Assuming that the migrating snail must travel two meters, then two meters down the tree and then find the next tree within two meters, a snail making a straight-line trip from the opposite side of the earth to the Middle East, a distance of 20,000 kilometers, would have to travel a true distance of 60,000 kilometers. At 8 centimeters per minute, the snail would take 1,426 years to make the trek. Thus the snail must start his trek almost the day of creation in order to make its way to the ark. But a terrestrial snail cannot take the most direct route because it cannot cross rivers without drowning. It must make numerous detours around creeks, lakes and rivers. A snail which lived on the opposite side of the earth could not reach the ark in the available time. Other snails, living a little closer to the ark must have begun their migration immediately upon their creation. And since snails do not live as long as 1,400 years the descendant of the snail that started the trek would have to finish it.[7]

He compounds these ridiculous impossibilities in referring to earthworms, tree sloths, herbivorous mammals, mice, amphibians, the giant panda, and kangaroos. Ross, on the other hand, deals with these supposed difficulties by arguing that only birds and mammals were taken onto the Ark.[8] He does this via a study of the Hebrew words used in Genesis 6-9 to describe the animals that went aboard the Ark. However, some of the Hebrew words are very broad in their usage, and thus restricting them to just describing birds and mammals is really a reflection of Ross's choice to keep details acceptable to, and consistent with, his local flood bias.

All these attempts at ridiculing the difficulties of animal migration to the Ark are flawed for a number of reasons. First, the Genesis account nowhere suggests that Noah was to take only domesticated animals into the Ark. The stated purpose of the Flood was to destroy everything on the earth, including "man," "beasts," "creeping things," and "fowls of the air" (Genesis 6:7), and "to destroy all flesh, wherein is the breath of life, from under heaven; and every thing that is in the earth shall die" (Genesis 6:17; also note Genesis 6:12-13, 19-21; 7:2-4, 8, 14-16; 8:1, 17-19; 9:8-17). These are exactly the same terms used in Genesis 1 to describe the various kinds of land animals which God created. If only domesticated animals

---

7   Morton, 1995, 68-69.

8   Ross, 1998, 162-163.

were to be taken into the Ark, are we then to assume that only domesticated animals were created by God in Genesis 1? This consideration also demolishes Ross's efforts to limit the Hebrew words used to just birds and mammals. The fact is that no clearer terms could have been employed by the Holy Spirit in directing the human writer than those which He did employ to express the idea of *the totality of air-breathing, land-dwelling animals in the world*. Once this point is conceded, surely all controversy about the global geographical extent of the Flood must end, because surely no one would maintain that all land animals were confined to the Mesopotamian Valley in the days of Noah!

A second and equally serious fault is that it begs the question of the extent and effects of the Flood. It assumes, for example, that climatic zones were exactly the same before the Flood as they are now, that the various animals inhabited the same areas of the world as they do now, and that the geography and topography of the earth are essentially the same now as they were before the Flood. However, a catastrophic, global flood with accompanying tectonic upheavals, massive erosion and sedimentation, etc., would have profoundly altered all these conditions. Arctic and desert zones may never have existed before the Flood, nor the great intercontinental barriers of high mountains, impenetrable jungles, and open seas (as between Australia and southeast Asia today, and Siberia and Alaska). Indeed, it is quite likely that there was only one very large continental landmass prior to the Flood. On this basis, it is quite probable that animals were more widely distributed than now, with representatives of each created kind of land animal living in that part of the single landmass where Noah was building the Ark. Furthermore, it is highly likely that specialization amongst animals, such as the narrowing of their ecological niches and/or the limiting of their diets as in the cases of tree sloths, giant pandas, and koalas, only occurred after the Flood due to the rapid development of post-Flood climatic zones, the rapid dispersal patterns of flora and fauna to the many separate post-Flood continental landmasses, and the genetic "bottleneck" at the Flood and rapid post-Flood speciation.

Thus, all manner of animals may well have been living in proximity to the Ark and wouldn't have had far to travel to go abroad. In any case, the scriptural account does not suggest that Noah had to go out and gather all the animals, rounding them up and bringing them to the Ark. On the contrary, it is clearly stated in Genesis 6:19-20 that "two of every sort shall come unto thee," meaning the animals would come to Noah to board the Ark, undoubtedly directed by God.

21

THE CAPACITY OF THE ARK

Just how large was the Ark? Critics charge that the capacity of the Ark could not have been sufficient for all of the animals. Noting that the Ark was a gigantic barge-like structure, advocates of a local flood resort to various methods of "multiplying the species" in order to make it impossible for any ark, however large, to carry two of each kind of creature. One method has been to take the phrase "by sevens, the male and his female" (Genesis 7:2-3) to mean seven pairs or fourteen clean animals, instead of "by sevens." Some have even tried to compound the perceived problem further by classifying all the birds amongst the clean animals and inflating the number of species to 15,000, thereby insisting that about 210,000 birds had to be placed on the Ark![1]

However, even assuming that there were 15,000 different species of birds in the days of Noah, that is still far too many birds needing to go aboard the Ark. Apart from the fact that the estimated number of species of birds is closer to 8,600 to 8,700, the Hebrew phrase "by sevens, the male and the female" no more means fourteen than does the parallel phrase "two and two" (Genesis 7:9, 15) means four! Indeed, what is meant by the phrase "two and two" is unmistakably clarified in Genesis 7:2 when Noah is commanded to take of the unclean beasts "by two, the male and his female." Furthermore, the context of Genesis 7:2-3 demands that the birds were to likewise be classified into "clean" and "unclean," just like the other animals, as is specifically stated in Leviticus 11. Leupold states:

> The Hebrew expression "take seven seven" means "seven each" (Koenig's *Syntax* 85; 316b; Gesenius' *Grammatik* Revised by Kautzsch 134q). Hebrew parallels support this explanation. In any case, it would be a most clumsy method of trying to say "fourteen." Three pairs and one supernumerary make the "seven." As has often been suggested, the supernumerary beast was the one Noah could conveniently offer for sacrifice after the termination of the Flood. In verse 3 the idea of "the birds of the heavens" must, of course, be supplemented by the adjective "clean," according to the principle laid down in verse 2. The birds are

---

1   J. Lever, 1958, *Creation and Evolution*, Grand Rapids, MI: Grand Rapids International Publications, 17.

separately mentioned so that Noah might not be left to his own devices in fixing the limits of what verse 2 included.[2]

Yet in order to continue championing the perceived impossibilities by wrongly inflating the calculations, Morton still insists:

> There is some disagreement as to exactly how many animals this refers to. …most people believe that it means two pair of the unclean and seven pair of the clean animals.[3]

Ironically, Morton quotes Genesis 7:2-3 from the New International Version of the Scriptures, which states "seven of every kind," thus making it quite clear what the Hebrew meant.

In addition, some identify the "species" of modern taxonomy with the "kinds" of Genesis. John Pye Smith was one of the first to do this, taking delight in pointing out that the Ark was too small for such a cargo, for "the innumerable millions upon millions of animalcules must be provided for; for they have all their appropriate and diversified places and circumstances of existence."[4] Even though this ploy has long been discredited, it has continued to be utilized to lampoon a supposedly overcrowded Ark by modern anti-creationists, such as Futuyma, Moore, McGowan, and Plimer,[5] and by skeptical Christians such as Morton.[6] In their zeal to ridicule God's Word, these skeptics have endeavored to exaggerate manufactured problems with the Ark's cargo by ignoring what the Scriptures clearly specify. Thus, Moore declares that the Ark had to carry deep-sea fish, while McGowan puts whales and sharks on the Ark. Futuyma adds to the farce by insisting all the millions of plant and animal species went on the Ark, while Plimer extends such rationalistic arguments against the Ark to the point of absurdity by suggesting it even had to carry cultures of microorganisms!

One hundred and fifty years of investigations in zoology and genetics have revealed the boundaries of genetic variability and the amazing potentialities for diversification with which the Creator endowed the Genesis kinds. These "kinds" have never evolved or merged into each other by crossing over the divinely-

---

2   Leupold, 1980, 290. Morris adds: "The three pairs were to encourage the relatively greater numerical proliferation of the clean animals after the Flood (on a par with man, with his three surviving families) and perhaps also to allow for a greater variety of genetic factors, so that more varieties could be developed later as needed." Morris, 1976, 191. The three pairs would in fact have provided Noah's three sons with a breeding pair each.

3   Morton, 1995, 67.

4   J. P. Smith, 1854, 144.

5   D. J. Futuyma, 1983, *Science on Trial*, New York: Pantheon Books; R. A. Moore, 1983, The impossible voyage of Noah's Ark, Creation/Evolution, 11: 1-43; C. McGowan, 1984, *In the Beginning: A Scientist Shows Why the Creationists are Wrong*, New York: Prometheus Books; I. R. Plimer, 1994, *Telling Lies for God*, Sydney, Australia: Random House.

6   Morton, 1995, 67-68.

established lines of demarcation,[7] but they have been diversified into so many varieties and sub-varieties (like the ethnic groupings and families of humanity) that taxonomists continue even today with the enormous task of recognizing and classifying them.[8]

Frank L. Marsh was a pioneer in recognizing and promoting the concept of the Genesis kinds, which he called *baramins* (from *bara*—"created," and *min*—"kind"). Marsh highlighted the fact that over 500 varieties of sweet pea have been developed from a single type since the year 1700, and that over 200 distinct varieties of dogs, as different from each other as a dachshund and a collie, have been developed from just a few wild dogs. Knowing this, Marsh proposed that the *baramins* became diversified both before and after the Flood.

> In the field of zoology a very good illustration of descent with variation is furnished by the domestic pigeon. The diversity in form and temperament to be found among strains of pigeons would stagger our belief in their common origin if we did not know that they have all been developed from the wild rock pigeon of European coasts, *Columbia livia*. It is extremely interesting to see the variations from the ancestral form which are exhibited in such strains as the pouter, the leghorn runt, the fantail, the tumbler, the owl, the turbit, the swallow, the carrier, the nun, the Jacobin, and the homer. Different "species" names and possibly even different "generic" names would certainly be assigned to some of these if it were not known that they are merely strains of a common stock.[9]

Woodmorappe has pointed out that calculating the numbers of animals that were taken on the Ark requires not only analysis of their taxonomic identity, but also taxonomic rank.[10] Not surprisingly, anti-creationists such as Awbrey and Moore,[11] along with Ross,[12] audaciously accuse creationists of having invented

---

7 Robert E. D. Clark concluded: "Every theory of evolution has failed in this light of modern discovery and, not merely failed, but failed so dismally that it seems almost impossible to go on believing in evolution!" R.E.D. Clark, 1958, *Darwin: Before and After,* Grand Rapids, MI: Grand Rapids International Publications, 145. More recently, Michael Denton has written: "Whatever view we wish to take of the current status of Darwinian theory….There can be no doubt that after a century of intensive effort biologists have failed to validate it in any significant sense….Ultimately the Darwinian theory of evolution is no more nor less than the great cosmogenic myth of the twentieth century." M. Denton, 1985, *Evolution: A Theory in Crisis*, London: Burnett Books, 357-358.

8 Thodosius Dobzhansky, 1951, *Genetics and the Origin of Species,* third ed., New York: Columbia University Press, 3-10; and Ernst Mayr, 1969, Principles of Systematic Zoology, New York: McGraw-Hill Book Company, 1-15.

9 F. L. Marsh, 1947, *Evolution, Creation and Science,* Washington: Review and Herald Publishing Association, 29, 351.

10 J. Woodmorappe, 1996, *Noah's Ark: A Feasibility Study,* Santee, CA: Institute for Creation Research, 5-8.

11 F. T. Awbrey, 1981, Defining 'kinds'—do creationists apply a double standard?, *Creation/Evolution,* 5: 1-6; and Moore, 1983, 1-43.

12 H. N. Ross, 1994, *Creation and Time: A Biblical and Scientific Perspective on the Creation-Date Controversy,* Colorado Springs, CO: NavPress, 73.

the concept of *baramins* as an *ad hoc* device to reduce the numbers of animals on the Ark, when the term is merely a direct translation of the Hebrew words, and the concept clearly and repeatedly presented in the Genesis creation account, as has already been noted. These critics also seem willingly ignorant of the many evidences that the *baramins* are broader than the species. The fact that the genus is the smallest divisions of plants and animals that can usually be identified without scientific study[13] could indicate that the *baramins* could be at the genus level. As Woodmorappe maintains, the Scriptures were written to be understood without modern scientific training or other knowledge unavailable to the ancients, so the *baramin* must be a real entity, as demonstrated by Jones.[14] Thus, largely using scriptural evidence (for example, the animal lists in Leviticus), Jones demonstrated that the *baramin* could be approximately equivalent to the sub-family or family, at least in the case of birds and mammals.[15] Scherer has arrived at the same conclusion, but on the basis of scientific evidence, such as numerous documented cases of interbreeding between individuals of different species and genera.[16] Considerable research has been conducted by creationist scholars over the last decade on this question of identifying the *baramin*, which has spawned a whole new field of study, baraminology.[17] In the case of cats, Robinson and Cavanaugh have shown that the cat *baramin* is at the family level and includes not only the lion and tiger, but the cheetah, cougar, and even the spotted hyena. On the other hand, there is still debate as to the taxonomic ranks included in the turtle *baramin*. Nevertheless, it is quite clear that in estimating the number of animals that had to go on board the Ark, it would be very conservative to place the *baramins* at the genus level, recognizing that even then the final calculated number of animals would probably be an excessive overestimate.

Thus, it is totally unwarranted to insist that all the present species, not to mention

---

13 A. J. Cain, 1956, The genus in evolutionary taxonomy, *Systematic Zoology,* 5: 97-109.

14 A. J. Jones, 1972, A general analysis of the Biblical "kind" (min), *Creation Research Society Quarterly,* 9(2): 53-57.

15 A. J. Jones, 1972, Boundaries of the min: an analysis of the Mosaic lists of clean and unclean animals, *Creation Research Society Quarterly,* 9(2): 114-123.

16 S. Scherer, 1993, Basic types of life, in *Studium Integrale,* ed. S. Scherer, Berlin: Pascal-Verlag, 1-19; and S. Scherer, 1998, Basic types of life: evidence for design from taxonomy? in *Mere Creation: Science, Faith and Intelligent Design,* ed. W. A. Dembski, chapter 8, Downers Grove, IL: InterVarsity Press, 195-211.

17 K. P. Wise, 1990, Baraminology: a young-earth creation biosystematic method, in *Proceedings of the Second International Conference on Creationism,* ed. R. E. Walsh and C. L. Brooks, vol. II, Pittsburgh, PA: Creation Science Fellowship, 345-360; W. J. ReMine, 1990, Discontinuity systematics: a new method of biosystematics relevant to the creation model, in *Proceedings of the Second International Conference on Creationism,* ed. R. E. Walsh and C. L. Brooks, vol. II, Pittsburgh, PA: Creation Science Fellowship, 207-216; W. Frair, 1991, Original kinds and turtle phylogeny, *Creation Research Society Quarterly,* 28(1): 21-24; D. A. Robinson, 1997, A mitochondrial DNA analysis of the testudine apobaramin, *Creation Research Society Quarterly,* 33(4): 262-272; D. A. Robinson and A. Cavanaugh, 1998, A quantitative approach to baraminology with examples from the catarrhine primates, *Creation Research Society Quarterly,* 34(4): 196-208; D. A. Robinson and A. Cavanaugh, 1998, Evidence for a hollobaraminic origin of the cats, *Creation Research Society Quarterly,* 35(1): 2-14; P. J. Williams, 1997, What does min mean? *Creation Ex Nihilo Technical Journal,* 11(3): 344-352; K. P. Wise, 1992, Practical baraminology, *Creation Ex Nihilo Technical Journal,* 6(2): 122-137.

all the varieties and sub-varieties, of animals in the world today needed to be represented on board the Ark. Nevertheless, as a gigantic barge, with a volume of approximately 1.45 million cubic feet or about 41,000 cubic meters (assuming 1 cubit = 18 inches or 45 centimeters), the Ark had a carrying capacity probably equal to that of 270 or more standard freight cars as used by modern American railroads, or of six freight trains each with 45 such cars![18] Moore has berated the comparison between livestock on railroad freight cars and the confinement of animals on the Ark, claiming that animals require large floor areas, based on the experiences of zoos.[19] However, Woodmorappe has correctly argued that a zoo is a very inappropriate and misleading analogy for the housing requirements of the animals on the Ark.[20] A zoo is a facility for the public display of captive animals in relatively comfortable confinement on a permanent basis, with provision for breeding in captivity. On the other hand, the Ark represented a temporary confinement of animals in an emergency situation without the need for breeding. The Ark was thus not a floating zoo, but instead analogous to an intensive livestock unit or "factory farm" where animals are held in intensive confinement for months or even years, commonly with few or no opportunities for them to leave their enclosures.

So how many animals needed to be taken on board the Ark? Ernst Mayr, who probably has been America's leading systematic taxonomist, listed the following numbers for animal species according to the then best estimates of modern taxonomy:

Mammals	3,700
Birds	8,600
Reptiles	6,300
Amphibians	2,500
Fishes, etc.	20,600
Tunicates, etc.	1,400
Echinoderms	6,000
Arthropods, etc.	838,500
Mollusks	107,250
Worms, etc.	34,700
Coelenterates, bryozoans, etc.	9,600

---

18   *Encyclopaedia Britannica,* 1962, vol. 14, 943 stated that a typical American boxcar of that era had a capacity of 45 tons of lading and a cubic capacity of 4,860 cubic feet, which would make the Ark's cubic capacity equivalent to about 287 of such railroad boxcars. However, the *New Encyclopaedia Britannica,* Macropaedia, 1985, vol. 28, 792 notes that most new American freight cars are designed for capacity of 50 or more tons, so calculated proportionally such freight cars would have a cubic capacity of at least 5,400 cubic feet, and thus the Ark's cubic capacity would be equivalent to about 268 such modern railroad freight cars.

19   Moore, 1983, 16-17.

20   Woodmorappe, 1996, 15-16.

Sponges	4,800
Protozoans	28,350
TOTAL ANIMALS	1,072,300[21]

More recent estimates vary little from these figures.[22] It should be remembered that these estimated numbers refer to species, but even then one wonders about "the innumerable millions upon millions of animalcules" which Pye Smith insisted the Ark had to carry, especially considering that of this total there was no need for Noah to make any provision for *fishes* (20,600 species), *tunicates* (marine chordates like sea squirts—1,400), *echinoderms* (marine creatures like starfishes and sea urchins—6,000), *mollusks* (mussels, clams, oysters, etc.—107,250), *coelenterates* (corals, sea anemones, jellyfishes, hydroids—9,600), *sponges* (4,800), or *protozoans* (microscopic, single-celled creatures, mostly marine—28,350). This eliminates 178,000 species of marine creatures. In addition, some *mammals* are aquatic (whales, seals, dolphins, etc.); the *amphibians* need not all have been included, while some *reptiles* are similarly aquatic (turtles, alligators, etc.); a large number of the *arthropods* (838,500 species), such as lobsters, shrimps, crabs, water fleas, and barnacles, are marine creatures, while the *insects* (750,000 species) among these arthropoda are usually very small; and many of the 34,700 species of *worms*, as well as many of the insects, could have survived outside of the Ark. When it is also considered that Noah was not required to take aboard the largest or even adult specimens of each created "kind," and that comparatively few were classified as "clean" birds and beasts, then the supposed space problem vanishes.[23] Lever thus completely missed the mark when he stated that "the lowest estimate of the number of animals in the ark then would be fully 2,500,000,"[24] and Morton likewise ignores the Scriptures with his estimate that "the grand total of animals needing to be on the ark is somewhere around 1.7 million individuals."[25]

If, as the preponderance of evidence shows, the "created kind" or *baramin* was possibly equivalent in most instances to the family (at least in the case of mammals and birds),[26] then there would have only been about 2,000 animals on the Ark.[27] On the other hand, the total number of species of mammals, birds, reptiles, and

---

21   Mayr, 1969, 11-12.

22   For example, the *Encyclopaedia Britannica*, 1982 lists 4,000 species of mammals, 6,000 species of reptiles, 2,400 species of amphibians, and 8,700 species of birds.

23   Woodmorappe, 1996, 8-10 discusses in detail which animals were classified as "clean" and suggests that the "clean" animals would have amounted to approximately thirteen genera of mammals and perhaps only a few tens of genera at most of birds.

24   Lever, 1958, 17.

25   Morton, 1995, 68. Anti-creationist Plimer suggests 30 million! (Plimer, 1994, 123).

26   A. J. Jones, 1973, Boundaries of the min: an analysis of the Mosaic lists of clean and unclean animals, *Creation Research Society Quarterly*, 9(2): 114-123; Scherer, 1993; and Robinson and Cavanaugh, 1998.

27   A. J. Jones, 1973, How many animals on the Ark? *Creation Research Society Quarterly*, 10(2): 102-108.

amphibians listed by Mayr is only 21,100, so for all practical purposes one could say that 43,000 individual vertebrate animals would be the maximum number which would have needed to have been on the Ark. Therefore, it is most likely that the number of animals on the Ark was somewhere between these two extremes, and so Woodmorappe has suggested that if we adopt the genus as the taxonomic rank of the *baramin,* then approximately 16,000 animals would have been on the Ark, based on the land animals whose existence we know of, either as living animals or fossils.[28]

Assuming the average size of these animals to be about that of a sheep (there are only a few very large animals, of course, and even those could have been represented on the Ark by juveniles, rather than the larger adults), the space needed to accommodate the animals on the Ark can be calculated using the following information:

> The number of animals per car varies greatly, depending on the size and age of the animal…reports of stock cars and railroads show that the average number of meat animals to the carload is for cattle about 25, hogs in single deck cars about 75 and sheep about 120 per deck.[29]

This would mean that at least 240 animals of the size of sheep could be accommodated in a standard two-decked freight car. Thus, if there were as many as 16,000 animals to be carried on the Ark, then at the very most these animals would fit into 67 such freight cars, representing only a quarter of the carrying capacity of the Ark, equivalent to approximately 270 such freight cars. In other words, all the animals would fit into less than one of the three decks of the Ark. Furthermore, even if there had to be as many as 43,000 animals to be carried on the Ark, then those animals could still fit into only 180 such railroad freight cars, which would represent two-thirds of the 270 freight car carrying capacity of the Ark, meaning two of the three decks of the Ark would have carried the animals.[30]

---

28 Woodmorappe, 1996, 7.

29 H. W. Vaughan, 1945, *Types and Market Classes of Live Stock,* Columbus, OH: College Book Co., 85. With the increase in the sizes of modern "cars" used on railroads in the last five and a half decades, this estimate of the number of animals per freight car would be very conservative, but will still suffice for the purpose of showing that there would have been ample room on the Ark for the animals.

30 Extinct animals such as dinosaurs would also have been represented on the Ark. Given the tendency for dinosaur names to be proliferated because new names are often assigned to each new discovery of a few pieces of bone, or a skeleton that looks similar to one that is a different size or in a different country, then there were probably fewer than 50 dinosaur *baramin* and perhaps as few as 20. Amongst the largest dinosaurs, the sauropods, of the 87 genera commonly cited, only 12 are "firmly established." Only a few dinosaurs grew to large sizes, the average size of the dinosaurs, based on the fossilized skeletons found, being about the size of a sheep. In any case, it is more than likely the pairs of animals that went aboard the Ark were juveniles, given that they were to be preserved on the Ark in order to reach their prime immediately after the Flood and thus repopulate the post-Flood earth with their kind. Thus, juvenile dinosaurs would have been much smaller than their older "parents" and "grandparents." Indeed, dinosaurs (like all reptiles) hatched out of eggs, which were often about the size of a football or less, and then probably grew all their lives. Thus, young adult dinosaurs coming into their reproductive prime would still have been relatively small and would not have been a problem spacewise on the Ark. The

In any case, Woodmorappe has shown from a detailed analysis of the body-mass categories into which these 16,000 animals would fit that the vast majority were small, and even without allowing for large animals to be represented by juveniles, the median size of the animals on the Ark would have been the size of a small rat.[31] Thus, the above calculations based on the average animal size on the Ark being that of a sheep are overly generous, because Woodmorappe's calculations show that only about eleven percent of the animals on the Ark were substantially larger than sheep. It is therefore abundantly clear that with a few simple calculations this trivial objection can be disposed of once and for all.

Morton makes much of the vast numbers of species of terrestrial invertebrates, such as snails (22,000 species), insects (750,000 known species), spiders (30,000 species), centipedes (280,000 species), earthworms (180,000 species), millipedes (8,000 species), and mites (20,000 species), and insists that because the vast majority of these species would not be able to survive in the Flood waters then all these creatures would likewise have to be taken on board the Ark.[32] However, such an objection is easily dismissed. First, the number of such invertebrates needing to go on the Ark is drastically reduced by again recognizing that only two of each *baramin,* rather than species, needed to go aboard the Ark, particularly if the taxonomic rank of these invertebrate *baramin* was at the genus or even family level. Second, the vast majority of these invertebrates are very small creatures, so that if the space occupied by each individual averaged two inches squared, then only twelve more railroad freight cars would be needed to carry over a million such creatures. This, of course, is a gross overestimate using the number of species in the calculations, and therefore the required number of two creatures from each terrestrial invertebrate *baramin* would easily be accommodated on the Ark, with abundant room to spare for the food which also needed to be stored aboard the Ark, and lots of room left over for Noah and his family.

Morton is also greatly troubled that 1.7 million animals could not be loaded on to the Ark in the allotted one-week period, for this would equate to a rate of three animals per second entering the Ark for all of that 7-day period![33] Once again, when the numbers of animals to board the Ark are correctly calculated by recognizing that the biblical *baramins* correspond to at least the taxonomic rank of genus rather than that of the species, then this alleged problem also vanishes. The probable 16,000 or fewer animals that had to go on board the Ark would

---

fossilized dinosaurs represent those that perished during the Flood, while the dinosaurs that came off the Ark then probably died out in subsequent centuries because of hostile environmental conditions after the Flood and other factors, such as removal of their habitats and direct hunting of them by the expanding human population. For a fuller treatment of this subject, see "What really happened to the dinosaurs?" in K.A. Ham ed., 2006, *The New Answers Book,* Green Forest, AR: Master Books, 149-176.

31   Woodmorappe, 1996, 10-13.

32   Morton, 1995, 68.

33   Morton, 1995, 68. Even more absurd is the claim by Plimer that 30 million species would have to board the Ark at a rate of nearly 500 pairs per second! (Plimer, 1994, 123-124.)

embark at an average rate of fewer than fifty pairs of animals per hour, hardly an arduous feat for eight adults to cope with, particularly if all these animals were able to be housed on just one deck of the Ark.

One last consideration is important here because there is yet another objection relevant to the capacity of the Ark and the numbers of animals that went aboard raised by those who want to relegate the Genesis Flood to a myth—the survival of the creatures and the plants that the Scriptures clearly state were not needed aboard the Ark. The usual objection raised is that of not only terrestrial organisms in the waters of the Flood, but also how both marine and non-marine creatures could survive the envisaged mixing of fresh and salt water, not forgetting all the sediment carried by the Flood waters.

With respect to the survival of plants through the Flood, Whitcomb and Morris reported comments from Lammerts, horticulturalist and geneticist:

> I am convinced that many thousands of plants survived either as floating vegetation rafts or by chance burial near enough to the surface of the ground for asexual sprouting of new shoots. I am, of course, aware that objections could be raised on the idea that long exposure to salt water would be so harmful to any vegetation as to either kill it or so reduce its vitality as to make root and new shoot formation impossible. However, I see no reason at all to postulate that the salt content of the ocean at the time of the Flood was as high as it is now.[34]

Marsh further suggested that :

> There was doubtless a considerable number of plants which were carried through the Flood in the form of seeds which composed a portion of the large store of food cached in the Ark. But most of the vegetation sprang up here and there wherever the propagules were able to survive the Flood.[35]

Howe went a step further and conducted experiments, from which he concluded:

> Finally, the results of this present study indicate that the seeds of certain plants will grow after soaking for as long as 140 days in various water baths. It may be argued that the Flood waters were almost as salty as our ocean waters of today, or it may be possible that they had a far lower saline content. In either case, the data of my study demonstrate that three out of five species tested germinated after long soaking periods in sea, mixed

---

34   Whitcomb and Morris, 1961, 70; as quoted from a letter dated November 27, 1957.

35   Marsh, 1947, 213.

or tap water….It may be concluded that seeds of many flowering plants could have resisted the direct contact of Flood waters and germinated vigorously after the Flood.[36]

Woodmorappe has extensively discussed these issues and with extensive documentation answered all the difficulties raised by critics, presenting a range of solutions for the survival of seeds and floating plant debris through the Flood so that the vegetation would have regenerated when the Flood waters subsided.[37] Some seeds would have undoubtedly floated on the Flood waters, only to be beached when the waters receded, there to germinate and grow. Those seeds which sank and were buried in sediments could have in some instances been re-exposed by the erosion caused by the retreating Flood waters, thereby subsequently germinating then growing. There would also have been a lot of floating vegetation masses or mats, and debris such as logs, carrying seeds, roots, and even insects and their eggs with them. Spores and pollens could have survived there too, or have been carried aloft into the atmosphere, there to drift until the storms of the Flood year subsided. And of course, it is well known that many plants and trees are easily propagated from cuttings, so that it is eminently reasonable to postulate that with the retreating of the Flood waters much of the floating vegetative debris would be beached in the soft sediments left behind and therefore would readily propagate. Indeed, the Genesis account provides a specific example of just that happening, namely the olive tree from which the dove sent out by Noah plucked a leaf and brought it back to the Ark (Genesis 8:10-11).

Even though Whitcomb and Morris dealt with the significance of this olive leaf in some detail, pointing out that the Scriptures are clear that it was an olive *leaf* and not an olive *branch* as wrongly asserted by Charles Lyell in the 1830s,[38] the anti-creationist Plimer still made the same mistake.[39] Lyell was advocating a tranquil flood in which the waters simply rose to cover olive trees without destroying them and simply subsided again, the dove bringing back the "olive branch" indicating dry land was soon to appear again. However, Whitcomb and Morris clearly explained, with supporting documentation, that the fresh olive leaf plucked off by the dove (as indicated in the Hebrew word *taraph* in Genesis 8:11, in contrast to an old water-logged leaf) could have come from a newly grown plant propagated from olive wood debris floating on the Flood waters and beached when they retreated. The olive tree is extremely hardy and would have been able to grow and thrive on almost barren, rocky slopes as soon as adequate sunlight was available. This is in keeping with the way olive trees are propagated in plantations today from cuttings, with only a few months being needed from the time of implantation to

---

36   G. F. Howe, 1971, Seed germination, sea water and plant survival in the Great Flood, in *Scientific Studies in Special Creation,* ed. W.E. Lammerts, Grand Rapids, MI: Baker Book House, 296-297.

37   Woodmorappe, 1996, 153-162.

38   Whitcomb and Morris, 1961, 104-106.

39   Plimer, 1994, 91.

the sprouting of leaves. Indeed, it was 135 days after the waters began to "assuage" when the dove episode took place, and the fact that the dove could only find a living leaf from one of the hardiest of all plants is in fact eloquent testimony in itself to the vast destructiveness of the Flood.

In response to subsequent ridicule from Moore,[40] Woodmorappe[41] has provided even more documentation of the hardiness of the olive tree and its ability to reproduce by vegetative propagation. As well as being able to survive diseases, drought, high soil salinities, toxins in soils, and wide ranges in soil pH, olive trees can grow where there is little soil and water, in stony ground, and also under precipices, and can be regenerated from just about any piece of olive-tree debris, even from bark fragments. Such is the documentation now available that any doubts about the ability of plants and trees to have survived the Flood can be dispelled. Domestic cereal plants used for animal and human food would have of course been taken aboard the Ark, but all other plants outside the Ark were left to be devastated by the Flood waters, only to be regenerated from the seeds, debris, and floating vegetation beached and exposed to germinate and sprout in the sediments and rocky slopes left behind by the retreating Flood waters. The scriptural reference to the freshly grown olive leaf is ample testimony to the reality of this explanation.

The fact that marine creatures were not included by God in the animals He brought to Noah to take aboard the Ark clearly indicates that it was intended sufficient numbers of them would survive in the Flood waters to repopulate the post-Flood world. However, many of today's fish species, for example, are specialized and do not survive in water of radically different saltiness to their usual habitat, so skeptics argue that with the mixing of fresh and salt waters during the Flood, fish and other aquatic creatures would not have survived. Of course, we do not know how salty the sea was prior to the Flood, but in all probability the pre-Flood oceans were less salty and salt was in fact added to the oceans during the Flood, particularly due to the erosion accompanying the retreating Flood waters. In any case, as argued by Woodmorappe, it is probable that most kinds of marine organisms did not survive the Flood, precisely because most of the Flood waters were intolerable for them.[42] Indeed, given the claim that there are far fewer species of aquatic invertebrates and plants in contrast to terrestrial invertebrates,[43] and given the huge numbers of marine creatures fossilized in the geologic record, present-day marine life seems to be but an impoverished remnant of that which had originally been created and had existed before the Flood.

In any case, many of today's marine creatures, especially estuarine and tidal pool

---

40   Moore, 1983, 12-13, 43.

41   Woodmorappe, 1996, 161-162.

42   Woodmorappe, 1996, 142.

43   J. C. Briggs, 1994, Species diversity: land and sea compared, *Systematic Biology,* 43(1): 130-135.

species, are able to survive large changes in salinity. For example, both starfish and barnacles can tolerate seawater with less than twenty percent its normal saltiness. There are migratory fish that travel between salt and freshwater, such as salmon, striped bass, and Atlantic sturgeon, which spawn in freshwater and mature in saltwater. Eels reproduce in saltwater and grow to maturity in freshwater streams and lakes. Thus, many fish are able to adjust to both fresh and saltwater.

Remembering that the *baramin* in many instances may coincide with the taxonomic rank of family, it is thus significant that most families of fish contain both fresh and saltwater species—for example, toadfish, garpike, boffin, sturgeon, herring/anchovy, salmon/trout/pike, catfish, cling fish, stickleback, scorpion fish, and flat fish.[44] This suggests that the ability to tolerate large changes in salinity was present in most fish at the time of the Flood, and that specialization (through natural selection) may have resulted in the loss of this ability in many species since then. For example, the Atlantic sturgeon is a migratory salt/freshwater species, but the Siberian sturgeon (a different species in the same *baramin*) lives only in freshwater. Similarly, hybrids of wild trout (freshwater) and farmed salmon (migratory species) have been discovered, suggesting that the differences between freshwater and marine types may be quite minor, the differences in physiology being largely in degree rather than kind. Indeed, fish can adapt to the prevailing water conditions if the salinity is changed slowly enough. Thus, many species have the ability to adapt to both fresh and saltwater within their own lifetimes, making it possible for them to survive through the Flood.

Woodmorappe has dealt at length with how organisms would have survived outside the Ark during the Flood, including the biological effects of the mixing of fresh and salt waters.[45] Extensive documentation supports the evidence that most aquatic organisms were biologically capable of handling water conditions during the Flood. It is not just a question of the salinity of the Flood waters, but also how organisms would have survived where the waters were muddy from their suspended sediment loads. However, turbidity currents are an excellent example of how the sediment load can be unevenly distributed in the water column. The sediment particles are so concentrated that the sediment load flows as a slurry, but above the turbidity current the water is virtually clear. Similarly, there is also the possibility that separate stable fresh and saltwater layers would have developed during the Flood and persisted through the Flood in some parts of the ocean. Freshwater layers are capable of sitting on top of saltwater for extended periods of time, provided turbulence is minimal. Temperature and therefore density differences will assist the permanence of such layering. Bottom topography can also play a role. For example, relatively dense, highly saline water is known to stagnate for months or years in fiords. Thus, it is entirely feasible that some

44   D. Batten, ed., 1999, How did fresh- and salt-water fish survive the Flood? *The Answers Book*, chapter 14, Brisbane, Australia: Answers in Genesis, 175-178; K.B. Cumming, 1991, How Could Fish Survive the Genesis Flood?, *Acts & Facts*, 20 (12).

45   Woodmorappe, 1996, 139-152.

sheltered regions could have formed on the ocean bottom during the Flood, allowing high salinity waters with their fauna to be protected from mixing with less saline waters above them, particularly at high latitudes where turbulence may have been sufficiently low. Furthermore, for it to be claimed that all the ocean bottoms were intolerably muddy during the Flood, thus destroying the habitats of bottom-dwelling marine invertebrates by giving them nowhere to survive, it should be remembered that eggs and larvae are well able to survive drifting in the ocean waters, particularly if attached to floating debris and vegetation. Thus, in spite of innumerable difficulties and uncertainties faced by all types of aquatic creatures outside the Ark, there seems no reason why some representatives of each *baramin* could not have been able to survive through the Flood.

Clearly the Genesis account requires only certain animals going on board the Ark, and the rest of the animals and plants being left to survive in the Flood waters, despite what perceived problems skeptical scholars may attempt to introduce. The Scriptures provide sufficient details and the relevant scientific evidence is robust enough to satisfy any honest inquiring mind. There was sufficient room on the Ark to carry all the animals and creatures God stipulated should be aboard, while most of those left outside the Ark, including the plants, were well able to survive in sufficient numbers to repopulate the post-Flood earth.

22

CARING FOR THE ANIMALS IN THE ARK

Granted, then, that the Ark was large enough to carry representatives of every kind of terrestrial animal, how could Noah and his family have cared for them all during the year of the Flood? Ramm feared that "the task of carrying away the manure, and bringing food would completely overtax the few people in the Ark,"[1] while Custance multiplies the difficulties even more:

> Many commentators have calculated the size of the Ark and the total number of species in the world, and spoken freely of its capacity to carry them. What they do not always remember is that such animals need attention and food, the carnivorous ones, if they existed as such, requiring meat which would have to be stored up for one whole year. In any case, a sufficient supply of water for drinking would probably have to be taken on board since the mingling of the waters in a worldwide Flood would presumably render it unfit to drink…it is rather difficult to visualise a Flood of worldwide proportions but with so little turbulence that four men (perhaps helped by their women folk) were able to care for such a flock. It would take very little unsteadiness to make the larger animals almost unmanageable. It becomes even more difficult to conceive how proper provision could have been made for many animals which spend much of their time in the water, such as crocodiles and seals.[2]

---

1   Ramm, 1964, 167.

2   Custance, 1979, 36-37. Of course, it would have been quite logical for Noah to have obtained the necessary drinking water from the rain that fell, though Woodmorappe, 1996, 17-21 has calculated how much water would be needed for the 16,000 animals taken aboard the Ark for a year and shown that the capacity of the Ark was more than adequate for that amount of water to be safely stored. Either explanation is adequate in itself to refute Custance's perceived difficulty. Similarly, in the original 1958 edition of his *Doorway Papers #41*, Custance imagined that the "rarefied atmosphere" at elevations above that of Mt. Everest, if the Flood covered the mountains, would "render all but a few creatures insensible in a very few moments for the lack of oxygen." He particularly expressed concern about Noah and his sons having to climb between the Ark's three decks at such high elevations! Of course, he had overlooked the elementary fact that atmospheric pressure depends on elevation *relative to sea level*. As pointed out by Whitcomb and Morris, 1961, 71, the air column above the raised sea level during the Flood was just as high, and the resulting sea level atmospheric pressure just as great, as the present sea level pressure. It is thus significant that in the 1979 edition of *Doorway Papers #41 (The Flood: Local or Global?*, Grand Rapids, MI: Zondervan Publishing House), Custance has realized his error and removed these

Similarly, Youngblood asks:

> How could a mere eight people feed [tens of thousands of species from all
> over the world] and care for them? How could those people—or a much
> larger group of people, for that matter—provide the special diets and
> varied environments necessary?[3]

It is, of course, disappointing that Christian scholars conceive of such objections
having sufficient merit to render the Genesis Flood account just an unbelievable
story contrived by the ancient Hebrews from the mythology of their Babylonian
captors. But it is worse still when these same objections are repeated by anti-
biblical skeptics who lampoon and ridicule the God-given Genesis Flood account.
Thus, Moore raises all manner of perceived problems, ranging from the feeding
of all the animals generally, as well as those with supposed special dietary needs,
with the storage of food and water, sanitation and water disposal, ventilation,
and light and temperature levels in the Ark.[4] Plimer repeats Moore's objections
but elaborates with derisive ridicule.[5] For example, Plimer supposes that if the
crew of four males worked twenty-four hours a day for the 371 days at sea, then
each animal would have received a total of six seconds of attention for the whole
year. Of course, such a calculation is based on Plimer's insistence that pairs of 30
million species were aboard the Ark, including whales. Sadly, Morton likewise
continues to repeat these exaggerated problems.[6] Thus, based on Whitcomb
and Morris' estimate of 35,000 sheep-sized animals on board the Ark, Morton
supposes that 78,750 litres of urine would be produced and need to be disposed
of daily, and that over 10 million calories of heat would be generated every hour
by the animals, needing an efficient ventilation system to remove. Critics have
tried their utmost to discredit the scriptural account of Noah and the animals
aboard the Ark for the Flood year.

However, all of these perceived difficulties can be, and have been, adequately
answered. To begin with, most of the supposed problems evaporate when, after
reading the actual stipulations in the Genesis account as to which animals were to
be taken aboard the Ark, and then the ramifications of the scriptural description
of what constitutes a created kind or *baramin*, it is realized that there were not 30
million pairs from each species on board the Ark, but a mere 16,000 animals in
total, with their average size that of a rat. As Woodmorappe ably points out, based
on actual manpower studies the people could definitely have taken care of these

---

comments. While this retraction is commendable, it is nonetheless a pity he and other critics have not
withdrawn all their other perceived difficulties which have likewise been adequately disposed of.

3   Youngblood, 1980, 131-132.

4   Moore, 1983, 25-33.

5   Plimer, 1994, 121-131.

6   Morton, 1995, 70-71.

16,000 animals *en masse*.[7] Providing extensive documentation, Woodmorappe elaborates upon labor-saving devices and practices, labor-saving interior configuration of the Ark, self-feeding devices, and the most efficient method of providing potable water. He also thoroughly deals with all aspects of waste management, handling, and disposal, including the use of appropriately-designed pens and stalls,[8] and how the issues of heating, ventilation, and illumination in the Ark could easily have been dealt with.[9] It should be remembered that God gave Noah specific instructions to construct a window one cubit (approximately 18 inches or 45 centimeters) high extending around the full circumference of the Ark above the third story for ventilation and light (Genesis 6:16), ventilation in the Ark being driven by the winds encountered during the Flood as quantified by Woodmorappe, and by the airflow due to the drifting of the Ark on the surface currents of the Flood waters.

Other presumed difficulties often raised by skeptics and critics that have been studied by Woodmorappe include the preservation of feed stuffs on the Ark, the supposed colossal bulk of hay required for large herbivores, feeding challenges for animals that eat fresh or live food, and feeding challenges for animals with specialized diets.[10] Noah was clearly commanded by God to take on board the Ark sufficient appropriate food for the animals and his family (Genesis 6:21), but actually what food was taken aboard can only be based on assumptions regarding what the animals at that time presumably ate. Thus, it is commonly assumed that because today there are animals with specialized diets such as the giant panda (bamboo) and the koala (eucalyptus leaves), and because other animals today are carnivorous or only eat fresh fruit or insects, that therefore Noah had to provide all these food needs on the Ark. However, as Woodmorappe has documented, all these different categories of animals even today can subsist on alternative foods which would have been easier for Noah to take aboard the Ark and keep preserved. In any case, since dietary choices and specialization primarily develop genetically before being environmentally acquired, it is quite possible such dietary preferences and specializations developed after the Flood and were thus not present in the representatives of those *baramin* aboard the Ark.

However, since the Bible does not give us any details about life on the Ark once Noah, his family, and the animals were aboard, it is not possible to be dogmatic about the methods that were used in caring for the animals. Nevertheless, there is an additional overriding factor that was probably at work assisting Noah and his family in minimizing the required care for the animals during the year-long voyage on the Ark: hibernation, as suggested by Whitcomb and Morris.[11] There

---

7   Woodmorappe, 1996, 71-81.

8   Woodmorappe, 1996, 23-35, 76-80.

9   Woodmorappe, 1996, 37-44.

10   Woodmorappe, 1996, 91-117.

11   Whitcomb and Morris, 1961, 71-75.

are various types of dormancy in animals, with many different types of physiologic and metabolic responses, but it is still an important and widespread mechanism in the animal kingdom for surviving periods of climatic adversity:

> Still another mechanism used by some organisms to avoid stressful environmental conditions is that of dormancy, an inactive state accompanied by a lower than normal rate of metabolism—the chemical processes responsible for the activity, nourishment, and growth of an organism—during which an organism conserves the amount of energy available to it and makes few demands on its environment. Most major groups of animals as well as plants have some representatives that can become dormant, however.[12]

Hibernation is usually associated with "winter sleep," and estivation with escape from summer heat and drought. Other factors also apparently are often involved, such as food shortage, oxygen and carbon dioxide in the environment, and accumulation of fat. Practically all reptiles and amphibians have the capacity of hibernation. Mammals, being warm-blooded, do not have as great a need for it, and so at present relatively few practice it:

> The zoological dispersion of hibernation among mammals is not especially illuminating, since closely allied forms may differ radically in this respect. Hibernation is reported for the orders *Monotremata, Marsupiala, Insectivora, Chiroptera, Rodentia,* and *Carnivora.*[13]

Furthermore:

> Although certain mammals are said to hibernate, they do not necessarily enter a state of deep hibernation during winter. Instead for weeks at a time they may be inactive and lethargic in behaviour, with a slightly depressed body temperature....Superficial hibernation, apparently a compromise between the minimum energy requirements of a deep hibernator and the high energy expended by an animal that remains active during the winter, saves energy without the stress of hibernation. The animal can thus conserve food.[14]

Thus, it is probable that the latent ability to hibernate in one form or another is present in practically all mammals.

Similarly, many of the invertebrates hibernate in some fashion for long periods. Although it is sometimes said that birds do not hibernate, it is now known that

---

12   *The New Encyclopaedia Britannica,* 1985, Macropaedia, Vol. 14, 670, article on "Dormancy."

13   W. C. Alee et al, 1949, *Principle of Animal Ecology,* Philadelphia, PA: W.B. Saunders Co., 106.

14   *The New Encyclopaedia Britannica,* 1985, 674.

at least one bird, the poor-will, does so, and each night the hummingbird also exhibits many of the characteristics of hibernation,[15] so that fundamentally it can be said that birds also possess the latent capacity of hibernation. It is likely that the reason more of them do not practice it is that their power of flight makes long migrations a more effective means of coping with adverse weather and other conditions.

It is of course well known that many species of birds migrate thousands of miles, with unerring accuracy, between their summer and winter homes. On the other hand, it is not so well known that many kinds of mammals also migrate many long distances to escape unfavorable weather. The homing instinct also seems strongly developed in many mammals. Both for birds and mammals, however, the mechanism for the migratory instinct is one of the great unsolved puzzles in biology:

> The study of behavior has frequently revealed capabilities that at the time they are discovered cannot be easily explained by any known sensory mechanisms....In most instances further investigation has shown a reasonable sensory basis for these capabilities. In at least one case, however, the mystery remains. This is the ability of animals to travel long distances to the correct destination through totally unfamiliar territory during migration or homing.[16]

Similarly, the phenomena of hibernation and estivation are still not understood:

> There is an enormous literature on the physiology of mammalian hibernation, and an almost embarrassing wealth of descriptive information on cardio-vascular activity, spontaneous and induced nervous activity, biochemistry, and endocrinology is available. Two of the few general conclusions that can be drawn from this plethora of data are
>
> (1) that the patterns of regulation of adaptive hypothermia [hibernation] are both complex and variable, and
> (2) that it is of polyphyletic origin.[17]

Despite this "plethora of data," the comment of another authority over fifty years ago is still valid:

> Our knowledge of this mechanism is very incomplete....Various theories have been proposed to account for hibernation, and it seems likely that

---

15   *The New Encyclopaedia Britannica*, 1985, 673-674.

16   M. S. Gordon et al, 1982, *Animal Physiology: Principles and Adaptations*, fourth ed., New York: McMillan Publishing Co., Inc., 517.

17   Gordon et al, 1982, 397.

the controlling stimuli may vary with different animals.[18]

It appears, therefore, that the animal world has two powerful means for coping with unfavorable environmental conditions, namely, hibernation and migration. It is likely that all animals possess these powers in latent form, some of them still in active form. Thus far, at least, science has been unable to fully explain them, in spite of their great importance in animal physiology and ecology.

> It was pointed out that an organism has but three choices available when exposed to adversity: it may die, adjust or migrate. Hibernation and estivation are broad adjustments to adverse weather or climate. Migration or emigration are still different ways of avoiding unfavorable conditions.[19]

It is again suggested, as previously by Whitcomb and Morris, that these remarkable abilities of animals were unusually intensified during the Flood period. In fact, it may well have been at this time that these powers were first implanted in the animals by God. It seems rather likely that climatic conditions before the Flood were so equable that these particular abilities were not needed then. Perhaps it is significant that after the Flood, God's pronouncement that "cold and heat, and summer and winter" (Genesis 8:22) would henceforth come in regular cycles is immediately followed by statements concerning the animals that seem to imply changes in animal natures and behavior, and in relationships to mankind (Genesis 9:2-5).

Even as God instructed Noah, by specific revelation, concerning the coming Flood and his means of escape from it, so He could easily have instructed certain of the animals—by implanting a migratory directional instinct in them that would afterward be inherited in greater or lesser degree by their descendants—to flee from their then native habitats to the place of safety, the Ark built by Noah perhaps not all that distant in the same or nearby regions of that one pre-Flood supercontinent. Then, having entered the Ark, they also received from God the ability to become more or less dormant, in various ways, in order to be able to survive for the year in which they were to be confined within the Ark while the storms raged outside:

> Hibernation is generally defined as a specific physiological state in an animal in which normal functions are suspended or greatly retarded, enabling the animal to endure long periods of complete inactivity.[20]

After leaving the Ark at the end of the Flood, this ability would then have been

---

18   M. Bates, 1956, 'Hibernation', Collier's Encyclopedia, vol. 7, 11.

19   Alee et al, 1949, 539.

20   Bates, 1956, 11.

inherited, in greater or lesser degree, by the descendants of those animals that survived the Flood.

Many of today's scientists are ruled by rationalistic naturalism, and sadly many Christian scholars have likewise been compromised. These doubtless deride evidence and explanations with the epithet of "supernaturalistic." But that is precisely the point! The Bible plainly says that God directed the animals to come to Noah, rather than Noah having to go out in search of them (Genesis 6:20; 7:9, 15). It also indicates that God continued to keep special watch over the occupants of the Ark during the Flood while He controlled all that was happening around the earth (Genesis 8:1).

But if the anti-supernaturalistic uniformitarian protests the ascription of the migration of the animals to the Ark and their dormancy in the Ark to abilities implanted in them by God, he needs to instead offer a better comprehensive explanation of these same abilities even as they exist today! As already demonstrated, no complete or consistent explanation has yet been forthcoming, and thus one might even be justified in saying that the marvelous migratory instinct and the equally remarkable power of hibernation can only be explained teleologically.

It is not denied, of course, that some truly physiological explanation of these capacities may some day be fully developed, but even this would only constitute a description of that which God Himself originally endowed. Again, it must be said that it is not really known how all this was accomplished, since the Bible is silent on these matters, but this is a very possible and plausible explanation, so that there is no longer any justification for the critic to profess incredulity about the animals on the Ark!

However, even Christians have been critical of this suggestion that God imposed a year-long hibernation or estivation experience, whereby bodily functions were reduced to a minimum. Morton has said:

> While this is certainly possible if it was miraculous, there is little evidence that most carnivores are able to hibernate. Besides, the Biblical record clearly states that Noah was to take on board enough food for the animals. If they were hibernating, why would they need food?[21]

This echoes the same comment made by Youngblood.[22] However, such an objection ignores the fact that the animals boarded the Ark over a seven-day period before the Flood actually began, during which time they still needed to eat. At least some of the animals would have been exhausted and hungry when they arrived at the Ark, and therefore they would need to have eaten well from the food Noah had

---

21   Morton, 1995, 70.

22   Youngblood, 1980, 132.

stored in the Ark at God's command as they settled into the "rooms" (Genesis 6:14) in the Ark as constructed by Noah under divine instructions. If all the animals had eaten well by the time the Flood commenced, then they would be ready to become dormant.

Nevertheless, Moore raises numerous objections and difficulties with the animals on the Ark being dormant during the Flood year.[23] Of course, these perceived difficulties with hibernation are based on his perceptions of animal behavior today and by assuming that behavior has always been the same in the past. However, Woodmorappe has more than adequately dealt with all objections and perceived difficulties with the question of dormancy of the animals on the Ark.[24] For example, Moore maintains that if the animals hibernated for the full year of the Flood without eating, then the loss in body weight would cause severe deterioration and a high mortality rate. But this is based on a distorted view of hibernation which many have, including scientists:

> The view of hibernation held by most people, and constantly reinforced by children's stories and superficial nature programs, is of a state of deep sleep which starts in autumn and ends in spring. The hibernator is thought to select a site which will permit it to survive throughout the winter. This view has many serious flaws in it, and though they have been pointed out by a number of scientists after conducting field studies in various parts of the world over many decades, it persists.[25]

In fact, hibernating animals today do not sleep continuously all winter, and still need to eat periodically, so the food that Noah was instructed to store on board the Ark would have also been available for any such feeding periods during the year-long voyage.

Woodmorappe provides extensive documentation to show that in fact many animals don't even need winter-like conditions to hibernate. They can enter short bouts of torpor instead of deep hibernation, can become inactive and/or reduce feeding without entering any apparent state of dormancy, and under the right conditions have been known to hibernate for an entire year. The evidence also clearly indicates that animals can hibernate under various conditions. Even when temperatures fluctuate, both wild and captive animals can become torpid if not enough food is available. Furthermore, once animals are in a state of hibernation or torpor, they are not easily aroused by constant motion, excessive and loud noises, or handling. Also, animals which today never hibernate still often go into bouts of torpor for periods up to weeks when denied food. In fact, the captivity of the animals on board the Ark under conditions of constant motion, continuous

23   Moore, 1983, 25-27.

24   Woodmorappe, 1996, 127-135.

25   R. Ransome, 1990, *The Natural History of Hibernating Bats*, London: Christopher Helm, 81.

monotonous sounds, and the essential removal of the normal diurnal changes in light levels would have been ideal for facilitating long bouts of torpor or dormancy for all sizes of animals, even up to the largest ones. And this has all been documented from observations in field and laboratory studies today. Thus, with the addition of God's intervention in supervising and caring for the Ark and its animal cargo, His putting the animals into lengthy bouts of dormancy is entirely believable, guaranteeing the survival of the animals during the Flood year and ensuring Noah and his family were fully able to therefore care for the animals and themselves more than adequately for the entire year of the Flood.

23

THE "NATURAL-SUPERNATURAL" PHILOSOPHY OF MIRACLES

It is both strange and exceedingly sad when those who defend a limited or local flood—including more and more evangelicals—have sought to win the argument over the geographical extent of the Flood by disallowing the right to appeal to God's overruling power in the events related to the Flood catastrophe! For example, notice carefully the line of reasoning followed by Ramm, whose book is still influential today (e.g., see Briscoe,[1] and Youngblood[2]):

> One point must be clearly understood before we commence these criticisms: *the flood is recorded as a natural-supernatural occurrence*. It does not appear *as a pure and stupendous* miracle. The natural and supernatural work side by side and hand in hand. If one wishes to retain a universal flood, it must be understood that a series of stupendous miracles are required. Further, one cannot beg off with pious statements that God can do anything....
>
> Again, there is no question what Omnipotence can be, but the simplicity [?] of the flood record prohibits the endless supplying of miracles to make a universal Flood feasible.[3]

Because this type of objection is still very common among evangelicals, it is imperative to examine and deal with it before proceeding. The first and foremost criticism of this attitude is that it fails to take into account the fact that the Word of God makes ample provision for, and reference to, miraculous elements in connection with the gathering and keeping of the animals. For example, God told Noah that "two of every sort *shall come unto thee*" (Genesis 6:20); and then we read that "*they went in unto Noah into the Ark*, two and two of all flesh, wherein is the breath of life" (7:15), and finally that "*the LORD shut him in*" (7:16). Jamieson admitted that the animals "must have been prompted by an overruling Divine

---

1   S. Briscoe, 1987, *Mastering the Old Testament, Volume 1*, Genesis, Dallas, TX: Word Publishing.

2   Youngblood, 1990, *The Genesis Debate*.

3   Ramm, 1964, 165, 167. Italics are his.

direction, as it is impossible, on any other principle, to account for their going *in pairs*."[4]

On the other hand, if it is insisted that the gathering of the animals be made entirely reasonable to the unregenerate mind by eliminating all supernatural elements, then all we have succeeded in doing is making the biblical account completely unreasonable. Note, for example, the explanation used by Filby:

> In cases of impending danger, animals, particularly younger ones, look for someone to protect them. We can well believe that with a raging storm outside, and warmth, food, comfort and safety within the Ark the attitude of most of the animals to Noah (even apart from any Divine over-ruling which could certainly have been exercised) would have been that of pets looking to their owners for protection and friendship.[5]

But would all of these animals have suddenly become docile pets just because of a storm? In any case, the text of Genesis informs us that the storm did not begin until after all the animals were in the Ark!

Unfortunately, the catastrophist, Patten, falls into the same "trap" when he attempted to explain the gathering of the animals without appealing to God's miraculous intervention. After giving several examples of the abnormal behavior of animals just prior to natural catastrophes, he stated:

> Animals spoken of in the Genesis account, domestic and probably wild ones as well, entered the Ark seven days prior to the Flood—seven days before the rain commenced and surging waters from the oceans began to heave. Apparently there were significant forewarnings, microvibrations or minute foreshocks of the coming catastrophe, seismic in nature.[6]

His theory is therefore that only two of each of all kinds of air-breathing creatures and only seven each of the kinds acceptable for sacrifice were impelled toward the Ark (while all the other animals were not) by a series of microvibrations in the earth's crust caused by the planet Mercury as it swept past the earth into its present orbit. But this is absurd and not the kind of help that the modern secular, scientific mind needs to persuade it to take the Genesis account seriously. Pondering such "harmonizations" between science and Scripture, it is easy to concur with the judgment that "each mixes up more or less of science with more

---

4   *Jamieson, Fausset and Brown Commentary,* vol. I, 1948, reprinted ed., Grand Rapids, MI: Wm B. Eerdmans Publishing Co., 95.

5   Filby, 1970, 86.

6   D. W. Patten, 1967, *The Biblical Flood and the Ice Epoch,* Seattle, WA: Pacific Meridian Publishing Co., 64.

or less of Scripture, and produces a result more or less absurd."[7] Why must so many Christian scholars hesitate to cut the Gordian knot of endless speculation and instead simply acknowledge that God, and God alone, had the power to bring two each of the basic kinds of air-breathing creatures to the Ark?

Furthermore, having directed Noah to construct the Ark and then led him into this situation by supernatural means, would God's power be withdrawn and no longer available to sustain him (consider Philippians 1:16; Galatians 3:3)? An analogous situation was faced by Moses, the compiler of the book of Genesis, many years later when he led his people out of bondage in Egypt by the supernatural help of God, only to face the barren wilderness and the apparently hopeless situation of finding food and water there for millions of people. Did the supernatural provisions of God fail Moses and his people then? Therefore, we must not underestimate the implications of Genesis 8:1: "And God *remembered* Noah, and every living thing, and all the cattle that was with him in the ark." This statement refers to the time when the waters were still at their maximum height and the fountains of the deep had not yet been stopped (Genesis 8:2). It is important to realize that the word "remember" (*zakar*) in this context does not imply that God had forgotten the Ark and its occupants during the first five months of the Flood! According to Hebrew usage, the primary meaning of *zakar* is "granting requests, protecting, delivering," when God is the subject and persons are the object.[8] As Kidner has stated:

> When the Old Testament says that *God remembered*, it combines the ideas of faithful love (*cf.* Jeremiah 2:2; 31:20) and timely intervention: "God's remembering always implies His movement towards the object of His memory" (*cf.* Genesis 19, 29; Exodus 2:24; Luke 1:54, 55).[9]

Yet Youngblood's response is:

> It will do no good to observe that "God remembered Noah" (8:1)... because the sentence of which that phrase is a part is connected with the receding of the waters rather than with their rising.[10]

In other words, God's special protection of the Ark and its occupants presumably only occurred during the last half of the Flood year! Without such divine control during the early months of the Flood year, Youngblood assures us:

> Swiftly rising waters [which the universal Flood view requires] would

---

7   White, 1955, 234.

8   F. Brown, S. R. Driver and C. A. Briggs, 1907, *A Hebrew and English Lexicon of the Old Testament*, Grand Rapids: MI: Baber Book House, 270, cited by Leupold, 1942, 308.

9   B. Kidner, 1980, Genesis: An Introduction and Commentary, Leicester, U.K.: Inter-Varsity Press, 92.

10   Youngblood, 1980, 129-130.

have generated powerful currents that would have smashed the Ark to smithereens against a cliff wall or mountainside.

Youngblood concludes that it must have been only a local flood, and Noah and his family were thus fully capable of taking care of a few animals in (perhaps) a small Ark without God's special help within the first five months of the Flood! This is hardly a theologically credible approach to the Genesis account, for Genesis 8:1 clearly implies that God's protective hand was on the Ark and all its occupants *throughout the entire year of the Flood.* If the Flood had covered only a limited region, it seems strange that God's special help would have been available only during the last few months of the Flood year, when, presumably, the situation was less dangerous than at the beginning.

Furthermore, the inconsistency of those who teach a local flood becomes more evident when it is discovered that they, too, must acknowledge God's special control over the animals at the time of the Flood. For example, Ramm says that the animals which came to Noah were "prompted by a divine instinct."[11] Once we grant God's power in bringing the animals *to* the Ark, we have no right to deny His power over the animals while they were *in* the Ark. In fact, it is simply not possible to have *any* kind of Genesis Flood without acknowledging the presence of supernatural elements.[12]

On the other hand, it is far from necessary to indulge in an "endless supplying of miracles to make a universal Flood feasible." That God intervened in a supernatural way to gather the animals into the Ark and to keep them under control during the year of the Flood is explicitly stated in the text of Scripture. Furthermore, it is obvious that the initiation of the Flood, including the breaking up of "all the fountains of the great deep," was a supernatural act of God, particularly including the precise timing of it all.

However, throughout the entire process, the waters that covered the earth *acted according to the known laws of hydrodynamics and hydrostatics.* They eroded, churned up, carried away and deposited sediments according to natural hydraulic processes, moving at velocities and in directions that were perfectly normal under such conditions. To be sure, the sudden and powerful upsetting of the delicate balances in the pre-Flood world brought into play hitherto unknown tectonic

---

11   Ramm, 1964, 169. We have already noted that Jamieson (Jamieson, Fausset and Brown, 1948, 95) concluded that "they must have been prompted by an overruling Divine direction, as it is impossible on any other principles, to account for their going out *in pairs.*"

12   This statement is fully supported by Psalm 29:10, which definitely speaks of Noah's Flood because the Hebrew word *mabbul,* used exclusively in Genesis 6-9, is again used here: "The LORD sitteth upon the Flood; yea, the LORD sitteth king forever." The entire psalm emphasizes the *omnipotence* of God and is climaxed by this reference to His greatest manifestation of omnipotence in the Flood. Lange notes that "the history of the Flood is an *hapax legomenon* in the world's history analogous to the creation of Adam, the birth and history of Christ, and the future history of the world's end." Lange, *A Commentary on the Holy Scriptures: Genesis,* 295.

and aqueous movements while new sets of balances and adjustments were being achieved. But such adjustments would, of course, be described as natural and not supernatural.[13]

An example of the basic misconceptions underlying this entire controversy is the assertion by Ramm that a universal flood would necessitate "a great creation of water" because "all the waters of the heavens, poured all over the earth, would amount to a sheath seven inches thick" and "to cover the highest mountains would require eight times more water than we have now."[14] For such an objection to be valid, it would have to be assumed that the earth's topography was unaltered by the Flood. In other words, we would have to assume the truth of uniformitarianism in order to prove the impossibility of catastrophism! As shall be described later in more detail, the Flood cataclysm involved tectonic changes of a massive scale that broke apart a pre-Flood supercontinent, moved the resulting continental blocks apart by thousands of miles, and replaced the entire pre-Flood ocean floor with the new ocean floor that underlies all of today's ocean basins. All of today's high mountain ranges, including the Himalayas, Alps, Andes, and Rockies, are the direct result of the tectonic catastrophism of the Flood. These mountain ranges did not even begin to appear until the end of the cataclysm. So the global Flood described in Scripture does not require the volume of water that would be needed to cover the mountains of our present world. Indeed, there appears to be no need for more water than exists in today's oceans.[15]

However, while there was no doubt great tectonic activity during the Flood, the Bible clearly emphasizes the volume and destructive power of the water in what was primarily a global cataclysmic judgment by water (2 Peter 3:6). Therefore, if the biblical testimony is accepted concerning the waters of "the great deep" bursting forth as fountains when the earth's pre-Flood crust was broken up, so that the waters catapulted high into the atmosphere fell as global torrential rain through "the windows of heaven" (Genesis 7:11; 8:2), then there were adequate sources for the waters of a universal flood. Furthermore, such passages as Genesis 8:3 and Psalm 104:6-9 confirm that today's new ocean basins formed as a result of the Flood and are deeper than those of the pre-Flood world, thus providing adequate storage space for the additional waters that had been in "the great deep" from their creation to the time of the Flood, while at the close of the Flood new mountain ranges rose to heights never attained during the pre-Flood era.

---

13   However, we read in Genesis 8:1 that "God made a wind to pass over the earth, and the waters assuaged." Judging from the effects produced, it would seem that this must have been more than merely a natural wind. Leupold, 1980, 309 has stated: "But, we are sure, as an element of the miraculous entered into the matter of the coming of the Flood, so a similar element contributed to its abatement."

14   Ramm, 1964, 165-166. It is tragic that a misconception like this on the part of a Christian scholar has then been magnified to the point of being used to ridicule the Scriptures by anti-creationist scientists such as Plimer, who has claimed: "Some 4.4 billion cubic kilometres of water would have to be added to the ocean for Mt. Everest and other large mountain ranges to be covered" (Plimer, 1994, 101).

15   These important details are discussed from a scientific standpoint in chapters 86-87.

It is a serious mistake, therefore, to assume and assert that the concept of a universal Flood involves "an endless supplying of miracles." A few biblical analogies are helpful in illustrating this point. When the Israelites crossed the Red Sea and the Jordan, God held back the waters supernaturally in both cases.[16] But once His hand was released in both instances, the waters hurried back to their appointed bounds in accordance with the normal laws of gravity. Likewise, the stones in the walls of Jericho fell to the ground by gravitational force; but it was evidently the unseen hand of God that first shook the foundations.

It is, of course, agreed that the Flood was "a natural and supernatural occurrence," with "the natural and the supernatural working side by side and hand in hand." But the claim by Ramm that this militates against its universality is far from obvious. One cannot help but suspect that the real thrust of Ramm's objection lies at a deeper level than that of a mere demand for "natural" as well as "supernatural" elements in the Flood." What he, and others who have followed his lead, really seem to be demanding is a removal of anything in the Flood narrative that might conflict with, and therefore offend, modern uniformitarian geologists and evolutionary scientists generally. In other words, God is permitted to intervene supernaturally for the purpose of destroying some godless men; but in this supernatural intervention, He is not permitted to go so far as to upset the general processes of nature operating in the earth as we know them today. What is tragic is that those who have followed Ramm and built upon his objections have removed all "supernatural" elements from the Flood entirely, thus relegating it in large measure to the status of a minor event or even an exaggerated story, so that many Christian leaders and evangelical Christians no longer care or even believe that the Flood was an actual historical event![17]

Now if this is the underlying motivation of Ramm's "natural-supernatural" argument, then he is not only completely at variance with the biblical testimony

---

16 The "strong east wind" of Exodus 14:21 could hardly have been merely a natural wind, for not only did it blow at the right time, but it must have blown in opposite directions at the same time to make the waters "a wall unto them on their right hand, and on their left" (Exodus 14:22, 29; 15:8 and Psalm 78:13), and yet not hinder the people as they walked across "dry ground." It is also important to note that the Jordan River's waters were stopped at flood-time (Joshua 3:15). It is most unlikely that blockage by a mere landslide upstream could have done this, as is often supposed. God was supernaturally involved because we read that the waters "rose up upon an heap" and the children of Israel crossed the bed of the Jordan River "on dry ground" (Joshua 3:16, 17).

17 That this assessment is valid can be clearly verified by surveying all the commentaries on Genesis and Bible dictionaries, etc., which are available to the evangelical Christian public in Christian bookstores today, and to read therein the comments made about the Flood which are so often couched in language analysing the scriptural account and what it means without emphasizing that this was actually a historical event. Furthermore, a survey of the positions held by theological seminaries, Bible colleges, and their faculties with respect to the Flood would reveal that most avoid teaching that the Flood was a literal, historical event, instead bypassing it as a sober story probably derived by demythologizing the Babylonian flood story, removing its grotesque and polytheistic elements to conform to Israelite monotheism. Such a position, of course, does not conflict with modern uniformitarian geology, but rather than making the Flood account palatable to evolutionary scientists, it is simply ignored by them generally, while some scoff at those Christians who still stand for a literal global Flood with catastrophic geological consequences, a fulfilment of Peter's prophecy (2 Peter 3:3-7).

concerning the Flood, but also can be accused of inconsistency in his approach to the issue of biblical miracles in general. For example, in the case of Jonah being swallowed by the great fish, Ramm clearly "solves his difficulties by recourse to the miraculous or to the sheer omnipotence of God," just as he accused Rehwinkel of doing in connection with the Flood.[18] Writing of Jonah and the fish, Ramm stated:

> The record clearly calls the creature a *prepared fish* and if this means a special creature for a special purpose we need not search our books on sea creatures to find out the most likely possibility. *It would be a creature created of God especially for this purpose, and that is where our investigation ends.* The evangelical accepts the supernatural theism, and the centrality of redemption and moral values. The necessity of getting the message of redemption to Nineveh *is sufficient rationale for God to have made such a creature.*[19]

So if getting Jonah to Nineveh to preach the message of redemption was "sufficient rationale" for God to create a special fish, then what right do we have to question God's "rationale" in bringing into operation forces of destruction and providence never before seen by man, for the purpose of wiping out a hopelessly corrupt race and preserving the Messianic line through Noah? Since God's *thoughts* (or "rationale") and God's *ways* (including miracles) are higher than ours, even the employment of a universal flood and an ark to accomplish these purposes could have been wholly in accord with the mind of God, even though they might cause offense because of scientific difficulties to the mind of modern man.

Therefore, it must be recognized that the efforts which some evangelical Christians have exerted to write off the universality of the Flood by appealing to supposed *a priori* principles of Divine methodology in the performing, or not performing, of miracles, stand condemned by the testimony of the Word of God itself. Whether or not such a concept can be adjusted harmoniously into one's theological or philosophical presuppositions, it happens to be true nonetheless that the Flood was an utterly unique and never-to-be-repeated phenomenon, a year-long demonstration of the omnipotence of a righteous God which mankind has never been permitted to forget, and a crisis in earth history that is comparable in Scripture only to the creation and to the final renovation of the earth by fire at the end of the age (2 Peter 3:3-7). It is because the Bible itself teaches us these things that we are fully justified in appealing to *the power of God*, whether or not He used means amenable to our scientific understanding, for the gathering of two of every created kind of animal into the Ark and for the care and preservation of those animals in the Ark during the 371 days of the Flood.

---

18   B. Ramm, 1954, *The Christian View of Science and Scripture,* Grand Rapids, MI: Wm B. Eerdmans Publishing Co., 244.

19   Ramm, 1964, 207-208, emphasis added. Ramm's analysis of this "problem" is agreed with, but one wonders how it would impress uniformitarian biologists. The fact of the matter is that consistent uniformitarianism can allow for *no* biblical miracles whatever.

24

POST-FLOOD ANIMAL DISTRIBUTION—
THE AUSTRALIAN MARSUPIALS

Another "problem" raised by skeptics and local flood advocates which is closely related to the issue of the animals on the Ark just discussed, and which thus now demands separate attention, is that of animal distribution throughout the earth since the time of the Flood. To put the issue succinctly, if the Flood was geographically universal, then all the terrestrial animals not aboard the Ark perished, and thus the present-day animal distribution must be explained on the basis of migrations from the mountains of Ararat where the Ark landed at the end of the Flood (Genesis 8:4).

In order to best focus on this perceived problem, just two groups of animals will be primarily discussed here—the *edentates* and the *marsupials*. The edentates are slow-moving, nearly toothless animals, some of which are today found in the jungles of South America (tree sloths, armadillos, and anteaters). The marsupials are pouched mammals, such as the kangaroos and koalas, only found today in Australia. How could these animals have traveled so far from the Near East to their current remote and isolated locations, cut off by water? These are the examples usually cited, by local flood proponents and rationalist skeptics alike, of animals whose migrations from the mountains of Ararat to their current locations after the Flood are regarded as impossible.[1] How then are these peculiarities of animal distribution to be explained?

Three Major Views

There are three generally accepted views as to how such animal distribution came about. First, there is the evolutionary and uniformitarian view, which explains the present-day animal distribution on the basis of gradual processes of migration over millions of years on slowly drifting continents, together with the evolution of totally new animal species in geographically isolated areas. This explanation is also accepted by those Christian scholars who maintain that God must have used evolutionary processes in order to "create" the earth and all the animals and

---

1   Moore, 1983, 34-36, and Morton, 1995, 68-70.

plants over millions of years. Second, there are evangelical Christian advocates of a local flood who would claim that most of these animals were probably created in the ecological niches where they are now found. Some who hold this view would argue that the creation of the animals was progressive over the millions of years of earth history.[2] And third, there are the advocates of a global flood, who thus believe that these animals must have reached their present locations by waves of migration during the centuries that followed the Flood, together with rapid speciation and specialization within the created kinds, or *baramins,* leading to diversification into different ecological niches as the animals migrated.[3]

It is ironic that even with this division of opinion, in certain respects most advocates of a universal flood join the evolutionists in contending for the migration of animals to distant areas, as opposed to the theory of the special creation of animals in their *present* (post-Flood) ecological zones. Both the evolutionist and the global Flood advocate maintain that intercontinental land bridges aided animals in their migratory movements across the face of the earth, although lately evolutionists have emphasized the role of continental drift.[4] Both schools of thought also agree that speciation has occurred amongst the animals during their migrations, so that differences have become established as the various animals became isolated in their different ecological niches. As far as the global Flood advocate is concerned, however, there is still a limit to the amounts of the changes that have occurred during such speciation, those limits having been fixed at the boundaries of the original created kinds, or *baramins.* On the other hand, there is a crucial difference in the timescales envisaged for these animal migrations and the speciation concurrent with it. Whereas the evolutionist allows for millions of years, the global Flood advocate envisages a timescale of only a few thousand years at most, with most of the migratory movements and genetic "shuffling" taking place in the first thousand years or so immediately after the global flood catastrophe.

The controversy between the different viewpoints increases in complexity when proponents of a local flood appeal to the evolutionary timescale to emphasize the impossibility of the migration of animals since the Flood to their present distribution. They are willing to use intercontinental land bridges to explain the distribution of some animals, but claim that others, such as the edentates of South America and the marsupials of Australia, were created and placed on the continents where we now find them. For example, Mixter is a local flood advocate who has written on this topic:

---

2   For example, Ross, 1998.

3   Another possible theory that was once advocated was that the animals were re-created after the Flood in their present ecological niches. However, this expedience would eliminate the need for an Ark to preserve the animals through the Flood, and of course is not suggested in the biblical account.

4   For example, J. C. Briggs, 1987, *Biogeography and Plate Tectonics,* Amsterdam: Elsevier Scientific Publishers B.V.

If kangaroos were in the Ark and first touched land in Asia, one would expect fossils of them in Asia. According to Romer, the only place where there are either fossil or living kangaroos is in Australia. What shall we conclude? If the fossil evidence means that there never have been kangaroos in Asia, then kangaroos were not in the Ark or if they were, they hurried from Australia to meet Noah, and as rapidly returned to their native land. Is it not easier to believe that they were never in the Ark, and hence were in an area untouched by the Flood, and that the Flood occurred only in the area inhabited by man?[5]

Since arguments of this type, based upon perceived problems of biogeography, have been considered by many evangelicals to be conclusive, it is imperative that they be examined at some length. However, it needs to be stated at the outset that the objective cannot be to *prove* that all modern animals have migrated from the Near East, because little is known about animals' movements in the past from either science or Scripture. It is only necessary to show that a general migration of animals from the Near East since the Flood is both possible and reasonable.

Australian Marsupials

The marsupials of Australia are very distinct animals, yet most have parallel representatives among the placental mammals. For example, there are marsupial *moles*, marsupial *anteaters*, marsupial *mice*, marsupial *rats*, marsupial *squirrels* (flying phalangers), marsupial *sloths* (koalas), marsupial *gophers* (wombats), marsupial *cats* (dasyures), marsupial *wolves* (thylacines), marsupial *monkeys*, marsupial *badgers* (Tasmanian devils), *rabbit-like* marsupials called bandicoots, and of course the distinctive kangaroo and wallabies. In addition, Australia boasts the only living monotremes (egg-laying mammals) in the world: the duck-billed platypus and the echidna (spiny anteater).[6]

On the assumption that the terrestrial animals of the present world (almost exclusively terrestrial mammals and reptiles) can trace their ancestry back to those pairs representing each *baramin* within the Ark, how can we explain the observation that these marsupials and monotremes are today found nowhere else in the world except in Australia, and that by contrast very few of the placentals ever succeeded in reaching that continent?[7] Klotz has suggested:

It may be that these forms have become extinct in Asia and along the

---

5   R. L. Mixter, 1950, *Creation and Evolution*, American Scientific Affiliation, Monograph Two, 15.

6   *The New Encyclopaedia Britannica*, 1985, Macropaedia, vol. 23, 399ff.

7   It was originally thought that the only placentals that reached Australia by their own means were bats, rats, and mice. The dingoes (native dogs) appear to have been introduced by the Australian Aborigines. Recently-discovered fossil fragments have been identified as those of a tiny placental mammal (on the basis of a few teeth), which is interpreted as being already in Australia before the marsupials arrived (R. Monastersky, 1992, Tiny tooth upends Australian history, *Science News*, 141(15): 228).

Malay Peninsula. Possibly they were able to live in some of these areas for only a very short time and travelled almost immediately to those places included in their present range. The evolutionary scheme itself requires that animals have become extinct in many areas in which they once lived.[8]

Shull, an evolutionist, has presented an apparent solution to this problem:

> The marsupials spread over the world, in all directions. They could not go far to the north before striking impossible climate, but the path south was open all the way to the tips of Africa and South America and through Australia....The placental mammals proved to be superior to the marsupials in the struggle for existence and drove the marsupials out...that is, forced them southward. Australia was then connected by land with Asia, so that it could receive the fugitives....Behind them the true mammals were coming; but before the latter reached Australia, that continent was separated from Asia, and the primitive types of the south were protected from further competition.[9]

Since fossil marsupials have been found in Europe and Africa, as well as in Australia, North and South America, and Antarctica, it is very evident that they have migrated rather widely in the past. It has been suggested on the basis of the fossil evidence and uniformitarian dating methods that they probably reached Europe from North America, but whether they originated in North America, South America, or Australia is a matter for guesswork in view of the small amount of evidence. Indeed, Archer has said:

> Unfortunately, at present, this question of northern or southern origins has no answer. The Cretaceous fossil mammal record from South America is too poor to provide much help and that from Antarctica and Australia is (unfortunately) non-existent.[10]

It should be noted that because of the lack of fossil evidence of marsupials in Asia, evolutionary paleontologists have suggested that the migratory path from North America to Europe was through Greenland, given the presumed juxtaposition of Greenland to both North America and Europe prior to the opening up of the Atlantic Ocean basin and the drifting of North America and Europe away from one another and Greenland.[11] However, fossil marsupials have not been

---

8   J. W. Klotz, 1970, *Genes, Genesis and Evolution*, second revised ed., St Louis, MO: Concordia Publishing House, 211.

9   A. F. Shull, 1951, *Evolution*, second ed., New York: McGraw-Hill Book Co., Inc., 60.

10   M. Archer, 1984, The Australian marsupial radiation, in *Vertebrate Zoogeography and Evolution in Australasia*, ed. M. Archer and G. Clayton, Perth, Australia: Hesperian Press, 788. Archer goes on to suggest that there is still a reasonable case to be made for a North American origin for marsupials!

11   Archer, 1984, 788-789.

found in Greenland either, so the migratory path could just have easily been through Asia. Thus, it cannot be insisted that other marsupials could not have migrated through Asia to Australia just because of the lack of fossil evidence for marsupials in Asia.[12] Therefore, since there is such a small amount of evidence to explain marsupial migrations anyway, and the "question of northern or southern origins has no answer," who is to say that marsupials could not have migrated into Australia via Asia? The Old Testament informs us that the kingdom of Israel was infested with lions for centuries (Judges 14:5; 1 Samuel 17:34; 2 Samuel 23:20; 1 Kings 13:24; 20:36; and especially 2 Kings 17:25), but there is no fossil evidence of lions having been in Palestine.[13] It is a well-known fact that at today's rates of geological processes animals leave fossil remains only under rare and special conditions. Therefore, the lack of fossil evidence of marsupials in Asia cannot be used as proof that they have never been in that region of the world.[14]

Whether the migration of the marsupials across Asia and into Australia was assisted by competition with placental mammals may be debatable, but it is not necessarily required as an explanation for the marsupial migration. Archer has concluded:

> Marsupial inferiority, as a sweeping generalization, does seem to be an indefensible point of view in terms of modern biology. Our knowledge of Australia's marsupials, as meagre as it is, generally tends to reinforce this marsupial self-respect renaissance....On balance, however, marsupials and placentals seem to be reasonably well matched. Both teams, when confronted, have had wins and both have suffered losses. So there is probably no basis for, or for that matter, purpose served by trying to generalize about relative superiority.[15]

Morton, like Mixter, has no warrant whatsoever for his assertion that:

> The only place on earth that fossil kangaroos are found is in Australia. If, as most global flood advocates believe, this represents the location in which pre-flood kangaroos lived, then the kangaroo must have traveled

---

12 There is fossil evidence that at least some marsupials once lived, even until fairly recent times, on the Indonesian island of Halmahera in the North Moluccas group (P. Flannery et al, 1995, Fossil marsupials [Macropodidae, Peroryctidae] and other mammals of Holocene Age from Halmahera, North Indonesia, *Alcheringa*, 19: 17-25).

13 Whitcomb and Morris, 1961, 83 refer to a personal communication dated April 20, 1959, from Palestinian archaeologist Nelson Glueck, who stated: "I do not believe that any fossils of lions have ever been found in Palestine, although the fossils of elephants and other animals have been discovered."

14 An even more familiar example is that of the American bison or buffalo. "The buffalo carcasses strewn over the plains in uncounted millions two generations ago have left hardly a present trace. The flesh was devoured by wolves or vultures within hours or days after death, and even the skeletons have now largely disappeared, the bones dissolving and crumbling into dust under the attack of the weather." C. O. Dunbar, 1949, *Historical Geology*, New York: Wiley, 39.

15 Archer, 1984, 790-791.

from Australia to the ark. Then, when the flood was over and Noah released the animals from Ararat, the kangaroos must have traveled back to Australia again. With a global flood, this is the only way to explain the distribution of fossil and present day kangaroos.[16]

The global flood concept by no means involves such absurdities. In the first place, no one can prove that the Ark was built in the same region of the world as that in which it landed.[17] As a matter of fact, if the Flood was global, pre-Flood geography would have been totally different from that of the present earth, since the tectonic forces unleashed during the Flood, and the massive erosion of the pre-Flood geography followed by deposition of great thicknesses of fossil-bearing sedimentary layers, would have guaranteed a total reshaping of the geography and topography of the earth's surface. In the second place, no one can prove that kangaroos and the other Australian marsupials were confined to Australia *before* the Flood.[18] And if not, then none of the chosen pairs of marsupials would have had to "hurry" to get from Australia to the Ark during the decades that it was under construction. In fact, it is possible that kangaroos and other marsupials may have been living in the same region as Noah. In the third place, it is not necessary to suppose that the very same pair of kangaroos that were in the Ark had to travel all the way to Australia after the Ark landed in the mountains of Ararat. Marsh has made some relevant comments:

> The journeys from the mountains of Ararat to their present habitats were made in an intermittent fashion, most generations sending representatives a little farther from the original home. The presence of tapirs today only in South America and the Malayan islands, opposite sides of the earth, is indicative of the fact that animals migrated in more than one

---

16   Morton, 1995, 70.

17   The fact that Genesis 2:14 mentions the Tigris (Hiddekel) and Euphrates Rivers is certainly not conclusive evidence to the contrary, for these and other geographical names could have been perpetuated by Noah's family into "the new world" even as happens in modern times. If the modern Tigris-Euphrates region was the area where the Ark had been built, then the other two rivers mentioned in Genesis 2:14 should still be there too, but they are not.

18   Although no fossil kangaroos have been found in Australia earlier than the late Oligocene, no one can prove that any of the kangaroo fossils found are in fact pre-Flood. See F. Flannery, 1984, Kangaroos: 15 million years of Australian bounders, in *Vertebrate Zoogeography and Evolution in Australasia*, ed. M. Archer and G. Clayton, Perth, Australia: Hesperian Press, 817-835, and T. H. Rich, 1991, Monotremes, placentals, and marsupials: their record in Australia and its biases, in *Vertebrate Palaeontology of Australasia*, ed. Vickers-Rich, J. M. Monaghan, R. F. Baird and H. Rich, Melbourne, Australia: Pioneer Design Studio Pty Ltd and Monash University Publications Committee, 893-1070. Ultimately, it all depends on where the Flood/post-Flood boundary is placed in the geologic record. If the Flood/post-Flood boundary were placed in the mid Tertiary, then all those kangaroo fossils are post-Flood, fossilization occurring after the kangaroos arrived in Australia from the Ark as a result of minor residual burials in isolated locations. Furthermore, as has already been pointed out, the absence of kangaroo fossils in Asia does not prove that they have never been there. Also, it must be kept in mind throughout this entire discussion that the question of paleontological dating methods is being held in abeyance for later discussion. On the basis that a global flood has occurred, there can be no assurance whatever that the fossil-bearing strata must be dated according to the uniformitarian scheme.

direction. The creationist holds that there is no reason for believing that this distribution of animals was accomplished by any other processes than those employed in distribution today....Increase in numbers of individuals of any one kind causes a necessity for spreading outwards toward the horizon in search of food and homes....Their arrival in new areas may be a result of deliberate individual endeavor or it may be that they arrive as wave-tossed survivors of some coastal accident.[19]

It should be noted that today the prevailing view among biogeographers, and paleontologists as already noted, is that the marsupials arrived in Australia from South America via Antarctica, because the three continents were believed to be joined at that time and only since have drifted apart. As Briggs has succinctly said:

It was in South America that the marsupials enjoyed their longest tenure—from the beginning of the Cenozoic until recent time. And, according to modern consensus, it was from South America that some marsupials invaded Australia in the early Tertiary by way of Antarctica.[20]

However, other biogeographers remain somewhat skeptical. For example, Brown and Gibson have commented:

Interpreting Australian patterns has always resulted in controversy. For years the field was dominated by scenarios in which the marsupials and placentals arrived from southeast Asia via island hopping....Throughout, however, some authors have attempted to move marsupials to Australia via the Antarctic connection with South America. When continental drift clearly demonstrated this passage was available until the lower Eocene and that the climate was warm enough for forest plants and animals, the southern route became acceptable. Authors (e.g., Patterson, 1981) still argue whether the primitive forms lived in South America or Australia and whether marsupials ever lived in Africa and therefore represent a broader Gondwanaland pattern. Moreover, no one has ever elucidated why placental mammals never made the southern trek across Antarctica.[21]

Indeed, the Antarctic connection becomes very tenuous when it is realised that:

The Antarctic record of marsupials, and all terrestrial mammals for that matter, is restricted to a single site on Seymour Island, which is south of

---

19   Marsh, 1947, 291.

20   Briggs, 1987, 69.

21   J. H. Brown and A. C. Gibson, 1983, *Biogeography*, St Louis, MO: The C.V. Mosby Co., 337.

the southern tip of South America.[22]

Could not these fossils be more simply explained as the remains of some mammals that island hopped? The proximity of Seymour Island to the southern tip of South America is compatible with this explanation. Furthermore, a single site so positioned hardly supplies conclusive proof of marsupial migration to Australia from South America via Antarctica.

So why not island hopping from Asia to Australia? Even Briggs has admitted:

> Although the earliest marsupials might have been more widespread, it is probably significant that Cretaceous marsupials are known only from North and South America. In the Eocene, marsupials reached Europe and by the early Oligocene had penetrated to Asia and North Africa.[23]

If the marsupials did reach Asia as Briggs admits (agreeing with the earlier contention made above), then it is conceivable that they did cross to Australia from Asia. Briggs later remarks about the placental rodents in Australia:

> It seems clear that they reached there by island hopping down the East Indian chain.[24]

So if the placental rodents island hopped to Australia, then it also seems clear that marsupials could have too. The rejection of this migration path in favor of the Antarctic connection with South America is only because the three continents appear to have once been connected, but as has been shown the fossil evidence for such a migration route is very tenuous.[25] Thus, the island hopping route from Asia to Australia is still viable, and still favored for some marsupials, so why not all?

---

22   Rich, 1991, 911.

23   Briggs, 1987, 69.

24   Briggs, 1987, 71.

25   Since continental breakup and subsequent drift would have occurred during the Flood, the possibility that South America, Antarctica, and Australia were once joined thus allowing marsupial migration is irrelevant to the question of post-Flood marsupial migrations. If the present continental configuration was essentially in place when the animals came off the Ark in the mountains of Ararat, then the marsupials had to migrate to Australia via Asia.

25

POST-FLOOD ANIMAL DISTRIBUTION—
RAPID ANIMAL DISPERSION

It is also quite unnecessary to assume that hundreds, or even scores, of thousands of years were required for animals to attain their present geographical distribution. In fact, there is much evidence available to show that animals could have reached their present habitats with astonishing speed, crossing vast continents and even wide stretches of open sea on their way.

In the year 1883, the island of Krakatoa in the Sunda Strait, between Java and Sumatra, was almost destroyed by a volcanic explosion which shook that entire part of the world. For twenty-five years afterwards practically nothing lived in the remnant of that volcanic island. But

> then the colonists began to arrive—a few mammals in 1908; a number of birds, lizards, and snakes; various molluscs, insects, and earthworms. Ninety percent of Krakatoa's new inhabitants, Dutch scientists found, were forms that could have arrived by air.[1]

Brown and Gibson also noted:

> By 1933, only 50 years after the eruption, Krakatoa was once again covered with a dense tropical rainforest, and 271 plant species and 31 kinds of birds were recorded on the island. Where did these organisms and numerous invertebrates come from and how did they get there?... They dispersed across the water gap from the large islands of Java and Sumatra, which lie 40 and 80 km, respectively, from Krakatoa.[2]

Moody has told how large land animals have been able to cross oceans on natural rafts and "floating islands:"

---

1   R. L. Carson, 1961, *The Sea Around Us,* revised ed., New York: Oxford University Press, 92. "riding on the winds, drifting on the currents, or rafting in on logs, floating brush, or trees, the plants and animals…arrived from the distant continents" (90).

2   Brown and Gibson, 1983, 314.

In times of flood large masses of earth and entwining vegetation, including trees, may be torn loose from the banks of rivers and swept out to sea. Sometimes such masses are encountered floating in the ocean out of sight of land, still lush and green, with palms 20-30 feet tall. It is entirely probable that land animals may be transported long distances in this manner. Mayr records that many tropical ocean currents have a speed of at least 2 knots; this would amount to 50 miles in a day, 1000 miles in three weeks.[3]

Brown and Gibson also reported another possibility:

Stories about swimming terrestrial vertebrates have appeared repeatedly in the literature and, as absurd as some reports may seem, we cannot deny that these occasionally occur. A well-documented case is the elephant, which enjoys being in water. However, who would think that an elephant would be found in the ocean? Odd as it may seem, actual reports are well authenticated. For example, a cow and her calf not only were photographed voluntarily swimming at sea in fairly deep water off the coast of Sri Lanka but were also followed and timed, showing that they made a return trip (Johnson, 1978, 1980, 1981). Johnson and others believe that elephants have been able to traverse narrow straits between islands and mainlands in search of new food supplies and therefore are not reliable indicators of a solid land connection. Other large vertebrates, such as tigers and terrestrial snakes, have been spotted over a kilometre at sea, but in many cases the organisms were probably not there by choice, having been washed out to sea during a torrential storm.[4]

Brown and Gibson continued: "No biogeographer today wants to believe that swimming was the means used by organisms to cross wide oceans." This, of course, shows their bias, but they admitted that "a more plausible means for achieving dispersal over water is by rafting," and they went on to agree with Moody's earlier cited comments: "These rafts have been reported drifting hundreds of kilometers out at sea."[5] Then they concluded:

For the majority of terrestrial animals having long-distance dispersal capabilities, one very successful method has been passive dispersal by

---

3   A. Moody, 1953, *Introduction to Evolution*, New York: Harper and Brothers, 262. Romer has also stated: "It seems certain that land animals do at times cross considerable bodies of water where land connections are utterly lacking....Floating masses of vegetation, such as are sometimes found off the mouths of the Amazon, may be one means of effecting this type of migration. Even the case of the entry of hystricoids [porcupine-like rodents] into South America may be a case of this sort...and one successful crossing might populate a continent." A.S. Romer, 1955, *Vertebrate Paleontology*, second ed., Chicago, IL: University of Chicago Press, 513.

4   Brown and Gibson, 1983, 314.

5   Brown and Gibson, 1983, 314.

being carried by larger creatures, especially externally on the feathers or the feet of flying birds or the fur of mammals.[6]

Shull observed:

> [T]he fauna of Madagascar is most similar, not to that of its continental neighbour Africa, but to that of Asia, the gap being bridged over by the Seychelles Islands whose animals are similar to those of Madagascar.[7]

However, the Seychelles Island are 700 miles (1,125 km) north of Madagascar, and the Asian mainland is another 1,500 miles (2,415 km) beyond the Seychelles! The monkey-like *lemur* is practically the only mammal found in Madagascar. So if the evolutionist Shull is right, the lemurs had to find their way across 2,200 miles (3,540 km) of the Indian Ocean in order to reach the island which is now their home.[8] However, more recently it has been suggested that for the slow-moving and sloth-like lemurs,

> ...the only possible means of access to Madagascar was by "rafting": floating across the Mozambique Channel from Africa on matted tangles of vegetation.[9]

In this case the distance thus traveled by "rafting" is reduced to only 250 miles (400 km) from the African mainland, but the question remains as to why lemurs like those in Madagascar are today not to be found in Africa.

The reality and potential of such rafts of matted vegetation or "floating islands" to transport large terrestrial animals across vast stretches of ocean are further illustrated by the observation of how green iguanas first colonized the island of Anguilla in the Caribbean. About a month after hurricanes had blown across the Caribbean in 1995, at least fifteen green iguanas were seen coming ashore on Anguilla's eastern beaches.[10] The "raft" of matted vegetation that they had traveled on was up to 30 feet (9 m) across and their voyage of over 190 miles (300 km) had lasted for a month. Follow-up studies have confirmed that these iguanas are now well established on their new island home, and that they similarly reached two other islands in the vicinity.

While it is thus true that even the open sea has proven to be no final barrier to animal migrations, land bridges have still been the principal means of animal

---

6   Brown and Gibson, 1983, 315.

7   Shull, 1951, 70.

8   See also P. Almasy, 1942, Madagascar: mystery island, *National Geographic*, 81(6): 798, 802.

9   J. Tattersall, 1993, Madagascar's lemurs, *Scientific American*, 268(1): 90-97.

10   E. J. Censky, K. Hodge, and J. Dudley, 1998, Over-water dispersal of lizards due to hurricanes, *Nature*, 395 (6702): 556.

distribution around the world. Marsh has summarized the significance of these continental connections:

> One glance at a world map will show that, with the exception of the narrow break at the Bering Strait, a dry-land path leads from Armenia to all lands of the globe except Australia. In the case of the latter the East Indies [the islands of Indonesia] even today form a fairly continuous bridge of stepping-stones to that southern continent. As regards the Bering Strait, there is no doubt that a land connection once existed between Asia and North America. With the Strait closed, the cold waters of the Arctic would have been prevented from coming south, and the Japan Current would have curved around the coast line farther north than today. The washing of those shores by the warm waters of this current would have produced a dry-land route that even tropical forms could have used.[11]

No biogeographer today denies the significance of this land bridge for animal migrations. Known as the land of Beringia, it provided a connection more than 1,500 km wide.[12] Analysis of core samples from the sea floor beneath the Bering Strait has revealed that

> ...shrub-tundra was widespread across the land bridge in all time periods; birch was important...and heaths and shrub willows were locally abundant. The central and northern sectors were characterized by fewer birch shrubs and more abundant grasses.[13]

Thus, it was concluded that a land-bridge was available for human and animal migration, and that the "insect evidence suggests that summer temperatures at that time were substantially warmer than now."

The existence today of some deep-water stretches along the migration route from Asia to Australia does not preclude the possible existence of a complete dry-land passage at the time the marsupials traveled to Australia. Because the region northwest of Australia linking it to southeast Asia through the islands of Indonesia is still tectonically active, it is conceivable that subsequent to the existence of a complete land bridge, tectonic activity resulted in the sinking of sections of the land bridge to become the sea floor of today's deep-water stretches.

Of course, it is unnecessary to suppose that the pairs of marsupials, for instance, that came off the Ark in the Ararat region had to make the long journey all the way to Australia themselves. Even though there have been isolated reports of individual animals making startling journeys of thousands of kilometres, such

---

11   Marsh, 1947, 291-292.

12   Colinvaux, 1996, Low-down on a land bridge, *Nature*, 382: 21.

13   S. A. Elias et al, 1996, Life and times of the Bering land bridge, *Nature*, 382: 60-63.

abilities are not required for the migration of the animals from Ararat to Australia. Rather, populations of animals may have taken centuries to migrate slowly and over many generations. Thus, for example, as a result of early settlers in Australia releasing just a very small number of rabbits, in less than 150 years wild rabbits were to be found all over the continent.

Another facet of this issue concerns the vegetation needed to feed these marsupials, for example, koalas, during their migration across Asia to Australia. As already noted, the absence of marsupial fossils in southeast Asia does not rule out marsupials having migrated through that area on their way to Australia. Similarly, the fact that eucalyptus trees are not found in southeast Asia today does not mean that they didn't grow in that region at some time in the recent past. It is now well established that changing climatic conditions lead to changes in vegetation patterns and the distribution of different types of plants. Current climate models indicate that the world is generally much drier now than in the recent past, when the Sahara region in Africa was well vegetated where now there is desert, and central Australia had a moist, tropical climate.[14] Thus, the distribution of eucalyptus trees in the past may have been quite different. We know that marsupials also migrated in other directions from the Ararat region because their fossils are found on most of the other continents, but it is in Australia where they primarily survived.

Rapid Breeding and Diversification

Two other important issues related to the post-Flood migration of animals to their current habitats across the earth's surface must be discussed here to completely expound upon the reliability of the scriptural account and to defend its scientific veracity. The first issue is that when two of each created kind, or *baramin,* of terrestrial animals disembarked from the Ark in the Ararat region, they obviously needed to breed rapidly in order to then migrate and fill each ecological niche on every continent across the globe in the time since the Flood. The second issue is that during that rapid post-Flood breeding, diversification and "speciation" had to also occur rapidly so as to produce all the different varieties within the *baramin* that we see today. Both Moore[15] and Morton[16] briefly raise these issues and claim that the magnitude and impossibility of this task of rapid breeding, diversification, and migration makes the scriptural Flood account incomprehensible and therefore absurd to the modern scientific mind.

Woodmorappe has extensively dealt with most aspects of these issues, providing copious technical documentation.[17] The ability of single pairs to give rise to growing and relatively permanent populations is not merely a theoretical possibility, but

---

14   M. E. White, 1994, *After the Greening: The Browning of Australia,* Sydney, Australia: Kangaroo Press.

15   Moore, 1983, 6-8, 14-15, 34-36.

16   Morton, 1995, 68-72.

17   Woodmorappe, 1996, 175-213.

a demonstrated fact. A crucial factor in the immediate post-Flood world was the absence of competitors. As the animals migrated in all directions away from the Ararat region, they moved into relatively empty habitats where there was no competition, and this is of crucial importance in the successful establishment of a breeding population to enable it to grow quickly to a large size. Such rapid population growth also greatly reduces the loss of genetic variability. Indeed, many animals appear to have a built-in mechanism to take advantage of empty niches, with the capacity to have many more offspring than usual when food sources are abundant and competitors few. Woodmorappe provides extensive documentation of many examples that confirm these statements. For example, four collared doves introduced to Britain grew to at least 19,000 birds within nine years, amounting to a 100 percent annual increase.[18] Similarly, the population of macaques on Mauritius Island numbers 25,000 to 35,000, and they are all descendants of just a few individuals introduced by sailors some 400 years ago.[19]

The argument that the descendants of single pairs could not possibly have the built-in potential to suffice for the post-Flood world, let alone produce descendants as ecologically variable as seen within modern families, or even genera, ignores the basics of population biology and the significant ecological changes that are routinely observed to occur in organisms in a matter of generations. In fact, introduced birds have repeatedly adapted to new environments, with changes in plumage, beak morphology, etc., in a matter of generations.[20] Similarly, an introduced population of rock wallabies, started by a single pair, became so differentiated from its parent stock in only several decades that classification as a new species was considered.[21] Thus, if the *baramins* on the Ark were at the level of the genus, it follows that the species found today must have arisen in the approximately 5,000 years since the Flood. Both fluctuating physical environments and environmental stresses, characteristic of the immediate post-Flood period, are known to trigger rapid speciation. Jones,[22] Lester and Bohlin,[23] Brand and Gibson,[24] and Briggs[25] have compiled numerous examples of various invertebrates and vertebrates giving rise to new species and even genera in thousands of years or less. Furthermore, it

18   R. Hudson, 1972, Collared doves in Britain and Ireland during 1965-70, *British Birds,* 65: 139-155.

19   S. H. Lawlor, R. W. Sussman, and L.L. Taylor, 1995, Mitochondrial DNA of the Mauritanian macaques *(Maca fascicularis),* an example of the founder effect, *American Journal of Physical Anthropology,* 96: 133-141.

20   J. Diamond et al, 1989, Rapid evolution of character displacement in myzomelid honeyeaters, *American Naturalist,* 134(5): 675-708.

21   S. Comant, 1988, Saving endangered species by translocation, *BioScience,* 38(4): 254-257.

22   A. J. Jones, 1982, The genetic integrity of the "kinds" *(baramins):* a working hypothesis, *Creation Research Society Quarterly,* 19(1): 13-18.

23   L. P. Lester and R. G. Bohlin, 1989, *The Natural Limits to Biological Change,* second ed., Grand Rapids, MI: Baker Book House.

24   L. R. Brand and L. J. Gibson, 1993, An interventionist theory of natural selection and biological change within limits, *Origins,* 20(2): 60-82.

25   J. C. Briggs, 1974, *Marine Zoogeography,* San Francisco, CA: McGraw-Hill Book Company, 442-443.

has been shown that some cichlid fish species have arisen in merely 200 years.[26]

Inbreeding is known to occur whenever close relatives sire offspring and has been blamed on the expression of the "genetic load," including many previously-accumulated deleterious recessive alleles. However, owing to the rapid growth of post-Flood animal populations, matings between close relatives would have been largely limited to the first post-Flood generation or so, and in any case, any potential for inbreeding is only likely to have occurred if small populations were sustained, which they weren't. Nevertheless, because deleterious recessive alleles accumulate with time, increasing the genetic load, it is certain that those animals that disembarked from the Ark approximately 5,000 years ago were less burdened with these genetic problems and were thus unlikely to experience inbreeding problems. Furthermore, to the extent that God Himself selected the animals for the journey on the Ark, He would have obviously chosen those pairs He knew would not have to contend with genetic problems during rapid breeding to populate the post-Flood world.

For the same reason, those animals placed on the Ark by God would have been carriers of adequate genetic diversity. In any case, evidence is steadily accumulating that a few individuals can carry sufficient genetic variation for their descendent populations to function in new environments.[27] Additionally, the importance of genetic variation remains essentially unquantified for almost all organisms,[28] and there is still much that we do not even know about genes themselves and how they interact to manifest themselves in the physical characters of descendent organisms. Any suggestion that a minimum of fifty animals are needed to commence a genetically viable breeding population, as argued by Morton,[29] is extremely inaccurate and misleading, because it has been found that a single pair of animals most definitely *can* have the same genetic diversity as fifty individuals, and without any miraculous or unusual procedures:

> Hence, a founder population of two lizards collected from different local populations would display more genetic variation for all diversity measures with the possible exception of N than a sample of 50 lizards from a single local population.[30]

26 R. B. Owen et al, 1990, Major low levels of Lake Malawi and their implications for speciation rates in cichlid fishes, *Proceedings of the Royal Society of London*, B240: 519-553.

27 L. A. Pray and C. J. Goodnight, 1995, Genetic variation in inbreeding depression in the red flour beetle Tribolium castaneum, *Evolution*, 49(1): 176-188, and citations therein.

28 M. Brakefield and I. J. Saccheri, 1994, Guidelines in conservation genetics and the use of population cage experiments with butterflies to investigate the effects of genetic drift and inbreeding, in *Conservation Genetics*, ed. V. Loweschcke, J. Tomiuk and S.K. Jain, Basel, Switzerland: Birkhauser Verlag, 165-179.

29 Morton, 1995, 71.

30 A. R. Templeton, 1994, Biodiversity at the molecular genetic level: experiences from disparate macroorganisms, *Philosophical Transactions of the Royal Society of London*, B345: 59-64.

Thus, it is unnecessary for God to have further intervened miraculously to restore genetic diversity and overcome any genetic load in the post-Flood animal populations to make them viable and able to diversify and speciate to fill all ecological niches in the post-Flood world in the centuries following the Flood. Woodmorappe has adequately documented how perceived genetic difficulties for maintaining genetic diversity in post-Flood animal populations are far from insurmountable, in spite of the genetic "bottleneck" at the time of the Flood.[31]

As animals began migrating away from the Ararat region and rapidly breeding as they traveled, mutation rates would have increased as stressful environments were encountered.[32] Such environmental stresses coupled with mutations would not only lead to rapid speciation, but specialization to deal with unique or special conditions for survival. This can result from a loss in genetic information, from thinning out of the gene pool, or by degenerative mutation. Thus, for example, many modern breeds of dog whose character traits were selected by man are much less able to survive in the wild than their "mongrel" ancestors. The St. Bernard carries a mutational defect, an overactive thyroid, which means it needs to live in a cold environment to avoid overheating, and so as a result of that mutation has become specialized. Similarly, the specialized diet of the koala may be due to a mutational defect, while the koala's ancestors that disembarked from the Ark may actually have been more hardy and able to survive on a much greater range of vegetation. Another potential example of specialization would be the very slow-moving sloth, whose ancestors from the Ark were possibly not as specialized as their descendants, who now carry only a portion of their *baramin's* original gene pool. The present-day sloths would seem to require much more time than the Genesis account allows for them to make the journey from Ararat to their present home in South America, but their less specialized ancestors were likely faster-moving, making the journey in a much shorter time.

It needs to be remembered that these genetic changes do not require much time to have an effect upon a rapidly growing population of animals under migrating pressures. As the growing populations that descended from the pairs of each *baramin* that disembarked from the Ark began to diversify and specialize as they migrated, they would also tend to break up rapidly into daughter populations going in different directions, each carrying only portions of the gene pools of the original pairs. Some of these daughter populations may have eventually become extinct due to the environmental pressures encountered during their migration, thus leaving only populations of specialized types. In other cases, new species survived and proliferated even though they migrated in different directions, so that today we find a tremendous diversity among some groups of animals which are very obviously related, being apparently derived from the same *baramin* and yet being found in ecological niches far apart from each other, even on different

---

31   Woodmorappe, 1996, 187-213.

32   Brand and Gibson, 1993, 72.

continents.

Therefore, in conclusion, the more the fascinating details of animal migrations and distribution around the earth are studied, the more convincing it becomes that these migration waves of all the variegated life forms which moved outward in all directions from the Ararat region across the continents and seas have really not been a chance and haphazard phenomenon. Instead, God's hand would seem to have been involved in guiding and directing these creatures in ways that man, with all his ingenuity, has not yet been able to fathom, in order to ensure that His great commission to the post-Flood animal kingdom might be carried out, and "that they may breed abundantly in the earth, and be fruitful, and multiply upon the earth" (Genesis 8:17).

26

SUMMARY AND CONCLUSIONS

This section has dealt with the further argument against a global flood that Noah and his family could never have gathered nor cared for the animals if two of *every* Genesis kind (*baramin*) were on board the Ark. In response, the tremendous capacity of the Ark was quantified; the likely taxonomic rank of the *baramin* was identified, and the number of *baramins* was thus determined. We observed how few terrestrial animals actually had to go aboard the Ark, especially relative to the number of species estimated to exist on the earth today. We noted especially that no provision in the Ark needed to be made for the large number of marine creatures. Given the probable existence of a single pre-Flood supercontinent with totally different topography, climate, and zoogeographical conditions before the Flood, we pointed out that terrestrial animals destined to go aboard the Ark may have lived in the same region as Noah and therefore no insurmountable obstacles may have existed to their successful migration to the Ark. We discussed that the task of caring for the animals on the Ark was partly mitigated by the small number of animals involved and possibly also by many of them entering a state of dormancy. Moreover, it was pointed out that God probably imparted to the animals migratory instincts and powers of dormancy in order to achieve the gathering and caring for the animals during that year of global catastrophic crisis.

Finally, in response to skepticism concerning post-Flood animal migrations and the resulting present-day biogeography, it is by no means unreasonable to assume that all terrestrial animals in the world today have descended from their ancestors that disembarked from the Ark in the Ararat region. Even though there is a lack of fossil evidence of marsupials having once lived in Asia, it is still conceivable that the marsupials could have reached Australia by rapidly migrating across Asia to Australia via a land bridge and/or island hopping before the two continents were separated by water. Comparatively little is known of animal migrations in the past, but what observational evidence there is indicates very clearly the possibility of rapid colonization of distant areas, even when oceans have to be crossed in the process. Thus, it would not have required many centuries even for animals like the edentates to migrate from the Ararat region across Asia to South America over the Bering land bridge. Inbreeding as animal populations rapidly grew from the pairs of each *baramin* that disembarked from the Ark would not have been a problem, because those few progenitors possessed all the genetic potential for the genetic diversity currently found in their descendants. Population and environmental pressures would have resulted in diversification, specialization, and speciation as populations split and became geographically isolated from one another in the search for new homes. Thus, impelled by God's command to the animal kingdom (Genesis 8:17), every part of the habitable earth was soon filled with birds, beasts, and creeping things.

The teaching of Scripture concerning the Flood is unmistakeably clear. Except for Noah's family, the entire pre-Flood human population, widespread and hopelessly wicked, was destroyed by water. All the world's air-breathing terrestrial animals were also engulfed by this watery cataclysm, except for those gathered into the Ark and sustained there by the power of God. The utter global devastation submerged all the then highest mountains for 110 days and finally left the Ark stranded on the mountains of Ararat.[1] From the occupants of the Ark have descended all men and terrestrial animals in the world today.

However complex, difficult, or obscure the problems may seem to be, with respect to the date of the Flood, the exact distribution of the pre-Flood human population, the number of "created kinds" of terrestrial animals in the days of Noah, and the migration of animals from the Ark to the ends of the earth, the fact remains that the Genesis Flood was geographically universal. "Whereby the world that then was, being overflowed with water, perished" (2 Peter 3:6); and it is in the light of that tremendous biblical truth that all investigations into the past history of the earth and its inhabitants must be pursued.

---

1   Reports of the sighting of the Ark, preserved high on the snow-covered slopes of Mt. Ararat, have been published from time to time (for example, LaHaye and Morris, 1976, *The Ark on Ararat*), but none of the many expeditions to Mt. Ararat over the last four decades has identified any remains whatever of the Ark there. The reason may well be, as evidence strongly suggests, that Mt. Ararat is a volcano, most of which formed *after* the Flood! That, of course, does not rule out the possibility that the Ark or its remains may yet be found somewhere in "the mountains of Ararat" where the Bible says the Ark landed (Genesis 8:4). These are in a different location to the Mt. Ararat volcano, and most of them are *not* volcanic. Lack of success to date emphasizes the difficulties of locating it, even if some remains have indeed been preserved. But the finding of the Ark is not essential to consideration of Noah's Flood as a historical event, since the record of the Scriptures is sufficient in and of itself.

Section IV

The Framework
for a Biblical Geology

27

INTRODUCTION

The hostility of geologists today toward the concept of a universal flood as described in Genesis is a somewhat curious phenomenon in contemporary geologic thought. Geologic evidence for the Flood cannot be understood because the possibility of such a catastrophe in the past has been ruled out of their interpretive framework on the basis of *a priori* philosophical reasoning. Hence, for most modern geologists, any suggestion that the recent, global, biblical Flood could have been responsible for reshaping the earth's surface and building a substantial portion of the geologic record is complete anathema.

Though written some seventy years ago, the words of L. Merson Davies, a then prominent British field and laboratory paleontologist, are still highly relevant. In a paper presented to the Victoria Institute, in which he pointed to this remarkable antipathy of geologists to the subject of the biblical Flood, Davies wrote:

> Here, then, we come face to face with a circumstance which cannot be ignored in dealing with this subject…namely, the existence of a marked *prejudice* against the acceptance of belief in a cataclysm like the Deluge. Now we should remember that, up to 100 years ago [i.e., 1830], such a prejudice did not exist…as a general one, at least. Belief in the Deluge of Noah was axiomatic, not only in the Church itself (both Catholic and Protestant) but in the scientific world as well. And yet the Bible stood committed to the prophecy that, in which it calls the "last days," a very different philosophy would be found in the ascendant; a philosophy which would lead men to regard belief in the Flood with disfavour, and treat it as disproved, declaring that "All things continue as from the beginning of the creation" (2 Peter 3:3-6). In other words, a doctrine of uniformity in all things (a doctrine which the Apostle obviously regarded as untrue to fact) was to replace belief in such cataclysms as the Deluge.[1]

Davies then proceeded to show how this remarkable prophecy of the apostle Peter had begun to find its fulfillment in the 19th century with the doctrines of uniformitarianism and evolution, as set forth by Hutton, Lyell, and Darwin,

---

1   L. Merson Davies, 1930, Scientific Discoveries and their Bearing on the Biblical Account of the Noachian Deluge, *Journal of the Transactions of the Victoria Institute*, vol. LXII, 62-63 (italics are his).

supplanting those of earlier thinkers.

> And so, after 18 centuries, we at last find the ancient prophecy fulfilled
> before our eyes; for here is, as foretold, where opposition to belief in the
> Flood lies today. There is no mistaking a fact. It stares us in the face,
> *anyone, today, who argues in favour of belief in the Flood, at once encounters
> opposition upon these long-foretold lines.*[2]

Before 1800, some of the outstanding theologians of the church were convinced
that the Genesis Flood was not only universal in extent, but was also responsible
for reshaping the earth's surface, including the formation of sedimentary strata.
Among those who held this view were Tertullian, Chrysostom, Augustine, and
Luther.[3]

Even though the Flood as a key element in the interpretive framework of geology
had to overcome some serious opposition in the 17th century, it nevertheless
became generally accepted by scientists and theologians in the Western world.
Indeed, during the last twenty years of the 17th century, a new enthusiasm for
Flood geology swept England and the continent through the influence of three
Cambridge scholars: Thomas Burnet, *A Sacred Theory of the Earth* (1681); John
Woodward, *An Essay Toward a Natural Theory of the Earth* (1693); and William
Whiston, *A New Theory of the Earth* (1696).[4] So great was the impact of these
volumes upon the thinking of western Europeans in those days that in 1697 it
could be written that "all sober and judicious men are now convinced that the
exuviae of sea animals, so plentifully found at this day in the strata of the earth,
and in the most hardened solid stone and marble, are the lasting proof of the
Deluge itself and of its universality."[5]

Throughout the entire 18th century, and well into the 19th, an imposing list of
scientists and theologians produced works in support of Flood geology. Thus, it
was accepted almost without question in the Western world during that period that
the Flood was both universal and responsible for the major geologic formations of
the earth. In the words of Gillispie:

> There was no question about the historical reality of the flood. When the
> history of the earth began to be considered geologically, it was simply
> assumed that a universal deluge must have wrought vast changes and
> that it had been a primary agent in forming the present surface of the
> globe. Its occurrence was evidence that the Lord was a governor as well

---

2   Davies, 1930, 63 (italics are mine).

3   Nelson, 1968, 7-10, see quotations from the writings of these men on the subject of the Flood.

4   B. C. Allen, 1949, *The Legend of Noah*, Urbana, IL: University of Illinois Press, 66-112, provides a
    thoroughly documented history of the Flood controversy during the Middle Ages.

5   J. Harris, quoted in Nelson, 1968, 51.

as a creator.[6]

However, over the past two centuries the development of modern geology has been accompanied by a gradual rejection of the scriptural revelation of the early history of the earth, including its geological implications. Except for occasional abortive attempts to harmonize the sequences of Creation Week with those of the geological ages, modern geology has now all but universally repudiated the book of Genesis as far as any geological significance is concerned. Even though written over five decades ago, the following comments are still very typical today:

> Early geologists fought to free people from the myths of biblical creation. Many millions still live in mental bondage controlled by ignorant ranters who accept the Bible as the last word in science, and accept Archbishop Ussher's claim that the earth was created 4004 BC. Attempts to reconcile Genesis with geology lead to numerous contradictions. Also the theory of evolution greatly affects modern thinking. Man's rise from simple life forms even today causes much controversy among "fundamentalists" who cling to a literal belief in the Bible.[7]

Similarly, former Harvard paleontologist George Gaylord Simpson, in an important speech delivered at the Darwinian Centennial Convocation in 1959 at the University of Chicago, said:

> With the dawning realization that the earth is extremely old, in human terms of age, came the knowledge that it has changed progressively and radically but usually gradually and always in an orderly, natural way. The fact of change had not earlier been denied in Western science or theology—after all, the Noachian Deluge was considered a radical change. But the Deluge was believed to have supernatural causes or concomitants that were not operative through earth's history. The doctrine of geological uniformitarianism, finally established early in the 19th century, widened the recognized reign of natural law. The earth has changed throughout its history under the action of material forces, only, and of the *same* forces as those now visible to us and still acting on it. The steps that I have so briefly traced reduced the sway of superstition in the conceptual world of human lives.[8]

The Flood was once believed to be the explanation for the formation of much of the geologic record; later it was regarded as one of a series of geological cataclysms that were the key features in geologic interpretation; then it was thought to explain only certain of the surficial deposits of the earth's surface; and finally, it

---

6   C. C. Gillispie, 1951, *Genesis and Geology*, Cambridge, MA: Harvard University Press, 42.

7   D. Hager, 1957, Fifty years of progress in geology, *Geotimes*, 2 (2): 12.

8   G. G. Simpson, 1960, The World into Which Darwin Led Us, *Science*, 131: 967.

was either dismissed as legendary or interpreted as a local flood in Mesopotamia, thus stripping it of all geological consequence. One may search modern geological textbooks or reference works from one end of an academic library to the other and find in every work consulted either no mention of the biblical Flood at all, or else perhaps a patronizing reference in some historical note on the rise of modern geology.

A Bible-believing Christian thus faces a serious dilemma. When many thousands of trained geologists, sincere and honest in their conviction of the correctness of their interpretation of the geological data, present an almost unanimous verdict against the biblical accounts of creation and the Flood, we must of course feel very reluctant to oppose such an impressive array of scholarship and authority.

On the other hand, when confronted with the biblical evidence for a global flood of tremendous geological potency, a Bible-believing Christian is still more reluctant to reject the Bible's testimony. This is no problem, of course, for those who do not accept the inspiration of the Bible or the authority of Jesus Christ. But the genuinely committed Christian knows that the evidence for full divine inspiration of Scripture is far weightier than the evidence for any supposed facts of science. When confronted with the consistent biblical testimony to a global flood, the believer must certainly accept it as unquestionably true.

Some Christians have attempted to escape this dilemma by various stratagems of harmonizing the Genesis record of creation and the Flood with the modern interpretive scheme for the geological data. However, at least as far as the Flood is concerned, all such attempts have proven to be quite futile due to distortion or entire neglect of certain biblical details. There is an obvious incompatibility of the modern interpretive framework for the geological data with the details of the Genesis account.

Thus, the decision must be faced: either the biblical record of the Flood is false and must be rejected, or else the interpretive system used in modern geology that seems to have discredited the Scriptures is wrong and must be changed. The latter alternative would seem to be the only one which a biblically and scientifically instructed Christian could honestly take, regardless of the barrage of scholarly wrath and ridicule that taking such a position might bring upon him.

However, taking this position does not in any way mean that the actual observational data of geology are to be rejected. It is not the observed facts and experimentally-reproducible data of geology that are at variance with the Scriptures, but only the interpretive framework into which those facts and data have been placed. This interpretive framework or system involves a commitment to the principle of uniformity of geological processes and to evolutionary theory for evaluation of the geological data to produce what is claimed to be a coherent picture of the geological history of the earth. The field of historical geology is only one of the many specialties within the earth sciences. Nevertheless, its perspective has become interwoven into so many other areas of geological study that changing the interpretive framework would require nothing short of a complete revolutionary upheaval. At present, the proposition of using a biblically-based interpretive framework for historical geology is both absurd and anathema to both professional and academic geologists alike.

This is not said in a critical vein, nor with specific personalities in mind. Furthermore, an adherence by present-day orthodox geologists to the uniformity principle is only rarely attributable to an anti-Christian bias. However, the uniformitarian geologists of the 19th century rejected the biblical testimony of deterioration and catastrophe and all the geological implications thereof, and accepted instead the philosophy of evolutionary naturalism, building their system of historical geology within that interpretive framework. In recent years, it has been increasingly accepted among geologists that the uniformity of geological processes also involves the occasional catastrophe, such as violent and widespread volcanic eruptions, meteorite impacts, and local flooding, producing upheavals on the earth's surface and sometimes extinctions amongst the earth's animal inhabitants.

Nevertheless, such catastrophes are viewed as part of the natural order and not as negating the normal reign of slow-and-gradual geological processes. The geological record overall is still interpreted according to evolutionary naturalism as representing countless millions and billions of years of earth history and not guided by the Creator's unseen hand. It is in this context that modern geologists should be seen as the products of a particular background, conditioned by education and group pressure to think always in terms of evolution and uniformity. Many geologists may even be sincerely religious, feeling more or less satisfied that these concepts are basically harmonious with theism and perhaps even with the Bible. If interviewed, most geologists would probably respond that the Bible and/or religious commitment are simply not relevant to geological science and its practice, because they sincerely believe the history of the earth and the evolutionary origin and development of its inhabitants have been satisfactorily explained by science without any recourse to the Bible or any religious belief.

It is also important to note that in many of the descriptive disciplines of geology where experiment and observation are used to gather the geological data, the interpretive framework often plays only a relatively minor role. In the disciplines of mineralogy, petrology, economic geology, exploration geophysics, petroleum geology, structural geology, seismology, geochemistry, marine geology, engineering geology, environmental geology, and ground-water geology, work usually proceeds largely independent of the evolutionary uniformitarian interpretive framework, as is also the case in the descriptive aspects of physical geology/geomorphology, stratigraphy, and paleontology. Thus, it is only the evolutionary uniformitarian framework for integrating the geological data from all these disciplines together into a comprehensive scheme for the historical development of the earth that is the focus of criticism here. Indeed, it is argued that a complete reorientation of historical geology is quite possible without any serious effect at all on most of the other disciplines of geology. In fact, such a complete reorientation offers the prospect of an even better understanding of the earth's history and thus a more successful discovery and exploitation of the earth's natural resources for the benefit of mankind.

Biblically-committed geologists believe that this can be done only by means of the clear statements and legitimate implications of biblical revelation. After all, any real *knowledge* of origins or of earth history antecedent to human historical records can be obtained only through divine revelation. Whereas the geological data of the descriptive disciplines of geology are based on currently observable and reproducible objects, processes, and events, historical geology purports to be able to reconstruct the unobservable past in a reliable way, drawing only on these present observations and processes. Yet it is *manifestly impossible* ever to *validate* by the scientific method of experimentation and observation alone any hypothesis outside of recorded human history.

Because it is highly important for man to understand the nature of his origin, as well as that of the earth on which he dwells, and because of the impossibility of his ever really *knowing* about these matters otherwise, it is eminently reasonable that his Creator would in some way reveal to him at least the essentials concerning them. Christians and Jews (and Muslims in a derivative manner) have for millennia believed that this revelation is given in the book of Genesis ("Beginnings"), with its sober yet majestic, realistic, and straightforward description of the origin and early history of the earth and its inhabitants. Indeed, there is no serious rival claim to this revelation anywhere else in the religious books of mankind. It is sad, therefore, to see the unrealistic, distorted, mythical, and often orally-transmitted stories associated with the religions of other people groups given the same status as the written record of Genesis, as if all were equally true as a religious explanation, as opposed to the true scientific explanation (based on evolutionary naturalism and uniformitarianism). This, of course, represents a downgrading of the book of Genesis to myth and legend. It occurs today largely because so many people have been led to believe that modern science has shown the biblical account of the earth's history to be irrelevant.

Consequently, it is imperative, and there is ample warrant both spiritually and scientifically, that a new scientific model of earth history be built on the framework divinely revealed in the Scriptures, rather than on uniformitarian and evolutionary assumptions. We must first start with the Scriptures to build our model of earth history before investigating how the geological data fit that model, recognizing that the geological data have to be stripped of and separated from their evolutionary and uniformitarian accompaniments. Building a truly scriptural scientific model of earth history should be done, not with the attitude of trying to make the biblical accounts fit into the data and theories of science, but rather of letting the Bible speak for itself and then seeking to understand the geological data in the light of its teachings.

28

THE SCRIPTURAL DIVISIONS OF GEOLOGIC HISTORY

There is no warrant for presuming that the Genesis Flood, which has been the focus of attention thus far, produced all the strata of the geologic record. On the contrary, the Bible plainly implies that there were five significant periods of earth history, during each of which substantial portions of the geologic record could have been produced.

The First Creative Act

"In the beginning," the Bible says, "God created the heaven and the earth" (Genesis 1:1). This initial act of creation on Day One may well have resulted in a fully-formed silicate (rocky) earth with an internal structure already differentiated into the three major divisions of core, mantle, and crust. Yet the first description given of the earth's appearance after this first act of creation is that of water ("the deep") covering its surface, which itself was also enveloped in darkness (Genesis 1:2). It seems reasonable also that, even if the earth's creation was accomplished with an instantaneous act, its internal heat from nuclear transformations of some elements and the waters across its surface would immediately have begun to accomplish work of profound geological significance.

The Work of the Six Days of Creation

On Day Two, mention is made of a division of the waters that covered the entire earth's surface at the time of creation. God divided it into two portions separated by the "firmament" or "expanse," which He then calls "heaven," or *shamayim* in Hebrew (Genesis 1:8). While many have interpreted the "firmament" or "expanse" to be the earth's atmosphere, from the description of God's placement of the sun, moon, and stars "in the firmament of the heaven" (both in Genesis 1:15 and 1:17), the text seems to be requiring that the "firmament" or "expanse" correspond to "interstellar space" beyond the atmosphere. The Hebrew word translated as "firmament," *raqia*, can also be translated "stretched out thinness." Elsewhere in the Old Testament (e.g., Job 9:8; Psalm 104:2; Isaiah 40:22; 42:5; 44:24), God is extolled and praised as the One "who stretches out the heavens." These passages all seem to be referring to the starry heavens. This lends support to the conclusion that the *raqia* is the realm in which the stars were created. The probable implication is that the waters which were "above the firmament" were not waters just above the earth's atmosphere, but instead are waters that even now may be beyond the most distant galaxy (see Psalm 148:3-4).

On Day Three, especially, an enormous amount of geological work must have been accomplished. The Genesis account tells us that on that day God commanded the dry land to appear from under the globe-encircling waters, which were pushed aside and gathered together into ocean basins. This can only mean that a great orogeny occurred, so that the rocks of the earliest-formed crust were deformed dramatically as they were lifted above sea level. As the uplift occurred, the waters being pushed aside would have to drain off the newly emerging land surface. This process would have been accompanied by great erosion, transport of sediments, and deposition of those sediments as the waters flowed down into the new ocean basins.

On the same day, Genesis records that God made vegetation of all kinds to appear on the now dry land surface, implying that by that time it had been covered by a mantle of fertile soil (Genesis 1:9-13). Then on Day Four, God established the sun and moon in their functions with respect to the earth. Because the sun now provides a substantial portion of the energy required to power the earth's surface geological processes, this event also had profound geological implications. Undoubtedly, there were also many other creative and developmental processes which took place during these six days of creation as the entire earth was being prepared by God as a wonderfully harmonious "dominion" for man to "subdue" (Genesis 1:28).

The Pre-Flood Period

As a result of the Fall of man, a whole new order of things began, not only in God's spiritual economy with respect to man, but also with respect to the operation of the earth itself, which we are told was "cursed for man's sake" (Genesis 3:17; 5:29). The whole creation was delivered into a bondage of corruption, that is, "decay," groaning and travailing in pain (Romans 8:21-22). The pre-Flood earth had mountains (Genesis 7:20), rivers (Genesis 2:10), and seas (Genesis 1:10), and so must have experienced geological processes and activities somewhat like those of the present era. On the other hand, there are implications that some significant differences may have existed as well.

One significant difference that likely existed in the pre-Flood period was the distribution of land on the earth's surface. Today there are many continents separated by ocean basins, whereas Genesis 1:9-10 states that God gathered together the waters "unto one place" so as to "let the dry land appear." This suggests that the dry land might also have been in one place, meaning that there was a single large continental landmass in the pre-Flood period. If this were the case, then this would have had an effect on terrestrial climates and geological activity, including where the activity occurred.

Some have suggested that Genesis 2:5 might mean that during this time rainfall was not experienced on the earth, but the text simply states that the Lord "had not caused it to rain upon the earth" in the days of the Creation Week before there was "a man to till the ground." This then does not necessarily imply that no rain at all fell during the pre-Flood period.

The Flood

It has been demonstrated already that the Flood was a global catastrophe, and therefore it must have had a global cause and produced worldwide geological effects. It clearly rivals the geological upheavals of the third day of the Creation Week as the greatest physical convulsion that has ever occurred on the earth. Indeed, since the creation of life itself, it is undoubtedly the greatest physical convulsion, because it in fact all but obliterated everything living on the face of the earth! There is no escaping the conclusion that if the Bible is true and if the Lord Jesus Christ possessed divine omniscience, the Flood was the most significant event, geologically speaking, that has ever occurred on the earth since its creation. (The Bible has more chapters and verses detailing the Flood than the creation of the universe, while Jesus also referred to Noah and the Flood more times than He did the creation.) *To be totally consistent with the geological data and thus qualify as true, any scientific model of the geological history of the earth must, therefore, give a prominent place to this event in its framework for systematizing the geological data.*

The Post-Flood Period

At the conclusion of the Flood, God promised that no more such earth-destroying watery cataclysms would ever be visited on the earth as long as it remained (Genesis 8:22). In general, uniform processes of nature would henceforth prevail. Thus, the geological principle of uniformity should be applied to the study of this period. However, there remain certain limitations. When using the geological principle of uniformity, there must still be acknowledgment of catastrophes occurring in the post-Flood period. These are recorded in Scripture, ancient mythologies (where they are based on actual historical occurrences), and in the resultant geologic deposits themselves. In fact, it is likely that even a large proportion of present geological work is accomplished during brief, intense periods of earth activity—in floods, hurricanes, earthquakes, volcanic eruptions, and similar events—a reality which increasingly is being recognized by uniformitarian geologists.

General Comments

All of the earth's geological features must have been formed during one of these periods in the earth's history. It should be possible, at least in a general way, to determine what geological formations and phenomena are attributable to each of these periods that constitute the scriptural framework for earth history. Of course, it is obvious that a really detailed reinterpretation of the incredible mass of geological data now available, accumulated by many thousands of geologists and other investigators over the past two centuries, is well beyond the scope of these volumes. That task will require the focused attention of many specialists within each of the various sub-disciplines of geological research for many years.

However, these specialists must first be convinced that the Bible, especially the early chapters of Genesis, is genuine God-given testimony concerning terrestrial and human origins, and as such provides the only true and reliable framework within which earth history can possibly be interpreted. Indeed, they must be convinced that this framework is the only sound basis for a true understanding of geological data and that the scriptural framework indeed makes sense of all the evidence. They must believe that using the scriptural framework is both philosophically possible and reasonable, and even absolutely necessary. Again, the principal defining issue is the reliability and applicability of the scriptural record.

Unless scholars are fully persuaded of this absolute priority, then their thinking can be influenced by the apparent success of the uniformitarian-evolutionary framework in providing the illusion of a coherent and detailed account of earth history. They need to recognize that the framework built upon the assumptions that matter is the totality of reality and that naturalistic processes are all that are required to explain the origin, history, and operation of the world around us is, first, utterly opposed to the God-given scriptural record. Moreover, they must recognize that the materialistic framework is actually full of contradictions that are generally glossed over or ignored completely. They need to see plainly the hopeless inadequacies that render the geological data totally inconsistent within that framework, even when some catastrophic events and processes are included. However, in order to gain the attention of such specialists to these problems, and therefore the importance of rejecting the uniformitarian-evolutionary framework, it must be shown convincingly that a new approach, based on the scriptural framework, provides a far better explanation of the geological data and demonstrates superior consistency with the observational evidence.

It is hoped, perhaps rather naively, but certainly with sincerity, that what is presented in this study will attract the attention of a new generation of such specialists and colleagues, persuading them to take up the challenge of further, more extensive studies for the purpose of building a comprehensive Creation-Flood scientific model that is thoroughly consistent both with the framework of earth history supplied by the Scriptures and with the voluminous amount of geological data now available.[1] The impetus for such further investigations would be more than just gaining new scientific knowledge and insight, though that is

---

1   A large number of those currently engaged in building or promoting the Creation-Flood model of earth history were convicted, or have been greatly influenced, by the ground-breaking treatise *The Genesis Flood* by Drs. Whitcomb and Morris, the forerunner of this present study.

highly worthwhile in itself. It might well be possible to eventually reconstruct the nature of the pre-Flood earth, at least with respect to the configuration of its continental landmass and its constituent geology, and perhaps even some details of the associated climatology. Furthermore, it might also be possible to produce a detailed description of the geological processes at work during the Creation Week, and then later during the Flood. This would obviously lead to a far better understanding of the state of the earth today, to a better understanding of the physical phenomena currently in operation, and to better management and stewardship of the earth and its resources. Perhaps most important of all, it could lead to the realization by people everywhere that the rocks of the earth bear eloquent testimony to the power and holiness of Almighty God, the Creator, and ultimately to the realization that He is both Judge and Redeemer.

It is readily recognized that the following detailed suggestions and the Creation-Flood scientific model presented are tentative, ever subject to revision and modification as more data become available and better understanding of that data unfolds. The purpose here is to construct the Creation-Flood scientific model in such a way that will serve as a stimulus to further study and investigation and demonstrate that there is at least one possible way to understand the geological data in the scriptural framework of a literal six-day creation and a universal flood.

29

THE BEGINNING OF CREATION

The opening verse of the biblical record can literally be translated "Initially (or first, to start with) God created the heaven and the earth."[1] Note that no attempt is made to prove that God exists; the verse simply states that He exists already as the eternal, omnipotent Creator. In the Hebrew, the divine name used is *Elohim*, which stresses God's majesty and omnipotence. He is also transcendent to, and separate from, the universe and everything in it that He then created. In consequence, He is not bound to act and to operate within the natural laws and processes that He built into the universe, which He brought into being. This opening verse of the book of Genesis describes the absolute origin of the universe and everything in it.

Contrast this to all ancient pagan mythologies, as well as modern scientific naturalism, which all begin with the space-time-matter universe *already existing* in a primeval state of chaos, and which continue with speculations as to how that chaos might have "evolved" into the universe we presently observe. Modern scientific naturalism begins with a singularity in space, time, and matter/energy. Then as a result of a "big bang," this singularity unfolds through mere natural forces and eventually into complex living systems. Similarly, pagan pantheistic mythologies also began with elementary matter in various forms evolving into complex systems by the forces of nature, personified as different gods and goddesses.

However, Genesis 1 begins with God creating the universe literally out of nothing by a specific act of creation. The Hebrew word *bara*, translated "created" in the text of Genesis 1:1, is exclusively used to describe the work of God. God is always the subject of this verb. It is a special word that has no other usage than for the creative agency of God, distinguishing it from any sort of human making and shaping.[2] Since this verb is reserved exclusively for God, this realm of divine creation activity lies outside human experience and is therefore beyond complete human conceptualization. Even though *bara* does not express specifically the method of creation, it does refer precisely to God's extraordinary, sovereign,

---

1   Hamilton, 1990, 104.

2   H. H. Schmidt, 1997, in *Theological Lexicon of the Old Testament*, E. Jenni and C. Westermann, eds., M. E. Biddle, trans., Peabody, MA: Hendrickson Publishers Inc., 255.

unhindered creative activity. That God did create the heaven and the earth out of nothing—that is, called into existence that which previously had no existence—is clearly affirmed by other Old Testament passages that connect His creative action to His spoken Word, such as "by the word of the LORD were the heavens made; and all the host of them by the breath of his mouth" (Psalm 33:6); and "let them [i.e., the sun, moon, and stars] praise the name of the LORD: for he commanded, and they were created" (Psalm 148:5). This concept is also emphasized in Hebrews 11:3: "The worlds were framed by the word of God, so that things which are seen were not made of things which do appear." The work of creation, therefore, is uniquely a work of God, who spoke into existence something whose materials had no previous existence, except in the mind of God.

Of the two entities God spoke into existence, the first in the Hebrew is *shamayim*, which can be translated either as "heaven" or "heavens" depending on the context. Since it is here created by God without any prior existence, it cannot be referring to "heaven" in the context of God's abode, but is instead a created entity into which the stars are placed after being made on the fourth day of creation (Genesis 1:16). In Genesis 1:1, the Hebrew word *eretz,* translated "earth," is linked to *shamayim*, "heaven," and together they constitute the entire universe or cosmos.[3] Thus, the context of the word indicates it is being used cosmologically to specify the earth, rather than one of the other common meanings of this Hebrew word *eretz*, such as dry land (in contrast to water or waters), the ground on which one stands, individual regions and parcels of land, or governed areas and countries. Given the context and the frequent use in the Old Testament of "heaven and earth" together, here in Genesis 1:1 the term "earth" would seem not to be referring to matter in a general way as a component of the universe, or even the basic elements of matter, but referring to the earth itself, the globe we now call planet earth. However, at the time of this initial creation, there were no planets, stars, galaxies, or other material bodies in the universe because they are specifically recorded as not being made until the fourth day of creation (Genesis 1:14-19).

That this is the legitimate understanding of *eretz* in Genesis 1:1 is confirmed by the same usage and meaning of "earth" immediately following in Genesis 1:2: "And the earth was without form, and void; and darkness was upon the face of the deep." It is significant, in fact, that every verse in Genesis 1 (except verses 1 and 27) begins with the conjunction "and" (Hebrew *waw*). This sentence construction clearly implies that each statement is in turn sequentially and chronologically connected to the statements before and after it, each action described following directly from the action described in the statement preceding it. Thus, it is grammatically correct to translate the Hebrew sentence structure, as has traditionally been done, to imply that verse 2 is a description of the earth which God had just created in verse 1, there being no room for any chronological gap whatsoever between these first two verses of Genesis. In other words, the condition of the earth as described

---

3   Schmidt, 1997, 172-179.

in verse 2 follows immediately from the creative act of verse 1. Therefore, because there is no dispute among Hebrew and biblical scholars that "earth" as translated here in verse 2 clearly refers to planet earth, then we are correct in understanding that it is planet earth which God created as the starting point in His creation of the universe (verse 1).

Furthermore, consistent with this is the translation of the Hebrew verb *hayetha* as "was." This verb is the regular Hebrew verb of being and does not denote any change of state. If that's what the Holy Spirit, as the author of Scripture, had wanted us to understand, then the word here would have been the Hebrew verb *haphak*, normally used to denote a change of state. Thus, it is inappropriate to translate the Hebrew verb here as "became" rather than "was," which some past commentators have suggested in order to accommodate their intent to place a significant time gap between Genesis 1:1 and 1:2. This is entirely ruled out by the use of the Hebrew word *waw* ("and") at the beginning of the clause in the text, grammatically known as a disjunctive clause that only adds explanatory details to the narrative.[4]

Thus, the text in verse 2 describes the condition of planet earth when God created it. The Hebrew words used are *tohu waw bohu*, which have been traditionally translated as "without form and void." However, numerous scholars, believing the narrative can only be understood in the context of the pagan mythologies which surrounded the ancient Hebrews, have insisted these Hebrew words should instead be translated as "waste, chaos, disorder, and void," or "a desert and a wasteland," or even "ruined and desolate." Such commentators ignore the likelihood that God's account of creation here in Genesis 1 was in fact revealed to Adam, rather than being some story generated by Hebrew priests for God's people as an antidote to the pagan mythologies (such as the Babylonian *enuma elish*).

Some commentators have used such translations to imply that the perfect earth which God had created had somehow been ruined and reduced to chaos in a supposed time gap between verses 1 and 2 of Genesis 1. This view is often called the Gap Theory. It postulates that the original creation of Genesis 1:1 occurred in the primeval past. Then Satan rebelled against God and was thrown out of heaven to the earth, where there was a cataclysmic judgment on Satan's sin that left the earth in ruin and darkness, covered by water (Genesis 1:2). God then re-created the earth, as described in Genesis 1:3 onwards. This view is otherwise known as the Ruin-Reconstruction Theory and was initially proposed to accommodate the conventional geologic ages within the gap, the fossils being due to destruction of the earlier creation by "Lucifer's Flood."

---

4   Wenham, 1987, 15; and W. W. Fields, 1976, *Unformed and Unfilled*, Nutley, NJ: Presbyterian and Reformed Publishing Company, 75-112. This latter reference is a very detailed and extensive treatment of the translation of the Hebrew in Genesis 1:1-2, refuting any concept of a gap and firmly establishing the continuity of verse 2 as a circumstantial statement expressing additional details concomitant to the principal statement in Genesis 1:1.

Such negative interpretations of Genesis 1:2 are rather forced and unnatural. The word *tohu*, for example, can carry various shades of meaning in the twenty places it occurs in the Old Testament, and so it has been translated in no fewer than ten different ways in the King James Version. On the other hand, the word *bohu* only occurs three times in the Old Testament together with *tohu*. This association is said to be an excellent example of hendiadys, the expression of a complex idea by two words connected with "and," forming a unit in which one member of the pair is used to qualify the other member.[5] Proper translation of this double expression depends on its specific context, particularly at its first occurrence, which is here in Genesis 1:2. In the King James Version, this expression has been translated "without form and void," while in the New International Version the translators have chosen "formless and empty." Both these translations accurately portray the description of the earth as an unformed and unshapened mass[6] that was unformed and unfilled.[7] These translations are logical in the context of Genesis 1:1-2, where the essential meaning is that in the beginning, when God created the earth in space, it was at first an unformed, shapeless mass that was uninhabited. God's purpose was to shape the earth and prepare it as a habitation for man, filling it with plants and animals, just as the rest of Genesis 1 describes for us. Indeed, Isaiah 45:18 specifically says that "God himself that formed the earth and made it; he hath established it, he created it not in vain [Hebrew *tohu*], he formed it to be inhabited." The creation account in Genesis 1 then continues by telling us the steps God took to bring form to the initially unformed planet earth, and then bring living inhabitants to its empty surface. The state of the initial creation as described in Genesis 1:2 was imperfect only in the sense that it was not complete. It was perfect as the first stage in His six-day plan for the creation of the entire universe and everything in it. This is why it is contradictory and inappropriate to translate the Hebrew words with terms such as chaos, waste, and desolate, because these have negative connotations which should not be regarded as inherent in God's handiwork.

Similarly, when we are next told in Genesis 1:2 "and darkness was upon the face of the deep," the presence of darkness should not be interpreted as implying that there was anything wrong or imperfect with the earth as God had initially created it. In Isaiah 45:7, God Himself declares, "I form the light, and create darkness," and in Psalm 104, in which the psalmist extols the virtues of God's creation and God's wisdom revealed therein, we are told, "Thou makest darkness, and it is night....O LORD, how manifold are thy works! in wisdom hast thou made them all: the earth is full of thy riches" (Psalm 104:20, 24). The reality being expressed in Genesis 1:2 is simply that God chose to create this initial incompletely formed earth without inhabitants and in the absence of physical light, which is all that darkness is. No inherent evil is implied. God would next choose to create light

---

5   Fields, 1976, 124.

6   Leupold, 1942, 46.

7   Fields, 1976, 124.

(Genesis 1:3) and thus begin the pattern of darkness (night) followed by light (day) that then characterized each of the days of creation (Genesis 1:5: "And the evening and the morning were the first day").

We are also told that darkness was "upon the face of the deep. And the spirit of God moved upon the face of the waters." The "deep" (Hebrew *t'hôm*) can be readily identified as the waters of the ocean, not only through the usage of the word elsewhere in the Old Testament, but because of the description here of "the waters," with both the darkness and the Spirit of God moving upon the face or surface of these waters. The expression is rather aptly given to today's ocean waters. The description here of the unformed, uninhabited, and incomplete earth being covered in water is corroborated by the apostle Peter using the same picture in 2 Peter 3:5: "the earth standing out of the water and in the water." Many commentators have interpreted *t'hôm* as primeval waters according to an ancient worldview stemming from Babylonian myths; but it is absolutely clear in the Old Testament that the word specifically describes the deep ocean waters which God created and does not signify a force opposed to God in some personified or mythical function.[8] Similarly, the Hebrew word *panim,* translated "face," is correctly understood in context to mean the surface of these ocean waters.[9]

Finally, we are told that "the Spirit of God moved upon the face of the waters." The word "Spirit" is the Hebrew *ruach*, which is also the word for "wind" and "breath." Of course, the context determines the correct meaning, so here in Genesis 1:2 there can be no doubt that a Person, the Holy Spirit, and His creative activity, are being spoken of and not merely a wind. Again, as in Genesis 1:1, the name for God used in the Hebrew is *Elohim*, the divine name which stresses His majesty and omnipotence. The *im* ending signifies the plural in Hebrew, so *elohim* can actually mean "gods." However, here throughout the first chapter of Genesis, the verbs used with *Elohim* are in the singular, so that the three Persons of the Godhead are given a plural name but act in concert with a singularity of purpose. Here in Genesis 1:2, the third person of the Godhead (the Holy Spirit, as He is called later in the New Testament) is described as moving on and across the surface of the deep waters covering the earth in its initially created condition. The word "moved" in the Hebrew is *rachach*, which in its other two occurrences in the Old Testament is translated "shake" (Jeremiah 23:9) and "fluttereth" (Deuteronomy 32:11).[10] Thus, the word seems to portray the idea of rapid back and forth motion, which in modern scientific terminology would best be translated as "vibrated" or "energized." The fact that we are specifically told that the Spirit of God was intimately involved in acting upon the surface of the waters in the darkness emphatically removes any notion whatsoever that at this stage of

8   See C. Westermann, 1997, *t'hôm* flood, in *Theological Lexicon of the Old Testament*, ed. E. Jenni and C. Westermann, trans. M. E. Biddle, Peabody, MA: Hendrickson Publishers, Inc., 1410-1414.

9   A. S. van der Woude, 1997, *panim* face, in *Theological Lexicon of the Old Testament*, ed. E. Jenni and C. Westermann, trans. M. E. Biddle, Peabody, MA: Hendricksen Publishers, Inc., 995-1014.

10   Morris, 1976, 52.

creation the earth was somehow in an imperfect condition with connotations of chaos and evil.

Finally, it is also important to note that there is no hint that the initial state of what God created was not that of ordinary matter. Genesis 1:2 refers to the Spirit of God moving "upon the face of the *waters*." Similarly, 2 Peter 3:5 speaks of the originally created earth "standing out of the water and in the water." There is no suggestion in these passages that the original state of the matter comprising the earth was a high energy ionized plasma or a state so energetic that even neutrons or protons could not form. This is in stark contrast to the secular ideas of a "big bang" in which all the matter in the present cosmos was in a volume smaller than that of an atom at an incredibly high state of excitation. Thus, we find a sharp dichotomy between the speculations of modern cosmologists as to how the cosmos began and God's account of what actually occurred.

30

THE FIRST DAY

Many commentators have traditionally regarded Genesis 1:3-5 as describing God's creative work on the first day of the Creation Week, thus only attributing the creation of light to the work of that first day.[1] This view puts the creation of the heaven and the earth in Genesis 1:1 prior to the Creation Week, which leaves unanswered the question of when "in the beginning" actually occurred. Such a reading of the text has, in the past, allowed for the date for the creation of the heavens and the earth to be set at billions of years ago, and then a gap of billions of years placed between verses 1 and 2 of Genesis 1—the so-called Gap or Ruin-Reconstruction Theory. Though this theory has now largely been abandoned by conservative, Bible-believing Christian scholars and lay people, this reading of the text has persisted, allowing scholars in some Christian circles to suggest that the universe and its material elements—including those that make up the earth—were initially created billions of years ago. Thus, while claiming the earth is billions of years old, they would insist that the earth's biosphere is nonetheless young, on the order of 6,000 to 7,000 years, in keeping with the young earth creationist viewpoint. These scholars feel comfortable in accepting the radioisotopic dating of rocks and meteorites at billions of years, but would insist that the creation of plants, animals, and man occurred in six literal days, only 6,000 to 7,000 years ago. Can this reading of the text be sustained on biblical grounds?

There are two clear reasons directly from the Scriptures to support the view that the Creation Week began in Genesis 1:1—"in the beginning"—and that the record of the first day of the Creation Week spans Genesis 1:1-5.

First, in Exodus 20 God declares through Moses that the children of Israel were to keep the Sabbath day holy (v. 8), working for six days (v. 7) and then refraining from work on the seventh day (v. 10). Here God is reminding Israel of the pattern He established for them during the Creation Week: work six days, rest the seventh. As He says in Exodus 20:11, "For in six days the LORD made heaven and earth, the sea, and all that in them is, and rested the seventh day: wherefore the LORD

---

1   For example, Kidner, 1967, 46; Briscoe, 1987, 36; Wenham, 1987, 17-18; and Hamilton, 1990, 118-119. Unfortunately, J. M. Boice, 1998, *Genesis: An Expositional Commentary*, Volume 1, Genesis 1-11, Grand Rapids, MI: Baker Books, 80-86, and Morris, 1976, 53-81, also maintain this view that the record of the first day of the Creation Week begins in Genesis 1:3.

blessed the sabbath day, and hallowed it." Clearly the Lord is emphasizing that He made the heaven, the earth, the sea, and everything in them in those six days of creation. Thus, when we compare this Scripture with Genesis 1 to determine when it was that God made the heaven, the earth, and the sea, it is immediately obvious. This took place in Genesis 1:1-2, placing these creative acts within the six days of the Creation Week, indeed, at the beginning of the first day of that week which ended in Genesis 1:5. In Exodus 31:17-18, God repeats the fact that in six days He made the heaven and earth, but this time actually writing these words with His finger on the tablets of stone. The comparison of Genesis 1 with the passages in Exodus is inescapable. God confirmed His own Word with His own writing. If God cannot be trusted to tell us the truth here, to write down accurately what He meant, then what basis is there for any absolute, God-given truth?

The second scriptural support for the view that the Creation Week began with Genesis 1:1 is that on this first day God commanded light into existence, dividing the light from the darkness that already existed, calling the light "day" and the darkness "night" (Genesis 1:3-5). As though in anticipation of future misunderstanding, God carefully defined the terms He used. Then having separated night and day, God completed His first day's work, which closes with the pronouncement "And the evening and the morning were the first day" (Genesis 1:5). The same formula for this pronouncement is used at the conclusion of each of the successive five days, so it is obvious that God intended us to understand that the duration of each of these days, including the first, was the same. The formula may in fact be rendered literally: "And there was evening, then morning—Day One," and so on. Thus, just as this first day of God's creative activity began with darkness, now with the coming of dusk and the end of the daylight comes the end to this first day of God's activity, and so this first day is pronounced as finished. Because the formula God used for His pronouncement matches the progression from darkness (Genesis 1:2), which God called "night" (Genesis 1:5), to light (Genesis 1:3-4), which God called "day" (Genesis 1:5), it is logical to conclude that God intended us to understand that this first day and the Creation Week began with the period of darkness, called night, which was "in the beginning" when God created the heaven and the earth (Genesis 1:1-2).

This reckoning of the night-day (darkness-light) cycle, constituting a normal day in earth time, was the same pattern adopted at God's direction by the children of Israel (Leviticus 23:32), and which was used by the Jews at the time when the Lord Jesus Christ was crucified on the hill of Calvary just outside the city wall of Jerusalem. It is stated in John 19:31 and Mark 15:42 that as nightfall approached on the day the Lord Jesus Christ was crucified, it was mandatory to determine that He was dead and that His body be removed from the cross before the commencement of the special Sabbath day and the preparation for it, as well as the need to follow God's instruction that the body of an executed criminal should not remain hanging all night in the place of execution (Deuteronomy 21:22-23). Thus, it is clear from both the Old and New Testament Scriptures that

God and His people regarded the Sabbath day as commencing at nightfall, in the "evening," which finds its original basis in the pattern established in Genesis 1 during Creation Week.

Furthermore, as noted previously, every verse in Genesis chapter 1 (except verses 1 and 27) begins with the conjunction "and" (Hebrew *waw*), a structure that clearly establishes that each statement is to be understood as connected sequentially and chronologically to the statements (verses) before and after. Thus, each of God's creative acts follows directly from the action described in the verse preceding it without any significant time gap whatsoever between the actions being implied. When God commanded the light into existence, He heralded the dawn and the morning of that first day, following sequentially from the darkness of the night that had begun when God created the heaven and the earth at the outset of this first day.

Leupold emphatically maintains that to try to make this evening and morning formula mean that the day began with evening "fails utterly," even though he admits later that Jewish reckoning of days followed this pattern, as per God's command in Leviticus 23:32.[2] Quite correctly, he maintains that Genesis 1:5 reports the conclusion of the first day's work after a progression of described activities, which includes the creation of heaven and earth in the "rough," then the creation of light, the approval of light, and the separation of day and night. However, he wrongly maintains that because an evening may only be stretched to include four hours and a morning could be said to be four, even six, hours long, then the addition of these timespans, according to the supposed formula of evening plus morning equals one day, just does not add up to twenty-four hours. It is nowhere implied in the text of Scripture that this expression is meant to be understood as a precise formula. Nevertheless, in context, Genesis 1:1-5 describes the establishment of the period of darkness, which God names night, followed by the period of light, which God calls day, together constituting the 24-hour day. So it is logical that at the end of this first day of activity, God should record in the Scriptures this summary of this passage of time as He created it: "And the evening and the morning were the first day." The repetition of this summary on each of the successive days serves as a reminder of this darkness-followed-by-light cycle that God had initiated on the first day to mark the passage of time on earth. Thus, Leupold's objection cannot be sustained logically, particularly as he agrees that the first day of the Creation Week began with the creation of the heaven and the earth in Genesis 1:1.

Morris has commented that the use of evening and morning in that order is significant. As God apparently accomplished each day's work during the daylight, there was nothing to report between "evening and morning." The beginning of the next day's activity began with the next period of light, after the morning, or

---

2   Leupold, 1942, 56-57.

better, the dawning. Thus, the literal sense of the expression after each day's work could be rendered: "Then there was dusk, then dawn, ending the first day." [3]

Furthermore, it is relevant to comment here on the use of the Hebrew word *yom*, translated "day" in Genesis 1:5, as this is its first occurrence in Scripture and its meaning is critical in defending the timespan in which God's work of creation was done. Indeed, to avoid confusion and misunderstanding, God specifically defines His use of the word *yom*, which in the first instance is used to name "the light" in the cyclical succession of darkness and light, and which has ever since He instituted it here "in the beginning," constituted what initially was an earth day, but later in the Creation Week became a solar day. Since the same word is used in defining all later occurrences of *yom* in the Creation Week as is used for the *yom* to define this first day, it is absolutely beyond dispute that God intended us to know that the days of the Creation Week were of the same duration as any natural solar day. Indeed, in Genesis 1:5 the word *yom* is used in exactly the same way by God as the word "day" is routinely used in the English language; that is, both for the daylight portion of a solar day and for the combination of light and darkness which constitutes the solar day itself.

Furthermore, the word *yom* throughout the Old Testament is used almost always in this natural sense and is never used to mean any definite time period other than a literal day. This is especially so when *yom* is preceded by or described with a numeral, as in "the first day," or is described with definite bounds, as in "the evening and the morning were the first day." Neither of these usages found in the Old Testament allow for non-literal meanings or interpretations.

The word *yom* is occasionally, though rarely, used symbolically or in the sense of indefinite time, as in the expression "the day of the Lord" (for example, Isaiah 13:6), but such usage in the Hebrew is always evident from the context itself, as it is in English or other languages. Thus, here in Genesis 1, in spite of the repeated claims of those who seek to compromise Scripture in order to accommodate the billions-of-years uniformitarian geological history of the earth, God has Himself defined that the word *yom* means a literal day. He ensured there would be no doubt by reminding us, both verbally and in His own handwriting in Exodus 20:11 and in Exodus 31:17, that the basis for our calendar week with its seven literal days is identical to His Creation Week, also of seven literal days, and that our literal day set aside as the Sabbath and as a rest from our work follows exactly the pattern of God working for six literal days and resting on the seventh literal day.

Some have objected that the first three days of the Creation Week could not have been literal days because the sun wasn't created until the fourth day, becoming the provider of daylight for a solar day. However, each of the first three days is described as having an evening and a morning in exactly the same way as the

---

3   Morris, 1995, 4.

second three days. As already noted, God also used the word *yom*, identically defined for all six days in which He created all things. It is irrelevant that the sun was not created until the fourth day, because God was not dependent on the sun to provide light upon the newly created earth, just as He will not be dependent on the sun to provide light on the new earth to come (Revelation 22:5). Genesis 1:3 does not tell us the source of the light which God commanded into existence. However, all that is needed to produce the cycle of darkness (night) followed by light (day) characteristic of a literal earth day is a source of light shining upon the earth, while the earth itself rotates. This is conceivable, given that Genesis 1:2 describes the Spirit of God moving upon the surface of the water-covered earth, potentially implying He energized the earth's rotation. Nevertheless, God describes this first day in exactly the same way as the fourth day after He had then created the sun "to give light upon the earth" and "to rule the day" (Genesis 1:15-16).

31

THE SECOND DAY

Having created the earth without form, empty, and covered with water, on this second day, God turned His creative ability to the process of providing form to the earth in order to make it fit for habitation. Again God speaks to bring into existence a "firmament" to divide the waters covering the earth's surface into waters above the firmament and waters below the firmament. The word "firmament" in the Hebrew is *raqia*, which means "expanse." It comes from the root meaning "to hammer," "to spread out," or "to stretch out," so an expanse would be a spread-out or stretched-out "thinness." God called this firmament "Heaven" (Genesis 1:8), which has previously been noted as essentially synonymous with the modern technical term "space." In the Scriptures, three particular "heavens" are mentioned—what we call the *atmosphere* ("all the birds of the heavens"—Jeremiah 4:25), what we would call *outer space* ("the stars of heaven and the constellations thereof"—Isaiah 13:10), and what we call *heaven*, referring to the place of God's throne (Hebrews 9:24). Likewise, the term "firmament" is used in each of these same three ways—the birds fly in (or more literally, "on the face of") the firmament (Genesis 1:20), the sun, moon, and stars were placed in the firmament (Genesis 1:14, 15, 17), and the place where the four living creatures appeared in Ezekiel's vision where God's glory was present (Ezekiel 1, especially verses 22-26), otherwise called "the third heaven" by the apostle Paul (2 Corinthians 12:1-4).

Exactly what this firmament was is difficult to determine from the Scriptures, though it is clear what it is not. Unfortunately, the English word "firmament" came from the translation of the Latin Vulgate *firmamentum*. This word involved the idea of something that is firmly put in place, so those critical scholars with a propensity to see the Genesis 1 account as influenced by, and written subsequent to, Babylonian mythology have interpreted the firmament as referring to a solid dome or vault across the sky, reinforcing the contention that the Genesis creation account was birthed in a pre-scientific era, which is logically erroneous. More distressing are the views of present-day evangelical Christian scholars, who are trusted as "Bible-believing" but who still accept this discredited, outdated assessment of the creation account in Genesis 1 in order to maintain credibility with secular academia who regard the billions-of-years of uniformitarian earth history as proven and above reproach. However, as many of these scholars know, neither the original Hebrew word nor any of the passages in which it occurs suggest any such idea. A "firmament" is simply a "thin, stretched-out expanse."

Nevertheless, what the "firmament" represents in modern scientific terms is somewhat conjectural. Because Genesis 1:20 describes the birds being created to "fly above the earth in the open firmament of heaven," many have identified the firmament simply as the earth's atmosphere. However, as noted above, the more literal rendering of the Hebrew of this verse indicates the birds were created to "fly above the earth *on the face* of the firmament of heaven." Moreover, as already noted, Genesis 1:14-17 stipulates that it was into the firmament that God placed the sun, moon, and stars when He created them, so that it seems the primary meaning of "firmament" or "expanse" is outer space. The difficulty then becomes identifying the nature and location of the waters that God tells us He placed "above the firmament."

Water still remained covering the earth's surface with a universal ocean, but the record clearly states that "God made the firmament, and divided the waters which were under the firmament from the waters which were above the firmament" (Genesis 1:7), so the upper waters could not simply be clouds, as many commentators have often stated,[1] because the clouds are in the atmosphere rather than above it (the firmament) as stipulated in the text. It has been suggested by many that if the firmament describes the atmosphere, then the "waters above the firmament" probably constituted a vast blanket of water vapor above the troposphere, and possibly above the stratosphere as well, in the high-temperature region now known as the ionosphere, and perhaps even extending far out into space beyond.[2] On the other hand, since Genesis 1:14-17 indicates that the sun, moon, and stars are also in the firmament, it would seem logical to assume that the waters which God placed above the firmament must have been put beyond outer space at the limits of the universe.[3] This is no easy matter to resolve scientifically. However, the biblical data on this matter are paramount.

It is therefore noted that the Hebrew word translated "firmament" means a thin, stretched-out expanse that God put in place as a division between the waters covering the earth's surface and the waters above the firmament. A crucial clue in the text as to the position of the firmament is that the sun, moon, and stars are in it. Once the firmament was in place, made by God at His command, and named "Heaven" by God, the second day of work was completed, and "the evening and the morning were the second day" (Genesis 1:8).

---

1   For example, R. Forster and P. Marston, 1999, *Reason, Science and Faith*, Crowborough, East Sussex, England: Monarch Books, 248.

2   For example, Whitcomb and Morris, 1961, 240-241, 255-257; Morris, 1976, 58-61; and Morris, 1995, 4-5.

3   D. R. Humphreys, 1994, A Biblical Basis for Creationist Cosmology, *Proceedings of the Third International Conference on Creationism*, R.E. Walsh, ed., Pittsburgh, PA: Creation Science Fellowship, 255-266.

32

THE THIRD DAY

At the outset of the third day of the Creation Week, the earth was still unformed and empty, its surface covered by water ("the deep"). Now God begins the work of preparing the earth to fill with inhabitants. God commences this creative work by first of all issuing a command for yet another division. On the first day when God made the light, it was to divide the darkness. On the second day He made the firmament to divide the waters. Now He commands the waters under the firmament which covered the earth's surface to "be gathered together unto one place, and let the dry land appear" (Genesis 1:9). While we are not specifically told, the expression "let the dry land appear" could imply that the land—that is, a rocky earth—already existed but was covered over by the waters of the deep. If that were so, then it is conceivable that this "gathering together of the waters," which God called "Seas" (Genesis 1:10), could have been accomplished by great earth movements which raised the land surface and produced basins into which the ocean waters could be gathered. Another possible implication of the wording here is that since the waters were "gathered together unto one place," then the dry land which God called "Earth" may similarly have been in one place as one landmass or supercontinent. Regardless of whether this is a legitimate implication of the text, it would nevertheless be true that once the waters had been gathered in numerous ocean basins, they could be deemed as being in "one place." The name given by God, "Seas," is a plural term to describe this single entity, hinting at a concept of numerous, distinct, interconnected ocean basins. It needs to be noted, of course, that these seas need not have been in the same locations as our present oceans, since the pre-Flood arrangement of continental and marine areas may well have changed at the time of the Flood.

Elsewhere in the Scriptures, such as in Psalm 102:25, Job 38:4, Zechariah 12:1, and Isaiah 48:13, "the foundation(s) of the earth" are referred to as having been laid by God, obviously during the Creation Week. Here in Genesis 1:10, God calls the dry land "Earth." The Hebrew word used is *eretz* and is the same word used in Genesis 1:1-2. Since the dry land made on this third day would obviously have been composed of rock strata, etc., it is conceivable that even when the earth was created at the beginning of the first day, it still somehow had a rocky consistency and was yet unformed and covered in water. It also would be consistent and logical for the expression "the foundations of the earth" to be referring to God laying the earth's rocky foundations (core, mantle, and a primeval crust) "in the beginning" on the first day of the Creation Week. Similarly, the use of *eretz* for "earth" in verses 1 and 10 can be argued to show that it was the same matter that constituted solid ground or dry land exposed after the waters were gathered into the seas.

Having formed the dry land, God now turned His attention to the next stage of making the land habitable. God commanded the earth to "bring forth grass, the herb yielding seed, and the fruit tree yielding fruit after its kind, whose seed is in itself…and it was so" (Genesis 1:11). Though we are not explicitly told, the text would seem to indicate that at God's command the earth responded immediately and "brought forth grass, and herb yielding seed after his kind, and the tree yielding fruit, whose seed was in itself, after his kind" (Genesis 1:12). Again the word "and" is used to begin the sentence describing the results of the command God had given as recorded in the previous sentence, so this message emphasizes that the action flowed in sequence without a time gap. Consequently, "God saw that it was good" (Genesis 1:12). God expressed His satisfaction with the work accomplished and the quality of the plants He had created. The measure of that quality was His own perfect character, there being no other objective standard against which God could measure the perfection of all that He had created.

Whatever the presumed scientific difficulties might seem to be for those who would seek to reconcile the biblical account of God's creative activity with a naturalistic uniformitarian explanation of earth history, there are a number of profound implications of the text here. When God's work of making the dry land appear had been completed, there must have been a thick blanket of fertile soil containing abundant chemical nutrients and moisture in readiness for the next task of bringing forth the grass, herbs, and trees. It matters not that in terms of human observation and experience, the formation of soil from the rock and mineral substrate would seem to take countless thousands and even millions of years, because here the Scriptures are reporting *God's* creative activity. That is not to say that God may not choose to use processes in His creative activity that can today be understood scientifically, but it is absolutely wrong, and in a sense somewhat arrogant and blasphemous, to insist, as many compromisers do, that God should have been restricted to *our* perception of the processes involved, as typified by the need for soil to have formed on the newly exposed land surface for the plants to grow in.

Second, the biblical text clearly describes God creating plants within the time constraints of the daylight portion of this third literal day, it being significant that these plants were not made as seeds, but as full-grown plants whose seed was in them. Indeed, fruit trees were created already bearing fruit. Thus, all the vegetation had an appearance of age, but *only* according to present human observations and experience. This concept of creation, "apparent age," does not in any way suggest deception on God's part, because it is a necessary accompaniment of genuine supernatural creative activity. (When Jesus Christ created wine from water [John 2:1-11], the resultant wine similarly had a "mature" appearance.) The processes operating in the Creation Week were not the processes of the present era, but were processes of God creating and making. Again, they were not at all commensurate with present processes. In this instance, the trees were created fully grown, fully developed, and functioning right from the beginning of their existence. God created them that way, choosing not to begin from seeds. The vegetation, when created, had all the appearance of grass, herbs, and trees that in our normal experience today would have taken years to grow from seeds and develop to maturity. It must be stressed that there is absolutely no deception involved on God's part. He has clearly communicated that this is the way He created, in this case the plants, even though their "apparent age" calculated in terms of present processes would undoubtedly be vastly different from their "true age" as revealed by the Creator Himself.

Third, with the creation of the plants we have the first mention of both "seed" and "kind." The meaning of the word "seed" in Genesis 1:11-12 can be clearly understood from its context and usage as identical to the seeds present in plants today. Thus, God implanted in each created plant a seed, programmed to enable its reproduction. In terms of modern scientific understanding of heredity and genetics, a seed having its own uniquely structured, extremely complex DNA can only specify the reproduction of that same plant type. The scriptural expression used here is "after his kind." This phrase occurs ten times in Genesis 1, so by such repetition God was emphasizing that He created each organism to reproduce after its own kind, not after some other kind. The Hebrew word translated "kind" is *min*. Precisely what is meant by this Hebrew term is not fully clear, but the expression does emphatically place limitations on the tremendous amount of variational potential within each type or kind of organism God created. Exactly what the created "kind" corresponds to in terms of the modern biological classification system is still a matter of present creation science research, but already it is apparent that the *min* may be identical with the genus or even the family. This would not allow interrelation of all living things by common ancestry and descent as modern evolutionary dogma insists.

Furthermore, observational evidence clearly demonstrates the incredible potential for variation in living things, the interplay of natural selection (survival and natural breeding in the struggle of life amidst environmental pressures and competition) with genetics to produce distinct individuals and even many varieties within each "kind." Because new varieties do develop, which can be classified as "species" in the modern classification system, it is evident that the created "kinds" in Genesis do not generally correspond to the man-made system of naming "species." The great many changes that occur in living things, however, provide for "horizontal" variation within distinct boundaries imposed by the Creator. No "vertical" changes are observed to occur in the living organisms, nor is there any evidence in the fossil record of these kinds of changes having occurred in the past. This pronouncement by the Creator that all living things would reproduce after their kinds, recorded here in Genesis, is well supported by all established scientific observations made to date. Furthermore, the permanence of these created kinds is reiterated in 1 Corinthians 15:38-39, while the term "kind," as applied to animals at least, is amplified in Leviticus 11:13-32.

It should also be noted that on the third day God created all forms of plants, even such complex forms as fruit trees, before the creation of any form of animal life. Of course, it was quite logical to create the food first in readiness for the animals that would need it. However, this totally contradicts the accepted evolutionary progression of life forms that has marine animals, both invertebrates and vertebrates, evolving hundreds of millions of years before the appearance of fruit trees and other complex plants. Furthermore, because many plants require pollination by insects, the fact that God did not create the insects until the sixth day of creation further argues against these days of creation being long ages.

When creating the plants, God describes them as belonging to three main types: grasses, herbs, and trees. This classification does not correspond to the modern, man-made taxonomic nomenclature, but these God-given biblical divisions seem obvious and natural. All types of plants are covered by these obvious comprehensive categories. The term "grass" would include all spreading, ground-covering vegetation, while "herbs" would be bushes and shrubs. The "trees" would refer to all large woody plants, including all fruit-bearing trees. God then once more "saw that it was good" (Genesis 1:12). This was the same pronouncement that God made after His work of bringing light to the earth (Genesis 1:4), and after His work of dividing the waters and establishing the dry land surfaces (Genesis 1:10).

Having declared the perfection of the plant cover He had made for the land, God closes the third day's work of creation with "And the evening and morning were the third day" (Genesis 1:13). It is worth noting that the terms "evening" (Hebrew *ereb*) and "morning" (Hebrew *boqer*) each occur more than 100 times in the Old Testament and always have the same literal meaning according to their common, natural usage. Since the days of creation consist of literal evenings and literal mornings, then logically the "days" are also literal. While it may seem impossible to our minds to visualize the land, seas, and all plants being formed in one literal day, that is nevertheless exactly what the Scriptures record! Secular scientific minds cannot grasp how this can be and thus deride the biblical account as unfounded mythology, while compromising Christians try to accommodate these Scriptures to the story of long ages by categorizing them as allegorical or poetic. However, since this is the record given by the Creator Himself, we are not justified, in any way, either in questioning His power to do this or His truthfulness in telling us that He did. With the discoveries of molecular biology over the last fifty years and the subsequent awareness we now have of the staggering complexity of living systems, the only conceivable manner for such systems to come into existence, from the standpoint of modern science (if one is to be honest), is just the sort of instantaneous, supernatural creation described on the opening page of the Bible!

33

THE FOURTH DAY

Whereas on the first day God created the light and divided it from the darkness, on the fourth day of creation He turned His attention to creating the visible, physical bodies in the heavens which now provide light to the earth. Thus He commanded, "Let there be lights in the firmament of the heaven" (Genesis 1:14). The Hebrew word translated "lights" is *maor*, which literally means "light-givers," which aptly describes their God-given function "to give light upon the earth" (Genesis 1:17). And just as the chief purpose of the light that shone upon the earth during the first three days of the Creation Week was to "divide the light from the darkness" (Genesis 1:4), so too were these light-givers now created on this fourth day. They took over the function of bearing the light that had already been created "to divide the day from the night" (Genesis 1:14) and "to divide the light from the darkness" (Genesis 1:18). This identical purpose and the continuity between them can only mean that the two regimes were essentially identical, the duration of the days and nights being the same in each case, and the direction of primary light emanation to the earth from space being the same in each case. The light rays would have to have been impinging on the earth from a particular direction as it rotated on its axis during the first three days to provide the sequence of day-night cycles; it would have essentially the same direction as would now characterize these light-giving heavenly bodies that God created and put in space on this fourth day. Thus, during the first three days light would have been coming during the day as though from the sun, even though the sun had not yet been made. While these concepts sound strange to the natural mind, we need to remind ourselves that none of this is impossible for God.

However, these "light-givers" or luminaries were also given three more general functions besides the division of the day from the night. Genesis 1:14 records God's command "and let them be for signs, and for seasons, and for days, and years." The Hebrew word *owth*, translated "signs," literally means "a signal, as with a flag, beacon or monument as a mark or token"[1] and is here used in the broadest possible sense.[2] Thus, the luminaries are signs in a number of ways. First, they are signs that declare the glory of their Creator (Psalm 8:1-3 and 19:1-6). Second,

---

1   J. Strong, *A Concise Dictionary of the Words in the Hebrew Bible; With Their Renderings in the Authorized English Version*, McLean, VA: MacDonald Publishing Company, 10, Word no. 226.

2   Leupold, 1942, 73.

they are signs by which navigators can get their bearings by day or by night. Third, they may convey signs in reference to future events (Matthew 2:2 and Luke 21:25). Fourth, they may be signs of divine judgments (Joel 2:30 and Matthew 24:29). Fifth, they furnish quite reliable signs for determining in advance the weather to be expected (Matthew 16:2-3). Thus, it is clear from Scripture, and from experience, that the sun, moon, and stars serve well as signs in all these capacities.

The use of the stars for signs is most naturally interpreted as a reference to the various star groupings which can serve both for easy visual recognition of the advancing days and years, and also by extension for tokens of the advancing stages of God's purpose in creation.[3] As has often been the case, what God created and intended for man's good has, in turn, been corrupted. When He had created the sun, moon, and stars for signs, God declared that it was good (Genesis 1:18), but because of sin and rebellion, these signs, even those of the zodiac, were soon corrupted into pagan astrology. Nevertheless, we should not allow man's corrupt use of what God created for our good to make us ignore or overlook what God intended. The fact remains that men always have and, in manifold ways, still do use the luminaries for signs.

These "light-givers" were also to be used to denote the "seasons." The Hebrew word translated "seasons" is *mow'adah* from the root *ya'ad*, which means "to fix upon by agreement or appointment" or "to set (a time)." Thus, the Hebrew word "seasons" in this context means appointed or fixed times, in the context of the seasons of the year. Of course, the luminaries do serve as indicators of such fixed, appointed times, and there is no reason to exclude what we normally think of as the seasons of the year in the meaning of the word here. Therefore, "seasons" or times in the widest sense should be thought of as agricultural seasons (or "feast days") (Hosea 2:9, 11; 9:5), and seasons for beasts and birds (Jeremiah 8:7), as long as they are times that are fixed and come with stated regularity. Furthermore, while the Genesis record of God's creative activity clearly implies that from the beginning there were distinct seasons throughout the year, this could imply that the earth's axis of rotation was inclined, but whether at the same angle as at present is obviously conjectural.

Finally, God declares that He created these "lights" or luminaries to be "for days, and years." These are respectively the shortest and the longest measures of time definitely fixed by the movements of these heavenly bodies. No one can possibly dispute that the usage of the Hebrew word *yom* translated "day" here definitely means a 24-hour day, and the year is likewise to be understood literally. Of course, we are not told here what the exact length of this year is. However, it is possible to infer from the timetable given for the Flood event as recorded in Genesis 6-8 that at that time there were twelve lunar months each of 30 days length, giving a year

---

3   Morris, 1976, 67-68.

totaling 360 days; so it is possible that this was originally the length of the year at the time of creation, but clearly we can't be adamant about this.

God also declared, "And let them be for lights in the firmament of the heaven to give light upon the earth; and it was so" (Genesis 1:15). This obviously was the primary purpose for these light-givers. Again, note that these luminaries were placed "in the firmament of the heaven." This is the realm which we know as the inner space of the solar system and the outer space beyond to the stars and galaxies.

The phrase "and it was so" occurs here for the fourth time in Genesis 1. It is found a total of six times in verses 7, 9, 11, 15, 24, and 30. God is unmistakably stressing that what He says, He also does. Furthermore, the phrase "and God said" occurs ten times in verses 3, 6, 9, 11, 14, 20, 24, 26, 28 and 29; and the first seven of these are followed by a creative command from God, beginning with the imperative word, "Let...!"

"God made two great lights; the greater light to rule the day, and the lesser light to rule the night" (Genesis 1:16). God now furnishes us with more details by describing the two great or "chief" luminaries He made—"chief" as far as the earth is concerned. This means they are the two great luminaries in reference to the earth and also in view of how they appear to man. This is not a description of the greatest or largest of the heavenly bodies in any absolute sense. That a comparison is being made is borne out by the use of comparative expressions, namely, that the greater luminary would rule the day (obviously, the sun), and the lesser luminary would rule the night (the moon). The fact that both the sun and the moon are called "light-givers" does not in itself suggest that they are of the same substance. Whereas one actually generates light, the other only reflects light; yet both "give light" as far as their functions relative to the earth are concerned.

Almost as if it were an afterthought on God's part, we are next told that "he made the stars also" (Genesis 1:16). Of course, this was no mere afterthought on God's part, but it does give perspective on God's creative ability and His awesome power, simply because we now do know something of the incredible number and variety of stars and galaxies that adorn the almost unfathomable vast reaches of the universe. Again, the perspective here is comparative, and in reference to the earth and to man, so in that sense the stars do seem very much inferior in size and light-giving ability compared to the sun and the moon. Now, of course, we know how important the stars are, and how large and intensely burning they are in comparison to the sun. Yet God's purpose here was principally to state how the stars originated, and the account is contrary to today's models of cosmological and stellar evolution.

God not only made the stars, but also set them, as well as the sun and the moon, "in the firmament of the heaven to give light upon the earth...and to divide the light from the darkness" (Genesis 1:17-18). The timeframe in which God created the sun, moon, and stars is identical to the activities of the other days of the Creation Week, because this fourth day is similarly described—"And the evening and the morning were the fourth day" (Genesis 1:19). Thus, unlike the modern evolutionary stellar and cosmological models, which require countless millions of years for stars to develop and give light, God makes it absolutely clear that He created the stars within the timeframe of an ordinary day—indeed, within the daylight portion of that fourth day, and by implication in the text, instantaneously by God's command. Thus, it did not take billions of years for the light of stars billions of light years distant from the earth to reach the earth after the stars were created.

However God accomplished the feat, it is emphatically clear from the Genesis account, as has already been noted, that God had on the first day already created light to shine upon the earth to dispel the darkness and to establish the day-night cycle of a literal day. Thus, when God created the stars on this fourth day, they, along with the sun and the moon, took over the role of giving light upon the earth, to rule over the day and the night. In other words, the light was already in place before the stars themselves were created! Furthermore, just as the fruit trees, created on the third day, were already bearing fruit and thus "full grown" from the beginning, God did not require millions of years to develop the stars into their intended useable form. The purpose of the stars was "to give light upon the earth," so they were immediately created fully-formed and fully-functioning from the very beginning to fulfill that role. Thus, like the fruit trees, it is to be expected that the stars also have an appearance of age, in this case vast ages, if present-day observed naturalistic processes are assumed to have been solely responsible for their formation.

From a purely naturalistic scientific perspective, the biblical account would seem impossible to reconcile with models of cosmological and stellar evolution and the timeframe associated with them. This apparent conflict may possibly be resolved in a number of ways. One solution is to claim that the Genesis account of creation should be dismissed as "naïve" and as having "an innocent lack of awareness of certain auxiliary information that must be incorporated into the process of biblical interpretation."[4] In that view, Genesis 1 is merely "primeval history" that should not be regarded as having any credible scientific application. Instead, this view contends that it is to modern science that we should turn to understand the make-up of the universe, how it operates, and its history.[5] The underlying fallacy of this approach is that these models are built on the *a priori* assumption or belief in uniformitarian naturalism which, by definition, not only excludes divine intervention in the course of the history of the universe, but excludes God altogether.

---

4   H. J. Van Till, 1986, *The Fourth Day: What the Bible and the Heavens are Telling Us About the Creation*, Grand Rapids, MI: William B. Eerdmans Publishing Company, 76.

5   Van Till, 1986, espouses this view, devoting three chapters to the presentation of the conventional, naturalistic models of cosmological and stellar evolution.

The other solution is to accept God's Word and question uniformitarian assumptions. One corollary to the uniformitarian naturalistic assumption underpinning modern astronomy is the assumption that light has always traveled at the same speed. But what if this uniformitarian assumption is not true? If light did travel faster in the past, say near infinity at the time of creation, then light from the farthest stars would have reached the earth in very much less than a literal day.[6] Alternately, it has been suggested that since a large number of verses refer to God "stretching out" or "spreading out" the heavens, and on the second day God refers to His making of the "firmament," which is a thin, stretched-out expanse, then it is possible that the universe, when God first created it, was small, but then He stretched it out, and the light with it, so that light always reached the earth but was red-shifted by the expansion.[7] Examples of some of the seventeen verses in the Old Testament that refer to God "stretching out" or "spreading out" the heavens include: "which alone spreadeth out the heavens" (Job 9:8); "who stretchest out the heavens like a curtain" (Psalm 104:2); and "It is he…that stretcheth out the heavens as a curtain, and spreadeth them out as a tent to dwell in" (Isaiah 40:22).

Whichever of these is the true explanation to resolve this apparent dilemma is still to be resolved, and it may even be that the final explanation is yet to be discovered. Thus, what needs to be emphasized is that just because we may think there is no solution to an apparent conflict between scientific observations and what God has clearly told us in the Scriptures, it does not mean that there is no solution or that we have to abandon our understanding of the Scriptures in favor of current scientific models. Rather, it should be obvious that the dilemma exists simply because we haven't yet found the solution, which does in fact exist. This is illustrated by the fact that thirty years ago neither of these options were available, yet now there are at least two viable options that are being researched that show promise of bringing resolution to what for many has been a great stumbling block. Yet these options have only been discovered because researchers involved remained absolutely faithful to the Genesis record as God's Spirit-breathed, trustworthy record of the literal history of His work in creating the universe, the earth, and everything in them. Our allegiance should be, without question, first and foremost to the Scriptures and not to the interpretations made by finite, fallible men who do not acknowledge either God or His work in creation.

As the fourth day's work came to a close, we read that "God saw that it was good" (Genesis 1:18). In other words, there was at that time nothing on any of the stars,

---

6   T. Norman and B. Setterfield, 1987, *The Atomic Constants, Light, and Time.*

7   D. R. Humphreys, 1994, *Starlight and Time: Solving the Puzzle of Distant Starlight in a Young Universe,* Colorado Springs, CO: Master Books. This book also contains two relevant technical papers: D. R. Humphreys, A Biblical Basis for Creationist Cosmology, 1994, *Proceedings of the Third International Conference on Creationism,* R.E. Walsh, ed., Pittsburgh, PA: Creation Science Fellowship, 255-266; D. R. Humphreys, 1994, Progress Toward a Young-Earth Relativistic Cosmology, *Proceedings of the Third International Conference on Creationism,* R.E. Walsh, ed., Pittsburgh, PA: Creation Science Fellowship, 267-286.

planets, satellites, or other heavenly bodies, or in the universe as a whole, that was out of place and not satisfying to God, as judged by His perfect character. There was perfect harmony and everything was in working order, just as He had planned it. Whatever remaining dilemmas we might have in understanding what God did and how He did it, God had executed His plans according to His purposes.

34

THE FIFTH DAY

God had established the atmosphere above the earth's surface waters on the second day. He brought the dry land up from under those surface waters on the third day and covered it with all manner of plants and trees. After filling the heavens with luminaries on Day Four, God next proceeds to make animal life suited for inhabiting the atmosphere and the earth's surface waters on the fifth day. All the necessities for these living creatures were now present on the earth—the day-night cycle ruled by the sun, moon, and stars, the seasons, air, water, soil, nutrients, plants, fruit, and more. Since God had formed the earth to be inhabited (Isaiah 45:18), He now turned His attention to creating inhabitants for this earth and placing them, suitably endowed, into their appropriate ecological niches.

"And God said, Let the waters bring forth [literally, and more correctly translated, *swarm* or *team*] abundantly the moving creature that hath life, and fowl that may fly above the earth in the open firmament of heaven" (Genesis 1:20). The first animal life, therefore, that God created was not some fragile blob of protoplasm that just simply happened to come together in response to electrical discharges over the primeval ocean. Neither was it the result of molecules being trapped by clay particles and heated in hydrothermal vents on the ocean floor, as proposed by scientists who accept only naturalistic explanations for the origin of life. Of course, neither observational evidence nor experimental work has in any way demonstrated that either of these scenarios is even remotely possible, in spite of the confident assertions of some scientists. Sadly, such assertions have served to convince many that the origin of life has been naturalistically explained without the need of God. In sharp contrast, the Bible states that the surface waters of the earth suddenly swarmed abundantly with swarming creatures at God's command.

The Hebrew word translated "moving creature" is *sherets*, which in eleven other occurrences is translated "creeping thing." Another Hebrew word, *rémes,* is also translated "creeping thing" in Genesis 1:24, 26, so the two Hebrew words would seem to be essentially synonymous. Nevertheless, here in Genesis 1:20 it would have to be referring to all kinds of marine and freshwater animals, both invertebrates and vertebrates, including fish, amphibians, and reptiles. Here also the Hebrew word *nephesh* occurs for the first time, translated "life," but the same word is translated "soul" in other places. This word *nephesh* frequently designates both the soul of man and the life of animals, and the fact that this same word is not used in the Scriptures to refer to plants indicates that in a biblical sense plants do not have life, in the sense of consciousness, as both men and animals do. Understanding this distinction is critical to understanding that from God's perspective, there was no death and suffering in the world prior to the Fall.

God also created the birds to fly above the ground, "across the face" of the firmament of the heavens, which is a better translation of the Hebrew. The perspective is that of a human observer on the earth's surface. The firmament is regarded as having a face, that is, a side turned toward the earth and thus "facing" it.

God having given the command, we are immediately told "And God created great whales [literally, sea monsters], and every living creature that moveth, which the waters brought forth abundantly, after their kind, and every winged fowl after his kind" (Genesis 1:21). Here, for the second time in the creation account, the Hebrew word *bara* (translated "created") is used, being the word that is only ever used to describe the creative work of God. This is significant, because here God is for the first time creating animal life with a consciousness or soul, as distinct from His previous creative activity, which had involved only the material or physical elements. Consciousness could not merely be developed by complex organization of these basic physical elements, so God once more acted to create what He alone could create: creatures with conscious life in integral partnership with their physical bodies. So God created swarms of living souls, moving creatures, an apt and graphical description of all forms of life that love to move in continual agitation in water, a clear reference to schools of fish and the like, marked by their pronounced gregarious instinct.

The first animals specifically mentioned as the product of this act of special creation were "great whales," or literally "great sea monsters," as most translations render the Hebrew word *tannin*. Its root indicates a creature of some length, hence the translation "whales" in some Bible translations, but the word also encompasses larger marine animals like sharks, and no doubt also crocodiles. It is perhaps significant that in older English translations, this same word was most frequently translated "dragons." This is not surprising, given the many early records and traditions surviving from many early nations of large sea monsters and fearsome land creatures often called "dragons." The descriptions of these creatures are often reminiscent of dinosaurs, so these stories and the occasional drawings that have been found should not be simply shrugged off as myths. It is thus highly likely that they represent memories of dinosaurs handed down from generation to generation after they had been encountered prior to their extinction. Thus, the word used here in the Hebrew allows for a wide range of water-dwelling creatures.

The expression "winged fowl" is literally rendered "bird of wing," which would seem to be a superfluous description given that all birds have wings. It is possible, because the Scripture is using the broadest of class distinctions, that the expression is meant to include every type of creature that has wings, both small and large creatures, and not only what we call birds.

In summary, it is clear that the types of animals mentioned here are intended to include every type of creature that inhabits the earth's surface waters and its atmosphere. Furthermore, we are once more told that God made all these creatures to reproduce "after their kind." As in the case of the various plants, God had programmed the actual biochemical reproductive systems of these animals to assure the fixity of the different "kinds." Thus, the DNA molecule of heredity for each kind allows for wide individual variations only within these boundaries and not beyond the structures of the kinds themselves, as ordained by God. This is also clearly demonstrated by all the available scientific evidence from the study of genetics.

After His creation work on Day Five, God not only declared that His work was good (Genesis 1:21), but He also pronounced a blessing on all these animals He had created: "And God blessed them, saying, Be fruitful, and multiply, and fill the waters in the seas, and let fowl multiply in the earth" (Genesis 1:22). The implication of this statement is that while God had created so many creatures that swarmed in the waters and flew across the atmosphere, there was still tremendous variability within the many kinds of creatures He had created to reproduce and further populate the earth. Furthermore, God was expressing His caring concern for all these animals, just as we are reminded in Matthew 10:29 that not even a sparrow falls to the ground without God noticing and caring, and in Matthew 6:26 that He continually provides food for them all.

It is extremely important to note, once more, how obvious it is that the theoretical evolutionary development of life is not the same as the order of creation recorded here in Genesis. According to evolutionary theory, marine invertebrate organisms evolved first, followed by marine vertebrates, then land plants, later still land animals, then birds, and finally, mammals. However, the Genesis creation account, provided by God, clearly stipulates that land plants came first, then marine creatures of all kinds and birds, simultaneously. Indeed, the largest sea animals, including the whales which are mammals, were created at the same time as the smallest marine invertebrates. These details render it impossible to equate the biblical order with the evolutionary scheme, which is unfortunately what many well-meaning Christians have suggested in their efforts to somehow reconcile the claims of modern science with the Genesis record. Such compromises, whether labeled theistic evolution, day-age creation, or progressive creation, all utterly fail because the evolutionary order simply does not match the God-given record of creation.

"And the evening and the morning were the fifth day" (Genesis 1:23). Just as God had made the expanse or "firmament" on the second day to divide the waters above the firmament from the waters that remained on the earth's surface, now on this fifth day, God filled the waters and the atmosphere above it with inhabitants, after having provided all kinds of plants for food on Day Three.

35

THE SIXTH DAY—LAND ANIMALS AND MAN

One final task remained to prepare the earth for mankind: to create land animals that would fill the earth's land surfaces. Thus, we read: "And God said, Let the earth bring forth the living creature after his kind, cattle, and creeping thing, and beast of the earth after his kind: and it was so" (Genesis 1:24). Once more, God issues a command to the earth to produce, or cause to come forth, all manner of land animals. Obviously, God could have called these creatures into existence by His mere word, but instead He speaks to the earth, commanding the ground to bring them forth. In other words, their bodies were composed of the same elements as the earth; they would have a kinship with the ground, to which they would return when they died.

Verse 25 reiterates what God had accomplished: "And God made the beast of the earth after his kind, and cattle after their kind, and every thing that creepeth upon the earth after his kind." It is noteworthy that the text says that God "made" (Hebrew *asah*) these land animals, whereas He was said to have "created" (Hebrew *bara*) the sea creatures and the birds. Some would argue that the two Hebrew words are used somewhat synonymously throughout Genesis 1 because everything that God did involved His creative word. However, as already noted, the second use of *bara*, in Genesis 1:21, marked God's special activity in creating the first living creatures with *nephesh*, or soul, as distinct from all previous creation that was only made up of the physical elements. God had already established this soul dimension in the biological life He created on the fifth day, so no further mention of this was required. During the making of these further living creatures, their creation simply followed the pattern already set. The creation of these land creatures did not require new or higher levels of creativity. It merely involved new types of organization of the materials already in existence, including the *nephesh*.

The land animals at the outset of this sixth day are categorized in three classes— cattle, creeping things, and beasts. The description would seem to be intended as a comprehensive list of all land animals. The Hebrew word *behemah*, translated "cattle," probably refers to more than simply cattle, but domestic animals generally (the root of the Hebrew word meaning "to be dumb," thus our colloquial expression "dumb brutes"). The second class is described in the Hebrew as *rémes*, which comes from the root meaning "to move about lightly" or to "glide about." Thus, "creeping things" refers to all animals, whether large or small, that crawl or creep close to the surface of the ground. The third class of land animals is called "beast of the earth" (Hebrew *chayyath ha'árets*, literally "wild beasts of the earth"), which are clearly large wild animals, the modifying phrase "of the earth" designating that these beasts have freedom of movement upon the earth. Of course, this classification list has no correlation with the man-made taxonomy system (amphibians, reptiles, mammals, insects), but would seem to be a more natural classification system, based on the relationship of the animals to man's interests. Thus, the "beasts of the earth" would include the large mammals such as lions and elephants, and probably also the dinosaurs. "Creeping things" would probably have included the insects and smaller reptiles, most of the amphibians, and many small mammals (for example, moles, mice—see Leviticus 11:29-31).

The listing of these three categories of land animals is twice recorded here, but each time in a different order, so the order does not indicate a sequence and therefore it is reasonable to conclude that all these land animals were made by God simultaneously. Furthermore, this rules out any possible correlation with an evolution-based order for the development of life (that is, insects, then amphibians, then reptiles, and finally all mammals). In any case, the fact that Genesis records the birds being created a day before the land reptiles immediately makes comparison impossible.

"And God saw that it was good" (Genesis 1:25). God surveyed the results of His handiwork and was completely satisfied that everything He had created was good and in harmony, perfect when measured against His holiness and pure character. This statement is important because there could not have been any violence, bloodshed, and death as a result of some evolutionary struggle for existence among these animals, which would have been entirely inconsistent with, and contrary to, God's assessment of what He had created. Furthermore, any concept of evolutionary development is refuted by the statement declaring that God separately created all these animals "after their kind."

The creation of these land animals must have only taken a small portion of this sixth day, because now we read about the Persons of the Godhead discussing among themselves their plans for their final act of creation: man. That God took as long as six days seems to be for the purpose of providing a divine pattern for the seven-day week, man's six days of work followed by a day of rest.

Whereas previously God gave commands that were followed immediately by acts of creation, we next read of God speaking in divine council: "And God said, Let us make man in our image, after our likeness" (Genesis 1:26). This divine council clearly and very strongly emphasizes the dignity of man as the climax and crown of creation.

To whom is God speaking? He could not have been speaking to the angels, because man was not going to be created in their likeness, but in the likeness of God (Genesis 1:27). Rather, this is a clear reference to the plurality of the Godhead, with one Person clearly addressing one or both of the other two in the Trinity. Indeed, the Genesis account has already recorded the involvement of the Holy Spirit in the processes of creation (Genesis 1:2). In the New Testament we read that the Lord Jesus Christ was intimately involved with every aspect of the creation of the world (John 1:1-3; Colossians 1:15-17; and Hebrews 1:2-3).

On this sixth day, the three Persons of the Trinity took council together and announced their plan to make man, or in the Hebrew *'adham,* a term whose root significance must very likely be sought in the cognate word *'adhamah,* which refers to soil capable of cultivation. Since man's body would be formed from "the dust of the ground" (Genesis 2:7), he would, therefore, be "the cultivator of the soil."[1]

The double modifying phrase "in our image, after our likeness" (Genesis 1:26) emphatically declares the singular dignity of man, for man is not only made after the deliberate plan and purpose of God, but is also very definitely patterned after Him. "Image" is the Hebrew word *tsélem,* whose root means "to carve" or "to cut off."[2] Of course, we cannot and should not go so far as to imply from this word that there is somehow a *physical* similarity with God, but at least the term refers to concrete similarity, whereas the second Hebrew word *demûth,* translated "likeness," refers more to similarity in the abstract or in the ideal. Some have asked the question, since God in His omnipresence is not corporeal but is Spirit (John 4:24), then how could man's body be made in God's image? On the other hand, we find in Revelation 4 and 5 a description of "him that sat on the throne" in heaven, who is the object of unceasing worship and adoration. In His hand is the book sealed with seven seals. Only the Lamb, who is also the Lion of the tribe of Judah and the Root of David, is found worthy to take this book and open its seals. Yet God designed man's body to function physically in ways in which He functions.[3] Interestingly, various passages reveal that God can see (Genesis 1:10, 18, 21, 25, 31; 16:13), hear (Exodus 3:7), smell (Genesis 8:21), touch (Genesis 32:30-32), and speak (Exodus 3:4-6; 20:1; Matthew 17:5; 2 Peter 1:17-18). Furthermore, whenever He has chosen to appear visibly to men, He has done so in the form of a human body (Genesis 18:1-2; 32:24-30). There is something about the human body, therefore, which is uniquely appropriate to God's manifestation of Himself, so it seems clear that He designed man's body with this in mind. Accordingly, He designed it with an erect posture, with an upward gazing countenance, capable of facial expressions corresponding to emotional feelings, and with a brain and a tongue capable of articulate, symbolic speech. Man was not created as another "animal."

---

1   Leupold, 1942, 88.

2   Leupold, 1942, 88.

3   Morris, 1976, 74.

It is stated for a second and third time in Genesis 1:27 that God created man in His image: "So God created man in his own image, in the image of God created he him." God now acts and creates man, twice more repeating that man is created in His image so as to emphasize this point.

Here again the Hebrew word for special creation, *bara,* is used, because quite clearly a specific act of special creation was needed for man to be made in the image and likeness of God Himself! Man was to be the highest and most complex of all the creatures made by God, yet his body was formed in the same way as the bodies of the animals had been formed (Genesis 1:24; c.f. Genesis 2:7). Similarly, man was given the "breath of life" like the animals (Genesis 2:7; c.f. Genesis 7:22), and in him was given the "living soul" like the animals (Genesis 1:24; c.f. Genesis 2:7). Thus, though man's structure, both physical and mental, was to be far more complex than that of the animals, it was still to be of the same basic essence, so God therefore proposed to "make [Hebrew *asah*] man in our image" just as He made (*asah*) the land animals.

However, God planned man to be far more than a very complex and highly organized animal. There was to be something in man that was not only quantitatively greater, but qualitatively distinctive, something not possessed in any degree by the animals. Man was "created" (Hebrew *bara*) in God's image, so he was both made and created in the image of God. This is profound, and virtually impossible to fully comprehend. Man was given a "spirit," which in the Old Testament is the Hebrew *ruach*, commonly translated "wind" and "breath." The "breath of life" (literally, "spirit of lives") is the possession of animals as well as man, but when the term "spirit" is used to define that aspect of man which is like God ("the likeness of God"), then it is referring to the eternal spirit that possesses aesthetic, moral, and spiritual attributes. The spirit of man, like God Himself, is an eternal spirit, whereas the spirit of an animal ceases to exist when the body dies (Ecclesiastes 3:21) and goes back to the earth. There can be little doubt that the "image of God" in which man was created must include those aspects of human nature which are not shared by animals, attributes such as moral consciousness, the ability to think abstractly, an understanding of beauty and emotion, and above all, the capacity for worshipping and loving God. This eternal and divine dimension of man's being must be the essence of what is involved in the likeness of God. None of this was part of the animal *nephesh,* the "soul," so it required a special act of creation by God.

It is also made very clear in Genesis 1:27 that "man" is being used as a generic term which includes both male and female—"male and female created He them." Both man and woman were thus created in God's image, both equally possessing an eternal spirit capable of personal fellowship with their Creator. Thus, Genesis 2 is unequivocally in perfect harmony with Genesis chapter 1; there is no contradiction, as Genesis 2 is an elaboration of the events of the sixth day, adding many more details not present in Genesis 1, where the focus is an overview of the six days of creation from the perspective of the origin of the universe and the earth. Chapter 2 has as its focus the origin and history of man.

In Genesis 1:26, when the divine council declared God's intention to "make man in our image, after our likeness," God also declared what man's relationship would be to the rest of God's creation: "and let them have dominion over the fish of the sea, and over the fowl of the air, and over the cattle, and over all the earth, and over every creeping thing that creepeth upon the earth." Then having created man, God repeats this as an instruction: "and God said unto them,…have dominion over the fish of the sea, and over the fowl of the air, and over every living thing that moveth upon the earth" (Genesis 1:28). God, the sovereign owner of all that He created, delegates to man the dominion over all of creation, a stewardship requiring accountability to God. Furthermore, man is clearly capable of exercising this delegated dominion over creation because of being created in God's image.

The expression "have dominion" is the Hebrew verb *radhah*, which signifies "to trample down" or "to master."[4] This should not be misconstrued to imply that man's dominion over the earth should involve ruthless exploitation without regard for the consequences. On the contrary, delegated stewardship with accountability to God requires that man exercises care for the earth and its creatures, developing and utilizing the earth's resources so as not to despoil and deplete them through selfishness. Man's dominion was to be exercised "over all the earth" and was to include all the "fish," "fowl," "cattle," and "every creeping thing that creepeth upon the earth." These are the classes of animals and living creatures previously described as having been created by God, though there is some slight modification of terminology. Furthermore, the absence of some classes of animals, for example, the beasts of the earth, should not be misconstrued to imply that man's dominion does not include such creatures. To the contrary, the classes of creatures listed indicate that man was to have mastery over the sea, air, land, and all the creatures therein, as confirmed by the all-encompassing expression "over all the earth." This implies that every type of being, and indeed the earth itself, was to be subservient to man. The delegation of such phenomenal, wide-ranging powers to man is again an indication of man's singular nobility and of his being created in the image and likeness of God, the Creator.

In Genesis 1:28, God not only instructs man to have dominion over the earth, but to "subdue" it. The Hebrew word translated "subdue" is *kabhash*. It has a slightly different meaning than "have dominion" (*radhah*) in that its root implies "to knead" or "to tread." Both of these words are like military terms—first conquer, and then rule—but should not be misconstrued as synonymous with ruthless exploitation. In context, no conflict between man, the earth's creatures, or the earth is suggested, since God had repeatedly pronounced all that He had made as "good," implying harmonious interrelationships and interworking of the earth's processes with all

---

4   Leupold, 1942, 91.

of its creatures. Rather, God's instructions here are best understood as giving man a mandate using these very expressive words to encourage an intense study of the earth (with all of its intricate processes and complex systems) and its creatures, and then to utilize that knowledge for the optimum benefit of the earth and its inhabitants, both mankind and all the animals. In modern terminology, this is God's commission to man authorizing both science and technology to be used for the greater good of all the earth's inhabitants.

The extent of this God-given dominion mandate could be perceived as rather limited if it were inferred from the biblical record that God only created a few pairs of each kind of creature, and thus there were very few animals to begin with. However, just as God commanded the ground everywhere to bring forth the plants (Genesis 1:11-12), God commanded the earth's surface waters and the ground everywhere to bring forth all the moving and living creatures (Genesis 1:20, 24). This in itself implies that God created many pairs of each of the animal kinds all over the earth and in the waters. Though this is not stated explicitly, it can be clearly inferred from the use of such terms as "swarms" and "abundantly." Then having been created to reproduce after their kinds, they had been blessed and told to be fruitful and multiply, and to fill the waters and multiply in the earth (Genesis 1:22).

36

THE SIXTH DAY—ADAM AND EVE

In contrast to the swarms of animals God made prior to man, Scripture makes it absolutely clear that He created only one man and one woman, Adam and Eve. God provides more details in Genesis chapter 2. There we are told: "And the LORD God formed man of the dust of the ground, and breathed into his nostrils the breath of life; and man became a living soul" (verse 7). The Hebrew word translated "formed" is *yatsar,* which means to "mold" or "form," and is the word that specifically describes the activity of a potter forming a pot (Jeremiah 18:2-4). The idea being emphasized is that God exercised meticulous care and personal attention to His task of making man's body from "the dust of the ground."[1] Then God "breathed into his nostrils the breath of life," a profoundly personal act of the Creator imparting life to man's body, formed from the basic physical elements of the earth and completely equipped with bones and organs, including nostrils and lungs, but lifeless until energized with life from God. It was only to man that God directly (rather than at a distance, as it were, by His spoken word) "breathed" in the "breath of life." It was in this way that man "became a living soul," referring to man's consciousness and the realm of the mind and emotions. Thus, man received his "spirit of life" directly from God rather than from any animal ancestry via some postulated evolutionary process.

Having created the first man, God placed him in the Garden of Eden (Genesis 2:15). This first man, Adam, was there alone with the birds and animals, "And the LORD God said, It is not good that the man should be alone; I will make him an help meet for him" (Genesis 2:18). Here God acknowledges that His work of creation is incomplete, because Adam is alone and incomplete without a woman. The phrase "not good" does not mean evil, but is only being used in the sense of unfinished. All the animals had been made both male and female (Genesis 6:19) so as to multiply on the earth after their kinds (Genesis 1:22, 24). Man alone had no such companion, so God now set about to personally make "an help meet for him" (literally, "a helper like man"). However, first God arranged for Adam to become familiar with many of the animals in the garden by personal inspection, so that in exercising his rulership over them he would realize that not one among them qualified to be a helper suitable for his needs or to have fellowship with him. During this time, Adam would realize that he was incomplete and would then

---

1   Leupold, 1942, 115.

be ready for God to perform the required act of creation to provide him with a suitable helper.

Since the account in Genesis 2 is not a chronological record, but a recounting of what happened in the latter part of the sixth day from the perspective of Adam, Genesis 2:19 should quite legitimately be translated "out of the ground the Lord God *had* formed every beast of the earth and every fowl of the air" (emphasis mine). Neither is the listing here meant to be exhaustive, because what God is endeavoring to demonstrate to Adam could readily be achieved by bringing to Adam just the animals and birds in the garden which God had previously created on Day Five and early on Day Six. It was only necessary to bring to Adam one male-female pair of each kind for the purpose God had in mind, which included having Adam name them.

How many kinds that would have involved we have no way of knowing, but it was a small enough number that they could have been examined within a few hours at most. It is not unreasonable to suggest that Adam, with his incredible God-given intellect as "the son of God" (Luke 3:38), could have noted and named perhaps as many as ten kinds each minute. At that rate, about 3,000 kinds could have been identified in five hours. Such a number would seem more than adequate for God's purposes here, particularly as we can't be sure whether there were as many as 3,000 kinds among the land animals and the birds in the Garden of Eden. The high level of intelligence Adam possessed is at once evident from his capacity to undertake this task, because inherent in the Hebrew word "name" is the idea of "giving a designation expressive of the nature or character of the one named."[2] These names were appropriate and significant names for the various creatures, in keeping with Adam's intelligence. This is confirmed by the statement recorded here by the Holy Spirit that "whatsoever Adam called every living creature, that was the name thereof" (Genesis 2:19). However, as the animals passed by him, no doubt in male-female pairs, Adam's aloneness became more and more evident. Each animal had its mate, but for Adam, there was no one suitably like him as a helper for him. He was unique in intelligence and spirituality, so there was clearly no kinship between him and any of the animals; none were able to provide him the fellowship or companionship he needed.

We are not told whether God explained to Adam what He was about to do next. However, immediately after God created Eve from Adam's side, Adam seemed to understand clearly what God had done. We read: "And the LORD God caused a deep sleep to fall upon Adam, and he slept: and he took one of his ribs, and closed up the flesh instead thereof; And the rib, which the LORD God had taken from man, made he a woman, and brought her unto the man" (Genesis 2:21-22). The "deep sleep" into which God placed Adam was not some hypnotic trance, but akin to the sleep caused by an anesthetic, a sleep that envelopes man's

---

2   Leupold, 1942, 131.

feelings and consciousness. And while Adam slept, God performed a marvelous surgical operation. It is likely that the word "rib" is a poor translation. Although the Hebrew word *tsela* definitely bears this meaning, it appears thirty-five times in the Old Testament and this is the only time it has been translated "rib."[3] In at least twenty of its occurrences, the word simply means "side." Of course, a "side" would include both flesh and bone, as well as blood, which was quite logically the case because Adam later said, "This is now bone of my bones, and flesh of my flesh" (Genesis 2:23).

This account is often ridiculed as some unscientific myth, because a man does not have one less rib than a woman, but this ignores the well-established fact that such "acquired characteristics" are never inherited. Adam and Eve's descendants received from their parents the genetics for a full complement of ribs. In any case, it is also well-established that of the bones in the human body, the ribs have been known to regenerate if a piece of bone has been removed. This divine act emphasizes the absolute unity of the human race, establishing its descent from only one ancestor, Adam. Indeed, all other men have been born of women, but the first woman was made from man, absolutely contradicting the evolutionary theory for the origin of man and any notion that the biblical account is an allegorical description of God allegedly using evolutionary processes to bring man into existence.

The true dignity of women is also stressed, because Eve was made neither from Adam's head nor his feet, for she is neither superior nor inferior to man. The truest of kinship with man is absolutely established, for she is of his bone and flesh, made from his side, indicating equality and companionship at exactly the same level with him.

When Adam awoke from his deep sleep after God had finished forming Eve, God "brought her unto the man." It is clear in the Hebrew that there is a certain animation prominent in Adam's exclamation: "This is now bone of my bones, and flesh of my flesh: she shall be called Woman [Hebrew *isha*], because she was taken out of Man [Hebrew *ish*]" (Genesis 2:23). Of course, the original language used here by Adam has in all probability been lost, so that the Hebrew must approximate the thought as nearly as its elements allow. Nevertheless, it can still be seen that the Hebrew has the same clever play upon words that has been retained in the English translation—ish/isha, man/woman. The intimate kinship of this first man and woman is expressed even with a kinship of sound.

Having made Adam and Eve, God now establishes the first marriage with the declaration, "Therefore shall a man leave his father and his mother, and shall cleave unto his wife: and they shall be one flesh" (Genesis 2:24). The Lord Jesus Christ based His own teaching about marriage on the creation account in Genesis. He combined the previously quoted verse with a verse from Genesis

---

3   Morris, 1976, 100.

chapter 1, thereby signifying that He regarded these passages as complementary and not separate contradictory accounts of creation. In Matthew 19:4-5, He said: "Have ye not read, that he which made them at the beginning made them male and female [quoting Genesis 1:27], And said, For this cause shall a man leave father and mother, and shall cleave to his wife: and they twain shall be one flesh? [quoting Genesis 2:24]." Jesus obviously regarded the creation account of the first two chapters of Genesis as absolutely historical and in no way allegorical or contradictory. Indeed, the whole basis for the declaration that when a man and a woman are married they become "one flesh" is the historical reality that Adam and Eve were literally "one flesh," Eve having been made from the flesh and bone of Adam's side. Otherwise, there is no absolute basis for marriage as one man and one woman for life outside of this historical reality of the literal "one flesh" in Genesis 2:21-24.

We read in Genesis 1:28 "And God blessed them, and God said unto them, Be fruitful, and multiply, and replenish the earth, and subdue it." Here God ordained family life and pronounced His blessing on the children of this first marriage and their future descendants. The Hebrew word translated "replenish" is *male'*, which does not contain the connotation to "refill" that the word brings to the minds of most speakers of modern English. The Hebrew word should more correctly be translated as "fill," which was the original meaning of the old English term "replenish." There is no suggestion that the earth had once been filled and now needed to be filled again. God is simply telling Adam and Eve that they have His blessing, that they are to have many descendants, and that those descendants are to spread out across the earth to fill it while exercising dominion over it and all its creatures. Again it needs to be stressed that man's subjugation of the earth and all its creatures was intended by God to be delegated stewardship with accountability to Him so that man's actions would produce the best results for the earth and its inhabitants.

God now assured Adam and Eve of His provision of food for them and all the animals: "And God said, Behold, I have given you every herb bearing seed, which is upon the face of all the earth, and every tree, in the which is the fruit of a tree yielding seed; to you it shall be for meat. And to every beast of the earth, and to every fowl of the air, and to every thing that creepeth upon the earth, wherein there is life, I have given every green herb for meat: and it was so" (Genesis 1:29-30). Here is one of the few times God tells us *why* He created something. In this instance, we are told that all the plants were created to be food for man and the animals. (Earlier we were told that God created the sun, moon, and stars to be the bearers of the light He had already created.)

The instruction here is very specific. The perfect tense of the verb translated "have given" is the "usual construction in ordinances or abiding decrees and giving the impression of a rule firmly fixed and already unwavering."[4] Man is permitted by God to use a great variety of plants for his diet. Two classes of plants are stipulated—"every herb bearing seed" and "every tree, in the which is the fruit of a tree yielding seed" (every tree upon which there is seed-bearing fruit). There can also be no doubt that in this instruction about what food was permissible was also the complete guide from God of what man was allowed to eat. There is no mention of man being permitted to eat animals as food. This is in contrast to the specific instruction allowing the eating of meat in Genesis 9:3, which was not until after the Flood many years later. Each of these commands is very specific; God absolutely rules out the eating of meat, which clearly was not His original intention as part of the "good" world He had created. This has definite implications regarding God's instructions for man's dominion over the beasts, cattle, birds, and fish. This dominion very definitely did not permit man to kill these creatures for food. Undoubtedly Adam and Eve followed the very letter of God's command and stayed strictly within the limits He had stipulated, but whether some of their descendants in the pre-Flood era disobeyed God's command we are not told, although it is a possibility since it is said of Jabal that he raised cattle (Genesis 4:20).

God also gave as food for the beasts, birds, and all creeping things "every green herb," evidently meaning all green plants, including grasses. It is clear that God not only did not intend for man to eat the animals, but He also never intended that the animals should prey upon and kill one another for food. This was part of the perfect harmony prevailing in the animal world and implied by His pronouncement that all the animals He had made were "good" (Genesis 1:25). This is not to suggest that among the animals God had created there were not those which would later become carnivorous, behavior which was clearly evident in the world just before the Flood (Genesis 6:11-12). Desire for meat most likely was a later development, perhaps at the time of the Curse (discussed below). Even today, carnivorous animals can and will, if they have to, live on a vegetarian diet. Sharp teeth which today are used for ripping the flesh of other animals could have originally been used only for ripping the plants of a vegetarian diet. An example of an animal today with sharp teeth that primarily has a vegetarian diet is the giant panda. The giant panda usually uses his sharp teeth to shred raw bamboo (which is very tough), but can also use the same sharp teeth to eat small mammals such as rodents. On the other hand, such structures as fangs and claws could have been the result of the expression of recessive features which only became dominant due to selection processes later, or were mutational features following the Curse instead of originally created equipment. This is really only speculation, but these possibilities are entirely feasible and are consistent with the details supplied in Scripture.

Similarly, based on the understanding of the "balance-of-nature" arrangements in

---

4 Leupold, 1942, 97.

today's various environments, whereby predators keep in check large numbers of other animals that would otherwise proliferate in plague proportions, we can only speculate as to how such balances would have been maintained in God's perfectly created world. However, the Bible is clear that predation and carnivory were not characteristic of the animals when God created them. First, the Scriptures predict that in the world of the future, after the Lord Jesus Christ has returned and restored the earth in part to its original perfection, there will once again be no predation, carnivory, or struggle between animals, or between animals and man, as recorded, for example, in Isaiah 11:6-9 and Hosea 2:18. Indeed, in the first of these passages we read that the wolf and the lamb will dwell together, the leopard will lie down with the kid, a little child shall lead, and the lion will eat straw just as an ox does—that is, there will be no predation and carnivory, for the animals will dwell in perfect harmony and be herbivorous again, just as they were originally. Second, immediately following God's specific instructions that both man and the animals were to be strictly vegetarians, we read: "And God saw every thing that he had made, and, behold, it was very good" (Genesis 1:31). As if to ensure that there would be absolutely no doubt regarding the status of His created world, God insists here with emphasis that there was no imperfection in anything that He had made and that by His pronouncement, as measured against His holiness, the whole creation was "very good." Six times previously, God had seen that what He had made was "good," but now that it was complete, with every part in perfect harmony with every other part, all perfectly formed and with an abundance of inhabitants, He saw with great joy that it was all (literally) "exceedingly good." It is quite clear that God's instruction that both man and the animals were to be strict vegetarians is emphatically underlined by this immediate pronouncement that His creation was now "very good," with absolutely no imperfection.

God's work was now completed. As on the previous five days, the day closes with the pronouncement: "And the evening and the morning were the sixth day" (Genesis 1:31). Even though there had been much creative activity on this day, with the creation of all the land animals, the creation of Adam, Adam naming all the animals, and then finally the creation of Eve from Adam's side; the repetition of this "formula" of evening and morning reminds us that this sixth day was of exactly the same duration as the previous five days. The only difference was that at the end of this sixth day, God completed His work of creation and declared it all "very good"—complete and perfect.

37

THE SEVENTH DAY

As the seventh day begins, we are reminded that God had now completed His work of creating and making all things, so the Genesis record provides us with a marvelous assertive summary: "Thus the heavens and the earth were finished, and all the host of them" (Genesis 2:1). It is clear that "the heavens and the earth" refer to the work of the first two days of creation, and work of Days Three to Six are covered by the expression "and all the host of them," meaning all the works found in heaven and on earth—the land and plants, the sun, moon, and stars, all the birds and fish, and the land animals and man.

God was fully satisfied with the completeness and perfection of all that He had created; now on this seventh day, having ended His work, He rested: "And on the seventh day God ended his work which he had made; and he rested on the seventh day from all his work which he had made. And God blessed the seventh day, and sanctified it: because that in it he had rested from all his work which God created and made" (Genesis 2:2-3). Four times it is emphasized that God had finished His work ("finished," v. 1; "ended," v. 2; and "rested," twice in vv. 2-3), and three times it is emphasized that this included *all* His work. It was not that God was weary and needed to rest and be refreshed as man requires today. The primary meaning of the verb used here translated "rested" (Hebrew *shabhath*) is "to cease" or "desist" from exertion or work. The "work" that He desisted from is described by the Hebrew term *mela'khah*, meaning a special task He had set for Himself. Thus, God desisted from His work of creation on this seventh day simply because no more work was required to be done; there was nothing more to be completed, as He had already declared. Therefore, God blessed or consecrated the seventh day and set it apart as a holy day and as a commemoration of the completion of His work of creation. This seventh day became known as the Sabbath (Hebrew *shabbath*), which is derived from the same primary root of the Hebrew verb *shabhath*.

This theme is taken up by God in His instruction through Moses to the children of Israel to keep the Sabbath day. In Exodus 20:8-11, we read: "Remember the sabbath day, to keep it holy. Six days shalt thou labour, and do all thy work: But the seventh day is the sabbath of the LORD thy God: in it thou shalt not do any work, thou, nor thy son, nor thy daughter, nor manservant, nor thy maidservant, nor thy cattle, nor thy stranger that is within thy gates: For in six days the Lord made heaven and earth, the sea, and all that in them is, and rested the seventh day: wherefore the Lord blessed the sabbath day, and hallowed it." God's words here echo the text in Genesis 2:1-3. The whole basis of the Sabbath is God resting. It is patterned after God's creative work over six days when He made heaven, earth, the sea, and everything in them. He then ceased from His work because it had been completed, and so He consecrated that seventh day as a day when we likewise would not work but cease from our regular labor. Thus, the Sabbath as instituted here was a commemoration of creation, and the whole basis for the seven-day week that we still abide by.

These instructions are repeated in Exodus 31:13-17. We are further told that God not only gave us these instructions through Moses, but He also wrote these words with His finger on stone tablets (31:18). No honest biblical scholar could possibly deny that God's instructions to the children of Israel were referring to six literal days of work and a seventh literal day of rest, which God both says and writes, with His own finger, are identical to the six days in which He made everything in the heaven and earth and the sea (which covers the totality of all that He created in the universe). If the days of creation in the Genesis account are merely allegorical or represent long periods of time, these passages would not make sense.

The fact that this seventh day as recorded in Genesis 2:1-3 is not formally summarized and closed with the formula "the evening and the morning were the seventh day" as are the other six days, certainly does not imply, as some today suggest, that the seventh day is still continuing. The Bible does not say, "He is resting on the seventh day," but rather, "He rested on the seventh day." In Exodus 31:17, we are even told that "on the seventh day he rested, and was refreshed." His work of creation was finished, but that does not imply He failed to continue other aspects of His work, such as the maintenance of His creation and His planned work of redemption, which is the central theme that runs throughout Scripture. The Creator, the Author of the Bible, is not the god of the deist, who winds up the universe to set it running and then takes his hands off of it and shows no further interest in it. On the contrary, as we read on in the Genesis record, God is active in having fellowship with Adam and Eve, speaking with them, pronouncing judgment, etc., intimately involved in all that He had created, including men and women, and the operations of the world around them, as so graphically illustrated in the judgment of the Flood.

We can accept the Genesis account as a strict, factual reporting of what actually transpired in the manner in which it transpired. It is not some picture devised later by human ingenuity, conveying truth by its general outlines or basic thoughts expressed in highly figurative terms. To the contrary, the creation account, as it stands, expects the impartial reader to accept it as entirely literal and historical. There are hundreds of cross references to this Genesis account found throughout the rest of the Bible. Each reference treats Genesis as sober, historical fact. The value of the Genesis account of creation lies both in the basic truths it embodies, and in the details by which these truths are conveyed. The details are truthful, exact, and essential, being in all their parts proof itself that God did indeed create everything in six literal days and then rested on the seventh day because His work had been completed.

38

THE FALL

Our purpose in examining the account of the temptation of Adam and Eve and the Fall, as recorded in Genesis 3, will be to highlight those details which are relevant to our consideration of the geology of the earth and its history. We are not specifically told how much time elapsed between the end of the Creation Week and the events recorded in Genesis 3, but there are some indirect hints in the text that would suggest that the elapsed time was short. What we can be adamant about is that at the close of Genesis 1-2, God's six-day work of creation was completed and everything in the world was "very good"—complete and perfect. There was nothing out of order—no pain, no suffering, no disease, no struggle for existence, no disharmony, no sin or evil, and above all, no death.

God had planted a garden and there He placed Adam and Eve "to dress it and to keep it" (Genesis 2:15). The Hebrew words used could be translated to till or tend and to watch, guard, or look after. The thought in mind is that Adam and Eve were to exercise careful and loving stewardship over the garden, keeping it beautiful and orderly, with every component in place and in harmonious relationship with the whole. God's command was to keep the ecology, not to destroy it, which belies the accusation that the concept of man's dominion has led to the exploitation of the earth's resources. To the contrary, it has been in his rebellion against God that man has exploited and destroyed. This was never God's intention.

God also made provision for Adam and Eve to freely eat of every tree in the garden, except for one: "the tree of the knowledge of good and evil" (Genesis 2:16-17). This tree is not identified by any other designation, so we are not at liberty to speculate as to which of our modern trees it might have been. Indeed, it is more than likely that this tree no longer exists because it probably was found only in the Garden of Eden, and the Garden of Eden was washed away and destroyed by the Flood. God warned Adam and Eve not to eat of this tree, "for in the day that thou eatest thereof thou shalt surely die" (Genesis 2:17). There is no suggestion here that the fruit contained some magical substance that would impart such knowledge when eaten. Indeed, this may have been an ordinary-looking tree with ordinary fruit that was no more attractive than any other tree or any other fruit, given that it was only after Eve was tempted that the tree and its fruit appealed to her (Genesis 3:2-6). Nevertheless, eating the fruit of this tree after it had been specifically forbidden by God would indeed give Adam and Eve a very real knowledge of "evil," which can be defined simply as rejection of God's will. By participating in such disobedience, evil is experimentally experienced and the difference between that which is "evil" and that which is "good" becomes known. All Adam and Eve had so far seen and experienced was perfection, so if they rejected God's instructions regarding this tree, they would experience evil, and the knowledge of it would be conveyed to them. Thus, partaking of the forbidden fruit would surely give Adam and Eve knowledge of good and evil, as well as the difference between them, in the most intensely real way.

With a single minor restraint, this absolute restriction of eating of the tree of the knowledge of good and evil was designed by God as a test of man's love for Him. Adam and Eve were free to chose, and this gave them the opportunity to reject God's Word. It would have been altogether natural, reasonable, and appropriate for Adam and Eve to have been so grateful to God for all that He had done for them—giving them life, a beautiful home in the Garden of Eden, an abundance of good food in profuse variety so that they had everything they would ever need or want—that their own love for God in return would cause them to gladly follow His will in all things. Surrounded by evidence of God's love, surely Adam and Eve would assume that any instruction coming from God would be a further demonstration of His love, and therefore willingly obey it. This one restriction was entirely appropriate for its purpose. There was every reason, based on love and not fear, for Adam and Eve to conform to God's command, and no reason to disobey Him. There could be no excuse. However, they did have a choice and so were truly "free moral agents" before God.

It should have been sufficient for Adam and Eve to have obeyed God merely as an expression of their love. However, God graciously provided them with even more incentive by giving them a clear warning of the consequences of disobedience. Disobedience would demonstrate a rejection of God's love, raise a barrier of doubt on Adam and Eve's part before God, and thus the sweet fellowship which they had enjoyed with God would be broken. The penalty for disobedience was death. Since God was the source of life itself, real life was found only in communion with God. Furthermore, the essence of death, which is the opposite of life, is therefore separation from God.

The Hebrew translation of this penalty would more accurately be rendered "dying, thou shalt die!" Undoubtedly, this refers to spiritual death or separation from God that would immediately take place the very moment Adam and Eve broke their bond of love with God. However, physical death would also take place, since God is the source of physical life as well as spiritual life. If Adam and Eve chose to disobey God, then in that moment, the principle of physical decay and death would begin in their bodies, particularly if they were then also unable to eat of the tree of life which was also in the Garden of Eden (Genesis 3:22). Adam and Eve could continue living because of continued biological functions, but the warning was clear: if they ate of the tree of the knowledge of good and evil, they would die spiritually through separation from God, and at the same time they would begin to die physically. The day of their physical deaths would be sealed. (More on this below.)

Adam and Eve lived a unique existence at the end of Creation Week, in harmony with God and with one another. God had provided a perfect home in the Garden of Eden; a perfect job, tending and keeping the garden; and perfect, unbroken fellowship with God. They could eat the fruit of any tree in the garden, except the fruit of the tree of the knowledge of good and evil, but they had no reason to doubt that this restriction was also "good" for them. They were living in complete innocence, "both naked, the man and his wife, and…not ashamed" (Genesis 2:25). Nothing had transpired to make them feel any sense of guilt. Indeed, they had no consciousness of sin or moral guilt, and thus any sense of shame or embarrassment would have been entirely unnatural in their state of perfection. Everything was in complete harmony, including Adam and Eve's relationship with each other and with God.

It is not known exactly how long after the end of the Creation Week that circumstances changed, but the Bible introduces the next phase of human history in Genesis 3. "Now the serpent was more subtil [subtle] than any beast of the field which the LORD God had made. And he said unto the woman, Yea, hath God said, Ye shall not eat of every tree of the garden?" (Genesis 3:1). This could hardly be simply a talking snake; it was Satan himself (Revelation 12:9; 20:2). As a "beast of the field," the physical "serpent" (Hebrew *nachash*, possibly originally meaning a shining, upright creature) was clever and possibly able to stand upright, eye-to-eye with man. Its bright and beautiful coloration, and smooth and graceful movement, made it an attractive animal, so in her innocence Eve was dazzled and mesmerized by this subtly attractive and deceptive creature.

It would seem that Satan himself must have entered into the serpent's body to possess it and then use it as his means of deceiving Eve. Satan had originally been created as Lucifer, the highest of all the angels, the anointed cherub covering the very throne of God in heaven (Ezekiel 28:13-15). Exactly when Lucifer and all the other angels were created we are not told. However, Lucifer was initially perfect in his ways, but became proud of his beauty and own wisdom, attempting a rebellion against God by exalting himself (Ezekiel 28:15-17; Isaiah 14:12-15). Consequently, he and the angels that rebelled with him were expelled from heaven. Lucifer, now known as Satan, was cast to the ground (Isaiah 14:12), most likely the earth. Now, as God's enemy, he immediately sought to disrupt God's plan on earth.

It is not at all clear whether the serpent naturally had the ability to speak with man in some way, or whether it was the result of Satan possessing this beautiful creature's body and using its mouth that he was able to speak. We have no way of knowing whether other animals in the Garden of Eden were able to communicate with man in some way, but it is clear that Eve was neither startled nor surprised by this talking serpent. Remember, everything—every plant, tree, fish, reptile, and mammal—existed in perfection, and Adam and Eve had no cause to fear anything. It may simply be that Eve, in her innocence, did not yet know that the animals around her in the Garden of Eden were incapable of speaking, and so was not alarmed when the serpent spoke to her. None of this is complete speculation, because we know that great physiological changes did take place in both the animal and plant kingdoms at the time of the Curse (Genesis 3:14-19).

These considerations raise the question as to whether this passage in the Genesis record is an actual narrative of facts, or perhaps a skillful allegory, or merely a pictorial representation intended to convey some general impressions.[1]

The cardinal rule of biblical interpretation is that the Scriptures were written to be understood by ordinary people, not just scholars, and, therefore, the text should normally be taken literally unless the context indicates a non-literal meaning and also makes it clear what the true meaning is intended to be. Thus, without a doubt, the events and details recorded here are just as they actually transpired, and find support in New Testament passages such as 2 Corinthians 11:3 and 1 Timothy 2:13-15.

The approach of Satan through the serpent to Eve was clearly a masterpiece of effective deception. He caught her when she was alone without Adam to counsel and warn her, probably as she was admiring the beautiful fruit trees in the Garden. He first offered something that neither she nor Adam had even imagined before, namely, that it was possible for a creature to question the Creator: "Yea, hath God said?" In other words, Satan said, "Did God *really* say that?" Besides questioning God's truthfulness, Satan was attempting to cast suspicion upon God's goodness. The fact that Adam and Eve were barred from one tree is magnified into a grievous and very unwelcome restraint. The subtle innuendo behind Satan's question could be paraphrased: "He has not allowed you to eat the fruit of *every* tree, has He? Why do you suppose He is withholding something like that from you?" The inference is that God is not quite as good and loving as they thought, all of which is a subtle and deceitful twisting of the truth, and thus a downright lie.

Eve's response to the serpent was clearly aimed at correcting Satan. After all, God had allowed them to eat of the fruit of the trees of the garden, and it was only the one tree in the midst of the garden that was off-limits to them. However, that Eve had obviously been caught off guard is evident from her response, because her recollections of God's command were not entirely accurate. "We may eat of the fruit of the trees of the garden: But of the fruit of the tree which is in the midst of the garden, God hath said, Ye shall not eat of it, neither shall ye touch it, lest

---

1   Leupold, 1942, 140.

ye die" (Genesis 3:2-3). In her attempt to correct Satan's subtle insinuations, Eve demonstrates that his verbal maneuvering had worked its deadly effect on her. In her reply, she both added to and subtracted from God's actual words, making God seem less generous and more demanding than He really was. God had said that Adam and Eve could *freely* eat of *all* the trees, but Eve reduced God's specific instructions to "we may eat of the fruit of the trees of the garden." Furthermore, God had told Adam and Eve that they should not eat from this one tree in the midst of the garden, but Eve now added that God had supposedly said they were not to touch it. This was simply not true, because God had not said anything about touching the fruit, so they were not specifically forbidden from doing so. Why would Eve have stumbled here? Clearly, Satan was successfully distracting Eve from the simplicity of the facts, from what God had commanded the couple when He placed them in the garden (cf. 2 Corinthians 11:3).

Satan enticed Eve to question God's authority and goodness, and then to augment and dilute God's spoken words before tightening his grip on Eve's thought processes: "Ye shall not surely die: For God doth know that in the day ye eat thereof, then your eyes shall be opened, and ye shall be as gods, knowing good and evil" (Genesis 3:4-5). The fact that God had warned Adam and Eve that eating the fruit of this tree would result in death was blatantly contradicted. Satan rather suggested that God Himself was afraid they would learn too much! A masterstroke of Satan's cunningness was his insinuation that God was withholding from Adam and Eve something that would give them higher understanding and even an equality with God (something that Satan had failed to obtain in heaven). Indeed, it is true that when one denies God's Word, one is in effect claiming the right to decide truth for oneself, which is aspiring to be one's own god. Furthermore, in one sense Satan's promises were true, because in coming to know both good and evil their eyes would indeed be opened. However, the result of Satan's deceit was that they would not become gods, but simply rebellious sinners before a holy God.

Doubt gave way to pride as Eve continued to gaze at the forbidden tree, her mind and emotions now fully influenced by Satan's insinuations, deceit, and lies. The fruit of the tree blazed with appeal: "And when the woman saw that the tree was good for food, and that it was pleasant to the eyes, and a tree to be desired to make one wise, she took of the fruit thereof; and did eat" (Genesis 3:6). The deed was done. Satan's temptation not only appealed to her appetite, but to her emotions and aesthetic senses, to her mind and spirit. Pride now desired knowledge and spiritual insight.

But Eve did not stop there. She "gave also unto her husband with her; and he did eat" (Genesis 3:6). This brief account of what subsequently happened raises questions about what was happening with Adam and how he became involved. Did he come along to join Eve just after she had taken the fruit and eaten it, or had she plucked more of the fruit from the tree and found Adam to give it to him to eat also? We can't be sure. Likewise, we can't be sure whether Satan was also involved in convincing Adam to eat of the fruit or whether it was just Eve telling him about what had happened that enticed him to eat the fruit also. Either way, Adam would have been faced with the same arguments, insinuations against God, and downright deceit that Satan had used on Eve. When Adam ate the fruit, it would have been as a result of a conscious decision. And besides, he could see that having eaten the fruit, Eve had apparently not suffered any harmful effect. Eating the forbidden fruit would seem no different from eating any other fruit in the garden, adding plausibility to Satan's cunning and deceitful lies. Nevertheless, Adam was fully aware of all of God's specific instructions. Additionally, he had experienced God's marvelous provision when Eve was made out of his side to be a helper for him. His sin was deliberate, wicked, and inexcusable.

The consequences of Adam and Eve's disobedience and rebellion against God were immediate: "And the eyes of them both were opened, and they knew that they were naked; and they sewed fig leaves together, and made themselves aprons" (Genesis 3:7). God had called this tree "the tree of the knowledge of good and evil," and the eating of the tree's fruit did deliver that knowledge to them. However, instead of becoming like gods as Satan had promised, the realization of what they had done immediately became apparent to them and an awful sense of shame overpowered them. Whereas previously their innocence made them not ashamed of their nakedness, now their eyes were opened; they recognized their nakedness and were embarrassed and ashamed. They sought to cover their nakedness, attempting to cover their shame and overwhelming sense of guilt. Hastily, they sewed fig leaves together to make crude aprons. This task would have required considerable ingenuity and intelligence, that is, to sew fig leaves together without needle and thread, so Adam and Eve were hardly primitive people!

Adam and Eve may have thought they could escape God's judgment by fashioning these garments and hiding their nakedness and shame. They very quickly discovered that they could not hide from God. Indeed, we read: "And they heard the voice of the LORD God walking in the garden in the cool of the day: and Adam and his wife hid themselves from the presence of the LORD God amongst the trees of the garden. And the LORD God called unto Adam, and said unto him, Where art thou? And he said, I heard thy voice in the garden, and I was afraid, because I was naked; and I hid myself" (Genesis 3:8-10). Previously, they had enjoyed unhindered fellowship with God, who must have regularly come walking in the garden "in the cool of the day" (literally, at the time of the breeze). This time when they heard God's voice as He walked toward them, they hid themselves among the trees in the garden. The almost casual way in which this Scripture describes God walking in the garden indicates that this was a normal event rather than the first time this had happened. Perhaps this was a daily appointment when they met with God for communion and fellowship. Furthermore, this was thus no crude anthropomorphism, but a repeated appearance of the Almighty in some form analogous to the human form in order to communicate, commune, and have fellowship with Adam and Eve. How long this period of fellowship between God and Adam and Eve had lasted was not specified. It would have begun on the sixth day when God had created Adam and Eve, and now it was probably only a few days or weeks later, because Adam and Eve had not yet had any children. Even though Adam and Eve had been instructed by God to be fruitful and multiply (Genesis 1:28), it wasn't until after these events in the Garden of Eden that Eve conceived a child (Genesis 4:1).

The attempt by Adam and Eve to hide from God was foolish. Coming out of hiding, Adam offered a weak excuse that he was hiding because of his nakedness. Of course, this had never been a problem before. Now he was acutely conscious of being naked in God's presence due to the sense of shame and guilt of flouting God's specific instruction. Sin had completely destroyed his innocence. When Adam mentioned his nakedness to God, he was in effect admitting his sinful disobedience. God, therefore, immediately asked him how he had discovered his nakedness and whether he had eaten of the one forbidden tree (Genesis 3:11). Because of God's love and mercy, these questions would have been asked by God in order to give Adam the opportunity to confess his sin and to ask forgiveness. Sadly, the effects of sin had so rapidly permeated the hearts of both Adam and Eve that they did not confess. Instead, without a moment's hesitation, and almost instinctively, Adam blamed his wife, and then Eve blamed the serpent (Genesis 3:12-13). Neither was willing to acknowledge their personal guilt. In fact, Adam, by implication, had the audacity to cast the blame on God Himself, emphasizing that it was after all because of "the woman whom thou gavest to be with me."

Of course, God's questions were not designed to obtain information, because He already knew what Adam and Eve had done. Rather, He was endeavoring to encourage Adam and Eve to acknowledge and repent of their disobedience and sin. Their responses to God's questions clearly indicated that they were only sorry they had been discovered. Although they would obviously have been fearful of the consequences of their actions, the record God has given us of this event shows no indication of true repentance on the part of Adam and Eve, only attempts to justify themselves. Their feeble excuses—given in a cowardly fashion, avoiding any admission of guilt, followed then with the vile attempt to blame God—were not worthy even of refutation or defense on God's part. Without confession and repentance, there was no other course of action God could have taken. He now moved to initiate punishment, not only for just retribution and correction, but also to show mercy by foreshadowing His provision of redemption.

39

THE CURSE

Man's fall from his created state of innocence to a state of disobedience and rebellion against God—a pivotal event in the course of earth history—could only result in an equally pivotal effect upon not only Adam and Eve, but their descendants and the whole of the earth itself. What is commonly called the Curse represents the various curses God placed on all of His creation because of what Adam and Eve had done. These are described in Genesis 3:14-19 and include the Curse on the animal kingdom, the Curse on the serpent, the special curse on Eve and all women descended from her, the Curse on Adam and his descendants, and the Curse on the very elements of the ground itself.

First, the serpent, as an animal, was cursed "above all cattle, and above every beast of the field," not because of direct culpability on its part, but rather as a perpetual reminder to man that it had been the instrument of his downfall and that Satan himself will ultimately be destroyed. Whatever may have been the serpent's beauty and posture before Satan used it to tempt Eve, henceforth it would glide on its belly and be an object of dread and loathing. It is unclear whether it is meant that the serpent would literally eat dust. It is more likely to be referring to the fact that the serpent would have to eat its prey directly off the ground in front of it because snakes do not eat dust, even though their tongues do sense the environment around them. Furthermore, it would certainly mean humiliation, since the expression "eat dust" would seem identical to the expression "lick dust" elsewhere in Scripture (Micah 7:17; Isaiah 49:23; Psalm 72:9), where in every case it means to be humbled or to suffer defeat. This is a graphic figure of speech indicating the humiliation of continual defeat throughout its existence, in addition to the humiliation of its mode of locomotion. Of course, the serpent, as an animal, was not to be blamed for Satan's apparent corrupt possession of its body, yet God was not unjust in His punishment, because all the other animals were also brought under the Curse at this time, though none of them had "sinned" either.

The serpent was merely cursed "above all" the rest, but every beast henceforth was cursed with the sentence of death, all due to Adam and Eve's sin. Man had been given dominion over all of creation and, therefore, he bore the responsibility for overseeing it and caring for it on behalf of God. When man failed, the consequences of his sin not only brought punishment upon himself, but upon his dominion—the creation. Adam had been appointed to exercise dominion over the earth, and since he was to begin to die, his dominion also would begin to die. "For the creature was made subject to vanity, not willingly, but by reason of him who hath subjected the same in hope, Because the creature itself also shall be delivered from the bondage of corruption into the glorious liberty of the children of God. For we know that the whole creation groaneth and travaileth in pain together until now" (Romans 8:20-22). God was not being capricious, for it was Adam and Eve who were responsible by their rebellion for bringing the bondage of corruption or decay on all of the creation, and thus all of the animals were made subject to the same futility.

It must also be noted that if indeed the serpent had used a different means of locomotion prior to this curse (as may be suggested by the possibility of the Hebrew word for serpent, *nachash,* originally meaning "shining, upright creature"), then the result of this curse in consigning the serpent to slither on its belly across the ground implies that notable biological changes likely occurred within the serpent. These would have included genetic changes so that its descendants would also henceforth slither on their bellies. While this is only an inference from the text, certainly if God chose to make design and genetic changes to the serpent, He was, as the Creator, fully capable of doing so. Furthermore, if He did so to the serpent with this curse, then He could have done so to other animals as part of the Curse on them as well.

Though the first part of the Curse was outwardly pronounced on the serpent, God next directed the Curse towards Satan, who was controlling the serpent's body and speech. By persuading Adam and Eve to follow his word instead of God's word, Satan had probably convinced himself that if he won their allegiance, they (and thus also their descendants) would be his allies in his continuing rebellion against God. Also, Eve had already demonstrated an ability to influence Adam, who had eaten the forbidden fruit when she gave it to him. Thus, with Adam and Eve under his control, their dominion over the earth now became his, which now made Satan the "god of this world" (2 Corinthians 4:4).

However, if Satan had thought he had won this round in his fight against God, then he had deceived himself, because God was going to make sure Eve and her descendants would not become his willing allies. "I will put enmity between thee and the woman," God said to Satan. Neither would Eve rule over her husband, because God told her, "Thy desire shall be to thy husband, and he shall rule over thee." Furthermore, conception and childbirth would not be easy and rapid, for God said to Eve, "I will greatly multiply thy sorrow and thy conception; in sorrow thou shalt bring forth children" (Genesis 3:15-16). Thus, Eve specifically was also the subject of the Curse. Pain and sorrow would be "greatly multiplied" in conception and childbirth. Since Eve was to be the "mother of all living" (Genesis 3:20), her children in the generations to come would also suffer under the Curse, their very entrance into the world being marked by unique suffering that would serve as a perpetual reminder of the awful effects of her sin. And because she had acted independently of her husband in her fateful decision to eat the forbidden fruit, Eve would henceforth exercise her desire only to her husband, who would rule over her. Sadly, throughout human history men have subjugated and humiliated women with little regard for their personal feelings and needs, yet God in His judgment on Eve did not cancel the "one flesh" relationship in marriage (Genesis 2:21-24). In other words, Eve's equality was not being taken away from her; this curse simply required submission on her part and loving leadership on the part of her husband (Ephesians 5:22-33; 1 Peter 3:1-7; and other Bible passages).

However, God also declared that ultimately Satan would be completely defeated and destroyed. "I will put enmity…between thy seed and her seed; it shall bruise thy head, and thou shalt bruise his heel" (Genesis 3:15). The "seed" of the woman would appear at first glance to be referring to her descendants (plural), but God stipulated an individual by using the singular ("it" and "his") when referring to "her seed." Thus, God was promising that there would come an individual descendant of Eve who would do battle with Satan, and even though Satan would succeed in grievously, but not fatally, injuring him ("bruise his heel"), this individual would completely crush Satan ("bruise thy head"). To crush Satan, the powerful fallen angel, would require more than just an ordinary man. By defeating Satan, this promised one would save Adam and Eve's descendants from Satan's grip. Furthermore, this promised redeemer could only be the seed of the woman, and thus, though born of a woman, could not be the seed of the man (but rather, "her seed"). The promised redeemer can, of course, only be the Lord Jesus Christ, who though He appeared to be mortally wounded when He died on the cross, nevertheless rose again to both defeat Satan and conquer death, which was the punishment for disobedience and sin as stipulated by God. He would be born to a virgin, as also prophesied in Isaiah 7:14, and would die in Adam's place for his sin, and thus also for all of Adam's descendants and their sin. "For as in Adam all die, even so in Christ shall all be made alive" (1 Corinthians 15:22). This was indeed good news!

Nevertheless, the full force of this curse would fall on Adam, and would include all his descendants (even Eve who was "of" him), as well as his entire dominion, which was the earth: "cursed is the ground [the same Hebrew word *eretz* which can also be translated "earth"] for thy sake," said God to Adam (Genesis 3:17). Even the "dust of the earth," the very elements out of which all things had been made, was brought into bondage to decay and disintegration. The ground which had previously cooperated readily as man cultivated it (Genesis 2:5, 15) now would become reluctant to yield his food. Instead, the earth would begin to yield thorns and thistles (noxious weeds), which would require toil, sweat, and tears before man could "eat of it" (Genesis 3:17-19). And then finally, in spite of all his struggle, death would triumph over man's life and his body would return to the dust from which it was taken.

It does not seem likely that God would have created thorns, thistles, and other noxious weeds as a result of His cursing the ground. The only hint that God could have formed the thorns and the thistles is the use of the expression "bring forth," which is parallel to God's command on the third day of the Creation Week for the earth to "bring forth" the plants (Genesis 1:11). However, since God clearly announced at the end of the sixth day that He had finished all His work of creating, it is questionable whether the use of this same expression "bring forth" here does mean an act of creation was involved with the thorns and thistles. Perhaps all we can infer is that as God evidently caused changes in the serpent as a result of His curse on it, God also caused changes to occur in some of the plants, that is, mutational changes that now made them noxious weeds. This may simply have involved God "allowing" certain plant structures, which previously were beneficial, to deteriorate into malevolent characteristics. Quite obviously, that deterioration would have had to have been very rapid at first, so as to become noxious and make the ground less productive for Adam. If this deterioration process was in the form of random changes in the molecular structure of the genetic systems, otherwise known as mutations, then the deterioration could have subsequently tapered off into a much more gradual process. On the other hand, God may have simply flipped some "genetic switches" present in His original design that caused these changes to appear immediately.

Furthermore, if God used such genetic switches to cause physical changes in some plants in response to the Curse, then it would seem reasonable that He caused similar changes in the animals. Thus, we could speculate that if smoothly rounded structures in plants were transformed to produce thorns, then perhaps teeth in the mouths and nails on the feet of animals designed for a herbivorous diet transformed into fangs and claws respectively, which in combination with a dietary deficiency of proteins and other essentials, rapidly generated carnivorous appetites in certain animals. Similarly, it is possible that bacteria and other microorganisms designed originally to serve essential functions in soil maintenance and supply nutrients, etc., also underwent genetic changes, which in many cases proved harmful and even lethal to other organisms that might eat them, as well as reducing the productive efficiency of the soil. This in turn would have made it harder for Adam to cultivate the soil and produce his food, which God said would be the net result of the Curse. As a result of such genetic changes, some organisms may have developed their current parasitic behavior. In other words, it would appear from the biblical data that whereas God had pronounced everything at the end of the Creation Week as "very good," now, as a result of the Curse, all the ecological imbalances and threats to health that we currently experience came into being either immediately after it was pronounced by God or subsequently to His pronouncement.

It should be noted that in pronouncing the Curse as a punishment on man, and as a consequence on the whole of creation, God was in fact acting in mercy. He declared that the Curse on the ground was for man's sake (Genesis 3:17). It was no longer fitting that an imperfect man dwell in the midst of a perfect dwelling place, and therefore it was entirely reasonable that man's outward circumstances be made to correspond to his inward state. It would be better for suffering and death to accompany sin than for rebellion to be permitted to thrive unchecked in a "very good" world. Without death, men would have proliferated in number and thus wickedness would grow without limits or boundaries. Presumably, the same would be true of the animals and plants, particularly as far as their numbers were concerned, but there was also the potential for man to use them in the pursuit of his rebellion and wickedness. Thus, God pronounced the Curse on man and on his whole environment. This would force him to recognize the serious consequences of his sin, as well as his helplessness to save himself and his dominion from the ravages of decay and death. The necessity of hard work just to keep alive would thus inhibit further rebellion and, of course, reinforce in his mind that Satan's tempting promises were all lies. Since Adam and Eve had been reluctant to repent and seek forgiveness, these conditions would now encourage repentance and a turning to God for deliverance from the wretched state in which they now had to labor for survival. Likewise, in the animal and plant kingdoms limitless proliferation would be kept in check by new factors of disease, predation, parasitism, and so on. Thus, the entire creation "was made subject to vanity" (Romans 8:20).

It should be noted that the Curse on man himself was fourfold: (1) sorrow, resulting from continual disappointment and futility; (2) pain and suffering, signified by the thorns that intermittently hinder man in his efforts to provide for his family; (3) sweat or tears, resulting from the intense struggle against a hostile environment; and finally (4) physical death, which would eventually triumph over all of man's efforts, with his physical body returning to the simple elements of the earth in the dust of the ground.

Though spoken to Adam and Eve, the pronouncement of the Curse was not addressed to them merely as individuals but as progenitors of the human race, as is amply demonstrated by experience not long after this event. Indeed, all the descendants of Adam and Eve have found themselves suffering the same consequences. Nevertheless, suffering and death are not due to blind fate, but to human rebellion and guilt. Divine punishment explains man's lot, but it was consequent to man's disobedience. Therefore, man is ultimately responsible for the harsh world with which he struggles.

However severe God's punishment may seem, it cannot be emphasized enough that in satisfying His justice, God exercised great mercy. This included God's necessary provision for man's physical well-being. Adam and Eve's self-made fig leaf aprons were entirely inadequate, so God graciously provided a covering for their nakedness by making "coats of skin" to clothe them (Genesis 3:21). By so doing, God acknowledged the sense of shame that had led Adam and Eve to cover their nakedness. Perhaps they silently, and sorrowfully, watched as God selected animals and slew them there, thus shedding innocent blood before their eyes, learning that a suitable and durable covering (or "coats," Hebrew *koot-o'-neth*, from the root meaning to "cover," compared to the atonement, Hebrew *kippur* or *kaphar*, to "cover") for sin could only be provided by God and through the shedding of blood, which is the life of the flesh (Leviticus 17:11). Since the slaying of the animals for man's need was thus sanctioned by God, this may have been where God instituted animal sacrifices, teaching Adam and Eve that the deaths of the animals were substitutes for them because of their sin. Whether these garments provided by God from the animal skins were actually coats or just tunics, this reveals God's standard for adequate clothing to cover man's nakedness, a standard that has nowhere in the Scriptures been revoked by God.

Now once more a divine council was held by the three Persons of the Godhead (Genesis 3:22). They recognized that man had "become as one of us, to know good and evil." This is a sad statement for God to have made, for man had once known only His goodness, but now he had come to know, by experiment and experience, the evil inherent in rejecting God's word, including the resultant spiritual and physical suffering.

God also announced the decision of the divine council to drive Adam and Eve from the Garden of Eden, "lest he put forth his hand, and take also of the tree of life, and eat, and live for ever" (Genesis 3:22). The Scriptures do not describe for us the tree of life, or its fruit, or by what medicinal powers it enabled its eater to continue living indefinitely in perfect health, but God had the power to endow it with this capacity and His own testimony is that He did so. The existence of this tree of life in the Garden of Eden implies that while Adam and Eve were in the garden eating of its fruit, they would have lived forever. Thus, in order to carry out His punishment of the Curse of physical death upon Adam and Eve and their descendants, God chose to prevent Adam and Eve from eating the fruit from the tree of life, removing them from the Garden of Eden altogether. It would have been calamitous had they continued in a perfect environment as sinful people, eating of the tree of life and living indefinitely in such a condition.

Perhaps Adam and Eve were repentant after God had pronounced the Curse, when they realized they had disobeyed God and couldn't escape the consequences, as well as the fact that they had been deceived by Satan. We are not told. However, understandably, they were probably reluctant to leave their garden home and face an unknown and harsh world outside. They also may have feared they would never see God again, since the garden was the only place they had fellowshipped with Him. Furthermore, the prospect of now having to till the ground outside the garden, to obtain their bread by the sweat of their brow, was quite obviously not a pleasant prospect in comparison to freely eating all the fruit of the trees in the garden. They probably hesitated at God's command to leave. At any rate, the Scripture states, "he drove out the man" (Genesis 3:24) and his wife from the garden.

God also ensured that they would stay out by placing at the east of the garden cherubim, described as having flaming swords which turned every way (Genesis 3:24), evidently involving sword-like flames flashing around them like lightning bolts. These cherubim, from the descriptions given in Ezekiel 1:4-28, 10:1-22, and Revelation 4:6-8, are the highest in the hierarchy of angels, and God placed them at the entrance of the Garden of Eden so as to guard the way to the tree of life. As cherubim are always associated closely with the throne of God, it is likely that God's presence was particularly manifest at the tree of life.

How long the Garden of Eden continued to exist after this we are not told. Perhaps Adam and Eve did return at intervals to the entrance of the garden to meet with God there. Eventually, the Garden of Eden, or its remnant, would have been washed away by the Flood. However, we are told that the tree of life still exists "in the midst of the paradise of God" (Revelation 2:7) and will be beside the river proceeding out of the throne of God on the new earth where the Curse has been removed (Revelation 22:1-2).

40

THE PRE-FLOOD WORLD

In a world now subject to the Curse, Genesis 4:1-2 describes the next phase in earth's history: "Adam knew Eve his wife; and she conceived, and bare Cain, and said, I have gotten a man from the LORD. And she again bare his brother Abel. And Abel was a keeper of sheep, but Cain was a tiller of the ground." While there is no indication of time between banishment from the garden to Eve's conception, it likely was not long, perhaps only a matter of days or weeks at most. God had commanded Adam and Eve to "be fruitful and multiply," and in their initial state of fellowship and obedience they would have set about immediately to follow this command, now likely more inclined to obey God right away.

When Cain was born, Eve exclaimed, "I have gotten a man from the LORD" (Cain literally means "acquisition"). God had promised Eve that she would bear children, and no doubt the birth of Cain, her firstborn, was a sign of hope to her and Adam. God had also promised redemption from the Curse through her "seed," but she had no way of knowing when that event would take place. It would not be unreasonable to assume that she placed a certain amount of that hope in Cain, at least until Abel was born. She must have wondered which of her boys would become that deliverer. Only the years would reveal the truth to her. However, her testimony of praise to God at Cain's birth gives proof that in spite of her sin, Eve still believed and trusted in God and His promises. Though she had now experienced the pain associated with childbirth as pronounced by God in the Curse, she had also seen God's faithfulness in allowing her to fulfill His primary command to be fruitful and multiply.

Again, the timeframe is unknown, but Eve conceived again and bore another son, Abel. As the boys grew, Cain became a farmer producing vegetables and fruit for the family's food, while Abel became a shepherd, no doubt providing clothing for the family. There is no suggestion here of the animals being used for food, because man was not authorized to do so until after the Flood (Genesis 9:3). Rather, the animals would have, in addition, been used for sacrifices, as indicated by Abel bringing the "firstlings of his flock and of the fat thereof" as an offering unto the Lord (Genesis 4:4). The fact that both Cain and Abel knew to bring sacrifices to the Lord indicates that they had been so instructed by their parents. It also reinforces the inference that when God killed the animals to provide coats of skin to clothe Adam and Eve that He had instructed them in the necessity of bringing a sacrifice, so that the shedding of the blood of the animal would be a covering (atonement) for their sin.

The Scriptures here do not actually say, specifically, whether such sacrifices had been commanded by God, but it would be difficult otherwise to understand why God was not pleased with Cain's offering of the fruit of the ground compared with Abel's slain lamb, as found in Genesis 4:3-5. This entire episode can really only be understood if God had originally given instructions on the necessity of a substitutionary animal sacrifice as a prerequisite to approaching Him. It is clear that Cain's actions were disobedient. All of this adds weight to the speculation that the appointed place of approaching God could well have been at the entrance to the garden, where the cherubim guarded the way to the tree of life and God's presence there. It would seem closely parallel to the mercy seat on the Ark of the Covenant in the Holy of Holies in the tabernacle, which was overshadowed by two golden representations of the cherubim (Exodus 25:17-22 and Hebrews 9:3-5).

Cain was bitter and resentful when his offering of produce was not respected by God while Abel's offering of a lamb was accepted. As a result, we read that out of anger, Cain murdered his brother Abel (Genesis 4:5-8). But again, sin produced consequences, in this case additional curses on Cain. The ground would no longer yield its produce to him, and he would wander the earth as a fugitive, away from the presence of the Lord (Genesis 4:9-15). Driven away from the Lord, from Eden, and from his parents, Cain traveled eastward into a region that came to be known as "Nod" (Genesis 4:16), which means "wandering." However, Cain did not go alone; he took his wife.

This is the first mention of anyone else apart from Adam, Eve, Cain, and Abel. Some Bible scholars have wildly suggested that God must have originally made other people besides Adam and Eve from whose descendants Cain obtained his wife. However, as we have already noted, Eve's name was given to her by Adam "because she was the mother of all living" (Genesis 3:20). Furthermore, in Genesis 5:4 we are told that Adam and Eve had sons and daughters in addition to Cain, Abel, and Seth, the only children specifically named. Since Adam lived 930 years (Genesis 5:5), many children could have been born, especially in light of God's command to be fruitful and multiply. There is no reason why after Cain and Abel were born that Adam and Eve did not also have many daughters, one of whom became Cain's wife.

Initially, there would not have been any problems with brother-sister marriages, because Adam and Eve's children would have few, if any, mutant genes, and thus no genetic harm could have resulted from such marriages. God's blueprint for marriage was one man and one woman for life, so at this stage in history a brother-sister marriage still followed that pattern. However, many generations later, during the time of Moses when God knew that the accumulated mutations were now genetically dangerous in close marriages, He prohibited such unions in the Mosaic laws and this became an ongoing standard. Thus, it is perfectly logical, and totally reasonable, both biblically and scientifically, to assume that Cain married one of his sisters.

Cain resided long enough in the one location to build a city. We are told "he builded a city" and named it after his son, Enoch, to whom his wife had given birth (Genesis 4:17). Rather than trying to defy God's prophecy that he would be a wanderer, the Hebrew verb here should be rendered "was building," probably suggesting that though he may have started the building work, he may not have finished it. Perhaps Cain moved on, leaving his son Enoch to complete the job of building this city that was named after him. Some suggest there weren't enough people to inhabit a city. Again it should be remembered that Adam and Eve had many sons and daughters, who obviously married one another and in turn had many more children. As we are not told how old Cain was when he murdered Abel, became a wanderer, and then built this city, it is entirely reasonable to suggest that some of his brothers and sisters and their families may have migrated with Cain and his wife away from Adam and Eve and their other brothers and sisters. This could have resulted from the upheaval, anger, and recriminations that must have occurred due to the tragedy of Abel's murder. Under these circumstances, it is to be expected that when Cain began building the city, his brothers and sisters and their families joined him, thus establishing a large enough number of dwellings for it to be identified as a city.

From the details provided about Cain's descendants in Genesis 4:18-24, we find further evidence of the development of technology in the pre-Flood world. Not only did Cain and his contemporaries build a city, but in the sixth generation descended from Cain, the record highlights Jabal and his family, who dwelt in tents and herded; Jubal and his family, who were musicians skilled in playing "the harp and organ" (literally, the lyre and pipes); and Tubal-cain, who was an instructor of craftsmen working in brass and iron (literally, Tubal the smith, the hammerer of every cutting device of bronze and iron). The use of such metals indicates that technology had advanced to the stage where metal ores were mined and the metals smelted. Thus, the pre-Flood people enjoyed a high standard of living, with metallurgy and metal-working technology providing all manner of cutting instruments and utensils, and support for music and more aesthetic pursuits allowing inventive genius to develop both stringed and wind musical instruments. All these developments, including agriculture, animal domestication, urbanization, and metallurgy, flourished within six generations after Adam and Eve's expulsion from the Garden of Eden in a matter of 500 to 600 years, while Adam was still living.

The history of Adam's family and the list of his descendants until the time of Noah and the Flood are provided for us in Genesis 5: "This is the book of the generations of Adam" (v. 1). The Hebrew word translated "book" is *cépher*, which refers to any document, long or short, as long as it is complete in itself. In other words, this record was originally a written document. That Adam could have kept written records is totally reasonable in the light of his ability to name the animals in the Garden of Eden within a few hours on the sixth day of Creation Week, and in the light of his descendants building cities, inventing musical instruments, mining, smelting, and metal-working. Thus, this chapter of Genesis reads as a sober, reliable account of the family history.

Adam was 130 years old when his son Seth was born as a designated replacement for Abel, whom Cain had murdered. Adam then lived a further 800 years, during which time many more sons and daughters were born, so that he lived for a total of 930 years (Genesis 5:3-5). Then follows a repetitive and cyclical listing of all pre-Flood patriarchs in the lineage from Adam through Seth to Noah—their names, their ages at the birth of those sons who continued faithful in worship of God and who were thus in the godly line of promise, the fact that each had sons and daughters, and finally their ages at death. There were ten of these patriarchs. The data provided in Genesis 5 is summarized in the following table:

Patriarch	Year of Birth	Age at Birth of Next Patriarch	Total Age	Year of Death
Adam	1	130	930	930
Seth	130	105	912	1042
Enos	235	90	905	1140
Cainan (Kenan)	325	70	910	1235
Mahalaleel	395	65	895	1290
Jared (Zared)	460	162	962	1422
Enoch	622	65	365*	987*
Methuselah	687	187	969	1656**
Lamech	874	182	777	1651
Noah	1056	500	950	2006

*Enoch did not die but was translated and taken to heaven by God.
**Methuselah died in the very year that the Flood came.

There is absolutely no reason to assume the existence of gaps in this record, or that the years are anything other than normal years (except for the likelihood that the original year was only 360 days long, as discussed previously). The record given is perfectly natural and straightforward, obviously intending to give both the necessary genealogical data and a reliable chronological framework for the pre-Flood period of history. The Hebrew construction of the record is an exact genealogical formula that signifies a father-son relationship and not just a general line of descent that could allow for gaps. In any case, any argument about the authenticity of this genealogical record is conclusively settled by the fact that the names of all these patriarchs are repeated in the correct order in 1 Chronicles 1:1-4 and Luke 3:36-38. Thus, assuming no gaps in these genealogies, there was a total of 1,656 years from creation to the Flood. The recorded lifespans of the patriarchs are somewhat larger in the Septuagint and certain other ancient versions of the Scriptures, but most scholars believe these have been somewhat artificially elongated and that the Masoretic text preserves the original numbers. The account is written and ordered as a complete chronology—marking the actual lapse of time. Any "claim that the Scriptures do not give a complete and accurate chronology for the whole period of the Old Testament that they cover is utterly wrong, dangerous, and mischievous."[1]

Assuming the numerical data are both literal and absolutely reliable, it is interesting to note that Adam lived until Lamech, the eighth generation of his descendants and the father of Noah. Lamech was 56 years old when Adam died, and Noah was born only 14 years after the death of Seth. Thus, the preservation of the written family history and any other oral instructions for the preserving and promulgating of God's Word would have been guaranteed, since Adam would have been able to hand them directly to Lamech, who then would have passed them on to Noah, who would then have preserved them through the Flood. Lamech died five years before the Flood and Methuselah (whose name means "when he dies, judgment") died in the year of the Flood. That means that all of the godly patriarchs died by the time the Flood came and thus did not face the judgment of the Flood, as did the ungodly descendants of Cain. Since both Enoch and Lamech were outlived by their fathers, there were only seven men in the line before Noah who had primary responsibility for preaching God's Word to their contemporaries. The accuracy of the Scriptures is exemplified in 2 Peter 2:5, where Noah is called "the eighth person, a preacher of righteousness" in the "old world."

The lifespans of these patriarchs, discounting Enoch, averaged 912 years. As astounding as this might seem, it is not entirely unreasonable, given that the world before the Flood was very different from the world in which we now live (2 Peter 3:5-7). There are observations that suggest that there was only one supercontinental landmass prior to the Flood, perhaps with a gentler topography and mountain ranges of lower elevations than in the present world. In a congenial mild-to-warm climate, there could have been lush vegetation and abundant animal life all over that supercontinental landmass. The volume of plants and animals fossilized in the geologic record would seem to support this contention. With nutrient-rich soils, these pre-Flood patriarchs and their families would have enjoyed very healthy lives, particularly if much of the harmful cosmic radiation that we now experience was not experienced at that time. If we compare the lifespans of the post-Flood patriarchs, as recorded in Genesis 11:10-32, with the lifespans of the pre-Flood patriarchs in Genesis 5, it is immediately evident that

---

1   Leupold, 1942, 238.

after the Flood there was a rapid and steady decline in lifespans, which may in large part be connected to the changed post-Flood climatic and environmental conditions.

However, the most likely explanation for this rapid decline from the longer lifespans before the Flood is a large amount of ionizing radiation and consequent genetic mutation during and after the Flood. As will be discussed in later chapters, there is considerable evidence that nuclear decay rates were extremely high during the Flood cataclysm. Even though water is a good shield against such radiation and thus Noah, his family, and the animals on board the Ark would have been afforded considerable protection because of the water between the Ark and the radioactive crustal rocks, nevertheless this protection would not have been perfect. Moreover, it is possible that radiation levels continued to be elevated relative to those of today for the first few centuries after the Flood. The accumulating genetic damage, or "genetic load," would have had a profound effect on human and animal lifespans. On the other hand, the pre-Flood patriarchs, as the immediate descendants of Adam and Eve who were created with pure genetics, would have had very few mutant genes. The plausibility of this human longevity is also seen in the details of how old these patriarchs were when their first children were born, which is an indication of when they reached adulthood. Their long timespans from birth to maturity are in the same proportion to the same average timespans in the present population, where the time to maturity is much shorter, but so are lifespans. Furthermore, the Flood was clearly what is known as a "genetic bottleneck." Only a subset of the genetic variation found in the human population in the pre-Flood world survived in the eight people in the Ark. In the small population immediately after the Flood, with individuals marrying close relatives, the resulting higher expression of recessive mutations accentuates the impact of the increasing genetic load. Although changed environmental conditions after the Flood certainly played some role in lifespans, it seems likely that a dramatic increase in the frequency of mutated genes in the human population played the leading role in the decline in lifespans. Thus, there is nothing mythological in these genealogical records in the Scriptures as compared to the totally unbelievable lifespans recorded in the well-known Babylonian list of its first ten kings, lifespans said to have reached up to 65,000 years![2]

Another pre-Flood earth condition was possibly the existence of one supercontinental landmass. The argument for this is based on the command by God on the third day of creation: "Let the waters under the heaven be gathered together unto one place, and let the dry land appear" (Genesis 1:9). It might possibly be inferred from this that if the waters were gathered together into one place to form the seas, the land might also have been in one place as a vast supercontinental landmass. This is only a speculative inference from the Scriptures, so we should not be dogmatic, but the possibility is not unreasonable.

---

2   C. Wilson and B. Wilson, 1997, *The Bible Comes Alive: A Pictorial Journey Through the Book of Books*, vol. 1, Adam to Joseph, Green Forest, AR: New Leaf Press, 41-42.

However, the Scriptures do supply some details concerning the pre-Flood water cycle. In Genesis 2:5-6, the text states that before man was created to till the ground, and before even the plants were created to grow across the surface of the earth, God had not caused it to rain, but instead a mist rose from the earth and spread across the face of the ground to water it. There has been some debate about this. One thought is that this Scripture implies that there was no rainfall upon the earth right through the pre-Flood era. This would have been due to some sort of greenhouse effect that inhibited normal rainfall. The greenhouse effect would maintain an approximately uniform temperature worldwide, with no great airmass movements capable of carrying clouds to precipitate rainfall. The other view of the phrase "for the Lord God had not caused it to rain upon the earth" is that it does not imply that the there was no rainfall during the 1,656 years between creation and the Flood. It would seem that the most reasonable understanding of this clause is that there hadn't been any rain on the earth until this time during the third day of the Creation Week, before the plants had been created. Rain subsequently fell upon the earth and did so all through the pre-Flood era. (The relevance of the rainbow in Genesis 9:8-17 to this view will be discussed later.)

However, while there was no rainfall at this early stage of the Creation Week, there was nevertheless a mist which watered the ground. The Hebrew word here is *'ed,* which is correctly translated as a mist in the sense of a fog or vapor.[3] Translators of the Septuagint guessed at the meaning of this difficult word and translated it as "spring," and this translation is consistent with the etymology of the word from Sumerian/Akkadian, with the connotation of ground water feeding the spring.[4] However, because the singular is used for the word, it is hardly likely that one spring would water "the whole face of the ground" across the earth. On Day Three of the Creation Week, when the landmass rose from under the original global ocean (literally, compacted out of the water and made to stand up above the water, according to 2 Peter 3:5), it is reasonable to infer that the ground of the newly-emerged landmass would be saturated with water, and the soils and many of the rock strata below would be fully charged with ground water. Under these circumstances, with the change in temperatures between daytime and nighttime, there would be continuous evaporation daily, and then condensation as dew and fog (mist) in the evening or morning. Such an effect would occur right across the earth's land surface and thus "the whole face of the ground" would be "watered."

This water cycle situation contrasts to God's provision in the Garden of Eden. "And a river went out of Eden to water the garden; and from thence it was parted, and became into four heads" (Genesis 2:10). It is not clear whether the source of

---

3   J. Strong, *A Concise Dictionary of the Words in the Hebrew Bible with their Renderings in the Authorized English Version,* McLean, VA: MacDonald Publishing Company, entry no. 108.

4   Wenham, 1987, 58.

the river was just within the Garden of Eden or just outside of it. However, the river flowed through the garden to water it. The water flow must have been very large, because after traversing the garden it separated into four "distributaries," each of which was itself a long and large river. Of course, those four rivers must then have emptied into the pre-Flood seas. Since nothing more is said about the daily mist watering the ground, it is unclear whether the daily cycle producing the mist was still operating, additionally to these rivers coming out of Eden. In any case, the text of Scripture does not describe the source of the water, which must have been prodigious to supply four large rivers. Even if there was regular rainfall, it would seem far more likely to assume that this mighty river with four distributaries had its source in a spring.

To explain a large spring with such a voluminous output does not require subterranean reservoirs in the form of huge caverns and chambers connected by channels, as some previous writers have suggested. On the contrary, even in Australia's Great Artesian Basin today, natural artesian springs are known to produce copious flows of water which then flow in channels, like rivers, great distances to water the ground. This artesian water is originally rain falling in Australia's eastern highlands close to the eastern seaboard. As the water percolates down into porous sedimentary rocks, it flows downhill across the basin, then emerges again where the ground surface has eroded down to the aquifer. A somewhat comparable situation could well have existed in the pre-Flood world when the rock strata formed as the pre-Flood landmass was uplifted from under the global ocean and would have been saturated in ground water. Where strata were tilted, the ground water in them would flow downhill and could thus be released at lower elevations to springs. Any pre-Flood rainfall in upland areas would then recharge aquifers and hydraulic gradients to ensure continued discharge of the springs. Thus, there is an entirely reasonable model for the spring which fed the large river flowing through Eden, a model that does not require any geological configurations for a water cycle that is different from the one found in the present post-Flood world.

The names of the four distributary rivers are given in the text, along with the geographical regions they flowed through. The four rivers were the Pison, the Gihon, the Hiddekel, and the Euphrates. In Assyrian monuments, Hiddekel is the name given to the Tigris River. Therefore, scholars have traditionally believed the Garden of Eden was located somewhere in the Mesopotamian region. They try to identify the Gihon as possibly the Nile River and the Pison as either the Ganges or Indus Rivers. However, such identifications are futile, as these pre-Flood rivers and the Garden of Eden would have been destroyed and washed away, and the topography and geography entirely changed, by the globe-encircling waters of the Flood. Nevertheless, because the text of Scripture in Genesis 2:10-14 mentions both the land of Ethiopia and Assyria, which were post-Flood geographical regions, many scholars still insist that these same geographical regions and these four rivers were the same in both the pre-Flood and post-Flood world. This is a convenient argument used to downgrade the geographical extent and devastation caused by the Flood. However, the description given in Genesis 2:10-14 provides many details that are totally inconsistent with the present post-Flood geography.

The most obvious is that the present Tigris and Euphrates Rivers do not have a common source in a river that starts from springs and then divides into these four rivers. The Pison is described as encircling the whole land of Havilah, which is of uncertain geography and may or may not be identified with Arabia in the post-Flood world. The Gihon is described as encircling the land of Ethiopia, but neither the Indus, the Ganges, nor the Nile encircle these lands, nor do they have the same source as the Tigris and Euphrates. Furthermore, the Tigris (Hiddekel) is described as going eastward of Assyria, whereas the Tigris of known history flows within Assyria. Thus, it is evident that the geography described in these verses does not exist in the present world, nor has it ever existed since the Flood. The rivers and countries described were pre-Flood geographical features familiar to Adam, who was the original recorder of this part of the narrative, and to his contemporaries and descendants.

It is obvious, therefore, that those names and geographical features known in the present post-Flood world (Ethiopia, Assyria, Tigris, Euphrates) were originally pre-Flood names and geographical features known to Noah and his sons before they entered the Ark. When these survivors of the Flood disembarked from the Ark after the Flood and ventured into the post-Flood world, they would have assigned those same names to places and geographical features in the post-Flood world, perhaps where and when the places and features somehow reminded them of the pre-Flood world. An obvious analogy is what happened when explorers and settlers left the "old world" of Europe to settle and explore the "new world" of North America and elsewhere. They gave names to places and geographical features in the "new world" which reminded them of places and geographical features in the "old world." Thus, it needs to be reiterated that those who have placed the Garden of Eden in the present Tigris-Euphrates region have ignored important details in the text. They have failed to realize that these pre-Flood rivers would have been completely obliterated by the Flood and have no physical connection whatsoever with their namesakes in the present world.

The river which flowed through the Garden of Eden originated from voluminous outpourings of a spring which split into four large distributary rivers outside of Eden. It is not unreasonable to expect that some of the other rivers in the pre-Flood world originated the same way. The Garden of Eden was a special place prepared by God as a home for Adam and Eve. Its particular river system was designed by God to enhance its beauty and to water it. However, this need not imply that conditions outside of the Garden of Eden were less than optimal during the period prior to the Curse. The Scriptures clearly indicate that when Adam and Eve were driven out of the garden after the Curse, where they would procure their living from the ground would be hard work. This was not necessarily because the world outside of the Garden of Eden was not equally a paradise. Adam and Eve were driven out of the Garden of Eden from God's presence so they would not eat of the tree of life. Thus, even though we are not told, probably all the land surface outside of the Garden of Eden was also covered in lush vegetation and well-watered by rivers that flowed from sources in upland areas out to the pre-Flood seas. Some of these rivers could well have been also fed by springs, while others may have been supplied by water directly from rainfall, just as most rivers are today.

Finally, the land of Havilah is described as having been a land rich in gold, precious stones (though the exact nature of what has been translated as "onyx stone" is uncertain), and a material called "bdellium," which evidently was a precious gem similar in color to the bread called "manna" that was sent from heaven to feed the Israelites in the wilderness (Numbers 11:7). Mention of these commodities, particularly the gold and precious stones, is consistent with the description later in Genesis 4:22 of Tubal-cain as a craftsman using brass and iron, all of which is indicative of the natural resources present in the pre-Flood world.

41

THE FLOOD

It is hardly surprising that "with the long lifespans of the patriarchs, and with the large number of children born to them, the population of the pre-Flood world grew exponentially, so that in the days of Noah some 1,500 years after Creation the world population could have numbered in the hundreds of millions, or even billions."[1] That there had been an explosion in the population numbers is evident from these repeated references in Genesis 6: "and it came to pass, when men began to multiply on the face of the earth" (v. 1), and "the earth was filled with violence…for all flesh had corrupted his way upon the earth…for the earth is filled with violence through them" (vv. 11-13).

The tragedy was that in spite of the witness and influence of the godly patriarchs, wickedness and rebellion against God was rife and had greatly increased so that the earth became filled with violence and corruption. "And GOD saw that the wickedness of man was great in the earth, and that every imagination of the thoughts of his heart was only evil continually" (Genesis 6:5). "The earth also was corrupt before God, and the earth was filled with violence. And God looked upon the earth, and, behold, it was corrupt; for all flesh had corrupted his way upon the earth" (Genesis 6:11-12). The universality of human wickedness and depravity is repeatedly emphasized here. God had commanded man to fill the earth, and this he had obeyed. However, man also filled the earth with violence. God had clearly instructed man in the way He required man to live, but now "all flesh had corrupted his way." The word translated "corrupt" is the Hebrew *shachath*, which is a very strong expression often translated "destroy." The thought is that in turning aside to follow their own ways, all men had thoroughly rebelled against God and were literally destroying themselves.

To say that God was displeased with these developments would be an understatement. "And it repented the LORD that he had made man on the earth, and it grieved him at his heart. And the LORD said, I will destroy man whom I have created from the face of the earth; both man, and beast, and the creeping thing, and the fowls of the air; for it repenteth me that I have made them" (Genesis 6:6-7). Such was the state of depravity and anarchy that filled human society across

---

1   H. M. Morris, 1973, World population and Bible chronology, in *Scientific Studies in Special Creation*, W. E. Lammerts, ed., Grand Rapids, MI: Baker Bookhouse, 198-205.

the face of the earth, God was so grieved in His heart about man's rebellion and corruption that He "repented" (changed His mind) about having created man. Since man had changed his attitude toward God, God was justified in changing his attitude toward man. Although God had made a perfect world for man and had been patient with him in his disobedience and rebellion, there finally came a time when, in justice to His own holiness, He had to terminate man's boundless wickedness. Man's outward wickedness had become "great in the earth" because his inward imaginations had become completely and continually evil.

The remedy for worldwide wickedness would have to be a worldwide judgment. Regretfully, therefore, a worldwide judgment on man would, as a consequence, also destroy all the land animals. Thus, God pronounced His judgment that He would destroy the beasts, birds, and creeping things, along with man, from the face of the earth. Since God had created the beasts, birds, and creeping things as part of man's dominion, it was His prerogative to destroy them. Note that God did not pronounce this judgment of destruction on the fish.

However, among the countless millions of people inhabiting the pre-Flood world, there was one exception. "But Noah found grace in the eyes of the LORD….Noah was a just man and perfect in his generations, and Noah walked with God" (Genesis 6:8-9). God had every right to destroy everyone and everything on the face of the earth because the violation of His holiness demanded justice. Nevertheless, out of love for man whom He had created, God sought to extend mercy. Thus, in sovereign mercy God extended grace to Noah, whose heart had been prepared to respond in obedient faith. So Noah first "found grace" to become "a just man" (that is, justified or declared to be righteous), so that he was "perfect in his generations" (that is, complete in so far as God is concerned) and therefore was able to "walk with God." Among all his contemporaries, over the many generations of a long life, Noah was the only one since Enoch, according to the record we have, who "walked with God." He also was a "preacher of righteousness" (2 Peter 2:5), but in all his years of preaching, as far as we know, there were no converts except his own family—his wife, his three sons, Shem, Ham, and Japheth, and their wives.

Yet, in spite of the total depravity of mankind, God was still patient and ready to extend grace, as in the case of Noah, to anyone prepared to turn to Him. However, a time limit would be set in place, after which the judgment for man's wickedness would come. "And the LORD said, My spirit shall not always strive with man, for that he also is flesh: yet his days shall be an hundred and twenty years" (Genesis 6:3). God was still going to allow a further 120 years for the Holy Spirit to do His work of convicting of sin. As the moral and spiritual character of the pre-Flood world degenerated, it was apparent that people had become so hopelessly corrupt as to be beyond reclamation. They had completely and irrevocably resisted the Spirit's witness, so that it was futile any longer for Him to "strive with man" (the Hebrew word for strive, *doon*, possibly includes the idea of "judging"). That same God has always been longsuffering, even under such awful conditions as prevailed in the days of Noah (1 Peter 3:20). Though all mankind rejected Him, He still granted 120 years to mankind in light of the possibility that at least some might "come to repentance" (2 Peter 3:9). This striving of God's spirit with man was undoubtedly accomplished through the preaching of Noah, though Methuselah and Lamech were still alive for most of this period and also had been faithful witnesses to God's grace.

Having set a time limit on the days of grace and therefore when the worldwide judgment on man would come, God now made the necessary preparations for the salvation of Noah and his family. He made Noah aware of the nature of the coming judgment. God spoke to Noah with specific instructions:

> Make thee an ark of gopher wood; rooms shalt thou make in the ark, and shalt pitch it within and without with pitch. And this is the fashion which thou shalt make it of: The length of the ark shall be three hundred cubits, the breadth of it fifty cubits, and the height of it thirty cubits. A window shalt thou make to the ark, and in a cubit shalt thou finish it above; and the door of the ark shalt thou set in the side thereof; with lower, second, and third stories shalt thou make it. And, behold, I, even I, do bring a flood of waters upon the earth, to destroy all flesh, wherein is the breath of life, from under heaven; and every thing that is in the earth shall die. But with thee will I establish my covenant; and thou shalt come into the ark, thou, and thy sons, and thy wife, and thy son's wives with thee. And of every living thing of all flesh, two of every sort shalt thou bring into the ark, to keep them alive with thee; they shalt be male and female. Of fowls after their kind, and of cattle after their kind, and every creeping thing of the earth after his kind; two of every sort shall come unto thee, to keep them alive. And take thou unto thee of all food that is eaten, and thou shalt gather it to thee; and it shalt be for food for thee, and for them. (Genesis 6:14-21)

In order to preserve both human and terrestrial animal life on earth, God instructed Noah to build a huge barge-like structure called "an ark," in which the occupants would be saved from destruction in the coming flood of waters. According to God's instructions, the Ark was designed for capacity, and stability in floating, rather than for speed or navigability. The dimensions given to Noah for the Ark was 300 cubits long, 50 cubits wide, and 30 cubits high—approximately 450 feet or 135 meters long, approximately 75 feet or 22.5 meters wide, and approximately 45 feet or 13.5 meters high. It was to have three stories, rooms, a door set in the side, and a window around its circumference near the roof for light and ventilation. (These and other details have already been discussed in full in Chapter 5.)

The exact nature of "gopher wood" is unknown today, though it is believed to have been some type of dense, hard wood. One suggestion is that it was cypress.[2] When constructed, the Ark was to be made waterproof and resistant to decay by impregnation inside and outside with "pitch." The Hebrew word used here for "pitch" is *kopher*, which is different from the word used in other places in the Old Testament for "pitch." It is related to the Hebrew *kaphar* ("to cover") and as a noun simply means a "covering."

Many critics have automatically identified this "pitch" with tar or bitumen derived as residues from petroleum and have decried the accuracy of the Genesis account here for two reasons—(1) petroleum was really not discovered and used commercially until the 19th century, although seepages of tar were discovered and used much earlier; and (2) since petroleum is now known to be derived from the mass burial of marine algae and land plants, how could petroleum exist in the pre-Flood world if the mass burial of the algae and plants did not take place until the Flood itself? However, what the critics regard here as absurd or impossible is easily explained by the fact that there was a well known procedure for making "pitch" in the Middle Ages which could easily have been the procedure used here. Sap was first collected from pine trees, which were then cut down and partly burnt to produce charcoal. The charcoal was then crushed to a powder and mixed with the sap. Then the mixture was boiled. The product was pitch, and those who produced it were called "pitchers," which is where we derive, in English, the family name Pitcher. So whether Noah and his sons used this procedure to make pitch, or whether there was a readily available resinous substance of some kind in the pre-Flood world, we cannot be sure, but at God's direction it was the right material to use as a covering for the Ark.

God also gave Noah the reason why he had to build this Ark. He was going to bring a mighty flood of waters (Hebrew *mabbul mayim*) upon the earth. This Hebrew word *mabbul* is used here in the Scriptures for the first time. Apart from being used in Genesis 6-9, it is found nowhere else in the Old Testament except Psalm 29:10, which also is a reference to the Flood, so the use of this unique word describes a unique event—a watery cataclysm. As such, it would cover the whole globe, and therefore all people and all air-breathing land animals would be swept away and perish. Thus, it was essential that Noah build and furnish the Ark so that life could be preserved through the coming Flood. Specifically, God said that only eight people would go aboard the Ark: Noah and his three sons, and all their wives. Additionally, Noah was to take into the Ark two (a male-female pair) of every kind of air-breathing, land-dwelling animal ("fowls," "cattle," and "every creeping thing of the earth") and to keep them alive in order to repopulate the post-Flood world. Finally, all the necessary food for Noah's family and the animals was to be gathered and stored in the Ark. Noah neither questioned nor complained, but simply obeyed and did "according to all that God commanded him" (Genesis 6:22).

---

2   Strong, *Concise Dictionary of the Words in the Hebrew Bible*, word no. 1613.

We are not told exactly when it was that God gave Noah these instructions to build the Ark and the warning of the coming Flood, but it is not unreasonable to infer that it could have been soon after God's pronouncement that He would give people 120 more years of grace to repent (Genesis 6:3) before sending the Flood. On the other hand, we are told that Noah was 500 years old, exactly 100 years before the Flood, when the first of his three sons was born (Genesis 5:32), and it would seem that Noah's three sons were born before God gave Noah the building instructions for the Ark (Genesis 6:9-16). Whichever is the case, Noah would still have had almost 100 years to organize the building of the Ark. The record makes no mention of any further communication by God to Noah after Noah had received the instructions to build the Ark, so it is quite possible that there was almost a century of silence in which he faithfully went ahead and steadily built the Ark, all the while preaching and warning of the judgment to come.

Then seven days before the Flood was due to begin, God again spoke to Noah with instructions for him and his family to go aboard the Ark and to take all the assembled animals into the Ark with them (Genesis 7:1-3). Noah once more did exactly what God had commanded him and went into the Ark with his family, taking aboard all the clean and unclean beasts, the fowls and "every thing that creepeth upon the earth" exactly as instructed by God (Genesis 7:5, 7-9). Furthermore, it was the seventeenth day of the second month in the six hundredth year of Noah's life that he and his family, and male-female pairs of all the animals, finished boarding the Ark, just as God commanded. Then the Scriptures record that God shut the door (Genesis 7:11, 13-16).

On exactly the same day that Noah, his family, and all the animals were aboard the Ark and God had shut them in, the Flood began. It was the seventeenth day of the second month of the six hundredth year of Noah's life, 1,656 years after creation, when "all the fountains of the great deep [were] broken up, and the windows of heaven were opened" (Genesis 7:11). The breaking up of all the fountains of the great deep is recorded first. This could imply a sequence of events, with the windows of heaven opening subsequently to the breaking up of the fountains. Alternately, since both are mentioned together, both physical phenomena may have occurred simultaneously. So what exactly were these physical phenomena?

Most Hebrew scholars and commentators agree that the Hebrew word *t'hôm*, translated "deep" in Genesis 7:11, has the primary meanings of (1) "deep, of subterranean waters," (2) "sea," and (3) "primeval ocean, deep."[3] Leupold refers to the "great deep" as being subterranean water,[4] while Wenham suggests that there was a "great subterranean ocean."[5] Furthermore, there seems to be little doubt that the *t'hôm rabbâh* ("great deep") here is the same *t'hôm* as in Genesis

---

3   Brown, Driver, and Briggs, 1906, 1062.

4   Leupold, 1942, 295.

5   Wenham, 1987, 181.

1:2 that describes the depths of the universal ocean which covered the entire earth, which were then confined as seas on Day Three. Thus, the primary meaning of *t'hôm* undoubtedly is the ocean depths. These fountains would have to have been springs on the pre-Flood ocean floor, and "breaking up" would signify the rupturing of the ocean floor in a vast upheaval. However, a secondary meaning, that of "subterranean waters," including waters stored deep in the earth's crust in the landmass of the pre-Flood world, cannot be ruled out. Because the river flowing through the Garden of Eden seems to have had as its source in a spring (or "fountain") which delivered subterranean waters to the land surface, there obviously were vast amounts of subterranean waters stored in the rocks of the pre-Flood landmass.[6] Therefore, the rupturing of the landmass and the release of these subterranean waters at the commencement of the Flood cannot be entirely ruled out, either. Nevertheless, as explained previously, it would seem unwarranted to postulate huge open caverns acting as subterranean reservoirs connected by conduits for the storage of these waters, because the rock strata of the earth's crust, even today, have the capacity for the storage of significant amounts of water, even to great depths, as indicated in recent decades by deep drilling of the earth's continental crust. It is likely that most of the subterranean waters in the continental crust of the pre-Flood landmass were trapped and thus stored in the rock strata when God made the dry land on Day Three of the Creation Week. We are not told what triggered the upheaval that broke up these fountains, but it is clear that global-scale forces must have been involved.

Whereas the literal meaning of "the fountains of the great deep" is easily recognized, understanding what is meant by the expression "the windows of heaven" is a little harder to fathom. This expression is sometimes translated as "the floodgates of heaven" and obviously means sustained heavy rainfall. Indeed, "the rain was upon the earth forty days and forty nights" (Genesis 7:12). Obviously, from our observations and experience in the present world, there are no literal "windows" or "sluice gates" in the heavens through which water pours down onto the earth, so this must be a figurative expression. In any case, the Hebrew words themselves do not seem to imply anything about the source of the water which fell as sustained, heavy rainfall. We do know that on the second day of the Creation Week, some of the primeval ocean waters of Day One were placed above the firmament created on that day, but it is not possible to be dogmatic that it was these "waters above" which were the source of this torrential rainfall. An idea that became popular at the end of the 19th century was that these "waters above" existed in the pre-Flood world as some form of water vapor canopy above the atmosphere. But this understanding of the "waters above" seems to be less likely if the "firmament," or *raqia*, corresponds to interstellar space as we have previously discussed.

---

6   D. M. Fouts and K. Wise, 1998, Blotting out and breaking up: miscellaneous Hebrew studies in geocatastrophism, in *Proceedings of the Fourth International Conference on Creationism*, R.E. Walsh, ed., Pittsburgh, PA: Creation Science Fellowship, 217-228.

Another possibility we shall describe later is that the intense rainfall was a result of steam jets emerging from where the ocean floor was splitting apart, which would have been like huge fountains rising out of the great deep. The water that these jets entrained would then fall back to the earth as intense and sustained rainfall. However, because these considerations cannot be determined from the Hebrew text, further elucidation is probably best left to later discussion of scientific models.

What we can be emphatic about from the text is that because it rained torrentially and globally for forty days and forty nights, a weather phenomenon not experienced in the post-Flood world, a unique source (or sources) for this vast amount of water must have either existed in the pre-Flood world, or a unique mechanism (or mechanisms) was triggered at the onset of the Flood to supply such sustained rainfall globally. Thus, the mention first of the breaking up of the fountains of the great deep may still be significant, because the "cleaving open" (the literal translation) of these fountains of the great deep may have been the initial action which then triggered the opening of these "windows of heaven."[7]

Once the Flood began, it rained for forty days and forty nights, but the waters increased and prevailed upon the earth for 150 days. "And the rain was upon the earth forty days and forty nights....And the flood was forty days upon the earth; and the waters increased,...And the waters prevailed, and were increased greatly upon the earth;...And the waters prevailed upon the earth one hundred and fifty days" (Genesis 7:12, 17-18, 24). It was only at the end of this 150-day period of prevailing Flood waters that the "fountains also of the deep and the windows of heaven were stopped, and the rain from heaven was restrained" (Genesis 8:2). Thus, it would seem from this description that after the initial period of forty days and forty nights of global torrential rainfall, further "rain from heaven" continued from "the windows of heaven" for a further 110 days until they were restrained and stopped. The mention of the fountains of the deep together with the windows of heaven in the cessation of the rain in this passage may hint of a causal connection between the phenomena.

It would therefore seem eminently reasonable to conclude from the text of Scripture that we can subdivide the flooding event into two parts. It began with an initial 40-day period, during which the Flood waters would have continued to increase greatly upon the earth's surface due to the fountains of the great deep and the torrential global rainfall. Subsequent to this there was a 110-day period in which the waters reached their maximum and prevailed across the earth's surface as a global ocean, with lesser amounts of water coming from the fountains of the great deep and more intermittent rainfall from the windows of heaven. It would seem also from the biblical text that by the beginning of this 110-day period, "the waters prevailed exceedingly upon the earth; and all the high hills, that were under

---

7   Morris, 1976, 196-197.

the whole heaven, were covered. Fifteen cubits upward did the waters prevail; and the mountains were covered" (Genesis 7:19-20). In other words, as a result of the forty days and forty nights of torrential global rainfall and the activity of the fountains of the great deep, the Flood waters had covered all the pre-Flood hills and mountains right around the globe to a depth of at least "15 cubits" (approximately 22 feet or 7 meters). These two periods then of forty days and 110 days make up the total of 150 days of prevailing Flood waters as described in Genesis 7:24. Because it was only after this 150-day period that the fountains of the great deep and the windows of heaven were stopped (Genesis 8:1-2), it would seem that the Flood waters continued to rise throughout this 150-day period of prevailing, even though the rate of rising would have been much slower in the 110-day period of continued prevailing after the initial 40-day period of intense global rain.

After the 150 days of the waters "prevailing," "God made a wind to pass over the earth, and the waters assuaged [literally, calmed or soothed]" (Genesis 8:1). This was the turning point of the Flood year. This was also when God stopped the fountains of the great deep and the windows of heaven so that the rain was restrained (Genesis 8:2). It was now the seventeenth day of the seventh month, five months or 150 days after the Flood began, when the waters were abated and began to return from off the earth continually. The Ark, as a result, came to rest on "the mountains of Ararat" (Genesis 8:3-4). This is the first mention in the Scriptures of "the mountains of Ararat." The Ark coming to rest there coincided with the fountains of the great deep and the rain being stopped, when the Flood waters were probably at their zenith. Since the mountains of Ararat are still with us today, along with many other mountain ranges that were not present in the pre-Flood world, it would seem possible to infer that the uplifting of these mountain ranges had begun at this turning point in the Flood year at the end of 150 days of the waters "prevailing."

The Scriptures record that it took 221 days (more than seven months) for the Flood waters to completely abate and for the surface of the ground to dry out sufficiently for Noah, his family, and the animals to leave the Ark. During this period of 221 days, there were a number of stages detailed in the biblical narrative. First, there was a 74-day period in which "the waters decreased continually" (Genesis 8:5), and at the end of that period "the tops of the mountains" were visible. This would mean that during this two and a half month period, the water level relative to the Ark dropped thousands of feet so that various mountain peaks of different altitudes could now be seen. Of course, it may not have just been the water level dropping, but the mountain peaks themselves were almost certainly rising from under the Flood waters due to tectonic movements (to be discussed further later). Noah still waited another forty days before he opened the window of the Ark in order to send out the raven (Genesis 8:6-7). Noah sought to gain information about the nature of these exposed mountain peaks, and the raven's failure to return to the Ark was a good sign, meaning this hardy bird was surviving on carrion even though the exposed ground on these mountain tops was probably still inhospitable to other creatures.

After sending out the raven, Noah waited seven days before sending out a dove. It could not find a suitable place to land because of the waters still covering the ground across the earth's surface, so it returned to the Ark (Genesis 8:8-9). Subsequently, seven more days later, Noah sent the dove out again and the dove returned to him at the end of the day, this time with a freshly plucked olive leaf in its beak (Genesis 8:10-11). Thus, Noah knew that the waters had abated sufficiently to expose more of the ground surface, into which floating sprigs and seeds of hardy plants such as olives had become embedded and then sprouted. Thus, in the fifty-four days since "the tops of the mountains" were seen, the water level continued to drop and the wind (Genesis 8:1) began to rapidly dry out the ground. Sufficient soil had developed, rich enough in nutrients for the olive plant, from which the dove plucked a leaf, to have grown rapidly in that seven-day period between the dove's excursions from the Ark. Noah then waited another seven days before sending the dove out again. This time it didn't return, obviously having found sufficient food for its needs and a comfortable resting place to set down on (Genesis 8:12).

Still, Noah waited another twenty-nine days until the first day of the first month in the 601st year of his life, exactly 314 days after the Flood had begun, before he "removed the covering of the Ark" (presumably a part of the roof) in order to observe the ground surface for himself (Genesis 8:13). "The face of the ground was dry," but he must have observed that there was still much water about and that the landscape in general looked forbidding and barren, because it took another fifty-seven days before Noah considered the earth sufficiently dry for him and his family, and the animals, to leave the Ark and begin life in the new world (Genesis 8:14). It was now 371 days since the Flood began (compare Genesis 8:14 with Genesis 7:11). That these time periods while Noah waited were successive assuaging and drying stages is attested to by the successive descriptions in the text—"the waters were abated from off the earth" (Genesis 8:11), "the face of the ground was dry" (Genesis 8:13), and "the earth [was] dried" (Genesis 8:14). Yet even then, Noah did not presume to decide of his own accord to leave the Ark, but waited for God's instructions. Indeed, just as God had instructed them to board the Ark and then He closed the door, God now spoke to Noah, 371 days after the Flood had begun, instructing him to take his family and disembark the Ark with all the animals (Genesis 8:14-17). As on previous occasions, Noah did exactly what the Lord instructed him to do (Genesis 8:18-19).

42

THE POST-FLOOD WORLD

The earth was not annihilated by the Flood, but it was drastically changed. The land surface that had previously been covered in lush vegetation and profusely populated with animals and people now appeared rather desolate, with new vegetation just starting to establish itself. The geography and topography of the post-Flood world was different, due to the total restructuring of the earth's surface by the geological processes unleashed during the Flood. Newly uplifted mountain ranges would have meant new river systems, and there would have been a new configuration of land areas and ocean basins, the latter possibly being deeper to accommodate waters which had been added to the earth's surface from the subterranean reservoirs. The earth's weather patterns and its climate would probably have also been drastically altered, so that the total environment was now rendered less congenial to man and animals, unlike the pre-Flood world. Nevertheless, God still commanded and expected that, as they went forth from the Ark, all the fowl, cattle, and creeping things would "breed abundantly in the earth, and be fruitful, and multiply upon the earth...after their kinds" (Genesis 8:17, 19).

In obvious gratitude to God for preservation and safe deliverance through the Flood and into the new world, and being glad to be back on dry land again, Noah built an altar and sacrificed to the Lord burnt offerings of every clean beast and every clean fowl that left the Ark with him (Genesis 8:20). Since the clean animals and birds, presumably, represented the domesticated varieties, Noah was in effect making an offering to God of one-seventh of all his flocks, a very considerable and generous sacrifice on Noah's part. This demonstrated his gratitude and his strong faith in God to preserve and bless his family and all the animals in this new world.

God was clearly pleased with this demonstration of Noah's devotion to Him. He responded by immediately dealing with any apprehensions about the future, promising not to curse the ground anymore for man's sake, and never again to destroy all life by smiting the earth with such a devastating cataclysm as it had just experienced (Genesis 8:21). It was not that the Curse of Genesis 3:16 would no longer operate, but that God would not again add to that curse by sending another Flood to again destroy every living thing. Instead, God promised that in this new world, there would be uniformity of natural and physical processes. While the earth, as it now existed, continued to operate, there would be "seedtime and harvest, and cold and heat, and summer and winter, and day and night," none of which would cease (Genesis 8:22). On the basis of God's Word, therefore, we can confidently assert that it is only in the post-Flood world that "the present is the key to the past," but beyond that, it is the Flood, in particular, which helps us to understand why the world is the way it is today. In fact, "the past is the key to the present." Thus, the essential constancy of the earth's rotation and its solar orbital revolution, controlling all diurnal and annual cycles, especially the new hydrological and climatological cycles, would be guaranteed by God to be uniform from the beginning of the post-Flood world through to the present day. Thus, though heavy rains and local floods might occur, God was promising never again to destroy all life on the land with a worldwide flood. Man and the animals could depend on a regular order of nature, with a fixed sequence of seasons and a fixed day-night cycle.

Furthermore, God renewed with Noah the original divine mandate given to Adam and Eve: "Be fruitful, and multiply, and replenish [correctly translated, fill] the earth" (Genesis 9:1). Thus, it was again God's design that man would quickly spread over the entire habitable earth in order to exercise proper dominion over it, under His sovereignty. However, man was no longer to exercise direct authority over all the animals, as had previously been his prerogative. Rather, there was to be fear manifested by the animals, indeed, dread or terror, rather than obedience and understanding (Genesis 9:2). This would be for the benefit of both mankind and the animals. On the one hand, the fear of man among the animals would be for man's protection against attack from large populations of marauding animals. On the other hand, because God was now delivering every beast of the earth, every fowl of the air, all that moves upon the earth, and all the fishes of the sea into man's hand for meat (food) (Genesis 9:2-3), it would be for the benefit of the animals to be fearful of man so that it was harder for man to catch them.

Although God now authorized man to eat meat, along with "the green herb" which God had previously given to man for food, God still prohibited the eating of blood with the flesh of the animals, because the blood represented the life (Hebrew *nephesh*) of the flesh (Genesis 9:3-4). Furthermore, because of the rampant violence going unpunished before the Flood, God now insisted that the taking of another man's life, by shedding his blood, would now be punishable by the execution of the murderer (Genesis 9:5-6). God was thus insisting on the sanctity of all life, and particularly man's life, as man alone was made in the image of God. God then repeated His command to Noah and his sons to be "fruitful, and multiply; bring forth abundantly in the earth, and multiply therein" (Genesis 9:7), insisting that man spread across the earth's surface to populate it and exercise dominion over it.

Further, to reassure Noah and his sons, God announced the establishment of a covenant with them and their descendants, and indeed, with every living creature (fowl, cattle, and every beast of the earth) that had been on the Ark. He would never send another Flood to destroy the earth (Genesis 9:8-11). This would be an unconditional covenant with them "for perpetual generations." As a "token" or sign of the covenant, God designated the rainbow seen in the clouds, so that when both He and they saw the rainbow, it would remind each of them of this everlasting covenant that God had made with them (Genesis 9:12-17).

The rainbow, of course, appears in the clouds as sunlight is reflected from them, refracted through the water droplets. Since God refers to the rainbow as "my bow" (Genesis 9:13), it has been argued that this must be the first time a rainbow was seen in the clouds. This could imply that there were no clouds in the skies in the pre-Flood world, for otherwise rainbows would have been seen previously, even by Noah and his sons before they went on the Ark. Genesis 2:5 is often cited in support of this view, which would insist that there was no rain before the Flood and hence no clouds or rainbows. However, the context of Genesis 2:5, and the tense of the verb used there, implies that there had not been any rain on the earth only up to this particular point in time, which is about halfway through Day Three of the Creation Week. Thus, there would have been rain and clouds in the pre-Flood world. If that were the case, then God would now be investing in the rainbow a symbolic meaning—a sign and remembrance of His covenant with Noah, his family, his descendants, and all living creatures that He would never again send another global flood. The view that this was the first time Noah and his sons had seen a rainbow, and that there had not been clouds or rain in the pre-Flood world, would seem compelling, but it is not inconsistent for God to choose to invest a meaning in something that has already existed. For example, Jesus took elements of the last Passover meal shared with His disciples to institute the communion meal in remembrance of Him, giving the elements new meaning (Matthew 26:17-20, 26-30). Fortunately, even though there may be some geological implications regarding rainfall or no rainfall in the pre-Flood world, dogmatism on these points is not crucial. The rainbow, spanning from horizon to horizon in the clouds, is a sign given by God as a reminder of His covenant that He will never destroy the earth and all flesh on it again by a global flood.

The history of Noah, his sons, and their descendants which follows in the biblical record contains details that are both instructive and relevant to the framework for a biblical geology. Indeed, the people on the earth today are the descendants of Noah and his three sons, Shem, Ham, and Japheth, so that it can truly be said that "of them was the whole earth overspread" (Genesis 9:18-19). In Genesis 10:1-5 are listed the sons and grandsons of Japheth and "By these were the isles of the Gentiles divided in their lands; every one after his tongue, after their families, in their nations." The sons and grandsons of Ham are next listed, and one of the grandsons is Nimrod, who became the founder of a kingdom that included the cities of Babel, Erech, Accad, and Calneh, built on the plain of Shinar

(Genesis 10:6-10). The record continues with the listing of many other nations that developed from Ham's descendants. Finally, Shem and his descendants are listed "after their families, after their tongues, in their lands, after their nations" (Genesis 10:21-31).

Of significance is the life of the great-great grandson of Shem, Peleg, because the record states "for in his days was the earth divided" (Genesis 10:25). Indeed, the name Peleg means "division" and is related to the Hebrew word *palag* which is here translated "divided." A different Hebrew word (*parad*) is translated "divided" in Genesis 10:5 as quoted above, and in 10:32: "These are the families of the sons of Noah, after their generations, in their nations: and by these were the nations divided in the earth after the flood." Some have suggested that the use of these different Hebrew words implies two different types of division, *parad* in Genesis 10:5, 32 clearly referring to the division of peoples and nations across the face of the earth, whereas *palag* in Genesis 10:25 could be referring to the division of the earth by continental drift. However, the tectonic splitting-up of a landmass would have been an especially catastrophic event, given that the rate of separation would have to have been incredibly rapid to produce, within a few years, the present configuration of the continents. Such rates of separation would have involved continuous earthquakes with magnitudes far exceeding the worst earthquakes experienced today, and therefore would have resulted in devastating consequences for all life on the earth's surface. There is no description of such an event seen in Scripture. Actually, the evidence is compelling that a dramatic amount of continental "sprint" and plate tectonics occurred during the Flood, during which the record even states that the "fountains of the great deep" were "broken up." Many lines of evidence indicate that large continental displacements were taking place simultaneously with the catastrophic deposition of fossil-bearing sediments on the surfaces of the continents.

There is no mistaking the fact that Eber, Peleg's father, named his son to commemorate a significant event, "for in his days was the earth divided" (Genesis 10:25). The most obvious understanding of this event is that it refers to the division of peoples at the Tower of Babel, as described in Genesis 11:1-9. As a result of that event, people were divided on the basis of languages they spoke, and such a division is mentioned in Genesis 10:5: "divided in their lands; every one after his tongue." All references to "division" in these verses are to a linguistic and geographic division, rather than to an actual splitting of the earth. Indeed, this division, according to the nation, is described in Genesis 10:32 as "divided in the earth," so the fact that the earth is likewise referred to as being divided in the days of Peleg can justifiably be understood to simply be a linguistic and geographic division. Thus, it can be argued that these two Hebrew words, *parad* and *palag*, are essentially synonymous.

Nimrod, the grandson of Ham, was the founder of the city of Babel, and he would have lived about the same time as Eber, the great grandson of Shem. Thus, it is reasonable to infer that the division at the Tower of Babel took place when both Nimrod and Eber were mature men, and that Peleg was probably born about the time of the dispersion of people from the Tower of Babel. It is not surprising that Eber would commemorate such a momentous event in the naming of his son. Otherwise, it is difficult to understand why God would record the meaning of "Peleg," since this was not done in the case of the other names listed in Genesis 10, the so-called Table of Nations.

A feature of the Genesis record, which has already been noted with respect to Genesis 1 and 2, is that after a general overview of a topic in one chapter, the next chapter focuses in and concentrates upon a particular topic or aspect dealt with in the previous chapter. Genesis 2 focuses in and concentrates upon the history of man, after the general overview in Genesis 1 of the history of the world. Thus, it can be argued that Genesis 10 gives a general overview of the history of the post-Flood families of Noah's three sons and the development of the nations from them, whereas Genesis 11 focuses in and concentrates upon the post-Flood patriarchs descended from Shem and leading to Abram (Abraham). Also, having mentioned the division of the earth in the days of Peleg in Genesis 10:25, God now, at the beginning of Genesis 11, focuses in and elaborates upon this event. This is another argument supporting the contention that the earth division referred to in the days of Peleg was, in fact, just the linguistic and geographic division resulting from the Tower of Babel event, now described in Genesis 11:1-9.

Genesis 11:1 records that after the Flood, "the whole earth was of one language, and of one speech." The immediate descendants of Noah, being all of the one family, of course, spoke the same language, the language that had been spoken by everyone in the pre-Flood period. It is probable that this was a Semitic language (perhaps even Hebrew), since the proper names of men and places in the pre-Flood to Babel period all have meanings only in Hebrew and its cognate languages.[1] Also, it seems unlikely that Shem participated in the Babel rebellion, so it is probable that his own language was not affected by the resulting confusion of languages. Consequently, Shem's family would have continued speaking the same language they had always spoken.

As the families of Noah's sons grew, they began to migrate from the initial area in the mountains of Ararat where Noah and his sons had settled after coming off the Ark. Thus, "it came to pass, as they journeyed from the east [or probably better translated, eastward[2]], that they found a plain in the land of Shinar; and they dwelt there" (Genesis 11:2). Thus, it was that many of Noah's descendants settled in the land of Shinar, the name then given to the fertile Mesopotamian plain. It obviously reminded them of what Noah, Shem, Ham, and Japheth had told them about their pre-Flood world, because they named the two rivers flowing

---

1   Morris, 1976, 267.

2   Morris, 1976, 266.

through this region the Tigris and Euphrates after two of the rivers that had once flowed out of the Garden of Eden. A leader named Nimrod asserted himself, the grandson of Ham and a mighty hunter, who (as noted earlier) established a kingdom in the land of Shinar and built the cities of Babel, Erech (Uruk), Accad, and Calneh (Genesis 10:8-10). With food production guaranteed on the fertile Tigris-Euphrates plain, urban development was possible. Evidently Nimrod sought to establish a strongly centralized, controlled society and self-sufficient civilization, rather than obeying God's command to systematically colonize and develop all parts of the earth ("fill the earth," Genesis 9:1). Thus, Nimrod and his community leaders developed a kiln-fired brick-making industry, and with "slime" for mortar began building the city of Babel (Genesis 11:3).

However, they went a step further in outright rebellion against God and decided to build not only a mighty city, but a huge tower, "whose top may reach unto heaven." Thus, they were seeking to make a name for themselves and to avoid being scattered across the face of the whole earth (Genesis 11:4), which was absolutely contrary to God's command. It would appear that this great tower was designed to be a focal point for the political and religious life of the population of the city, and a symbol of unity and strength in defiance against God. That the tower was built for religious motives is evident from the literal translation "tower unto heaven" or "a tower dedicated to heaven," which would mean that it was a great temple with its apex providing a place for sacrifices and worship. However, this tower was designed to exalt man and not the true Creator God of heaven, because all of this activity was done in disobedience to God.

Understandably, God was not pleased with this act of defiance and rebellion, which threatened to corrupt the entire population in much the same way as the pre-Flood people had. Thus, while God is longsuffering and normally allows men and nations to pursue their own ways without supernatural interference, the threat to His purposes now required divine intervention. God had promised to Noah and his descendants that He would never again send a global flood to destroy all flesh upon the earth, so a different strategy was required. Thus, God "came down to see the city and the tower," a figurative expression indicating that the time had come for God to officially and judicially observe the situation and consider His course of action (Genesis 11:5). The divine council pronounced its assessment: "Behold, the people is one, and they have all one language; and this they begin to do: now nothing will be restrained from them, which they have imagined to do" (Genesis 11:6). The problem, in God's estimation, lay in the unity of the people, a unity which was made possible only by a common language. Thus, practically the entire population was supporting this establishment of an autonomous, man-centered civilization in direct defiance of God's command. Under Nimrod's evil leadership there would be virtually no limits to what this rebellion could achieve.

The plan of the divine council was simple: "let us go down, and there confound their language, that they may not understand one another's speech" (Genesis

11:7). The key to the rebellion of these people was their ability to cooperate and organize together, which enabled them to formulate and implement complex plans; and all this was dependent on their ability to communicate with each other. They had one language and vocabulary, so they spoke with the same sounds and formulated their thoughts in the same way. Thus, to thwart this rebellion against God's command to Noah and his descendants, this key needed to be removed. God decided to "confound their language" (their ability to make the same sounds with their lips) so that they would not "understand one another's speech." The result was swift. "So the LORD scattered them abroad from thence upon the face of all the earth: and they left off to build the city. Therefore is the name of it called Babel; because the LORD did there confound the language of all the earth: and from thence did the LORD scatter them abroad upon the face of all the earth" (Genesis 11:8-9).

Surprised confusion quickly spread through the whole population of Babel. Presumably, individual members of each family group could still understand each other, but otherwise everyone else was talking what seemed nonsense. Order among the populace would have immediately broken down. Loud, incoherent arguments would erupt as people tried to communicate with one another. This would obviously lead to fully-fledged chaos. With no further cooperation possible between families, it would be immediately obvious that survival depended on each family group fending for itself; and to do so they must leave Babel. Thus, God achieved His purpose of making the post-Flood people obey His command to spread across the face of the earth to fill it. Of course, how God confused their tongues is unknown, but it is clear that it was a miracle (direct divine intervention). The word "confound" is the Hebrew *balal*, while the name "Babel" means "confusion." Obviously the sounds emanating from the confused throngs of people at Babel were like unintelligible babblings, so the name of the city in the minds of those who left it became "the city of babbling or confusion."

This, then, is how the nations of the earth were established. Even though the entire human population was still one in kind, it was now divided into "tongues, in their lands, after their nations" (Genesis 10:31). However, God's plan to provide the Redeemer promised to Adam and Eve, the One who would crush the serpent, begins to unfold. The line of the promised Seed is preserved through the line of Shem, so the Genesis record focuses on the patriarchs descended from him. Shem's genealogy from the Flood to the time when God called out Abram (Abraham) to establish the nation of Israel is listed in Genesis 11:10-32. Assuming no gaps in these genealogical records, the chronological figures indicate that Shem lived until after the death of Terah, the ninth generation after the Flood, so that Terah had ample opportunity to talk with Shem and so ensure that the family records were accurate. Again assuming no gaps, even Noah, who lived 350 years after the Flood (Genesis 9:28), lived until Terah was 128 years old. Indeed, many of these post-Flood patriarchs were contemporaries with Noah and Shem throughout most of this period, ensuring that accurate records were passed on to Abraham's father, Terah.

Some suggest that these incredible overlaps in the lives of these patriarchs instead indicate there might be gaps in the genealogies, particularly as in the repetition of this genealogy in Luke 3:36 the name of Cainan is inserted between Arphaxad and Salah. However, the name of Cainan is not included in the other repetition of this genealogical record in 1 Chronicles 1:18, nor is Cainan given as a son of Arphaxad in Genesis 10:24. Thus, confusion remains about this much-debated inclusion of Cainan in Luke 3:36, though it is possible to argue that this insertion is the result of "a copyist's error" in early manuscripts.[3] In any case, the language formula used in the genealogical record of Genesis 11 is identical to that used in Genesis 5 for the pre-Flood patriarchs, that is, a direct father-son relationship. This denotes a "tight" chronology (with no gaps) for these genealogical records.

The major reason for the overlap of so many generations in this genealogy is the decreasing lifespans of these post-Flood patriarchs. All the relevant data are summarized in the following table:

Patriarch	Year of Birth (Since Creation)	Age at Birth of Next Patriarch	Total Age	Year of Death (Since Creation)
Noah	1056	502	950	2006
Shem	1558	100	600	2156
Arphaxad	1658	35	438	2096
Salah	1693	30	433	2126
Eber	1723	34	464	2187
Peleg	1757	30	239	1996
Reu	1787	32	239	2025
Serug	1819	30	230	2049
Nahor	1849	29	148	1997
Terah	1878	70	205	2083
Abram (Abraham)	1948	100	175	2123

Note: The Flood occurred 1,656 years after creation.

Excluding Noah, who lived most of his life before the Flood, it is very obvious that there was a rapid decline in the lifespans of the post-Flood patriarchs from Shem onwards (Figure 1, page 441). There is also a drop in the age of each patriarch at the birth of the next patriarch, strongly suggesting that the age at maturity had dropped dramatically. People matured more quickly in the post-Flood world, with their age at maturity proportionate to their lifespans. This adds credence to the account as an eyewitnessed, literal, historical record. According to the chronology of this genealogical record, the Tower of Babel dispersion event, occurring about the time of Peleg's birth, must have been about 101 years after the Flood. Then there were approximately 191 years from the Tower of Babel until Abraham's birth

---

3   Morris, 1976, 281-282.

292 years after the Flood. The chronology of this genealogical record connects the dates for the Tower of Babel event, the Flood, and creation with the biblical chronology that begins at the time of Abraham. All the relevant archaeological evidence supports the biblical chronology from Abraham onwards.

One other consideration is worth noting here. Some would ask if the Babel dispersion event occurred just 100 years after the Flood, would there have been enough descendants from the eight survivors of the Flood to have built the Tower and inhabited the city? It could be that the population increased rapidly in that first century because it would have been an advantage for each family to have as many children as possible to assist with survival in the new world. There was also God's command to be fruitful and multiply in order to fill the earth. Shem, Ham, and Japheth had a total of 16 listed sons, but there may well have been others who were not listed, and there would presumably have been at least as many daughters. Even Noah may have had other unnamed children after the Flood. In the first generation after the Flood, then, there would have been, conservatively, at least 32 people, an increase of 533 perecent over their original six parents.[4] Assuming this portion remained the same (and this is a conservative assumption, given that the record continually repeats that each patriarch had sons and daughters), then the second generation would have had at least 171 people, and the third generation at least 912 people, making for a total of at least 1,120 mature adults at the time of the dispersion from Babel. Additionally, many of the young men of the fourth generation would also have been old enough to help in the construction work. In any case, it is quite possible that each family had many more children than the numbers calculated above. A growth rate of only 8 percent annually would produce a population of 9,000 by the time of the dispersion from Babel, just over 100 years after the Flood. The genealogical details given in the Genesis record do not claim to constitute a complete listing, but only gives the details of selected families originating from Noah's three sons. Thus, it is easily possible for the earth to have had a population of many thousands at the time of the building of the Tower of Babel and the city surrounding it, so these considerations are far from being an impediment to the historicity of this period.

One final consideration remains, as some additional details regarding the immediate post-Flood period are provided in the book of Job. The internal evidence within this book—the details of creation, the Fall, the Curse, and the Flood—strongly suggests that Job lived before the time of Abraham, and thus was a contemporary of many of the post-Flood patriarchs. What is of interest and import here are the hints scattered throughout the book of Job of a post-Flood Ice Age. For example, "Out of the south cometh the whirlwind: and cold out of the north. By the breath of God frost is given: and the breadth of the waters is straitened" (Job 37:9-10). This is reminiscent of the cold weather associated with an Ice Age. But particularly critical are the direct words of God Himself to Job

4   Morris, 1976, 282-283.

in His speech from the whirlwind. "Hast thou entered into the treasures of the snow? or hast thou seen the treasures of the hail, Which I have reserved against the time of trouble, against the day of battle and war?" (Job 38:22-23). Then in Job 38:29-30, there is perhaps an even more significant comment, at least with respect to Job's obvious awareness of ice-covered lakes and seas during such an ice age: "Out of whose womb came the ice? and the hoary frost of heaven, who hath gendered it? The waters are hid as with a stone, and the face of the deep is frozen." Though it is possible to interpret all these passages in other ways, because there are also many references throughout the book of Job to the Flood and various details concerning it, it would seem reasonable to understand these references to cold weather, snow, and ice as indications of their presence in the area and time that Job lived. One reasonable explanation for that would be a post-Flood Ice Age. This would suggest that between the end of the Flood and the time of Abraham, there was cold weather, snow, and ice at the low latitudes where Job and his other post-Flood contemporaries lived. This will obviously prove to be an important component of the scriptural framework for earth history.

43

CONCLUDING COMMENTS

The extensive discussion of the details within the biblical framework for earth history has been necessary to show the cohesion and flow of the Genesis record. Thus, in the biblical geological model of earth history to be presented later, the inclusion of many necessary geological inferences from the text can be more readily justified. One of the most crucial aspects of this framework is the time constraints placed on earth history. Depending on the exact time placement of Abraham based on the biblical record, corroborated in part by the available archaeological data, and assuming no gaps in the genealogical records, the date for the Flood would be about 2350 BC, or approximately 4,350 years ago. That would place the Tower of Babel dispersion event at around 2250 BC. And finally, the creation of the world itself would thus have occurred a little before 4000 BC, or just over 6,000 years ago. Six thousand years of human history is an incredibly long time, particularly when one looks at it in the perspective of the population explosion and man's achievements in just the last century, the 20th century AD. However, when viewed from the perspective of modern evolutionary geologists, 6,000 years is an incredibly short timespan which cannot be reconciled with the claimed 4.5-billion-year time framework insisted upon by the modern uniformitarian model for earth history. Proposing a defendable creation-Flood model for earth history that reconciles the actual geological data within the biblical time framework is the challenge before us in the remainder of this book.

The detailed discussion of the Creation Week will prove to have been necessary as we seek to unravel the geological data available to us from the earth's early history. Critical details in the creation account include:

1. The earth was covered in water when it was first created.
2. The subsequent development of dry land, possibly as one supercontinental landmass, potentially involving tectonic processes, erosion, and sedimentation as the land surface rose above the waters.
3. The creation of vegetation to cover the land surface, well before the subsequent creation of fish and birds, followed then by land animals.
4. The creation of the sun, moon, and stars after the land was formed, the plants created, and before the creation of the fish, birds, and land animals. The order of these creation events will prove crucial when we look at the

geological data for the earth's early history.

Conditions and processes operating in the pre-Flood world will be crucial to unraveling just how much geological work, and therefore how many geological strata, could have formed between the end of the Creation Week and the onset of the Flood. Finally, deciding on whether the division of the earth in Peleg's day was just a linguistic and geographic division of peoples, or a tectonic splitting and division of the earth itself, poses constraints on the geological work which transpired during the immediate post-Flood period and the geological record produced by it. Thus, in the subsequent investigations of the geologic record, it will prove necessary to refer back repeatedly to this biblical framework as a geological model is constructed upon this literal God-given history of creation, the Curse, the Flood, and the Tower of Babel.

SECTION V

THE MODERN
GEOLOGICAL SYNTHESIS

44

INTRODUCTION

Having surveyed the details provided by the Genesis record of the scriptural framework for earth history and a biblical geology, it is appropriate now to examine the available geologic data. It is important here to distinguish between the terms "data" and "evidence," because they are often used interchangeably. The term "data" shall be used in its usual scientific sense to refer to measurements or observations that have little interpretational content attached to them. The term "evidence," on the other hand, usually carries with it the sense of something that might be introduced in a court of law in order to bolster one of two opposing points of view. The term "evidence," although it generally appeals to data, usually also includes an interpretation of the data that is designed to persuade and that usually involves crucial assumptions and logical inferences. What sometimes is labeled as evidence, and trumpeted dogmatically as proof contrary to the biblical account of earth history, is most often laden with interpretation. Such so-called evidence invariably involves *a priori* assumptions utterly contrary to God's revealed Word. Sadly, many Christians insist that the opening chapters of the Bible are inconsistent, or even in conflict, with the modern geological synthesis. They maintain that the Bible, therefore, needs to be reinterpreted to make it compatible with man's understanding of earth history as "read" in the rocks. In so doing, they have failed to grasp and appreciate the fundamental thought processes by which verifiable observations (data) become evidence. An example will help illustrate this fundamental distinction.

Geologists often describe different sandstone layers as having been deposited in a desert environment in some instances, or by fluvial processes in others. Thus, it is argued that an aeolian sandstone formed in a desert environment, perhaps even between other sediment layers deposited by water in marine environments, is totally incompatible with the global Flood as described in the Scriptures. However, what is not explained, and thus what is not readily apparent to lay people and those not schooled in the art of geologic reasoning, is that desert or marine environments are never actually observed in the rocks. The wind and/or water which deposited the sand grains are no longer observed, having completed their work in the unobservable past. What we do observe, however, are the shapes of the sand grains, how they are stacked with respect to one another, and various structures in the rock layers produced by the depositional processes. Such observations are *data* and are distinct from any interpretation imposed on them that is claimed to be *evidence* against the global Flood.

Of course, such interpretations do have some validity attached to them, but when used as evidence to claim "proof" that the biblical record is wrong, untrustworthy, and/or needing reinterpretation to produce compatibility with the said evidence, one should carefully examine the assumptions that underlie the interpretations. Thus, in the example of the aeolian and marine sandstones, the key *a priori* assumptions applied to the raw data (observations) to produce the resulting interpretations include: (a) the belief that only presently observable processes are responsible for sedimentation; and (b) the belief that only presently observed rates of sedimentation processes have operated in the past. It should be immediately apparent that neither of these assumptions is in any way provable, yet they are routinely applied by the geological community to deny that there is any evidence in the rocks of the global Flood. After all, we do not observe a global flood in action today to enable us to see and record its effects. So how then can the global Flood be so dogmatically dismissed as a model for explaining what we observe in those sandstone layers? On the other hand, there can be validity in using present-day observable processes to understand how these sandstone layers may have been deposited, since present-day processes may duplicate the features we observe in the sandstones; but this does not "prove" that the sandstone layers were not deposited during a global Flood.

Thus, the assumptions one adopts in order to interpret the observable data are a matter of choice, since there is no external objective scientific yardstick for determining which assumptions are the best to adopt. Of course, to admit that the observable data could be explained by the global Flood is tantamount to accepting the reliability of the early chapters of the Bible as a literal record of earth history, which in turn makes God sovereign over man and man accountable to Him. The bias exhibited by one's choice of assumptions may not simply be a matter of objective science, but rather primarily of one's subconscious spiritual condition.

Implicit in the assumptions upon which the modern geological synthesis is built is the belief that the earth's history spans billions of years. After all, presently observable geological processes acting continuously at current rates would seemingly have taken countless years to generate just one thick widespread sandstone layer. When the timespans represented by successive layers in the rock record are summed, it seems quite logical to derive the millions of years claimed for the accumulation of a local sequence of sedimentary rock layers, then billions of years for the earth's history when all the successive local sequences are summed on a global scale. As impressive as the modern geological synthesis may seem, it needs to be emphasized that much of the edifice consists of interpretations built on a foundation of assumptions that are not provable on the basis of observations or scientific objectivity. Nevertheless, observable data do form the building blocks of this imposing edifice, and thus it is crucial that the data be distinguished from interpretations so that as the edifice is dismantled, the building blocks can be retained in order to use them in building the creation/Flood model for a biblical geology within the scriptural framework of earth history.

The modern geological synthesis has two critical components. The first of these is the *geologic column*, which was established more or less in its present form during the 19th century. The second is *plate tectonics*, which was developed in the 1960s and early 1970s and which now provides the global tectonic framework for describing and integrating all scales of geological processes. Therefore, in seeking to distill the data in the modern geological synthesis from that which is based on interpretations, it is of the utmost importance that these two crucial components be closely examined.

45

THE GEOLOGIC COLUMN

No one disputes that exposed rock layers observable all over the earth's surface, seen stacked on top of one another as they often are in hillsides and cliffs, lend themselves to being "read" like the pages of a book. In the early days of the development of geology as a science, interest in studying and characterizing individual rock layers was often rather localized and frequently in the immediate vicinity where mining activity was taking place. However, it was not long before efforts were undertaken to compare and correlate rock layers from location to location to produce regional geologic maps. As these efforts spread, the local sequences of rock layers began to be correlated from region to region across most of Europe. The eventual result became known as the geologic column.

It needs to be emphasized that the rock layers making up the pages of this "book of earth history" are not all found exposed to view at any one spot on the earth's surface. Instead, this "book" is a composite of many local rock strata sequences, partial by themselves, that must be correlated with one another based on portions of the vertical sequence they share in common to form the whole "book." Furthermore, because of the geological processes required to produce the sequences of rock strata, there is a time factor implied. However, the amount of elapsed time is a matter of interpretation.

When the geologic column was being developed, there was considerable debate about whether the rock layers had been deposited catastrophically (during the biblical Flood), or whether deposition had occurred at presently observed rates of sedimentation. The outcome was in favor of "the present is the key to the past," rather than a continued recognition that the unobservable past could only be understood from the eyewitness revelation given us in Scripture by God. Invoking the argument that observed natural laws were inviolable, advocates trumpeted this new outlook as a victory for human reason over Scripture. Accordingly, it was not necessary to look beyond presently observed environments and processes of sedimentation, and observable rates of these processes, to explain the formation of the rock strata. Again, this choice was not based ultimately on objective scientific inquiry, but rather on a philosophical preference. The crucial assumption that presently observed geological processes can be extrapolated reliably into the unobservable past (uniformitarianism), however, can be tested. We shall see in subsequent chapters that from the observations we have today, the case is overwhelming that this assumption is demonstrably false.

Historical Development

Nevertheless, the basic principles embodied in the geologic column are based on observational data that at face value imply relative age relationships between strata, but not necessarily the millions-of-years interpretation imposed on the strata by the uniformitarian assumption. Foundational to any understanding of the sequential order of rock layers is the principle of superposition, which states that in any sequence of flat-lying rock strata, the oldest layers are at the bottom and the youngest at the top. Based on the observed deposition of sediment layers, this principle ought to apply regardless of whether the deposition is slow and gradual or extremely rapid as in a global watery cataclysm (e.g., the Genesis Flood). This principle of superposition was first enunciated in a book by Nicolaus Steno published in 1669.[1] Steno had studied the rocks of Tuscany in northern Italy, but in keeping with other naturalists of his day, he envisaged the sequential deposition of the strata during the Flood of Noah's day. Steno also stated that when any series of strata are deposited, they must be nearly horizontal; tilted and deformed strata are the result of displacement by earth movements after deposition.

The first systematic attempts to formalize a system of correlating strata regionally were made just after the middle of the 18th century. Johann Lehmann (1756) applied the superposition principle on a wide scale in northern Germany to establish the order of his three main classes of "mountains."[2] Distinguished by the rocks from which they are composed, he considered them to represent three different periods of deposition, from oldest to youngest:

1. "Mountains" formed at the formation of the earth and consisting of crystalline rock with steep and unsystematic layering;
2. "Mountains" formed during Noah's Flood and consisting of non-crystalline rocks with regular, horizontal, or near-horizontal layers of fossiliferous sediments; and
3. "Mountains" formed since the Flood by local events (earthquakes, volcanic eruptions, flooding by rivers and the sea) and consisting of unconsolidated materials.

Meanwhile, Giovanni Arduino (1760) in Italy came to similar conclusions regarding the three kinds of "mountains" formed of the three classes of rocks,

---

1   W. B. N. Berry, 1968, *Growth of a Prehistoric Time Scale Based on Organic Evolution*, San Francisco, CA: W. H. Freeman and Company, 24-25.

2   C. O. Dunbar and J. Rodgers, 1957, *Principles of Stratigraphy*, New York: John Wiley & Sons, Inc., 289–290; Berry, 1968, 28–31; S. Boggs, Jr, 1995, *Principles of Sedimentary and Stratigraphy*, 2nd ed., Saddle River, NJ: Prentice Hall, Upper, 4–5.

but he named them the Primitive, the Secondary, and the Tertiary.[3] Also, George Füchsel (1761) in Germany divided the Flood rocks into nine rock units which he called series.[4] Füchsel's work was extraordinary in that it contained a remarkable geologic map (drawn in perspective) and a cross-section that showed he understood the full implication of dipping rock layers.

During the rest of the 18th century, considerable success was achieved in tracing beds by their lithologic characters over large areas in northern Germany, in northern France, and in southern England; and the law of superposition was expanded, due to the influence of the German Abraham Werner (1787), into the principle that the age of rocks everywhere can be told from their lithologic characters.[5] Applied universally, however, this Wernerian principle soon ran into grave difficulties, and in the first years of the 19th century it was discarded in favor of the Law of Faunal Succession, that the relative ages of the rocks everywhere can be told from their fossil content.[6] This relationship became apparent as many collectors of the time noted that fossils they obtained from stratigraphically lower layers in any succession of rocks were different from those collected from the upper layers. Based on these observations, Frenchman Georges Cuvier (1817) concluded that several revolutions had been produced on the earth's surface by great catastrophes, and that these had led to profound changes in the nature of the rocks and of such fossils as they contained.[7] Because the presence of certain fossils permitted the conclusion that the rocks containing them had been deposited from a fluid, Cuvier thought the fossils were the remains of once-living organisms that had been annihilated during the catastrophes. New organisms had been created following each catastrophe, so that the succession of catastrophes killed off one set of creatures and a new set was created after each catastrophe. The catastrophes were concluded to have been sudden in occurrence. In strict adherence to biblical tenets, Cuvier believed the last of them had been the Genesis Flood. Thus, because new organisms were created after each catastrophe, each new creation was characterized by new associations of organisms, which explained the faunal succession in successive groups of rock layers.

However, in spite of Cuvier's theories, no general principle was induced from the empirical observations of fossils until the work of William Smith in England.[8] Though Smith received only limited schooling and was employed by a surveyor while in his late teens, he became so proficient in his surveying duties that he was soon entrusted with numerous engineering tasks as well. In 1793, he did

---

3   Berry, 1968, 33–34; Dunbar and Rodgers, 1957, 290; Boggs, 1995, 4–5.

4   Berry, 1968, 31–33; Dunbar and Rodgers, 1957, 290.

5   Berry, 1968, 34–39; Dunbar and Rodgers, 1957, 290; W. C. Krumbein and L. L. Sloss, 1961, *Stratigraphy and Sedimentation,* 2nd ed., San Francisco, CA: W.H. Freeman and Company, 10–11.

6   Berry, 1968, 50–53; Boggs, 1995, 6.

7   Berry, 1968, 43–44.

8   Berry, 1968, 53–59; Krumbein and Sloss, 1961, 12; Boggs, 1995, 6.

the survey work for a canal in Somerset and supervised its construction. This gave him ample opportunity to work out the stratigraphic succession of the rock layers above the coal beds in that area, and because fossils were plentiful in many layers, he collected them and observed the aggregates in each layer. His studies soon revealed that each rock unit was typified by a definite fossil aggregate (or assemblage). Smith made notes on the local stratigraphic sections. He knew how to identify strata by their fossils, so he could determine a particular stratum's position in a succession of strata by its fossils, even where the relationships were otherwise obscured. Hindered by a lack of time and by his poor education, Smith did not push toward publishing his ideas, but he realized that he could demonstrate his knowledge in map form. He pursued this objective with zeal and developed geologic maps of the area around Bath during the 1790s, depicting on them four units now known as the Coal Measures, the Trias, the Lias, and the Oolite.

When his employment with the canal-building firm terminated in 1799, Smith worked on a series of civil engineering jobs in many different parts of Britain; and wherever he traveled he made notes of the rock successions and the fossils contained in each unit. Before long, his notes had grown so voluminous and his ideas so exciting to him that his professional work became only a means to an end—that of completing a geologic map of England and Wales. During the first few years of the 19th century, Smith made small maps on which only a few formations were portrayed, but progress toward publication of a comprehensive geologic map of England and Wales was slow. His circle of friends continued to encourage him with the project. One of them had a large collection of fossils from northern Somerset, was well-read in science, and had accompanied Smith on several trips to see for himself the succession of strata, each typified by a faunal aggregate (assemblage). When given the opportunity, Smith was able to arrange his friend's collection of fossils according to the strata from which they had come, assuring him that throughout the entire area the same strata were always found in the same superpositional sequence, typified by the same distinctive fossil aggregates.

Thus, in 1799 Smith's friends had coaxed him into dictating a list of the strata succession in northern Somerset with details of the lithologic aspect of each unit, the fossils they contained, their thicknesses, and the localities at which each unit might be studied. This list was widely circulated soon thereafter and demonstrated that Smith had not only grasped, but also had used, the principle of faunal succession in a certain area before the year 1800. While Jean Louie Giraud-Soulavie (1779) in France had recognized that rock layers in a local stratigraphic section were characterized by distinctive fossil aggregates,[9] Smith had gone further than that by demonstrating that particular strata intervals could be recognized over a broad area by their unique fossil assemblages. Using the knowledge of faunal succession that he had so carefully gleaned in his surveying duties, Smith

---

9   Berry, 1968, 51–52, 56.

was able to place any fossiliferous rock formation in its proper superpositional relationship by examination of its fossils and comparison of its faunal assemblage with others whose stratigraphic position he knew. Smith thus made use of the principle of superposition to enable him to determine the relative relationship of one fossiliferous bed to another, and therefore one fossil assemblage to another. Once the relative relationship of fossil-bearing beds had been established, Smith could then use any given isolated fossil aggregate to determine the position of the rocks bearing it in an overall rock succession.

Smith continued to travel, work, study, and compile data; his burning desire was to finish his colored geologic map.[10] In 1812 with the aid of about 400 subscribers, headed by Sir Joseph Banks, the printing of his map was begun, and finally, on May 23, 1815, the first copy of *The Geological Map of England and Wales* was presented by Smith to a meeting of the Board of Agriculture. Unhappily, Smith's great accomplishment was ignored at the time of its publication by most of those who would have been considered geologists, but this does not diminish his contribution to geology in demonstrating through his geologic map that the hypothesis he had formulated regarding faunal succession was a broadly applicable general truth—a principle. It was not until February 1831 that Smith received appropriate acknowledgment as the "Father of English Geology" when he was presented with the Geological Society of London's first award of its Wollaston Medal by the society's president, Cambridge University geology professor Adam Sedgwick.

As a consequence of Smith's work early in the 19th century, geologists using the principle of faunal succession were able to demonstrate the existence of a sequence of large magnitude fossil aggregates coinciding with the succession of rock strata. Each aggregate (or assemblage) was first studied in an area in which its position in the overall sequence of such aggregates could be established, and in which there were a relatively large number of the fossils taken to constitute the diagnostic aggregate. This sequence of fossil assemblages thus provided the essential key to geologists in different countries, enabling them to correlate between their local strata sequences. Indeed, during the latter part of the 18th century and into the 19th, geologists in nearly every country of Europe were engaged in tracing strata, collecting fossils from them, and establishing local strata sequences. For example, Cuvier and Alexandre Brongniart studied the rocks in the Paris Basin, and using the chalk as their starting point, worked out the stratigraphic order of the rock units throughout the basin based on both the lithological and paleontological characteristics of each unit.[11]

During the early 19th century when geologists were correlating local strata sequences to develop the geologic column and produce geologic maps, the

---

10   Berry, 1968, 57–59.

11   Berry, 1968, 61.

major divisions of the rocks of the earth's crust were still considered to be those recognized by Lehmann, Arduino, and Werner, namely the Primitive, Secondary, and Tertiary (or in some places, Primitive, Transition, Secondary, and Tertiary).[12] These major divisions were equated with the biblical divisions of earth history— creation (Primitive), the Flood (Secondary), and post-Flood (Tertiary). The timescale assigned to strata sequences was relative and also complied with the biblical timescale for earth history, with the Secondary rocks being assigned to the Flood year.

Individual rock bodies ("formations" in today's usage) were assigned to one of these major divisions according to their general appearance and, to some extent, on their strata superpositional relationships. Groups of formations were sometimes classified as "series," such series being considered as first-order subdivisions of the major divisions. As work with strata units developed during the 19th century, formations came to be thought of as second-order subdivisions. No interpretation was needed to recognize any of these strata units; that is, they were all descriptive rock units. The fossils in the rocks were used in the same manner as the sizes of the grains forming the rock units, or their colors—descriptively—to denote and map a unit. Fossils were not interpreted for their time significance until after William Smith demonstrated the principle of faunal succession, which he demonstrated in compiling his geologic map.

Furthermore, the rock units that are today called formations, and the groups and series of such formations, were then only descriptive units, having no place in a timescale based upon interpretation of fossils; so the names attached to many of these rocks units were widely used and well-known to geologists before Smith demonstrated the validity of the principle of faunal succession. Because of this, many of these same names were later used for interpretative units in the geological timescale that was developed. Many of these widely-used descriptive rock units did contain fossils, and the recognition of diagnostic fossil aggregates (assemblages) in these mappable rock units was not, in any way, a matter of interpretation dependent upon any uniformitarian or evolutionary assumptions. Strata sequences could be walked and mapped in the field, and so the transition in fossil content of these units was an empirical observation.

It was only subsequently, with the popularizing of uniformitarianism and Darwin's evolution theory, that the faunal succession of fossils was interpreted as an evolutionary sequence over millions of years. The geological timescale was thus constructed and imposed on the empirically-developed geologic column as an interpretation arising from uniformitarian and evolutionary assumptions.

---

12   Berry, 1968, 61–63.

Terminology Used

As geologic mapping accelerated and the rock units were not only being studied across Europe but in North America and elsewhere, there was a proliferation of terms being used to describe and group the basic rock units. Thus, the need for greater uniformity and standardization of terminology became evident. As a result of a motion put forward by a group of American geologists, the First International Geological Congress was convened in 1878 in Paris to study "uniformity in geologic reports with respect to nomenclature and map symbols."[13] International commissions were appointed to consider these matters, and national committees to work with the commissions. These commissions reported to the Second Congress, held in Bologna in 1881. Their reports were vigorously debated and the proposals in them put to the vote, one by one. The decisions reached there resulted in a dual hierarchy of terms—physical, mappable rock unit terms, devoid of absolute time and evolutionary connotations; and interpretive time unit terms—which have been in standardized usage in geologic science ever since.

Of course, discussion and debate have continued over definitions and terms in subsequent International Geological Congresses, and International Commissions on Stratigraphy have continued to meet to resolve problems arising from geologists' attempts to apply the standardized terminology and procedures in their field mapping. Thus, according to the *International Stratigraphic Guide* of 1994,[14] the primary formal unit of lithostratigraphic classification used to map, describe, and interpret the geology of a region is still the formation, which is a cohesive body of rocks identifiable by its lithologic character and stratigraphic position. Two or more formations make up a group, while several associated groups with significant lithologic properties in common can be termed a supergroup. For convenience, a group of formations may also be divided into subgroups. Within a formation, a named lithologic entity is called a member and a distinctive layer within a member of a formation is called a bed.

This hierarchy of terms, according to the scale of the rock units mapped, is applied to give descriptive coherency to what is known as the lithostratigraphic or geologic column. Its development has a historic basis, as just outlined, which involved empirical observations, a process which continues to this day. In recent years, the need has arisen for another type of rock unit to be recognized on a regional scale which transcends the parallel hierarchy of lithostratigraphic units described above. These are termed "unconformity-bounded units," and are defined as bodies of rocks bounded above and below by specifically designated, significant, and demonstrable discontinuities in the stratigraphic succession (angular unconformities, disconformities, etc.), preferably of regional or interregional

---

13   Dunbar and Rodgers, 1957, 290.

14   A. Salvador, ed., 1994, *International Stratigraphic Guide: A Guide to Stratigraphic Classification, Terminology, and Procedure*, 2nd ed., Trondheim, Norway: The International Union of Geological Sciences, and Boulder, CO: The Geological Society of America, 31–36.

extent.[15] The diagnostic criteria used to establish and recognize these stratigraphic units are their two designated bounding unconformities. These also are mappable stratigraphic units and are generally composed of diverse types of rocks. Again, it should be emphasized that these are mappable units based on empirical observations and are not derived by interpretation based on assumptions.

Distinct from, but parallel to and imposed upon, the stratigraphic or geologic column made up of physical, mappable rock units is the geological timescale or chronostratigraphic column, with its own hierarchy of interpretative time-rock units.[16] Thus, the basic working unit of chronostratigraphy is the stage, which can be subdivided into substages, or alternately, several adjacent stages, which may be grouped into a superstage. Two or more stages grouped together are called a series, while several series can be grouped together into a system. The parallel equivalent chronologic unit terms are age (stage), epoch (series), and period (system). Yet another hierarchy of terms are those for what are called biostratigraphic units, which are bodies of rock strata that are defined or characterized on the basis of their contained fossils.[17] Even though they are defined by empirical observations of fossil assemblages in rock units, these biostratigraphic units are distinct from the lithostratigraphic units of the geologic column.

There is good reason to be specific here about the official definitions of all these terms, and the significance of this procedure will be apparent shortly. The *International Stratigraphic Guide* clearly distinguishes between these different types of units and describes very clearly the relationship between them. As stated previously:

> Lithostratigraphic units are the basic units of geologic surface or sub-surface mapping....Lithostratigraphic units are based primarily on the lithologic properties of rocks—sedimentary, igneous, and metamorphic. The fossil content of lithostratigraphic units may in certain cases be an important distinguishing element in their recognition, not because of the age significance of the fossils but because of their diagnostic lithologic (physical) properties....Inasmuch as each stratigraphic unit was formed during a specific interval of geologic time…the concept of time, however, properly plays little part in establishing or identifying lithostratigraphic units and their boundaries. Lithologic character is generally influenced more strongly by conditions of formation than by time of origin; similar rock types are repeated time and again in the stratigraphic sequence.[18]

---

15   Salvador, 1994, 45–48.

16   Salvador, 1994, 77–85.

17   Salvador, 1994, 53–64.

18   Salvador, 1994, 99.

The *Guide* goes on to describe biostratigraphic units as

> ...based on the fossil content of the rocks. The selection and establishment of biostratigraphic units are not determined by the lithologic composition of the rock strata, except that the presence or absence of fossils and the kinds of fossils present may be related to the type and lithofacies [the collective lithologic character] of the rocks in which they are found. Lithostratigraphic and biostratigraphic units are fundamentally different kinds of stratigraphic [rock] units and are based on different distinguishing criteria....Both lithostratigraphic and stratigraphic units reflect the environment of deposition, but [only] biostratigraphic units are influenced by, and indicative of, geologic age."[19]

> Chronostratigraphic units are defined as encompassing all rocks formed during certain timespans of Earth history regardless of their compositions or properties. By definition, these units everywhere include rocks of only a certain age, and their boundaries are everywhere isochronous [formed at the same time]. This is in contrast with lithostratigraphic units that can be objectively recognized wherever there are rocks....Whereas other kinds of stratigraphic units are largely established and distinguished on the basis of observable physical features, chronostratigraphic units are identified on the basis of their time of formation—an abstract character [subject to interpretation].[20]

Thus, based on the careful definitions of these terms and the relationship between them, it can be emphasized, yet again, that there is a clear distinction between the lithostratigraphic (rock) units of the geologic (rock) column, based on empirical observations and mapping, and biostratigraphic (fossil) and chronostratigraphic (time-rock) units of the geological timescale, which are based on reasoning and interpretation subject to uniformitarian and evolutionary time assumptions. It is possible to name, describe, and discuss the lithostratigraphic units of the geologic column as distinct from, and without the interpreted time constraints of, the geological timescale.

Unfortunately, confusion can be engendered by the fact that there is a single system of names for this dual system of rock and time-rock units. Indeed, among the major units of the interpretative geological timescale, which were originally descriptive rock units of the geologic column, are the Cambrian, Carboniferous, Jurassic, Cretaceous, and Tertiary.[21] Thus, if Jurassic rock units are being discussed, the terminology refers to lithostratigraphic units of the Jurassic "system-group" section of the geologic column, without necessarily referring to the interpreted

---

19   Salvador, 1994, 100.

20   Salvador, 1994, 101–102.

21   Berry, 1968, 63.

timespan for the Jurassic period in the geological timescale. It is imperative that this distinction, which is made by definition in the *International Stratigraphic Guide*, be recognized, understood, and maintained. If we wish to refer to the empirical data of the lithostratigraphic (geologic) column, we can do so without accepting and/or implying the millions of years dictated by the interpretative geological timescale imposed on it.

46

A CLASSIC EXAMPLE OF A LOCAL GEOLOGIC COLUMN

As indicated earlier, there is no one place on the earth's surface where the rock units making up every part of the lithostratigraphic or geologic column (Figure 2) are all found in the correct sequence, one on top of the other. However, there are a number of areas in different parts of the world where there is a good sampling of a relatively large portion of the column, making it available for study. One such area is in northern Arizona and southern Utah.

In the Inner Gorge at the bottom of the Grand Canyon are exposed the crystalline Precambrian rocks, which would have been classified by early geologists as "Primitive" (Figure 3 on page 441). These rocks consist of metamorphosed sedimentary and volcanic rocks intruded by a variety of granitic rocks.[1] Exposed in a number of places in the bottom of the Grand Canyon, particularly in the eastern Grand Canyon, are sediments and lava flows of the upper Precambrian Grand Canyon Supergroup that unconformably overlie the crystalline basement (Figure 3). These sediments are generally devoid of any fossils, though a few trace fossils and/or *problematica* have been reported but seem to be very scarce.[2] The best known genuine fossil in these rocks are stromatolites and associated microfossils in the Kwagunt Formation of the Chuar Group near the top of the Grand Canyon Supergroup sequence.[3] These strata were variously tilted prior to being eroded, because the flat-lying Cambrian rock units unconformably overlie them (Figure 3). This unconformity is known regionally as the Great Unconformity.

Above the Great Unconformity, the overlying Cambrian rock units exposed in the walls of the Grand Canyon are similar to Cambrian rocks elsewhere in the world in that they contain a great diversity of fossils, including all major phyla of animals. This is in stark contrast to the scarcity of fossils in the voluminous

---

1 S. S. Beus and M. Morales, ed., 2003, *Grand Canyon Geology,* 2nd ed., New York: Oxford University Press.

2 S. A. Austin, 2000, The pre-Flood/Flood boundary: Correcting significant misunderstandings, *Creation Ex Nihilo Technical Journal,* 14 (2): 59-63.

3 T. D. Ford and C. M. Dehler, 2003, Grand Canyon Supergroup: Nankoweap Formation, Chuar Group, and Sixtymile Formation, in *Beus and Morales,* 53-75.

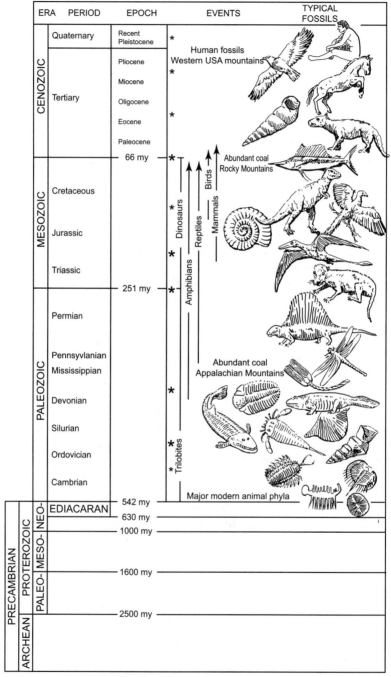

Figure 2. The geologic column as it appears in many textbooks, showing its standard named subdivisions. The alleged geologic timescale for some of the key strata boundaries, and some of the representative fossils found in this rock record, are also shown. The asterisks mark the locations of alleged "mass extinctions."

underlying Precambrian sedimentary rocks. Except for some fish scales,[4] the animals fossilized in the Cambrian rocks are marine invertebrates. Above the Cambrian rock units in the walls of the Grand Canyon is an apparent gap, with no Ordovician or Silurian rock units, and only thin and discontinuous Devonian rock units (Figure 3). There is evidence of erosion into the topmost Cambrian rock unit, but it is unclear whether Ordovician and/or Silurian layers were originally deposited on top of the Cambrian rock units and then eroded away, or whether there was just a cessation of sedimentation in this area. Elsewhere, Ordovician and Silurian rock units contain fossilized fish and invertebrates, but these fossils are first abundant in Devonian rock units. Fossilized trilobites are a widespread, very diverse, and unique part of the fossil assemblages in the so-called Paleozoic sedimentary rock units. Sitting on top of the Devonian rock units in the walls of the Grand Canyon are Mississippian, Pennsylvanian, and Permian rock units; the Mississippian and Pennsylvanian together are elsewhere called the Carboniferous (named after the many extensive coal beds in this part of the geologic column sequence). Pennsylvanian and Permian rock units contain fossils of more invertebrates, amphibians (first found in Devonian rock layers), reptiles (represented by their fossilized footprints), and land plants. A Permian rock unit forms the rim of the Grand Canyon, so all the rocks in the Grand Canyon are either Precambrian or belong to the so-called Paleozoic section of the geologic column sequence.

However, to the north of the Canyon, where the Paleozoic rock units exposed in the walls of the Canyon dip toward the north, Triassic rock units are present on top of them.[5] These include the brown Moenkopi Formation and the very colorful Chinle Formation in the Vermillion Cliffs (Figure 4). These Triassic rock layers contain dinosaur remains and other fossils not present in the Paleozoic rock units. A little further north up the so-called "Grand Staircase," Jurassic rock layers appear on top of the Triassic strata. The most prominent Jurassic formation is the Navajo Sandstone, which is spectacularly exposed in Zion National Park as part of cliffs up to 2,000 feet (610 meters) high. Above them are other Jurassic and Cretaceous rock units. Fossils of dinosaurs and a number of other extinct reptiles are found only in these so-called Mesozoic strata. In some places, the first mammal and bird fossils are also found in the lower to middle Mesozoic rock units; these bird and mammal fossils never are common and all represent extinct groups. The Mesozoic strata also contain many invertebrate and plant fossils, as well as the first flowering plant fossils in Cretaceous rock units.

Even further north in Utah are some rock units above the Cretaceous layers that represent the so-called Cenozoic portion of the geologic column sequence (Figure 4). These rock units include the Eocene Wasatch Formation that forms the colorful

4   J. E. Repetski, 1978, A fish from the Upper Cambrian of North America, *Science* 200: 529-5311.

5   M. Morales, Mesozoic and Cenozoic strata of the Colorado Plateau near the Grand Canyon, in *Beus and Morales,* 2003, 212–221.

cliffs and ridges in Bryce Canyon National Park, and a volcanic layer on top of the Wasatch. The uppermost sedimentary rock units in the sequence are localized Pleistocene and Holocene deposits. These Cenozoic rock layers, including the Wasatch Formation, contain many fossils of plants, invertebrates, and vertebrates (including birds and mammals), representing types not found lower down in the rock sequence. Human fossils are found only in the Pleistocene rock layers at the top of the rock sequence in this geologic column.

In northern Arizona and southern Utah, successive rock layers spanning much of the sequence of rock units making up the geologic column are exposed in a series of cliffs and hillsides, beginning in the walls of the Grand Canyon and then upward in the stratigraphic sequence as one travels northward to the Bryce Canyon area. Figures 3 and 4 are cross-sections through this area, showing the rock layers dipping to the north and extending beneath the next exposure above and to the north of them. Not only is this sequence evident in the rock layers exposed at the surface in cliffs and canyon walls, but the drilling of oil wells has confirmed that this same sequence of rock units exists beneath the surface throughout the region. The rock chips recovered during drilling confirms that the rock layers are where they should be underground, consistent with the observed sequence of rock layers in the Canyon walls and cliff exposures.

In the Grand Canyon-Bryce Canyon region and other places across the earth's surface, the major rock units of the geologic column are exposed in order, layer upon layer (Figure 2). In many other places, only a part of the rock sequence of the geologic column is present. Where large portions of the geologic column are present, the rock layers with their fossils are found in a consistent sequence, unless faults and overthrusts have caused layers to be moved around. Thus, the geologic column itself is not an imaginary construct—not an abstract representation of interpretation built upon unprovable assumptions about timescale and geological processes in the past—but instead is based on the empirical data of field observations and careful geologic mapping.

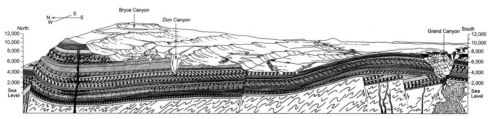

Figure 4. An extended geologic cross-section from the Grand Canyon (right) to Bryce Canyon (left), showing the "Grand Staircase" of progressively stepped, colored cliffs from the North Rim of Grand Canyon up through Zion Canyon to Bryce Canyon.

47

CORRELATION OF STRATA BETWEEN LOCAL GEOLOGIC COLUMNS

As noted twice already, the complete sequence of rock units that make up the geologic column is not found in any one place or region on the earth's surface, even though much of it is present in some places, as can be seen in the northern Arizona-southern Utah area. This raises the question: How did the details of the complete rock unit sequence of the geologic column become standardized? And how is it decided where any isolated local sequence of rock units fits into the standardized geologic column? The answer is, of course, that strata are correlated with one another, from the known to the unknown. But on what basis?

Stratigraphic correlation is the demonstration of equivalency of stratigraphic (rock) units.[1] The methods of correlation are either direct (formal) or indirect (informal). Direct correlation can be established physically and unequivocally. Physical tracing of continuous stratigraphic units is the only unequivocal method of showing correspondence of a rock unit in one locality to that of another. On the other hand, indirect correlation can be established by numerous methods, such as visual comparison of instrumental well logs (drill-hole records) or fossil assemblages. However, such comparisons have different degrees of reliability and therefore can never be entirely unequivocal.

The process of correlation must of necessity begin with the formal definition of rock units, for which there are two chief requisites, namely, mappability and lithologic constancy. Such formally defined rock units must be readily identified by objective lithologic criteria and should be easily delineated in the vertical sequence or succession in which they occur by surfaces representing changes in lithologic character or breaks in the depositional continuity at, for example, bedding planes. Lithologic constancy in a rock unit may be expressed by a single dominant rock type or by a distinctive intercalation of several lithologies, but in either case there is lateral continuity of the lithologic character. In areas of either monotonously homogeneous or excessively heterogeneous rock unit sequences, it is often crucial for correlating rock units to find a rock layer that can be delimited

---

1   Dunbar and Rodgers, 1957, 271–278; Krumbein and Sloss, 1961, 332–351; Boggs, 1995, 519–529.

by an easily recognizable, distinctive lithology that can be readily traced over a vast lateral extent. These are called *marker beds*.

The object of correlation is to establish the equivalency of rock units and strata sequences separated geographically. Of course, direct, continuous tracing of a lithostratigraphic (rock) unit from one locality to another is the only correlation method that can establish the equivalence of such a unit without doubt. This correlation method can be applied only when strata are continuously or nearly continuously exposed. An excellent example of this is in the Grand Canyon, where the rock units exposed in the walls of the Grand Canyon may be physically traced continuously for more than 130 miles (210 kilometers) laterally from east to west. Outcrops as continuous as those of the Grand Canyon are, of course, rare, but even with discontinuous outcrops, a rock unit, usually a formation or member within a formation, can often be traced satisfactorily by assuming its continuity, an assumption that has proved correct in most cases where it could be tested in drill-holes or mines. Alternately, if physical continuity is not reliable for correlation because of discontinuous outcrops and/or faulting, then correlation must depend on the matching of strata from one area to another on the basis of lithologic similarity and stratigraphic position. The success of such correlation depends upon the distinctiveness of the lithologic attributes used for correlation, the nature of the stratigraphic succession, and the presence or absence of lithologic changes from one area to another.

Lithologic similarity can be established on the basis of a variety of rock properties. These include gross lithology (e.g., sandstone, shale, or limestone), color, heavy mineral assemblages, or other distinctive mineral assemblages; primary sedimentary structures such as bedding, cross-lamination, ripple marks, and the like; even thickness and weathering characteristics. Obviously, the greater the number of properties that can be used to establish a match between strata, the more reliable the match can be. A single property such as color or thickness may change within a given rock unit, but a suite of distinctive lithologic properties is less likely to change. Fossils and fossil assemblages may also contribute to the lithologic identities of rock units. This is particularly true of rock units that are largely composed of fossil fragments, such as limestones. Thus, for example, a particular limestone that may be identified by the large number of crinoid columnals of which it is composed, might serve to distinguish it from other limestones in the stratigraphic sequence.

However, the most reliable lithological correlations are often made when it is possible to match not just one or two distinctive rock units, but a succession of several distinctive units. Thus, another crucial aspect for accurate correlation of rocks units by lithologic identity is the importance of the position of rock units in the stratigraphic succession. Under normal circumstances, each lithological unit possesses a unique position with reference to other units above and below, so that once the stratigraphic succession is established in any area under study, then succession itself becomes a primary tool in correlation. Thus, where the lithology of a rock unit is not sufficiently distinctive to permit correlation from place to place, the position of the unit in the local stratigraphic succession may be the only satisfactory method.

Another way in which position in a stratigraphic succession is important has to do with establishing correlation of strata by relation to some highly distinctive and easily correlated unit or units. Such distinctive marker beds serve as control units for correlation of other strata above and below. For example, a thin volcanic ash bed may be easily recognized throughout a particular region, and if it is the only such bed in the stratigraphic succession in that region and cannot therefore be confused with any other bed, it can serve as a distinctive marker bed. Strata immediately above or below this control unit can be correlated with a reasonable degree of confidence with strata that are in a similar stratigraphic position with respect to the control unit in other areas.

These were the means used for correlating rock units by early geologists in the late 18th century and early 19th century. For example, William Smith used lithologic character and fossil assemblage content to correlate rock units in England and Wales to produce his geologic map of 1815. Indeed, along the coast of southern England, the Cretaceous and Jurassic rock units are well exposed and easily identified by their distinctive lithologic features, including fossil assemblages; and many of these units can be traced northwards because of physical continuity and/ or their distinctive lithologic features and fossil assemblages.[2] Other correlations could be made across northern Europe. Of course, in the Grand Canyon the strata exposed in its walls are physically continuous along its length, but many of the formations have distinctive lithologic and other features in addition to their unique sequence of stacking. Thus, where these rock units outcrop in other areas, in cliffs or on hillsides, they can be readily identified, even where there may have been thickening or thinning of the formations, or where some are absent, because of their distinct lithologic features and the constancy of the overall stratigraphic sequence. The same is true not only for the Paleozoic rock units of the Grand Canyon, but for the Triassic and Jurassic formations of the Colorado Plateau, which stretches northward from the Grand Canyon area across Utah and eastward into Colorado. These Triassic and Jurassic formations consist of a highly distinctive succession of largely red-to-green siltstone and mudstone units interstratified with red-to-white, cross-bedded sandstones. This succession of formations is so distinctive that it can be recognized and correlated lithologically with considerable confidence over wide areas of the Colorado Plateau (Figure 5), even where some of the formations thin and become absent.

---

2   M. House, 1989, *Geology of the Dorset Coast,* London: The Geologists' Association.

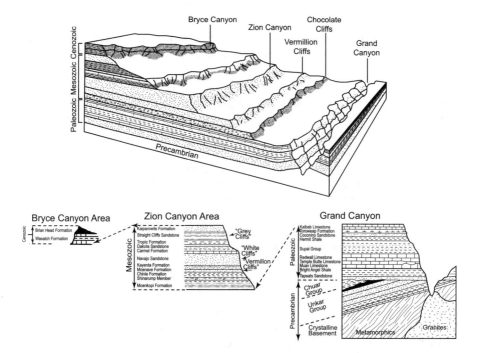

Figure 5. The succession of named rock layers making up wide areas of the Colorado Plateau, from the Grand Canyon northwards up the colored cliffs of the Grand Staircase to Bryce Canyon.

It is important to recognize that fossils and fossil assemblages are an important lithologic feature that historically was used to correlate strata. This was prior to the time when uniformitarian and evolutionary assumptions gained ascendancy in the ruling paradigm that has become the modern geological synthesis. Indeed, as a common working man, detached from the philosophical discussions of his day (arguments over the uniformitarian ideas of Hutton which were progressively popularized by Playfair and then Lyell), Smith successfully compiled his geologic map of England and Wales simply because he focused on the observational data of his field work. The empirical data he accumulated confirmed the principle of faunal succession, which he espoused. This was no "armchair" interpretation of the data, which is why the rock unit details of his geologic map have remained essentially the same since his time. This is true even though within the uniformitarian evolutionary paradigm, the fossils and fossil assemblages in these rock units are interpreted in terms of the geological timescale and the assumed operation of geological processes over millions of years. It is thus both feasible and possible to use fossils and fossil assemblages for correlation of the rock strata containing them without encumbrance by or commitment to the geological timescale.

With the growth of the oil industry and the development of new technologies, dramatically more information is now available from the subsurface on rock unit sequences in geographic localities that would not otherwise be available for study due to the lack of outcrop. Not only can the rock chips recovered from drill-holes be studied, but after drilling, a variety of instruments can be lowered down the drill-hole to measure the rock properties of the different units intersected by the hole. The data obtained from these measurements are often referred to as "well logs," which are digital records of variations in rock properties such as electrical resistivity, sound wave speed, and adsorption and emission of nuclear radiation in the surrounding rocks. These variations reflect changes in gross lithology, mineralogy, fluid content, porosity, and other properties in the subsurface formations. Thus, while correlation by use of well logs is not based directly on lithology, most of the properties measured by well logs are closely related to it.

Characteristically, the well log data from adjacent drill-holes are very similar, but the degree of similarity tends to decrease in more distant holes. By working with a series of closely-spaced drill-holes, however, it is possible to correlate across an entire sedimentary basin, even when pinch-outs or facies (lithology and rock characteristics) changes occur. Lithologic information obtained from actual drill cores, as well as from the rock chips recovered during the drilling, can be extremely important in this correlation process because well logs by themselves in general do not uniquely constrain the actual lithology. This is because variations in the well log data often may be influenced more by generic rock properties such as porosity and fluid content instead of more lithology-specific properties. Correlation by well logs is usually based more on the positions of individual rock units in the overall succession of units, rather than on the specific characteristics of any individual unit. Correlation by well logs is thus the approximate subsurface equivalent of correlation of surface sections by position in the regional stratigraphic succession.

Another modern correlation technique used extensively to build a "picture" of subsurface rock sequences is the *seismic reflection method*, in which waves created by an explosion are reflected from subsurface rock interfaces back to the surface.[3] Appropriately designed detectors pick up the reflected waves, and the signals are processed to produce, in cross-section, a graphical representation of the subsurface strata sequence and structure. The method is based on the principle that elastic or seismic waves travel at known velocities through rock materials, with characteristic velocities associated with each type of rock—for example, shale 3.6 km/s, sandstone 4.2 km/s, limestone 5.0 km/s. Seismic waves are reflected strongly from discontinuities such as bedding planes and unconformities, and the travel time of the elastic waves enables accurate calculation of the depths to such discontinuities.

Primary seismic reflections occur in response to the presence of significant density-velocity changes at either unconformity or bedding surfaces. In particular, reflections are generated at unconformities, because unconformities separate rocks

---

3   Boggs, 1995, 532–543.

having different structural attitudes or physical properties, particularly different lithologies. Similarly, reflections are generated at bedding surfaces because, owing to lithological textural differences, a velocity-density contrast exists between some sedimentary beds. The seismic records produced as a result of these primary reflections from unconformities and bedding surfaces have distinctive characteristics that can be related to depositional features such as lithology, bedding thickness and spacing, and continuity.

Generally, the first step in the interpretation process is to identify the major large-scale stratification patterns in the seismic records. Parallel patterns, including subparallel and wavy patterns, are generated by strata that would appear to have been deposited at uniform rates. Divergent patterns are characterized by wedge-shaped units in which lateral thickening of the entire unit is caused by thickening of individual reflection sub-units within the main units, signifying lateral variations in rates of deposition. Prograding patterns are generated by strata that were deposited by lateral outbuilding or progradation to form gently-sloping depositional surfaces, such as along the front of a delta. Erratic patterns represent a disordered arrangement of reflection surfaces owing to penecontemporaneous, soft-sediment deformation, or deposition of strata in a variable, high-energy environment. On the other hand, reflection-free areas on seismic records represent homogeneous, non-stratified units, such as igneous masses or thick salt deposits, or highly contorted or very steeply dipping strata.

In the conventional structural application of seismic data, seismic reflections are used to identify and map the structural dispositions of subsurface sedimentary rock layers, which can then be traced and correlated between outcrops and drill-holes across sedimentary basins. By contrast, the subsequently developed technique of seismic stratigraphy uses seismic reflection correlation patterns to identify depositional sequences, which will often consist of packages of rock units related to one another. These "packages" of strata are often separated by unconformities.

Seismic sequence analysis involves the identification of these major reflection "packages" that can be delineated by recognizing surfaces of discontinuity, chiefly unconformities, which are surfaces of erosion or non-deposition that represent major hiatuses.[4] These packages of rock units represent depositional sequences, which are defined as stratigraphic units composed of relatively conformable successions of genetically related strata, bounded at their tops and bottoms by unconformities or their correlative conformities.[5] As such, these "packages" are unconformity-bounded units, as defined earlier. Depositional sequences are found

---

4   Boggs, 1995, 511–519, 547–552.

5   R. M. Mitchum, Jr, R. Vail and S. Thompson, III, 1977, Seismic stratigraphy and global change of sea level, Part 2: The depositional sequence as a basic unit for stratigraphic analysis, ed. C.E. Payton, *Seismic Stratigraphy - Applications to Hydrocarbon Exploration*, American Association of Petroleum Geologists Memoir 26, 53–62.

in two forms—transgressive sequences and regressive sequences.[6] Transgression refers to what appears to be the movement of a shoreline in a landward direction, the vertical succession of sedimentary units thus produced beginning with coarser-grained sediments fining upwards into finer-grained sediments superimposed on top of them. Regressive sequences result from the apparent seawards movement of a shoreline, leading to a vertical superposition of contiguous lateral facies (rock types) in which coarser-grained sediments become progressively stacked on top of finer-grained sediments, leading to a coarsening-upwards succession.

In depositional sequences, there exists a well-demonstrated relationship between lateral facies and vertically stacked or superimposed successions of strata. This concept was first formally stated by Johannes Walther in 1894 and is now called the law of the correlation (or succession) of facies, or simply Walther's law.[7] It states that those facies found in conformable vertical successions of strata also occurred as laterally adjacent facies. This relationship can be seen in both transgressive and regressive depositional sequences (Figure 6 on page 442), which are interpreted as being produced by rising water levels and falling water levels respectively.

The advent of the seismic reflection method has revolutionized the analysis of strata sequences and correlation of them across and between sedimentary basins. Because the seismic reflection method can "see" through enormous thicknesses and lateral extents of rock units and sequences, it has been possible to analyze sedimentation patterns on regional and continental scales. As a result, various orders of stratigraphic cycles in the geologic column have been recognized, ranging in scale from transgression-regression cycles to the megasequences recognized by Sloss in North America as early as 1963.[8] These are major rock-stratigraphic units defined as being larger than a group or supergroup, of inter-regional scope, and traceable over large areas of the continent, being separated, delimited, and bounded by unconformities of inter-regional scope. Six of these megasequences have been recognized across North America, each separated by demonstrable regional unconformities that can be traced from the Cordilleran region in the west to the Appalachian Basin in the east. Each megasequence represents a major cycle of transgression and regression. Recognition of these megasequences is based on physical relationships among the rock units. Thus, for example, the Tonto Group in the Grand Canyon, comprising the Cambrian strata of the Tapeats Sandstone, the Bright Angel Shale, and the Muav Limestone (Figure 3), represents in this region the Sauk megasequence. To the extent that these megasequences physically exist on such a large scale must be significant, given also that they represent the rising and falling of the waters responsible for deposition of their sedimentary rock units.

---

6   Boggs, 1995, 501–507.

7   Boggs, 1995, 501.

8   L. L. Sloss, 1963, Sequences in the cratonic interior of North America, *Geological Society of America Bulletin*, 74: 93–114.

48

THE PRECAMBRIAN OF THE GEOLOGIC COLUMN

As a result of physically tracing sequences of rock units from sections in canyon walls, cliffs, and hillsides, and using sound principles of correlation, including newer technologies, it has been firmly established that the geologic column is a physical reality, at least for the fossil-bearing sequences and megasequences, from Cambrian to Recent rock units. But what of the Precambrian? In those parts of the earth's surface where Precambrian rocks are exposed to view, the strata are often deformed and metamorphosed to varying degrees, which can make it difficult to unravel the original strata sequences. Furthermore, while there are extensive exposures of Precambrian rocks in several places on the earth's surface, such as in Canada, Australia, and southern Africa, the complexity of most Precambrian rock sequences, together with their isolation from one another, makes correlation among these occurrences much more challenging. Indeed, while lithologic properties are still useful for correlation, very few fossils are present in these rocks and only of a few different types, so the law of faunal succession is not applicable. Physical continuity for tracing strata can often be difficult due to the deformation and frequent metamorphism.

Yet the thicknesses of the Precambrian strata sequences are enormous, even greater than the cumulative thicknesses of Cambrian-Recent strata. Furthermore, numerous geological processes seem to have been involved in producing these strata sequences, sometimes with several episodes of deformation followed by erosion, further deposition, and then further deformation. Thus, the geologic column which has been constructed for the Precambrian would seem to incorporate a longer geologic history than that for the Cambrian-Recent strata. But have these correlations been made on a sound basis? Is the Precambrian part of the geologic column as trustworthy a physical reality as the Cambrian-Recent portion?

Some examples will help to put these issues into perspective. In the walls of the Grand Canyon, the Cambrian-Permian strata together amount to a total thickness of about 1,340 meters (4,400 feet), and to the north traversing up the "Grand Staircase" of southern Utah, the Triassic-Cretaceous strata have been measured in total as approximately 1,585 meters (5,200 feet) thick. The overlying Tertiary strata comprise a thickness of at least 183 meters (600 feet), so the total cumulative thickness of Cambrian-Recent strata in the regional geologic column of the Grand Canyon-Bryce Canyon area totals at least 3,110 meters (10,200 feet).[1] By contrast, the Precambrian portion of the local Grand Canyon geologic column is comprised of the crystalline basement unconformably overlain by the sedimentary rock strata and basalt flows of the Grand Canyon Supergroup. In the crystalline basement, granitic rock masses have been demonstrated to have intruded into metamorphosed sedimentary and volcanic rocks. Once known as the Vishnu Schist complex, these metamorphic rocks have been more recently renamed and subdivided into three mappable units—the Rama, Brahma, and Vishnu Schists, collectively named the Granite Gorge Metamorphic Suite.[2] While the complexities of metamorphism and deformation of the original sedimentary and volcanic rock units make it difficult to quantify the original thicknesses, it is nevertheless estimated that the total thickness of these sedimentary and volcanic rock units was more than 12,200 meters (40,000 feet). Subsequent to metamorphism and deformation, erosion occurred, so that the Grand Canyon Supergroup sediments and lava flows accumulated unconformably on this crystalline basement. The thickness of these strata has been measured at 3,960 meters (13,000 feet), which means that the total original thickness of sedimentary and volcanic rock strata in the Precambrian portion of the geologic column represented in the Grand Canyon amounts to at least 16,160 meters (53,000 feet), a much greater thickness than that of the Cambrian-Recent strata of this local geologic column.

However, even greater thicknesses of rock units are known in Precambrian strata sequences in Australia. For example, in the Hamersley Basin of Western Australia (Figure 7 on page 442) the sedimentary and volcanic rock strata (including the Wyloo Group) are estimated at almost 21,500 meters (70,500 feet) thick.[3] The rock strata of the adjoining Bangemall Basin overlie, with an angular unconformity, the strata of the older Hamersley Basin, and in the western portion of the Bangemall Basin, the total thickness of the sedimentary rock units is about 13,700 meters (45,000 feet). Thus, the total cumulative thickness of these successive sequences of Precambrian rock strata represented in these sedimentary basins alone is approximately a staggering 35.2 kilometers (35,200 meters, 115,500 feet, or almost 22 miles)!

Similarly, in the Pine Creek Basin in northern Australia, which is unconformably overlain by the McArthur Basin (Figure 7),[4] there is a total thickness of sedimentary

---

1   Beus and Morales, 2003, *Grand Canyon Geology.*

2   E. R. Ilg, K. E. Karlstrom, D. Hawkins and M. L. Williams, 1996, Tectonic Evolution of Paleoproterozoic Rocks in the Grand Canyon: Insights into Middle-Crustal Processes, *Geological Society of America Bulletin,* 108(9): 1149-1166.

3   A. D. T. Goode, Proterozoic Geology of Western Australia, in Hunter, D. R., ed., 1981, *Precambrian of the Southern Hemisphere,* Amsterdam: Elsevier, 105-203; A. F. Trendall, The Hamersley Basin, in A. F. Trendall and R. C. Morris, ed., 1983, Iron-Formation: Facts and Problems, Amsterdam: Elsevier, 69-129.

4   K. A. Plumb et al, The Proterozoic of Northern Australia, in Hunter, 1981, 205-307.

rock strata of about 14 kilometers (46,000 feet). These strata are overlain by up to 1.2 kilometers (3,900 feet) of predominantly acid volcanics, and intruded by up to 500 meters (1,640 feet) of diabases. Thus, the total thickness of Proterozoic strata in the Pine Creek Basin is about 15.7 kilometers (51,500 feet). In the unconformably overlying McArthur Basin, there is a total thickness of sedimentary rock units of at least 12 kilometers (39,000 feet). Thus, the total cumulative thickness of all the successive rock units in these two basins is approximately 27.7 kilometers (90,500 feet, or 17.1 miles). Furthermore, the lateral extent of individual rock units is not insubstantial. In the Pine Creek Basin, for example, several thick units of black shales and carbonaceous schists can be correlated across the basin over a distance of about 200 kilometers.[5]

Additionally, in the example of the Hamersley and Bangemall Basins, the Hamersley Basin strata sequence unconformably overlies the granite-greenstone terrane of the Pilbara Block (Figure 7).[6] The regional geology comprises granitoid-gneiss complexes and intervening belts of shallowly-dipping to tightly-folded volcanic and sedimentary rocks that have suffered only low-grade metamorphism. The succession of rock units in these so-called greenstone belts has been postulated to have a maximum thickness of between 20 and 30 kilometers, although the maximum true thickness preserved in any single area is believed to be about 15 kilometers.[7] Thus, if this conservative estimate of 15 kilometers thickness for the rock units of the strata sequence in the Pilbara Block is added to the thickness estimates for the strata sequences in the successively overlying Hamersley and Bangemall Basins, then the total cumulative thickness of the rock units in these sequences of successive Precambrian sedimentary and volcanic rocks total about 50 kilometers (about 164,000 feet, or 31 miles)! Quite clearly, the regional geologic column in this area of Western Australia has a cumulative sequence of rock units, based on the empirical observations, which is about sixteen times thicker than the approximate 3.1-kilometer-thick rock unit sequence in the local Cambrian-Recent geologic column of the Grand Canyon-Bryce Canyon area of the southwestern United States.

These examples alone should be sufficient to prove that there is a substantial record of Precambrian rock units that surpasses in magnitude the Cambrian-Recent rock unit sequence. However, these cited examples are not isolated occurrences. There are other extensive and thick Precambrian rock sequences in other parts of Australia. And across most of Canada, it is Precambrian rock sequences that are exposed at the surface. Indeed, there are Precambrian terranes exposed over large

5   R. S. Needham, 1980, I. H. Crick and G. Stuart-Smith, Regional geology of the Pine Creek Geosyncline, in *Uranium in the Pine Creek Geosyncline*, ed. J. Ferguson and A. B. Goleby, Vienna: International Atomic Energy Agency, 1-22.

6   A. F. Trendall, 1990, Hamersley Basin, in *Geology and Mineral Resources of Western Australia*, Geological Survey of Western Australia, Memoir 3: 163-189.

7   B. Krapez, 1993, Sequence stratigraphy of the Archean Supracrustal Belts of the Pilbara Block, Western Australia, *Precambrian Research* 60: 1-45.

areas on every continent, including Antarctica, and some important Precambrian rock sequences are found along the coasts of Greenland. The same sound principles of correlation have been studiously applied in field mapping of the rock units in these Precambrian sequences, so that one can have a high level of confidence at least in the physical reality of the local geologic columns for each of these Precambrian terranes.

The question then remains as to whether the composite geologic column for the Precambrian, built up by correlating among all the local geologic columns of these Precambrian terranes worldwide, can be trusted equally well as physical reality?

Perhaps the clearest response to that question can be illustrated from the examples in Western Australia already discussed, namely, the extensive, thick sequences of rock units in the greenstone belts of the Pilbara Block, in the Hamersley Basin, and in the Bangemall Basin, which unconformably overlie one another in what therefore represents an extremely thick continuous geologic column encompassing all the rock units sequentially in these adjoining Precambrian terranes. Similar cumulative rock unit sequences are found in other adjoining Precambrian terranes worldwide, such as the McArthur Basin unconformably overlying the Pine Creek Basin in northern Australia, the Transvaal, Witwatersrand and related rock unit sequences unconformably overlying the Kaapvaal Craton in South Africa, and the Grenville Province rock unit sequences unconformably overlying the Superior Province greenstone belts in Canada.

Thus, within the Precambrian terranes, the same sound principles of correlation used to establish the Cambrian-Recent rock unit sequence of the geologic column as a physical reality have been successfully applied, in correlation with careful field work that has established in a number of instances a relationship between various adjoining Precambrian terranes. The result is a confident recognition of the Precambrian section of the standardized geologic column as a physical reality, even if the complete sequence of Precambrian rock units is not present in any one region on the earth's surface.

Correlation of rock units between non-adjoining Precambrian terranes has primarily depended upon lithological similarities. For example, granite-greenstone belt terranes are typical of, and are confined to, the Precambrian shields in every continent. These can be demonstrated to be the basement to other adjoining and nearby Precambrian terranes, making these granite-greenstone belt terranes the first-formed and oldest rock unit sequences in the Precambrian geologic record.[8] Thus, it seems eminently reasonable to equate all these granite-greenstone belt terranes worldwide as belonging to the same section of the Precambrian geologic column. Another example of similar lithology used for correlation among Precambrian terranes are the highly distinctive, banded-iron formations that are

---

8   K. C. Condie, ed., 1994, *Archean Crustal Evolution*, Amsterdam: Elsevier; K. C. Condie, 1997, *Plate Tectonics and Crustal Evolution*, 4th ed., Oxford, England: Butterworth-Heinemann.

found in the Hamersley Basin of Western Australia, the Transvaal Group of South Africa, and the Mesabi Iron Range of northern Minnesota, for example, all in rock unit sequences overlying granite-greenstone belt terranes.[9]

Further up the Precambrian geologic column are rock units with a scattered worldwide occurrence called *diamictites*,[10] which contain large angular boulders and rock fragments supported in a very fine matrix. These have been conventionally interpreted as evidence of globally widespread glaciation, but which could all reasonably be interpreted as the result of submarine debris flows.[11] Again, such a correlation worldwide is quite logical and proves to have useful ramifications. Furthermore, such a global correlation of these diamictite units in the Precambrian does have a precedent in the Cambrian-Recent part of the geologic column, where there are similar diamictite units, for example, in Permian rock sequences.

Yet another useful lithologic feature that has aided correlation, primarily in upper Precambrian rock units, has been fossil content. As stated previously, fossils are extremely rare in Precambrian rock units, but with the intensity of study applied to Precambrian terranes in recent years, some distinctive fossils have been found in rock units that have been correlated with one another as belonging to the upper Precambrian portion of the geologic column. Thus, stromatolites, the fossilized remains of sedimentary structures apparently built by colonies of cyanobacteria, have been found in distinctive forms characteristic of particular rock units that have then been correlated.[12] There is also the distinctive Ediacara megascopic fossil assemblage, first found in South Australia, but then found in a similar stratigraphic position in similar rock unit sequences in other parts of the world (for example, in the Wood Canyon Formation in the rock unit sequence of the Death Valley area of California).[13] This fossil assemblage has been found in a number of locations worldwide in rock units not far below Cambrian rock units, and has proven useful in correlating rock units worldwide and relating them to the uppermost portion of the Precambrian rock record.

It is also relevant that radioisotopic dating, particularly of volcanic and intrusive rock units, has been extensively used in Precambrian terranes as a correlation tool,

9   A. F. Trendall et al, Precambrian Iron-formation, in Eriksson, G. et al, ed., 2004, *The Precambrian Earth: Tempos and Events*, Amsterdam: Elsevier, 403-421.

10   L. A. G. Schermerhorn, 1974, Late Precambrian mixtites: glacial and/or non-glacial? *American Journal of Science*, 74: 673-824; N. Eyles, 1993, Earth's glacial record and its tectonic setting, *Earth Science Reviews*, 35: 1-248; N. Eyles and N. Januszczak, 2004, "Zipper-rift": a tectonic model for Neoproterozoic glaciations during the breakup of Rodinia after 750 Ma, *Earth-Science Reviews*, 65:1-73.

11   Schermerhorn, 1974; M. J. Oard, 1997, *Ancient Ice Ages or Gigantic Submarine Landslides?*, Chino Valley, AZ: Creation Research Society, Monograph 6.

12   J. Kazmierczak, S. Kempe and W. Altermann, Microbial origin of Precambrian carbonates: lessons from modern analogues, in Eriksson, 2004, 545-564; W. Altermann, 2004, Precambrian stromatolites: problems in definition, classification, morphology and stratigraphy, in Eriksson, 2004, 564-574.

13   G. M. Narbonne, 1998, The Ediacara biota: a terminal Neoproterozoic experiment in the evolution of life, *GSA Today*, 8 (2): 1-6.

and very recently the technique has been also applied to Precambrian sedimentary rock units. Notwithstanding other considerations that will be discussed later, the use of this tool in correlation between Precambrian rock sequences likely can be justified; this is because the radioisotopic ratios which are the basis of the interpreted "ages" can instead simply be used as further geochemical "fingerprints" characteristic of these rock units and, in some instances, the minerals within them (e.g., zircon).[14] The measured radioisotopic ratios are empirical data in the same way as other geochemical analyses for major and trace elements in the rocks. Thus, the use of radioisotopic ratios in correlating Precambrian rock units should not automatically be scorned and disregarded simply because vast "ages" are commonly derived from them (by interpretation using in-built uniformitarian assumptions, which will be discussed later). In any case, the validity of radioisotopic "dating" (based directly on radioisotope ratios) as a correlation tool for rock units within and between Precambrian terranes has been established by the empirical observation that the results obtained are consistent, and do strongly agree, with correlations established by physical continuity in the field, and correlations according to lithological similarities. Thus, for example, where a succession of rock unit sequences unconformably overlie one another, as in the case of the greenstone belts in the Pilbara Block being unconformably overlain by the rock sequences of the Hamersley Basin, which are in turn unconformably overlain by the rock unit sequences in the Bangemall Basin, the radioisotopic "dates" do correctly follow the progression of the rock sequences from oldest to youngest "ages."[15] Similarly, radioisotopic "dating" of volcanic units in the greenstone belts of the Pilbara Block correlate with volcanic units in the greenstone belts of the Superior Province of Canada with similar "ages," which is as expected based on the lithological similarities between the rocks in these greenstone belts at the base of these Precambrian rock sequences.[16]

The sum total of these considerations, therefore, inevitably leads to the conclusion that the Precambrian portion of the geologic column is as much a physical reality as the Cambrian-Recent portion of the geologic column. For some, this may at first be hard to accept because of the complexities in many Precambrian terranes, the poor outcrop in some instances, the physical separation of the different Precambrian terranes from one another globally, plus the use of radioisotope dating in correlation. However, intense study of these metasedimentary terranes globally in recent decades—with modern saturation technology such as satellite imagery, airborne geophysics, deep seismic probing methods, plus exhaustive field work and many drill-holes—has produced an incredible array of empirical data that has overwhelmingly confirmed and added to initial correlations; so that the

---

14   A. A. Snelling, Geochemical processes in the mantle and crust, in L. Vardiman, A. A. Snelling and E. F. Chaffin, ed., 2000, *Radioisotopes and the Age of the Earth*, El Cajon, CA: Institute for Creation Research, and St. Joseph, MO: Creation Research Society, 123–304.

15   A. D. T. Goode, Proterozoic geology of Western Australia, in Hunter, 1981, 105-203.

16   C. Thurston and L. D. Ayres, Archaean and Proterozoic greenstone belts: setting and evolution, in Eriksson, 2004, 311-333.

physical reality of the Precambrian rock record can no longer be in question. Of course, this does not mean that all the finer details of the geologic column have been irrevocably established; future study using evermore powerful modern technology will inevitably produce results that will cause some of the finer details to be modified. However, what we can conclude is that the overall "big picture" of the global sequences of rock strata and their relationship to one another as expressed in the standard geologic column is a physical reality that is a reliable record of the earth's geologic history.

49

IMPLICATIONS OF THE GEOLOGIC COLUMN

That the standard geologic column is a genuine physical reality and represents a reliable record of the earth's physical history has a number of far-reaching implications. Foremost among these is the implication that just as the order of physical rock units throughout the whole geologic column is real, then so also is the sequence of different fossils and fossil assemblages found in the rock units of which the geologic column is comprised. Recognizing this, however, emphatically does not imply or require an acceptance of the fossil sequence as being a record of the evolutionary development of life over millions of years of geologic time. The sequence of fossils and fossil assemblages is simply an objective empirical observation. The evolutionary theory of the development of life over millions of years, by contrast, is an interpretation imposed on that empirical data. Thus, disagreement with the evolutionary interpretation of the fossils should not and does not prevent us from recognizing that the sequence of fossils and fossil assemblages in the rock record is genuine and derived from real empirical observations.

As we have seen, where large portions of the geologic column are represented, such as in the Grand Canyon-Bryce Canyon region, the layers with their fossils and fossil assemblages are found in a consistent sequence, except, of course, where faults have caused rock layers to be transposed. In fact, the original study and description of the divisions of the geologic column, particularly the Cambrian to Recent strata, were done largely by creationists, who believed that the fossils and fossil assemblages they were describing in the strata sequences were a record of death and destruction that occurred during the Genesis Flood. Whereas scientific theories and the resultant interpretation changed because of the influence of Lyell and Darwin, the original recognition and description of the rock unit sequences and the fossils and fossil assemblages they contained have remained largely unchanged and essentially correct. In other words, what changed was not the observational data but rather the *interpretation* of how the rocks and fossils were produced and the timescale over which the postulated processes occurred.[1]

---

1   D. M. Raup, 1983, The geological and paleontological arguments of creationism, in *Scientist Confront Creationism*, ed. L. R. Godfrey, New York: W.W. Norton, 147-162.

Because the sequence of fossils and fossil assemblages as represented in the geologic column is based on empirical data, that sequence of fossils and fossil assemblages provides obvious and significant clues as to the geological processes operating during the Genesis Flood. This sequence of fossils provides critical information as to how and when the various fauna and flora were progressively buried and preserved during the Flood. The occurrence and sequence of the fossils and fossil assemblages also provide crucial clues for determining where in the geologic column the record of the Flood begins and ends, as well as where in the geologic record the Creation Week ended, and which strata are the result of geological processes in the pre-Flood era.

Another equally important implication of the physical reality of the geologic column is that the geologic column represents an objective record of geological processes and events in a sequence that actually unfolded in the earth's past. Again, this by no means requires one to accept the notion that geological processes have been operating for millions of years or that a billions-of-years geological timescale for earth history, which is based on a uniformitarian interpretation of the rock record, has validity. However, rejection of the billions-of-years geological timescale imposed on the observational data of the rock record should not cause us to deny or ignore the real geological history recorded in the rock sequences of the geologic column. These empirical data still need to be accounted for within whatever interpretive framework a person might choose.

Accounting for this history is not a simple matter. Attention to detail in geologic mapping of the rock units in each region across the earth's surface has revealed that the geological history recorded in the geologic column is highly complex, based on the relationships of all the various rock units to one another in terms of a relative time sequence (Figure 8 on page 443). Thus, metamorphism of sedimentary and volcanic rocks has occurred over large areas at different relative times, followed by erosion and deposition of further sediments and eruption of further volcanics, with subsequent intrusion of granites. There have been repeated cycles of erosion and deposition, such as the six megasequence cycles identified across North America.[2] These imply a repeated rising and falling of relative water levels. Even in Precambrian rock sequences, sedimentation cycles have been identified, such as the four megasequences in the greenstone belts of the Pilbara Block of Western Australia,[3] and the nine unconformity-bounded supersequences identified for the Calvert and Isa Superbasins of northern Australia (Figure 7).[4]

It is completely understandable, therefore, that once the physical reality of the

---

2   Sloss, 1963.

3   B. Krapez, 1993, Sequence stratigraphy of the Archean supracrustal belts of the Pilbara Block, Western Australia, *Precambrian Research*, 60:1-45.

4   N. Southgate et al, 2000, Chronostratigraphic basin framework for Palaeoproterozoic rocks (1730-1575Ma) in northern Australian and implications for base-metal mineralisation, *Australian Journal of Earth Sciences*, 47 (3):461-483.

geologic column, from Precambrian rock sequences to the Cambrian-Recent rock units, is recognized, then the sheer magnitude of the apparent long and complex geological history for the earth might seem to lend strong support to the uniformitarian interpretation of a billions-of-years geological timescale. In other words, if one looks only at the present slow rates of geological processes, then even allowing for the occasional catastrophe (e.g., flooding, volcanic eruptions, meteorite and asteroid impacts, etc.), it is not hard to be persuaded that the earth's geological history might have spanned billions of years. Of course, that does not prove that the conventional geological timescale is true, but it honestly recognizes why the geological community generally is convinced of it. The implication of these considerations is that to construct a viable and convincing creation-and-Flood framework for earth history requires that we grapple honestly and earnestly with the observational data of the geologic column. These data include both the sequence of fossils and fossil assemblages that occur systematically in the rock unit sequences, as well as the complexities of repeated episodes of metamorphism, deformation, and/or magmatism between repeated cycles of sedimentation and erosion with fluctuating relative water levels.

So, for example, under what conditions does metamorphism occur regionally over hundreds and thousands of square kilometers? Careful mapping in regional metamorphic terranes has demonstrated that they are generally zoned, with the metamorphic rocks in each zone characterized by different mineral assemblages, as demonstrated in the Scottish Highlands as early as 1893 (Figure 9 on page 444).[5] Experimental data on these metamorphic mineral assemblages indicate they formed in response to progressively higher temperatures and pressures having been applied to the precursor sedimentary and volcanic rocks. The highest grade mineral assemblages of the sillimanite zone appear to have reached temperatures and pressures of about 650°C and 6 kb, respectively.[6] The simplest way to have reached these temperatures and pressures is for the precursor sedimentary and volcanic rocks to have been buried to depths of 15 to 20 kilometers. This in turn implies that more than 15 kilometers of erosion have subsequently occurred for these metamorphic rocks to now be exposed at the earth's surface. Of course, some aspects of this scenario are inferred, but the pressure and temperature conditions are consistent with experimental data for high-grade mineral assemblages.

In other regionally metamorphosed terranes, the temperatures and pressures appear to have reached such high levels that the minerals in the rocks with the lowest melting points (quartz and feldspars) actually melted and then recrystallized

---

5   G. Barrow, 1893, On the intrusion of muscovite-biotite gneiss in the southeastern Highlands of Scotland, and its accompanying metamorphism, *Quarterly Journal of the Geological Society of London*, 49: 330–356; G. Barrow, 1912, On the geology of Lower Dee-side and the Southern Highland Border, *Proceedings of the Geologists' Association*, 23: 274–290.

6   F. S. Spear, 1993, *Metamorphic Phase Equilibria and Pressure-Temperature-Time Paths*, Mineralogical Society of America, Washington; K. Bucher and M. Frey, 1994, *Petrogenesis of Metamorphic Rocks*, Berlin: Springer-Verlag.

in segregated light-colored bands alongside dark-colored bands made up of the minerals which did not melt (biotite, hornblende, etc.), producing a rock known as migmatite. Or at slightly higher temperatures, the melt migrated and segregated nearby to recrystallize as a granitic mass (containing a mixture of both these dark and light-colored minerals). Experimental data have shown that this partial melting can occur at temperatures as low as 750°C, but melting temperatures are often higher depending on how much water is present.[7] Huge masses of granitic rocks with surface exposures measuring tens of square kilometers are found in many parts of the world, intruding rock unit sequences at many levels in the geologic column. These upwelling granitic bodies usually leave unequivocal field evidence of having intruded into these other rocks, primarily sedimentary and metamorphic rocks.[8] Sometimes the contact zones outcrop so that the contact metamorphic effects of the heat of the intruded magma on the surrounding host rocks can clearly be seen.[9] Again, the data produced from experiments on the mineral assemblages found in these contact metamorphic zones confirm the temperatures and pressures postulated for the cooling granitic magmas and the effects of the hot water released at the same time.

Large-scale deformation seems to have often accompanied metamorphism and/or magmatism. Strata over extensive areas have suffered intensive folding and faulting, in some cases drastically shortening the dimensions of the original sedimentary and volcanic rock units so that the folding and faulting have caused the upthrusting of huge blocks of deformed rocks to produce mountain ranges.[10] Sometimes the deformation has been so intense that overthrusting has occurred, so that enormous blocks of rocks have sometimes been pushed up over other deformed rocks and moved along a fault plane up to tens of kilometers. As with the episodes which repeatedly produced metamorphic rocks, and sometimes also granitic and other intrusions, deformation events appear to have occurred at many different levels of the geologic column, in rock unit sequences at different locations around the globe. Thus, for example, the American Appalachians are the result of the deformation and uplift of Paleozoic rock strata, whereas the Rockies are deformed and uplifted Mesozoic rock strata. This difference signifies that the respective deformation and mountain-building events occurred at different levels, and therefore at different times, in the rock record. Consequently, any model of earth history needs to account for these different and often large-scale, high-intensity deformation events within the relative time sequence. Some sort

7   W. Johannes and F. Holtz, 1996, *Petrogenesis and Experimental Petrology of Granitic Rocks,* Berlin: Springer-Verlag.

8   F. J. Turner, 1968, *Metamorphic Petrology: Mineralogical and Field Aspects,* New York: McGraw-Hill Book Company; W. S. Pitcher, 1993, *The Nature and Origin of Granite,* London: Blackie Academic and Professional.

9   D. M. Kerrick, ed., 1991, *Contact Metamorphism,* Reviews in Mineralogy Volume 26, Mineralogical Society of America, Washington.

10   F. Press and R. Siever, 1986, *Earth,* 4th ed., New York: W.H. Freeman and Company; S. M. Stanley, 1989, *Earth and Life Through Time,* 2nd ed., New York: W.H. Freeman and Company.

of real physical processes were responsible for these deformation events and their associated metamorphism and magmatism, processes that occurred in different places at different relative times. Various physical processes were also responsible for producing economic accumulations of minerals and metals in ore deposits that tend to be concentrated at certain zones in the rock record and at diverse geographic locations. Thus, the recognition of the geologic column as a real and reliable composite record of accumulation of rock units globally in a relative time sequence carries with it the implication that the earth has a complex history involving many diverse physical processes, including cycles of deposition of sediments, burial of fossils and fossil assemblages, rising and falling global water levels, rock deformation, metamorphism and magmatism, and the formation of ore deposits.

50

PATTERNS AND TRENDS IN THE GEOLOGIC COLUMN—
INVOLVING DIFFERENT ROCK TYPES

There can be no doubt that the conventional geological community has been highly successful in systematizing the empirical observations of the rock record by constructing their geologic model of earth history which incorporates the manifold features of the geologic column. Of course, the billions-of-years geological timescale has been imposed upon this relative time sequence of events that produced this rock record. However, rejecting that timescale, and the uniformitarian assumption for the generally slow rates of past geologic processes that underlies that timescale, does not allow us to ignore the empirical data of the rock record and the relative time sequence of geological processes and events that produced it. To the contrary, there are good reasons for accepting the veracity of the rock record as documented by the conventional geological community, as well as for affirming the relative time sequence for geological processes and events responsible for producing that record and all its associated features.

Such recognition means that there is essential consensus on the empirical data that needs to be explained in any geologic model of earth history, including the biblical geologic model based on the scriptural framework of creation and the Flood. It should be self-evident that if the biblical geologic model provides an even better explanation of the empirical data than the modern geological synthesis, then apart from spiritual issues, the rules of science should mandate that the biblical paradigm ought to supersede and replace the uniformitarian-evolutionary paradigm. Moreover, recognition of the validity of the empirical data allows for acceptance of patterns and trends that are evident in the data. Such patterns and trends obviously need to also be explained within the biblical framework of earth history, but their existence potentially provides clues as to how the various geological processes can be understood within the biblical geologic model and provides indications of, for example, conditions in the pre-Flood world; the nature of the processes and conditions God used during the creation of the earth, its surface and its inhabitants; and the relative time sequence of geological processes and their operation during the Flood event.

Patterns Involving Sedimentary Rocks

The first group of patterns and trends we observe in the rock record is the occurrence and relative abundance of different rock types, which are not uniformly distributed through the rock sequences of the geologic column. Figure 10 (page 444) depicts the relative abundance of banded-iron formations at various geographic locations through the geologic column.[1] It is immediately apparent that these distinctive rock units are found only in the Precambrian part of the record and, in fact, occur predominantly in upper Archean and lower Paleoproterozoic sequences, peaking in relative abundance in the Hamersley Basin of Western Australia, the Transvaal Group of South Africa, and in the Lake Superior region of the United States, in the lowermost Paleoproterozoic part of the record. Such a distinctive pattern of occurrence is surely significant.

These banded-iron formations are usually classified as chemical sediments, meaning they apparently precipitated from water, presumably from the ocean, but it is also now recognized that submarine volcanic activity was mostly responsible for supplying the billions of tons of iron required to generate these enormous iron ore rock units. Typical banded-iron formations are thin-bedded or laminated with >15 percent iron content, but they commonly also contain interbedded layers of chert.[2] Many banded-iron formations are characterized by thin wave-like laminations that can be correlated over hundreds of kilometers,[3] and the dominant iron oxide mineral is magnetite. It also seems to be significant that redbeds, detrital sedimentary rocks with red ferric oxide cements, do not appear in the geologic record before middle Paleoproterozoic rock sequences, which is just after the peak in abundance of banded-iron formations in lower Paleoproterozoic rock units.[4] Similarly, the sulfate minerals gypsum and anhydrite, which occur in chemical sedimentary rocks known as evaporites (a term implying an interpreted mode of formation that can be disputed), although known in Archean rock units, do not become important in the geologic record until after the middle Paleoproterozoic rock unit sequences, when the deposition of banded-iron formations was rapidly declining.[5]

1   C. Klein and N. J. Beukes, 1992, Time distribution, stratigraphy, and sedimentologic setting, and geochemistry of Precambrian iron-formations, in *The Proterozoic Biosphere*, ed. J. W. Schopf and C. Klein, Cambridge: Cambridge University Press, 139-146.

2   C. Klein and N. J. Beukes, 1992, Proterozoic iron-formations, in *Proterozoic Crustal Evolution*, ed. K. C. Condie, Amsterdam: Elsevier, 383-417.

3   A. F. Trendall, 1973, Precambrian iron formations of Australia, *Economic Geology*, 68: 1023-1034; A. F. Trendall, The Hamersley Basin, in Trendall and Morris, 1983, 69-129.

4   G. Eriksson and E. S. Cheney, 1992, Evidence for the transition to an oxygen-rich atmosphere during the evolution of redbeds in the lower Proterozoic sequences of South Africa, *Precambrian Research*, 54: 257-269.

5   M. Solomon and S.-S. Sun, 1997, Earth's evolution and mineral resources, with particular emphasis on volcanic-hosted massive sulphide deposits and banded iron formations, *AGSO Journal of Australian Geology and Geophysics*, 17 (1): 33-48.

In contrast to the banded-iron formations, manganese-rich sedimentary rock units are not only found in upper Archean rock sequences, but occur regularly throughout the Paleoproterozoic and the rest of the Precambrian, and are prolific among Cambrian-Recent rock sequences, being most common in the Mesozoic and Cenozoic rock records (see Figure 26c, page 453).[6] On the other hand, even though phosphorites are known in Paleoproterozoic rock units, these phosphate-rich sedimentary rock units are most abundant worldwide in Neoproterozoic-Cambrian rock sequences, with another occurrence peak in middle Paleozoic-Mesozoic rock sequences (see Figure 26c).[7] However, it has been demonstrated that sedimentary phosphate rock units have an episodic distribution in the Cambrian-Recent (Phanerozoic) rock record, with well-defined periods of major phosphate deposition in late Neoproterozoic-early Cambrian, late Permian, late Jurassic, late Cretaceous-early Tertiary and Miocene rock sequences (Figure 11, page 445).[8] The prolific occurrence of sedimentary phosphate rock units at the bases of Cambrian rock unit sequences is particularly intriguing and appears to be the largest of several peaks in phosphorite occurrences near the Cambrian-Precambrian boundary in the rock record.[9]

Interestingly, deposition of evaporite rock units (which should instead be known as precipitites to avoid interpretative connotations) is likewise prolific around the Precambrian-Phanerozoic boundary in Neoproterozoic-Cambrian rock sequences (Figure 12 on page 445). Their deposition was also sharply episodic through the Cambrian-Recent rock record, with peaks in occurrence of such units in Devonian, Permian-lower Jurassic, middle Cretaceous and Miocene rock sequences.[10] Yet another potentially significant trend is that the ratio of dolomite to calcite in sedimentary carbonate rock units (limestones) decreases upwards through the rock record, from entirely dolomitic carbonates in Archean rock sequences to Recent limestones that are wholly calcitic.[11] Furthermore, Archean carbonate rock units are scarce, and while there are short-term variations in the dolomite/calcite ratio in Cambrian-Recent rock sequences, dolomitic carbonates are widespread in Permian rock sequences where evaporite rocks are also prevalent.[12]

---

6   S. Roy, 1992, Environments and processes of manganese deposition, *Economic Geology,* 87: 1218-1236; Solomon and Sun, 1997.

7   J. Cook, J. H. Shergold, W. C. Burnett and S. R. Riggs, 1990, Phosporite research, a historical overview, in *Phosporite Research and Development*, ed. A. J. G. Northolt and I. Jarvis, Geological Society of London, 1-22.

8   J. Cook and M. W. McElhinny, 1979, A re-evaluation of the spatial and temporal distribution of sedimentary phosphate deposits in the light of plate tectonics, *Economic Geology,* 74: 315-330.

9   J. Cook, 1992, Phosphogenesis around the Proterozoic-Phanerozoic transition, *Journal of the Geological Society of London,* 149: 615-620.

10   W. T. Holser, 1984, Gradual and abrupt shifts in ocean chemistry during the Phanerozoic time, in *Patterns of Change in Earth Evolution*, ed. H. D. Holland and A. F. Trendall, Berlin: Springer-Verlag, 123-143.

11   H. D. Holland, 1984, *The Chemical Evolution of the Atmosphere and Oceans*, Princeton, New Jersey: Princeton University Press.

12   S. Q. Sun, 1994, A reappraisal of dolomite abundance and occurrence in the Phanerozoic, *Journal of*

Patterns Involving Igneous Rocks

Patterns of occurrence through the geologic column are not confined just to chemical sedimentary rocks, but they are also apparent among some igneous rocks. Archean terranes are virtually unique, consisting of sequences of volcanic and sedimentary rocks in greenstone belts surrounding dome-shaped complexes of granitic gneisses. While greenstones are found throughout the geologic record, they are much more abundant in Precambrian rock sequences. After the granitic gneiss complexes, greenstones make up most of the balance of the Archean rock sequences (Figure 13 on page 445).[13] Furthermore, although many Archean greenstones differ from younger greenstones by the presence of komatiite (an extremely high melting temperature ultramafic igneous rock with a very high MgO content formed by a high degree of partial melting of mantle rock), the proportion of basalt also is greater in Archean greenstones. In most Archean greenstones, the volume of basalt plus komatiite exceeds that of intermediate plus felsic volcanics; whereas on the whole, Proterozoic greenstones, for which data are available, have smaller proportions of basalt (and usually no komatiite) and range from 20 to 50 percent of felsic volcanics plus andesite. Phanerozoic greenstones are more variable than Precambrian greenstones and are not as prevalent. There is also a broad inverse correlation between the abundances of *greywackes* (sandstones consisting of rock and mineral grains) and basalt plus komatiite in greenstone belts, with most Phanerozoic greenstones having a high proportion of greywacke, and Archean greenstones being dominated by basalt plus komatiite. Furthermore, although there is a great deal of overlap in the proportion of flows to fragmental volcanics in greenstone belts, the flow/fragmental ratio is generally higher in Archean greenstones than in post-Archean greenstones. There also appears to be an absence of Archean greenstone rock sequences with flow/fragmental ratios less than one. This consistently high flow/fragmental ratio in Archean greenstone belt rock sequences appears to be consistent with the lavas having been erupted chiefly as submarine flows in deep water, whereas a great proportion of post-Archean greenstone belt volcanics seems to have been erupted in shallow water.

Perhaps the most distinctive volcanic rock in Archean rock sequences is *komatiite*.[14] Indeed, one of the striking differences between Archean and post-Archean rock sequences is the relative importance of komatiites in Archean greenstone belt rock sequences (Figure 14 on page 446). Komatiites are ultramafic (very low silica) lava flows (or hypabyssal intrusives) that exhibit what is known as a spinifex texture and contain >18 percent MgO. Although komatiites are common in some Archean greenstone successions, they are uncommon in Proterozoic rock sequences, and very rare among Cambrian-Recent strata. It is the high MgO content of komatiites, occurring primarily in the mineral *olivine*, that makes them

---

Sedimentary Research, A64: 396-404.

13   K. C. Condie, Greenstones through time, in Condie, 1994, 85-120.

14   N. T. Arndt, Archean komatiites, in Condie, 1994, 11-44.

distinctive from basalts. The high MgO content implies that the temperatures at which mantle rock melted to generate these magmas were very high. The hottest modern magmas are basaltic komatiites (with 20 percent MgO) that have erupted on Gorgona Island (near Columbia, South America) at temperatures of 1400°C. By contrast, typical basalts (with an MgO content of around 10 percent) erupt at temperatures of around 1250°C. Thus, it is estimated that a komatiite with a 30 percent MgO content, the lowest value for the least altered komatiites, may well have had an eruption temperature as high as 1600°C.[15]

Granitic rocks associated with Archean greenstone belts fall into one of three categories: granitic gneiss complexes and batholiths, diapiric plutons of variable composition which were intruded during deformation of the greenstone belts, and subsequent discordant granite plutons.[16] The gneissic granitoid complexes and batholiths make up the majority of the preserved Archean rocks exposed at the earth's surface today, and are dominantly composed of tonalite, trondhjemite, and granodiorite, thus being referred to as the TTG suite. They contain large infolded remnants of overlying crustal rocks, as well as numerous inclusions of the surrounding greenstone belts. Contacts between TTG complexes and greenstone belts are generally intrusive and usually strongly deformed. All the TTG complexes and the diapiric granitic plutons are geochemically similar to the felsic volcanic rocks in the greenstone belts, suggesting they are genetically related, the felsic volcanics being derived from the same magmas that produced the TTG complexes and diapiric plutons. Furthermore, of significance is the fact that there are several important geochemical differences between Archean and post-Archean TTG granitic rocks. As reflected by their large sodium-plagioclase content, Archean TTGs are relatively high in Na compared to K and Ca (Figure 15 on page 446). In fact, almost all Archean TTGs fall in the tonalite-trondhjemite field, have a limited compositional distribution, and are I-type granitoids. On the other hand, post-Archean granitoids are dominantly calc-alkaline, ranging in composition from diorite to granite, with an abundance of granite-granodiorite. The most striking difference among the trace elements in these rocks is the relative depletion in yttrium and heavy rare earth elements in Archean TTGs compared to post-Archean TTGs. This distinction is particularly well-defined on a La/Yb versus Yb plot (Figure 16 on page 447).[17] The Archean rare earth element patterns are strongly fractionated with low Yb contents, whereas by contrast, post-Archean TTGs show only moderate rare earth element fractionation and a broad range of Yb values. These stark differences suggest that the Archean and post-Archean TTGs were derived from different sources. Experimental data are consistent with this inference, which might be significant in terms of which geological processes were operating to produce these Archean rocks compared with their post-Archean

---

15   E. G. Nisbet et al, 1993, Constraining the potential temperature of the Archean mantle: A review of the evidence from komatiites, *Lithos*, 30: 291-307.

16   H. Martin, Archean grey gneisses and the genesis of continental crust, in Condie, 1994, 205-260; J. Sylvester, Archean granite plutons, in Condie, 1994, 261-314.

17   Martin, 1994.

counterparts.

Anorthosites are coarse-grained intrusive igneous rocks composed of more than 90 percent plagioclase. They frequently are found interlayered with diverse sorts of gabbros and norites in large layered intrusions, but they are also found on their own in completely separate intrusions within Precambrian rock sequences. However, anorthosite intrusions occurring in, or associated with, Archean greenstone belt sequences are distinct from the anorthosite intrusions in Proterozoic rock sequences. Archean anorthosites typically have large equi-dimensional plagioclase crystals, 5 to 30 cm in diameter, of very calcium-rich composition in a mafic groundmass.[18] Field, textural, and geochemical relationships are consistent with most of these Archean anorthosite intrusions being genetically related to the basalts in the greenstone belts where they occur. Typically, they are also relatively small, commonly only a few hundred square kilometers in area. In contrast, the anorthosite massifs that intrude Proterozoic rock sequences are generally much larger, often thousands of square kilometers in area, and appear to be spatially associated with granitic and related intrusions. Furthermore, these Proterozoic anorthosites have plagioclase crystals with roughly equal amounts of calcium and sodium.[19] The close association of granites and Proterozoic anorthosites seems to suggest a genetic relationship between them, but geochemical and isotopic studies indicate that they were not derived from the same parent magma. Thus, it is not clear why there is a difference between Archean and Proterozoic anorthosites. However, this difference does appear to highlight a further fundamental difference between the geological processes that produced the Archean rock sequences compared to the geological processes responsible for the Proterozoic rock record.

Alkaline igneous rocks, including kimberlites and related rocks that host diamonds, as well as carbonatites, do not become important in the geologic record until the upper Mesozoic (Figure 17 on page 447).[20] Although alkaline igneous rocks have been recorded in upper Archean greenstone belt rock sequences, they are extremely rare, and only a relatively small number of occurrences are known in the Proterozoic and Paleozoic. Of course, because the alkaline igneous volcanic centers are usually small, they could easily have been removed by erosion, but they do appear to be significantly absent from Archean rock sequences (Figure 17). This could likewise be significant in the light of other known differences between the Archean and post-Archean rock records.[21]

Moreover, it has been established that for basalts with the same relative Mg content, those from Archean rock sequences are enriched in Fe, Ni, Cr, and Co and depleted

---

18   L. D. Ashwal and J. S. Myers, Archean anorthosites, in Condie, 1994, 315-355.

19   R. A. Wiebe, Proterozic anorthosite complexes, in Condie, 1992, 215-261.

20   Condie, 1997, 168–169.

21   Solomon and Sun, 1997.

in Al compared to most basalts in post-Archean rock sequences.[22] Trace element contents of Archean basalts are also very different from those of post-Archean basalts. Further, the recognized types of basalts present in Archean greenstone belt rock sequences contrast with those present in Proterozoic greenstone belt rock sequences. All of these differences suggest that different sources and geological processes were responsible for these Archean and post-Archean basalts.[23] Similar differences are also observed in mafic dike swarms that cross-cut Archean and post-Archean rock sequences. The trace element geochemistry of these mafic dike swarm rocks is different for those intruding Archean rock sequences compared with those cross-cutting Paleoproterozoic rock sequences. It may also be significant that the trace element geochemistry of mafic dike swarms that cross-cut Neoproterozoic rock sequences is different yet again.[24]

In contrast to the predominance of greenstone belt rock sequences in the Archean geologic record, the rock sequences known as *ophiolites* are marked by their absence (Figure 18 on page 448). The succession of rock strata in complete ophiolite rock sequences has been well-defined from good exposures of such rock strata sequences, particularly those found in the Cambrian-Recent geologic record. This distinctive succession consists of five rock units that clearly represent a cross-section through present-day oceanic crust, as exposed, for example, on Macquarie Island in the southern Pacific Ocean between Australia and Antarctica.[25] Thus, as strictly defined, the earliest known ophiolites in the geologic record occur in upper Paleoproterozoic rock sequences. Although some Archean ophiolites have been described, they lack one or more of the ophiolite components and so may not be fragments of oceanic crust, as seen exposed today on Macquarie Island.[26] Considering the detailed geologic mapping in Archean greenstone belts, it is becoming less and less likely that ophiolites have somehow been overlooked and not identified as such. Thus, it may be possible to conclude that if Archean rock sequences do preserve remnants of what may have been oceanic crust at that time in the geologic record, then the Archean oceanic crust must have been different from remnants preserved in ophiolites in upper Paleoproterozoic-Recent rock sequences.[27]

---

22   N. T. Arndt, 1991, High Ni in Archean tholeiites, *Tectonophysics* 187: 411-420.

23   K. C. Condie, 1989, Geochemical changes in basalts and andesites across the Archean-Proterozoic boundary: identification and significance, *Lithos*, 23: 1-18.

24   K. C. Condie, 1997, Sources of Proterozoic mafic dyke swarms: Constraints from Th/Ta-La/Yb ratios, *Precambrian Research*, 81: 3-14.

25   B. J. Griffin and R. Varne, 1980, The Macquarie Island ophiolite complex: Mid-Tertiary oceanic lithosphere from a major ocean basin, *Chemical Geology*, 30: 285-308; E. M. Moores, 1982, Origin and emplacement of ophiolites, *Reviews of Geophysics and Space Physics*, 20: 735-760.

26   M. J. Bickle, E. G. Nisbet and A. Martin, 1994, Archean greenstone belts are not oceanic crust, *Journal of Geology*, 102: 121-137.

27   Condie, 1997, *Plate Tectonics*, 70-74, 169.

A Pattern Involving Metamorphic Rocks

Finally, there is also a pattern in the rock record of a particular type of metamorphic rock, namely, *blueschists*. Based on experimental data for the formation of their constituent minerals, they appear to have formed at high pressures but relatively low temperatures. It has long been recognized that blueschists occur only in rocks above the lower Neoproterozoic part of the geologic record and seem to be absent in the entire earlier part of the rock record below them.[28] Another noteworthy feature is that blueschists containing minerals reflecting the highest pressures are restricted to the Jurassic-Recent part of the record.[29] Two possible explanations have been proposed for the absence of blueschists in the rock record below the Neoproterozoic. The first possibility is that, subsequent to their formation at high pressures (consistent with deep burial), uplift and erosion of overlying rock units reduced the confining pressures and caused these metamorphic rocks to recrystallize into lower-pressure mineral assemblages, that is, into non-blueschist types of metamorphic rock. The second possibility is that erosion has entirely obliterated the blueschists from the earlier part of the record. Nevertheless, the presence of blueschists in Neoproterozoic-Recent rock sequences is real, and their apparent absence from the earlier rock record may well be an important clue in correctly reconstructing the physical history of our planet.

---

28   W. J. Ernst, 1972, Occurrence and mineralogic evolution of blueschist belts with time, *American Journal of Science,* 272: 657-668.

29   Condie, 1997, *Plate Tectonics,* 173.

51

PATTERNS AND TRENDS IN THE GEOLOGIC COLUMN—
INVOLVING RELATIVE SEA-LEVEL CHANGES

It has been noted how the use of the seismic reflection method in the exploration of sedimentary basins by the oil industry had revolutionized both the correlation of strata in rock sequences across sedimentary basins and led to recognition of larger-scale features in the sedimentary strata record, such as the six megasequences across the North American continent. Furthermore, using seismic sequence analysis, it was possible to delineate unconformity surfaces between strata representing erosion or non-deposition of sediments.[1] Such unconformities appear to be major hiatuses in sediment deposition that represent dramatic declines in the water level, with retreat of water that had been responsible for deposition of the preceding sedimentary rock units. When it was recognized that the next sequence of sedimentary rock layers overlying these unconformities represented rising water levels, it became apparent that sequence stratigraphy could potentially be used to map fluctuations in water levels during deposition of sedimentary rock sequences. When applied on a continental scale, this would seem to imply that these unconformities equated to the rising and falling of sea level globally.[2]

Consistent with these conclusions was the recognition that fining-upwards successions of sedimentary strata above unconformities represented transgressive sedimentation, while coarsening-upwards sequences are consistent with regressive depositional sequences due to falling water levels. However, estimating relative sea level simply by correlating transgressive and regressive strata sequences ignores the possibility that such strata sequences can also result from downwarping or uplifting of the surface on which sedimentary strata are being deposited, apart from any rising or falling of the absolute water level. Nevertheless, using the concepts of sequence stratigraphy to identify transgressive and regressive sedimentation patterns and unconformities in seismic reflection profiles over large geographic regions on different continents, attempts have been made to estimate the changes of sea level that appear to have been recorded in the sedimentary rock sequences

---

1   Boggs, 1995, 511–519, 547–552.

2   Boggs, 1995, 552–561.

of the geologic column.[3]

Figure 19 (page 448), produced by Vail and Mitchum,[92] shows the estimated long- and short-term relative changes in sea level during the deposition of Cambrian-Recent rock sequences. There is, of course, an element of interpretation of depositional features in the Cambrian-Recent strata sequences, but the resulting curve of long-term changes in sea level appears to be consistent with the available observational data of depositional sequences in the rock record. Indeed, the long-term component in sea level change as recorded in the Cambrian-Recent strata seems to be agreed upon by most investigators, whereas the short-term components and amplitudes of variation remain uncertain.

However, what is potentially significant is that according to this evidence, there was a major transgression as sea level rose during the deposition of Cambrian rock strata, with sea level beginning at a level well below the present sea level.[4] Furthermore, sea level apparently never fell to its present level until after the deposition of the Tertiary rock sequences. Even though sea level apparently fluctuated through the Ordovician-Triassic part of the record, the sea level never again fell to the level from which it rose when the Cambrian transgression began. A second major transgression is recorded in Jurassic rock sequences, and the sea level appears to have reached its highest peak by the end of the deposition of Cretaceous rock sequences. Sea level then apparently fell rapidly during the deposition of Tertiary rock units. Estimates of the amplitude of the Cretaceous sea level rise range from 100 to 350 meters above present sea level, while estimates of the sea level rise during deposition of the Cambrian strata are generally in the range of tens of meters.[5]

These are only estimates, for while the Vail sea level curve has been widely accepted, the amplitudes are subject to uncertainty. Therefore, differences in sea levels for the different rock sequences of the Cambrian-Recent geologic column, though significant, can really only be regarded as relative. It needs to be noted also that sea level changes can be influenced significantly by tectonic processes that alter the height of the earth's surface, both of the ocean bottom as well as the surfaces of the continents. For example, it has been estimated that the rise of the Himalayas, while Tertiary rock sequences were being deposited elsewhere on the earth's surface, may well have produced a drop in sea level of about 50 meters.[6] Similarly, dramatic changes in the topography of the ocean floor from Cambrian to Recent almost certainly influenced the relative sea level.

---

3   P. R. Vail and R. M. Mitchum, Jr., 1979, Global cycles of relative changes of sea level from seismic
     stratigraphy, *American Association of Petroleum Geologists Memoir 29,* 469-472; M. Steckler, Changes in
     sea level, in Holland and Trendall, 1984, 103-121.

4   Vail and Mitchum, 1979.

5   T. J. Algeo and K. B. Seslavinsky, 1995, The Paleozoic world: Continental flood, hypsometry, and sea
     level, *American Journal of Science,* 295: 787-822.

6   Condie, 1997, *Plate Tectonics,* 195-196.

In conclusion, while this evidence relating to sea level change is based on interpretation of observational data, it nevertheless is generally accepted as part of the modern geological synthesis. Because flooding of the continents is such a prominent and essential feature of a biblical understanding of earth history, this evidence would appear to be highly significant to the quest to develop a comprehensive and consistent biblical geologic model of earth history.

52

PATTERNS AND TRENDS IN THE GEOLOGIC COLUMN— INVOLVING THE FOSSIL RECORD

It is crucial to recognize that the order of occurrence of fossils in the rock record is based on real and verifiable observational field data and does not depend in any way on the evolutionary interpretation which the conventional geological community imposes on the fossil record. Although the rock sequences and the order of occurrence of the fossils in them clearly imply a relative time sequence, this recognition in no way requires one to accept the uniformitarian geological timescale of billions of years. Nevertheless, in recognizing the reality of the fossil data and the reality of the order of occurrence of the fossils, as well as their geographic distribution, the paramount requirement to account for these observations within any credible geologic model for earth history can be acknowledged at the same time. This certainly includes any model based on Scripture that treats both creation and the Flood as authentic history. Thus, it is important that the pattern of occurrence of fossils be closely examined, because not only do the details need to be explained within the biblical geologic model, but they likely will assist in the construction of that model.

While fossils may seem to be rare in Precambrian sedimentary rock sequences, these rocks are in no way devoid of apparent fossil evidence, even in the earliest-formed lower Archean rock sequences. Two types of evidence are available for identifying what sorts of living creatures were in existence at the time the lower Archean rock units were deposited early in earth history—microfossils and organic geochemical signatures.[1] Many microstructures preserved in rocks can be mistaken for cell-like objects, and metamorphism can produce structures that look remarkably organic, but at the same time can destroy real microfossils. Nevertheless, the oldest well-described assemblage of microfossil-like structures is found in lower Archean chert strata in the Barberton greenstone belt in South Africa.[2] Three types of microstructures, ranging in size from <1 mm to approximately 20 mm, have

---

1   J. W. Schopf, The oldest known records of life: Early Archean stromatolites, microfossils, and organic matter, in S. Bengtson, ed., 1994, *Early Life on Earth*, New York: Columbia University Press, 193-206.

2   A. H. Knoll and E. S. Barghoorn, 1977, Archean microfossils showing cell division from the Swaziland system of South Africa, *Science*, 198: 396-398.

been reported from the Barberton rock sequence and from other lower Archean sediments, such as those of the Warrawoona Group in the Pilbara Block of Western Australia.[3] These are rod-shaped bodies, filamentous structures, and spheroidal bodies, all generally interpreted as prokaryotic bacteria cells. Confirmation that these are in fact fossil bacteria comes from the isotopic signatures of the preserved carbon. Identical organic geochemical evidence has been found in carbonaceous inclusions preserved within grains of apatite in banded-iron formations from the Isua Belt and Akilia Island, west Greenland, claimed to be the oldest known lower Archean sedimentary rocks.[4] There may be reasons to question the validity of some of these observational and experimental data, but the most straightforward interpretation of them strongly implies that at least bacteria were likely living at the time of deposition of these lower Archean sediments very early in the earth's history.

The oldest unambiguous megascopic structures of apparent organic origin are stromatolites in chert and dolostone units in the lower Archean Warrawoona Group in the Pilbara Block of Western Australia.[5] Stromatolites are finely-laminated sediments composed chiefly of carbonate minerals that have formed by the accretion of detrital and biochemical precipitates on successive layers of micro-organisms (commonly cyanobacteria). They exhibit a variety of domical forms and are found in rock sequences from the lower Archean to the Recent. Two parameters appear to be especially important in stromatolite growth—water currents and sunlight. However, there are serious limitations in interpreting ancient stromatolites in terms of modern ones, because the latter are not well understood, even though they occur in a great variety of aqueous environments.[6] Fossil stromatolites are found in increased numbers and complexity in Paleoproterozoic and Mesoproterozoic rock sequences, but then they decrease rapidly in Neoproterozoic rock sequences and are rarely found in Cambrian-Recent strata (Figure 20). Even the conventional geologic community is unsure of the cause or causes of this decline in fossil stromatolites, but one widely suggested and possible explanation is that the chemistry of the ocean waters changed, with decreasing saturation of carbonate resulting in decreased stabilization of algal mats by precipitated carbonate.[7]

---

3   S. M. Awramik, J. W. Schopf and M. R. Walter, 1983, Filamentous fossil bacteria from the Archean of Western Australia, *Precambrian Research*, 20: 357-374; J. W. Schopf, 1993, Microfossils of the early Archean Apex Chert: New evidence of the antiquity of life, *Science*, 260: 640-646.

4   S. J. Mojzsis et al, 1996, Evidence for life on Earth before 3,800 million years ago, *Nature*, 384: 55-59.

5   R. Buick, J. S. R. Dunlop and D. I. Groves, 1981, Stromatolite recognition in ancient rocks: An appraisal of irregularly laminated structures in an early Archaean chert-barite unit from North Pole, Western Australia, *Alcheringa*, 5: 161-181; M. R. Walter, Stromatolites: the main geological source of information on the evolution of the early Benthos, in Bengtson, 1994, 270-286; H. J. Hofmann et al, 1999, Origin of 3.45Ga coniform stromatolites in Warrawoona Group, Western Australia, *Geological Society of America Bulletin*, 111 (8): 1256-1262.

6   Walter, 1994.

7   Condie, 1997, *Plate Tectonics*, 214.

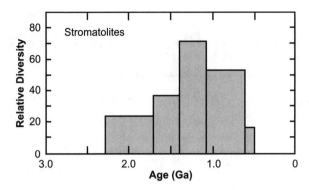

Figure 20. Relative diversity of stromatolites through the geologic record (after Walter, 1994).

The earliest-known fossils of eukaryotic algae are *Grypania* found in a middle Paleoproterozoic banded-iron formation in Michigan.[8] This fossil appears to have been a coiled, cylindrical organism that grew up to about 50 cm in length and 2 mm in diameter. Although it has no certain living relatives, it is generally regarded as having been a eukaryotic alga because of its complexity, structural rigidity, and large size. However, fossil eukaryotes do not have a more widespread distribution in the geologic record until the uppermost Paleoproterozoic and lowermost Mesoproterozoic rock sequences (Figure 21). Indeed, it is not until upper Mesoproterozoic that the first well-preserved multicellular algae fossils are found.

In contrast to bacteria and algae, metazoans are multicellular animals characterized by specialization of cells for different functions, allowing for increased sizes of organisms. Fossil evidence of metazoans comes in two forms—body fossils, where whole organisms have been fossilized; and trace fossils, where trails and traces left behind by the activities of the organisms have been fossilized. The trace fossil record suggests that metazoans existed widely in large numbers and in great diversity when the lower Neoproterozoic rock sequences were deposited (Figure 21). However, the discovery of leaf-shaped fossils in an uppermost Paleoproterozoic rock unit in north China suggests that metazoans probably also existed when Paleoproterozoic rocks were being deposited.[9] Of course, the paucity of fossils in what appears to be an extremely sparse Precambrian fossil record might also be consistent with poor conditions for fossilization, so it is difficult to know with certainty whether these multicellular organisms might not have also co-existed with, for example, stromatolites during deposition of lower Paleoproterozoic rocks. Nevertheless, in the fossil record as currently known, metazoan fossils are not widely preserved until the Neoproterozoic.

---

8   B. Runnegar, Proterozoic eukaryotes: evidence from biology and geology, in Bengtson, 1994, 287-297.

9   Z. Shixing and C. Huineng, 1995, Megascopic multi-cellular organisms from the 1700-My-old Tuanshanzi Formation in the Jixian area, North China, *Science*, 270: 620-622.

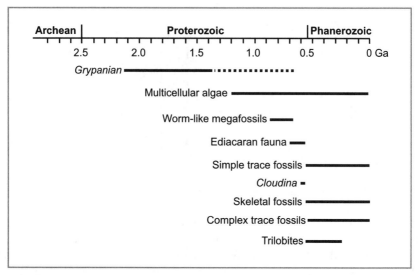

Figure 21. Distribution through the geologic record of various Precambrian fossil groups (after Condie, 1997, *Plate Tectonics*, 168-169).

In uppermost Neoproterozoic rock units, just below the Precambrian-Cambrian boundary, a unique fossil assemblage has been preserved. Found first in the Ediacara area of South Australia, it is now known from similar rock units at the same stratigraphic level in numerous locations worldwide, as far away as Namibia in southwest Africa, as Russia, and as the Death Valley area of California.[10] Although most paleontologists regard the Ediacaran fossils as metazoans, some have suggested that some or all may represent extinct animals with a construction rather like an air mattress, living with symbiotic algae in their tissues.[11] However, similarities between the Ediacaran fossils and invertebrates seem almost indisputable. The thirty-one Ediacaran species that have been described from their widespread fossil record include forms similar to flatworms, coelenterates, annelids, soft-bodied arthropods, and soft-bodied echinoderms.[12] The most convincing evidence that animals were active in the waters responsible for depositing the upper Neoproterozoic sedimentary rocks units comes from trace fossils associated with the Ediacaran fossils, such as looping and spiraling trails up to several millimeters in width, and strings of fecal pellets. One other interesting metazoan fossil found worldwide in uppermost Neoproterozoic rock units just below the Precambrian-Cambrian boundary is the tubular fossil *Cloudina* (Figure 21), the oldest known metazoan with a mineralized exoskeleton.

---

10 G. M. Narbonne, 1998, Ediacara biota: A terminal Neoproterozoic experiment in the evolution of life, *GSA Today,* 18 (2): 1-6; G. J. H. McCall, 2006, The Vendian (Ediacaran) in the geological record: Enigmas in geology's prelude to the Cambrian explosion, *Earth-Science Reviews,* 77: 1-229.

11 A. Seilacher, Early multicellular life: Late Proterozoic fossils and the Cambrian explosion, in Bengtson, 1994, 389-400.

12 Runnegar, 1994; S. Weiguo, Early multicellular fossils, in Bengtson, 1994, 358-369.

However, beginning with the deposition of the first Cambrian rock units, the Ediacaran assemblages cease to appear any further in the record. Instead, for the first time all of the major invertebrate phyla (except the Protozoa) appear abruptly and abundantly, a feature which is sometimes referred to as the "Cambrian explosion."[13] This "sudden" increase in numbers and diversity of organisms fossilized is matched by a sharp increase in the diversity of trace fossils and the intensity of bioturbation (the churning of subaqueous sediments by burrowing organisms). Moreover, in the Cambrian rock sequences, many of the fossilized animals have calcareous and siliceous skeletons, the first, apart from *Cloudina*, to be found in the record (Figure 21). Thus, something significant happened at that Precambrian-Cambrian boundary, because not only is there a dramatic change in the types and numbers of organisms fossilized, but there is also a physical break, a widespread unconformity, in the rock record itself, and the very rock types themselves also suddenly change. Whereas stromatolites had continued to be fossilized abundantly in uppermost Neoproterozoic rock sequences, above in the Cambrian rock sequences such fossils are rare, and instead, large deposits of phosphate-rich sediments appear over wide areas.

In some of the very first rock units deposited at the base of the Cambrian rock sequence appears an unusual fossil suite of small animals with shells, together with sponges and the sponge-like archeocyathids.[14] Most of these fossilized small shells are tiny cones and tubes. Paleontologists are still studying these to understand them, but they were obviously complex animals, and some were definitely mollusks. This assemblage of small fossils at the base of Cambrian rock sequence has been given the name Tommotian, which name has also been applied to the rock units in which this fossil assemblage is found. This same set of small shelly fossils called the Tommotian is now known worldwide. It is overlain by rock units in the Cambrian rock sequence containing a much larger variety of larger marine creatures, particularly trilobites, brachiopods, and echinoderms, but also mollusks, conodonts, and ostracods.

Soft-bodied animals were also buried and fossilized in some Cambrian rock units. The most famous of these is the Burgess Shale in the Rocky Mountains of southern British Columbia, Canada.[15] This rock unit contains a unique fossil assemblage with a spectacular abundance of soft-bodied animals. Many of the animals have been preserved with their soft parts intact, often with food still in their guts, indicating instant death and immediate burial in the fine mud.[16] All together, arthropods make up nearly 40 percent of the Burgess Shale fossil

---

13   Weiguo, 1994; S. Bengtson, The advent of animal skeletons, in Bengston, 1994, 412-425.

14   R. Cowen, 1990, *History of Life,* Boston: Blackwell Scientific Publications, 85; Stanley, 1989, 312–313.

15   S. J. Gould, 1991, *Wonderful Life: The Burgess Shale and the Nature of History,* London: Penguin Books; D. E. G. Briggs, D. H. Erwin and F. J. Collier, 1994, *The Fossils of the Burgess Shale,* Washington: Smithsonian Institution Press.

16   Cowen, 1990, 90–93.

species, and worms make up more than 25 percent. As many as 86 percent of the preserved fossil genera in this shale are without a biomineralized skeleton and are therefore generally not represented in fossil assemblages at most other Cambrian localities. Typically, Cambrian fossil assemblages are dominated by trilobites (approximately 60 percent) and brachiopods (approximately 30 percent), and the shelly component of the Burgess Shale assemblage does resemble these more usual Cambrian assemblages. There are at least thirty other localities worldwide where some of these Burgess Shale fossil animals are also found, including North America, Greenland, China, Australia, Siberia, Spain, and Poland, yet many of the fossilized soft-bodied animals remain unique to the Burgess Shale.

It is also in lower Cambrian rocks that the first possible vertebrate fossils are found.[17] These potentially indicate that while vertebrates may only rarely have been buried in Cambrian strata, they were nonetheless living at the time those rocks were being deposited.

Above the Cambrian rock sequence in the geologic column is the Ordovician rock sequence, and most of the common invertebrate classes that are found in the ocean today are well represented in its fossil record.[18] A great variety of shapes, sizes, and shell ornamentation of fossilized trilobites is found in Ordovician rock sequences; also, bryozoans are first found fossilized there. Increasing numbers of fossilized graptolites, cephalopods, crinoids, echinoderms, mollusks, corals, and fish are also found in Ordovician rock sequences. Marine algae and bacteria fossils are the plant remains found in these lower Paleozoic rock sequences.

In upper Paleozoic rock sequences, plant and vertebrate fossils are found in increasing numbers and varieties, whereas fewer numbers of fossils of many invertebrate groups are present.[19] Nevertheless, brachiopod, coelenterate and crinoid fossils all increase in abundance in upper Paleozoic rocks, only to be followed by a precipitous decrease in numbers at the top of the Permian sequences. At the Permian-Triassic boundary, trilobite, eurypterid, and many coral and bryozoan fossils disappear from the rock record, which the conventional geological community interprets as a mass extinction. Insects first appear as fossils in upper Devonian strata. Fish fossils are found in greatly increased abundance in Devonian and Mississippian (lower Carboniferous) rock sequences, while amphibian fossils first appear in Mississippian rock units, and reptile fossils first in Pennsylvanian (upper Carboniferous) strata. Increasing numbers of plant fossils are found in the upper Paleozoic, including fossils of plants that would be regarded as being terrestrial. Psilopsids are important fossils in the Devonian, while lycopsids, ferns, and conifers are important fossils in the overlying Carboniferous and Permian

---

17   X. G. Zhang and X.-G. Hou, 2004, Evidence for a single median fin-fold and tail in the lower Cambrian vertebrate, *Haikouichthys ercaicunensis, Journal of Evolutionary Biology,* 17: 1162-1166.

18   Condie, 1997, *Plate Tectonics,* 217–218.

19   Condie, 1997, *Plate Tectonics,* 217–218.

rock sequences. Fossils of seed plants become more numerous relative to fossils of spore-bearing plants in the upper Paleozoic and lower Mesozoic.

Enormously increased numbers of gymnosperm fossils are then found in Mesozoic strata, with cycads, ginkgos, and conifers being the most important plant fossils.[20] It is not until the lower Cretaceous rock units that angiosperm (flowering plant) fossils make their first appearance in the rock record, but their numbers increase rapidly upwards in the rock sequences thereafter. Fossils of marine invertebrates, which decreased in numbers at the top of the Permian, increase in numbers again in the Mesozoic (such as bryozoan, mollusk, echinoderm, and cephalopod fossils). Fossils of gastropods, pelecypods, foraminifera, and coiled cephalopods are particularly important invertebrate fossil groups in Mesozoic strata. Fossil arthropods in the form of insects, shrimp, crayfish, and crabs are also found in increased numbers in Mesozoic rock sequences. A great variety of groups of reptile fossils, including dinosaurs, are also found throughout the Mesozoic, and it is not until the lower Jurassic strata that fossils of birds and mammals are found. Only in the Cenozoic are large numbers of groups of mammal fossils found, while the vertebrate groups found fossilized in Mesozoic rock sequences are also found in increased numbers in the Cenozoic. The number of angiosperm fossils increase exponentially upwards through the Cenozoic strata. Undisputed human fossils are first found in Pleistocene strata.

This analysis of the fossil record clearly demonstrates that there is a distinctive order of first appearance of the fossils of the various groups of animals and plants in the rock record. Figure 22 summarizes this order of first fossil appearance of the different groups of animals and plants.[21] This pattern holds true at the lower taxonomic levels of genus and species as well. From Figure 22, we observe that fossilized bacteria and algae appear first in the rock record, followed by soft-bodied metazoan fossils, and then invertebrate animal fossils, while fossils of the more structurally complex types appear in successively higher strata in the rock record. It has been noted earlier that this same pattern of fossil occurrence occurs also on a more localized scale, as in the example given of the Grand Canyon-Bryce Canyon area, which reinforces the reality that the geologic column's fossil sequence can be verified and confirmed at the local and regional scale. While it is generally true that this pattern of occurrence in the fossil record fulfils the expectations of the evolutionary theory for the supposed development of life, this should not surprise us nor prompt us to deny that this pattern exists. It is important to recognize that the correlation between evolutionary theory and the fossil record occurs in large part because evolutionary theory has been crafted to include and reflect the order of first appearance actually observed in the fossil record. That is, the assumption has been applied that the observed order in the fossil record must logically be the order of evolutionary development. Our challenge, however, is to

---

20   Condie, 1997, *Plate Tectonics*, 217–218.

21   Adapted from Condie, 1997, 218.

seek a better and more robust explanation for these observational data within a biblical geologic model for earth history based on the scriptural details of creation and the Flood.

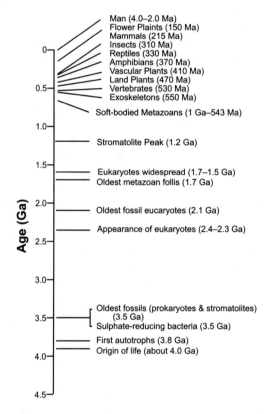

Figure 22. Biological "benchmarks" in the geologic record marking the first appearances of various fossil groups (after Condie, 1997, 168-169).

Another pattern that should be noted is that there is the ever-increasing percentage of extinct groups as one goes further back in the fossil record (Figure 23 on pages 449-450).[22] When the stratigraphic distribution of the major groups of animals and plants in the fossil record is examined, including the distribution of extant and extinct forms, it is obvious that the groups of animals and plants that live today are common as fossils only in Pleistocene and upper Tertiary strata. Commonly, groups lower in the rock record tend not to be found higher in the record. The conventional geological community interprets these data as indicating evolution through time, necessitating a different explanation in the biblical geologic model

---

22   Adapted from L. Brand, 1997, *Faith, Reason and Earth History*, Berrien Springs, MI: Andrews University Press, Figure 9.18, 143-144. The data used to construct this diagram are based on N. J. Benton, ed., 1993, *The Fossil Record 2*, New York: Chapman and Hall, with the data for flowering plants from W. B. Harland, ed., 1967, *The Fossil Record*, London: Geological Society of London.

for this important pattern in the fossil record.

Yet another general trend evident in the fossil record, both regionally in the Grand Canyon-Bryce Canyon area as well as globally, pertains to the environments in which the fossilized plants and animals presumably lived. Most fossils found in Paleozoic rock sequences, especially in lower Paleozoic strata, represent organisms that lived in marine environments. The fossils found in the Mesozoic, on the other hand, are a mixture of organisms that lived in marine and terrestrial environments. By contrast, the fossils found in the Cenozoic represent organisms that lived mostly in terrestrial environments. A high percentage of fossils in the Paleozoic rock sequences are in extinct groups, while the percentage of modern groups increases strongly towards the upper part of the fossil record (Figure 23). This predominance of fossils in Paleozoic strata that represent organisms that lived in marine environments is also reflected in the dominant rock types. Limestone is abundant in Paleozoic rock sequences, while the amount of it decreases higher in the geologic column, with very little limestone being formed today.

Trace fossils were discussed previously in the context of invertebrates, but vertebrates also leave behind footprints, tracks, and other traces that can be fossilized (Figure 21). Fossilized footprints and tracks of vertebrates are indeed found in the rock record, and the pattern of their stratigraphic distribution potentially has important significance. Figure 24 (page 451) summarizes the available data on the stratigraphic distribution of fossilized vertebrate footprints.[23] Many additional fossil track sites have been reported in the literature since the analysis summarized in Figure 24 was completed, but these new discoveries only reinforce the stratigraphic distribution pattern already depicted in the diagram. Fossilized amphibian footprints are almost entirely limited to the upper Paleozoic rock sequences and the Triassic and lower Jurassic strata. These fossilized footprints are the right size and shape to have been made by the labyrinthodonts and other now extinct amphibians (Figure 23b). Beyond the top of the lower Jurassic rock sequences, it is rare to find fossilized amphibian footprints; only a very few have been identified in the upper Jurassic-Recent strata. This is both puzzling and potentially significant, given that body fossils of amphibians are still found in reasonable numbers in these sequences that are higher in the record.

On the other hand, the greatest diversity of fossilized reptile footprints occurs in Triassic and lower Jurassic strata, while reptile body fossils (bones) are most abundant higher up in Cretaceous and Tertiary rock sequences. When the data pertaining to reptiles is split into the two subsets, dinosaurs and other reptiles (Figure 24a), it can be seen that the great diversity of fossilized reptile tracks in Triassic and lower Jurassic strata is dominated by fossilized dinosaur tracks, and yet, the greatest diversity of dinosaur body fossils is in Cretaceous strata. Fossilized dinosaur tracks are very abundant and have yielded many insights into the lives

---

23   L. R. Brand and J. Florence, 1982, Stratigraphic distribution of vertebrate fossil footprints compared with body fossils, *Origins*, 9: 67-74.

of these animals.[24] Fossil tracks of small dinosaurs and other reptiles almost cease to occur above mid-Jurassic strata, but abundant large dinosaur tracks are found in the late Mesozoic, only to disappear abruptly at the top of Cretaceous strata, as do the body fossils of all dinosaurs. The reason why so few fossilized amphibian or reptile tracks (compared with those in Paleozoic and Mesozoic strata) have been found preserved in all of the Cenozoic rock sequences is an unresolved mystery in the uniformitarian model.

By contrast, a great diversity of mammal and bird fossils occurs only in Cenozoic rock sequences, although even here bird fossils tend to be rare. Furthermore, the greatest abundances of mammal and bird trace fossils are found only in upper Tertiary and Quaternary strata (Figure 24b). Such trace fossils include fossilized corkscrew-shaped burrows of extinct giant beavers. Many types of fossilized mammal footprints have been found, almost all of them made by carnivores, ungulates (hoofed mammals), or elephants. Fossilized bird footprints are not as common. Since there are mammal and bird body fossils in Mesozoic rock sequences, it is curious why so few fossilized bird and mammal tracks have been found in Mesozoic strata. Furthermore, there are at least two reports in the literature of trace fossils that appear to be bird tracks, but since they are found in Paleozoic rock strata (where they were not supposed to be, according to evolutionary theory), they were labeled merely as unidentified tracks.[25]

One other set of relevant observations that is somewhat challenging to explain within a biblical geologic model for earth history involving the Genesis Flood involves the presence of fossilized reptile eggs, sometimes containing fossil embryos, which are commonly interpreted as fossilized reptile nests full of fossilized eggs. Indeed, abundant fossilized dinosaur "nests," eggs, and eggshell fragments have been found on several continents, sometimes in successive sedimentary layers.[26]

Finally, there is one last observation to be made with respect to patterns in the fossil record: mass extinctions. These are understood by the conventional geologic community to be extinctions of many diverse groups of organisms over short periods of time (relatively speaking). These mass extinction events are believed

24   D. D. Gillette and M. G. Lockley, 1989, *Dinosaur Tracks and Traces,* New York: Cambridge University Press; M. G. Lockley, 1991, *Tracking Dinosaurs,* New York: Cambridge University Press; M. Lockley and A. Hunt, 1995, *Dinosaur Tracks and Other Fossil Footprints of the Western United States,* New York: Columbia University Press; T. Thulborn, 1990, *Dinosaur Tracks,* New York: Chapman and Hall.

25   C. W. Gilmore, 1927, Fossil Footprints from the Grand Canyon: Second contribution, *Smithsonian Miscellaneous Collections,* 80 (3): 1-78; C.M. Sternberg, 1933, Carboniferous tracks from Nova Scotia, *Geological Society of America Bulletin,* 44: 951-964.

26   J. R. Horner, 1982, Evidence of colonial nesting and 'site fidelity' among ornithischian dinosaurs, *Nature,* 297: 675-676; J. R. Horner and D. B. Weishampel, 1989, Dinosaur eggs: the inside story, *Natural History,* 98: 61-67; D. D. Gillette, and M. G. Lockley, 1989, *Dinosaur Tracks and Traces,* New York: Cambridge University Press, 87-118; K. Carpenter, K. F. Hirsch and J. R. Horner, ed., 1994, *Dinosaur Eggs and Babies,* New York: Cambridge University Press; K. F. Hirsch, 1994, The fossil record of vertebrate eggs, in *The Palaeobiology of Trace Fossils,* ed. S. K. Donovan, Baltimore: The Johns Hopkins University Press, 269-294.

to have occurred at eight different times (levels) in the Cambrian-Recent rock sequence.[27] These events seem to have affected a great diversity of organisms, those that would have been living in both marine and terrestrial environments, both stationary and swimming forms, carnivores and herbivores, protozoans, and metazoans. Hence, the processes responsible for these events do not appear to have been restricted in their scope or range of effect to specific ecological, morphological, or taxonomic groups.

Figure 25 depicts the patterns of animal and plant family extinctions recorded in Cambrian-Recent strata sequences.[28] In terms of actual observational data, it is more accurate to describe this diagram as depicting only where in the rock record we observe the last occurrence of fossils of animal and plant families. Hence these "mass extinctions" are in reality the locations in the rock record where, *en masse,* we observe the last appearances of so many animal and plant families. It is, of course, true to say that these animal and plant families are no longer alive and therefore they must have become extinct. However, they could have lived on for some time after fossils of many of them were entombed in the rock record, except that they have left no fossil record of that continued existence. This may be considered pedantic, but it is a point worth noting that may have some significance.

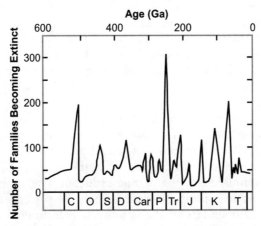

Figure 25. Patterns of animal and plant family extinctions through the Phanerozoic geologic record (after Benton, 1995).

Nevertheless, eight important mass extinctions have been recognized in the Cambrian-Recent (or Phanerozoic) rock record, and the same peaks are found for both terrestrial and marine organisms. This implies that the major extinctions affected organisms on land and in the sea concurrently.[29] The extinctions recorded

27   D. J. McLaren and W. D. Goodfellow, 1990, Geological and biological consequences of giant impacts, *Annual Review of Earth and Planetary Sciences,* 18: 123-171.

28   M. J. Benton, 1995, Diversification and extinction in the history of life, *Science,* 268: 52-58.

29   J. J. Sepkoski Jr, 1989, Periodicity in extinction and the problem of catastrophism in the history of life, *Journal of the Geological Society of London,* 146: 7-19; Benton, 1995.

in the Carboniferous, upper Jurassic, and lower Cretaceous rock sequences were more devastating for terrestrial than for marine organisms. The apparently high extinction rate recorded in lower Cambrian strata may not be real, since it probably reflects the low diversity of fossilized organisms in these strata. Five major mass extinctions are recognized in the data depicted in Figure 25—in upper Ordovician, upper Devonian, upper Permian, upper Triassic, and upper Cretaceous rock sequences. Of these, the extinction rate at the Permian-Triassic boundary is the highest, with a mean family extinction rate of 61 percent for all life, 63 percent for terrestrial organisms, and 43 percent for marine organisms.[30]

The second highest extinction rate occurs at the Cretaceous-Tertiary (K/T) boundary, but this mass extinction has captured the most attention because it is claimed that this event brought about the extinction of the dinosaurs, perhaps due to the earth being impacted by an asteroid.[31] Although most, or all, of the dinosaurs do not appear to have survived beyond the K/T boundary, numerous terrestrial species, such as lizards, frogs, salamanders, fish, crocodiles, alligators, and turtles, were not affected by this extinction event, because their fossilized remains continue to be found in lower Tertiary strata above this boundary.[32] At the taxonomic level of genus, the K/T extinction of terrestrial forms was actually only about 15 percent. Teeth of twelve dinosaur genera have been described above the K/T boundary in Paleocene sedimentary strata in eastern Montana.[33] Suggesting these fossilized dinosaur teeth are not the result of later reworking of earlier remains is the fact that reworked fossilized remains of a widespread species of mammals commonly found in the underlying upper Cretaceous strata are not found in these lowermost Paleocene rock units of Montana. If these fossilized teeth are truly in place, then they clearly indicate that at least some dinosaurs survived the K/T extinction. Indeed, other possible lowermost Tertiary fossilized dinosaur remains are known from India, Argentina, and New Mexico.[34] On the other hand, the marine extinction at the K/T boundary is far more spectacular than the terrestrial extinction, as it involves many more species and groups of animals.[35] At the family level, the marine extinction rate is about 15 percent, while at the generic and specific levels it is about 70 percent. Major groups to disappear at the K/T boundary are the ammonites, belemnites, inoceramid clams, rudistid pelecypods, mosasaurs, and plesiosaurs. Calcareous phytoplankton and

---

30   Benton, 1995.

31   McLaren and Goodfellow, 1990; W. Alvarez Asaro and A. Montanari, 1990, Iridium profile for 10 million years across the Cretaceous-Tertiary boundary at Gubbio (Italy), *Science*, 250: 1700-1702; A. R. Hildebrand et al., 1991, Chicxulub crater: a possible Cretaceous/Tertiary boundary impact crater on the Yucatan Peninsula, Mexico, *Geology*, 19: 867-871.

32   Condie, 1997, *Plate Tectonics*, 220–221.

33   R. E. Sloan et al, 1986, Gradual dinosaur extinction and simultaneous ungulate radiation in the Hell Creek Formation, *Science*, 232: 629-633.

34   Condie, 1997, *Plate Tectonics*, 220.

35   McLaren and Goodfellow, 1990; D. H. Erwin, 1993, *The Great Paleozoic Crisis,* New York: Columbia University Press.

planktonic foraminifera show sharp extinctions. Indeed, upper Cretaceous rock sequences are characterized by thick strata of chalk, which predominately consists of fossilized remains of calcareous phytoplankton.

53

PATTERNS AND TRENDS IN THE GEOLOGIC COLUMN— INVOLVING METAL ORE DEPOSITS

The processes which formed many of the earth's mineral resources are closely linked to the physical processes that shaped the earth, including geological processes. Many mineral deposits are sensitive signatures of particular geological phenomena, such as volcanism and magmatism, that release hydrothermal fluids that carry and concentrate metals and precipitate them in high enough accumulations to form economic metal deposits. It is thus likely that patterns in the distribution of mineral deposits in the rock record may be significant in understanding when the relevant geological processes occurred and also the scales of those processes. A number of compilations and reviews of mineral deposit distribution throughout the geologic column have been published,[1] and the results are summarized and depicted in Figure 26 (pages 452-453).

Some patterns are clearly evident in Figure 26. Note that the vertical bars for each type of ore deposit is proportional to the estimated quantity of ore formed in that interval of the rock record compared with the total estimated amount for that type of deposit throughout the entire record. Thus, it is apparent that there are major occurrences of particular ore types in upper Archean rock sequences, namely, Abitibi-type Zn-Cu volcanic-hosted massive sulfide ores, hydrothermal gold and base metal veins, Kambalda-type nickel ores in komatiite lava flows, and gold and uranium ores in conglomerate units (the most notable example of which is in the Witwatersrand Basin of South Africa). This means that there was significant volcanic activity with large hydrothermal systems active during the time these upper Archean rock sequences were formed, but there was also active erosion to produce conglomerates that hosted the gold and uranium minerals. There is still debate about the gold and uranium minerals in the conglomerates of the Witwatersrand. The traditional view is that the gold and uranium mineral

---

1   C. Meyer, 1985, Ore metals through geologic history, Science, 227: 1421-1428; C. Meyer, 1988, Ore deposits as guides to geologic history of the earth, *Annual Review of Earth and Planetary Sciences*, 16: 147-171; M. E. Barley and D. I. Groves, 1992, Supercontinent cycles and the distribution of metal deposits through time, *Geology*, 20: 291-294; I. B. Lambert et al, 1992, Proterozoic mineral deposits through time, in *Proterozoic Biosphere*, ed. J. W. Schopf and C. Klein, Cambridge: Cambridge University Press, 59-62; R. V. Kirkham and S. M. Roscoe, 1993, Atmospheric evolution and ore deposit formation, *Resource Geology Special Issue*, 15: 1-17; Solomon and Sun, 1997.

particles were of detrital origin and thus deposited with the conglomerates, whereas the minority view is that the gold and uranium were introduced via hydrothermal fluids to the conglomerates subsequent to their deposition. It is also in late Archean rock sequences that banded-iron formations become more prevalent and larger in extent. Increasingly, it is being suggested that the formation of banded-iron formations is linked with volcanic and hydrothermal activity.[2] This is consistent with the volcanic and hydrothermal activity responsible for volcanic-hosted massive sulfide Abitibi ores and the gold and base metal veins in late Archean rock sequences. This could therefore be a significant correlation that needs to be accounted for in a biblical geologic model of earth history.

As noted previously, there are distinct differences in the rock types between upper Archean rock sequences and the overlying lower Paleoproterozoic rock sequences. Thus, while banded-iron formations increased in prevalence and size, and manganese-rich strata were also being deposited, the volcanic activity and hydrothermal systems responsible for the volcanic-hosted massive sulfide Abitibi-type ores and the gold and base metal veins appear to have abruptly ceased. The absence of Kambalda-type nickel ores also reflects the dramatic decline in komatiite lava flows in lower Paleoproterozoic greenstone belt sequences (Figure 26). Minor quantities of gold and uranium ores hosted by conglomerates are recorded primarily in the Huronian lower Paleoproterozoic conglomerate strata in Canada. Perhaps of significance are the layered mafic intrusions hosting chromite ores, which appear to have formed at the time of the boundary between the upper Archean and the lower Paleoproterozoic rock sequences. However, the peak in occurrence of chromite ores in layered mafic intrusions is at the time when middle Paleoproterozoic rock sequences were being deposited. These data are shown in Figure 26 and are dominated by the enormous Bushveld Complex in South Africa, which is a major host to chromite and platinum group element ores. Also at this relative time is the large Palabora carbonatite intrusion which hosts a giant copper deposit. In the upper part of some middle Paleoproterozoic rock sequences, there are again large quantities of banded-iron formations, as well as copper ores in clastic sedimentary rocks, such as the giant basin deposits of Udokan in Siberia. Subsequently, there is a sudden cessation of deposition of banded-iron formations, and instead lead-zinc ores are deposited with clastic sediments in a number of large basins, particularly in Australia in the Mount Isa, McArthur River, and Broken Hill areas. Otherwise, renewed volcanic activity in some areas appears to have been responsible for further formation of volcanic-hosted massive sulfide Abitibi-type deposits.

At the relative time of deposition of the uppermost Paleoproterozoic rock sequences

---

2   M. E. Barley, A. L. Pickard and J. Sylvester, 1997, Emplacement of a large igneous province as a possible cause of banded iron formation 2.45 billion years ago, *Nature*, 385: 55-58; T. S. Blake et al, 2004, Geochronology of a late Archean flood basalt province in the Pilbara Craton, Australia: constraints on basin evolution, volcanic and sedimentary accumulation, and continental drift rates, *Precambrian Research*, 113: 143-173.

and the beginning of deposition of the lowermost Mesoproterozoic, there was in some areas renewed hydrothermal activity, as evidenced by the hydrothermal uranium ore deposits in northern Australia and northern Saskatchewan, Canada, as well as giant Olympic Dam-type copper-uranium deposits associated with granitic intrusives (Figure 26). Then, during the deposition of the Mesoproterozoic strata, there was a peak in the intrusion of numerous large anorthosite plutons hosting ilmenite ore, as well as an episode of intrusion of carbonatites, kimberlites, and related rocks, the latter two carrying diamonds. Straddling the Mesoproterozoic-Neoproterozoic boundary are clastic sedimentary rock sequences that host copper ore, the most prominent of which is in the Katanga Basin of central Africa. Otherwise, Neoproterozoic rock sequences are not noted for hosting major metal deposits, but they do contain a few minor banded-iron formations and phosphate-rich strata, as well as being noted for further manganese-rich sedimentary strata.

At the Precambrian-Cambrian boundary there is a dramatic change, with many new styles of ore deposits occurring in Cambrian-Recent rock sequences (Figure 26). In particular, throughout the Phanerozoic (Cambrian-Recent) it is likely there were repeated cycles of intense magmatic, volcanic, and hydrothermal activity. Copper, molybdenum, and tin-tungsten ores are hosted by numerous granitic intrusions. Porphyry copper deposits reached their peak in terms of distribution, size, and numbers in the Mesozoic and particularly the Tertiary, and appear to be associated with the rising mountain belts of the Andes in South America and the Rockies in North America, as well as in the western Pacific (the New Guinea area and the Philippines) and the Middle East (Iran). Extensive volcanic activity is evident from the widespread occurrence of volcanic-hosted massive sulfide ore deposits, particularly of the Kuroko/Rosebery type, deposits of which occur throughout Cambrian-Recent strata sequences, but are particularly prevalent in Cambrian-Ordovician rock sequences. The other types of volcanogenic massive sulfide deposits are dispersed periodically through Paleozoic strata, with a peak in Cyprus-type deposits associated with upper Cretaceous-lower Tertiary strata. Extensive, intense hydrothermal activity must have accompanied the formation of the ore deposits associated with both the granitic intrusives and the volcanics, but it was also responsible for the formation of more gold and base metal veins in Paleozoic-lower Mesozoic rock sequences and hydrothermal uranium deposits in the upper part of the Mesozoic. Additionally, there was renewed intrusion of pipes of kimberlites and related rocks carrying diamonds together with some carbonatites, while minor mafic layered intrusions accumulated chromite ore deposits (Figure 26). A contrasting type of chromite ore accumulation—podiform chromite ore deposits only previously seen in lower Archean strata—are widely found in Cambrian-Recent rock sequences, but here in ophiolites, which we have already noted are not present in Archean rock sequences. And finally, various metals were accumulated in particular units of sedimentary rock sequences, such as copper sulfide ores and lead-zinc sulfide ores in some Paleozoic clastic sedimentary strata.

Another class of sediment-hosted massive sulfide ore deposits that is almost exclusively found in Cambrian-Recent strata sequences are lead-zinc sulfide ores in carbonate rock units, the classic location being in the Mississippi valley of the United States. Because carbonate strata are prolific in Paleozoic rock sequences, this class of sediment-hosted massive sulfide ore deposits is found predominantly in upper Paleozoic carbonate strata.

From the foregoing discussion, it is clear that there are numerous patterns in the distribution and occurrence of many types of metal ore deposits in the rock record, which in turn is consistent with patterns of distribution and occurrence of different rock types, as well as of magmatism, and volcanism, in the strata sequences of the geologic column. As with the trends and patterns of fossil occurrences evident in the rock record, the evidence strongly suggests that various geological processes were operating with varying levels of intensity and scale as the geologic record accumulated, which means that these patterns and trends are potentially significant clues to unraveling and understanding earth history. The next question is whether there might be some larger-scale driving mechanism for these geological processes that could account for these global patterns over the course of earth history but within a shorter span of time, such as given in the Genesis account of creation and the Flood.

54

A Brief History of Plate Tectonics

The sudden emergence of the concept of plate tectonics in the 1960s fostered a revolution in the earth sciences because it resolved so many long-standing puzzles. The term "tectonics" is a term that had long been used to describe the movements of the earth's crust, such as when strata are folded and deformed and when uplifting occurs to produce mountain ranges. Accordingly, the term "plate tectonics" was adopted to refer to processes that involve motions of large patches of the earth's rigid outer surface layer known as the lithosphere, "plates" that had been discovered to move in relation to one another. Whereas continents were once thought to be locked in place because of the strength of the mantle rock beneath them, the theory of plate tectonics holds that continents can and do move across the earth's surface because they form parts of moving plates. Moreover, because continents are parts of moving plates, they occasionally can break apart and at other times collide and fuse together to form larger continents. This theory of plate tectonics gained widespread acceptance as part of the modern geological synthesis because it successfully and powerfully explained so much geological data, such as why most volcanoes and earthquakes occur along curved belts on the sea floor, why mountain belts tend to develop along the edges of continents, and why the present ocean basins appear to be very young relative to continental rocks.

For many years, the idea that continents had moved horizontally over the surface of the earth, a concept known as continental drift, failed to receive general support amongst geologists in Europe and North America. Indeed, as recently as 1944 one prominent geologist went so as far to assert that the idea of continental drift should be abandoned outright, because "further discussion of it merely encumbers the literature and befogs the minds of students."[1] Thus, until the late 1950s little attention generally was given to the possibility that continental drift was a real phenomenon. The idea had generated considerable discussion earlier in the 20th century, attracting widespread attention primarily as a result of the arguments of two scientists, Alfred Wegener in Germany and Alexander du Toit of South Africa. Yet they were not the first to notice fairly obvious circumstantial evidence

---

1   S. M. Stanley, 1989, *Earth and Life Through Time*, second ed., New York: W.H. Freeman and Company, 165.

for continental drift and suggest it in print. Indeed, the observation that the coasts on the two sides of the Atlantic Ocean fitted together like separated parts of a jigsaw puzzle constituted rather clear evidence that the continents might have at some point in earth history broken apart and moved across the surface of the earth. For centuries, map readers had noted with curiosity that the outline of the west coast of Africa seemed to match that of the east coast of South America. But it wasn't until 1858 that Antonio Snider-Pellegrini published a book in which he suggested that a great continent had once broken apart and that the Atlantic Ocean had formed by powerful forces applied from within the earth.[2] What is not usually recognized is that Snider's book proposed that the horizontal divergence of the continental blocks had been rapid and had occurred during Noah's Flood. Snider may have been the first to propose some of the main elements of modern plate tectonics theory, but he did so in the context of catastrophic Flood geology, which is probably why his work was little known and almost entirely ignored.

Conventional "wisdom," however, continued to insist that larger blocks of continental crust could not move over the face of the earth. So when the distributions of certain living and extinct (fossilized) animals and plants across the earth's surface began to suggest former connections had existed between presently separated landmasses, most geologists tended to assume that great corridors of felsic rock (the most abundant material in the continental crust) had once formed land bridges that connected continents but later subsided to form portions of the modern sea floor, an idea that we now know from modern exploration of the seafloor to be demonstrably wrong. But until the mid-20th century, when sonar technology developed during World War II allowed detailed mapping of the deep ocean floor for the first time, speculation continued about ancient land bridges.

An example of the observations driving such speculation was the similarity between the present fauna of the island of Madagascar and that of India, which are separated from one another by an expanse of ocean nearly 4,000 kilometers (approximately 2,000 miles) across. Madagascar does not have zebras, lions, leopards, gazelles, apes, rhinoceroses, giraffes, and elephants that characterize nearby Africa. Instead, some of its native animals closely resemble those in India. So there was speculation that a land bridge had once existed between India and Madagascar. Similarly, during the 19th century the coal beds in the upper Paleozoic strata sequences of India, South Africa, Australia, and South America were found to contain a group of fossil plants that were collectively designated the *Glossopteris* flora, after their most conspicuous genus, a variety of seed fern. The *Glossopteris* flora was later discovered in coal beds in Antarctica also. The occurrence of this fossil flora on these widely separated landmasses was one of the facts that led Eduard Suess to suggest that land bridges had once connected all of these continents. It was Suess who introduced the term *Gondwanaland* as the name of the hypothetical continent consisting of these landmasses and the land

---

2　　A. Snider-Pellegrini, 1859, *La Création et ses Mystères Dévoilés,* Paris: A Franck et E. Dentu.

bridges that he believed once connected them (Gondwana is a locality in India where coal seams yield fossils of the *Glossopteris* flora).

In 1908 the American geologist Frank D. Taylor proposed that the continents had once lain side-by-side as components of very large landmasses which eventually broke apart and moved across the earth's surface to their present positions. The particulars of Taylor's hypothesis are no longer accepted, but he correctly suggested that the immense submarine mountain chain now called the Mid-Atlantic Ridge marks the line along which one ancient landmass ruptured to form the Atlantic Ocean.

Though first published in 1915, it was not until the third edition of the book on the origin of continents and oceans was translated into many languages, including English, in 1924 that the ideas of German meteorologist Alfred Wegener became the subject of extensive debate. Wegener presented evidence that virtually all of the large continental areas of the modern world were united at the time of deposition of late Paleozoic strata as a single supercontinent which he called Pangaea. In essence, Wegener viewed Gondwanaland as part of the large landmass of Pangaea. He assumed that felsic land bridges could not possibly account for ancient land connections, since they could not have descended into the more dense oceanic crust. Thus, Pangaea must have broken apart to form today's continents, which then drifted to their present positions. As well as emphasizing the jigsaw-puzzle fit of today's continents now separated by ocean basins, Wegener noted that there were numerous geologic similarities between eastern South America and western Africa. He also called attention to the many similarities between the fossil biotas of these two widely separated continents. Several extinct groups of fossilized animals and plants were found to occur in the fossil records of two or more Gondwanaland continents, and this led Wegener to argue that these continents must once have been joined together. He showed that even living animal and plant groups appear to exhibit a "Gondwanaland" pattern, with individual species widely distributed across the southern continents.

Wegener's arguments were more fully developed by South African geologist Alexander du Toit. With others, he publicized a wealth of circumstantial evidence favoring the idea of continental drift, both before Wegener's death in 1930 and during the three decades of controversy that followed. For example, one genus of earthworm was found to be restricted to the southern tips of South America and Africa, areas which lay close together in Wegener's Gondwanaland construction. Furthermore, another genus was identified in southern India and southern Australia, and it was argued that these soil-dwelling animals could only have such strange distributions in the modern world if the land areas they inhabit today had once been connected.

The evidence from the fossil record seemed even more compelling. For example, twenty of the twenty-seven species of fossilized land plants recognized within the *Glossopteris* flora of Antarctica were also found as far away as India. It might be argued that winds could have spread the plants that far by transporting their seeds. However, the seeds of the genus *Glossopteris* are several millimeters in diameter, much too large to have been blown across wide oceans. Thus, when the distribution of the *Glossopteris* flora was plotted on a map of the southern continents, it seemed more logical and natural for Gondwanaland to consist of these continents, not where they are today but in a tight cluster. Similarly, du Toit noted that fossils of the reptile *Mesosaurus* occurred in strata at or near the Carboniferous-Permian boundary in both Brazil and South Africa. On both continents, fossils of *Mesosaurus* occur in dark shales along with fossil insects and crustaceans, so it would seem more logical for deposition and fossilization to be contemporaneous in adjoining areas, rather than for such identical fossil assemblages somehow to have been deposited contemporaneously in the same rock type separated by a distance as broad as the present Atlantic Ocean.

The nature of the strata sequences themselves in which the *Glossopteris* flora and *Mesosaurus* are encountered also offered evidence supporting the existence of Gondwanaland. Specifically, the Carboniferous and Permian rock units that yield the *Glossopteris* flora, now known as the Gondwana sequence, occur with remarkable similarity in South America, South Africa, India, and Antarctica. For example, the Gondwana sequence of Brazil bears an uncanny resemblance to the Karoo sequence of South Africa. At the base of both sequences are *diamictites* (a non-sorted or poorly-sorted sedimentary rock containing a wide range of particle sizes, typically angular pebbles or boulders in a fine-grained muddy matrix), often interpreted as glacial tillites. Above these are found dark shales containing *Mesosaurus* fossils. There are adjacent coal beds in both sequences. Hundreds of species of fossil reptiles are found in the overlying sandstones, and finally, the sequences on both continents are capped by extensive basalt flows. Very similar Gondwana sequences are found in Antarctica and India; the only component missing from these sequences are the *Mesosaurus* fossils.

Du Toit also recognized that if South America, Antarctica, and Australia were assembled as Gondwanaland, the mountain belts along their margins would line up. Even the small Cape Fold Belt at the tip of South Africa would form a link in this chain. Du Toit also plotted other structural trends, including regional strikes of folds and faults, and found that these ancient geologic features on these now separate continents would match when the continents were placed in their Gondwanaland positions.

Despite mounting evidence favoring Wegener's and du Toit's ideas, northern hemisphere geologists continued to view the theory of continental drift with considerable skepticism. The primary source of their dissatisfaction lay in the absence of a demonstrated mechanism by which continents could move over long distances. Wegener favored the pole-fleeing force, which pulls objects near the North and South Poles toward the equator because the earth's rotation creates an equatorial bulge that deflects the pull of gravity slightly toward the equator at most latitudes. Other geophysicists of his day could readily calculate that this force could have but a minuscule effect. Seismologists such as Sir Harold Jeffreys pointed out, based on the way which seismic waves propagate through the mantle, that the strength of mantle rock is comparable to that of steel and that it was therefore utterly absurd to imagine continents ploughing their way laterally through the mantle rock beneath them and around them.[3] This is especially true if they were driven only by the weak pole-fleeing force.

Questions about the mechanism of continental drift were not the only issue that troubled geologists. Many were reluctant to adopt the continental drift hypothesis simply because its chief proponent, Wegener, was a meteorologist! Nevertheless, two eminent geologists of Wegener's time—Reginald Daly, an American, and Arthur Holmes of Britain—supported the drift hypothesis, but their views seemed to have little influence on the opinions of most of their northern hemisphere contemporaries. Interestingly, it was Arthur Holmes in the 1940s who suggested a much more potent mechanism for continental drift, namely, mantle convection, proposing that the ocean floor spread apart at the top of a mantle convection cell, carrying the continents with it. However, the continental drift hypothesis continued to maintain a significant degree of popularity in South America, South Africa, and Australia, where the remarkable resemblance between the various Gondwana sequences could be observed firsthand.

Continental drift theory made no effort to explain the locations of either volcanoes or earthquakes, except where the earthquakes were located along mountain fronts. On the other hand, Wegener proposed that continents moved westward through or over the basement rocks of the ocean basins, and the frictional drag created by this movement was presumed to cause a "wrinkling" into mountains along the leading margins of the continents. However, such motion should produce a major zone of slippage that either surrounds or lies beneath each continent, where it either pushes through or slides over the basement rocks of the ocean floor, but no evidence for such a zone could be found from geophysical investigations.

Prior to the emergence of "The New Global Tectonics," by which plate tectonics was known in the early 1960s, other explanations were advanced to account for the earth's prominent tectonic features such as mountain ranges. Most mountain belts are relatively long and narrow features. In many cases, they are observed to be composed of thick sequences of deformed sedimentary strata. These observations were commonly explained by "geosynclinal theory."[4] According to this conceptual framework, geosynclines were understood to be elongated belts of deep subsidence in which thick sedimentation had occurred. Subsequently, according to the theory,

---

3   See for example N. Oreskes, 1999, *The Rejection of Continental Drift: Theory and Method in American Science,* New York: Oxford University Press, 85-86.

4   Krumbein and Sloss, 1961.

the thick geosynclinal strata were folded and metamorphosed, and then uplifted and eroded to form the mountain belts.

In the early to mid-20th century, field observations from many mountain ranges had been accumulated and compared. One key observation noted that there appeared to have been two parallel geosynclines side by side—one in which the sediments were very thick and strongly deformed (eugeosyncline), and a second belt that exhibited a thinner sequence of sediments that were largely undeformed (miogeosyncline). The nature of the sediments filling the basins of these two geosynclinal types were different. The miogeosynclinal succession contained mature (characterized by stable minerals and well-sorted but sub-angular to angular grains), undeformed sandstones and limestones, with plentiful fossils. Eugeosynclinal rocks were characterized by immature (characterized by relatively unstable minerals, the presence of weatherable materials such as clay, and poorly sorted and angular grains) sediments and submarine volcanic rocks, and the sediments appeared to have been deposited rapidly in very deep marine water. Thus, miogeosynclines were interpreted to be shallow marine settings, but the eugeosynclinal deposits presented a difficult problem. Fossils of shallow marine creatures found in some of the eugeosynclinal sedimentary strata were consistent with deposition close to continental shelves, but such sedimentary environments in the modern world commonly lack active volcanism, in contrast to the volcanic deposits in the eugeosynclinal environment which implied volcanism there. Moreover, advocates for this idea were unable to relate the strong deformation of these eugeosynclinal sequences to any known mechanism.

This was the status of geological ideas in the late 1950s, when marine geophysicists began to analyze information from the world's ocean floors, including magnetic measurements, determinations of the topography of the ocean floors, and actual sampling of the rocks beneath the oceans. Astonished researchers found features that ushered in an entirely new understanding of the earth's large-scale tectonic features, as well as how they must have unfolded in the past. Consequently, geosynclinal theory for mountain-building was superseded. It was clear that geosynclines had been a heroic attempt to explain valid geologic observations but with an inadequate model. At that point, it was recognized that miogeosynclinal sediments represent passive continental margin sedimentation, apparently the kinds of sedimentary sequences that we find today around the edges of continents away from plate margins. On the other hand, eugeosynclinal deposits appear to be composites of deep marine sediments, volcanics, and material derived from the continents that accumulate at convergent plate margins ("active" continental margins).

Also in the late 1950s, interest in large-scale continental displacements was renewed as a result of new evidence derived from paleomagnetism, that is, the magnetization of rocks at the time of their formation. Geophysicists were discovering from paleomagnetic measurements on rocks from around the world that the earth's north and south magnetic poles had not only reversed their positions many times in the past, but also apparently had wandered about along complex paths. Paleomagnetism in a rock is similar to a compass needle. Magnetic minerals within a rock often tend to display both a detectable inclination and dip. By measuring these angles relative to the orientation of the rock in its geological setting, it is possible to determine the apparent direction of the north magnetic pole at the time when the rock was first magnetized, as well as the rock's apparent paleolatitude. However, neither a compass needle nor the paleomagnetism of a rock reveals anything about longitude (position in an east-west direction).

When geologists first began measuring rock magnetism, they found that igneous rocks that had cooled and crystallized in the very recent past exhibited magnetism consistent with the earth's current magnetic field. However, the magnetism in older rocks often displayed other orientations. As data accumulated, it began to appear that the earth's magnetic pole had wandered. A plot of the pole's positions for rocks from various strata sequences of different relative ages in North America and in Europe showed that the pole seemed to have moved to its present position from much farther south, in the Pacific Ocean. However, doubt was cast on this hypothesis because the path obtained from European rocks differed in detail from that obtained from North American rocks. Nevertheless, it was recognized that this pattern might actually reflect a history in which the North Pole did not wander at all. Instead, as Wegener had suggested, the continents of Europe and North America might possibly have moved relative both to the pole and to one another, carrying with them rocks that had been magnetized when the continents were in different positions from where they are today. This possibility led to the use of the cautious phrase "apparent polar wander" to describe the pathways that geophysicists plotted. Tests were then conducted to examine the possibility that continents rather than the magnetic poles had moved. Thus, if North America and Europe had once been united and had drifted over the surface of the earth for a while joined together, they should have developed identical paths of apparent polar wander during their joint voyage. The test was to fit the outline of North America and Europe together along the mid-Atlantic ridge to determine whether, with the continents in this position, their paths of apparent polar wander coincided. When this was done, the apparent polar wander paths of North America and Europe did coincide almost exactly for both Paleozoic and lower Mesozoic rock sequences, thus strongly suggesting that these continents had indeed once been joined together but later drifted apart, carrying their earlier magnetized rocks with them.

55

THE DEVELOPMENT OF THE PLATE TECTONICS THEORY

During the late 1950s, these new paleomagnetic data generated widespread discussion of continental drift, but most geologists continued to be skeptical. Many paleomagnetic measurements were known to be imprecise, and the belief persisted that no natural mechanism could move the continents relative to the very strong mantle rock beneath them. However, in 1962 American geologist Harry H. Hess proposed a solution, suggesting that the felsic continents had not ploughed their way through adjacent ocean floor rock., but instead a section of outer shell of the earth that included the continent as well as the adjacent ocean floor had moved due to sea-floor spreading.[1]

Hess assembled circumstantial evidence to construct his sea-floor spreading theory. Following World War II, the sonar technology developed to detect submarines was applied in extensive sonar surveys to produce detailed maps of the ocean floor, and as a result some unusual topographic features were discovered. For example, Hess discovered flat-topped seamounts rising from the floor of the deep ocean. Named *guyots*, these were demonstrated to have been volcanic islands that had been truncated by wave erosion near sea level, but the ocean floor on which they sat must have subsided subsequently to great depths, thus submerging the flat tops well below sea level.

It was also discovered that the ocean basins were relatively youthful, with only a thin veneer of deep-sea sediments averaging only 1.3 kilometers (less than 1 mile) in thickness, whereas on the basis of an estimated sedimentation rate of about 1 cm (approximately ½ inch) per thousand years, it had been expected that through the assumed billions of years of earth history, the deep sea sediment layer could be as much as 40 kilometers (approximately 25 miles) thick. Consistent with this estimated youthfulness of the ocean floor was the discovery of only about 10,000 volcanic seamounts (volcanic cones and guyots) in all the world's oceans, many of which appeared to have been formed only recently.

---

1   H. H. Hess, 1962, History of ocean basins, in *Petrological Studies: A Volume in Honor of A.F. Buddington*, ed. A. E. J. Engel, H. L. James and B. F. Leonard, Geological Society of America, 599–620.

Hess again noted the central location of the Mid-Atlantic Ridge, and also observed that other mid-ocean ridges tended to also be centrally located within ocean basins. The "best fit" restoration of continents along the Mid-Atlantic Ridge had been refined in the 1950s by Edward C. Bullard, an English geophysicist, who, realizing that shorelines are transient features and thus a poor outline upon which to attempt a fit between continents, instead drew maps on which the edges of the continents were defined by the edges of the continental shelves at the base of the continental slopes. Hess noted four curious facts about the mid-ocean ridges that seemed significant:

1. They are characterized by a high rate of upward heat flow from the mantle to neighboring segments of the sea floor.
2. Seismic waves from earthquakes move through the ridges at unusually low velocities.
3. Along the crest of each ridge there is a deep valley.
4. Volcanoes frequently rise up from mid-ocean ridges.

All these observations were consistent with Hess's sea-floor spreading hypothesis. Essentially, Hess suggested that mid-ocean ridges represent narrow zones where oceanic crust forms as material from the mantle moves upward and under lower pressure undergoes partial melting to form basalt that rises to the surface and cools as new crust. As this material rises, he maintained, it carries heat from the mantle to the surface of the sea floor. Moreover, because warmer rock has a lower density than colder rock, the warm rock in these narrow zones stands up higher than the adjacent cooler sea floor due to the principle of isostasy forming the ridge. Furthermore, Hess revived Holmes's idea that material within the earth's mantle flows like a very viscous fluid due to large-scale thermal convection. Radioactive decay within the mantle maintains its high temperatures, but it is also cooled from above by loss of heat through the crust. Consequently, the upper surface layer of the mantle, being cooled, is more dense than the regions below it and thus tends to sink, while the regions below in the deeper mantle are hot and tend to rise, resulting in convection. Hess proposed that the mantle is divided into huge convection cells and suggested that the spreading apart at the mid-ocean ridges is somehow associated with the upwelling flow in these vast convection cells. The new oceanic crust, produced by cooling of basaltic magma at the ridge, then moves laterally, forming new ocean floor. The valley down the center of many ridges Hess explained as the site where the newly-formed crust separates and flows laterally in opposite directions. Similarly, the localized melting beneath the ridge naturally forms volcanoes along the ridge, while the low velocity observed for seismic waves passing beneath a ridge is consistent with the fact that temperatures are higher there.

In Hess's explanation of mid-ocean ridges, the sea floor adjacent to a mid-ocean ridge (together with anything attached to the sea floor) moves laterally away from the zone of spreading. Sometimes a volcano along a mid-ocean ridge grows upward above sea level, as is the case with Ascension Island in the Atlantic. As such a volcano moves laterally away from the ridge, along with the crust on which it formed, it also moves away from the source of the lava that produced it and so becomes an inactive seamount. Usually, its tip is quickly planed off by erosion. Because the sea floor continues to cool as it moves away from the ridge, its depth below sea level increases as the rock comprising the seafloor cools and contracts. The truncated seamount is gradually transported into deeper and deeper water as if it were on a conveyor belt, and thereby becomes a guyot.

Hess also suggested that continents can be viewed as enormous bodies that, because of their lower density, float in the mantle rock beneath them and ride along passively like the guyots. He reasoned that when mantle convection cells change their locations, the upwelling "limbs" of two adjacent cells must sometimes come to be positioned beneath a continent. Convective spreading would then rift the continent into two blocks and move them away from the newly-formed spreading center, with new ocean floor subsequently forming at the same rate on each side of the spreading center between the two continental blocks. The spreading center would continue to operate along the mid-line of the new ocean basin and persist as a mid-ocean ridge, as long as the convective cells maintained their general positions in the mantle below.

However, if oceanic lithosphere (consisting of about 5 to 6 km of basaltic crust overlying typically 50 to 80 km of cold, stiff mantle rock) flows laterally, it must eventually disappear somewhere. Thus, Hess postulated that it must be swallowed up again by the mantle along the trenches that had been found on the ocean floors at the margins of the ocean basins. This postulated movement of ocean lithosphere into the mantle along one side of the trench provided a ready explanation for the unusually weak gravitational field there and the presence of low-density sediments in the trenches. Assuming a calculated spreading rate of about 1 cm per year operating uniformly, Hess estimated that the formation of new ocean lithosphere along mid-ocean ridges and the simultaneous disappearance of ocean lithosphere into the trenches would have recycled the entirety of the world's ocean floor into the mantle in less than 200 million years.

Hess's sea-floor spreading hypothesis, by asserting that continents move as part of a lithospheric plate that normally also has some portion of oceanic lithosphere, overcame the objection that continents could not move through the mantle. Furthermore, the hypothesis was consistent with a variety of observations that had not previously made sense. However, despite the strong circumstantial evidence, his concepts initially made little impact on the thinking of the geological community. What was needed was a really convincing test of this hypothesis.

In 1963, British geophysicists Fred Vine and Drummond Matthews reported that newly-formed rocks along the axis of the central ridge of the Indian Ocean were magnetized while the earth's magnetic field was in its present polarity.[2] This in itself was not surprising, because it was already known that such "normal" magnetization also characterized other mid-ocean ridges. However, Vine and Matthews found that seamounts on the flanks of the Indian Ocean ridge were magnetized in the reverse way, an observation they concluded might confirm Hess's sea-floor spreading hypothesis. They reasoned that if crust is now forming along the axis of any mid-ocean ridge, it must become magnetized with the field's present polarity as it crystallizes from the molten mantle. However, given that the earth's magnetic field has periodically reversed its polarity, based on observations of repeated lava flows on the flanks of various volcanoes around the world, older crust lying some distance from the ridge should exhibit reversed polarity, and in even older crust further away, the polarity should be normal again.

This idea was soon tested by a major magnetic survey and sample-collecting expedition along the Mid-Atlantic Ridge south of Iceland. Results of this survey, published in 1967, conclusively demonstrated that magnetic banding or "striping" is symmetrical on the two sides of the Mid-Atlantic Ridge.[3] Moreover, the sequence of polarity reversals recorded in the ocean floor basalts was found to be identical to the magnetic reversal stratigraphy already documented by other researchers, including the potassium-argon radioisotopic dating of the polarity reversals in lava flows on land, in places such as the Hawaiian Islands and Reunion Island.[4] However, because of inhomogeneities in the oceanic crust, the magnetic anomalies were found to not form perfectly smooth striping patterns on the sea floor. Furthermore, it was then found that the relative widths of the sea floor magnetic stripes were proportional to the time intervals these stripes were thought to represent, that is, presumed long intervals of normal polarity were represented by broad stripes, while narrow intervals were represented by narrow stripes.

Following the publication of Hess's sea-floor spreading hypothesis, the deep trenches on the ocean floor also attracted much interest as the sites where the oceanic plate was believed to be descending back into the mantle by the process which became known as *subduction*. In the decade before Hess developed his ideas, the geophysicist Hugh Benioff and others had noted that two other geological features were associated with the trenches, namely, volcanoes and deep-focus earthquakes.[5] The latter are earthquakes that originate more than 300 kilometers (approximately 190 miles) below the surface of the earth. In areas distant from the deep ocean trenches, deep-focus earthquakes are rare. However, near the trenches

2   F. J. Vine and D. H. Matthews, 1963, Magnetic anomalies over oceanic ridges, *Nature*, 199: 947-949.

3   A. Cox, G. B. Dalrymple and R. R. Doell, 1967, Reversals of the earth's magnetic field, *Scientific American*, 216: 44-54.

4   I. McDougall and D. H. Tarling, 1963, Dating of polarity cones in the Hawaiian Islands, *Nature*, 200: 54-56; F. H. Camalaun and I. McDougall, 1966, Dating geomagnetic polarity epochs in Reunion, *Nature*, 210: 1212-1214.

5   H. Benioff, 1954, Orogenesis and deep crustal structure: additional evidence from seismology, *Bulletin of the Geological Society of America*, 65: 385-400.

both shallow- and deep-focus earthquakes occur frequently.

The typical spatial relationship found between trenches, volcanoes, and earthquake foci is shown in Figure 27 (page 454). Earthquakes involve the sudden release of stored elastic energy in brittle rock when a rupture occurs. Most earthquakes in the world today occur near plate boundaries and involve sudden slippage along a fault along or near a plate boundary. If two adjacent plates are moving such that, averaged over time, there is a relative velocity between them, the displacement at their common boundary is usually not smooth and continuous, but instead discontinuous, with the two plates locked together most of the time and the relative motion between the places taking place episodically, in localized sudden jumps, that is, as earthquakes. When one plate subducts beneath another, the earthquake foci fall along a narrow, nearly planar zone that plunges downward at an angle from the trench along the boundary between the two plates. It was soon discovered that there were earthquakes occurring in the subducting oceanic plates at depths much greater than the thickness of the overriding plate. Some of these deeper earthquakes, known as deep-focus earthquakes, were found to be occurring at depths of more than 600 km, apparently within the subducted plate itself. The mechanism that would cause rock to rupture at these depths and high pressures remained a mystery for many decades. The current consensus is that these deep-focus earthquakes are the result of a sudden change of phase within the cold slab of subducting rock. The mineral olivine that is stable at depths above 410 km normally changes to a denser mineral phase, a phase generally referred to as spinel, just below 410 km. However, at the low temperatures that are typical in subducted slabs, this reaction can be quite slow, such that the phase transformation does not take place before the slab sinks to depths of 600 km or more. Olivine is a major mineral component of oceanic lithosphere. The transformation to spinel is an exothermic reaction, in other words, the reaction releases energy. So if there is a significant volume of metastable olivine within a slab that has subducted, say, to 600 km depth, a relatively low energy trigger can set off a sudden reaction in which the phase transformation occurs suddenly and catastrophically, resulting in a significant change in volume and rapid displacement of material in the slab, producing a deep-focus earthquake. The discovery of these deep-focus earthquakes and their association with trenches and a plane of earthquakes at shallower depths was early evidence that slabs of oceanic lithosphere indeed were penetrating deep into the earth.

Chains of volcanic islands were found often to run parallel to the deep ocean trenches. The reason for their existence and the source of the magma to feed the volcanoes that made them could also now be explained. The volcanic islands are so positioned because wet sediments and basaltic crust on the top surface of the descending slab of lithosphere tend to melt at depths of about 100 km, and the resulting magma, because its density is significantly lower than the surrounding mantle rock, rises readily toward the surface. Some of this magma can solidify within the continental crust to form intrusive igneous bodies called plutons, while the magma that reaches the surface builds volcanoes and the volcanic islands. The deep ocean trenches and the chains of volcanoes associated with them tend to exhibit arcuate shapes, so island chains formed by volcanoes that rise above sea level are known as island arcs.

56

Global Plate Tectonics: The Unifying Model

During the first half of the 20th century, the majority of earth scientists had been very skeptical of the theory of continental drift, and at first the same was also true with its successor, the theory of global plate tectonics. But as a flood of new data began to be gathered and reported in the early 1960s—data that strongly supported the new theory—a major revolution in geological thinking took place. The revolution occurred not because of a vocal majority who were championing an outrageous idea, but because the rapidly accumulating weight of evidence displayed an amazing level of internal consistency, answered many questions that had previously been unsolved puzzles, and unified a vast and diverse body of geological and geophysical observations into a coherent and workable conceptual framework for geological processes on a global scale. In a span of just ten years, the decade of the 1960s, the prevailing outlook in the earth sciences went from earnest skepticism to widespread acceptance. Of course, all theories continue to be tested, even after they have gained general acceptance, and the validation of a good theory is its predictive power to account for more and more observational data. Because the theory still does not adequately explain some details, refinements continue to be made in order to encompass such data. To be sure, plate tectonics theory still has a few detractors, but their numbers have decreased markedly over the past decades. As a unifying conceptual framework for global tectonic and geological processes, plate tectonics theory has proven itself extremely powerful and therefore has become an integral part of the modern geological synthesis. Because it plays such a central role in modern geological thinking, it, along with its supporting observations, need to be thoroughly evaluated and understood if a successful biblical geologic model for earth history is to be constructed within a scriptural framework of creation and the Flood.

A key foundational assumption of plate tectonics theory, as in the modern geological synthesis generally, is that tectonic and geological processes have been uniformly slow in their operation through time, generally similar to the rates these processes display in our world today. This assumption, of course, does not rule out occasional catastrophes, but such events are believed to be generally rare and interspersed within the conventional uniformitarian timescale for earth history that spans some four and a half billion years. Indeed, what most earth scientists consider to be one of the strongest arguments that uniformitarianism is true and that the standard geological timescale is correct is the amazing agreement between the rates of past plate motion inferred from radioisotope dating, combined with the plate displacements implied by plate tectonics theory, and the rates of plate motion actually measured for the earth today. GPS and other sophisticated satellite technology together with earth-bound instruments that can measure, among other things, slip rates at plate boundaries, such as across the San Andreas Fault in central California, yield rates and directions of plate movements very close to the rates and directions provided by plate tectonics theory for the past few millions of years in the assumed uniformitarian timescale. Any successful model for earth history consistent with the account of creation and the Flood of Scripture and its timescale must account for this astonishing agreement.

To be able to understand the theory of plate tectonics in a more concise way, let us define some important terms and summarize some pertinent aspects of earth structure. For plate tectonics, one of the most important features of earth structure is that of the lithosphere. The lithosphere is the rigid layer of rock, typically about 100 km thick, that includes the crust and top part of the upper mantle. This outermost mechanically strong shell of rock is broken into a dozen or so rigid plates whose outlines are shown in Figure 28 (page 455). The plates slide over a mechanically much weaker zone immediately beneath it known as the asthenosphere in the general directions shown. The weakness of the asthenosphere is almost certainly due to the presence of a significant amount of water (on the order of a few percent) within the crystalline structure of the minerals that comprise the rock in this part of the upper mantle. The asthenosphere also tends to be weak because in most places its temperature is not too far below the point at which some of its minerals would begin to melt. It is important to emphasize, however, that the asthenosphere, except for tiny volumes in certain special places, is solid and *not liquid magma*, as many people today somehow have been led to think. However, relative to the temperatures that exist inside the earth, the earth surface is very cold. Hence, the rock near the earth's surface down to depths of 50 km or so also tends to be much cooler and more rigid than the rock at greater depths. Plate-like motion occurs because of the rigidity of the lithosphere, which enables plates with horizontal dimensions of thousands of kilometers to move more or less as distinct, mechanically rigid units. According to the relative motions of adjacent plates, three kinds of plate boundaries have been defined:

(1) Divergent, or spreading, boundaries, exemplified by the mid-ocean ridges;
(2) Transform boundaries, involving horizontal shearing motion across a vertical fault, such as the San Andreas fault in California, and in fracture zones on the ocean bottom; and
(3) Convergent boundaries, such as where an ocean plate subducts beneath another plate or where two continents collide (Figure 29 on page 456).

Because of the movements between the plates, the plate boundaries are marked by earthquakes and so are readily identified on maps of the global distribution of earthquakes (Figure 30 on page 456). This is an example of data explained by plate tectonics theory.

Divergent boundaries occur where plates move apart from one another. In the process of plate separation, partially molten mantle material rises beneath linear segments of the resulting mid-ocean ridges, and new lithosphere is created within the rift zones, or grabens, along the axes of the ridges. Such boundaries are characterized by active basaltic volcanism, shallow-focus earthquakes caused by tensile (stretching) stresses, and high rates of heat flow. The outpouring of magma along mid-ocean ridges and the building of the ocean lithosphere are volumetrically the most significant form of volcanism on earth.

Transform faults form the boundaries along which plates slide past one another, usually with neither creation nor destruction of lithosphere. Sometimes marked by scarps, transform faults are characterized by shallow-focus earthquakes with horizontal slips. Occasionally there occur "leaky" transforms, in which some volcanism and slight plate separation accompany the transform. An example is shown in Figure 29.

Convergent boundaries occur when plates move toward one another. The most common type of convergent boundary involves subduction of one plate beneath another. The subducting plate is almost always of the ocean type, that is, without the thick layer of lower density continental crust that characterizes continental lithosphere. Because the average chemistry of oceanic lithosphere is similar to that of the underlying mantle, its lower temperature means that its density is higher than the underlying mantle, and hence it is able to sink largely unhindered into the mantle. Indeed, it is the weight of the sinking plate (due to its higher density) which acts to pull the entire plate toward the subduction zone and then downward that serves as the primary driving mechanism of plate tectonics.

The water which is associated with the top surface of the subducting plate tends to lower the melting temperature of adjacent rock, and the melting that occurs at about 80 km depth commonly produces volcanic island arcs when the opposite plate is oceanic (Figure 31 on page 457) and chains of basaltic and andesitic volcanoes when the opposite plate is continental. Subduction zones are clearly distinguished by the presence of deep ocean trenches, as well as by shallow- and deep-focus earthquakes. Usually, when there is convergence between two regions of continental lithosphere, that collision has been preceded by subduction of oceanic lithosphere that is still driving the convergence. When plate convergence occurs at the edge of a continent, the associated subduction and crustal deformation usually produce adjacent mountain ranges of folded and faulted rocks, and also both basaltic and andesitic volcanism.

Each tectonic plate is bounded by some combination of these three generic kinds of boundaries (Figure 32 on page 458). For example, the Nazca plate in the Pacific is bounded on three sides by zones of divergence along which new lithosphere is forming, and on one side by the Peru-Chile trench where lithosphere is being consumed. Continental margins may or may not coincide with plate boundaries. When they do, the continents tend to remain "afloat" because the thick layer of buoyant continental crust normally makes that lithosphere too buoyant to subduct. Where two plates with continents at their leading edges converge (collide), the crust is crumpled, deformed, and thickened to form great mountain ranges like the Himalayas.

Figure 31 depicts some of the structural details of the rigid lithospheric slab, a plate, from the region of its generation at a ridge axis to its disappearance from the surface at a subduction zone, where it plunges into the deeper mantle. Either oceanic or continental crust may cap the plate. Where a continent is embedded in the moving plate, it is carried along passively by it. Thus, continental drift is simply a consequence of plate movements. Beneath the plates is the plastic, much weaker asthenosphere. Its weakness is due to the presence of water in the crystalline lattice of its constituent minerals. The water and small amount of sediment on the top of the subducted lithosphere lowers the melting temperature of the adjacent rock, which becomes a source of magma that rises to feed the overlying volcanic arc. A large amount of heat emerges along the ridge axis, less from the older, cooled subducting slab, and more from the volcanic arc of the subduction zone and the marginal basement behind it, where a small region of secondary spreading is occurring.

Geophysicists have conducted theoretical studies and generated computer models of the development of a plate, from its generation from hot, upwelling mantle at ocean ridges, through its spreading and cooling phase, to its subduction, with reheating and final resorption in the underlying mantle. Such models help explain some important geological and geophysical observations—the major features of the ocean floors, the variation of heat flow from the ocean floor, the occurrence of volcanism at plate margins, and the location and mechanism of earthquakes in the subducted slab. However, almost all of these models are based on the assumption of uniformitarianism, which does not account for the evidence that there has been an episode of extremely rapid plate motion in the recent past, with little resorption of the subducted lithosphere since that event.

Ocean depths increase with relative age of the ocean floor in a simple relationship, derived from projection of spreading rates and distance from the spreading ridge. For some distance from the spreading center, the data fit the curve in which the ocean depth increases as the square root of the relative age, which is precisely the relationship predicted if a plate cools and contracts as it spreads. At the furthest distances from the spreading ridge, the ocean depths tend to flatten out compared to the theoretical cooling curve, as would be expected if a small amount of heat is flowing into the plate from the underlying hot asthenosphere. The deepening of the ocean floor with relative age is another one of the important lines of evidence in support of the concept of sea-floor spreading.

When a cold plate is subducted, it remains cooler than the surrounding hot mantle for a considerable relative timespan, only gradually warming as it penetrates more deeply. The occurrence of earthquakes within these slabs at depths between 400 and 700 kilometers has puzzled earth scientists for a long time. The consensus now seems to be that these earthquakes are a consequence of a volume of material within the slab undergoing a rapid change in phase, with constituent minerals changing from a less dense structure to new minerals with a more dense structure. At normal mantle temperatures, this transition in mineral phase would normally occur spontaneously at about 410 km depth. However, because the rock in the sinking slabs is cold, rates of processes are much lower and the phase changes may not take place at all, leaving the minerals in their low-pressure, low-density state as the slab penetrates to greater and greater depths. This leads to the potential of a sudden extremely rapid event that results in an earthquake, sometimes very large in magnitude, as large volumes of material in the low-density state undergo a rapid change of phase. The observation that such earthquakes never seem to occur below a depth of 700 kilometers is explained by the fact that still other major phase transitions take place at this depth. While the phase transitions between 400 and about 700 are exothermic, that is, release energy when they occur, the ones at about 700 kilometers' depth are endothermic and require an input of energy. This seems to be the likely explanation for the fact that no earthquakes occur below 700 kilometers.

As can be seen from Figures 27, 28, and 32, the boundaries of plates do not necessarily correspond to the boundaries of continents, and this is the major distinction between plate tectonics and the older concept of continental drift. Crust (continental and oceanic) and mantle are distinguished on the basis of composition, whereas lithosphere and asthenosphere are distinguished on the basis of mechanical properties. The lithospheric plates "slide" over a zone of weakness beneath them known as the asthenosphere, which earlier had been identified as a region of low seismic wave velocity and called the low velocity zone. Where lithospheric boundaries do correspond to the edges of continents, such as along the western edge of South America (Figure 28), the continental margin is referred to as active. In contrast, a passive continental margin occurs where the edge of the continent, which corresponds roughly to the junction between continental and oceanic crust, is not located at a plate boundary—for example, the east coast of the USA. Plates typically are moving today at rates of 0.1 to 10 centimeters per year, as measured using the Global Positioning System.

Where three plates meet, their boundaries converge at a single point called a triple junction. If the plates at the triple junction continue to move without changing the geometry, that is, the relative positions of the three plates, then the triple junction is termed stable. If not, it is termed unstable. The stability of triple junctions is limited by the relative motion among the plates. Stability should not be interpreted to mean that the junctions may not move, for in fact stable triple junctions can be quite mobile. It is the relationship among the plates that is termed stable or unstable.

It has already been noted that plate tectonics theory explains both the occurrence and global distribution of both earthquakes and volcanoes. Indeed, both earthquakes and volcanoes are known to occur adjacent to the boundaries between plates, and especially around the rim of the Pacific Ocean basin, which has long been called the "ring of fire" because of its abundant volcanoes. The rim of the Pacific basin is different from the "Atlantic Rim" in a very important way. The Pacific Basin is surrounded by plate margins and the rim consists of a series of subduction zones and transform faults (Figure 28). In contrast, the Atlantic Basin is largely bounded by passive continental margins, which tend to be tectonically quiet.

However, there are instances of earthquakes and volcanism occurring well away from plate margins. Indeed, some of the earth's large, currently active volcanoes are located near the centers of plates, such as the volcanoes on the Hawaiian Islands. Such magmatism is referred to as a hotspot, a small geographic area where heating and igneous activity occur within the crust. Another hotspot is located in the Yellowstone area of Wyoming, where geysers and volcanoes have long been present. Many of these hotspots result from what are known as mantle plumes. These are important components of the mantle "plumbing," being concentrated regions of hot (and therefore low density) upwelling material, which can be considerable distances from plate boundaries. Hot ascending material from the deep mantle in these plumes melts only when it reaches the very shallow mantle, there producing basaltic magma, which rises rapidly to the surface to erupt as volcanoes.

Mantle plumes arise from deep in the mantle (most likely from the core-mantle boundary). In their positions, these plumes appear to have been relatively stationary over long periods of time. In contrast, the lithospheric plates on the earth's surface move relative to each other and relative to the underlying mantle. Thus, the plates must move over the plumes, and as they do so, chains of volcanoes are produced which are known as hotspot trails. Indeed, the volcanoes formed by a hotspot in the interior of a plate are commonly arranged in a linear chain in which the volcanoes become progressively older along the chain in a direction away from the currently active volcano.

More than a century ago, American geologist James Dwight Dana argued that the Hawaiian Islands increase in age toward the northwest because erosion has had an increasingly pronounced effect in this direction (the islands are progressively more eroded and smaller). This observation was curious at the time and generally defied explanation until it was put into a plate-tectonic context. The Hawaiian

Island-Emperor Seamount Chain in the middle of the Pacific plate is perhaps the best known example. The volcanoes are not only more eroded in a northwesterly direction, but in the extreme northwestern part of the chain they are deeply eroded, inactive, and mainly submerged as seamounts. There is also a bend in the hotspot trail as the Hawaiian Islands pass into the submerged Emperor seamounts. A similar bend occurs in other hotspot trails in the South Pacific, thus indicating that the Pacific plate changed its direction of movement at some time in the past. These observations provide important evidence for the way plates have moved in the past.

It is not surprising that many hotspots are situated on or very near mid-ocean ridges, given that mantle plumes may in some cases be responsible for initiating active spreading ridges. Thus, where a mantle plume rises under continental lithosphere, the resultant upwelling may cause rifting to develop. This is because continental lithosphere is typically thicker than oceanic lithosphere, where mantle plumes may simply produce volcanoes. If the continental crust remains nearly stationary for some time over a hotspot, it is suggested that doming and then rifting would tend to develop, because the heat beneath it is more effectively trapped, bowing up the lithosphere and rupturing it by rifting. A prime example of this is the mantle "superplume" under Africa that appears to have produced the East African Rift system with its associated volcanism, where there is also evidence of doming. On the other hand, the general correlation of hotspots with mid-ocean ridges may be more a result that subducted material beneath subduction zones tends to cool and insulate the core-mantle boundary and preferentially cause mantle plumes to form away from such regions where significant volumes of subducted material has accumulated at the base of the mantle.

What drives the motion of the plates, and by what mechanism does plate tectonics occur? The basic answer is that gravity acts on density variations in the mantle, causing colder, more dense rock to sink and hotter, less dense rock to rise. These motions of rock in the mantle act on the lithospheric plates at the surface, causing them to move.

The forces that drive the plates today appear to be in balance; that is, plates appear to be neither accelerating nor decelerating. Should two continents collide, the plates that are involved would decelerate, which appears to be what has occurred in the past when India collided with Asia. But in today's world, the plates seem to be traveling at constant velocity. Plates are the cool upper layer of the global convection system. The subducting oceanic plates represent the return flow of cool material that sinks in the mantle due to gravity because the cold plate is denser than the warm mantle. The tug of gravity pulling these subducting plates downward is balanced mostly by horizontal forces from other plates acting at the plate boundaries, and secondarily from viscous drag of the asthenosphere on the bottom of the plate.

Actually, the overall driving effects of gravity can be divided into three categories: slab pull, ridge push, and slab suction. Slab pull arises from old oceanic lithosphere (a slab) plunging into the mantle at a subduction zone and literally pulling the remainder of the plate in behind it. This force is usually the most important of the forces acting on plates. Ridge push is a consequence of the higher average temperature of rock beneath a spreading ridge and the height of the mid-ocean ridges being elevated. Furthermore, the newly formed oceanic lithosphere thickens steadily from a value near zero at the ridge crest to as much as about 100 kilometers at a subduction zone. This varying topographic height and the varying pressure at depth associated with it exerts an outward horizontal force on the plate, tending to push it away from the ridge. Ridge push is the sum total of this force across the full topographic structure. Finally, slab suction is the result of interaction between two plates at a convergent margin. Slabs not only typically plunge at an angle into the mantle at a subduction zone, but their vertical component of sinking normally continues right up to the subduction zone itself. This results in a backward migration of the subduction zone itself. In so doing, the sinking slab acts like a paddle sweeping down and back through the mantle, with the effect of creating a suction on the overriding plate. As a result, the subduction zone migrates in the opposite direction to that of plate movement, and the suction force pulling on the overriding plate tends to move it toward the trench and can even rift it apart.

Plates are thus usually subjected to the forces of ridge push, slab pull, and slab suction, which are balanced by friction with other plates at plate boundaries and by viscous drag in the asthenosphere. Which of these driving forces dominates in a given situation depends on multiple factors, such as height of the ridge, angle of subduction, temperature of the mantle, and the temperature and density of the plate. Certainly, plate tectonics would not exist without slab pull, which is responsible for the return flow of the overall mantle circulation. The importance of slab pull is illustrated through observations from several present-day plates of the clear relationship between the plate migration rates and the proportional amount of plate margin associated with a subduction zone. Rapid plate movement occurs where a subduction zone along one edge of the plate involves more than 20 percent of the plate edge.

As the downgoing slab sinks into the asthenosphere, several related phenomena occur. The cold slab is enclosed in hot asthenosphere and effectively cools off a portion of the surrounding asthenosphere. At the same time, the slab itself is heated by the surrounding hot material. Because the slab is thick and rocks are good insulators, the slab remains cool for a relatively long period of time, extending the duration of the negative buoyancy necessary for continued sinking into the deeper mantle. Furthermore, as the slab sinks below about 400 km, transformations to denser mineral phases occur in response to the increased pressure. For example, at a depth of 410 kilometers the mineral olivine changes to the more compact spinel structure. The thermodynamics of this phase transition acts to increase the negative buoyancy of the slab. However, at a depth of 660 kilometers, which is the base of the upper mantle, the additional phase transition from the spinel structure to perovskite and magnesiowuestite exerts a resistive force on the slab. Although there was once debate over whether slabs push directly through this transition or are sufficiently impeded to remain in the upper mantle, the seismic evidence is now clear that slabs have indeed penetrated this boundary, with large volumes of cold slab material now located just above the core-mantle boundary. The seismic evidence, however, also suggests strongly that presently slab material tends to pile up above this transition boundary until the accumulated weight becomes large enough for the cold mass to punch through the boundary and then sink like an avalanche to the core-mantle boundary.

Finally, hot, narrow, jet-like plumes are known to rise from the bottom of the mantle, which closes the circuit of flow in mantle circulation. Even though this rock is hot and readily deformed on scales of kilometers, it nevertheless is solid, not liquid. Evidence at the earth's surface today indicates that the head of a plume, formed when a new plume emerges from the base of the mantle, causes doming and rifting as it approaches the earth's surface, with extensive partial melting of the asthenosphere. The result is a massive outpouring of basaltic magma at the earth's surface, expressed as a flood basalt on a continent or by formation of an ocean plateau in an ocean basin. Fortunately, formation of new plumes and the catastrophic consequences when the plume head reaches the earth's surface seem to be limited to the earth's past. In today's world, we see evidence only of old plume conduits expressed in hot spot volcanism as observed in Hawaii, Iceland, and Yellowstone.

57

PLATE TECTONICS:
CONTROLLING THE FORMATION
OF THE ROCK RECORD—
DIVERGENT PLATE MARGINS AND THE OCEAN FLOOR

The theory of plate tectonics has not only provided a conceptual framework for understanding topographic and geologic features of the earth's surface and the current operation of many geological processes, but can also be used as a basis for understanding the operation of geological processes in the past, and thus the development through time of the rock record. The conventional geological community rigorously applies the principle of uniformitarianism, which asserts that all the geologic processes that we observe today—including volcanic activity, magmatism, metamorphism, and faulting—occurred in the distant geologic past as well, and for the same reasons and by the same mechanisms. In isolation from the eyewitness revelation of the catastrophic events in earth history given us in the Scriptures, this assumption is not unreasonable, particularly as there is also a biblical basis for continuity in the operation of natural processes that the Creator set in operation after He had created the earth. Of course, what is at issue is the timescale of earth history. Nevertheless, because the conceptual framework of plate tectonics has become an integral part of the modern geological synthesis in explaining the development of the rock record, it is important to understand how the plate tectonics theory is used in conjunction with the geologic column to build a picture of the operation of geological processes and events in the past that have left their record in the earth's strata sequences. In turn, because of the obvious connection of the past to the present, it may be that if plate tectonics has explanatory power for understanding the rock record in the uniformitarian geological timescale context, then it may also have relevance to understanding the rock record of earth history within the scriptural framework of creation and the Flood.

The evidence for the existence of lithospheric plates on the earth's surface today is now generally well established, and the movements of these plates have been measured, the movement rates and directions being consistent with those predicted by other geological evidence. If the measured plate movements were to be reversed, then the present configuration of plates and continents would be moved back in time to eventually reassemble, more or less, in the configuration first suggested by Wegener into the supercontinent which he called Pangaea, made up of the southern continents combined as Gondwana and the northern continents combined as Laurasia (Figure 33 on page 459). As already noted, circumstantial evidence for this supercontinent reconstruction resulted from the jigsaw fit across the Atlantic Ocean of North and South America, and Greenland with Africa and Europe. Additional evidence surfaced from the matching of different rock types (such as coal seams) and fossil assemblages among the southern continents reassembled as Gondwana.

With this reconstruction of Pangaea, several other major correlations and geological relationships are established. For example, in closing the Atlantic Ocean basin to join Greenland and North and South America with Europe and Africa, the Appalachian Mountain range in North America and its northeasterly extension in eastern Greenland join and become coincident with the Caledonian Mountain range of Scandinavia, Scotland, and Ireland. Furthermore, the extensive flows of Parana basalts on the southern Atlantic coast of South America line up with and match the corresponding extensive flows of Etendeka basalts on the southern Atlantic coast near the tip of southern Africa, making just one enormous basalt province. These basalts have become known as flood basalts, because vast lava flows appear to have rapidly erupted over a relatively short period of time, believed to be the result of an upwelling hot mantle plume causing extensive melting of the asthenosphere, producing huge volumes of basaltic magma. Given then that the Parana and Etendeka flood basalts were contemporaneous outpourings in an original single province (and other evidence supports this), then the same mantle plume responsible for the outpourings of flood basalts must have domed underneath the supercontinent in this area, causing an upward bulge and an uplift, creating a weakness that caused rifting. Subsequently, before rifting began in the extreme north of what was to become the North Atlantic basin, another mantle plume was responsible for more outpourings of flood basalts, which today are found around the southeastern coast of Greenland, across northern Ireland, and northwestern Scotland. These also correlate as one original flood basalt province, so the mantle plume responsible for it would then have initiated the rifting that caused the opening up of the northernmost Atlantic Ocean (Figure 34 on page 460).

Thus, the opening of the Atlantic Ocean basin, and indeed the entire break-up of Pangaea and subsequent movements to produce the present continental and plate configuration, began by rifting to produce divergent plate margins. Therefore, oceanic rifts between the separating continents started as continental rifts. Upwelling hot asthenosphere, often the result of mantle plumes, began exploiting the weak continental crust, causing rifting and block faulting, which eventually produced a central graben, a valley between the two separating pieces of a continental rift. As the continental rifting continued, the upwelling asthenosphere produced more basaltic lavas until all the continental crust had been pushed aside, and in fact, new oceanic lithosphere formed in the rift. The end result was that a new ocean basin began to form, with the upwelling asthensophere producing new oceanic crust at the mid-ocean ridge; and ridge push moving the oceanic lithospheric plates on either side of the axial valley, resulting in sea-floor spreading.

A divergent plate margin, then, forms when a plate splits and the two pieces separate. On continents, the valley floor that forms as the two pieces separate is called a continental rift. A giant fault-bounded graben, it can become loaded with sediments and can extend to a depth of six kilometers. If a plate splits on the ocean floor, an oceanic rift forms. Recently-formed major rifts generally lie on top of broad ridges, supported by the low-density mantle material of the upwelling asthenosphere. Most oceanic rifts probably started as continental rifts, so that as the continental plates separated, new oceanic lithosphere formed in the rift from the upwelling mantle material in the asthenosphere. Eventually a new ocean basin was formed with its own mid-ocean ridge. Once formed, oceanic lithosphere tends not to rift, whereas continental lithosphere does. Furthermore, oceanic lithosphere can subduct, but continents are too buoyant to subduct and instead rift apart. Topographic profiles across slow-spreading continental rifts resemble profiles across oceanic rifts, even though continental-plate separations occur at a rate that is ten times slower than that of oceanic rifting.

After new oceanic lithospheric plates are formed at mid-ocean rifts, they cool, thicken, and subside as they move away, until they are eventually consumed at subduction zones. Investigations, including deep-sea drilling, have shown that the oceanic lithosphere is approximately 100 kilometers thick, the top 7 kilometers being oceanic crust overlying sub-oceanic mantle lithosphere. In the oceanic crust, the first layer consists of up to several hundred meters of sediments sitting on top of a second layer formed by about a kilometer thickness of pillow basalts. Below this is a third layer consisting entirely of a sequence of vertical basalt dikes, known as a sheeted dike complex, below which are layered gabbros down to the base of the oceanic crust. Upward movement of hot mantle peridotite due to mantle convection causes decompression, the decrease in pressure lowering the melting point to initiate partial melting. The molten basalt formed forces its way up and out through channels in the solid peridotite to form a magma chamber at the base of the oceanic crust below the mid-ocean rift, where the space has been made available by the stretching and rifting of the oceanic crust due to the convective flow of the mantle underneath it (Figure 35 on page 461). Magma from the chamber repeatedly intrudes the rift between the spreading plates above and solidifies as vertical sheets or dikes, with dikes intruding dikes to form a structure like a pack of cards standing on edge. It is these dikes that record the direction of the earth's magnetic field at the time they solidify and thus give the ocean floor its characteristic magnetic stripes, each corresponding to the polarity of the geomagnetic field at the time of its formation. When the basalt magmas from the dikes erupt onto the surface of the ocean floor, they are quenched by the cold seawater to form pillow basalts characteristic of submarine volcanism. Meanwhile, at the roof of the magma chamber, circulatory seawater cools the adjacent magma, which crystallizes and plates to the roof as a coarse-grained gabbro below the sheeted dikes. At the same time, magma freezes to the walls of the chamber and crystals settle to its floor, crystallizing to form layered gabbros and peridotites below the chamber size keeping, on average, constant over time. A thin blanket of deep-sea sediments covers the pillow basalts at the top of the oceanic crust. The thickness of the sediments increases with distance from the mid-ocean ridge as the oceanic crust gets systematically older, allowing more time for sediments to accumulate. As rifting and sea-floor spreading continue, the newly-formed oceanic crust with its zones of lavas, dikes, gabbros, and peridotites is transported away from the mid-ocean ridge where this unique sequence of rocks has been assembled. Meanwhile, the magma chamber is periodically replenished by fresh injections of molten basalt from partial melting of the mantle to keep this process going.

Combined sequences of deep-sea sediments, pillow basalts, sheeted dikes, and mafic igneous intrusions, identical to cross-sections through the oceanic crust, have also been found on land in various parts of the world. Known as ophiolites, or ophiolite suites, they were a puzzle to geologists for over 100 years until plate tectonics theory provided the explanation for them. These rocks, otherwise exotic in the contexts in which they are found, are slices or fragments of the oceanic crust of old sea floors which have been transported by sea-floor spreading and were raised above sea level in an episode of plate collision, being thrust up (obducted) onto the continents. For example, the narrow ophiolite zones found in convergence features like the Alpine-Himalayan belt and the Ural and Appalachian belts would be slices of former oceanic crust and mantle thrust onto the continents when former ocean basins finally disappeared as continents collided (discussed below). It was this recognition of what ophiolites represented that, in conjunction with deep-sea drilling, enabled geologists to reconstruct the process of the formation of the oceanic crust at and below mid-ocean ridges.

Several consequences result from the contact between the hot pillow basalts and seawater at mid-ocean ridges. Not only are reactions between the basalt and seawater fundamental to changing the composition of both the basalt and the seawater itself, but the heating of seawater is the major mechanism for dissipation of the earth's internal heat. Sediments and fractured rocks near the ridge crest are permeable, so water flows through them via cracks and pores. This permeability allows seawater sufficient penetration into the oceanic crust so that it approaches the magma chamber and is heated. Boreholes drilled near the crests of active ridges found the oceanic crust to be quite cold to depths of 1 to 2 kilometers. Such observations are consistent with large hydrothermal circulation cells penetrating to these depths, indicating that hydrothermal circulation represents a very important cooling mechanism.

The interactions between the down-welling seawater in the oceanic crust and the hot basalt of the mid-ocean ridges trigger extensive chemical changes. Some chemical components are leached out of the basalts and replaced by components from seawater, with the most commonly leached elements being silicon, iron, sulfur, manganese, copper, calcium, and zinc. Basalt incorporates magnesium and sodium, which is dissolved in seawater as a result of continental weathering and erosion. Chlorine combines with sodium, remaining in the seawater to form dissolved salt. Thus, both the basalt and seawater are profoundly changed by this interaction. Given the quantities of water cycled through these hydrothermal systems at mid-ocean ridges, it is possible that the basalt-seawater interaction occurring there represents a primary mechanism contributing dissolved salts to the oceans. Within the basalt, primary mineral components are altered to become new mineral assemblages. Plagioclases are metamorphosed from a high-calcium content to a high-sodium one, which results from the loss of calcium and the addition of sodium during the water-rock hydrothermal reaction. Rock formed by this process is called *spilite*. The formation of spilites had been a puzzle to geologists for years, and would have remained so without the observations of sea floor interactions between basalt and seawater.

The hydrothermal fluids produced by the seawater percolating down into the hot basalt circulate in the oceanic crust, and then rise along fractures and conduits to be discharged as hot springs on the ocean floor along the axis of the mid-ocean ridge. These discharging hydrothermal fluids are heavily mineral-laden due to all the metals leached from the basalts, so when these hot springs were first observed from submersible mini-submarines, they looked like black smoke pouring out of chimneys sitting upright on the sea floor, and hence were named "black smokers." Temperatures as high as 450°C have been measured, although they are more commonly about 350°C. Thus, the hot water, black because of its mineral content, rises through the discharge openings and chimneys. It immediately begins dispersing into the cold ocean water, whereupon the dissolved iron, copper, zinc, and other metals quickly precipitate as sulfides on the sea floor surface adjacent to the black smokers, and along channels or pipes that develop in the rock which has carried this hot, mineral-laden water upward through the basalt. In this way, rich mineral deposits of iron, copper, and other metal sulfide minerals and calcium sulfate (anhydrite) are found adjacent to and within the black smoker systems. Any further release of basalt lavas could then bury the massive sulfide deposits, making them volcanic-hosted—identical to volcanic-hosted massive sulfide deposits found in the geologic record, as described previously. Thus, these metal deposits on the ocean floor can be viewed as modern analogs of the volcanic-hosted massive sulfide deposits in the geologic record, which in turn could imply that where volcanic-hosted massive sulfide deposits are found in the geologic record, they indicate that a mid-ocean ridge system, complete with basalt volcanism and hydrothermal massive sulfide accumulation, was active at that geographic location and stratigraphic level in the geologic record.

Also discovered were previously unknown marine organisms flourishing around these hot springs—tube worms, crabs, mussels, and other organisms that were living around the vents of the black smokers. Nearly identical organisms have been found fossilized in close spatial relationship to volcanic-hosted massive sulfide metal deposits, such as the Cretaceous sulfide deposits in ophiolites in Oman and Cyprus, the Carboniferous Navan deposit of Ireland,[1] and an Archean deposit in the Pilbara Block of Western Australia.[2] Again, there is an unmistakable relationship between these fossilized organisms and corresponding ore deposits comparable with the volcanic-hosted massive sulfide ore deposits forming today on the ocean floor due to the hydrothermal circulation systems in the axial valleys of the mid-ocean ridges. This strongly suggests that these ore deposits in the geologic record formed in a similar manner, which in turn implies hydrothermal convection systems associated with volcanism were active at those times and in those places in earth history.

As noted previously, continental rifts are expressed by a central graben bounded by normal faults and containing faulted sediments. Rift volcanism occurs as fissures and central volcanoes along the rift. Erosion of the rift walls, volcanoes, and rim mountains provide the sediments which begin to fill the graben, and volcanic eruptions pour lavas also into the graben, which along with the sediments form alternating layers of volcanic and sedimentary rocks. As the graben deepens and widens, the sedimentary and volcanic infill, itself, undergoes faulting. The shoulders, or edges, of continental rift grabens are usually at a higher elevation than that of the surrounding plateau. This shoulder uplift is attributed to two sources: doming of the plateau, possibly prior to the rifting, that continues during the rifting process; and the result of volcanic eruptions along the rift margins building up large volcanoes. In some cases, rifting and doming occur in continental regions that have undergone plateau uplift over hundreds to thousands of square kilometers. The driving force of continental rifting must explain these three phenomena: plateau uplift on a broad scale, shoulder uplift, and graben formation in the rift zone.

Although the topography of continental rifts bears a striking similarity to that of mid-ocean ridges, heat flow is quite different. Within the rift valleys themselves, heat flow is generally high, but on either side of the rift, the heat flow is not significantly greater than that measured in stable continental regions. Because a thermal anomaly would only become apparent in regions where actual upward motion of hot mantle material brings heat near the surface—for example, in the rift zones themselves—it is apparent that the rifting must be due to localized

1   R. M. Haymon, R. A. Koski and C. Sinclair, 1984, Fossils of hydrothermal vent worms from Cretaceous sulfide ores of the Samail Ophiolite, Oman, *Science*, 223: 1407-1409; C. T. S. Little et al, 1999, Late Cretaceous hydrothermal vent communities from the Troodos ophiolite, Cyprus, *Geology*, 27: 1-27-1030.

2   B. Rasmussen, 2000, Filamentous microfossils in a 3,235-million-year-old volcanogenic massive sulphide deposit, *Nature*, 405: 676-679.

convection of upwelling mantle material. As hot convective plumes of upper mantle rock develop and push upwards, they cause doming of the continental crust above. When the doming becomes sufficiently extreme, cracks in the surface are formed, typically three cracks radiating out from the dome at about 120° to each other. Like the mid-ocean ridges, the elevated topography above the elevated asthenosphere gives rise to a continental ridge push, though probable subduction at distant plate edges also causes the continental lithosphere to be pulled apart. As favorably aligned pairs of cracks from the domal uplifts propagate toward each other, they link up to form a continental rift and eventually a divergent margin. The remaining crack or rift of the original three that radiated out from the doming becomes inactive and cools, subsides, and is filled with sediments to become a failed rift, called an *aulocagen*. There is abundant evidence of failed rifts now filled with sedimentary strata preserved in the geologic record—for example, the Mid-Continental Rift of the central United States. What conditions cause a continental rift to continue spreading and become a fully-fledged divergent plate margin, or to cease spreading and become a failed rift, are not clear, but one suggestion is that one of the rift flanks must be pulled by a subducting slab for a continental rift to make the transition to an ocean basin.

Continental rifts can be separated into two types: passive rifts and active rifts. An example of a passive rift is the Rio Grande Rift of the southern United States. It is suggested that remote subduction forces have extended the crust and associated faulting has resulted in graben formation. On the other hand, active rifts occur where active motions in the mantle, upwellings of hot material such as mantle plumes, are primarily the cause of rifting. An example would be the East African Rift. Thus, passive rifting occurs above normal mantle and is driven by plate forces, whereas active rifting is driven by convection in the mantle beneath the rift. In both cases, mantle upwelling beneath the continental lithosphere causes thinning and doming, so that continental rifts form when fractures associated with the doming link together.

58

PLATE TECTONICS:
CONTROLLING THE FORMATION
OF THE ROCK RECORD—
PLATES THAT COLLIDE: CONVERGENT MARGINS

Much of the tectonic activity on the earth's surface today occurs at convergent plate margins, including volcanoes, earthquakes, and crustal deformation. Convergent margins occur where one plate sinks or subducts beneath the other due to the dense oceanic lithosphere sinking back into the mantle, largely under its own weight. Two possible structures characteristic of convergent plate margins are shown in Figure 36 (page 462)—oceanic lithosphere can subduct beneath oceanic lithosphere at an oceanic convergent margin, or oceanic lithosphere can subduct beneath continental lithosphere at a continental convergent margin (which would also be termed an active continental margin). The subducting, or sinking, plate is always oceanic, whereas continental lithosphere, which contains a thick section of continental crust far less dense than the mantle, is too buoyant to sink back into the mantle.

The site where two plates meet is commonly marked by a topographic depression on the ocean floor called a trench, produced by the subducting oceanic lithospheric plate. The other most obvious expression of a subduction zone is a volcanic arc, which is developed on the upper or overriding plate. Plutons of intrusive rocks are abundant in the continental crust below the volcanic arc, which is thus often called a magmatic arc. At continental margin arcs (Figure 36b), the volcanoes commonly form a significant mountain range, such as the South American Andes. In contrast, the volcanoes at an oceanic convergent margin are built on oceanic lithosphere, and it is only the peaks of the highest volcanoes that usually emerge above sea level to form a chain of volcanic islands known as an island arc (Figure 36a).

Between the volcanic arc and the trench is a region in which sediments may accumulate, called a fore-arc basin. Sediments accumulate there from both erosion of the active volcanic arc and the actual transport of ocean floor sediments toward the trench on the subducting plate. The area on the other side of the volcanic arc away from the trench is known as the back-arc region, where in some cases a back-arc basin forms. Such a basin is similar to a mini-ocean basin, where sea-floor spreading takes place on a small scale (Figure 36a). Thus, the processes occurring there (volcanism, sediment accumulation) are analogous to those at mid-ocean ridges and in true ocean basins. Of course, it seems incongruous if two plates are moving toward one another at a subduction zone that one of them could be also breaking apart only a short distance away behind the volcanic arc. However, the upper plate is coupled to the subducting slab through slab suction, so if the upper plate is not overriding the subducting slab, the downward pull of the subducting slab will pull the upper plate toward the trench and the arc will be under tension. The weakest part of the upper plate is along the line of the volcanic or magmatic arc, so if the upper plate is under tension it will break along the arc and rift into two pieces, with the formation of sea-floor spreading of a back-arc basin between the two pieces. The piece of volcanic arc left on the trenchward side remains the site of active volcanism, whereas the other volcanic arc fragment becomes an inactive remnant arc on the opposite side of the back-arc basin. Alternately, if the dominant force is caused by the upper plate overriding the subducting slab, the overall effect will be a compressional stress, so the arc may instead be subjected to deformation, such as folding and thrusting, rather than extension and rifting.

Earthquakes are associated with subduction zones and are a direct result of the stresses generated when one plate moves beneath the other. Nearly all of the focal points of the earthquakes (where the rupturing or slippage is taking place) are located on the upper part of the subducting plate within 300 kilometers of the trench, and they form an inclined array defining what is called the Benioff zone, which dips beneath the volcanic arc. Seismic imaging of subduction zones reveals that the subducting slab is a region of higher seismic-wave velocities because it is cold and dense, and accordingly stronger than the surrounding mantle, whereas the seismic waves are slower in the hotter mantle, particularly in the mantle wedge above the subducting slab and beneath the volcanic arc. The subducting slab is cold relative to the mantle because it has been at the earth's surface, and as it sinks it does not heat up quickly enough to reach the same temperature as the surrounding mantle, thus forming a cold sheet penetrating the hot mantle. The cool temperatures in the slab not only mean that it will be dense, which is why it sinks, but also that it is unlikely to melt.

Volcanic arcs at convergent margins obey a rather consistent relationship with the geometry of subduction zones. The upper surface of the subducting slab is typically located at a depth of 100-150 kilometers beneath the volcanoes. The width of the fore-arc, the distance between the trench and the volcanic arc, therefore varies according to the dip of the subducting slab. The systematic and almost universal association of volcanism with subduction zones links the process of subduction to magma generation. It was originally thought that a subducting slab melts as it sinks down into the hot mantle, but more recent investigations indicate that the cold slab is slow to heat up to the temperatures sufficient for it to start to melt.

Instead, water, driven off from the subducting oceanic crust, lowers the melting point of the mantle wedge immediately above it, beneath the volcanic arc, causing partial melting.

In tectonic environments other than convergent margins, such as divergent margins and intraplate settings, magmas are dominantly basaltic in composition, reflecting their derivation directly as partial melts of the peridotite mantle. On the other hand, the compositions of magmas erupted at, or intruded into, convergent margin magmatic arcs are, on the whole, more differentiated, though some basalt lavas are also extruded in magmatic arcs. Due to the structure of the arc environment, the ascent of magmas is impeded. At continental margin arcs in particular, magmas cannot rise easily through the thick, low-density continental crust, so melts accumulate in magma chambers where they differentiate, dense minerals crystallizing in the magma chambers, leaving a less dense, more buoyant residual magma, which then can rise further into the crust. In contrast, basalt magmas can ascend easily at mid-ocean ridges (divergent margins) where the crust is basaltic, thin, and relatively dense.

Batholiths are spectacular manifestations of the huge quantities of differentiated rocks generated at magmatic arcs. They are actually composed of many individual plutons (Figure 36b), and although they are loosely termed granites in composition, most batholiths, such as those of California's Sierra Nevada, are generally in the compositional range of diorite to granodiorite. Three main ways are postulated for the generation of the granitic magmas that formed these batholiths—fractional crystallization of basaltic magmas originally derived from the mantle, or by the melting of lower crustal materials such as sedimentary rocks, or by a combination of these two processes. If the granitic magmas had been generated by fractional crystallization of a basaltic magma derived from partial melting of the mantle, more than twice the volume of the granite would have to be removed as gabbro in order to leave behind a residual granitic magma, so large bodies of gabbro should be found below the granitic batholiths. However, while gabbro plutons are indeed found associated with many granitic batholiths, they are generally not in the volumes needed if the associated granites had been generated by fractional crystallization of basalt magmas. On the other hand, the occurrence of migmatites, produced by partial melting in metamorphic rocks, and xenoliths of crustal rocks often found in granites, are both consistent with granitic magmas being generated by partial melting of crustal rocks. Thus, the currently preferred model is that heating of the lower crust by basalt magmas derived from the mantle causes partial melting of crustal rocks to generate granitic magmas, although the basalt magmas may also tend to undergo some fractional crystallization and then mix with the crustal melts.

The full compositional range of volcanic rocks are found extruded in the volcanic arcs at convergent margins, though andesites and dacites are particularly prevalent. Nevertheless, convergent margin volcanism is commonly dominated by explosive eruptions and the accumulation of their volcanic products. Indeed, in terms of the total volume of erupted material, many major eruptions in recent history have been associated with subduction and have been pyroclastic in nature. The eruptions of Mount St. Helens in 1980 and Mount Pinatubo in the Philippines in 1991 are typical examples. In the past 200 years, large eruptions have occurred at Tambora and Krakatoa in Indonesia (1815 and 1883, respectively) and at Katmai, Alaska (creating the "Valley of Ten Thousand Smokes," 1912). These eruptions produced up to 30 km^3 of ash and other pyroclastic deposits. These volumes, however, pale in comparison with the hundreds to thousands of cubic kilometers erupted in places such as the western United States and the Andes, as now preserved in the geologic record.

Although pyroclastic eruptions can also occur at divergent plate margins or in intraplate settings, they are much less frequent in those locations. Magmas at volcanic arcs tend to be rich in dissolved gases, and they tend to be viscous because of their high silica contents. As a result, explosive pyroclastic eruptions are common. Varying in style and magnitude, they can produce deposits that are described and classified both in terms of the size and type of fragment (clast), and in terms of the way in which the deposit was formed. Pyroclastic materials range in size from large blocks or volcanic bombs (10 centimeters or larger) that are ejected into the air, to smaller, pebble-size fragments, to finer-grained ash (less than 2 millimeters). Pyroclastic deposits, which are generally termed tuffs when lithified, are classified by the way in which they were formed. Pyroclastic fall deposits form when pyroclastic material is ejected into the air and falls back to the ground. Layers of fall deposits, therefore, tend to be well sorted and can be spread over a wide area, covering the topography almost like snow. Ashfall deposits from ancient eruptions can be traced over large areas. Because they are deposited very quickly, ashfall layers are useful time markers in the geologic record. On the other hand, pyroclastic flows commonly form when the material from a rising ash-eruption column suddenly collapses and falls to the ground. The flows follow pre-existing valleys as they travel downhill at very high speeds and form poorly-sorted deposits.

Many large-volume eruptions, such as those at Crater Lake in Oregon and Lake Taupo in New Zealand, have produced widespread ash-flow tuffs or *ignimbrites*, pyroclastic flows formed of ash and pumice. The heat and weight of these pumice and ash deposits have typically caused them to compact and fuse together to form a hard rock called a welded tuff. At certain times in earth history, continental arcs must have produced huge volumes of ignimbrites from large volcanic complexes. Very large magma chambers are required to erupt such large volumes, and it is possible that the root zones of large caldera complexes are the plutonic and batholithic complexes exposed in eroded continental arcs. Hundreds of thousands of cubic kilometers of ignimbrite layers are found in the western United States, with individual ignimbrite sheets each comprising volumes up to 3,000 km^3 in the case of the Fish Canyon Tuff, and distributed over thousands of square kilometers.

Even as far back in the geologic record as the Ordovician, the Millbrig Tuff can be traced over more than a million square kilometers of the eastern United States and correlates with an identical tuff bed in Europe, the total volume being in the order of a million cubic kilometers.[3] Thus, it is possible to regard tuff and lava beds in strata sequences of the geologic column as recording the volcanism in past volcanic and continental margin arcs.

There is commonly an abundant supply of sediments in volcanic arcs. The sediments accumulate in the trench, where plate convergence forms a characteristic structure known as an accretionary wedge, a structure which is not found in any other tectonic environment. Sediments are supplied to an accretionary wedge from both the volcanic arc and the subducting plate. Sediments derived from the arc are volcanic material, particularly fragmented pyroclastics that have been erupted at the arcs and that erode very easily, accompanied by sediments eroded from other igneous, sedimentary, and metamorphic rocks that make up the basement of the arc. The sediments on the subducting plate are typically fine-grained pelagic (deep sea) mud, consisting mainly of microscopic plankton skeletons and fine, windblown dust, deposited on top of the igneous oceanic crust, which carries them in conveyor-belt fashion toward the subduction zone, where they may be scraped off by the upper plate. The predominant sediments in an accretionary wedge are greywackes, immature sandstones and mudstones containing clay minerals and volcanic rock fragments, reflecting the source of the sediments and the short transport distances to the trench that limit the degree of sorting and decomposition. The sediment supply at continental margin arcs may be greater than that at island arcs simply because more land is exposed, allowing for more erosion and a greater proportion of the sediments to originate from sedimentary and metamorphic sources.

An accretionary wedge forms at a subduction zone in a manner similar to the action of a bulldozer. At the trench, the sediment is scraped off the sinking plate by the upper or overriding plate, and it piles up there. Continuing subduction pushes additional sediment underneath the accumulating pile, so that the sedimentary mass is progressively lifted up and increases in volume, forming a characteristic wedge shape. Sedimentary material is carried down within the wedge itself short distances by the subducting plate, and then pushed back upward on thrust faults, or in some cases, some of the sedimentary material can be carried down to substantial depths and by this mechanism be overridden by hot asthenosphere. At some subduction zones, though, very little sediment accumulates, either because not much is available (continental sediment sources are far away) or because it is subducted beneath the arc rather than scraped off at the trench. On the other hand, in some accretionary wedges, so much sediment accumulates that the pile

---

3   W. D. Huff, S. M. Bergström and D. R. Kolata, 1992, Gigantic Ordovician volcanic ash fall in North America and Europe: biological, tectonomagmatic, and event-stratigraphic significance, *Geology*, 20: 875-878; D. R. Kolata, W. D. Huff and S. M. Bergström, 1996, Ordovician K-bentonites of eastern North America, *Geological Society of America Special Paper*, 313.

rises above sea level. For example, the Caribbean island of Barbados is the tip of an accretionary wedge formed at the Lesser Antilles subduction zone. The sediment pile is more than 5,000 meters thick at the trench, where it appears that approximately 85 percent of the sediment is scraped off the lower plate by the overriding plate and the remaining 15 percent is carried into the subduction zone. Thus, the mechanics of subduction determine how much sediment ultimately accumulates at the trench, and how much is subducted to greater depths.

Deformation and squeezing of the wet sedimentary accumulation cause some parts of the accretionary wedge to be very fluid-rich and low in density, and as a result buoyant forces cause the intrusive rise of mud diapirs within the wedge. Temperatures within subduction zones are anomalously low because of the cooling effect of the subducted oceanic crust. Given that the subducting slab penetrates hot mantle, the subducted succession will alter to moderately high-grade metamorphic rocks, but in the core of the subducted sediment package, protected and insulated from contact with the hot asthenosphere, there is probably a sequence of much less altered, relatively buoyant rocks capable of flowing back out of the subduction zone. This counterflow process may thus result in complex mechanical mixing, so that within the portion of the accretionary prism that becomes stacked up at the trench, deformation can be so extreme that the sedimentary material becomes pervasively sheared and folded on every scale. Subduction mélange (from the French word "mixture") is the name given to these strongly deformed and usually jumbled sedimentary materials that have accumulated within the accretionary wedge. A mass of sediment effectively rolls around, caught between the grip of the downgoing slab and the buttress of the overlying plate. The resulting mélange consists of tectonically mixed assemblages of lower- and higher-grade metamorphic rocks embedded within a matrix of pervasively sheared, slightly metamorphosed mudstones. Overall, the metamorphism is characteristically high pressure-low temperature, because the material may be carried relatively rapidly to depths as great as 30 kilometers, where recrystallization occurs in the environment of the cold slab. Furthermore, parallel to the mélange is the magmatic belt of the island arc or continental margin arc made up of an arcuate system of volcanoes, intrusions, and metamorphic rocks formed on the edge of the overriding plate. Here, conditions are dominated by the rise of magmas from the descending plate, characteristically erupting andesitic lavas and intruding granitic plutons. In contrast to that in a mélange, the metamorphism in the magmatic belts is typically the result of recrystallization under conditions of high temperatures and low pressures. The overall result is paired belts of mélange and magmatism (Figure 37 on page 463), the characteristic signature of subduction.

The essential elements of these features of collisions have been found in many places in the geologic record. For example, there is the mélange in the Franciscan belt of the California Coastal Ranges and magmatism in the parallel belt of the Sierra Nevada to the east. This pair of metamorphic belts would seem to mark the boundary where, in the past, the Pacific and North American plates have collided, with the Pacific plate being subducted under the North American continental margin. Another example of paired metamorphic belts is in Japan, where subduction has occurred under a volcanic arc, the collision producing the paired and parallel Sanbagawa and Abukuma metamorphic belts.[4] Until the advent of plate tectonics theory, this feature of paired metamorphic belts remained an unsolved enigma, but the conceptual framework of the theory has now elegantly solved the puzzle. Thus, the presence of these paired metamorphic belts at various levels within the geologic column and various geographical locations gives clear testimony to similar geological processes occurring through earth history.

In complete contrast to the subduction of an oceanic plate underneath a continental margin arc or a volcanic island arc, the low density of the continental crust of a continental plate makes it isostatically buoyant, which prevents it from being subducted. Thus, whereas oceanic crust is continually recycled, once continental crust has been generated it remains, apart from loss by erosion and deposition as ocean floor sediments, which may then be subducted. Thus, fragments of continental crust produced in the earliest phases of earth history have survived to the present. A second important consequence is that when two plates of continental lithosphere converge, they will eventually collide and be crushed together, or sutured. The crust folds and fractures in response to the huge forces involved in the collision, and a mountain belt forms along the line of collision. Thus, the growth of mountain belts at convergent plate margins, in response to both magmatic additions at volcanic arcs and the deformation associated with lithospheric plates converging and colliding, is known as *orogenesis*. Furthermore, the elongate tracts of igneous rocks and deformational structures formed at convergent margins are known as orogens. The compressional forces involved when two continents collide can give rise to significant vertical displacement of strata. This explains how, in the collision of India and Asia that formed the Himalayas, rocks originally deposited on the ocean floor containing fossils of sea shells came to be exposed near the top of Mt. Everest, some 9 kilometers above sea level. Indeed, careful measurements show that the Himalayas are still being uplifted at a rate of about one centimeter annually.

The evidence of plate movements which produced the present plate configuration indicates that the Indian continent traveled northward toward the Asian landmass, convergence being made possible by subduction along southern Asia, and possibly at a number of island arcs in the intervening ocean. Subduction beneath Asia appears to have given rise to a huge continental volcanic arc, much like the Andes today. However, the northern edge of India seems to have been a passive continental margin. As the two continents approached each other, sediments accumulated in the intervening ocean basin. When all of the oceanic lithosphere between them had been subducted, the continental lithospheres of India and Asia came into contact, so that as the ocean finally closed, the sediments were squeezed

---

4   A. Miyashiro, 1973, *Metamorphism and Metamorphic Belts,* London: George Allen and Unwin Ltd.

and folded between the two continents in the collision. The softer, weaker material at the southern edge of the Asian plate was forced upwards to form the Tibetan Plateau, the extreme elevation of it and of the Himalayas being a direct reflection of the crustal thickening that occurred as a result of this continental collision. The crust forced up in the Himalayas was shortened by folding and faulting to accommodate the convergent movement, huge slices of this crust even being transported tens to hundreds of kilometers southward over the advancing Indian continental plate.

During collisions, tectonic forces dominate and the mountains produced grow taller, but as uplift occurs the mountains are subjected to faster erosion rates. However, erosion may actually increase the rate of uplift. More rapid downcutting in response to uplift removes mass from the mountains, which in turn produces broad isostatic uplift that then accentuates tectonic uplift. The overall effect is to produce extreme topographic relief, with high mountain peaks and deep valleys. Huge accumulation of sediments on the ocean floor in the Indus and Bengal Fans testify to the impressive amount of material that has been eroded from the Himalayas. Eventually, the lithosphere will adjust to the Indian and Asian continents being jammed together, the mountains will settle into isostatic equilibrium as they are worn down, and the crust will eventually return to normal thickness.

Erosion gradually wears down mountains, and given time they are reduced to nearly a flat surface. The Appalachians are an example of the results of such processes. The Appalachians appear to have formed as a result of a collision between the North American continent and the joined continents of Europe and Africa, when Pangaea was originally formed. The Appalachians would probably have been nearly as high at the time as the Himalayas are today, but erosion has worn them down, in places to gentle rolling hills. The Rockies resulted from another collision more recent than that which produced the Appalachians, because the Rockies are higher and are still being eroded. Thus, mountain belts, or orogens, are formed when continents collide; the orogens then are worn down by erosion. Recognition of orogens in the geologic record indicates that this cycle of mountain-building and erosion has been repeated a number of times during earth history.

When continental crust collides with continental crust, most of the deformation structures produced reflect large-scale compression. In the upper layers of the crust, where the rocks are brittle, thrust faulting is very common and tracts of strata can be moved tens or even hundreds of kilometers by thrust faults. Tight folds are also produced where the rocks respond in a more ductile or plastic way, and continued compression may overturn these folds. If a fold becomes increasingly stretched, the limbs may be sheared off completely, giving rise to nappe structures, which are a combination of a large fold and a thrust. Deep within the center of the collisional mountain belt, the rocks are subjected to increasing temperatures and intensities of deformation, so the metamorphic grade of the rocks also increases. Typically exposed in the heart of a mountain are granulites and migmatites, the result of high pressures and temperatures. Indeed, the temperatures can become sufficiently high to cause partial melting of the crust, the magma produced forming large granite plutons, which are common in collisional mountain belts. Nevertheless, chemical compositions of such granites differ from the compositions of those formed during a subduction episode at the active continental margin preceding continental collision. For example, large volumes of granitic crustal melts were formed and emplaced in the Himalayas immediately following the most intense period of collision between India and Asia.

When two continents converge and collide, the entire ocean basin is largely eradicated, because most of the ocean floor that was originally between the continents has been subducted and returned to the mantle. The only clues to the former existence of an ocean basin are in the deformed ocean sediments and other rocks that were scraped off the subducted slab or trapped in the suture between the plates. Most important among these remnants are slithers of ocean floor, ophiolites, caught up and deformed between the colliding plates. In older, largely eroded mountain belts, outcrops of ophiolite indicate the sutural zone along which two plates were joined. Also, rocks on either side of the suture are typically very different in character and may contain different fossil types. These are patterns of occurrence in the rock record that are consistent with the operation of these same geological processes during periods of earth history.

The mechanisms of deformation during the collision of two continental plates are extraordinarily complex, only being decipherable from the rocks and structures exposed in mountain belts due to erosion. The bulk of the crust is generally crystalline igneous or metamorphic material called basement, whereas the cover is the younger, more stratified overlying sedimentary (or metamorphosed sedimentary) strata. Where deformation occurs in the cover, which is just a thin skin on top of the basement, and there is in effect a detachment between the cover and the underlying basement, it is called thin-skinned tectonics. In contrast, if the basement is deformed along with the cover so that thrust faults and folds affect both, then the deformation is called thick-skinned tectonics. During continent-continent collisions, both types of deformation may occur. Within the interior of orogens, in the vicinity of the suture, the deformation is typically very intense and the basement is folded and thrust along with the overlying cover. On the other hand, thin-skinned deformation is commonly found in the outer zones of the mountain belts, where the uppermost layers have simply been pushed outward across the basement. In the Appalachians, drilling and seismic reflection surveys have shown that the deformation responsible for the mountain-building is probably thin-skinned tectonics.

As a result of continent-continent collisions, the crust is thickened considerably during the mountain-building. Pressures calculated in some rare metamorphic rocks from the European Alps, for instance, indicate they were probably formed at depths of about 100 kilometers, so the crust beneath the Alps must have been very thick when the Alps were formed, in contrast to normal continental crustal thicknesses of 30 to 40 kilometers. Some of this increase in crustal thickness in orogenic belts would have been the result of the intrusion of mantle-derived magmas, but the majority of the thickening probably occurred in response to compression and shortening applied in the horizontal direction. If the mass of crust remains the same before and after collision, then any shortening in the horizontal direction must produce uplift and thickening.

Within orogenic belts of continents, blocks of strata sequences have been found that are internally consistent, but are abruptly discontinuous and alien to their surroundings. They are variable in size and contrast sharply with rocks of adjacent areas in their strata sequences, fossil contents, structures, and apparent magmatic and metamorphic histories. The mismatch of rock units across the boundaries of these blocks is also reflected in their paleomagnetism. These blocks are referred to as terranes. These are now believed to be fragments of other continents, island volcanic arcs, or slices of oceanic crust that were sutured or accreted onto a continent in the process of numerous plate collisions. For example, along the western edge of North America there are many such distinct terranes, each containing certain packages of rocks and types of fossils that can be mapped, but do not cross the boundaries into adjacent terranes. Many of these terranes do not appear to have been part of the original North American plate, although they are part of it now. These blocks have evidently been added to the continent at various times in earth history and so are known as exotic terranes, because they appear to have a different history and origin from most of North America. The assembling of several of these terranes over a period of relative time is referred to as collage tectonics.

Prior to the advent of plate tectonics theory, these exotic terranes were a puzzling problem, but understanding plate tectonics processes supplies an explanation, which again suggests the operation of these geological processes in various stages of earth history. It is thus suggested that these terranes were assembled and accreted primarily due to subduction. Island arcs are difficult to subduct because they constitute a fragment of thicker, lower-density crust. Thus, as an ocean basin closes due to subduction of the oceanic crust, any arcs formed within the basin will eventually collide with a continent. The arc becomes sutured to the continent, and the collision causes deformation, although less deformation than would occur in the collision of two continents. Of course, the rocks of the island arc forming an accreted terrane may have formed thousands of kilometers away, and thus will record distinct and different paleomagnetic directions. There may also be fossils that are distinctly different between the arc and the continent. After the arc collided, there may have been a rearrangement of the plate boundary, and the subduction zone may then have moved to the other side of the now-accreted terrane in order to allow convergence to continue with additional subduction of oceanic lithosphere.

Another way of accreting exotic terranes is by transform faulting, sliding along strike-slip faults. In fact, based on paleomagnetic data, it has been suggested that many of the terranes that make up western North America may have moved hundreds to thousands of kilometers north or south into their current locations. While these terranes are now part of the North American plate, originally these terranes were not equivalent to plates in their own right. Many were probably island arcs or small continental fragments that were part of much larger plates, most of which were probably subducted (if it was oceanic lithosphere) or broken away along transform faults during the accretion process.

59

PLATE TECTONICS:
CONTROLLING THE FORMATION
OF THE ROCK RECORD—
TRANSFORM PLATE MARGINS AND PLATE INTERIORS

Transform Plate Margins

The physical feature associated with transform margins are transform faults, a name that was coined because it describes the nature of the fault termination. These faults do not continue for long distances, with movement gradually diminishing. Instead, they end abruptly at a plate margin, where the lateral motion of the fault terminates either an oceanic spreading ridge or a subduction zone. At a spreading ridge, the fault motion is transformed into the generation of new lithosphere, whereas at a subduction zone, the fault motion is transformed into destruction of old lithosphere. Thus, activity along transform faults is confined to the interval between the axes of spreading ridges or subduction zones. The Alpine fault, which traverses lengthwise the South Island of New Zealand, links two subduction zones. The San Andreas fault of California links a spreading ridge to a subduction zone/transform boundary at a triple junction. Major transform faults represent approximately 15 percent of the total length of plate margins worldwide. However, the most common expressions of transform faulting are small offsets along spreading ridges on the ocean floor. Worldwide, there are only fourteen transform faults of sufficient length to be considered of major importance.

Thus, in most cases, transform faults laterally offset segments of spreading ridges, though a few transform faults offset segments of subduction zones. Furthermore, transform faults at transform plate margins are characterized by strike-slip motion, shallow earthquake foci, and an absence of magmatism. They are conservative boundaries because lithosphere is neither generated nor consumed. Nevertheless, the energy released along transform faults at ridges by strike-slip earthquakes is much greater than the energy released by the normal faulting in the axial rifts of mid-ocean ridge spreading centers.

Continental transform faults are large strike-slip faults with up to hundreds of kilometers of offset. These faults are near-surface expressions of transform plate margins. In general, these faults are nearly vertical, and the depth to which they extend is a matter of controversy. Indeed, to qualify as a plate boundary, the discontinuity involved must penetrate completely through the lithosphere. Earthquake activity along the San Andreas fault extends to depths of approximately 12 to 15 kilometers, and both the distribution and the nature of the earthquakes are consistent with a vertical fault trace. Below 15 kilometers, the crust is ductile and the relative motion of the remainder of the lithosphere probably occurs by ductile flow. Thus, it is inferred from indirect evidence that the fault extends through the lower crust and upper mantle, possibly as a shear zone, but the deep structure of this fault is still the subject of ongoing research.

Large strike-slip faults, such as transform faults, tend to be slightly sinuous or to split into several traces. If the fault trace curves so that movement along the fault compresses the two sides together, it is a confining bend. If the curvature is opposite, it is a releasing bend. Both translational and compressive stresses (transpression) occur in a confining bend of a strike-slip fault. Results of transpression include uplift, folding, and thrust faulting. Releasing bends in the trace of a strike-slip fault experience both translational and extensional stresses (transtension). These bends result in subsidence and, therefore, become small depositional basins. The sediments are commonly provided by the erosion of uplifts at confining bends. Pull-apart basins are specifically related to large strike-slip faults where the crust has been thinned by substantial fault offset. The crust may be sufficiently thinned that volcanism occurs early in the basin history. Two examples of pull-apart basins are the Dead Sea basin in Israel, and the Salton Sea trough in southern California. Duplex structures result from the duplication of a fault trace into a braided pattern of several fault traces and may be either compressional or extensional. The relevance of all these features is in providing the explanations for small fault-bounded depositional basins and their strata sequences, which are sometimes found in the geological record.

Plate Interiors

Plate interiors are tectonically quiet today, typically not being associated with active deformation, earthquakes, or volcanoes. However, what is now a plate interior could have been a plate margin in the past.

Most of the continental crust consists of crystalline (igneous and metamorphic) basement covered by a thin veneer of younger sedimentary strata. The two major structural components distinguished at the surface are mountain belts, which are generally young, and by comparison older regions, referred to as cratons. The mountain belts are largely the result of relatively recent plate-collision processes. Some older mountain belts, though, such as the Appalachians, do not coincide with current plate boundaries but are inferred to mark the locations of older margins, which have since become sutured. Where extensive tracts of low-lying, relatively ancient continental crusts are exposed at the earth's surface, they are referred to as shields, although the terms shields and cratons are often used interchangeably. More commonly, though, the cratons are covered by layers of sedimentary strata, and under those circumstances they are referred to as platforms. The older crustal fragments have often been subjected to repeated periods of deformation and metamorphism, which can be difficult to distinguish from one another as each event overprints and masks the effects of previous events. Currently, lithospheric material is being added to the continents at magmatic arcs, which will eventually be sutured to the edges of continents. Thus, the continents grow by lateral accretion, which explains the presence of discrete terranes along active continental margins.

A passive continental margin represents what was originally one side of a continental rift. The crust grades from fully continental on land, to fully oceanic; that is, from less dense to more dense material. After continental rifting has occurred and the two segments of the continent have diverged, as the new ocean basin forms and grows, the receding continental margins subside gradually as the underlying lithosphere cools and contracts. Passive continental margins are characterized by a shoreline, a continental shelf, a continental slope, and a continental rise. The continental shelf slopes gently away from the shore and extends an average of 65 kilometers out into the ocean, although in some places it extends out to a distance of several hundred kilometers. The continental shelf reaches an average depth of 130 meters and, in some cases, attains a maximum depth of 650 meters. At the edge of the shelf, the sea floor becomes steeper and is called the continental slope. The continental rise lies at the base of this slope and consists of sediments that have moved down the continental slope to accumulate at the edge of the ocean basin. The rise can stretch out for hundreds of kilometers until it finally becomes the floor of the ocean basin, or the abyssal plain.

Ultimately, most of the sediments produced by erosion of the continents are deposited in the oceans surrounding the continents, primarily on the continental shelves. Continental shelf deposits are sedimentary rock assemblages that are laid down in an orderly sequence under tectonically quiet conditions, because volcanism and earthquakes do not commonly occur at receding passive continental margins. In time, a wedge-shaped deposit of sediments eroded from the nearby continent and carried out into the shallow water of the offshore shelf builds up into a thick sequence of sedimentary strata in what used to be called a geosyncline. Because the trailing edge of the continent slowly subsides, the geosyncline continues to receive sediments for a long time. The load of the growing mass of sediment further depresses the crust isostatically, so that the geosyncline can receive still more material from the adjacent land. For every three meters of sediments received, the crust sinks two meters. The result of these two effects is that the geosynclinal deposits can accumulate in an orderly fashion to thicknesses of 10 kilometers or more. At the same time, the supply of sediments is sufficient to maintain the shallow-water environment of the geosyncline, or more correctly, the *miogeosyncline*. Thus, the miogeosynclinal deposits show all of the characteristics of shallow-water conditions. As the miogeosynclinal shelf deposits build up, deposition can become dominated by shales and carbonate platform deposits, indicators of a decrease in the supply of detritus from the continent.

As explained previously, geologists had been puzzled for a long time by the juxtaposition of miogeosynclinal and eugeosynclinal sequences observed in old mountain belts. In eugeosynclinal sequences, the sedimentary strata were very thick and were characterized by immature sediments that appeared to have been deposited rapidly in very deep marine water, and yet contained shallow marine fossils and submarine volcanic rocks. The undeformed miogeosynclinal sequences were readily interpreted to be the shallow marine settings comparable to today's continental shelf deposits, due to the undeformed sandstones and limestones in them and plentiful fossils. Why were these two parallel geosynclines with totally different strata sequences found side by side in old mountain belts? An understanding of these juxtaposed strata sequences in the geologic record only became apparent with the advent of the conceptual framework of plate tectonics. Whereas the miogeosynclinal sediments represent the passive continental margin sedimentation of continental shelf deposits, the eugeosynclinal deposits are composites of deep marine sediments, volcanics, and material derived from the continents that accumulate at convergent plate (active continental) margins. The eugeosyncline concept is effectively replaced by the oceanic trench that marks convergent plate boundaries, characterized by volcanism. Eugeosynclinal deposits, in fact, are not a continuous depositional sequence, but a tectonic stacking of material scraped off the oceanic crust at a subduction zone, where there is also the volcanism of a nearby island or continental margin arc. This explains the mixture of shallow marine, deep marine, and volcanic deposits that have been tectonically deformed. Plate tectonics thus also explains the juxtaposition of miogeosynclinal and eugeosynclinal sequences observed in the geological record of old mountain belts, the two very different environments having been brought together in mountain-building continental collisions, as ocean basins that originally separated them eventually closed because of continued subduction. With the suturing of these two juxtaposed parallel strata sequences in the mountain belts, they subsequently became part of the interiors of continental plates as part of the geologic record of earth history.

A significant portion of continental crust at passive continental margins is covered by the sediments deposited on continental shelves, which are covered by the water of the oceans. The amount of the continents covered by the ocean waters, or the extent of the continental shelves surrounding the continents, is of course determined by sea level. Indeed, the thickness of the sediment sequences accumulating on the continental shelves, the amount of sediment that can accumulate, and the extent of the continental shelves, also depend on sea level, which has risen and fallen during the earth's history, just as it has been observed to do in recorded human history. As was noted earlier, the sedimentary strata sequences of the geologic record can be divided into transgressive and regressive sequences that were deposited as a result of the level of water responsible for deposition rising or falling respectively, which equates to the rising and falling of sea level, where the continental shoreline moves inland in a transgression and retreats to expose more land in a regression. Transgressive strata sequences initially begin with unconformities, and the sedimentary strata in them become finer-grained upwards through the sequence. In contrast, regressive strata sequences are recognized by the grain sizes in the sedimentary strata coarsening upwards, and the succession finishing with an unconformity at the top. Careful correlation of sedimentary strata sequences using these observational principles has suggested that there have been global transgressions and regressions during deposition of the geologic record, with at least six major unconformities recognized in rock successions worldwide that correspond to the suggested rising and falling of water levels.[1] These six unconformity-bounded rock successions, which represent relative times of higher sea level and consequent sedimentation, constitute important subdivisions of the sedimentary record (Figure 38 on page 464).

Within these globally recognized megasequences of the Cambrian-Recent geologic record, and in the sedimentary strata successions and megasequences recognized in the global Precambrian geologic record, geologists attempt to determine under what conditions each sedimentary rock unit was originally deposited. This is accomplished by studying the geological processes in modern environments where sediments are being deposited, by comparing the characteristics, sedimentary structures, and features of modern sediments with those of the sedimentary strata of the geologic record. This method is not unreasonable. However, if geological processes in the past occurred on a more catastrophic scale than we observe today, then our modern analogs may not be adequate to explain some of the geologic data. Indeed, there is a difference between the observational data (such as the way modern sedimentation processes operate, and the characteristics and features of modern sediments and ancient sedimentary strata) and the interpreted sedimentation processes by which ancient sedimentary strata were deposited. Therefore, any claim that we know under what environmental conditions certain sedimentary rocks were deposited becomes an interpretation based on the observational data that we have.

For example, prior to 1950, sedimentary strata composed of coarse-grained, graded beds, such as those in the Ventura Basin in California, were believed to have been deposited slowly in shallow water. Indeed, the available evidence at that time indicated that it would have taken several years to deposit each layer in shallow water, so with hundreds of these graded beds in the Ventura Basin, the timescale involved for deposition was interpreted in terms of thousands of years.[2] Then in 1950, the discovery of a previously unknown phenomenon

---

1   Sloss, 1963.

2   J. E. Eaton, 1929, The by-passing and discontinuous deposition of sedimentary materials, *American*

was reported—turbidity currents.[3] Turbidity currents were found to be rapid underwater mudflows that can deposit a layer of graded sediments over a large area. Thus, the layers produced by turbidity currents became known as turbidites. Consequently, turbidity currents provided an even more satisfactory explanation for the graded beds in the Ventura Basin, and the entire sequence of layers was reinterpreted as a series of turbidites, with each graded bed now being understood to have been deposited in minutes rather than years, and in deeper water.[4] Whereas previously the observational data of sedimentary environments had been used to interpret these graded beds as slowly-deposited, shallow-water sediments, a change of interpretation was brought about by the accumulation of new data and the discovery of previously unknown processes.

Thus, while the interpretations of the conditions under which ancient sedimentary strata were deposited in terms of modern sedimentary environments are useful, they are nonetheless limited by the observational data we have available, and by the philosophical framework in which the interpretations are made (for example, assumptions about past and present rates of geological processes). Nevertheless, when modern analogs are compared with the sedimentary strata in the geologic record, an attempt is made to interpret where and how the sediment was deposited, where it came from, and how it was transported to its site of deposition. The principal types of observational data that help in reconstructing sedimentary environments are sedimentary textures, sedimentary structures, facies relationships, mineralogy, and fossil types.

Sedimentary textures include grain size, shape, and orientation. Grains may be oriented randomly or in a particular plane by the water current or wind that has transported them. Sedimentary structures are features like cross-beds or parallel bedding, and ripple marks. Facies relationships are the horizontal spatial relationships between different types of sediments deposited adjacent to each other during the same period of time. Thus, for example, a unit might be composed of sandstone in one area and shale in another, interfingering where they meet, the sandstone and shale being two different facies of the same strata unit. This unit could thus resemble deposits that form just offshore in a body of water, where sand is deposited near the shore and mud is deposited at the same time further offshore.

The types of minerals found in sedimentary rocks, as with the facies, may provide important indicators of the depositional environments. For example, sediment containing calcite would probably have been deposited in a marine or alkaline

Association of Petroleum Geologists' Bulletin, 13: 713-761.

3   H. Kuenen and C. I. Migliorini, 1950, Turbidity currents as a cause of graded bedding, *Journal of Geology,* 58: 91-127.

4   M. L. Natland and H. Kuenen, 1951, Sedimentary history of the Ventura Basin, California, and the action of turbidity currents, *Society of Economic Paleontologists and Mineralogists Special Publication,* 2: 76-107.

lake environment, whereas dolomite, similar to limestone, possibly formed in hypersaline water (water with a higher salt content than normal seawater).

Finally, the types of fossils in sedimentary strata can also give clues about the depositional environments, though care needs to be exercised in interpreting the data because an organism may have been carried from its original habitat and deposited in an environment in which it normally does not live. Nevertheless, in general, strata containing marine fossils would suggest that the sediments were deposited in the ocean, while fossils of terrestrial mammals would suggest the sedimentary strata were deposited in a terrestrial environment, such as a river bed, lake, or floodplain. However, most reliable interpretations of the depositional environments of sedimentary strata are based on a combination of these different types of observational data.

There are, of course, a large number of widely different sedimentary environments in the modern world, ranging from channels and floodplains of rivers in their valleys; sand dunes, alluvial fans, and playa lakes of desert environments; to deltas and lagoons of coasts and continental shelves. Yet as already described, the validity of these interpreted depositional environments and conditions for individual sedimentary strata, or even strata sequences, is overshadowed by the global scale of rising and falling water levels depositing megasequences made up of these individual sedimentary rock units and strata sequences (Figure 38).

Finally, while a very strong correlation exists between the locations of volcanoes and plate margins, there are nonetheless many volcanic centers located far from plate margins. This intraplate magmatism is commonly associated with hotspots generated by mantle plumes, which transport hot material from deep within the mantle and are a critical element in mantle convection within the earth. Plumes may rise from a range of depths in the mantle, those originating at the core-mantle boundary being an important mechanism for heat loss from the core. As already described in detail, mantle plumes may trigger the rifting of continents. Indeed, the initial stages of plume activity might also be accompanied by voluminous basaltic outpourings that form what are known as continental flood basalts. The scale of these eruptions, and the size and volume of these basalt flows, make them significant rock units in the geologic record as indicators of the presence and action of mantle plumes during earth's history.

60

Concluding Comments

There are, of course, many more descriptive details and observable data that together underpin the modern geological synthesis. Our purpose here has of necessity focused on a broad overview of the major elements of the modern geological synthesis and the important data. Evidence and interpretations have led to the success of the modern geological synthesis in bringing about a revolution in the earth sciences, with a conceptual framework for integrating and explaining so much disparate data. For complete immersion in the descriptive details and observational data of the many branches of the earth sciences, and how they are fully integrated in the modern geological synthesis, study of any one of the currently available comprehensive geology textbooks is recommended.

Our purpose here has been to highlight relevant data, interpretations, and the conceptual framework of the modern geological synthesis that are directly relevant to an understanding of earth history and the rock record that has been produced by it. Of course, the modern geological synthesis is built on the alleged evidence that the earth's history and the development of the rock record span a timescale measured in billions of years, in stark contrast to the biblical framework for earth history encompassing creation and the Flood on a timescale that spans only thousands of years. How, then, may these two frameworks for earth history be reconciled? An answer to that question is the subject of the next sections and their chapters.

SELECTED
BIBLIOGRAPHY

Selected Bibliography

Alee, W. C. et al, 1949, *Principle of Animal Ecology*, Philadelphia, PA: W.B. Saunders Co.

Allis, O. T., 1951, *God Spake by Moses*, Philadelphia, PA: The Presbyterian and Reformed Publishing Co.

Archer, Jr, G. L., 1974, *A Survey of Old Testament Introduction*, revised ed., Chicago, IL: Moody Press.

Archer, M., 1984, The Australian marsupial radiation, *Vertebrate Zoogeography and Evolution in Australasia*, M. Archer and G. Clayton, eds., Perth, Australia: Hesperian Press.

Austin, S. A., 2000, The pre-Flood/Flood boundary: Correcting significant misunderstandings, *Creation Ex Nihilo Technical Journal*, 14 (2): 59-63.

Awbrey, F. T., 1981, Defining 'kinds' – do creationists apply a double standard?, *Creation/Evolution*, 5: 1-6.

Baxter, J. S., 1960, *Explore the Book: A Basic and Broadly Interpretive Course of Bible Study from Genesis to Revelation*, Grand Rapids, MI: Zondervan Publishing House.

Bengtson, S., ed., 1994, *Early Life on Earth*, New York: Columbia University Press.

Benton, M. J., 1995, Diversification and extinction in the history of life, *Science*, 268: 52-58.

Berry, W. B. N., 1968, *Growth of a Prehistoric Time Scale Based on Organic Evolution*, San Francisco, CA: W. H. Freeman and Company.

Beus, S. S. and M. Morales, eds., 2003, *Grand Canyon Geology*, 2nd ed., New York: Oxford University Press.

Boardman, D. C., 1990, Did Noah's Flood cover the entire world?, *The Genesis Debate: Persistent Questions about Noah and the Flood*, R. F. Youngblood, ed., Grand Rapids, MI: Baker Book House.

Boggs, Jr., S., 1995, *Principles of Sedimentary and Stratigraphy*, 2nd ed., Upper Saddle River, NJ: Prentice Hall, Upper.

Brand, L., 1997, *Faith, Reason and Earth History*, Berrien Springs, MI: Andrews University Press.

Brand, L. R. and J. Florence, 1982, Stratigraphic distribution of vertebrate fossil footprints compared with body fossils, *Origins*, 9: 67-74.

Briggs, J. C., 1974, *Marine Zoogeography*, San Francisco, CA: McGraw-Hill Book Company.

Briggs, J. C., 1987, *Biogeography and Plate Tectonics*, Amsterdam: Elsevier Scientific Publishers B.V.

Bright, J., 1942, Has archaeology found evidence of the Flood?, *The Biblical Archeologist*, V(4): 56, 58-59.

Briscoe, S., 1987, *Mastering the Old Testament, Volume 1, Genesis*, Dallas, TX: Word Publishing.

Brown, F., S. R. Driver and C. H. Briggs, 1906, *A Hebrew and English Lexicon of the Old Testament*, Boston, New York and Chicago: Houghton, Mifflin and Company.

Brown, J. H. and A. C. Gibson, 1983, *Biogeography*, St Louis, MO: The C.V. Mosby Co.

Burton, C., 1845, *Lectures on the Deluge and the World After the Flood*, London: Hamilton, Adams and Co.

Carson, R. L., 1961, *The Sea Around Us*, revised ed., New York: Oxford University Press.

Cassuto, U., 1961, *A Commentary on the Book of Genesis*, Jerusalem: Magnes Press.

Cassuto, U., 1964, *A Commentary on the Book of Genesis 1-11*, vol. 2, trans. I. Abrahams, Jerusalem: Magnes Press.

Condie, K. C., ed., 1992, *Proterozoic Crustal Evolution*, Amsterdam: Elsevier.

Condie, K. C., ed., 1994, *Archean Crustal Evolution*, Amsterdam: Elsevier.

Condie, K. C., 1997, *Plate Tectonics and Crustal Evolution*, 4th ed., Oxford, England: Butterworth-Heinemann.

Cook, J. and M. W. McElhinny, 1979, A re-evaluation of the spatial and temporal distribution of sedimentary phosphate deposits in the light of plate tectonics, *Economic Geology*, 74: 315-330.

Cowen, R., 1990, *History of Life*, Boston: Blackwell Scientific Publications.

Custance, A. C., 1972, Flood Traditions of the World, *A Symposium on Creation IV*, D. W. Patten, ed., Grand Rapids, MI: Baker Book House.

Custance, A. C., 1979, *The Flood: Local or Global?*, vol. IX: The Doorway Papers, Grand Rapids, MI: Zondervan.

Davidson, F., ed., 1953, *The New Bible Commentary*, Grand Rapids: Wm. B. Eerdmans Pub. Co., 84-85.

Davies, L. Merson, 1930, Scientific Discoveries and their Bearing on the Biblical Account of the Noachian Deluge, *Journal of the Transactions of the Victoria Institute*, vol. LXII, 62-63.

Delitzsch, F., 1899, *A New Commentary on Genesis*, S. Taylor, trans., New York: Scribner and Welford.

Denton, M., 1985, *Evolution: A Theory in Crisis*, London: Burnett Books.

Dods, M., 1890, *The Book of Genesis*, vol. I of *The Expositor's Bible*, W.R. Nicoll, ed., fourth ed., London: Hodder and Stoughton.

Driver, S. R., 1904, *The Book of Genesis*, London: Methuen and Co.

Dunbar, C. O. and J. Rodgers, 1957, *Principles of Stratigraphy*, New York: John Wiley & Sons, Inc.

Elias, S. A. et al, 1996, Life and times of the Bering land bridge, *Nature*, 382: 60-63.

Eriksson, G. et al, ed., 2004, *The Precambrian Earth: Tempos and Events*, Amsterdam: Elsevier.

Fields, W. W., 1976, *Unformed and Unfilled*, Nutley, New Jersey: Presbyterian and Reformed Publishing Company.

Filby, F. A., 1970, *The Flood Reconsidered: A Review of Evidences of Geology, Archaeology, Ancient Literature and the Bible*, London: Pickering and Inglis Limited.

Flood, J., 1987, *Archaeology of the Dreamtime*, Sydney, Australia: Lansdowne Press.

Forster, R. and P. Marston, 1989, *Reason and Faith: Do Modern Science and Christian Faith Really Conflict?*, Eastbourne, Sussex, U.K.: Monarch Publications Ltd.

Forster, R. and P. Marston, 1999, *Reason, Science and Faith*, Crowborough, East Sussex, England: Monarch Books.

Fouts, D. M. and K. Wise, 1998, Blotting out and breaking up: miscellaneous Hebrew studies in geocatastrophism, *Proceedings of the Fourth International Conference on Creationism*, R.E. Walsh, ed., Pittsburgh, PA: Creation Science Fellowship.

Frazer, J. G., 1919, *Folk-Lore in the Old Testament*, vol. I, London: Macmillan and Co. Ltd.

Free, J. P., 1956, *Archaeology and Bible History*, 5th ed. revised, Wheaton, IL: Scripture Press.

Futuyma, D. J., 1983, *Science on Trial*, New York: Pantheon Books.

Gillispie, C. C., 1951, *Genesis and Geology*, Cambridge, MA: Harvard University Press.

Gordon, M. S. et al, 1982, *Animal Physiology: Principles and Adaptations*, 4th ed., New York: McMillan Publishing Co., Inc.

Gould, S. J., 1989, Grimm's greatest tale, *Natural History*, 98(2): 22, 27-28.

Green, M., 1968, *The Second Epistle General of Peter and the General Epistle of Jude: An Introduction and Commentary*, Tyndale Testament Commentaries, London: InterVarsity Press.

Green, W. H., 1979, *The Unity of the Book of Genesis*, Grand Rapids, MI: Baker Book House (originally published by Charles Scribner's Sons, 1895).

Hager, D., 1957, Fifty years of progress in geology, *Geotimes*, 2 (2): 12.

Ham, K., A. A. Snelling and C. Wieland, 1990, *The Answers Book*, Brisbane, Australia: Creation Science Foundation.

Hamilton, V. P., 1990, *A New International Commentary on the Old Testament: The Book of Genesis Chapters 1-17*, Grand Rapids, MI: Eerdmans Publishing Company.

Harris, R. Laird, 1955, Racial dispersion, *Journal of the American Scientific Affiliation*, 7(3): 52.

Hasel, G. F., 1978, The Genealogies of Genesis 5 and 11 and Their Alleged Babylonian Background, *Andrews University Seminary Studies*, 16: 361-374.

Heidel, A., 1949, *The Gilgamesh Epic and Old Testament Parallels*, 2nd ed., Chicago: University of Chicago Press.

Hitchcock, E., 1852, *The Religion of Geology and Its Connected Sciences*, Boston: Phillips, Sampson and Co.

Holland, H. D. and A. F. Trendall, eds., 1984, *Patterns of Change in Earth Evolution*, Berlin: Springer-Verlag.

Holser, W. T., 1984, Gradual and abrupt shifts in ocean chemistry during the Phanerozoic time, *Patterns of Change in Earth Evolution*, H. D. Holland and A. F. Trendall, eds., Berlin: Springer-Verlag, 123-143.

Hong, S. W. et al, 1994, Safety investigation of Noah's Ark in a seaway, *Creation Ex Nihilo Technical Journal*, 8(1): 26-36.

Howe, G. F., 1971, Seed germination, sea water and plant survival in the Great Flood, *Scientific Studies in Special Creation*, W.E. Lammerts, ed., Grand Rapids, MI: Baker Book House.

Howells, W., 1947, *Mankind So Far*, New York: Doubleday and Co.

Hunter, D. R., ed., 1981, *Precambrian of the Southern Hemisphere*, Amsterdam: Elsevier.

Isaacs, J., 1987, *Australian Dreaming: 40,000 Years of Aboriginal History*, Sydney, Australia: Lansdowne Press.

Jamieson, R., A. R. Fausset and D. Brown. 1948, *Critical and Experimental Commentary*, vol. I, Grand Rapids, MI: Wm B. Eerdmans Publishing Co.

Johnson, M. R., 1988, *Genesis, Geology and Catastrophism: A Critique of Creationist Science and Biblical Literalism*, Exeter, U.K.: The Paternoster Press.

Jones, J. C., 1897, *Primeval Revelation: Studies in Genesis I-VIII*, New York: American Tract Society.

Kalisch, M. M., 1858, *Historical and Critical Commentary on the Old Testament*, London: Longman, Brown, Green, et al.

Keil, C. F., 1875, *Biblical Commentary on the Old Testament (Genesis)*, Edinburgh: T. and T. Clark.

Keil, C. F. 1951, *Biblical Commentary on the Old Testament*, vol. I, J. Martin, trans., vol. I, Grand Rapids, MI: William B. Eerdmans Publishing Company.

Kidner, B., 1967, *Genesis: An Introduction and Commentary*, The Tyndale Old Testament Commentaries, Leicester, U.K.: Inter-Varsity Press.

Kidner, B., 1980, *Genesis: An Introduction and Commentary*, Leicester, U.K.: Inter-Varsity Press.

Kiel, F. and F. Delitzsch, 1949, *Biblical Commentary on the Old Testament: The Pentateuch*, James Martin, trans., Grand Rapids, MI: Eerdmans.

Klein, C. and N. J. Beukes, 1992, Time distribution, stratigraphy, and sedimentologic setting, and geochemistry of Precambrian iron-formations, *The Proterozoic Biosphere*, J. W. Schopf and C. Klein, eds., Cambridge: Cambridge University Press, 139-146.

Klotz, J. W., 1970, *Genes, Genesis and Evolution*, 2nd revised ed., St Louis, MO: Concordia Publishing House.

Koehler, L. and W. Baumgartner, 1953, *Lexicon in Veteris Testamenti Libros*, vol. II, Grand Rapids, MI: Eerdmans Publishing Company.

Kroeber, A. L., 1948, *Anthropology*, New York: Harcourt, Brace and Co.

Krumbein, W. C. and L. L. Sloss, 1961, *Stratigraphy and Sedimentation*, 2nd ed., San Francisco, CA: W.H. Freeman and Company.

LaHaye, T. F. and J. D. Morris, 1976, *The Ark on Ararat*, Nashville, TN: Thomas Nelson Inc. Publishers, and San Diego, CA: Creation-Life Publishers.

Lange, J. P., ed., *A Commentary on the Holy Scriptures: Genesis*, Grand Rapids, MI: Zondervan Publishing House.

Leupold, H. C., 1980, *Exposition of Genesis*, vol. 1, Grand Rapids, MI: Baker Book House (originally published by The Wartburg Press, 1942).

Lever, J., 1958, *Creation and Evolution*, Grand Rapids, MI: Grand Rapids International Publications.

Lloyd-Jones, D. M., 1983, *Expository Sermons on 2 Peter*, Edinburgh: The Banner of Truth Trust.

MacRae, A. A., 1950, The relation of archaeology to the Bible, *Modern Science and Christian Faith*, 2nd ed., Wheaton, IL: Van Kampen Press.

Marsh, F. L., 1947, *Evolution, Creation and Science*, Washington: Review and Herald Publishing Association.

Martin, H., 1994, Archean grey gneisses and the genesis of continental crust, *Archean Crustal Evolution*, K. C. Condie, ed., Amsterdam: Elsevier, 205-260.

Mayr, E., 1969, *Principles of Systematic Zoology*, New York: McGraw-Hill Book Company.

McGowan, C., 1984, *In the Beginning: A Scientist Shows Why the Creationists are Wrong*, New York: Prometheus Books.

McLaren, D. J. and W. D. Goodfellow, 1990, Geological and biological consequences of giant impacts, *Annual Review of Earth and Planetary Sciences*, 18: 123-171.

Miller, H., 1857, *The Testimony of the Rocks*, New York: Gould and Lincoln.

Miller, H., 1875, *The Testimony of the Rocks*, New York: Robert Carter and Brothers.

Mixter, R. L., 1950, *Creation and Evolution*, American Scientific Affiliation, Monograph Two.

Moody, A., 1953, *Introduction to Evolution*, New York: Harper and Brothers.

Moore, R. A., 1983, The impossible voyage of Noah's Ark, *Creation/Evolution*, 11: 1-43.

Morris, H. M., 1971, The Ark of Noah, *Creation Research Society Quarterly*, 8(2): 142-144.

Morris, H. M., 1973, World population and Bible chronology, *Scientific Studies in Special Creation*, W. E. Lammerts, ed., Grand Rapids, MI: Baker Bookhouse.

Morris, H. M., 1976, *The Genesis Record: A Scientific and Devotional Commentary on the Book of Beginnings*, Grand Rapids, MI: Baker Book House.

Morris, H. M., 1984, *The Biblical Basis of Modern Science*, Grand Rapids, MI: Baker Book House.

Morris, H. M., 1995, *The Defenders Study Bible*, Grand Rapids, MI: World Publishing.

Morton, G. R., 1995, *Foundation, Fall and Flood: A Harmonization of Genesis and Science*, Dallas, TX: D.M.D. Publishing Company.

Nelson, B. C., 1968, *The Deluge Story in Stone*, Minneapolis, MO: Augsburg Publishing House and Bethany Fellowship Inc.

Olsson, I. U., ed., 1969, *Radiocarbon Variations and Absolute Chronology*, Stockholm: Almqvist and Wiksel, and New York: Wiley Interscience.

Osgood, A. J. M., 1988, A better model for the Stone Age - Part 2, *Ex Nihilo Technical Journal*, 3: 73-95.

Patten, D. W., 1967, *The Biblical Flood and the Ice Epoch*, Seattle, WA: Pacific Meridian Publishing Co.

Payne, J. B., 1960, Hermeneutics as a cloak for the denial of Scripture, *Journal of the Evangelical Theological Society*, 3(4): 94.

Pieters, A., 1947, *Notes on Genesis*, Grand Rapids, MI: Eerdmans.

Plimer, I. R., 1994, *Telling Lies for God*, Sydney, Australia: Random House.

Ramm, B., 1954, *The Christian View of Science and Scripture*, Grand Rapids, MI: Wm B. Eerdmans Publishing Co.

Ramm, B., 1964, *The Christian View of Science and Scripture*, Exeter, U.K.: The Paternoster Press.

Ramm, B., 1971, *The Christian View of Science and Scripture*, 5th ed., Exeter, U.K.: The Paternoster Press.

Ransome, R., 1990, *The Natural History of Hibernating Bats*, London: Christopher Helm.

Ratzsch, D., 1996, *The Battle of Beginnings: Why Neither Side is Winning the Creation-Evolution Debate*, Downers Grove, IL: InterVarsity Press.

Rich, T. H., 1991, Monotremes, placentals, and marsupials: their record in Australia and its biases, *Vertebrate Palaeontology of Australasia*, Vickers-Rich, P. et al, eds., Melbourne, Australia: Pioneer Design Studio Pty Ltd and Monash University Publications Committee.

Romer, A.S., 1955, *Vertebrate Paleontology*, 2nd ed., Chicago, IL: University of Chicago Press.

Ross, A. P., 1996, *Creation and Blessing: A Guide to the Study and Exposition of Genesis*, Grand Rapids, MI: Baker Book House.

Ross, H. N., 1994, *Creation and Time: A Biblical and Scientific Perspective on the Creation-Date Controversy*, Colorado Springs, CO: NavPress.

Ross, H. N., 1998, *The Genesis Question: Scientific Advances and the Accuracy of Genesis*, Colorado Springs, CO: NavPress.

Runnegar, B., 1994, Proterozoic eukaryotes: evidence from biology and geology, *Early Life on Earth*, S. Bengtson, ed., New York: Columbia University Press.

Ryan, W. and W. Pitman, 1998, *Noah's Flood: The Scientific Discoveries about the Event that Changed History*, New York: Simon and Schuster.

Salvador, A., ed., 1994, *International Stratigraphic Guide: A Guide to Stratigraphic Classification, Terminology, and Procedure*, 2nd ed., Trondheim, Norway: The International Union of Geological Sciences, and Boulder, CO: The Geological Society of America.

Sauer, E., 1964, *The Dawn of World Redemption*, G.H. Lang, trans., Exeter, U.K.: Paternoster Press.

Schaeffer, F. A., 1972, *Genesis in Space and Time: The Flow of Biblical History*, London: Hodder and Stoughton.

Schermerhorn, L. A. G., 1974, Late Precambrian mixtites: glacial and/or non-glacial? *American Journal of Science*, 74: 673-824.

Schmidt, H. H., 1997, *Theological Lexicon of the Old Testament*, E. Jenni and C. Westermann, eds., M. E. Biddle, trans., Peabody, MA: Hendrickson Publishers Inc.

Schulz, S. S., 1955, The Unity of the Race: Genesis 1-11, *Journal of the American Scientific Affiliation VII*, 52.

Scroggie, W. G., 1953, *The Unfolding Drama of Redemption*, vol. I, London: Pickering and Inglis.

Shull, A. F., 1951, *Evolution*, 2nd ed., New York: McGraw-Hill Book Co., Inc.

Simpson, G. G., 1960, The World into Which Darwin Led Us, *Science*, 131: 967.

Sloss, L. L., 1963, Sequences in the cratonic interior of North America, *Geological Society of America Bulletin*, 74: 93–114.

Smalley, W. A., 1950, A Christian View of Anthropology, *Modern Science and Christian Faith*, 2nd ed., Wheaton, IL: Van Kampen Press.

Smith, J. P., 1854, *The Relation Between the Holy Scriptures and some parts of Geological Science*, 5th ed., London: Henry G. Bohn.

Snider-Pellegrini, A., 1859, *La Création et ses Mystères Dévoilés*, Paris: A Franck et E. Dentu.

Solomon, M. and S.-S. Sun, 1997, Earth's evolution and mineral resources, with particular emphasis on volcanic-hosted massive sulphide deposits and banded iron formations, *AGSO Journal of Australian Geology and Geophysics*, 17 (1): 33-48.

Stanley, S. M., 1989, *Earth and Life Through Time*, 2nd ed., New York: W.H. Freeman and Company.

Strong, J., *A Concise Dictionary of the Words in the Hebrew Bible; With Their Renderings in the Authorized English Version*, McLean, VA: MacDonald Publishing Company.

Sutcliffe, E. F., 1953, *Genesis, A Catholic Commentary on Holy Scripture*, New York: Thomas Nelson and Sons.

Tattersall, J., 1993, Madagascar's lemurs, *Scientific American*, 268(1): 90-97.

Templeton, A. R., 1994, Biodiversity at the molecular genetic level: experiences from disparate macroorganisms, *Philosophical Transactions of the Royal Society of London*, B345: 59-64.

Thomas, W. H. Griffith, 1946, *Genesis: A Devotional Commentary*, Grand Rapids, MI: Eerdmans.

Tigay, J., 1982, *The Evolution of the Gilgamesh Epic*, Philadelphia, PA: University of Pennsylvania Press.

Trendall, A. F. and R. C. Morris, eds., 1983, *Iron-Formation: Facts and Problems*, Amsterdam: Elsevier.

Turner, C. G., 1989, Teeth and prehistory in Asia, *Scientific American*, 260(2): 70-77.

Unger, M. F., 1956, *Archaeology and the Old Testament*, 3rd ed., Grand Rapids, MI: Zondervan Publishing House.

Vail, P. R. and R. M. Mitchum, Jr., 1979, Global cycles of relative changes of sea level from seismic stratigraphy, *American Association of Petroleum Geologists Memoir 29*, 469-472.

Van Till, H. J., 1986, *The Fourth Day: What the Bible and the Heavens are Telling Us About the Creation*, Grand Rapids, MI: William B. Eerdmans Publishing Company.

Vardiman, L., A. A. Snelling and E. F. Chaffin, eds., 2000, *Radioisotopes and the Age of the Earth: A Young Earth Creationist Research Initiative*, El Cajon, CA: Institute for Creation Research, and St Joseph, MO: Creation Research Society.

Vaughan, H. W., 1945, *Types and Market Classes of Live Stock*, Columbus, OH: College Book Co.

Vos, H. F., 1982, *Everyman's Bible Commentary: Genesis*, Chicago, IL: Moody Press.

Walter, M. R., 1994, Stromatolites: the main geological source of information on the evolution of the early Benthos, *Early Life on Earth*, S. Bengtson, ed., New York: Columbia University Press, 270-286.

Walton, J., 1981, The Antediluvian Section of the Sumerian King List in Genesis 5, *Biblical Archaeologist*, 44: 207-208.

Weiguo, S., 1994, Early multicellular fossils, *Early Life on Earth*, S. Bengtson, ed., New York: Columbia University Press.

Wenham, G. J., 1978, The Coherence of the Flood Narrative, *Vetus Testamentum*, 28: 336-348.

Wenham, G. J., 1987, *Word Biblical Commentary, Volume 1, Genesis 1-15*, Waco, TX: Word Books.

Whitcomb J. C., and H. M. Morris, 1961, *The Genesis Flood: The Biblical Record and Its Scientific Implications*, Philadelphia, PA: Presbyterian and Reformed Publishing Company.

Whitcomb, J. C., 1988, *The World That Perished*, revised ed., Grand Rapids, MI: Baker Book House.

White, A. D., 1955, *A History of the Warfare of Science with Theology and Christendom*, New York: George Brazillier.

Wiseman, P. J., 1936, *New Discoveries in Babylonia About Genesis*, London: Marshall, Morgan and Scott.

Woodmorappe, J., 1996, *Noah's Ark: A Feasibility Study*, Santee, CA: Institute for Creation Research.

Young, D. A., 1977, *Creation and the Flood: An Alternative to Flood Geology and Theistic Evolution*, Grand Rapids, MI: Baker Book House.

Young, D. A., 1995, *The Biblical Flood: A Case Study of the Church's Response to Extrabiblical Evidence*, Grand Rapids, MI: William B. Eerdmans Publishing Company, and Carlisle, U.K.: The Paternoster Press.

Youngblood, R. F., 1980, *How It All Began*, Ventura, CA: Regal Books.

Youngblood, R. F., 1985, *In the NIV Study Bible*, K. Barker, ed., Grand Rapids, MI: Zondervan Bible Publishers.

Youngblood, R. F., ed., 1990, *The Genesis Debate: Persistent Questions about Noah and the Flood*, Grand Rapids, MI: Baker Book House.

FOR MORE INFORMATION

Sign up for ICR's FREE publications!

Creation? Evolution? Intelligent Design?

Which theory is correct? Six days or six billion years? Does it matter?

Find out with your free subscription to *Acts & Facts* magazine from the people who ignited the creation science movement over 40 years ago—the Institute for Creation Research.

The Institute for Creation Research equips believers with evidence of the Bible's accuracy and authority through scientific research, educational programs, and media presentations, all conducted within a thoroughly biblical framework.

Our monthly *Acts & Facts* magazine offers fascinating articles and current information on creation, evolution, and more. With your free subscription comes the complimentary *Days of Praise*, a quarterly booklet providing daily devotionals—real biblical "meat"—to strengthen and encourage the Christian witness.

Sign up for ICR's FREE publications today—call 800.337.0375, visit our website at www.icr.org, or write to the address below.

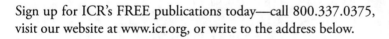

INSTITUTE
for CREATION
RESEARCH

P. O. Box 59029
Dallas, TX 75229
800.337.0375
www.icr.org

FOR MORE INFORMATION

Visit ICR online

ICR.org offers a wealth of resources and information on scientific creationism and biblical worldview issues.

✓ Read our daily news postings on today's hottest science topics

✓ Explore the Evidence for Creation

✓ Investigate our graduate and professional education programs

✓ Dive into our archive of 40 years of scientific articles

✓ Listen to current and past radio programs

✓ Order creation science materials online

✓ And more!

For a list of ICR resources, visit icr.org/store

INSTITUTE *for* CREATION RESEARCH

P. O. Box 59029
Dallas, TX 75229
800.337.0375
www.icr.org

Notes

Notes

Notes

Notes

Notes

Notes

COLOR FIGURES

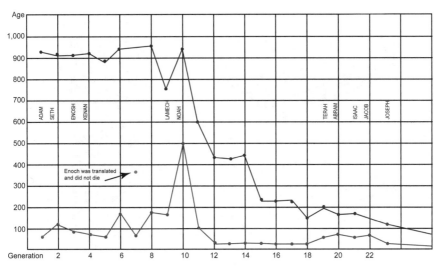

Figure 1. Graph showing the sudden decrease in the age of the patriarchs (at maturity and at death) after the Flood. The horizontal "generation" scale is not intended to be an accurate time representation but an arbitrary assigned "generation number" (after Whitcomb and Morris, 1961).

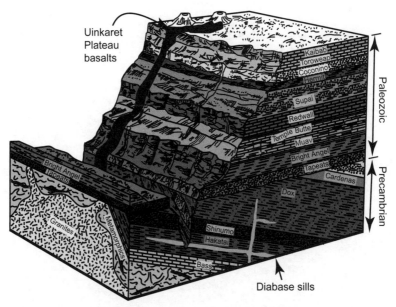

Figure 3. A block diagram to represent the geology of the Grand Canyon, showing the relationships between many of the named rock units exposed in the Canyon. The Bass to Cardenas make up the Unkar Group, while the overlying Chuar Group layers are not shown.

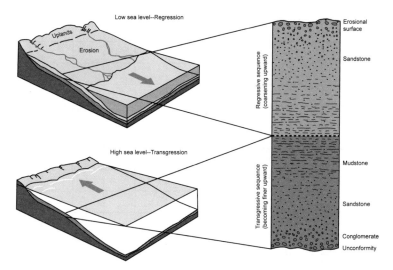

Figure 6. Transgressive and regressive depositional sequences. The block diagrams to the left show the direction of the rising and falling sea levels with respect to a continental margin, while the strata column to the right depicts the sediments which are deposited accordingly.

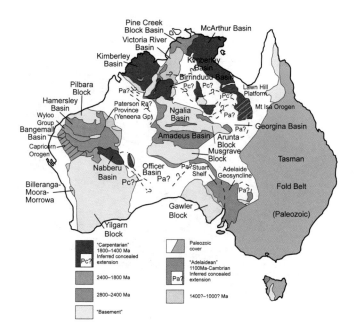

Figure 7. Map of Australia showing the continent's Precambrian geology, both exposed and inferred. The alleged geologic ages of the named basins and Archean basement blocks are indicated.

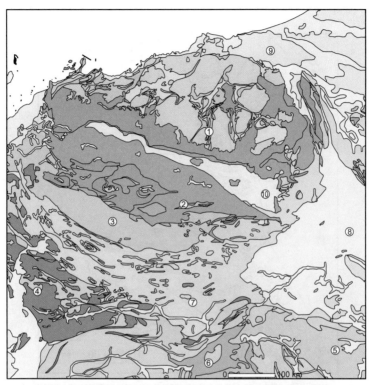

Age	Map Reference	Tectonic Element	Principal Lithologies and Relationships
Archean	1	North Pilbara Terrane	Granite-greenstone with some komatiite
Paleoproterozoic	2	Hamersley Basin	Volcanosedimentary succession, including banded iron formation. Unconformably overlies granite-greenstone terrane which has generally subdued paleotopography
	3	*Capricorn Orogen (3–6):* Ashburton Basin	Deformed low-grade metasedimentary and metavolcanic rocks. Unconformably overlies the Hamersley Basin
	4	Gascoyne Complex	High-grade metasedimentary rocks, orthogneiss and graniotoid rocks. To the east is overlain by Gangemall Basin rocks.
	5	*Nabberu Basin (5–6):* Earaheedy Basin	Eeraheedy Group consists of clastics, carbonate and cherty iron formation
	6	Yerrida Basin	Sedimentary and volcanic rocks
Mesoproterozoic	7	Bangemall Basin	Mainly clastic sedimentary rocks and large volumes of basaltic intrusives. Angular unconformity with underlying Ashburton Formation.
Neoproterozoic	8	Officer Basin	Sedimentary and some volcanic rocks. Unconformably overlies basement.
Paleozoic (and Mesozoic)	9	Canning Basin	Sedimentary and some volcanic rocks
Cretaceous to Recent	10	Fortescue River valley	Alluvial valley fill

Figure 8. Relative time sequence of the local geologic column as mapped in the Pilbara area of Western Australia.

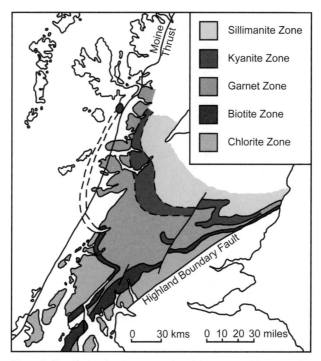

Figure 9. Simplified regional representation of the metamorphic zones of the Grampian Caledonides in the Highlands of Scotland.

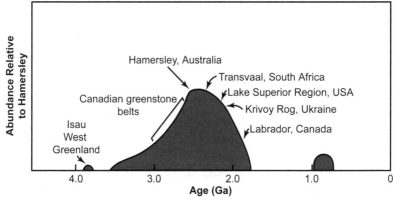

Figure 10. Abundance of banded-iron formations in the geologic record relative to the giant banded-iron formations of the Hamersley Basin, Australia (after Klein and Beukes, 1992, 139-146).

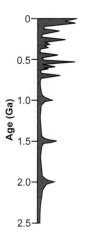

Figure 11. Variations in sedimentary phosphate deposition through the geologic record (after Cook and McElhinney, 1979, 315-330).

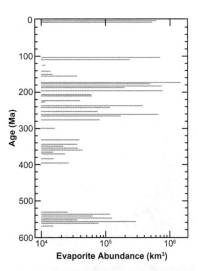

Figure12. Estimated abundances of marine evaporites (or precipitites), NaCl + CaSO$_4$, during the Phanerozoic of the geologic record (adapted from Holser, 1984, 123-143).

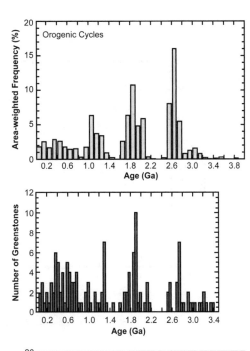

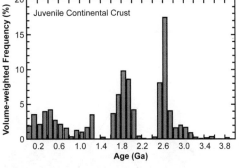

Figure 13. Top: Histogram showing distribution of U-Pb zircon ages in continental crust through the geologic record. Zircons are from syntectonic granitoids, and areas are weighted by areal distribution of crustal provinces. **Middle:** Episodic distribution of greenstone U-Pb zircon ages through the geologic record. Each age represents one greenstone belt, with no more than one age from any given terrane or stratigraphic succession. **Bottom:** Distribution of juvenile continental crust through the geologic record. Frequency is weighted by volume of crust produced in 100-million-year windows (after Condie, 1997, 168-169).

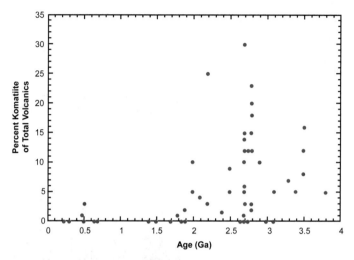

Figure 14. Distribution of komatiites through the geologic record as a percentage of the total volcanics (adapted from Condie, 1997, 168-169).

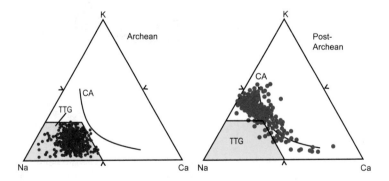

Figure 15. Potassium-sodium-calcium (K-Na-Ca) diagrams showing the distribution of Archean and post-Archean granitoids. TTG=tonalite-trondhjemite-granodiorite field, and CA=calc-alkaline trend (after Martin, 1994, 205-260).

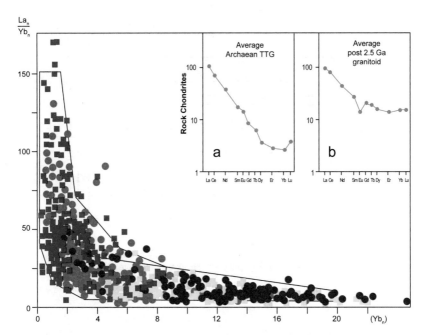

Figure 16. La$_n$/Yb$_n$ ratio versus Yb$_n$ content of TTG. La$_n$ and Yb$_n$ are the lanthanum and ytterbium values normalized to chondritic meteorites. Solid symbols are Archean, and open symbols are post-Archean (after Martin, 1994, 205-260).

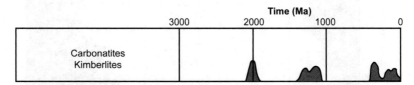

Figure 17. Distribution and frequency of alkaline igneous rocks, especially carbonatites and kimberlites, through the geologic record (after Solomon and Sun, 1997). The vertical bars represent the approximate proportions of the total tonnage.

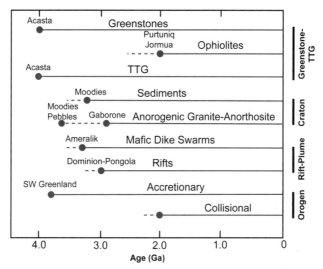

Figure 18. Distribution of tectonic rock sequences through the geologic record, especially comparing ophiolites with greenstones (after Condie, 1997, 168-169).

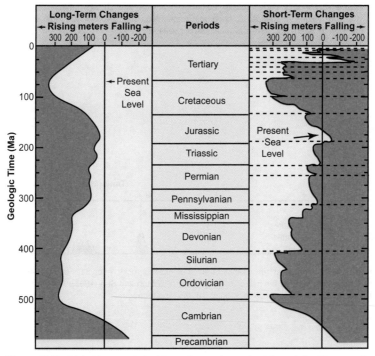

Figure 19. Postulated long- and short-term changes in sea level through the Phanerozoic geologic record (modified after Vail and Mitchum, 1979, 469-472).

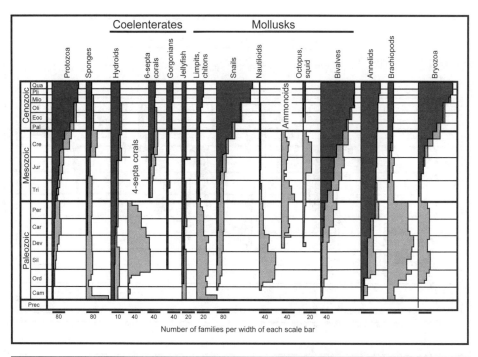

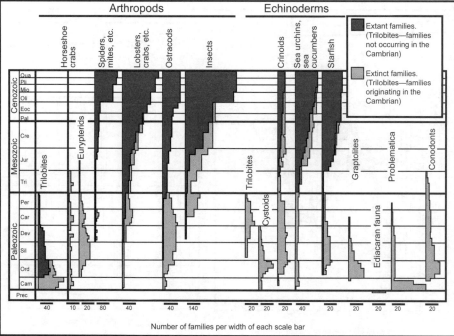

Figure 23a. Stratigraphic distribution of major groups of invertebrate animals in the fossil record, showing the distribution of extant and extinct forms (adapted from Brand, 1997, 143-144).

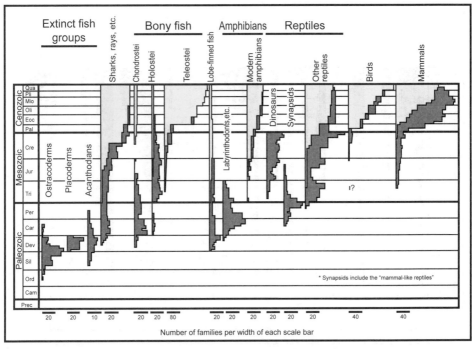

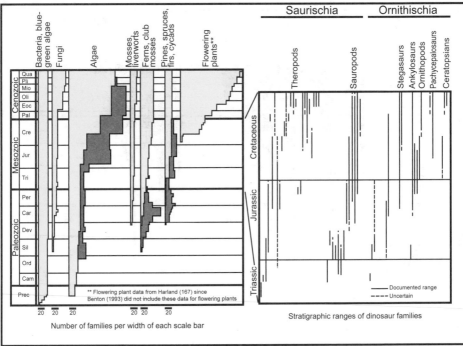

Figure 23b. Stratigraphic distribution of major groups of vertebrates and plants in the fossil record, showing the distribution of extant and extinct forms, and the straigraphic ranges of dinosaur families (adapted from Brand, 1997, 143-144).

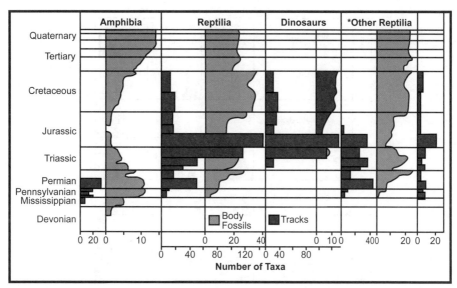

Figure 24a. Stratigraphic distribution of fossil amphibian and reptile tracks and body fossils (after Brand and Florence, 1982, 67-74).

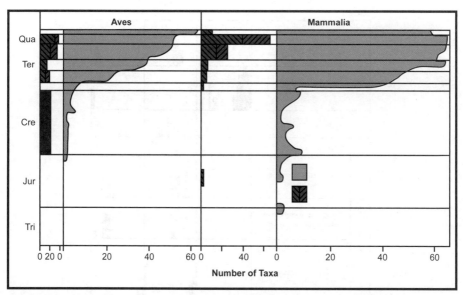

Figure 24b. Stratigraphic distribution of fossil bird and mammal tracks and body fossils (after Brand and Florence, 1982, 67-74).

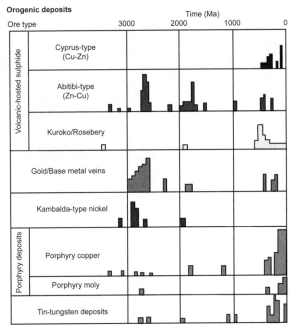

Figure 26a.

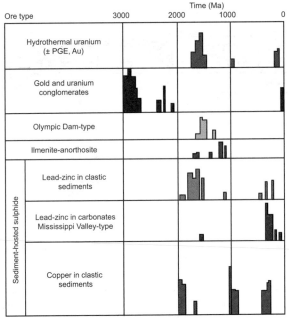

Figure 26b.

Other deposits

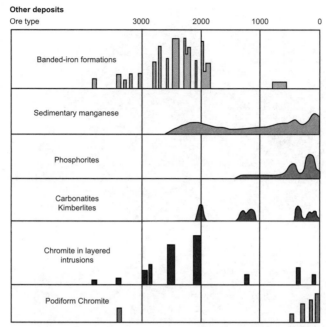

Figure 26c. The distribution through the geologic record of some important types of mineral deposits (after Solomon and Sun, 1997). The vertical bars for each ore type represent the approximate proportions of the total tonnage.

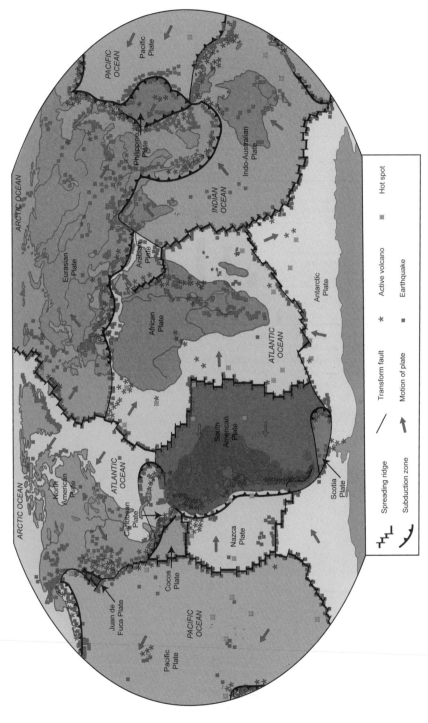

Figure 27. Map of the world indicating the distribution of earthquakes, volcanoes, and trenches (subduction zones) at the margins and boundaries of the tectonic plates.

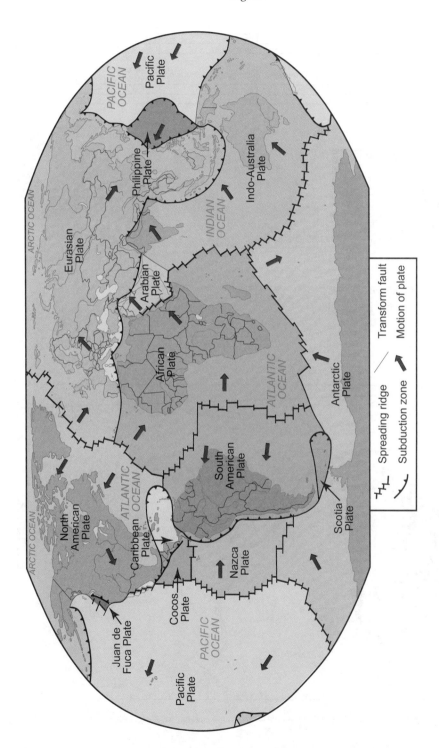

Figure 28. Map of the world showing how the lithospheric plate boundaries are defined by subduction zones, spreading ridges, and transform faults.

Type of Margin	Divergent	Convergent	Transform
Motion	Spreading	Subduction	Lateral sliding
Effect	Constructive (lithosphere created)	Destructive (lithosphere destroyed)	Conservative (lithosphere neither created or destroyed)
Topography	Ridge/Rift	Trench	No major effect
Volcanic Activity?	Yes	Yes	No

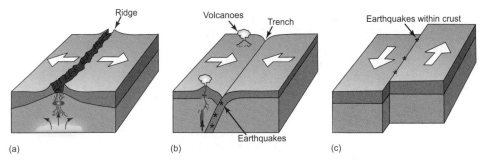

(a)   (b)   (c)

Figure 29. The three types of plate margins or boundaries—divergent, convergent, and transform.

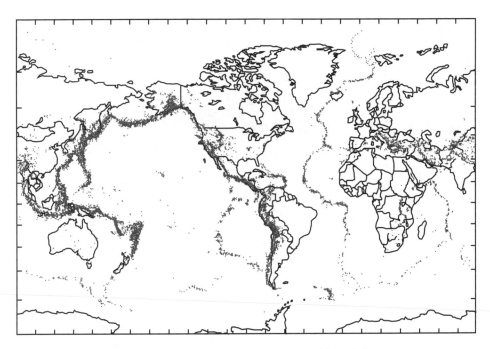

Figure 30. Global distribution of earthquakes (1961-1969) (after Condie, 1997, 168-169).

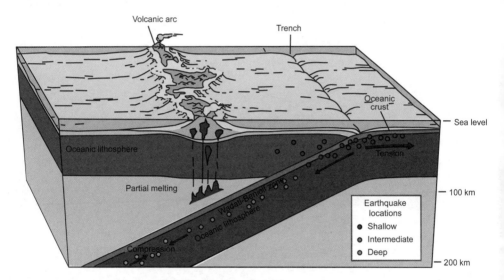

Figure 31. The collision boundary at a subduction zone where a volcanic island arc has developed.The distribution of earthquakes at various depths is shown.

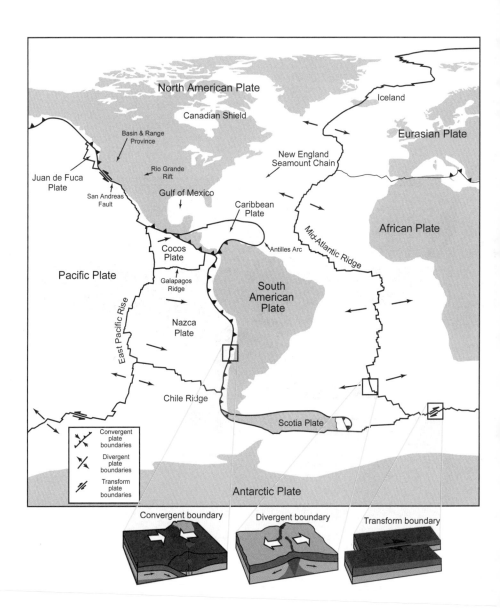

Figure 32. The three kinds of boundaries around lithospheric plates, as illustrated around the eastern Pacific and Atlantic Oceans.

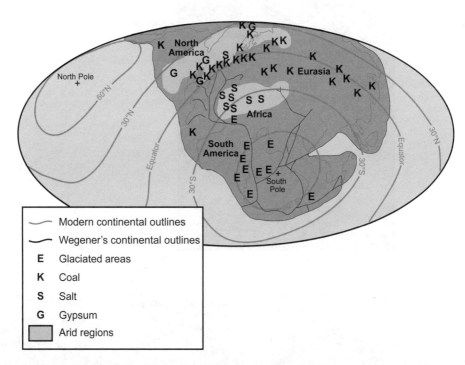

Figure 33. Wegener's reconstruction of the continents as the combination called Pangaea, which contained his "Gondwanaland." He based his reconstruction on the distribution of glacial features (E), coal (K), and salt (S), gypsum (G), and sand dune deposits (supposed arid regions).

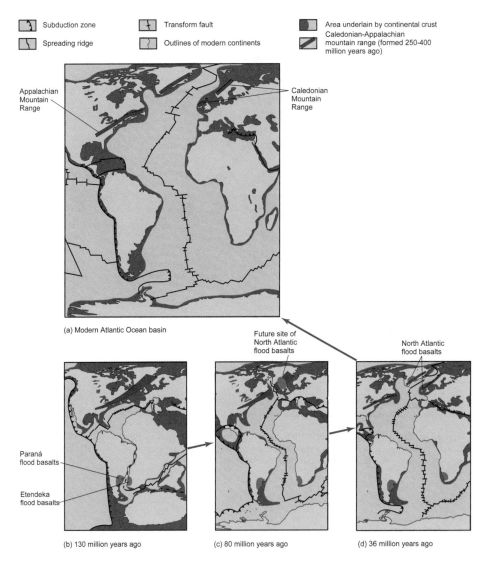

Figure 34. The opening of the Atlantic Ocean basin at different alleged time markers compared to the modern basin, showing the correlation of flood basalts and mountain ranges on either side of the basin.

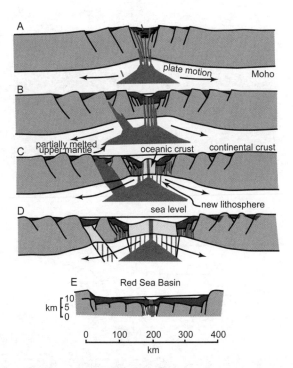

Figure 35. Stages in the stretching, rupture, and fragmentation of a continent or oceanic crust and the development of a new oceanic ridge due to upwelling convective mantle flow underneath it (after Condie, 1997, 168-169).

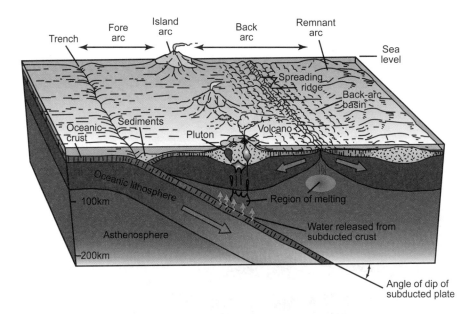

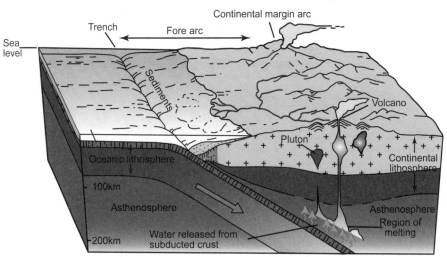

Figure 36. Structures of convergent plate margins: (A) An oceanic convergent margin with volcanoes emerging above sea level to form an island arc, showing a back-arc basin with active sea-floor spreading. (B) A continental convergent margin with volcanoes above plutons intruded into the continental margin arc.

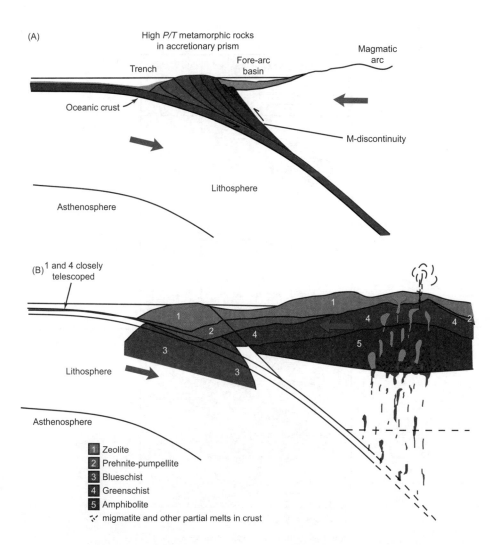

Figure 37. Schematic cross-sections through a continental margin subduction zone showing typical settings for regional and contact metamorphism. (A) Underthrust imbrication (stacking) of slices of arc-trench sediments and scraped-off oceanic lithosphere builds an accretionary prism or wedge. (B) Distribution of metamorphic facies in an orogenic (mountain-building) belt or orogen.

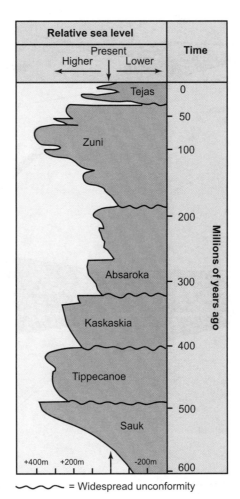

= Widespread unconformity

Figure 38. Variations in global relative sea level as reflected in the sedimentary record, showing the six named unconformity-bounded megasequences of the geologic record, representing major sedimentary depositional cycles and sequences.

EARTH'S
CATASTROPHIC
PAST

GEOLOGY, CREATION
& THE FLOOD

VOLUME 2

EARTH'S CATASTROPHIC PAST

GEOLOGY, CREATION & THE FLOOD

VOLUME 2

ANDREW A. SNELLING

INSTITUTE
for CREATION
RESEARCH

Dallas, Texas
www.icr.org

EARTH'S CATASTROPHIC PAST
GEOLOGY, CREATION & THE FLOOD
VOLUME 2
by Andrew A. Snelling

First printing: December 2009
Second printing: February 2011

Copyright © 2009 by Andrew A. Snelling

All rights reserved. No portion of this book may be used in any form without written permission of the publisher, with the exception of brief excerpts in articles and reviews.

Published by Institute for Creation Research
P. O. Box 59029, Dallas, TX 75229
www.icr.org

ISBN: 978-0-932766-94-6
Library of Congress Catalog Number: 2009922120

Please visit our website for other books and resources: www.icr.org.

Printed in the United States of America.

CONTENTS

VOLUME 2. GEOLOGICAL IMPLICATIONS OF THE BIBLICAL RECORD FOR A BIBLICAL GEOLOGIC MODEL FOR EARTH HISTORY

SECTION VI. GEOLOGICAL IMPLICATIONS OF THE BIBLICAL GEOLOGIC MODEL FOR EARTH HISTORY

SECTION VIII. PROBLEMS IN BIBLICAL GEOLOGY SOLVED —RADIOACTIVE DATING AND GEOCHRONOLOGY

SECTION IX. CONTRADICTIONS IN GEOCHRONOLOGY—SUPPORT FOR BIBLICAL GEOLOGY

SECTION X. PROBLEMS FOR BIBLICAL GEOLOGY SOLVED —FORMATIONS IMPLYING SLOW DEPOSITION

Concluding Challenges

Selected Bibliography

Index

Color Figures

SECTION VI

GEOLOGICAL IMPLICATIONS OF THE BIBLICAL GEOLOGIC MODEL FOR EARTH HISTORY

61

GEOLOGICAL IMPLICATIONS
OF THE BIBLICAL RECORD

The task before us now is to construct a biblical geologic model of earth history, taking the data of the geologic record and placing them within the scriptural framework for earth history. To achieve this goal, extreme care must be taken not to either force scientific details from the Scriptures or to manipulate the geological data to achieve agreement between the geologic and biblical records. The Bible was not written in scientific language and terminology from the standpoint of modern scientific endeavor to provide a science textbook. Instead, it was written under God's direction as His communication to common people, revealing in an understandable manner His provision for and dealings with man. Of course, this in no way implies that the early chapters of Genesis are couched in sub-scientific, conceptual language for the benefit of supposedly primitive people. Instead, the record indicates that Adam and his descendants were anything but primitive, with an ability and capacity to understand God's works in creation, and to apply that knowledge and understanding technologically. God's communication through the Scriptures was also not just intended for the children of Israel at the time of Moses and the immediate centuries that followed. It was intended to be timeless, communicating the truth to all people throughout history, including those of our modern scientific age. Furthermore, because God is all-knowing and infallible, His communication by and through the Scriptures, though not exhaustive in the details provided, must nonetheless be accurate and trustworthy when it touches on matters of science and history.

It should also be stressed that due care must be exercised in the levels of certainty and dogmatism attached to our understandings of the scientific information and implications that we might derive from the Scriptures. Thus, where the text of the Scriptures is clear and unambiguous in providing scientific and historical details, we have every reason to be dogmatic and assertive in applying those details in the construction of a biblical geologic model. We should not therefore be surprised when the geologic data are readily consistent with those details of the scriptural framework. However, it is abundantly clear that the Scriptures are far from exhaustive in the scientific and historical details provided, so there is always the temptation to fill in the "gaps" with inferences and suppositions. While this may be regarded as a legitimate process, such inferences and suppositions are to be held more tentatively and less dogmatically, and be subjected to more critical appraisal, particularly when applying them to the geologic data. There are definitely details and statements provided in the Scriptures that have clear implications of a scientific nature, and where that is the case we can usually be confident. However, a measure of caution is nonetheless warranted lest we read additional information into the text. Finally, in other places we endeavor to draw scientific inferences and suppositions from the text that may seem warranted to us, but are nonetheless speculative and open to challenge.

With these considerations and caveats in mind, attention is now directed to the stated task. First, it is important to highlight the geological implications that can be drawn from the biblical record and to confirm that the geologic data are consistent with them. Then, it is important to survey the available evidence that the geologic data, rightly understood, are in fact more consistent with the scriptural framework of earth history than the uniformitarian framework of the modern geological synthesis. Having satisfied ourselves, and thus established the superior explanation and consistency of the geologic data within the biblical framework of earth history, we are then well-positioned to construct a truly biblical geologic model and to elaborate upon how the geologic data, and the patterns and trends found in the geologic column, fit into this biblical geologic model of earth history.

Some geological implications have already been drawn from the biblical text in our earlier considerations of the relevant passages of Scripture, but it is instructive to gather them together here, along with other geological implications, so that their collective import may be established. Thus, the following geological implications would appear to be legitimately inferred from the biblical record of creation and the Flood.

The Uniqueness of the Creation Week

The Bible repeatedly emphasizes that, during this first week of the earth's history, God's supernatural acts of creation were responsible for bringing into existence the earth and all its basic features, such as the land and the oceans, all forms of life upon the earth, the rest of the solar system, and the stars and galaxies in outer space beyond. This would not have meant the total suspension of the rule of so-called natural laws. Those laws were also instituted by God during His supernatural creative acts for the ongoing operation and maintenance of what He had created, so it could be argued that any distinction may be somewhat arbitrary. Nevertheless, a fundamental difference between supernatural and so-called natural processes is the rates at which they occur, though this should not be misconstrued to infer that supernatural processes are only natural processes that operated at almost infinitely rapid rates. What is clear from the biblical record is that the perception of a human observer on the earth during the Creation Week would have been that countless millions of years of earth history at uniformitarian rates had been compressed into six days of normal human existence.

Furthermore, while the implication is that a different regime of geological processes was operating on the earth during those supernatural acts of creation, there was nevertheless continuity in the operation of those geological processes between what could be termed supernatural and natural rates. An example, by way of illustration, will help to avoid any misunderstanding or misconception.

When we read that, on the third day of the Creation Week, God commanded the dry land to appear, the implication is that earth movements occurred rapidly and the waters also rapidly drained from off the emerging land surface, thus undoubtedly causing extremely rapid erosion. However, that erosion did not simply cease when the process of formation of the dry land had occurred. Instead, erosion rates decreased rapidly to rates that would be considered normal under today's conditions. Thus, while a different regime was in operation while the dry land was rapidly being formed, there was nonetheless continuity between the erosion processes then operating, and those operating subsequently. It could almost be argued that to a human observer the erosion rates during this supernatural formation of the land were *catastrophic*. Nevertheless, because the Creation Week was a unique period in the earth's history, we should expect that some of the features and strata of the rock record produced in that period should likewise be unique, distinctive from features and strata of the subsequent rock record.

Enormous Geological Work Accomplished During the Creation Week

The implication in the biblical record is that by the end of the Creation Week there was one interconnected supercontinental landmass, fully vegetated and populated with animals and man, surrounded by seas. We are specifically told that, in the initial act of creation on Day One, the earth was created covered in water, and by inference there was a rocky earth underneath the waters, presumably already with its internal structure developed or developing. Whatever was then happening underneath the waters through the remainder of Day One and through Day Two, we are next told that on the third day of the Creation Week, God made the dry land to appear from under the globe-encircling waters. This implies an enormous amount of geological work was then accomplished as the waters were pushed aside by great earth movements that buckled the earlier-formed crust and uplifted its rock strata above the waters. As the uplift of this great orogeny occurred, the waters being pushed aside would have to drain off the newly emerging land surface, so this process was inevitably accompanied by a great amount of catastrophic erosion, transport of sediments, and then deposition of sediments as the waters flowed down into the new ocean basins.

Since these geological processes occurred at unprecedented rates with such profound results in such a brief period of time, the rock strata produced by these geological processes cannot be understood in terms of presently observed rates for these processes. Thus, not only would the features and strata of the rock record produced during this unique event defy explanation within the uniformitarian philosophical framework, they would not have their counterparts in the modern world, because the geological processes that produced them are no longer operating at the scale and intensity at which they operated during Creation Week.

It is also an implication from the biblical record that once the dry land surface was established, it stabilized sufficiently to be vegetated. Furthermore, once the major erosion that had shaped the land surface was completed, it tapered off rapidly to minimal levels. This would not have precluded continued geologic activity in the ocean basins, although even there a measure of stability would have been achieved by Day Five, when the ocean waters were populated with all manner of living creatures requiring a stable environment in which to live. Thus, it is likely that geological processes subsided rapidly in the latter part of the Creation Week to levels and rates more typical of geological processes as they occur today.

A Stable Pre-Flood World

The pre-Flood world was, by implication from the text of Scripture, tectonically quiet and geologically stable, living conditions being ideal for the animals and man on the land surface, and for the fish and other sea creatures in the ocean basins. However, the implication from 2 Peter 3:6-7 is that the pre-Flood world, "the world that then was," in contrast to "the heavens and the earth which are now," was different from the world that exists today. Thus, we could expect that the features and strata of the pre-Flood rock record are different from the rock record produced by the Flood, with features even different from what is being produced by geological processes operating today. It is even unclear whether uniformitarian rates of geological processes, or even exactly the same geological processes, were operating during the pre-Flood period as those operating today. Indeed, judging from the large numbers of plants and animals that have become extinct, there was obviously a far greater biodiversity in the pre-Flood world. Conditions then must have been more conducive for those plants and animals, perhaps even with environments that are no longer inhabited today in the same way as they were in the pre-Flood world.

Tremendous Erosion from the Rainfall During the Early Stage of the Flood

Speaking metaphorically to make the description more graphic, the Scriptures report that at the beginning of the Flood the "windows (or floodgates) were opened." In other words, great quantities of water poured down onto the earth from the skies, not in the form of gentle drizzle, but as a torrential global downpour that continued without ceasing for forty days and nights. The impact on the earth's surface of this intense pounding rain would first be prodigious rock and soil erosion, easily visualized from the effects of localized torrential downpours experienced in today's world. Falling raindrops, observed in today's torrential downpours, are a very significant factor in the initiation of erosion, as soil and rock particles are dislodged from the ground surface. As the raindrops then coalesce on the ground surface and the water begins to flow from higher to lower elevations, the loosened soil and rock particles are carried with the water. This sedimentary load, already contained in these surface run-off waters, then aids the further erosive action of the run-off by the mechanisms of turbulence and attrition as it flows *en masse* across the ground surface, or is channelized to form rivulets. The water then runs finally to the nearest stream, but in the process deepens the channels it flows through by further erosion. Thus, great gullies are carved out, often to great depths, even in a single storm today. However, the intensity of this unique, global, torrential downpour in the first forty days and nights of the Flood has to be visualized as somewhat analogous to the effects of the most intense localized torrential downpour today multiplied on a global scale. Under such conditions, the combined processes of raindrop impact, sheet erosion, and gully erosion would have catastrophically excavated and transported prodigious quantities of earth and rock, even if no other agencies had been available for sediment transport.

Clouds Not the Major Source of the Flood Rainfall and Waters

Intense, global, torrential rainfall continuing for forty days, as described in the biblical record, would have required a completely different mechanism, and an additional water source, for its production than is available for the localized intense storms experienced today. This is evident from the fact that if all the water in our present atmosphere were to be precipitated *en masse*, it would barely suffice to cover the ground to an average depth of less than 2 inches (5 centimeters). Furthermore, the normal process of evaporation could not have been effective during this intense, global, torrential rainfall at the beginning of the Flood, because the atmosphere immediately above the earth's surface would have been already at saturation level. Thus, the normal hydrologic cycle would not have been capable of supplying the tremendous amounts of water required to maintain this intense, global, torrential rainfall. The implication, therefore, is that there had to be an additional source of water, and a transfer mechanism to the atmosphere of an entirely different type and order of magnitude than now exists.

Some have suggested that the climatology and meteorology of the pre-Flood world were much different from today's world.[1] This is based on the contention that some form of water vapor canopy existed above the atmosphere in the pre-Flood world, because we are told in the biblical record that on the second day of the Creation Week some of the primeval ocean waters of Day One were placed above the firmament, also created on that day. Thus, it is argued, these "waters above" could have been the major source of the torrential, global rainfall for the first forty days

---

1   J. C. Whitcomb and H. M. Morris, 1961, *The Genesis Flood: The Biblical Record and its Scientific Implications,* Philadelphia, PA: The Presbyterian and Reformed Publishing Company.

and nights of the Flood, the expression "the windows of heaven" referring to the catastrophic collapse of this water vapor canopy, which precipitated as sustained, heavy rainfall. However, the Hebrew words for the "windows [or sluice-gates] of heaven" do not seem to imply anything about the source of the water for the rainfall. Furthermore, given that the firmament or "stretched-out thinness" more likely refers to interstellar space than to the earth's atmosphere, the "waters above" referred to in Genesis 1:7 would have been far removed from the earth at that point. If so, these "waters above" would not be referring to a water vapor canopy immediately above the earth's atmosphere. Apart from the issue of the identity and location of the "waters above," scientific considerations place severe restrictions on the amount of water vapor that could have been maintained in position above the atmosphere according to known physical laws. One consideration is that much more than a few inches of liquid water equivalent in a vapor canopy appears to lead to a runaway greenhouse effect.[2] A second is that the amount of latent heat released from the condensation of water vapor limits the amount of condensation that can occur during the Flood without boiling the oceans and killing all the life on earth because of the high temperatures required to radiate the latent heat to space at a sufficient rate. These considerations imply that even if a water vapor canopy did exist above the atmosphere, it could not have contained sufficient water vapor to have sustained forty days and nights of intense, global, torrential rainfall.[2]

There is, however, another source for the Flood waters described in the biblical record. Genesis 7:11 states that "all the fountains of the great deep [were] broken up" at the initiation of the Flood. The primary meaning of the Hebrew words translated "great deep" is undoubtedly the waters of the ocean depths, so these fountains would have primarily been springs on the pre-Flood ocean floor. Thus, the breaking up of them would have been the rupturing of the ocean floor in a vast upheaval. However, because a secondary meaning of the expression is simply "subterranean waters," water stored deep in the supercontinental crustal landmass of the pre-Flood world could possibly also be included. Thus, the breaking up at the commencement of the Flood might also refer to the rupturing of this supercontinental landmass to release these subterranean waters.

We are not told what triggered this upheaval that broke up all these fountains on the ocean floor and possibly also on land. It is conceivable that pressure built up inside the earth due to internal heat, so once the first fountain had cracked open, the water surging through would immediately weaken the adjacent crust, whether continental or oceanic crust, resulting in a rapid worldwide chain reaction that cleaved open "all the fountains of the great deep" right around the globe. If heat was involved as the driving force, then it is likely that much of the water was released as steam. This would have burst from this global network of cleaved

2   D. E. Rush and L. Vardiman, 1990, Pre-Flood vapor canopy radiative temperature profiles, *Proceedings of the Second International Conference on Creationism*, ed. R.E. Walsh and C.L. Brooks, Pittsburgh, PA, 231-245.

fountains as jets, catapulting it high into the atmosphere, where it condensed and fell as rain. Indeed, whereas the intense, global, torrential rainfall is described in the text as falling for forty days and nights, the fountains of the great deep were open for 150 days. Thus, the implication is that these fountains of the great deep were the major source of water not only for the Flood rainfall, but for the Flood event itself.

Enlarged Ocean Basins as a Result of the Flood?

Given the duration of the intense, global, torrential rainfall at the beginning of the Flood, the mass of waters that fell to the earth's surface could hardly have been elevated back up into the atmosphere after the Flood, because that quantity of water is simply not there in the atmosphere today. Similarly, if a large volume of subterranean waters actually were released through the fountains of the great deep during the first 150 days of the Flood, these also could not all be returned to the inside of the earth at the end of the Flood. Only a small portion of these waters became trapped in the sediments, and thus in the strata of the earth's crust, formed during the Flood.

Thus, the overall result of the Flood was that most of the Flood waters remained on the earth. Whether or not the volume of the ocean basins was greater after the Flood than before depends on the amount of new water added to the earth's surface. If some of the water that emerged from the fountains of the great deep was simply water from the pre-Flood ocean that flashed to superheated steam as it came into contact with molten rock rising to fill the gap as ocean plates pulled apart at mid-ocean ridges and emerged as supersonic steam jets, which in turn entrained more liquid water from the ocean to produce the forty days and nights of heavy rainfall, then perhaps little new subterranean water from the earth's interior was actually added to the earth's surface during the Flood. In this case, most of the water of the Flood was water that had been present in the pre-Flood ocean basin. On the other hand, it is likely that at least some new water was added to the earth's surface, and this implies that at least some of the waters of our present oceans entered at the time of the Flood. This, in turn, implies three possibilities: either the proportion of land area to water area was larger before the Flood; the ocean basins were shallower before the Flood, in contrast to their depth today; or there was a combination of more land area and shallower ocean basins. In any case, there is much evidence now that today's ocean basins are much younger features on the earth's surface than the continents, with only a relatively thin veneer of sediments on the ocean floors. This is consistent with great tectonic movements and isostatic adjustments having taken place toward the end of the Flood, in order for land to appear again from under the Flood waters and to form ocean basins sufficient to contain them.

This seems to be implied in the poetic reflection about the Flood in Psalm 104:5-9, where we read: "Who laid the foundations of the earth, that it should not be removed for ever. Thou coveredst it with the deep as with a garment: the waters stood above the mountains. At thy rebuke they fled; at the voice of thy thunder they hasted away. They go up by the mountains: they go down by the valleys unto the place where thou hast founded them. Thou hast set a bound that they may not pass over; that they turn not again to cover the earth." This passage of Scripture refers to the Flood, rather than to the events of Days One to Three of the Creation Week, because the last verse refers to God's promise that a globe-covering Flood would never again occur on the earth (Genesis 9:11). Also, to underline the implication of these verses to the tectonics of the Flood, a literal translation of Psalm 104:8 would be "the mountains rose, the valleys sank down." Thus, the biblical record makes it abundantly plain that the processes responsible for the Flood, and associated with it, were of immense geologic potency, and therefore caused profound geological changes.

Volcanic and Seismic Upheavals During the Flood

The statement in Genesis 7:11, that "all the fountains of the great deep [were] broken up," appears to suggest that the cleaving open of the earth not only involved the release of water and steam, but also the release of magmas (molten rock) through great volcanic explosions and eruptions. These would have been triggered by the cleaving open of the earth's crust, and undoubtedly would have also contributed to the initiation of that process. Not only would some water have been released from solution in the magmas themselves, but where the molten rock came in contact with cold ocean water, vast quantities of supercritical steam would be generated. The energy of this steam, given the temperature of the molten rock and pressure at the ocean bottom, is sufficient to accelerate it to supersonic velocity as it rises toward the ocean surface. It also has sufficient energy to entrain vast amounts of liquid water and carry it into the stratosphere, where it falls to produce the intense, global, torrential rainfall. Similarly, where cleaving of the earth's crust occurred on land, there would also have been volcanic eruptions accompanied by vast outpourings of lavas. Furthermore, it is entirely reasonable to make comparisons with the phenomena associated with volcanism today, and therefore to expect that there must have also been great earthquakes and tsunamis (popularly known as tidal waves) generated by this explosive volcanic activity around the globe during the Flood. The intensity and global scale of these eruptions, earthquakes, and tsunamis would have been catastrophic, wreaking havoc and thus accomplishing great amounts of geologic work directly, as well as augmenting the destructive effects of the Flood waters themselves.

Unprecedented Sedimentary Activity Again During the Flood

The biblical record of the Flood clearly implies that enormous quantities of earth and rock must have been excavated by the Flood waters to produce vast quantities of sediments, that were then transported and deposited in thick sequences of sedimentary strata. Unprecedented sedimentary activity, compared to the slow and gradual sedimentation observed today, had occurred already on Day Three of the Creation Week due to the catastrophic erosion caused by the retreating ocean waters as earth movements uplifted the earth's crust to form the dry land. The same factors that had operated during Creation Week, catastrophic erosion and sedimentation, would have been also operating during the Flood. However, many additional factors would have contributed during the Flood to the devastation and reshaping of the earth's surface and the catastrophic deposition of new sedimentary strata—in particular, the driving rains and the raging streams resulting from them, the volcanic eruptions, and accompanying earthquakes and powerful tsunamis, resulting from the cleaving open of the earth's crust. Furthermore, later in the Flood there would have been waves and other currents generated by tectonic processes again uplifting land surfaces and deepening the ocean basins.

Additionally, there would have perhaps been many other factors and their effects in operation during this unique catastrophic event that we cannot now know or study, because in today's slow and gradual regime of geological processes we cannot study the catastrophic geological processes that would have been uniquely in operation on a global scale during the Flood. Apart from the profoundly catastrophic geologic activity and shaping of the earth and its surface during the early part of Creation Week, there could never have been such extensive erosion of soil and rock strata on a global scale as during the Flood. The materials that were eroded would, of course, have formed prodigious quantities of sediments that eventually had to be re-deposited as new sedimentary rock strata in thick sequences on a vast scale. This is exactly what we find everywhere today in huge sedimentary basins that blanket the earth's surface.

Ideal Conditions for the Formation of Fossils During the Flood

It would seem that biodiversity in the pre-Flood world was much richer and more varied than in our present world. This can be inferred from the great numbers and varieties of flora and fauna found fossilized in the geologic record that have become extinct. This inference is supported by evidences that the pre-Flood climate was very different and more conducive globally to such a rich and varied biodiversity. Indeed, the fossil record provides evidence of what were probably whole ecosystems that are no longer found in today's world. (There will be more discussion of these details later.)

In any case, the stated purpose of the Flood was to destroy all life on the earth, that is, at least on the dry land ("And all flesh died that moved upon the earth... All in whose nostrils was the breath of life, of all that was in the dry land, died," Genesis 7:21-22), except, of course, the passengers on the Ark. Thus, an incredible number of living creatures, as well as plants, were likely swept away by the Flood waters, and then trapped and eventually buried in the huge, moving masses of sediments under conditions that were eminently conducive to fossilization. Indeed, never before or since could there have been such favorable conditions for the formation of fossiliferous strata. The uplift of the dry land and its catastrophic erosion on Day Three of the Creation Week occurred before the plants had been created to vegetate that dry land, and well before the creation of the land animals and man on Day Six. Therefore, even though the devastating erosion on Day Three of the Creation Week had produced catastrophic sedimentation conducive to fossilization, no mass destruction and fossilization of life occurred then. This implication of the biblical record will be utilized later in a biblical geologic model of earth history consistent with what is found in the geologic record.

Uniformitarianism Also Undermined by the Flood

In view of the global nature of the Flood catastrophe and the magnitude of the tectonic, volcanic, geophysical, erosion, and sedimentation phenomena accompanying it, the Flood constituted a profound discontinuity in the normal operation of all geological processes. Any deposits formed before the Flood, even the rocks and strata formed catastrophically during the Creation Week, would almost certainly have been changed, or even severely altered, by the catastrophic hydrodynamic and tectonic forces unleashed during the Flood period. The fundamental conceptual principle that the conventional geological community uses to build its reconstruction of earth history is uniformitarianism, encapsulated in the maxim "the present is the key to the past." However valid it may be for the study of rocks and strata formed since the Flood, the implication of the biblical record is that it cannot be legitimately applied before that time, that is, to the Flood and Creation Week periods. The catastrophism of the Flood period is especially important when considering the so-called absolute geological chronometers which the conventional geologic community uses to interpret observational and geochemical data to assign vast ages to the various strata and to the earth itself.

62

THE RENEWED RECOGNITION
OF CATASTROPHISM

All these geological implications of the biblical record of the Flood are generally supported by, and are consistent with, the actual details preserved in the rock record. Almost all of the sedimentary rocks, which are the strata containing fossils and from which the conventional interpretation of the earth's history has been largely deduced, were laid down by moving water. This is obvious and universally accepted. Sedimentary rocks by definition are those that were originally deposited as layers of sediments, which are defined as "solid fragmental material that originates from weathering of rocks and is transported or deposited by air, water, or ice, or that accumulates by other natural agents, such as chemical precipitation from solution or secretion by organisms, and that form in layers on the earth's surface at ordinary temperatures in a loose unconsolidated form; for example, sand, gravel, silt, mud, till, loess, alluvium. Strictly speaking, solid material that has settled down from a state of suspension in a liquid...material held in suspension in water or recently deposited from suspension."[1] Thus, the great masses of sediments that now make up the earth's sedimentary rocks must first have been eroded from previous locations, transported, and then deposited (perhaps even more than once). This is exactly what would be expected to occur in any flood, and would obviously have occurred on a uniquely grand scale during the Genesis Flood.

As noted earlier, by the end of the 17th century and throughout the 18th century it was generally accepted, almost without question, by scientists in the western world that not only had the biblical Flood been global, but it was the key element in the biblical framework of earth history, having been responsible for the major geologic formations of the earth. However, during the 19th century a complete revolution occurred, the catastrophic geology of the biblical Flood being abandoned for the slow and gradual geological processes of the uniformitarian philosophy for interpreting the formation of rock strata through the earth's history.

---

1   R. L. Bates and J. A. Jackson, ed., 1980, *Glossary of Geology*, second edition, Falls Church, VA: American Geological Institute, 566.

It was Scottish geologist James Hutton who is often regarded as the founder of modern geology. His work paved the way for the revolution in geological thinking that followed. In 1785 he communicated to the Royal Society of Edinburgh his *Theory of the Earth*, presenting what was regarded as "an irrefutable body of evidence to prove that the hills and mountains of the present day are far from being everlasting, but have themselves been sculptured by slow processes of erosion such as those now in operation."[2] Hutton also showed that the alluvial sediment continually being removed from the land by rivers is eventually deposited as sand and mud on the sea floor. He observed that the sedimentary rocks of the earth's crust bear all the hallmarks of having accumulated exactly like those now being deposited, so he insisted that the vast thicknesses of these older sedimentary rocks implied the operation of erosion and sedimentation throughout a period of time that could only be described as inconceivably long. Thus, he declared that "the present is the key to the past," that "the past history of our globe must be explained by what can be seen to be happening now."[3] Hutton expressed his faith in the orderliness of nature when he wrote, "No powers are to be employed that are not natural to the globe, no action to be admitted except those of which we know the principle."[4] He insisted that the ways and means of nature could be explained only by observation, and that the same processes and natural laws prevailed in the past as those we can now observe or infer from observations. So Hutton did not exclude temporary and local natural catastrophes, such as earthquakes or volcanic eruptions. This interpretative principle became known as uniformitarianism, or actualism to those who did not like that term, and was based on a rejection of the supernatural global catastrophism of the Genesis Flood. In his book, also entitled *Theory of the Earth* and published in 1795, Hutton recorded that however far we penetrate back into the past in our study of the earth's rocks, we can find "no vestige of a beginning."

Far from being welcomed, Hutton's theory was regarded by most of his contemporaries with righteous horror, because it was in direct and open conflict with the prevailing and entrenched views of Flood geology and a young earth. Nevertheless, Hutton's assault was continued after his death by John Playfair, whose *Illustrations of the Huttonian Theory of the Earth* was published in 1802. However, it was not until the publication of the famous textbook *Principles of Geology* (subtitled *Modern Changes of the Earth and its Inhabitants Considered as Illustrative of Geology*) in 1830-1833 that the tide of the debate began to turn in favor of Hutton's uniformitarianism. The author was a young English attorney, turned geologist, Charles Lyell, who enthusiastically accepted and vigorously promoted Hutton's doctrine of gradual geological changes. It was in fact Lyell who introduced the term uniformitarianism, championing not only the uniformity of natural law, but also the uniformity of the rates of geological processes. Indeed,

---

2　　A. Holmes, 1965, *Principles of Physical Geology*, second edition, London: Thomas Nelson and Sons, 43.

3　　Holmes, 1965, 142.

4　　Holmes, 1965, 44.

Lyell went further than his predecessors in his insistence that all geologic processes had been very gradual in the past, and in his utter abhorrence of anything suggestive of sudden catastrophes:

> [T]he earlier geologists had not only a scanty acquaintance with existing changes, but were singularly unconscious of the amount of their ignorance. With the presumption naturally inspired by this unconsciousness, they had no hesitation in deciding at once that time could never enable the existing powers of nature to work out changes of great magnitude, still less such important revolutions as those which are brought to light by Geology....never was there a dogma more calculated to foster indolence, and to blunt the keen edge of curiosity, than this assumption of the discordance between the ancient and existing causes of change. It produced a state of mind unfavourable in the highest degree to the candid reception of the evidence of those minute but insistent alterations which every part of the earth's surface is undergoing...for this reason all theories are rejected which involve the assumption of sudden and violent catastrophes and revolutions of the whole earth, and its inhabitants— theories which are restrained by no reference to existing analogies, and in which a desire is manifested to cut, rather than patiently to untie, the Gordian Knot.[5]

Lyell was thus intent on removing any trace of the catastrophic biblical Flood from the study of geology, which was one of the main reasons why uniformitarianism was so quickly adopted by those intent on being freed from all biblical constraints. Furthermore, as a disciple of Lyell, Darwin built his theory of organic evolution upon the uniformitarian foundation which Lyell had laid. In *The Origin of Species,* Darwin acknowledged his debt of gratitude to Lyell when he referred to "Sir Charles Lyell's groundwork on the *Principles of Geology,* which the future historian will recognize has having produced a revolution in natural science."[6]

It is beyond dispute that Lyell's uniformitarianism has provided the interpretative framework for the geological study of earth history for almost 200 years. Nevertheless, recognition of catastrophism in the geologic record was not completely extinguished by Lyell's rigid insistence on the uniformity of the rates of geological processes. Indeed, in the last forty years there has been a renewed acceptance of the role of catastrophes in generating the rock record, although geologists still strictly adhere to accepting natural causes operating over the same recognized geological timescale for earth history. This change has been bolstered by the recognition that uniformitarianism has historically been a dual concept— substantive uniformitarianism (a testable theory of geologic change postulating

---

5   C. Lyell, 1872, *Principles of Geology,* eleventh edition, vol. 1, London: John Murray, 317-318.

6   C. Darwin, 1979, *The Origin of Species by means of Natural Selection,* reprinted first ed., New York: Avenel Books, 293.

uniformity of rates or material conditions), and methodological uniformitarianism (a procedural principle asserting spatial and temporal invariance of natural laws).[7] Thus, Stephen Jay Gould maintained that substantive uniformitarianism, which denies catastrophism, is an incorrect theory and should be abandoned. Furthermore, while methodological uniformitarianism enabled Lyell to exclude the miraculous from geologic explanation, "its invocation today is anachronistic, since the question of divine intervention is no longer an issue in science," so it is a superfluous term that is best confined to the past history of geology! Other geologists have also questioned uniformitarianism, calling it an "ambiguous principle,"[8] a "dangerous doctrine,"[9] a principle that is "vaguely formulated,"[10] a doctrine that is "largely superfluous,"[11] and a term that "should be abandoned when describing formal assumptions used in modern geological enquiry."[12]

So what has brought about these reactions and the shift within the modern geological synthesis to accept catastrophism within the range of geological processes that have shaped the earth and left their record in the geologic column? Albritton wrote:

> Those who oppose substantive uniformity [that is, the belief in the uniformity of the rates of geological processes] tirelessly point out that the present condition of the earth, with its high-standing continents and remnants of vast continental glaciers, must be quite atypical of average conditions through geologic time, so that the present cannot be a very reliable key to the past. These opponents have no difficulty in classifying substantive uniformity; it is a discredited scientific hypothesis, an *a priori* assumption, or an anti-historical dogma.[13]

As Austin also wrote, "if the term [uniformitarianism] is understood to require temporal uniformity of rates or conditions, it is refuted by geological data, and is therefore false."[14] And Shea has written:

> Contrary to all these historical modern examples, contemporary

---

7   S. J. Gould, 1965, Is uniformitarianism necessary? *American Journal of Science*, 263: 223-228.

8   C. C. Albritton, 1967, Uniformity, the ambiguous principle, in *Uniformity and Simplicity, a Symposium on the Principle on the Uniformity of Nature*, C. C. Albritton, Jr, ed., Geological Society of America Special Paper 89: 1-2.

9   P. D. Crynine, 1956, Uniformitarianism is a dangerous doctrine, *Journal of Palaeotology*, 30: 1003-1004.

10   M. K. Hubbert, 1967, Critique of the principle of uniformity, in *Uniformity and Simplicity, a Symposium on the Principle of the Uniformity of Nature*, C. C. Albritton, Jr, ed., Geological Society of America Special Paper 89: 3-33.

11   H. B. Baker, 1938, Uniformitarianism and inductive logic, *Pan-American Geologist*, 69: 161-165.

12   S. A. Austin, 1979, Uniformitarianism—a doctrine that needs rethinking, *Compass*, 56: 29-45.

13   Albritton, 1967, 1.

14   Austin, 1979, 42.

uniformitarianism (or actualism) does not require that past processes or conditions be duplicated today. We now realize that Earth *has evolved* and that at least some past conditions and processes were quite different from those of today. However, this does not stop us from proposing reasonable, though unobserved, processes to explain geologic features, such as astroblemes, whose natural formation has not been observed.... The modern concept of uniformitarianism says nothing about the rate of processes but leaves such substantive matters to be determined by the evidence in the rock record....Fortunately, modern geology has long since outgrown any tendency to reject natural catastrophes out of hand (see, for example, Cloud, 1961, p. 156), and many examples can be cited of scientific, reasonable (that is, uniformitarian) geologic catastrophes whose occurrence is almost universally accepted (for example, the Spokane Flood, the refilling of the Mediterranean Basin after desiccation, numerous astroblemes, the formation of extensive ignimbrites, the extrusion of flood basalts, the 1929 Grand Banks turbidity current). Furthermore, if one follows the usual procedure of consulting authoritative recent sources, one finds that "gradualism" is simply not a part of modern uniformitarianism. Goodman (1967), for example, referred to this fallacy as a "blatant lie"....The definitive modern works reject the substantive idea of constancy of conditions. In addition to being physically impossible (Hubbert, 1967, p. 29), this approach involves assuming what we want to find out, namely the condition of Earth at various times in the past. Furthermore, the geological literature offers numerous examples where a uniformitarian interpretation of empirical evidence suggests that past conditions were radically different from those of today....[15]

Elsewhere, Shea has also written:

Unfortunately, we have overreacted...and have adopted an excessively gradualist view of earth history, refusing in many cases to consider catastrophic events...even when the evidence clearly suggests that sudden, violent, cataclysmic events have occurred. This attitude is changing, however, and we need to free ourselves completely from the artificial constraints of the fallacious dogma that would preclude any possibility of natural catastrophes having occurred, even if the postulated catastrophes are perfectly rational and supported by strong evidence.... In short, the time has surely come for sedimentologists to free themselves of all remaining traces of constraining dogmas of uniformitarianism and to become true scientists free to go where observation, experimentation,

---

15   J. H. Shea, 1982, Twelve fallacies of uniformitarianism, *Geology*, 10: 455-460. The references he cites are: E. Cloud, Jr, 1961, Paleobiogeography of the marine realm, *Report of the American Association for the Advancement of Science*, 151-200; N. Goodman, 1967, Uniformity and simplicity, in *Uniformity and Simplicity*, C.C. Albritton, Jr, ed., Geological Society of America Special Paper 89: 93-99; Hubbert, 1967.

and reasonable theory take us.[16]

As a consequence, catastrophes, initially unrivalled in modern geological processes, have now become an acceptable and necessary part of the modern geological synthesis:

> This process brings with it visions of random violence to the Earth on a scale never before contemplated: meteorite or comet impacts scar the lithosphere and generate towering tsunamis; exceptional impacts trigger magmatism, or shroud the globe in darkness and cold, poisoning life on land and in the sea or igniting wildfires that incinerate the world's flora to ash....Once the full implications of bolide impact are clearly understood, geologists will realize that this violent force carries with it a far more revolutionary departure from classical geology than did plate tectonics. The idea of instantaneous change triggered by projectiles from space runs counter to every tenet of uniformitarianism. To be sure, the ubiquity of impact scars on planets and satellites throughout the Solar System may seem to demonstrate a uniformity of process that brings bolide impact into conformity with the principle of uniformitarianism. But to regard the cataclysmic geologic effects of bolide impacts as uniformitarian is an exercise in "new speak," whereby we would impose a 1980s usage on an 1830s term, which since the time it was coined, has donated the exact opposite of cataclysmic. Impact-generated craters, eruptions, wildfires, and extinctions, whether they are sporadic or periodic, have a place in the serene uniformitarian world of Hutton and Lyell, the world that has been envisioned by the geological community for the past two centuries. Rather than to invert the definition of the venerable word, it is time to recognize that bolide impact is a geologic process of major importance, which by its very nature demolishes uniformitarianism itself as the basic principle of geology.[17]

Both William Whewell and C. S. Peirce criticized Lyell's induction on grounds that he sought facts to support his theory of a uniformitarian Earth. They believed, instead, that nature's facts should be the only guide to scientific inference. For example, if the geomorphic facts or results observed in the Scablands of Washington State imply a floodwaters of magnitude greater than any ever observed in the present, we should trust what nature tells us. Assuming only that the fundamental principles of hydraulics have been uniform in kind through time, we can infer the nature of such an unwitnessed historical event—even quantitatively!

---

16   J. H. Shea, 1982, Editorial: Uniformitarianism and sedimentology, *Journal of Sedimentary Petrology*, 52: 701-702.

17   U. B. Marvin, 1990, Impact and its revolutionary implications for geology, in *Global Catastrophes in Earth History: an Interdisciplinary Conference on Impacts, Volcanism and Mass Mortality*, V. L. Sharpton and D. Ward, ed., Geological Society of America Special Paper 247: 147-154.

This process of reasoning, whereby we observe historical effects and then infer past causes or past conditions, Peirce termed *retroduction*, in contradistinction to *induction*. Whereas Lyell's induction sought facts to support his theory, retroduction uses facts to seek a theory. The difference is profound, even if subtle. It allows us to accept unwitnessed cataclysmic events, and believe that Earth was bombarded by countless bolides in the past....Finally, it even means that catastrophism, in the sense of not straining the intensities of processes, was a better premise than Lyell's uniformitarianism (Baker, 1998)![18]

Perhaps the data of the rock record that have been most influential in bringing catastrophism back into respectable contention and acceptance as the explanation for those data were the observations and careful recording of the first and last appearances of animal and plant families in the strata sequences of the geologic column. This data led to the recognition of mass extinctions and then catastrophic causes for them.[19] This development has led to a plethora of articles and books on the subject of catastrophes as the explanation for the mass extinctions recognized as being preserved in the rock record.[20]

This revolution in invoking catastrophism to explain features found in the rock sequences of the geologic column has not just been confined to fossils, but to the rock strata themselves. Recall the account of how the hundreds of graded beds in the Ventura Basin of California were originally interpreted as requiring several years to deposit each layer in shallow water. However, when the phenomenon of turbidity currents was discovered and understood, then it was realized that these graded beds had each been deposited within minutes in deeper water.[21] Indeed,

---

18   R. H. Dott, Jr, 1998, What is unique about geological reasoning?, *GSA Today*, 8 (10): 15-18. The reference he cites is: V. R. Baker, 1998, Catastrophism and uniformitarianism: Logical roots and current relevance in geology, in *Lyell: the Past is the Key to the Present*, A. C. Scott and D. Blundell, ed., Geological Society of London Special Publication 143.

19   N. D. Newell, 1963, Crises in the history of life, *Scientific American*, 208: 77-92; N. D. Newell, 1967, Revolutions in the history of life, in *Uniformity and Simplicity, A Symposium on the Principle of Uniformity of Nature*, C. C. Albritton, Jr, ed., Geological Society of America Special Paper 89: 63-91.

20   Some examples are M. Allaby and J. Lovelock, 1983, *The Great Extinction*, London: Secker and Warburgh; D. M. Raup, 1986, *The Nemesis Affair*, New York and London: Norton; C. C. Albritton, Jr, 1989, *Catastrophic Episodes in Earth History*, London: Chapman and Hall; S. K. Donovan, ed., 1989, *Mass Extinctions—Processes and Evidence*, London: Bellhaven Press; V. L. Sharpton and D. Ward, ed., 1990, *Global Catastrophes in Earth History*, Geological Society of America Special Paper 247; W. Glen, ed., 1994, *The Mass Extinction Debates*, Stanford, CA: Stanford University Press; D. H. Erwin, 1995, *The Great Paleozoic Crisis—Life and Death in the Permian*, New York: Columbia University Press; G. R. McGhee, 1996, *The Late Devonian Mass Extinction—The Frasnian-Famennian Crisis*, New York: Columbia University Press; A. Hallam and B. Wignall, 1997, *Mass Extinctions and their Aftermath*, Oxford: Oxford University Press; Palmer, 1999, *Controversy, Catastrophism and Evolution: The Ongoing Debate*, New York: Kluwer Academic/Plenum Publishers.

21   J. E. Eaten, 1929, The by-passing and discontinuous deposition of sedimentary materials, *American Association of Petroleum Geologists Bulletin* 13: 713-761; H. Kuenen and C. I. Migliorini, 1950, Turbidity currents as a cause of graded bedding, *Journal of Geology*, 58: 91-127; M. L. Natland and H. Kuenen, 1951, Sedimentary history of the Ventura Basin, California, and the action of turbidity currents, *Society of Economic Paleontologists and Mineralogists Special Publication* 2: 76-107.

turbidity current deposition represents a catastrophic event, in that each graded bed represents a single depositional episode.[22] A turbidity current can deposit one of these turbidite layers, that is more than a meter thick, as an enormous lobe of sediment covering thousands of square kilometers, but the length of time required for this deposition might be only a few minutes.

The first direct measurement of a turbidity current speed was facilitated by an earthquake on November 18, 1929, on the continental slope southwest of the Grand Banks, off the south coast of Newfoundland. The earthquake triggered a sudden slump of the sediments on the continental slope, which became a slide, and then as the sediments were thrown into suspension, a turbidity current. That turbidity current flowed rapidly downslope, causing breaks in the trans-Atlantic communication cables on the continental slope, and then further down the continental rise onto the abyssal plain. The times at which communications were interrupted by the sequence of different cables breaking enabled measurement of the turbidity current speed at an average of between 45 and 60 kilometers per hour.[23] It is also estimated that the quantity of sediment carried by this turbidity current and deposited as a turbidite unit on the abyssal plain amounted to a volume of 200 cubic kilometers.[24]

Another, more recently discovered, turbidite bed has been found on the deep abyssal plain floor of the western Mediterranean Sea.[25] What is exceptional about this turbidite unit is its scale. It is 8 to 10 meters thick and covers an area of some 60,000 square kilometers, with an estimated volume of 500 cubic kilometers. However, the evidence of episodic catastrophic sedimentation on a large scale is not just confined to finer sediments, since debris of immense sizes are now known to be capable of being transported in submarine debris flows. For example, giant submarine landslide deposits have been recognized off Hawaii, in which blocks of rock up to 10 kilometers long have been transported more than 50 kilometers.[26] Some of these landslides have flowed over 200 kilometers, and some have debris volumes exceeding 5,000 cubic kilometers. Another well-known set of submarine landslides is that known as the Storegga ("Great Edge") suite. These slides have an immense headwall, nearly 300 kilometers long, which runs roughly along the edge of the continental shelf of Norway.[27] Debris, up to 450 meters thick, is spread

22   J. Davidson, W. E. Reed, and M. Davis, 1997, *Exploring Earth: An Introduction to Physical Geology*, Upper Saddle River, NJ: Prentice Hall, 349.

23   C. R. Longwell, R. F. Flint, and J. Sanders, 1969, *Physical Geology*, New York: John Wiley and Sons, Inc., 360-364; Holmes, 1965, 864-870; Davidson, Reed, and Davis, 1997, 349.

24   E. G. Nisbet and D. J. W. Piper, 1998, Giant submarine landslides, *Nature*, 392: 329-330.

25   R. G. Rothwell, J. Thomson, and G. Kähler, 1998, Low-sea-level emplacement of a very large Late Pleistocene "megaturbidite" in the western Mediterranean Sea, *Nature*, 392: 377-380.

26   J. G. Moore et al, 1989, Prodigious submarine landslides on the Hawaiian ridge, *Journal of Geophysical Research*, 94: 17,465-17,484; J. G. Moore, W. R. Normark and R. T. Holcomb, 1994, Giant Hawaiian underwater landslides, *Science*, 264: 46-47.

27   Nisbet and Piper, 1998.

over a distance of 800 kilometers out to the abyssal plain floor. Why are there so few large landslide deposits similar to those described here recognized in the geologic record? It has been suggested that perhaps geologists have misinterpreted the evidence.[28]

In his ground-breaking book *The Nature of the Stratigraphical Record*, the late Derek Ager, Professor at the University College of Swansea, Wales, presented his field observations from many parts of the world that compelled him to conclude that the rocks recorded a somewhat catastrophic picture of earth history, challenging some of the assumptions of uniformitarian stratigraphy at that time.[29] His discussion of abundant field data in each chapter is drawn together in concluding statements that summarize the thrust of the book:

> At certain times in earth history, particular types of sedimentary environment were prevalent over vast areas of the earth's surface. This may be called the *Phenomenon of the Persistence of Facies*.

> Palaeontologists cannot live by uniformitarianism alone. This may be termed the *Phenomenon of the Fallibility of the Fossil Record*.

> The sedimentary pile at any one place on the earth's surface is nothing more than a tiny and fragmentary record of vast periods of earth history. This may be called the *Phenomenon of the Gap Being More Important than the Record*.

In a subsequent book, Ager again emphasizes the importance of violent catastrophic events in building the geologic record:[30]

> The sedimentation in the past has often been very rapid indeed and very spasmodic. This may be called the *Phenomenon of the Catastrophic Nature of much of the Stratigraphical Record*.

> The periodic catastrophic event may have more effect than vast periods of gradual evolution. This may be called the *Phenomenon of Quantum Sedimentation*.

> Most sedimentation in the continental areas is lateral rather than vertical and is not necessarily directly connected with subsidence. This may be called the *Principle of the Relative Independence of Sedimentation and Subsidence*.

---

28 N. H. Woodcock, 1979, Size of submarine slides and their significance, *Journal of Structural Geology*, 1: 137-142.

29 D. V. Ager, 1973, *The Nature of the Stratigraphical Record*, London: MacMillan.

30 D. V. Ager, 1993, *The New Catastrophism: The Importance of the Rare Event in Geological History*, Cambridge: Cambridge University Press.

In conclusion, Ager made the oft-quoted statement that "the history of any part of the earth, like the life of a solider, consists of long periods of boredom and short reigns of terror."[31] Of course, he still maintains that earth history has spanned countless millions of years. Nevertheless, Ager concludes:

> [I]t is obvious to me that the whole history of the earth is one of short, sudden happenings with nothing much in particular in between. I have often been quoted for my comparison of earth history with the traditional life of a soldier, that is "long periods of boredom separated by short periods of terror."[32]

Indeed, Ager reinforces this claim with copious examples of fossils and geological deposits that could not have formed by any other means than by sudden catastrophes or disasters that occurred in fleeting moments of time. However, he claims that these "episodic catastrophes" were separated by immense eons, when virtually no geological deposits and contained fossils were being formed, suggesting that there are "more gaps than record." Or to put it another way, the bulk of geological time occurred during the gaps in the record! "It may be said that Earth history is not a record of what actually happened," but "is a record of what happens to have been preserved."[33] Of course, this merely begs the question as to how Ager and the conventional geological community know that the gaps in the record represent vast eons of time. If neither the gaps nor the eons of geological time claimed to be associated with them are in the rock record, then one is left only with a record of brief catastrophic geologic processes!

---

31   Ager, 1973, 13, 26, 34, 42, 50, 59, 100.

32   Ager, 1993, 197-198.

33   Ager, 1993, 14.

63

Evidences of Catastrophism in the Geologic Column—Rate of Sediment Accumulation and Widespread Rapidly-Deposited Strata

Rate of Sediment Accumulation

The average thickness of the sediments on all of the continents is approximately 1,500 meters, although in some places the sedimentary rock sequences can be up to 10,000 meters or more thick. How long did it take to deposit the sediments that now make up these sedimentary rocks? Observations of present-day sedimentation rates have only been made for a relatively short time, but in conventional geology present observed rates of sedimentation are extrapolated into the past. Of course, variations in the rate of sedimentation and catastrophic events are now recognized as having happened in the past, but it is claimed that over the allegedly billions of years of earth history, the average rate of sedimentation has been more or less the same. On the other hand, it is quite obvious that in any biblical geologic model of earth history, sedimentation rates would have to have been cataclysmic during part of Day Three of the Creation Week and during the year-long Flood event. Do the sedimentary rocks themselves, therefore, provide any evidence of past sedimentation rates that would be definitive in favoring the scriptural timeframe of earth history compared to that of the modern geological synthesis?

Sediments are known to be deposited much faster today than they have supposedly accumulated in the geologic record according to conventional geologic reasoning.[1] Sedimentation rates were measured and estimated in meters of sediment per thousand years over different timespans and are plotted in Figure 39 (page 1079). Of course, the sedimentation rate measured over a one-minute period during a flash flood is extremely high; indeed, it can be more than a staggering 1 million meters per thousand years. In other words, if a flash flood continued steadily at its peak flow rate for 1,000 years, it would deposit sediment one million meters thick! On the other hand, if the measurements were averaged over a few hours, the rate would probably be lower, because flood water does not flow continuously

---

1   M. Sadler, 1981, Sediment accumulation rates and the completeness of stratigraphic sections, *Journal of Geology,* 89: 569-584.

at peak rates. Thus, a rate measured over a month is significantly lower, because a local flood occurs for only part of that time. Furthermore, the most realistic measurement to obtain for an average sedimentation rate at the present time would be to probably take a measurement over several years, because that would then reflect the changes in sedimentation through the seasons, and would average that for several yearly cycles. Of course, such rates actually can and have been measured today.

Needless to say, sedimentation rates over significantly longer timespans must be determined in a different way, such as by measuring the thickness of sediment between two radioisotopically dated layers. If it is assumed that the radioisotopic dates are correct (these are, of course, also based on assumptions and will be discussed later), then the amount of time for the measured thickness of sediments, and thus a rate in meters per thousand years, can be calculated. It is not surprising that calculated sedimentation rates for sedimentary strata in the rock record that are dependent on the radioisotopic dating methods are extremely low compared to measured modern sedimentation rates.

Figure 39, where the data are plotted on a log/log scale, indicates that the longer the timespan over which sedimentation rates are calculated, the slower are those sedimentation rates. The same data when plotted on a log/linear scale in Figure 40 (page 1079) more clearly reveal that sedimentation rates today are extremely rapid in comparison with ancient sedimentation rates calculated from sedimentary rock strata. From these data it is logical to conclude that:

1. Sedimentation occurred at a much slower rate in the past; or
2. Much of the ancient sediments originally deposited has not been preserved in the geologic record; or
3. The geological timescale is not correct, being a gross overestimate of the elapsed time of earth history.

If the present is indeed the key to understanding the past, then option 1 is not only an unlikely hypothesis, but is untenable by definition. Calculated sedimentation rates over a timespan of one million years average about 0.01 meters per thousand years, whereas the average sedimentation rate actually measured today over a period of one year is approximately 100 meters per thousand years. Thus, as recognized by Ager (cited earlier), the time over which the rock record has accumulated is only a small fraction of the claimed available time of the geological timescale. Indeed, even with all the possible claimed breaks in strata sequences, the accumulation of the rock record would still only have required less than ten percent of the claimed available time of the geological timescale. The universality, and especially the magnitude, of this shortfall are both startling and staggering (for the conventional geological community). Thus, option 2 is all too readily appealed to, with the claim that many cycles of sedimentation have occurred, erosion of most of those sediments having taken place before the next cycle of sedimentation began, so most of the ancient sediments originally deposited have not been preserved in the rock record. However, the field evidence for those proposed erosional breaks generally is not detectable (to be further discussed). Nevertheless, the startling shortage of sediments still remains after the detectable erosional breaks are accounted for, so option 2 is likewise untenable and inconsistent with the data.

Even if we assumed modern sedimentation rates (the present is the key to the past) had produced the Phanerozoic strata sequences in one or even ten percent of the geological time usually assigned to those rocks, it would still have taken between 5.45 and 54.5 million years. However, modern sedimentation rates fall drastically short of the sedimentation that would have been occurring during the global cataclysmic Flood. Therefore, the following conditions are assumed to have applied during the global cataclysmic Flood event, to demonstrate both the feasibility and compatibility of a biblical geologic model with the observational data:

1. Almost all deposited sediments have been preserved in the geologic record as extensive cycles of deposition, and erosion did not occur (discussed further below).
2. All Paleozoic and Mesozoic strata sequences were deposited during the Flood, while the Cenozoic strata were deposited post-Flood (this is only a first approximation for the sake of the argument).
3. These Flood strata sequences (Paleozoic and Mesozoic) average a thickness of about 700 meters on the continents.
4. During the Flood, the volume and speed of the flowing water were sufficient to sustain, on average, the same sedimentation rate as an average modern flash flood.

The modern geological synthesis allocates 480 million years for the accumulation of these Paleozoic and Mesozoic strata sequences, so the time required at modern depositional rates for those sedimentary rock sequences would be only 4.8 to 48 million years (that is, one to ten percent of the claimed time, assuming the claimed erosional breaks in the geologic record represent the passage of millions of years during which no sediment was preserved). However, the average deposition rate in a modern flash flood, measured over one hour (see Figure 39), is one million meters of sediment per thousand years, or 1,000 meters per year. Consequently, if the waters of the Flood only equaled a modern flash flood continuously covering all the earth, it would only have taken 8.4 months to deposit all the Paleozoic and Mesozoic strata sequences. Of course, in some places the sedimentary rock layers are much more than 700 meters thick.

For example, in northern Arizona and southern Utah the Paleozoic and Mesozoic strata sequences are approximately 2,925 meters thick.[2] To deposit all these

2   S. S. Beus and M. Morales, ed., 2003, *Grand Canyon Geology,* 2nd ed., New York: Oxford University Press.

sedimentary rock layers in just one year would require the waters of the Flood to be flowing on average only 1.7 times faster than the rate used in the previous calculation, as the sediment-carrying capacity of flowing water varies as the square of its flow rate. However, the required flow rate would not need to be that much faster if the Flood waters were deeper. In any case, this flow rate is still below the maximum flow rate for modern flash floods (Figure 39). Of course, the assumptions used in these calculations are only rough approximations, but they do suggest the possibility that the waters of the Flood could have deposited the thickness of sedimentary rock strata found in the geologic record. It is also realistic to assume that the waters of the Flood were deeper than those of any modern flash flood, and like a modern flash flood the waters would not necessarily have been flowing at a constant rate all the time. This not only demonstrates that realistic sedimentation rates could feasibly have produced the sedimentary rock record left behind by the Flood year, but more than adequately responds to those who have claimed otherwise.[3]

Widespread, Rapidly Water-Deposited Strata

If a rate of sedimentation equivalent to that in a modern flash flood, with the sediment-carrying capacity of deeper water, is capable of depositing the rock sequences preserved in the geologic record of the Flood within the scriptural time framework of the Flood year, then there should be evidence in the strata themselves of their rapid deposition by water on a widespread scale. In other words, if the biblical account and description of a cataclysmic global flood are both true and relevant to our understanding of the geologic record, then the strata in that record should show evidence of cataclysmic water deposition on a global scale.

The required evidence is not only observed in the strata sequences of the rock record, but it has already been recognized in the conventional geologic community. For example, note again the comments made by Derek Ager that catastrophic deposition has had more effect than any vast periods of gradual evolution, that particular types of sediments are prevalent over vast areas of the earth's surface, and that most sedimentation in the continental areas is lateral rather than vertical.[4] Ager provides numerous examples of globally extensive, unique strata at various levels in the geologic record. Most noteworthy are the examples of very thin units that persist over fantastically large areas in particular sedimentary basins, such as rock units with thicknesses of 30 meters or less in the Permian strata sequences of western Canada that persist over areas up to 470,000 square kilometers, and the thin layer only about one meter thick that can be found all around the Alpine chain of Europe.[5] In the United States, the Dakota Formation of the western

---

3   For example, A. N. Strahler, 1987, *Science and Earth History—The Evolution/Creation Controversy,* Buffalo, NY: Prometheus Books, and I. R. Plimer, 1994, *Telling Lies for God—Reason vs Creationism,* Sydney: Random House.

4   Ager, 1973, 1-13, 43-50, and 51-59.

5   Ager, 1973, 13.

United States (a sandstone), with an average thickness of 30 meters, covers an area of some 815,000 square kilometers.[6] Even more remarkable is the Brockman Iron Formation in the Paleoproterozoic rock sequences of the Hamersley Basin of Western Australia in which there are bands about 2 centimeters thick that are able to be correlated over an area of almost 52,000 square kilometers. Even microscopic "varves" within those bands can be traced laterally over almost 300 kilometers.[7]

There are also numerous examples of discontinuous, but yet spectacular, distributions of similar, or even identical, synchronous deposits. Perhaps the most distinctive are the familiar white chalk beds in the upper Cretaceous strata sequences of northwest Europe, with their layers of black flint nodules and characteristic fossils. The most familiar images of these chalk beds are the white cliffs along the channel coast of England. However, these beds extend from the Antrim area of Northern Ireland, via England and northern France, through the Low Countries, northern Germany and southern Scandinavia to Poland, Bulgaria, and eventually to Georgia in the south of the Commonwealth of Independent States. There are also records of these same white chalk beds on the Black Sea coast of Turkey, and at the other extreme end of the belt, in southwest Ireland, and also covering extensive areas of the sea floor south of Ireland. However, identical chalk beds are also found in Egypt and Israel, but more remarkably, they are also found on the other side of the Atlantic in Texas, as well as in Arkansas, Mississippi, and Alabama. Even more surprising are identical chalk beds, complete with the same black flint nodules and the same familiar fossils, on the coast of Western Australia just north of Perth, overlying glauconitic sands, as in northwest Europe.[8] This global distribution of such uniform beds with the same characteristics and fossils is astounding, given that the chalk is an extremely pure coccolith-bearing limestone that is unique to this level in the geologic record.

Two other examples will suffice here. The strata sequences making up the three-fold division of the Triassic geologic record in Germany are so distinctive that they can also be readily recognized in the English Midlands, in eastern Spain, and north of Sofia and elsewhere in Bulgaria at the other end of Europe.[9] Furthermore, the sedimentary strata of the Newark Group of the eastern seaboard of the United States are exactly like the Triassic strata of northwest Europe, even to the extent that the brown sandstone near Birmingham, England, is remarkably like the brown sandstone of New York. Similarly, the distinctive red and green marls of these German Triassic strata sequences may also be instantly recognized

---

6   A. A. Roth, 1998, *Origins: Linking Science and Scripture,* Hagerstown, MD: Review and Herald Publishing Association, 218.

7   Ager, 1973, 13; A. F. Trendall, 1968, Three great basins of Precambrian banded iron formation deposition: a systematic comparison, *Bulletin of the Geological Society of America* 79: 1527-1544.

8   Ager, 1973, 1-2.

9   Ager, 1973, 4-6.

in southern Spain, and in the southwestern United States, where the red and green marls and thin sandstones with layers of gypsum of the Moenkopi and associated formations of northern Arizona are identical to the Triassic strata exposed along the banks of the River Severn in England.

Yet another distinctive and unique example is the remarkable similarity of the upper Carboniferous (Pennsylvanian) Coal Measures on both sides of the Atlantic Ocean, in North America and in Europe. The plant fossils of the British Coal Measures are just as easy to identify in the diverse fossil flora of the coal beds in the Illinois Basin.[10] Certainly there are some differences, such as more sedimentary strata containing marine fossils in the American Pennsylvanian, but just as with the plant fossils, the non-marine bivalve fossils of the coal measures in the American Mid-West are very much like those found in the coal measures that extend from Ireland to Russia. Whatever the vertical and lateral changes in the upper Carboniferous strata sequences of the coal measures, the rock types, their features, and their contained fossils are essentially the same all the way from Texas to the Donetz Coal Basin, north of the Caspian Sea in the former USSR, an extent amounting to some 170° of longitude.

However, it is not just the widespread extent of the same strata and strata types that is consistent with global sedimentation patterns during the biblical Flood (and earlier at the end of the Creation Week in the case of the Hamersley Basin of Western Australia), but evidence of widespread sedimentary strata deposited rapidly by water that is of most importance in our quest to demonstrate the biblical geologic model of earth history. It is therefore imperative that numerous examples of the deposition or formation of such strata of many different rock types be documented.

---

10   Ager, 1973, 6-7.

64

THE WIDESPREAD, RAPIDLY WATER-DEPOSITED, PALEOZOIC STRATA OF THE GRAND CANYON, ARIZONA—LIMESTONES

Of the many places on the earth's surface that have been well studied, the Grand Canyon area of northern Arizona probably ranks among the most intensively investigated. The Paleozoic strata exposed in the walls of the Canyon and in surrounding areas have been thoroughly documented, and are well-known as examples of the principal sedimentary rock types—limestones, sandstones, and shales. These rock units are also widespread, extending more than 300 kilometers from one end of the Canyon to the other and beyond to surrounding areas, usually in all four directions. The evidence within them for their rapid deposition has been thoroughly discussed and well-documented by Austin.[1]

The shallow-water lime muds accumulating in tropical oceans today are usually believed to provide an excellent example of how ancient lime mudstones (micritic limestones) such as those in Grand Canyon accumulated. Modern lime muds are formed mainly by mechanical breakdown of the carbonate-containing remains of sea creatures, and they accumulate at an estimated average rate of 0.33 meters thickness per thousand years. Thus, for example, it is insisted that simply comparing the texture of the cliff-forming Redwall Limestone of Grand Canyon with modern lime muds provides the convincing evidence that this and other Canyon limestone strata required millions of years to be deposited.[2]

However, modern, shallow-water lime muds are dominated by silt-sized crystals (approximately 20 microns in diameter) of aragonite (most contain 60-90 percent aragonite, and 0-10 percent calcite), derived from disaggregation or abrasion of skeletons of marine organisms.[3] On the other hand, the ancient lime mudstones (micritic limestones) abundant in Grand Canyon are dominated by clay-sized

---

1   S. A. Austin, 1994, Interpreting strata of Grand Canyon, in *Grand Canyon, Monument to Catastrophe*, S. A. Austin, ed., Santee, CA: Institute for Creation Research, 21-56.

2   D. E. Wonderly, 1977, *God's Time-Records in Ancient Sediments*, Flint, MI: Crystal Press, 138-145.

3   R. Steinen, 1978, On the diagenesis of lime mud: scanning electron microscopic observations of subsurface material from Barbados, W.I., *Journal of Sedimentary Petrology*, 48: 1140.

crystals (less than 4 microns in diameter) of calcite (nearly 100 percent calcite and/or dolomite), with sand-sized and larger skeletal fragments floating in the fine crystal matrix.[4] These textural, mineralogical, and chemical differences between modern lime muds and many ancient limestones have been emphasized: "Micritic limestones, composed essentially of calcite, have textures quite different from those of the aragonite-dominated modern lime muds that have long been regarded as their precursors."[5] "Modern carbonate sediments contrast sharply in their chemistry and mineralogy with ancient carbonate rocks."[6] Even the shapes of the grains in modern lime muds are very different from those in these ancient limestones: "Furthermore, the grain (crystal) size distribution and grain (crystal) shape characteristics of modern lime-mud sediment are very different from their lithified counterparts."[7]

Nevertheless, could recrystallization after deposition be responsible for transforming modern, coarser-textured, aragonite muds into the ancient, finer-textured, calcite limestones? No, the recrystallization process makes larger crystals from smaller crystals, so coarse-grained lime muds simply do not recrystallize into finer-grained limestones. It was once argued that the microcrystalline-calcite (micrite) of ancient limestones formed by direct precipitation from seawater,[8] and not from recrystallization or even extensive abrasion of skeletons of marine organisms, a process much different from the slow processes in modern oceans. Thus, the scientific evidence does not support the contention that ancient fine-grained limestones were derived from lime muds resembling those being deposited slowly in modern tropical seas. Indeed, as the compositions and textures of modern lime muds and fine-grained limestones have been thoroughly investigated, the "lime mud problem" has become more apparent and "the origin of micrite is far from clear."[9]

Whereas many modern lime muds do accumulate very slowly, there are some modern examples of rapid lime mud accumulation. For example, hurricanes in the Florida-Bahamas area have been observed to move and redeposit large quantities of fine, laminated, carbonate mud. Flats above normal high-tide level receive carpets of laminated mud after hurricanes, and offshore mud deposits have been observed to form rapidly.[10] Of particular interest are layers of creamy-white

---

4   E. D. McKee and R. G. Gutschick, 1969, History of the Redwall Limestone in northern Arizona, *Geological Society of America Memoir* 114: 103.

5   Z. Lasemi and A. Sandberg, 1984, Transformation of aragonite-dominated lime muds to microcrystalline limestones, *Geology*, 12: 420.

6   R. M. Garrels and F. T. MacKenzie, 1971, *Evolution of Sedimentary Rocks*, New York: W.W. Norton, 215.

7   Steinen, 1978, 1139.

8   R. L. Folk, 1959, Practical petrographic classification of limestones, *American Association of Petrologists Bulletin*, 43: 8.

9   F. J. Pettijohn, 1975, *Sedimentary Rocks*, third ed., New York: Harper and Row, 334.

10   M. M. Ball, E. A. Shinn and K. W. Stockman, 1967, The geologic effects of Hurricane Donna in south Florida, *Journal of Geology*, 75: 583-597; R. W. Perkins and Enos, 1968, Hurricane Betsy in the Florida-

mud with the consistency of toothpaste found in tidal channels between islands in the Bahamas. These are lime muds dominated by silt- and clay-sized needles of aragonite in beds 2.5-5 centimeters thick within a 1-meter-thick deposit described as "a high-energy bank margin environment not usually considered to be the site of mud-sized particle deposition."[11] Subsequent investigations have revealed that these lime mud layers associated with tidal channels formed by direct precipitation of aragonite during storms.[12]

These observations of lime mud deposits within environments of rapid accumulation would appear to be puzzling. After all, modern mud-sized particles are observed to settle very slowly, and only in quiet water, so how could fine mud particles settle quickly from turbulent, fast-flowing waters? The answer: microscopic examination of lime muds from the tidal channels in the Bahamas washed by a gentle stream of water revealed that the mud particles had aggravated into pelletoids.[13] Evidently, these pelletoids of flocculated aragonite particles exhibit the hydraulic characteristics of sand, allowing aggregates of particles to settle quickly. Thus, these new discoveries "mandate caution when using these features as indicators of shoreline or quiet water in ancient carbonate deposits."[14]

The rapid accumulation of fine-grained lime muds in modern sedimentary environments suggests that many fine-grained ancient limestones would similarly have accumulated rapidly. Probably the most significant limestones often claimed to have formed by extremely slow deposition are the so-called "lithographic limestones," which have an extremely fine texture and extraordinary fossil preservation. These limestones appear to have formed as animals were smothered in lime mud.[15] The most famous lithographic limestone is that found at Solnhofen in Germany, which includes fossils of the bird *Archaeopteryx*. Another fine-grained limestone containing the "world's most perfect fossils" is the Santana Formation of northeast Brazil, where the fossil fish in it have been described: "… lithification was instantaneous and fossilization may even have been the cause of death."[16] Yet

Bahamas area—geological effects and comparisons with Hurricane Donna, *Journal of Geology*, 76: 710-717; E. A. Shinn et al, 1993, Lime-mud layers in high-energy tidal channels: a record of hurricane deposition, *Geology*, 21: 603-606.

11 R. F. Dill and R. Steinen, 1988, Deposition of carbonate mud beds within high-energy subtidal sand dunes, Bahamas, *American Association of Petroleum Geologists Bulletin* 72: 178-179.

12 E. A. Shinn et al, 1989, a sedimentologic dilemma, *Journal of Sedimentary Petrology*, 59: 147-161; J. D. Milliman et al, 1993, Great Bahama Bank aragonitic muds: mostly inorganically precipitated, mostly exported, *Journal of Sedimentary Petrology*, 63: 589-595.

13 Dill and Steinen, 1988, 179; R. F. Dill, C. J. S. Kendall, and E. A. Shinn, 1989, Giant subtidal stromatolites and related sedimentary features, *American Geophysical Union, Field Trip Guidebook,* T373: 33.

14 Dill and Steinen, 1988, 179. See also Shinn et al, 1993, 605-606.

15 C. E. Brett and A. Seilacher, 1991, Fossil largerstätten, a taphonomic consequence of event sedimentation, in *Cycles and Events in Stratigraphy*, G. Einsele, W. Ricken and A. Seilacher, ed., New York: Springer-Verlag, 296.

16 D. M. Martill, 1989, The Medusa Effect: instanteous fossilization, *Geology Today*, 5: 201.

another excellent example of a lithographic limestone that must have accumulated rapidly as fine lime mud because of the extraordinarily preserved fossils in it is found in Mexico.[17] Clearly, catastrophic depositional processes are required to produce these fine-grained limestones.

Many abundantly fossiliferous limestones are claimed to be organically constructed limestone "reefs," which accumulated slowly in shallow ancient seas. It is alleged that it must have taken thousands of years to construct the huge, wave-resistant frameworks of these limestone "reefs," as innumerable generations of marine organisms chemically cemented themselves one on top of another. Thus, if there were large, organically-bound structures ("reefs") within the Grand Canyon limestones, they would seemingly be evidence that the lime muds making up these limestones must have accumulated slowly and *in situ* on the floors of ancient tranquil seas.

In the most extensive study of a Grand Canyon limestone, it was admitted: "Coral reefs are not known from the Redwall Limestone."[18] Concerning laminated algal structures (stromatolites) in the Redwall, which might have formed slowly in tidal flat environments, it was reported: "The general scarcity or near absence of bottom-building stromatolites suggests that places generally above low tide are not well represented."[19] Yet these cautious statements concerning algal structures in the Redwall Limestone have still been used to imply that the presence of some algal structures indeed represent *in situ* ocean floor.[20] However, the reported laminated algal structures typically show concentric structure (oncolites), and are best interpreted as algal masses that were transported by rolling. Thus, the claim that the Redwall Limestone represents an *in situ* ocean-floor deposit has not been proven by any empirical evidence.

In many modern reefs, sponges, as well as corals and algae, are responsible for building the rigid-growth frameworks, but sponge frameworks are not found in Grand Canyon limestones. Instead, small broken fragments of sponges have been described in the Redwall, but the largest sponges occur in the lower part of the Kaibab Limestone. Nevertheless, a recent report on the Kaibab admits: "Discrete organic build-ups, such as sponge patch reefs, have not been documented."[21] The absence of any coral or sponge-reef structures in all the limestones of the Grand Canyon strongly mitigates against any claim of slow *in situ* accumulation of these limestones on ancient ocean floors.

---

17   D. M. Martill, 1989, A new "Solnhofen" in Mexico, *Geology Today,* 5: 25-28.

18   McKee and Gutschick, 1969, 557.

19   McKee and Gutschick, 1969, 546.

20   D. E. Wonderly, 1987, *Neglect of geologic data: sedimentary strata compared with young-earth creationist writings,* Hatfield, PA: Interdisciplinary Biblical Research Institute, 17.

21   R. L. Hopkins, 1990, Kaibib Formation, in *Grand Canyon Geology*, S. S. Beus and M. Morales, ed., New York: Oxford University Press, and Flagstaff: Museum of Northern Arizona Press, 243.

However, there is a significant fossil deposit within the Redwall Limestone that provides relevant evidence of the mode of deposition of the limestone. Numerous, large orthocone nautiloids, marine mollusks in the class Cephalopoda, which includes the living octopuses, squids, and cuttlefishes, are found fossilized within a thin but extremely persistent bed in the basal member of the Redwall Limestone throughout the length of the Grand Canyon.[22] These are distinctive cigar-shaped fossils that are up to 0.6 meters in length and up to about 10 centimeters in diameter. Their chambered calcium carbonate shells are straight, unlike those of the modern coiled nautilus. Like its modern counterpart, the fossil nautiloid had a squid-like animal living in the last (largest) chamber of its shell, the other chambers being pressurized and used to compensate for buoyancy in a fashion similar to a submarine. This construction allowed the animals to swim freely, probably at great speed, through the deep ocean.

The two-meter-thick, coarse-grained, medium-gray dolomite bed in which these large fossil nautiloids are found is at the top of the Whitmore Wash Member within the Redwall Limestone. The fossil nautiloids are within this upper half of this bed, and always as a single layer. In the far eastern Grand Canyon the density is greater than one fossil nautiloid per four square meters, and similar nautiloid density is seen at outcrops in both the central Grand Canyon and in the type section at Whitmore Wash in the western Grand Canyon. This fossil-nautiloid-containing bed also extends into the Monte Cristo Limestone, which is equivalent and directly correlatable to the Redwall Limestone, as far as the Las Vegas area in southeastern Nevada. With such a fossil density laterally over a distance of more than 220 kilometers, the number of these fossil nautiloids is conservatively estimated at more than a billion. How then could so many of these free-swimming, deep-sea animals become buried and fossilized in fine-grained lime mud at this one particular horizon over such a large area?

The orientations or alignments of 160 of these fossil nautiloids have been measured and plotted on a rose diagram, which shows the compass-direction alignment of the long axes of the shells. The long axes of most of the fossilized nautiloids are aligned primarily in a northwest-southeast direction. Simple probability analysis indicates an extremely low chance that such an arrangement of shells could be generated by random falling of dead nautiloids over an extended period of time onto a motionless and static, deep ocean floor. On the other hand, it is known that long, cigar-shaped objects tend to align themselves in the direction of minimum resistance to flowing water, so it can be inferred that the long axes of these nautiloid shells in the Redwall Limestone were aligned in the direction of the prevailing current. However, any current able to induce orientation of large shells on the deep ocean floor would also be able to move and deposit fine-grained lime mud. Therefore, these fossil nautiloids indicate that the lime mud entombing them

---

22   S. A. Austin, A. A. Snelling and K. Wise, 1999, Canyon-length mass kill of orthocone nautiloids, Redwall Limestone (Mississippian), Grand Canyon, Arizona, *Geological Society of America Annual Meeting Abstracts*, Volume A: 421.

was moved and accumulated by the current catastrophically. Indeed, the sizes of the fossil nautiloids are log-normally distributed, indicating a life assemblage and therefore a mass-kill event involving a single species. Furthermore, shell implosion structures and the shell orientations are consistent with their bodies being present in many of the shells during the burial event. The chert directly overlying this bed is chemically distinctive, suggesting deposit-length toxic marine conditions as the cause of the mass-kill event. Mounds within the chert above, as well as the orientations of the fossil nautiloids, indicate a bi-directional current during rapid sedimentation and deposition of the fine-grained lime mud that entombed the nautiloids. Thus, a gigantic population of orthocone nautiloids was overcome by a catastrophic event that buried them in fine-grained lime mud over an area exceeding several thousand square kilometers.

What is also significant about this fossil nautiloid bed within the Redwall Limestone is that, except for the fossil nautiloids, it resembles many other limestone beds within the Redwall Limestone and other Grand Canyon limestones. Indeed, the fine-grained composition and bedded structure of the bed containing the fossil nautiloids is typical of the Redwall generally. Thus, it is reasonable to infer that many of the other fine-grained limestone layers were also rapidly accumulated, as lime muds were moved by water currents, and not by the slow and steady rain of fine lime debris in calm and placid seas.

However, not all Grand Canyon limestones are fine-grained. Some contain coarse, broken fossil debris, which appears to have been sorted by strong currents. The Redwall Limestone contains coarse, circular discs (columnals) from the stems of crinoids (sea-lilies). Vigorous current-washing to disaggregate these marine animals into fragments must have occurred, followed by winnowing away of the finer sediment to leave a "hash" of crinoid debris. Occasionally, the heads of crinoids are found embedded with the coarse, circular discs in the limestone. Sometimes these occur where the limestone is cross-bedded, which implies strong currents. Because modern crinoid heads in the ocean today are susceptible to rapid breakdown when these organisms die,[23] we can conclude that rapid burial was required to fossilize these crinoid heads.

Cross-bedded limestone layers sometimes reach great thicknesses. In the Redwall Limestone, cross-beds have been reported from several locations.[24] One set of cross-beds in the Redwall Limestone has a vertical thickness of almost ten meters. This implies that these beds represent the remnants of large (up to 20-meter-high) sand waves (underwater dunes) composed of coarser lime sediment, which were shaped by vigorous and sustained ocean currents moving at 1-1.5 meters per second. Thick cross-beds also occur within limestone members of the Esplanade

---

23   D. L. Meyer and K. B. Meyer, 1986, Biostratonomy of recent crinoids (Echinodermata) at Lizard Island, Great Barrier Reef, Australia, *Palaios*, 1: 294-302.

24   McKee and Gutschick, 1969, 111.

Sandstone in the western Grand Canyon.

Evidence of current transport of lime sediments is also provided by quartz sand grains, which are found embedded in the fine-grained matrix of many Grand Canyon limestones. These quartz sand grains are common in the Kaibab Limestone and limestones of the Supai Group. Because quartz sand grains cannot be precipitated from seawater, they must therefore have been transported from some other location. Any water current fast enough to move sand grains would also be able to move lime mud. Thus, these quartz sand grains are convincing evidence that the Kaibab Limestone and Supai Group limestones accumulated by deposition of sediments transported by moving water, and not simply by slow, steady, gravity settling of lime muds on the floors of calm and placid seas.

Thus, the evidence in the Grand Canyon limestones overwhelmingly points to the lime sediments of which they are composed having been deposited after rapid transport, and this implies that the limestones were derived from pre-existing sediments elsewhere. Rapid transportation would explain the broken fossil fragments that compose an important part of these limestones. Nevertheless, some of the lime muds were derived simply by precipitation of calcium carbonate from seawater, which explains some of the very fine micrite particles.

65

THE WIDESPREAD, RAPIDLY WATER-DEPOSITED, PALEOZOIC STRATA OF THE GRAND CANYON, ARIZONA—SANDSTONES

If the sedimentary strata of the Grand Canyon were deposited by advancing and retreating seas through millions of years, as is claimed by the conventional geologic community, then clay-rich mud and quartz sand would have been deposited in these oceans by rivers. As rivers enter the ocean they typically form deltas, triangular-shaped (map view) sediment deposits that thin abruptly and become finer grained under the sea in the direction of deeper water. The clay, silt, and sand so deposited when buried and cemented would form strata of shale, siltstone, and sandstone, with distinctive geometry. The sediments deposited in a delta would be wedge-shaped in cross-section, and individual sandstone beds would represent either the distributary channels of the river on the delta or the sand bars at the front of the delta where the sand is deposited where the river enters the ocean.

If Grand Canyon sandstones had accumulated in river deltas, there ought to be evidence of these deltas, where "marine limestones" are interlayered with "terrestrial sandstones." In Grand Canyon, the most obvious candidate would be the Supai Group, repeating layers of sandstone, siltstone, shale, and limestone. Furthermore, these strata contain fossils of both marine and terrestrial animals, as might be expected in the sediments of ancient river deltas.[1] However, although the river-delta model for accumulation of the Supai Group strata has long been considered by the conventional geologic community, most geologists remain skeptical. McKee, who has published the most data relevant to the Supai Group, wrote an entire paper on these strata without using the word "delta."[2] Another geologist who has also extensively studied these strata has questioned the delta model:

Numerous previous workers have loosely assigned Supai deposition to a deltaic

---

1   W. J. Breed, V. Stefanic and G. H. Billingsley, 1986, *Geologic Guide to the Bright Angel Trail*, Grand Canyon, Arizona, American Association of Petroleum Geologists, Tulsa, Oklahoma, 20.

2   E. D. McKee, 1979, Characteristics of the Supai Group in Grand Canyon, Arizona, in *Carboniferous Stratigraphy in the Grand Canyon Country, Northern Arizona and Southern Nevada*, ed. S.S. Beus and R.R. Rawson, Falls Church, VA: American Geological Institute, 105-113.

environment. Both stratigraphic and sedimentological data gathered in this study contradict these earlier findings. Vertical sequences typical of deltaic environments are not abundant and paleogeography and basin analysis do not support major deltaic episodes of deposition....The sand was probably distributed, deposited, and reworked by shallow marine currents.[3]

The exceptionally extensive nature of the individual sandstone layers is perhaps the most obvious problem with the delta model.[4] In fact, the sandstone units within the Supai Group are remarkably thin, and some extend the whole length of the Grand Canyon. These units are not wedge-shaped, as are sand layers in modern deltas. Furthermore, channels that might represent rivers or distributary channels of river systems are unknown.

The failure of the delta model for the Supai Group sandstones has only heightened the prevailing controversy over their formation. An alternative depositional model is that these sandstones represent shallow marine sand deposits,[5] perhaps moved by intense tides, storms, or floods. Another suggestion is accumulation as terrestrial sand dunes in a desert.[6] Thus, no consensus has been reached, even within the conventional geologic community, about the deposition of these sandstone strata, though there is considerable doubt about river accumulation and the delta model. Instead, the controversy that rages is whether the Grand Canyon sandstones were deposited by water or by wind.

Within many of the large-scale horizontal sandstone beds are distinctly inclined cross-beds, most obvious in the Coconino Sandstone (Figure 41, page 1080), but also a dominant property of Supai Group sandstones. For many years these cross-beds have been compared with sand dunes in modern deserts, which are dominated by quartz sand and have inclined internal sand beds. It has been proposed that the Coconino Sandstone, for example, accumulated in an immense windy desert as a result of migrating sand dunes. The cross-beds supposedly accumulated over many thousands of years on the down-wind side of dunes as sand was deposited there. A large number of fossilized footprints, usually in sequences called trackways, are also found in the Coconino Sandstone, and these appear to have been made by four-footed vertebrates moving across the original inclined sand surfaces. Because these fossil-footprint trackways seem similar to the tracks made by reptiles on

3   R. C. Blakey, 1979, Stratigraphy of the Supai Group (Pennsylvania-Permian), Mogollon Rim, Arizona, in *Carboniferous Stratigraphy in the Grand Canyon Country, Northern Arizona and Southern Nevada*, ed. S.S. Beus and R.R. Rawson, Falls Church, VA: American Geological Institute, 102-108.

4   E. D. McKee, 1982, *The Supai Group of Grand Canyon*, US Geological Survey Professional Paper 1173: 1-504.

5   McKee, 1982.

6   R. C. Blakey, 1990, Supai Group and Hermit Formation, in *Grand Canyon Geology*, ed. S.S. Beus and M. Morales, New York: Oxford University Press, and Flagstaff: Museum of Northern Arizona Press, 167-168.

desert sand dunes,[7] it has been assumed that these fossilized footprints in the Coconino Sandstone must have been made in dry desert sands, which were then covered up by wind-blown sand and subsequently cemented. Additionally, the sand grains from modern desert dunes studied under a microscope often show pitted or frosted surfaces, so when similar grain-surface textures were observed in the very thick cross-bedded Coconino Sandstone, it strengthened the argument that the Coconino Sandstone was originally deposited slowly as dunes in a dry desert.

Above the Coconino Sandstone is the Toroweap Formation and below is the Hermit Formation (Figure 41), both of which consist of sediments that were clearly deposited in water.[8] How then could there have been a period of dry, desert conditions depositing the Coconino Sandstone between these water-deposited sediment layers, particularly if all these Grand Canyon strata were deposited during the Genesis Flood? This seeming problem is recognized by certain Christian geologists in the conventional geologic community who argue against the Flood depositing the Coconino Sandstone, and who instead argue for the desert dune interpretation:

> The Coconino Sandstone contains spectacular cross bedding, vertebrate track fossils, and pitted and frosted sand grain surfaces. All these features are consistent with the formation of the Coconino as desert sand dunes. The sandstone is composed almost entirely of quartz grains, and pure quartz sand does not form in floods…no flood of any size could have produced such deposits of sand.[9]

However, the fossilized footprint trackways in the Coconino Sandstone have been re-examined in the light of experimental studies.[10] Observations and measurements were performed on 236 trackways made by living amphibians and reptiles in experimental chambers. These tracks were formed on sand beneath water, on moist sand at the water's edge, and on dry sand. The sand surface was mostly sloping at an angle of 25°, although some observations were made on slopes of 15° and 20°, for comparison. Observations also were made of the underwater locomotion of five species of salamanders (amphibians) both in the laboratory and in their natural habitat, and measurements were again taken of their trackways.

7   E. D. McKee, 1947, Experiments on the development of tracks in fine cross-bedded sand, *Journal of Sedimentary Petrology*, 17: 23-28.

8   Blakey, 1990, 176-178; C. E. Turner, 1990, Toroweap Formation, in *Grand Canyon Geology*, ed. S.S. Beus and M. Morales, New York: Oxford University Press, and Flagstaff: Museum of Northern Arizona Press, 203-223.

9   D. A. Young, 1990, The Discovery of Terrestrial History, in H.J. Van Till et al, *Portraits of Creation*, Grand Rapids, MI: William B. Eerdmans, 72-73.

10 L. R. Brand, 1979, Field and laboratory studies on the Coconino Sandstone (Permian) vertebrate footprints and their paleoecological implications, *Palaeogeography, Palaeoclimatology, Palaeoecology*, 28: 25-38.

Careful surveying and detailed measurements of 82 fossilized vertebrate trackways in the Coconino Sandstone were then made. A detailed statistical analysis of all these data led to the conclusion, with a high degree of probability, that the fossil footprints in the Coconino Sandstone must have been made underwater.

Furthermore, whereas the animals had produced footprints under all experimental conditions, both up and down the 25° slopes of the laboratory "dunes," all but one of the fossil trackways could have been only made by the animals in question climbing "uphill" underwater. Indeed, whereas fossilized footprints have generally distinct toe imprints, the dry-sand, uphill tracks made in the animal experiments were usually just depressions, with no details. Of added interest were the observations that living salamanders all spent the majority of their locomotion time by walking on the bottom, underwater, rather than by swimming.

When all these observations were put together, the overwhelming conclusion was that the configurations and characteristics of the animals' trackways made on the underwater sand surfaces most closely resembled the fossilized quadruped trackways in the Coconino Sandstone. Furthermore, the fossilized trackways are best understood as suggesting that the animals were entirely underwater (not swimming at the surface) and moving upslope (against the current), in an attempt to get out of the water. This evidence is thus consistent with water deposition of the Coconino Sandstone during the Flood, under conditions of water flow which overwhelmed even four-footed reptiles and amphibians that normally spend most of their time in water.

These initial studies were pursued with further research,[11] the results of which were so significant that brief reports of them were subsequently published elsewhere.[12] Careful analysis of even more fossilized trackways in the Coconino Sandstone again revealed that all but one had been made by animals moving up cross-bed slopes. Furthermore, these additional tracks often showed that the line of the trackway was in one direction, while the animals' feet and toes were pointing in a different direction, indicating that the animals had been walking in a current of water, not air. Other trackways started and stopped abruptly, with no sign that the animals' missing tracks were covered by some disturbance such as shifting sediments, consistent with these animals having simply swum away from the sediment.

Because many of the tracks have characteristics that are virtually impossible to explain unless the animals were moving underwater, it was suggested that newt-like animals made the tracks while walking underwater and being pushed by a current. To test these ideas, living newts were videotaped while walking through

11 L. R. Brand and T. Tang, 1991, Fossil vertebrate footprints in the Coconino Sandstone (Permian) of northern Arizona: evidence for underwater origin, *Geology*, 19:1201-1204.

12 R. Monastersky, 1992, Wading newts may explain enigmatic tracks, Science News, 141: 5; Anonymous, 1992, Wet tracks, *Geology Today*, 8: 78-79.

a laboratory tank with running water. All 238 trackways made by the newts had features similar to the fossilized trackways in the Coconino Sandstone, and their videotaped behavior, while making the trackways, thus indicated how the animals that made the fossilized trackways might have been moving. These additional studies confirmed the conclusions of the earlier research. Thus, it was concluded that all data suggest the fossil tracks are not evidence of desert-wind deposition of dry sand to form the Coconino Sandstone, but instead are conclusive evidence for underwater deposition.

The desert sand-dune model for the origin of the Coconino Sandstone has been challenged also by the observations that large storms, or amplified tides, today produce submarine sand dunes called "sand waves."[13] These modern sand waves on the sea floor contain large cross-beds composed of sand with very high quartz purity. The Coconino Sandstone has thus been interpreted as a submarine sand-wave deposit accumulated by water, not wind. Furthermore, the average angle of slope of the Coconino cross-beds is about 25° from the horizontal, less than the average angle of slope of sand beds on the down-wind side of most modern-desert sand dunes. Those sand beds usually slope at an angle of more than 25°, with some beds inclined as much as 30-34°—the angle of rest of dry sand. Thus, the lower average angle of the Coconino Sandstone cross-beds matches those of modern oceanic sand waves.

Other positive evidence for accumulation of the Coconino Sandstone in water is the feature within it known as "parting lineation," which is commonly formed on sand surfaces during brief erosional bursts beneath fast-flowing water.[14] In fact, parting lineation is not known from any desert sand dunes. Thus, this feature is evidence of vigorous water currents having accumulated the sand that now forms the Coconino Sandstone. Furthermore, the different grain sizes of sand within the sandstone are a reflection of the process that deposited the sand. Thus, when sand grain-size analyses of the Coconino Sandstone, desert sand dunes, and modern sand waves were performed, it was found that the Coconino Sandstone does not compare favorably to dune sands from modern deserts.[15] Instead, the bimodal character of the grain-size distribution in the Coconino Sandstone resembles the sand accumulated underwater as sand waves.

The pitting and frosting of sand grains, claimed to prove wind deposition, has also been investigated further. It now has been found that not only is the pitting

13   G. S. Visher, 1990, *Exploration Stratigraphy,* second edition, Tulsa, OK: Penn Well Publishing Co., 211-213.

14   J. R. L. Allen, 1984, *Sedimentary Structures: Their Character and Physical Basis,* second ed., New York: Elsevier Science Publishers, 259-266.

15   Visher, 1990, 213; W. E. Freeman and G. S. Visher, 1975, Stratigraphic analysis of the Navajo Sandstone, *Journal of Sedimentary Petrology,* 45: 651-668; G. S. Visher and J. D. Howard, 1974, Dynamic relationship between hydraulics and sedimentation in the Altamaha estuary, *Journal of Sedimentary Petrology,* 44: 502-521.

not diagnostic of the last process to have deposited the sand grains (pitting can, for example, form first by wind impacts, followed by redeposition by water), but pitting and frosting of sand grains can form outside a desert environment.[16] For example, it has been described how pitting on the surface of sand grains can form by chemical processes during the cementation of sand.

There is now considerable evidence that most of the Grand Canyon sandstones were deposited by the ocean. The Tapeats Sandstone, the Supai Group sandstones, the Toroweap sandstones, the sandstones within the Kaibab Limestone, and the Coconino Sandstone are all characterized by cross-bedding that was produced by transport and deposition of the sand in dune-like sand waves by ocean currents.[17] The water current moves over the sand surface, mounding up the sand into the dune-like sand waves (Figure 42, page 1080).[18] The current erodes sand from the back of the sand wave, and deposits it in the zone of reverse flow as the inclined layers of the cross-beds on the front of the sand waves. The current moves the sand waves forward, eroding sand from the backs and tops of the sand waves as the inclined layers continue to be deposited. Only the fronts of the sand waves are usually preserved as the cross-beds, and usually just the lower half of the original dune fronts. Thus, the heights of the cross-beds preserved are just a fraction of the original sand-wave heights. If the current and sediment supply continue, a second series of sand waves migrating over the area of sand already deposited produces a second layer of sand containing another set of cross-beds.

Sand waves have been observed forming under laboratory conditions in large flumes, and also on certain parts of the ocean floor and in rivers. Experimentally-produced sand waves have been used to demonstrate that sand-wave wave height is related to water depth.[19] As the water depth increases, so does the height of the sand wave which is produced. The empirically-derived relationship between sand-wave height and water depth is shown graphically in Figure 43 (page 1081), on the left side.[20] Sand-wave height is thus approximately one-fifth of the water depth. These laboratory studies have also helped delimit the hydrodynamic conditions under which sand waves and cross-beds form. As a water current flowing over sand reaches a critical velocity, small ripples form. As the water velocity increases, the ripples grow larger and become sand waves that form cross-beds. Observations of sand waves in San Francisco Bay have also been related to the sand waves made in flumes.[21] In Figure 43 the graph on the right side shows the stable bedforms

---

16   P. H. Kuenen and W. G. Perdok, 1962, Experimental abrasion—frosting and defrosting of quartz grains, *Journal of Geology*, 70: 648-658.

17   For a summary on sand waves, see C. L. Amos and E. L. King, 1984, Bedforms of the Canadian eastern seaboard: a comparison with global occurrences, *Marine Geology*, 57: 167-208.

18   Austin, 1994, 33, Figure 3.11.

19   J. R. L. Allen, 1970, Physical Processes of Sedimentation, London: George Allen and Unwin Ltd, 76-80.

20   Austin, 1994, 34, Figure 3.12.

21   D. M. Rubin and D. S. McCulloch, 1980, Single and superimposed bedforms: a synthesis of San

produced in fine sand at various water depths and water velocities. Cross-beds form within the stability field of sand waves.

Very thick cross-bed sets have been found in the fine-grained sandstone strata of Grand Canyon. Cross-beds sets in Supai sandstones are up to five meters thick,[22] while the quartz sandstone at the base of the Kaibab Limestone has individual cross-beds up to six meters thick.[23] Among the thickest sets of cross-beds are those in the Coconino Sandstone, where a thickness of nine meters has been reported.[24] Even coarse-grained lime sediments contain thick cross-bedding, the most extraordinary examples being in the Redwall Limestone, where nine-meter-thick cross-beds have been described.[25] These great thicknesses of individual cross-beds imply enormous heights of sand waves. Because erosion removed the sand from the tops of the sand waves during deposition, the true height of the sand waves could have been double the present cross-bed thickness. Thus, in the case of the sand waves that formed the cross-beds in the Supai and Kaibab sandstones, the sand-wave heights could have been ten meters, while those that deposited the Coconino Sandstone could easily have been eighteen meters high.

Using the sand-wave heights for the cross-beds in the Supai and Kaibab sandstones, the current velocity that deposited the sand in them can be estimated. For the sand-wave height of ten meters the water depth on the curve in Figure 43 (left side) is 54 meters. Then in Figure 43 (right side) the stability field of sand waves at a water depth of 54 meters is bounded by minimum and maximum water current velocities of 90 centimeters per second and 155 centimeters per second respectively. Thus, cross-beds five meters high were produced from sand waves ten meters high, which would require a water depth of 54 meters and a current velocity between 90 and 155 centimeters per second. Similarly, the nine-meter-thick cross-beds in the Coconino Sandstone were produced by sand waves eighteen meters high, in a water depth of between 90 and 95 meters by a water current velocity between 95 and 165 centimeters per second.[26]

The large-scale cross-beds in Grand Canyon sandstones thus indicate that high

---

Francisco Bay and flume observations, *Sedimentary Geology*, 26: 207-231. For a survey of flume studies of bed configuration, see J. B. Southard and L. A. Boguchwal, 1990, Bed configuration in steady unidirectional water flows. Part 2. Synthesis of flume data, *Journal of Sedimentary Petrology*, 60: 658-679.

22   McKee, 1979, 110, 112.

23   J. W. Brown, 1969, Stratigraphy and petrology of the Kaibab Formation between Desert View and Cameron, Northern Arizona, in *Geology and Natural History of the Grand Canyon Region, Four Corners Geological Society Guidebook*, Fifth field conference, 172.

24   S. S. Beus, 1979, Trail log—third day: South Kaibab trail, Grand Canyon, Arizona, in Carboniferous Stratigraphy in the Grand Canyon Country, Northern Arizona and Southern Nevada, ed. S. S. Beus and R. R. Rawson, Falls Church, VA: American Geological Institute, 16.

25   McKee and Gutschick, 1969, 111.

26   A. A. Snelling and S. A. Austin, 1992, Startling evidence for Noah's Flood! Footprints and sand "dunes" in a Grand Canyon sandstone, *Creation Ex Nihilo*, 15 (1): 46-51.

velocity water currents deposited them as enormous sand waves. Sustained, unidirectional currents of 90 to 155 centimeters per second occurred in deep water. Modern tides and normal ocean currents do not have these velocities in the open ocean, but deep-sea currents have been reported to attain velocities of 150 centimeters per second in the Norwegian Sea, more than 100 centimeters per second out of the Mediterranean Sea, and more than 50 centimeters per second out of the Red Sea.[27] On the bottom of San Francisco Bay at the Golden Gate, currents have been measured at over 250 centimeters per second.[28] However, these high velocities are caused by the flow of tides through restrictions of the ocean within straits, whereas the Grand Canyon strata provide no evidence of having been deposited where there were geographic restrictions. On the other hand, catastrophic events can also produce high-velocity ocean currents. For example, hurricanes are thought to make small sand waves, but hurricane-driven currents approaching 100 centimeters per second in water over 50 meters deep have not been measured. The most severe ocean currents known are generated during a tsunami ("tidal wave"). In shallow oceans, tsunami-induced currents can exceed 500 centimeters per second, and unidirectional currents have been sustained for hours.[29] Such an event would move large quantities of sand, and in its waning stages build huge sand waves in deep water. Thus, tsunamis could have formed the large-scale cross-beds in Grand Canyon sandstones.

From what source was the sand transported to be deposited as these Grand Canyon sandstones? As the quartz and feldspar grains that constitute most of the Grand Canyon sandstones could not have been precipitated from water, these grains had to be derived either by erosion of crystalline basement rocks such as granite, gneiss, or schist, or by reworking of earlier sandstones and sand deposits. The grains in the Tapeats Sandstone were derived from both sources. This sandstone rests directly, with an erosional contact, on both crystalline basement and beveled sandstones, and at its base in some places it contains boulders up to three and five meters in diameter that have been eroded and moved 500 meters from their source in the strata beneath.[30] Thus, this erosion and these boulders are evidence of catastrophic underwater debris flows.

The cross-beds in the Supai Group sandstones dip southeast, indicating that the current that moved the sand flowed southeast.[31] However, there is no acceptable source of quartz sand grains for these Supai strata to the northwest of Grand Canyon. Everywhere north and west, the Supai Group overlies the Redwall

---

27   P. Lonsdale and B. Malfait, 1974, Abyssal dunes of foraminiferal sand on the Carnegie Ridge, *Geological Society of America Bulletin*, 85: 1697-1712.

28   Rubin and McCulloch, 1980, 207.

29   P. J. Coleman, 1978, Tsunami sedimentation in *The Encyclopedia of Sedimentology*, R. W. Fairbridge and J. Bourgeois, ed., Stroudsburg, PA: Dowden, Hutchison and Ross, 828-831.

30   A. V. Chadwick, 1978, Megabreccias: evidence for catastrophism, *Origins*, 5: 39-46.

31   McKee, 1982, 218-242.

Limestone, which is an extraordinarily pure carbonate with extremely rare sand grains. Furthermore, the Supai sandstones laterally change northwestward, grading into limestone.[32] Therefore, there is no nearby source for quartz sand for the Supai Group sandstones to the west or north of the Canyon. This sand-source problem is recognized:

> Full interpretation of the Supai-Hermit sequence is thwarted by some puzzles. For example, throughout the Grand Canyon region the typically aqueous cross-bedding in the Supai consistently dips toward the south and southeast, indicating that this was the general direction of the depositing currents. Yet, it is difficult to find an adequate northern or northwestern source for such quantities of sand and mud; those that lie in the right direction seem either to have been underwater or composed predominantly of limestone at the appropriate time. [33]

This evidence clearly indicates that the Supai sand grains were transported a great distance by ocean currents, and not by a river. Northern Utah, and even Wyoming, have been postulated as the nearest sources for the Supai sand.[34] However, there is no evidence of a great, ancient river system that eroded and transported the Supai sand grains from Wyoming. Instead, the limestone deposits of an ocean are directly on the path from Wyoming to the Grand Canyon.

The Coconino Sandstone is part of a vast blanket of sandstone extending eastward from Arizona into New Mexico, Colorado, Kansas, Oklahoma, and Texas (Figure 44, page 1082).[35] The area covered by the Coconino and its correlating sandstones is about 520,000 square kilometers, and the sand volume in the sandstones is estimated at about 42,000 cubic kilometers. The cross-beds within the Coconino Sandstone (and the Glorieta Sandstone of New Mexico and Texas) dip toward the south, indicating that the sand came from the north. However, along its northern occurrence the Coconino rests directly on the Hermit Formation, which consists of silt and mud. Thus, it would not be an ample erosional source of sand grains for the Coconino. Therefore, the source of this colossal quantity of sand must be further northward beyond the underlying Hermit Formation and its lateral equivalent in southern Utah. Thus, there is no obvious, nearby source for the Coconino sand grains, and again, this means a very distant source must be postulated.

---

32   McKee, 1982, 335-359.

33   J. S. Shelton, 1966, *Geology Illustrated*, San Francisco, CA: W.H. Freeman, 280.

34   Blakey, 1979, 102.

35   R. C. Blakey and R. Knepp, 1989, Pennsylvanian and Permian geology of Arizona, in *Geologic Evolution of Arizona*, ed. J. Jennie and S. J. Reynolds, Arizona Geological Society Digest, 17: 313-347; D. L. Baars, 1962, Permian system of Colorado Plateau, *American Association of Petroleum Geologists Bulletin* 46: 200-201; J. M. Hills and F. E. Kottlowski, 1983, Correlation of Stratigraphic Units of North America—Southwest/Southwest Mid-continent Region, American Association of Petroleum Geologists, Tulsa, Oklahoma.

In conclusion, the combined evidence indicates that the colossal quantities of sand grains in Grand Canyon sandstones had to be transported and deposited by tsunami-generated ocean currents, which had to also erode and transport the sand over great distances from distant source areas. It is also abundantly obvious that uniformitarian models of desert dunes or river erosion, transport, and sedimentation are woefully inadequate as explanations for these sandstone strata. Instead, abundant evidence for catastrophic, inter-regional erosion, transport, and sedimentation is far more consistent with the biblical description of the Flood and its geological implications.

66

THE WIDESPREAD, RAPIDLY WATER-DEPOSITED, PALEOZOIC STRATA OF THE GRAND CANYON, ARIZONA—SHALES

Rather than always being rich in lime (calcium carbonate), many muds are dominated by microscopic particles of clay minerals. Rivers carry enormous amounts of clay, much of which comes from weathered materials on the continents. Indeed, clay-rich muds are distinctive of continents and shale is generally assumed to be their sedimentary-rock counterpart. The conventional geologic community favors the delta model for deposition of clay-rich shale, especially if the shale contains fossils of terrestrial plants and animals. However, the delta model for the deposition of Grand Canyon shales has proven inadequate, because of the tremendously extensive nature of these strata and the absence of the necessary sand-channel systems suggestive of rivers. Nevertheless, the belief persists that the Grand Canyon shales represent very slow accumulation of muds in quiet water. Three main lines of evidence are claimed to indicate very slow deposition of muds to form shales—thin laminae, burrows of organisms, and shrinkage cracks.

Laminae are defined as sedimentary layers less than one centimeter thick. They are frequently abundant in fine-grained, clay-rich rocks such as shales. The conventional geologic community often makes the assumption that great periods of time are required to deposit thinly laminated sediments. Usually, each lamina is regarded as representing a seasonal alternation of sedimentary conditions, a feature known in some modern lake sediments. Thus, a single lamina, or pair of laminae, is supposed to represent the alternation between summer and winter deposition over a one-year period. The boundary between successive laminae is claimed to represent a break in sedimentation, perhaps at times caused by a drought. Thousands of laminae, stacked one on top of each other as they are in many shales, are thus supposed to represent thousands or even millions of years of slow accumulation. Furthermore, the conventional geologic community maintains that catastrophic sedimentary action would homogenize fine clay-rich sediments, and thus would deposit massive, non-laminated strata.

The thinly laminated sediments of the Green River Formation of Colorado, Utah, and Wyoming are usually regarded as a classical example of thin laminae that represent yearly alternations in sedimentation (called varves):

> There are more than a million vertically superimposed varve pairs in some parts of the Green River Formation. These varve deposits are almost certainly fossil lake-bottom sediments. If so, each pair of sediment layers represents an annual deposit....The total number of varve pairs indicates that the lakes existed for a few million years.[1]

This slow-and-gradual notion of laminae formation has consequently had a powerful impact on the interpretation of many sedimentary deposits.

However, a large body of experimental and observational data refutes this claim that laminae in shales generally formed slowly.[2] In fact, new evidence demonstrates just the opposite, that fine-grained laminated sediments can, and do, form by rapid sedimentation. Indeed, rapid deposition of laminae has been observed in some modern situations, and laboratory experiments have documented how extremely thin laminae form rapidly.

In 1960, Hurricane Donna created surging ocean waves that flooded inland up to eight kilometers for six hours along the coast of southern Florida.[3] The hurricane deposited a 15-centimeter-thick mud layer, with numerous thin laminae. In Colorado, a storm in June 1965 caused flooding of Bijou Creek, and fine lamination was produced in the resultant sediments.[4] The June 12, 1980, eruption of Mount St Helens produced a hurricane-velocity, surging flow of volcanic ash, which accumulated in less than five hours as a 7.6-meter-thick layer of laminated fine-grained volcanic ash.[5] A Swiss lake, which was thought to accumulate one pair of laminae each year, was shown to accumulate up to five laminae pairs per year by a rapid, turbid-water, underflow process.[6] Indeed, one layer within the Swiss lake that dates from the year 1811 was observed in 1971 (160 years later) to be buried beneath 300 to 360 varve-like silt laminae.

Laboratory experiments have also enabled researchers to observe this process. Horizontal laminae were produced in fine-grained sediment by a high-velocity

---

1   Young, 1990, 77.

2   For a summary of the literature, see S. A. Austin, 1984, *Catastrophes in Earth History*, El Cajon, CA: Institute for Creation Research.

3   Ball, Shinn and Stockman, 1967.

4   E. D. McKee, E. J. Crosby and H. L. Berryhil, Jr, 1967, Flood deposits, Bijou Creek Colorado, June 1965, *Journal of Sedimentary Petrology*, 37: 829-851.

5   S. A. Austin, 1986, Mount St Helens and Catastrophism, in *Proceedings of the First International Conference on Creationism*, vol. 1, Pittsburgh, PA: Creation Science Fellowship, 3-9.

6   A. Lambert and K. Hsu, 1979, Non-annual cycles of varve-like sedimentation in Walensee, Switzerland, *Sedimentology*, 26: 453-461.

current in a circular flume.[7] The high-velocity currents had sorted and deposited the sediment grains by weight, density, and shape. The grain segregation occurs as a turbidity current loses velocity, producing a succession of thin, parallel laminae. However, laboratory experiments have also shown that a current is not needed to form laminae. Both in water and air, rapidly deposited homogenized, heterogranular clay and silt is deposited *en masse*, but separates just after deposition to form very thin laminae.[8] Evidently, the laminae form rapidly just below the sediment-water or sediment-air interface by a grain-penetration process, the coarse silt particles penetrating downward a certain distance through the clay particles until they meet the resistance of more compacted clay. Similar, more recent experiments have confirmed that heterogranular mixtures spontaneously segregate in the absence of external perturbations into alternating laminae of smaller and larger grains, this spontaneous stratification being related to the occurrence of avalanches.[9]

This rapid grain-segregation has also been demonstrated to have potentially been responsible for forming laminae in some ancient rocks.[10] Two laminated sedimentary rocks were carefully disaggregated then rapidly redeposited in a laboratory sedimentation apparatus, where the laminae of the original rocks were reproduced without requiring long periods of time.

The claim that the laminae in shales formed by slow deposition has also been disputed as a result of field research on such rocks. Marine black shales in Scotland were found to intertongue with large boulders.[11] It was suggested that the boulders were moved during a submarine earthquake, and that an enormous tsunami rapidly deposited shallow marine organisms in clay-rich muds on top of the boulders. Similarly, large boulders have also been reported within the Bright Angel Shale of the Grand Canyon, and these would also appear to have required rapid accumulation of the shale. Rapid deposition of laminated shales and mudstones has been documented in Ireland, England, and Canada.[12] It was proposed that the laminae were deposited from high-velocity, dense suspensions of sediment and water that moved over the ocean floor. In Washington state, thin laminae in beds of clay, silt, and sand more than 90 meters thick called the Touchet beds were

7   P. H. Kuenen, 1966, Experimental turbidite lamination in a circular flume, *Journal of Geology*, 74: 523-545.

8   G. Berthault, 1986, Experiments on lamination of sediments resulting from a periodic graded-bedding subsequent to deposition—a contribution to the explanation of lamination of various sediments and sedimentary rocks, *Compte Rendus Académie des Sciences, Paris*, 303: 1569-1574; G. Berthault, 1988, Sedimentation of a heterogranular mixture: experimental lamination in still and running water, *Compte Rendus Académie des Sciences, Paris*, 306: 717-724.

9   H. A. Makse et al, 1997, Spontaneous stratification in granular mixtures, *Nature*, 386: 379-382; J. Fineberg, 1997, From Cinderella's dilemma to rock slides, *Nature*, 386: 323-324.

10   Berthault, 1986.

11   E. B. Bailey and J. Weir, 1932, Submarine faulting in Kimmeridgian times, East Sutherland, *Transactions of the Royal Society of Edinburgh*, 57: 429-454.

12   D. J. W. Piper, 1972, Turbidite origin of some laminated mudstones, *Geological Magazine*, 109: 115-126.

once supposed to have been deposited slowly by gradual water fluctuations in an ancient lake, but were later reinterpreted as slack-water sediments associated with the catastrophic floods that formed the famous Channeled Scabland of eastern Washington.[13]

The Green River Formation in Wyoming is dominated by oil shale containing very thin laminae. The popular opinion is that each pair of laminae represents a varve deposited during a one-year period. These very thick laminated oil shales are claimed to represent slow deposition on a lake bottom over millions of years. However, this varve interpretation fails a crucial test.[14] Near Kemmerer, Wyoming, the Green River Formation contains two tuff beds, each 2 to 3 centimeters thick, representing the synchronous deposits of two volcanic eruptions. The two tuff beds are separated by 8.3 to 22.6 centimeters of laminated oil shale. According to the varve interpretation, the number of years between the two tuff beds should be exactly the same over the wide area the tuff beds cover, so the number of varves between the tuff beds should be the same over the entire area. Furthermore, the average thickness and composition of the laminae should be nearly constant over this same wide area. However, the number of laminae counted between the two tuff beds varies from 1,160 to 1,568, with an overall increase of laminae number (up to 35 percent) and laminae thickness, from basin center to basin margin. The kerogen content of the oil shale also decreased from basin center to basin margin. Quite clearly, these observations are inconsistent with the varve model of deposition of the Green River Formation in a stagnant lake:

> The differences in laminae count, laminae thickness, unit thickness, and kerogen content can be accounted for by a model evoking more voluminous sedimentation and more frequent sedimentation "events" nearer the lake margins than center. The "varve" model is not adequate to explain these differences because it would predict the same number of laminae lake-wide as well as consistent unit thickness and kerogen content.[15]

More recent flume experiments have demonstrated that clay particles flocculate in larger "clumps" to be transported and deposited at flow velocities similar to sand.[16] The experimenters found that deposition-prone floccules formed over a wide range of experimental conditions, and floccule ripples developed into low-angle

13   R. J. Carson, C. R. McKhann and M. H. Pizey, 1978, The Touchet beds of Walla Walla Valley, in *The Channeled Scabland*, ed. V. R. Baker and D. Nummedal, Washington, D.C.: National Aeronautics and Space Administration, 173-177.

14   H. Buchheim and R. Biaggi, 1988, Laminae counts within a synchronous oil shale unit: a challenge to the "varve" concept, *Geological Society of America Abstracts with Programs*, 20: A317.

15   Buchheim and Biaggi, 1988.

16   J. Schieber, J. Southard, and J. Thaisen, 2007, Accretion of mudstone beds from migrating floccule ripples, *Science*, 318: 1760-1763; J. H. S. Macquacker and K. M. Bohacs, 2007, On the accumulation of mud, *Science*, 318: 1734-1735.

foresets so that the resulting mud beds appeared laminated after postdepositional compaction. It was concluded that laminated mudstones (and shales) can therefore be deposited under far more energetic conditions than conventionally assumed. Furthermore, since mudstones make up the majority of the sedimentary record (about two-thirds), a total reappraisal is required of the rate at which many sedimentary strata sequences accumulated.

Burrows are the tubes left by organisms that live within sediments. Many terrestrial and marine organisms occupy burrows and leave obvious evidence of their activity by disrupting layering, especially lamination in clay-rich muds. Modern marine and terrestrial organisms are "biological bulldozers," so thoroughly reworking and burrowing recent sediments that stratification is often completely homogenized. For example, the distinctive five-centimeter-thick, graded sand, silt, and mud layer deposited offshore of the central Texas coast by Hurricane Carla in 1961 had been so thoroughly burrowed by marine organisms that 20 years later it was unrecognizable.[17]

Therefore, if the burrowing in sediments on land and under the sea is so intense, how could any laminae be preserved in the strata record if sediments accumulated very slowly and were in contact with burrowing organisms for so long? It has been proposed that the deep-burrowing activity of organisms had not yet evolved when most Grand Canyon strata were deposited.[18] However, this view has been strongly challenged by deep-burrow structures found even in Cambrian strata.[19] On the other hand, the reason why major laminae have not been severely burrowed may be because the thick sequences of strata were deposited rapidly, not slowly. The sediments would only have been in contact with burrowing organisms for very short periods of time, ensuring the probability of burrowing was low.

While the evidences of rapid sedimentation in the Bright Angel Shale (Cambrian) of Grand Canyon are obvious, it is still claimed that some horizons where trackways and burrows occur represent long time periods.[20] Of course, burrows and trackways are regarded as features produced by normal life activities of organisms, with some burrows representing feeding, and others representing resting. Thus, burrows and trackways might indicate cessation of sedimentation, which is not consistent with a single flood forming great thicknesses of strata.

---

17   R. H. Dott, Jr., 1983, Episodic sedimentation—How normal is average? How rare is rare? Does it matter?, *Journal of Sedimentary Petrology*, 53: 12.

18   C. W. Thayer, 1979, Biological bulldozers and the evolution of marine benthonic communities, *Science*, 203: 458-461.

19   M. F. Miller and C. W. Byers, 1984, Abundant and diverse early Paleozoic infauna indicated by the stratigraphical record, *Geology*, 12: 40-43; M. Sheehan and D. R. J. Schiefelbein, 1984, The trace fossil *Thalassinodes* from the Upper Ordovician of the Eastern Great Basin: deep burrowing in the early Paleozoics, *Journal of Paleontology*, 58: 440-447.

20   D. K. Elliott and D. L. Martin, 1987, A new trace fossil from the Cambrian Bright Angel Shale, Grand Canyon, Arizona, *Journal of Paleontology*, 61: 641-648.

However, trackways of trilobites on bedding surfaces in the Bright Angel Shale did not necessarily require long periods of time to form. Modern marine arthropods move rapidly across sediment surfaces and form short trackways in seconds. Both horizontally and vertically oriented burrows are in the Bright Angel Shale. Each of the three types of horizontal burrows (*Palaeophycus, Phycodes,* and *Teichichnus*) observed in the Bright Angel Shale are formed by marine organisms burrowing while entirely buried within the sediment. Thus, because these horizontal burrows had no connection with the overlying water column, the organisms that produced them did not require cessation of sedimentation, and their activity would not have been restricted by the overlying sedimentation, whether slow or fast.

On the other hand, the two types of vertically oriented burrows (*Dipolocraterion* and *Skolithos*) observed in the Bright Angel Shale have direct bearing on the rate of sedimentation question, because they connected vertically to the water column that overlaid the sediments. If these vertical burrows were the dwellings of the organisms, then they represent occupation levels upon which these marine burrowers lived and died. This would suggest long time periods elapsed at each burrowing level, an interpretation favored by the conventional geological community that would cast doubt on the sedimentation being due to catastrophic flooding. However, instead of representing occupation or dwelling-sites of organisms, these vertical burrows may have been excavated by organisms escaping vertically from rapid sediment burial. The modern worm-like organism *Phoronopsis viridis* constructs burrows that closely resemble *Skolithos.*[21] Laboratory experiments show that burial induces an escape response from the organism, which can produce either vertical or horizontal burrows.[22] *Dipolocraterion,* the commonest vertical burrow in the Bright Angel Shale, could have been made also by upward movement of an organism in response to rapid sedimentation. It has been admitted that "... *Dipolocraterion* cannot be dismissed as an escape trace."[23] If vertical burrows in shale are regarded as the traces of animals escaping from sediment that was rapidly burying them, then the long time periods needed for their formation disappears. Instead, they become evidence for rapid burial.

Shrinkage cracks are the third line of evidence claimed to indicate great periods of time within sedimentary layers. Clay-rich muds often shrink when they lose water and form cracks on the bedding surfaces. Many different strata surfaces within the Grand Canyon sedimentary sequence display irregular and polygonal cracks. These are especially abundant within the Hakatai Shale, Supai Group, and Hermit Formation. Interpreted as shrinkage cracks, they resemble those commonly seen in the beds of dry lakes and ponds, or on mud flats on modern deltas. Thus, it has been proposed that these Grand Canyon shales were alternately wet and dry

---

21   Miller and Byers, 1984, 40.

22   T. E. Ronan, Jr, 1975, Structural and paleoecological aspects of a modern marine soft-sediment
       community: an experimental field study, Ph.D. dissertation, University of California, Davis.

23   Miller and Byers, 1984, 41.

during deposition, like a modern delta or mud flat. When the surface was wet, water brought in clay-rich muds. Then, when drying of the mud began, shrinkage of mud occurred and a layer of cracks formed. This repeated wetting and drying formed the different layers of cracks in the Supai Group and Hermit Formation, the desiccation process claimed to require enormous amounts of time.[24] Thus, no single flood could be responsible for depositing these shales:

> Mudcracks commonly develop on tidal flats or the shores of lakes when mud dries out. As the mud dries, it shrinks and cracks into individual plates that curl up with increased drying. Obviously, mudcracks could not have formed during flood conditions, but only afterward. The Supai Group within the Grand Canyon contains numerous layers with abundant mudcracks, as do the Moenkopi, the Chinle, and the Morrison Formations. Each of these formations had to experience several episodes of wetting and extended drying out. They cannot be global flood deposits.[25]

However, a cross-sectional view of the shrinkage cracks in the Hermit Formation reveals that the cracks frequently occur in clay-rich shale where it contacts thinner silty or sandy layers. After the clay-rich layer contracted and cracked, silt or sandy material, which had not shrunk as much, filled in the cracks. The reason why these shrinkage cracks are apparent in the Hermit Formation is that the silty or sandy material that fills in the cracks is of a different color and resistant to erosion. The desiccation hypothesis for these shrinkage cracks requires that each clay-rich layer dried and cracked before the silt or sand layer was deposited on top of it. This requires that the infilling of the cracks was from above, and that the cracks only penetrate downward. However, the Hermit Formation shrinkage cracks are from above and from below. This downward and upward filling of cracks occurs where two clay-rich shale layers have been penetrated by a much thinner sandy layer which lies between them. Thus, logic requires that the lower and upper clay-rich layers shrank and cracked simultaneously. Furthermore, the principle of cross-cutting relationships requires that the thin sandy and upper clay-rich layers were on top of the lower clay-rich layer when the clay-rich layers cracked. Thus, no period of desiccation of the lower clay-rich layer would have been required to shrink and crack it before the sandy layer infilled it. This evidence, therefore, requires that the cracks in the Hermit Formation formed while the clay-rich layers were buried, and not while they were drying at the surface.

It is now widely recognized that shrinkage cracks can form in clay-rich sediments without desiccation.[26] Both modern subaqueous natural environments and

---

24 Wonderly, 1987, 6-10.

25 Young, 1990, 74.

26 W. A. White, 1961, Colloid phenomena in sedimentation of argillaceous rocks, *Journal of Sedimentary Petrology*, 31: 560-570; L. Dangeard et al, 1964, Triggers et structures observes au cours du passement des vases sous l'eau, *Compte Rendus Académie des Sciences, Paris*, 258: 5935-5938; J. F. Burst, 1965.

laboratory experiments have demonstrated that wet, clay-rich sediments commonly develop shrinkage cracks. That evidence documents the process of *syneresis*, a volume reduction that occurs as clay-rich sediments lose water in a subaqueous or subsurface environment. Numerous examples of such shrinkage cracks in shales that have been filled from above and below have been documented.[27] Indeed, the "from-above-and-below" filling is diagnostic of syneresis cracks. They are common in the geologic record and form in a substrata environment without the desiccation process. Such research, experiments, and field observations discount the long-age interpretation of the shrinkage cracks in the Hermit Formation shales. Thus, all claimed evidence for slow-and-gradual deposition of the shales in the Grand Canyon strata sequence has proved incorrect by both experimental and field observations. Instead, these data remain consistent with catastrophic flood deposition of these shales.

Subaqueously formed shrinkage cracks in clay, *Journal of Sedimentary Petrology*, 35: 348-353; P. H. Kuenen, 1965, Value of experiments in geology, *Geologie en Mijnbouw*, 44: 22-36; P. S. Plummer, 1978, The upper Brachina Subgroup: a late Precambrian intertidal deltaic and sandflat sequence in the Flinders Ranges, South Australia, Ph.D. dissertation, University of Adelaide, Adelaide, Australia.

27   P. S. Plummer and V. A. Gostin, 1981, Shrinkage cracks: desiccation or synaeresis?, *Journal of Sedimentary Petrology*, 51: 1147-1156.

67

OTHER EXAMPLES OF WIDESPREAD, RAPIDLY WATER-DEPOSITED STRATA

The detailed discussion of the Grand Canyon strata demonstrates in a conclusive manner that the evidence associated with these limestone, sandstone, and shale strata strongly favors their catastrophic deposition by water on a grand scale over a widespread area, contrary to the oft-repeated claims that these strata were deposited during long ages of slow-and-gradual deposition. Indeed, for such rapid sedimentation to have occurred on a widespread scale, the evidence points to the ocean having been over the continent, the sediments being transported very long distances after erosion in great quantities from source areas. The sum total of evidence in these strata is thus very compelling for their flood deposition. However, it also needs to be recognized that many of these same features found in these strata that are consistent with catastrophic flood deposition are also found in similar and other types of strata in many other parts of the world. Thus, it is important to describe other examples of widespread, rapidly water-deposited strata of other rock types from other parts of the world.

The Shinarump Conglomerate, Utah

The Shinarump Conglomerate has an average thickness of about 15 meters and covers more than 260,000 square kilometers in Utah and neighboring states. This formation is composed of sand and rounded pebbles, like those often found in many stream beds. Indeed, this conglomerate looks very much like a river deposit. The usual interpretation is that a network of braided streams flowed over this vast area, slowly and gradually depositing pebbles and sand over a long period of time. Of course, the stream beds of a braided system frequently change as the stream changes course, so it is argued that as these streams migrated they gradually covered this entire vast area with stream deposits.[1]

However, the Shinarump Conglomerate does not match any modern depositional environment, and especially does not compare to the modern analog of a braided

---

1   R. F. Dubiel, 1994, Triassic deposystems, Paleogeography and Paleoclimate of the western interior, in *Mesozoic Systems of the Rocky Mountain Region, USA*, M. V. Caputo, J. A. Peterson and K. J. Franczyk, ed., Denver, CO:Rocky Mountain Section, Society for Sedimentary Geology, 133-168.

stream system. Specifically, where is there any place in the world today where streams are depositing sand and conglomerate of such massive uniform thickness like this over such a vast area of 260,000 square kilometers, or even close to that? There is simply not one known. Streams make deposits that meander through a valley, but they don't create uniform deposits over tens of thousands of square kilometers. Thus, it is far more realistic to explain this conglomerate formation as deposited by a massive sheet of rapidly flowing water *en masse*, in what therefore had to be a catastrophic event over such a vast area in a very short time. Such conditions are totally consistent with Flood deposition.

The Uluru Arkose and Mt. Currie Conglomerate, Central Australia

Technically known as an inselberg, Uluru is an isolated rock-mass or monolith that rises steeply on all sides to a height of about 340 meters above the surrounding desert plain of central Australia. It is, in effect, an enormous outcrop of beds of arkose, a coarse sandstone consisting of poorly sorted, jagged grains of other rock types, and feldspar. The arkose occurs in multiple layers that together form a cohesive massive rock unit, and these beds dip at 80-85°. The cumulative thickness of the arkose through the entire length of Uluru is at least 2.5 kilometers, but from drilling below the surrounding desert sands, the total thickness of this arkose has been determined at almost 6,000 meters. Its full lateral extent is poorly known, due to paucity of other outcrops, but the Uluru Arkose is very conservatively estimated at covering an area of at least 30 square kilometers.[2]

Thirty kilometers west of Uluru is Kata Tjuta, a series of huge, rounded, rocky domes, the highest being Mt. Olga about 600 meters above the desert floor. These spectacular domed rock-masses cover an area of about 40 square kilometers (8 km x 5 km), and consist of layers of conglomerate dipping at 10-18° to the southwest, with a total cumulative thickness of 6,000 meters. This massive conglomerate unit, known as the Mt. Currie Conglomerate, extends under the desert sands to other outcrops over an area of more than 600 square kilometers. The conglomerate is poorly sorted and contains boulders up to 1.5 meters in diameter, as well as cobbles and pebbles, held together by a matrix of finer fragments and cemented sand, silt, and/or mud. The pebbles, cobbles, and boulders are generally rounded and consist mainly of granite and basalt, but also some sandstone, rhyolite, and several kinds of metamorphic rocks.

Though the outcrops of the Uluru Arkose and the Mt. Currie Conglomerate are isolated from one another, the available evidence clearly suggests that both rock units were formed at the same time and in the same way. Conventional geologic

---

2   D. J. Forman, 1965, *Ayers Rock, Northern Territory 1:250,000 geological map series plus explanatory notes,* Canberra, Australia: Bureau of Mineral Resources; A. T. Wells et al, 1970, Geology of the Armadeus Basin, Central Australia, *Bureau of Mineral Resources Bulletin 100,* Canberra, Australia; I. Sweet and I. H. Crick, 1992, Uluru and Kata Tjuta: a geological history, *Australian Geological Survey Organisation,* Canberra, Australia.

explanations for these rocks units, which are now regarded as uppermost (or terminal) Neoproterozoic, have changed. They were once regarded as having been deposited by massive glacial action during a claimed "late Precambrian ice age,"[3] but are now believed to be the products of rapid erosion and deposition in alluvial fans adjacent to mountains in an arid landscape. Occasional flash floods are believed to have scoured the mountain ranges and carried the rubble many tens of kilometers out onto the adjoining alluvial flats, where the two separate deposits of arkose and conglomerate are supposed to have progressively accumulated, slowly and gradually, with successive flash floods over many thousands, or perhaps even millions, of years. Of course, the streams had to be very swiftly flowing in order to carry boulders up to 1.5 meters across, and the stream channels needed to be large and form a vast network in order to deposit the conglomerate and arkose over such vast areas.

While large alluvial fans are known on the earth's surface today, none are forming over such vast areas with such massive thicknesses, or with the scale and intensity of the sheet flooding that would have been required to transport such enormous quantities of conglomerate and sand such long distances with a ferocity capable of carrying boulders up to 1.5 meters across. Furthermore, if deposition had been episodic over millions of years, there ought to be evidence of erosion (such as channels) and weathering surfaces between the layers within both the conglomerate and the arkose, while some compositional and fabric variations would be expected between successive layers. However, in the exposures at Uluru and Kata Tjuta, the arkose and conglomerate compositions, respectively, and their fabrics, are uniformly similar throughout the 2.5-kilometer thickness at Uluru and the 1.8-kilometer thickness exposed at Kata Tjuta, and the layering is extremely regular and parallel. In contrast, where there are large alluvial fans on the earth's surface today, deposition on them is only occurring at a greatly reduced rate and scale, and most of the water flow across them in flash floods erodes channels in the earlier deposits.

Furthermore, the ubiquitous fresh feldspar crystals in the Uluru arkose would never have survived the claimed millions of years of deposition, as feldspar deposited in sheets of sand only centimeters thick spread over many tens of square kilometers and exposed to the sun's heat, water, and air over countless years would decompose relatively quickly to clays. Additionally, sand grains that are moved over long distances and periodically swept further and further by water over vast time periods would lose their jagged edges to become smooth and rounded. Moving water would also produce sorting of the sands. Thus, fresh feldspar crystals and jagged, unsorted sand grains are more consistent with the Uluru Arkose having accumulated rapidly.

The implication of all this evidence is that the deposition of the arkose and the

---

3   Holmes, 1965, 737-740.

conglomerate concurrently as lateral equivalents required an amount and force of water sufficient to erode, transport, and deposit at least 4,000 cubic kilometers of boulders, pebbles, cobbles, and sand distances of at least tens of kilometers in successive continuous pulses, so as to stack the resultant layers to a thickness of 6,000 meters over at least 600 square kilometers, all probably in a matter of hours or days at the very most![4] This description is consistent with what we know of turbidity currents and submarine debris flows. However, the scale, intensity, and rapid repetition would not only have required cataclysmic flooding, but repetitive fault movements and earthquakes to trigger the currents and flows responsible for the rapid successive pulses of erosion, transport, and deposition.

Kingston Peak Formation, Southeastern California

Another graphic example of catastrophic deposition is the Kingston Peak Formation in the eastern Mojave Desert of southeastern California. In its type section in the northern Kingston Range, the Kingston Peak Formation is dominated by very coarse clastics, with clasts ranging from pebble size to enormous blocks greater than 1.5 kilometers wide.[5] More than twelve such megaclasts, with their main axes greater than 200 meters long, occur along a 17-kilometer exposed strike length within the Kingston Peak Formation. Each gigantic megaclast often consists of portions of the dolomite units that underlie the Kingston Peak Formation. Two of these megaclasts seem to have been rotated into place, while the other ten megaclasts occur at various levels with bedding concordant to the surrounding Kingston Peak Formation. Directly associated with the large megaclasts are lithology-matching, clast-supported megabreccias. Away from these gigantic megaclasts, the sizes of the clasts in these megabreccias, and their angularity, decreases, matrix/clast ratio increases, and clasts of other lithologies become more common. Several of the largest megaclasts sit directly on top of thick, massive, carbonate-rich, matrix-supported conglomerates, which are sometimes called "pudding stones," but which are often known as *diamictites*. These pudding stones have been interpreted as long-runout, matrix-supported submarine debris flows that carried sedimentary blocks (including the carbonates and many of the largest megaclasts) into a depositional basin. Multiple stratigraphic levels of megaclast emplacement, deformation of the upper part of the underlying rock unit in the basal section of the Kingston Peak Formation, and the breccia facies associations within the formation, all indicate a brief depositional period from the upper portion of the underlying rock unit through the entire Kingston Peak Formation.

The observational data support a catastrophic sedimentary-tectonic model for

---

4   A. A. Snelling, 1984, The origin of Ayers Rocks, *Ex Nihilo*, 7 (1): 6-9; A. A. Snelling, 1998, Uluru and Kata Tjuta: testimony to the Flood, *Creation*, 20 (2): 36-40.

5   K. P. Wise and S. A. Austin, 1999, Gigantic megaclasts within the Kingston Peak Formation (upper Precambrian, Pahrump Group), south-eastern California: evidence for basin margin collapse, *Geological Society of America Abstracts with Programs 31*, A455-A456.

deposition, with gravitational collapse of a basin margin generating mass-flow deposits, turbidites, high-energy currents, and enormous megaclasts. The sandy and limey debris flows that produced the pudding stones are estimated to have moved at a rate of 15-30 meters per second, after being instantly generated by the onset of massive local faulting.[6] A displacement of 950 meters or more in some areas along the giant fault scarp would have changed the gentle slope of the continental shelf depositional environment to a slope approaching 60°. This would have resulted in flows of fluidized rock masses cascading down this slope and flowing across the depositional basin below at 50-100 meters per second. Large-scale slumping would have occurred in deeper areas, as huge megaclasts or slabs hundreds of meters long slid downslope within a succession of high concentration turbidites.

The Kingston Peak Formation has traditionally been interpreted as a tillite, and therefore of glacial origin.[7] However, there is now abundant observational data that is far more consistent with this formation being a submarine landslide deposit, as described above. Paleomagnetic and fossil data, and the presence of carbonates, suggest a low-latitude, warm water, position for this area during deposition of the Kingston Peak Formation, which is an improbable glacial environment.[8] Furthermore, the faceted and striated boulders in the Kingston Peak Formation could have been produced during conditions of catastrophic mass movement, while pillow lavas and ripple marks throughout the formation are unequivocal evidence of subaqueous deposition. Indeed, dish structures, inverse to normal-graded beds, turbidites, flame structures, and convolute lamination all indicate not just subaqueous, but also rapid deposition, consistent with debris flows resulting from a submarine landslide. Thus, the Kingston Peak Formation would be better described as a diamictite.

The Kingston Peak Formation is only one of many upper Precambrian diamictites that are conventionally thought to be glacial deposits. In western North America, the Kingston Peak Formation apparently correlates with other similar formations from Mexico northward through the western United States and Canada up to

6   R. Sigler and V. Wingerden, 1998, Submarine flow and slide deposits in the Kingston Peak Formation, Kingston Range, Mojave Desert, California: evidence for catastrophic initiation of Noah's Flood, in *Proceedings of the Fourth International Conference on Creationism*, R. E. Walsh, ed., Pittsburgh, PA: Creation Science Fellowship, 487-502.

7   J. M. G. Miller, L. A. Wright and B. W. Troxel, 1981, The Late Precambrian Kingston Peak Formation, Death Valley Region, California, in *Earth's Pre-Pleistocene Glacial Record: International Geological Correlation Program Project 38: Pre-Pleisotocene Tillites*, M. J. Hanbrey and W. B. Harland, ed., Cambridge University Press, 745-748; J. M. G. Miller, 1985, Glacial and syntectonic sedimentation: the upper Proterozoic Kingston Peak Formation, southern Panamint Range, eastern California, *Geological Society of America Bulletin*, 96; 1537-1553.

8   S. A. Austin and K. P. Wise, 1994, The pre-Flood/Flood boundary: as defined in Grand Canyon, Arizona and eastern Mojave Desert, California, in *Proceedings of the Third International Conference on Creationism*, R. E. Walsh, ed., Pittsburgh, PA: Creation Science Fellowship, 37-47.

at least Alaska.[9] Upper Proterozoic diamictites have also been recognized in at least 100 other formations located in at least fifteen countries around the globe, including other parts of the United States, southern Australia, and southern Africa.[10] These correlated diamictites that dot the globe are commonly associated with low-latitude indicators, so these deposits may also have not been produced by glaciation.[11]

Essentially coarse conglomerates, diamictites are the product of substantial mechanical erosion and are commonly deposited during tectonic disturbances. The lithological character and gross dimensions of the Kingston Peak Formation and the upper Proterozoic diamictites are comparable to features in modern giant submarine landslide deposits. For example, off Hawaii, blocks of rock up to 10 kilometers long have been transported more than 50 kilometers, and off Norway, where an immense headwall nearly 300 kilometers long defines the source area, the debris is up to 450 meters thick and spread over a distance of 800 kilometers.[12] Thus, these submarine debris flows duplicate most, if not all, the features unique to these diamictites. Consequently, the major diamictites found not only in the upper Proterozoic, but at other levels in the geological record, all around the globe can be interpreted more consistently as having been produced by giant submarine landslides or debris flows.[13] Because the Kingston Peak Formation and all these other upper Proterozoic diamictites it correlates with globally at the same level in the geologic record are best understood as submarine debris flow/ landslide deposits, there must have been a tectonic disturbance of catastrophic global dimensions.

Hawkesbury Sandstone, Sydney Basin, Australia

The Hawkesbury Sandstone dominates the landscape within a 100 km radius of the city center of Sydney. It is a flat-lying layer of sandstone with an areal extent of about 20,000 square km and a maximum thickness of 250 m.[14] Rather

---

9   J. H. Stewart, 1972, Initial deposits in the Cordilleran Geosyncline: evidence of a late Precambrian (<850m.y.) continental separation, *Geological Society of America Bulletin*, 83: 1345-1360.

10 W. B. Harland, 1983, The Proterozoic glacial record, in *Proterozoic Geology: Selected Papers from an International Proterozoic Symposium*, Geological Society of America Memoir, 161: 279-288.

11 L. J. G. Schermerhorn, 1974, Late Precambrian mixtites: glacial and/or nonglacial?, *American Journal of Science*, 274: 673-824.

12 J. G. Moore et al, 1989, Prodigious submarine landslides on the Hawaiian ridge, *Journal of Geophysical Research*, 94: 17,465-17,484; E. G. Nisbet and D. J. W. Piper, 1998, Giant submarine landslides, *Nature*, 392: 329-330.

13 M. J. Oard, 1994, Submarine mass flow deposition of pre-Pleistocene 'Ice Age' deposits, in *Proceedings of the Third International Conference on Creationism*, R. E. Walsh, ed., Pittsburgh, PA: Creation Science Fellowship, 407-418; M. J. Oard, 1997, Ancient ice ages or gigantic submarine landslides?, *Creation Research Society Monograph 6*, Chino Valley, AZ: Creation Research Society Books.

14 P. J. Conaghan, 1980, The Hawkesbury Sandstone: gross characteristics and depositional environment, in *A Guide to the Sydney Basin*, C. Herbert and R. Helby, ed., Geological Survey of New South Wales, Bulletin 26, 188-253.

than consisting of just one sandstone bed encompassing its total thickness, the Hawkesbury Sandstone is made up of three principal rock types—sheet sandstone, massive sandstone, and relatively thin mudstone. Conventionally, this formation is designated as middle Triassic, and has variously been attributed to having been deposited in sedimentary environments ranging from shallow marine and littoral (intertidal) to estuarine, fluvial, and lacustrine, and even aeolian. Based on studies of present-day depositional environments and the depositional features within the Hawkesbury Sandstone, the current favored explanation for deposition of the Hawkesbury Sandstone is deposition by a low-sinuosity river such as the Brahmaputra River in Bangladesh.[15]

However, that view has been challenged, because key depositional features in the Hawkesbury Sandstone do not match those in the Brahmaputra River floodplain. For example, the frequent cross-bedding, generally 2-5 m high, but sometimes up to 8 m high,[16] has foresets dipping at between 20 and 30°, usually averaging about 25°, which contrasts with the maximum dip of 18° recorded for sand-wave cross-beds in the banks of the Brahmaputra River, where even lower average foreset dips of 3-7° are common.[17] Furthermore, the sand waves are distinct, in that they are two-dimensional forms with straight to sinuous crests, with no examples of lunate sand waves having been identified, for example, in the Brahmaputra River floodplain, regardless of channel size or discharge, whereas the sand waves responsible for generating the cross-bedding in the Hawkesbury Sandstone, as evident from the foresets in plan view, were straight-crested and lunate.

Even more significant is the fact that the Hawkesbury Sandstone is composed of well-sorted and rounded, generally fine to medium (massive sandstone) or medium to coarse (sheet sandstone) quartz sand. Rounding and sorting of this type is not known to occur in rivers today, unless derived from a source that is already a rounded and sorted sand.[18] For instance, the detritus of the Mississippi River at its delta end is generally more angular than near its source, after being transported thousands of kilometers down the river. In contrast, the only rounded quartz sands occur on the beaches and barrier bars offshore from the main Mississippi deltas. Indeed, such sediment is well known from studies in modern sediments, and is generally deposited in the barrier bar-tidal delta environment.[19] The sediments

---

15   P. J. Conaghan and J. G. Jones, 1975, The Hawkesbury Sandstone and the Brahmaputra: a depositional model for continental sheet sandstones, *Journal of the Geological Society of Australia*, 22 (3): 275-283; Conaghan, 1980.

16   J. C. Standard, 1969, Hawkesbury Sandstone, in The Geology of New South Wales, G. H. Packham, ed., *Journal of the Geological Society of Australia*, 16 (1): 407-417; B. G. Jones and B. R. Rust, 1983, Massive sandstone facies in the Hawkesbury Sandstone, a Triassic fluvial deposit near Sydney, Australia, *Journal of Sedimentary Petrology*, 53 (4): 1249-1259.

17   G. M. Ashley and I. J. Duncan, 1977, The Hawkesbury Sandstone: a critical review of proposed environmental models, *Journal of the Geological Society of Australia*, 24 (2): 117-119.

18   J. R. Conolly, 1969, Models for Triassic deposition in the Sydney Basin, *Special Publications of the Geological Society of Australia*, 2: 209-223.

19   J. R. L. Allen, 1970, *Physical Processes of Sedimentation*, London: Allen and Unwin.

in such environments are well-sorted and rounded sands, containing little or no siltstone or mudstone supposedly derived from levies, back swamps, lakes, or bank or splay deposits found in normal river delta systems that feed from the land and in braided river systems, even those of low sinuosity such as the Brahmaputra River. Thus, the general lack of silt and clay within the Hawkesbury Sandstone, and the excellent rounding and sorting of the quartz grains, would appear to be more consistent with a barrier bar-tidal delta depositional environment.[20]

The nature of the cross-bedding in the Hawkesbury Sandstone also provides important clues to the mode of deposition of what are enormous thick and wide blankets of very pure quartz sand. Each blanket or cross-bedded unit overrides the underlying unit by advancing of the foresets in a simple deltaic-like fashion. The units are generally trough-shaped in plan view, the troughs being commonly 90-360 m across. These are much larger than those found in point-bar sands in present-day braided river systems, but they are similar to those found in present-day tidal sand sheets behind barrier bars in shallow marine waters. Also characteristic of the Hawkesbury Sandstone are many erosion surfaces with reliefs of between three and six meters. These surfaces are continuous over distances of up to at least 0.8-1.5 km. These have been interpreted as channels that formed during ebb-flow through the interpreted tidal delta system. In present-day tidal-flat environments, most deposition occurs during flood tides when the sand sheet builds landward, whereas the strong ebb currents may cut channels but deposit little sand on the seaward side of the sand sheet. Thus, the barrier bar-tidal delta model envisages that it was in this manner the bulk of the Hawkesbury Sandstone was redeposited. Because cross-bedding measurements indicate a pattern of paleocurrents in the general northerly to northeasterly direction,[21] the blanket sands are interpreted as having formed by the coalescing of a series of interlocking tidal deltas that spread in a general northward to northeasterly direction away from the presumed sea. The degree of variation in the direction of the paleocurrents is remarkably small. This is not what would be expected from redeposition in either a braided or meandering river, whereas it is very consistent with unidirectional marine currents influenced by ocean swells.

However, it has been claimed that the "complete lack of marine fossils" is a problem for the barrier-bar tidal delta marine depositional model for the Hawkesbury Sandstone.[22] Nevertheless, while it is true there is an apparent lack of fossils, in general, in the massive and sheet sandstones of the formation, the siltstone/mudstone or shale lenses, that may be up to 35 m thick and up to several kilometers in extent, contain a mixture of diverse marine/estuarine and freshwater

20   Conolly, 1969; J. R. Conolly and J. C. Ferm, 1971, Permo-Triassic sedimentation patterns, Sydney Basin, Australia, *Bulletin of the American Association of Petroleum Geologists,* 55: 2018-2032; Ashley and Duncan, 1977.

21   Standard, 1969; Conolly, 1969.

22   Ashley and Duncan, 1977.

fossils.[23] Indeed, the abundance of fish fossils on single bedding planes in some of these shale lenses indicates mass mortality in what are known as fossil graveyards, some spectacular examples of which have been found in the Hawkesbury Sandstone. Many varieties of fish and even sharks are preserved in patterns consistent with their sudden burial under catastrophic conditions.[24] The list of fossils found in these mudstone/shale lenses includes more than twenty genera of fish (both freshwater and marine), a shark, insects, freshwater-marine arthropods, crustaceans, amphibians (for example, labyrinthodonts), bivalves, and gastropods, as well as amphibian footprints. These mudstone/shale lenses also contain abundant plant microfossils and plant debris, including horsetails (*Phyllotheca*), tree ferns, and seed ferns (*Dicroidium*).[25] Organic remains within the sheet and massive sandstones are scarce, but those that occur consist predominantly of fragments of fossil wood, commonly coalified.[26] All of these fossils, including the plant debris and wood fragments, and the mixture of both freshwater and marine creatures, are evidence for the rapid deposition of the Hawkesbury Sandstone, both the sheet and massive sandstones, and the mudstone/shale lenses.

Just how rapidly the water currents responsible for deposition of the Hawkesbury Sandstone were flowing can be quantified from the height of the cross-beds in the sandstones, as discussed earlier. It has been empirically demonstrated that the heights of the sand waves, of which the cross-beds are remnants, were originally double the cross-bed thickness, and the heights of the sand waves are directly related to the water depth and the velocities of the water currents moving the sand waves along (see Figure 43 again). The cross-beds in the Hawkesbury Sandstone are up to 8 m high, with average heights between 2 m and 5 m. The original sand-wave heights would thus have averaged 4 to 10 m, up to a maximum of 16 m, with the water depths between approximately 20 m and 54 m, up to as much as 90 m. Sand waves 10 m high would require water currents flowing at velocities of between 0.9 m per second and 1.55 m per second, while sand waves 16 m high would require water current velocities approaching 1.7 m per second to move the sand along. In context, we have to therefore envisage sustained, unidirectional currents of around 1 m per second occurring in deep water over some 20,000 square kilometers in order to deposit the flat-lying sandstone layers that together make up the Hawkesbury Sandstone.

We know of such high velocities occurring because of the flow of tides through restrictions of the ocean within straits, such as at the entrance to the Mediterranean

23   C. Herbert, 1997, Sequence stratigraphic analysis of Early and Middle Triassic alluvial and estuarine facies in the Sydney Basin, Australia, *Australian Journal of Earth Sciences*, 44: 125-143.

24   A. A. Snelling, 1988, An exciting Australian fossil fish discovery, *Creation*, 10 (3): 32-36.

25   Standard, 1969; R. J. Helby, 1969, Plant microfossils in the Hawkesbury Sandstone, in *The Geology of New South Wales*, G. H. Packham, ed., *Journal of the Geological Society of Australia*, 16 (1): 417; M. E. White, 1986, *The Greening of Gondwana*, Sydney: Reed Books, 135-155.

26   Conaghan, 1969; A. A. Snelling, 1999, Dating dilemma: fossil wood in ancient 'sandstone,' *Creation*, 21 (3): 39-41.

Sea, so to generate such high velocity, sustained, unidirectional ocean currents over such a large area would require a mechanism of catastrophic proportions. The only modern analogue would be the severe currents generated during a tsunami, when unidirectional currents exceeding 1 m per second are known to have been sustained for hours while moving large quantities of sand and building huge sand waves in deep water in its waning stages. The recent discovery of recumbent or overturned cross-beds within the Hawkesbury Sandstone has provided convincing evidence that a succession of catastrophic, massive flood waves, possibly as high as 20 m and up to 250 km wide, carried billions of tons of sand at enormous speed and dumped it to form the massive sandstone units.[27] This admission recognizes that the extent and volume of these massive sandstones have no equal or comparison among the sandy sediments deposited by rivers in the present world. The huge volumes and velocities necessary to explain the water and sediment flows to deposit these sandstone beds over these vast areas required catastrophic conditions in the past on a scale not experienced in the present world.

Megasequences of North America

The advent of the seismic reflection method to recognize and delineate strata sequences, and correlate them across and between sedimentary basins, has made it possible to analyze the sedimentation patterns on regional and continental scales. Thus, as a result of the extensive use of the seismic reflection method and the concurrent emphasis on sequence stratigraphy, various orders of strata sequence cycles in the geologic record have been recognized, including continent-wide, unconformity-bounded packages of sedimentary strata known as megasequences. Six such megasequences traceable across North America have been identified, and can be traced from the Cordilleran region in the west to the Appalachian Basin in the east.[28] Recognition of these megasequences is based on physical relationships among the rock units, each megasequence representing a major cycle of transgression and regression.

The first and lowermost of these North American megasequences has been called the Sauk Megasequence. A typical exposure of it occurs in the Grand Canyon, where it is known as the Tonto Group. The Cambrian strata compromising this group are, from the base of the sequence upwards, the Tapeats Sandstone, the Bright Angel Shale, and the Muav Limestone, which represents a fining upwards sequence produced by a transgression.[29] As the ocean waters from the southwest flooded northeastwards onto what had been land, they and their sediment load eroded that land surface as they surged over it. A prograding, fining-upwards

---

27   J. Woodford, April 30, 1994, Rock doctor catches up with our prehistoric surf, *The Sydney Morning Herald*, 2.

28   L. L. Sloss, 1963, Sequences in the cratonic interior of North America, *Geological Society of American Bulletin*, 74: 93-114.

29   S. A. Austin, A creationist view of Grand Canyon strata, in Austin, 1994, 67-70. Note especially Figure 4.12 on 69.

sequence of sediments was deposited as the waters flooded further and further inland. The different strata units were deposited side-by-side laterally and stacked vertically at the same time. The result was deposition of the Tapeats Sandstone, Bright Angel Shale, and Muav Limestone contemporaneously to form the Tonto Group over a vast area, separated from the underlying basement rocks by an angular unconformity.

At the base of the sequence where the surging waters were at their fastest, boulders with a diameter of up to 4.5 m and weighing up to 200 tons eroded from the basement strata were carried along by the advancing waters and then deposited at the unconformity.[30] Just above in the water column where the current was not quite as fast, sand was carried landwards to be deposited on top of the basal boulders of the Tapeats Sandstone as the waters transgressed further inland. In the relatively quieter waters oceanward, clay and lime muds were deposited to form the Bright Angel Shale, and Muav Limestone, respectively. The Tapeats Sandstone varies in thickness between 38 and 99 meters, the Bright Angel Shale is between 106 and 122 meters thick, while the Muav Limestone thickens westwards from 106 meters to 305 meters.[31] The majority of the Tapeats Sandstone consists of beds typically less than 1 meter thick, with planar and trough cross-stratification and crudely developed horizontal stratification, features comparable to storm-generated sand beds. Similarly, horizontal laminations, small- to large-scale planar, tabular, and trough cross-stratification, and wavy and lenticular bedding, in the Bright Angel Shale have been described as suggesting "deposition by storm-enhanced currents."[32]

The vertical sequence consisting of the Great Unconformity, Tapeats Sandstone, Bright Angel Shale, and Muav Limestone has enormous horizontal extent, which can be measured in terms of many hundreds of kilometers. However, the Sauk Megasequence, which consists of these Tonto Group strata in the Grand Canyon region, has been traced right across the North American continent, because strata units similar to those which make up the Tonto Group can be correlated with one another over such an enormous lateral extent. Indeed, it is possible to map the occurrence of all the sandstone strata that correlate with the Tapeats Sandstone, which together are known as the basal sandstone lithosome of the Sauk Megasequence. Distribution of this basal sandstone lithosome appears to form a single sandstone body that blankets a major portion of North America, extending along the Mexico border from southern California to Texas northwards across Montana and much of North Dakota through to Canada, and from southern California and Nevada right across to the Mid-West and the New England including Maine (Figure 45, page 1082). As such, this enormous blanket

---

30 Austin, 1994, 46, Figure 3.23.

31 L. T. Middleton and D. K. Elliott, 2003, Tonto Group, in *Grand Canyon Geology*, 2nd ed., S.S. Beus and M. Morales, ed., New York: Oxford University Press, 90-106.

32 Middleton and Elliot, 2003.

of sandstone right across North America represents a major flooding of the land, the evidence in the Tapeats Sandstone implying that it was a rapid, storm-driven inundation, such as that which occurred at the initiation of the cataclysmic Flood event.

68

FOSSILIZATION

Although it cannot be categorically said that no fossils are now being formed in currently accumulating sediments, it is nevertheless emphatically true that there are no modern parallels for the formation of the fossil assemblages found in great numbers in various parts of the geologic record. Actually, the formation and preservation of fossils is rare, and requires special conditions:

> All kinds of agents may destroy or damage organisms beyond recognition, before they can become fossils or while they are fossils. After death the soft parts of organisms may rot or be eaten, and any hard parts may be dissolved by water, or broken or crushed and scattered by scavengers, or by storms, flood, wind, and frost. Remains must be buried to become part of the rock, but the very process of burial may cause cracking and crushing. After burial, groundwater seeping through the sediment may dissolve bones and shells. Earth movements may smear or crush the fossil beyond recognition or may heat them too much. Even if a fossil survives and is eventually exposed at the earth's surface, it is very unlikely to be found and collected before it is destroyed by weathering and erosion.[1]

> [M]any marine organisms secrete shells of calcium carbonate, and many marine and terrestrial animals secrete skeletons of calcium phosphate…. Despite the relative resistance of these shells and bones to bacterial decay and their lack of appeal to predators and scavengers, only a small proportion of such hard parts formed by organisms are entombed in sediments to become part of the fossil record….In order for hard parts to enter the permanent record, they must be protected from these destructive processes by being covered rapidly with sediment. This cycling of both soft and hard parts is the normal condition in most environments; removal of the remains from the recycling agents, enabling them to be preserved in the fossil record, is an exceptional event.[2]

---

1   R. Cowen, 1990, *History of Life*, Boston, MA: Blackwell Scientific Publications, 33.

2   C. W. Stearn and R. L Carroll, 1989, P*aleontology: The Record of Life*, New York: John Wiley and Sons, Inc., 6-7.

The full significance of the fossils preserved in the geologic record can only be fully appreciated when it is understood how these fossils have been preserved and the conditions responsible. There are numerous ways in which animal and plant remains may be preserved as fossils.[3]

Preservation of Unaltered Remains

Few organisms are entombed and persist to the present day essentially complete, with little change of form or composition. Mammoths found frozen in the tundra of North America and Siberia are so little changed that their flesh has been reported still palatable to wild animals, and their last meals remained undigested in their stomachs. Estimates of the remains buried all along the coastline of northern Siberia and into Alaska are as high as 5 million mammoths.[4] The great number of bones interred with them in the same sediments cannot be explained easily apart from a widespread catastrophic event. Among other examples are a rhinoceros preserved intact in a Polish oil seep, because petroleum penetrating the flesh retarded bacterial decay, while similar preservation has occurred of numerous animals in the La Brea tar pits of Los Angeles. Another spectacular example of the exquisite preservation of unaltered tissues are the insects and other organisms preserved in unsurpassed detail in amber (tree resin), the most famous deposits of which are found around the Baltic Sea area and in the Dominican Republic, though other deposits are found in New Jersey.[5] These examples are all exceptionally rare, and are not representative of normal conditions of preservation.

Of particular interest are certain details about the insects that have been preserved in amber, such as in the Baltic Sea area:

> In the pieces of amber, which may reach a size of 5 kilos or more, especially insects and parts of flowers are preserved, even the most fragile structures. The insects are of modern types and their geographical distribution can be ascertained. It is then quite astounding to find that they belong to all regions of the earth, not only to the Palaeoarctic region, as was to be expected....The geological and palaeobiological facts concerning the layers of amber are impossible to understand unless the explanation is accepted that they are the final result of an allochthonous process, including the whole earth.[6]

---

3   Stearn and Carroll, 1989, 7-11.

4   H. H. Hopworth, 1887, *Mammoth and the Flood—An Attempt to Confront the Theory of Uniformity with the Facts of Recent Geology*, London: Sampson Lowe, Marston Searle and Risington, provides a very detailed description of these deposits. Other estimates of fossil numbers and the references to them are provided in M. J. Oard, 2000, The extinction of the woolly mammoth, was it a quick freeze?, *Creation Ex Nihilo Technical Journal*, 14 (3): 24-34.

5   A. Henwood, 1993, Still life in amber, *New Scientist*, 137 (1859): 31-34; D. A. Grimaldi, 1996, Captured in amber, *Scientific American*, 274 (4): 70-77.

6   N. Heribert-Nilsson, 1953, *Synthethische Artbildung*, Sweden: Verlag C.W.E. Gleerup, Lund, 1194-1195.

An allochthonous process is one which transports materials from a source area (or areas) and finally deposits them elsewhere, more often than not by the agency of flowing waters. Though at most amber shows signs that it was moved by water before it settled into the sediment in which it now lies.[7]

Just as astounding is the claim that large segments of DNA were recovered and sequenced from a termite fossilized in Dominican amber claimed to be 25 million years old.[8] Subsequent research challenged this claim by demonstrating that when an organism dies the DNA rapidly breaks down.[9] Then painstaking and exhaustive experiments to replicate the original DNA results failed completely.[10]

After the soft parts decay, the hard parts of many organisms can still be preserved essentially unaltered in sedimentary rocks. For example, the shells of many marine organisms, once they have been entombed in sediments, are relatively stable. Thus, some fossil shells claimed to have been formed millions of years ago cannot be distinguished from modern shells. An example of this phenomenon occurs near Wootton Bassett, near Swindon in Wiltshire, England, where oozing mud springs are bringing to the surface "pristine fossils" from Jurassic strata about 13 meters below.[11] Among these fossils, claimed to be 165 million years old, are specimens of the ammonite *Rhactorhynchia inconstans*—many still with "shimmering mother-of-pearl shells," their iridescence retained because "their original shells of aragonite" have been retained—and "the shells of bivalves which still have their original organic ligaments."[12]

Preservation by Permineralization

The most common type of fossil found, especially bones and shells, is where only the hard parts of the organisms have been preserved. Most shells and bones are not solid, but contain canals and pores. The bones of land animals, for example, are generally highly porous, particularly in their central regions where marrow fills the voids when the animals are alive. When organisms die, if they are buried in sediments the soft parts decay, but the pores in the bones and shells are filled with water that often contains dissolved minerals. Such ground waters may then

---

7   Henwood, 1993, 32.

8   R. DeSalle, J. Gatesy, W. Wheeler and D. Grimaldi, 1992, DNA sequences from a fossil termite in Oligo-Miocene amber and their phylogenetic implications, *Science*, 257: 1933-1936.

9   Lindahl, 1993, Instability and decay of the primary structure of DNA, *Nature*, 362: 709-715.

10   J. J. Austin et al, 1997, Problems of reproducibility—does geologically ancient DNA survive in amber–preserved insects?, *Proceedings of the Royal Society of London, B*, 264: 467-474.

11   A. A. Snelling, 1997, A "165 million year" surprise, *Creation*, 19 (2): 14-15, and references contained therein.

12   Dr. Neville Hollingworth, paleontologist with the Natural Environment Research Council, as quoted in N. Nuttall, May 2, 1996, Mud springs a surprise after 165 million years, *The Times*, London, 7; Anonymous, 1995, Iridescent fossils rise up from volcano, *New Scientist*, 148 (1998): 10.

precipitate calcium carbonate or silica in the pores of the shells or bones, reinforcing and solidifying them. The fossilized remains of many organisms, including almost all fossils in sedimentary strata deemed to be old, are subject to this process, which is called permineralization, but is sometimes called petrification or petrifaction. For example, coniferous logs in the Petrified Forest of Arizona have been preserved through the infiltration of silica into the original cellular structure of the wood, with so little disturbance that the microstructure appears to be that of a living tree.

Preservation by Recrystallization

After a shell, for example, has been covered with sediment and possibly also infiltrated with mineral matter via the process of permineralization, the crystals that were secreted to form the shell originally may be changed in form and size, without changing in composition. In calcium carbonate shells, the original minute crystals often increase in size until the texture of the shell is instead a coarse calcite mosaic. Forms of the shells may remain faithfully defined, but the microstructure secreted by the organisms has been destroyed. Such fossils are said to be recrystallized.

Preservation by Replacement

The ground water seeping through sedimentary rocks that contain fossil bones and shells may dissolve some of the hard parts, and at the same time replace them with the minerals it carries in solution. The effect is to substitute another material for the original hard parts without changing the form of the shells or bones. "Paleontologists cannot duplicate these processes, nor do they fully understand them, but the fossil record leaves no doubt that they occur."[13] Commonly, the replacing mineral is silica in its fine, crystalline form known as chalcedony. Delicate spines and fine structures on silicified shells have been revealed by dissolving the limestone that encases them in dilute hydrochloric or acetic acid. Many other minerals can also replace fossils. In shales, for example, shells are commonly replaced by the iron sulfide mineral, pyrite. Thus, delicate structures of organisms may be replaced by pyrite and preserved, as in the Hunsrück Slate in western Germany. The iron oxide, hematite, may also replace fossils, and under rare conditions, both the soft and hard parts of animals may be replaced by calcium phosphates. In all, about twenty different minerals are known to have replaced fossils.

Preservation of Only the Original Forms in Casts and Molds

Instead of replacing fossil shells, ground water passing through sediments may dissolve them completely. If the sediments packed around the shells have been

---

13   Stearn and Carroll, 1989, 7.

consolidated into rocks before the shells are dissolved, voids will be formed. The walls of the voids may preserve impressions of the faces of the shells, which can be examined when the voids are broken open. These impressions are called molds. Their relief is opposite to that of the shells themselves: knobs on the shells are represented by depressions and vice versa. If conditions change and the ground water deposits minerals into the voids where the shells have been dissolved, the molds may be filled. The resultant mineral deposits will take from the molds the external forms of these fossils they have inherited, but will have none of their internal structures. Thus, this is not a replacement of the shells, but casts that duplicate the shells after the originals have been destroyed. The casts are replicas of the dissolved fossils. The molds are negative impressions of their surfaces.

Preservation of Carbon Only (Carbonization)

Plants are commonly fossilized by being preserved as thin forms of carbon pressed between the bedding planes of sandstones and shales. When plants die and are covered with sediments, the volatile constituents of the various carbohydrates of which they are composed (for example, hydrogen and oxygen) largely disappear by being dispersed, leaving behind a residue of coal-like carbon, a black film that preserves forms of the original leaves, stems, or even fruits. Similarly, the soft parts of marine animals have also been preserved in the fossil record. Such preservation of soft parts rarely takes place, but when it does, it has to have been due to burial where bacterial decay was inhibited by lack of oxygen. An excellent example of where this has occurred are the black shales that are so prevalent in the geologic record.

Preservation of the Tracks and Trails

Animals crossing the surfaces of sediments may leave behind footprints or impressions of parts of their bodies. These are then preserved when the sediment hardens to rock. Similarly, animals living or feeding within sediments leave behind burrows and tunnel systems that may then be preserved, for example, by infilling with other material at the time of burial, or by minerals that have crystallized in the voids from percolating ground waters after burial. These types of fossils are called *ichnofossils*, or trace fossils.

Related to animal tracks and traces that have been thus preserved are the many instances of the preservation of ripple marks produced by water flowing across sediment surfaces, or of raindrop impressions. That such ephemeral markings have been preserved in great numbers, particularly ripple marks, and in such perfection, is truly remarkable, all the more so because there appears to be no modern parallel phenomenon. Indeed, our observations in today's world overwhelmingly indicate that impressions like this in soft mud or sand are very quickly obliterated. It would seem, therefore, that the only way raindrop impressions could be preserved as fossils is by rapid lithification of the sediments (which would have to be by the rapid reaction to harden a chemical cement), followed by rapid burial of the sediment surface and the now fossilized prints. Such rapid burial would necessitate rapid sediment transport and deposition by fast moving water.

While there are the following seven ways in which fossils are preserved—unaltered, permineralized, recrystallized, replaced, carbonized, as molds and casts, and as ichnofossils—each requires specialized conditions. The frequent occurrence of fossils, especially in large accumulations called fossil graveyards, suggests specialized conditions repeatedly on large scales. However, it is virtually impossible to find specific present-day depositional areas where fossils are forming that are analogous to the fossil deposits found in the rock record. Land animals, amphibians or fish, whole bodies or just their bones, may occasionally be trapped in sediments and buried, but this is not a normal or frequent occurrence, even where mass destruction and mortality occurs in some localized catastrophe. Usually, the bones remain in land or sediment surfaces until they gradually disintegrate.

69

FOSSIL GRAVEYARDS

Great "graveyards" of organisms buried together undergoing fossilization and preservation are not found in the world today. However, this is exactly what must have happened in the past, because of the frequent fossil graveyard deposits found in many places around the world in the rock record. Many examples could be cited, but just a few examples, and details concerning them, will suffice.

The Cambrian Burgess Shale, British Columbia, Canada

More than 120 species of marine invertebrates have been preserved at various closely-spaced stratigraphic levels within this shale in the Canadian Rockies. Most of these were soft-bodied animals, but they have been preserved with soft parts intact, often with food still in their guts. Arthropods make up nearly 40 percent of the fossil species, including trilobites, while worms of various types make up more than 25 percent.[1] Other animals preserved in the shale include four species of coelenterates, at least four species of echinoderms, three species of mollusks, and eighteen species of sponges, plus five species of chordates and hemichordates, and species from ten or more previously unknown phyla. Many thousands of specimens of these fossils have been collected from small quarries in the shale since their discovery in 1909.

Usually found squashed flat into thin films, these animals were not fossilized in their normal life position, and though difficult to interpret, it is believed that more than 40 percent were mobile bottom dwellers and around 30 percent were fixed bottom dwellers, the remaining 30 percent representing free swimmers and burrowers. It is believed that the Burgess Shale animals lived on a quiet muddy sea floor. Submarine landslides swept the animals into a deeper basin where there was no oxygen, where they were killed instantly and buried immediately in fine

1   S. Conway Morris and H.B. Whittington, 1982, The animals of the Burgess Shale, in *The Fossil Record and Evolution*, Readings from *Scientific American*, San Francisco, CA: W. H. Freeman and Company, 70-80; Cowen, 1990, 90-93; S. J. Gould, 1991, *Wonderful Life, The Burgess Shale and the Nature of History*, London: Penguin Books; D. E. G. Briggs, D. H. Erwin and F. J. Collier, 1994, *The Fossils of the Burgess Shale*, Washington and London: Smithsonian Institution Press; S. Conway Morris, 1998, *The Crucible of Creation: The Burgess Shale and the Rise of Animals*, Oxford, England: Oxford University Press.

mud. Indeed, the turbulent flow is evidenced by the disposition of the fossils in the rock, the animals being dumped at a variety of angles to the bedding.[2] The Burgess Shale is, therefore, an enormous fossil graveyard, produced by countless animals living on the sea floor being catastrophically swept away in landslide-generated turbidity currents, and then buried almost instantly in the resultant massive turbidite layers, to be exquisitely preserved and fossilized.

The Ordovician Soom Shale, South Africa

The Soom Shale member of the Cedarberg Formation in the Table Mountain Group outcrops in the Cedarberg Mountains of the Cape Province of South Africa.[3] The Soom Shale is only 10 m thick and thinly laminated, the mud and silt laminae being normally less than 1 mm thick (rarely up to 10 mm) and laterally persistent and undisturbed by any penetrative bioturbation. This is consistent with rapid deposition and lithification, before burrowing organisms could obliterate the laminae. Thousands of exceptionally preserved fossils have been found throughout this shale unit at several locations hundreds of kilometers apart, which suggests that this shale unit is an incredibly large and widespread fossil graveyard. Among the identified fossils are brachiopods, straight-shelled nautiloids, various arthropods, worms, conodonts, chitinozoan chains, and a number of enigmatic organisms, including one represented only by scattered spines.

The most spectacular fossil specimens are those of arthropods called eurypterids. They not only display complete cuticular skeletons, but also show the sensory chelicerae and walking appendages that are normally lost to early decay after death. The preservation of some of the fibrous muscular masses that operated these appendages is particularly remarkable. A spiral food tract is also sometimes visible at the rear of the head, and there are well-preserved gill tracts and dendritic structures in the pre-abdomen. Trilobites are rare. Nautiloids are characteristic members of this fossil assemblage, several being found colonized by inarticulate brachiopods. Other inarticulate brachiopods are the most common isolated shells in the shale, some displaying exquisite preservation of the shell ornament. A few completely soft-bodied organisms, which are represented by carbon films or mineral replacements, are currently enigmatic.

Conodonts are extinct soft-bodied vertebrates, normally represented in the fossil record only by the scattered phosphatic elements of their feeding apparatuses, which are generally about 1 mm in length and microscopic. In the Soom Shale, however, the conodont elements in individual specimens are up to 20 mm long, so are easily visible on the bedding planes. Of great significance is the fact that most of the conodonts are represented not by scattered elements, but by complete

2   Cowen, 1990, 90; Briggs, Erwin and Collier, 1994, 27.

3   R. J. Aldridge, J. N. Theron and S. E. Gabbott, 1994, The Soom Shale: A Unique Ordovician Fossil Horizon in South Africa, *Geology Today*, 10 (6): 218-221.

feeding apparatuses. These show that the conodont animals must have been buried alive in the shale and become fossilized without any disturbance from water currents, scavengers, or burrowers. Even more important is the fact that several of these apparatuses are associated with traces of the soft tissues of the conodont animals, with the eyes, in particular, commonly well preserved. The evidence is clearly consistent with catastrophic burial of countless thousands of these organisms over thousands of square kilometers, which implies that the shale itself had to be catastrophically deposited and covered under more sediments before burrowing organisms could destroy the laminations.

The Devonian Thunder Bay Limestone, Michigan

Outcropping along the western shore of Lake Huron south of Alpena, Michigan, the Thunder Bay Limestone is at least 4 meters thick and stretches laterally for many hundreds of kilometers. It dips westward into the Michigan Basin, which covers many hundreds of square kilometers right across Michigan. Of particular interest are the fossilized corals and brachiopods that occur in profusion in the limey shale and crystalline limestone portions of this rock unit.[4] A full list of fossils found in this limestone include colonial corals, solitary corals, bryozoans, crinoids, stromatoporoids, brachiopods, blastoids, and conodonts.

Most of the fossil remains in this limestone are fragments and broken pieces of the hard parts of the original organisms, such as the disks or columnals of crinoids' stems or stalks, which were connected and stacked on top of one another in the living crinoids. After death, crinoids fall apart very quickly, so it is common to find abundant fossilized columnals from broken stalks scattered and jumbled indiscriminately through limestones such as this Thunder Bay Limestone. This limestone, like so many other limestones in the geologic record, is largely composed of the debris and broken remains of all these marine organisms. They were destroyed then transported by fast-moving water before being dumped and buried in what is an enormous fossil graveyard. Thus, the Thunder Bay Limestone contains countless billions of fossils that have been catastrophically buried over many hundreds of square kilometers across Michigan.[5]

The Carboniferous Montceau Shale, Central France

This shale, in the Montceau Basin of central France, is associated with coal seams, and so far has yielded the fossilized remains of nearly 300 species of plants and

---

4   R. C. Gutschick, 1987, Devonian shelf-basin, Michigan Basin, Alpena, Michigan, *Geological Society of America Centennial Field Guide—North-Central Section*, Boulder, CO: Geological Society of America, 297-302; D. M. Ehlers and R. V. Kesling, 1970, *Devonian Strata of Alpena and Presque Isle Counties, Michigan*, Guidebook prepared for the North-Central Section, Boulder, CO: Geological Society of America, and the Michigan Basin Geological Society, 1-130.

5   P. A. Catacosinos and P. A. Daniels, Jr, ed., 1991, *Early Sedimentary Evolution of the Michigan Basin*, *Special Paper* 256, Boulder, CO: Geological Society of America; A. A. Snelling, 1998, Thundering burial: a fossil graveyard in Michigan gives another example of Flood catastrophism, *Creation*, 20 (3): 38-41.

pollen, and 16 classes of animals representing about 30 genera.[6] These animals and plants are found flattened within the shale between layers of silt, or in nodules that are believed to have formed as a result of finer sediments accumulating around the organisms as they were buried and fossilized. Among the fossilized plants are giant seed ferns and conifers, the former represented by specimens that must have grown as tall as trees, judging by the trunks found fossilized. Fossilized leaves and thorns are plentiful.

Arthropods are by far the most numerous and well-preserved animals in this fossil graveyard, crustaceans alone representing about 33 percent of the fossil fauna. These include the shrimp-like syncarids, and ostracods and estherians, both minute crustaceans with bivalve shelves. Other aquatic arthropods included the euthycarcinoids (resembling millipedes with tails), and xiphosurans, believed to be related to the horseshoe crabs. Among the terrestrial arthropod fossils are millipedes, spiders, and scorpions, the latter in many cases being beautifully preserved, complete with their venomous vesicle and sting. Representatives of eight orders of insects, including cockroaches, are present, many of the insects being found as nymphal forms. Due to the exceptional preservation, even the soft tissues of polychaete annelids (segmented worms) have been fossilized, along with rare specimens of onychophores, animals that bear a superficial resemblance to large caterpillars. Other invertebrates include bivalve mollusks, which are found at Montceau in great abundance.

The vertebrates found belong to at least four classes—bony fishes, cartilaginous fishes, amphibians, and reptiles. Fish are the most numerous, including small sharks. The fossil amphibians resemble small salamanders, and dual-bearing larvae, similar to the tadpoles of extant amphibians, are also found fossilized here. While only fragments of larger skeletons have been preserved, numerous footprints of amphibians and reptiles have been found, complete with finger and claw marks, and sinuous lines made by tails trailing in the mud. Even raindrop imprints and ripple marks have been found preserved, signifying that burial and lithification must have been extremely rapid. Similarly, the preservation of the fragile hinges in the bivalve mollusk fossils suggests that these animals were not transported before burial, but were entombed abruptly by rapid deposition of sediment. As this fossil graveyard contains a mixture of freshwater, marine, and terrestrial animals and terrestrial plants, some rapid transport of organisms had to take place, along with the rapid sedimentation and burial. Such a mixture of organisms from vastly different habitats buried catastrophically together is consistent with conditions during the Genesis Flood.

The Carboniferous Francis Creek Shale, Mazon Creek Area, Illinois

A similar diverse array of organisms is found in the fossil graveyard in the Francis

---

6   B. Heyler and C. M. Poplin, 1998, The fossils of Montceau-Les-Mines, *Scientific American*, 259 (3): 70-76.

Creek Shale, associated with coal seams in the Mazon Creek area near Chicago. More than 100,000 fossil specimens representing more than 400 species have been recovered for study, and these belong to 14 phyla, more than 33 classes, and about 100 orders, including forms that are otherwise unknown outside of their modern counterparts.[7] These organisms are found spatially distributed in two overlapping groups—a terrestrial assemblage of ferns, insects, scorpions, and tetrapods, and an essentially marine assemblage dominated by jellyfish, but also consisting of abundant mollusks, crustaceans of various types, and fish.

Arthropods, and all of their major sub-phyla (except trilobites), are again particularly well represented by marine, freshwater, and terrestrial forms, the latter including spiders, scorpions, millipedes, centipedes, giant arthropleurids, and insects (some 150 species). The crustaceans include a host of shrimp-like forms, stromatopods, isopods, clam-like conchostracans, ostracods, and barnacles. Many varieties of worms are also present. The comparatively rare vertebrates are well represented by a variety of fish, including lampreys, hagfishes, sharks, and spiny jawed fish. At least four orders of amphibians are also present, including an extremely rare, tiny salamander-like fossil, preserved in such exquisite detail that it even shows partially digested food within its gut. Finally, some small, extraordinarily rare lizard-like reptiles are also found in the nodules.

The remains of all these organisms were evidently buried rapidly in the silty and muddy sediments, with the exquisite preservation of lightly skeletonized, and even soft, body parts in traces being paradoxically the result of their incipient decay. Bicarbonate produced as a by-product of their anaerobic decay led to the entombment of the organism remains as nuclei of the iron carbonate (siderite) concretions or nodules. Strikingly similar to the Montceau fossil graveyard, this Mazon Creek fossil graveyard also contains a mixture of terrestrial, freshwater, and marine organisms that show evidence of being rapidly buried in order for the exquisite preservation of even the soft part details of these fossils.

The Triassic Mont San Giorgio Basin, Italy-Switzerland

The shales of Mont San Giorgio are in a basin that is estimated to have been from 6 to 10 kilometers in diameter and only approximately 100 meters deep. Yet thousands of well-preserved fossils in a diverse assemblage of fish and reptiles have been found in these bituminous shales.[8] Once buried in the fine-grained muds, compression flattened the animal skeletons as they petrified. In some instances, the force of compression crushed the skeleton so severely that interpretation of fine anatomical detail is difficult, if not impossible. However, most of the fossils are well preserved, so that delicate bones and fine details, such as tiny spines and

---

7   C. W. Shabika and A. A. Hay, ed., 1997, *Richardson's Guide to the Fossil Fauna of Mazon Creek*, Chicago, IL: North-eastern Illinois University; C. E. Brett, 1998, Picture of an ancient world, *Science*, 279 (5358): 1868-1869.

8   T. Bürgin et al, 1989, The fossils of Monte San Giorgio, *Scientific American*, 260 (6): 50-57.

scales, are still distinctly visible. It is readily apparent that a wide variety of animal species were buried and preserved in this basin.

In terms of fish diversity alone, the fossil assemblage in these shales is analogous to a modern coral reef. Five species of sharks have been identified so far, four of them being small, yet robust in shape, with crushing teeth that suggest they ate shellfish. The San Giorgio specimens are represented mostly by teeth and occasional fin spines or backbones (sharks, unlike bony fish, have skeletons made of cartilage and deteriorate rapidly after death). Yet several almost complete shark specimens have been found, providing further testimony to the exceptional preservation in this fossil graveyard. A limited number of lobe-finned fish specimens tend to be complete, because their heavy, enamel-like scales have resisted decay. They fall into three distinct size categories. The largest ones measure about 70 cm in length, and in contrast, the smallest ones are only 20 cm long. More than 550 well-preserved specimens of ray-finned fishes (the group to which the majority of living fish belong) have been catalogued. The exquisite preservation of these San Giorgio fossils is exemplified by some of these ray-finned fishes, with fine details, such as the tail fins and elongate snout of the lizard fish *Saurichthys* being visible. Even more remarkable is the presence of two embryos inside the abdomen of a female, evidence that these fish gave birth to live young. Many of these fish are believed to have been ocean-dwelling, fast-swimming forms, based on comparison with their modern counterparts.

Most abundant and perhaps best studied of the reptile fossils are the amphibious nothosaurs. They are thought to have moved forward through water by lateral undulations of the trunk and tail. In addition to having elongate, flattened tails, most of these fossil reptiles have long, flexible necks. These nothosaurs vary in shape and size, from three meters in length to a dwarf lizard which averaged only about 30 cm in length. All together some 400 specimens, representing each stage of the life cycle from embryo to adult, have been documented. It has been possible to study the development of these animals, because, like all cold-blooded reptiles, they grew by adding new bone in the form of annual growth rings. Thus, thin cross-sections of their bones, about 50 microns thick, have been examined microscopically, and the number of growth rings counted, extensive analysis revealing the animals lived to a maximum of six years. The genera of placodonts, short, stout marine reptiles that had large, flattened teeth, are known from Monte San Giorgio, while a group of reptiles known as archosauromorphs are well represented. The most bizarre of these fossil reptiles is the 4.5 meter giraffe-necked saurian, *Tanystropheus*, which had an absurdly long neck more than twice the length of its trunk. Only one true archosaur (the group to which dinosaurs belong) has been found in this fossil graveyard. The animal, which was about 2.5 meters long, is believed to have been a ferocious terrestrial carnivore. Thalattosaurs, another enigmatic group of marine reptiles, are also represented in the San Giorgio shales by three genera, the largest specimen of which measures about 2.5 meters in length and has a long, narrow skull. Ichthyosaurs, a group of marine reptiles that were similar in size and shape to modern dolphins, having paddle-shaped limbs and distinct snouts, are also represented by three genera here. Some specimens have been found that contain the remains of unborn young, so it is surmised that the eggs must have developed within the mother's body, and that the young were born live.

As for how this great diversity of vertebrates came to be fossilized together, it is conventionally suggested:

> The bottom of the (San Giorgio) basin consisted of fine-grained mud, and when the animals that lived in the basin died they sank to the bottom. There conditions were anoxic (without oxygen), so their remains, which would normally be broken down by aerobic bacteria and other scavengers, were protected from decay, thus exquisitely preserving even fine details.[9]

However, fish, like so many other creatures, do not naturally become entombed like this, but are usually devoured by other fish or scavengers after dying. Furthermore, when most fish die their bodies float. In the fossil assemblage at Mont San Giorgio are some indisputable terrestrial reptiles among the marine reptiles and fishes. Thus, to fossilize all those fish with the large marine *and* terrestrial reptiles, so that they are all exquisitely preserved, would have required a catastrophic water flow to sweep all these animals together and bury them in fine-grained mud.

The Triassic Cow Branch Formation, Cascade, Virginia

The fossiliferous shales of the Cow Branch Formation in the Virginia-North Carolina border area contain an abundance of complete insects, and preserve even the soft-part anatomy of some vertebrates, along with an unusual diversity of flora.[10] The sediments of this formation are markedly cyclical and fossiliferous throughout, including plants and abundant plant fragments, together with ripple marks and what are interpreted as mudcracks. However, it is in the microlaminated, organic-rich shales that the great diversity of fossilized insects has been found, together with the articulated remains of the tanystropheid reptile, *Tanytrachelos*, complete with impressions of soft tissue, and the best preserved plant remains. The matrix is an exceptionally fine-grained black shale that shows no evidence of bioturbation, and the insects are preserved as two-dimensional silvery images. Microscopic details are preserved with great fidelity, and the resolution of preserved detail is approximately 1 micron.

The most abundant fossilized insects are aquatic sucking bugs, two families being represented by numerous nymphal and adult specimens. The next most common order of insects in the fossil assemblages is leaf-hoppers, and at least six families

---

9   Bürgin et al, 1989, 52.

10   N. C. Fraser et al, 1996, A Triassic Lagerstätten from eastern North America, *Nature*, 380: 615-619.

of flies are also represented here. Single specimens of a thrip, a caddis-fly, and of a new family of the super-family of moths and sandflies, are also found in these shales. Finally, a single large specimen of an extinct family of beetles, specimens unquestionably belonging to a huge living family of beetles, and a representative of an undetermined family of cockroaches, complete the list of insect taxa found in this significant fossil deposit. Despite lacking cuticle (typically a diagnostic feature of fossil plants), the plant remains show a remarkable diversity. Ferns, cycadeoids, and conifers predominate, but also present are lycopods, scouring rushes, gingko, and cycad-like seed plants, as well as a number of seeds.

Many articulated specimens of the aquatic reptile *Tanytrachelos* have been described from these black shales. Many more specimens have been recovered in the latest excavations, including some spectacular individuals complete with ghosts of the muscles on the tails, and ligaments in the webbed hind feet. Fragmentary remains of two as-yet undescribed tetrapods have also been found. Also, numerous specimens of bony fishes, both ray-finned and lobe-finned, have been recovered from these black shales, along with an isolated shark tooth. It is this mixture of organisms (terrestrial, freshwater, and marine) buried together, fossilized and so well preserved, that again is consistent with very rapid deposition and burial, repeatedly during this cyclical sedimentation to produce this fossil graveyard. Insects do not simply die, fall into a body of water, and slowly sink to be gradually covered up by slowly accumulating sediments, even if anoxic conditions prevailed. There are still bacteria which operate under those conditions that would destroy the insects before they could be preserved in such exquisite detail.

The Cretaceous Santana Formation, Brazil

The Santana Formation of Brazil possibly represents the finest fossil locality in the world, due to the incredible preservation of fishes and other animals.[11] The strata hosting the fossils consists of lithographic limestones (compact, dense, homogeneous, exceedingly fine-grained), and shales with nodular calcium carbonate concretions. It is in these concretions that many of the fish have been so well preserved that it is often concluded fossilization must have been instantaneous (the so-called "Medusa effect"). The fossil assemblage is dominated by fishes, including numerous species of armored fishes and ray-finned bony fishes, with rare sharks, a skate, and two species of coelacanth. Associated with the fishes are rare crocodiles, frogs, turtles, dinosaurs, and pterosaurs, particularly pterodactyls with wingspans of over three meters. The invertebrate fauna includes shrimps (crustaceans), ostracodes, bivalves, gastropods, echinoderms, rare foraminifera, insects, and spiders. Fossil plants are also present.

The most spectacular of the fossil fishes are the three-dimensional specimens that are found in the calcium carbonate nodules. Some display large patches of

11　　D. M. Martill, 1989, The Medusa effect: instaneous fossilization, *Geology Today*, 5 (6): 201-205; P. G. Davis, 1992, Geological miracles, *Nature*, 355: 218.

buff-colored calcium phosphate, which must have formed before the fishes were buried in the sediment, and before any decomposition could occur. Sometimes the calcium phosphate replaces the soft tissues of the fishes at the molecular level. Preservation has been so rapid, and so perfect, that structures such as muscle fibers with banding present, some displaying ultrastructure, fibrils, and even cell nuclei arranged in neat rows, have been fossilized. Underneath the scales, small pieces of skin are preserved and show thin sheets of muscle and connective tissue. In a female specimen the ovaries have been preserved with developing eggs inside, and one egg even had phosphatized yolk. Many specimens display the stomach wall with all its reticulations, and often with the last meal still in the stomach. One specimen has no fewer than 13 small fish in its alimentary tract, with a number of shrimps, that even had their compound eyes preserved with the lenses in place. But the most spectacular tissues found in these fish specimens are the gills, many having the arteries and veins of the gills preserved with the secondary lamellae intact.

These tissues are very useful for estimating the speed of the phosphatization process. After the death of a fish, blood pressure is reduced and the secondary lamellae collapse within one to three hours. In the Santana fossil fish, the secondary lamellae are intact, with very little sign of collapse, cells are inflated, but the ultrastructure is not preserved. It is clear, therefore, that the fossilization process took place moments after the fish had died, and was completed within only a few (probably less than five) hours. It is truly remarkable that if a phosphatized fish becomes the nucleus for a carbonate concretion, these phosphatized soft tissues remain in an uncrushed condition, and can be examined today as though they were from a fresh fish! However, the fishes are not the only animals whose remains have been phosphatized. For example, ostracodes are found phosphatized, with the tiny animal still inside with its hairy legs preserved. However, even more spectacular are the phosphatized wings of pterosaurs, which somewhat unusually are the most abundant reptiles in the Santana Formation. Preserved in an uncrushed condition, the bones can be extracted from the matrix and related to each other to work out how they functioned, including the aerodynamics of pterosaur flight. Even better still, the Santana Formation has yielded pterosaurs with phosphatized wing membrane, which has been cross-sectioned to reveal a highly complex organ consisting of a variety of tissue types, including skin, a vascular layer, and muscle tissue.

It is abundantly clear from examination of the incredible preservation of so many fossils in the Santana Formation that this fossil graveyard represents a spectacular catastrophic event, given that flying reptiles and terrestrial dinosaurs, plants, insects, and spiders are found buried together and exquisitely preserved as fossils with fish of many types, crocodiles, turtles, and various marine invertebrates. Burial had to be very rapid, because scavenging and water current activity did not disturb the carcasses, which had to be phosphatized rapidly between death and their very rapid burial. The carbonate concretions also had to form rapidly around the phosphatized carcasses, before overburden pressures squashed the carcasses flat. Obviously, to produce this fossil graveyard required a catastrophic mass-mortality event to virtually instantaneously kill and bury all these organisms together.

The Cretaceous Tepexi Limestone, Mexico

Fissile red limestone near the town of Tepexi southwest of, and close to, Mexico City contains a fossil graveyard with an assemblage of organisms not too dissimilar to the Santana fossil graveyard in Brazil.[12] Fishes are again the most prominently represented, with more than thirty new species. This fact, coupled with the exceptional preservation of the specimens, makes Tepexi a spectacular fossil fish site. For some species the site has yielded a complete developmental series from hatchling to adult. Numerous species of bony, ray-finned fishes are found fossilized with deep-bodied, armored fish with crushing dentitions that are thought to have inhabited coral reefs, while many more specimens remain to be satisfactorily identified. Several thin spines have also been found, indicating the presence of sharks. The fish fossils are probably more abundant here than at many famous fossil fish localities (estimated at about one fossil per cubic meter), although they do not cover entire bedding planes as they do in some other localities, such as the Eocene Green River Formation in Wyoming. Usually the fish are astonishingly well preserved in their entirety, fully articulated, with every bone, scale, and fin in place. Some specimens have been preserved with their last meals still in their guts, and these often include other fishes. The generally perfect preservation of the fish shows that no scavenging took place as the fish died.

Furthermore, the limestone hosting the fossils does not represent deposition on an inhabited sea floor, because the fossilized invertebrate fauna is dominated by free-swimming, pelagic forms, compared to benthic (bottom living) forms, which although present, are extremely rare. The invertebrate fauna is diverse, although somewhat sparse, and is dominated by mollusks. Several ammonites have been discovered, along with rarer bivalves and gastropods. Many new species of invertebrates have been revealed, including crabs. A number of other crustaceans have been found, as have the spines of regular echinoids, and small but complete brittle-stars. Even soft-bodied organisms have been found, among them anemones, some extremely rare sea-cucumbers, and a segmented, bristle-bearing worm. Fish are not the only vertebrates found in this fossil graveyard, as there are also extinct reptiles, including lizards, a turtle, a new type of crocodile, a pleurosaur, and a pterosaur (some isolated bones are attributed to pterodactyls, although no complete specimens have yet been found).

The most puzzling fossils are what have been called "assorted fronds," several different types of which have been found. Some may merely be solution features or dendrites, but a number are certainly of organic origin. A segmented frond

---

12   D. M. Martill, 1989, A new "Solenhofen" in Mexico, *Geology Today*, 5 (1), 25-28.

might be a gymnosperm, but it is only preserved as an impression or an external mold. Other frond-like structures, varying in size and degree of branching, might be organic-walled bryozoa (lace corals), hydroid coelenterates, or algae. Otherwise, trace fossils are relatively common, such as the impressions of ammonites where the shell hit the sediment surface, and feeding traces of worm-like animals. Coprolites, presumably from the fish, are also quite common, in some cases showing that the fish were eating foraminifera.

Most of the fossil-bearing horizons in the limestone are laminated micrites (carbonate mud with crystals less than 4 microns in diameter), often with slightly coarser bases. The width of the laminae is highly variable, with individual laminae often only 1 to 2 mm thick, but the rock usually splits in slabs 1 to 3 cm thick. Throughout the succession there are thin clay partings, which appear to represent volcanic ash falls. It has been suggested that the individual laminae may represent micro-turbidite sequences generated during storms. The direction of flow of the turbidites appears to be reflected in the various current-formed sedimentary structures that have been found, along with indicators of current movements preserved on some of the fossils, such as faint drag marks made by the trailing arms of a fossilized free-swimming crinoid. It is quite obvious that a catastrophic process was involved in transporting and depositing a diverse mixture of organisms, from flying and terrestrial reptiles, to fish and marine organisms. Turbidity currents carrying fine lime-mud were interspersed with falls of volcanic ash, so that the organisms were killed, squashed together, and rapidly buried so as to be well preserved in this fossil graveyard.

The Cretaceous Djadokhta Formation, Nemget Basin, Ukhaa Tolgod Area, Mongolia

In the Ukhaa Tolgod area of the Gobi Desert of Mongolia, an unmatched abundance of well-preserved vertebrate fossils are found in the Djadokhta Formation, including the highest concentration of mammalian skulls and skeletons from any Mesozoic site.[13] From an area of about four square kilometers, the recovered and uncollected articulated skeletons of theropod, ankylosaurian, and protoceratopian dinosaurs represent over 100 individuals. Specimens collected also include skulls, many with associated skeletons, of over 400 mammals and lizards, and include the first known skull of the bird *Mononykus*. Certain sites have been interpreted as nests, because fossilized eggs at these sites contain what are believed to be theropod dinosaur embryos. A distinctive feature of this Ukhaa Tolgod fossil graveyard is the marked diversity and abundance of small vertebrates. Also striking is the preservational quality of these delicate specimens. Many skulls are virtually complete with lower jaws still in articulation, and tympanic rings and ear ossicles well preserved. Postcranial skeletons associated with the mammal skulls provide evidence of anatomical regions that have not been preserved at

---

13   D. Dashzeveg et al, 1995, Extraordinary preservation in a new vertebrate assemblage from the Late Cretaceous of Mongolia, *Nature*, 374: 446-449.

comparable sites. Indeed, five well-preserved skeletons of a placental mammal species were found *in situ*, close together. Thus, this fossil graveyard represents an unprecedented aggregate of mammal skeletons in Mesozoic strata.

The excellent preservation of these vertebrate fossils at Ukhaa Tolgod prompts questions concerning the mode of their death, burial, and preservation. Given that the well-preserved fossils are all found in a distinctive sandstone layer, it is obvious that this fossil assemblage resulted from rapid post-mortem *in situ* burial in sand. Evidence for this is the abundant articulated skeletons, which suggest minimal post-mortem surface weathering and transport, positions of skeletons that suggest "death struggles," and monospecific death assemblages for certain dinosaurs such as *Protoceratops* and *Pinacosaurus*. Many of the small mammals may simply have been buried in their burrows. Above the fossiliferous sandstone layer is a moderately coarse conglomerate bed, which is indicative of high-energy water deposition. Furthermore, the structureless (non cross-bedded) sandstone in which all the vertebrate fossils are found contains pebbles and abundant coarse sand.[14] Because of the perfect articulation of the fossil skeletons entombed within the sandstone, its structureless nature is interpreted as being depositional, and not the result of bioturbation. Thus, to virtually bury alive such large animals as dinosaurs implies rapid water flow and catastrophic deposition of the sand. Interbedded with the fossil-bearing, structureless sand units are further sandstone layers with large-scale cross-bedding, which has resulted in these sandstone layers being interpreted as aeolian (produced by desert dunes). Enclave-up downfolds seen in vertical cross-section on the cross-bed surfaces in these sandstones have been interpreted as the tracks of large vertebrates. Although most of these tracks are represented by smooth folds, some show distinct toe and claw indentations. While it hasn't been possible to identify the makers of the tracks, on the basis of the fossils found in the structureless sandstone units, the tracks were probably made by larger dinosaurs such as ankylosaurs or *Protoceratops*. Invertebrate burrows are also present in great abundance.

There is, however, an alternative explanation for the cross-beds in these sandstone units, which is more consistent with what we know of present-day depositional environments and with the evidence in the fossil-bearing, structureless sandstone units. In a desert environment the cross-beds produced by sand dunes are at an angle of 30-34°, the angle of repose for sand. However, the cross-beds produced by underwater sand waves are consistently at an angle of 25°. Thus, the cross-beds in these sandstones being at an angle of 25° are more consistent with an underwater sand-wave origin, which is also consistent with the rapid transport of the sand that catastrophically buried the vertebrates in the associated, structureless sandstone units. Thus, all the evidence surrounding this Ukhaa Tolgod fossil vertebrate graveyard points to catastrophic burial under rapidly water-transported sand.

---

14   D. B. Loope et al, 1998, Life and death in a Late Cretaceous dune field, Nemegt Basin, Mongolia, *Geology*, 26 (1): 27-30.

70

COAL BEDS—FOSSIL GRAVEYARDS OF PLANTS TRANSPORTED AND DEPOSITED BY WATER

Coal is formed from the accumulation and compaction of dead plant material. It consists of nearly pure carbon, from carbon compounds that made up the plants.[1] Even though the oxygen and hydrogen largely disappear from the original plant remains leaving only the carbon, the original plant structures are usually beautifully preserved, so it is easy to identify coal as the end product of the metamorphism of enormous quantities of plant remains buried under sediments and transformed by temperature, pressure, and time. Thus, coal beds qualify as fossil graveyards, where huge masses of plants have become fossilized, their original constituents still often visible within the coal at macroscopic and microscopic scales. Many plant remains such as leaves, stems, and tree trunks are still visible macroscopically in the coal, while under the microscope, wood, leaves, spores, and other components of plants can be readily identified.

Coal beds are first found in the geologic record among Carboniferous strata, and are then found all through the strata sequences above, right up to among Miocene strata, close to the present. Coal beds are found in all parts of the world, on every continent, including Antarctica. In the United States alone, the coal reserves have been estimated by the U.S. Geological Survey to be 7.64 trillion tons,[2] but huge coal reserves occur in China, Canada, Australia, and South Africa. Many coalfields contain multiple coal seams interbedded with other sedimentary strata, each coal seam having a thickness that may vary from a few centimeters to more than a meter. Each meter of coal is thought to represent 4 to 6 meters of plant remains,[3] so the great thicknesses of coal seams testify to the former existence of almost unimaginably massive accumulations of buried plants.

---

1   Davidson, Reed and Davis, 1997, 92, 422-424.

2   Davidson, Reed and Davis, 1997, 423.

3   E. Stach et al, 1982, *Stachs' Textbook of Coal Petrology*, third revised and enlarged edition, Berlin: Gebrüder Borntraeger, 17-18.

Theories of Origin

Historically, geologists have been divided into two camps: those favoring the autochthonous (growth-in-place) theory for the origin and formation of coal, and those favoring the allochthonous (transport and deposition) theory. However, because of the ascendancy of consistent uniformitarianism in geological reasoning over the last century or more, today it is almost universally accepted and taught that the coal-forming plants grew in swamps that slowly over thousands of years accumulated peat layers, which were subsequently buried by other sediments (sands, muds, etc.), to be compressed and biochemically transformed (coalified) to eventually form coal seams.[4] Modern peat-forming swamps, usually cited as examples of what the postulated ancient coal-forming swamps must have been like, include the Dismal Swamp near the coast in the Virginia-North Carolina border area, the swamps and marshes along the Gulf of Mexico coast associated with the Mississippi River delta, and the Okefenokee Swamp and the Everglades of Florida. The great thicknesses of coal seams in coal measure sequences are thus accounted for by assuming a continuous subsidence of the land, more or less at the same rate as the slow accumulation of plant remains in a swamp.

The sedimentary strata interbedded with the coal seams, some of which often contain fossils of marine organisms, are explained by alternating marine incursions over the swamps, and the resulting periods of sediment deposition. A wide variety of sedimentary strata have been found between coal seams, but these are typically explained in terms of cyclothems, recurring cycles of deposition of different sediments, corresponding to the various stages of marine transgressions and regressions. The "ideal" cyclothem is defined on the basis of ten different sedimentary units in sequence in the western part of the Illinois Basin,[5] but the exact cycle found at any one locality is always different from the cycle at any other locality:

> The concept of the ideal cyclothem was developed to represent the optimum succession of deposits during a complete sedimentary cycle. The ideal cyclothem has not been observed fully developed in any one locality.[6]

In fact, a typical cyclothem is usually missing one or more of the strata in the ideal sequence, and/or the order of strata may be reversed. Alternately, coal seams may be interrupted, or disappear laterally, being replaced by massive limestone or being marginally supplanted by shale. Thus, the coal seams appear to constitute a regular part of the deposition that has produced the sequences of sedimentary

---

4   Stach et al, 1982; C. F. K. Diessel, 1992, *Coal-bearing Depositional Systems*, Berlin: Springer-Verlag.

5   J. M. Weller, 1930, Cyclical sedimentation of the Pennyslvanian Period and its significance, *Journal of Geology*, 38: 97-135.

6   W. C. Krumbein and L. L. Sloss, 1963, *Stratigraphy and Sedimentation*, second edition, San Francisco, CA: W.H. Freeman and Company, 536-537.

strata. Indeed, the coal beds are commonly associated above and below with strata that clearly consist of transported sedimentary material.

In any one locality in a coal-bearing sedimentary basin, the cyclothems are commonly repeated tens of times, with each cycle of deposition having accumulated on the previous one. Thus, for example, there are fifty successive cycles in the Illinois Basin, and over one hundred in West Virginia. Although the coal seam in a typical cyclothem may be quite thin (commonly a few centimeters to a few meters thick) compared with the other sedimentary strata, the lateral extent of the coal is often incredible. For example, detailed stratigraphic research has found that the Broken Arrow coal seam of Oklahoma can be correlated with the Croweburgh Seam (Missouri), the Whitebreast Seam (Iowa), the Colchester No. 2 Seam (Illinois), the Coal IIIa Seam (Indiana), the Schultztown Seam (west Kentucky), the Princess No. 6 Seam (east Kentucky), and the Lower Kittanning Seam (Ohio and Pennsylvania).[7] Thus, these seams together form a single, vast bed of coal exceeding 260,000 square kilometers in area in the central and eastern United States. No modern swamp has an area even remotely similar to that of these Carboniferous coal seams.

If the autochthonous (growth-in-place) model for coal formation is correct, a very unusual sequence of circumstances must have occurred. An entire region, often encompassing tens to hundreds of square kilometers, had to be raised simultaneously relative to sea level in order to allow a vast swamp to develop and accumulate peat, and then lowered to permit the ocean to flood the area to deposit the successive sedimentary strata in the cyclothem sequence. If the land surface on which the swamp and its forest had developed was raised too far above sea level, the swamp and its antiseptic water necessary for peat accumulation would have been drained, thus destroying the swamp and the forest. On the other hand, if during peat accumulation the ocean invaded the swamp, then the marine conditions would have killed the plants, and other sediments would have been deposited instead of peat. Thus, according to this almost universally-held conventional model, the formation of a thick bed of coal would require the maintenance of an incredible balance, over many thousands of years, between the rate of peat accumulation, and the rising and falling of sea levels. One or two, or even three, coal seams formed by such alternate stages of swamp growth and peat accumulation, followed by marine transgression, and then subsequently regression, might be believable, but the insistence that this cycle was repeated scores of times on the same spot, and over an enormous area, over a period of perhaps millions of years, is not only most improbable and thus not easy to accept, but simply impossible, there being no modern parallel. Depending on the compaction ratio,

---

7   C. R. Wright, 1965, Environmental mapping of the beds of the Liverpool Cyclothem in the Illinois Basin and equivalent strata in the northern Mid-continent Region, unpublished Ph.D. thesis, University of Illinois; R. M. Kosanke, 1973, Palynological studies of the coals of the Princess Reserve District in north-eastern Kentucky, US Geological Survey, Professional Paper 839; S. E. Nevins, 1976, The origin of coal, Impact Series No. 41, Santee, CA: Institute for Creation Research.

each meter thickness of coal seam could represent five, six, or even twelve meters thickness of accumulated plant remains,[8] so seams of up to ten meters thickness would have supposedly required up to one hundred or more meters thickness of accumulated plant remains, and this cycle at many sites needed to be repeated up to one hundred or more times!

Though almost universally accepted and dogmatically championed, the autochthonous peat swamp model for coal formation utterly fails to explain even one coal seam, because the evidence associated with coal seams, when carefully examined, is utterly inconsistent with the model. Decades of concerted scientific research has not changed this assessment. One of the most respected authorities on coal geology in the 1940s said:

> Though a peat-bog may serve to demonstrate how vegetal matter accumulates in considerable quantities, it is no way comparable in extent to the great bodies of vegetation which must have given rise to our important coal seams....There is sufficient peat in the temperate regions of the world today to form large amounts of coal, if it were concentrated into coal seams, but no single bog or marsh known would supply sufficient peat to make a large coal seam.[9]

More than fifty years later, a comparable scientific authority commented in the introduction to a major textbook:

> Development of actualistic models of peat formation has led to a rejection of the delta environment as the most likely birthplace of major coal deposits....Yet most of today's peat deposits can be compared, in time and volume, only with the (often quite dirty) bottom portion of many economic coal seams. The origin of the up to 80-m-thick anthracite seam (Grande Couche) in the Hongai Coalfield of Vietnam's Tongking Basin (Dennemberg 1937), or the composite thickness of the 300 m of brown coal in a mere 800 m of coal measures in the Latrobe Valley of Victoria, Australia (George 1982), to mention only two of many examples, require conditions in time and space for which there are no current equivalents on Earth.[10]

The Dismal Swamp of coastal Virginia-North Carolina, perhaps one of the most frequently cited examples of a swamp producing a peat layer that could potentially become a coal seam, has formed only an average of just over two

---

8   R. A. Gastaldo, 1999, Debates on autochthonous and allochthonous origin of coal: empirical science versus the diluvialists, in *The Evolution-Creation Controversy II: Perspectives on Science, Religion, and Geological Education*, W.L. Manger, ed., The Palaeontological Society Papers, 5: 135-167.

9   E. S. Moore, 1940, *Coal: Its Properties, Analysis, Classification, Geology, Extraction, Uses and Distribution*, second edition, New York: Wiley, 146.

10   Diessel, 1992, 3-4.

meters of peat, hardly enough to make a single respectable coal seam if the compaction ratio requires 5 to 6 or up to 12 meters of peat to form a one-meter-thick coal seam. However, if the calorific values of equal volumes of coal and peat are compared, then the peat-to-coal compaction ratio would only be 2.3 to 1, while comparing the specific weight of these two, the ratio would come down to 2.2 to 1.[11] In other words, to produce a one-meter-thick coal seam would only require a 2.3-meter-thick layer of peat, which is comparable to the peat layer that has formed beneath the Dismal Swamp. Indeed, field evidence from the geometry of penecontemporaneous channel sandstones in contact with coal seams, and dinosaur tracks in the roofs of coal mines, show that peat-to-coal ratios of 1.2-2.2 to 1 are more realistic estimates of the magnitude of compaction.[12] Furthermore, these data also indicate that virtually all of the compaction occurs at the surface, or within the upper few meters of burial.

However, this evidence does not in itself give credence to the peat swamp model for coal formation, because there is so much evidence associated with coal seams that is far more consistent with the allochthonous (transport and deposition) model. Coal seams are an integral part of the sedimentary sequences in which they occur, and are commonly associated with, and enclosed by, sedimentary strata consisting of transported sediments. For example, sandstones may occupy as much as 80 percent of the total thickness of strata in coal measure sequences, the sand having been moved and deposited by water, as evidenced by cross-bedding. Conglomerates, even with large boulders and wood debris, are not uncommon. In the Newcastle Coal Measures of the Sydney Basin, eastern Australia, conglomerate beds make up 29 percent of the coal measure strata (sandstones make up another 23 percent), and some of these conglomerate beds are cross-bedded and directly overlie coal seams.[13] Even fine-grained siltstones and shales, usually even-bedded, often contain evidence of rapid deposition by water, such as aligned fossilized plant remains, flute casts, and the general absence of bioturbation. Often coal seams are abruptly overlain by sedimentary strata interpreted as distinctly marine, because of the marine fossils found in them. There is a complete lack of any intervening transitional brackish-water deposits, which would be expected with the gradual change in salinity if the ocean had gradually encroached upon the enormous freshwater swamps and bogs, in which the peat for the coal seams was supposedly formed.

Some coal seams when followed laterally are found to split into two seams, separated by strata consisting of transported marine sediments. This can only indicate that the deposition of the plant remains making up the coal and the

---

11   J. Scheven, 1981, Floating forests on firm grounds: advances in Carboniferous research, *Biblical Creation*, 3 (9): 36-43.

12   G. C. Nadon, 1998, Magnitude and timing of peat-to-coal compaction, *Geology*, 26 (8): 727-730.

13   C. F. K. Diessel, 1980, Newcastle and Tomago coal measures, in *A Guide to the Sydney Basin*, C. Herbert and R. Helby, ed., *Geological Survey of New South Wales Bulletin*, 26: 100-114; Diessel, 1992, 330-335, 361-374.

associated marine sediments had to be coeval. In the west European coalfields, coal seams not only coalesce or split over a distance of only a few kilometers, but cases are known where two separate well-defined seams are connected by a sloping third coal seam, producing what is termed a Z-connection. Coal seams themselves are usually bedded, with laminations marked by slight changes in color, and break apart on certain planes, like shale that is regarded as being of transported origin. Indeed, many coal seams, particularly thick coal seams, contain one or more shale or siltstone bands that are often consistent for tens of kilometers or more. Thus, the actual physical evidence associated with coal seams is very strongly consistent with the plant remains, which formed the peat precursor to the coal, having been transported and deposited by water flow, just as the sediments in the inter-seam strata have been water-deposited. Simplicity and consistency would both suggest that the plant remains were also water-borne and deposited.

The microscopic texture and structure of peat and coal have been investigated, as part of a comparative structural study between modern autochthonous (growth-in-place) mangrove peats, and a rare modern allochthonous (transported and deposited) beach peat from southern Florida.[14] It was found that most autochthonous peats had plant fragments showing random orientation within a dominant matrix of finer material, while the allochthonous peat showed current orientation of elongated axes of plant fragments generally parallel to the beach surface, with a characteristic lack of the finer matrix. Also, the poorly-sorted plant debris in the autochthonous peats had a massive structure, due to the intertwining mass of roots, while the allochthonous peat had characteristic micro-lamination, due to the absence of intergrown roots. It was concluded:

> A peculiar enigma which developed from study of the allochthonous peat was that vertical microtome sections of this material looked more like thin sections of Carboniferous coal than any of the autochthonous samples studied.[15]

It was also noted that the characteristics of this allochthonous peat (orientation of elongated fragments, sorted granular texture with general lack of finer matrix, micro-lamination with a lack of matted root structure) are also the general characteristics of Carboniferous coals, the world's major coal deposits in North America and Europe.

Not only are coal seams interbedded with sedimentary strata containing marine fossils, but marine fossils have also been found in the coal seams themselves:

> The small marine tubeworm, *Spirorbis*, is abundant in the fossil record.

---

14   A. D. Cohen, 1970, An allochthonous peat deposit from southern Florida, *Geological Society of America Bulletin*, 81: 2477-2482.

15   Cohen, 1970, 2480.

No member of this genus is found in a fresh-water habitat. Since *Spirorbis* tubes are found as a constituent of Carboniferous coal, they are strong evidence for the allochthonous, or transported, origin of much of the coal.[16]

These marine tubeworms must have become attached to the drifting plants that now make up the coal, because they are commonly found attached to the plant remains in the Carboniferous coals of Europe and North America. Furthermore, it is not uncommon to find various marine fossils within what are known as "coal balls," which are rounded masses of matted and exceptionally well-preserved plant and animal fossils, cemented with mineral matter. The marine animals found fossilized in these coal balls include sponges, corals, crinoid stems, bryozoa (lace corals), brachiopods, mollusks, arthropods, conodonts, and even fish.[17] Furthermore, the mineral cement of these coal balls requires a salt-water environment for their formation.[18]

One of the most striking inorganic features of coal seams is the presence of boulders. These have been observed in coal beds all over the world, including Europe and North America, for well over one hundred years. In a survey of the many erratic boulders found in the Sewell Seam in West Virginia, the average weight of forty boulders collected was 5.44 kg, with the largest weighing just over 73 kg.[19] Many of the boulders were igneous and metamorphic rocks, unlike any rock outcrops in West Virginia. The nearest possible source for some of them was almost 100 km away. It has been suggested that the boulders must have been transported from their distant source areas as they were entwined in the roots of trees. Thus, the occurrence of these boulders in the coal seams would seem to favor the allochthonous model.

---

16   H. G. Coffin, 1968, A paleoecological misinterpretation, *Creation Research Society Quarterly*, 5: 85.

17   S. H. Mamay and E. L. Yokhelson, 1962, *Occurrence and significance of marine animal remains in American coal balls*, US Geological Survey Professional Paper, 354-I: 193-224.

18   L. R. Moore, 1968, Some sediments closely associated with coal seams, in *Coal and Coal-bearing Strata*, D. Murchison and T.S. Westoll, ed., New York: American Elsevier Publishing Company, 105-107.

19   P. H. Price, 1932, Erratic boulders in Sewell Coal of West Virginia, *Journal of Geology*, 40: 62-63.

71

COAL BEDS—FOSSIL GRAVEYARDS OF PLANTS THAT GREW FLOATING ON WATER

The types of fossil plants found in coal seams do not readily, or necessarily, support the autochthonous (growth-in-place) model for coal seam formation. The fossil plants in the North American and European Carboniferous coals are dominated by fossil lycopods trees (for example, *Lepidodendron* and *Sigillaria*), and giant ferns (especially *Psaronius*). While it is claimed these plants may have had some ecological tolerance to swampy conditions, other Carboniferous coal plants, such as the conifer *Cordaites*, the giant scouring rush *Calamites*, and the various extinct seed ferns, by their basic construction must have preferred well-drained soils, not swamps.

However, the anatomy of these plants needs to be carefully reconsidered. The huge, fossilized trunks of these Carboniferous trees, as exposed in outcrops and in coal mines, are not solid wood, but casts of hollow stems. Indeed, all the trees whose remains are either found in the Carboniferous coal seams, or associated with them, are either hollow or otherwise lightly-built structures.[1] The lycopods, *Lepidodendron*, *Sigillaria*, and related genera, giant relatives of the clubmosses, were supplied with mineral nutrients and water through a central cylinder, while a tough and ever-widening ring of bark rendered structural support. The space between the bark and the central cylinder was largely filled with aerenchyma (air tissue). In the fossil state, these tree trunks are found either flattened or, if buried erect, filled with sediment, which on occasion has been found to have entombed gastropods, worms, and even reptiles.[2] These tree-sized lycopods are known to have grown to heights of up to 45 meters,[3] their trunks rising above four cross-shaped, equally air-filled, main roots, which in turn were forked dichotomously, and extended away from the stem by as much as 20 meters horizontally. Apart from a spongy central cylinder, these structures were also essentially hollow, so like

---

1   Scheven, 1981, 40-41; J. Scheven, 1990, Stasis in the fossil record as confirmation of the belief in Biblical Creation, in *Proceedings of the Second International Conference on Creationism*, volume 1, R. E. Walsh and C. L. Brooks, ed., Pittsburgh, PA: Creation Science Fellowship, 197-215.

2   J. W. Dawson, 1866, On conditions of the deposition of coal, more especially as illustrated by the coal formations of Nova Scotia and New Brunswick, *Quarterly Journal of the Geological Society*, 22: 95-104.

3   White, 1986, 75.

the trunks, they are also preserved either flat or as casts. The central cylinder usually became compressed after burial, which left a characteristic groove on the top sides of many of these roots resulting from this compression. These air-filled root axes, known as *Stigmaria*, were covered all around with radiating appendices, that is, pencil-thick organs up to 0.5 m long, which again seem to have contained little but air. Frequently they are preserved in their original lamp-brush position, which is a growth pattern characteristic of plant organs submerged in water, whereas roots growing in soils are always predominantly geotropic. These *Stigmarian* axes thus formed a network of roots in water, over which the tall trunks of the lycopods could stand erect, the leaf tops of the trees probably being quite small. The fact that disused appendices of older *Stigmaria* fell off at tree-formed abscission layers, leaving behind the well-known circular scars seen on the bark of fossilized trunks, is further proof that the coal-forming lepidophytes never grew in soils on firm ground, but must have been floating adherently on water surfaces.

That the flora found fossilized in the Carboniferous coals was originally a floating vegetation ecosystem was first recognized more than a century ago.[4] The principal constituent of a Carboniferous coal seam appears to have been these criss-crossing, intertwined lycopod roots (*Stigmaria*), as determined through the study of coal balls. Furthermore, the remains of trunks have been found fossilized, buried in the upright living position, apparently rooted in the coal seams themselves, having grown in the peat that developed on the floor of this floating-forest vegetation, supported by the entangled *Stigmaria*. Nevertheless, the most common plant fossils found in the shales, which often overlie the coal seams, are the leaves of seed-bearing ferns, the stems of which grew several meters high. The roots of these seed ferns are never encountered in the so-called underclays, where lycopod roots are usually found in abundance. Instead, the roots of the seed ferns are found only in the coal seams themselves, and thus the seed ferns seem to have been rooted above the matted and interwoven *Stigmaria*-tangle in the thick-layered peat formed from leaf and other litter. The seed ferns, therefore, probably represented the undergrowth in the floating forest's decay system. Similarly, the roots of the conifer *Cordaites* are not found in the underclays among the *Stigmaria*, so it seems certain that the *Cordaites* trees also grew on the peat layer accumulating above the *Stigmaria* roots, rather than from the level of those roots that became buried in the underclays. Tree trunks of *Cordaites* enclosed a wide pith, which thus lessened their weight. Some Carboniferous coal-bearing strata contain a greater percentage of fossilized giant horsetails, commonly *Calamites*, whose stems were essentially hollow, greatly reducing their bulk weight. Cross-sections of the roots of *Calamites*, also sometimes found in coal balls within coal seams, reveal that they also consisted of large air spaces, which means that these roots can likewise be interpreted as submerged organs. Thus, the giant horsetails were probably also growing as part of this floating-forest ecosystem, perhaps sometimes growing by themselves.

4   O. Kuntze, 1895, *Geogenetische Beitrage. Sind Carbonkohlen autochthon, allochthon oder pelagochthon?*, Leibzig, Germany.

The coal seams of the southern hemisphere continents plus India, that are said to have been joined together in a Gondwana supercontinent, are all Permian, in contrast to the North American and European coals, which are Carboniferous. These Gondwana coals also are made up of a different fossil flora, dominated by fossilized *Glossopteris* leaves. The common lack of underclays, or so-called fossil soils, beneath the Gondwana coal seams has in the past been convincing evidence that the plant remains were transported and deposited to form the coal seams:

> In the case of the Permo-Carboniferous of India, the Barakar Series and the Damuda Series, overlying the Talchir Boulder Bed, include numerous coal seams, some up to 100 feet thick, occurring in a well-developed and oft-repeated cycle of sandstone, shale, coal.... The vegetation is considered to be drift accumulation.[5]

However, such is the strength of the prevailing paradigm, shaped by the interpretation of the evidence associated with the Carboniferous coals, that the Permian Gondwana coals are nevertheless still almost universally regarded to have been produced by peat swamps that grew in place.[6] That assertion, though, depends heavily on the assumption that the *Glossopteris* flora found fossilized associated with, and in, the coal seams is of autochthonous origin. Yet the fossil *Glossopteris* flora is poorly understood, because what has been preserved is almost exclusively fossilized leaves.

The name *Glossopteris* refers to the tongue-shaped outline of these detached leaves, but the overall appearance of the plants has not yet been conclusively elucidated due to the lack of complete fossils, and in spite of claims to the contrary.[7] To identify *Glossopteris* leaves on a specific level is practically impossible, given the range of shapes and venations found in fossil specimens. Without a pronounced mid-rib such fossil leaves are referred to the genus *Gangamopteris*. There are, however, so many intermediates between this absence of a mid-rib through to the mid-rib in *Glossopteris* leaves, and an arrow-shaped *Glossopteris* leaf from India has an outline similar to the leaf of an arum lily.[8] Without the support of this mid-rib (which is actually only a concentration of parallel veins), these leaves may even have grown underwater. There are perhaps fewer than one dozen descriptions of fossil twigs with *Glossopteris* leaves connected to them.[9] It appears that the leaves grew

5   S. E. Hollingsworth, 1962, The climatic factor in the geological record, *Quarterly Journal of the Geological Society of London*, 118: 13.

6   For example, Diessel, 1992.

7   For example, White, 1986, 99-121.

8   J. Scheven, 1992, *Gleanings from Glossopteris*, Fifth European Creationist Congress, Biblical Creation Society and Creation Science Movement, England.

9   J. Etheridge, 1905, Sub-reniform-ovate leaves of *Glossopteris*, *Records of the Geological Survey of New South Wales*, Sydney; E. Dolianiti, 1954, *A Flora do Gondwana Inferior Em Santa Catarina IV*. Notas Preliminares e Estudos, Ministry of Agriculture, Rio de Janeiro; E. P. Plumstead, 1958, The habitat of growth of *Glossopteridae*, *Transactions of the Geological Society of South Africa*, 61: 81-96; D. D. Pant,

in whorls, perhaps comparable to some conifers like *Araucaria*. The compressed reproductive organs have been given various names, and are so different from one another that their relationships are difficult to elucidate with certainty.[10] The striking uniformity of leaf shapes may have been imposed by an environmental factor, or may be internally controlled. Its nearest replication is among numerous recent ferns.[11]

The only fossilized, stem-like structures found with *Glossopteris* leaves are flat ribbon-like impressions that are vaguely reminiscent of bones in the human vertebral column, so they have been given the name *Vertebraria*. Although usually much rarer, the fact that they occur in conjunction with *Glossopteris* leaves probably means that both are just different organs of the same type of plant. A number of reconstructions of *Vertebraria* postulate large serial air spaces along their axes, which would explain the invariably flattened appearance of the *Vertebraria*.[12] Thin threads, that are apparently genuine roots, are sometimes visible where they emerge from the main axes at the junction between neighboring air spaces. It also appears as if there are two modifications of *Vertebraria* axes—the thin and inflated horizontal rhizome-like structures, and the more solid, upright version, which would appear to have carried the foliage. The chambered axes with their air spaces clearly point to an aquatic mode of life, which would suggest only moderate growth, perhaps with a semi-herbaceous, water-borne habit.

Despite the almost total absence of fossilized *Glossopteris* leaves attached to fossilized branches and tree stumps, it has been claimed that the *Glossopterids* were woody plants, presumably of all sizes from shrubs to large trees.[13] However, the fossilized tree stumps and prone logs found associated with coal seams, and at various levels within the inter-seam sedimentary strata of the coal measures in the Sydney Basin, eastern Australia, have been assigned to the genus *Dadoxylon*, related to the conifers of the *Araucaria* because of their woody structure with many distinct growth rings.[14] It should, therefore, be obvious that these woody

1977, The plant of *Glossopteris*, *The Journal of the Indian Botanical Society*, 56 (1): 1-23.

10   E. P. Plumstead, 1958, Further fructifications of the *Glossopteridae* and a provisional classification based on them, *Transactions of the Geological Society of South Africa*, 61: 51-79, M. E. White, 1978, Reproductive structures of the *Glossopteridales* in the plant fossil collection of the Australian Museum, *Records of the Australian Museum*, 31 (12): 473-505; M. E. White, 1986, 108-121.

11   Scheven, 1992.

12   J. M. Schopf, 1965, Anatomy of the axis in *Vertebraria*, in *Geology and Palaeontologies of the Antarctic*, Antarctic Research Series, 6: 217-228; R. B. Gould, 1975, A preliminary report on petrified axes of *Vertebraria* from the Permian of eastern Australia, in *Gondwana Geology*, K. S. W. Campbell, ed., Canberra: Australian National University Press, 109-115; Pant, 1977; White, 1986, 102-109; P. G. Neish, 1993, A. N. Drinnan and D. J. Cantrill, Structure and ontogeny of *Vertebraria* from silicified Permian sediments in east Antarctica, *Review of Palaeobotany and Palynology*, 79: 221-244.

13   Pant, 1977; White, 1986, 102-3, 108.

14   W. B. Clarke, 1884, Awaba fossil forest, *Annual Report of the Department of Mines, New South Wales*, 156-159; T. W. E. David, 1907, The geology of the Hunter River coal measures, New South Wales, *Geological Survey of New South Wales, Memoir 4*; Diessel, 1992.

tree stumps and logs cannot be the same as, or even related to, these *Vertebraria* with their chambered air spaces that are undoubtedly related to the ubiquitous *Glossopteris* leaves found with them. The other fossil flora that accompanies *Glossopteris* in association with the Gondwana coals include some lycopods, horsetails, ferns, and seed-ferns. Thus, this fossil floral assemblage, ostensibly from mixed habitats, though dominated by water-borne varieties, is more consistent with an allochthonous origin for these Gondwana coals.

Because "the composite thickness of the 300 m of brown coal in a mere 800 m of coal measures in the Latrobe Valley of Victoria, Australia" required "conditions in time and space for which there are no current equivalents on Earth,"[15] it is important to also review the fossil flora found in these thick (up to 165 m) lignite seams. These seams are considered to be autochthonous in origin, requiring a coal-forming swamp that occupied an area of at least 50 x 25 km, in which there were a number of changing plant communities. These ranged from a swamp lake and moors, to swamp forests, supposedly similar to the vegetation claimed to be in the coal-forming swamps responsible for producing the Tertiary brown coals of the Lower Rhineland area of Germany.[16] Yet the list of trees whose wood is found in the Latrobe Valley coal seams includes the conifers *Agathis* (Kauri), *Araucaria* (Hoop Pine), *Dacrydium* (Huon Pine), *Phyllocladus* (Celery-top Pine), and *Podocarpus* (Totara), all in the families *Araucariaceae* and *Podocarpaceae*, and the angiosperms *Casuarina*, *Nothofagus*, and *Banksia*.[17] Other plant groups, including the *Ericales*, *Myrtaceae*, *Oleaceae*, and *Proteaceae*, are assumed to be present in the brown coal because of the occurrence of their pollen there.

It has been concluded that the forests from which the brown coal was formed were most purely coniferous, and hardwoods, although occasionally present, were somewhat accidental. Furthermore, the coal seams consist largely of tree trunks, some with their roots upright, there being a general absence of mineral matter. Nevertheless, it is insisted that all these conifers, and hardwoods, grew in a huge forest in a swamp. However, these trees today are known to only grow in rainforests.[18] Indeed, many of these trees cannot tolerate swampy conditions, as is evidenced by where their descendants grow today, namely, in soils on firm ground that is not swampy. Some grow in the same area today, but the Kauri and most of the other pines, for example, prefer more subtropical-tropical environments. Thus,

---

15   Diessel, 1992, 4.

16   M. Teichmüller, 1958, Reconstruction of the various moor types in the mainland Coal Seam of the Lower Rhineland, *Fortschrieft Geologische Rhineland und Westfalen*, 2: 599-612; A. M. George, 1975, Brown coal lithotypes in the Latrobe Valley deposits, *State Electricity Commission of Victoria, Petrological Report*, 17: 32-35.

17   I. C. Cookson and S. L. Duigan, 1951, Tertiary Araucariacae from south-eastern Australia, with notes on living species, *Australian Journal of Scientific Research*, B (4): 415-449; R. T. Patton, 1958, Fossil wood from Victorian brown coal, *Proceedings of the Royal Society of Victoria*, 70 (2): 129-143; George, 1975.

18   Patton, 1958; I.R.K. Sluiter et al, 1995, Biogeographic, ecological and stratigraphic relationships of the Miocene brown coal floras, Latrobe Valley, Victoria, Australia, *International Journal of Coal Geology*, 28: 277-302.

it is evident that the brown coal formed as a result of transport and deposition of all this plant material, leaving prone logs and tree stumps with roots upright as unequivocal evidence.

Underclays—Fossil Soils?

Among the strongest evidences claimed for the autochthonous (growth *in situ*) model for coal formation is the widespread presence, under the Carboniferous coal seams of North America and Europe, of what are called underclays or seat-earths. These are regarded as the fossilized remains of the substrate or soil in which ancient vegetation once germinated and flourished in a swamp, and then died to accumulate the peat. The presence of *Stigmaria*, the fossilized roots of the lycopods found fossilized in association with the coal seams, projecting out from under the coal seams into these underclays, is claimed to be *prima facie* evidence that these lycopods grew *in situ* in these underclays in coal-forming swamps. However, the *Stigmarian* roots of the lycopods are the only plant organs commonly found in these underclays. Other roots, for example, of ferns, seed-ferns, horsetails, and the conifer *Cordaites*, which are well known within the coal seams, are completely absent in the underclays.[19] This is the principal difference between the *Stigmarian* roots of the lycopods and the roots of other constituents of the coal-forming vegetation. In contrast, in any modern plant community the member plants are rooted side-by-side in the substrate soil. Because this is not the case with the underclays, the obvious conclusion is that the plant communities of these Carboniferous coal-forming forests were not rooted in soils, and the underclays are thus not fossilized soils.

Additional confirmation of this is the hollow structure of the *Stigmarian* roots and of the trunks of the lycopods (as already elaborated above), which conclusively demonstrate that these trees (giant clubmosses) must have grown in water in a unique floating-forest ecosystem that is now extinct.[20] Thus, the presence of the fossilized *Stigmaria* in the underclays is because they became entombed in these clays as the peat layers they supported, by their intertwined network generated by the floating forests, were buried by the sediments being deposited on top of them. The evidence for these *Stigmaria* not being soil-penetrating roots but hollow structures for supporting the lycopod trees in water is irrefutable, because of the careful investigation of well-preserved *Stigmaria* in coal balls.[21] Indeed, the name "stigmaria" is derived from the presence of numerous scars spirally distributed all

---

19   J. Scheven, 1996, The Carboniferous floating forest—an extinct pre-Flood ecosystem, *Creation Ex Nihilo Technical Journal*, 10 (1): 70-81.

20   K. P. Wise, 2003, The pre-Flood floating forest: a study in paleontological pattern recognition, in *Proceedings of the Fifth International Conference on Creationism*, R. L. Ivey, Jr., ed., Pittsburgh, PA: Creation Science Fellowship, 371-381.

21   J. Frankenberg and D. A. Eggert, 1969, Petrified *Stigmaria* from North America: part 1. *Stigmaria ficoides*, the underground portions of lepidodendraceae, *Palaentographica Abt.*, B 128: 1-2, Stutgart; J. R. Jennings, 1973, The morphology of stigmaria stellata, *American Journal of Botany*, 60 (5): 414-425.

over the surface of the cylindrical roots where aging rootlets were shed, just like foliage discarded on branches, a procedure that does not occur in roots that grow in soils, but is consistent with their growth in water.

Much research has shown conclusively that these underclays are not fossilized soils. For example, the chemical and physiological nature of the underclays reveals no soil profile similar to that found in modern soils:

> The relationships between underclays and coals indicate that the underclays formed before the coals were deposited. Furthermore, lack of a soil profile similar to modern soils and similarity of the mineralogy of all rock types below the coals indicate that underclay materials were essentially as they were transported into the basin. ... The underclays were probably deposited in a loose, hydrous flocculated state, and slickensides developed during compaction.[22]

Numerous other scientific papers reporting research on these underclays over five decades repeatedly conclude that the underclays are not the product of atmospheric weathering, show no soil profiles, and are in fact transported sediments.[23] Indeed, some of the minerals found in the underclays are not those that would be expected in a soil. Probably the most widespread type of underclay is a purplish-black mudstone, thickly permeated from flattened *Stigmaria* and their adhering appendices. Most common are underclays consisting of laminated siltstone or of pure sandstone. In some instances, it has been observed the lithology of an underclay may vary below a seam over some distance. Furthermore, an underclay may also consist of limestone. How could these underclays therefore be fossilized soils, as no living plant is known that would tolerate such a diversity of "soils," from nutrient rich to sterile, and from utterly acidic to utterly alkaline? The different lithologies around the lycopod roots are therefore simply the product of the deposition of different sediments, and no relationship exists between the uniform coal-forming vegetation and the varying compositions of these underclays that have been claimed to be fossil soils. In any case, many coal seams do not rest on underclays, even being found to overlie granite or schist where there is no evidence whatsoever of a former soil. Other coal seams, such as the Gondwana coals that rival the Carboniferous coals of North America and Europe, are rarely underlain by these underclays, with siltstones, sandstones, and even conglomerates and tuffs, being far more prevalent beneath the coal seams than shales or mudstones.[24]

Where underclays contain a component of sand or silt they are commonly laminated or stratified, due to the differential segregation of the different sized

---

22 L. G. Schultz, 1958, Petrology of underclays, *Geological Society of America Bulletin*, 69 (4): 391-392.

23 Scheven, 1996, 72, Table 1.

24 For example, Diessel, 1992, 362-365, Figure 7.9, which is a detailed stratigraphic section of the Tomago and Newcastle Coal Measures in the Sydney Basin, eastern Australia.

sediment particles during the settling process. Many typical underclays of the northwest European coal basins are between two and three meters thick, and are distinctly more coarse-grained toward their bases. In other examples there is evidence of clay flocculation. These are all simple sedimentary features that always form in water-accumulated layers. Furthermore, the laminations, stratification, and graded bedding have in no way been disturbed by the *Stigmaria* entombed in the underclays, in comparison to a true soil where growing roots will destroy any such original structures. Thus, the coal-forming vegetation did not take root on the surfaces of the underclays after the underclays formed, so the latter were not soils, but just sediments that buried the *Stigmaria*. Also relevant is the observation that, although the Carboniferous underclays are devoid of root organs other than the *Stigmarian* axes belonging to lycopods, there are numerous fine examples of fern pinnules and even parts of whole fronds found in some underclays, as well as lepidophyte bark and fossilized marine organisms. A fresh fern frond in soil will decompose within a very short time, yet these fern fronds are identical to those ordinarily found in the roof shales above the coal seams, so both must therefore have been buried in the same manner by sediment deposition. The persuasive clarity of all this evidence has convinced serious investigators for more than a century that these ubiquitous underclays beneath Carboniferous coal seams are not soils in which vegetation grew *in situ*, but are very clearly water-laid sediments.[25]

It was the *Stigmaria* in the underclays beneath the Carboniferous coal seams of Nova Scotia, studied by Charles Lyell and J. W. Dawson almost 160 years ago, that were considered to provide definitive proof that the coal-forming vegetation grew in place.[26] However, this same Nova Scotia coal sequence was restudied 125 years later, and four types of sedimentary evidence for the allochthonous origin of the *Stigmaria* in the underclays were documented.[27] The *Stigmaria* were found to be only fragments, and rarely attached to a lycopod tree trunk. The *Stigmaria* in each sampling location also showed a preferred orientation of their long axes, unequivocal evidence of current action during deposition. Furthermore, the *Stigmaria* were filled with sediment unlike the immediately surrounding sedimentary rock, and they were often found on multiple horizons in beds that were entirely penetrated by upright fossilized lycopod tree trunks. Thus, it was concluded that these *Stigmaria* studied, and their enclosing sedimentary strata, must have been transported by water and deposited in their present locations, rather than having grown in place. However, this is not the only coal measure sequence where these observations have been made, because the *Stigmarian* axes

---

25   W. S. Gresley, 1887, Notes on the formation of coals seams as suggested by evidence collected chiefly in the Leicestershire and South Derbyshire coalfields, *Quarterly Journal of the Geological Society of London*, 43: 671-674.

26   C. Lyell, 1844, On the upright fossil-trees found at different levels in the coal strata of Cumberland, Nova Scotia, *Annals and Magazine of Natural History, Companion: Botanical Magazine N.S.*, 17: 148-151.

27   N. A. Rupke, 1969, Sedimentary evidence for the allochthonous origin of Stigmaria, Carboniferous, Nova Scotia, *Geological Society of America Bulletin*, 80: 2109-2114.

associated with coal seams in other places have occasionally been found to be in drift-aligned positions, while the surrounding appendices have been found compressed on split rock surfaces contrary to their natural arrangement of growth.[28] All of these observations, taken together, plus the fact that underclays may also occur on top of coal seams, demonstrate conclusively that underclays were deposited in the normal sedimentary deposition cycle of the other strata in coal measure sequences, including the coal seams themselves.

Upright Fossilized Trees

One of the most fascinating types of fossils associated with coal seams are upright tree trunks, which often penetrate several to ten or more meters perpendicular to the stratification, such fossils being known as polystrate (many strata). These upright tree trunks are frequently encountered in strata associated with coal, often sitting directly on top of the coal seams, and on rare occasions are found in the coal itself. It was in the 1830s that the so-called fossil forest at Joggins, Nova Scotia, was first noticed, and following detailed mapping in the early 1840s, was frequently visited by Lyell and Dawson, who both regarded these fossilized upright lycopod tree trunks, along with the *Stigmaria* in the underclay, as conclusive proof of the autochthonous (growth-in-place) model for coal-seam formation.[29]

Among the important discoveries also made was the occurrence of vertebrate and invertebrate fauna within the erect tree stumps, the hollow insides of which had been infilled with sediments that had entombed these animals. Eleven vertebrate genera have so far been identified, including amphibians and reptiles (over 100 individuals), as well as snails, millipedes, worms, and even a may-fly.[30] In recent years, fauna previously found only in the fossilized tree trunks has been discovered external to them, including an amphibian skull, and a fully articulated reptile skeleton. "Many of the trunks are up to 5 m tall and 75 cm in diameter, and the nature of the sediments within the trunks suggest that at some periods the trunks may have been submerged in more than 5 m of water."[31] Sediments that fill the hollow lycopod trunks to make the cast of them are commonly unlike the immediately surrounding sedimentary strata, but there is also evidence that, after

28   Scheven, 1981, 39; Gastaldo, 1999, 151, Figure 4.1.

29   Lyell, 1844; C. Lyell and J. W. Dawson, 1853, On the remains of a reptile (*Dendrerpeton acadianum* Wyman and Owen), and of the land shell discovered in the area of an erect fossil tree in the coal measures of Nova Scotia, *Geological Society of London Quarterly Journal*, 9: 58-63; J. W. Dawson, 1866, On the conditions of the deposition of coal, more especially as illustrated by the coal formations of Nova Scotia and New Brunswick, *Quarterly Journal of the Geological Society*, 22: 95-104; J. W. Dawson, 1882, On the results of recent explorations of erect trees containing animal remains in the coal-formation of Nova Scotia, *Philosophical Transactions of the Royal Society of London*, 173 (II): 621-654.

30   M. R. Gibling, J. H. Calder and R. D. Naylor, 1992, Carboniferous coal basins of Nova Scotia, *Geological Association of Canada and Mineralogical Association of Canada, Joint Annual Meeting*, Wolfville '92, Field trip C-1, guidebook, 21-29; A. C. Scott and J. H. Calder, 1994, Carboniferous fossil forests, *Geology Today*, 10 (6): 213-217.

31   Scott and Calder, 1994, 215.

the hollow lycopod trunks were surrounded by sediment, the bark surviving long enough to keep the hollow inside unfilled, the sediment layer being washed in above slumped into the hollow trunks to infill them, taking with them the animals that had been trapped within those sediments due to the speed of the deposition.[32] Also confirming the rapid rate of transport and deposition of these sediments that buried and infilled these lycopod trunks is the presence of cross-bedding in the sandstones inside some of the casts of the fossilized lycopod trunks.[33]

The "fossil forest" of upright, polystrate tree trunks associated with the Carboniferous coal seams at Joggins, Nova Scotia, is not unique. Numerous other examples have been found in North America and Europe. Some examples include the "fossil forests" at Kupferdray near Essen in Germany,[34] at Weaklaw near North Berwick on the Scottish coast just east of Edinburgh, on the northeast corner of the island of Arran off the west coast of Scotland, at Table Head near Sydney on Cape Breton Island, at Mary Lee in the Warrior Basin of northwestern Alabama, [35] and along Sand Mountain in the Plateau coalfield of northeastern Alabama.[36] However, these "fossil forests" are not confined to Carboniferous coal measure sequences, but have also been found in Permian Gondwana coal measure sequences, such as in the Newcastle and Wittingham Coal Measures in the Sydney Basin of Australia's east coast.[37] Indeed, in the Newcastle Coal Measures there are repeated horizons with fossilized upright tree stumps and prone logs, but here the wood of the trees, which are usually *Dadoxylon* (probably belonging to the *Araucariaceae*), is either coalified or petrified. Some of these tree trunks are sitting on top of one coal seam penetrating the strata above and right up through the next coal seam (Figure 46, page 1083). Miners have reported such upright coalified logs being tens of meters long, and penetrating several coal seams and the strata between them.[38] Most of these fossilized logs and tree stumps have no roots, because they have been broken off (Figure 47, page 1084).

In each case, the sediments that make up the strata in which these fossilized trees are entombed must have amassed rapidly in a short time to cover the trees before

32 Scheven, 1996, 76-77, Figures 5-7; H. G. Coffin, 1969, Research on the classic Joggins petrified trees, *Creation Research Society Quarterly*, 6 (1): 35-44, 70.

33 Diessel, 1992, 390, Figure 7.30; Scheven, 1996, 77, Figure 7.

34 H. Klusemann and R. Teichmüller, 1954, Begrabene Wälder im Rurhkohlenbecken, *Natur und Volk*, 84: 373-382; Stach et al, 1982, 7, Figure 1.

35 R. A. Gastaldo, T. M. Demko, and Y. Liu, 1993, The application of sequence and genetic stratigraphic concepts to Carboniferous coal-bearing strata: an example from the Black Warrior Basin, USA, *Geologische Rundschau*, 82: 212-226; Scott and Calder, 1994; Gastaldo, 1999, 150, Figure 3.1.

36 R. A. Gastaldo, M. A. Gibson and T. B. Gray, 1989, An Appalachian-sourced deltaic sequence, northwestern Alabama, USA: biofacies-lithofacies relationships and interpreted community patterns, *International Journal of Coal Geology*, 12: 225-257.

37 David, 1907; I. G. Percival, 1985, *The Geological Heritage of New South Wales*, volume 1, New South Wales National Parks and Wildlife Service, Sydney, 2-3, 81-89; Diessel, 1992, 312-329, Figures 6.33, 6.41 and 6.42, 360-371, Figures 7.9 and 7.18, and 388-393, Figures 7.29, 7.31 and 7.32.

38 Personal communication from Bruce Clark in 1998 in reference to the West Wallsend Colliery.

they could rot and fall down:

> In 1959 Broadhurst and Magraw described a fossilized tree, in position of growth, from the coal measures at Blackrod near Wigan in Lancashire. This tree was preserved as a cast, and the evidence available suggested that the cast was at least 38 feet (almost 12m) in height. The original tree must have been surrounded and buried by sediment which was compacted before the bulk of the tree decomposed so that the cavity vacated by the trunk could be occupied by new sediment which formed the cast. This implies a rapid rate of sedimentation around the original tree.[39]

> It is clear that trees in position of growth are far from being rare in Lancashire (Teichmüller, 1956, reaches the same conclusion for similar trees in the Rhein-Westfalen Coal Measures), and presumably in all cases there must have been a rapid rate of sedimentation.[40]

It is also noteworthy that even though many of these fossilized tree trunks may be six to nine meters high, the tops of the trees have never been found preserved also. In every case, the tops of the trees have been broken off, and often at the bottom as well, being devoid of both branches and roots. The fossilized tree trunks are not always found erect either, occurring in positions at all angles to the enclosing strata, and some even appear to be upside down, with their root end uppermost.[41] A striking example of an inclined fossilized trunk was found in a sandstone quarry near Edinburgh, Scotland, this fossilized log being 25 m long, leaning at an angle of about 40°, and intersecting ten or twelve different strata.[42] Other similar examples have been recorded, in one case with the comment: "In such examples, the drifted trees seem to have sunk with their heavy or root end touching the bottom and their upper end pointing upward in the direction of the current."[43] Just as noteworthy is where upright trees appear to be rooted in the growth position in one stratum, which is entirely penetrated by a second upright tree.[44]

Thus, in conclusion, the evidence unequivocally favors the contention that these

---

39 F. M. Broadhurst and D. Macgraw, 1959, On a fossil tree found in an opencast coal sight near Wigam, *Lancashire, Liverpool and Manchester Geological Journal*, 2: 155-158; F. M. Broadhurst, 1964, Some aspects of the paleoecology of non-marine faunas and rates of sedimentation in the Lancashire coal measures, *American Journal of Science*, 262: 865.

40 R. Teichmüller, 1956, Die Entwicklung der Subvariscishen Vortiefe und der Werdegang des Ruhrkarbons, Z, *Dtsch Geol. Ges.*, 107: 55-65; Broadhurst, 1964, 866.

41 N. A. Rupke, 1966, Prolegomena to a study of cataclysmal sedimentation, *Creation Research Society Quarterly*, 3: 16-37.

42 W. E. Tayler, 1857, *Voices from the Rocks (or proving the existence of man during the Paleozoic or most ancient period of the earth): A Reply to the late Hugh Miller's Testimony of the Rocks*, London.

43 A. Geikie, 1903, *Textbook of Geology*, fourth edition, London: MacMillan, 655.

44 Rupke, 1966.

polystrate tree fossils in the strata associated with coal seams were buried rapidly, and thus the sediments making up the strata enclosing them had to also be rapidly deposited. Of even further significance is that not only are the polystrate tree fossils found over wide areas in many places, but they occur over thick vertical strata successions, such as Joggins, Nova Scotia, where these erect fossilized tree trunks have been found at twenty horizons distributed at intervals through about 750 m of strata.[45] Thus, these polystrate tree trunks are also significant as evidence for rapid deposition of thick sequences of strata and the coal seams found in these coal measure sequences. Furthermore, the coal seams represent the fossil graveyards of countless billions of tons of plant remains.

---

45   C. O. Dunbar, 1960, *Geology*, second edition, New York: Wiley, 227.

72

FURTHER EXAMPLES OF FOSSIL GRAVEYARDS

The geologic record consists of many fossil graveyards and their enclosing strata sequences that show convincing evidence of rapid and catastrophic deposition of sediments on an enormous scale. Examples of fossil graveyards already described above, including the coal beds, are but a few of the many that could be cited. A few more examples, therefore, will suffice to underscore how prevalent fossil graveyards really are.

In the lower Devonian Hunsrück Slate of Germany, the non-biomineralized tissues of organisms with exceptional detail are preserved by replacement with pyrite, including trilobites, nautiloids, star-fishes, and other invertebrates.[1] It is considered even more remarkable that the finest details of arthropod trackways and other trace fossils are so well preserved, along with the pyritized soft-bodied fossils, in what are regarded as storm-induced, rapidly-deposited, fine-grained turbidites.[2]

Upper Devonian strata are also known for their abundant fish fossils, often found in mass mortality layers, such as that found near Canowindra in the central west of New South Wales, Australia—thousands of fossilized armored and lobe-finned fishes, the latter up to 1.5 m long, with head, skull, and gill regions superbly preserved in three dimensions.[3] Testimony to the immensity of this fossil fish graveyard is that the first discovered slab of sandstone, two meters by one meter, had 114 fossilized fish, most of them complete, beautifully preserved on its surface, and the thousands of fossilized fish specimens so far recovered have all come from

1   D. E. G. Briggs, R. Raiswell, S. H. Bottrell, D. Hatfield and C. Bartels, 1996, Controls on the pyritization of exceptionally preserved fossils: an analysis of the lower Devonian Hunsrück Slate of Germany, *American Journal of Science*, 296: 633-663; C. Bartels, D. E. G. Briggs and G. Brassel, 1998. *The Fossils of the Hunsrück Slate: Marine Life in the Devonian*, Cambridge, England: Cambridge University Press.

2   A. Seilacher et al, 1985, Sedimentological, ecological and temporal patterns of fossil Lagerstätten, *Royal Society of London Philosophical Transactions B*, 311 (1148): 5-23; O. E. Sutcliffe, D. E. G. Briggs and C. Bartels, 1999, Ichnological evidence for the environmental setting of the Fossil-Lagerstätten in the Devonian Hunsrück Slate, Germany, *Geology*, 27 (3): 275-278.

3   A. Ritchie, 1994, The Canowindra fish kill, *Australasian Science*, Summer Issue: 17-18; J. Cribb, 1996, A prize catch, Australian Geographic, 43: 100-115.

a twenty meter section of this extensive sandstone layer.

An equally impressive upper Devonian fossil fish graveyard with three-dimensionally, perfectly preserved, armor-plated, jawed fishes is found in the limestones of the Gogo Formation of northern Western Australia.[4] Also well preserved in the Gogo fossil fish graveyard are ray-finned fishes, lung-fishes, and megamouth-toothed, lobe-finned fishes.

Yet another Australian fossil fish graveyard is a shale lens in the Triassic Hawkesbury Sandstone at Somersby in the Sydney Basin, where in a volume of shale, measuring 100 meters by 60 meters to an average depth of 2 meters, it was estimated that over 1,200 well-preserved fossil fish were found, including more sharks and lung-fishes.[5] As many as six or seven fossilized fish were found per square meter of shale in morality zones, where the occurrence of associated sand and pebbles confirms the catastrophic death and burial of these fish.

Another spectacular fossil graveyard of incredible extent, somewhat comparable to coal seams, are the Cretaceous chalk beds that consist of the tiny calcium carbonate shells (or tests) of countless trillions of microscopic foraminifera and coccolithophores (calcareous algae). In southern England the chalk beds are estimated to be about 405 m thick, and from there they extend inland across England to the Antrim area of Northern Ireland, southwest Ireland, and to extensive areas of the sea floor south of Ireland. In the opposite direction they extend from northern France across northern Germany and southern Scandinavia, to Poland, Bulgaria, and eventually to Georgia in the south of the Commonwealth of Independent States.[6] However, identical chalk beds are also found in Egypt and Israel. On the other side of the Atlantic Ocean the same chalk beds are found in Texas, through to Alabama, Arkansas, Mississippi, and Tennessee, in Nebraska and adjoining states, and in Kansas. Incredibly, identical chalk beds, complete with the same black flint nodules and the same fossils, are found in the Perth basin of Western Australia. As well as the countless microfossils, this fossil graveyard of global distribution contains many macroscopic fossils, including barnacles, crustaceans, brachiopods, oysters, gastropods, pelecypods, cephalopods, ammonites, bryozoans, echinoids, corals, crinoids, and even fish, as well as abundant trace fossils, particularly burrows.[7] That catastrophic deposition rates were involved in forming these thick chalk beds is evident from the size of some of the ammonite fossils (which may be up to one meter in diameter), and the large *Mosasaurus* skull found near Maastricht (The Netherlands), as well as by

---

4   J. A. Long, 1988, Late Devonian fishes from the Gogo Formation, Western Australia, *National Geographic Research*, 4: 436-450.

5   F. Holmes, 1987, Somersby – Paradise for "Palaeofisherman," *The Fossil Collector*, 21: 23-28; Mann, 1987, Fossil find rewrites Australia's past, *Omega Science Digest*, January/February: 14-21.

6   D. V. Ager, 1973, *The Nature of the Stratigraphical Record*, London: MacMillan; A. A. Snelling, 1994, Can Flood geology explain thick chalk layers?, *Creation Ex Nihilo Technical Journal*, 8 (1): 11-15.

7   H. Zijlstra, 1995, *The Sedimentology of Chalk*, Berlin: Springer-Verlag.

the recognition of storm-deposited tempestite layers within the chalk.

Other famous fossil graveyards in Mesozoic strata include the upper Jurassic Solnhofen Limestone of Bavaria, Germany, which has yielded some of the world's most perfect fossils and some of its rarest, including those of the fossil bird *Archaeopteryx*. This limestone was deposited as a very fine lime-mud which was capable of preserving exceptional details, such as the impressions of feathers and skin, among the small dinosaurs, crocodiles, lizards, fish, crustaceans, and other fossils found in it.

Also of a spectacular nature are the fossil graveyards of dinosaur bones in the upper Jurassic Morrison Formation, which persists over an area of more than 1.5 million square kilometers in thirteen U.S. states and three Canadian provinces, stretching from Manitoba to Arizona, and Alberta to Texas.[8] In the United States alone, dinosaur bones have been found at 353 sites in the Morrison Formation, including 141 principal dinosaur bone sites and quarries.[9] Other dinosaur fossil graveyards are found in the upper Cretaceous Hell Creek and Lance Formations in Montana and Wyoming, and adjoining areas of southern Canada. One of these fossil graveyards consists of a bone-bed containing a transported assemblage of disarticulated bones in all size categories, ranging from small bone chips and ossified tendons to whole femora, all dinosaur remains from the genus *Edmontosaurus*.[10] With these dinosaur bones are fragments of turtle and fish bones, fish scales, and numerous teeth, not only those of *Edmontosaurus*, but also from several other species of dinosaurs (including *Triceratops*, *Tyrannosaurus*, *Troodon*), as well as those from crocodilians, fish, mammals, and other forms still under study. It is evident that this fossil graveyard is part of a high-energy debris accumulation, the extent of which is still being determined.

Tertiary strata also abound with fossil graveyards, such as that found in the Green River Formation of Wyoming, Utah, and Colorado. Some of the most perfect specimens of fossil fish and plants in the world are found there—palm leaves more than two meters long and about one meter wide, sycamore, maple, poplar, and other leaves, flowers, and pine fruit and needles, gar-pike up to two meters long, sunfish, deep-sea bass, chubs, pickerel, herring, and others—buried with birds up to the size of today's domestic chickens, some with feather impressions, alligators, turtles, mollusks, crustaceans, lizards, frogs, snakes, crocodiles, bats, and numerous mammals, and many varieties of insects, including beetles, flies,

---

8   J. A. Peterson, 1972, Jurassic System, in *Geological Atlas of the Rocky Mountain Region*, Denver, CO: Hirschfeld Press.

9   C. E. Turner and F. Peterson, 1999, Biostratigraphy of dinosaurs in the upper Jurassic Morrision Formation of the Western Interior, USA, in *The Morrison Formatin Extinct Ecosystems Project, Final Report*, C.E. Turner and F. Peterson, eds., National Parks Service, United States Geological Survey Joint Project, unpublished report.

10   L. Spencer, L. E. Turner and A. V. Chadwick, 2001, A remarkable vertebrate assemblage from the Lance Formation, Niobrara County, Wyoming, *Geological Society of America Annual Meeting Abstracts with Program*.

dragonflies, grasshoppers, moths, butterflies, wasps, ants, and others.[11] Numerous attempts have been made to explain the "uniform" process by which hundreds of thousands of modern and extinct fishes, birds, reptiles, mammals, insects, and plants could have been piled together, buried, and preserved in exquisite detail, as is often the case, but inevitably the only explanation consistent with the state of this fossil assemblage is catastrophic entombment.

Similar catastrophic burial also explains the myriad of a wide variety of insect fossils preserved in minute perfectional detail in shales with a volcanic component, near Florissant, Colorado:

> Although insect remains are by far the most numerous of the animal fossils preserved at Florissant, other groups are also represented. The shells of tiny freshwater mollusks are not difficult to find entombed in the rock and occasionally even the skeletons of fish and birds are seen. Several hundred species of plants have been identified from these shales, usually from leaves, but fruits (that is, nuts) and even blossoms have also been found....Insect life around and above Lake Florissant must have been abundant, for it is not unusual to find on a single piece of shale from one of the richer fossiliferous layers several individuals within two to three inches of each other. This life was also extremely varied, with the total number of species running into the hundreds.[12]

In southern Alberta, Canada, a layer of silty mudstone only a few centimeters thick in the lower part of the Paskapoo Formation contains thousands of complete skeletons of fossil fishes, primarily species in the trout-perch family.[13] There is little disarticulation and no sign of scavenging, and the fishes occur in distinct size classes, tend to be clumped together on a scale of a few meters or less, and tend to lie with their heads facing one or perhaps preferred directions. All of these findings are consistent with this fossil graveyard representing a mass-death event with extremely rapid burial. Although the fishes occur without other kinds of fossils in this distinctive layer, other layers in the same outcrop have yielded abundant remains of plants, insects, mollusks, and mammals.

At Grube Messel, about 30 km southeast of Frankfurt in western Germany, articulated skeletons of various fish, salamanders, frogs, turtles, lizards, snakes, crocodiles, birds, and mammals, as well as several hundred insects and plant remains, have been found in an oil shale of the Messel Formation.[14] The

---

11   L. Grande, 1984, Palaentology of the Green River Formation, with a review of the fish fauna, second edition, *Geological Survey of Wyoming, Bulletin*, 63.

12   R. D. Manwell, 1955, An insect Pompeii, *Scientific Monthly*, 80 (6): 357-358.

13   M. V. H. Wilson, 1996, Taphonomy of a mass-death layer of fishes in the Paleocene Paskapoo Formation at Joffre Bridge, Alberta, Canada, *Canadian Journal of Earth Sciences*, 33: 1487-1498.

14   J. L. Franzen, 1985, Exceptional preservation of Eocene vertebrates in the lake deposit of Grube Messel (West Germany), *Philosophical Transactions of the Royal Society of London B*, 311: 181-186.

quality of preservation is truly exceptional, for in many cases not only are the skeletons articulated, but the outlines of the entire bodies are preserved as black silhouettes, and sometimes even the contents of the digestive tracts are available for investigation.

Also in Germany, the lignite beds of Geiseltal are an incredible fossil graveyard:

> Here, too, there is a complete mixture of plants and insects from all climatic zones and all recognized regions of the geography of plants or animals. It is further astonishing that in certain cases the leaves have been deposited and preserved in a fully fresh condition. The chlorophyll is so well preserved that it has been possible to recognize the alpha and beta types....An extravagant fact comparable to the preservation of the chlorophyll, was the occurrence of preserved soft parts of the insects: muscles, corium, epidermis, keratin, color stuffs as melamine and lipochrome, glands, and the contents of the intestines. Just as in the case of chlorophyll we are dealing with things that are easily destroyed, disintegrating in but a few days or hours. The incrustation must therefore have been very rapid.[15]

> More than 6000 remains of vertebrate animals and a great number of insects, mollusks, and plants were found in these deposits. The compressed remains of soft tissue of many of these animals show details of cellular structure and some of the specimens had undergone but little chemical modification....Well-preserved bits of hair, feathers and scales probably are among the oldest known examples of essentially unmodified preservation of these structures. The stomach contents of beetles, amphibia, fishes, birds and mammals provide direct evidence about eating habits. Bacteria of two kinds were found in the excrement of crocodiles and another was found on the trachea of a beetle. Fungi were identified on leaves and the original plant pigments, chlorophyll and coproporphyrin, were found preserved in some of the leaves.[16]

It is inconceivable that fossil graveyards like this could be somehow due to normal, slow autochthonous processes, for even a putrid swamp has bacteria at work in it, and this would not also explain how bats and birds became similarly entombed with horses, mollusks, and palm trees. Instead, unusual transport and rapid burial mechanisms would have been required.

Finally, on the northwest coast of Tasmania, Australia's island state, is a headland called Fossil Bluff, due to the fossil graveyard in the calcareous sandstone layers exposed there. The lowermost sandstone layer is composed of coarse sand and

---

15   N. Heribert-Nilsson, 1953, *Synthetische Artbildung*, Lund, Sweden: Verlag CWK Gleerup, 1195-1196.

16   N. O. Newell, 1959, Adequacy of the fossil record, *Journal of Paleontology*, 33: 496.

broken shells, with rounded quartz pebbles. The number of fossil species decreases upwards as the grain size of the sandstones also decreases, with particular horizons containing distinctive bands of just the one fossil species.[17] Fossils found in this graveyard include 267 species of mollusks (gastropods, cephalopods, and pelecypods), corals, bryozoans, brachiopods, barnacles, sea urchins, sharks' teeth, leaves, decomposed wood, brown coal fragments, and the skeletal remains of a toothed whale and a possum-like marsupial (mammal). The grading of the sediment and fossils, the stratification of the sandstone and some of the fossils, the broken shells, and the mixture of fossils, including the land-dwelling marsupial and the ocean-dwelling toothed whale, are all clear testimony to this fossil graveyard, which is exposed for more than one kilometer, having resulted from catastrophic water transport and sediment burial.

Mass Extinctions

The succession of fossils found in the sequences of rock strata making up the geologic record is primarily a record of death and the sequence in which the animal and plant remains were buried. Fossil graveyards found throughout the geologic record, in strata from the uppermost Precambrian upwards in many places around the globe, demonstrate the rapid and catastrophic processes that had to be operating to transport, bury, preserve, and fossilize such an abundance of animal and plant remains on a global scale. Such has been the scale of destruction recognized at various levels in the geologic record that even the conventional geological community has recognized what have been called mass extinctions. Eight such "mass extinctions" have been recognized in the Cambrian to Recent strata sequence (see Figure 25, page 357).[18] At these levels in the geologic record a great variety of organisms, those that would have been living in both marine and terrestrial environments, both stationery and swimming forms, carnivores and herbivores, protozoans and metazoans, were buried on a global scale, so the catastrophic processes involved transcended specific ecological, morphological, and taxonomic groupings of organisms simultaneously on the land and in the sea.

To explain these global mass destructions, the conventional geological community has accepted the possibility of global catastrophes, such as the earth being impacted by asteroids or comets.[19] Thus, while fossil graveyards are usually only

17   R. Tate and J. Dennant, 1896, Correlation of the marine Tertiaries of Australia. Part III. South Australia
       and Tasmania, *Transactions of the Royal Society of South Australia*, 20 (1): 118-148; N. R. Banks, 1957,
       The Stratigraphy of Tasmanian Limestones, in *Limestones in Tasmania*, vol. 10, T. D. Hughes, ed.,
       Mineral Resources of Tasmania, 39-85; A. A. Snelling, 1985, Tasmania's Fossil Bluff, *Ex Nihilo*, 7 (3):
       6-10.

18   S. M. Stanley, 1987, *Extinction*, New York: Scientific American Books, W.H. Freeman and Company;
       J. J. Sepkoski Jr, 1989, Periodicity in extinction and the problem of catastrophism in the history of life,
       Journal of the Geological Society of London, 146: 7-19; M. J. Benton, 1995, Diversification and extinction
       and the history of life, *Science*, 268: 52-58.

19   C. Stearn and R. Carroll, 1989, *Paleontology: The Record of Life*, New York: John Wiley and Sons, 368-

of local to regional extent, though still requiring catastrophic and rapid transport and burial of sediments and organisms, the recognition of "mass extinction" on a global scale in the geologic record extends the evidence for catastrophic transport and deposition of sediments and organisms to a global scale. Asteroid or comet impacts, and/or catastrophic volcanic outpourings, as explanations for this global catastrophism have evidence to support them, and both are consistent with the global catastrophic Flood within the biblical framework for earth history.

371; D. J. McLaren and W. D. Goodfellow, 1990, Geological and biological consequences of giant impacts, *Annual Review of Earth and Planetary Sciences*, 18: 123-171; K. C. Condie, 1997, *Plate Tectonics and Crustal Evolution*, fourth edition, Oxford, England: Butterworth-Heinemann, 218-225.

73

THE RATE OF FOSSILIZATION

Once the plants and animals have been buried catastrophically, processes of fossilization need to be operative to ensure preservation of these animal and plant remains in the resultant sedimentary strata. The different fossilization processes have already been discussed earlier, but the mechanisms and rates of the fossilization processes are crucial, not only because of the exquisitely preserved details in so many fossils, as seen already in many of the fossil graveyards discussed above, but because of the limited timeframe for these processes to have occurred during the year of the Genesis Flood, and in the overall biblical framework for earth history.

Petrification by Silicification

Rapid petrification of wood has long been demonstrated and understood. For example, silica deposition rates into blocks of wood lowered into alkaline springs in Yellowstone National Park, Wyoming, have been reported at being between 0.1 and 4.0 mm/yr.[1] Petrification of wood is considered to take place in five stages:

1. Entry of silica in solution or as a colloid into the wood
2. Penetration of silica into the cell walls of the wood's structure
3. Progressive dissolving of the cell walls, which are at the same time replaced by silica, so that the wood's dimensional stability is maintained
4. Silica deposition within the voids within the cellular wall framework structure
5. Final hardening (lithification) by drying out[2]

This understanding of the petrification process is solidly based on experimental evidence. For example, small branches were partially silicified by placing them in

---

1   A. C. Sigleo, 1978, Organic geochemistry of silicified wood, Petrified Forest National Park, Arizona, *Geochimica et Cosmochimica Acta*, 42: 1397-1405.

2   G. Scurfield and E. R. Segnit, 1984, Petrification of wood by silica minerals, *Sedimentary Geology*, 39: 149-167.

concentrated solutions of sodium metasilicate for up to 24 hours,[3] while fresh wood was immersed alternately in water and saturated ethyl silicate solutions until the open spaces in the wood filled with mineral material, all within several months to a year.[4] As early as 1950 it had been shown that the sorption of silica by wood fibers from solutions of sodium metasilicate, sodium silicate, and activated silica sols (a homogeneous suspension in water) at only 25°C (77°F) was as much as 12.5 moles of silica per gram of wood within 24 hours, the equivalent of partial silicification/petrification.[5] It has thus been concluded: "These observations indicate that silica nucleation and deposition can occur directly and rapidly on exposed cellulose [wood] surfaces."[6] Indeed, a patent has even been issued for the artificial petrification of wood.[7] More recent experiments, where pieces of wood were suspended in hot spring water in Japan, for up to seven years, showed complete silicification of wood was a rapid process under natural conditions requiring only years.[8]

However, perhaps these processes observed in experiments are not really applicable to conditions and processes in the natural world? To the contrary, there is much anecdotal evidence that petrification of wood can occur rapidly, even in soils:

> [F]rom Mrs McMurray [of Blackall, southwestern Queensland, Australia], I heard a story that rocked me and seem to explode many ideas about the age of petrified wood. Mrs McMurray has a piece of wood turned to stone which has clear axe marks on it. She says the tree this piece came from grew on a farm her father had at Euthella, out of Roma, and was chopped down by him about 70 years ago. It was partly buried until it was dug up again, petrified. Mrs McMurray capped this story by saying that a townsman has a piece of petrified fence post with the drilled holes for wire with a piece of the wire attached.[9]

Piggott writes of petrified wood showing axe marks and also of a petrified fence post. This sort of thing is, of course, quite common. The Hughenden district, N.Q. [north Queensland], has...*Parkensonia* trees washed over near a Station [ranch] homestead and covered with silt by a flood in 1918

3   R. W. Drum, 1968, Silification of Betula woody tissue in vitrio, *Science*, 161: 175-176.

4   R. F. Leo and E. S. Barghoorn, 1976, *Silification of Wood*, Harvard University Botanical Museum Leaflets No. 25, 1-47.

5   R. C. Merrill and R. W. Spencer, 1950, Sorption of sodium silicates and silicate sols by cellulose fibers, *Industrial Engineering Chemistry*, 42: 744-747.

6   Sigleo, 1978, 1404.

7   H. Hicks, 1984, Mineralized sodium silicate solutions for artificial petrification of wood, U.S. patent no. 4612050, filed October 12, 1984, and issued September 16, 1986.

8   H. Akahane, T. Furano, H. Miyajima, T. Yoshikawa and S. Yamamoto, 2004, Rapid wood silification in hot spring water: An explanation of silicification of wood during Earth's history, *Sedimentary Geology*, 169: 219-2287.

9   R. Piggott, 1970, Petrified wood, *The Australian Lapidary Magazine*, 6 (6): 9.

[which] had the silt washed off by a flood in 1950. Portions of the trunk had turned to stone of an attractive colour. However, much of the trunks and all the limbs had totally disappeared. On Zara Station [ranch], 30 miles [about 48 km] from Hughenden, I was renewing a fence. Where it was dipped into a hollow the bottom of the old posts had gone through black soil into shale. The Gidgee wood was still perfect in the black soil. It then cut off as straight as if sawn, and the few inches of post in the shale was pure stone. Every axe mark was perfect and the colour still was the same as the day the post was cut.[10]

Wood is not the only material that has been observed to have rapidly petrified. Laboratory experiments have also demonstrated that unicellular bacteria can be readily silicified in silicate solutions.[11] However, *in situ* silicification of bacteria in natural hot spring waters has been also observed and studied.[12] Microbial mats were observed growing as hard, finely-laminated crusts on ledges within the outflow channel of the Strokkur Geyser in south Iceland, and samples examined by electron microscopy revealed that the filamentous bacteria making up the mat had undergone rapid silicification in the hot spring water. The silica mineralization association with the cells occurred both extra-cellularly, within and on the external sheaths of the bacteria, and intra-cellularly, within the cytoplasm. The exceptional preservation of the bacterial sheaths was found to be due to the presence of distinct mineral nucleation sites, which had resulted in the production of silica casts of the bacteria remarkably similar to microbial remains in microfossil assemblages preserved in the geologic record.[13] It was concluded that the observed silicification in a natural environment represents an important link between laboratory experiments of microbial silicification and observational studies of ancient microfossils assemblages. Furthermore, the observed rapid *in situ* silicification of the bacteria is regarded as a prerequisite to preservation of cell structure as a microfossil.

Fossilization by Phosphatization

In some fossil graveyards, some of the most remarkable fossils have preserved

10 R. C. Pearce, 1970, Petrified wood, *The Australian Lapidary Magazine*, 6 (11): 33.

11 J. H. Oehler and J. W. Schopf, 1971, Artificial microfossils: experimental studies of per-mineralisation of blue-green algae in silica, *Science*, 174: 1229-1231; F. G. Ferris, W. S. Fyfe and T. J. Beveridge, 1988, Metallic binding by *Bacillus subtilis*: implications for the fossilizations of microorganisms, *Geology*, 16: 149-152; M. M. Urrutia and T. J. Beveridge, 1993, Mechanism of silicate binding to the bacterial cell wall in *Bacillus subtilis*, *Journal of Bacteriology*, 175: 1936-1945.

12 S. Schultze-Lam, F. G. Ferris, K. O. Konhauser and R. G. Wiese, 1995, *In situ* silification of an Icelandic hot spring microbial mat: implications for microfossil formation, *Canadian Journal of Earth Sciences*, 32: 2021-2026.

13 E. S. Barghoorn and S. A. Tyler, 1965, Microorganisms from the Gunflint chert, *Science*, 147: 563-577; J. W. Schopf and B. M. Packer, 1987, Early Archean (3.3-billion to 3.5-billion-year-old) microfossils from the Warrawoona Group, Australia, *Science*, 237: 70-73; J. W. Schopf, 1993, Microfossils of the Early Archean Apex Chert: new evidence of the antiquity of life, *Science*, 260: 640-646.

cellular details of soft tissues because of being replaced by calcium phosphate. This process had been assumed to require elevated concentrations of phosphate in sediment pore waters. However, in decay experiments, modern shrimps became partially mineralized in amorphous calcium phosphate, preserving cellular details of muscle tissue, particularly in a system closed to oxygen.[14] The source for the formation of the calcium phosphate fossilization was the shrimp itself. Mineralization commenced within two weeks, and increased in extent for at least four to eight weeks. The mechanism observed in the laboratory halts the normal loss of detail of soft-tissue morphology before fossilization. Thus, it was concluded that for the first time success had been achieved in phosphatizing soft tissue in laboratory experiments, which had demonstrated that the process occurs relatively rapidly, requiring only the phosphate present in the carcasses, although it was reasoned that elevated phosphate concentrations may be necessary to explain the more extensive phosphatization seen in fossils.

In these laboratory experiments it was also shown how bacteria can turn flesh into stone, in only a few weeks managing to mimic a mineralization process that supposedly takes millions of years "in nature."[15] The key was allowing the freshly killed shrimps to decay in closed experimental vessels of seawater. The researchers placed the carcasses in containers of artificial seawater, then inoculated the containers with water from the Firth of Tay in Scotland, a site characterized by the activity of both aerobic and anaerobic bacteria. Because the containers were airtight, an anoxic environment could be built up and the initial fall in acidity was slightly reversed. The result was that blocks of muscle tissue, individual muscle fibers, and eggs were replaced by calcium phosphate particles ("microspheres") less than one micron across.

The experiments were also designed to investigate the role of bacteria, which were expected to play a role in this extraordinary process of preservation of anatomical details found in certain fossils in some fossil graveyards. The role of bacteria in post-mortem decay is well known, and there is fossil evidence of bacteria themselves being preserved. The researchers had developed biochemical models, using our understanding of how it is possible for bacteria to concentrate, oxidize, and precipitate mineral ions on soft tissue surfaces. They found that the smaller the aggregations of calcium phosphate particles precipitated in their experiments, the greater the fidelity of morphological preservation, and the highest fidelity occurred where the bacteria themselves, present in the sealed containers in the experiments, are not replicated, even though the precipitation of the calcium phosphate had been bacterially induced. Furthermore, the soft tissue phosphatized in their laboratory experiments closely resembled the fossil phosphatized soft tissues in the remarkably preserved fossil fish from the fossil graveyard in the Santana

---

14　D. E. G. Briggs and A. J. Kear, 1993, Fossilization of soft tissue in a laboratory, *Science*, 259: 1439-1442.

15　D. E. G. Briggs, A. J. Kear, D. M. Martill and P. R. Wilby, 1993, Phosphatization of soft-tissue in experiments and fossils, *Journal of the Geological Society*, London, 150: 1035-1038; D. Palmer, 1994, How busy bacteria turn flesh into stone, *New Scientist*, 141 (1917): 17.

Formation of Brazil, indicating that similar processes must have been involved in the fossilization of the fish. Indeed, in mineral composition, textures, and features, the laboratory phosphatized shrimps were very similar to the fossilized shrimps found in the stomachs of the fossil fish from the Santana Formation.

While the mineralization of soft tissue in the laboratory was not "instant," taking several weeks (it may even take months if decay is inhibited), the experiments did produce mineralized "fossils" without having to wait hundreds of millions of years. It was concluded that, while extensive phosphatization of larger carcasses may necessitate the build-up of phosphate concentrations in the sediment beforehand, this is not the case for phosphatization of small quantities of soft tissue, because the phosphate content of the carcass itself is adequate for starting the process. Of significance also was the determination in the experiments that the precipitation of associated calcium carbonate is controlled by shifts in pH in response to the decay process, thus showing how the precipitation of the calcium carbonate nodules, in which many of the Santana fossil fish are found, may have been initiated. In conclusion, these experiments have unmistakably demonstrated that the delicate fossilization of even soft tissues, as seen in many fossil graveyards, can be a rapid process that takes weeks, rather than millions of years.

Although limited phosphatization of soft tissues may be sourced from within the carcasses themselves, simple mass-balance calculations indicate that more phosphorus is present in extensively phosphatized fossils than would have originally been present in the living animal, so an external source of phosphorus would have been required. Microbial mats are one of the factors most widely invoked to explain exceptional fossil preservation, because they are believed to prevent carcasses from floating, and to protect them from scavengers and currents. Microbial mats have also been recorded in several fossil graveyards where phosphatized soft tissues have been preserved, including the Solnhofen Limestone of Germany, and the Santana Formation of Brazil. Nevertheless, the precise means by which microbial mats create a suitable chemical environment for the phosphatization of soft tissues had not been determined, until tested by chemical analyses of the Jurassic limestones of Cerin, France, where phosphatized soft tissues are also abundant, and are also associated with unequivocal microbial mats.[16] It was found from these analytical results that the sedimentary distribution of phosphorus, potassium, and iron following deposition of the limestone was controlled by the presence of the microbial mats, the phosphorus concentrations in the mats approaching 2.5 times those elsewhere in the sediments. Indeed, the highest phosphorus concentrations correlated precisely with the occurrence of phosphatized soft tissues in fossil fish and crustaceans. This analytical evidence thus demonstrates the fundamental geochemical role for microbial mats in localizing the mineralization that preserves the soft tissues during fossilization. The microbial mats may not only function to trap phosphate, but also control the pH, which laboratory experiments have

---

16   P. R. Wilby, D. E. G. Briggs, P. Bernier and C. Gaillard, 1996, Role of microbial mats in the fossilization of soft tissues, *Geology*, 24 (9): 787-790.

shown is a critical factor in the soft-tissue phosphatization process.

Fossilization by Biofilms

Terrestrial leaf fossils often form through authigenic preservation, in which the leaf surface is coated by a variety of minerals, especially iron oxides, such that leaf venation patterns, stomatal morphology, and even epidermal hairs are often well preserved. However, the hydrophobic, waxy cuticles covering the surfaces of most leaves results in leaf surfaces themselves not being able to readily bind metal ions as the direct mechanism involved in this authigenic fossilization process. Under normal circumstances, leaves and other plant detritus are colonized and decomposed by a variety of microorganisms and macro-invertebrates, but in aquatic environments, these and other objects are quickly colonized by bacteria that form surface-adherent biofilm communities. It has now been demonstrated that these diverse bacterial species, which rapidly colonize leaf surfaces and form biofilms within days of the leaves falling into water, enhance the fossilization of these leaves.[17]

Leaves, from living counterparts of plant genera commonly preserved as iron-encrusted impressions in the fossil record, were used in controlled experiments to show that mineralization does not form on leaves without biofilms, whereas leaves with biofilms rapidly adsorb metal ions such as Fe^{3+} onto the biofilm surface (which is anionic), where the ions form ferrihydrite. It was concluded that once such mineralized leaves are buried by sediment, they are more likely to be converted to fossils than non-mineralized leaves, because this early mineralization would ensure the integrity of the leaf is maintained during subsequent mineralization and fossilization, so that small-scale structures can be preserved. Furthermore, examination by scanning electron microscopy of some iron-encrusted fossil leaves, showing fine-scale surface details, showed bacteria-sized structures resembling those found in biofilms. Thus, it was concluded that these experimental data imply that bacterial colonization of leaves may be an essential prerequisite for authigenic preservation. Furthermore, because these bacterial biofilms and the early mineralization they adsorb form within a few days, it is evident that leaf fossilization can also be relatively rapid.

It is evident, therefore, that microbial mats play a major role in the formation of exceptionally preserved fossil deposits, by overgrowing and binding organic remains and sedimentary particles, which minimized hydrodynamic and biological disruption of dead organisms and sedimentary laminae. The microbial agent is usually prokaryotic cyanobacteria, the presence of which likely also assists in locally controlling the pH and the concentration of ions. It is equally significant that the exceptionally well-preserved macrofossils in the Florissant (Colorado) fossil graveyard are enveloped in matted aggregations of mucous-secreting, pinnate

17   K. A. Dunn, R. J. C. McLean, G. R. Upchurch and R. L. Folk, 1997, Enhancement of leaf fossilization potential by bacterial biofilms, *Geology*, 25 (12): 1119-1122.

diatom frustules.[18] It has thus been suggested that the macrobiota became entrapped in mucous-secreting mats of surface water blooms of planktonic diatoms, and as the mats and the incorporated macrobiota were subsequently sedimented out of the water column, the mucosic mats and their associated bacterial communities arrested decay and promoted preservation of refractory tissues as organisms were fossilized. Thus, it would appear that, by a completely different mechanism, the diatom mats fulfilled the same preservational role as already demonstrated for cyanobacterial mats, and may be an important causative factor in the formation of some exceptionally preserved fossil biotas.

Fossilization by Pyritization

Whereas in animals the highest fidelity in fossil preservation of soft tissues is retained in calcium phosphate (apatite), and pyritized soft tissue is relatively rare, pyritization of plants is more common. However, the process has been poorly understood.[19] Where pyritization has occurred, it is unclear how the plant tissues became fossilized, whether pyritization is selective to specific biopolymers, or whether original organic constituents survive. Consequently, laboratory experiments have been used to replicate the fossilization process, by using both microbial and chemical approaches to pyritize plant debris. The experimental results demonstrated that initial pyritization can be an extremely rapid process (within 80 days), and is driven by anaerobic bacterial-mediated decay. The outcome was pyritization of the plant debris, very similar to that found in fossilized plants.

It would appear that, initially, pyrite precipitates on and within plant cell walls, and in the spaces between them. Further decay and infilling at all scales preserve broad cellular anatomy. Thus, pyritization does not seem to involve direct replacement of the original organic material, but precipitation on, and impregnation of, the cell walls, plus rapid filling of intracellular spaces, provide sufficient strength to preserve detailed plant morphology as burial proceeds. As microbial decomposition of organic material continues, even after burial, more space is made available within which pyrite crystallizes, to produce a cast of the original plant material. The decaying plant materials provides a locus for pyritization, because the enhanced nucleation of pyrite on organic substrates as the concentration of decomposable organic matter increases stimulates bacterial activity, and thus anoxia, sulfate reduction, and sulfide formation. These experimental results thus demonstrate that pyritized plant fossils can be produced rapidly in a matter of weeks, rather than requiring millions of years.

---

18   I. C. Harding and L. S. Chant, 2000, Self-sedimented diatom mats as agents of exceptional fossil preservation in the Oligocene Florissant Lake beds, Colorado, United States, *Geology*, 28 (3): 195-198.

19   P. Kenrick and D. Edwards, 1988, Anatomy of the lower Devonian *Gosslingia breconensis* Heard based on pyritised axes with some comments on the permineralisation process, *Linnean Society Botanical Journal*, 97: 95-123; D. E. G. Briggs, R. Raiswell, S. H. Bottrell, D. Hatfield and C. Bartels, 1996, Controls on the pyritization of exceptionally preserved fossils: an analysis of the Lower Devonian Hunsrück Slate of Germany, *American Journal of Science*, 296: 633-663.

Coalification

When plant remains accumulate in great thicknesses to form peat, subsequent burial of it beneath layers of sediments causes it to be compacted due to the pressures, plus the heat at depth dries out the water and gases in the original plant material in a manner that progressively enriches the peat with carbon, until it finally forms coal.[20] The rank (quality) of the resultant coal is a measure of carbon content, which depends on the amount of volatiles (mainly CO_2 and NH_3) and moisture that have been removed from the coal during this coalification process. The rank varies from lignite (or brown coal), which contains only about 30 percent carbon, to sub-bituminous to bituminous coal, the latter containing about 87 percent carbon, and then to anthracite, which contains about 94 percent carbon.

It is often claimed that rank increases with time and depth of burial, but there isn't always a systematic increase in the rank of coal with increasing age. Some blatant contradictions include lignites (low rank) in some of the oldest coal measure strata sequences, and anthracites (highest rank) occurring in some of the youngest coal measure strata. However, pressure likewise cannot be the major factor in metamorphosis of peat to coal, because the rank of coal does not increase in highly-deformed and folded strata. Furthermore, laboratory experiments have demonstrated that increasing pressure can actually retard the chemical alteration of peat to coal.[21] The most important factor in coal metamorphoses is now regarded as temperature. The effect of igneous intrusions on coal seams has confirmed that elevated temperatures can cause coalification. Nevertheless, these three factors, namely, time, pressure, and temperature, must work together to transform the plant debris of a peat into coal. Indeed, compaction of peat and its transformation to lignite have been observed to occur below depths of only six and eleven meters.[22]

Laboratory experiments have been quite successful in artificially producing coal-like materials relatively rapidly, under conditions designed to simulate those present in sedimentary basins where coal measure strata have accumulated. For example, artificial coal has been produced by rapidly applying vibrating pressures to wood.[23] In this experiment, the prolonged series of brief violent shocks (rather than the application of continuous pressure) altered the molecular arrangement of the organic matter so that it resembled coal, and this was produced within hours and days. In different experiments, a substance like anthracite was manufactured in just a few minutes by rapid application of intense heat, much of the heat

---

20   J. Davidson, W. E. Reed and P. M. Davis, 1997, *Exploring Earth: An Introduction to Physical Geology*, Upper Saddle River, NJ: Prentice-Hall, 422.

21   S. E. Nevins, 1976, The Origin of Coal, *Acts & Facts*, 5 (11): 41.

22   Nadon, 1998, 729.

23   J. Carlweil, 1965, Kolloquim Chemi und Physik dar Systinkhole, *Erdol und Kohle-Erdgas Petrochemie*, 18 (7): 565.

involved being generated by the cellulosic material being altered.[24] While both of these studies used simulated conditions that are applicable to the coalification of buried peat layers in areas of tectonism and volcanism, other laboratory studies have wider application.

A research team at the Argonne National Laboratory in Illinois made insoluble material resembling coal macerals (components) by heating lignin with clay minerals at 150°C for 2 to 8 months in the absence of oxygen.[25] It was discovered that the longer heating times produced higher rank coal macerals, and the clays appeared to serve as catalysts that speed the coalification reactions, given that the lignin was fairly unreactive in their absence. The clay mineral montmorillonite was primarily used in the experiments, but using kaolinite or illite, independently or mixed with montmorillonite, produced similar results. It was also demonstrated that in the presence of clay minerals activated by acid, the reaction of lignin to form coal macerals was highly accelerated (four weeks instead of 2 to 4 months), even at only 150°C. Furthermore, loss of catalytic action of the clay minerals occurred when the reaction was carried out in the presence of air. The overall conclusion was that coal macerals can be produced directly from biological source material via clay-catalyzed thermal reactions in periods from only one to four months. It is relevant, therefore, that clay minerals often account for up to 80 percent of the total mineral matter associated with the plant debris that has formed the coal. Indeed, clay minerals are found in coal as fine inclusions, layers, and partial or complete fillings of plant cell cavities. Thus, with the presence of clay minerals obviously dispersed through the original peat, clay-catalyzed thermal reactions would easily be achieved after burial of the peat to induce rapid coalification. Other experiments have confirmed that clay mineral particles act as catalysts in what is a rapid coalification process.[26]

Pressure has always been considered crucial to the coalification process, given that once buried, peat layers are subject to overburden (or lithostatic) pressures. Thus, uniaxial pressure devices have routinely been used in artificial coalification experiments, which invariably are conducted at temperatures ranging from 100 to 400°C over periods of from one to eight days.[27] The result of such experiments on wood samples was the transformation of the wood into materials similar in microscopic appearance to the maceral components of naturally-formed coals. This was also confirmed by chemical analyses. However, temperatures above 200°C in the natural coalification process can be definitely discounted, because at temperatures of 220°C and above, clay minerals such as montmorillonite and

24   G. R. Hill, 1972, Some aspects of coal research, *Chemical Technology*, May: 292-297.

25   R. Hayatsu, R. L. McBeth, R. G. Scott, R. E. Botto and R. E. Winans, 1984, Artificial coalification study: preparations and characterization of synthetic macerals, *Organic Geochemistry*, 6: 463-471.

26   J. D. Saxby, P. Chatfield, G. H. Taylor, J. D. FitzGerald, I. R. Kaplan and S.-T. Lu, 1992, Effect of clay minerals on products from coal maturation, *Organic Geochemistry*, 18 (3): 373-383.

27   A. Davis and W. Spackman, 1964, The role of the cellulosic and lignitic components of wood in artificial coalification, *Fuel*, 43: 215-224.

kaolinite are metamorphosed to chlorite and pyrophyllite,[28] whereas the clay minerals montmorillonite and kaolinite are routinely found in coal seams and associated with them, rather than chlorite and pyrophyllite. These clay minerals, principally kaolinite, are found in tonstein layers that are important as marker horizons within coal seams, and for correlation of coal seams within and between coal basins, even over distances of several hundred kilometers, such as in the northern European coal belt.[29] These tonsteins are widely regarded as having originated as ash-fall tuffs.[30] Thus, the presence of clay minerals in these tonsteins intimately associated with coal seams indicates the temperatures involved in coalification must have been less than 200°C. More recent coalification experiments have tried to more closely simulate the natural geologic conditions, with temperatures of only 125°C in both lithostatic and fluid pressures equivalent to burial under 1,800 meters of wet sediments, yet maintained as a geologically open system which allowed by-products that may retard coalification to escape.[31] In that experiment, after only 75 days, the original peat and petrified wood had been transformed into coalified peat and coalified wood, comparable chemically and structurally to lignite and coalified wood from the same geographical region as the original peat and petrified wood samples.

It is thus certain that, because these artificial coalification experiments have demonstrated the process under simulated natural conditions, coalification is a quick process that does not require long periods of time to be achieved. Therefore, there is no reason to insist that coalification under natural conditions must take millions of years. Indeed, the many examples of dislocated fragments of mature coal being found enclosed in sandstones, which are nearly contemporaneous with the nearest coal seam above or below, emphatically demonstrate that not only is coalification extremely rapid, but neither deep burial nor elevated temperatures and pressures are required for coalification.[32] Similarly, rounded pebbles of mature coal are known to occur in a conglomerate bed less than half a meter vertically from the underlying coal seam (Figure 48, page 1084). Whatever then are the natural conditions under which coalification occurs, such evidence demands that the process is rapid in terms even of days at or close to the earth's surface.

28   Stach et al, 1982, 84-86.

29   Stach et al, 1982, 158-164.

30   N. B. Price and P.McL. D. Duff, 1969, Mineralogy and chemistry of tonsteins from Carboniferous sequences of Great Britain, *Sedimentology*, 13: 45-69; Stach, 1982, 158-164; Diessel, 1982, 140-149, 312-329.

31   W. H. Orem, S. G. Neuzil, H. E. Lerch and C. B. Cecil, 1996, Experimental early-stage coalification of a peat sample and a petrified wood sample from Indonesia, *Organic Geochemistry*, 24 (2): 111-125.

32   Scheven, 1981, 42.

74

ARE THERE LONG AGES BETWEEN THE STRATA?

Even though the conventional geological community now generally recognizes that some strata may have been catastrophically deposited, it is still argued that long periods of geologic time are accounted for by gaps between the strata in the geologic record. However, the magnitude of these time gaps between strata, required by the conventional geological community, become larger than the time supposedly represented by the strata themselves when modern sedimentation rates are taken into account. Calculated sedimentation rates over a timespan of 1 million years average about 0.01 meters per thousand years, whereas the average sedimentation rate actually measured today over a period of one year is approximately 100 meters per thousand years. Thus, the calculated and measured sedimentation rates data (see Figures 39 and 40)[1] indicate that the geologic record contains only a small fraction of the sedimentary strata that would be predicted as having been deposited over geological time based on modern sedimentation rates. Expressed another way, these data indicate that the time over which the rock record would have accumulated is only a small fraction of the claimed available time according to the geological timescale.

The proposed answer to this problem is that either the geologic record consists of brief periods of sedimentation separated by long periods of inactivity, or there may be long periods in which sediments are deposited, and then much or all of the sediments are eroded before the next sediments arrive.[2] Similarly, it has been claimed that the whole history of the earth has been one of short, sudden happenings with nothing much in particular in between, so that these "episodic catastrophes" were separated by immense eons when virtually no geologic deposits and contained fossils were being formed, suggesting that there are "more gaps than record," and that therefore the bulk of geological time occurred during the gaps in the record![3] The corollary to this is the claim that, therefore, earth history

---

1   P. M. Sadler, 1981, Sediment accumulation rates and the completeness of stratigraphic sections, *Journal of Geology*, 89: 569-584.

2   T. H. van Andel, 1981, Consider the incompleteness of the geological record, *Nature*, 294: 397-398.

3   D. V. Ager, 1993, *The New Catastrophism: The Importance of the Rare Event in Geological History*, Cambridge, MA: Cambridge University Press.

is not a record of what actually happened, but is a record of what happens to have been preserved.

However, if there are many gaps between different strata in the geologic record that represent more geologic time than the strata themselves, then there ought to be some record that can be detected of the events that occurred in these time gaps. In particular, there ought to be some evidence of erosion, soil formation, or burrowing by animals. However, there is generally a lack of such evidence, which is puzzling for the conventional geological community. After all, if the present is the key to the past, then in the present, land surfaces have been carved by erosion into an irregular topography, with upland areas being deeply eroded and the sediments deposited in lowland basins, principally by water. This is not to deny that there are erosion surfaces buried and preserved in the geologic record, but often it is claimed that there are time gaps between consecutive strata without any evidence of erosion, or any other events that might have occurred in the time represented by the gaps.

Two examples will graphically illustrate this problem. In Venezuela, two thin coal seams separated by 30 cm of gray clay were, respectively, assigned to the lower Paleocene and upper Eocene.[4] Even though the outcrops are excellent, very close inspection of them failed to identify the precise position of the claimed 15 million year time gap. In the central United States, the Pliocene Ogallala Formation, dated at 2 to 5 million years old, covers an area of 150,000 square kilometers and lies directly on top of the Triassic Trujillo Formation, regarded as 208 million years old.[5] If indeed 200 million years had passed before deposition of the Ogallala Formation on top of the Trujillo Formation, then there should surely have been erosion of valleys, gullies, or even canyons, as well as soil formation and plant growth. However, the contact between these two formations is very flat, with only slight evidence of erosion, even though there are soft layers in the Trujillo that should have eroded easily.

There are, of course, many significant erosion surfaces in the geologic record, and these are known as unconformities. These do show evidence of erosion and/or uplift of sedimentary layers before the next layers were deposited. A good example occurs in the Grand Canyon, where a prominent erosion surface called the Great Unconformity cuts across tilted upper Precambrian strata with some topography evident on that surface (for example, hills of the harder Shinumo Quartzite), which is covered by the flat-lying Cambrian Tapeats Sandstone and the Paleozoic rock sequence above it. The time gap involved is claimed to be perhaps 200 million years,[6] during which time gentle weathering and slow erosion is claimed to have

4   Van Andel, 1981, 398.

5   A. A. Roth, 1988, Those gaps in the sedimentary layers, *Origins*, 15: 75-92.

6   T. D. Ford and C. M. Dehler, 2003, Grand Canyon Supergroup: Nankoweap Formation, Chuar Group, and Sixtymile Formation, in *Grand Canyon Geology*, second edition, S. S. Beus and M. Morales, eds., New York: Oxford University Press, 53-75.

occurred: "The observed features indicate that the Unconformity is an ancient land surface that experienced gentle weathering and erosion over a long period of time before being submerged beneath a gradually encroaching sea."[7]

However, geologists have been divided on whether gentle weathering occurred at this Great Unconformity. Some have maintained that extensive chemical weathering occurred because of a prevailing humid climate, yet the very granular detritus at the boundary is structureless and not at all consistent with different chemical weathering zones expected in a residual soil.[8] Other geologists have disputed the claims of extensive chemical weathering, of either the bedrock or of the debris incorporated into the base of the Tapeats Sandstone.[9] Indeed, there are minerals in some areas of the bedrock that would be unstable during long exposure in a humid climate, and instead, there is evidence of considerable physical disintegration without chemical effects. Large boulders of Shinumo Quartzite and sand-filled great channels occur in places directly at the Great Unconformity, and these have been wrongly interpreted as "fossil soils."[10] However, boulder and sand beds that cover hills in the bedrock at the Unconformity are more consistent with catastrophic underwater debris flows, which were able to move boulders 20 meters in diameter more than half a kilometer.[11] Such processes unmistakably require conditions that would be very erosive to bedrock, so rather than there being evidence of "gentle weathering and erosion" at the Great Unconformity over many millions of years, the observed features are only consistent with significant erosion occurring catastrophically while the Great Unconformity was underwater, rather than being an exposed and elevated land surface.

So even where there are angular unconformities in the geologic record, catastrophic erosion rules out that these time gaps represent millions of years. However, the problem of the supposed time gaps in the geologic record is far more acute for the conventional geologic community, because after the evident unconformities have been accounted for, there is still a general lack of evidence for the many claimed erosional gaps that remain in the geologic record. For example, between the ten major Paleozoic formations that constitute the walls of the Grand Canyon are nine boundaries, five of which are claimed to represent time gaps. There is certainly some erosion at the top of the Cambrian Muav Limestone, because there are channels up to 120 meters wide and 30 meters deep in various parts of the eastern Grand Canyon, which are filled with the Devonian Temple Butte

7   D. A. Young, 1990, The discovery of terrestrial history, in *Portraits of Creation*, H. J. Van Till, R. E. Snow, J. H. Stek and D. A. Young, eds., Grand Rapids, MI: William B. Eerdmans, 68.

8   R. Sharp, 1940, Ep-Archean and Ep-Algonkian erosion surfaces, Grand Canyon, Arizona, *Geological Society of America Bulletin*, 51: 1235-1270.

9   N. E. A. Hinds, 1935, *Ep-Archean and Ep-Algonkian Intervals in Western North America*, vol. 1, Carnegie Institution of Washington Publication, 463.

10   S. A. Austin, 1994, Interpreting strata of Grand Canyon, in *Grand Canyon: Monument to Catastrophe*, S. A. Austin, ed., Santee, CA: Institute for Creation Research, 46-47.

11   A. V. Chadwick, 1978, Megabreccias: evidence for catastrophism, *Origins*, 5: 39-46.

Formation.[12] However, such minor erosion with insignificant topographic relief could easily be catastrophically eroded, instead of supposedly taking the best part of 80 million years. There are also places in the Canyon where the overlying lower Carboniferous Redwall Limestone lies directly on the Cambrian Muav Limestone in an apparent conformable relationship, without any trace of significant erosion to represent the claimed time gap of more than 140 million years.

The upper surface of the Redwall Limestone has been identified as a disconformity, that is, where parallel strata occur above and below the boundary, but where discordance of bedding is still apparent. In places there is a slight degree of relief on top of the Redwall, and broad channels commonly 45 to 60 meters deep are filled with the Surprise Canyon Formation.[13] Elsewhere the uppermost strata of the Redwall Limestone are very level and continuous, being overlain by the thick limestone sequence of the Watahomigi Formation, which forms the base of the Supai Group. Of particular significance is the evidence of buried and infilled caves found in places at the top of the Redwall Limestone, which contain lenticular deposits resembling the overlying Supai lithology. These buried caves and associated solution deposits clearly formed as a result of chemical weathering and erosion producing a karst topography.

It is assumed by the conventional geological community that this chemical weathering and solution occurred in a time gap between deposition of the Redwall Limestone and the overlying Supai Group, that is, while the Redwall Limestone was an exposed land surface prior to inundation by the ocean that deposited the overlying Supai Group sediments.[14] However, there are hundreds of solution and collapse structures (breccia pipes) in strata above the Redwall Limestone, many having filled horizontally with radiating solution drainage channels in the uppermost Redwall, but containing fragments of formations overlying the Supai Group.[15] Many of these solution collapse structures, which have been mined for copper and uranium, contain breccia fragments of Coconino Sandstone and even Kaibab Limestone, conclusively demonstrating that the solution of the Redwall Limestone occurred after the rest of the Grand Canyon strata were deposited, and not in any claimed time gap between deposition of the Redwall Limestone and Supai Group sediments. Furthermore, in many other places it is difficult to locate the disconformity exactly and prove that it exists, especially where limestone overlies limestone. Thus, most solution and infilling features are localized, and

12   S. S. Beus, 2003, Temple Butte Formation, in *Grand Canyon Geology*, second edition, S. S. Beus and M. Morales, eds., New York: Oxford University Press, 107-114.

13   S. S. Beus, 2003, Redwall Limestone and Surprise Canyon Formation, in *Grand Canyon Geology*, second edition, S. S. Beus and M. Morales, eds., New York: Oxford University Press, 115-135.

14   E. D. McKee and R. G. Gutschick, 1969, History of the Redwall Limestone in Northern Arizona, *Geological Society of America Memoir*, 114: 74-85.

15   K. J. Wenrich and P. W. Huntoon, 1989, Breccia pipes and associated mineralization in the Grand Canyon region, northern Arizona, in *Geology of Grand Canyon, Northern Arizona*, D. Elston, G. H. Billingsley and R. A. Young, eds., Washington D.C.: American Geophysical Union, 212-218.

appear to have formed after the deposition of the Grand Canyon strata sequence, so that the evidence for solution having occurred is not evidence for a time gap of millions of years at this strata boundary.

Siltstones and shales of the Hermit Formation overlie the Esplanade Sandstone, the uppermost formation of the Supai Group, with a boundary claimed to be an unconformity of regional extent, representing an extended period of non-deposition due to uplift, weathering, and erosion.[16] However, abundant field evidence does not substantiate this claim. There is a general lack of conglomerate at the boundary, signifying the claimed time gap was so short that the Esplanade Sandstone did not become lithified prior to Hermit Formation deposition.[17] In many areas there is no obvious relief, on what is an even, flat contact. Furthermore:

> In a number of areas no evidence of a physical break has been detected, and at these places a boundary between formations can be established only by placing it arbitrarily where a lithologic change occurs. Thus, the significance of the surface as a record of regional erosion seems questionable.[18]

At many locations there is a definite transition with intertonguing of the two units, and where channels are found they are related to deposition of the Hermit Formation.[19] "A relatively sharp contact is between the two units in some areas, whereas gradation and probable intertonguing is observed elsewhere."[20] Thus, the evidence unequivocally shows that there is no claimed unconformity with a time gap between these two strata units. The intertonguing and transitional gradation between them resulted from continuous sedimentation.

There is an extraordinarily flat surface, free of any channel erosion, between the Hermit Formation and the overlying Coconino Sandstone. No soil or weathering profile is known at the top of the Hermit Formation, nor are pebbles of lithified Hermit siltstone known from the base of the Coconino. Instead, the uppermost Hermit Formation contains elongated cracks filled from above with Coconino Sandstone (clastic dikes). It would thus appear that the uppermost Hermit was not lithified when deposition of the Coconino began.[21] However, the discovery of the thick Schnebly Hill Formation between the Hermit Formation and the

---

16   L. F. Noble, 1923, A section of Paleozoic formations of the Grand Canyon at the Bass Trail, *U.S. Geological Survey Professional Paper*, 131-B: 63-64; E. D. McKee, 1982, The Supai Group of Grand Canyon, *U.S. Geological Survey Professional Paper*, 1173: 169-171; Young, 1990, 68-69.

17   McKee, 1982, 171.

18   McKee, 1982, 202.

19   R. C. Blakey, 2003, Supai Group and Hermit Formation, in *Grand Canyon Geology*, second edition, S. Beus and M. Morales, eds., New York: Oxford University Press, 136-162; Austin, 1994, Figure 3.26: 50.

20   R. C. Blakey, 1990, Stratigraphy and geologic history of Pennsylvanian and Permian rocks, Mogollon Rim region, central Arizona and vicinity, *Geological Society of America Bulletin*, 102: 1205.

21   Austin, 1994, 49.

Coconino Sandstone in central and eastern Arizona has prompted the conventional geological community to insert a significant paraconformity between the Hermit and Coconino: "The sharp contact may be a major regional unconformity though sufficient paleontological evidence to confirm this hypothesis is not yet available."[22] If "there is no evidence of prolonged weathering or extensive erosion" at this boundary,[23] then insertion of a time gap is neither necessary nor mandatory. Usually the sole reason for defining a paraconformity is different biostratigraphic (fossil) ages for the strata on either side of the contact, the absence of the appropriate fossils between the strata defining the time gap, even though no physical evidence of subaerial exposure or erosion is present to confirm the claimed millions of years between the strata. In this instance, if the Schnebly Hill Formation did not exist, then "sufficient paleontological evidence" would not be sought to define a time gap and a paraconformity. Thus, this supposed time gap at the Coconino-Hermit contact is an artifact of theory, and not based on the observable field evidence.

The fifth boundary in the Grand Canyon Paleozoic sequence where a time gap is postulated is the contact between the Toroweap and Kaibab Formations. Because the Toroweap Formation is absent from between the Kaibab Formation and Coconino Sandstone east of the Grand Canyon, and because at rare locations there are small channel-like "erosional structures" filled with broken clasts of Toroweap lithology at the contact with the Kaibab, it has long been conjectured that a significant paraconformity or disconformity exists at the Kaibab-Toroweap boundary.[24] Such was the confidence that a time break existed at this boundary, it was held up as a "textbook" example:

> The relative importance of a hiatus is immediately evident if the beds above and below bear fossils by which they can be assigned to their proper position in the geologic column. In most instances this is the final and the only criterion that gives quantitative results for the large unconformities. In the Grand Canyon walls, for example, where the Redwall limestone can be dated as lower Mississippian and the underlying Muav limestone as Middle Cambrian, we know that the paraconformity represents more than three geologic periods, yet the physical evidence for the break is less obvious than for that which separates the Toroweap and the Kaibab limestones, both of which are Middle Permian. Many large unconformities would never be suspected if it were not for such dating of the rocks above and below.[25]

The implication of this claimed regional unconformity is that, after marine

---

22   Blakey, 1990, 164.

23   J. S. Shelton, 1966, *Geology Illustrated*, San Francisco: W.H. Freeman, 283.

24   E. D. McKee, 1938, *The Environment and History of the Toroweap and Kaibab Formations of Northern Arizona and Southern Utah*, Washington: Carnegie Institute, Publication 492, 1-268.

25   C. O Dunbar and J. Rodgers, 1957, *Principles of Stratigraphy*, New York: John Wiley and Sons, 127.

deposition of the Toroweap limestone, the ocean responsible supposedly retreated, and an epoch of subaerial exposure followed, in which cementation occurred, followed by weathering and erosion of the lithified, uppermost surface of the Toroweap. Then this land surface had to subside, for the ocean to rise again to cover the region in order for the Kaibab limestone to be deposited. So is there really physical evidence for an epoch of subaerial erosion between the Kaibab and Toroweap? The Kaibab-Toroweap contact has now been declared as conformable, because no erosional channels have been found.[26] Furthermore, the channel erosion at the top of the Toroweap was found to be very localized and limited, while the broken clasts of Toroweap lithology at the top of the Toroweap and the associated "erosional channels" were found to have formed by underground solution and collapse of limestone, not by subaerial weathering and channel erosion.[27] So the Kaibab-Toroweap boundary is now regarded as conformable, or only locally disconformable, so no time gap of any significance can be inserted between these two formations.

Thus, it can be shown that there are real problems for the conventional geological community regarding these claimed time gaps between consecutive strata, as illustrated from the walls of the Grand Canyon. The physical evidence is absent or minimal at best, being more consistent with continual deposition of the strata. On a global scale this problem is greatly expanded, for if this phenomenon were rare, it might easily be passed over as an oddity not pertinent to explaining the geologic record in general. However, these gaps are characteristic of what is found frequently in the geologic record globally.[28] As has been stated:

> The difficulty with the extended passage of time proposed for various gaps in the sedimentary record is that we find neither deposition, nor is much erosion evident. If there is deposition, there is no gap, because sedimentation continues. If there is erosion, one would expect abundant channeling and the formation of deep gullies, canyons and valleys, yet the contacts (gaps), sometimes described as "continent-sized," are usually "near planar" (flat). It is difficult to conceive of little or nothing happening for millions of years on our planet's surface. Over time either deposition or erosion will occur.... The question of the assumed gaps in the sedimentary layers witness to a past that differed greatly from the present. We can easily reconcile that difference with catastrophic models such as the Genesis flood that propose rapid deposition of the layers with

---

26   Austin, 1994, 48, and references contained therein.

27   C. W. Cheevers and R. R. Rawson, 1979, Facies analysis of the Kaibab Formation in northern Arizona, southern Utah, and southern Nevada, in *Permianland Guide Book for the Ninth Field Conference Four Corners Geological Society*, Durango, CO, 105-113; R. L. Hopkins, 2003, Kaibab Formation, in *Grand Canyon Geology*, second edition, S. S. Beus and M. Morales, eds., New York: Oxford University Press, 196-211.

28   Roth, 1998.

no extended time periods between them.[29]

To add visual impact to the significance of this problem, Figure 49 (page 1085) compares the erosion that might be expected if long time periods had passed between sedimentary formations with the characteristic appearance of the geologic record, especially in the Paleozoic and Mesozoic, where there has been minimal erosion between formations. Some erosional channels are evident, as seen between some of the Grand Canyon strata, but the amount of relief is surprisingly small compared to modern topography produced by erosion with the passage of time.

Figure 50 (page 1086), a geological time cross-section through southeastern Utah, illustrates how common these gaps are in the geologic record in a well-studied area just to the north of the Grand Canyon. The presumed time gaps are shown in black, but of course, in reality, the formations lie on top of one another over large areas without significant erosion between them. They are relatively thin, widespread layers (the vertical exaggeration in the diagram is 16x), with some of them laterally correlating with one another. It is clearly evident that the claimed time gaps between these strata represent more geological time than that claimed for the deposition of these strata themselves (more than 60 percent of the Phanerozoic geologic record represented in this diagram is claimed time gaps). Yet there is little to virtually no erosion on the strata surfaces below the claimed time gaps, as has already been well documented for that part of this strata sequence that outcrops in the walls of the Grand Canyon.

Attempts to explain how the surfaces of these layers below each of the time gaps have remained uneroded during the claimed millions of years, when deposition was supposed to not be occurring, have not withstood critical analysis. Apparently, no modern analog exists for these very flat areas with little or no erosion.[30] However, some very arid areas of Australia, which are quite flat and featureless, are believed to represent areas that have been uneroded for millions of years. Perhaps the most extreme case would be Kangaroo Island, off the coast of South Australia, which is 140 x 60 kilometers in area, is extremely flat, and has a land surface believed to have been undisturbed for at least 200 million years.[31] However, the very arid condition of this and other parts of Australia today is not at all comparable to the apparent climatic conditions believed to have been operating during accumulation of the geologic record, including those parts containing the claimed time gaps, and even during the supposed 200 million years there at Kangaroo Island and other parts of Australia. Furthermore, these relatively flat land surfaces in arid areas of Australia are not characteristic of the expected results of normal geological processes, but are oddities which are "in some degree an embarrassment to all the

---

29   Roth, 1998, 229.

30   Roth, 1998.

31   B. Daily, C. R. Twidale and A. R. Milnes, 1974, The age of the lateritized summit surface on Kangaroo Island and adjacent areas of South Australia, *Journal of the Geological Society of Australia*, 21 (4): 387-392.

commonly accepted models of landscape development."[32] On the other hand, the land surface of an area like Kangaroo Island is much more easily explained by a timespan for its existence of only thousands of years. After all, it stretches scientific credulity to suppose that a land surface was exposed for more than 200 million years without leaving any trace of any significant weathering and erosion.

The far simpler scientific explanation, that is elegantly consistent with the scientific evidence, is that the rocks beneath such land surfaces formed during the Genesis Flood, and that the land surfaces themselves were formed at the end of the Flood only thousands of years ago. This explains why there has been so little modification by weathering and erosion subsequently. Similarly, the catastrophic geological processes operating during the Genesis Flood offer a more scientifically reasonable explanation for these presumed time gaps in the geologic record. The timespans represented by the genuine gaps would vary from days to weeks if during the Flood, or to years or hundreds of years, at most, if generated subsequent to the Flood. Of course, the geologic record sometimes does contain evidence for erosion between some strata, as has already been described—in localized erosion channels within the Cambrian Muav Limestone, which are filled with Devonian Temple Butte Limestone at the boundary with the overlying lower Carboniferous Redwall Limestone. However, notwithstanding the geological ages assigned to these strata, the actual physical evidence at this and other boundaries between strata in the Grand Canyon sequence is far more consistent with the elapsed timespan for this erosion having been only hours or days during the catastrophic geological processes of the Genesis Flood, rather than the claimed 100 or more million years. Indeed, it is only to be expected that the global geological catastrophe represented by the Genesis Flood would have at times resulted in erosion of significant amounts of sediments, including erosion of strata already deposited during the catastrophe. Current geological processes on the present earth, even at their comparatively slow rates, cannot explain the small amounts of erosion at many strata boundaries in the geologic record in the presumed passing of extremely long periods of time, measured in millions of years.

Additionally, where there has been no erosion at strata boundaries, yet the geological ages assigned to the strata imply the absence of sedimentation and erosion for presumed millions of years, the physical evidence is really only consistent with deposition having been continuous. Thus, the presumed time gaps of millions of years are eliminated, and bringing into question the conventional geologic age dating. Instead, this evidence supports the role of the global Genesis Flood catastrophe in depositing the strata sequences.

Another related observation is that on top of some strata sequences are enormous, fairly flat erosion surfaces. An excellent example is the extensive, fairly flat erosion surface that occurs above most of the strata units found in the Grand Canyon,

---

32   C. R. Twidale, 1976, On the survival of paleoforms, *American Journal of Science*, 276 (1): 77-95 (81).

and forms the upper surface of many of the most prominent plateaus of northern Arizona. In the Grand Canyon area this erosion surface is most commonly seen as the upper surface of the Coconino and Kaibab Plateaus, and the Kaibab Limestone is the most prominent formation observed at this surface, which intersects the rim of the Canyon itself (see Figures 3 and 4, pages 441 and 312). The Kaibab Limestone is the prominent formation at the Canyon rim and is the most prominent formation observed across the erosion surface at the top of the surrounding plateau country. That other formations were originally deposited on top of the Kaibab Limestone can be seen in two erosionally isolated remnants that consist of the overlying Moenkopi Formation and the Shinarump Conglomerate Member of the Chinle Formation. North of Grand Canyon the same erosion surface is just above the level of the Navajo Sandstone in the strata sequence above the Kaibab Limestone.

This physical evidence for extensive removal of most of the units in the strata column above the Kaibab Limestone is best explained as being the result of sheet erosion, by an enormous body of water that uniformly swept across the vast area. Furthermore, this enormous sheet of water would have been retreating from this area, and the strata eroded and removed must have been poorly consolidated after only having been recently deposited, that is, relative to the flooding of the area by this extensive sheet of water. This broad sheet-flood erosion of these elevated plateaus of northern Arizona stands in stark contrast to the channelized erosion that forms the present topographic profile within the Canyon, the latter erosion being more recent than the extensive sheet-flood erosion of the plateaus. There is really no modern counterpart to this catastrophic flooding, and movement of the resultant vast body of water responsible for such sheet erosion, to produce such extensive fairly-flat surfaces. This evidence is again consistent with the waters of the Genesis Flood when they retreated, being responsible for this sheet erosion across Arizona and elsewhere.

75

Soft-Sediment Deformation Features

Most sedimentary strata today, even when exposed at the earth's surface, are hard and brittle, because after deposition the sediment grains were cemented together, turning the soft sediment into hard rock. The processes are called diagenesis and lithification. In conventional geologic thinking, the layers of sedimentary strata in any given strata sequence, such as that exposed in the walls of the Grand Canyon, were deposited consecutively over millions of years, with the deposition of each conformable layer separated in time, perhaps also by millions of years. Diagenesis and lithification are also said to have perhaps taken millions of years, as chemicals in the water trapped between the sediment grains precipitate and crystallize to form the cement that binds the grains together. The strata sequence was then probably deformed, by being folded and faulted, probably millions of years after deposition finished and diagenesis and lithification had occurred, as has happened to the strata sequence in the Grand Canyon. Because in conventional geologic thinking deformation would thus have taken place after the sediment layers had already hardened into solid rocks, there should have been brittle failure of those rocks in response to the deformation.

It is known from experimental evidence that, under severe pressure and moderate temperature conditions, rocks can be made to deform and flow as if they were plastic, similar to modeling clay. However, when that happens, there is also evidence of the rocks being mineralogically and physically transformed, that is, metamorphosed. Nevertheless, many sedimentary strata sequences have not been so metamorphosed, and even though the strata are now brittle, they appear to have only suffered plastic deformation. The only way this could have occurred, without the tell-tale signs of metamorphism, is when the sediments were still soft after deposition, but prior to diagenesis and lithification. Yet even where the strata show compelling evidence of this having occurred, conventional geologic thinking discounts this evidence, because it automatically accepts the millions-of-years geologic timescale for the deposition of the sequences of sedimentary strata and their subsequent deformation.

On the other hand, this evidence of soft-sediment deformation is precisely what would be expected if the sedimentary sequences were rapidly deposited and then deformed in the year-long Genesis Flood, only thousands of years ago. Since the sediment layers at the base of strata sequences would generally have been deposited early in the Flood, then even if considerable thicknesses of other sediments were deposited on top of them, there would not have been the time or appropriate conditions for diagenesis and lithification to have fully occurred in the subsequent months of the Flood year, when deformation would have occurred while all the sedimentary strata were thus still soft and plastic.

This raises the question as to how long it takes for diagenesis and lithification of sediment layers to occur. Unfortunately, because there are a lot of variables involved, and each sediment layer experiences different conditions, there is no one specific answer. Important factors include the type of sediment, the amount of water in pore spaces, the type and amount of cement in solution, and the depth of burial (which determines the pressure and temperature conditions). If a sediment layer is buried deeply enough, then confining pressure will force the trapped water out of the pore spaces between the sediment grains, and the increased temperature will help precipitate the cement to bind the sediment grains together. Because conditions are unique to each sediment layer, in any particular strata sequence some sedimentary rock units are softer than others, while some may not have yet completely lithified, for one reason or another. Nevertheless, all sedimentary strata do become lithified, hard, and brittle, because under normal conditions sediments lithify relatively quickly, often in a matter of years, but at the most perhaps hundreds of years. Given ideal conditions, lithification can happen within days. The lithification process is somewhat analogous with a man-made mixture of gravel, sand, Portland cement, and water that lithifies to produce concrete, because the chemical present in the cement reacts with the water as the mixture dries. The process only takes hours to days.

A natural example of lithification illustrates how rapidly the process can occur. Following the explosive eruption of Mount St. Helens in Washington state on May 18, 1980, up to 600 feet (180 meters) of strata accumulated from the primary air blast, landslides, pyroclastic flows, mudflows and air falls.[1] The resultant strata, having been deposited catastrophically, appear essentially the same as other strata in the geologic record that are claimed to have been deposited over thousands and millions of years. After being deposited by the volcanic activity of Mount St. Helens, these sediment layers have subsequently not been subjected to optimum conditions for lithification, even suffering severe erosion as a result of a mudflow on March 19, 1982, eroding deeply into them to form a canyon system over 100 feet (30 meters) deep. Yet within five years of having been deposited, these sediment layers had been lithified sufficiently for them to support near-vertical cliffs in this canyon system. Thus, lithification can be a relatively rapid process, even at the earth's surface.

---

1   S. A. Austin, 1986, Mount St Helens and catastrophism, *Proceedings of the First International Conference on Creationism*, vol I, 3-9, Pittsburgh, PA: Creation Science Fellowship.

Thus, once sediment layers become lithified, the resultant sedimentary rocks are extremely difficult to bend and deform without being broken and shattered. The rocks are hard and brittle, which is in stark contrast to their soft and plastic, more pliable, condition soon after sediment deposition, and prior to lithification. If deformation of a rock has occurred after its lithification, then the effects of the deformation on the mineral grains making up the rock can clearly be seen upon microscope examination. Many sedimentary strata sequences appear to have been deformed while the sediments were still soft and pliable, yet in conventional terms the sediments were deposited and supposedly lithified millions of years before deformation occurred. Thus, since lithification had occurred millions of years before deformation, the rocks were hardened when deformation occurred, and should have behaved in a brittle fashion. However, both at the macroscopic and microscopic scales, evidence implies plastic deformation has occurred when the sediments were still soft and pliable after deposition, thus challenging the claimed millions-of-years timeframe for the deposition of the sedimentary strata sequences and the subsequent deformation.

An excellent example of this soft-sediment deformation, which challenges the conventional timeframe for a sedimentary strata sequence, is found in the Grand Canyon area. The Grand Canyon itself has been carved through a 7,000-8,000 foot (2,150-3,450 meter) high plateau, and in the walls of the Canyon the sedimentary strata beneath the plateau are exposed. However, to the east, the same rock units that crop out at the rim of the Grand Canyon are found at a lower elevation. Indeed, some 250 miles (400 kilometers) to the east the same rock units are a mile or so (more than 1,600 meters) lower in elevation, so the plateau through which the Grand Canyon has been carved was uplifted to its current elevation by earth movements during tectonic adjustments of the earth's crust. In conventional terms, this is claimed to have occurred some 70 million years ago, during the Laramide Orogeny when the Rocky Mountains were also being formed. This pronounced elevation difference, due to uplift of what is known as the Kaibab Plateau, was achieved by upwarping in the eastern Grand Canyon, where the strata have been bent to form a fold structure called a monocline. The axis of the fold is called the East Kaibab Monocline, and its surface expression is a bending/folding of the Kaibab Limestone through an elevation difference of 3,000 feet (more than 900 meters). The fact that the Kaibab Limestone has been folded rather than altered indicates that it was still soft and pliable when the deformation occurred supposedly 70 million years ago. However, the Kaibab Limestone is supposed to be 250 million years old, more than enough time for it to have lithified in the claimed 180 million years since its deposition.

The other rock units in the sequence below the Kaibab Limestone have also been folded during this deformation event responsible for the Kaibab Upwarp, and the most extreme example is the Tapeats Sandstone at the base of the strata sequence. In the hinge zone of the monocline, the Tapeats Sandstone has been severely deformed, the internal layering being bent and twisted to be oriented almost vertically (Figure 51, page 1087). In conventional terms, the Tapeats Sandstone is claimed to be around 540 million years old, so that at least 470 million years had supposedly elapsed by the time of the Laramide Orogeny 70 million years ago. Since there was also at least 4,000 feet (1,200 meters) thickness of other sedimentary layers stacked on top of the Tapeats Sandstone for 180 million years (that is, after deposition of the Kaibab Limestone), there was ample time and sufficient confining overburden pressure to have resulted in the lithification of the Tapeats Sandstone by the time the deformation occurred. Thus, it would be expected that the lithified Tapeats Sandstone suffered brittle failure during deformation, if the millions of years are the correct time framework for these events.

However, the bending of the sandstone in the hinge area of the monocline does not show any sign of brittle failure (Figure 51), but instead the sandstone appears to have been in a soft, pliable condition when the bending occurred. Thus, lithification of the sandstone had not yet taken place, and therefore, there could not have been millions of years between deposition of the sandstone and the deformation event. Furthermore, close examination of the sandstone does not reveal any evidence of elongated sand grains, or of broken and recrystallized cement, both brittle deformation features that would be expected if the sandstone was fully lithified when the bending occurred. The Tapeats Sandstone obviously was thus still soft and pliable when the deformation occurred, even though the confining pressure of the overlying sediments must have compacted the sandy sediment, so the process of lithification had begun. There can't have been much time, therefore, between deposition of the Tapeats Sandstone, deposition of the overlying sediment layers, and then the deformation of the entire strata sequence.

It cannot be denied that if a rock is buried deeply, and thus experiences confining pressure from all directions surrounding it, then bending can occur in an otherwise brittle rock. Nevertheless, in a hard, lithified sandstone, such as the Tapeats Sandstone, such bending always results in elongated sand grains, and/ or recrystallization of broken cement, neither of which has been found in the deformed Tapeats Sandstone in the Grand Canyon. There is a limit to how much strain (or deformation) a rock can endure under a given stress.[2] Deformation occurs when stress is applied to a rock, and if the stress is maintained at a constant level, the rock will continue to deform or "creep." If the rock experiences additional stress, it will suffer failure because it is brittle and will fracture. On the other hand, if a constant stress is maintained, at a value below that failure point, deformation will continue in most rocks, until a terminal value is reached where the rock will either become stable or will fracture. For most rocks there is a limit to the amount of creep that can occur over time, because they cannot undergo unlimited deformation, and will eventually rupture.

---

2   R. E. Goodman, 1980, *Introduction to Rock Mechanics*, New York: John Wiley and Sons, 74.

In the example of the Tapeats Sandstone in the Grand Canyon, in the hinge area of the East Kaibab Monocline where the folding is greatest, the sandstone is bent at an approximate 90° within a distance of about 100 feet (30 meters). In the folding process, the sandstone in the outer half of the fold would have been under tension, while in the inside part of the fold the sandstone would have been under compression. Lithified rock is notoriously weak under tension, invariably failing by fracturing, yet at places within the hinge zone of the monocline, it can be seen that entire layers within the sandstone have thinned as they were stretched during bending. This is visible confirmation that the sandstone must have still been relatively soft and plastic under the stress of the deformation event, which must therefore have occurred soon after deposition of the sandstone, not 470 million years later. Lithified sandstone could otherwise have not withstood the amount of stretching involved in this folding, even under the confining pressures involved, because experimental work has demonstrated that lithified rock simply does not stretch and thin in the way observed in the Tapeats Sandstone. Thus, this observed soft-sediment deformation of the Tapeats Sandstone, in the hinge zone of the East Kaibab Monocline in the eastern Grand Canyon, is irrefutable testimony that the sequence of events, beginning with deposition of the Tapeats Sandstone and the overlying 1,200-meter-thick sedimentary strata sequence, followed by the deformation event that folded this strata sequence along this monocline during the uplift of the Kaibab Plateau, could not have occupied hundreds of millions of years, but rather an extremely short timeframe, which implies that deposition and deformation of this sedimentary strata sequence were catastrophic events.

Added powerful confirmation that this is the correct interpretation of the observed evidence is the faulting of the metamorphic rocks below the folded Tapeats Sandstone to Kaibab Limestone strata sequence along the East Kaibab Monocline. During the Kaibab Upwarp event, the same applied stress that stretched and thinned the Tapeats Sandstone as it was folded, caused fracturing and faulting of the schists and other metamorphic rocks in the basement complex directly underlying the Tapeats Sandstone. This implies that, by the time deposition of the Tapeats Sandstone-Kaibab Limestone sediments was occurring, these metamorphic rocks were hard and brittle, which in turn implies that sufficient time had previously elapsed for these rocks to have reached this condition. This is, therefore, consistent with their formation prior to the Genesis Flood, even dating back to the events of the Creation Week itself. Seismic studies have demonstrated that the fracturing of these brittle metamorphic rocks resulted in a vertical displacement of at least 5,000 feet (1,500 meters) along faults located underneath the East Kaibab Monocline. Thus, while the previously hardened brittle metamorphic rocks in the basement complex were faulted by the deformation produced by the Kaibab Upwarp, the Tapeats Sandstone-Kaibab Limestone sedimentary sequence catastrophically deposited on top of the basement complex during the Flood was only folded, because the strata were still soft and pliable due to the upwarp occurring so soon after deposition that lithification had not fully taken place. However, the subsequent faulting with much less displacement, for example, along the Bright

Angel Fault, which fractured and faulted the entire Tapeats Sandstone-Kaibab Limestone strata sequence, implies that the lithification of these sediments was soon completed after the major deformation of the Kaibab Upwarp.

This dramatic example of soft-sediment deformation in the Grand Canyon is definitely not unique, because there are almost countless other examples in other places where strata have been deformed while still soft and pliable. In the United States alone, both the Appalachian Mountains and the Rocky Mountains are full of such occurrences. Several examples in the Rocky Mountains are associated with the Ute Pass Fault, west of Colorado Springs.[3] The Front Range of the Rocky Mountains in Colorado was formed by large reverse faults, with vertical displacements of as much as 21,000 feet (6,400 meters). The very abrupt margin of the Front Range, with Pikes Peak (more than 14,000 feet or 4,250 meters elevation) on the west and Colorado Springs (6,000 feet or 1,830 meters elevation) on the east, is caused by the Ute Pass Fault, a prominent north-trending reverse fault more than 40 miles (64 km) in length. On the west side of the fault is the upthrown Pikes Peak granite and associated Precambrian metamorphic rocks, all sedimentary strata overlying them having been removed by erosion. On the east side of the Ute Pass Fault there are about 12,000 feet (3,650 meters) of Phanerozoic sedimentary strata overlying the Precambrian basement, so the vertical displacement on the fault is about 20,000 feet (6,100 meters). The Ute Pass Fault truncates, or folds, Cambrian to Cretaceous strata, so it must therefore be Cretaceous or post-Cretaceous. Field relationships confirm that all of the very intense deformation associated with the Ute Pass Fault is thus assignable to the Laramide Orogeny, which was responsible for the formation of the Rocky Mountains and for the uplift of the Kaibab Plateau in the Grand Canyon area.

Characteristic of the Ute Pass Fault is the intensity of folding of the strata on its east side, where there is an eroded remnant of an enormous monocline involving about two miles (more than 3 km) of structural relief. Approaching the flank of the Front Range, within three miles (almost 5 km) of the exposure of the Precambrian basement on the other side of the fault, the 14,000 feet (more than 4,200 meters) of sedimentary strata are bent into nearly vertical orientation. The Ute Pass Fault appears to be concealed at depth in the Precambrian basement, but this thick overlying sedimentary rock cover did not fault, and so must not have then been fully lithified. Instead, these sedimentary strata were plastically deformed by vertical displacement on the Ute Pass Fault to form this spectacular monocline.

Further evidence of soft-sediment deformation are the tight drag folds very close to the Ute Pass Fault, such as the very strong folding of the Fountain Formation

---

3   S. A. Austin and J. D. Morris, 1986, Tight folds and clastic dikes as evidence for rapid deposition and
     deformation of two very thick stratigraphic sequences, *Proceedings of the First International Conference on
     Creationism*, vol II, 3-15, R. E. Walsh, C. L. Brooks and R. S. Crowell, eds., Pittsburgh, PA: Creation
     Science Fellowship.

sandstone in contact with the fault near Manitou Springs. The sandstone dips at 35°NE just 80 feet (24 meters) northeast of the Ute Pass Fault, but at the fault it is overturned and dips about 60°NW. This folding was caused by drag of the strata against the upthrown west side of the fault. Field observations clearly reveal that the sandstone was not able to transmit stress away from the fault, so was not internally faulted as it was folded, which is consistent with the strata being ductile and not solidly cemented when deformed. However, this Fountain Formation sandstone is Pennsylvanian-Permian, so in conventional terms it is regarded as 300 million years old, whereas the Laramide Orogeny is supposed to have occurred less than 70 million years ago. Therefore, how could this sandstone have remained ductile for those claimed 230 million years? That ductile flow was the mechanism for the tight drag folds has long been recognized from field observations of several outcrops on the Ute Pass Fault:

> These examples demonstrate that the drag effect in Fountain arkoses can be very local. The drag is accomplished with few visible fractures. The shape of the beds is apparently altered by ductile flow, that is, by small translation and rotation of individual grains of the arkoses and conglomerates.[4]

Translation and rotation of individual grains could be easily accomplished if the sandstone was not yet cemented when deformed. If the sandstone was cemented and fully lithified when Ute Pass Fault was formed, significant modifications to the shapes of individual grains within the sandstone due to the stress of the folding should now be observed. Furthermore, there should also have been significant faulting due to brittle failure.

Other soft-sediment deformation features that are even more significant are the clastic dikes of quartz sandstone associated with the Ute Pass Fault and many other reverse faults of the Front Range.[5] More than 200 sandstone dikes were mapped in one study alone, the dikes varying from a fraction of an inch to miles in length, from a fraction of an inch to 300 feet (over 90 meters) in width, and penetrating up to 1,000 feet (305 meters) or more through the surrounding bedrock, which is usually Precambrian basement (Pikes Peak granite or associated metamorphic rocks). The dikes occur most frequently on the upthrown (hanging wall) side of the Ute Pass Fault, within one mile (1.6 km) west of the fault, having been injected downwards from sandstone overlying the Precambrian basement (now eroded away) along extension fractures in the hanging wall of the convex-upward

4   J. C. Harms, 1965, Sandstone dikes and their relation to Laramide Faults and stress distribution in the southern Front Range, Colorado, *Geological Society of America Bulletin*, 76: 989.

5   W. Cross, 1894, Intrusive sandstone dikes in granite, *Geological Society of America Bulletin*, 5: 225-230; P. W. Vitanage, 1954, Sandstone dikes in the South Platte area, Colorado, *Journal of Geology*, 62: 493-500; G. R. Scott, 1963, Geology of the Kassler Quadrangle, *U.S. Geological Survey Professional Paper*, 421-B: 125pp; Harms, 1965, 981-1002; L. S. Kost, 1984, Paleomagnetic and petrographic study of sandstone dikes and the Cambrian Sawatch Sandstone, east flank of the southern Front Range, Colorado, University of Colorado, unpublished M.S. thesis, 173 pp.

reverse fault. Virtually all the dikes strike parallel to the strike of the main reverse fault, and because of their coincidence with, and relationship to, the structures generated by the Laramide Orogeny, it is only reasonable to conclude that they are Laramide dikes. These sandstone dikes are remarkably uniform in composition, with greater than 90 percent quartz by volume, less than 5 percent feldspar, and less than 5 percent clay-size matrix. Xenoliths of granite from the wall-rock are common. Among investigators of these clastic dikes there is agreement that the Sawatch Sandstone (the Cambrian sandstone immediately overlying the basement) is the source. Not only is the Sawatch the closest sandstone to the dikes, but there is nearly identical compositional and textural similarity.

The evidence that the sand of the dikes was unconsolidated when injected has been widely recognized. There is little evidence of breakage of sand grains as if they were cemented before injection, and there is a lack of fine matrix, which would have formed from disaggregation of the sandstone had it been lithified. On the other hand, the long axes of granite xenoliths are oriented parallel to the dike walls, and the dikes themselves show laminated flow structures, with segregation of sand by size as if forcefully injected. Even dikes only a fraction of an inch wide are completely filled with sand, testimony to the great fluidity of the injected material.

Having agreed upon the source of the sand in these clastic dikes along the Ute Pass Fault, there is a divergence of opinion as to when their intrusion occurred. Of course, some investigators have recognized the fundamental impossibility of the Cambrian Sawatch Sandstone (supposedly 500 million years old) remaining unlithified while deeply buried for 430 million years until the Laramide Orogeny (assumed to be late Cretaceous about 70 million years ago or less). To avoid this obviously embarrassing problem, important field relationships are overlooked in order to suggest that the dikes were actually intruded in the Cambrian while the Sawatch Sandstone was unconsolidated. However, there is no evidence of tectonic movements in the Cambrian or Ordovician of a magnitude able to open up extension fractures hundreds of feet (tens of meters) wide along the Ute Pass Fault. Instead, the actual field data strongly support the Laramide intrusion of the dikes. The Laramide Orogeny was not only of sufficient magnitude to open up the large extension fractures, but the coincidence of the dikes along the Ute Pass Fault, a proven Laramide structure, cannot be accidental. Furthermore, one of these quartz sandstone bodies penetrates the Pennsylvanian-Permian Fountain Formation sandstone, so this dike cannot be Cambrian or Ordovician, but is related to the Laramide Ute Pass Fault.

In conclusion, it is abundantly clear that the total time required for deposition of the sequence of 14,000 feet (more than 4,200 meters) of sedimentary strata overlying the Precambrian basement, for regional flexing, for faulting, and for the development of the local deformation features, must have been less than the time it took for this entire thick sequence of soft sediments, complete with their contained water and mineral cement content, to lithify and completely harden to rock. This implies catastrophic deposition of these strata, and that tectonism immediately followed deposition before lithification of even the sand layer at the base of the 14,000-feet-(more than 4,200 meters) thick sequence of sediments. On the other hand, the conventional view is that this 14,000-feet-(more than 4,200 meters) thick sequence of strata along the Ute Pass Fault in Colorado accumulated from the Cambrian through to the Cretaceous, from supposedly 500 million years ago through to 70 million years ago, a total deposition time of some 430 or more million years. However, as amply demonstrated by the field observations of numerous investigators, there are numerous soft-sediment deformation features (monoclines, tight drag folds, and clastic dikes) among the strata along the fault which are associated with the Laramide Orogeny that supposedly occurred less than 70 million years ago, so how could this thick sequence of sediments escape lithification after deep burial through a duration of up to 430 million years? Without a doubt, the answer is that the evidence overwhelmingly supports the conclusion that the entire thick sequence of sediments was catastrophically deposited, and then immediately deformed, on a timescale consistent with the Genesis Flood, rather than the conventional view that claims deposition over 430 million years.

These two examples of soft-sediment deformation features that question the conventional claims of hundreds of millions of years for deposition of thick sequences of sedimentary strata should suffice. One or two such occurrences might be discounted as simply anomalies, but when there are numerous similar examples of soft-sediment deformation in many similarly deformed terrains all over the world, the overwhelming conclusion must be that the conventional timescale is wrong. The catastrophic deposition of these thick sequences of sedimentary strata was followed immediately by deformation before the sediments were lithified, on a timescale that must have been brief, because lithification can occur in only days or weeks. This is all consistent with the biblical account of the Genesis Flood.

76

SUMMARY

This discussion and documentation of many detailed examples of distinctive features of the geologic record have been necessary to demonstrate the overwhelming evidences of catastrophic accumulation of the rock record and these distinctive features. Furthermore, it has been easily demonstrated that, even in the conventional geologic community, there has been renewed recognition of the evidence for catastrophism in the geologic record. These evidences for catastrophism in the geologic record include:

1.   The rate of sediment accumulation

When actual sedimentation rates have been measured, they far exceed the sedimentation rates conventionally claimed for accumulation of the sedimentary strata of the geologic record, often by many orders of magnitude. Thus, it has been recognized that a single flash flood could deposit as much sediment in a few hours as that which is conventionally claimed to have been deposited over thousands, and even millions, of years. Thus, it was concluded that even if the waters of the Genesis Flood were like those of a modern flash flood, there would have been ample time in the biblical timescale for the Flood to have accumulated the sedimentary strata sequences we find worldwide in the geologic record. Therefore, realistic sedimentation rates would feasibly have produced the sedimentary rock record within the year of the Genesis Flood.

2.   Widespread, rapidly water-deposited strata

Whereas today's sediments accumulate intermittently on a local scale, the numerous thick sediment strata with amazing horizontal continuity, even on a continental scale, are overwhelming testimony to catastrophic deposition of sediments on the continental scale that would be expected to result from the global inundation of the Genesis Flood. It has also been demonstrated that even for different sediment types, as diverse as limestones from sandstones and shales, the nature of these sediments as preserved, and the internal structures within them, can only be explained by catastrophic accumulation rates. Furthermore, the depths of water and the velocities of the water currents involved, and the catastrophic widespread deposition of the sedimentary strata of the geologic record, plus the regular occurrence of marine fossils in many strata now exposed on the continents, even at elevations thousands of meters above sea level, are testimony that the ocean waters in the past covered the continents, just as recorded in the Scriptures with respect to the Genesis Flood. The sediments in these thick widespread strata spanning all regions of continents, and even across continents, show no evidence of having been derived by erosion and transport of the materials immediately underlying them, which implies that the sources of such sediments were at some distances from the regions now blanketed by these strata. This thus implies enormous distances for transport of such sediments, even on a continental scale, evidence that is not consistent with conventional explanations, but instead with the catastrophic, inter-regional erosion, transport, and sedimentation clearly implied from the scriptural record of the Genesis Flood.

3.   Fossil graveyards

The presence of so many fossils, often preserved in exquisite detail, throughout the geologic record on every continent, are testimony to the rapid burial of countless animals and plants during the catastrophic sedimentation of these strata. The detailed descriptions of some of the many spectacular fossil graveyards, found at all the various levels within the sedimentary rock record, serve to emphasize the catastrophic rates at which the sediments accumulated to bury such huge masses of animals and plants on a global scale. Indeed, the presence of many thick coal beds on every continent, with the types of plant fossils found in them, and the way these plant fossils have accumulated and been buried, is not consistent with the growth of countless plants *in situ* over millions of years, but instead with the catastrophic destruction and burial of forests with their accumulated peats on a global scale. It can also be demonstrated that the fossilization processes were extremely rapid, so as to preserve the exquisite details of fossils found in the fossil record, just as the conversion of plant material to coal has also been shown to occur in only a matter of weeks or months, a timescale consistent with the year of the Genesis Flood, only thousands of years ago.

4.   Rapid erosion and/or time gaps

The conventional view—based as it is on timescales of millions of years for strata accumulation with contained fossils characteristic of each epoch, period, and era—is that in many instances there are significant time gaps between strata in the geologic record. This is not only where some erosion is clearly evident between strata, but even where strata boundaries are flat and featureless with knife-edge clarity, because stratigraphic and biostratigraphic dating dictate the time gaps. However, while there are many locations in the geologic record where significant erosion has occurred at unconformities, such erosion can be shown to have been catastrophically rapid, thus ruling out the necessity of long ages between these strata. Furthermore, in those places where there has been minor erosion at strata boundaries, the relief is miniscule, compared to that found on the present-day land surface, if the proposed millions of years for these time gaps really did occur. If both stratigraphic and biostratigraphic dating were ignored, then the scale of erosion at these boundaries, and where so many strata boundaries are flat, featureless and knife-edge, would indicate that the rapid accumulation of the sediments in these strata would merely have been continuous, as dictated by the field evidence. Thus, the millions of years for each of the many claimed time gaps between strata in the geologic record has not been documented, but instead, the continuous catastrophic deposition of the sediments is consistent with the Genesis Flood. Furthermore, where there are water-eroded surfaces still evident on the earth's surface today, these were produced by regional-scale sheet erosion, consistent with the retreating waters at the end of the Genesis Flood.

5.   Soft-sediment deformation

Following the deposition of many thick sequences of sedimentary strata, the whole sequences were deformed by earth movements that uplifted the strata to form plateaus and mountains. Whereas this resulted in fracturing and faulting of strata, primarily in the older Precambrian basements, often the overlying sedimentary strata were bent into monoclines, and even tight folds, without evidence of the brittle fracture and failure that would be expected if the deformed sedimentary strata had already been lithified and hardened. Clastic dikes also intrude along tension fractures where faulting of strata has occurred. These soft-sediment deformation features are often found in sedimentary strata that were deposited hundreds of millions of years before the deformation events, according to conventional dating. Thus, the field evidence consistently implies that these sediment sequences thousands of meters thick had to be deposited and remain unlithified so as to subsequently deform while still soft and pliable, which automatically discounts the claimed hundreds of millions of years from the beginning of deposition to the deformation events. Thus, the timescale for accumulation of the sedimentary record is consistent with the timescale for the year-long Genesis Flood only thousands of years ago.

These summarized conclusions, based on field and laboratory evidence, give overwhelming testimony that the conventional view, which claims the geologic record required hundreds of millions, and even billions, of years to accumulate, is not only misleading, but in error because of the interpretative framework assumed and applied. Even conventional geologists are increasingly recognizing the evidences of catastrophism in the geologic record. Their uniformitarian assumptions, however, blind them to insisting that catastrophism was periodic, punctuating millions and millions of years of little to no geologic activity. This survey of the evidences for catastrophism in the geologic record, on the other hand, uninhibited by these uniformitarian assumptions, clearly demonstrates that most of the geologic record must have accumulated catastrophically, particularly that portion of the record containing fossils. All this evidence is exactly what one would expect to find in the geologic record based on the details given in the biblical record in Genesis of creation and the Flood. All that now remains to cement this demonstrated consistency between the biblical record of earth history and the geologic data is to systematize the latter within a biblical geologic model of earth history.

Section VII

A Biblical Geologic Model
of Earth History

77

THE CREATION WEEK

In the scriptural account of earth history, there are four major time periods in which the geologic record accumulated. These in order are: the Creation Week era, the pre-Flood era, the Flood era, and the post-Flood era. The durations of these eras are markedly different, and the eras themselves can be readily subdivided.

The Creation Week involves but six days of God's creating a fully-functioning mature earth with a fully operational biosphere, hydrosphere, and atmosphere, followed by God's day of rest—referred to as the "Sabbath" day. In this short timespan, the earth was created and established, with an almost incomprehensible amount of geological work completed in order to produce as much as half or more of the geologic record. By contrast, the pre-Flood era that followed lasted for approximately1,656 years, and the pace of geological processes would have to have been much, much slower in order to ensure the earth was habitable for its biosphere that was teeming with all manner of life. On the other hand, during the year-long Flood era, catastrophic geological processes were responsible for the wholesale destruction, burial, and fossilization of the pre-Flood biosphere, so again a major portion of the geologic record was built in a relatively short period of time. Finally, the post-Flood era commenced at the close of the Flood about 4,500 years ago, and has continued to the present day. In the early years of the post-Flood era the residual effects of the Flood would have been significant enough to have left behind a detectable portion on the geologic record, in sharp contrast to the slow and gradual geological processes now operating that barely leave behind any geologic record at all.

Within this broad outline it is necessary to build a comprehensive geologic model of earth history that can account for the preserved geologic record we observe today, and that upholds the veracity and integrity of both the historical record in Scripture and all the geologic data. Each of these eras therefore needs to be extensively examined in light of the data supplied by both the biblical and geologic records.

The Creation Week Processes Unique

Reading the account of the Creation Week in Genesis 1-2, one immediately observes the specific sequence in which God performed His acts of creation of different entities that eventually joined together to make a completed and integrated whole. The description in Genesis is of unequivocal acts of fiat creation that, from a human perspective, would be observed as instantaneous, simply at God's command. Psalm 33:6, 9 declare: "By the word of the LORD were the heavens made; and all the host of them by the breath of his mouth....For he spake, and it was done; he commanded, and it stood fast." Nevertheless, the text of Genesis 1 not only refers to God's commands, but also His acts of creating and making, while Genesis 2:2 refers to God ending His work. Thus, it can be argued that God's acts of creating and making involved the unleashing and setting in motion of processes that accomplished what God had commanded. However, this does not imply that these processes were anything other than unique to the Creation Week era, when God was bringing matter into existence and then organizing, ordering, and energizing it to establish the universe, the earth, and life itself. It is abundantly clear in the Genesis record that the processes used by God in creation were utterly different from the processes that now operate in the universe. That the Creation Week era was unique, entirely incommensurate with this present world, is unmistakably emphasized by divine revelation, which concludes in Genesis 2:1-2 with the words: "Thus the heavens and the earth were finished, and all the host of them. And on the seventh day God ended his work which he had made; and he rested on the seventh day from all his work which he had made." In view of these strong and repeated assertions in God's Word, it is highly presumptuous for any scientist to imply that the origin and early history of the earth can be elucidated and studied in terms of present geological and other processes.

Yet herein lies the basic fallacy of modern conventional geological research and the model for earth history it has developed, based as they both are on the belief that geological processes have been uniform in scope and operation throughout the earth's history, and indeed during its origin. It may seem reasonable to use the principle of the uniformity of natural processes as a key to deciphering the geologic record that has been produced since the end of the Creation Week, except that the scale and intensity of present-day geological processes could not have been uniform throughout the earth's history because of their acceleration during the Flood year. Obviously, the geologic record does provide much valuable information concerning earth history subsequent to the close of the Creation Week, after God finished His work of creating the "heaven and earth, the sea, and all that in them is," as summarized in Exodus 20:11. However, it is not legitimate for the uniformity principle to be used, as it has been by the general scientific community, to attempt to establish a long history for the origin and development of the creation itself over billions of years. God has plainly said that the processes He used during the creation no longer operate, a fact that is thoroughly verified by the two universal laws of thermodynamics that are intrinsic to the creation as designed by God.

The Laws of Thermodynamics

The two most fundamental and certain of all laws of modern physics are the first two laws of thermodynamics. The well-known first law of thermodynamics is the law of energy conservation, confirming that although energy can be converted from one form to another, the total amount remains unchanged, because energy is neither being created out of nothing nor totally destroyed at the present time. Matter may be transformed into energy and energy into matter, but neither creation nor annihilation occurs. The second law states that, although the total amount of energy remains unchanged, there is always a tendency for it to become less available for useful work. In other words, in any closed system in which work is being accomplished through energy conversions, the "entropy" increases, where entropy is essentially a mathematical formulation of the non-availability of the energy of the system to it.

The importance of the universal application of these laws has never been in doubt:

> The two laws of thermodynamics are, I suppose, accepted by physicists as perhaps the most secure generalizations from experience that we have. A physicist does not hesitate to apply the laws to any concrete physical situation in the confidence that nature will not let him down.[1]

These two laws operate through the whole modern scientific enterprise, and the technology it has spawned. The operation of all geological processes, as well as all other physical and biological processes, is governed by these laws, without exception. In none of them is any energy or matter (matter being one form of energy) being created. However, during the six days of creation, both matter and energy were being created, so God's creative activity was entirely different from all current geological, physical, and biological processes.

Still more significantly, this newly-created matter and energy were being organized into increasingly complex and highly energized systems, emphatically the opposite to the universal tendency toward disorganization and de-energization experienced in all processes at the present time:

> Another way to explain the meaning of entropy is to compare it to the property of "randomness." This conclusion leads to the generalization that every system that is left to itself will, on the average, change toward a condition of maximum randomness. The implication of this statement that the entropy of a system increases spontaneously...when entropy

---

1   P. W. Bridgman, 1953, Reflections on thermodynamics, *American Scientist*, 41: 549.

is thought of as randomness, it can be recognized in many natural phenomena.[2]

[E]ntropy is the supreme law of nature and governs everything we do.[3]

Randomness, of course, is synonymous with disorder, disorganization, disintegration, and degeneration. Furthermore, this is an absolutely universal rule of nature at the present time, as demonstrated and verified by countless scientific observations.

However, in spite of this unequivocal recognition of the universality of the entropy principle in all natural processes operating today, as repeatedly tested by experiments and confirmed by every scientific observation, the conventional scientific community today presupposes that the universe, the earth, and all living things on it, have developed by means of the supposed universal principle of evolution (for example, stellar evolution, planetary evolution, biological evolution). Numerous attempts have been made to harmonize, and even to equate, entropy and evolution in order to overcome this profound dilemma. The standard "answer" provided by the conventional scientific community has long been the insistence that this conflict is resolved by the fact that the earth is an "open system," with the incoming energy from the sun able to sustain evolution throughout the geological ages, in spite of the natural tendency of all systems to deteriorate toward disorganization:

> The total of living material forms a very thin layer on the surface of the earth, the *biosphere*, which is continually being degraded and reconstituted out of the same mass of chemical constituents. The work involved in this reconstitution and those evolutionary changes that go on in the biosphere is supported by photosynthesis, the process through which a small fraction of the energy of sunlight is captured: thus the biosphere system is dependent upon energy exchange in the Sun-Earth system of which it is a part. The energy of sunlight received by the Earth is ultimately reradiated to space; consequently the Earth's temperature remains nearly constant. But the outgoing quanta are smaller in size and greater in number than the incoming, this representing a continuing increase in entropy of the Sun-Earth system. Since any increase in order within the biosphere must be very small compared to the increase of entropy in the Sun-Earth system there is no reason to think that evolution controverts the second law of thermodynamics, even though it may appear to do so if viewed as a thing apart.[4]

---

2   G. Faure, 1998, *Principles and Applications of Geochemistry*, second edition, Upper Saddle River, NJ: Prentice Hall, 162.

3   J. Rifkin, 1980, *Entropy*, New York: Bantam Books.

4   H. F. Blum, 1968, *Times Arrow and Evolution*, third edition, Princeton, NJ: Princeton University Press, 200-201.

This, of course, does not solve the problem of entropy at all, because it does not explain the origin of the machinery of photosynthesis that is able to increase the local order in an open system. Simply saying that the earth is open to the energy from the sun says nothing about how that raw solar heat is converted into increased complexity in any system, open or closed. The fact is that the best known, and most fundamental, equation of thermodynamics states that the influx of heat into an open system will increase the entropy of that system, not decrease it:

> Evolution produces temporary structures of subtle and beautifully ordered complexity, but the Second Law ensures that their net contribution will be a permanent increase in the entropy and disorder of the Universe.[5]

The above claim is made as if evolution is a fact, even though it naively ignores that no explanation, apart from creation by design, has yet been forthcoming to explain the complexity of the machinery of photosynthesis. Nevertheless, mainstream scientists still continue to defend what they think is the "natural processes' ability to increase complexity" by insisting that there is a "flaw" in "the arguments against evolution based on the second law of thermodynamics":

> Although the overall amount of disorder in a closed system cannot decrease, local order within a larger system can increase even without the actions of an intelligent agent.[6]

However, all known cases of decreased entropy (or increased organization) in open systems involve a guiding program of some sort, and one or more energy conversion mechanisms. Indeed, it is the origin of the complexity that permeates all living organisms that continues to confound all attempts at naturalistic explanations, for even in the building block of life, the cell, and its intricate biochemical workings, are many examples of "irreducible complexity" in the machinery and their operation.[7] Each of the claimed evolutionary processes, for which there is no general consensus in the scientific community, has neither a guiding program nor energy conversion mechanisms. Mutations are not "organizing" mechanisms, but disorganizing (in accordance with the second law of thermodynamics). They are commonly harmful, sometimes neutral, and never beneficial (at least as far as observed mutations are concerned). Furthermore, natural selection cannot generate order, but can only "sieve out" the disorganizing mutations presented to it, thereby conserving the existing order, but never generating new order. Natural selection can only work on the existing genetic and biochemical information in the cells of an organism—it cannot "create" new information. Thus, it is barely conceivable that evolution could even occur in open systems, in spite of the tendency of all systems to disintegrate sooner or later.

---

5   S. Adams, 1994, No way back!, *New Scientist*, 144 (1948), Inside Science 75: 4.

6   N. A. Johnson, 2000, Design flaw, *American Scientist*, 88 (3): 274.

7   M. J. Behe, 1996, *Darwin's Black Box: The Biochemical Challenge to Evolution*, New York: The Free Press.

Failing the advent of the "chaos theory," some evolutionists are now arguing that the apparent underlying order in chaotic systems, instead of complete randomness, may somehow generate a higher stage of evolution: "In far from equilibrium conditions, we may have transformation from disorder, from thermal chaos, into order."[8] The fact is, however, that except in the very weak sense, it has not been demonstrated that dissipation of energy in an open system produces order, because in the chaotic behavior of a system in which a very large energy dissipation is taking place, certain temporary structures (called "dissipative structures") form and then soon decay. They have never been shown, even mathematically, to reproduce themselves or to generate still higher degrees of order. It is very significant that all discussions, of how chaotic systems (which are of course still perfectly consistent with the laws of thermodynamics) supposedly generate a higher order required by evolutionary theory, have been purely philosophical and mathematical—not experimental. Such phenomena as these, which evolutionary theorists attempt to call evolution from chaos to order, may be manipulated on paper or on a computer screen, but not in real life.

Not even the first, absolutely critical, step in the evolutionary process, that of the self-organization of non-living molecules into self-replicating molecules, can be explained in this way:

> The problem of biological order involves the transition from the molecular activity to the supermolecular order of the cell. This problem is far from being solved....However, we must admit that we remain far from any quantitative theory.[9]

Yet the naïve claim continues to be made that since life "appeared" on earth very early in geologic history, it must have been the result of spontaneous self-organization. This claim still awaits objective scientific demonstration, as opposed to circumstantial interpretation of the geologic record. "In short, chaos theory cannot explain complexity."[10]

Sadly though, in spite of the overwhelming objective scientific evidence of the serious implications of entropy for claimed biological evolution, most evolutionists continue to simply ignore the problem of entropy, or continue to blandly assert that the second law is refuted by the "fact of evolution." However, this second law of thermodynamics has always proved valid wherever it has been tested, and this law of increasing entropy continues to be, by any measure, one of the most universal best-proved laws of nature. It still applies, not only in physical and chemical systems, but also in biological and geological systems, without exception:

---

8   I. Prigogine and I. Stengers, 1984, *Order out of Chaos*, New York: Bantam Books, 12.

9   Prigogine and Stengers, 1984, 175-176.

10   P. Bak, 1996, *How Nature Works: The Science of Self-Organized Criticality*, New York: Springer-Verlag, 31.

No exception to the second law of thermodynamics has ever been found —not even a tiny one. Like conservation of energy (the "first law"), the existence of a law so precise and so independent of details of models must have a logical foundation that is independent of the fact that matter is composed of interacting particles.[11]

This comment is, of course, referring primarily to physics, but it is stated that the second law is "independent of details of models." In any case, practically all evolutionary biologists insist that all biological processes are explicable in terms of physics and chemistry alone. Therefore, biological processes also must operate in accordance with the laws of thermodynamics, and practically all biologists acknowledge this. The same, of course, applies to geological processes.

The incredible enigma is that mainstream biologists (and geologists) are unable to see that this insurmountable impasse is not due to difficulties with the second law of thermodynamics, but is rather a consequence of their assumption of universal evolution, for which there has never yet been offered even a shred of any genuine, experimental, laboratory proof! The evidences for speciation, including mutations and natural selection, are irrelevant, because there is no experimental or observational justification for extrapolating these processes as somehow proof of the macro-evolutionary changes required between the entirely different body plans of different phyla. These natural processes are themselves subject to increasing entropy, as mutations result from new combinations of the existing genetic information that can lead to degeneration. Natural selection also acts only on what is already present. Neither of these processes, therefore, leads to the greater order and complexity required by macro-evolution in the opposite direction to the overwhelming, universally demonstrated, downward influence of the second law of thermodynamics. This basic and absolute disharmony between the evolutionary model and the real-world scientific laws governing all natural processes cannot be disposed of simply by pointing to small systems that temporarily receive external stimuli retarding, or apparently reversing, their normal tendency toward deterioration. Any claimed circumstantial evidence will never overcome the almost infinite accumulation of improbabilities in the biological evolution model, which is nothing less than an absolute denial of the second law of thermodynamics, despite the fact that the second law has been always verified by observation and experimentation wherever tested.

Let it be emphasized again, lest there is a misunderstanding on this point, that there is no dispute over the fact that natural processes operating today do cause biological changes, which are patently obvious from observations and experiments. However, it is the quality and direction of these changes, which only result in conservation or deterioration, that emphatically rule out the postulated changes required by biological evolution theory, which are supposed to be progressing

---

11   E. H. Lieb and J. Yngvason, 2000, A fresh look at entropy and the second law of thermodynamics, *Physics Today*, 53 (4): 32.

toward increasing order and complexity.

The creation of all living things (or what mainstream biologists imply by "evolution") was actually accomplished by means of creative processes that, according to the first, or conservation, law of thermodynamics, no longer operate. Indeed, rather than creative processes, what we observe in the world around us are the deteriorative processes of increasing entropy implicit in the second law of thermodynamics. Every living organism eventually dies, at which point the highly developed order of organisms is reduced to random and disorderly collections of molecules. Yet despite this being the universal experience of every living creature, including man, demonstrated by observation and experimentation of relentless overall deterioration, contemporary biologists insist that their model of biological evolution is a fact, despite the complete absence of any experimental evidence supporting it. Indeed, they simply assume evolution as the universal overriding principle of change in nature, despite all the evidence from observation and experimentation demonstrating the very opposite, that is, disorganization and deterioration. Simply stated, they refuse to accept God's emphatic statement that the creation of the world and its living creatures was accomplished by processes no longer in operation. In man's quest to explain the origin and operation of everything around him in the cosmos in terms of what he can comprehend and quantify, man refuses to acknowledge that there is a Creator to whom he is accountable. Therefore, he has to find an explanation for his origins that does not require a Creator. He even builds this exclusion of God into his definition of science.

Just how did the "curse" in Eden affect these principles of science? Some have suggested that the universal domination of overall increasing entropy must have been established as part of God's "curse" on the earth and the whole of the cosmos as a result of the entrance of sin (Genesis 3:17) and represents the "bondage of decay" to which the entire creation has been "subjected" by God (Romans 8:20-22). Death did indeed begin as a result of sin and the Curse. This is a fundamental truth of Scripture. However, the second law of thermodynamics is also fundamental to the proper functioning of almost every physical process, and it is difficult to conceive that it was not included, in some form, in God's original design of this creation. The thermodynamics of all systems, the metabolism of our bodies, and even the movement of heat from warm regions to colder ones, depend critically on the second law. But how did this law operate on these systems during a state of absolute perfection in the environment and in Adam and Eve? There may be no direct statement in the text of Scripture of God altering the physical laws governing His creation when He pronounced the Curse. However, it is clear from Scripture that life in Eden was conserved in an absolutely perfect manner. Then when the Curse came, decay, loss, and death ruled over all of creation.

It is important to remember that the real understanding of origins requires the testimony of an eyewitness who was present at the time the earth and its living creatures came into existence, and this has been provided in the divine revelation of the Genesis record. God in His greatness has provided this revelation to satisfy the inquisitiveness that He created in us. Yet men refuse to believe it and insist this record must be wrong, which in effect implies that God is a liar. It is no wonder that in denying reality, contemporary scientists ultimately face contradictions and irreconcilables in their reasoning! We must therefore approach the study of the origin of the universe, the earth, and all life on it, strictly from the perspective of the God-given biblical revelation, and emphatically not by a projection of present natural processes back into the past, and particularly not into these six days of the Creation Week. It is precisely this sort of illegitimate presumptions by scientists and philosophers that led to the theories of biological and geological evolution that are now regarded as fact, and to the various theological devices that have been conceived for harmonizing these theories with the biblical revelation. However, since God's revealed Word describes the creation of the universe, the world, and all living things, as taking place in six literal days, and since there apparently is no contextual basis for understanding these days in any sort of symbolic sense, it is an act of both faith and reason grounded in the authority and truth of God's Word to accept them literally, as real days.

Furthermore, while rejecting the assumption that present geological processes can be extrapolated back to the origin of the earth to explain how the earth formed and the timescale it formed in, God's use of creation processes during the Creation Week would nevertheless have left behind details now preserved in the geologic record. Since the geologic record of the Creation Week and Scripture must be completely compatible with one another, because God is the originator of both, then it is legitimate to carefully study the details preserved in the early part of the geologic record, and guided by Scripture to use those details to unravel the earth's early history. Because there was a progression through the six days in God's creative activities, the geologic record should reflect this. While the geologic evidence will never explain the creation processes that God used (our finite minds would never be able to grasp the activity of the infinite), geologic evidence is the product of those creation processes. It is, then, with great caution in total submission to the scriptural record, that the geologic record can give us clues to the history of the earth during the Creation Week, somewhat similar to how the rest of the geologic record must accurately reflect the rest of the earth's history, through the pre-Flood, Flood, and post-Flood eras.

78

THE FIRST TWO DAYS

The First Day

Whatever scientists and philosophers may speculate in their many theories regarding the origin of the universe, the sun, and the solar system, the opening sentences of God's infallible and authoritative revelation states that, at the beginning of this first day of the Creation Week, God created the matter of the earth in empty space, with the earth's surface empty and uninhabited, but covered in water (Genesis 1:1-2). This was a once-for-all event, never repeated and not observed by man. Our only real knowledge of the mode of origin of the universe and the earth must be therefore by means of this divine revelation. Although secondary processes are not precluded by Scripture here, the most obvious meaning of the text would be that God instantaneously, by divine omnipotence, called space ("the heaven") into existence and the earth as a discrete entity within it. Perhaps the earth was even placed at the center of what was to become the universe, because the earth from God's perspective was to be the focal point of His creative activities and of His dealings with man through history. Similarly, Psalm 33:6 declares: "By the word of the LORD were the heavens made; and all the hosts of them by the breath of his mouth." Not only is this the most obvious meaning of these passages, but there is nothing whatever in science (as opposed to philosophical and scientific speculations) or theology to prevent us from accepting this obvious meaning simply as written under the direction of God's Spirit. Nevertheless, if this initial creation involved secondary processes, they would still have to have been in the category of creative processes, that is, processes involving the actual creation of matter and energy as well as processes, that put order and complexity into what was created. These would not have been the same processes we observe in operation today, which conserve matter and energy and are accompanied by deterioration and disorganization as the available energy is less able to accomplish work.

While it is impossible to deduce from present processes and their rates the manner in which the earth was originally created, we can most certainly ascertain the make-up and condition of this newly-created primeval earth because of the present structure of the earth and the earliest details in the geologic record. The majority of conservative Christian Old Testament scholars maintain that the biblical text can be understood to imply that in its original state on this first day, the earth was already rocky, even though the earth was not yet completed as far as God's ultimate purposes were concerned.[1] Indeed, Hebrew scholars are comfortable that the biblical text allows the earth at creation to be differentiated into core, mantle, and crust, with a rocky surface covered in water. There are also good scientific reasons for postulating that God differentiated the earth into core, mantle, and crust, much as it is today, right at the outset of the Creation Week. First, under any known natural conditions, core/mantle differentiation would destroy all evidence of life on earth completely. The current earth has a core/mantle/crust division according to the successively lower density of its components. If this differentiation had occurred by any natural means, the gravitational potential energy released by the heavier elements relocating to the earth's interior would produce enough heat to melt the earth's crust and vaporize the earth's oceans. If differentiation of the earth's elements did occur with its associated natural release of energy, it is therefore reasoned that it most certainly had to have occurred before the creation of organisms, at the latest on Day Three of the Creation Week. Second, even though such differentiation could have been performed by God without the "natural" release of gravitational potential energy, the already-differentiated earth's interior has subsequently provided a natural driving mechanism for the rapid tectonics (earth movements) that primarily occurred on Day Three of the Creation Week, and then during the Flood (to be described below).[2]

Of course, it is entirely reasonable based on the biblical record to just say that the core and mantle were simply created at the outset in essentially their present form. Perhaps these are the "foundations of the earth" about which the Bible often speaks (e.g., Jeremiah 31:37; Isaiah 48:13). It is of course questionable whether man will ever be able to observe directly the nature of these "foundations" in the earth's deep interior, although in the last few decades great strides have been made in understanding the probable make-up of the earth's interior based on carefully considered inferences drawn from both direct and indirect investigations. For example, seismic tomography has enabled the earth's interior to be imaged using the characteristics of seismic waves generated by earthquakes as these waves propagate through the earth. Moreover, large numbers of rock samples and minerals from deep within the earth's mantle have now been recovered from lava flows and from materials erupted onto the earth's surface by volcanoes, and these have carefully been tested and analyzed. Furthermore, it is known that volcanic rocks on the sea floor and on ocean islands were produced from magmas forced

---

1 J. C. Whitcomb, Jr., 1986, *The Early Earth*, revised edition, Grand Rapids, MI: Baker Book House, 39, 149; Whitcomb and Morris, 1961, 219-221; E. J. Young, 1964, *Studies in Genesis 1*, Philadelphia, PA: Presbyterian and Reformed Publishing Company, 34, 35, 91.

2 S. A. Austin, J. R. Baumgardner, D. R. Humphreys, A. A. Snelling, L. Vardiman and K. P. Wise, 1994, Catastrophic plate tectonics: a global Flood model of earth history, in *Proceedings of the Third International Conference on Creationism*, R. E. Walsh, ed., Pittsburgh, PA: Creation Science Fellowship, 609-621.

from different levels deep within the earth's mantle. Therefore, they represent an important direct chemical profile of the earth's mantle. Detailed analyses of these rocks, especially their trace element and radioisotopic compositions, have provided a wealth of insight concerning the composition and differentiation of the earth into its core, mantle, and crust. In particular, these data have revealed that the earth seems to be made from the same recipe of higher melting temperature elements as those observed in the sun and in most meteorites, presenting a strong case for the earth to have undergone significant chemical differentiation during its earliest history, when segregation of much of the iron to the center of the earth formed the core. Furthermore, these chemical data strongly suggest that the earth's continental crust has been extracted via partial melting processes from the silicate-mineral-based mantle that remained after the metallic core had segregated. These partial melting processes also appear to have extracted and concentrated into the continental crust a large fraction of the mantle's incompatible elements, elements that are excluded from the normal crystal lattice structures of the minerals found in the mantle due to their large ionic radii and high ionic charges, and these include the major heat-producing radioactive elements.[3]

So just how realistic and robust is the evidence that the earth's major chemical/ structural divisions, that is, its crust, mantle, and core, are the result of chemical differentiation processes very early in the earth's history? There are two basic features of the geochemical data that would seem to argue forcefully that a significant amount of chemical differentiation has indeed occurred during the earth's early history. These are the complementary abundances of the incompatible elements between the continental crust, and the mantle below that is depleted in these same elements, and the complementary abundances of siderophile elements (those that are readily soluble in molten iron, that is, they are "iron-loving") between the core and the mantle. The implications are very real, because the extraction of the core from an initially undifferentiated earth is not a trivial process that occurs in a few hours time, according to the physical processes we currently observe. Likewise, the chemical segregation of the continental crust via partial melting of mantle rock, assisted by the presence of water, also seems to require much more than a few hours time in the framework of presently observed physical laws.

However, this is precisely what we would expect to have happened during this first day of the Creation Week, where the Scriptures clearly indicate that God employed special means to accomplish changes such as these, by methods outside the physics we observe today, that is, by creative processes. The scientific data upon which our understanding of the earth's internal chemistry and structure is based, and the conjectures regarding the chemical differentiation to form the core, mantle, and crust internal structure, are all based on present-day observations and

---

3   J. R. Baumgardner, 2000, Distribution of radioactive isotopes in the earth, in *Radioisotopes and the Age of the Earth: a Young-Earth Creationist Research Initiative*, L. Vardiman, A. A. Snelling and E. F. Chaffin, eds., El Cajon, CA: Institute for Creation Research and St. Joseph, MO: Creation Research Society, 49-94.

analyses of rock and mineral samples, and seismic data, so that the basic conclusions drawn are not dependent on any interpretations of a great age for the earth, or the extrapolation of any known present-day processes. Thus, as already conceded, it is possible that after the initial creative act of bringing the earth into existence covered by water, that God then used secondary creative processes to bring about the chemical differentiation of the earth's interior through the remainder of that first day. Whether this chemical differentiation process was completed by the end of the first day we have no way of knowing. We can also only speculate as to which part and how much of the actual geologic record corresponds to God's creative activities on this first day, particularly as it has proven very difficult to locate and identify the very earliest scant fragments in the geologic record that belonged to this earliest period of earth history, which the conventional geologic community has called the Hadean. Of course, given all the geologic work that was accomplished by God in the remainder of the Creation Week, and then the massive geologic upheavals of the Flood (soon to be discussed), the earliest part of the geologic record would have subsequently been reworked, perhaps several times, so that it is no longer in the pristine state in which it was created. Thus, we have no way of knowing now what the initially created rocky materials would have looked like.

The only other detail we are given in the Scriptures of this first day is God's command for light to shine on the earth, to dispel the darkness that enshrouded the earth when He first created it (Genesis 1:3-5). This light could not have been from the sun, because the sun was not created until the fourth day, so we have no way of knowing for sure the nature of this light, except that it was a special provision of God at this time and instituted the day-night cycle and the literal day, just as we know and continue to experience today. We do not need to speculate the source of this light, as God does not need a source to provide light apart from Himself if He so chooses. After all, we are told in Revelation 21:23 and 22:15 that in the holy city of the new heaven and new earth, there will be no need for either the sun or moon and there will be no night there, because God Himself will provide the light of His glory through His Son, the Creator Jesus Christ. Since light would be considered the most basic and all-pervasive form of energy, its introduction to the surface of the earth might well have been the physical manifestation of God energizing the primordial earth that He had just created, so as to bring about this internal reorganization through chemical differentiation. However, what we can be certain about is that, despite the presence of light shining on the waters covering the earth's surface, there was no life within those waters to utilize the light energy, because God had not yet created any form of life. This also applies to those rocks forming in the earth's earliest crust as a result of the initiation of this chemical differentiation process, if that's how God created the earth's basic internal chemical/structural divisions. Because there were no life forms of any type, there would also not have been any bacteria or other life forms that today we find are able to live within the rocks deep within the earth's surface. Thus, any strata now found in the earliest part of the geologic record that contain fossils, or any evidence of life, cannot have been produced during this first day of the Creation Week era.

The Second Day

On the second day of the Creation Week, the waters covering the earth's surface were divided into two great reservoirs, by God commanding into existence a firmament (or "expanse") "in the midst of the waters" (Genesis 1:6-8). As we have mentioned previously, various lines of evidence suggest that the Hebrew word *raqia* translated "firmament" or "expanse" refers almost certainly to what we today call interstellar space, where God on Day Four created the sun, moon, and stars. If so, this means that a large mass of water that earlier deeply enveloped the earth was now separated from it by this expanse, a region God calls "heaven" in Genesis 1:8. The water that remained on the earth became the seas on Day Three.

If God initiated on the first day the secondary creative processes of chemical differentiation inside the earth, to chemically and structurally divide it into the core, mantle, and crust, then such processes would appear to have not only required the cycling of a large fraction of the mantle's silicate rock, via rapid thermal convection to very near the earth's surface (where two stages of partial melting plus interaction with the water covering the earth's surface could take place), but also a significant amount of accompanying radioisotopic "decay." (The use of the term "decay" is somewhat misleading, as it unfortunately gives the impression of imperfection in God's "very good" creation. A better, less emotive, descriptive term would be "transmutation.") The amount of convective circulation in the mantle involved with the extraction of the continental crust implies a vast amount of heat extraction from the earth's interior. Furthermore, it is the elements whose radioisotopes undergo transmutation that are among those elements that are incompatible with the mantle silicate minerals, and so have been partitioned into the earth's crust, particularly the continental crust where the nuclear transmutations generate further heat. The convective circulation in the mantle, of course, also provides the means for removal of the heat from this nuclear transmutation. Quite obviously, the heat from both chemical differentiation and nuclear transmutation would, by convective circulation in the mantle, be transferred to the earth's surface, where it would have come in contact with the water covering the earth's surface. Thus, it is conceivable that this rapid application of tremendous amounts of heat on a global scale to this surface water would have caused intense boiling of the water at the crust/water interface and rapid weathering of the earth's surface rocks.

Regarding the formation of the earth's atmosphere, it is also likely that, in addition to the convective circulation in the mantle bringing heat to the earth's surface, it would also have brought gases to be released above it and accumulate as the atmosphere. Today gases are added to the atmosphere from the earth's deep interior, primarily due to volcanic activity, which is also believed to be largely due to convective transfer of heat in the mantle. However, if God used this secondary creative process to put the atmosphere in place, the speed at which the gases were expelled from the earth's interior to accumulate as the atmosphere would have been incredibly rapid, as the whole task was completed in the biblical timeframe before the end of the second day.

In what are regarded as the earliest rocks found in the geologic record, there is abundant evidence for high temperatures within the earth. It is important to reiterate that, if God was using secondary creative processes to generate the chemical/structural divisions within the earth, then convective circulation in the mantle, partial melting, and magma generation would have occurred at rates many orders of magnitude faster than the rates of similar processes observed today. This would also have applied to other processes in operation contemporaneously, such as magma cooling, sedimentation, metamorphism, and nuclear transmutation. What are perceived to be the earliest known mineral grains are zircons from metamorphosed sandstone in Western Australia, whose radioisotopic ratios have been interpreted as "dating" these grains as being around 4.2 billion years old.[4] This is graphic testimony that, at this early stage of the earth's history only thousands of years ago, the radioisotopic transmutation rates were incredibly rapid as a result of the creative processes God was using to form the earth's crust, beginning on the first day and continuing into the second day of the Creation Week. It is also significant that zircons are among the earliest mineral grains detected in the geologic record, and that they are in a sedimentary rock, because this means they were eroded from an earlier crystalline rock. Such would have likely been a granitic rock, from a suite of granitic rocks that are almost unique to the earliest part of the geologic record, the so-called tonalite-trondhjemite-granodiorite (TTG) suite, with their geochemistry suggesting that they were produced by partial melting of a wet, mafic crust. That would be the composition expected for the earliest crust forming by extraction from the mantle by chemical differentiation.

The other dominant rock types in this earliest section of the geologic record, known as the Archean, are basaltic lavas with a very high and unusual Mg content called komatiites. These are again almost unique to the Archean section at the base of the geologic record, and all the evidence points to these being derived at very high temperatures deep within the earth's mantle, after which they were extruded onto the earth's surface as lavas at very high temperatures, much higher than experienced when normal basaltic lavas are extruded today. This is exactly what would be expected to have been happening at this very earliest stage of earth history, as a result of this convective circulation in the mantle moving heat to the earth's surface and establishing the earth's earliest crust.

---

4   D. O Froude, T. R. Ireland, P. D. Kinny, I. S. Williams, W. Compston, I. R. Williams and J. S. Myers, 1983, Ion microprobe identification of 4100-4200 Myr-old terrestrial zircons, *Nature*, 304: 616-618; R. Maas, P. D. Kinny, I. S. Williams, D. O. Froude and W. Compston, 1992, The earth's oldest known crust: a geochronological and geochemical study of 3900-4200 Ma old detrital zircons from Mt. Narryer and Jack Hills, Western Australia, *Geochimica et Cosmochimica Acta*, 56: 1281-1300.

Once these granitic rocks were intruded to near the earth's surface and were cooling rapidly along with these komatiite lava flows that were beginning to form the earth's earliest crust, contact with the water covering the earth's surface would have induced rapid chemical weathering and erosion, so that sediments began forming sedimentary rocks. It is no surprise, therefore, that we find also in the Archean geologic record, interbedded with komatiite and basaltic lavas, a variety of different sediment types, particularly volcanic tuffs and breccias that have resulted from explosive eruptions of more felsic (granitic-like) magmas, chemical sediments such as cherts, carbonates, banded-iron formations, unusual shales, "immature" sandstones, and conglomerates. In those Archean terranes exposed today, such as in Western Australia and Canada, these sedimentary rocks are found in wide linear belts of strata dominated by komatiites and basalts known as greenstone belts that surround large circular exposures of these TTG granitic rocks.

As well as magmas being expelled onto the earth's surface and intruded into its rapidly forming crust, massive amounts of hot water must likewise have been expelled from the earth's deep interior, carrying with it dissolved chemicals such as silica, carbonate, and iron, that then precipitated as the expelled hot waters mixed with the waters God had created covering the earth's surface. In so doing, these chemical sediments would have been rapidly formed. The heat being released as these granitic magmas intruded into these sediments and volcanics, crystallized, and cooled, would have metamorphosed the strata in contact with them, and the hydrothermal fluids from the cooling granitic magmas would have rapidly carried the heat away, resulting in metamorphism on a regional scale. It must be emphasized, though, that these were potential outworkings of God using secondary creative processes that He had initiated on the first day, and that continued through this second day, building the earth's early crust by geological processes that unfolded at rates many orders of magnitude higher than any similar conceivable geological processes today. As can be seen, these details are consistent with what are regarded as the earth's earliest rocks in the geologic record. It is worth noting that even mainstream geologists recognize that many of these rocks, as described here, are unique to this Archean section of the geologic record, meaning that we know of no geological process occurring today at today's rates that would have been capable of producing these rocks. Furthermore, the fact that the radioisotopic ratios found in these rocks are able to be interpreted in terms of "ages" of 3.5 to 4.0 billion years indicates that extremely rapid nuclear transmutations must have occurred to give these rocks such extraordinarily old apparent "ages."

By the end of the second day, the work of forming the earth's earliest crust by convective circulation within the mantle, which was being formed distinct from the core by chemical differentiation, would almost have been complete. At no point was God not in control, as He was fashioning the earth by His creative activity to prepare it for the next stages of His plans.

79

THE THIRD DAY

God's secondary creative geological processes now reached their climax and culmination in the early part of the third day. God's command, "Let the dry land appear" (Genesis 1:9), is interpreted by most conservative Christian Old Testament scholars as an unveiling of previously created crustal rock, suggesting that a continent (or continents) were uplifted on this third day out of the water that had previously covered the whole, rocky earth.[1] "The waters, which were still covering everything under the heavens, were to be concentrated in one place, and, as a result, the solid matter hidden beneath them would be revealed in the remaining areas."[2] To make the "dry land" appear from under the waters, heretofore covering the earth's surface, must have required earth movements on the scale of global tectonics at an extremely rapid or catastrophic rate. The earth's buoyant continental crust would have been gathered together in some parts of the earth's surface, while the complementary areas would have been swept clean of this continental material, so that the surface waters could in turn be gathered together in ocean basins to allow a dry land surface on a continent (or continents) to be exposed. If God was continuing to use secondary creative processes, then based on what we know of the early geologic record in the Archean, plus what we can infer about the global tectonic processes resulting from both the chemical differentiation of the earth's internal structure and the convective circulation in the mantle, there would have to have been an early form of plate tectonics at work, catastrophically resulting in what could termed the first great "orogeny" or mountain-building episode.

The reason continents sit on the earth's surface above sea level today is because they are composed of continental crust of an overall felsic (granitic or sialic) composition, compared to the denser oceanic crust of mafic (basaltic) composition. The denser oceanic crust sinks relative to the less dense continental crust, thus forming the ocean basins.[3] Just how this distinct horizontal differentiation of the

---

1   Whitcomb and Morris, 1961, 229-232; Young, 1964, 91; Whitcomb, 1986, 39.

2   U. Cassuto, 1978, *From Adam to Noah*, Part One, Jerusalem: Magnes Press, 34; See also H. C. Leupold, 1942, *Exposition of Genesis*, Columbus: T. Wartburg Press, 63-66.

3   Austin et al, 1994, 609-621.

early earth's crust into oceanic and continental crust might have been achieved is unclear. However, one possibility is that, as the chemical differentiation and mantle convection processes began, the first-formed crust globally around the earth's surface was entirely mafic oceanic crust, and then, as these processes continued, partial melting took place to generate lighter felsic magmas, which intruded that early-formed oceanic crust in some places to produce the buoyant TTG granitic plutons. Because of their buoyancy, these plutons would tend to clump together above the zones of downwelling of the large-scale mantle convection pattern. The initial continental crust would have begun to thicken in those areas and to rise relative to other areas where only denser mafic oceanic crust was present. This process of sections of the earth's crust adjusting in surface height according to their densities is known by geologists as *isostasy,* meaning "equal weights." It is now a well-known basic process in global tectonics that has even been enunciated in the Scriptures as a process the Creator used and put into operation: "[God] hath measured the waters in the hollow of his hand and metered out heaven with the span, and comprehended the dust of the earth in a measure, and weighed the mountains in scales, and the hills in a balance" (Isaiah 40:12).

Hence, there was almost certainly a significant component of horizontal tectonics at work in order to bring together and concentrate all the less dense felsic rock materials into the continental crust, relative to the denser mafic oceanic crust. Given the convective circulation in the mantle, driven by the heat generated from the chemical differentiation and nuclear transmutations occurring there, it is highly likely that there would have been some catastrophic form of what is now known as plate tectonics. This directly follows from the convective upwelling of heat in the mantle, which would cause partial melting to produce new oceanic crust where the upwelling met the earth's surface. Therefore, there could have been horizontal spreading of oceanic crust, which then pushed together those areas where granitic magmas had intruded. Both horizontal and vertical tectonics would have resulted, therefore, in distortion and buckling to bring together and concentrate the felsic rock materials into a less dense crust, to form the continent or continents that God had commanded to rise from under the globe-encircling waters on this third day. Any subduction of oceanic crust under this newly forming continental crust, as a result of these horizontal tectonic movements, would only have caused further partial melting of that subducted oceanic crust to produce new magmas, which intruded into, and extruded onto, the newly-forming continent (or continents).

This uplift, through the waters that then parted as land surfaces became exposed, would have resulted in an enormous amount of catastrophic erosion, which would of course result in the widespread deposition of thick sequences of sedimentary strata. Furthermore, accompanying the upwelling of magmas into both the oceanic and continental crusts would have been large amounts of hydrothermal fluids, which would have carried in solution incredible amounts of different chemicals. Thus, as the hydrothermal fluids came in contact with the cooler surface waters, the dissolved chemical species would have precipitated to produce chemical sediments, such as chert, carbonates (dolomites and limestones), and banded-iron formations, as well as metal ore deposits from the other metals carried in the fluids. Where the hydrothermal fluids intruded into the continental crust there would also have been a change in temperature, which would have triggered precipitation of dissolved chemical species and metals, again leading to the formation of metal ore deposits that would later prove valuable for man's use. There would also have been accompanying explosive volcanic eruptions from water and gases being released from the earth's interior, and this would have contributed large volumes of volcanic fragmental materials to the sedimentary rocks being deposited.

This scenario is not simply speculative, because the details match what is found in the geologic record, particularly in the Archean section of that record. A crucial marker point in this rock record, as we attempt to align it with the scriptural account, would be the first, and therefore earliest, record of fossilized former living organisms. It was only on this third day, after God had commanded the dry land to appear from under the waters, which were now gathered together in "one place," that God created the first life. He commanded the earth to "bring forth grass, herb yielding seed, and the fruit tree yielding fruit after his kind, whose seed is in itself" (Genesis 1:11-12). Thus, the earliest fossilized evidence of living organisms would have to be plants, or plant-related organisms (as opposed to animals), and such fossilized remains would have to date to the middle and later part of this third day of the Creation Week era. This would correspond in the geologic record to after the tectonic upheavals, magmatism, sedimentation, and metamorphism responsible for building the continental crust that became the first continent (or continents). There is still some dispute in the conventional geological community over the validity of several claims of the fossilized evidence for the earliest life,[4] but there is general agreement that the structures known as stromatolites, first found in chert conventionally dated at almost 3.5 billion years old in the Pilbara region of Western Australia, were built by *cyanobacteria*.[5] These cyanobacteria are a form of blue-green algae, and they evidently built the

---

4   S. J. Mojzsis, G. Arrhenius, K. D. McKeegan, T. M. Harrison, A. P. Nutman and C. R. L. Friend, 1996, Evidence for life on Earth before 3800 million years ago, *Nature*, 384: 55-59; J. M. Hayes, 1996, The earliest memories of life on Earth, *Nature*, 384: 21-22; Y. Sano, K. Terada, Y. Takahashi and A. P. Nutman, 1999, Origin of life from apatite dating?, *Nature*, 400: 127; S. J. Mojzsis, T. M. Harrison, G. Arrhenius, K. D. McKeegan and M. Grove, 1999, Origin of life from apatite dating?, *Nature*, 400: 127-128; S. M. Awramik, J. W. Schopf and M. R. Walter, 1983, Filamentous fossil bacteria from the Archean of Western Australia, *Precambrian Research*, 20: 357-374; R. Buick, 1984, Carbonaceous filaments from North Pole, Western Australia: Are they fossil bacteria in Archean stromatolites?, *Precambrian Research*, 24: 157-172; J. W. Schopf, 1993, Microfossils of the early Archean Apex Chert: new evidence of the antiquity of life, *Science*, 260: 640-646; M. D. Brasier, O. R. Green, A. P. Jephcoat, A. K. Kleppe, M. J. Van Kranendonk, J. F. Lindsay, A. Steele and N. V. Grassinean, 2002, Questioning the evidence for earth's oldest fossils, *Nature*, 416: 76-81.

5   B. R. Lowe, 1980, Stromatolites 3400-Myr old from the Archean of Western Australia, *Nature*, 284: 441-443; M. R. Walter, R. Buick and J. S. R. Dunlop, 1980, Stromatolites 3400-3500 Myr old from the North Pole area, Western Australia, *Nature*, 284: 443-445; H. J. Hofmann, K. Grey, A. H. Hickman and R. I. Thorpe, 1999, Origin of 3.45Ga coniform stromatolites in Warrawoona Group, Western Australia, *Geological Society of America Bulletin*, 111 (8): 1256-1262.

stromatolite structures as a result of their mat-like growth at the sediment-water interface. Other undisputed fossilized stromatolites are also found in the Archean rock record, so the presence of these fossils is thus consistent with this portion of the Archean rock record being a result of God's creative activities in the middle and latter part of this third day of the Creation Week.

Such a correlation between the geologic and scriptural records does, though, raise one very critical question, namely, if the scriptural account specifies grasses, herbs, and fruit trees as having been created by God on this third day, then why are not these plants found fossilized this early in the rock record instead of just bacteria and stromatolites? The answer lies in recognizing that the fossils found at any level in the rock record only represent those creatures that were in environments and locations where they could be buried and fossilized. Many other creatures and organisms would likely have been alive at the same time, but in other areas of the earth's surface where they were not prone to burial and fossilization. If this is the case at other levels in the rock record, then it is likely to be the same here in the Archean rock record. Indeed, all the available evidence indicates that the stromatolite-growing cyanobacteria lived in hypersaline waters fed by hydrothermal springs, where chemical sediments were being precipitated and where sulfide ores were accumulating due to the volcanic activity that was producing the hydrothermal fluids.[6] The stromatolites and their cyanobacteria-builders thus lived in an environment where they were automatically prone to fossilization, due to the chemical sedimentation continually going on around them. The fact that stromatolites and these bacteria are among the major fossils of the Precambrian rock record, and then are virtually absent in Phanerozoic rocks and are rare today, suggests that these stromatolites were a significant part of an important late Creation Week/pre-Flood hydrothermal biome.[7]

Fossils of the plants created on the third day, and the creatures created later in the Creation Week, are not found preserved in the rock record that probably dates back to the Creation Week and early pre-Flood eras. This suggests that conditions on the land surface exposed by the tectonic upheavals in the early part of the third day were quite stable, and free from catastrophic destruction, by the time God created the grasses, herbs, fruit trees, and other plants later that day, and that these conditions remained stable and conducive for life for the remainder of the Creation Week and on into the pre-Flood era. Of course, one could argue that many fossils of other plants and creatures, which might have formed after the Creation Week, were subsequently destroyed by catastrophic erosion during

6   G. P. Glasby, 1998, Earliest life in the Archean: rapid dispersal of CO_2-utilizing bacteria from submarine hydrothermal vents, *Episodes*, 21 (4): 252-256; B. Rasmussen, 2000, Filamentous microfossils in a 3235-million-year-old volcanogenic massive sulphide deposit, *Nature*, 405: 676-679; E. G. Nisbet and N. H. Sleep, 2001, The habitat and nature of early life, *Nature*, 409: 1083-1091; Y. Shen, R. Buick and D. E. Canfield, 2001, Isotopic evidence for microbial sulphate reduction in the early Archaean era, *Nature*, 410: 77-81.

7   K. P. Wise, 2003, Hydrothermal biome: a pre-Flood environment, In *Proceedings of the Fifth International Conference on Creationism*, R. L. Ivey, Jr., ed., Pittsburgh, PA: Creation Science Fellowship, 359-370.

the Flood, but this argument from the absence of evidence would seem to be discounted by the enormous thicknesses of sedimentary strata in the Precambrian rock record. The deposition of these strata would easily have been conducive for the fossilization of plants and animals if there had been catastrophes across the earth's surface capable of their destruction and burial.

Thus, once the land surface was exposed, God established stable conditions on it before creating all the plants upon it. First, there was the catastrophic tectonic upheaval that built the continental crust, which then rose from under the waters. There is the distinct possibility that there was just one supercontinent formed as a result, because it can be argued that since God commanded all the waters to be gathered together into one place to form the seas, then the land may also have been in one place. However, it may otherwise be argued that this expression "one place" may simply refer to the waters being gathered into the newly-formed ocean basins whose geographical distribution has not been stipulated, just as today's ocean waters could be argued as being in the one place, namely, the ocean basins that are in any case interconnected with one another. With the retreating of the globe-encircling waters from the emerging land surface of the newly-formed continental crust, there would have been enormous catastrophic erosion, and this event could be given the name "the Great Regression." Once the land surface was exposed, further erosion and sedimentation would have been confined to the continental shelf and slope areas adjoining the exposed continental land surface, and on the floors of the ocean basins.

As the land surfaces would likely have been saturated with water, the subsequent intense drying out would have initiated deep chemical weathering, so that very thick soil soon blanketed the entire land surface. This is not to suggest that God was somehow dependent on the natural rate at which such a drying out process occurs today, because this was still part of His creative activity. Therefore, these secondary creative processes would have been occurring at supernatural rates, outside of the operation of the laws of physics as we know them today. Once this thick, nutrient-rich soil was ready, then God covered it in all types of grasses, herbs, fruit trees, and other trees and plants. This would also have included all types of bacteria, in all types of environments and ecological niches, including those that live deep within the rocks below the earth's surface, and those in the hydrothermal biome responsible for building stromatolites in the warm hypersaline waters in shallow marginal seas adjacent to the continent or continents, and perhaps even where hydrothermal springs may have occurred within continental areas. These hydrothermal springs may well have been "the fountains of waters" referred to in Revelation 14:7 in connection with God also making "heaven, and earth, and the sea." Since these springs would be gushing hot waters, they may likewise have been responsible for the "mist from the earth" that "watered the whole face of the ground" (Genesis 2:6).

Thus, by the end of the third day, the chemical differentiation process of internally structuring the earth into core, mantle, and crust would have been completed, and the convective circulation in the mantle would have slowed. All the heat having been generated by these processes and by nuclear transmutations would have largely been released from inside the earth and dissipated from the earth's surface, so that conditions were now ideal for life on both the exposed land surface and in the oceans. There would now also be a distinct horizontal differentiation between oceanic and continental crust, very much as there is today. As well as being sialic (essentially on average granitic) in composition, the continental crust would also have been stabilized into a craton or cratons that would suffer little deformation through subsequent earth history. Thus, it is suggested here, the remnants of this Creation Week continental crust are found in the cratonic Archean shield areas still exposed at the earth's surface today in the continental nuclei (Figure 52, page 1088). Since much Archean sialic material still survives today, its existence by the middle of the Creation Week would have meant that it was then available for erosion and sedimentation in the pre-Flood era and beyond.

The existence today of low-density, low-temperature "keels" beneath these Archean cratons implies that they have persisted more or less in their present form since their differentiation in these first three days of the Creation Week.[8] This also suggests that little or no mantle convection has disturbed the upper mantle beneath these cratons since their formation. Furthermore, if these Archean cratons were sialic and the adjoining oceanic crust was mafic, then the buoyancy forces due to the density differences would provide a natural means of supporting the cratons above sea level, with isostatic adjustments thus producing the dry land on the continents on this third day. That the oceanic crust has always been mafic (basaltic) is suggested by ophiolites (containing pillow basalts and presumed ocean sediments), which are thought to represent pieces of ocean floor that were subsequently thrust up and accreted onto the continents, found in the Archean rock record.[9] Additionally, if the oceanic crust were mafic in contrast to a sialic continental crust, then the denser oceanic crust would sink as the continental crust rose, thus providing natural basins for the ocean waters to drain into, so that sea level would be lower than the exposed continental crust land surface. At the end of the third day this process of cratonizing continental crust would have been completed, so that it became stabilized, and the Great Regression would have completed its erosive leveling of that land surface. Residual erosion and sedimentation would still occur, though around the marine margins of the continent or continents. After drying out and deep chemical weathering to form a thick soil, all manner of plants had been created to vegetate the entire land surface.

Just exactly what level in the rock record represents the end of this third day can

---

8   P. H. Jordon, 1978, Composition and development of the continental tectosphere, *Nature*, 274: 544-548; Austin et al, 1994, 611.

9   T. M. Cusky, J-H. Li and R. D. Tucker, 2001, The Archean Dongwanzi ophiolite complex, North China craton: 2.505-billion-year-old oceanic crust and mantle, *Science*, 292: 1142-1145.

only be speculated, given that very few specifics are given in the scriptural account. Any strata containing indisputable fossilized bacteria and related microorganisms, as well as the stromatolites built by cyanobacteria mats, have to post-date the creation of plants in the latter part of this third day. This would make the Hadean and early Archean section of the rock record remnants of the earliest continental crust produced by God's creative processes during the early part of the Creation Week, up until He created the plants in the middle or latter part of this third day. The first undisputed fossilized bacteria and stromatolites are in strata of the Pilbara region of Western Australia, that are conventionally "dated" at 3.5 billion years old, so if there is any systematic correlation between such "dates" and the scriptural record (to be discussed later), then this point in the rock record would have to be placed in the middle or latter part of the third day of the Creation Week era.

It is also highly likely that the ramifications of God's creative activities to form and uplift the continental crust and produce the dry land surface did not cease as a result of the Great Regression, as it is likely that catastrophic geologic activity continued on through the remainder of the third day, and even through the rest of the Creation Week into the pre-Flood era. While the geological processes occurring at supernatural rates would have climaxed with the uplifting of the continental crust, formation of the ocean basins, and the Great Regression, the tempo of that activity would perhaps have continued to gradually decline in intensity and scope from the latter part of this third day onwards. This may then account for the middle and late Archean rock record, and some of the overlying Proterozoic, and such rocks would have to have been formed in areas adjacent to, but away from, the exposed vegetated land surfaces. The rock record seems to support this pattern, because most of the early Archean cratons are surrounded by middle-late Archean rocks accreted to them, and subsequently cratonized (Figure 52). Furthermore, in many instances these Archean cratons are surrounded by adjoining Proterozoic sedimentary basins, whose strata unmistakably overlie these Archean cratons at their margins. An excellent example of this is the Proterozoic sedimentary basins that are marginal to, and surround, the Pilbara Archean craton of Western Australia (Figure 53, page 1089). The original nature of these rocks early in the geologic record has been transformed by metamorphism, and their original extent has been modified by subsequent erosion, so how extensive they originally were, and the relationship of these original Archean cratons to one another, has been destroyed, perhaps even as early as the Great Regression during the third day of the Creation Week.

This scenario is also consistent with the presence in the middle-late Archean and early Proterozoic rock sequences of further volcanic rocks and lava flows, chemical sedimentary rocks such as carbonates, cherts, and banded-iron formations, and sedimentary rocks composed of volcanic fragments and normal detritus derived from erosion of land surfaces. It is conceivable that there would have been continued volcanic activity in the shallow ocean basins adjoining the exposed continent or continents, and hydrothermal springs would have continued to precipitate chemical sediments that were then deposited in alternation with lava flows, volcanic fragmental sediments, and detritus washed from margins of the nearby land surfaces. The presence of fossilized bacteria and stromatolites in these sequences testifies to their deposition and formation in the latter part of the third day of the Creation Week, after the plants and the bacteria were created.

80

THE FOURTH DAY TO THE END
OF THE CREATION WEEK

During the remainder of the Creation Week following the close of the third day, the Bible is silent with respect to any ongoing geological processes as part of God's creative activities. However, it is possible to make some reasonable, logical speculations which are consistent with the details preserved in the geologic record. It is possible that marginal continental areas were still rising and surfaces being eroded prior to stabilization, soil formation, and growth of vegetation. Further volcanic activity and hydrothermal springs on continental shelves, and in shallow marine areas adjoining the continents, would have continued to release heat from inside the earth and chemicals to precipitate chemical sediments, such as the extensive and enormous banded-iron formations and associated cherts, as well as the carbonates with fossilized stromatolites, and the interbedded volcanics and other fragmental sediments. Such a strata sequence is seen in the early Proterozoic (Paleoproterozoic) Hamersley Basin of Western Australia, which is marginal to and overlies the Pilbara Archean craton. Some tectonic adjustments could well have continued through this period, particularly away from the exposed and vegetated land surfaces where such would not disturb God's continuing creation of other life forms.

During the fourth day, the focus of God's creative work was on providing the sun, moon, and stars to rule the day and the night, and to be for signs and seasons (Genesis 1:14-19). The light that God had provided for daylight on the first three days was now replaced with light from the sun. This provides significant evidence that these days of the Creation Week were literal, approximately 24-hour days, because the plants created on Day Three would only have endured approximately twelve hours of darkness (night) before the light of this fourth day dawned, and the daylight was then provided by the sun. However, if these were only figurative "days" that were in fact millions of years long, as proposed by those who advocate the day-age, progressive creation, and theistic evolution views, then the plants would have somehow had to have survived millions of years of darkness (the figurative "night") before the fourth figurative "day" dawned. Of course, the reality is that these views simply propose these figurative "days" to represent millions of years in which there were countless regular days, so that the plants had the benefit of the regular, more or less normal length, day-night cycle for millions of years before the next stage of God's "progressive creation," or instead "theistic evolution," activity. However, this only leads to further inconsistencies and complications. For example, the insects (whether they are categorized as "winged fowl" or "creeping things") were not created ("evolved") until either the fifth or sixth figurative "day," so this begs the question as to how the plants could have survived through the intervening millions of years without the insects available to pollinate them.

The truth is that the order of God's creative activities as outlined in the biblical text can in no way be made to fit the order described by both the progressive creation and theistic evolution views, which blindly follow the claimed order of development of the universe, the earth, and all life upon it as insisted by the conventional scientific community. Their version of earth history is largely atheistic, because assigning any of this "development" to the work of God in the scientific literature is ruled as inadmissible by all, and heretical by some. After all, the conventional scientific world insists that the sun was formed billions of years after the universe began, and the earth developed subsequent to the sun. This in no way can be reconciled with the order in the biblical record, where it is clearly stated that the earth was created at the beginning at the same time as the universe, and then the sun and the stars were created four days later. Thus, the day-age, progressive creation, and theistic evolution attempts to unify the Scriptures and conventional science, by insisting the two are really telling us the same "story," are merely wishful thinking. Such attempts to marry the Scriptures and conventional science can only lead to compromises that do violence to the Scriptures or conventional science, or both, because how "can two walk together, except they be agreed?" (Amos 3:3). The tragedy is that when faced with being unable to reconcile the order in the Genesis record with the order insisted upon by the conventional scientific community of astronomers, geologists, and biologists, the proponents of these alternative views end up compromising by "trashing" the text of Scripture, bending or "reinterpreting" it to make it fit what the conventional scientific community insists is "fact." However, it is insisted here that the Genesis record is the infallible account of the early history of the earth and the universe provided by the Creator Himself, who was there at creation and who cannot lie. Therefore, the interpretations of the fallible, finite conventional scientists, who were not there, must be questioned if they conflict with the scriptural account. Furthermore, it is here maintained that the data, as opposed to conventional scientific interpretations, are not in conflict with the details given in the Scriptures.

Thus, substantial, wide-scale geologic activity could have continued at catastrophic supernatural rates right through this fourth day, marginal to the vegetated continent (or continents) on the surrounding continental shelves and in the shallow ocean basins. There would have been no problems engendered by the large areas where the marine environment was rendered hypersaline and/or toxic by the enormous quantities of chemicals issuing into them from the hydrothermal springs and volcanic activity that produced the interbedded chemical sediments, lavas, and volcanic fragmental sediments, because no marine creatures had yet been created. This is confirmed by the absence of fossilized marine creatures in these strata. Neither the heating locally of the ocean waters by the hydrothermal springs and volcanic activity, nor the turbulent water filled with choking sediments washed by erosion from the continental margins, would have killed off marine creatures or then have potentially buried and fossilized them.

However, these considerations imply that the scale of these secondary creative processes must have became greatly reduced by the dawn of the fifth day, when "God created great whales and every living creature that moveth, which the waters brought forth abundantly, after their kind" (Genesis 1:21). The fact that the text insists that there was no animal death and bloodshed prior to the Fall in God's very good creation clearly implies that no marine creatures were buried and fossilized by geologic activity during this fifth day and the remainder of the Creation Week. In contrast, in God's reckoning plants don't "die" in the same way as animals do, and the plants were created for food that was eaten prior to the Fall, so the fossilization of plants (bacteria and stromatolites) is allowed by Genesis during the Creation Week.

Also created on the fifth day was "every winged fowl after his kind" "that may fly above the earth in the open firmament of heaven" (Genesis 1:21, 20). Then on the sixth day, God created "the beast of the earth after his kind, and cattle after their kind, and every thing that creepeth upon the earth after his kind," followed by the creation of man in His image (Genesis 1:25, 27). Thus, during these fifth and sixth days, no geologic activity could have occurred to violently disturb the atmosphere or the land surface to kill and bury any birds or land creatures. Thus, for example, any violent volcanism and/or catastrophic flooding and erosion on the land surface are ruled out. As on the third and fourth days, on these fifth and sixth days, God declared both His creative activities and the products of them to be "good" (Genesis 1:10, 18, 21, 25, 31), clearly implying that nothing had occurred during these Creation Week days that was inconsistent with God's standards of perfection.

Just what portion of the geologic record corresponds to the Creation Week era is open to reasonable, logical speculation, based on the implications of the data of the rock record in accordance with the biblical account. The latter, though, does not provide the required specific geological details. Nevertheless, it is imperative to emphasize that just because continued secondary geological creative processes are not specifically mentioned in the Genesis account for the fourth through the sixth day, that does not mean that such were not occurring. Indeed, it is not until the end of the sixth day, and the dawning of the seventh day, that the biblical text stipulates God's declaration that "the heavens and the earth were finished," because God had "ended his work which he had made" so He "rested from all his work which God had created and made" (Genesis 2:1-3). Thus, if Scripture does not specifically discount the possibility of continued creative geological processes during the latter half of the Creation Week, then we may speculate that such secondary geological creative processes could have continued right through this period, but would have done so at supernaturally-directed and catastrophic rates. This means that the data of the geologic record corresponding to this second half of the Creation Week must not be viewed in terms of today's slow-and-gradual rates of geologic processes. Indeed, today's imperceptibly slow geologic processes would conceivably have taken hundreds of millions, and even billions, of years to accomplish what God's secondary creative geologic processes would have achieved in just these few days of the Creation Week.

So just what can we glean from the data of the geologic record? First, it has already been noted (Figure 15, page 446) that the granitic rocks in the Archean belong to the tonalite-trondhjemite-granodiorite (TTG) suite, and these are significantly different geochemically and mineralogically from post-Archean TTGs, which are in contrast calc-alkaline and predominantly granite-granodiorite. Second, Archean greenstone belts are characterized by the presence of komatiites, and the volume of basalt plus komatiite exceeds that of intermediate plus felsic volcanics, whereas on the whole, Proterozoic greenstones have smaller proportions of basalt (and usually no komatiite), and range from 20 to 50 percent felsic volcanics plus andesite. Also of significance is the evidence that the lavas in Archean greenstone belts have been erupted chiefly as submarine flows in deep water, whereas a great proportion of post-Archean greenstone belt volcanics would seem to have been erupted in shallow water. These observations alone would suggest a fundamental change in the nature and style of the operating geologic processes, as well as significant changes on the earth's surface and in the mantle, perhaps related to a change in the convective circulation there. Because the first genuine fossilized stromatolites and bacteria are also found in these Archean strata sequences, it seems evident that the formation of these Archean cratons has to have been the work of the third day of the Creation Week, with the transition into the Proterozoic strata sequences marking the transition into the fourth day. At this point in the late Archean rock record, there is evidence of rapid growth of new continental crust, in conjunction with many intrusions of granitoids during the development, metamorphism, and cratonization of surrounding greenstone belts (Figure 13, page 445). This period also coincided with the formation of many volcanic-hosted metal sulfide ore deposits, gold/base metal veins, Kambalda-type nickel sulfide deposits, and massive gold and uranium-bearing conglomerates (see Figure 26, pages 452-453). There was also a pronounced rapid increase in the development of banded-iron formations, climaxing at the beginning of the Proterozoic with the formation of the giant, iron-rich, banded-iron formations of the Hamersley Basin of Western Australia, the Transvaal Group of South Africa, and in the Lake Superior region of the United States (see Figure 10, page 444). This reflects the coincidence of the generation of copious quantities of hydrothermal fluids that then deposited these enormous quantities of chemical sediments, with the peak in granitoid magmatism, volcanism, and the formation of volcanic-related metal ore deposits, plus the generation of new continental crust that continued to be eroded, exposed, and vegetated in the closing stages of the third day. Thus, the end of the third day and the beginning of the fourth day may arbitrarily be placed at the Archean/Proterozoic boundary in the geologic record, conventionally dated at around 2.5 billion years ago.

It is in the Proterozoic rock record that algal mats and their stromatolite structures are found fossilized in increased numbers and complexity (see Figure 20, page 349), which reflects the importance of this hydrothermal biome in conjunction with the hydrothermal springs that were producing copious quantities of chemical sediments in the shallow waters of the continental shelves, and in the marine basins adjoining the continent (or continents) that had been produced on the third day. During the fourth day there were still no creatures living with the plants anywhere on the earth's surface, in its atmosphere, or in the oceans, so vigorous volcanic, magmatic, hydrothermal, and sedimentation activity on the continental shelves and in the ocean basins could have continued through the fourth day. However, they would need to have come to an end by the fifth day, when God created the marine creatures. Figure 10 indicates that there was a dramatic decrease in the generation of banded-iron formations, and thus the hydrothermal activity responsible for them, in the latter part of the early Proterozoic (Paleoproterozoic) rock sequence, at a level conventionally "dated" at around 1.7-1.8 billion years ago. This level in turn corresponds to another peak in the generation and intrusion of granitoids into contemporaneously extruded volcanics and deposited sediments in further greenstone belts, that were consequently metamorphosed and cratonized as new continental crust (see Figure 13). However, the volume of activity and strata produced by these secondary creative geologic activities was not as large at the close of this fourth day as in the latter part of the third day. This is consistent with the inference from the biblical record that the third day was the climax in these secondary creative activities, which would then have begun to wane progressively during the second half of the Creation Week.

Even though there was a rapid decline in hydrothermal activity producing banded-iron formations, other volcanic activity at this time was still responsible for further development of volcanic-hosted metal sulfide ore deposits, while hydrothermal fluids began depositing metal sulfides in the thick sedimentary strata sequences that had resulted from the continued erosion and sedimentation adjacent to the continental margins. Thus, it may be possible to place the end of the fourth day at the level in the geologic record marked by the end of the Paleoproterozoic, perhaps even at the level conventionally dated at 1.6 billion years ago. Of course, it needs to be emphasized that these are not here regarded as "absolute ages," these quoted conventional figures having been produced by accelerated nuclear transmutations, coupled with inheritance from mantle sources and consequent contamination/mixing (to be discussed in detail later).

From this level upwards in the geologic record, there is a continued marked decrease in the formation of new continental crust, and in the generation and intrusion of granitoid magmas, compared with the volume produced at the closing stages of the third and fourth days (see Figure 13). There seems to have been almost a complete cessation of secondary creative geologic processes in the lower part of the middle Proterozoic (Mesoproterozoic) rock record, possibly coinciding with the commencement of the fifth day when marine and flying creatures were created. However, hydrothermal activity must have continued, with increasing fossilization of the algae and stromatolites of the hydrothermal biome in the carbonate sediments precipitated from the hydrothermal springs, while at depths within the crust the hydrothermal fluids precipitated uranium deposits, with or without gold and platinum group elements, and copper sulfides were precipitated with associated uranium, gold, and rare earth elements in an iron-oxide matrix within brecciated granitic rocks to form Olympic Dam-type ore deposits (see Figure 26). Circulating hydrothermal fluids also continued to precipitate metal sulfide ore deposits within the fragmental sediments being deposited. There had also been a change in the type of chemical sediments being deposited, with virtually no more precipitation of banded-iron formations, but manganese-rich sediments, which had begun to be deposited in Paleoproterozoic rock sequences, continued being deposited in the Mesoproterozoic strata record.

There seems to be no obvious feature (or features) in the subsequent Mesoproterozoic rock record that might indicate the boundary between the fifth and sixth days. However, this is not unreasonable, given that once set in motion, these secondary creative geologic processes would just have continued producing the rock record as they progressively waned during these closing days of the Creation Week. The focus of God's primary creative activity was on the creation of all manner of marine and flying creatures on the fifth day, and then all manner of land creatures and man on the sixth day. So long as these secondary creative geologic processes were not bringing death and destruction to the creatures God was creating and placing in the ocean waters, in the atmosphere, and on the land surfaces, they would have been allowed to continue their work of building and shaping the earth's crust, and furnishing it with the rock and mineral resources man would need to use in exercising the dominion over the earth that God was to give him. Perhaps it might be easier to identify the level in the rock record where the sixth day, and thus the Creation Week era, ends, because that is where all of God's creative activities ceased, and where supernaturally directed process rates operating outside of today's God-ordained physical laws also ceased. From this time onwards the pre-Flood era began, in which God's involvement in His creation was one of conservation, using the physical laws He had built into His creation. Thus, geological and other processes then simply continued according to those physical laws, more or less at today's "natural" process rates as recognizable today. Because the products of the Creation Week processes appear to be exactly comparable to the products of today's "natural" geologic processes, there would have been continuity across this Creation Week/pre-Flood boundary between these respective geologic processes. However, there could still be features in the rock record that would indicate at which level this Creation Week/pre-Flood boundary occurs.

The first clues are probably found in the fossil record. Figure 20 shows that fossilized stromatolites increased in numbers and complexity through the Paleoproterozoic and Mesoproterozoic, to reach their peak in relative diversity at the level in the geologic record that is conventionally "dated" at about 1.2 billion years ago, after which there was a rapid decrease in their fossilization in Neoproterozoic rock sequences. It is conceivable that because there were such prodigious volumes of hydrothermal fluids being discharged through springs onto the shallow continental shelves and ocean floors, with large quantities of carbonates being precipitated in the latter part of the Creation Week, these conditions were ideal for both the rapid growth and diversification of the stromatolite-building cyanobacterial and microbial mats, and for their rapid burial and fossilization. With the close of the Creation Week and the waning of the supernaturally-directed rate of discharge of these hydrothermal springs, and precipitation of carbonate sediments, into the God-ordained "natural" rate of these same processes, it is also conceivable that there was a decline in the growth, diversification, and fossilization of the stromatolites, and their cyanobacterial and microbial builders. These considerations would thus suggest that the level in the rock record that might represent the boundary between the strata of the Creation Week era and those formed during the pre-Flood era might coincide with where this distinct change in fossilized stromatolite abundance occurs, which is conventionally "dated" at approximately 1.2 billion years ago, near the end of the Mesoproterozoic geologic record. This is the same level above which fossils of multicellular algae begin appearing in the rock record (see Figure 21, page 350), but is still well below where worm-like megafossils, and subsequently the fossilized Ediacaran fauna, are found.

Another clue that is consistent with this choice for the Creation Week/pre-Flood boundary is that this level in the upper Mesoproterozoic rock record is where sedimentary phosphate rock units start appearing in strata sequences. This is a significant change that strongly suggests a change in geologic processes, and in ocean water chemistry due to the supply of nutrients to the ocean basins (see Figure 11, page 445). This might perhaps be explained by the life cycles of marine creatures becoming established, as they flourished in the pre-Flood seas, their deaths contributing their remains to the ocean waters and the sediments accumulating on the ocean floors. Otherwise, at this same level in the upper part of the Mesoproterozoic rock record, there is another, but much smaller, peak in the number of granitic magmas generated and intruded, but interestingly, this does not coincide with any major generation of new continental crust (Figure 13). This implies that these secondary creative geologic processes were rapidly diminishing and waning, which is exactly what would be expected at the close of the sixth day and the Creation Week. Thus, on balance, the end of the Creation Week might possibly coincide in the geologic record with the top of the Mesoproterozoic rock sequences, which have been conventionally "dated" at around 1 billion years ago.

81

CREATION OF "APPEARANCE OF AGE"

This attempt at reconciling the details preserved in the geologic record with the scriptural account of the creation of the earth, the land, the vegetation, all the animals and man, during the six days of the Creation Week, is at best very sketchy and somewhat tentative. Despite the wealth of data now available on the large volume of rocks that make up the Archean and Proterozoic strata sequences, there are still a lot of unknowns and puzzles in deciphering what these strata sequences and rock units mean in terms of the earth's early history, with the relationships between strata and strata sequences often being determined by reliance on radioisotopic dating. On the other hand, we are given so few details in the Genesis record of the Creation Week that it is difficult to be any more than very tentative about these correlations with the early geologic record. All we have are some guidelines that constrain these tentative correlations, which will likely remain tentative, even as advances continue to be made in unraveling the geologic details of the Archean and Proterozoic rock record, and their apparent implications for the earth's early history.

However, there is one extremely important implication that remains very significant. The scriptural account of God's creative activities in the six days of the Creation Week unmistakably describes the results of God's creative work on each day as fully-functioning, complete, and pronounced "good" by God Himself. From a human perspective, even though there is a hint of progressive processes involved, at each stage God created what to us would be termed a mature creation, with an appearance of age in terms of our understanding and experience. This is a fundamental principle clearly implied in the Genesis record, which is of paramount importance in applying the scriptural account to the rock record. This principle is a direct consequence of God accomplishing by creation in an instant of time, as now measured in our human existence, what our experience today suggests would take years, decades, and even perhaps millions of years, to be accomplished by today's "natural" processes operating over such timescales. Expressed another way, the earth, the land, the vegetation, and all the animals and man, were created virtually instantly with the appearance of a long history, as we would perceive it, that did not occur over such human-measured timescales, and which in fact did not at all occur as such. As this concept may be difficult to grasp, or may seem far-fetched, and perhaps even straining the biblical text, some illustrations and elaborations will help.

In John 1:1-3, Jesus is identified as in very nature and essence both truly God and the Creator of all things. Even in human flesh He never ceased to be God (John 1:14), or the Creator. The miracles He performed testified to this. Indeed, His very first miracle, recorded in John 2:1-11, was the creation of wine from water at the marriage feast in Cana. Jesus told those serving at the feast to fill six "water pots of stone" with water, and then draw from them a sample of the created wine for the master of the feast to taste. The master's response was that it seemed to be the best quality wine that had been served during the whole of the feast, and he declared that to the bridegroom, without inquiring of the servants as to where the wine had come from. He, of course, assumed that because of the quality of this wine it was of natural origin, having come from grapes that had been grown on vines, nurtured by soil and water, and then crushed to extract the juice, which was then stored to ferment and mature, a process well known in human experience that required years for the best wines to be produced. However, only minutes before being served to the master of the feast this wine had been water, and Jesus the Creator had performed this transformation within a split second, without any hint of how He did it. Note that this had to be a miracle of creation, because whereas there were only water molecules to begin with, a split second later there were now more complex molecules, also containing carbon atoms when carbon atoms had not been present before. The product of Jesus' creative miracle was a wine with the "appearance of age," and of a history as measured in human terms. Note that there was no deception here, because the master of the feast, even though he didn't see the miracle take place, could have asked the attendants who served the wine to him as to where the wine came from, and they as the eyewitnesses of Jesus' miracle could readily have told him. There is no hint whatsoever of any deception on the part of Jesus, who quite openly instructed the attendants, who in obeying His instructions witnessed the water pots being filled with water, and then the serving of the wine minutes later to the master of the feast. In doing so, they witnessed the transformation.

The parallels to God's miracles of creation during the Creation Week as recorded in Genesis should now be obvious. For example, when God created the plants on the third day, certain absolutely necessary environmental components had to be put in place, so that once created the plants would continue to grow—soil, water, light, chemical nutrients, etc. Whereas the biblical text mentions the creation of water and light on the first day, no details are provided as to the provision of the soil and its contained chemical nutrients, so we can only surmise that the provision of soil is implied when God made the dry land appear, in readiness for the land surface to be vegetated, all on the third day. Yet in our human experience soil requires a long period of development before being able to support plant growth. However, here in the Genesis record, the creation of the soil on the newly exposed land surface must have been virtually instantaneous, yet from God's perspective this is not even significant enough to rate a specific mention! Whether God created the soil instantaneously, or used secondary creative processes of chemical weathering at supernaturally accelerated rates, we are not told, except that the end result was a land surface blanketed by thick, nutrient-rich soil with an appearance of being "old," when it was still just new. It was created with an "appearance" of age, without having gradually developed over centuries of chemical weathering of bedrocks, alluvial deposition, etc. Furthermore, there is no deception on God's part in creating new soil that from a human perspective looked "old," because as the eyewitness present when He created the soil, God has told us the timeframe in which the creation of this soil took place.

The same is also true with respect to the plants that were subsequently created on the third day. The biblical account states that after God issued the command, "the earth brought forth grass, and herb yielding seed after his kind, and the tree yielding fruit, whose seed was in itself, after his kind" (Genesis 1:12). The implication is that all these plants were created instantly. Furthermore, these plants included mature fruit trees already yielding fruit. Similarly, the fish and birds were created on the fifth day, and the land animals, insects, and man were created on the sixth day, each "full grown" and placed in environments already perfectly suited to them. This rapid, almost instantaneous, attainment of maturity is simply stated as implicit in the text of Scripture. Special emphasis and some more details are provided in the case of the first man, who is said to have been directly formed by God out of the same elements ("the dust") as are found in the earth (Genesis 2:7), but was then endued with the breath of life. Then the first woman was fashioned by God out of man's side (Genesis 2:21-22).

Without doubt, this clear implication of a "mature creation" with an "appearance of age" is a tremendously significant truth that cannot be overemphasized. Many details about how God created, and further descriptions of what was created, are not given to us in the Genesis record, because finite humans, locked into our space-time existence locally on the surface of planet earth, cannot possibly comprehend the infinite Creator God who exists in eternity outside of the entire universe that He created. However, God considers that He has revealed enough for us to accept, and know beyond any doubt, that at the end of these six days the creation of "heaven and earth, the sea, and all that in them is" was complete and perfect, being "very good" in God's assessment (Genesis 1:31). Everything was in harmony, with each of God's creatures fully grown and placed in environments perfectly suited to them, with interlocking relationships. Thus, for example, there had to be fully-grown grasses and fruit trees bearing fruit at the end of the third day, so that flying creatures created on the fifth day, and the land animals and man on the sixth day, would have food to eat. Furthermore, to emphasize that the first man, Adam, was fully mature and intelligent, rather than a baby who still had to grow and develop, we are told that after he was placed in the Garden of Eden, he "gave names to all cattle, and to the fowl of the air, and to every beast of the field" there within less than a few hours, before God created Eve from his side (Genesis

2:20). Adam was thus created with the full capacity to speak a language and to think, as well as to have dominion over the creation and maintain the Garden of Eden, right from the very time he was created on the sixth day.[1]

However, simple acceptance of genuine creation by the all-powerful, infinite Creator God of the Bible, as revealed in the person of His Son Jesus Christ, has not only become extremely difficult for modern man in general, but is anathema to the scientific intelligencia of our day. Of course, this is not just simply a rejection of genuine creation, but of the Creator Himself, who is deemed irrelevant and unnecessary, because modern science now claims to be able to explain the origin of the universe, the earth, and all life on it by so-called natural processes. Evolutionary theories are not just a phenomenon of the modern era, because even in ancient times, philosophers were continually devising varied and sundry schemes of evolution to explain how the world might have gradually developed from primeval chaos into its present state of high organization and complexity. Such evolutionary theories may perhaps reflect faintly the actual creation revelation recorded in the Scriptures, according to which God in six days did build up the universe from an initial formless state into a primeval order of high perfection. However, the great error made by scientists and philosophers in the last 200 to 300 years has been the refusal to recognize that this original creation was completed at the end of the sixth day of the Creation Week, and that modern natural processes are not the continuation of the processes God used in creation.

Modern man generally rebels at any suggestion of an original complete creation, desiring instead to push the divine Creator as far back in time as possible, so as to conceive Him as being as little concerned as possible with, and even irrelevant to, His creation. Any concept of a creation and a Creator, in any vital sense of the words, is assiduously avoided and vehemently opposed in all scientific literature, apart from very rare exceptions in some very recent scientific literature allowing the promotion of New Age, pantheistic "mother earth," or Gaia hypotheses. Geological evolution over billions of years is proclaimed as the explanation for the origin and formation of the earth, its rock strata, and its landscapes, while biological evolution is all but universally accepted today as the sufficient explanation for the origin and formation of all living organisms, including men, as well as the evolution of life itself from inorganic compounds. The most absurd improbabilities have been considered more probable than the alternative of real

---

1 These details, which are clearly explicit in the Genesis account of a mature creation with an appearance of age, have led to questions on non-consequential issues that we can merely speculate about when searching for answers. For example, some might ask whether because the trees were created fully mature and fruit-bearing on the third day, did they then have growth rings? Similarly, did Adam and Eve have navels? We are, of course, not told, so we are left to speculate. Logically the answer in both instances would likely be "no," because on the one hand the trees did not take years to grow (growth rings generally correlating with the seasons of the year), and on the other hand, Adam and Eve did not come into existence as babies birthed from a mother's womb, where they would have required umbilical cords. These answers would seem to be correct and logical implications of what we are given in the biblical text, and yet they are not specifically stated there. Thus, these are inconsequential issues where the answers are not really important, one way or the other.

creation. For example, a former professor of biology at Harvard University, when discussing the extreme complexity of even the simplest living organisms, and the almost infinite improbability that such systems could ever arise spontaneously from living systems, still confessed:

> One has only to contemplate the magnitude of this task to concede that the spontaneous generation of a living organism is impossible. Yet here we are—as a result, I believe, of spontaneous generation.[2]

This Harvard biology professor, only a few paragraphs before making the above quoted statement, had admitted that the only alternative to belief in spontaneous generation was "to believe in a single, primary act of supernatural creation," which he admitted most modern biologists are unwilling to accept. Yet, in spite of decades of research, in conjunction with many hopeful experiments, the impossible improbabilities remain:

> The chance that higher life forms might have emerged in this way is comparable with the chance that "a tornado sweeping through a junkyard might assemble a Boeing 747 from the materials therein."[3]

So how have biochemists and other scientists today, researching how life may have spontaneously evolved, overcome these probabilities? In summary, they have faith in the ability of inanimate molecules to generate life:

> Most researchers agree with Hoyle on this point (although on little else). The one belief almost everyone shares is that matter quickened through a succession of steps, none of which is widely improbable.[4]

Furthermore, their faith position has become essential, because even ingenious experiments have not demonstrated how life could have begun:

> The full details of how the RNA world, and life, emerged may not be revealed in the near future. Nevertheless, as chemists, biochemists and molecular biologists co-operate on ever more ingenious experiments, they are sure to fill in many missing parts of the puzzle.[5]

Such is the confidence of modern scientists in their own abilities, that they believe it is only a matter of time doing more experiments before they will then eventually be able to work out how life began, and so "create" themselves. As a consequence,

---

2   G. Wald, 1954, The origin of life, *Scientific American*, 191 (2): 47.

3   The late Sir Fred Hoyle, Professor of Astronomy at Cambridge University, England, as quoted in Hoyle on evolution, 1981, *Nature*, 294: 105.

4   J. Horgan, 1991, In the beginning…, *Scientific American*, 264 (2): 102.

5   L. E. Orgel, 1994, The origin of life on the earth, *Scientific American*, 271 (4): 61.

they proudly denounce those Christians who maintain that it was God who created life, and God alone who can create it:

> The debate about life's origins has deep resonance in our society. Those who work in this field frequently find their search challenged in assaults on empirical natural science. Judeo-Christian thought must accept convincing evidence from nature: denial is both destructive of faith and dangerous to science. To find the fragments of fact, and to attempt to understand them, is a powerful response to the creationist heresy. Not only fact and honest interpretation, but also orthodox theological argument reject creationism.[6]

The modern scientific intelligensia arrogantly asserts, and has convinced most in society, that nature "created" itself, all of which seems to be a sad but up-to-date commentary on a well-known biblical passage, describing man and his drift into polytheistic pantheism:

> For the invisible things of him from the creation of the world are clearly seen, being understood by the things that are made, even his eternal power and Godhead; so that they are without excuse: Because that, when they knew God, they glorified him not as God, neither were thankful; but became vain in their imaginations, and their foolish heart was darkened. Professing themselves to be wise, they became fools, and changed the glory of the uncorruptible God into an image made like to corruptible man, and to birds, and fourfooted beasts, and creeping things. (Romans 1:20-23)

---

6   E. G. Nisbet and N. H. Sleep, 2001, The habitat and nature of early life, *Nature*, 409: 1090.

82

COSMOLOGICAL EVOLUTION AND THE "BIG BANG"

The evolutionary philosophy does not only purport to explain the origin of life and the development of living organisms. The denial of true creation extends into the inorganic realm, encompassing the origin of stars and galaxies, and even eventually all the elements that make up the physical universe. In the last fifty years, there have been two competing cosmologies vying to successfully explain the origin of the universe and the matter in it—the so-called "steady-state" and "big bang" cosmologies.

The first of these, the steady-state cosmology, obtained a large following among scientists and philosophers when first proposed fifty years ago. Carrying the principle of uniformitarianism to its ultimate extreme, this theory was often called (really a misnomer) the "continuous creation" theory, because its key feature was the concept of the continual evolution (not creation in the real biblical sense) of matter out of nothing, at many places at the same time in the vast universe! The philosophy of this theory has been described in the following terms:

> This idea requires atoms to appear in the Universe continually instead of being created explosively at some definite time in the past. There is an important contrast here. An explosive creation of the Universe is not subject to analysis. It is something that must be impressed by an arbitrary fiat. In the case of the continuous origin of matter on the other hand the creation must obey a definite law, a law that has just the same sort of logical status as the laws of gravitation, of nuclear physics, of electricity and magnetism.[1]

The extreme uniformitarianism of this theory is even more evident in the statement:

> The old queries about the beginning and end of the universe are dealt with in a surprising manner—by saying that they are meaningless, for the reason that the Universe did not have a beginning and it will not

---

1   F. Hoyle, 1955, *Frontiers of Astronomy*, New York: Harper's, 317-318.

have an end.[2]

It is obvious that the concept of a Creator God and a real creation have no place in this interpretation of the universe. It is also obvious that the basic reason for replacing the concept of creation with that of an eternal "steady-state" is not scientific at all, but purely the desire to conform all things in the universe to man's understanding in terms of present physical processes. This has been perceptively noted:

> So far as I can judge, the authors of this new cosmology are primarily concerned about the great difficulty that must face all systems that contemplate a changing universe—namely, how can we conceive it to have begun? They are not content to leave this question unanswered until further knowledge comes; all problems must be solved now. Nor, for some reason, are they content to suppose that at some period in the distance past something happened that does not continually happen now. It seems to them better to suppose that there was no beginning and will be no ending to the material universe, and therefore, tacitly assuming that the universe must conform to their tastes, they declare that this must have been the case.[3]

However, in the years that followed, an alternative theory became so prominent, that it was for a time presented as almost the only contender that explained the origin and history of the universe. For some years now, the big bang cosmology has been promoted by astronomers and cosmologists in the media as a virtual fact, so that most in our society now accept this theory as "the explanation" for the origin and history of the universe. This cosmology maintains that:

> Fifteen billion years ago, a Universe erupted out of nothing in a titanic explosion that we now call the big bang. Everything—all matter, energy, even space and time—came into being at that instant. Ever since, the stuff of the Universe has been expanding and cooling. In the earliest moments of the big bang, the Universe occupied a tiny volume and was unimaginably hot. It was a blistering fireball of radiation mixed with microscopic particles of matter, but eventually, the universe cooled enough for atoms to form. Gradually, these clumped together under gravity to make billions of galaxies, great islands of stars of which our own galaxy, the Milky Way, is but one.[4]

Enthusiastic support has been given to this big bang cosmology by some Christian astronomers, as if it were a confirmation of the biblical account of the origin

---

2   Hoyle, 1955, 321.

3   H. Dingle, 1954, Science and modern cosmology, *Science*, 120: 519.

4   M. Chown, 1994, Birth of the universe, Inside Science 69: 1, *New Scientist*, 141 (1914).

and history of the universe and the earth.[5] However, the reality is that this big bang cosmology is also purely evolutionary and naturalistic, because the initial state of the universe is not conceived in any way as a time of divine creation. Indeed, no allowance or mention of a divine Creator appears anywhere in the scientific literature discussing the origination of this big bang, and where the word "creation" is used, it in no way is meant to imply divine creation, but is a play on words, in all probability to appease man's religious consciousness. Rather than a beginning as such, other descriptions are used:

> If we run the expansion of the Universe backwards to the moment of creation itself, we find that the Universe was compressed into an impossibly small volume, was infinitely dense and infinitely hot. In mathematical jargon, the Universe was a singularity. Singularities are a disaster in any physical theory. They are a warning that we have gone terribly wrong with our description of nature. We need a better theory and that theory is a "quantum" theory of gravity. Quantum theories have been hugely successful in describing the other three forces of nature... so there is great confidence that they will be successful in describing gravity as well....in any quantum theory, the idea of an exact position in space is jettisoned because of the Heisenberg uncertainty principle. The implication is that if the Universe were to be run backwards in time it would never quite reach the stage where all of creation is compressed into a single point. Something would happen to prevent the formation of a singularity.[6]

> By applying quantum mechanics to the universe as a whole, cosmologists hope to look beyond the very instant of creation....So we arrive at a possible answer. According to the picture afforded by quantum cosmology, the universe appeared from a quantum fuzz, tunneling into existence and thereafter evolving classically. The most compelling aspect of this picture is that the assumptions necessary for the inflationary universe scenario may be compressed into a single, simple boundary condition for the wave function of the universe.[7]

---

5   H. N. Ross, 1994, Cosmology's holy grail, *Christianity Today*, 38 (14): 24-27. In Ross's words: "And if the universe is 'exploding' there must have been a start and a Starter to that explosion. As Genesis reveals, the universe had a beginning—hence, an Initiator, one who existed before and outside of the universe, as the Bible uniquely declares." (p. 26) "The scientific underpinning for correlating the big bang with Jesus Christ lies in a set of mathematical equations, the equations of general relativity" (pp. 25-26). "How awesome to consider that God caused the big bang and all its components, including exotic matter and over 10 billion trillion stars..." (p. 27). What Ross fails to acknowledge is that the Genesis account of God creating the universe begins with God creating the earth "in the beginning" on the first day, with the sun and other stars, and the galaxies not being created until four literal days later, specific details given by God which are totally in conflict with the claims of the big bang cosmology, both in terms of the timescale and in the order in which creation took place. In order to maintain this compromised position, the Scriptures ultimately suffer, as the biblical text is reinterpreted to fit finite, fallible man's scientific ideas.

6   Chown, 1994, 4.

7   J. J. Halliwell, 1991, Quantum cosmology and the creation of the universe, *Scientific American*, 265 (6):

Thus, there is no more room in the big bang cosmology for a genuine divine creation than there is in the steady-state cosmology.

What compromising Christian astronomers need to remember is that finite, fallible, science theories usually end up eventually being discarded, because new observations and data in conflict with those theories invariably accumulate. If the Bible has then been reinterpreted so as to accommodate finite, fallible man's theories, then when those theories are abandoned, the Scriptures are further discredited and are regarded increasingly as irrelevant. As a matter of fact, the once discredited and largely discarded steady-state cosmology is now making a comeback, as observations and data that conflict with the big bang cosmology have increasingly accumulated.

More than a decade ago it was stated:

> The relativistic…Big Bang model for the expanding Universe has yielded a set of interpretations and successful predictions that substantially outnumber the elements used in devising the theory, with no well-established empirical contradictions. It is reasonable to conclude that this standard cosmology has developed into a mature and believable physical model.[8]

Yet only seven years later there was a different assessment being made:

> The "Big Bang" model includes a few unknown numbers that determine the size, shape and future of the Universe. In the past few years our measurements of these three parameters have begun to rule out the old picture of the Universe dominated by cold dark matter. What will take its place?…Theoretical slack in the Big Bang model is being tightened all the time, and we should soon pin down the floating parameters with acceptable confidence. But perhaps none of the available family of models will fit all the new data.[9]

Indeed, even when the big bang cosmology was being trumpeted as being the best and virtually only viable theory, severe doubts about it were being raised:

> The above discussion clearly indicates that the present evidence does not warrant an implicit belief in the standard hot Big Bang picture….As a general scientific principle it is undesirable to depend crucially on what is unobservable to explain what is observable, as happens frequently in

---

28, 35.

8   P. J. E. Peebles, D. N. Schramm, E. L. Turner and R. G. Krom, 1991, The case for the relativistic hot Big Bang cosmology, *Nature*, 352: 769.

9   P. Coles, 1998, The end of the old model Universe, *Nature*, 393: 741, 744.

Big Bang cosmology. Geology progressed variably from the time Hutton's principle of uniformity was adopted, according to which everything in geology is explained by observable ongoing processes. One can suspect that cosmology and cosmogony would profit similarly from the adoption of the same principle, as the view proposed here does.[10]

So what alternative cosmological theory is now being proposed? In fact, the steady-state cosmology has been revived:

> Note that in the steady-state theory the Universe expands because of the creation of matter within it. The space-time structure of each near creation unit makes room for itself by shouldering aside the products of previously existing units, a process that requires each creation unit to expand with just sufficient energy to fit itself into the general Hubble flow of the Universe...the conventional critic may argue that from the standpoint of economy of postulates the idea of "many" creation events is a lot worse than the notion of the single creation event (the Big Bang). We disagree. The "many" events in our alternative theory are potentially observable and satisfy the repeatability criterion of physical theories. The Big Bang satisfies neither of these requirements, and hence as a scientific hypothesis fails to compete with the alternative proposed here.[11]

Meanwhile, attempts are being made to adjust the big bang cosmology to overcome some of the recent conflicting observations:

> The evolution of inflationary theory has given rise to a completely new cosmological paradigm, which differs considerably from the old big bang theory and even from the first versions of the inflationary scenario. In it the universe appears to be both chaotic and homogeneous, expanding and stationary. Our cosmic home grows, fluctuates and eternally reproduces itself in all possible forms, as if adjusting itself for all possible types of life that it can support.[12]

There is neither room nor scope for the divine Creator in this cosmology, so how will compromising Christian astronomers reinterpret the biblical text of Genesis to accommodate the Scriptures to this cosmology? The end result is total capitulation that relegates the Genesis record to nothing more than an historically-based myth!

Furthermore, just how empirically verifiable and valid are the claims made by the

---

10   H. C. Arp, G. Burbidge, F. Hoyle, J. V. Narlikar and N. C. Wickramasinghe, 1990, The extragalactic Universe: an alternative view, *Nature*, 346: 810, 812.

11   Arp et al, 1990, 811-812.

12   A. Linde, 1994, The self-reproducing inflationary universe, *Scientific American*, 271 (5): 39.

scientists championing these cosmologies? Of course, it is sheer wishful thinking to suppose that observations made today can establish the conditions at the beginning, and the means by which the universe came into existence:

> How can one verify a law of initial conditions?…because it is so hard to verify quantum cosmology, we cannot conclusively determine whether the no-boundary or the tunneling proposals are the correct ones for the wave function of the universe. It could be a very long time before we can tell if either is an answer to the question, "Where did all this come from?"[13]

Moreover, when honest enough to admit it, even the scientists involved in constructing these cosmologies admit to the paucity of hard data available to construct their theories:

> Cosmology is unique in science in that it is a very large intellectual edifice based on very few facts. The strong tendency is to replace a need for more facts by conformity, which is accorded the dubious role of supplying the element of certainty in peoples' minds that properly should only belong to science with far more extensive observational support. When new facts do come along, as we believe to be the case with anomalous redshifts, it is a serious misprision to ignore what is new on the grounds that the data do not fit established conformity. Certainty in science cannot be forthcoming from minimal positions such as those which currently exist in cosmology.[14]

If this then is the true state of these cosmological theories, admitted to be based on only a few scarce real facts, it is totally illogical, out of order, and absurd to compromise the God-provided eyewitness account of His supernatural creation of the universe, the earth, and all life, by attempting to reinterpret the biblical text to accommodate finite, fallible man's woefully inadequate cosmological theories.

It should now be obvious, therefore, that when one decides to reject the concept of real creation, there is no scientific stopping-point short of totally rejecting any role for the divine Creator, in what then amounts to atheism, or increasingly, animistic pantheism. Not only various types of living creatures, but even life itself, and then everything in the physical universe from the simplest atom to the greatest galaxy, must be incorporated into the all-encompassing cosmic evolutionary hypothesis! One searches in vain for any acknowledgement of the Creator God of the Bible and His creative power in all these theories. Everything can be "scientifically" explained, so what need is there for a Creator?

---

13   Halliwell, 1991, 35.

14   Arp et al, 1990, 812.

However, the conviction of so many scientists in the mainstream scientific community (especially those quoted above), that evolution is the explanation of all things, must obviously arise from outside the domain of verifiable science, because the evidence for it is only circumstantial at best, and in the main highly speculative and conjectural. It thus has to be, in fact, much more of a faith or belief system than is creationism. It is a belief exercise, in spite of all the evidences of the most basic and best-validated scientific laws that are absolutely contrary to it. On the other hand, creation as a fact revealed by God both in the biblical text of Genesis and in the miracles performed by the Creator Himself, Jesus Christ, is at least very strongly supported by the law of cause and effect,[15] by the first and second laws of thermodynamics, and by other basic truths of demonstrable science.

Men complain, however, that God would be dishonest to create the universe, the earth, and all life on it with an appearance of age. If God is Truth, then how could He cause things to look as though they were old with a history, and had come into their present forms by long processes of growth and development, when actually they had just been created? To do this would be deceptive, and therefore this is impossible for God to do. After all, God would not lie, for in fact, He has specifically condemned lying (Exodus 20:16), as well as punishing those who have lied to Him (e.g., Acts 5:1-11).

This sort of reasoning, however, is entirely unworthy of reasonable men, especially scientists who pride themselves on their skepticism of any argument or claim that will not stand up to scrutiny unless supported by valid evidence and observable, reputable data. Such reasoning is essentially an affirmation of atheism, a denial of the possibility of a real creation. If God actually created anything at all, even the simplest atoms, then those atoms, or whatever it was He created, would necessarily have an immediate appearance of some age to us, as human observers bound by our finite understanding of the processes operating around us today. This is exactly how the master of the marriage feast in Cana saw the wine that our Creator Jesus Christ had just created from water. There could be no genuine creation of any kind without an initial appearance of age inherent in it. Of course, it would still be possible to interpret this newly-created matter in terms of some

---

15 The law of causality or cause and effect is very much a part of the empirical basis of the scientific method. It affirms that like causes produce like effects, and that every effect must have an adequate cause. No effect can be quantitatively greater than or qualitatively divergent from its cause. Thus, for example, if the personality of man is regarded as an effect, his intelligence requires a Cause possessed of intelligence, man's power of choice implies a Cause possessed of volition, and his moral consciousness must be explained in terms of a Cause possessed of morality. Similarly, the intelligibility of the physical universe implies an intelligent Designer, and so on. Thus, the law of causality, though admittedly not philosophically impregnable, is at least very strong circumstantial evidence of the existence of a great First Cause, a personal Creator-God. This has again, very recently, been powerfully argued in W. A. Dembski, 1998, *The Design Inference: Eliminating Chance through Small Probabilities*, Cambridge, UK: Cambridge University Press; W. A. Dembski, 1999, *Intelligent Design: The Bridge between Science and Theology*, Downers Grove, IL: InterVarsity Press; W. A. Dembski and J. M. Cushiner, eds., 2001, *Signs of Intelligence: Understanding Intelligent Design*, Grand Rapids, MI: Brazos Press, Baker Book House.

kind of previous evolutionary history. However, if God is able to create the simplest atoms with an appearance of age—in other words, if God exists—then there is no reason why He could not, in absolute conformity with His character as the Truth, instantaneously create a whole universe full-grown and fully functioning.

Obviously, if God did this, there would be no way by which any of His creatures could deduce the age or manner[16] of creation, by the study of the laws of maintenance of His creation that have operated since He completed His creation. This information could only be obtained, correctly, through God Himself revealing it! Furthermore, if God has revealed how and when He created the universe and its inhabitants, then to charge God with falsehood in creating His creation with "apparent age" is presumptuous and arrogant in the extreme—even blasphemous. It is not God who has lied, but rather those who have called Him a liar by rejection of His revelation of creation, as given in Genesis and verified by the Lord Jesus, the Creator Himself!

However, if we are willing to accept in faith the biblical account of creation as simple, literal truth, then we immediately have a powerful tool for understanding all the observations and data of geology in proper perspective. We can study the earth, starting with the concept that its internal constitution, the rocks and minerals of its crust, and the various necessary geologic entities, were all brought into existence by God during the six days of the Creation Week, using unique creative processes that resulted in the earth and its surface being eminently and perfectly suitable for man's habitation and dominion. Of course, the original form and appearance of the creation is now much masked, because of the subsequent entrance of sin, decay, and death into the creation, and very much altered by the subsequent upheavals associated with the Flood. Not only mankind, but also "the whole creation," has been delivered into the "bondage of decay," and has ever since been "groaning and travailing together in pain" (Romans 8:21, 22). Recognition of all these basic facts must ultimately lead to a far more satisfactory, scientific explanation of all the observed geologic field relationships than any evolutionary/ uniformitarian synthesis can ever do.

---

16   F. A. Schaeffer, 1969, The universe and two chairs, in *Death in the City*, Chicago: Inter-Varsity Press, 110-127; A. E. Wilder-Smith, 1987, Materialism in the light of an analogy and of some practical examples, in *The Scientific Alternative to Neo-Darwinian Evolutionary Theory: Information Sources and Structures*, Costa Mesa, CA: TWFT Publishers, 109-129.

83

THE PRE-FLOOD ERA—THE "WATERS ABOVE THE FIRMAMENT"

The Fall and the Beginning of the Pre-Flood Era

The Genesis record does not state how long it was between man's creation and the Fall and the entry of death into the world. It may not have been all that long, though, between the end of the Creation Week and when Satan came to tempt Adam and Eve, because Eve did not become expectant of her firstborn son until after the Fall (Genesis 4:1). Indeed, it is unlikely Adam and Eve had been unresponsive to God's admonition to be fruitful and multiply (Genesis 1:28) before the Fall, in view of Adam's delight at God's provision of Eve and God ordaining the first marriage (Genesis 2:21-25).

Fossils are a notable aspect of the rock record. So an important issue in our comparison of the rock record with Scripture is the point in the record where animal fossils appear, since fossils of living creatures other than plants plainly record suffering, bloodshed, and death. Plants do not contain blood, and they do not suffer or experience "death" in the same way as living creatures. In any case, God provided them for food, including for man's consumption, even during the Creation Week when it was all declared by God to be "very good" (Genesis 1:29-31). Although the sentence of death was specifically pronounced only on man, and on the serpent used by Satan as the vehicle of his temptation, the most obvious implication is that this curse on the master of creation extended likewise to his dominion. This fact is also strongly implied by the New Testament expositions on the Fall. Paul says, "By man came death" (1 Corinthians 15:21); and in another place, "By one man, sin entered into the world, and death by sin" (Romans 5:12). Similarly, in Romans 8:20 we are told that "the creation was subject to vanity."

Most of the fossil deposits display evidence of the sudden burial of animals and plants of all kinds, and they therefore often indicate a watery catastrophe of some kind. The whole appearance of the rocks containing animal fossils seems completely out of harmony with the system of creation that God so many times pronounced as "good." Therefore, it would seem compelling to date all rock strata with contained fossils of once-living creatures as subsequent to Adam's Fall. This is certainly consistent with our analysis already of the content of the overall fossil record. As depicted in Figures 20 and 21, only algae and stromatolite fossils are found in Archean, Paleoproterozoic, and Mesoproterozoic strata, so it is possible to consign these to the Creation Week era, whereas worm-like megafossils and other animal fossils only begin appearing in Neoproterozoic and later strata, which should thus be consigned to the pre-Flood era subsequent to the Fall and beyond, for the reasons just given.

Furthermore, it seems likely that relatively few of these animal fossil-bearing strata, if any, should be dated to the period between Adam's Fall and the Flood, that is, to the 1,650 or more years of the pre-Flood era. This is primarily because geologic activity would seem to have been very mild during this period of time, because otherwise there would have been the capacity to produce fossil deposits of at least some animals in pre-Flood strata, for example, of marine invertebrates in shallow marginal marine environments, where they would normally be susceptible to burial by sediments eroded and transported from off the adjacent continental margins. Of course, it is also possible that any such fossil deposits that did form in the pre-Flood era would most likely have been reworked, or even destroyed, during the initial stages of the Flood. The conclusion that the pre-Flood era was probably one of relative inactivity, geologically, has traditionally been argued from the relevant Scripture passages,[1] so these arguments need to be examined.

The "Waters Above the Firmament"

It is beyond dispute that, on the second day of the Creation Week, God elevated some of the water covering the earth's surface, from when He created the earth on the first day, and placed a "firmament" (literally, a stretched out thinness) between these "waters above" and the waters left on the earth's surface. It has frequently been argued that this "firmament" was the atmosphere, because on the fifth day God made "fowl that may fly above the earth in the open firmament of heaven" (Genesis 1:20). However, it has recently been proposed that this "firmament" or "expanse" was instead interstellar space, which would then require that these "waters above the firmament" be cosmic in scale and represent an outer boundary for interstellar space.[2] If this interpretation is correct, then this would place these "waters above" well beyond any further consideration with respect to their involvement in the earth's atmosphere and climate system and in the Flood.

Otherwise, it has been suggested that these were waters that existed above the atmosphere, apparently in the form of a great vapor canopy around the earth of unknown (but possibly very great) extent. Of course, in the form of water vapor this canopy would have been quite invisible, but nevertheless it is claimed that it would have had a profound effect on the earth's climate and meteorological

---

1   Whitcomb and Morris, 1961, 240-243, 255-258.

2   D. R. Humphreys, 1994, A Biblical basis for Creationist cosmology, in *Proceedings of the Third International Conference on Creationism*, R. E. Walsh, ed., Pittsburgh, PA: Creation Science Fellowship, 255-266.

processes.[3] However, before it is appropriate to discuss the climatic and meteorological effects of such a water vapor canopy, it is necessary to investigate the scientific feasibility of such an entity. Such a water vapor canopy would have been put in place supernaturally while natural physical laws were suspended during the Creation Week. Once in place, it would have to be maintained there subsequently, as well as operating, under the same natural physical laws that govern the earth's atmospheric processes today.

Dillow determined from his expository studies of the biblical text, and general physical reasoning, that these "waters above" were probably in vapor form, and had originally rested on top of the earth's atmosphere.[4] He preferred to use a two-layer model of the earth's atmosphere in his scientific analysis, with pure water vapor above resting on top of the air compressed below. Dillow also assumed that the amount of water vapor in the canopy was a column equivalent to 40 feet (about 12 meters) of liquid water. He obtained this estimate from an assumed rainfall rate of 0.5 inches (12.7mm) per hour over a period of forty days and nights during the initial stage of the Flood. Such a rainfall rate would be considered a heavy rainfall rate today, particularly if it occurred uniformly over a large area. The Bible indicates that the rainfall was heavy during the first forty days and nights of the Flood. If this quantity of water was in such a canopy, and was converted to rain over the entire earth during these forty days and nights at the beginning of the Flood, then the canopy would have produced 40 feet (about 12 meters) of water on the ground. Dillow also justified this figure of 40 feet (about 12 meters) of water, contained in his vapor canopy model, by recognizing that the weight of water vapor in this canopy would have increased the pressure of the atmosphere at the earth's surface. A column of water 34 feet (over 10 meters) high would produce one atmosphere of pressure (approximately 1,013 millibars) at the bottom of such a column, so 40 feet (just over 12 meters) of water in a vapor canopy on top of the air in the atmosphere would increase the total pressure (of the atmosphere plus the vapor canopy) at the earth's surface to a little more than two atmospheres (more than 2,026 millibars). He also found that another factor constraining the total pressure, and therefore the amount of water vapor that could have been in such a canopy, was that a pressure much greater than two atmospheres would have caused oxygen poisoning of human and animal life on the earth's surface.

Dillow realized that the major problem for his vapor canopy model was that there simply seemed to be no apparent mechanism by which the atmosphere, as it is presently constructed, could either hold within it, or support above it, anywhere near the required 40 feet (over 12 meters) of water as vapor. For example, it is easy to demonstrate that for a saturated atmosphere, with a sea-level temperature of 28°C (82.4°F) and in saturation-adiabatic equilibrium, the total

3   Whitcomb and Morris, 1961, 240-241, 255-258; J. C. Dillow, 1981, *The Waters Above: Earth's Pre-Flood Vapor Canopy*, Chicago: Moody Press.

4   J. C. Dillow, 1981.

precipitable water that such an atmosphere could hold is only 10.54 cm (about 4 inches).[5] Furthermore, if a massive amount of water vapor was placed above the atmosphere, distributed in hydrostatic equilibrium throughout the gravity field, it would immediately begin to diffuse toward the earth's surface, condensing and so precipitating out as rain. Thus, some kind of support mechanism would have to have held up this large amount of water vapor in such a canopy above the atmosphere that prevented downward diffusion of the water vapor. The key factor would be temperature, because higher temperatures increase the saturation vapor pressure, so that more water vapor can be maintained in each unit of volume. However, this requires the pre-Flood atmosphere to have been characterized by a different temperature structure from today's atmosphere, without the turbulent atmospheric mixing that occurs today. Indeed, because a vapor canopy would very effectively absorb infrared radiation coming upward from the earth's surface, and to a lesser degree some of the solar radiation coming down from above, a vapor canopy would automatically be much hotter than the earth's surface. Under these conditions, the changing temperature with altitude (known as the lapse rate) in the lower atmosphere would have been reversed from that experienced today, namely, the temperature would have increased with altitude from the earth's surface to the base of the canopy, rather than decrease with altitude upwards as it normally does today.

The crucial issue then becomes the question of whether under such canopy conditions the earth's surface temperature would be habitable for life, including a climate acceptable for human habitation. Thus, Dillow found that under a cloudless sky, such a vapor canopy may have resulted in the earth's surface temperature having been as high as 314°C (597°F). Nevertheless, he argued that once convection cells began to redistribute the heat of the canopy, a radiative-convective equilibrium profile would be established, with a canopy base temperature considerably less than this. Furthermore, the presence of a discontinuous cloud layer at the top of the canopy could have had the effect of reducing the solar input into the canopy-atmosphere system by as much as 35 percent, while in the lower regions of the canopy, where convective cells could have produced cloud formation, up to a 100 percent cloud layer could have been established, which would have raised the albedo of the earth considerably and thus further reduced the earth's surface temperature. With these constraints, Dillow was able to propose a temperature structure for the pre-Flood atmosphere and vapor canopy commencing with a temperature at the earth's surface of 23°C (73.4°F), and rising upwards through the atmosphere to 100°C (212°F) at the base of the vapor canopy at an altitude of 6 to 7 km (about 4 miles), before decreasing upwards through the vapor canopy at a lapse rate of 1 to 2°C per kilometer. This vertical temperature structure would have been hot enough to keep the vast amounts of water in the canopy in the form of steam vapor, and massive temperature inversion as a result of this structure would have eliminated any diffusion of vapor down into the atmosphere. The

---

5   H. R. Byers, 1974, *General Meteorology*, fourth edition, New York: McGraw Hill, 113.

daytime cloud cover would maintain pleasant temperatures at the earth's surface for human habitation, but would have cleared at night to provide uninterrupted viewing of the stars.

Nevertheless, Dillow found a major problem with his vapor canopy model. There first has to be a mechanism for providing sufficient condensation nuclei to precipitate the water vapor in the canopy as heavy continuous rainfall for forty days and nights. However, it is the total resulting heat load on the atmosphere, generated by the condensation of the vapor canopy, which causes a serious difficulty. Indeed, the latent heat of condensation of the water vapor in the canopy would have potentially resulted in the temperature of the atmosphere, as the canopy precipitated as rain, being raised by as much as 1,600°C (about 2,900°F). This is clearly intolerable! Dillow thus explored various heat loss mechanisms to alleviate the severity of this problem, such as heat loss by atmospheric expansion, by radiation, by droplet formation, by mass transport, and perhaps even by some pre-Flood cooling. Dillow also argued that the increased atmospheric pressures under the canopy would not have led to oxygen toxicity for human and animal life, and that with the resultant drop in pressure as the canopy collapsed during the early stages of the Flood, there would have been no decompression problems for Noah and his family.

Having established the potential scientific viability of his vapor canopy model, Dillow also drew on circumstantial evidences for the existence of a pre-Flood vapor canopy. Perhaps the most compelling of these circumstantial evidences is the incredible longevity of the pre-Flood patriarchs compared to their post-Flood descendants.[6] The average lifespan of the pre-Flood patriarchs (excluding Enoch) was more than 900 years, but from the time of the Flood onwards there was a dramatic decrease in the lifespans of the post-Flood patriarchs, eventually to a new equilibrium level of around 70 years. The implication is that something extremely significant happened to the earth and to man at the time of the Flood to cause this dramatic change in human lifespans. The collapse and removal of this water vapor canopy at the time of the Flood has thus been cited as the chief candidate, because it has also been argued that the existence of the vapor canopy in the pre-Flood era would have shielded the pre-Flood patriarchs from harmful cosmic radiations, which today are known to significantly contribute to the aging process. Thus, it was maintained, that the collapse of the water vapor canopy during the Flood would have removed that protection, so the genetic effects of cosmic radiations steadily accumulated in the post-Flood human population to produce the decline in lifespans that steadily increased in successive generations.

Confirmation of both the longevity of the pre-Flood human population, and of the existence of the pre-Flood vapor canopy, can be found in the mythologies of the early post-Flood civilizations. Furthermore, if there was indeed a pre-Flood

---

6   Whitcomb and Morris, 1961, 23-25, 399-405.

vapor canopy, with associated daytime cloud cover and nighttime mists, then the condensation of that vapor canopy at the time of the Flood would have left an indelible impression on the minds of Noah and his family, as they remembered the appearance of the pre-Flood heavens in comparison to the heavens after the Flood. Indeed, it is possible that, with the canopy gone, thousands of additional stars would have been visible in the post-Flood night sky, while the sun would have become a bright yellow ball, in contrast to the reddish disk in the pre-Flood cloud-covered sky. Dillow thus argued that these profound changes may well explain the prevalence of worship of the sun and stars by almost all the early post-Flood civilizations, practices that were then subsequently passed on to succeeding civilizations, even (sadly) to our present society. Finally, the higher atmospheric pressure produced by the pre-Flood vapor canopy, Dillow argued, was consistent with giantism in the fossil record; the higher atmospheric pressure produced more efficient oxygen diffusion in animal metabolism, resulting in some animals growing to giant proportions, compared to body sizes today—for example, the large dinosaurs. Furthermore, the higher atmospheric pressure would be consistent with the aerodynamics of the wingspans of gigantic flying reptiles, such as the pteranodons, the higher air pressure evidently enabling these creatures with wingspans of up to 16 meters to have taken off and flown in gentle breezes, in contrast to the strong breeze that would seem to be required by these same creatures if they were alive today.

As impressive as these arguments, circumstantial evidences, and scientific details are for the pre-Flood vapor canopy as presented by Dillow, more recent analyses have continued to raise serious problems for this vapor canopy model.[7] In these analyses of the vapor canopy, a two-layer model was chosen with an assumed surface temperature of 30°C (90°F), and a temperature at the base of the canopy of 100°C (212°F). Because the weight of the overlying water vapor in the canopy compresses the air below in the atmosphere, the base of the canopy at the top of the atmosphere was found in these analyses to occur at only about 7 km (4.35 miles), the resulting pressures being one atmosphere at the base of the canopy and two atmospheres at the earth's surface. As a result of attempting to estimate the rate of molecular diffusion of water vapor downward, which may have existed in such a vapor canopy, it was found that this vapor canopy was indeed stable, with molecular diffusion unlikely to remove a significant quantity of water vapor from it.

Even more critical is whether this vapor canopy could have been maintained in a

7   L. Vardiman, 1986, The sky has fallen, in *Proceedings of the First International Conference on Creationism*, Basic and Educational Sessions, vol 1, Pittsburgh, PA: Creation Science Fellowship, 113-119; D. E. Rush and L. Vardiman, 1990, Pre-Flood vapor canopy radiative temperature profiles, in *Proceedings of the Second International Conference on Creationism*, vol. 2, R. E. Walsh and C. L. Brooks, eds., Pittsburgh, PA: Creation Science Fellowship, 231-246; L. Vardiman and K. Bousselot, 1998, Sensitivity studies on the vapor canopy temperature profiles, in *Proceedings of the Fourth International Conference on Creationism*, R. E. Walsh, ed., Pittsburgh, PA: Creation Science Fellowship, 607-618; L. Vardiman, 2001, A vapor canopy model, in *Climates Before and After the Flood: Numerical Models and their Implications*, El Cajon, CA: Institute for Creation Research, 7-21.

balance between radiation coming from the sun, and infrared radiation coming from the earth's surface, without collapsing, and whether the resultant surface temperature conditions could have been livable under such extreme greenhouse conditions. Using computer simulations of vapor canopies containing the equivalent of 4 inches (10 cm), 20 inches (51 cm), 40 inches (102 cm), and 34 feet (more than 10 meters) of liquid water, it was found that, while vapor canopies of any magnitude could be maintained by solar radiation, only thin vapor canopies would allow livable conditions on the earth's surface. Any canopy containing more than about 20 inches (51 cm) of water produced such a strong greenhouse effect that surface temperatures became unsuitable for life, although cirrus clouds forming near the top of the canopy could possibly have alleviated this strong greenhouse effect.

With the aim of determining whether a vapor canopy could have held larger quantities of water while surface temperatures were still livable, this vapor canopy model was subjected to sensitivity studies for the effects of five constants related to the radiation balance—the solar constant (the rate of heating of the earth by the sun), the albedo (the average percent of reflective energy from the earth's surface), the solar zenith angle (the angle of the sun from the vertical), and the cirrus cloud height and thickness. Computer simulations of a vapor canopy containing the equivalent of 4 inches (10 cm) of liquid water revealed that temperatures on the earth's surface would have been most strongly affected by changes in the solar constant, a 50 percent reduction in that constant reducing the earth's surface temperature under the canopy from 60°C (140°F) to −31°C (-25°F). While the albedo, solar zenith angle, and cirrus cloud thickness also produced strong effects on the earth's surface temperature, none of the effects were dramatic enough to eliminate the concern over the water content of the canopy being limited because of resultant hot temperatures on the earth's surface. Even when all five parameters were introduced simultaneously into computer simulations, such that the earth's surface temperature was minimized, it was estimated that the water content of the canopy would only be increased to about 1 meter (about 3 feet), less than 10 percent of the water content in Dillow's vapor canopy model. Thus, in order for there to have been livable temperatures at the earth's surface, the amount of water that could have been held in a vapor canopy would not have been sufficient to contribute significantly to the rainfall, and thus the waters of the globe-encircling, mountain-covering Genesis Flood. However, there were other sources available when the Flood was initiated for both the intense global rainfall and the surface waters required to Flood the pre-Flood continent or continents (to be discussed later).[8]

---

8   J. R. Baumgardner, 1986, Numerical simulation of the large-scale tectonic changes accompanying the Flood, in *Proceedings of the First International Conference on Creationism*, vol. 2, R. E. Walsh, C. L. Brooks and R. S. Crowell, eds., Pittsburgh, PA: Creation Science Fellowship, 17-30; J. R. Baumgardner, 1990, 3-D finite element simulation of the global tectonic changes accompanying Noah's Flood, in *Proceedings of the Second International Conference on Creationism*, vol. 2, R. E. Walsh and C. L. Brooks, eds., Pittsburgh, PA: Creation Science Fellowship, 35-45; Austin et al, 1994, 609-621.

84

THE PRE-FLOOD ERA—CLIMATE CONDITIONS BEFORE THE FLOOD

If there was indeed a vapor canopy above the earth's atmosphere in the pre-Flood world, even if it only contained the equivalent of 1 meter (about 3 feet) or less of liquid water, it would still have had a profound impact on the climate in the pre-Flood world, such as large differences in temperature, atmospheric stability, cloud formation, and precipitation from that experienced in today's climate.[1] Indeed, it has been suggested that there are a number of references, in the scriptural account of the pre-Flood world, to climate factors that can be used as circumstantial evidence for the existence then of a vapor canopy.

Perhaps the most quoted biblical passage, that is regarded as both relevant and significant, is Genesis 2:5-6, where we read, "For the LORD God had not caused it to rain upon the earth, and there was not a man to till the ground. But there went up a mist from the earth, and watered the whole face of the ground." The context, as well as the text itself, indicates that these verses apply specifically to the initial completed creation, but because there is apparently no mention made subsequently in the text of these early chapters of Genesis after the Fall of any change in this climate factor, it has been argued that there was thus no rainfall at all in the pre-Flood world.[2] Furthermore, it has often been argued that this inference of no rainfall before the Flood is supported also by the mention of the rainbow in Genesis 9:11-17 after the Flood as a new sign from God to man, which in turn is interpreted as strongly implying that rain as we know it today, and thus the rainbow produced when the sun is reflected through the water droplets, were then only experienced for the first time.[3]

This specific statement in Genesis 2:5-6 unquestionably states that up until the end of the Creation Week, when man had been created and placed in the Garden of Eden, there had not been any rain. However, is there scientific support for the interpretation that there was then no rainfall subsequently in the pre-Flood world, until the Flood itself began? If a pre-Flood vapor canopy did exist, then

---

1   Vardiman, 2001, 21.

2   Whitcomb and Morris, 1961, 241-242; Dillow, 1981, 77-93.

3   Whitcomb and Morris, 1961, 241; Dillow, 1981, 93-98.

the computer simulations substantiate the claim that under canopy conditions it is quite likely that there would have been no rain on the earth's surface prior to the Flood.[4] Indeed, there is a consensus that under canopy climatic conditions, the earth's surface would have been watered by "mists," exactly as stated in Genesis 2:6. Described as going up from the earth, it has been implied that these mists may have been due to the process of evaporation from both land and water surfaces on the pre-Flood earth.[5] Indeed, because the temperatures at the earth's surface would have been colder than temperatures higher in the atmosphere under the vapor canopy, the water vapor produced by evaporation near the earth's surface would be retained there, because to transport the water vapor upward toward the canopy would require temperatures on the earth's surface higher than those at the base of the canopy.[6] However, the calculations show that there would have been some diffusion of water vapor downward from the base of the vapor canopy. Furthermore, because the temperature decreases rapidly in the atmosphere beneath the canopy base, the water vapor that diffused downward would most likely have condensed out as rain, and fallen to moisten the lower atmosphere.[7] Whether this implies that there could actually have been rainfall under a vapor canopy in the pre-Flood world via this means would depend on how much water vapor diffused down into the atmosphere. If the quantity of the water vapor was small, then its condensation in the lower atmosphere may have simply added to the water vapor evaporated from the earth's land and water surfaces to enhance the mist described in Genesis 2:6.[8]

However, the geologic record may perhaps shed some light on these questions. Of primary significance is what clearly appears to be fossilized raindrop imprints preserved in Precambrian fine-grained, water-deposited volcanic ash and sandstone beds, found deep in the geologic record in South Africa and Norway, respectively.[9] In conventional terms, these occurrences are "dated" at 2.7 billion

---

4   Dillow, 1981, 280-283; Vardiman, 2001.

5   Whitcomb and Morris, 1961, 241.

6   Vardiman, 2001, 12.

7   Vardiman, 2001, 12-13.

8   However, if as already indicated there is only a limited amount of liquid water equivalent that can be stored as vapor in the canopy to ensure livable temperatures at the earth's surface, then even with an extremely small diffusion rate of water vapor downward below the vapor canopy base there is the real possibility that in the 1,650 or more years between the Creation Week and the beginning of the Flood the entire vapor canopy may have diffused downward into the atmosphere below. For example, Vardiman (2001, pages 13 and 21) has indicated that the liquid water equivalent content of the vapor canopy could possibly be raised to as much as 1 meter (about 3 feet) without making the temperatures on the earth's surface intolerable for life, and yet he also indicates that the total amount of water vapor that might diffuse downward from the base of the vapor canopy in the 1,650 or so years in the pre-Flood era could be about 100 cm, which is exactly 1 meter (about 3 feet)! In other words, by the end of the pre-Flood era, the vapor equivalent to 1 meter of liquid water originally in a viable canopy would have all diffused down into the atmosphere, leaving no canopy at all by the time of the Flood! Any advantages to the pre-Flood climate would also have dissipated with the loss of this vapor canopy.

9   J. P. Singh, 1969, Primary sedimentary structures in Precambrian quartzites of Telemark, southern Norway, and their environmental significance, *Norsk Geologisk Tidsskrift*, 49: 1-31; W. A. Van Der

years (South Africa) and between 1.5 and 0.9 billion years (Norway), so they are here designated as belonging to the pre-Flood era. Of course, these trace fossils cannot be proved to be raindrop imprints, but careful comparison of them with present-day raindrop imprints on the surfaces of muddy sediments, complete with comparable desiccation cracks, shows a remarkable similarity that makes the case compelling. These would then be *prima facie* evidence of rainfall in the pre-Flood world. In any case, it is not unreasonable to expect that there was rainfall in the pre-Flood era, if the postulated water vapor canopy was of negligible thickness, or if the "waters above" were instead in the outer reaches of the universe.

The Hebrew word *ed* is usually translated as "mist," but old translations such as the Septuagint, Syriac text, and the Vulgate all translate the word as "spring."[10] Such a translation would seem relevant in the light of other biblical evidence for the existence of terrestrial and oceanic springs.[11] In Revelation 14:7, an angel declares, "Worship him that made heaven, and earth, and the sea, and the fountains of waters," which suggests that fountains or springs were an integral part of the created earth. It would have been the same fountains that were then "broken up" at the beginning of the Flood (Genesis 7:11, "were all the fountains of the great deep broken up"). The connotation in both the Greek and Hebrew words used in these verses, respectively, is of gushing springs where water bursts forth from inside the earth. It is also the connotation of a different Hebrew word used in Job 36, usually translated as "springs." Some, who have contended that Genesis 2:5 implies that there was definitely rain in the pre-Flood era, have thus suggested that the river that flowed through the Garden of Eden to water it, and that then split into four rivers (Genesis 2:10-14), had to be fed by these fountains or springs.[12] Of course, the biblical record does not specifically say there was a connection between these fountains or springs and the rivers on the pre-Flood earth. However, since the existence of these springs and fountains on both the land surface and the ocean floor are clearly mentioned in the Scriptures, then it is not unreasonable to expect at least some of the rivers on the pre-Flood earth were fed by springs. Furthermore, even though the Hebrew *ed* in Genesis 2:6 is probably correctly translated as "mist," the existence of springs and fountains on the pre-Flood earth is clearly mentioned in the other passages.

Westhuizen, N. J. Grobler, J. C. Loock and E. A. W. Tordiffe, 1989, Raindrop imprints in the Late Archaean-Early Proterozoic Ventersdorp Supergroup, South Africa, *Sedimentary Geology*, 61: 303-309.

10   G. J. Wenham, 1987, *Word Biblical Commentary*, vol. 1, Genesis 1-15, Waco, TX: Word Books, 58; V. P. Hamilton, 1990, *The New International Commentary on the Old Testament, The Book of Genesis chapters 1-17*, Grand Rapids, MI: William B. Eerdmans, 154.

11   For a fuller discussion on this topic in the light of relevant Hebrew words, see D. M. Fouts and K. P. Wise, 1998, Blotting and breaking up: miscellaneous Hebrew studies in geocatastrophism, in *Proceedings of the Fourth International Conference on Creationism*, R. E. Walsh, ed., Pittsburgh, PA: Creation Science Fellowship, 217-228.

12   J. Scheven, 1990, The geological record of Biblical earth history, *Origins (BCS)*, 3 (8): 8-13; J. Scheven, 1990, Stasis in the fossil record as confirmation of the belief in Biblical creation, in *Proceedings of the Second International Conference on Creationism*, vol. 1, R. E. Walsh and C. L. Brooks, eds., Pittsburgh, PA: Creation Science Fellowship, 197-215.

Nevertheless, we cannot be dogmatic that there was no rain for the entire pre-Flood era, even though Genesis 2:6 indicates that the mist "watered the whole face of the ground." In this way the pre-Flood land surface must have been well-watered and have produced lush vegetation. The latter, is of course, attested to by the huge volume of the coal beds in the geologic record. Thus, climate conditions in the pre-Flood era would seem to have been ideal for animal and human habitation across the face of the earth, and must have been generally warm and humid. Though the Scriptures are silent on the subject, it could perhaps also be inferred that there may not have been the same extremes of weather conditions that we experience on today's post-Flood earth.

It has also been claimed that, along with there being no rain prior to the Flood, there were also no climatic seasons, with a mist watering the land surface and a global greenhouse environment. However, whereas the biblical evidence for the lack of rain is somewhat equivocal, there are specific references to seasons in the pre-Flood world. In Genesis 1:14, God specifically stipulates that the "lights in the firmament of the heaven" were not only to "divide the day from the night," but were to be for "signs and for seasons, and for days, and years." Furthermore, when God spoke to Noah when he left the Ark after the Flood, we read in Genesis 8:21-22 that He reassured Noah that "while the earth remaineth, seedtime and harvest, and cold and heat, and summer and winter, and day and night shall not cease." Noah was thus reassured that, even though the world he had been familiar with before the Flood had been destroyed, and he had now alighted onto a new harsh landscape, the pattern of the days, years, and seasons he had been familiar with in the pre-Flood world would continue in the post-Flood world. This mention of cold and heat, and summer and winter, would seem to confirm that the seasons God instituted at creation did include the associated climatic changes in the pre-Flood world. Furthermore, the trees that are fossilized in what seem to be Flood sediments, and that therefore grew in the pre-Flood world, have growth rings preserved in them.[13] Because these tree rings record changes in growth rates, they indicate that at least some areas of the earth's pre-Flood land surface experienced temperate conditions before the Flood (there are characteristic patterns in the tree rings of tropical and temperate climate trees). Although there is some evidence in those same fossilized pre-Flood trees that the earth may have been a bit warmer back then compared to today, there is also evidence of wet seasons and dry seasons, and even early and late frosts. This thus indicates that there couldn't have been a global greenhouse climate on the pre-Flood earth, and this is evidence of not only seasons, but of climatic zonation.

Furthermore, the growth rings in the fossilized pre-Flood trees thus also provide evidence of rainfall that watered the ground, in addition to the mist referred to in Genesis 2:6. It has been argued that when God designated the rainbow as a sign to Noah and his family of His covenant, "the water shall no more become

---

13   K. P. Wise, 1992, Were there really no seasons? Tree rings and climate, *Creation Ex Nihilo Technical Journal*, 6 (2): 168-172.

a flood to destroy all flesh" (Genesis 9:12-17), this implies that Noah and his family had not previously seen a rainbow in the pre-Flood world, and therefore, there could not have been clouds and rainfall in the pre-Flood world. However, God refers to clouds covering the earth during Creation Week (Job 38:9). In any case, it is not unusual in Scripture for the sign of a covenant to already be occurring prior to its appropriation and designation by God.[14] Examples include the practice of circumcision prior to the covenant with Abraham, the practice of the Sabbath instituted and followed at creation (Genesis 2:1-3; Mark 2:27) prior to the covenant with Israel at the giving of the law (Exodus 16:23, 20:8-11), and the breaking of bread and drinking of wine as a normal activity prior to them being designated as a sign of the new covenant by Christ (Matthew 26:26-29).

Thus, all the evidence taken together from Scripture and the geologic record would strongly suggest that there was rainfall in the pre-Flood world, and that there was climatic zonation from the equator to the poles, and according to topography. There were also seasons. We are given no hint as to by how much the topography varied, except that the Garden of Eden was at a high elevation, due to the river flowing from it dividing into four other rivers as it flowed downhill (Genesis 2:10-14). Perhaps the climatic differences between geographical regions were not as extreme as those we experience today, but we cannot be sure. Perhaps the elevated regions obtained higher rainfall and caused drier inland regions, in much the same way as happens today. Just where the pre-Flood continent(s) were situated relative to the equator and the poles is very uncertain, but if continent reconstructions based on the unraveling of the geologic record are in any way feasible, it may be that the pre-Flood land surface was largely concentrated in a supercontinent (conventionally called Rodinia) centered over the tropical to temperate portion of one half of the Southern Hemisphere.[15] This would be consistent with the climate data available from the growth rings in fossilized trees. Note also that there is no evidence to suggest that there were polar ice caps or glacial conditions anywhere on the pre-Flood earth surface.

---

14   K. P. Wise, 2002, *Faith, Form, and Time*, Nashville, TN: Broadman and Holman Publishers, 265.

15   Wise, 2002, 151. This theoretical supercontinent of Rodinia is in conventional terms dated to the earlier Neoproterozoic, which would be consistent with the interpretation here of that part of the geologic record that pertains to the pre-Flood world.

85

THE PRE-FLOOD ERA—THE BIOLOGY AND GEOLOGY

Some Unique Pre-Flood Biological Communities

The brief description of selected aspects of the pre-Flood earth given in the Scriptures can potentially be augmented by details preserved in the geologic record. Among the many fossils found in the post-Cambrian strata are some unusual plants that make up many of the coal beds of the Northern Hemisphere. Most of these plants are now extinct, though some of their relatives have survived into the present world but are today diminutive and minor compared to the huge volume of these plants found almost exclusively making up the thick coal beds, which stretch across many parts of the Northern Hemisphere. These plants had hollow roots and hollow trunks, but nevertheless grew to heights of ten meters and more, judging from the sizes of trunks found preserved, many times buried in upright positions. Such huge trees could not have grown in soils, for their roots would have been crushed. Instead, they must have grown in water. Indeed, the coal beds composed of the fossilized remains of these plants are buried by, and are interbedded with, sediments containing fossils of sea creatures, which indicates that these plants must have grown in the ocean basins of the pre-Flood world.

Based upon these observations, it has been proposed that these plants formed the basis of a large floating forest community (or biome) that grew on the pre-Flood ocean surface.[1] Given the lateral extent of the coal beds containing the fossilized remains of these plants, these floating forests may have been sub-continent-size, or even continent-size, which would in turn suggest that enormous stretches of the pre-Flood ocean surface were covered with these floating forests. These were perhaps similar in basic structure to what are known today as "quaking bogs," which are floating vegetation mats with outer edges made up of aquatic plants. Such plants expand the edge of the mat by means of root-like rhizomes. In from the edge of the mat, where the plants have been growing for some time, the

---

1   J. Scheven, 1981, Floating forests on firm grounds: advances in Carboniferous research, *Biblical Creation (Journal of the Biblical Creation Society)*, 3 (9): 36-43; Wise, 2002, 170-173; K. P. Wise, 2003, The pre-Flood floating forest: a study in paleontological pattern recognition, in *Proceedings of the Fifth International Conference on Creationism*, R. Ivey, ed., Pittsburgh, PA: Creation Science Fellowship, 371-381.

rhizomes have become so intertwined that they are dense enough to have captured some soil, in which land plants can then grow. In the center of the floating mat, where it is thicker and has been established longer, enough soil accumulates for larger plants to grow, so that full-sized trees and all the understory plants of the entire forest would have developed. Of course, such a floating forest would have formed an entire complex ecosystem, complete with everything from bacteria and fungi to other plants and also animals.

The existence of this floating forest biome in the pre-Flood world also has implications for the prevailing weather patterns. Given that the stormy seas during the Flood must have broken up and destroyed these floating forests, so that they were buried to become the coal beds, their absence in the post-Flood world would suggest that the choppy seas we experience today as a result of weather patterns were not conducive to these floating forests being able to grow again under such conditions. This in turn implies that the weather was not stormy enough, nor the seas choppy enough, in the pre-Flood world to disrupt the existence of these huge floating forest mats. In any case, if much of the ocean surface was covered with these floating forests, then the winds would generally not have had the open stretches of water to blow across and thus generate large waves. This in turn suggests that weather conditions in the pre-Flood world were generally calm, without the extremes we now experience, such as hurricanes that form over tropical ocean surfaces.

This pre-Flood floating-forest biome explains a number of features observed in the fossil record. The various members of this ecosystem are found buried in the Paleozoic portion of the geologic record, deposited during the Flood. From then on, most of these seemingly land plants and animals are absent from the record and are extinct today. It would be expected that, as the Flood began to destroy these pre-Flood floating forest mats, the edges would be broken off first, and thus buried first, while the centers of the mats would be last to be destroyed and buried. This explains the fossil progression observed in the Paleozoic geologic record. Plants on the edges of such floating forests were plants that love water, required standing water for reproduction, and were short. On the other hand, plants at the centers of these floating forests needed less water to survive, and less standing water for reproduction, as well as being tall. Such a progression is seen in plant fossils up through the Paleozoic strata, and in the presumed land animals that were associated with the different plants in this ecosystem (for example, certain now extinct tetrapods and amphibians, and well as large insects, that are unique and confined to the Paleozoic fossil record). Most of the fossil plants in Paleozoic strata have, instead of roots, rhizomes that are root-like structures incapable of penetrating through soils, but capable of intertwining with the rhizomes of other plants to have created the floating forests. Furthermore, many of these Paleozoic plants, especially the large ones, have rhizomes, branches, and even trunks that are largely hollow due to huge cavities, an ideal design for the entire plant to weigh less so that it would float in water. Indeed, *Stigmaria*, the most common rhizome in the plants that make up the coal beds, is hollow and circular in cross-section, with small, hollow rootlets branching off them. Neither these rhizomes nor the rootlets seem capable of penetrating soils, but would be ideal to support the floating in water of the large hollow trunks of the coal plants.

Another biological community that must have been unique to the pre-Flood era is that made up of the dinosaurs, and the plants and other animals found fossilized with them, in the Mesozoic portion of the geologic record.[2] Since the dinosaurs were land animals, they must have been created on Day Six of the Creation Week, and thus have lived on the earth at the same time as man in the pre-Flood world, only to be subsequently buried in sediments and become extinct due to the Flood. In the strata in which we find the dinosaurs fossilized are found other fossilized animals and plants that are either extinct or seen only infrequently. Among these fossilized animals are those that have been classified as mammals based upon their teeth, but they are strange mammals that are now extinct. Flowering plants are only rarely found fossilized with dinosaurs. Instead, the "naked seed" plants, or *gymnosperms*, that do not have flowers (like cycads and ginkgos), are found fossilized with the dinosaurs. It appears the dinosaurs probably ate gymnosperms rather than flowering plants, unlike humans. Thus, the gymnosperms probably formed the basis of a biome with dinosaurs separate from the one in which humans lived with flowering plants. Furthermore, it is likely that this gymnosperm-dinosaur biome was located at a lower altitude to the angiosperm-human biome, because the inference from Scripture is that the Garden of Eden and surrounding areas were at a high point geographically, as the river that flowed out of Eden split into four rivers in the surrounding areas (Genesis 2:10-14), and water flows downhill.

The existence of springs on the sea floor is mentioned in Job 38:16, which must surely identify the nature of some of the "fountains of waters" referred to in Revelation 14:7. For much of the Precambrian rock record, the only fossils found are generally dome-shaped structures known as stromatolites, which are made up of layers of organic material alternating with sediment particles, often lime sand. Indeed, these fossilized stromatolites are prolific in the Proterozoic portion of the geologic record, but are virtually absent from the Cambrian upwards. They have only survived to be relatively rare and small in the present world, where they tend to grow in extreme environments, such as hot springs or salty bays. The organic layers of modern stromatolites are composed of communities of cyanobacteria or blue-green algae that grow as an organic mat on a limey sediment surface, where they would provide food for any browsing animals that could survive in the hot and salty conditions. Since the springs on the ocean floor today are salty, hot water (hydrothermal) springs, and since the fossilized stromatolites are usually preserved

---

2   Wise, 2002, 173-174.

in limey sedimentary rocks that also show signs of having been deposited from hydrothermal waters, it seems reasonable to postulate a stromatolite hydrothermal biome in the pre-Flood world.[3] Indeed, the limestones of the Precambrian rock record are dominated by dolomites (magnesium-rich limestone), rather than the usual limestones that are calcium-rich, and this is a puzzle that is solved once it is recognized these dolomites were deposited from hydrothermal springs.

The peak occurrence of fossilized stromatolites in the Precambrian rock record is in the middle to upper Mesoproterozoic and the Neoproterozoic, from around 1,400 to 600 million years ago in conventional dating (see Figure 20), which is the level in the rock record that seems to equate to sedimentation on the pre-Flood ocean floor. Many sites where fossilized stromatolites are found in these sediments tend to have a lot of evidence of hot spring activity, and seem to be located near what could have been the margins of the pre-Flood continent(s). It is thus postulated that around the pre-Flood continent(s) there existed offshore a long, wide zone of hot springs, which generated ideal living conditions for algae and bacteria to produce extensive fringing stromatolite reefs. These springs may have been related to the "fountains of the great deep" that were broken up at the onset of the Flood (Genesis 7:11). That catastrophic break-up would have destroyed those stromatolite reefs, and the hot springs, so that those stromatolite reefs no longer exist in the present world. The influence of these hot springs upon sedimentation on the pre-Flood ocean floor is also potentially illustrated by the occurrence of hydrothermally-deposited banded-iron formations in this part of the geologic record (see Figures 10 and 26). Furthermore, the offshore stromatolite reefs would have protected a lagoon between the reefs and the shoreline, where many multicellular organisms would have lived, leaving traces of their existence in the quiet sedimentation on the shallow sea floor, and perhaps occasionally their remains were buried and fossilized (see Figure 21).

The existence in the pre-Flood world of these distinct and geographically separated biological communities or biomes suggests that there was strong ecological zonation related to altitude, topography, and climatic zones. This would have its ramifications subsequently, when during the Flood the waters steadily rose up onto the pre-Flood continent(s) to progressively inundate these biomes and fossilize their animals and plants. This may potentially explain the order we see in the fossil record (to be further discussed later).

Geologic Activity in the Pre-Flood World

While the Scriptures are obviously silent on this issue, because of their abbreviated description of earth history (three chapters describing more than 1,650 years),

---

3   Wise, 2002, 174-175; K. P. Wise, 2003, The hydrothermal biome: a pre-Flood environment, in
     Proceedings of the Fifth International Conference on Creationism, R. Ivey, ed., Pittsburgh, PA: Creation
     Science Fellowship, 359-370; K. P. Wise and A. A. Snelling, 2005, A note on the pre-Flood/Flood
     boundary in the Grand Canyon, *Origins (Geoscience Research Institute)*, 58: 7-29.

it is still possible to infer that the pre-Flood earth was stable with no major catastrophe, and the geologic record would seem to confirm this. We are told in Genesis 7:11 that the Flood began with the breaking up of "the fountains of the great deep," a vivid description of catastrophic geologic activity. This implies that whatever caused this "breaking up" was restrained in the pre-Flood world. The Hebrew phrase translated "the great deep" is used in Scripture to refer to both oceanic and subterranean waters (Isaiah 51:10 and Psalm 78:15, respectively),[4] so as indicated previously, "the fountains of the great deep" were oceanic and terrestrial springs that clearly tapped the plentiful waters then residing within the earth's crust. Thus, the geologic activity referred to by the term "breaking up" must imply deep fracturing of the earth's crust, dramatic earth movements, and devastating earthquakes. Such geologic activity on a global scale must have been restrained and thus absent in the pre-Flood world.

Nevertheless, we cannot be so dogmatic about geologic activity in the pre-Flood world on a local scale, except to infer from the geologic record that any such activity had to be mild in its effects, otherwise there would have been some destruction of larger multi-cellular organisms, which would thus be found in the geologic record pertaining to this era. The fossil record in the Mesoproterozoic and Neoproterozoic consists almost exclusively of stromatolites, whose fossilization and preservation was a consequence of their growth in the sediments being deposited adjacent to the hydrothermal springs, due to the precipitation of calcium and magnesium carbonates and silica from the spring waters, and detrital material being washed onto the shallow sea floor from the adjacent land surfaces by rivers and tidal action. There is thus good reason to suppose that there was an ongoing steady accumulation of thick sequences of sediments on the pre-Flood ocean floor, especially carbonates and cherts in association with hydrothermal springs, but with the detrital contribution from weathering and erosion of the pre-Flood land surface. Where the prolific moist climatic conditions occurred, continuing deep chemical weathering would have been facilitated, and both the springs and the rainfall would have facilitated erosion of detritus into the pre-Flood rivers, which washed the sand, silt, and mud out to the ocean, just as happens in the present world. Nevertheless, the unique catastrophic conditions necessary for burial and fossilization of larger multi-cellular organisms were absent. Only bare traces of the passage across the sea floor of the occasional browsing organism have been preserved in the resulting rock record.

It is abundantly evident that by the time of the Flood there was a significant thickness of all types of sediments available on the earth's surface.[5] There are three reasons for believing this to be the case. First, the biologically optimum terrestrial and marine environments created during the Creation Week would have resulted

---

4   Whitcomb and Morris, 1961, 242; D. M. Fouts and K. P. Wise, 1998, Blotting and breaking up: miscellaneous Hebrew studies in geocatastrophism, in *Proceedings of the Fourth International Conference on Creationism*, R. E. Walsh, ed., Pittsburgh, PA: Creation Science Fellowship, 222.

5   Austin et al, 1994, Catastrophic plate tectonics, 611.

in at least a small amount of sediment of each type having been created, in just the same way as God prepared the soil on the land surface for the plants He then created. Second, Archean and Proterozoic sediments, most of which date from the Creation Week and pre-Flood eras, contain substantial quantities of all types of sediments. Third, there is the practicality that it may not be possible to derive all the Flood sediments from igneous and/or metamorphic precursors by chemical weathering and physical erosion processes in the course of a single year-long flood. Indeed, substantial quantities of very fine detrital carbonate sediment must have existed in the pre-Flood oceans, primarily because not enough bicarbonate could have been dissolved in the pre-Flood ocean waters to produce the carbonate strata deposited during the Flood, unless substantial quantities were provided by outgassing of mantle and crustal fluids during the Flood. The existence of large quantities of mature, or nearly mature, pre-Flood quartz sand would certainly explain the otherwise puzzling clean, mature nature of the sandstones in the early Paleozoic portion of the geologic record, deposited early in the Flood (see below).

If as suggested such large quantities of very fine detrital carbonate sediments existed on the pre-Flood ocean floor, then there would have been a substantial chemical buffer in the pre-Flood ocean, perhaps contributing to very stable pre-Flood ocean water chemistry. This in turn would suggest that the water in the pre-Flood ocean was somewhat salty. However, just how saline is unknown. Salt crystals have been found in sedimentary strata that are believed to have been sediments on the pre-Flood ocean floor, but it may be that the salinity was only high in the region where these sediments were deposited in proximity to the hydrothermal springs.[6] Alternately, if the oceans were originally created with fresh water, then their saltiness today could have been caused during the Flood with all the volcanic emissions and erosion. However, it is more likely the pre-Flood oceans were originally saline, though not as salty as the ocean waters are today. Organisms that can only live in salt water today, for example, are very common as fossils in the sedimentary strata attributed to the Flood. Nevertheless, the many varieties of each kind of organism we see today are testimony to the fact that organisms were created with great potential for change. Thus, we find that some kinds of organisms have varieties that live in fresh water today and have closely related varieties that live in salt water, while some organisms can live in both fresh and salt water, and some can even migrate between the two. Thus, it is entirely possible that freshwater organisms before the Flood were able to adapt to salt water after the Flood. However, it is most likely the pre-Flood ocean water was salty, not only because of the evidence of saltiness found in pre-Flood sediments, but because this would require less biological transformation after the Flood.

While it is clearly evident that extensive sedimentation occurred on the pre-Flood ocean floor, it is not possible to be as dogmatic about the level of volcanic and/

---

6   Wise, 2002, 152; Wise and Snelling, 2005.

or tectonic activity in the pre-Flood world. Obviously, any volcanic or tectonic activity in the pre-Flood world would have to have been minimal, so as not to threaten the human population, at the very least. However, there must have been some volcanic activity, because we do find the remains of lava flows buried among the pre-Flood sediments, and there appear to be granites and other igneous rocks intruded into them. This is consistent with the operation of the hydrothermal springs ("fountains of the great deep") that would have required active heat sources to drive their water flow, in much the same way as hot water springs do today. Minor igneous activity in the pre-Flood world is not unreasonable as an aftermath to the much more extensive volcanic and igneous activity that must have occurred early in the Creation Week, during the formation of the earth's crust and the building of the dry land, as is evident from the rock record pertaining to that period of earth history. Perhaps most or all the volcanic and intrusive activity, and the associated tectonic movements, occurred in the ocean basins, and the areas proximal to the continental margins.

What is abundantly clear from the geologic record pertaining to the pre-Flood era is that much geologic activity, including the erosion and deposit of sediments, could in no way have been catastrophic in intensity or in geographical extent, for otherwise conditions suitable for fossilization would have resulted. Indeed, the most significant aspect of the pre-Flood geologic record is the almost total absence of fossilized organisms. Thus, in spite of erosion and deposition of sediments, and occasional somewhat muted volcanic, intrusive, and tectonic activity, the affects of these geologic processes were either sufficiently reduced in intensity, or remote geographically, to have had no destructive effect on all pre-Flood animal and plant life, except for some bacteria and algae, and some microorganisms. Nevertheless, in spite of the comparative quiescence geologically of the pre-Flood era, implied by the brief biblical record of it, there must still have been a steady build-up during the pre-Flood era of heat, magmas, and tectonic forces, held under restraint in readiness to be catastrophically unleashed at just the precise moment in earth and human history to trigger the Flood judgment under God's ultimate control.

86

THE FLOOD—A GLOBAL TECTONIC CATASTROPHE

There can be no doubt as to exactly how the Flood began, because the Scriptures give us a vivid description of the defining moment. In Genesis 7:11 we read, "The same day were all the fountains of the great deep broken up, and the windows of heaven were opened." Here the Bible claims that all these fountains were broken up on a single day to trigger the commencement of the Flood, the major geologic event in the history of the earth, second only to the creation of the earth itself during the Creation Week. The sense of the Hebrew word for "breaking up" appears to be that of cleaving open and shattering of the earth's crust. The description in Genesis 7:11 would also seem to imply that breaking up the earth's crust around these fountains almost simultaneously triggered the opening of "the windows of heaven," or the flood-gates, resulting in global torrential rainfall for forty days and nights.

As to exactly what was responsible for causing "the fountains of the great deep" to be broken up, the Scriptures are silent. Therefore, this has been the subject of much speculation, both reasonable and fanciful. Suggestions have included the passage of the earth through a meteorite storm, and sudden volcanic explosions that propelled large amounts of volcanic dust high into the atmosphere,[1] the impact or near-miss of an astronomical object(s), such as asteroids, meteorites, a comet, another moon of the earth, or even Venus, Mars, or Jupiter,[2] the natural collapse of rings of ice that were once around the earth, or perhaps even just radioactive heat build-up within the earth until a critical level was reached.[3] Of

---

1   Whitcomb and Morris, 1961, 258.

2   D. W. Unfred, 1984, Asteroidal impacts and the Flood-judgment, *Creation Research Society Quarterly*, 21 (2): 82-87; W. S. Parks, 1989, The role of meteorites in a creationist cosmology, *Creation Research Society Quarterly*, 26 (4): 144-146; D. W. Patten, 1966, *The Biblical Flood and the Ice Epoch: A Study in Scientific History*, Seattle, WA: Pacific Meridian; R. L. Whitelaw, 1983, The fountains of the great deep and the windows of heaven: a look at the canopy theory, and a better alternative, in *Science at the Crossroads: Observation or Speculation?*, Papers of the 1983 National Creation Conference, Minneapolis, MN: Bible-Science Association, 95-104.

3   J. F. Henry, 1992, Space age astronomy confirms a recent and special creation, in *Proceedings of the 1992 Twin-Cities Creation Conference*, St. Paul, MN: Twin Cities Association, 88-90; For full referencing of all these and other suggestions, see Austin et al, 1994, 609-621.

course, it cannot be ruled out that God directly intervened.[4] In any case, whether God directly or indirectly intervened, numerous Scriptures insist that God was (and is) always ultimately in control according to His sovereign will, even if some apparently natural means was involved. The result was the same—catastrophic cracking and movement of the earth's crust surrounding springs on the pre-Flood ocean floor and possibly also the land surface, which by implication produced a simultaneous release and outpouring of water, steam, and molten rock, with the accompanying explosions blasting volcanic ash and pulverized rock into the earth's atmosphere, where it would have combined with the steam and water to produce heavy, sustained rainfall.

A Global Tectonic Catastrophe

Tectonics refers to the development and relationship of the larger structural and deformational features of the broad architecture of the outer part of the earth. Thus, given the description in Genesis 7:11 of the breaking up of the earth's crust wherever the fountains or springs were located qualifies as a significant tectonic event. The earth's cold outer layer, known as its *lithosphere*, is broken into a number of different pieces or plates that today exhibit imperceptibly slow residual movement along their boundaries relative to one another. At these boundaries, or adjacent to them, the motions of the plates relative to one another generate earthquakes and volcanic activity. The theory of plate tectonics has been developed to describe and explain the motion of these plates and has been successful in building a consistent explanation of many of the earth's current surface, and internal structural and geophysical, features.[5] The fact that the case is strong that all the present igneous ocean floor has been formed by sea floor spreading at mid-ocean ridges since much of the fossil-bearing sedimentary rock sequence had already been deposited on the continents means that a large amount of sea floor spreading and plate motion must logically have been an integral part of the Flood catastrophe. This implies that the entire pre-Flood ocean floor and much of the sea floor formed during the early stages of the Flood must have been recycled into the earth's interior in a very rapid manner. It can be shown that the gravitational potential energy associated with the pre-Flood ocean lithosphere is indeed capable of driving such a cataclysm. This model for the global Flood catastrophe has come to be called *catastrophic plate tectonics*,[6] with the gradual motions of crustal plates

---

4   G. R. Morton, 1980, Prolegomena to the study of the sediments, *Creation Research Society Quarterly*, 17 (3): 162-167; G. R. Morton, 1987, *The Geology of the Flood*, Dallas, TX: DMD.; J. R. Baumgardner, 1987, Numerical simulation of the large-scale tectonic changes accompanying the Flood, in *Proceedings of the First International Conference on Creationism*, vol. 2, R. E. Walsh, C. L. Brooks and R. S. Crowell, eds., Pittsburgh, PA: Creation Science Fellowship, 17-30; J. R. Baumgardner, 1990, 3-D finite element simulation of the global tectonic changes accompanying Noah's Flood, in *Proceedings of the Second International Conference on Creationism*, R. E. Walsh and C. L. Brooks, eds., Pittsburgh, PA: Creation Science Fellowship, 35-45.

5   K. C. Condie, 1997, *Plate Tectonics and Crustal Evolution*, fourth edition, Oxford, UK: Butterworth Heinemann.

6   Austin et al, 1994.

today being merely residual effects of the cataclysm.

To understand how plate tectonics theory might be a viable framework for understanding the global Flood tectonic catastrophe, it is important first to describe the essential elements of that theory as it pertains to present-day observations. In today's ocean basins are found broad linear chains of mountains, approximately midway between the continents. These are called mid-ocean ridges, and they extend throughout the ocean basins, linking up with one another to encircle the globe. At the axes of these mid-ocean ridges are rift valleys, which are the sites of volcanic activity accompanied by earthquakes. The elevation of the mid-ocean ridges is due to uplift caused by hotter than average mantle rock beneath them These higher temperatures are the result of hot mantle rock rising from below to fill the gap caused by the diverging plates on either side of the ridge. Because the melting temperature of silicate minerals decreases with decreasing pressure, as this hot mantle rock rises, some of the minerals in the rising rock find themselves above their melting points, so they begin to melt and separate from the remainder of the rock, before the melting point of the entire rock is reached. The resulting partial melt does not contain all the minerals of the original rock, so it has a different composition. The lavas produced by the volcanic activity along the mid-ocean ridges are basalts, which have been demonstrated in the laboratory to form from the partial melting of the rocks that are known to exist in the earth's upper mantle. Thus, according to plate tectonics theory, mantle rock rising beneath the mid-ocean ridges undergoes partial melting along the rift zones at the mid-ocean ridge axes, and the resulting melt of basaltic composition is intruded and extruded to form new oceanic crust. The axial zones of the mid-ocean ridges are thus the boundaries between crustal plates on either side of them. New basaltic crust forms there as the plates on either side move apart from the axial rift zones, in what is thus known as sea floor spreading. Thus, the entire ocean floor underneath the thin veneer of sediments consists of basaltic oceanic crust, which is older the further away it is from the axes of the mid-ocean ridges. Just as the volcanic activity along the axial rift zones is fed by molten basalt from partially melted mantle rock, so likewise are other volcanoes across the ocean floor fed by basalt from partially melted mantle rock below them to produce the basalts that make up those volcanoes and volcanic islands (e.g., the Hawaiian Islands).

As the newly-forming oceanic lithosphere, capped with an approximately six-kilometer-thick basaltic crust, moves away from the active ridge, it cools, contracts, becomes denser, and therefore begins to sink and become lower in elevation relative to the active ridge. Ocean lithosphere consists of the surface layer of basaltic crust and a layer beneath it of relatively cool mantle rock that can vary in thickness from zero near the ridge axis to as much as 80 km at about 2,000 km or more away. The base of the lithosphere is defined by the transition from strong, mostly elastic/brittle behavior to weaker more plastic behavior due to higher temperature. As the oceanic lithosphere cools, shrinks, and ages as it spreads away from the mid-ocean ridge, any volcanoes on it that once stood up above the ocean water surface eventually sink also, becoming extinct as they are covered by ocean water to produce submarine mountains, or seamounts. If wave action erodes away their peak leaving them with a flat top, these seamounts are known as *guyots*. The older the oceanic lithosphere gets as it spreads away from the mid-ocean ridges, the more time there is for sediments to accumulate over it, so we observe that the total sediment thicknesses and the ages of the deepest sediments increase away from the mid-ocean ridges.

Since the warm oceanic lithosphere at the mid-ocean ridges is only newly formed, it has only cooled to shallow depth. Thus, the earthquakes that occur along the mid-ocean ridges, as a result of the masses of solid rock moving past one another, are restricted to shallow depths. As expected, these earthquakes along the ridge axes are extensional, reflecting the separation of the plates. It is common for a ridge axis to display abrupt jumps or offsets. Such offsets between segments of ridge axis create what are known as fracture zones. The sections of lithosphere on opposite sides of a fracture zone between segments of ridge axis move in opposite directions. As predicted by plate tectonics theory, the earthquakes caused by movement of the rocks sliding past one another along these features are restricted to the portions of the fracture zones found between the active spreading ridges, because only here does the side-by-side motion of the rocks occur.

A minor mineral within basalts is magnetite, an iron oxide mineral that is magnetic. As the molten basalt cools, magnetite grains form, and as they do they become magnetized in the direction of the earth's magnetic field prevailing at that time. Consequently, new basaltic oceanic crust forming in the rift zones along the spreading axes of the mid-ocean ridges records the present direction of the earth's magnetic field. As the newly formed crust moves away in both directions from the ridge because of sea floor spreading, the crustal rock at equal distance on either side of the spreading axis represents basalt formed at the same time and therefore will display the same orientation of its magnetic minerals. If the earth's magnetic field then changes its orientation, the magnetism recorded by the basalts forming at the spreading axis likewise changes its orientation. Many independent lines of evidence indicate the earth's magnetic field has reversed it polarity numerous times in the past. Multiple reversals have produced a series of bands (or stripes) of alternating magnetic orientations recorded in the basaltic ocean crust paralleling the mid-ocean ridges, and these parallel bands display a high degree of symmetry on opposite sides of the ridge. It was the discovery of this symmetric pattern of stripes of rock magnetized in alternating directions on opposite sides of the mid-ocean ridges in the early 1960s that provided some of the early persuasive support for the concept of sea floor spreading.

As the oceanic lithosphere cools, it becomes increasingly denser relative to the mantle rock beneath it, because of its cooler temperature. However, continental lithosphere has a much lower average density than oceanic lithosphere and also the underlying mantle because of the layer, typically about 35 km thick, of buoyant continental crust it includes that typically lies above a layer of cool mantle rock to form the lithospheric slab. Continental crust has a granitic composition that is typically about 20 percent less dense than mantle rock at the same temperature. The low density of the continental crust causes a column of continental lithosphere to "float" higher in the mantle than an equal mass column of oceanic lithosphere. This maintains continental land surfaces about 4 to 5 kilometers higher than the ocean bottom, and above sea level. On the other hand, because cold oceanic lithosphere is so much denser than the mantle beneath it, it has the natural tendency to peel away and sink into the mantle. This process is called *subduction*.

Where an oceanic plate plunges into the mantle, the ocean floor is also pulled downwards and becomes depressed to produce a long linear feature known as an ocean trench. That subduction is indeed occurring today is confirmed by the earthquakes generated as sinking slabs enter into the mantle. These earthquakes originate at the depths where the top of the sinking oceanic slab slides beneath the adjacent plate. As expected, the depths of these earthquakes increase as one moves beyond the trench in the direction of subduction. These earthquakes are compressional, as expected. The crustal portion of the subducting slab contains a significant amount of surface water, as well as water contained in hydrated minerals within the basalt itself. As the subducting slab descends to greater and greater depths, it progressively encounters greater temperatures and greater pressures that cause the surface rocks to release water into the mantle wedge overlying the descending plate. Water has the effect of lowering the melting temperature of the mantle wedge, thus causing it to melt. The magma produced by this mechanism varies from basalt to andesite in composition. It rises upward to produce a linear belt of volcanoes parallel to the oceanic trench. A good example of this is observed in the volcanoes of the Andes of South America, which parallel the trench offshore along the adjacent western coastline.

These and many other features of the present-day earth are explained by the theory of plate tectonics, particularly the geology and features of the earth's ocean basins. This huge number of diverse geological features readily explained by plate tectonics theory gives confidence in projecting motions of the earth's current plates backward in time. That plate tectonics is not only active today, but has been active in the earth's past, is indicated by the increasing "ages" of rocks on the ocean floor away from the mid-ocean ridges, and the accompanying parallel stripes of rocks magnetized with alternating magnetic polarity.

Furthermore, there is abundant evidence on the continents that they have moved across the earth's surface relative to one another. For example, it has long been recognized that the continents on either side of the Atlantic Ocean have complementary shapes, suggesting that at some time in the past they formed a single supercontinent, which subsequently broke apart, and as the continental fragments drifted apart, the Atlantic Ocean basin was formed. Supporting this conclusion are many geological features that can be matched across the continents on either side of the Atlantic Ocean, but are not found on the ocean floor. These include almost identical rock strata, fossils, directions of sediment transport, the occurrence of mountain fold belts, and mineral deposits. There are similar matchings between Antarctica and Australia, and between Antarctica and India. Between the continents on either side of the Atlantic Ocean, and between these other continent pairs, there are mid-ocean ridges and ocean sediments that increase in "age" away from those ridges. Moreover, these ridges and ocean sediments are younger than the geological features that match on the continents on either side of the ocean basins. This is precisely the evidence we would expect to find had these continents once been together but later became separated, with the generation of new oceanic crust as a result of sea floor spreading between them.

Further evidence in continental rocks for the movement of continents across the earth's surface is the history of the directions of the earth's magnetic field preserved in continental rocks. This record of changing magnetic field directions indicates that the continents have moved with respect to the earth's magnetic poles. The relative motions implied by this record of rock paleomagnetism are called polar wander curves, because they were interpreted originally to be a result of movements of the earth's magnetic poles with respect to the continents. However, it was then discovered that, if the continents themselves are assumed to have been motionless, the polar wander curves from different continents were in conflict with one another. If, on the other hand, the continents have moved with respect to one another, as indicated by much geological evidence, but the magnetic poles have remained nearly fixed in position, then it was found that the polar wander curves coincide, just as one would expect from plate tectonic theory.

Given the vast explanatory power that the plate tectonics theory provides in accounting for so many of the presently observed features of the earth, can this theory also provide any insights for what happened during the Flood, which, based on the scriptural description, certainly appears to have involved global tectonic upheaval? Because the same natural laws that govern the operation of geologic processes today may well have been in operation during the Flood, it is possible that the geologic processes and events that occurred during the Flood may be geological processes and events that we are familiar with today, except that during the Flood they operated on larger and more rapid scales. It is noteworthy that, even though the plate tectonics theory has been successful in explaining many diverse geological features, other geological evidence cannot so simply be explained by projecting present plate motions and processes uniformly back into the past. For example, in some ocean trenches the sediments are flat-lying and undisturbed, rather than being deformed due to ongoing plate motion as predicted by standard plate tectonics theory. Also, all the high mountain ranges of the world, including the Himalayas, Alps, Andes, and Rockies, rose at an extremely high rate during the Pliocene/Pleistocene epochs, in conflict with the near constant plate motions assumed by standard uniformitarian plate tectonics theory. Such evidences are sometimes used as reasons to reject plate tectonics completely, but a better explanation appears to be that plate tectonics operated differently during and immediately after the Flood than it does today.

87

CATASTROPHIC PLATE TECTONICS—THE DRIVING FORCE OF THE FLOOD

As has been pointed out earlier, many lines of evidence indicate that the basaltic crust of all today's ocean floor is younger than the Paleozoic portion of the continental fossil-bearing sediment record. This, together with the convincing evidence that the basaltic oceanic crust forms at mid-ocean ridges as the direct result of sea floor spreading, means that the case is strong that the Flood catastrophe, if the fossil record represents its signature, involved a huge amount of sea floor spreading. It logically implies that all the pre-Flood ocean lithosphere was recycled into the earth's interior during a few month's time, which in turn means that rapid plate motions and tectonic catastrophism occurred on a vast scale during the Flood.[1] Cold dense ocean lithosphere lying above much hotter and therefore less dense mantle rock beneath it represents a huge store of gravitational potential energy. The rapid sinking of the pre-Flood ocean lithosphere to the base of the mantle transforms this vast store of potential energy into heat and mechanical work. Even a tiny fraction of this energy unleashed at the earth's surface is capable of driving a staggering amount of geological process. Because plate tectonics processes account for so many of the earth's physical characteristics largely independent of the rates of these processes, it is proposed here also that a catastrophic version of plate tectonics, which we refer to as catastrophic plate tectonics, is a viable model that can plausibly explain the processes that operated during the Flood to produce the geologic record.

But a critical issue is how the mantle of the earth could possibly become weak enough to allow slabs of oceanic plate to sink through it in only a matter of a few weeks. On timescales on the order of a second or so, that is, on the timescales of seismic waves, the elastic strength of mantle rock is almost that of steel! This result, recognized in the early days of seismology, is obtained simply and directly from the speed of seismic waves through the earth. On longer timescales, however, mantle rock deforms in a plastic manner by the migration of defects at the atomic level, via a class of processes known as solid-state creep. One can characterize the strength of mantle rock in this creep deformation regime in terms of a shear

---

1   Austin et al, 1994, 609-621.

viscosity.

There are multiple ways for estimating the viscous strength of mantle rock. One approach is to measure the properties of its constituent minerals, or even entire samples of the rock itself, in the laboratory under the appropriate temperature and pressure conditions. Another approach has been to infer the viscous strength of the upper mantle from observations of glacial rebound rates in areas that were heavily glaciated during the Ice Age. Peak uplift rates in these areas are observed to be about 1 cm/year. Similarly, one can infer the average viscosity over the full depth of the mantle from observed surface plate velocities, which today are on the order of a few centimeters per year, by making just a few assumptions about the thermal contrast between the lithospheric plates and the mantle. The inferred average value for the mantle using this approach is approximately 10^{22} Pa-s. With the perspective that the present is the key to the past, uniformitarian earth scientists generally are persuaded that plate velocities in the past must have been not much different from the plate velocities observed today because they cannot conceive how the strength of mantle rock could have changed in any significant way since early in the earth's history.

But laboratory measurements on the behavior of mantle minerals under mantle conditions of stress and temperature also reveal that mantle rock can weaken dramatically, by some ten orders of magnitude, under the sorts of stress levels that can arise inside a planet with the mass and composition of the earth. These laboratory studies of the deformation properties of silicate minerals have been performed and their results duplicated in many different laboratories around the world over the past forty years. But how might these results apply in the context of the Flood? The answer is straightforward. The combination of a gravitational body force acting on a cold slab of ocean lithosphere that possesses potential energy to release as it sinks within a lower density medium that weakens as the stress level increases provides the essential elements needed for an episode of runaway sinking. If the initial conditions allow the slab to begin sinking at a rate sufficient to heat the material immediately surrounding the slab at a rate that exceeds the rate of heat loss by thermal diffusion, this surrounding zone weakens, allowing the slab velocity to increase, which increases the stress level, which weakens the zone further, which allow the slab velocity to increase further, ultimately resulting in sinking rates many orders of magnitude higher than the normal strength of the rock would allow.

At least as far back as the early 1960s it has been known that the phenomenon of thermal runaway can potentially occur in materials whose effective viscosity is described by an Arrhenius-like relationship, in which the viscosity varies as $e^{(E^*/RT)}$, where T is absolute temperature, E^* is the activation energy, and R is the gas constant. A large variety of materials, including silicate minerals, have viscosities that vary with temperature in this manner. In 1963 Gruntfest showed for a layer subject to constant applied shear stress and a viscosity with Arrhenius temperature dependence, both the deformation rate and the temperature within the layer can increase without limit, that is, run away.[2] The criterion for runaway to occur is that the time constant associated with viscous heating be much less than the characteristic thermal diffusion time of the layer.

Several investigators in the late 1960s and early 1970s explored the possibility of thermal runaway of lithospheric slabs in the mantle. Anderson and Perkins,[3] for example, suggested that the widespread Cenozoic volcanism in the southwestern U.S. might be a consequence of thermal runaway of chunks of lithosphere in the low-viscosity upper mantle. They conjectured that surges of melt associated with such runaway events might account for episodes of volcanism observed at the surface. Lithospheric slabs, because they display an average temperature some 1,000 K or more lower than that of the upper mantle but have a similar bulk chemical composition, are several percent denser than the surrounding upper mantle rock and therefore have a natural ability to sink. The gravitational body forces acting on a slab lead to high stresses, especially within the mechanical boundary layer surrounding the slab. As a slab sinks, most of its gravitational potential energy is released in the form of heat in these regions of high deformation. If conditions are right, the weakening arising from heating can lead to an increased sinking rate, an increased heating rate, and greater weakening. This positive feedback associated with thermal weakening can result in runaway, provided the criterion mentioned above is met.

Baumgardner[4] more recently has emphasized that silicate minerals weaken not only with increasing temperature, but also—and even more dramatically—with increasing levels of stress. He makes the point that the stress weakening leads to a spectacularly stronger runaway tendency. Baumgardner describes studies performed by many laboratories over the past forty years to measure the way silicate minerals deform under a wide range of temperature and stress conditions. He focuses attention on the fact that these laboratory studies demonstrate that silicate rocks can weaken by ten or more orders of magnitude for temperature and stress conditions that can exist inside the mantle of a planet like the earth. Baumgardner presents numerical results, using a viscosity law that depends both on temperature and on stress, which show that slab runaway causes the effective viscosity of the entire volume of the mantle to plummet by orders of magnitude

2   I. J. Gruntfest, 1963, Thermal feedback in liquid flow; plane shear at constant stress, *Transactions of the Society for Rheology*, 8: 195-207.

3   O. L. Anderson and P. C. Perkins, 1974, Runaway temperatures in the asthenosphere resulting from viscous heating, *Journal of Geophysical Research*, 79: 2136-2138.

4   J. R. Baumgardner, 2003, Catastrophic plate tectonics: The physics behind the Genesis Flood, in *Proceedings of the Fifth International Conference on Creationism*, R. L. Ivey, Jr., ed., Pittsburgh, PA: Creation Science Fellowship, 113-126.

during the runaway episode. Therefore, motions throughout the mantle, far from the immediate vicinity of the slab, rise to values similar to that of the sinking slab itself. Thus, instead of viscosities on the order of 10^{22} Pa-s inferred for the mantle today, these numerical studies indicate that viscosities some ten orders of magnitude smaller, on the order of 10^{12} Pa-s, can occur through large portions of mantle during a runaway event. This allows a slab of lithosphere to sink through the depth of the mantle in a matter of weeks instead of requiring on the order of a hundred million years.

So what about the actual Flood? Given the catastrophe to follow, on the day the Flood began it is at least conceivable that the earth was balanced critically on the edge of that catastrophe. Today, seismic images of the mantle show evidence of lithospheric slabs penetrating from the surface all the way to the core-mantle boundary only in an extremely limited area. Beneath most subduction zones there is little, if any, slab signature evident in the lower mantle, except for what appears to be a quite prominent slab graveyard at the very bottom. Although seismic imaging does show slab material beneath subduction zones in most of the upper mantle, the amount of slab material is certainly not sufficient to lead any earth scientists to have any concern about impending runaway. By using the present as the key to the past, conventional plate tectonics theory assumes the relatively small amount of slab present in the upper mantle involved with the very slow plate motions observed in the present world also characterizes the past. On the other hand, the thermodynamics of phase transitions that occur at about 600 km depth (the base of the upper mantle) are such that motion of a cold slab from the upper mantle into the lower mantle is impeded, though not prevented. Thus, there is a tendency for cold slab material to pond at this depth. It is therefore not beyond the realm of possibility that in the original earth that God created there was a ring of cold mantle rock, representing ocean lithosphere subducted on Day Three of creation when the waters that were below the heavens were gathered together into one place and the dry land appeared, rock that lay just above this phase boundary in the upper mantle and below the perimeter of the large newly emerged land mass. Because this cold rock would have been gravitationally unstable, held in check only by the resistance of the phase boundary, the earth could be viewed as being on the knife edge of catastrophe. Very little would have been required to lose it on a trajectory leading to the Flood cataclysm. Perhaps that release occurred at the time of the Fall and was so subtle that it was undetectable at the earth's surface. It would then take another 1650 years or so for gradual motions suddenly to give way to runaway catastrophe.[5] The runaway sinking of this cold ring of rock in the upper mantle, in turn, pulled in the oceanic slabs at the dormant subduction zones surrounding the pre-Flood continent, splitting apart the mid-ocean ridges, causing "all the fountains of the great deep" to be "broken up" or "cleaved apart." Numerical modeling of various aspects of the ensuing physical

---

5   M. F. Horstemeyer and J. R. Baumgardner, 2003, What initiated the flood cataclysm?, in *Proceedings of the Fifth International Conference on Creationism*, R. L. Ivey, Jr., ed., Pittsburgh, PA: Creation Science Fellowship,.155-163.

processes shows that a global Flood similar to that described in the Scriptures is the inevitable result.[6]

The numerical modeling reveals that, because the amount of deformational heating that arises during the runaway is proportional to the viscosity, the drastically reduced viscosity that accompanies the runaway and indeed makes it possible also reduces the deformation heating drastically to quite modest levels, such that little melting of the mantle occurs.

Because all the current oceanic crust seems to date from the Flood and post-Flood times, it is apparent that essentially all the pre-Flood oceanic lithosphere was subducted during the Flood. The gravitational potential energy released by the subduction of this oceanic crust would have been on the order of 10^{28} joules. This alone would probably have provided all the energy necessary to drive all the tectonic and geologic processes of the Flood event. The continental fragments on the same plates as the subducting slabs of oceanic crust would have been pulled toward the subduction zones, resulting in rapid horizontal displacement of these continental fragments at a rate of meters per second (several miles per hour). Subsequent collisions of continental fragments at subduction zones are the likely mechanism for the formation of mountain fold-and-thrust belts, such as the Appalachians, Himalayas, and the European Alps. The rapid deformation, burial, and subsequent erosion of early-formed mountain belts within the year of the Flood, at this orders of magnitude acceleration of geologic processes, would seem to provide the only adequate explanation for the existence of high-pressure, low-temperature minerals in the rocks in the cores of these deeply eroded mountain belts.

The subducting slabs of oceanic lithosphere, according to the catastrophic plate tectonics framework, would have sunk rapidly all the way to the bottom of the earth's mantle, accompanied by equally rapid large-scale flow throughout the entire mantle. The leading edges of present subducting slabs of oceanic crust reach deep into the mantle under the trenches, and are under compression, suggesting that the slabs are being resisted from passing through the phase boundary at the base of the upper mantle, which would thus seem to represent a barrier. Thus,

---

6   J. R. Baumgardner, 1987, Numerical simulation of the large-scale tectonic changes accompanying the Flood, in *Proceedings of the First International Conference on Creationism*, vol. 2, R. E. Walsh, C. L. Brooks and R. S. Crowell, eds., Pittsburgh, PA: Creation Science Fellowship, 17-30; J. R. Baumgardner, 1990, 3-D finite element simulation of the global tectonic changes accompanying Noah's Flood, in *Proceedings of the Second International Conference on Creationism*, vol. 2, R. E. Walsh and C. L. Brooks, eds., Pittsburgh, PA: Creation Science Fellowship, 35-45; J. R. Baumgardner,1994, Computer modeling of the large-scale tectonics associated with the Genesis Flood, in *Proceedings of the Third International Conference on Creationism*, R. E. Walsh, ed., Pittsbursh, PA: Creation Science Fellowship, 49-62; J. R. Baumgardner, 1994, Runaway subduction as the driving mechanism for the Genesis Flood, in *Proceedings of the Third International Conference on Creationism*, R. E. Walsh, ed., Pittsburgh, PA: Creation Science Fellowship, 63-75; J. R. Baumgardner, 2003, Catastrophic plate tectonics: the physics behind the Genesis Flood, in *Proceedings of the Fifth International Conference on Creationism*, R. Ivey, ed., Pittsburgh, PA: Creation Science Fellowship, 113-126.

some conventional slow-and-gradual plate tectonics models have suggested that subduction, flow, and circulation have at certain times been restricted to the upper mantle. In any case, according to conventional plate tectonics, even if the plates were to eventually penetrate this apparent barrier at the base of the upper mantle, they would be falling so slowly that they should have mostly equilibrated thermally with the surrounding hot mantle before reaching the bottom of the lower mantle. On the other hand, numerical modeling of catastrophic plate tectonics has demonstrated that the subducted slabs of oceanic lithosphere readily penetrate through this apparent barrier into the lower mantle, and because of the runaway rate, they sunk so quickly that they would have made it all the way through to the mantle/core boundary without any significant temperature increase. Indeed, it is a prediction of the catastrophic plate tectonic model that the subducted slabs of oceanic lithosphere should still be at the core/mantle boundary today and at near their original temperature, because their sinking occurred during the Flood only a few thousand years ago. Not surprisingly, recent seismic tomography studies have mapped zones of cooler material reaching down from the ocean trenches to the bottom of the mantle along the theorized paths of past subduction. This evidence confirms that large-scale flow occurred throughout the entire mantle, while cold material at the bottom of the mantle just above the core/mantle boundary indicates that oceanic lithosphere has sunk recently all the way through the mantle. Thus, the numerical modeling and predictions of catastrophic plate tectonics have been powerfully vindicated, and the expectations of conventional slow-and-gradual plate tectonics have been contradicted.

In the catastrophic plate tectonics framework for the Flood, as soon as the ocean's crust was broken up and oceanic lithosphere began to sink, mantle-wide circulation began. One important consequence of this mantle-wide flow would have been the transportation of shallower, cooler mantle material to lower positions in the mantle, right down to the core/mantle boundary. This process would thus have created different and cooler temperatures at the base of the mantle, which in turn would have had the effect of cooling the outer core, leading to strong convection within it. Because the outer core is liquid with a consistency similar to liquid water, if there were temperature differences in various places at the bottom of the mantle above it, the core material would have begun to circulate. Significantly, the earth's magnetic field is generated in the core, and thus convective circulation in the outer core would have caused the earth's magnetic field to rapidly and regularly reverse, in much the same way as the sun's internal circulation today causes the sun's magnetic field to reverse every eleven years.[7] However, the temperature contrasts in the earth's outer core suggested by the numerical modeling would have produced the reversals of the earth's magnetic field even more frequently,

7   D. R. Humphreys, 1987, Reversals of the earth's magnetic field during the Genesis Flood, in *Proceedings of the First International Conference on Creationism*, vol. 2, R. E. Walsh, C. L. Brooks and R. S. Crowell, eds., Pittsburgh, PA: Creation Science Fellowship, 113-126; D. R. Humphreys, 1990, Physical mechanisms for reversals of the earth's magnetic field during the Flood, in *Proceedings of the Second International Conference on Creationism*, vol. 2, R. E. Walsh and C. L. Brooks, eds., Pittsburgh, PA: Creation Science Fellowship, 129-142.

perhaps as often as a few days, a rate rapid enough to have generated most of the known reversals during the year of the Flood. Furthermore, the low electrical conductivity of the subducting plates of oceanic crust would have split up the lower mantle's high electrical conductivity, so as to have lessened the mantle's attenuation of the magnetic field reversals generated in the core. This would have thus allowed these rapid magnetic field reversals to be expressed and recorded in the rocks forming at the earth's surface.

In conventional thinking these reversals of the earth's magnetic field would have required hundreds to thousands of years to occur, in stark contrast to the timescale of days or weeks at most within the catastrophic plate tectonics model. Field observations are available to test the two models. In particular, if the magnetic reversals actually occur on timescales of days to weeks, then such reversals can potentially be recorded within thin (0.5 to 1 meter thick) basalt lava flows as they cool. This is possible, because as the lava cools, the magnetic particles that have been free in the magma to orientate themselves to the earth's magnetic field become "frozen" in place. Therefore, if the earth's magnetic field changes after the outer surfaces of the lava flows have cooled, then the insides of the flows that are still molten will, when they cool, preserve a different magnetic field direction. Since the cooling times for such lava flows are easily calculated, it is possible to determine how long it took for the magnetic field reversal to occur. Much to the surprise of conventional geophysicists, two separate such basalt lava flows that record magnetic field reversals within a span of a week or two have been identified, confirming the catastrophic plate tectonics model.[8]

As slabs of oceanic lithosphere subducted, elsewhere the tension ripped apart the pre-Flood ocean floor and produced rapid extension along globe-encircling linear belts. This rifting of the oceanic crust would have allowed mantle material to upwell, the partial melting of it producing new basaltic ocean crust as sea floor spreading progressed. Because this rifting was so catastrophic and rapid, the pressure drop experienced by the upwelling mantle material was also rapid, causing many of the minerals to find themselves above their melting temperatures, which in turn would have resulted in rapid partial melting. The hot magma rapidly rising to the ocean floor to cool as new oceanic crust would have come in contact with the ocean water, instantly forming superheated steam. Together with the volatiles degassing from the magma itself, the steam would have erupted from the V-shaped rifts on the ocean floor at supersonic speed as spectacular jets, rising high into the earth's atmosphere. These jets would have entrained large amounts of liquid sea water and carried it aloft high into the atmosphere. Thus, there would have been a linear chain of geyser-like fountains along the tens of thousands of kilometers of globe encircling mid-ocean ridge, matching closely the description provided in Genesis 7:11. The entrained water carried into the atmosphere would have then fallen back to the earth as intense global rain, which

---

8   R. S. Coe and M. Prevot, 1989, Evidence suggesting extremely rapid field variation during a geomagnetic reversal, *Earth and Planetary Science Letters*, 92: 292-299.

suggests that the opening of the "windows of heaven" of Genesis 7:11 is describing the rather sudden onslaught of torrential rain from the water carried aloft by the globe-encircling fountains arising out of the great ocean depths. The steam in the jets would have spread out in the earth's upper atmosphere, cooled by radiation into space, and condensed to fall back to the earth's surface again as additional rain. However, the rate at which the latent heat of condensation can be radiated away from the surface of the atmosphere is severely limited, so that the fraction of the overall rainfall resulting from condensed steam may have been relatively small. As already discussed, vapor canopy models do not appear capable of containing the water equivalent to 150 days of continuous rainfall (including the first forty days of the most intense rainfall). However, this globe-encircling chain of geysers that carry aloft huge volumes of ocean water, as postulated in the catastrophic plate tectonics model for the Flood, provide bountifully the water needed for this rainfall.

As new basaltic oceanic crust formed at the mid-ocean ridges encircling the earth, the direction of the prevailing magnetic field at the time was frozen into the basalt lava as it cooled. Conventional plate tectonics assumes that plates spread apart at a few centimeters every year and that each reversal of the earth's magnetic field takes around 1,000 years, so at these rates, only a few tens of meters of new oceanic crust should be produced during each field reversal, with a mixture of magnetic field directions preserved in it. In contrast to this comparatively brief reversal period, it is claimed that an average of a million years or more separated these reversals, during which time many tens of kilometers of new oceanic crust would have been produced with no evidence of mixed-up magnetic field directions, but instead only one uniform magnetic field direction preserved. Thus, if the conventional model were correct, amid the parallel bands of alternating paleomagnetic directions in the new oceanic crust produced by sea floor spreading, there would be far less than one percent of the ocean floor displaying mixed-up magnetic field directions. On the other hand, however, if the catastrophic plate tectonics model is correct, then because the new oceanic crust was being generated during the Flood at miles per hour, with reversals occurring on a timescale of days to weeks, it is likely that there were always patches of the oceanic crust that remained hot from one reversal to the next. Thus, this model would predict that all the ocean crust today should be magnetically mottled, with adjacent patches throughout the basalt having opposite magnetic orientations, and even vertical variations also through the oceanic crust. Indeed, such locally patchy distribution of paleomagnetic orientations does seem to exist across all of today's ocean crust, and the same mottling seems to exist vertically in the basalts of the oceanic crust in every one of the hundreds of holes drilled into them. Thus, the catastrophic plate tectonics Flood model is strongly supported by this evidence, while the same model for the earth's magnetic field uniquely explains the low intensity of the paleomagnetic data through the strata of the Phanerozoic of the geologic record, deposited during the Flood.[9]

---

9   D. R. Humphreys, 1988, Has the Earth's magnetic field flipped? *Creation Research Society Quarterly*, 25 (3): 130-137.

The rapid emplacement of warmer and isostatically lighter mantle material beneath the mid-ocean spreading centers would have raised the level of the ocean floor to produce a linear chain of mountains encircling the globe, similar to today's mid-ocean ridge system. Consequently, the warmer and more buoyant oceanic lithosphere would thus have displaced ocean water onto the continents, with a rise of sea level of possibly as much as one kilometer from this mechanism alone. This would thus have resulted in inundation of much of the continents, the primary objective of the Flood event. Heat from the magma emplaced at the spreading centers would have heated the ocean waters throughout the duration of the Flood. This heating is confirmed by the gradual increase in oxygen-18/oxygen-16 ratios in carbonate rock units, and in the shells and tests of fossilized invertebrates, progressively upwards through the Paleozoic and Mesozoic strata of the geologic record.

An understanding of how sediments would have been produced rapidly is critical to confirmation of the year-long Flood event having produced a significant portion of the strata in the geologic record. A major sediment type in that record are *carbonates* (limestones), and the catastrophic plate tectonics model for the Flood event provides suitable explanatory mechanisms for their production. Contributions to Flood carbonates probably came from at least four sources— carbon dioxide would have been released by degassing of the cooling magmas at the spreading centers; bicarbonate dissolved in the pre-Flood ocean water would have precipitated as the ocean water temperatures rose during the Flood (given that carbonate dissolution rates are inversely related to temperature); pre-Flood carbonates (dominant among pre-Flood sediments) would have been eroded and redeposited; and pre-Flood shell debris would have been pulverized and redeposited. The origin of micro-crystalline carbonate (micrite) in limestones is puzzling, and otherwise unknown in the conventional uniformitarian model for the formation of the geologic record. However, the ubiquity of this micro-crystalline carbonate in Flood sediments is consistent with the large-scale rapid precipitation of carbonate during the Flood from degassing magmas and from ocean-water bicarbonate, as predicted in the catastrophic plate tectonics model. Further confirmation is provided by the presence of high-magnesium carbonates (dolomites) only among the early Flood strata—the postulated carbonate precipitation would have included the magnesium, dissolved in the pre-Flood ocean water, early in the Flood.

The degassing of, and the water being expelled from, the rapidly emplaced and cooling magmas at the spreading centers and elsewhere would also have generated prodigious quantities of dissolved salts, so when these salt-laden magmatic waters mixed with the colder ocean waters, the salts would have precipitated to form cherts, fine-grained limestones, anhydrite, and salt deposits. Such rocks would be more accurately described as precipitites, that is, sediments precipitated directly from supersaturated brines. Only the catastrophic plate tectonics Flood model provides a mechanism for the generation of supersaturated brines, and thus these precipitite sediments in association with the rapid horizontal divergence of newly-generated oceanic crust. The association of rock salt and anhydrite deposits with active sea floor tectonics and volcanism has already been noted, and catastrophist models for their formation have been proposed.[10] Thus, hot-rock/ocean-water interactions during the Flood, including on the continents as they were inundated, would explain many of the bedded chert deposits and fine-grained limestones found in the geologic record, along with the many anhydrite and salt deposits.

It is evident that most of the rock strata deposited by the Flood are found on the continents and continental margins, and not on the ocean floor where sediments might be expected to have ended up (as they often do today).[11] The catastrophic plate tectonics Flood model provides a number of mechanisms for the transportation of sediments, which would have been on the pre-Flood ocean floor, onto the continents where such sedimentary strata are primarily found today. First, the rapid sea floor spreading and ocean-plate motion would have transported the ocean-floor sediments toward the subduction zones, where the slabs of oceanic crust were entering the mantle, and thus the sediments would have been moved mostly toward the continents in a conveyor-belt fashion. Second, as the weight of the oceanic lithosphere forced it to quickly bend as it sank and was subducted into the earth's interior, it would have warped upward on the ocean side of the trenches. This would have raised the deep-sea sediments of the pre-Flood ocean floor above the typical depth at which they had been deposited, and this in turn would have reduced the amount of work that would have been required to move the sediments from the ocean floors onto the continents. Third, the rapid subduction of the oceanic plates would have also warped downward the margins of the continental plates on the continent side of the ocean trenches. This would again reduce the amount of energy needed to move the sediments onto the continents from the ocean floors. Fourth, as more and more of the cold pre-Flood oceanic crust was replaced with the hotter new oceanic crust from partial melting of the upwelling mantle, the ocean floor would have generally been gradually elevated. Displacement of the ocean water, as the sea level consequently rose by the inundation of the continents, would have also reduced the depths of the ocean waters covering these pre-Flood ocean-floor sediments. This would have also reduced the amount of work required to move the sediments from the ocean floors up onto the continents. Fifth, as the oceanic crust was subducted, the ocean sediments would have been scraped off the sinking ocean floor to be accreted to the adjoining continental crust margins, and/or to be transported and redeposited on the inundated continents. Sixth, wave refraction on the continental shelves, where the shallowing water depth produces higher and higher waves and tsunamis, would have tended to transport the ocean floor sediments shoreward. Finally, seventh, it is possible that some amount of tidal resonance may have been

10   K. P Rode, 1944, On the submarine volcanic origin of rock-salt deposits, *Proceedings of the Indian Academy of Science*, 20 (B): 130-142; V. I. Sozansky, 1973, *Geology and Genesis of Salt Formations* (Russian), Kiev: Izd Naukova Dumka.

11   G. R. Morton, 1987, *The Geology of the Flood*, Dallas, TX: DMD.

achieved.[12] This would have resulted from the tidal surges across a global ocean eventually building on top of one another, to produce an even bigger surge with very strong currents. Such currents would have been dominantly east-to-west, and would have tended to transport any sediments accumulated on the eastern continental margins into the continental interiors.

The global Flood would have involved much larger scales for geologic processes, such that sedimentation, for example, would be expected to have impacted much larger areas, have involved much greater volumes of sediment, and moved the sediments much farther from their sources than the prevailing conventional uniformitarian view of earth history generally accepted. Significantly, the Paleozoic and Mesozoic strata consist of sediments that were often deposited in great thicknesses, with remarkably uniform compositions, extending over very large areas of regional, inter-regional, and even continental scales, and many times displaced many hundreds of kilometers from their source areas or are of unknown provenance.[13] These sedimentary units also contain abundant evidence of catastrophic deposition.[14] All these evidences are totally consistent with the catastrophic plate tectonics Flood model, and not as easily explained by the conventional uniformitarian model. Sedimentation today is very localized, with the only larger-scale deposition being on the continental shelves, particularly around deltas, and almost imperceptibly slowly on the ocean floor, none of which is comparable with the strata sequences in the geologic record, unless catastrophism is invoked. Furthermore, on the present earth, the sediments are being transported toward and within the ocean in all directions, so that the sedimentary structures that indicate the direction of currents (such as ripples marks, dune structures or drag marks) show a random pattern on every continent. However, extensive compilation of measured paleocurrent direction indicators in the Paleozoic and Mesozoic strata of the geologic record on all continents reveals that during the deposition of these rocks the water currents all around the globe were consistently flowing in one direction—more or less east-to-west.[15] These data are consistent with east-to-west-dominated currents generated by some sort of global forcing during the Flood to transport ocean floor and continental sediments such long distances and over such large areas.

---

12 M. E. Clark and H. D. Voss, 1985, Gravitational attraction, Noah's Flood, and sedimentary layering, in *Science at the Crossroads: Observation or Speculation?*, Papers of the 1983 National Creation Conference, Minneapolis, MN: Bible Science Association, 42-56; M. E. Clark and H. D. Voss, 1990, Resonance and sedimentary layering in the context of a global Flood, in *Proceedings of the Second International Conference on Creationism*, vol. 2, R. E. Walsh and C. L. Brooks, eds., Pittsburgh, PA: Creation Science Fellowship, 53-63; M. E. Clark and H. D. Voss, 1992, Resonance on flooded planet earth, in *Proceedings of the 1992 Twin-Cities Creation Conference*, St. Paul, MN: Twin-Cities Association, 30-33.

13 S. A. Austin, 1994, Interpreting the strata of Grand Canyon, in *Grand Canyon: Monument to Catastrophe*, S. A. Austin, ed., El Cajon, CA: Institute for Creation Research, 21-56.

14 D. V. Ager, 1973, *The Nature of the Stratigraphical Record*, New York: MacMillan.

15 A. Chadwick, 2001, Lithologic, paleogeographic and paleocurrent maps of the world, http:\\geology. swau.edu\index.html. This conclusion is based on 640,000 paleocurrent measurements.

The volcanism associated with the rapid tectonics of the catastrophic plate tectonics Flood model would have been substantial in magnitude and worldwide in distribution, but concentrated in particular zones and sites. Based on laboratory experiments as well as three-dimensional numerical modeling, the rapid subduction-induced mantle-wide flow rapidly generates mantle plumes, whose mushroom heads would rise to, and erupt at, the earth's surface. Thus, catastrophic plate tectonics during the Flood provides an explanation for flood basalts, kimberlites, and other extensive explosive volcanic activity that the conventional uniformitarian plate tectonics model cannot so readily explain, simply because the mantle moved so much more rapidly during the Flood than it does at the present. These rapidly upwelling mantle plumes would have produced extensive flood basalts through enormous catastrophic fissure eruptions. Flood basalts are very thick sequences of voluminous basalt lava flows that typically cover huge areas. Examples include the Karoo basalts of South Africa, the Deccan Traps in India, the Siberian flood basalts, the Parana basalts of South America and related Etendeka basalts of Africa, the Antrim Plateau basalts of northern Australia and the Karmutsen Basalt of Alaska/Canada. This correlation between the formation and upwelling of mantle plumes and the eruption of flood basalts is now well established, and various studies of many of these flood basalts have suggested very rapid eruption times, on the order of days to weeks. This is extraordinarily catastrophic, given that the basalt lava flows from these eruptions are on average 10 to 20 meters thick, and flowed out over areas of thousands of square kilometers, repeatedly over a matter of days to weeks, the successive flows being stacked on top of one another to produce lava piles hundreds of meters thick.[16] No remotely comparable eruptions and lava flows are seen today. Even one-meter-thick basalt lava flows are rare, and areal extents are typically limited to only a few tens of square kilometers. The supply of such voluminous quantities of magma within days to weeks from the mantle can only be explained by extremely rapid and catastrophic movement of these upwelling mantle plumes, and thus mantle motion much faster than at present, just as the modeling of catastrophic plate tectonics demonstrates.

Kimberlites are an unusual and rare type of volcanic rock, are usually found in pipe-like intrusions at or near the earth's surface, and often contain diamonds. They originate deep in the upper mantle, probably at depths of 150 to 400 kilometers, because it is only at those depths that the pressures are high enough to produce diamonds. After the kimberlite magmas form at those depths, they have to rise through fractures, taking any diamonds with them, to be emplaced at or close to the earth's surface. However, if the transit time is not exceedingly rapid, any diamonds in the kimberlite magmas would be unstable at the lesser pressures, and thus would transform to graphite. Thus, the emplacement of diamond-containing kimberlite magmas requires extremely rapid vertical ascent

---

16   S. A. Weinstein, 1993, Catastrophic overturn of the earth's mantle driven by multiple phase changes and
      internal heat generation, *Geophysical Research Letters*, 20: 101-104.

of the magma at speeds of 100 to 200 kilometers per hour.[17] Thus, the eruption of these kimberlites is explosive, their catastrophic ascent propelled by gases such as carbon dioxide under pressure from those mantle depths. The generation and emplacement of kimberlite magmas and their contained diamonds are thus more readily explained by the rapid motion of mantle flow during catastrophic plate tectonics.

The whole cycle of mantle-wide flow and plate motions of meters per second had been initiated by simultaneous triggering of the rifting of the pre-Flood oceanic and continental crust to produce plates, and to simultaneously commence sea floor spreading and thermal runaway subduction that reached speeds of meters per second. As slabs of the oceanic lithosphere were catastrophically subducted, not all the ocean-floor sediments were scraped from the slabs. The presence of water lowers the melting point considerably, so upon reaching depths of about 100 km, the subducted sediments readily melt. Simultaneous dehydration reactions also release water into the overlying mantle wedge that also induces some melting of the mantle rock just above the inclined subducting slab, and perhaps even melting of some of the former oceanic crust in the slab itself. Thus, various combinations of magmas rapidly generated from these sources produced explosive volcanism over the compositional range from andesites to rhyolites continent-ward of the subduction zones, such as that found today in the Andes of South America and the Cascade Mountains of the northwest United States, and, for example, through parts of the Paleozoic geologic record in southeastern Australia. The huge volumes of these lavas suggest that these eruptions were not only catastrophic, but occurred at an enormous scale, orders of magnitude greater than any comparable volcanic activity experienced today, so this evidence is again more readily explained by the catastrophic plate tectonics Flood model.

The very rapid motions of the continental portions of the lithospheric plates, as oceanic portions were subducted and new oceanic lithosphere formed at mid-ocean ridges, resulted in some cases in collision between continental blocks. The forces exerted on the lithosphere still at the earth's surface by the rapidly sinking slabs were sufficient to fold and deform rocks and to uplift them as mountains in the collision zones. As indicated previously, the gravitational potential energy released by subduction of the cold pre-Flood ocean crust is of the order of 10^{28} joules, which alone would be sufficient energy to drive the Flood dynamics, including continental collisions and mountain-building. This is energy not available in conventional uniformitarian plate tectonics, which is thus unable to provide an adequate explanation for continental collisions and mountain-building.

---

17   G. C. Kennedy and B. E. Nordlie, 1968. The genesis of diamond deposits, *Economic Geology*, 63 (5): 495-503; D. H. Eggler, 1989, Kimberlites: How do they form?, in *Kimberlites and Related Rocks*, vol. 1, J. Ross, A. L. Jaques, J. Ferguson, D. H. Green, S. Y. O'Reilly, R. V. Danchin and A. J. A. Janse, eds., Melbourne, Australia: Geological Society of Australia Special Publication No. 14 and Blackwell Scientific Publications, 489-504; A. A. Snelling, 1993, Diamonds: evidence of explosive geological processes, *Creation Ex Nihilo*, 16 (1): 42-45.

This energy would also have driven a large number of other high-energy geologic processes evidenced in the earth's rock record, which are thus better explained by the catastrophic plate tectonics Flood model than by any of the alternate conventional theories. For example, there is evidence of strong earthquakes resulting from the collapse of the continental margins, and huge mountain-size blocks thousands of meters thick of sedimentary strata having been uplifted, thrust over the top of these same sedimentary strata, and then sliding for tens of kilometers.[18]

These rapid continental collisions would have also had the potential to generate sufficient pressure to produce high-pressure minerals deep below the earth's surface, in the cores of the collision zones and the mountain belts produced. The subsequent rapid erosion within the Flood to unroof the cores of these mountain belts, where the high-pressure minerals were generated, before the minerals in these rocks could equilibrate again to the lower pressures and temperatures near the earth's surface, can only be explained by the catastrophic plate tectonics model. Conventional old-age models thus can't grapple with the evidence of rocks containing minerals formed at both high pressure and low temperature in the cores of mountain belts, now exposed at the earth's surface, evidence that is fully explainable by catastrophic exhumation following the rapid collisions of continental fragments in the catastrophic plate tectonics Flood model. Indeed, the millions of years required by conventional plate tectonics to generate the high pressures needed to produce the high-pressure minerals would have allowed the rocks to also reach high temperatures at the required depths. Thus, the existence of high-pressure/low-temperature minerals is a complete enigma to conventional theories, but is easily explained by the catastrophic plate tectonics Flood model.

Moreover, many of these processes during the Flood would have made substantial modifications to the thickness of the pre-Flood continental crust. This change in crustal thickness occurred through the redistribution of sediments, such as those rapidly transported from the pre-Flood ocean floor up and across the continental crust; by the moving of ductile lower continental crust by its subduction under adjoining continental crust; by the addition of molten material to the underside of the continental crust where it cools and crystallizes (underplating); by stretching (for example, due to spreading); and by compression (for example, due to continental collisions). These rapid changes in crustal thicknesses would have resulted in isostatic disequilibrium, which would subsequently have led to large-scale isostatic adjustments, with their associated earthquakes, frictional heating, and deformation. Many of these tectonic processes would thus have involved vertical motions of sequences of rock strata, so that a tectonically-controlled rock cycle would have been established, particularly in the latter half of the

---

18   K. P. Wise and S. A. Austin, 1999, Gigantic megaclast within the Kingston Peak Formation (Upper Precambrian, Pahrump Group), south-eastern California: evidence for basin margin collapse, *Geological Society of America Abstracts with Programs*, 31: A455-456; As seen at the Lewis Overthrust in Glacier National Park and surrounding areas.

Flood, with residual effects continuing into the early post-Flood period.[19] Even more spectacular expression of vertical tectonics driven by a return to isostatic equilibrium after the large changes in crustal thickness was the rapid uplift of the high mountain ranges of the world soon after the Flood, including the Himalayas, Alps, Andes, and Rockies.[20]

All of these details of the catastrophic processes involved in the catastrophic plate tectonics model, and the evidence consistent with them, form a coherent and integrated whole model for the Flood, which explains many more details preserved in the geologic record than can be explained by the conventional geological synthesis based on uniformitarian plate tectonics. The replacement of the cold pre-Flood oceanic lithosphere with more expanded hot oceanic lithosphere, by subduction and sea floor spreading, respectively, raised the ocean floor. The strong pull of the subducting oceanic lithosphere into the mantle dragged those portions of the earth's lithospheric plates down, as upwelling mantle material rose to fill the gaps along the spreading centers. The rising ocean floor displaced water onto the continents, raised the sea level more than a kilometer, and the inundation thus resulted in the Flood itself. The rising ocean waters, complemented by the intense global rainfall from the seawater entrained and lofted into the atmosphere by the geysers along the spreading centers, would thus have raised the Ark upon their surface, and ultimately carried it up over the tops of the highest pre-Flood mountains, as recorded in the Scriptures.

When all the pre-Flood oceanic lithosphere had been replaced with new, warm, less-dense, less-subductable oceanic lithosphere, rapid plate motion would have ceased. This brought sea floor spreading almost to a standstill and terminated the spreading-center-associated geyser activity, so the global rainfall would have ceased. This would probably correlate with the 150-day point in the Genesis chronology for the Flood, when "the fountains also of the deep and the windows of heaven were stopped, and the rain from heaven was restrained" (Genesis 8:2). After the rapid horizontal motion of the plates stopped, cooling increased the density of the new oceanic lithosphere, producing deepening oceans, until they reached their current depth. This sinking of the ocean floor would have caused the waters covering the continents to recede from the land, as contemporaneous isostatic adjustments caused the thickened continental crust, including new mountain belts, to rise. The most superficial, and therefore, least lithified, continental sedimentary deposits would have been eroded off the continents and deposited at the new continental margins and on the ocean floor, leaving an unconformity on the new continents not reflected in ocean-floor stratigraphy. This erosion by the receding Flood waters would have been wide-scale sheet erosion, which would be expected to have planed off a substantial percentage of the newly-emerging continental

19   D. J. Tyler, 1990, A tectonically-controlled rock cycle, in *Proceedings of the Second International Conference on Creationism*, R. E. Walsh and C. L. Brooks, eds., Pittsburgh, PA: Creation Science Fellowship, 293-299.

20   C. Ollier and C. Pain, 2000, *The Origin of Mountains*, London and New York: Routledge.

surfaces. This would explain such planar erosion features as the Canadian Shield, and the Kaibab and Coconino Plateaus of the Grand Canyon area, which cannot be so easily explained by the erosional processes available in the conventional uniformitarian model.

88

WHERE IS THE PRE-FLOOD/FLOOD BOUNDARY IN THE GEOLOGIC RECORD?

In the catastrophic plate tectonics model for the Flood event, the onset of the Flood was the fracturing and rifting of the pre-Flood oceanic lithosphere, as "the fountains of the great deep" were broken up, which was caused by the nearly simultaneous runaway of cold rock in the upper mantle, the commencement of subduction of the cold pre-Flood oceanic lithosphere, and consequent mantle-wide flow that set in motion globe-encircling sea floor spreading. This subsequently led to rising of the ocean floor, which progressively caused inundation of the continents. Thus, the onset of catastrophic plate tectonics is argued to have been the cause of the Flood event itself. However, is it possible to pinpoint in the geologic record exactly where the pre-Flood era ended and the Flood event began?

It has been proposed that the pre-Flood/Flood boundary in the geologic record should be associated with five geologic discontinuities.[1] These five criteria are summarized as follows:

A Mechanical-Erosional Discontinuity

Energized by the onset of global catastrophic tectonic activity, the early Flood waters would have caused some of the most substantial mechanical erosion in the earth's history. Thus, in any particular stratigraphic section or local geologic column, the pre-Flood/Flood boundary is likely to correspond to the most substantial (or one of the most substantial) and significant regional, mechanical-erosional unconformities.

A Time or Age Discontinuity

By the time the Flood began, the pre-Flood sediments would have had more than two orders of magnitude more time (more than hundreds of years) for lithification than any sediments formed subsequently, particularly early in the

---

1   S. A. Austin and K. P. Wise, 1994, The pre-Flood boundary: as defined in Grand Canyon, Arizona and eastern Mojave Desert, California, in *Proceedings of the Third International Conference on Creationism*, R. E. Walsh, ed., Pittsburgh, PA: Creation Science Fellowship, 37-47.

Flood. Even though many conglomerate strata would have been generated during the Flood, because of this factor just mentioned, conglomerates containing clasts of pre-Flood sediments would be expected to have been more common, thicker, of broader areal extent, and/or coarser than those conglomerates containing clasts of Flood-generated sediments. Furthermore, because later Flood deposition would bury pre-Flood source rocks, conglomerates with pre-Flood clasts are more likely to have been produced very early in Flood deposition in a given area. Thus, the pre-Flood/Flood boundary in any stratigraphic section is likely to be just beneath a conglomerate with clasts of underlying sediments units, particularly if it is associated with a dominant mechanical-erosional unconformity in the region, thus making the conglomerate unit the oldest preserved deposits of the Flood.

A Tectonic Discontinuity

The unparalleled magnitude of tectonism (earth movements) in the first moments of the Flood would be expected to leave a distinctive signature in many places across the earth's surface. Furthermore, the rapid plate motion of the ensuing catastrophic plate tectonics would have tended to leave the early Flood tectonism uniquely associated with the almost complete absence of volcanic rocks. Thus, the pre-Flood/Flood boundary in any stratigraphic section should be associated with evidences of tectonic disturbance in the region, such as rapid changes in the thicknesses of sedimentary units, conglomerates, breccias, megaclasts, megaslides, and detachment faulting, particularly if the greatest amount of this tectonic disturbance is accompanied by the dominant mechanical-erosional unconformities of that region.

A Sedimentary Discontinuity

As the Flood waters deepened at any given locality, the erosion at the onset of the Flood would have given way to deposition, so that the waning energies would be expected to deposit a megasequence of clastics fining-upward, to be capped by chemical sediments such as carbonates. Given that the unparalleled energies involved would likely have been unique to the onset of the Flood, and given the global extent of this surge of waters beginning the inundation of the continent early in the Flood, a transgressive megasequence should be the largest such sequence in local and regional stratigraphic columns, and should thus consist of sedimentary units that are identifiable regionally and inter-regionally. Thus, the pre-Flood/Flood boundary in any stratigraphic section would be where a dominant, fining-upward transgressive, clastic-to-chemical sedimentary megasequence sits on top of a dominant, mechanical-erosional onlap unconformity, particularly where this combination can be identified on a local and regional scale. The fining-upward sedimentary megasequence would thus represent the first sediments of the Flood in that region.

A Paleontological Discontinuity

Under the normal conditions in which animals and plants live and die, the probability of fossilization is proportional to the rate of sedimentation. Thus, in the pre-Flood world the slow deposition of sediments would have made fossilization of plant, animal, and fungal remains unlikely. Then, the initial erosion at the onset of the Flood would likely have destroyed or reworked many of the pre-Flood sediments, and thus any fossils contained in them. Consequently, sediments below the pre-Flood/Flood boundary capable of preserving fossils would probably only contain traces of the most abundant and easily fossilized life-forms, such as bacteria, algae, and protists, and probably in very low abundance. Plants, animal, and fungal fossils would thus be expected to only be found in high abundance above the pre-Flood/Flood boundary. Thus, the regional paleontology needs to be studied when the pre-Flood/Flood boundary is being defined in any stratigraphic section, and the abundance of fossils in each of the strata units should be noted, as well as how they were buried and fossilized. Consequently, where there is a dominant mechanical-erosional unconformity, which has (at most) uncommon fossils below it, and abundant plant, animal, and fungal fossils only above it, this is likely to represent the initial erosion at the onset of the Flood in that region.

Other than relying upon one criterion, the greatest strength of this analysis comes when all five criteria are applied simultaneously to the stratigraphic section of any region. Thus, the dominant, regionally-defined, mechanical-erosional unconformity that underlies a clastic unit incorporating the highest proportion of lithified clasts from below the boundary, has associated with it the greatest amount of tectonic disturbance, directly underlies the most dominant clastic-to-chemical sedimentary megasequence with regionally-deposited sediments, and which is underlain by low-abundance fossils of microorganisms, but overlain by high-abundance fossils of macroorganisms, can be confidently defined as the pre-Flood/Flood boundary in that region. Such an analysis has been used to define and correlate the pre-Flood/Flood boundary in the Grand Canyon region of northern Arizona and the Mojave Desert region of southern California.[2] By application of these five criteria, the pre-Flood/Flood boundary has been successfully identified as being at the unconformity beneath the Sixtymile Formation in the Grand Canyon, where the overlying Tonto Group is a fining-upward, clastic-to-chemical sediment megasequence, there is a paucity of microfossils below it, but an abundance of macrofossils above it, and this unconformity coincides with tectonic upheaval. In the Mojave Desert region of southern California, this unconformity, and thus the pre-Flood/Flood boundary, can be correlated with the unconformity within the Kingston Peak Formation, which is a substantial mechanical-erosional discontinuity where more than 3,000 meters of erosion has occurred in order to enclose clasts of underlying crystalline rocks in the megabreccia that immediately overlies it at the base of a fining-upward megasequence. In conventional terms,

---

2   Austin and Wise, 1994; Wise and Snelling, 2005.

this would place the pre-Flood/Flood boundary in the late Neoproterozoic, at around 700-740 billion years ago.[3] Significantly, this approximates the timing of the break-up of a postulated supercontinent called Rodinia, which may thus correlate with the initiation of catastrophic plate tectonics at the beginning of the Flood.

The defining of the pre-Flood/Flood boundary at this stratigraphic level within the geologic record is not all that far below the Precambrian/Cambrian boundary, the traditional placement of the beginning of the Flood.[4] Nevertheless, the lower stratigraphic placement of the boundary is justified by the five carefully defined criteria outlined above, and is consistent with the reasoning formerly used to place the boundary at the base of the Cambrian. There too, there is often a mechanical-erosional unconformity and a paleontological discontinuity, with the so-called "Cambrian explosion" of multi-cellular animal fossils. However, in recent decades, unusual multi-cellular animal fossils, the so-called Ediacara fauna, have been found in late Neoproterozoic sediments below the Precambrian/Cambrian boundary in those regions where the relevant portion of the geologic record has been preserved and exposed to view.[5] Furthermore, stratigraphically below those fossils, thick conglomerate units have been found that have been called diamictites, and interpreted as glacial deposits known as tillites, but which can equally be regarded simply as breccias that are consistent with a major tectonic disturbance. These units correspond to the Sixtymile Formation in the Grand Canyon, and the Kingston Peak Formation in the Mojave Desert region of southern California. They are also found in the Wasatch Mountains of central Utah, the MacKenzie Mountains of western Canada, in the Adelaidean and adjoining basins of southern and central Australia, and in the Otavi carbonate platform of the southern Kalahari craton of southern Africa.[6] Also of significance is the association with these diamictite units of carbonate strata that were deposited in warm water, which is hardly

3   K. E. Karlstrom, S. A. Bowring, C. M. Dehler, A. H. Knoll, S. M. Porter, D. J. Des Marai, A. B. Weil, Z. D. Sharp, J. W. Geissman, M. A. Elrick, J. M. Timmons, L. J. Crossey and K. L. Davidek, 2000, Chuar Group of the Grand Canyon: Record of breakup of Rodinia, associated change in the global carbon cycle, and ecosystem expansion by 740 Ma, *Geology*, 28 (7): 619-622. This paper reports a U-Pb zircon age of 742±6 Ma for an ash layer at the top of Chuar Group, just below the unconformity at the base of the Sixtymile Formation which has been identified as the pre-Flood/Flood boundary.

4   N. Steno, 1677, *De solido intra solidum naturaliter contento dissertationis prodomus [Prodomus to a Dissertation on a Solid Body Naturally Contained Within a Solid]*, Florence, Italy; Whitcomb and Morris, 1961.

5   V. M. Narbonne, 1998, The Ediacara biota: a terminal Neoproterozoic experiment in the evolution of life, *GSA Today*, 8 (2): 1-6.

6   P. F. Hoffman, A. J. Kaufman and D. J. Halverson, 1998, Comings and goings of global glaciations on a Neoproterozoic tropical platform in Namibia, *GSA Today*, 8 (5): 1-9; P. F. Hoffman, A. J. Kaufman, G. P. Halverson, and D. P. Shrag, 1998, A Neoproterozoic snowball earth, *Science*, 281: 1342-1346; M. J. Kennedy, B. Runnegar, A. R. Prave, K. H. Hoffmann and M. A. Arthur, 2000; C. M. Dehler, M. B. Elrick, K. E. Karlstrom, G. A. Smith, L. J. Crossey and J. M. Timmons, 2001, Neoproterozoic Chuar Group (≈800-742 Ma), Grand Canyon: A record of cyclical marine deposition during global cooling and supercontinent rifting, *Sedimentary Geology*, 141-142: 465-499.

consistent with these diamictites being interpreted as glacial deposits.[7] On the other hand, these warm-water carbonate rock units associated with these breccias at such distant locations around the global are consistent with the warm climate before the Flood, and with the warmth of the initial Flood waters from the warm water and steam that burst forth from the fountains of the great deep as they broke up. Therefore, these breccia units could well mark the tectonic upheaval that is to be expected for the onset of catastrophic plate tectonics, when the pre-Flood supercontinent and the pre-Flood ocean floor were broken up as the trigger for the commencement of the Flood.

---

7   Further discussion of the claimed Neoproterozoic Ice Age is in chapter 126.

89

THE DESTRUCTIVE POWER
OF FLOODS AND OCEAN WAVES

One thing is absolutely certain, if the biblical record of the Flood is true, as is strongly affirmed here, then the Flood was a cataclysm of absolutely enormous scope and such potency that it must have accomplished an immense amount of geologic work during the year in which it prevailed over the earth. It is unreasonable to reject the Bible's account as of no historical value whatever, so the facts must be acknowledged that many of the earth's present rock strata must have been produced by the Flood. It has already been shown that the Bible quite clearly and emphatically teaches the historic fact of a global Flood, and thus it should be immediately obvious that if such a global Flood occurred, it must have been the greatest geologic and geomorphic agent acting on the earth since the creation of the earth itself! Anyone who can conceive of a worldwide Flood as being "tranquil"and geologically impotent should be easily able to equate east with west and black with white!

Even the relatively trivial floods of modern experience exert tremendous erosive force and sediment-carrying power. Indeed, in the words of the late Derek Ager, former geology professor at the University College of Swansea in Wales:

> The hurricane, the flood or the tsunami may do more in an hour or a day than the ordinary processes of nature have achieved in a thousand years.[1]

It is precisely because disastrous floods are rare events, that even the power of local floods and the geologic work they accomplish is often forgotten:

> The astonishing power exerted by a flood of rushing water, both in scouring and in transporting material, is rarely fully appreciated even today.[2]

---

1   Ager, 1973, 49.

2   C. F. Fox, 1953, *Water*, New York: Philosophical Library, xiv.

Following is a striking account of floods and the carrying power of flooded streams in northeast India:

> [T]he water had risen only thirteen feet above the level at which it had stood a few days previously; the rush was tremendous—huge blocks of rock measuring some feet across were rolled along with an awful crashing, almost as easily as pebbles in an ordinary stream. In one night a block of granite, which I calculated to weigh upwards of 350 tons, was moved for more than 100 yards; while the current was actually turbid with pebbles of some inches in size, suspended almost like mud in the rushing stream.... In that region there now is practically no soil...and it is also noticeable that water carrying much mud in suspension (and its increased density therefrom) carries larger stones than clear water, for equal velocities.[3]

One must visualize flood action like this, not just in a limited area, but on a worldwide scale, not just for a few days or hours, but continuing for weeks and months, to appreciate the character of, and geologic work accomplished by, the biblical Flood.

From Utah comes an account of another modern flood:

> On this area the 1930 floods destroyed houses, broke in the east wall of the schoolhouse and deposited debris for a depth of several feet, including boulders of all sizes up to 20 tons in weight. Some larger boulders removed about 1000 feet from the canyon's mouth down a 4° gradient. Several of these weigh from 75 to 100 tons each, and two, previously mentioned, weight 150 and 210 tons respectively. The deep gorges freshly excavated for the full length of the flood canyons are no less impressive than the flood depositions in the valley. Cuts were made in typical canyon fill— in places to a depth of 70 feet. Long, continuous stretches of bedrock were exposed on the bottom of the channels. The canyon fill consisted of debris brought from further upstream by running water, and of materials collected from the adjacent canyon slopes. Included were boulders ranging up to 50 feet in diameter.[4]

Undoubtedly the most spectacular demonstration of the results of catastrophic water action is provided by the "Channeled Scabland" of the Pacific Northwest of the United States. This is a 16,000-square-mile area, mostly in eastern Washington state, that is essentially flat and underlain by thick and extensive basalt flows, with only a thin soil cover. However, into it has been eroded a braided pattern of deep, dry channels, with severely scrubbed bare rock surfaces. Geologists of the late

---

3   Fox, 1953, 70.

4   R. W. Bailey, C. L. Forsling and R. J. Becraft, 1934, *Floods and Accelerated Erosion in Northern Utah*, US Department of Agriculture Miscellaneous Publication 196, 9.

19th century thought that the large dry channels were eroded by streams very slowly during immense periods of time, when the region was more humid during the Ice Age, and when the edge of the great continental ice sheets and associated glaciers were in northern Washington.[5] In 1885 T. C. Chamberlain noted "a series of parallel water marks…sweeping around the valleys" in northwestern Montana, which he suggested were the remnants of an enormous lake that had been impounded by glacier ice. That drained lake became known as Lake Missoula. However, for more than 50 years geologists failed to make the connection between this former lake and the Channeled Scabland, except, that is, for J. Harlen Bretz, who in 1923 proposed a catastrophic flood hypothesis for the erosion of the channels in the scabland. He suggested that there had been a catastrophic drainage of Lake Missoula in Montana by breaching the glacier ice dam that had impounded the lake's waters, and thus water hundreds of feet deep had eroded the complex network of channels downstream catastrophically. But such was the stranglehold of uniformitarian orthodoxy on the geological establishment of the day that Bretz's hypothesis was considered outrageous and vigorously opposed. Undaunted, Bretz stood his ground in papers he wrote during the subsequent bitter debate, which spanned four decades, and yet single-handedly he eventually prevailed in the 1960s.[6]

It is estimated that ancient Lake Missoula covered an area of 3,000 square miles, having been formed by a glacier as much as 2,500 feet deep blocking a valley. The lake would have been at least 950 feet deep, where the town of Missoula now is. At an elevation of 4,200 feet above sea level, the lake was estimated to have had a volume of 500 cubic miles of water, about one-fifth the volume of Lake Michigan. When the ice dam failed catastrophically, it is estimated that 380 cubic miles of water were discharged in two days, the ice-charged waters surging across the Columbia Plateau of eastern Washington at an estimated rate of up to 10 cubic miles per hour. The Channeled Scabland was the 16,000-square-mile erosional product, from which an estimated 50 cubic miles of sediment and rock had been removed.

The surging floodwaters cut deep gorges or "coulees" in solid basalt, the largest of these being the Grand Coulee, which is 50 miles long and two miles wide, with walls up to 900 feet high. Almost ten cubic miles of solid basalt bedrock was removed to produce this enormous trench. There would also have been a series of great waterfalls, the best known being the Dry Falls in the Lower Grand Coulee,

---

5   See the discussion on the Ice Age in chapters 97-98.

6   J. H. Bretz, 1923, The Channeled Scabland of the Columbia Plateau, *Journal of Geology*, 31: 617-649; J. H. Bretz, 1927, Channeled Scabland and the Spokane Flood, *Washington Academy of Science Journal*, 17 (8): 200-211; J. H. Bretz, 1930, Lake Missoula and the Spokane Flood, *Geological Society of America Bulletin*, 41: 92-93; J. H. Bretz, 1959, Washington's Channeled Scabland, *Washington Division of Mines and Geology Bulletin*, 45; J. H. Bretz, 1969, The Lake Missoula Floods and the Channeled Scabland, *Journal of Geology*, 77: 505-543.

which are 350 feet high and three miles wide.[7] It is estimated that the flood of water as it flowed over Dry Falls would have been up to 300 feet deep and flowing at a rate of 386 million cubic feet (nearly 11 million cubic meters) per second, or about ten times the combined flow of all the rivers of the world! This great flood swept across eastern Washington at up to 45 miles per hour (more than 72 kilometers per hour). At Palouse Falls, a 180-foot-high waterfall was eroded, and now stands at the end of a 400-foot-deep gorge that is six miles long. If this flood lasted for as much as a week, the erosional retreat of the falls to carve the six-mile-long gorge into solid basalt would have averaged about 180 feet per hour, and the basalt would have been eroding at a rate of approximately 10 million cubic feet per hour! Yet this was only a local flood, so it is not difficult to conceive the erosional capacity of the year-long global Flood!

This controversy over the Channeled Scabland of eastern Washington centered on whether the catastrophic water flows could generate the magnitude and speed of erosion necessary to scour solid basalt bedrock to form what are today dry, deeply-incised channels.[8] Even some of the most famous geologists between 1930 and 1960 remained solidly uniformitarian and refused to believe in massive-flood erosion in eastern Washington:

> The role of floods in the erosion of stream channels has been one of the most controversial topics in fluvial geomorphology....Indeed, the famous Spokane flood debate, concerning the effects of the greatest known freshwater floods on the planet...centered on the issue of the erosive capability of running water....Those who disbelieved the flood theory of J. Harlen Bretz did so out of their experience that rivers did not behave as Bretz proposed. Subsequent work showed that their experience, not Bretz's theory, was inadequate.[9]

Investigations of the magnitude and speed of erosion of bedrock during catastrophic floods have determined that the processes of cavitation and plucking are dominant. Cavitation is a rock-pulverizing process associated with fluid flows greater than 30 feet per second (20 miles per hour), and occurs as the fluid detaches from irregularities in the bedrock, producing vacuum cavities ("bubbles") that implode (see Figure 54, page 1089). The cavitation process inflicts explosive, hammer-like blows on the bedrock surface, with pressures ranging as high as 30,000 atmospheres (440,000 pounds per square inch).[10] These extreme pressures, with

7   D. V. Ager, 1993, *The New Catastrophism: The Importance of the Rare Event in Geological History*, Cambridge, UK: Cambridge University Press, 19-22.

8   V. R. Baker, 1978, The Spokane flood controversy and the martian outflow channels, *Science*, 202: 1249-1256.

9   V. R. Baker, 1988, Flood erosion, in *Flood Geomorphology*, V. R. Baker, R. C. Cochel and P. C. Patton, eds., New York: John Wiley, 89.

10   H. L. Barnes, 1956, Cavitation as a geological agent, *American Journal of Science*, 254: 493-505; F. R. Young, 1989, *Cavitation*, New York: McGraw-Hill.

which cavitation literally hammers the rock, are many times greater than the rock's compressive strength, so the rock is literally pulverized and converted to powder.

Plucking is the second extremely rapid erosive process, whereby high-velocity flows are able to rip loose large blocks of bedrock along joint surfaces (see Figure 54). Once dislodged, the high-velocity flow is able to move and abraid the large blocks of bedrock. However, the most energetic phenomenon associated with the macro-turbulent flow in a catastrophic flood is a "kolk," a vortex of water with a very low pressure beneath the flowing water, the underwater equivalent of a tornado (see Figure 54).[11] The suction power of the kolk exerts intense hydraulic lifting forces, and can remove or pluck large slabs of bedrock. Thus, there can be no doubt that a catastrophic flood on a global scale is more than capable of eroding its way through thousands of meters of rock strata from the pre-Flood continental land surface.

Another agent of catastrophic erosion not usually considered, but relevant in the context of the Flood event, is explosive volcano activity. Just what a volcanic eruption can achieve is best illustrated by the extraordinary results of the May 18, 1980, and subsequent eruptions at Mount St. Helens in Washington state. There was exceptional variety in the major agents of erosion unleashed by the Mount St. Helens eruptions, concentrated within a limited and intensely-studied area:[12]

1. The direct blast—the 20-megaton-TNT equivalent, northward-directed steam blast at the onset of the May 18 eruption caused hot gas and rock fragments to abraid the slopes around the mountain.

2. Pyroclastic flows—explosive blasts on and after May 18 generated superheated, erosive "rivers" of ground-hugging volcanic ash and steam.

3. Debris avalanches—the movement of great masses of rock, ice, and debris over the ground surface next to the volcano caused significant abrasion of the ground surface.

4. Mudflows—viscous streams of mud gouged out soft volcanic ash deposits and, unexpectedly, even the hardest underlying rocks.

5. Water in channels—overland flow of water caused extraordinary rill and gully patterns to appear, even in nearly level slopes.

6. Water waves—enormous waves generated in nearby Spirit Lake by the avalanche on May 18 inflicted severe erosion on the slopes adjacent to the lake.

---

11   V. R. Baker, 1978, Paleohydraulics and hydrodynamics of scabland floods, in *The Channeled Scabland*, V. R. Baker and D. Nummedal, eds., Washington: National Aeronautics and Space Administration, 59-79.

12   S. A. Austin, 1984, Rapid erosion at Mt St Helens, *Origins (Geoscience Research Institute)*, 11 (2): 90-98.

7. Jetting steam—eruptions of steam from buried glacier ice reamed holes through hot volcanic ash deposits and formed distinctive explosion pits.

8. Mass wasting—gravitational collapse induced significant changes to unstable slopes, especially those areas sculptured by other agents, leaving behind a varied landscape.

The most fearsome sight would have been the colossal wave up to 650 feet high, generated on Spirit Lake by one-eighth of a cubic mile of avalanche debris from the summit and north slope of Mount St. Helens within the first minute of the May 18 eruption. This enormous water wave eroded the northern slopes of the lake, scouring it of soil and trees, and leaving a distinct clip line. Equally impressive were the mudflows that were responsible for the most extraordinary erosion features. On the slopes of the volcano, melted snow water mixed with volcanic debris formed mudflows that accelerated up to 90 miles per hour, causing very severe erosion, even into solid bedrock, on the flanks of the volcano. Two new canyons were catastrophically excavated to solid rock (old andesite lava flows) to depths of tens of feet, and one of these canyons is up to 700 feet deep (215 meters) and several miles long.

Two-thirds of a cubic mile of landslide debris from the May 18 eruption occupied 23 square miles in the valley to the north and west of the crater, deposited across its entire width for 16 miles. Averaging 150 feet in thickness, but reaching a maximum thickness of almost 600 feet near Spirit Lake, this debris blocked the natural drainage outlet from the Mount St. Helens and Spirit Lake area. Then an explosive eruption at Mount St. Helens on March 19, 1982, melted a thick snow pack in the crater, creating a destructive sheet-like flood of water that became a mudflow. This mudflow breached the deposits blocking the drainage in the valley, catastrophically downcutting through them to form anastomosing channels over much of the debris, and established a new dendritic pattern of channels, including a canyon system one-fortieth the scale of the real Grand Canyon in northern Arizona. Individual canyons have depths of up to 140 feet, with sheer cliffs of up to almost 100 feet high.

There is no doubt, therefore, that the great volcanic upheavals associated with the breaking up of the earth's crust at the onset of the Flood, and as a result of upwelling mantle, mantle plumes, and subducting oceanic crust due to catastrophic plate tectonics during the Flood, unleashed vast amounts of juvenile waters, and created profound disturbances both on the ocean floor and on the continental land surfaces as they were being inundated. So it must not be forgotten that catastrophic erosion at the onset on the Flood was not just due to the torrential rains pouring from the skies. Prodigious great tidal waves would have undoubtedly been generated by the earth movements and earthquakes associated with the fracturing of the earth's crust. Added to this, as the Flood progressed, the ocean waters would have been heated around the spreading centers encircling the globe, while the geysers blasting steam and water into the atmosphere would have generated extreme atmospheric turbulence. Thus, it has been postulated that exceedingly violent storms and catastrophic hurricanes ("hypercanes") would have been generated, producing enormous storm surges and storm waves, with incredible erosive potential as they reached the transgressing shorelines.[13]

Even the action of ordinary waves and littoral currents can, over relatively short periods of time, accomplish enormous amounts of erosion and/or deposition along coastlines, particularly when something happens to change the sediment balance normally existing:

> Any unusual conditions, whether natural or man-made, may upset the balance in such a way that what has been a very stable beach may quickly show significant erosion or accretion. For example, the hurricanes that at times sweep the Atlantic and Gulf Coasts of the United States frequently produce pronounced changes on the affected beaches.[14]

Obviously, the onset of the Flood would have presented profoundly "unusual conditions," and would have immediately resulted in the catastrophic erosion of the coastline of the pre-Flood continent(s). Furthermore, the destructive effect of ordinary storm waves is trivial compared to that of tidal waves or tsunamis, such as must have occurred with great frequency and complexity during the Flood. However, even ordinary waves display awesome power:

> Waves are seldom more than twenty-five feet high; but violent storms may raise them to sixty feet, and there are unverified reports of even greater heights…the immense striking power of a wave cannot be released until it hits an object that cannot float with it. Waves striking the shore of Terra del Fuego can be heard for 20 miles. Spray from a storm wave has been hurled to the top of a lighthouse nearly 200 feet above sea level. The force of waves striking the shore can be measured, and has been found to reach three tons per square foot.[15]

The immense erosive power of such wave forces should be obvious:

> Waves, particularly storm waves and tsunamis, are the most important agents of marine erosion. Smaller waves, such as those associated with surf, may carry on attrition of material and minor amounts of abrasion,

---

13   J. Woodmorappe, 1998, Hypercanes as a cause of the 40-day global Flood rainfall, in *Proceedings of the Fourth International Conference on Creationism*, R. E. Walsh, ed., Pittsburgh, PA: Creation Science Fellowship, 645-658; L. Vardiman, 2003, Hypercanes following the Genesis Flood, in *Proceedings of the Fifth International Conference on Creationism*, R. L. Ivey, ed., Pittsburgh, PA: Creation Science Fellowship, 17-28.

14   J. M. Caldwell, 1949, Beach erosion, *Scientific Monthly*, 69: 432.

15   T. Ting, 1953, *Water*, New York: McMillan, 49.

but, just as a stream during a single flood may do more geologic work than it will for months or years at low-water stage, so storm waves during a short period may effect more change than ordinary waves will in months.... The enormous force exerted by breaking waves is attested by recorded movements of masses weighing many thousands of pounds. Air in joints and cracks is suddenly compressed and acts as if a wedge were suddenly driven into them. Recession of the water is accompanied by sudden expansion of air with explosive force. This driving of water into cracks not only exerts great mechanical stress but in soluble rocks may greatly accelerate solution.[16]

Wind-generated waves exceeding 100 feet in height have been measured, and some examples of the immense destructive forces that storm waves can develop have been described:

At Sherbourg, France, a breakwater was composed of large rocks and capped with a wall 20 feet high. Storm waves hurdled 7,000-pound stones over the wall and moved 65-ton concrete blocks 60 feet...at Wick, Scotland, the end of the breakwater was capped by a 800-ton block of concrete that was secured to the foundation by iron rods 3.5 inches in diameter. In a great storm in 1872 the designer of the breakwater watched in amazement from a nearby cliff as both cap and foundations, weighing a total of 1350 tons, were removed as a unit and deposited in the water that the wall was supposed to protect. He rebuilt the structure and added a larger cap weighing 2600 tons, which was treated similarly by a storm a few years later.[17]

Probably the most destructive of all waves are tsunamis, caused by submarine earthquakes, volcanic eruptions, or debris slides. They have been known to attain velocities of 400 or more miles per hour and heights of 130 feet, traveling extraordinary distances.[18] The explosive volcanic eruption of Krakatoa in Indonesia on August 27, 1883, generated enormous waves at least 100 feet high and traveling up to 450 miles per hour, inundating neighboring islands, sweeping away a town and drowning nearly 40,000 people. A tsunami from this eruption was still two feet high as it passed Sri Lanka, and tidal gauges in South Africa, Cape Horn, and Panama (11,470 miles from Krakatoa) clearly recorded the progress of the sequence of waves! In April 1946, a tsunami originating from an earthquake and landslide in the trench associated with the Aleutian Islands traveled at 470 miles per hour across the Pacific and generated a 19-foot-high "tidal" wave on the shores of Hawaii, causing great destruction. At Scotch Cape in Alaska, the same tsunami

---

16   W. D. Thornbury, 1969, *Principles of Geomorphology*, second edition, New York: Wiley, 424-425.

17   W. Bascom, 1959, Ocean waves, *Scientific American*, 201 (2): 80.

18   P. H. Kuenen, 1950, *Marine Geology*, New York: Wiley, 80; F. P. Shepard, 1977, *Geological Oceanography*, Brisbane: University of Queensland Press, 50, 54.

destroyed a concrete lighthouse when a wave more than 100 feet high crashed onto the shore. A tsunami that swept across the Bay of Bengal in 1876 left 20,000 people dead.[19] Between 1900 and 1983 there were no fewer than 245 tsunamis that crossed the Pacific Ocean, an average of nearly three per year.[20] The tsunamis generated by the destructive Chilean earthquakes of 1960 demonstrate how their destructive power had widespread effects:

> The disastrous series of earthquakes that struck Chile late in May has brought death and destruction to countries on the perimeter of the entire Pacific. In the wake of the earthquakes, great tidal waves—up to 50 feet high and traveling at jet speeds of 525 miles an hour—caused extensive damage to Pacific ports, from Japan to California and from Alaska to New Zealand. The waves that wrecked the coastal villages of Japan a third of the way around the world were 32 feet high. In both Japan and Hawaii, which was struck by four waves, there was serious loss of life and extensive property damage.[21]

Thus, it is tsunamis like these, the most destructive of all types of waves, which would have been unleashed during the Flood by the breaking up of the earth's crust in continuing catastrophic earthquake activity and volcanic eruptions due to rapid plate motions, subduction, outpouring of lavas, etc. Furthermore, this breaking up of the earth's crust, with all its associated destructiveness, continued from the first day of the Flood (Genesis 7:11) through the same period of 150 days while the global rain fell, until both were stopped by God (Genesis 8:2). There can be absolutely no doubt about the destructive potential of this catastrophic global Flood to inflict the devastation intended by God as a judgment upon man, and upon the earth that he had corrupted.

---

19   Bascom, 1959, 81-83.

20   N. M. Ridgeway, 1984, Tsunamis—a natural hazard, *Pamphlet No 41*, New Zealand DSRI Science and Information Centre.

21   1960, Chile earthquake spreads disaster around the world, *Civil Engineering*, 30: 88.

90

SEDIMENTATION AND FOSSILIZATION DURING THE FLOOD

The overall picture is one of awesome proportions. Magma and superheated steam were bursting up through the fractured fountains on the ocean floor, with steam and water being catapulted high into the atmosphere. Powerful tsunamis were being generated by the associated earth movements and earthquakes, as the ocean lithosphere began to move and be subducted. High in the atmosphere, the water lofted by the chain of ocean geysers fell back to earth as intense global rain. On the exposed land surface, rivers and waterways would have become swollen and then raging torrents, initiating erosion and transportation of the captured sediment load. The ocean water displaced by the rising spreading centers would have, in concert with the tsunamis, moved as a surging current toward the shorelines, picking up the sediments being scraped off the subducting ocean floor and from the continental shelves.

This globe-encircling interplay of catastrophic diastrophic and hydrodynamic forces must, beyond any question, have profoundly altered the pre-Flood topography and geology of the earth's crust. The powerful ocean currents, tsunamis, and tidal and storm surges, in particular, would have surged onto the continental land surfaces, inundating them, and together with the intense rainfall would have been extremely potent agents of immense, catastrophic erosion that produced sediments that were transported and deposited. Under the action of this combination of effects, almost any sort of sedimentary deposit or depositional sequence would have been produced, so that an immense variety of sedimentary strata must finally have been the result as the Flood ran its course. Even in the strata sequences locally deposited, the raging Flood waters would erode the tops of them before the next sediment-laden surges would have deposited yet more sedimentary strata sequences unconformably on top of them. The progressive cycle of catastrophic plate tectonics would ensure, as continental fragments collided, these strata sequences were buckled and folded, faulted and uplifted, perhaps to be temporarily above the Flood waters, only to be eroded again as the Flood continued. It is thus easy to envisage catastrophic formation of the strata sequences we now see exposed to view across the surface of today's continents, as a result of this global, cataclysmic tectonic, year-long Flood event.

The speed at which tectonic upheavals, mass wasting, and rapid, turbulent water flows can carry and deposit enormous quantities of sediment into strata layers has been well documented. One reads of 170 feet of debris being deposited in an hour as a result of a cloud-burst, and in 1958, 40 million cubic meters of rock fell in a landslip into Lituya Bay on the coast of Alaska.[1] Rock strata produced by such debris flows are well known in the geologic record, such as the diamictite units previously mentioned that are postulated to have been the first-formed strata layers of the Flood. Hurricanes are known to also deposit extensive layers of sediment as they move toward coastlines. For example, a hurricane in 1960 generated surging ocean waves, which flooded inland along the coast of southern Florida for up to five miles for six hours, and deposited a six-inch-thick mud layer, even with numerous thin laminae.[2]

Furthermore, volcanic eruptions also demonstrate the catastrophic accumulation of sediments. Indeed, even though the 1980 eruptions of Mount St. Helens in Washington state were relatively small compared to the eruptions of other volcanoes elsewhere in the world in historic times, they were nevertheless responsible for forming a thickness of up to 600 feet of strata. These deposits accumulated from the primary air blast, landslide, the wave on Spirit Lake, pyroclastic flows, mudflows, air fall, and stream water. The most interesting accumulations were the pyroclastic flow deposits, best illustrated by the 25-feet-thick stratified deposit of June 12, 1980.[3] The collapse of the eruption plume of debris over the volcano generated hurricane-velocity, ground-hugging, fluidized, surging turbulent slurries of fine volcanic ash and debris that moved off the flank of the volcano. In less than five hours, 25 feet of very extensive strata had accumulated, even containing thin laminae and cross-bedding from 1 mm thick to >1 meter thick, each representing just a few seconds to several minutes of accumulation.

Another graphic example of the sedimentation resulting from catastrophic flooding is the deposits produced from the erosion debris scoured from the Channeled Scabland of Washington state during the catastrophic drainage of Lake Missoula. It is estimated that more than 50 cubic miles of sediment, soil, and solid-rock basalt flows were eroded from the Channeled Scabland, and then deposited downstream as the floodwaters slowed. Noteworthy are the thick deposits of silt, sand, gravel, and boulders in the Quincy Basin, just downstream from the Grand Coulee, and the thick, rhythmically-bedded layers of silt up to 300 feet thick over an area of 300 square miles in the Walla Walla Valley.[4]

---

1   Ager, 1973, 47-48.

2   M. M. Ball, E. A. Shinn and K. W. Stockman, 1967, The geologic effects of Hurricane Donna in South Florida, *Journal of Geology*, 75: 583-597.

3   S. A. Austin, 1986, Mount St Helens and catastrophism, in *Proceedings of the First International Conference on Creationism*, vol. 1, Pittsburgh, PA: Creation Science Fellowship, 3-9.

4   J. H. Bretz, 1929, Valley deposits immediately east of the Channeled Scabland of Washington, *Journal of Geology*, 37: 393-427, 505-541; J. H. Bretz, 1930, Valley deposits immediately west of the Channeled Scabland, *Journal of Geology*, 38: 385-422; R. J. Carson, C. F. McKhaun and M. H. Pizey, 1978, The

There can be no doubt, therefore, that in spite of the complexity of the physical agencies involved, the Flood event provides an adequate explanation for the formation of the sedimentary strata in the geologic record attributed to it. Furthermore, it would have been the catastrophic deposition of sediments that was the necessary condition for the rapid burial and fossilization of many animals and plants that had been living in the pre-Flood world. The creatures of the ocean floors would have been universally overwhelmed by the toxicity and violence of the volcanic eruptions, as the ocean floor was lifted and the spreading centers formed, and by the heat and bottom currents thereby generated. These upheavals would have dislodged and scoured the veneer of mixed organic and inorganic ocean-floor sediments, and transported them along with the overwhelmed sea creatures, the mixture eventually to be redeposited either elsewhere on the ocean floor, or ultimately on the pre-Flood land surfaces as they were progressively inundated by the rising sea level surging shorewards. In similar fashion, the fish and other organisms living within the ocean nearer the surface would subsequently have been swept with sediments washing up onto the land surface, as it progressively became the bottom of a global ocean. These sediments and the animal remains they carried would have been transported and deposited on top of other sediments already being laid down. On the remaining land surfaces, the raging torrents of grossly flooded rivers would have carried great quantities of detritus toward the encroaching seas, occasionally consuming animals, together with great rafts of vegetation. These would normally have been deposited finally in some more or less quiescent part of these streams, or have finally been laid down in the encroaching sea on top sediment layers and their contained organic remains, already laid down by the strong sediment-laden ocean water surges progressively inundating the land.

There can thus be no doubt that under such conditions during the Flood, as the torrential rains fell and the ocean waters surged to inundate the land surfaces, burial and fossilization of myriads of animals and plants *en masse* was guaranteed. Whereas burial and fossilization of even a single animal or plant is an exceedingly rare happenstance, the abundance of fossils preserved in the geologic record, often in massive numbers in what have aptly been called fossil graveyards, is unmistakable, powerful testimony to the destructive effects of the watery cataclysm described in the Scriptures. Even after the first forty days, when the greatest of the rains and upheavals diminished, the biblical record says that the waters of the then universal ocean "prevailed" across the earth's surface for a further 110 days before their abatement began. Furthermore, this 110 days, in which the waters of the universal ocean continued to flow and surge around the globe, with each successive regular tide, coincided with the continued operation of the catastrophic plate tectonics process of mantle upwelling and steam expulsion as new oceanic crust was generated to cause sea floor spreading, plate motion, subduction of oceanic crust, and continental collisions. This great dynamic imbalance imposed on the

Touchet beds of the Walla Walla Valley, in *Channeled Scabland*, V. R. Baker and D. Nummedal, eds., National Aeronautics and Space Administration, 173-177.

earth for such a long time would certainly imply that extensive hydraulic and sedimentary activity continued right through that period, with even early Flood sedimentary strata, especially those deformed and uplifted during continental collisions, being re-eroded and reworked. Thus, some sediments may well have been transported and deposited several times before reaching their final resting places. Furthermore, where magmas had been intruded into these sediments and cooled, or where the deep burial of sediments had resulted in metamorphism, these new magmatic and metamorphic rocks would have been exposed to erosion by the stripping of any overlying sediments, so that all these erosion products would have been included in new sedimentary strata. These processes continued, guaranteeing the destruction of the pre-Flood earth surface, and the burial and fossilization of the animals and plants that had inhabited it.

91

THE ORDER OF THE STRATA
DEPOSITED BY THE FLOOD

The foregoing description of global tectonics, sedimentation, and fossilization processes catastrophically operating during the Flood must, of course, be subject to testing by comparison with the field data of the geologic record, with a view to establishing the general adequacy of the scriptural framework for organizing and harmonizing the geologic data. Obviously, a very substantial portion of the earth's crustal geology must be explained in terms of the Flood, if the biblical record is true.

For example, the most obvious implication of the biblical account is that a very large proportion of the earth's fossil deposits must be associated with catastrophic aqueous action especially, or with volcanism. The vast extent of the sedimentary strata is indicated as follows:

> About three-fourths, perhaps more, of the land area of the earth, 55 million square miles, has sedimentary rock as the bedrock at the surface or directly under the cover of mantle-rock....The thickness of the stratified rocks ranges from a few feet to 40,000 feet or more at any one place....The vast bulk of the stratified rocks is composed of shallow-water deposits.[1]

This is exactly what would be expected if the waters of a universal flood had covered the earth. Similarly, recent volcanic deposits are widely distributed across the earth's surface, which is again just as the biblical account would imply.

However, it is crucial to consider the all-important question of the sequence of deposition of the strata preserved in the geologic record. Even though the order of strata has been made the basis of the conventionally-accepted system of geochronology and historical geology, the physical reality of the strata order is generally not in dispute. Local strata sequences can be physically compiled by field work, and careful correlations between local areas and from region to

---

1   O. D. Von Engeln and K. E. Caster, 1952, *Geology*, New York: McGraw-Hill, 129.

region have clearly established the robustness of the overall strata sequence of the geologic record. Indeed, careful correlations have shown the inter-regional and sub-continental extent of some of the strata, which then is totally inexplicable in terms of deposition of the sediments according to conventional uniformitarian thinking, but becomes powerful evidence of catastrophic deposition during the Flood. Thus, it is not the order of the strata in the geologic record that is in dispute, but rather the uniformitarian interpretation of the order of the strata, and of their contained fossils as the backbone of the theory of organic evolution, with its purported display of gradual development of all forms of creatures from simple cells, and of the various geological ages as supposedly shown in the fossils contained in the sedimentary strata. By the false belief in the perpetual uniformity of geologic processes, the very plainest testimony to the global cataclysmic Flood in which the "world that then was, being overflowed with water, perished" (2 Peter 3:6) has been transformed instead into a supposed rock record of gradual organic evolution!

Of course, the complete geologic record is hardly ever, if at all, found in any one place on the earth's surface. Usually several or many of the strata systems are missing compared to the overall geologic record, but usually over a given region there is more complete preservation of the record via correlation and integration. However, quite commonly there is little or no physical or physiographic evidence of the intervening period of erosion or non-deposition of the missing strata systems, suggesting that at such localities neither erosion nor deposition ever occurred there. However, this is exactly what would be expected in the light of the biblical record of the Flood and its implications! In some areas would be deposited one sequence of sedimentary strata with their contained fossil assemblages, and in other areas entirely different strata sequences, depending on the source areas and directions of the currents transporting the sediments. Some strata units would have been deposited over wider areas than others, with erosion in some areas but continuous deposition in others, even when intervening strata units were deposited elsewhere. Thus, as a result of the complex interplay of currents, waves, and transported sediments with their entombed organisms, a variety of different types of sedimentary rocks and strata sequences would have been laid down directly on the pre-Flood strata sequences, and particularly the crystalline basement that probably dates back to the Creation Week itself:

> Further, how many geologists have pondered the fact that lying on the crystalline basement are found from place to place not merely Cambrian, but rocks of all ages?[2]

This seems to have been a rhetorical question, which ought to have been puzzling to conventional geologists because of the immense eons of time thus represented at some strata boundaries, with the evidence of the presumed uniformity of geologic

---

2   E. M. Spieker, 1956, Mountain-building chronology and nature of geologic time-scale, *American Association of Petroleum Geologists' Bulletin*, 40: 185.

processes in space and time being almost entirely absent. On the other hand, this pattern of deposition of the sedimentary strata sequences is entirely consistent with the strata record the Flood would have been expected to have produced.

It is also important to note, in passing, that even though the Cambrian, and the underlying Vendian or latest Precambrian (where they occur), rocks are the oldest strata containing megascopic animal fossils (excluding the stromatolite-building algae and bacteria, and associated multi-cellular organic remains), the evolutionary interpretation still faces an unsolvable problem:

> Most paleontologists today give little thought to fossiliferous rocks older than the Cambrian, thus ignoring the most important missing link of all. Indeed, the missing Pre-Cambrian record cannot properly be described as a link for it is in reality about nine-tenths of the chain of life: the first nine-tenths.[3]

Indeed, apart from the megascopic Ediacaran fauna found in some Vendian strata, conventional paleontologists and geologists are puzzled by the so-called "Cambrian explosion," the sudden appearance in the fossil record of all the different invertebrate phyla with their different body plans, and with no apparent evidence in the Vendian and other Precambrian sedimentary strata of any ancestors to the animals in these phyla that might suggest how they evolved.[4] It has thus been noted:

> Granted an evolutionary origin of the main groups of animals, and not an act of special creation, the absence of any record whatsoever of a single member of any of the phyla in the Pre-Cambrian rocks remains as inexplicable on orthodox grounds as it was to Darwin.[5]

Nevertheless, if the order of the strata and their contained fossil assemblages is not generally in dispute, then that order in the strata sequences still must reflect the geological processes and their timing responsible for the formation of the strata and their order. If, as it is assiduously maintained here, the order in the fossil record does not represent the sequence of the evolutionary development of life, then the fossil order must be explainable within the context of the tempo of geological processes during the global Flood cataclysm. Indeed, both the order of the strata and their contained fossils could well provide us with information about the pre-Flood world, and evidence of the progress of different geological processes during the Flood event. There are a number of factors that have been suggested to

---

3   H. S. Ladd, 1957, Introduction, in *Treatise on Marine Ecology and Paleoecology*, vol. II, Geological Society of America Memoir 67: 7.

4   S. C. Meyer, M. Ross, P. Nelson and P. Chien, 2003, The Cambrian explosion: biology's big bang, in *Darwinism, Design and Public Education*, J. A. Campbell and S. C. Meyers, eds., East Lansing, MI: Michigan State University Press, 323-402.

5   C. N. George, 1960, Fossils in evolutionary perspective, *Science Progress*, XLVIII: 5.

explain the order in the fossil record, and these must now be considered.

Pre-Flood Biogeography

As has already been suggested in the foregoing discussion of the pre-Flood era, there could well have been distinct biological communities in the pre-Flood world, spatially and geographically separated from one another. For example, there is evidence of a floating-forest biome that existed as a distinct ecosystem on the surface of much of the pre-Flood ocean. This biome not only included the unique lycopods, trees of various sizes containing large hollow cavities and root-like rhizomes, and associated similar plants, but also some unique animals, mainly amphibians, that lived in these forests. Similarly, the evidence in the fossil record would suggest other unique pre-Flood ecosystems, such as the hydrothermal biome where stromatolites grew as reefs adjacent to hydrothermal springs, a gymnosperm-dinosaur biome, and an angiosperm-mammal-man biome.[6]

Based on the spatial separation of the fossil remains of these biomes in the geologic record, it is evident that these biomes must have been spatially and geographically separated and isolated from one another in the pre-Flood world. This would clearly have been the case with the floating-forest biome on the pre-Flood ocean surface spatially and geographically separated from the gymnosperm-dinosaurs and angiosperm-mammal-man biomes that inhabited the pre-Flood land surface. Similarly, the hydrothermal-stromatolite reef biome was confined to hydrothermal spring systems on the floors of the shallow seas fringing the pre-Flood continent(s), where waters were too shallow and perhaps too saline for the floating-forest biome to have been present on the water surfaces above the stromatolite reefs. On land, it is also likely that the gymnosperm-dinosaurs biome was located at a lower altitude, or closer to the shorelines of the pre-Flood continent(s). This is consistent with the description in Genesis of the river out of the Garden of Eden dividing into four rivers, which implies that the Garden of Eden, with its fruit trees and other angiosperms, mammals, and man, was at a high point geographically. Additionally, and perhaps even alternatively, perhaps one or more island continents housed the gymnosperm-dinosaurs biome in the pre-Flood world, while other island continents separately housed the angiosperm-mammal-man biome.

When the Flood began, and as it progressed, these distinct ecosystems would have been effected at different stages of the Flood due to their geographical separation. With the breaking up of the oceanic crust particularly, and the formation of the mid-ocean ridges, the sudden surge of strong ocean currents picking up sediments from the ocean floor and moving landwards would have first of all overwhelmed the stromatolite reefs in the shallow seas fringing the shorelines. This would have been facilitated by the crust supporting the hydrothermal springs also

---

6   Wise, 2002, 170-175.

breaking up, and thus wiping out that environment conducive to the growth of the stromatolite reefs. With the subsequent destruction of the protected lagoons between the stromatolite reefs and the shorelines by these severe storms, the strange animals that probably were unique to these stromatolite reefs thus ended up being preserved in the lowermost Flood strata. Then as the ocean surface was disturbed by increasing storms and tidal surges, with tsunamis generated by the earth movements, earthquakes, and volcanism on the ocean floor, the floating-forest ecosystem would have been progressively broken up, and huge rafts of vegetation swept landwards to be beached with the sediment load on the land surfaces being inundated. Thus, the floating-forest vegetation would have been buried higher in the strata record of the Flood, well above the stromatolites and the strange animals that lived with them. It would have only been later in this first 150 days of the Flood that, as the waters rose higher across the land surface, the gymnosperm-dinosaurs ecosystem was first swept away and buried, followed later by the angiosperm-mammal-man ecosystem that lived at higher elevations. Thus, the existence in the pre-Flood world of these geographically-separated, distinct ecosystems could well explain their spatial separation and order of fossilization in the geologic record. This thus might explain why, for example, man and dinosaurs were not buried and fossilized together in the geologic record (see Figure 23, pages 449-450), simply because they didn't live spatially together in the pre-Flood world. This existence of unique pre-Flood ecosystems, spatially and geographically separated in a distinctive pre-Flood biogeography, has previously been proposed as ecological zonation.[7]

Early Burial of Marine Creatures

Even a cursory examination of the fossils preserved in the strata of the geologic record reveals that the vast majority of them by number are the remains of shallow-water marine invertebrates (brachiopods, bivalves, gastropods, corals, graptolites, echinoderms, crustaceans, ammonites, etc.). Indeed, in the lowermost fossiliferous strata (Cambrian, Ordovician, Silurian, and Devonian), the contained fossils are almost exclusively shallow-water marine invertebrates, with fish and amphibian fossils only appearing in progressively sparser numbers in the higher strata. With reference to the Cambrian strata, the following statement provides corroboration:

> At least 1500 species of invertebrates are known in the Cambrian, *all marine*, of which 60% are trilobites and 30% brachiopods.[8]

The same could largely be said of the Ordovician, Silurian, and Devonian strata sequences as far as their fossil fauna are concerned, although the first fish fossils

---

7   H. W. Clark, 1946, *The New Diluvialism*, Angwin, CA: Science Publications.

8   M. Gignoux, 1955, *Stratigraphic Geology*, Full French edition, G.G. Woodford, trans., San Francisco: W. H. Freeman and Company, 46.

are found in the Ordovician, and in the Devonian are found amphibians and the first evidence of continental-type flora (see Figure 23).[9] It is not until the Carboniferous (Mississippian and Pennsylvanian) and Permian strata are reached much higher in the geologic record that the first land animals are encountered.

None of this is at all unexpected, but would be predicted from the implications of the biblical account of the Flood, and by the catastrophic plate tectonics Flood model. The Flood began with the breaking up of the earth's crust, particularly on the pre-Flood ocean floor, where geysers expelling prodigious quantities of steam and lavas flowed at the forming of the mid-ocean ridges, and the oceanic crust near continental margins began to sink and be subducted. Strong and destructive ocean currents were generated and moved landwards from the rising mid-ocean ridges, scouring the sediments on the ocean floor and carrying them and the organisms living in and on them. Thus, as these currents and sediments reached the shallower continental shelves, where the shallow-water marine invertebrates lived in all their prolific diversity, unable to escape, these organisms would have been swept away and buried in the sediment load as it was dumped where the water crashed onto the land surface it was progressively encroaching upon and inundating. The fact that the lower Paleozoic strata of the geologic record are marine strata containing these marine invertebrate fossils therefore corroborates this implication of the biblical record of the Flood.

Other writers have followed this hypothesis in a similar attempt to explain how the fossils were deposited in the order in which they are now found in the geologic record.[10] Possible reconstruction of the pre-Flood landscape, based on a synthesis of what can be gleaned from the biblical and fossil records, would postulate that there was a system of shallow seas bordered by lowland, swampy environments. Many of the marine creatures from these shallow seas, and almost all the plants and animals from that swampy, lowland habit, are now extinct. In warm, humid lowlands inland from the sea, the gymnosperm-dinosaurs ecosystem would have occurred, with pterosaurs and other extinct reptiles, and plesiosaurs and other now extinct aquatic reptiles living in adjacent bodies of water. The higher elevations were home to most of the mammals, birds, and angiosperms (flowering plants), plus man. It is at once obvious that this proposed pre-Flood ecological zonation is very different from the ecology of the present world, but based on the data from the fossil record, it is evident that this difference is because some of these pre-Flood habitats did not become re-established after the Flood. This would have been due to the Flood destroying those ecosystems and all the creatures in them, so that they did not survive into the post-Flood world, and/or those organisms

---

9   Further study of the fossil record has only confirmed this pattern of fossil occurrence, as can be verified by referring to current textbooks such as: S. M. Stanley, 1989, *Earth and Life Through Time*, second edition, New York: W. H. Freeman and Company; R. Cowen, 2000, *History of Life*, third edition, Oxford, UK: Blackwell Scientific Publications.

10   Whitcomb and Morris, 1961, 273, 275-281; L. Brand, 1997, *Faith, Reason and Earth History*, Berrien Springs, MI: Andrews University Press, 279-283.

and creatures could not survive on the changed, cooler earth after the Flood. Thus, the mammals (including man) and birds, the angiosperms, the modern groups of reptiles and amphibians, and some of the fish that lived in the cooler upland areas, were the ones that primarily re-populated the post-Flood world, because they were better prepared to survive on the cooler earth.

With this ecological zonation in mind, it is to be expected that as the sea level rose and the ocean waters began to inundate the land, the strong sediment-laden ocean currents would first have deposited their load in the shallow seas, burying the marine creatures there, before then destroying the lowland, swampy habitats and burying the amphibians and reptiles living near the shore. As the waters rose to higher elevations, the habitats containing the dinosaurs were next destroyed, and finally at the highest elevations the birds, mammals, and angiosperms were buried and fossilized. Thus, from the perspective of a broad overview of the fossil record, this pre-Flood ecological zonation and biogeographical model can explain the order of fossils in the geologic record. However, other factors do need to be considered that enhance the explanatory power of this model.

Hydrodynamic Selectivity of Moving Water

Another factor tending to ensure the deposition of the supposedly simple marine organisms in the first-deposited strata, now deep in the geologic record, is the hydrodynamic selectivity of moving water for particles of similar sizes and shapes, together with the effect of specific gravity of the respective organisms. The so-called "Impact Law" states:

> The settling velocity of large particles is independent of fluid viscosity; it is directly proportional to the square root of particle diameter, directly proportional to particle sphericity, and directly proportional to the difference between particle and fluid density divided by fluid density.[11]

These criteria are derived from consideration of hydrodynamic forces acting on immersed bodies and are well established. Moving water, or moving particles in still water, exerts "drag" forces on those bodies, which depend on the above quoted factors. Particles in motion will tend to settle out in proportion mainly to their specific gravity (or density) and sphericity. It is significant that the marine organisms fossilized in the earliest Flood strata, such as the trilobites, brachiopods, etc., are very "streamlined" and quite dense. The shells of these and most other marine invertebrates are largely composed of calcium carbonate, calcium phosphate, and similar minerals, which are quite heavy, heavier than quartz, for example, the most common constituent of many sands and gravels. This factor alone would have exerted a highly selective sorting action, not only tending to deposit the simpler (that is, the more spherical and undifferentiated) organisms first in the sediments

---

11   W. C. Krumbein and L. L. Sloss, 1963, *Stratigraphy and Sedimentation*, second edition, San Francisco: W. H. Freeman and Company, 198.

as they were being deposited, but also tending to segregate particles of similar sizes and shapes, which could have thus formed distinct faunal stratigraphic "horizons," with the complexity of structure of deposited organisms, even of similar kinds, increasing progressively upwards in the accumulating sediments.

It is quite possible that this could have been one of the major processes responsible for giving the fossil assemblages within the strata sequence a superficial appearance of "evolution" of similar organisms in the progressive succession upwards in the geologic record. Generally, the sorting action of flowing water is quite efficient, and would definitely have separated the shells and other fossils in just the fashion in which they are found, with certain fossils predominant in certain stratigraphic horizons, and the complexity of such distinctive, supposedly "index," fossils increasing in at least a general way in a progressive sequence upwards through the strata of the geologic record. Of course, these very pronounced "sorting" powers of hydraulic action are really only valid statistically, rather than universally. Furthermore, local variations and peculiarities of turbulence, environment, sediment composition, etc., would be expected to cause local variations in the fossil assemblages, with even occasional heterogeneous combinations of sediments and fossils of a wide variety of shapes and sizes. Nevertheless, transitional fossil forms that are true stratomorphic intermediates expected by the evolutionary theory are exceedingly rare, and are not found at all among the groups with the best fossil records (shallow-marine invertebrates like mollusks and brachiopods).[12] Indeed, even conventional evolutionary researchers have found that successive fossil assemblages in the strata record invariably only show trivial differences between fossil organisms, the different fossil groups with their distinctive body plans appearing abruptly in the record, and then essentially staying the same ("stasis") in the record.[13]

Behavior and Higher Mobility of the Vertebrates

It is entirely reasonable to also expect, in the light of the biblical record of the Flood, that vertebrates would be found fossilized higher in the geologic record than the first invertebrates. In fact, if vertebrates were to be ranked according to their likelihood of being buried early in the fossil record, then we would expect oceanic fish to be buried first, since they live at the lowest elevation.[14] However, in the ocean the fish live in the water column and have greater mobility, unlike the invertebrates that live on the ocean floor and have more restricted mobility, or are even attached to a substrate. Therefore, we would expect the fish to only be buried and fossilized subsequent to the first marine invertebrates. Of course, fish would

---

12 Wise, 2002, 196-200.

13 N. Eldredge and S. J. Gould, 1972, Punctuated equilibria: an alternative to phyletic gradualism, in *Mammals in Paleobiology*, T. J. M. Schopf, ed., San Francisco: Freeman, Cooper and Company, 82-115; S. J. Gould and N. Eldredge, 1977, Punctuated equilibria: the tempo and mode of evolution reconsidered, *Paleobiology*, 3: 115-151; S. J. Gould and N. Eldredge, 1993, Punctuated equilibrium comes of age, *Nature*, 366: 223-227.

14 Brand, 1997, 282-283.

have inhabited water at all different elevations in the pre-Flood world, even up in mountain streams as well as the lowland, swampy habitats, but their ranking is based on where the first representatives of fish are likely to be buried. Thus, it is hardly surprising to find that the first vertebrates to be found in the fossil record, and then only sparingly, are the ostracoderms in Ordovician strata.

Fish fossils are found in profusion in the Devonian, often in great "fossil graveyards," indicating violent deposition, often in what has been interpreted as freshwater deposits. It is obvious that fish do not usually die and become fossilized under normal conditions, but usually either float on the water surface until decomposed, or are eaten and destroyed by scavengers. Thus, fossil fish beds are convincing evidence of the violent burial of fish in large masses of rapidly-moving sediments, the source of which often appears to have been continental in nature. This is true of some of the most famous Devonian beds containing fossil fish graveyards, such as those of the Old Red Sandstone of Britain, and the corresponding strata in the Catskill Mountains of the United States. These strata can only be explained by torrential runoff into flooded streams carrying vast quantities of sediments and depositing them in ancient lakes and deltas, where they overwhelmed and buried hundreds of thousands of fish and other aquatic creatures. This is impossible to account for under normal conditions, except during extreme flooding, which of course is consistent with the sustained catastrophic conditions of the biblical Flood.

A second factor in the ranking of the likelihood of vertebrates being buried is how animals would react to the Flood. The behavior of some animals is very rigid and stereotyped, so they prefer to stay where they are used to living, and thus would have had little chance of escape. Other more intelligent and adaptable animals would have recognized something was wrong, and thus made an effort to escape. Fish are the least intelligent and adaptable in their behavior, while amphibians come next, and then are followed by the reptiles, birds, and lastly, the mammals.

The third factor to be considered is the mobility of land vertebrates. Once they became aware of the need to escape, how capable would they then have been of running, swimming, flying, or even riding on floating debris? Amphibians would have been the least mobile, with reptiles performing somewhat better, but not being equal to the mammals' mobility, due largely to their low metabolic rates. However, birds, with their wings, would have had the best expected mobility, even being able to find temporary refuge on floating debris.

These three factors tend to support each other, as shown in Table 2. If they had worked against each other, then the order of vertebrates in the fossil record would be more difficult to explain. However, since they all do work together, it is somewhat realistic to suggest that the combination of these three factors could have contributed significantly to producing the general sequence we now observe in the fossil record.

Table 2. Three factors for Flood burial of vertebrates.

	Ecology	Behavior	Mobility	Mean
Birds	4	4	4	4.0
Mammals	4	5	3	4.0
Reptiles	3	3	2	2.3
Amphibians	2	2	1	1.7
Fish	1	1	—	0.7

Numbers indicate rank order in which they would be expected to be buried, as predicted by the ecological zonation hypothesis. A low number indicates that the first burials of members of that class would be expected to occur early, in relation to first burials of other vertebrate groups, if the indicated factor was the determining one. Ecology = successive elevations in a hypothesized pre-Flood ecology; behavior = intelligence and behavioral adaptability (after Brand, 1997, 283, Table 15.1).

In general, therefore, the land animals and plants would be expected to have been caught somewhat later in the period of the rising waters of the Flood and buried in the sediments in much the same order as that found in the geologic record, as conventionally depicted in the standard geologic column. That is, overlying sediment beds burying marine vertebrates would be beds containing fossilized amphibians, then reptile fossils, and finally beds containing fossils of birds and mammals. This is essentially in the order:

(1) Increasing mobility, and therefore increasing ability to postpone inundation and burial;
(2) Decreasing density and other hydrodynamic factors tending to promote earlier burial; and
(3) Increasing elevation of habitat and therefore time required for the Flood waters to rise and advance to overtake them.

This order is essentially consistent with the implications of the biblical account of the Flood, and, therefore, provides further circumstantial evidence of the veracity of that account. Indeed, in no sense is it necessary to capitulate to the claim that the order in the fossil record is evidence of the progressive organic evolution of today's plants and animals through various stages over millions of years from common ancestors.

Of course, there would have been exceptions to this expected general order, both in terms of omissions and inversions, as the water currents waxed and waned with the twice daily tidal surges, and their directions changed due to obstacles and obstructions as the land became increasingly submerged and more and more amphibians, reptiles, and mammals were overtaken by the waters. Thus, in any one locality we would not necessary expect to find a continuous series of strata containing all possible types of fossils in the "ideal" sequence, because the actual deposits found would depend on the local circumstances of current directions, sediment source areas, and the manner in which these had changed during the course of the Flood event. Furthermore, some fossil groups are difficult to explain in terms of their burial according to ecological zonation. For example, since the flowering plants were present on the pre-Flood land surface, why do we not find pollen from the flowering plants in the strata below the Cretaceous, which represent the bulk of the Flood deposits? There have been claims of such pollen being found, even as low in the geologic record as the Cambrian strata, but these have not been unequivocally documented.[15]

And why aren't at least a few mice or sparrows in Paleozoic or Mesozoic deposits? In other words, why weren't animals and plants from "higher zones" mixed and fossilized with those in "lower zones" during the massive river and valley flooding that must have been occurring, even early in the Flood event?

Other factors must have been significant in influencing the time when many groups of organisms met their demise. As the catastrophic destruction progressed, there would have been changes in the chemistry of seas and lakes from the mixing of fresh and salt water, and from contamination by leaching of other chemicals into the water. Each species of aquatic organism would have had its own physiological tolerance of these changes. Thus, there would have been a sequence of mass mortalities of different groups as the water quality changed. Changes in the turbidity of the waters, pollution of the air by volcanic ash, and/ or changes in air temperatures would likely have had similar effects. So whereas ecological zonation of the pre-Flood world is a useful concept in explaining how the catastrophic geological processes during the Flood would have produced the order of fossils now seen in the geologic record, the reality was undoubtedly much more complex, due to so many other factors.

15　For example, some selected references (in chronological order) include: W. H. Lang and I. C. Cookson, 1935, On the flora, including vascular land plants, associated with *Monograptus*, in rocks of Silurian age, from Victoria, Australia, *Philosophical Transactions of the Royal Society of London B*, 224: 421-449; W. C. Darrah, 1937, Spores of Cambrian plants, *Science*, 86 (2224): 154-155; A. K. Ghosh and A. Bose, 1952, Spores and tracheids from the Cambrian of Kashmir, *Nature*, 169 (4312): 1056-1057; K. Jacob, C. Jacob and R. N. Shrivatsava, 1953, Spores and tracheids from the Vidhyan system, Indian: The advent of vascular plants, *Nature*, 172 (4369): 166-167; R. M. Stainforth, 1966, Occurrence of pollens and spores in the Roraima Formation in Venezuela and British Guyana, *Nature*, 210 (5033): 292-294; C. L. Burdick, 1966, Microflora of the Grand Canyon, *Creation Research Society Quarterly*, 3 (1): 38-46; C. L. Burdick, 1972, Progress report on Grand Canyon palynology, *Creation Research Society Quarterly*, 9 (1): 25-30; C. L. Burdick, 1975, Cambrian and other early pollen in the literature, *Creation Research Society Quarterly*, 12 (3): 175-176; A. V. Chadwick, 1981, Precambrian pollen in the Grand Canyon—a re-examination, *Origins*, 8 (1): 7-12; G. F. Howe, 1986, Creation Research Society studies on Precambrian pollen: Part I — A review, *Creation Research Society Quarterly*, 23 (3): 99-104; G. F. Howe, E. L. Williams, G. T. Matzko and W. E. Lammerts, 1988, Creation Research Society studies on Precambrian pollen: Part III: A pollen analysis of Hakatai Shale and other Grand Canyon rocks, *Creation Research Society Quarterly*, 24 (4): 173-182; W. E. Williams, 1997, Precambrian pollen—a response, *Creation Research Society Quarterly*, 33 (4): 239-242.

92

THE ORDER OF THE FLOOD STRATA—OTHER CONSIDERATIONS IN THE STRATA SEQUENCE

Bioturbation and Mass Extinctions

When the Flood began, the earth's geological balance was disrupted by the breaking up of "the fountains of the great deep," so new ocean currents began to transport sediments already on the ocean floor and redeposit them as the lower Paleozoic strata. The animals that could not escape were buried and preserved as fossils. Many others did escape initially, but were buried later. In the meantime, invertebrate animals would have still been alive and moving around, as demonstrated by the presence of abundant fossilized burrows and trails throughout the geologic record. These include many trilobite trails, feeding marks and burrows, escape burrows, and resting marks where the animals had dug into the sediment surface to rest while hidden in the mud.[1]

Animals that live within sediments continually burrow through them, destroying the original layering, an activity called bioturbation.[2] In the modern world, the activity of burrowing animals in underwater sediments results in a total bioturbation of those sediments, so that none of the original layering or other sedimentary structures remains (Figure 55, page 1090). For example, in 1961, Hurricane Carla deposited a thick layer of sediment on the continental shelf offshore of the central Texas coast, yet within twenty years subsequent bioturbation had obliterated all evidence of that bed.[3] In contrast, much of the sedimentary rock record has not been completely bioturbated, which therefore requires explanation. Indeed, trace fossils are only found in the top portions of some individual sedimentary rock units. Incomplete or no bioturbation would result if the sediments when deposited could not support animal life (for example, if they lacked oxygen), or if they were deposited so rapidly that the animals had no time to do their work.

---

1   E. N. K. Clarkson, 1993, *Invertebrate Palaeontology and Evolution*, third edition, New York: Chapman and Hall, 362-366.

2   R. G. Bromley, 1990, *Trace Fossils: Biology and Taphonomy*, Boston: Unwin Hyman.

3   R. H. Dott, Jr., 1983, Episodic sedimentation—How normal is average? How rare is rare? Does it matter?, *Journal of Sedimentary Petrology*, 53: 12

Most of the sedimentary rock units deposited during the global catastrophic Flood would have been deposited too quickly for complete bioturbation to have occurred. Those rock layers that have some bioturbation in their rock portions, however, would represent the passing of at least a few hours for the animals to have walked around and left their footprints and trails, or to have burrowed in the sediment surfaces before the next layers were deposited. These sedimentary rocks surfaces that are partially bioturbated with burrows, tracks, and other marks are sometimes referred to as "hardgrounds," and these have been suggested to be problematic for the year-long catastrophic Flood because of the time they supposedly require.[4] However, such claims grossly overestimate the time required for animals to make burrows, and leave tracks and marks, particularly as these animals would have been affected by the changing turbulent water conditions that only gave them brief times of respite to crawl across and burrow into sediment surfaces. To the contrary, the fact that there is so little bioturbation of sedimentary strata in the geologic record, and that it is only some strata surfaces that have burrows, tracks, and marks on and in them, is evidence for rapid deposition of the strata within a timeframe consistent with the global Flood catastrophe.

The first fish fossils found abundantly preserved in Silurian and Devonian strata were mostly armored, bottom-dwelling fish. Their probable behavior pattern of hiding from danger on the sea floor would not have been helpful for surviving the sudden influx of sediments, so they were the first vertebrates buried in large numbers.

The movement of water on a global scale would have deposited sediments over extensive areas, producing widespread sedimentary formations, which is consistent with the pattern observed in the geologic record of similar formations of the same geological "age" spread over many parts of the earth's surface. Furthermore, where there are claimed long gaps of many millions of years between strata in the geologic record, there is often little or no evidence of the passage of the claimed long periods of time at the strata boundaries. Indeed, most boundaries between sedimentary strata are planar, without relief from erosion or any of the weathering that should have occurred in the claimed long gaps of millions of years. Instead, these features of the geologic record are better explained by the sedimentary strata having been deposited in a rapid sequence of events, during which the most significant periods of time elapsed between deposition of the layers above and below the supposed gaps. The global scale of the geologic record with these features in it is thus consistent with the biblical Flood.

Investigations of the geologic record on a large geographic scale has identified an interesting pattern of six cycles of large-scale sedimentation across the North American continent known as megasequences, separated across the middle of the continent by unconformities, or supposed time gaps not represented by any

---

4   D. Tyler, 1996, A post-Flood solution to the chalk problem, *Creation Ex Nihilo Technical Journal*, 10 (1): 107-113.

rocks (Figure 38, page 464).[5] The same pattern continues worldwide with some variation in details, the major unconformities often coinciding with major mass extinctions. These phenomena have the potential to yield important insights into the large-scale processes operating during the global catastrophic Flood. For example, the unconformities would represent lowered water levels, or changes of the sediment source areas, resulting in no sediments at the unconformities without any long time periods elapsing. Of course, the so-called mass extinctions would be expected to coincide with these major unconformities, because the abrupt change in sedimentation, and/or lowered water levels, would likely have resulted in the mass burial of the creatures carried in each major wave of sedimentation, prior to different creatures being carried by the subsequent sedimentation.

Formation of Coal Beds

It is in the Permian and Carboniferous sedimentary strata, near the top of the Paleozoic sequence, that fossilized remains of land animals are first found. This obviously starts an important stage in the onset of the Flood waters over the land, when the smaller and less agile of the amphibians and reptiles were overtaken and buried in the Flood sediments. It is also at the same stage in the geologic record that vast quantities of plants have been buried *en masse* to form the vast coal measures. The Carboniferous (Mississippian and Pennsylvanian) coalfields of eastern North America appear to represent the remains of vast lowland swampy areas along the shores of the pre-Flood ocean, extending offshore to the open ocean. These areas were populated by some unique plants, amphibians, reptiles, and other animals, that together constituted a floating-forest biome, the progressive destruction and burial of which appears to explain the order in which these fossils are found in the geologic record.[6]

Many of these plants have features, such as roots with air spaces, which seem to indicate that they were more suited to growing in water, and therefore were floating plants unable to grow in soil. Furthermore, the vertical sequence of plant fossils in the strata record is consistent with a character trend toward increased resistance to desiccation (or increased terrestriality) that closely correlates with the stratigraphic order of both first appearance and maximum diversity. The rapid deposition and burial of plants and other fossils in the Flood model for these strata allows for the possibility that this pattern also represents horizontal succession of organisms in this pre-Flood floating-forest biome that was progressively destroyed by the Flood. It has therefore been suggested that in a fashion analogous to the plants of a quaking bog today, the floating-forest biome grew out over the pre-Flood ocean from the shores, through an ecological succession of rhyzomous plants of steadily increasing size that generated and thrived upon an increasingly

5   R. H. Dott and D. R. Prothero, 1994, *Evolution of the Earth*, fifth edition, New York: McGraw-Hill.

6   K. P. Wise, 2003, The pre-Flood forest: A study in paleontological pattern recognition, in *Proceedings of the Fifth International Conference on Creationism*, R. L. Ivey, ed., Pittsburgh, PA: Creation Science Fellowship, 371-381.

thick mat of vegetation and soil. There was thus a succession of plants from open water inward toward the shore to the full forest biome, which included herbaceous lycopods and ferns on the forest floor, seed ferns in the understory, and arborescent sphenophytes and more lycopods making up the canopy. It has also been suggested that living in these floating forests was a succession of animals (those "land" animals uniquely fossilized in Paleozoic strata). This would have included the large Paleozoic insects, as well as the unique Devonian aquatic tetrapods (like *Ichthyostega*) in pools on thinner portions of the forest floor, and a wide variety of large amphibians (including the labyrinthodonts) in the thicker sections of the forest.

With the onset of the Flood catastrophe, the turbulence of the ocean surface would have progressively disrupted and destroyed the shoreline-fringing floating forests from their open ocean side inwards, the plants and animals being buried in the sediments having been transported from the adjacent areas and accumulating on the sea floor beneath. Thus, not only does the Flood destruction of these floating forests explain the first appearance and maximum abundance order of these fossil plants and animals, it also explains the strong association of Paleozoic plants with marine sediments and fossils, and how the pre-Flood world could have supported the plant biomass now fossilized in the extensive coal beds. The eventual destruction of the cores of these floating forests, with their large, tall lycopods, would have generated extensive floating log mats of this plant debris. As these log and debris mats became water-logged, the logs and plant debris would have sunk and been buried by clastic sediments to form the coal beds. The continuance of these floating log and plant debris mats for some time on the surface of the Flood waters, with currents and winds able to move them around, would have resulted in cyclic repetition of sinking logs and plant debris forming coal seams buried by clastic marine sediments, thus explaining the generation of cyclothems in coal measure sequences. Finally, the complete destruction of this pre-Flood floating-forest biome during the Flood, and the residual catastrophism of the immediate post-Flood period preventing its restoration in the post-Flood world, resulted in the extinction of most of these Paleozoic plants and "land" animals, as their remains are not found in the post-Paleozoic fossil record.

The physical evidence within the coal measure sequences plainly and emphatically demonstrates that both the coal beds and the inter-seam sediments are water-laid deposits. The progressive breaking up and sinking of the logs and plant debris from these floating forests generated the repetition of coal beds, interspersed in cycles of marine sedimentation that was concurrently occurring below the floating log and plant debris mats. This is in stark contrast to the conventional peat swamp model for coal bed formation, the claimed supporting evidence for which includes upright tree trunks in apparent growth positions and *Stigmaria* ("roots") in underclays or seat earths ("fossil soils"). However, these evidences are equally well, or better, explained by the catastrophic Flood model. As observed at Spirit Lake after the devastation of the May 18, 1980, eruption of nearby Mount

St. Helens,[7] in a catastrophic flood waterlogged trees often sink vertically, the thicker ends first with roots broken off, but otherwise appearing to have been buried in their growth positions. Furthermore, within the floating-forest biome it is envisaged that, between the intertwined roots, a mat of soil developed, overlain by a peat layer of rotting vegetative debris, so that upon break-up of these floating forests during the Flood catastrophe, these large laterally extensive soil and peat mats would have sunk in their entirety, to be buried on the sea floor beneath by continuing deposition of marine sediments. This gives the impression that these soil and peat layers with roots, now forming many coal seams, had grown *in situ*.

On the other hand, the conventional uniformitarian peat swamp model does not explain how the rhyzomous aborescent lycopod "roots" could penetrate traditional soils, or indeed the aquatic-plant-like anatomy of the coal plants generally. Furthermore, the conventional uniformitarian peat swamp model does not explain how the coal beds could be so widespread, and so often interbedded with marine sediments, especially when marine fossils are sometimes found even within the coal beds themselves. The uniformitarian explanation, therefore, requires the impossible scenario of vast peat swamps sinking and being invaded by the sea, and buried until the land rises again to form new peat swamps, with this process being repeated tens of times in succession in order to generate the cyclothems and coal measure sequences. Yet the upright fossil trees often found sitting on top of coal beds sometimes pass through one or more of the overlying sediment layers, and even through overlying coal beds, which implies that all these overlying layers, including the coal beds, had to have been deposited rapidly or else these upright trees would have rotted rather than having been fossilized. Many of these upright fossil trees are lycopods and therefore hollow, and some have been found containing fossilized amphibians buried inside them. Thus, the evidence is overwhelmingly consistent with the vast masses of plant debris forming the coal beds having been washed in and buried during the Flood catastrophe, rather than having grown in place repeatedly before slow burial.

The question now arises as to whether the plant remains, once transported by water and buried, could have been metamorphosed into coal in the relatively brief period of time since the Flood. The prevailing perception is that immense ages are required for the coal to form from the vegetative debris after its burial, but both experimental and field evidence suggest the opposite. For example, in one series of experiments, woody materials were heated to temperatures of only 150°C, which in geological terms are low, being obtained just by deep burial, in the presence of water and clay, and material indistinguishable from natural black coal was produced in a matter of weeks.[8] In earlier experiments, uniaxial pressure (applied

---

7   H. G. Coffin, 1983, Erect floating stumps in Spirit Lake, Washington, *Geology*, 11: 298-299; S. A. Austin, 1986, Mount St Helens and catastrophism, in *Proceedings of the First International Conference on Creationism*, vol. 1, Pittsburgh, PA: Creation Science Fellowship, 3-9.

8   R. Hayatsu, R. L. McBeth, R. G. Scott, R. E. Botto and R. E. Winans, 1984, Artificial coalification study: Preparation and characterization of synthetic macerals, *Organic Geochemistry*, 6: 463-471.

from one direction) was sufficient to produce artificial coal from the components of wood, again at geologically low temperatures, but in just a few days.[9] Such experiments confirm earlier field observations of wooden bridge piles that had been rammed into the ground, and thus due to the compressive force, the wood at the bottom of the piles had been transformed into what resembled black and brown coal, both visually and compositionally.[10] Thus, it is not surprising that even before the advent of more modern experiments, it was conceded that,

> From all available evidence it would appear that coal may form in a very short time, geologically speaking, if conditions are favourable.[11]

Indeed, due to the presence of clay and water with the vegetative debris when buried acting as catalysts, it is totally conceivable that, as a result of the applied pressures of rapid burial and the easily obtainable low geological temperatures of 150 to 200°C, the plant remains were rapidly transformed into coal, particularly during the continuing catastrophic upheavals of the Flood.

9   A. Davis and W. Spackman, 1964, The role of cellulosic and lignitic components of wood in artificial coalification, *Fuel*, 43: 215-224.

10   O. Stutzer, 1940, *Geology of Coal*, A. C. Noe, trans., Chicago, IL: University of Chicago Press, 105-106.

11   E. S. Moore, 1940, *Coal*, second edition, New York: Wiley, 143.

93

ANIMAL TRACKS AND FOSSILS IN MESOZOIC STRATA

Fossil vertebrate footprints are common in upper Paleozoic sedimentary strata, indicating that such animals were quite active on the new sediment surfaces before they were killed or buried.[1] Numerous amphibians or reptiles left their footprints on Permian cross-bedded sandstones, such as the Coconino Sandstone of northern Arizona and related sandstones in Colorado and Utah, as well as in similar sandstones in Europe, Africa, and other places.[2] These tracks are always much the same wherever they are found around the world, most being in trackways that indicate the animals that made them were climbing up the slopes of underwater sand dunes. It would logically seem that during the Flood these animals were washed by water currents from their natural habitats into areas where pure sand was being deposited, so as these animals tried to escape to go back to where they came from, they often had to climb up the lee sides of sand dunes against the prevailing water currents. It is hardly surprising that these animals were subsequently overwhelmed by the prevailing Flood waters, which increasingly left them without any land surfaces they could re-inhabit, so they eventually were buried in the subsequently deposited sediments. This is confirmed by the observation that in the fossil record the body fossils of amphibians and reptiles are usually found in the same or subsequent strata to where their tracks are found (see Figure 24, page 451).

As the Flood continued, its waters reached beyond the floating-forest biome that fringed the shorelines to encounter life zones with other characteristic animals, such as the adjoining pre-Flood lowland areas dominated by dinosaurs and other large reptiles, which were thus buried in the so-called Mesozoic strata. It is likely that the dinosaurs and these other reptiles were not found as fossils in the Paleozoic because they lived inland of the floating-forest biome that was destroyed and buried in upper Paleozoic strata. They also may have been more mobile, and could thus have escaped further before being progressively overwhelmed by the Flood waters as they covered their habitats. However, at many different levels

---

1   L. R. Brand and J. Florence, 1982, Stratigraphic distribution of vertebrate fossil footprints compared with body fossils, *Origins (Geoscience Research Institute)*, 9: 67-74.

2   P. J. McKeever, 1991, Trackway preservation in Eolian sandstones from the Permian of Scotland, *Geology*, 19: 726-729.

in the Mesozoic sedimentary deposits, additional types of dinosaurs and other animals appear in the rocks for the first time as they were affected progressively by the Flood waters. These include swimming reptiles such as plesiosaurs and ichthyosaurs, and flying reptiles or pterosaurs. Deposition also continued in the adjoining marine areas, as evidenced by the many extensive Mesozoic strata containing characteristic fossilized marine organisms, such as ammonites.

The creatures whose fossilized remains have generally captured the most attention are the dinosaurs, primarily because of the enormous sizes of some of their representatives, and because of the apparent mystery of their sudden extinction. Various theories have been suggested within the conventional uniformitarian model for the geologic record, the most popular contenders being meteorite, comet, or asteroid impact(s), globally widespread explosive and voluminous volcanic eruptions, or a combination of these, coupled with the devastating climatic consequences that destroyed habitats. However, none of these competing theories has prevailed, due to the inadequacies of all of them to account for all the observed details in the fossil record. However, at least there is a consensus that a global catastrophe is ultimately responsible for the demise of the dinosaurs.

Dinosaur fossils are found at many different levels in Mesozoic strata, particularly in large numbers in what can only be described as great dinosaur graveyards, found in numerous places around the globe. The scale of entombment of such large numbers of these great creatures necessitates some form of catastrophic action. One such location is the Dinosaur National Monument in Utah, where the Jurassic Morrison Formation has yielded the remains of more than 300 dinosaurs from at least 10 different kinds. Excavations have exposed in a 50 feet by 150 feet quarry wall more than 2,000 bones in a jumbled mass, together with the fossilized remains of crocodiles, turtles, lizards, frogs, and clams:

> The quarry area is a dinosaur graveyard, not a place where they died. The majority of the remains probably floated down an eastward flowing river until they were stranded on a shallow sandbar. Some of them, such as the stegosaurs, may have come from far-away dry-land areas to the west. Perhaps they drowned trying to ford a tributary stream or were washed away during floods. Some of the swamp dwellers may have mired down on the very sand bar that became their grave while others may have floated for miles before being stranded.[3]

One could hardly ask for a better description of the way in which these large creatures must have been overwhelmed, drowned, and buried by the sediment-laden Flood waters. The fossils include well-worn bone fragments, and relatively pristine and semi-articulated skeletal segments, unmistakably aligned in an east-southeast preferred orientation, and buried in a conglomeratic sandstone that was

---

3   J. M. Good, T. E. White and G. F. Stucker, 1958, *The Dinosaur Quarry*, US Government Printing Office, 20.

deposited by water velocities of 1 to 2 meters per second.[4] Furthermore, some 141 dinosaur fossil sites have so far been found in the Morrison Formation in the Colorado Plateau area alone, yet the Morrison Formation has been traced over an area of 1.5 million square kilometers, covering thirteen U.S. states and three Canadian provinces from Manitoba to Arizona and Alberta to Texas, even though in most places it is 100 meters or less thick. Such a scale of deposition must surely be consistent with the catastrophic global Flood.

Many amphibians and reptiles were actively leaving footprints on the surfaces of the sediments being deposited during this middle to late stage of the Flood. Amphibian footprints are almost entirely limited to the upper Paleozoic, the Triassic, and the lower Jurassic, these early-middle Flood footprints being the right size and shape to have been made by the now extinct Paleozoic amphibians. After deposition of the lower Jurassic strata, almost no more amphibian footprints are found, very few having been fossilized in subsequent strata (see Figure 24). The greatest diversity of reptile footprints occurs in Triassic and lower Jurassic strata, but body fossils (bones) are most abundant higher up the strata sequence in Cretaceous and Tertiary strata. Dinosaur tracks are quite diverse in Triassic and lower Jurassic strata, but the greatest diversity of their body fossils is in the Cretaceous (see Figure 24). Dinosaur tracks are very abundant, though, and yield insight into the lives of these animals.[5] Fossil tracks of small dinosaurs and other reptiles are almost entirely absent in upper Jurassic and higher strata, but abundant large dinosaur tracks are found in Cretaceous strata. The overall picture is of abundant vertebrate animal activity recorded in the middle Flood deposits, but by the time the last Jurassic strata were being deposited, most of the vertebrates still making tracks were only the large dinosaurs. All other tetrapods were either mostly dead, their carcasses having been buried, or they were not in the areas where sediments were then being deposited. After deposition of the Cretaceous strata, even the large dinosaurs and their tracks are no longer found in subsequent strata.

Other evidence of normal behavior of animals during deposition of the sedimentary strata is the presence of fossilized reptile "nests" full of eggs, sometimes containing fossil embryos. Indeed, abundant fossilized dinosaur eggs in apparent nests have been found on several continents, sometimes on several successive sedimentary layers.[6] It has been suggested that this poses a serious objection to the Flood

---

4   W. A. Hoesch and S. A. Austin, 2004, Dinosaur National Monument: Jurassic Park or Jurassic Jumble?, *Acts & Facts*, 33 (4).

5   D. D. Gillette and M. G. Lockley, 1989, *Dinosaur Tracks and Traces*, New York: Cambridge University Press; A. Thulborn, 1990, *Dinosaur Tracks*, New York: Chapman and Hall; M. Lockley, 1991, *Tracking Dinosaurs*, New York: Cambridge University Press; M. Lockley and A. P. Hunt, 1995, *Dinosaur Tracks and Other Fossil Footprints of the Western United States*, New York: Columbia University Press.

6   J. R. Horner, 1982, Evidence of colonial nesting and 'site fidelity' among ornithischian dinosaurs, *Nature*, 297: 675-676; J. R. Horner and D. B. Weishampel, 1989, Dinosaur eggs: the inside story, *Natural History*, 98 (12): 61-67; Gillette and Lockley, 1989, 87-118; K. Carpenter, K. F. Hirsch and J. R. Horner, eds., 1994, *Dinosaur Eggs and Babies*, New York: Cambridge University Press; K. F. Hirsch,

model for catastrophic deposition of these strata, because dinosaurs laying eggs in nests requires time, and successive fossilized nests and eggs would perhaps require much more time that just a few weeks within the Flood year.[7]

However, how much time is required by dinosaurs to lay eggs in nests? Quite obviously, there are no observations to answer that question. What is known is that many dinosaurs were actively walking and running across the newly-deposited sediment surfaces on which eggs were laid. These animals would also have been under the considerable stress of continually having to find dry land on which to escape destruction by the Flood waters. Having retained their eggs within their bodies, perhaps until the eggs were almost ready to hatch, like some modern reptiles do, as their time approached the female dinosaurs would have been desperate to find places to build nests and lay their eggs, so as soon as there was a suitable land surface available above the Flood waters, they would have built their "nests" and laid their eggs. However, within hours the next inflow of sediments would have catastrophically buried those "nests," and the eggs within them. Indeed, "nests" of eggs, including embryos within the eggs, could only be preserved by such rapid burial. And if the eggs were laid just before they hatched, then this would also explain those "nests" where fossilized, newly-hatched dinosaur babies have been found. When a subsequent land surface was again exposed, more of the still-surviving female dinosaurs with eggs ready to hatch would build more "nests" and lay eggs. This could have happened repeatedly over a matter of days, resulting in several levels of "nests" and eggs, and even newly-hatched babies, in successive sedimentary strata in the same geographic area. Because preservation of the eggs and newly-hatched babies requires catastrophic burial, successive horizons of fossilized dinosaur "nests" and eggs are thus further evidence of Flood deposition of the sediments, rather than the elapse of large amounts of time.

Fossil tracks and burrows made by invertebrate animals are also common in Mesozoic marine strata, implying that even late in the Flood many invertebrate animals were still moving around. Because the marine environment was their natural habitat, they weren't all destroyed and buried in the early stages of the Flood. Many continued to survive well into the Flood, because they were able to burrow up through the sediments that were burying them. (Some even survived right through the Flood into the post-Flood world, and still survive today.) If there were quiet periods of time, even only a few hours between tidal surges, the live animals would have made new feeding burrows, and when the next sediments accumulated over those burrows, some would have burrowed up through those sediments, leaving escape burrows. Others would have swum up in the water and come down on top of the next layers.

1994, The fossil record of vertebrate eggs, in *The Palaeobiology of Trace Fossils*, S. K. Donovan, ed., Baltimore, MD: The Johns Hopkins University Press, 269-294.

7   P. A. Garner, 1996, Where is the Flood/post-Flood boundary? Implications of dinosaur nests in the Mesozoic, *Creation Ex Nihilo Technical Journal*, 10 (1): 101-106.

Marine deposits are more abundant among Cretaceous strata, including the extensive chalk beds, than in the underlying Mesozoic strata. In fact, it is likely that the Flood waters reached their highest point at about this time, destroying all the pre-Flood upland areas. Whereas the smaller dinosaurs had been increasingly overwhelmed and buried in Triassic and Jurassic strata, the larger dinosaurs that had survived a little longer, perhaps because of their size and strength, now too were suddenly destroyed and buried in the last of the Cretaceous strata, consistent with destruction of the last remaining upland habitats of the pre-Flood earth. The first mammals and birds encountered in the fossil record are buried in Mesozoic strata (see Figure 24). Bird fossils are rare in Mesozoic strata and belong to extinct orders. Similarly, the mammals found fossilized in Mesozoic strata are all small (mouse to rat size), are all in groups, and none are common as fossils. Furthermore, apart from a few rare mammal tracks, only body fossils of mammals and birds are found in Mesozoic strata, and then primarily in Cretaceous strata. Even many of the plants found fossilized in Mesozoic strata are in extinct groups, though they are more familiar than the plants in Paleozoic strata. Indeed, the flowering plants are not preserved in the fossil record until the Cretaceous strata. This is again consistent with these groups of animals representing the ones that could escape the Flood waters longer than others, and/or organisms that lived at higher elevations with these plants in cooler upland environments that were finally overwhelmed by the Flood waters as they reached their highest point.

94

THE FLOOD/POST-FLOOD BOUNDARY IN THE GEOLOGIC RECORD

There has been much discussion about what point in the geologic record constitutes the boundary between the Flood strata and post-Flood strata, but little consensus has been reached. Whitcomb and Morris regarded the Tertiary strata as final Flood deposits, with the mountain-building coinciding with upper Tertiary strata representing the time at the end of the Flood when the mountains rose and the valleys sank, so that the Flood waters drained off the earth (Psalm 104:7-9).[1] More recently, there are those who would still argue for the Flood/post-Flood boundary being at the Tertiary/Quaternary boundary in the geologic record,[2] but others who would place the end of the Flood at the Cretaceous/Tertiary boundary,[3] or even lower in the geologic record within middle Carboniferous strata.[4] That there could be such a divergence of opinion is somewhat puzzling, until it is realized that different weightings to the relevant geologic data, and some perceived problems, have greatly influenced these vastly different choices for the Flood/post-Flood boundary in the geologic record. This is, therefore, not a simple matter to resolve, yet it is important to do so, because the outcome determines just how much geology has to be accounted for in the post-Flood to present era, and how the fossils in the post-Flood geologic record may be related to the present flora and fauna. Thus, it is important to briefly consider the factors that have been variously used in determined this all-important boundary. Furthermore, if perceived problems are also resolved, then resolution of the controversy over this boundary might be possible.

1   Whitcomb and Morris, 1961, 281-288.

2   For example, R. D. Holt, 1996, Evidence for a late Cainozoic Flood/post-Flood boundary, *Creation Ex Nihilo Technical Journal*, 10 (1): 128-167.

3   Austin et al, 1994, 609-621.

4   For example, S. J. Robinson, 1996, Can Flood geology explain the fossil record?, *Creation Ex Nihilo Technical Journal*, 10 (1): 32-69; M. Garton, 1996, The pattern of fossil tracks in the geological record, *Creation Ex Nihilo Technical Journal*, 10 (1): 82-100; P. Garner, 1996, Where is the Flood/post-Flood boundary? Implications of dinosaur nests in the Mesozoic, *Creation Ex Nihilo Technical Journal*, 10 (1): 101-106; P. Garner, 1996, Continental Flood basalts indicate a pre-Mesozoic Flood/post-Flood boundary, *Creation Ex Nihilo Technical Journal*, 10 (1): 114-127.

Biblical Considerations

After the first 150 days of the Flood, the scriptural account indicates that the Flood waters generally began to subside. By day 314 it is recorded that the waters of the Flood were dried up from off the earth, and the face of the ground was dry (Genesis 18:13). However, it wasn't for another 57 days that the earth was dried (Genesis 8:14), and Noah was then instructed by God to leave the Ark, taking his family and also all the animals. These descriptions can't be referring to the entire planet earth having dried up, because 70 percent of the planet is still covered by ocean waters. On the other hand, at the very least, the description given would have been from the perspective of Noah and those on board the Ark, because the ground in the region of the planet where the Ark had come to rest needed to be dry enough for them to disembark. Thus, it would seem that the scriptural account does not preclude the possibility that some parts of the continental land surfaces may have still been immersed by residual Flood waters, where sedimentation may still have continued in local basins in subsequent decades and centuries. Furthermore, it cannot be asserted by inference from the scriptural account of the Flood that when Noah and the animals left the Ark all catastrophic geological activity immediately ceased. Unless God supernaturally intervened at that time to immediately change the rate of geological activities from catastrophic to present-day normal (and the Scriptures nowhere state that this happened), then it is likely that there was an exponential decay in most geological process rates. This has been demonstrated to have been the case with volcanic activity, the extent and power of which has exponentially declined, as quantified from preserved Cenozoic volcanic deposits.[5] Thus, if declining catastrophic geological activity continued on into the post-Flood era in areas other than where Noah, his family, and all the animals disembarked from the Ark, then it may be extremely difficult to find a geological boundary in the record of global extent that marks the end of the Flood.

However, from the 150th day of the Flood onwards, the scriptural account indicates that the Flood waters were retreating from off the face of the earth, increasingly exposing the mountains and then eventually the new continental land surfaces, with vegetation rapidly re-establishing itself thereon. In Psalm 104:7-9, there is the inference that the draining of the Flood waters off the surfaces of new continental lands was achieved with the help of vertical earth movements, in which mountains were uplifted, valleys eroded, and the new ocean basins subsided. Because this would have been on a global scale, this process therefore should have left a global signature in the geologic record.

Geological Considerations

Based upon a qualitative assessment of geological maps worldwide, it has been suggested that the Flood/post-Flood boundary could be defined at the termination

---

5   S. A. Austin, 1998, The Declining Power of Post-Flood Volcanoes, *Acts & Facts*, 27 (8).

of global-scale erosion and sedimentation, which appears to correspond approximately to the Cretaceous/Tertiary boundary in the geological record, where the types of rock strata change from being worldwide or continental in character in the Mesozoic, to local or regional in the Tertiary.[6] This corresponds to the time in the geologic record when in North America the Rocky Mountains formed, and when the last phase of catastrophic plate tectonics was producing other large-scale tectonic features that are still currently found at the earth's surface.

That catastrophic rates and scales of earth movements were involved in the formation of these most recent mountain chains is shown by the many overthrusts in them. For example, a large part of the Canadian Rockies appears to be a gigantic overthrust belt, in which older, Flood-deposited strata sequences thousands of meters thick over areas of thousands of square kilometers moved along thrust faults up and over younger strata deposited later in the Flood, with whole mountain ranges catastrophically sliding sometimes tens of kilometers. Similarly, in the southwestern United States we can still see today where whole ranges of mountains were apparently pushed tens of kilometers along low-angle to almost horizontal detachment faults. However, rocks have finite compressive strength, much lower than needed to support the horizontal forces required to move such large piles of sediment, if applied at their edges. The only conceivable way such massive blocks of rock can be moved in such a coherent way is by means of a *body force* that acts on each individual parcel of rock. The obvious candidate for the body force is gravity. That is, these overthrusts must be huge gravity slides. This means that when these thrusts occurred, the slope of the terrain was much higher than it is today. Only the catastrophic forces at work during a global tectonic upheaval such as the Flood can explain how whole mountain ranges slid "uphill" tens of kilometers along such fault planes over thousands of square kilometers, while leaving minimal evidence of imbrication, brecciation, and pulverizing of the rocks either side of these fault planes.

It is likewise evident that only catastrophic plate tectonics still operating at the close of the Flood can explain the formation of the Himalayas, where the Indian Plate has collided with the Eurasian Plate and been pushed up over it along a 1,500 kilometer or more front. As a result, sedimentary layers containing marine fossils, which obviously were originally deposited on the ocean floor, were thrust up to where they are now some nine kilometers above sea level.[7] To envisage this stupendous uplift and movement of countless millions of tons of rock strata over such a vast area at uniformitarian plate movement rates of 5 to 10 millimeters per year is clearly incredible, and totally unbelievable. Only the dramatic weakening of the mantle and lithosphere associated with the runaway conditions during the Flood allows for such catastrophic deformation and uplift of whole mountain chains such as the Himalayas.

---

6   Austin et al, 1994, 614.

7   J. P. Davidson, W. E. Reed and P. M. Davis, 1997, The rise and fall of mountain ranges, in *Exploring Earth: An Introduction to Physical Geology*, Upper Saddle River, NJ: Prentice Hall, 242-247.

Vast regions of the earth's surface were thus catastrophically uplifted at the end of the Flood to form the European Alps, the Himalayas, the Rockies, the Andes, and related mountain chains, along with plateaus such as the Tibetan Plateau and Colorado Plateau. As a result, the Flood waters would have been displaced, and huge amounts of moving water around the earth would have catastrophically eroded into the newly emerging mountains, carving out deep valleys and canyon systems. This is confirmed by experiments that indicate that, if a continental area were under water, and then the water level drops to expose the land surface again, then one result is the carving of canyons or valleys similar to the Grand Canyon, Arizona.[8] The intriguing aspect of these experiments is that the investigators didn't discuss the results in terms of catastrophic geological processes, yet a global catastrophe would be required to explain where all the water necessary for this erosion originated.

A number of objections to the placement of the Flood/post-Flood boundary at approximately the Cretaceous/Tertiary boundary in the geologic record have been raised on geological and related grounds. Among the most serious objections are those pertaining to how the fossil record can be explained in terms of the Flood. The dominant premise of these objections is that the Carboniferous coal seams of the Northern Hemisphere formed as a result of the "beaching" of the pre-Flood floating forests on emerging land surfaces, that therefore represents the end of the Flood and the uplift associated with it.[9] In this view, the amphibian and reptile fossils found in Devonian, Carboniferous, and Permian strata represent the fauna of the pre-Flood floating forests, while the terrestrial fossils found in upper Triassic and higher strata represent the recolonization of the post-Flood world by the animals that had disembarked from the Ark, and the associated flora represents the revegetation of the post-Flood land.[10] Geological evidence cited to support this view is the presence of vertebrate tracks that, it is claimed, could not have formed under the turbulent conditions of the Flood, and whose fossilization required time for hardening under sub-areal conditions, only in Permian and later strata.[11] It is also claimed that successions of multiple nests of dinosaur eggs in numerous stratigraphic sequences would have required considerable periods of dry land conditions unexplainable within the Flood.[12] These inferences are further supported by the claim that, even though continental flood basalts represent huge catastrophic outpourings of lavas, the evidence that they were extruded sub-aerially means that the continental land surfaces onto which they were extruded could not have been under water at those times. Thus, because these basalts are

---

8   J. E. Coss, F. G. Ethridge and S. A. Schumm, 1994, An experimental study of the effects of base-level change on fluvial, coastal plain and shelf systems, *Journal of Sedimentary Research*, B64: 90-98.

9   J. Scheven, 1996, The Carboniferous floating forest—an extinct pre-Flood ecosystem, *Creation Ex Nihilo Technical Journal*, 10 (1): 70-81.

10   Robinson, 1996.

11   Garton, 1996.

12   Garner, Where is the Flood/post-Flood boundary? Implications of dinosaur nests in the Mesozoic, 1996.

absent from Paleozoic strata and present within Mesozoic and higher strata, this implies that continental land surfaces were not under water from the end of the Paleozoic onwards, the claimed post-Flood period.[13] Furthermore, the thick chalk beds among Cretaceous strata are claimed to have required a timescale for deposition significantly longer than days, weeks, or even months, and so had to have been deposited after the Flood.[14]

However, all of these claims can be adequately dealt with based on all available evidence. The coal beds, formed from the break-up of the pre-Flood floating-forest biome, were deposited within sequences of sediments containing marine fossils, so both the coal beds and the sediment layers were deposited in marine environments, thus during the Flood. Strata with marine fossils are found in the Mesozoic record above the coal beds in many parts of the world, so marine sedimentation continued, while land surfaces continued to be inundated, with more and more land creatures being progressively swept away and buried as the Flood waters reached higher elevations (as discussed previously).

The preservation of animal footprints has to be rapid, immediately after being made, because otherwise they would be quickly obliterated, just as they are so easily obliterated on today's land surfaces. Exceptional circumstances are required for track preservation. Such were present during the Flood, when the trackways were left by animals fleeing the Flood waters, as evident from the trackways left behind by animals climbing the underwater sand dune surfaces now preserved in the Coconino Sandstone of the Grand Canyon area.[15] Furthermore, the footprints of animals are often found preserved in strata below where their body fossils are found (see Figure 24), testimony to the animals subsequently being overwhelmed by the Flood waters they were endeavoring to escape.[16]

Similarly, because of being extinct we can't observe the dinosaurs building "nests" and laying eggs, so it is impossible to insist that the "clutches of fossilized dinosaur eggs" found on multiple horizons are true "nests." It is equally valid to regard these "nests" as eggs that were hurriedly laid on temporarily exposed land surfaces by dinosaurs in panic, as they continued to flee from the repeated surges of the rising Flood waters that eventually swept them away and entombed their remains catastrophically in fossil graveyards. It should also not be overlooked that during the deposition of the sediments that entombed the dinosaurs, elsewhere over large areas all around the earth's surface marine deposition of chalk was occurring,

13   Garner, Continental Flood basalts indicate a pre-Mesozoic Flood/post-Flood boundary, 1996.

14   D. J. Tyler, 1996, A post-Flood solution to the chalk problem, *Creation Ex Nihilo Technical Journal*, 10 (1): 107-113; J. Scheven, 1990, The Flood/post-Flood boundary in the fossil record, in *Proceedings of the Second International Conference on Creationism*, vol. 1, R. E. Walsh and C. L. Brooks, eds., Pittsburgh, PA: Creation Science Fellowship, 247-266.

15   L. R. Brand and T. Tang, 1991, Fossil vertebrate footprints in the Coconino Sandstone (Permian) of Northern Arizona: Evidence for underwater origin, *Geology*, 19: 1201-1204.

16   Brand and Florence, 1982.

testimony to the global scale of what had to have therefore been the waters of the Flood. The purity of the chalk is testimony to the catastrophic rate of its deposition, while the oft-cited "hardgrounds" with their evidences of burrows, hardening, erosion, and encrustation, do not necessarily represent claimed long periods of time, given that all these features can be produced rapidly (to be discussed further below).[17]

Finally, even if the continental flood basalts were extruded sub-aerially, they nevertheless represent rapid catastrophic volcanism intimately associated with the break-up of continental plates during the catastrophic plate tectonics of the global Flood catastrophe. Furthermore, those continental flood basalts that are found among Tertiary strata are generally not as voluminous or extensive as their pre-Tertiary counterparts, and the use of the Tertiary fauna as evidence for sub-aerial extrusion to conclude that the earlier flows were also sub-aerial could well be inappropriate. Indeed, if most of the Tertiary strata are post-Flood, then it is to be expected that the continental flood basalts among them would have been extruded sub-aerially. On the other hand, there is definitive evidence that at least one pre-Tertiary continental flood basalt was extruded underwater.

In stark contrast are the reasons and evidences that have been given for the Flood/post-Flood boundary to be toward the top of the Tertiary strata record, perhaps even at the base of the so-called Quaternary.[18] An analysis of the sediments globally represented in the Phanerozoic (Cambrian to the present) geologic record would suggest that if the Flood/post-Flood boundary were placed within middle or upper Carboniferous strata, then the volume of sediment deposited in the post-Flood period would have been more than twice as much the volume of sediments deposited in the Flood itself. Therefore, the amount of catastrophism and rainfall in the post-Flood period would have had to eclipse the catastrophism and rainfall during the Flood! This observation alone would clearly rule out placement of the Flood/post-Flood boundary so low in the strata record. The largest volume of sedimentation would appear to have occurred with deposition of the Cretaceous and Tertiary strata. However, that analysis could be heavily biased because of the erosion and reworking of earlier deposited sedimentary strata. The estimates of sediment volumes in the earlier part of the strata record were based only on the strata that have been preserved in the record, there being no way of quantifying what volume of strata have been eroded away and redeposited as later strata. Nevertheless, the huge disproportionate volume of Cretaceous and Tertiary strata, compared to the rest of the Phanerozoic geologic record, is consistent with these strata having been deposited during the mountain-building phase at the end of the Flood, when the uplift was exposing the new land surface and the resultant catastrophic run-off was occurring as the waters of the Flood drained

17   A. A. Snelling, 1994, Can Flood geology explain thick chalk layers?, *Creation Ex Nihilo Technical Journal* 8 (1): 11-15; A. A. Snelling, 1995, Coccolithophores and chalk layers, *Creation Ex Nihilo Technical Journal*, 9 (1): 33-35.

18   Holt, 1996, 128-167.

from off the continents into the present ocean basins. It is likely that the erosion and sedimentation resulting from run-off of the Flood waters continued as it tapered off in the early post-Flood period, while Noah, his family, and the animals were re-establishing themselves on the new land surface. Thus, placement of the Flood/post-Flood boundary at the boundary between Cretaceous and Tertiary strata would seem to be feasible, although the author of the analysis still argued for placement at the Quaternary/Tertiary boundary.

The analysis of the volumes of volcanic rocks among Phanerozoic strata shows that there were huge volumes of catastrophic volcanism that occurred up until the Cretaceous/Tertiary strata boundary, consistent with placement of the Flood/post-Flood boundary at that level in the record. If instead the Flood/post-Flood boundary were to be placed in the middle of the Carboniferous strata, there would have been as much catastrophic volcanism in the post-Flood period as in the Flood itself. Any catastrophic volcanism in the post-Flood period would have seriously affected the survival of Noah, his family, and the animals, because of the choking volcanic dust and gases blasted into the atmosphere. Even the significantly reduced residual volcanism recorded in Tertiary strata could have been severely detrimental to post-Flood life, suggesting that a placement of the Flood/post-Flood boundary higher in the Tertiary strata record could potentially be more feasible.

Various attempts have been made to estimate the changes in the global sea level during deposition of the Phanerozoic strata record, based on the assumption that the presence of marine fossils in strata indicates these areas were covered by the oceans, while the presence of terrestrial fossils indicates land apparently above sea level. Additionally, sea level changes are inferred from the interpretation of marine transgressions and regressions within the strata record.[19] The resulting curves estimating the global changes in sea level during deposition of the Phanerozoic strata show two broad episodes of global inundation peaking during deposition of the Ordovician and Cretaceous strata, with probable widespread exposure of land surfaces during the Triassic. However, if as claimed the Permian and Triassic onwards represent strata deposited in the post-Flood period, then the inundation peaking in the Cretaceous would have globally covered the earth's surface with the same depth of water that it had been covered with during deposition of the Ordovician strata, thus covering the post-Flood world in as much water as during the Flood itself! In any case, from the perspective of the biblical global Flood catastrophe, the use of terrestrial fossils to indicate land exposed above sea level is rather questionable, given that the mere fact of the burial and fossilization of terrestrial animals on a large scale requires catastrophic flooding of land surfaces.

---

19 P. R. Vail, R. M. Mitchum, Jr. and S. Thompson III, 1977, Global cycles of relative changes of sea level, in *Seismic Stratigraphy and Global Changes at Sea Level*, Memoir 26, E. D. Payton, ed., Tulsa, OK: American Association of Petroleum Geologists, 83-97; A. Hallam, 1984, Pre-Quaternary sea-level changes, *Annual Reviews of Earth and Planetary Sciences*, 12: 205-243; B. U. Haq, G. Hardenbol and P. R. Vail, 1987, Chronology of fluctuating sea levels since the Triassic, *Science*, 235: 1156-1167.

On the other hand, given that these estimates of global sea level are likely to be more accurate for the period from the end of the Flood to the present, it is highly significant that these curves show a rapid drop in global sea level immediately after the deposition of the Cretaceous strata, tapering off to the present sea level through the Tertiary, consistent with a Flood/post-Flood boundary at the Cretaceous/Tertiary strata boundary or soon thereafter. Nevertheless, depending on the identification of the resting place of the Ark, and thus the area into which Noah, his family, and the animals disembarked from the Ark in the biblical "mountains of Ararat," the most likely suggested disembarkation areas consist of upper Tertiary strata, thus perhaps forcing a placement of the Flood/post-Flood boundary after deposition of those strata.[20]

Finally, if as claimed the Carboniferous and Permian coal beds are the result of the beaching, break-up, and burial of pre-Flood floating forests at the beginning of the post-Flood era, then even more coal beds were formed in the Jurassic, Cretaceous, and Tertiary strata later in the post-Flood period. If this were the case, then the origin of the biomass they represent remains problematic, as there would be insufficient time to have grown the required plants and then have them catastrophically uprooted and buried. Even more compelling are the data that show that if the Flood/post-Flood boundary is placed in the middle Carboniferous, then about three times the volume of oil and gas sources rocks would have been deposited during the post-Flood period compared to those source rocks deposited in the Flood itself![21] On the other hand, if the Flood/post-Flood boundary is placed at approximately the Cretaceous/Tertiary strata boundary, then more than 70 percent of all the coal beds, and more than 85 percent of all the oil and gas source rocks, would have been deposited under the catastrophic conditions prevailing during the Flood. The biomass thus involved would largely represent growth in the pre-Flood and Creation Week eras, with some potential growth of algae and bacteria, for example, during the Flood itself. Even though there are large volumes of coal beds, and oil and gas source rocks, particularly oil shales and tar sands, among Tertiary strata, the depositional basins involved are only of local and regional extent, compared with the continental and greater distribution of deposition of Cretaceous strata. Therefore, these localized Tertiary strata would still not preclude a Cretaceous/Tertiary Flood/post-Flood boundary.

On balance, therefore, it is almost certain from all the above geological considerations that the Flood/post-Flood boundary simply cannot be placed as low in the strata record as the middle Carboniferous without causing insurmountable geologic difficulties. Those include sediment volumes, rainfall and erosion, volumes of volcanic rock, choking volcanic dust and gases in the atmosphere, global sea levels, and the volumes of coal beds, and oil and gas source rocks, not to forget the relative position of the strata making up the likely candidates for

---

20   Holt, 1996, 145-149.

21   Holt, 1996, 153-161.

the "mountains of Ararat." However, what about the Flood/post-Flood boundary being as high in the geologic record as the Tertiary/Quaternary strata boundary, compared with being lower down at the Cretaceous/Tertiary strata boundary? The strong argument against a Tertiary/Quaternary Flood/post-Flood boundary is that the Pleistocene strata immediately above that boundary represent the record of the post-Flood Ice Age (to be discussed below), which did not commence immediately after the Flood ended, but instead required several centuries to be fully initiated.[22] The Flood ending at the end of the Cretaceous, instead, provides time for the Tertiary strata to have accumulated in those early centuries of the post-Flood era before the onset of the Pleistocene Ice Age. Furthermore, whereas those who have claimed a middle Carboniferous Flood/post-Flood boundary have appealed to the fossil record as their major piece of evidence, it is the fossil record that really does support a Cretaceous/Tertiary or later Flood/post-Flood boundary.

Of particular relevance is the observation that, subsequent to the burial of the fossils found in the uppermost Cretaceous strata, all of the large reptiles, including the dinosaurs, became extinct, along with the pterosaurs and the swimming reptiles such as plesiosaurs, ichthyosaurs, and others, as well as many types of marine invertebrates. This is consistent with those strata being deposited during the Flood, because unlike other reptiles, the dinosaurs didn't survive in the post-Flood world, in spite of their representatives that disembarked from the Ark. On the other hand, whereas mammal and bird fossils are rarely found in Cretaceous and earlier strata, mammal and bird fossils are abundant, more common, and diverse in Tertiary strata (see Figure 24).[23] Indeed, the fossil mammals are used as index fossils to define the various biostratigraphic stages in Tertiary strata, and to correlate those strata between sedimentary basins on all the continents. Furthermore, in ascending the sequence of Tertiary strata, the numbers of contained mammal fossils that are identical to their modern counterparts increases, implying a lineage connection between the fossil and living mammal populations.

This is supported in two ways. First, a large number of mammal families have their fossil record and modern distribution limited to only one continent. For example, kangaroos are only found in Australia, and so are their fossils, in upper Tertiary strata. It hardly makes sense to suggest that the kangaroo fossils represent kangaroos buried within the Flood, and that the extant kangaroos are thus back in Australia after having traveled there from the Ark after the Flood. On the contrary, it is logical that the kangaroo fossils represent kangaroos that were buried by local catastrophes after the kangaroos traveled to Australia from the Ark after the Flood. Thus, the upper Tertiary strata containing kangaroo fossils

---

22 M. J. Oard, 1987, An Ice Age within the Biblical timeframe, in *Proceedings of the First International Conference on Creationism*, R. E. Walsh, C. L. Brooks and R. S. Crowell, eds., Pittsburgh, PA: Creation Science Fellowship, 157-166; M. J. Oard, 1990, *An Ice Age caused by the Genesis Flood*, El Cajon, CA: Institute for Creation Research; L. Vardiman, 1993, *Ice Cores and the Age of the Earth*, El Cajon, CA: Institute for Creation Research.

23 Brand and Florence, 1982.

must be post-Flood, and the Flood/post-Flood boundary is therefore further down in the strata record. Second, it is within the Tertiary strata that we find stratomorphic series of mammal fossils that have been interpreted as representing post-Flood intrabaraminic diversification.[24] Confirmation of this comes from a baraminological analysis of nineteen fossil equid (horse) species, which found that they all belonged to a single monobaramin ("created kind").[25] The earliest of these fossil equids is found in Eocene strata, so since these fossil equids are clearly related to one another genetically as a stratomorphic series, they can be interpreted as rapid post-Flood genetic diversification. This suggests that the Flood/post-Flood boundary should be placed below those Eocene (lower Tertiary) strata.

On the other hand, there appears to be a strong constraint against placing most of the Tertiary strata and fossils after the Flood/post-Flood boundary. This constraint comes from the amount of Tertiary plate motion recorded in the sea floor rocks. From a map of sea floor age,[26] one readily observes that sea floor with Tertiary age exceeds more than a thousand kilometers on either side of a large portion of the mid-ocean ridge system. These sea floor ages are based on the microfossil content of cores from more than two thousand holes from the deep sea drilling project, from radioisotope dates from basaltic rocks dredged from the sea floor, from the magnetic reversal record obtained from surveys of the world ocean basins, and from the magnetic orientations of magnetic minerals in the deep sea sediment cores. It is only possible to have a large amount of sea floor spreading during the timescale of the Flood because of the dramatic weakening of the mantle that was part of the runaway of cold upper mantle rock and cold oceanic lithosphere. When this runaway shuts down, the viscosity of the mantle quickly recovers to its present high value. At the present value, plate velocities are on the order of a few centimeters per year. At a half spreading rate of five centimeters per year, there is only 215 *meters* of new ocean crust formed during the approximately 4,300 years since the Flood. So only a trivial amount of new sea floor forms after the mantle recovers its strength. Since it hard to imagine the mantle remaining weak more than a few months and at most only a few years after the runaway episode itself ended, it seems likely that most of the Tertiary sea floor was formed during the run-off stage during the year of the Flood.

Although there is still some dispute about where the Flood/post-Flood boundary should be placed in the geologic record, and thus further studies need to be conducted to allow for a more precise definition of this boundary, on balance the available evidence suggests that the Flood/post-Flood boundary certainly must be

---

24   K. P. Wise, 1994, *Australopithecus ramidus* and the fossil record, *Creation Ex Nihilo Technical Journal*, 8: 160-165; K. P. Wise, 1995, Towards a creationist understanding of 'transitional forms', *Creation Ex Nihilo Technical Journal*, 9 (2): 216-222.

25   D. P. Cavanaugh, T. C. Wood and K. P. Wise, 2003, Fossil equidae: A monobaraminic, stratomorphic series, in *Proceedings of the Fifth International Conference on Creationism*, R. L. Ivey, Jr., ed., Pittsburgh, PA: Creation Science Fellowship, 143-153.

26   For example, http://www.ngdc.noaa.gov/mgg/image/images/g01167-pos-a0001.pdf.

above the Cretaceous/Tertiary boundary in the strata record. This approximately corresponds to a transition from worldwide/continental to regional/local deposition and therefore possibly more correctly marks the transition point to the regression stage of the Flood. Vertical earth movements and isostatic readjustments (vertical tectonics) built mountains and elevated plateaus after the Cretaceous, while the sea level rapidly fell as the Flood waters drained from off the surfaces of the continents, accompanied by massive erosion that carved out valleys and canyons and deposited new sediments off the continental margins. Continued volcanic activity declined in power and effect, as the rates of global tectonic and all geologic processes also rapidly declined to provide a new stable world safe enough for Noah, his family, and the animals to disembark from the Ark and to spread across and repopulate the earth's surface again.

95

THE POST-FLOOD WORLD

Post-Flood Geology

After the global effects of the Flood had ended, the earth took considerable time to recover as it continued to experience several hundred years of residual catastrophism.[1] Colliding plates during the Flood had produced mountains in days, and then they were eroded in weeks by the rapidly moving Flood waters. Earthquakes had moved rock strata up and down by thousands of meters in seconds, minutes, and hours. Hundreds of meters of water had covered the continents, pressing them down, and now only months later they were rapidly being uncovered again. With the close of the Flood, and plate motion rapidly decelerating, the plates and the rocks comprising them were totally out of isostatic balance, being either too elevated or too depressed relative to the appropriate equilibrium surface for the earth's crust "floating" on the mantle beneath. So at the end of the Flood, the crustal plates, and the various separate terranes within them, began rebounding toward their appropriate equilibrium positions. However, because of the rheology of the mantle, these isostatic (vertical) adjustments would require thousands of years, with most of the motion probably occurring in the first few hundreds of years after the Flood. Thus, some of this vertical motion would still be occurring today, which would explain the active earthquakes in old mountain chains, such as the Appalachians, and still rising mountains, such as the Tetons. Thus, current geologic activity can be explained as the continued isostatic adjustments after the catastrophic global tectonics during the Flood.

Modern earthquake and volcanic activity is in some sense relict Flood plate tectonics. As rapid horizontal tectonics ceased, when all the cold oceanic lithosphere had sunk during the Flood into the mantle, in the months and years following the Flood new warm oceanic lithosphere would have cooled, particularly the oldest oceanic lithosphere distant from the mid-ocean ridges. Once having cooled, this oceanic lithosphere would be denser than the mantle beneath it, and so gravity is even now pulling these colder lithospheric slabs at the edges of plates downward.

---

1   J. R. Baumgardner, 1990, 3-D finite element simulation of the global tectonic changes accompanying Noah's Flood, in *Proceedings of the Second International Conference on Creationism*, R. E. Walsh and C. L. Brooks, eds., Pittsburgh, PA: Creation Science Fellowship, 35-45.

Thus, the limited plate motions that still occur today, as a result of the sinking of colder lithosphere, explain the position, depth, and nature of most of the world's earthquakes. Early in the post-Flood period, this limited horizontal plate motion would have combined with vertical motions of crustal rocks, isostatically readjusting, to produce rather dramatic results. Mountains would have actually broken off from their foundations along detachment faults, and slid along those fault surfaces for tens of kilometers, a phenomenon not easily explained in the uniformitarian model of earth history.[2] After the initial rapid release of energy early in the post-Flood period, the energy being released would have quickly lessened, bringing more stable conditions to the post-Flood earth. Thus, this biblical model of earth history explains what the uniformitarian model cannot, namely, the incredible amount of energy unleashed around the San Andreas Fault in the past. It also explains why the frequency and sizes of earthquakes has been decreasing over the period we have been able to measure them.[3]

The large changes in crustal thicknesses produced during the Flood not only left the earth in isostatic disequilibrium, but some rocks where the crust was thickest had been quickly buried deeper in the earth's interior. There, the increased temperatures and pressures caused them to begin melting, thus forming less dense magmas that rapidly rose toward the earth's surface. Some of the magmas generated volcanoes, while other magmas cooled under the surface as intrusions. The source of the magma would determine its composition and how explosive any volcanoes would be. If basaltic crust had been subducted, partial melting of the basalt would have produced explosive andesitic volcanism, as in the Andes of South America. Where buried andesites were partially melted, even more explosive rhyolitic volcanism would result, such as in the Yellowstone area and the Taupo Volcanic Zone of New Zealand. The huge volumes of volcanic ash thus generated would have been ideal for fossil burial and preservation, such as the petrified trees in the Yellowstone area. Where lower crustal rocks had melted to produce granitic magmas, these cooled as shallow intrusions, which explains the many Tertiary granitic plutons throughout the western United States. However, concurrent with the mantle heating of thickened or subducted crust, isostatic readjustments would progress, so that less and less magma would be generated with time. The thickened crust would cool, so volcanoes could be expected to decrease in size, intensity, and frequency through the post-Flood period to the present, which appears to be the case with Cenozoic sialic volcanism in the western United States.[4]

2   S. H. Rugg, 1990, Detachment faults in the southwestern United States – evidence for a short and catastrophic Tertiary period, in *Proceedings of the Second International Conference on Creationism*, R. E. Walsh and C. L. Brooks, eds., Pittsburgh, PA: Creation Science Fellowship, 217-229; E. H. Frost, S. C. Suitt and M. Fattahipour, 1996, Emerging perspectives of the Salton Trough region with an emphasis on extensional faulting and its implications for later San Andreas deformation, *Sturzstroms and Detachment Faults, Anza Borrego Desert State Park, California*, P. L. Abbott and D. C. Seymour, eds., Santa Ana, CA: South Coast Geological Society, 81-121.

3   S. A. Austin and M. L. Strauss, 1999, Are earthquakes signs of the end times?, *Christian Research Journal*, 21 (4): 30-39.

4   F. V. Perry, D. J. DePaolo and W. S. Baldridge, 1991, Isotopic evidence for a decline in crustal

Because of the frequency and intensity of residual catastrophism after the Flood, post-Flood sedimentary processes were predominantly rapid. However, the local nature of such catastrophism restricted sedimentation to local areas, which explains the basinal nature of most Cenozoic sedimentation. The heavy rainfall in the early post-Flood years (see below) eroded mountainsides, washing the sediments into lakes, such as those in Wyoming, Utah, and Colorado, into which the Green River Formation was rapidly deposited, preserving millions of fossil fish and some frogs, turtles, lizards, snakes alligators, crocodiles, birds, bats, other mammals, and many invertebrates and plants.[5]

Post-Flood Climate

Enormous amounts of heat came from inside the earth during the Flood, particularly with the extrusion of new oceanic crusts, but also as a result of the volcanic rocks extruded on the continents, and the granite and other intrusions. Although much of the heat was probably passed into space,[6] some of the heat had to be taken up directly by the Flood waters that covered the earth. By the time the Flood waters had settled into the post-Flood ocean basins, they had accumulated enough heat to make the ocean waters as much as 20°C or more warmer than today's ocean waters.[7] These warmer oceans might be expected to have produced a warmer climate on the earth in the immediate post-Flood period than is experienced on the earth now.[8] Furthermore, a warm ocean would have resulted in a higher evaporation rate, and thus a lot more water in the atmosphere. Away from the coast, the continental interiors would have cooled quickly at night below the ocean water temperature, so the cool air from the continents would have moved over the oceans to replace the warm air rising from their surface. Thus, the warm, moisture-laden air above the oceans would have moved over the continents to replace the air moving seawards. Over the continents, this moist air would have cooled, causing condensation and lots of heavy precipitation.[9]

---

contributions to Caldera-forming rhyolites of the western United States during the middle to late Cenozoic, *Geological Society of America Abstracts with Programs*, 23 (7): A441; Austin, 1998.

5   L. Grande, 1984, *Paleontology of the Green River Formation, with a Review of the Fossil Fish Fauna*, second edition, Geological Survey of Wyoming, Bulletin 63; J. H. Whitmore, 2006, The Green River Formation: a large post-Flood lake system, *Journal of Creation*, 20 (1): 55-63.

6   J. R. Baumgardner, 2003, Catastrophic plate tectonics: the physics behind the Genesis Flood, in *Proceedings of the Fifth International Conference on Creationism*, R. L. Ivey, Jr., ed., Pittsburgh, PA: Creation Science Fellowship, 113-126.

7   J. P. Kennett, R. E. Houtz, P. B. Andrews, A. R. Edwards, V. A. Gostin, M. Hajos, M. Hampton, D. G. Jenkins, S. V. Margolis, A. T. Ovenshine and K. Perch-Neilson, 1975, Site 284, *Initial Reports of the Deep Sea Drilling Project, 29*, J. P. Kennett et al, eds., 403-445; J. J. Shackleton and J. P. Kennett, 1975, Paleotemperature history of the Cenozoic and the initiation of Antarctic glaciation: oxygen and carbon isotope analysis in DSDP sites 277, 279, and 281, *Initial Reports of the Deep Sea Drilling Project, 29*, J. P. Kennett et al eds., 743-755; Vardiman, 1993.

8   Oard, 1990.

9   L. Vardiman, 1994, A conceptual transition model of the atmospheric global circulation following the Genesis Flood, in *Proceedings of the Third International Conference on Creationism*, R. E. Walsh, ed., Pittsburgh, PA: Creation Science Fellowship, 569-579; L. Vardiman, 1998, Numerical simulation of

However, over time the evaporation of water from the oceans would have gradually caused them to cool, resulting in progressively less precipitation being generated. Thus, in the centuries following the Flood, the entire earth would have gradually become drier.

In the early centuries of the post-Flood period, the warm oceans and cooler continental interiors would have resulted in a rather uniform warm climate along the continental margins, permitting a wider latitudinal range for temperature-limited organisms,[10] such as mammoths,[11] and tropical trees and forests.[12] The situation may have as a consequence facilitated the post-Flood dispersion of animals (to be further discussed below).[13] Furthermore, there would likely have been along the continental margins a rather high climatic gradient running from oceans toward the continental interiors, because the temperatures would have dropped further and faster than they do today from the coastlines inland. As a result of this temperature structure, there would have probably been different communities of flora and fauna closer to the coastlines than further inland. Furthermore, with the rapid temperature changes from the coastlines to the continental interiors, the biological communities would probably have been geographically narrow and overlapped with adjacent communities. This might explain why fossils of some Cenozoic plant communities found near the continental coastal margins include a mixture of plants and organisms from a wider range of climatic zones (that is, with different climatic tolerances) than we would expect to see today, for example, fossil Pleistocene communities,[14] and the Gingko Petrified Forest in Oregon.[15]

As the oceans and the earth cooled in the first few centuries after the Flood, the large amounts of water evaporated off the oceans decreased, so the precipitation rates over the cooler continental interiors gradually decreased. This cooling of the oceans is confirmed by oxygen isotope ratios in Cenozoic foraminifera of polar

precipitation induced by hot mid-ocean ridges, in *Proceedings of the Fourth International Conference on Creationism*, R. E. Walsh, ed., Pittsburgh, PA: Creation Science Fellowship, 595-605.

10   M. J. Oard, 1979, A rapid post-Flood Ice Age, *Creation Research Society Quarterly*, 16 (1): 29-37; M. J. Oard, 1987, An Ice Age within the Biblical timeframe, in *Proceedings of the First International Conference on Creationism*, R. E. Walsh, C. L. Brooks and R. S. Crowell, eds., Pittsburgh, PA: Creation Science Fellowship, 157-166; Oard, 1990.

11   C. E. Schweger et al, 1982, Paleoecology of Beringia – a synthesis, *Paleoecology of Beringia*, D. M. Hopkins et al eds., New York: Academic Press, 425-444.

12   K. P. Wise, 1992, Were there really no seasons?: Tree rings and climate, *Creation Ex Nihilo Technical Journal*, 6 (2): 168-172; C. Felix, 1993, The mummified forests of the Canadian Arctic, *Creation Research Society Quarterly*, 29 (4): 189-191.

13   J. Woodmorappe, 1990, Causes for the biogeographic distribution of land vertebrates after the Flood, in *Proceedings of the Second International Conference on Creationism*, vol. 2, R. E. Walsh and C. L. Brooks, eds., Pittsburgh, PA: Creation Science Fellowship, 361-367.

14   R. W. Graham and E. L. Lundelius, Jr, 1984, Coevolutionary disequilibrium and Pleistocene extinctions, *Quaternary Extinctions: A Prehistoric Revolution*, E. S. Martin and R. J. Klein, eds., Tuscon, AZ: University of Arizona, 223-249.

15   H. G. Coffin, 1974, The Gingko Petrified Forest, *Origins (Geoscience Research Institute)*, 1: 101-103.

bottom, polar surface, and tropical bottom waters,[16] and may have contributed to the general increase in the body sizes of vertebrates throughout the Cenozoic (what is known as Cope's Law).[17] As precipitation rates decreased, the earth dried and vegetation patterns changed. For example, the description in Genesis 13:10 of the Dead Sea region as well-watered everywhere "as the garden of the Lord" implies that there must have been higher precipitation rates there in Abraham's day, only a few centuries after the Flood. Furthermore, some 400 years later, the land of Canaan was still an incredibly fertile land described as flowing "with milk and honey" (Numbers 13:23-27). Today it is largely desert. It is to be expected that floral and faunal communities would have tracked this cooling of the oceans and the corresponding cooling and drying of the continents. This explains the trend in Cenozoic plant communities to progress from woodland that dwindled worldwide to be gradually replaced by extensive grasslands, as documented by the change in pollen in Tertiary sedimentary sequences.[18] As a consequence, there is a parallel trend in Cenozoic herbivores that change from browsers to grazers. Eventually, continued drying of the earth's surface generated the world's current deserts, which explains why beneath its wind-blown sands the Sahara Desert has evidence of being in the past a well-watered area with rivers and forests.[19]

The high precipitation rates in the early centuries after the Flood would have produced a greater volume of run-off water, which would have meant corresponding rates of both erosion and sedimentation. Such heavy rainfall concurrently over large areas would have resulted in peak flows of the water over the earth's surface, eroding sediments and strata in a planar fashion, rather than being channeled into streams. This would explain the widespread planar erosional surfaces found in Tertiary sedimentary strata. As they slowed down, these sediment-laden sheets of water would have deposited those sediments in sheets, consistent with the extensive, nearly-flat wedges of sediments found among Tertiary strata. As the rainfall decreased, deposition and erosion would have occurred over smaller areas, which would explain the large alluvial fans that cannot be produced under present climatic conditions. The higher rainfall would also have produced lakes into which sediments would have been deposited, such as the lakes cited earlier in which the Green River Formation was deposited.

---

16 Kennett et al, 1975; Shackleton and Kennett, 1975; L. Vardiman, 1996, *Sea-Floor Sediment and the Age of the Earth*, El Cajon, CA: Institute for Creation Research.

17 S. M. Stanley, 1973, An explanation of Cope's Rule, *Evolution*, 27 (1): 1-26.

18 B. E. Cerling and J. R. Ehleringer, 2000, Welcome to the C_4 world, in *Phanerozoic Terrestrial Ecosystems*, R. A. Gastaldo and W. A. DiMichele (convenors), The Paleontological Society, United States, 273-286.

19 J. F. McCauley et al, 1982, Subsurface valley and geoarcheology of the eastern Sahara revealed by shuttle radar, *Science*, 218: 1004-1020; H. J. Pachur and S. Kröplin, 1987, Wadi Howar: Paleoclimate evidence from an extinct river system in the southeastern Sahara, *Science*, 237, 298-300; R. A. Kerr, 1987, Climate since the ice began to melt, *Science*, 236: 326-327; This also provides a possible explanation for why the Sphinx shows signs of being eroded by water when younger Egyptian edifices such as the pyramids only have evidence of wind erosion: R. M. Schoch and J. A. West, 2000, Further evidence supporting a pre-2500BC date for the great Sphinx of Giza, Egypt, *GSA Abstracts with Programs*, 32 (7): A276.

With continued rainfall these post-Flood lakes may have overfilled, the excess water quickly cutting through whatever "dam" had held the lake-water in place and rapidly draining the lakes to catastrophically erode spectacular canyons. The most notable example is the lake system in which leftover Flood waters were impounded by the Kaibab Upwarp, as part of the Colorado Plateau, in northern Arizona. Subsequent post-Flood rainfall overfilled these lakes, so the excess water breached this natural dam, resulting in catastrophic draining of the lakes and erosion of the Grand Canyon.[20] Furthermore, with so much heavy rainfall in the early centuries of the post-Flood period, the resultant local catastrophic flooding would have meant that all the world's canyons were cut in those first centuries early in the post-Flood period. This explains why modern rivers are underfit, no longer downcutting into their basement rock, but merely eroding and readjusting their banks. Of course, during this intense period of canyon erosion, the sediments that were removed would have been deposited at the river mouths, thus forming deltas. This would explain the rapid origin of the great deltas at the mouths of the world's large rivers, including the huge deltas that have been built out onto the deep ocean floor. Finally, during this high-rainfall period it is possible that, with larger amounts of water percolating down into the ground, the large cave systems found today were carved out.

---

20   S. A. Austin, 1994, How was Grand Canyon eroded?, *Grand Canyon, Monument to Catastrophe*, S. A. Austin, ed., Santee, CA: Institute for Creation Research, 83-110.

96

THE POST-FLOOD ICE AGE—
A CONSEQUENCE OF THE FLOOD

Another feature of the earth's surface today, which therefore formed subsequent to the Flood during the post-Flood period to the present, are the deposits of glacial debris. These are found across North America, northern Europe, and northwest Asia in the Northern Hemisphere, and the southern half of South America, southernmost Africa, southeastern Australia and Tasmania, and New Zealand in the Southern Hemisphere, plus in many mountainous areas of the world, where glaciers do not exist today. Even in the tropics, glacial debris is found on the highest mountains, about 1,000 meters below existing glaciers. This debris consists of all different sizes of rock fragments chaotically mixed in a fine-grained matrix known as rock flour. End moraines similar to those associated with present-day mountain glaciers are abundant. Streamlined lens-shaped mounds called drumlins exist in large numbers, and large areas of North Dakota, Montana, and Saskatchewan, for example, are covered by parallel grooves with intervening ridges.[1] The hard-rock surfaces of some outcrops are also polished, scratched, and grooved, and so are called striated pavements. Rock protrudences known as *roche moutonnées* have one side smoothed with parallel scratches, and the opposing sides have plucked or sheared surfaces. All these landforms and features are difficult to account for except by means of the passage of glaciers across these land and rock surfaces, with rock debris in the ice capable of scratching and cutting hard rock. Indeed, there are many other abundant landforms that are indicative of glaciation.[2] The distribution of these various evidences thus indicates that the mid and high latitudes of the northern and southern hemispheres were once covered by large ice sheets, the remnants of which still cover Greenland, much of the Arctic Ocean centered on the North Pole, and Antarctica. Because these features are found on the land surface today, this glaciation had to have occurred after the Flood, so an explanation for this post-Flood glaciation is required.

In the conventional uniformitarian model of earth history, this period of the geologic record is known as the Ice Age within the Pleistocene Epoch, which

1   R. F. Flint, 1971, *Glacial and Quaternary Geology*, New York: John Wiley and Sons.
2   D. E. Sugden and B. S. John, 1976, *Glaciers and Landscape*, London: Edward Arnold.

supposedly spanned the period from 1.8 million to ten thousand years ago. Furthermore, it is claimed that during this period there were four advances and retreats of these continental ice sheets, which thus requires some explanation as to how the climate could have changed in such a cyclical manner to cause these continent-wide glaciations. Indeed, more than sixty theories have been proposed,[3] but all have serious difficulties:

> Pleistocene phenomena have produced an absolute riot of theories ranging from the remotely possible to the mutually contradictory and the palpably inadequate.[4]

It was once thought that colder winters were the main requirement for glaciation, but winters are still cold enough over areas that were once covered by ice sheets. In fact, winters are now too cold in places such as Siberia, where no glaciers now exist. Rather, to produce an ice sheet the winter snow must survive the summer and continue to accumulate year by year, so it is crucial that summers were colder than they are today for the snow to survive. For example, in Siberia today the summers are too warm for the snow to progressively accumulate year by year. Furthermore, enough snow must fall in the winter to survive through the cooler summer until the next winter. Thus, the requirements for an Ice Age would appear to be a combination of cooler summers and greater snowfall than today.[5] However, according to realistic climate simulations over snow cover, at least 10 to 12°C summers cooling and twice the snowfall are needed just to glaciate northeast Canada.[6]

However, such climate simulations still beg the question as to how such stringent requirements could have been initiated. Several proposed solutions are largely speculation. While many climate simulations indicate that an Ice Age could have developed easily with only a small change in higher latitude summer radiation, these climate simulations are crude, and glaciation is specified as a response to unrealistic variables.[7] The most popular proposal has been an extra-terrestrial explanation, namely, a decrease in solar output. Thus, probably the most widely adopted theory several decades ago was the "solar-topographic" hypothesis of the prominent Yale glacial geologist R. F. Flint, which tried to explain the glaciations in terms of the worldwide mountain uplifts toward the end of the Tertiary combined with assumed fluctuations in incoming solar radiation. Flint commented about

---

3   E. Eriksson, 1968, Air-ocean-icecap interation in relation to climatic fluctuations and glaciation cycles, in *Causes of Climatic Change*, J. M. Mitchell, Jr., ed., Meteorological Monographs, 8 (30), Boston: American Meteorological Society, 68-92.

4   J. K. Charlesworth, 1957, *The Quaternary Era*, London: Edward Arnold, 1532.

5   J. O. Fletcher, 1968, The influence of the Arctic pack ice on climate, in *Causes of Climatic Change*, J. M. Mitchell, Jr., ed., Meteorological Monographs, 8 (30), Boston: American Meteorological Society, 93-99.

6   L. D. Williams, 1979, An energy balance model of potential glacierization of northern Canada, *Arctic and Alpine Research*, 11: 443-456.

7   Oard, 1990.

his hypothesis:

> However, changes in the composition and turbidity of the atmosphere and changes in the earth's axis and orbit may have been factors.[8]

In the past twenty years, the astronomical theory of a mechanism for the Ice Age has grown immensely in popularity, so that many are now confident that the mystery of the Ice Age has been solved.[9] Commonly called the Milankovitch theory, this mechanism does not state how the Ice Age itself began, but it does suggest a solution to the glacial/interglacial fluctuations within the Ice Age. This astronomical theory suggests that periodic differences in the earth's orbit around the sun caused slight changes in the intensity of sunlight reaching the earth. The gravitational pull of the moon and the planets causes three orbital variations:

1. Slight changes in the eccentricity of the earth's orbit;
2. Small variations in the tilt of the earth's axis with the plane of the elliptic; and
3. The precession of the equinoxes.

It is the first variation that is considered to be the main cause of the glacial/ interglacial oscillations. Because the earth's orbit changes from nearly circular to slightly elliptical and back to nearly circular about every 100,000 years, the variations in the amount of sunlight at higher latitudes in summers are periodic, the cooler temperatures that trigger ice sheets being separated by interglacials at regular intervals of 100,000 years. First proposed in the late 1800s, and then developed by Milankovitch in the 1920s and 1930s, this astronomical theory was not "proven," and thus did not become popular until the 1970s, when the earth's orbital variations were matched with slight differences in the oxygen isotopic compositions of small planktonic shells fossilized in the ocean-floor sediments.[10] Now, as many as twenty or thirty glacial periods, separated by interglacials of complete melting, are regarded as having developed in succession during the supposed 1.8 million years of the Pleistocene epoch.[11]

However, many serious problems have been overlooked in the uniformitarian establishment's enthusiasm for this theory.[12] For example, the changes in summer

---

8   R. F. Flint, 1957, *Glacial and Pleistocene Geology*, New York: John Wiley and Sons, 509.

9   J. Imbrie and K. P. Imbrie, 1979, *Ice Ages: Solving the Mystery*, Short Hills, NJ: Enslow Publishers.

10   J. D. Hays, J. Imbrie and N. J. Shackleton, 1976, Variations in the earth's orbit: Pacemaker of the Ice Ages, *Science*, 194, 1121-1132.

11   J. P. Kennett, 1982, *Marine Geology*, Englewood Cliffs, NJ: Prentice-Hall.

12   M. J. Oard, 1984, Ice Ages: The mystery solved? Part I: The inadequacy of the uniformitarian Ice Age, *Creation Research Society Quarterly*, 21: 66-76; M. J. Oard, 1984, Ice Ages: The mystery solved? Part II: The manipulation of deep-sea cores, *Creation Research Society Quarterly*, 21: 125-137; M. J. Oard, 1985, Ice Ages: The mystery solved? Part III: Paleomagnetic stratigraphy and data manipulation, *Creation Research Society Quarterly*, 21: 170-181.

sunshine at higher latitudes postulated by the theory are actually too small to cause the dramatic changes needed to produce ice sheets, the actual development of which the theory does not explain. Furthermore, the heating at higher latitudes only partially depends on sunshine, the important equator-to-poles transport of heat by the atmosphere and oceans being largely neglected by the theory's proponents. This transport would lessen the cooling at higher latitudes caused by reduced sunshine, one weakness of the theory known by meteorologists. Additionally, the 100,000-year periodicity determined by statistical correlations in the ocean-floor sediment data only matches the eccentricity variation of the earth's orbit, the smallest by far of the three variations. In any case, many poorly known processes can influence the oxygen isotopes in the plankton shells in the ocean-floor sediments.[13] For instance, the water temperature when the shells formed in the past must be known within one or two degrees, yet these planktonic animals often live in the surface layer of the ocean that exhibits seasonal changes of 10°C or more at mid and high latitudes. However, these planktonic animals also at times change depths to where the ocean water is much cooler, especially at lower altitudes, which introduces another large unknown error. Additionally, once these plankton shells accumulate in the ocean-floor sediments, they are commonly subject to erosion by ocean currents, to mixing by abundant bottom-feeding worms, and to the dissolution of the calcium carbonate, which can even change the oxygen-isotope ratios by the dissolving of thinner shells that are isotopically lighter.[14]

Thus, the Milankovitch astronomical theory is subject to serious scientific difficulties in explaining the Ice Age. Nevertheless, although a uniformitarian Ice Age seems meteorologically impossible and proposed solutions are inadequate, atmospheric climate simulations have shown that the small changes in solar radiation proposed by the Milankovitch theory supposedly do cause glacial periods. However, the desired results are actually the consequence of radiation-sensitive initial conditions, such as ice sheets already in place, uncertain values for input variables, and by inexact statistical representations of other poorly understood variables in the models. One variable that is favorable for the development of an Ice Age in these climate models is the albedo of snow, but the value used to make the models work is far too high for melting snow, and is especially too high for exposed glacial ice. Similarly, these Ice Age climate simulation models have generally used unreasonably high values of precipitation, such as 1.2 meters/year for northeastern North America, a rate 2 to 6 times too high for the average values in different parts of this region. It is, therefore, hardly surprising that with such extremely high values for snowfall and snow albedo being used, these

---

13   W. H. Berger and J. D. Gardner, 1975, On the determination of Pleistocene temperatures from planktonic foraminifera, *Journal of Foraminiferal Research*, 5: 102-113.

14   J. Erez, 1979, Modification of the oxygen-isotope record in deep-sea cores by Pleistocene dissolution cycles, *Nature*, 281: 535-538; M. C. Bonneau, C. Bergnaud-Grazzini and W. H. Berger, 1980, Stable isotope fractionation and differential dissolution in recent planktonic foraminifera from Pacific box-cores, *Oceanologica Acta*, 3: 377-382.

simulation models do predict an Ice Age due to small changes in solar radiation that are correlated to the Milankovitch oscillations. Nevertheless, one such model predicts that we should be in an Ice Age at the present![15] Thus, there are very basic problems with all of these climate models, the results generated being severely distorted by the choice of input values to give the desired results. Furthermore, the crucial explanation of what actually initiated the Ice Age still remains elusive, the apparent contrived success of the popular Milankovitch theory notwithstanding.

The Ice Age as a Consequence of the Flood

The aftermath of the global biblical Flood actually provided the initial conditions that made the Ice Age inevitable. As a consequence of the prodigious volumes of hot water that gushed from inside the earth through the fountains of the great deep during the Flood, coupled with the enormous outpourings of hot volcanic lavas whose remains are still preserved over many large areas in thick piles within the strata record, the waters of the oceans were heated to a temperature some 20°C warmer than they are today. This claim is based on placement of the Flood/post-Flood boundary at the Cretaceous/Tertiary boundary in the strata record, and is evidenced in the temperature-related oxygen isotope ratios of the shells of single-celled marine organisms, which suggest that ocean temperatures increased during deposition of the Paleozoic and Mesozoic strata, and then decreased during Tertiary (post-Flood) deposition.[16] Significantly, the uniformitarian model of earth history has no comprehensive explanation for these data.

At the end of the Flood, as the waters drained off the emerging land surfaces, the mixing would have resulted in the ocean waters being universally warm from pole to pole, and from top to bottom. Even though there continued to be large volcanic eruptions as part of catastrophism residual to the global tectonics of the Flood event, these were on a decreasing scale, as indicated by the smaller volumes of lavas preserved in the Tertiary strata record. The dust and aerosols generated by this volcanism would have provided a measure of cooling during the summers over the mid and high latitude portions of the continents, by reflecting a relatively large percentage of the summer sunshine back into space.[17] However, as already discussed, the warm oceans greatly increased the evaporation rates, and with the cooler continental interiors the warm moist air moved landwards, producing heavy rainfall over the continental interiors. This heavy rainfall would have cleaned the air of the volcanic dust and aerosols, but the cloud cover would have added to the summer cooling. Eventual combination of cold land and warm oceans would have caused major storm tracks to develop parallel to the east coasts

15   M. J. Suarez and I. M. Held, 1976, Modelling climatic response to orbital parameter variations, *Nature*, 263: 46-47; M. J. Suarez and I. M. Held, 1969, The sensitivity of an energy balance climate model to variations in the orbital parameters, *Journal of Geophysical Research*, 84 (C8): 4825-4836.

16   T. F. Anderson, 1990, Temperature from oxygen isotope ratios, *Paleobiology: A Synthesis*, D. E. G. Briggs and P. R. Crowther, eds., Malden, MA: Blackwell, 403-406.

17   Oard, 1990.

of Asia and North America, and remain more-or-less stationary all year round. Storm after storm would have developed and dropped most of their moisture over colder land, while the strongest evaporation from the warm oceans would have occurred near the continents. This prodigious evaporation removed heat from the oceans, so they began to progressively cool. Eventually, the world's oceans cooled sufficiently for the precipitation over the continents to come down to high altitudes and latitudes as snow, particularly in northeastern North America, eastern Antarctica, and the mountains of Scandinavia, Greenland, west Antarctica, and western North America.

It was, therefore, the copious amounts of moisture evaporated from the warm oceans that eventually triggered the Ice Age. Because this moisture eventually came down so quickly as snow, the summer warmth in these cool continental areas was not able to melt all the snow that had fallen the previous winter. As a result, the snow built up and was compacted in some places into ice, which in turn thus accumulated into huge ice sheets, which became so thick that they flowed under their own weight, surging over areas where there was no ice. Many areas closer to the warm oceans, such as the British Isles and the lowlands of northwestern Europe, would have initially been too warm for glaciers, while the lowlands of eastern Asia and Alaska would have escaped glaciation all together. The oceans adjacent to the developing ice sheets and in the paths of storms would have continued to be warm, due to a vigorous horizontal and vertical ocean circulation. As the ocean water was cooled by evaporation and by contact with the cold continental air, it would have become more dense and sunk, being replaced by warmer water from deeper in the oceans. The ocean currents along the east coast of Asia and North America would have continually transported warmer water northward. As the deeper oceans cooled, the ocean surface and atmosphere at mid and high latitudes would have slowly cooled, as the Ice Age progressed and ice sheets expanded. Mountain ice caps in many areas would have coalesced and spread to lower elevations.

Based on starting with the oceans 20°C warmer than today, and the placement of the Flood/post-Flood boundary at the Cretaceous/Tertiary strata boundary in the geologic record, early results from numerical climate modeling studies have successfully shown that the ice accumulated in the places where we know it actually did, and all this happened in a matter of a few centuries.[18] Indeed, this numerical climate modeling, which fits the biblical timescale, seems to be the only such modeling that has successfully produced ice sheets where we know they were. The ice began accumulating over just a few centuries, during which the Tertiary strata were deposited. When the ice had accumulated sufficiently, it surged out in a couple of decades, and then melted in another couple of decades, equivalent to

18   Vardiman, 1993; L. Vardiman, 1994, An analytic young-earth flow model of ice sheet formation during the 'Ice Age', in *Proceedings of the Third International Conference on Creationism*, R. E. Walsh, ed., Pittsburgh, PA: Creation Science Fellowship, 561-579; L. Vardiman, 2001, *Climates Before and After the Genesis Flood: Numerical Models and Their Implications*, El Cajon, CA: Institute for Creation Research.

the Pleistocene epoch of the geological record. This rapid ice accumulation and melting demonstrated by this numerical climate modeling, based on the biblical timescale and boundary conditions, is of course too rapid for the uniformitarian theory of the Ice Age, which in any case cannot explain how the oceans became warm to be the driving force that initiated the ice accumulation. Furthermore, it has been suggested that because of its brevity, this rapid build-up and surging of ice would be more appropriately called an "Ice Advance," rather than an Ice Age.[19] This Ice Advance model, confirmed by the numerical modeling that also extends its explanatory power, has a lot of advantages, because it is consistent in not only explaining the same evidence explained by the conventional uniformitarian Ice Age model, but is also consistent with much more evidence beyond that.

It is estimated that due to the unique post-Flood climate, glacial maximum would have been reached very rapidly in about 500 years, based on the length of time the controlling conditions could have operated. The main variable determining this timespan would have been the ocean warmth, which generated the required copious moisture. Once the ocean water had cooled to some threshold temperature, the supply of moisture would have critically declined, and thus deglaciation would have begun. This estimated time of 500 years needed to cool the ocean water was calculated from the oceanic and atmospheric heat-balance equations applied to the post-Flood climate.[20] The available moisture for an Ice Advance not only would have come from the warm mid and high latitude oceans, but also from the poleward transported water vapor from lower latitudes by the atmospheric circulation. Indeed, the modeling has shown that enormous hurricane-like storm cells would have developed over the poles, drawing in the moisture and then precipitating it in spiral rain-bands around the central "eye."[21]

This Ice Advance model suggests that there was only one ice advance, with minor surges around the lobes of the ice sheets. In the conventional uniformitarian Ice Age model, multiple glaciations alternating with interglacial periods are postulated, but the number of glaciations has never been firmly established. The glacial sediments are so complex that a case could be made for from one to six or more separate glaciations. Four glaciations were initially agreed upon, based on investigations in the Swiss Alps, but recently glaciologists have revised that to twenty or thirty glaciations that developed and dissipated in succession, as correlated with the ocean-floor sediment data supposedly supporting the Milankovitch astronomical theory. However, abundant evidence is consistent with one ice advance only, particularly given the very radical requirements for

---

19   Wise, 2002, 215-216.

20   Oard, 1990.

21   L. Vardiman, 1994, A conceptual transition model of the atmospheric global circulation following the Genesis Flood, in *Proceedings of the Third International Conference on Creationism*, R. E. Walsh, ed., Pittsburgh, PA: Creation Science Fellowship, 569-579; Vardiman, 1993.

development of the ice advance[22] (including a warm ocean) were simply not repeatable. The glacial sediments have not been transported far, the till cover is only thin, especially over interior regions, and nearly all the till was deposited during the last supposed glaciation, all of which is more reasonably consistent with only one thin advancing and retreating ice sheet. Moreover, since practically all of the glacial period fossils are found south of the former northern hemisphere ice sheets, and most of the related major faunal extinctions were only the result of the last supposed glaciation, there most likely never were interglacial periods. Indeed, the evidence for the claimed multiple glaciations is only found at the peripheries of the ice sheet, evidence that is actually rare, such as fossils in ancient soils between sheets of till. Even recognizing an ancient soil is difficult, because there simply are too many poorly known variables that make identification speculative, let alone using their properties for dating. Instead, this claimed evidence for multiple glaciations is more simply and adequately explained by just one dynamic ice advance, in which the ice sheets, like modern glaciers, would advance, retreat and then surge again as dictated by climate variations. In the post-Flood Ice Advance model, the ice sheets would have moved rapidly at their peripheries and slowly in their interiors. Rapid oscillations at their peripheries would have caused stacked thin till sheets, with non-glacial deposits sandwiched between them, occasionally containing engulfed fossil remains.

Another consequence of the Ice Advance model is that the ice would have been much thinner, and would not have remained in position as long as claimed by the conventional uniformitarian model. Therefore, it more easily explains how there could be ice-free or "driftless" areas, such as in Wisconsin, which the periphery of the ice sheet completely surrounded but never covered in glacial ice. On the other hand, thick ice sheets advancing and retreating more than twenty times, as in the conventional uniformitarian model, would surely have not missed covering such areas. Furthermore, if thick ice had remained on the continents for a long time, it would have slowed the continents down under its own weight. Since it takes the earth some 25,000 years to recover completely from being depressed in this fashion, it should still be rebounding. However, most of Ohio, Indiana, and Illinois show very little to no rebound, as if the ice was either very thin, and/or it did not cover this area for very long.

The modeling of the ice advance also enables the thicknesses of the ice sheets to be calculated, based on the aerial distributions of the available precipitation. Thus, the best estimate for the average ice depth over the Northern Hemisphere was found to be about 700 meters, and over the Southern Hemisphere about 1,200 meters. Though these thicknesses seem large, they are significantly less and more soundly based than uniformitarian estimates. It is usually assumed that past ice sheets were similar to the current Antarctic ice sheets, but there is much evidence from the interior and margin of the Laurentide (North American) Ice Sheet that indicates it

---

22   Williams, 1979.

was actually comparatively thin. The fatal problem for the uniformitarian Ice Age model is that inflated ice sheet thickness estimates only exacerbate the difficulties of generating the required precipitation, not just for the ice sheets for one glacial episode, but repeatedly for twenty or more such episodes!

However, the uniformitarian model claims to have far more time available for the required precipitation to accumulate, because drilling into the Greenland and Antarctic ice sheets has shown the ice to consist of thousands of thin layers that have been equated with annual cycles of precipitation and thawing. While such thin ice layers can be visually recognized in the drill-cores from the tops of the ice sheets, with increasing depth the pressures have obliterated the visual layering, and so recognition of the layering depends on oxygen isotope variations[23] and on the calculated age-depth relationship incorporating the generally accepted ice flow model.[24] However, if the oxygen isotope data from the ice cores are interpreted within the biblical timeframe for the post-Flood Ice Advance model, rather than the uniformitarian age-depth relationship, an entirely different outcome is obtained that fits extremely well with the overall climate modeling of the single, short, post-Flood Ice Age.[25]

The calculated curve for the thickness of the ice sheets, and the accumulation of the layers as a function of time, shows a rapid build-up of most of the thickness in the first few centuries of the post-Flood period, and is consistent with the very high precipitation rates during that time. However, if it is assumed that the fluctuations in oxygen isotopes within the ice do delineate layers that represent annual precipitation and thawing with the changes of seasons, then even though the age-thickness relationship exactly fits the post-Flood Ice Advance model, many of these thin, proposed annual ice layers have to have formed each year during the rapid build-up of the ice sheets in the early centuries after the Flood.

This apparent contradiction is easily resolved by a correct understanding of the significance of the variations in the oxygen isotope ratios of the ice, and then by recognizing the affects of the individual storms that carried the moisture and precipitated it as snow on the growing ice sheets. Although the primary factor that causes the oxygen isotope ratio in precipitation to change is the influence of the formation temperature on the fractionation of the two oxygen isotopes,[26] the variation in oxygen isotope ratios is also a function of the distance of an observation site from the source of the moisture, the relative concentration of oxygen isotopes

23   S. J. Johnsen, W. Dansgaard, H. B. Clausen and C. C. Langway, Jr., 1972, Oxygen isotope profiles through the Antarctic and Greenland ice sheets, *Nature*, 235: 429-434.

24   W. Dansgaard, S. J. Johnsen, H. B. Clausen and C. C. Langway, Jr., 1971, Climatic record revealed by the Camp Century ice core, in *Late Cenozoic Glacial Ages*, K. K. Turekian, ed., New Haven and London: Yale University Press, 37-56.

25   Vardiman, 1993, 1994, and 2001.

26   H. Craig, 1961, Isotope variations in meteoritic water, *Science*, 133: 1702-1703.

at the source of moisture, and the type of precipitation process.[27] It has thus been shown that the observed oxygen isotope trends in the ice cores can be explained successfully in terms of the dispersion of oxygen isotope ratios as a function of the distance from the edge of a growing or retreating ice shelf.[28] Of course, the ice cores drilled in the Greenland and Antarctic ice sheets contain records of the oxygen isotope ratios in the snows that precipitated at those locations through a timespan in which the ice was accumulating. Thus, if the site of an ice core was a short distance from the open ocean (say 200 km) at the time the snow at the bottom of the ice core fell, then the value of the oxygen isotope ratio in that snow would be relatively high, compared to the value if an ice shelf was forming over the open ocean so that the distance was slowly increasing to 1,000 km. Moreover, if there was then a sudden reversal in the growth of the ice shelf, causing the distance to decrease rapidly to 400 km or so, then the value of the oxygen isotope ratio in the snow would increase rapidly to a moderate level. Finally, if the shelf were then to remain fixed at a constant distance from the ice core site, then the oxygen isotope ratios would level out at a constant value. This is exactly the overall pattern in the oxygen isotope ratio in the Greenland ice cores.

As for the thin ice layers delineated by the small-scale variations in the oxygen isotope ratios supposedly representing annual precipitation and thawing with the cycle of the seasons, the same pattern can be readily explained in terms of individual ice storms being responsible for each thin layer of precipitation.[29] Given that the climate modeling has shown that an enormous hurricane-like storm system was perpetually situated over each of the poles during the formation and growth of the ice sheets,[30] the spiral rain-bands imbedded in such systems would have brought periodic storms that repeatedly swept in from the open ocean across the ice sheets, dumping the moisture they carried as snow. As the snow precipitated the temperature would fall, only to rise again with the passing of each storm, which would be reflected in a difference between the oxygen isotope ratio values in the first snow precipitated compared to the snow at the surface that was affected by the temperature increase in the passing of the storm. Thus, if each of these thin ice layers defined by the change in the oxygen isotope values represent snow precipitation from individual storms, then it is to be expected that there were many such storms each year, particularly in the early stages of rapid accumulation of the ice sheets in those first few centuries after the Flood.

27   J. R. Petit, M. Briat and A. Roger, 1981, Ice Age aerosol content from east Antarctic ice core samples and past wind strength, *Nature*, 293: 391-394; R. Bowen, 1991, *Isotopes and Climate*, London: Elsevier Applied Science; J. R. Petit, J. W. C. White, N. W. Young, J. Jouzel and Y. S. Korotkevich, 1991, Deuterium excess in recent Antarctic snow, *Journal of Geophysical Research*, 96: 5113-5122.

28   Vardiman, 2001, 59-68.

29   J. Zavacky, 2003, M.S. thesis (unpublished), Santee, CA: Institute for Creation Research Graduate School.

30   Vardiman, 1993, 1994.

97

THE POST-FLOOD ICE AGE—GEOMORPHIC FEATURES AND ICE-AGE ANIMALS

The unique post-Flood climate during the accumulation of the ice sheets, and their pattern of growth, would explain some long-standing observations that have puzzled uniformitarians. For example, at that time many large lakes filled enclosed basins in what are now arid or semi-arid regions of the earth. One was the Great Salt Lake in Utah, which was 285 meters deeper at its peak and 17 times the size that it is now, a volume that would have required six times more precipitation then than in today's climate.[1] While these fluvial lakes would have actually been filled briefly by leftover waters from the Flood, there is evidence that they were partially maintained during the post-Flood Ice Age, which would have required during that period at least three times the current precipitation rate, contrary to uniformitarian theory that usually specifies very dry weather during the Ice Age.

Another puzzling observation is that cold-tolerant animals like reindeer lived at this time with warm-tolerant animals like the hippopotamus. Indeed, the latter even migrated into northern England, France, and Germany. However, the post-Flood Ice Advance model easily accounts for this unique distribution of animals, because winters would have been mild and summers cool, with northwest Europe being relatively warm at first, because of the surrounding warm ocean and the generally westerly onshore flow of air. Indeed, because of the huge volumes of moisture evaporated from the warm oceans and carried landwards to precipitate as snow to form the ice sheets, the sea level would have dropped sufficiently to expose land-bridges, for instance, across the Bering Strait and the English Channel, which would have aided rapid animal dispersion. The climate of Siberia and Alaska would also have been mild during the first few centuries of the post-Flood period, because the Arctic Ocean was relatively warm and thus not covered by sea ice, making the temperatures over the surrounding continents significantly warmer than at present.[2] The warm north Atlantic and north Pacific oceans also

---

1   G. I. Smith and F. A. Street-Perrott, 1983, Fluvial lakes of the western United States, *Late-Quaternary Environments of the United States*, vol. 1, H. E. Wright, Jr., ed., Minneapolis: University of Minnesota Press, 190-212.

2   R. L. Newson, 1973, Response of a general circulation model of the atmosphere to removal of the Arctic ice-cap, *Nature*, 241: 39-40.

would have contributed to the warmth in these regions, and precipitation would have been higher. Consequently, the woolly mammoth, whose fossil remains have been found as far south as Mexico, and therefore was actually a warm-tolerant animal, and many other types of animals would have been suitably at home with adequate food in Siberia and Alaska.

Once the warm ocean at the end of the Flood had cooled to some threshold temperature, the supply of moisture would have critically declined, so glacial maximum was then reached, and subsequently deglaciation would have begun. Glacial maximum has been estimated to have been reached about 500 years after the Flood. During deglaciation, with the oceans now cooler and moisture supply drastically reduced, summers over the mid and high latitudes of the northern hemisphere would have been warm, but the winters would have become very cold due to the continued cooling of the atmosphere by the ice sheets.[3] The cold climate would now have caused sea ice to develop on the Arctic Ocean, and it would have also become more extensive than it is today in the north Atlantic and north Pacific oceans. Due to the cooler temperatures and the greater extent of sea ice, the atmosphere would also have become drier than at present. The storm tracks, which had been responsible for delivering the snow to build the ice sheets, would now have been displaced southward, and dry, windy storms would have tracked south of the ice sheets, blowing dust that would result in extensive sand and loess sheets. With this changing climate, even though the winters were colder, the ice sheets would have begun melting in the summers. Even with the summer temperatures around the periphery of the ice sheets 10°C colder than summer temperatures at present, the energy-balance equation indicates not only the winter snow cover, but the ice sheets themselves, would melt rapidly at the peripheries in less than 100 years.[4] The interiors of the ice sheets, though, would probably have taken a little longer to melt, perhaps as much as 200 years. It should also be noted that these melting rates are not unrealistic, since they are close to the observed melting rates in the present climate. Consequently, the total time for the post-Flood Ice Age would have only been about 700 years.

The rapidly melting ice sheets would have caused rivers to overflow and become choked with sediments. River valleys, already deeply filled with alluvium, would thus have had terraces eroded into that alluvium at the high flow levels. Large river meanders, close to where the edges of the ice sheets were, attest to the large volume of run-off. Of course, some of these geomorphic features would have initially formed at the end of the Flood, due to the erosion of the retreating Flood waters, but this enormous volume of meltwater from the ice sheets at the end of the Ice Age would have surely added its imprint. It was at this time that the catastrophic outbursting of glacial meltwaters dammed up in the former Lake Missoula in Montana carved out the Channeled Scabland in Washington state,

---

3   Oard, 1990.

4   Oard, 1990.

as described earlier.

Another well-known and spectacular example of the excessive erosion due to the waters from the rapid melting of the ice sheets is the cutting of the Niagara Gorge and the recession of Niagara Falls on the U.S.-Canada border.[5] While erosion at the end of the Flood may have begun to form the Great Lakes, it was the erosion by the passage southwards of the Laurentide Ice Sheet that produced their present shape. Thus, at the end of the Ice Age, huge volumes of meltwater flowed out through these lakes and down into the St. Laurence River. The Niagara River flows from Lake Erie over Niagara Falls and on into Lake Ontario, but initially the Falls had flowed over the Niagara escarpment where the Niagara River flows into Lake Ontario, some seven miles downstream of their current position. Extrapolating the observed erosion rate of 4 to 5 feet per year,[6] the recession of Niagara Falls seven miles upstream from the Niagara escarpment would have taken about 7,000 to 9,000 years. However, this doesn't take into account the much greater erosion rate at the end of the Ice Age, when the discharge rate through the Niagara River was very much higher due to the huge volumes of glacial meltwaters. When this is taken into account, along with the more dependable estimate of the timespan of erosion along the sides of the Niagara Gorge itself, the more realistic estimate for the recession of Niagara Falls would be 4,000 years at most, consistent with the timescale back to the post-Flood Ice Age.

The rapid change in the climate at mid and high latitudes during this brief, 200-year deglaciation period would have had profound effects upon both flora and fauna, the cold, dry climate particularly causing great stress to the abundant megafauna that had flourished during the wet, warm climate in areas where the ice sheets were not accumulating. The rapid fall in temperatures at polar latitudes, for example, would have caused the freezing of surface sediments and soils, which have produced today's vast stretches of permanently frozen soils in the Arctic and sub-Arctic known as permafrost. Many animals would thus have become extinct due to the rapid loss of their habitats, and with the assistance of man, the hunter, in some cases. Indeed, embedded in the frozen mucks of the Arctic are large numbers of fossil mammals, apparently trapped and, in some cases, partially frozen before the soft parts had decayed:

> The extensive silty alluvium, now frozen, in central Alaska contains a numerous mammal fauna….Freezing has preserved the skin and tissue of some of the mammals. The faunal list includes two bears, dire wolf, wolf, fox, badger, wolverine, sabre-tooth cat, jaguar, lynx, woolly mammoth, mastodon, two horses, camel, saiga antelope, four bisons, caribou, moose,

---

5   For a fuller treatment of this issue see: I. T. Taylor, 1984, *In the Minds of Men: Darwin and the New World Order*, Toronto, Canada: TFE Publishing, 81-84; J. D. Morris, 1994, *The Young Earth*, Colorado Springs, CO: Master Books, 48-49; Oard, 1990, 69-172.

6   G. K. Gilbert, 1907, Rate of recession of Niagara Falls, *United States Geological Survey, Bulletin 306*, Washington, DC: US Government Printing Office.

stag-moose, elk, two sheep, musk-ox and yak types, ground sloth, and several rodents. The number of individuals is so great that the assemblage of the whole must represent a rather long time.[7]

It is quite obvious that these mammals, which were once living in forests and grazing on grassy meadows but are now fossilized in alluvium, represent a sharp change of climate:

> Vast herds of mammoths and other animals (the New Siberian Islands in the far north of Asia have yielded mammoth, woolly rhinoceros, musk ox, saiga antelope, reindeer, tiger, Arctic fox, glutton, bear and horse, among the 66 animal species) required forests, meadows and steppes for their sustenance…and could not have lived in a climate like the present, with its icy winds, snowy winters, frozen ground and tundra moss year round.[8]

The extinction of many members of this megafauna so suddenly at the end of the Ice Age still remains a mystery unexplainable by uniformitarian scenarios. The woolly mammoth is one member of this extinct megafauna, and the estimated number that were destroyed by this rapid climate change in Siberia and Alaska is at least hundreds of thousands, and likely more than a million. The extent and abundance of these mammoth deposits in the permafrost have often been understated:

> In Siberia alone some 50,000 mammoth tusks have been collected and sold to the ivory trade, and there are rare occurrences of whole animals being preserved in frozen ground.[9]

Indeed, the Arctic islands north of Siberia have been described as densely packed with the remains of elephants and other mammals, as well as dense tangles of fossil trees and other plants.

However, it is the frozen carcasses that have especially attracted attention. Although preserved only in permafrost areas, most of the mammoth carcasses are of animals that apparently were healthy and robust just before they died. Some had just eaten before their deaths, which at least in some cases was due to suffocation or asphyxia:

> The only direct evidence of the mode of death indicates that at least some of the frozen mammoths (and frozen woolly rhinoceroses as well) died of asphyxia, either by drowning or by being buried alive by a cave-in

---

7   Flint, 1957, 471.

8   Charlesworth, 1957, 650.

9   Flint, 1957, 470.

or mudflow. As stated above, sudden death is indicated by the robust condition of the animals and their full stomachs.[10]

Nevertheless, the number of frozen carcasses, indicating sudden death and burial before major decomposition had occurred, must be kept in perspective. By 1929 there were only 39 known carcasses of woolly mammoths and rhinoceroses, but only about half a dozen of those were actually complete, most being only a few small remnants of soft tissue attached to bones.[11] Since 1929 several more carcasses have been unearthed, including a baby mammoth discovered in 1977.[12]

Many more carcasses than those known must still exist in this remote, barren frozen ground of Siberia, because once exposed, carcasses would likely decompose and completely rot before being found. Thus, most carcasses that have become exposed would have completely decayed without leaving a record, so the number of carcasses with some remaining soft parts is probably hundreds or thousands times the number known. This number is still small compared with the million or more mammoths whose remains are estimated to be entombed in the permafrost, so most mammoths must have decayed completely before, or while, becoming interred. This is confirmed by the carcasses found with signs of partial decay having occurred before they were buried and frozen in the permafrost.

It is the stomach contents of a few mammoth carcasses that have heightened the mystery over the deaths of the mammoths. Stomach contents were only half digested, a condition believed to occur only if the mammoths cooled very quickly.[13] Indeed, many of the plants in these stomach contents could still be identified, though there has been some dispute over whether the plants indicated a much warmer climate, or represented plant types found in the current Arctic tundra. Based on the stomach contents, it has been concluded that the time of death was late summer or early fall, while the presence of beans and other vegetation found in the teeth of one carcass suggests that mammoth must have died while eating its last meal. Thus, whatever happened to kill and bury a million or more mammoths in the permafrost so quickly must have been a climatic catastrophe. Because the flesh has remained frozen, the animals had to be buried while the permafrost developed. Thus, there must have been a catastrophic change, from a climate in which the mammoths grazed on grasslands and experienced mild winters, to a climate with cold winters and barren frozen soil. However, because nearly all the mammoth flesh decayed before or during burial, the climate change

10   W. R. Farrand, 1961, Frozen mammoths and modern geology, *Science*, 133: 729-735 (quote on p. 734).

11   I. P. Tolmachoff, 1929, The carcasses of the mammoth and rhinoceros found in the frozen ground of Siberia, *Transactions of the American Philosophical Society*, 23: 11-74.

12   J. M. Stewart, 1977, Frozen mammoths from Siberia bring the Ice Ages to vivid life, *Smithsonian*, 8: 60-69; J. M. Stewart, 1979, A baby that died 40,000 years ago reveals a story, *Smithsonian*, 10: 125-126; N. A. Dubrovo et al,1982, Upper Quaternary deposits and paleogeography of the region inhabited by the young Kirgilyakh mammoth, *International Geology Review*, 24: 621-634.

13   Dillow, 1981, 383-396.

could not have been the equivalent of snap freezing. Rather, the small number of frozen carcasses suggests they resulted from rare conditions involving rapid burial. Furthermore, the famished condition of the baby mammoth found in 1977, and the putrefied, structureless contents of its skull, are both features that required some time to elapse during progression of this catastrophic climate change. Of course, many other types of animals lived with the mammoths, but most of the remains are only of mammoths, so the other animals being more fleet must have mostly escaped the catastrophic climate change, probably being able to migrate out of the area. Thus, the cooling of the climate was relatively rapid to kill a million or more well-fed mammoths, along with many other types of animals, preserving their remains in the developing permafrost, but not so rapid as to prevent most of the other animals except the slower mammoths from escaping. The catastrophic climate change would not have been the original quick freeze, because there are only a few frozen carcasses among the countless thousands of mammoth carcasses that had enough time for decomposition before burial and freezing of the ground. Thus, the change from mild weather to a very cold climate was relatively rapid, but permanent because freezing conditions have been maintained to the present day.

As already described, such a rapid climate shift would have occurred at the end of the relatively brief post-Flood Ice Age. Instead of the warmer temperatures and more moisture for plant growth in Siberia and Alaska during the Ice Age, the Arctic Ocean and the surrounding areas now gradually cooled, so the animals living there had to adapt. With the onset of deglaciation, the climate of Siberia and Alaska would have turned colder and drier. The melting ice sheets would have provided fresh water to the Arctic Ocean, which would float on the denser salt water and rapidly form sea ice, reinforcing the colder temperatures. Consequently, Siberia and Alaska, previously kept warm by the ice-free Arctic Ocean, now would have rapidly turned much colder. Many animals had enough time to migrate to a less severe climate, but many of the slower-moving mammals became trapped and perished. Migrating away from the continental interior toward the Arctic Ocean where the climate had been warmer, the mammoths in particular were caught in droves by the sudden climate shift and died in the cold. The carcasses found with partially digested food in their stomachs may have suffocated after the passage of a strong late-summer or early-autumn cold front, accompanied by strong winds, the wind-chill factor greatly enhancing the cooling efficiency of the freezing temperatures. Practically all the mammoths decayed before final burial and freezing of the soil that entombed them. However, some happened to be buried quickly enough to partially preserve their flesh. With the rapid melting of the ice caps in the Asian mountains, the rivers of Siberia would have been swollen with water and sediment, so that many of these animals that died of cold would have been buried in the sediment on what now became vast flood plains, with the water in the sediments freezing. Subsequent to the deglaciation when water volumes decreased, the rivers would have eventually eroded into their alluvial flood plains, forming valleys and terraces containing the mammoth remains, mostly where they are found today. Thus, modeling of the climate changes during the 500-year post-Flood Ice Age and 200-year deglaciation period provides adequate answers to the apparent riddle (in the uniformitarian Ice Age model) of the sudden demise of the mammoths in Siberia and Alaska.

With the melting of most of the ice sheets, the sea level would have risen to its current level. It had, of course, been higher at the end of the Flood prior to the onset of the Ice Age, because at that time neither the Greenland nor Antarctic ice sheets existed. The maximum lowering of sea level during the Ice Age would have been significantly less than suggested by uniformitarian estimates, which are based on excessive ice thicknesses and many other poorly known variables. Thus, the sea level immediately following the Flood would have been about forty meters higher than at present, while the lowest sea level at glacial maximum, when the largest volume of water was locked up as ice on land, would have been of the order of 50 to 60 meters below the current sea level.[14] This estimate is based on an ice volume less than one-half of uniformitarian estimates, because of the evidence that the ice sheets were that much thinner. In any case, uniformitarian methods of estimating sea levels are faulty, and just estimating ancient shorelines above the current sea level is a major problem.[15] Nevertheless, if "non-movable" sea-level indicators are used, then the estimated sea level during maximum glaciation would be at about 50 to 70 meters below the present sea level,[16] consistent with the estimate based on modeling within the context of the biblical post-Flood Ice Age. Of course, during deglaciation the melting of the glacial ice sheets would have resulted in a rapid rise in the sea level to the present shorelines, also rapidly flooding the continental shelf areas and land-bridges that had been exposed at glacial maximum.

Finally, 47 percent of the present ocean floor is covered in an average thickness of 200 meters of carbonate ooze, which consists of the shells of foraminifera and of the coccoliths (scales) of planktonic coccolithophores. At the current rate of such carbonate sedimentation, which is on the order of 1 to 3 cm/1000 years,[17] this ocean floor carbonate ooze would require millions of years to accumulate. However, that estimated sedimentation rate is actually inferred from steady-state conditions, in which the carbonate deposition rate is balanced by the amount of new material brought into the ocean by rivers. In contrast, with the higher sediment input to the oceans from rivers immediately after the Flood, and during the post-Flood ice advance and deglaciation due to a higher rainfall and erosion rates, the carbonate

---

14　Oard, 1990, 173-176.

15　J. Donner, 1995, Book review of *Shorelines and Isostasy*, D.E. Smith and A.G. Dawson, eds., *Boreas*, 14: 257-258.

16　P. W. Blackwelder, O. H. Pilkey and J. D. Howard, 1979, Lake Wisconsinan sea levels on the southeast US Atlantic shelf based on in-place shoreline indicators, *Science*, 204: 618-620.

17　Kennett, 1982, 464.

sedimentation rate would have been very much higher.[18] Furthermore, the larger influx of water and sediments into the oceans from rivers would also bring a large nutrient input, which combined with a rapid mixing of ocean waters, plus the warm temperatures of the ocean waters, would all have contributed to a large, sustained supply of foraminifera and coccoliths, enough to have accumulated the current thickness of calcareous ooze on the ocean floors in less than 1,000 to 2,000 years under ideal conditions and assuming no dissolution. However, some dissolution would invariably have occurred, but not at the current rate and current ocean depths, due to a greater supply of carbonate ions, the warmer water temperatures, the rapid sedimentation producing water flow through the accumulating sediments, and the more rapid circulation of the surface and deep ocean water, all reducing the amount of carbon dioxide in the deep ocean water where carbonate sediments were rapidly accumulating. Thus, these ocean-floor biogenic sediments can be readily accounted for on a sound scientific basis within the timeframe of the post-Flood ice advance and deglaciation period, plus the time to the present. This has been confirmed by numerical modeling, in which ocean-floor sediments accumulated rapidly in the initial post-Flood period, and then decreased exponentially to today's rate.[19]

---

18   A. A. Roth, 1985, Are millions of years required to produce biogenic sediments in the deep ocean?, *Origins (Geoscience Research Institute)*, 12: 48-56.

19   Vardiman, 1996.

98

From the Ice Age to the Present World

After the approximate 200-year period of deglaciation, the earth's climate had again changed, but now began to stabilize into the present general pattern. The ocean water had cooled to its current temperature and most of the continental ice sheets had melted, leaving Greenland and Antarctica still largely covered by ice, while the sea ice had developed in the Arctic Ocean. In mid to low latitudes the climate became warmer and drier, so that areas such as the Sahara and central Australia, which were once well-watered and lusciously vegetated, now progressively became deserts. With the reduction in rainfall rates there was a drastic decrease in run-off in river systems, and therefore in sediment transport. This is seen in a sudden change from the deposition of sand to silt in the Mississippi delta, while more or less simultaneous rapid desiccation is seen in the pluvial lakes in the western U.S. and elsewhere:

> [I]t is clear that a major fluctuation in climate occurred close to 11,000 years ago. The primary observation that both surface ocean temperatures and deep sea sedimentation rates were abruptly altered at this time is supplemented by evidence from more local systems. The level of the Great Basin lakes fell from the highest terraces to a position close to that observed at present. The silt and clay load of the Mississippi was suddenly retained in the alluvial valley and delta. A rapid ice retreat opened the northern drainage systems of the Great Lakes below and terrestrial temperatures rose…in each case the transition is the most obvious feature of the entire record.[1]

Some of these changes coincided with the deglaciation, and the uniformitarian "date" corresponds with the beginning of what is known as the Holocene Epoch, essentially the post-Ice Age period to the present. The sea level was rising rapidly in response to the melting of the ice sheets and glaciers, so that present shorelines became established.

---

1   W. S. Broeker, M. Ewing and B. C. Heeze, 1960, Evidence for an abrupt change in climate close to 11,000 years ago, *American Journal of Science*, 258: 441.

In the early centuries after the Flood, and right through the Ice Age period, the residual tectonic and volcanic effects of the Flood were still being experienced as localized and limited catastrophes. From the meters-per-second movement of the crustal plates during the catastrophic plate tectonics of the Flood, plate movements abruptly declined, and then tapered off to the current centimeters per year, resulting in a rapid decline in the numbers and intensities of earthquakes. During this process of decline, there were still earth movements and volcanic eruptions on a scale much less than the Flood, but still greater than experienced today:

> The Pleistocene was an Ice Age only in certain regions. Sub-crustal forces were also operative; signs of Pleistocene volcanicity and earth movements are visible in all parts of the world....the Pleistocene indeed witnessed earth movements on a considerable, even catastrophic, scale. There is evidence that it created mountains and ocean deeps of a size previously unequalled—a post-Tertiary age has been proved for at least one deep-sea trench...faulting, uplifting and crustal warping have been proved for almost all quarters of the globe.[2]

By the end of the Ice Age and the deglaciation period, these tectonic and volcanic disturbances would have been greatly reduced in their scale and frequency, although some minor earth movements continued, and there have been occasional localized volcanic eruptions up to the present time. Most of the earth movements have involved uplift, which in some measure has been isostatic rebound in response to the removal of the "weight" of the continental ice sheets.

As is to be expected, there is strong evidence that much more water once filled the lakes and flowed in the rivers of the earth than is true at present. Not only was this due to leftover waters from the Flood, but also due to the higher rainfall in the post-Flood Ice Age period. This is evidenced by the raised beaches and terraces found all over the world, as well as the evidence that deserts were once well-watered. For example, as already noted, in the time of Abraham, which remotely corresponds to the time of glacial maximum, the Jordan Valley and Dead Sea area were well-watered and lushly vegetated, whereas by the time of Jesus Christ the Dead Sea area was desolate and dry.

> Almost all the drainage basins of the closed lakes of the world bear, above the modern lake level, raised beaches which clearly testify to high lake levels at a previous time; Bonneville and Lahontan are only two of the more dramatic examples.[3]

That the rivers of the world once carried much larger volumes of water than

---

2   Charlesworth, 1957, 601, 603.

3   G. E. Hutchinson, 1957, *A Treatise on Limnology*, vol. 1, New York: Wiley, 238.

do their present remnants is evidenced both by the raised river terraces nearly always found along their courses, and by the extensive deposits of alluvium along their floodplains. Indeed, many streams are actually called "underfit," because the valleys they traverse are much too large to have been constructed by them:

> In a stream valley, the width of the channel occupied by the current may be only a small fraction of the width of the valley floor. Further, the banks of the channels are regularly low compared to the height of the valley sides. In a word, valleys commonly appear to be far too large to have been formed by the streams that utilize them. A first thought is to infer that the stream was once a much greater current.[4]

There is also little actual evidence of extensive lateral erosion by streams, especially when cutting through bedrock. Alluvial streams, such as the lower Mississippi, of course have wide meander belts, but the streams are cutting into alluvial fill that had already been deposited by earlier flows of greater magnitude, so that the floodplains themselves are basically plains of deposition rather than erosion:

> If rivers that flow across floodplains many times wider than their meander belts are observed, it will be found that in relatively few places are the streams actually against and undercutting the valley sides. This suggests at least that there may be a limiting width of valley flat beyond which lateral erosion becomes insignificant....The valleys of many, if not most, of the world's large rivers are so deeply filled with alluvium that it may seem inappropriate to consider their floodplains as veneers over bedrock valley flats. The alluvial fills in such valleys as those of the Mississippi, Missouri, and Ohio in places are several hundred feet thick.[5]

Further proof that rivers formerly carried much larger quantities of water is found in the great size of their original channels as cut out of the bedrock:

> As has already been stated, the bed widths of the filled channels are some ten times those of the present channels in the same localities....The whole of the present annual precipitation, with no loss to percolation or evaporation, could similarly have been run off in no more than five days. It is therefore necessary to postulate a former precipitation greater, and probably considerably greater, than that which is now recorded.[6]

Clearly, this geomorphic evidence points to greater volumes of water having flowed across, and carved out, the present land surface with the retreating waters

---

4   O. D. von Engeln and K. E. Caster, 1952, *Geology*, New York: McGraw-Hill Book Company, Inc., 256-257.

5   Thornbury, 1969, 129-130.

6   G. H. Dury, 1954, Contribution to a general theory of meandering valleys, *American Journal of Science*, 252: 215.

at the end of the Flood, and of the higher volumes of water flowing in river valleys during the higher rainfall of the immediate post-Flood period. The present river levels are therefore testimony to the warming and drying out of the earth's climate after the post-Flood Ice Age.

Mention should also be made of the old marine shorelines and raised beaches that are now found all around the world's seacoasts:

> In many parts of the world elevated strandlines exist which had a marine origin. If these features were local in extent they might be attributed to the effects of local diastrophism, but they are so widespread that they seem to be related mainly to eustatic rise of sea level rather than uplift of the land. In some areas, as in southern California, Pleistocene marine terraces exist at heights of 1300 to 1700 feet above sea level. Obviously Pleistocene seas never stood this much higher than present sea level and a good part of the height of the terraces here may be attributed to local diastrophism. In areas where local uplift has operated there is no consistency in the altitudes of the terraces from one point to another, but along coastlines that are relatively stable, such as the Atlantic and Gulf of Mexico coasts, we do find a considerable degree of consistency in terrace altitudes. Some elevated strandlines owe their present height above sea level to isostatic rebound from the load which was imposed upon the earth's crust by the Pleistocene ice sheets.[7]

Obviously, many of these elevated marine strandlines and terraces are the result of local uplift and/or isostatic rebound at the end of both the Flood and the post-Flood Ice Age. Furthermore, the only time that sea level was so much higher than at present, probably about 40 meters higher, was at the end of the Flood and the immediate post-Flood period, before the sea level dropped as ocean water evaporated to be precipitated as snow to form the continental ice sheets of the post-Flood Ice Age.

There is much evidence of a former lower sea level. The topography of the continental shelves, the irregularity of coastlines, the submarine canyons, the seamounts, and many other factors seem to indicate that they were formed, at least in part, at a time when the sea level was 50 to 60 meters lower during the post-Flood Ice Age. With the melting of the ice sheets, the oceans rose to their present level and, with minor fluctuations, have remained at that level since. Of course, as mentioned previously, with the lowering of the sea level during the post-Flood Ice Age, land-bridges were exposed where the oceans were shallow, such as across the Bering Strait between Asia and North America, the English Channel between England and France, and much of the ocean between the Indonesian islands. These land-bridges appear to have been successfully used by both animals and humans to

---

7   Thornbury, 1969, 408.

migrate across the globe, as they dispersed from where they disembarked from the Ark when it landed "in the mountains of Ararat" (Genesis 8:4), and subsequently from Babel. Growth in the animal population would have been rapid in those first few centuries after the Flood, as the animals that disembarked from the Ark moved into empty ecological niches without competitors. For example, even with a population doubling time of twenty years, there would be more than a million mammoths 500 years later at glacial maximum (before their extinction during deglaciation) that had descended from the representative pair of the elephant kind that disembarked from the Ark. At the same time, rapid intrabaraminic (within created kinds) diversification was occurring to produce many new varieties of animals and plants that split into sub-populations to establish and fill all the different new ecological niches in the post-Flood world.[8]

However, the existence of these land-bridges does not explain the biogeographic distribution of the majority of plants and animals in our post-Flood world. Even the best evolutionary biogeography models have neither successfully explained the multi-taxon concurrence of trans-oceanic range disjunctions, nor why areas of endemism exist where they do. In contrast, a rafting dispersal mechanism, in which plants and animals rafted across oceans on and among masses of logs, plant debris, and vegetation mats, in the immediate post-Flood world, has successfully explained not only the data explained by the best evolutionary models, but also data that such models fail to explain.[9] Some plants in the present world are known to float for decades, as indicated by the floating log mat in Spirit Lake since the eruption of Mount St. Helens.[10] Of course, the Flood destroyed all the world's pre-Flood forests, and many of the pre-Flood plants were buried either directly, or after subsequently becoming waterlogged and sinking, in the sediments that accumulated, including the extensive coal beds, during the Flood. However, based upon the flotation times of modern plants, it is expected that many pre-Flood plants would have still been floating on the ocean surface after the Flood ended. Indeed, given the global destruction of forests, each system of post-Flood ocean currents may have been carrying billions of logs in the immediate post-Flood world.

Therefore, these log mats immediately after the Flood may have been nearly as efficient in dispersal of some of the terrestrial organisms as was the land itself, carrying many organisms across the oceans in the post-Flood world. Furthermore, due to the high rainfall rates in the early centuries after the Flood, and the residual

---

8   T. C. Wood, 2003, Perspectives on aging, a young-earth creation diversification model, in *Proceedings of the Fifth International Conference on Creationism*, R. L. Ivey, Jr., ed., Pittsburgh, PA: Creation Science Fellowship, 479-489.

9   K. P. Wise and M. Croxton, 2003, Rafting: a post-Flood biogeographical dispersal mechanism, in *Proceedings of the Fifth International Conference on Creationism*, R. L. Ivey, Jr., ed., Pittsburgh, PA: Creation Science Fellowship, 465-477.

10   S. A. Austin, 1991, Floating logs and log deposits of Spirit Lake, Mount St Helens volcano national monument, Washington, *Geological Society of America Abstracts with Programs*, 23: 7.

catastrophism, it is likely that much mass-wasting occurred in early post-Flood times, including the dislodging and floating of vegetation mats, complete with resident animals, such as those that have been occasionally observed on today's oceans. In any case, most of the raft debris itself was probably plant material that was intended to survive the Flood outside the Ark, and these plants and other organisms would thus have experienced trans-global dispersal, even before land began rising out of the Flood waters, and long before the organisms on the Ark were able to join them on these floating vegetation rafts. It is possible by this means that even freshwater organisms were transported across bodies of salt water. Faster-moving organisms, such as marsupials that don't have to stop as long to care for their young, may have been the first in the post-Flood world to ride these rafts over oceanic barriers and thus colonize island continents such as Australia and Antarctica, and even South America, which probably was only joined to North America by the Panama Isthmus as a result of post-Flood tectonic and geologic activity. By the time slower organisms made it to key locations, the plant rafts may have been destroyed. Nevertheless, this rafting dispersal mechanism on the ocean currents of our post-Flood world can successfully explain the biogeographic distribution of most plants and animals today.

Finally, when Noah and his family disembarked from the Ark, they brought with them the culture and technology developed before the Flood to a new and totally different world, where the pre-Flood land had been faulted, flooded, eroded, and buried with an average of two kilometers of sediment. All lakes and rivers, hills and mountains, and even the air and the soil, were different. Plants and animals were assembling into new and different communities, and genetically were rapidly diversifying. Life would initially have been hard, though the domesticated animals and plants brought with them off the Ark would help them to quickly re-establish homes and a manageable lifestyle. Metals such as copper and iron would have to be searched for in new locations. However, in the meantime, even with their advanced cultural and technical abilities, Noah and his descendants immediately after the Flood would have used whatever resources were available to them, so food would have to be gathered where it could be found, and tools would have to be fashioned from crude materials. It is thus easy to envisage that, as conditions stabilized and resources were found, the lifestyles of Noah and his descendants changed from a hunting-gathering, stone-tooled-based, and even cave-dwelling society into an agricultural, copper- and then iron-tool-based city-dwelling society. However, these changes would have occurred within just a few decades, well within the course of a single human lifetime.

For the first 100 to 200 years after the Flood, Noah and his descendants lived in the one society, in essentially the same location, that culminated in the Babel civilization, contrary to God's specific command to spread out across the earth (Genesis 9:1). In rebellion against God, the Tower of Babel was built, so God judged them by confusing the language (Genesis 11:1-10). Because of this breakdown in communication between the different family groupings, now speaking different languages, they were forced to disperse from Babel and begin migrating across the earth, taking their individual genetic characteristics with them. Each family group as it migrated to new land would have found itself in the same situation again, lacking shelter, agriculture, and metal for tools. In each situation, agriculture, metal-working, and cities would have progressively developed independently, so the rate of cultural development and the rise of civilizations again would have varied considerably from location to location, some even never moving out of the hunting-gathering mode at all. However, overall, culture developed again through stages of stone tools, then to copper and bronze tools, and beyond with city civilizations of the different cultures and languages.

This migration from Babel would have started some 100 to 200 years after the Flood, when the ice sheets of the post-Flood Ice Age were advancing across northern Eurasia and North America, and when the sea level was lower, exposing land-bridges. Man had refused to disperse immediately after the Flood, so he would have arrived at distant locations long after most animals and plants already had. This would explain why human fossils are found in the local surficial sediments above ape fossils, and why it took a while for humans to acquire full evidences of culture. Furthermore, at the same time these events were occurring, both animals and humans were experiencing rapid genetic diversification, and humans at least were experiencing rapidly shortening lifespans. This would, in turn, explain the differences between the human fossils that have been found, particularly the brain size differences, as the non-skull bones can hardly be distinguished from modern humans.

Section VIII

Problems in Biblical Geology Solved—Radioactive Dating and Geochronology

99

The Radioactive Methods for Dating Rocks

In the preceding section a systematized outline of earth history was presented that explains the data of the geologic record in a comprehensive, but more consistent, fashion compared to the uniformitarian and evolutionary framework that has dominated geological thinking for the past 150 years or so. The basic rationale for this alternate framework for understanding earth history is the frank recognition of the literal character of all historical narrative in the unique revelation of the Judaeo-Christian Scriptures. It must first be realized that because uniformitarian models are based on the assumption that present processes must be utilized as the primary means of understanding the earth's history, they have not provided, and cannot provide, a scientifically valid explanation of the earth's origin, development, and history consistent with all geological, geophysical, and biological data. Instead, it must be recognized that all absolute knowledge of what has happened in the earth's past, when no human observers were present, must have necessarily come by way of divine revelation.

The unique claim of the Bible is that it embodies this divine revelation. This claim is supported by the testimony of Jesus Christ Himself and 2,000 years of Christian history. Thus, the Bible provides a more than adequate reason to base a framework for earth history on the factual details recorded therein. Accordingly, an attempt has been made to determine how the actual data of the geologic record can be understood in full harmony with these revealed factual details, especially regarding the creation of a mature, fully-operational universe, and the catastrophic earth-destroying Flood. It is claimed here that the data, at least in the broad outline presented in the preceding chapters, have been shown to be remarkably consistent with the biblical record. Such a demonstrated harmony does not, of course, indicate any particular insight or originality, but only gives testimony to the veracity and perspicuity of the inspired accounts in the Bible.

It is certainly recognized that not all questions have been answered, or all problems resolved. A complete reorientation of the entire, voluminous accumulation of pertinent data and published interpretations would not take a mere few hundred pages, but countless large volumes, and would require the intensive efforts of a great number of specialists trained in the various branches of the earth sciences.

However, the comprehensiveness of the biblical framework points the way forward for such studies, and provides the basic keys by which all such perceived problems can be ultimately resolved.

The chapters in this section can only deal with some of the critical aspects of the perceived major problems. However, if it has indeed been shown that the general features of the geological data all harmonize with the biblical outline of earth history, and if it can now be shown that the major apparent difficulties in interpreting the geologic record within this framework can likewise be resolved and understood in these terms, then it is reasonable to conclude that any remaining smaller problems will also be eventually solved by further research and study.

The Radioactive Methods for Dating Rocks

Without doubt, the most important and serious of these perceived problems is the question of time. There are, of course, many lines of geological evidence that appear to strongly imply that the earth and its various rock strata are millions, and even billions, of years old, immensely older than the straightforward biblical interpretation. The latter, as presented here, involves the relatively recent creation and subsequent Flood as the causes of most of the earth's geologic features.

There have been many different ways used by geologists in their attempts to measure the absolute age of the earth and its various strata, deposits, and features. In each such method, some physical or chemical process is involved whose present rate of activity can be measured. The total accumulation of the product from the process must also be measured. It is then a simple matter of calculating how long that process must have been in operation in order to have produced its present results. Some of the processes which have been used at various times as supposed geologic chronometers have included the influx of sodium and other elements into the ocean, lakes and rivers, the erosion of canyons or other areas by either flowing water, wind or glaciers, the building of deltas, the deposition of sedimentary strata, the growth of chemical deposits in soils, caves or other places, the moving of rocks, the growth of annual bands in trees, the accumulation of seasonal cycles of sediments on lake beds, or other entities whose appearance may be affected by seasonal changes, the escape of terrestrial gases into the atmosphere, addition to the earth's surface of connate waters through volcanism, and various other similar processes. There are also various chronometers in astronomy that have been used to determine absolute age, most of them being based on the rate of expansion of the universe and its various component parts, and on the velocity of the light coming from distant galaxies.

However, the most important geologic chronometers are, of course, those based on the radioactive decay of various chemical elements. Some isotopes of certain elements are radioactive, disintegrating continuously by various processes into isotopes of other elements. The present rates of disintegration of these isotopes can be measured, and if both the parent and daughter isotopes are found in measurable quantities in a rock, or mineral within a rock, being analyzed, then a relatively simple calculation yields the time period during which the daughter isotopes have apparently been accumulating due to radioactive decay. This is then declared to be the age of the rock. The most important and routinely used of these radioactive dating methods involve the disintegration of uranium and thorium into radium, radon, helium, and lead, of rubidium into strontium, of potassium into argon, and of samarium into neodymium. More specialized methods involve the disintegration of lutetium into hafnium, and of rhenium into osmium. All the parent isotopes in these methods disintegrate very slowly, so these methods are used to supposedly measure long ages of millions and billions of years for all but the most recent rocks. In contrast to these long-age methods is the short-age radiocarbon method, based on the formation of the radioactive isotope of carbon in the atmosphere by cosmic radiation, and its subsequent decay to a stable nitrogen isotope. Of course, because carbon is the element on which organic materials are built (in contrast to silicon being the primary basis of rocks), the radiocarbon method can only be used for "dating" organic-based materials. However, because the disintegration of the radioactive carbon isotope is relatively rapid, the method can only yield relatively short ages of thousands of years.

There is no question that the vast majority of the geochronometers mentioned above have given estimates for the age of the earth and its strata immensely greater than any possible estimate based on biblical chronology. In particular, the radioactive dating methods, except for the radiocarbon method, have usually yielded ages of hundreds of millions, and even billions, of years. Indeed, the accepted age for the earth of 4.55 (±0.07) billion years is based on the uranium-thorium-lead dating of meteorites.[1] However, no matter how accurate the analyses of these radioactive parent isotopes and their daughter isotopes in rocks, minerals, and meteorites, the significance of any or all of these measurements depends on, and is limited by, the assumptions that are made when interpreting the data. To obtain the most reliable and extensive overviews on all these radioactive dating methods, it is recommended that the best specialist textbooks are read,[2] as well as good, simplified summaries.[3]

---

1   C. C. Patterson, 1956. Age of meteorites and the earth, *Geochimica et Cosmochimica Acta*, 10: 230-237; R. H. Steiger and E. Jäeger, 1977, Subcommission on geochronology: convention on the use of decay constants in geo- and cosmochronology, *Earth and Planetary Science Letters*, 36: 359-362.

2   G. Faure and T. M. Mensing, 2005, *Isotopes: Principles and Applications*, third edition, Hoboken, NJ: John Wiley & Sons; A. P. Dickin, 2005, *Radiogenic Isotope Geology*, second edition, Cambridge, UK: Cambridge University Press.

3   S. A. Austin, 1994, Are Grand Canyon rocks 1 billion years old?, in *Grand Canyon: Monument to Catastrophe*, S. A. Austin, ed., Santee, CA: Institute for Creation Research, 111-131; D. DeYoung, 2000, Radioisotope datingreview, in *Radioisotopes and the Age of the Earth: A Young-Earth Creationist Research Initiative*, L. Vardiman, A. A. Snelling and E. F. Chaffin, eds., El Cajon, CA: Institute for Creation Research and St. Joseph, MO: Creation Research Society, 27-47.

The Assumptions of Radioactive Dating

The measurement of time by radioactive decay of a parent isotope is often compared to the measurement of time as sand grains fall in an hourglass (Figure 56, page 1090). The sand in the upper chamber of an hourglass represents a radioactive parent isotope, while the sand in the lower chamber is analogous to the respective daughter isotope. The sand grains fall from the upper chamber at a constant rate, said to be analogous to radioactive decay. If all the sand grains started in the upper chamber and then the number of sand grains were measured in the two chambers after some time elapsed, provided the rate at which the sand grains fall has been measured, simple mathematics can be used to calculate how long the hourglass has been in operation, and thus, the time when the process started. When applied to the radioactive decay "clock," this starting time is when the rock formed and is, therefore, its calculated age.

From this description of the analogy of the hourglass to radioactive decay of isotopes in rocks and minerals, it should be evident that the calculation of the "age" of a rock or mineral, based on the measurements of the quantities of the parent and daughter isotopes, and of the decay rate for the particular parent-daughter isotopes pair, requires three crucial assumptions:

1. The number of atoms of the daughter isotope originally in the rock or mineral when it crystallized can be known. In other words, it is assumed that we can know the initial conditions when the rock or mineral formed. In the potassium-argon method it is usually assumed that there was originally no daughter argon; therefore, all the argon measured in the rock or mineral was derived by radioactive decay from *in situ* parent potassium.

2. The numbers of atoms of the parent and daughter isotopes have not been altered since the rock or mineral crystallized, except by radioactive decay. In other words, it is assumed that the rock or mineral remained closed to loss or gain of the parent and/or daughter isotopes since crystallization.

3. The rate of decay of the parent isotope is known accurately, and has not changed during the existence of the rock or mineral since it crystallized.

These assumptions require careful evaluation for each rock or mineral being dated, and obviously impose certain restraints in the interpretation of the resultant calculated "ages." Indeed, these assumptions simply cannot be proven, because, when most rocks or minerals crystallized, no human observers were present to determine the original numbers of atoms of the daughter isotopes. Nor were human observers present throughout the histories of most rocks and minerals to determine whether the rocks and minerals have remained closed to loss or gain of parent and/or daughter isotopes, and if the rates of radioactive decay of the parent isotopes have not changed. Thus, it logically follows that these assumptions are, strictly speaking, not provable. It is often claimed that it is obvious where assumption two has failed, because anomalous results are obtained, that is, results not in agreement with the expected "ages." Otherwise, the calculated "ages" are often what are expected, and so the methods are confidently accepted as valid. Of course, this is uniformitarianism in the extreme, because it is assumed that decay rates measured in the present (over the past century) have been constant for millions and billions of years, an extrapolation of up to seven orders of magnitude!

When a radioactive dating determination is performed on an individual rock or mineral, the calculated result is called a "model age." Calculating the model age can only succeed if the original concentration of daughter isotope in the rock or mineral when it formed is known. In the case of potassium-argon dating, it is assumed that there was no daughter argon in the rock or mineral when it formed, because argon is an inert gas that would not have been chemically bonded within the rock or mineral. On the other hand, daughter strontium is usually included and chemically bonded into minerals and rocks when they formed, along with other isotopes of strontium not derived by radioactive decay. Since it is not known how much daughter strontium was incorporated in the mineral or rock when it formed, a method has been devised to determine that.

This is known as the "isochron age" method. At least four rock samples are obtained from the same geologic unit, or at least three minerals are separated from a single rock sample. It is safely assumed that these should have all formed at about the same time. However, the geologic processes that formed the sampled rock unit may have caused an uneven distribution in the rock unit of the parent rubidium and daughter strontium isotopes. When three or more minerals in a single rock are sampled, there will undoubtedly be different amounts of the radioactive parent and daughter isotopes, because the minerals have varying abilities to bind the chemically different elements in their crystal lattices. Nevertheless, it has to be assumed that within each rock sample or mineral there has been sufficient mixing to produce uniformity between the rock samples and the minerals with respect to the isotopic composition of the daughter strontium. Of course, over time the isotopic composition of the samples of the rock unit, and the minerals in each rock sample, will have been altered by radioisotope decay. However, for the isochron dating method to work, it is essential that all rock samples have to be from the same rock unit, and there has to be uniformity within the rock unit of the original daughter strontium isotope ratio. These two conditions replace the assumption about the original daughter isotope ratio being known (for example, no daughter argon originally), that has to be inserted into the "model age" calculation.

Figure 57 (page 1091) shows how the isochron method works. Here, hypothetical measurements of radioisotope ratios in six samples from the same rock unit are plotted, because all six samples are believed to have formed at the same time. A positive-sloping line can be plotted through the radioisotope measurements of five of the six rock samples, as shown in Figure 57(c). One of the six radioisotope analyses lies off the line described by the other five, and thus could be interpreted as having been altered by some geologic process. Such an outlier would usually be disregarded in the subsequent calculations. Therefore, the interpretation depicted in Figure 57(a) assumes the line through the five rock samples can provide an "age" for the rock unit represented by these five samples. Figure 57(b) shows how these five samples from the hypothetical rock unit can yield an "age" interpretation. When all parts of this rock unit formed at the same time, they all had the same abundance of the daughter isotope (zero time = zero slope). With the passage of time, the radioisotope decay of the parent increased the quantity of daughter in a uniform manner, according to the different abundances of the parent in the rock samples. Thus, all points of equal "age" lie on the same line. In Figure 57(b), it is evident that the slope or steepness of the line of "equal age" or "isochron" (from the Greek, *isos*, equal, and *chronos*, time) increases with elapsed time. The "isochron age" is calculated from the slope of the isochron line that best fits the radioisotope analyses of the rock samples, as shown in Figure 57(c).

The isochron method has become the most widely-used radioisotope dating technique among geologists for dating rocks. This is for two reasons. First, no assumption about the initial conditions is apparently necessary, because the isochron itself can be used to determine the initial daughter isotope abundance (see Figure 57). Second, if there has been any open-system behavior due to contamination, weathering, or other geologic processes, the rock samples in which that has occurred will not plot on the isochron line (or so it is assumed). Furthermore, the isochron method can be used for four or more samples from the same rock unit, or for three or more minerals from the same rock sample, the whole-rock radioisotope values also plotting on the resultant mineral isochron. The isochron method is primarily used in rubidium-strontium, samarium-neodymium, and uranium-thorium-lead radioisotope dating, but is also used in the lutetium-hafnium and rhenium-osmium radioisotope methods that have specialized applications.

100

THE PITFALLS IN THE RADIOACTIVE DATING METHODS—THE POTASSIUM-ARGON AND ARGON-ARGON METHODS

Both these methods suffer from the same problems, because they are both based on the radioactive decay of potassium (K) to argon (Ar), a gas which does not bond with other elements. The argon-argon method is a refinement, in that some of the potassium (^{39}K which is regarded as a proxy for radioactive ^{40}K) in a rock or mineral is first converted in a nuclear reactor to ^{39}Ar, a different isotope of argon compared to that produced by radioactive decay of ^{40}K, which is ^{40}Ar. This argon-argon method is now regarded as more reliable, because these two argon isotopes can be measured together in a mass spectrometer, whereas the traditional potassium-argon method requires separate measurements of potassium and argon, compounding the likely measurement errors. Nevertheless, the pitfalls with both these methods are the same and have already been elaborated.[1]

"Excess" or Inherited Argon

The basis for the potassium-argon (and also the argon-argon) method has been stated strongly:

> The K-Ar method is the only decay scheme that can be used with little or no concern for the initial presence of the daughter isotopes. This is because the ^{40}Ar is an inert gas that does not combine chemically with any other element and so escapes easily from rocks when they are heated. Thus, while a rock is molten the ^{40}Ar formed by decay of ^{40}K escapes from the liquid.[2]

However, many cases have been documented of recent historic lava flows which yielded grossly incorrect potassium-argon ages because they contained more argon

1   A. A. Snelling, 2000, Geochemical processes in the mantle and crust, in *Radioisotopes and the Age of the Earth: A Young-Earth Creationist Research Initiative*, L. Vardiman, A. A. Snelling and E. F. Chaffin, eds., El Cajon, CA: Institute for Creation Research and St. Joseph, MO: Creation Research Society, 123-304.

2   G. B. Dalrymple, 1991, *The Age of the Earth*, Stanford, CA: Stanford University Press, 91.

derived from radioactive potassium (^{40}Ar*) than expected. This has been called "excess argon." This was ^{40}Ar* initially in these rocks when they formed, and, therefore, it would have been inherited from the magma sources of the lavas, since it is often present in the gases released during volcanic eruptions. This violates the key assumption of non-zero concentrations of ^{40}Ar* for the potassium-argon and argon-argon methods. Many examples are now well documented of recent and young volcanic rocks that have yielded grossly inaccurate potassium-argon ages as a result of this excess and inherited ^{40}Ar*.[3]

After the May 18, 1980, eruption of Mount St. Helens in Washington state, a new lava dome began developing from October 26, 1980, onwards within the volcano's crater. In 1986, less than ten years after it flowed and cooled, a dacite lava from this dome was sampled and analyzed.[4] The lava flow yielded a potassium-argon "age" of 350,000 years for the whole rock, and the constituent minerals yielded potassium-argon ages up to 2.8 million years. Similarly, the June 30, 1954, andesite lava flow from Mt. Ngauruhoe, central North Island, New Zealand, yielded potassium-argon model "ages" up to 3.5 Ma (million years) due to excess ^{40}Ar*.[5] Furthermore, a separate split of that flow sample also yielded a model "age" of 0.8 Ma, which indicates the variability in the excess ^{40}Ar*. Investigators also have found that excess ^{40}Ar* is preferentially trapped in the minerals within lava flows, with one K-Ar "date" on olivine crystals in a recent basalt being greater than 110 Ma.[6] Even laboratory experiments have been used to test the solubility of argon in synthetic basalt melts and their constituent minerals, with olivine retaining as much as 0.34 ppm ^{40}Ar*.[7]

---

3   G. B. Dalrymple, 1969, ^{40}Ar/-^{36}Ar analyses of historic lava flows, *Earth and Planetary Science Letters*, 6: 47-55; G. B. Dalrymple and J. G. Moore, 1968, Argon-40: Excess in submarine pillow basalts from Kilauea Volcano, Hawaii, *Science*, 161: 1132-1135; D. Krummenacher, 1970, Isotopic composition of argon in modern surface volcanic rocks, *Earth and Planetary Science Letters*, 8: 109-117; R. P. Esser, W. C. McIntosh, M. T. Heizler and P. R. Kyle, 1997, Excess argon in melt inclusions in zero-age anorthoclase feldspar from Mt Erebus, Antarctica, as revealed by the ^{40}Ar/^{39}Ar method, *Geochimica et Cosmochimica Acta*, 61: 3789-3801; A. A. Snelling, 2000, Geochemical processes in the mantle and crust, in *Radioisotopes and the Age of the Earth: A Young Creationist Research Initiative*, L. Vardiman, A. A. Snelling and E. F. Chaffin, eds., El Cajon, CA: Institute for Creation Research and St. Joseph, MO: Creation Research Society, 123-304.

4   S. A. Austin, 1996, Excess argon within mineral concentrates from the new dacite lava dome at Mount St. Helens volcano, *Creation Ex Nihilo Technical Journal*, 10 (3): 335-343.

5   A. A. Snelling, 1998, The cause of anomalous potassium-argon 'ages' for recent andesite flows at Mt. Ngauruhoe, New Zealand, and the implications for potassium-argon 'dating', in *Proceedings of the Fourth International Conference on Creationism*, R. E. Walsh, ed., Pittsburgh, PA: Creation Science Fellowship, 503-525.

6   P. E. Damon, A. W. Laughlin and J. K. Precious, 1967, Problem of excess argon-40 in volcanic rocks, in *Radioactive Dating Methods and Low-Level Counting*, Vienna: International Atomic Energy Agency, 463-481. Also: A. W. Laughlin, J. Poths, H. A. Healey, S. Reneau and G. WoldeGabriel, 1994, Dating of Quaternary basalts using the cosmogenic ^{3}He and ^{14}C methods with implications for excess ^{40}Ar, *Geology*, 22: 135-138; D. B. Patterson, M. Honda and I. McDougall, 1994, Noble gases in mafic phenocrysts and xenoliths from New Zealand, *Geochimica et Cosmochimica Acta*, 58: 4411-4427.

7   C. L. Broadhurst, M. J. Drake, B. E. Hagee and T. J. Benatowicz, 1990, Solubility and partitioning of Ar in anorthite, diopside, forsterite, spinel, and synthetic basaltic liquids, *Geochimica et Cosmochimica Acta*, 54: 299-309; C. L. Broadhurst, M. J. Drake, B. E. Hagee and T. J. Benatowicz, 1992, Solubility and

The obvious conclusion most investigators have reached is that the excess ^{40}Ar* had to be present in the molten lavas when extruded, and they did not completely degas when they cooled. This resulted in excess ^{40}Ar* becoming trapped in constituent minerals and the rock fabrics themselves. However, from whence comes this excess ^{40}Ar*? This is ^{40}Ar, which cannot be attributed to atmospheric argon or *in situ* radioactive decay of ^{40}K, nor is it simply "magmatic" argon. The excess ^{40}Ar* in the 1800-1801 Hualalai flow, Hawaii, was found to reside in fluid and gaseous inclusions in olivine, plagioclase, and pyroxene in ultramafic xenoliths in the basalt, and was sufficient to yield "ages" of 2.6 Ma to 2,960 Ma.[8] Thus, because the ultramafic xenoliths and the basaltic magmas came from the mantle, the excess ^{40}Ar* must have initially resided there, having then been transported to the earth's surface in the magmas. Indeed, most investigators now concede that the excess ^{40}Ar* in all Hawaiian lavas, including those from the active Loihi and Kilauea volcanoes, is indicative of the mantle source area from which the magmas have come. This is also confirmed by the considerable excess of ^{40}Ar* measured in ultramafic mantle xenoliths from the Kerguelen Archipelago in the southern Indian Ocean, which is also regarded as being the result of extruding magmas from a mantle plume source.[9] Furthermore, data from single vesicles in mid-ocean ridge basalt samples dredged from the North Atlantic suggest the excess ^{40}Ar* in the upper mantle may be almost double previous estimates, that is, almost 150 times more than the atmospheric content (relative to ^{36}Ar).[10] However, another study on the same sample indicates the upper mantle content of ^{40}Ar* could be even ten times higher.[11]

Further confirmation comes from diamonds. Diamonds form deep in the mantle because of the required pressures, and are rapidly carried by explosive volcanism into the upper crust and to the earth's surface. When a K-Ar isochron "age" of 6 Ga (billion years) was obtained for ten Zaire diamonds, it was obvious excess ^{40}Ar* was responsible, because the diamonds could not be older than the earth itself.[12] These same diamonds produced ^{40}Ar/^{39}Ar "age" spectra yielding an isochron "age" of approximately 5.7 Ga.[13] It was concluded that the ^{40}Ar is an

partitioning of Ne, Ar, K and Xe in minerals and synthetic basaltic melts, *Geochimica et Cosmochimica Acta*, 56: 709-723.

8   J. G. Funkhauser and J. J. Naughton, 1968, Radiogenic helium and argon in ultramafic inclusions from Hawaii, *Journal of Geophysical Research*, 73: 4601-4607.

9   P. J. Valbracht, M. Honda, T. Matsumoto, N. Mattielli, I. McDougall, R. Ragettli and D. Weis, 1996, Helium, neon and argon isotope systematics in Kerguelen ultramafic xenoliths: Implications from mantle source signatures, *Earth and Planetary Science Letters*, 138: 29-38.

10   N. Moreira, J. Kunz and C. Allègre, 1998, Rare gas systematics in Popping Rock: Isotopic and elemental compositions in the upper mantle, *Science*, 279: 1178-1181.

11   P. Burnard, D. Graham and G. Turner, 1997, Vesicle-specific noble gas analyses of "Popping Rock": Implications for primordial noble gases in the earth, *Science*, 276: 568-571.

12   S. Zashu, M. Ozima and O. Nitoh, 1986, K-Ar isochron dating of Zaire cubic diamonds, *Nature*, 323: 710-712.

13   M. Ozima, S. Zashu, Y. Takigimi and G. Turner, 1989, Origin of the anomalous ^{40}Ar-^{36}Ar age of Zaire cubic diamonds, Excess ^{40}Ar in pristine mantle fluids, *Nature*, 337: 226-229.

excess component which has no age significance and is found in tiny inclusions of mantle-derived fluid.

All this evidence clearly shows that excess ^{40}Ar* is ubiquitous in recent and young volcanic rocks, because it has been inherited from the mantle source areas of the magmas. If this ^{40}Ar* in the mantle predominantly represents primordial argon that is not derived from *in situ* radioactive decay of ^{40}K, it has no age significance. Furthermore, if this is primordial argon emanating from the mantle, then it is possible that all other rocks in the earth's crust are also susceptible to "contamination" by excess ^{40}Ar*. If so, then both the K-Ar and Ar-Ar "dating" of all crustal rocks would be similarly questionable.

When muscovite (a common mineral in crustal rocks) is heated to 740° to 860°C under high argon pressures for periods of 3 to 10.5 hours, it absorbs significant quantities of Ar, producing K-Ar "ages" of up to 5 billion years, and the absorbed Ar is indistinguishable from radiogenic argon (^{40}Ar*).[14] In other experiments, muscovite was synthesized under similar temperatures and argon pressures, with the resultant muscovite retaining up to 0.5 wt % Ar, approximately 2,500 times as much Ar as is found in natural muscovite.[15] It has been found also that under certain conditions Ar can be incorporated into minerals which are supposed to exclude Ar when they crystallize.

It has been envisaged that noble gases from the mantle, including Ar, are migrating and circulating through the crust.[16] Noble gases in carbon-dioxide-rich natural gas wells confirm such migration and circulation. The isotopic signatures clearly indicate a mantle origin of the noble gases, including amounts of excess ^{40}Ar in some natural gas wells exceeding those in mantle-derived mid-ocean ridge basalts.[17] In fact, it has been estimated that the quantities of excess ^{40}Ar* in the continental crust are as much as five times that found in such mantle-derived, mid-ocean ridge basalts, strongly implying that excess ^{40}Ar* in crustal rocks and their constituent minerals could well be the norm, rather than the exception.

In reference to metamorphism and melting of rocks in the crust, it is well known that:

---

14   T. B. Karpinskaya, I. A. Ostrovsckiy and L. L. Shanin, 1961, Synthetic introduction of argon into mica at high pressures and temperatures, *Isu Akad Nauk S.S.S.R. Geology Series*, 8: 87-89.

15   T. B. Karpinskaya, 1967, Synthesis of argon muscovite, *International Geology Review*, 9: 1493-1495.

16   D. B. Patterson, M. Honda and I. McDougall, 1993, The noble gas cycle through subduction systems, in *Research School of Earth Sciences Annual Report 1992*, Canberra, Australia: Australian National University, 104-106.

17   P. Staudacher, 1987, Upper mantle origin of Harding County well gases, *Nature*, 325: 605-607; C. J. Ballentine, 1989, Resolving the mantle He/Ne and crustal ^{21}Ne/^{22}Ne in well gases, *Earth and Planetary Science Letters*, 96: 119-133; P. Burnard, D. Graham and G. Turner, 1997, Vesicle-specific noble gas analyses of "Popping Rock": Implication for primordial noble gases in the earth, *Science*, 276: 568-571; M. Moreira, J. Kunz and C. J. Allègre, 1998, Rare gas systematics in Popping Rock: Isotopic and elemental compositions in the upper mantle, *Science*, 279: 1178-1181.

If the rock is heated or melted at some later time, then some or all of the ^{40}Ar may escape and the K-Ar clock is partially or totally reset.[18]

Thus, ^{40}Ar* escapes to migrate in the crust to be incorporated in other minerals as excess ^{40}Ar*, just as ^{40}Ar* degassing from the mantle migrates into the crust. Excess ^{40}Ar* has been recorded in many minerals (some with essentially no ^{40}K) in crustal rocks, and the Ar-Ar method has also been used to confirm the presence of excess ^{40}Ar* in feldspars and pyroxenes.[19] Ten profiles across biotite grains in high-grade metamorphic rocks yielded 128 apparent Ar-Ar "ages" within individual grains ranging from 161 Ma to 514 Ma (Figure 58, page 1092).[20] This cannot be solely due to radiogenic build-up of ^{40}Ar*, but due to the incorporation of excess ^{40}Ar* by diffusion from an external source, namely, from the mantle and other crustal rocks and minerals. Indeed, excess ^{40}Ar* was found to have accumulated locally in the intergranular regions of a gabbro via diffusion from its hornblende grains according to a well-defined law.[21]

This crustal migration of ^{40}Ar* is known to cause grave problems in regional rock-dating studies. For example, in the Precambrian Musgrave Ranges Block of northern South Australia, a wide scatter of K-Ar mineral "ages" was found, ranging from 343 Ma to 4,493 Ma due to inherited (excess) ^{40}Ar*, so no meaningful age interpretation could be drawn from those rocks.[22] Likewise, when Ar "dating" was attempted on Precambrian high-grade metamorphic rocks in the Fraser Range of Western Australia, and on the Strangways Range of central Australia, it was found that important minerals contained excess ^{40}Ar* which rendered the Ar "dating" useless because it produced "ages" higher than expected.[23] It was concluded that this excess ^{40}Ar* was probably incorporated at the time of mineral formation, and calculations suggest that the Proterozoic lower crust of Australia (which extends over half the continent) contains so much of this excess ^{40}Ar* that it produces a partial pressure equivalent to approximately 0.1 atmospheres. This is consistent with an Ar-Ar "dating" study of Proterozoic high-grade metamorphic rocks in the Broken Hill region of New South Wales that documented widely distributed

---

18   G. B. Dalrymple, 1991, *The Age of the Earth*, Stanford, CA: Stanford University Press, 91.

19   J. G. Funkhauser, I. L. Barnes and J. J. Naughton, 1966, Problems in the dating of volcanic rocks by the potassium-argon method, *Bulletin of Volcanology*, 29: 709-717; A. W. Laughlin, 1969, Excess radiogenic argon in pegmatite minerals, *Journal of Geophysical Research*, 74: 6684-6690; M. A. Lanphere and G. B. Dalrymple, 1976, Identification of excess ^{40}Ar by the ^{40}Ar/^{39}Ar age spectrum technique, *Earth and Planetary Science Letters*, 12: 359-372.

20   C. S. Pickles, S. P. Kelley, S. M. Reddy and J. Wheeler, 1997, Determination of high spatial resolution argon isotope variations in metamorphic biotites, *Geochimica et Cosmochimica Acta*, 61: 3809-3833.

21   T. M. Harrison and I. McDougall, 1980, Investigations of an intrusive contact, north-west Nelson, New Zealand—II. Diffusion of radiogenic and excess ^{40}Ar in hornblende revealed by ^{40}Ar/^{39}Ar age spectrum analysis, *Geochimica et Cosmochimica Acta*, 44: 2005-2030.

22   A. W. Webb, 1985, Geochronology of the Musgrave Block, *Mineral Resources Review, South Australia*, 155: 23-27.

23   A. K. Baksi and A. F. Wilson, 1980, An attempt at argon dating of two granulite-facies terranes, *Chemical Geology*, 30: 109-120.

excess $^{40}Ar^*$.[24] Plagioclase and hornblende were most affected, step heating Ar-Ar "age" spectra yielding results up to 9.588 Ga (Figure 59, page 1092). Of course, such unacceptable "ages" were produced by release of excess $^{40}Ar^*$, this being obvious because of the expected interpreted "ages" of these rocks.

Domains within the mantle and crust have been identified, and the interaction between them described in terms of the migration and circulation of Ar (and therefore excess $^{40}Ar^*$) from the lower mantle through the crust.[25] In the proposed steady-state upper mantle model, at least some of the $^{40}Ar^*$ must be primordial, that is, not derived from radioactive decay of ^{40}K. But just how much is primordial is unknown, because primordial ^{40}Ar is indistinguishable from $^{40}Ar^*$. Therefore, because it is known that excess $^{40}Ar^*$ is carried from the mantle by plumes of basaltic magmas up into the earth's crust, it is equally likely that much of the excess $^{40}Ar^*$ in crustal rocks could also be primordial ^{40}Ar. Additionally, $^{40}Ar^*$ released from minerals and rocks during lithification and metamorphism adds to the continual migration and circulation of $^{40}Ar^*$ in the crust. Thus, when crustal rocks are analyzed for K-Ar and Ar-Ar "dating," one can never be sure if the $^{40}Ar^*$ in the rocks is from the *in situ* radioactive decay of ^{40}K since their formation, or if some or all of it came from the mantle or from other crustal rocks and minerals. Thus, we have no way of knowing if any of the $^{40}Ar^*$ measured in crustal rocks has any age significance at all.

Argon Loss

For the K-Ar and Ar-Ar "dating" methods to work successfully, the rocks and minerals to be dated must not contain any excess $^{40}Ar^*$ (whether inherited or primordial), but also they must have retained all of the $^{40}Ar^*$ produced within them by the radioactive decay of *in situ* ^{40}K. However, $^{40}Ar^*$ loss from minerals is claimed to be a persistent problem. Because Ar is a noble (non-reactive) gas, it does not form chemical bonds with other atoms in a crystal lattice, so no mineral locks Ar into its structure. Thus, it is often claimed that $^{40}Ar^*$ can be readily lost from the minerals where it was originally produced.[26] Yet this explanation is often resorted to in order to resolve conflicts between K-Ar and Ar-Ar "dating" results and the expectations based on the evolutionary timescale.

Nevertheless, a very good demonstration of apparent $^{40}Ar^*$ loss from different minerals in a thermal event is provided in the contact metamorphic zone

---

24   T. M. Harrison and I. McDougall, 1981, Excess ^{40}Ar in metamorphic rocks from Broken Hill, New South Wales: Implications for $^{40}Ar/^{39}Ar$ age spectra and the thermal history of the region, *Earth and Planetary Science Letters*, 55: 123-149.

25   B. Harte and C. J. Hawkesworth, 1986, Mantle domains and mantle xenoliths, in *Kimberlites and Related Rocks, Proceedings of the Fourth International Kimberlite Conference*, vol. 2, Special Publication No. 14, Sydney, Australia: Geological Society of Australia, 649-686; D. Porcelli and G. J. Wasserburg, 1995, Transfer of helium, neon, argon, and xenon through a steady-state upper mantle, *Geochimica et Cosmochimica Acta*, 59: 4921-4937.

26   Faure and Mensing, 2005, 116.

associated with the Eldora granite in the Front Range of Colorado.[27] The biotite, hornblende, and K-feldspar in the adjoining Precambrian metamorphic rocks were found to have lost varying amounts of $^{40}Ar^*$ at increasing distances from the contact with the intruded granite body (Figure 60, page 1093). This resulted in profound affects on the K-Ar mineral "ages," even though there were only very minor contact metamorphic effects. The fraction of $^{40}Ar^*$ lost from each mineral decreased as a function of distance from the contact, and the effects of this $^{40}Ar^*$ loss could be traced for more than two kilometers from the contact, well beyond the thermal contact zone of the intrusive granite body.

Such diffusion of $^{40}Ar^*$ from minerals as a result of heating is now in fact the basis of the Ar-Ar "dating" method. A K-bearing mineral is heated in the "dating" laboratory so that the $^{40}Ar^*$ accumulated escapes by diffusion and is then measured for the "age" calculation. Thus, the $^{40}Ar^*$ diffusion rates due to heating have been experimentally determined for the minerals relevant to the Ar-Ar "dating" method.[28]

Since recent lava flows often contain excess $^{40}Ar^*$, it is conceivable that "ancient" lava flows would likewise have initially had excess $^{40}Ar^*$. But because of the experimental evidence of $^{40}Ar^*$ diffusion and geological evidence of $^{40}Ar^*$ loss, whenever a K-Ar "date" for an "ancient" lava flow is not what is expected according to the uniformitarian timescale, the perceived discrepancy is usually attributed to net $^{40}Ar^*$ loss. This is the conventionally offered explanation for the apparent failure of K-Ar "dates" to match what is regarded as the acceptable Rb-Sr "date" for the middle Proterozoic Cardenas Basalt of the eastern Grand Canyon, Arizona.[29] Yet the 516 Ma K-Ar isochron "age," which is less than half the accepted uniformitarian "age" of 1,100 Ma, when plotted actually indicates some initial excess $^{40}Ar^*$. Therefore, if there has been no $^{40}Ar^*$ loss from these lava flows since their extrusion, then it could be argued that their K-Ar "age" is their maximum age, and that the uniformitarian timescale is hardly an objective yardstick for assessment of what constitutes valid "dates."

Nevertheless, there is a steady measured loss of $^{40}Ar^*$ from crustal rocks to the atmosphere of 1-6 x 10^9 atoms/m^2/sec, which is the result of degassing of

---

27   S. R. Hart, 1964, The petrology and isotopic-mineral age relations of a contact zone in the Front Range, Colorado, *Journal of Geology*, 72: 493-525.

28   T. M. Harrison, 1981, Diffusion of ^{40}Ar in hornblende, *Contributions to Mineralogy and Petrology*, 78: 324-331; T. M. Harrison, I. Duncan, and I. McDougall, 1985, Diffusion ^{40}Ar in biotite: Temperature, pressure and compositional effects, *Geochimica et Cosmochimica Acta*, 49: 2461-2468; M. Grove, and T. M. Harrison, 1996, $^{40}Ar^*$ diffusion in Fe-rich biotite, *American Mineralogist*, 81: 940-951.

29   E. H. McKee and D. C. Noble, 1976, Age of the Cardenas lavas, Grand Canyon, Arizona, *Geological Society of America Bulletin*, 87: 1188-1190; E. E. Larson, P. E. Patterson and F. E. Mutschler, 1994, Lithology, chemistry, age, and origin of the Proterozoic Cardenas basalt, Grand Canyon, Arizona, *Precambrian Research*, 65: 255-276; S. A. Austin and A. A. Snelling, 1998, Discordant potassium-argon model and isochron "ages" for Cardenas basalt (middle Proterozoic) and associated diabase of eastern Grand Canyon, Arizona, in *Proceedings of the Fourth International Conference on Creationism*, R. E. Walsh, ed., Pittsburgh, PA: Creation Science Fellowship, 35-51.

primordial [40]Ar and [40]Ar* from the mantle and crust.[30] Thus, even though this [40]Ar* flux produces a build-up of excess [40]Ar* in both mantle-derived and crustal rocks, [40]Ar* loss can clearly be a problem locally, resulting in "ages" much younger than conventionally expected. Therefore, when the [40]Ar* contents of rocks are measured, there is no way of determining categorically whether there has been [40]Ar* loss, or gain (by excess [40]Ar*), even when the calculated "ages" are compatible with other radioisotopic "dating" systems or conventional "ages" based on the strata record, all of which renders such K-Ar and Ar-Ar "dates" questionable at best.

---

30   J. Drescher, T. Kirsten and K. Schäfer, 1998, The rare gas inventory of the continental crust, recovered by the KTB Continental Deep Drilling Project, *Earth and Planetary Science Letters*, 154: 247-263.

101

THE PITFALLS IN THE RADIOACTIVE DATING
METHODS—THE RUBIDIUM-STRONTIUM
DATING METHOD

The rubidium (Rb)–strontium (Sr) radioisotope system is still one of the most widely used for rock and mineral "dating." However, the results are not always easy to interpret because of conflicting claims. On the one hand, it is claimed that both Rb and Sr are relatively mobile elements, so the isotopic system may be readily disturbed either by influx of fluids or by a later thermal event.[1] On the other hand, it has been stated that thermal inducement of radiogenic ^{87}Sr to leave its host mineral in quantities commeasurable to the loss of ^{40}Ar* under geologically feasible conditions has not been experimentally demonstrated, even though it is not uncommon to find minerals in nature which have lost both ^{40}Ar* and ^{87}Sr due to a thermal event.[2] Thus, the geological interpretation of Rb-Sr isochrons is guided by the required consistency with the uniformitarian timescale, in spite of numerous demonstrated problems.

Anomalous Rb-Sr Isochrons

The Rb-Sr isochron method presumes that a suite of rock samples from the same rock unit should all have the same "age" due to the entire rock unit being formed at the same time, should have the same initial ^{87}Sr/^{86}Sr ratio, and should have acted as a closed system. However, these basic assumptions have been questioned. It has become apparent that in an increasing number of geological situations the linear relationships between the ^{87}Sr/^{86}Sr and ^{87}Rb/^{86}Sr ratios sometimes yield anomalous isochrons that have no distinct geological meaning, even when there is an excellent goodness of fit of the isochrons to the data.[3] Thus, it is now recognized that basalt magma will invariably inherit the isotopic composition of its mantle

---

1 H. Rollison, 1993, *Using Geochemical Data: Evaluation, Presentation, Interpretation*, Harlow, UK: Longman.

2 G. N. Hanson and P. W. Gast, 1967, Kinetic studies in contact metamorphic zones, *Geochimica et Cosmochimica Acta*, 31: 1119-1153.

3 Y.-F. Zheng, 1989, Influences of the nature of the initial Rb-Sr system of isochron validity, *Chemical Geology*, 80: 1-16.

source, and, in some instances, also the parent/daughter ratio.[4] Indeed, when plotted on an isochron diagram, the Rb-Sr data for fourteen different ocean island basalts yielded a positive correlation with a slope "age" of approximately 2 Ga.[5] The basalts on individual ocean islands occasionally also define linear arrays with positive slopes. Because it was suggested that these apparent "ages" represented the time since the magma source areas were isolated from the convecting mantle, they were called "mantle isochrons."[6]

This mantle isochron concept was even found to apply to both volcanic and plutonic continental igneous rock suites. Although selected examples were all "ancient," unlike most of the recent ocean island basalts, when their measured $^{87}Sr/^{86}Sr$ ratios, corrected for their calculated initial ratios at the presumed time of the formation of these rocks, were plotted against their Rb/Sr ratios, the resultant data for each rock suite studied formed linear arrays that were termed "pseudo-isochrons."[7] Another example of correlated $^{87}Sr/^{86}Sr$ and $^{87}Rb/^{86}Sr$ ratios was reported for lava flows from two volcanic centers about 160 kilometers apart in east Africa.[8] They are known to be quite young because of volcanic activity in historic times, yet these lava flows yielded an apparent isochron "age" of 773 Ma. This isochron was interpreted as probably resulting from a mixing process in the mantle source region, because it could not be due to decay of ^{87}Rb in these rocks since their recent formation. Two other observed trends are worth noting. In modern volcanic rocks there is an overall approximate inverse correlation between their initial $^{87}Sr/^{86}Sr$ ratios and their Sr contents,[9] while in a general way the $^{87}Sr/^{86}Sr$ ratios of oceanic basalts correlate positively with their relative K contents.[10]

Yet another trend observed in some basaltic rocks is their $^{87}Sr/^{86}Sr$ ratios increase with their increasing SiO_2 contents, which has been suggested is due to crustal contamination.[11] Furthermore, apparently cogenetic (formed at the same time)

---

4   Dickin, 2005.

5   S. S. Sun and G. N. Hansen, 1975, Evolution of the mantle: Geochemical evidence from alkali basalt, *Geology*, 3: 297-302.

6   C. Brooks, S. R. Hart, A. Hoffmann and D. E. James, 1976, Rb-Sr mantle isochrons from oceanic regions, *Earth and Planetary Science Letters*, 32: 51-61.

7   C. Brooks, D. E. James and S. R. Hart, 1976, Ancient lithosphere: Its role in young continental volcanism, *Science*, 193: 1086-1094.

8   K. Bell and J. L. Powell, 1969, Strontium isotopic studies of alkalic rocks: The potassium-rich lavas of the Birunga and Toro-Ankole Regions, east and central equatorial Africa, *Journal of Petrology*, 10: 536-572.

9   G. Faure and J. L. Powell, 1972, *Strontium Isotope Geology*, Berlin: Springer-Verlag.

10 Z. E. Peterman and C. E. Hedge, 1971, Related strontium isotopic and chemical variations in oceanic basalts, *Geological Society of America Bulletin*, 82: 493-500.

11 G. Faure, R. L. Hill, L. M. Jones and D. H. Elliot, 1971, Isotope composition of strontium and silica content of Mesozoic basalt and dolerite from Antarctica, *SCAR Symposium*, Oslo, Norway: University Press.

suites of both oceanic and continental volcanic rocks have been found to have significant within-suite variations in their $^{87}Sr/^{86}Sr$ ratios.[12] It was suggested that in general these variations could have been caused by either differences in the initial $^{87}Sr/^{86}Sr$ ratios at the source regions of the rocks in the upper mantle and lower crust, or by variable contamination of their parent magmas with "foreign" Sr via bulk assimilation, wall-rock reaction, selective migration of radiogenic Sr, and/or isotopic exchange and equilibration. Thus, it has been argued that the assumption that all rocks in a co-magmatic igneous complex started with the same initial $^{87}Sr/^{86}Sr$ ratio may be invalid.[13] Indeed, variations in the initial $^{87}Sr/^{86}Sr$ ratios for suites of young lavas from a single volcano have been found.[14] Therefore, the assumption of a well-defined initial ratio for many suites of rocks is difficult to defend, and yet this is a crucial assumption for successful Rb-Sr isochron dating.

Magma contamination is a case in point. One cannot assume that all the Sr of the contaminants has been uniformly mixed into the magma; therefore, the assumption that all rocks in the same intrusive suite initially had the same $^{87}Sr/^{86}Sr$ ratio cannot be justified. Indeed, contamination is one of the main sources of mineralogical and geochemical variation in granitic rocks, and all main types of likely contaminant have compositions that would lead to an under-estimation of the initial $^{87}Sr/^{86}Sr$ ratio, and an over-estimation of the "age" of crystallization.[15] Obviously, the nature of the Rb-Sr system at the initial instant of time in the formation of a rock is of crucial importance in understanding the meaning of an isochron. Yet even suites of samples which do not have identical "ages" and initial $^{87}Sr/^{86}Sr$ ratios can be fitted to isochrons.[16] Furthermore, supposed multi-stage development of a geological system increases the complexity of interpreting Rb-Sr data for "dating" purposes. For example, a two-stage ^{87}Sr development for a rhyolite rock unit in the Lake District of England has been suggested in order to account for its anomalous whole-rock Rb-Sr isochron "age."[17] Also, the "rotation of the isochron" was used to describe the perceived distortion of the Rb-Sr system in some German volcanics, due to presumed post-magmatic processes.[18]

---

12   Faure and Powell, 1972.

13   P. S. McCarthy and R. G. Cawthorn, 1980, Changes in initial $^{87}Sr/^{86}Sr$ ratio during protracted fractionation in igneous complexes, *Journal of Petrology*, 21: 245-264.

14   M. Cortini and O. D. Hermes, 1981, Sr isotopic evidence for a multi-source origin of the potassic magmas in the Neapolitan area (S. Italy), *Contributions to Mineralogy and Petrology*, 77: 47-55.

15   A. Hall, 1996, *Igneous Petrology*, second edition, Harlow, UK: Addison Wesley Longman.

16   H. Cöhler and D. Müller-Sohnius, 1980, Rb-Sr systematics on paragneiss series from the Bavarian Moldanubium, Germany, *Contributions to Mineralogy and Petrology*, 71: 387-392; U. Haack, J. Hoefs and E. Gohn, 1982, Constraints on the origin of Damaran granites by Rb/Sr and $\delta^{18}O$ data, *Contributions to Mineralogy and Petrology*, 79: 279-289.

17   W. Compston, I. McDougall and D. Wyborn, 1982, Possible two-stage ^{87}Sr evolution in the Stockdale rhyolite, *Earth and Planetary Science Letters*, 61: 297-302.

18   H. Schleicher, H. J. Lippolt and I. Raczek, 1983, Rb-Sr systematics of Permian volcanites in Schwalzwald (S.W.-Germany) Part II. Age of eruption and the mechanism of Rb-Sr whole-rock age distortions, *Contributions to Mineralogy and Petrology*, 84: 281-291.

Because of the different geochemical behaviors of Rb and Sr, variations in initial $^{87}Sr/^{86}Sr$ ratios may result from Rb/Sr fractionation.[19] Furthermore, the three variables, ^{87}Sr, ^{86}Sr, and ^{87}Rb, are not independent of each other, and as a result the measured $^{87}Sr/^{86}Sr$ and $^{87}Rb/^{86}Sr$ ratios are not necessarily two dependent variables on an Rb-Sr isochron diagram, making invalid the "age" derived from the isochron.[20] Indeed, because a geological system cannot have had a homogenous ^{86}Sr distribution, and because the ^{86}Sr is used as a common variable in the conventional isochron equation, the observed correlation in the Rb-Sr isochron plot is enhanced. Given then that the present-day observed linear array on an isochron diagram is in fact the combination of the initial linear relationship between $^{87}Sr/^{86}Sr$ and $^{87}Rb/^{86}Sr$ ratios, corresponding to pseudo-isochrons, and the accumulation of radiogenic ^{87}Sr since the time of rock formation, the observed isochron can only be an apparent isochron. Therefore, it can be argued that the nature of the initial Rb-Sr system has considerable influence on the validity of an isochron, and this inherited initial Rb-Sr array may have rotated any valid present-day isochron, changing its slope and, therefore, the resultant calculated apparent "age."[21]

Open-System Behavior, Mixing and Resetting

The effects of some of these processes on a geological system are illustrated by granitic rocks of southeastern Australia. Regional variations of isotopic and chemical compositions of these granitic rocks are not too dissimilar to the granitic rocks of southern California. There has been much debate over the source rocks and mode of formation of these granitic rocks in southeastern Australia, which have been classified on the basis of their mineral and chemical compositions being derived either from the melting of mantle or sedimentary rocks. However, much evidence would suggest that many granite bodies are, in fact, blends or mixtures of both mantle and crustal sources, which has been demonstrated by radioisotope studies. For these granites in southeastern Australia, using the initial $^{87}Sr/^{86}Sr$ of each granite body as a measure of the mean $^{87}Sr/^{86}Sr$ of the source rocks at the time of their melting, a source Rb-Sr isochron diagram was plotted, from which a "source isochron" was derived for these source rocks that melted to form the granites.[22] However, whereas the age of these granites was regarded as 420 Ma, the source isochrons yielded an "age" for the source rocks of 1,100 Ma, consistent with the "ages" of supposedly inherited zircon grains in these granites.[23] This, of

19   C. E. Hedge and F. G. Walthall, 1963, Radiogenic strontium-87 as an index of geological processes, *Science*, 140: 1214-1217; C. J. Allègre, 1987, Isotope geodynamics, *Earth and Planetary Science Letters*, 86: 175-203.

20   Zheng, 1989.

21   Zheng, 1989.

22   W. Compston and B. W. Chappell, 1978, Estimation of source Rb/Sr for individual igneous-derived granitoids and the inferred age of the lower crust in southeast Australia, *US Geological Survey, Open-File Report 78-701*, 79-81.

23   Y. D. Chen and I. S. Williams, 1990, Zircon inheritance in mafic inclusions from Bega Batholith

course, suggests that Precambrian crustal material was incorporated in the granite magmas.

Other radioisotope investigations confirm this mixing of crustal and mantle components to form these granitic rocks. When the initial $^{87}Sr/^{86}Sr$ and $^{143}Nd/^{144}Nd$ ratios of some of these granitic rocks were used, they plotted along a curved trajectory typical of binary mixtures.[24] The granites in fact plotted in two overlapping clusters along the curved trajectory on this isotope correlation diagram (Figure 61, page 1093), which represents a mixing curve formed from crustal and mantle components. A subsequent study went further by showing that a three-component mixture of mantle-derived magma and two contrasting crustal components could successfully explain the radioisotope compositions of these southeastern Australian granites.[25] Indeed, it was possible to construct three-component radioisotope mixing curves that incorporated the radioisotope signatures of these granites, indicating that they all appear to be mixtures of a mantle component and two crustal components, one of which is the host sediments. Thus, it was suggested that the supposedly inherited zircon grains in these granites could instead be zircons that were originally inherited by the host sedimentary rocks during their sedimentation.

Magma mixing, therefore, as a major process of generating igneous rocks has received considerable attention, and contamination/assimilation of mantle-derived magma with crustal rocks during emplacement has now been accepted as the mixing mechanism. Furthermore, the resultant effects of this mixing on Rb-Sr "dating" have now been recognized.[26] The present-day measured Rb-Sr data may not define a valid isochron, but rather the production of an apparent isochron that can be a mixing isochron or an inherited linear array. Of course, this would only be realized if the isochron produced was not in accord with the expected "age" based on the uniformitarian timescale.

Mineral and whole-rock Rb-Sr radioisotope systems may respond differently to the heat and fluids during the metamorphism of a rock. ^{87}Sr tends to migrate out of crystals if subjected to a thermal pulse.[27] If fluids in the rock remain static, Sr released from Rb-rich minerals such as micas and K-feldspar will tend to be taken up by the nearest suitable mineral, such as plagioclase. Thus, individual minerals will be open systems during metamorphism. However, a whole-rock domain of a

granites, southeastern Australia: and ion microprobe study, *Journal of Geophysical Research*, 95: 17,787-17,796; I. S. Williams, 1992, Some observations on the use of zircon U-Pb geochronology in the study of granitic rocks, *Transactions of the Royal Society of Edinburgh*, 83: 447-458.

24   M. T. McCulloch and B. W. Chappell, 1982, Nd isotopic characteristics of S- and I-type granites, *Earth and Planetary Science Letters*, 58: 51-64.

25   S. Keay, W. J. Collins and M. T. McCulloch, 1997, A. three-component Sr-Nd isotopic mixing model for granitoid genesis, Lachlan Fold Belt, eastern Australia, *Geology*, 25: 307-310.

26   Zheng, 1989.

27   Dickin, 2005.

certain minimum size will remain an effective closed system during the thermal event, and thus, is regarded as "dating" the initial crystallization of the rock, provided there is no Rb remobilization, loss, or contamination.

A classic example of the effect of the temperatures of metamorphism is the apparent mineral "ages" with outward distance from the contact of the Eldora granite in the Front Range of Colorado (Figure 60).[28] The coarse biotites in the Precambrian metamorphic rocks intruded by the granite show even greater disturbance of the Rb-Sr system than the K-Ar system due to the heat of the intruding granite. Only 20 feet (just over 6 meters) from the contact, the coarse biotite has lost 88 percent of its radiogenic ^{87}Sr. In a subsequent study of the effect of thermal metamorphism, it was concluded that the relative stability of mineral "ages" in the contact metamorphic zone appeared to be hornblende K-Ar >muscovite Rb-Sr>muscovite K-Ar>biotite Rb-Sr>biotite K-Ar, although for the micas the Rb-Sr and K-Ar "ages" were essentially concordant.[29] Nevertheless, if uniformitarian timescale assumptions are ignored, and the isotopic ratios are simply interpreted as a geochemical signature of the rocks, then the heat from the intrusion studied was responsible for migration and redistribution of ^{87}Sr in commensurate quantities to ^{40}Ar*. It has also been found that Rb-Sr isotopic data require that Sr was redistributed during amphibolite facies (>650°C, >7kbar) regional metamorphism on a scale of at least tens of meters, fluid transport facilitating that Sr isotopic resetting.[30]

What is even of greater concern is how easily and quickly Rb and Sr can be leached from fresh rock. Experiments on granites have demonstrated that a mildly acidic solution will, in less than a day, leach large amounts of Rb from granite.[31] Rb was about ten times more leachable than Sr, and hence the ^{87}Sr/^{86}Sr ratio of the leaching solution was controlled by the leached Rb-fraction (and ^{87}Sr), which resulted in a higher ^{87}Sr/^{86}Sr ratio in solution compared to that in the rock. Thus, when the calculated isotopic compositions of the leached rock samples were plotted on an isochron diagram, they shifted along the isochron produced by the fresh rock samples. In other granites, Sr was up to fifty times more leachable than Rb, and hence the ^{87}Sr/^{86}Sr ratio of the solution was controlled by the Sr-fraction whose isotopic composition was that of "common" ^{86}Sr, similar to the initial ^{87}Sr/^{86}Sr ratio of the granite, and lower compared to the present-day fresh whole-rock ratio. Thus, the calculated isotopic composition of the leached rocks plotted away from the isochron produced by the fresh rock samples, effectively rotating the isochron.

---

28   Hart, 1964.

29   G. N. Hanson and P. W. Gast, 1967, Kinetic studies in contact metamorphic zones, *Geochimica et Cosmochimica Acta*, 31: 1119-1153.

30   S. C. Patel, C. D. Frost and B. R. Frost, 1999, Contrasting response of Rb-Sr systematics to regionally and contact metamorphism, Laramie Mountains, Wyoming, USA, *Journal of Metamorphic Geology*, 17: 259-269.

31   W. Irber, W. Siebel, P. Möller and S. Teufel, 1996, Leaching of Rb and Sr (^{87}Sr/^{86}Sr) of Hercynian peraluminous granites with application to age determination, in *V.M. Goldschmidt Conference, Journal of Conference Abstracts*, vol. 1 (1), 281.

Investigations of alteration sequences have thus shown that, during most common types of alteration, a spread of Rb/Sr whole-rock ratios occurs due to drastic loss of Sr, whereas the Rb increases due to formation of sericite (fine-grained white mica). Because such changes due to chemical weathering by the atmosphere and meteoritic water are systematic, false isochrons can be generated which, therefore, may not be distinguishable from the "true" isochrons and "ages."

Mounting evidence of whole-rock Rb-Sr open-system behavior has meant that the widely used whole-rock Rb-Sr method has lost credibility.[32] For example, Rb-Sr isochrons in metamorphic terrains can yield good linear arrays, whose slopes are, nevertheless, meaningless averages of the original rocks and metamorphic "ages." Whole-rock Rb-Sr systems can be disturbed and reset to give good-fit secondary isochrons, even by relatively low-grade metamorphism.[33] Indeed, the Rb-Sr systems in metamorphic rocks are complicated by two factors, namely, whether the initial $^{87}Sr/^{86}Sr$ ratios have been homogenized by the metamorphism, or whether the Rb and Sr elemental abundances have been redistributed during the metamorphism. In reality, few systems are perfectly homogenized during metamorphism. Furthermore, minerals separated from single whole-rock specimens may yield distorted internal mineral isochrons also dependent on the degree of Sr isotopic homogenization. In some cases, gain or loss of Rb and Sr from rocks is so regular that linear arrays can be produced on the conventional isochron diagrams, and biased isochron results give spurious "ages" and initial $^{87}Sr/^{86}Sr$ ratio estimates. Thus, it has been concluded that:

> As it is impossible to distinguish a valid isochron from an apparent isochron in the light of Rb-Sr isotopic data alone, caution must be taken in explaining the Rb-Sr isochron age of any geologic system....An observed isochron does not certainly define a valid age information for a geologic system, even if a goodness of fit of the experimental data points is obtained in plotting $^{87}Sr/^{86}Sr$ vs. $^{87}Rb/^{86}Sr$. This problem cannot be overlooked, especially in evaluating the numerical timescale.[34]

In conclusion, all of these considerations combine to cast a "shadow" over the Rb-Sr radioisotope system as a reliable geochronometer. The repeatedly demonstrated mobility of Sr and Rb in fluids, and at elevated temperatures, invariably disturbs the Rb-Sr systematics to yield invalid or meaningless "ages." Anomalous and false isochrons are prolific, their status only being apparent when such results are compared with other radioisotope systems, and/or the stratigraphic setting. Thus, recognition of inheritance, open-system behavior, contamination and mixing, and the later effects of weathering, together have increasingly caused Rb-Sr radioisotope "dating" to be regarded as unreliable.

---

32   Dickin, 2005.

33   Zheng, 1989.

34   Zheng, 1989, 14.

102

THE PITFALLS IN THE RADIOACTIVE DATING METHODS—THE SAMARIUM-NEODYMIUM DATING METHOD

Samarium (Sm) and neodymium (Nd) are light rare earth elements that occur in trace amounts in common rock-forming minerals, where they replace major ions. They may also reside in accessory minerals, particularly apatite and monazite (phosphate minerals), and zircon (zirconium silicate). Minerals exercise a considerable degree of selectivity in admitting rare earth elements into their crystal structures, affecting the rare earth element concentrations of the rocks in which the various minerals occur. Thus "age" determinations by the Sm-Nd radioisotope method are usually made by analyzing separated minerals of cogenetic suites of rocks in which the Sm/Nd ratios vary sufficiently to define the slope of an isochron. It is claimed that, because Sm and Nd are much less mobile than Rb, Sr, Th, U, and Pb during regional metamorphism, hydrothermal alteration, and chemical weathering, the Sm-Nd radioisotope "dating" method supposedly "sees through" younger events in rocks where the Rb-Sr and U-Pb isotopic chemistry has been disturbed. Furthermore, it is claimed that whole-rock Sm-Nd "dating" has an advantage over mineral Sm-Nd "dating," in that the scale of sampling is much larger (the meters or kilometers extent of a rock unit instead of the millimeters scale between minerals), so that the possibility of post-crystallization isotopic re-equilibration between samples is reduced.[1]

The chief limitations on the Sm-Nd technique are the long half-life of ^{147}Sm (106 billion years), and the relatively small variations in Sm/Nd ratios found in most cogenetic rock suites. It is often claimed that the long half-life limits the usefulness of this method to only "very old" rocks. The second limitation has led some investigators to combine a wide range of rock types on the same isochron in order to obtain a spread of Sm/Nd ratios.[2] However, such samples from different sources with very different histories plotted on the same isochrons have produced spurious results. Furthermore, it is difficult to obtain precise initial ^{143}Nd/^{144}Nd ratios, because no common minerals have their ^{147}Sm/^{144}Nd ratio

1   D. J. DePaolo, 1988, *Neodymium Isotope Geochemistry: An Introduction*, Berlin: Springer-Verlag.

2   Rollinson, 1993.

near zero. Therefore, on isochron plots, long extrapolations are usually required to determine the intercepts, which produce relatively large uncertainties.[3] Indeed, variations in initial ratios for suites of young lavas from a single volcano have been found, suggesting that the assumption of a well-defined initial ratio for many suites of rocks is difficult to defend.[4] This is a critical problem for Sm-Nd whole-rock "dating," because the relatively small range of $^{143}Nd/^{144}Nd$ ratios in most rock suites means that any differences in the initial ratios that are larger than the analytical uncertainties could substantially affect the calculated "age," leading to serious errors. For example, rocks from the Peninsula Ranges Batholith of southern California, which is supposed to be about 100 million years old, plot on an apparent Sm-Nd isochron of 1.7 billion years.[5] Even Archean rock suites yield an excellent whole-rock isochron with a grossly erroneous "age."[6]

The Sm-Nd method has frequently been applied to "dating" the "age" of the supposed original igneous rocks of what is now high-grade metamorphic basement, where other radioisotope systems have evidently been reset.[7] However, when this application to a suite of granitic and basaltic metamorphic rocks of different grades in northwest Scotland was further investigated, it was evident that the basaltic rocks had "retained" an older Sm-Nd isochron "age," whereas the Sm-Nd whole-rock systems in the non-basaltic rocks seemed to have been "reset" to the same "age" as the U-Pb zircon and other whole-rock radioisotope systems.[8] Thus, it was concluded that the Sm-Nd radioisotope system had only remained closed in the basaltic rocks during the metamorphic event, while the Sm-Nd radioisotope system in the other metamorphic rocks was disturbed. This is contrary to the usual claim that the less mobile Sm and Nd are not disturbed by events subsequent to the initial formation of their host rocks. Thus, if these isotopes are indeed mobile in ways similar to the other radioisotope systems, then the reliability of Sm-Nd "ages" is equally questionable.

It has now been clearly demonstrated that, under certain hydrothermal conditions, the mobility of rare earth elements perturbs the Sm-Nd radioisotope system.[9] The net result of hydrothermal alteration is leaching of the rare earth elements from the rocks. Furthermore, the perturbation of the Sm-Nd radioisotope system

3   DePaolo, 1988.

4   C.-Y. Chen and F. A. Frey, 1983, Origin of Hawaiian tholeiite and alkalic basalt, *Nature*, 302: 785-789.

5   D. J. DePaolo, 1981, A neodymium and strontium isotopic study of the Mesozoic calc-alkaline granitic batholiths of the Sierra Nevada and Peninsula Ranges, California, *Journal of Geophysical Research*, 86: 10,470-10,488.

6   C. Chauvel, B. Dupre and G. A. Jenner, 1985, The Sm-Nd age of Kambalda volcanics is 500 Ma too old!, *Earth and Planetary Science Letters*, 74: 315-324.

7   P. J. Hamilton, R. K. O'Nions, N. M. Evensen and J. Tarney, 1979, Sm-Nd systematics of Lewisian gneisses: Implications for the origin of granulites, *Nature*, 277: 25-28.

8   M. J. Whitehouse, 1988, Granulite facies Nd-isotopic homogenisation in the Lewisian Complex of northwest Scotland, *Nature*, 331: 705-707.

9   F. Poitrasson, C. Pin and J.-L. Duthou, 1995, Hydrothermal remobilization of rare earth elements and its effect on Nd isotopes in rhyolite and granite, *Earth and Planetary Science Letters*, 130: 1-11.

was found not to be solely due to significant modification of the Sm/Nd ratio after emplacement of the granitic rocks studied. Therefore, it was concluded that the isotopic compositions were modified by a component introduced from the hydrothermal fluid that had contrasting $^{143}Nd/^{144}Nd$ ratios. It was also found that rare earth elements were transported over distances exceeding several tens to hundreds of meters, even where mineralized fractures were absent. Indeed, isotopically perturbed samples could not be discriminated readily from unperturbed samples because of the lack of obvious indicators of different degrees of fluid-rock interactions. Thus, Sm and Nd are not as immobile as often claimed, nor does the Sm-Nd radioisotope system escape being significantly perturbed, which raises similar doubts about the reliability of the Sm-Nd "dating" system, as with other radioisotope dating systems.

Nevertheless, the Sm-Nd mineral isochron method has been widely applied to the "dating" of high-grade metamorphic rocks, because mineral isochrons have the advantage that variations in partition coefficients between minerals may have caused moderately large variations in Sm/Nd ratios. The best metamorphic mineral to use has been garnet. It has high Sm/Nd ratios in contrast to other metamorphic minerals. This results in a large range in Sm/Nd ratios, and thus better statistics, in the "age" determined from mineral isochrons using garnets, and one or more other metamorphic minerals. However, mineral systems may be opened sufficiently during metamorphism to disrupt the original mineral chemistry. It is claimed that certain minerals will close to element mobility at different so-called blocking temperatures, and the different radioisotope systems in the same mineral will also close at different closure temperatures, below which the radioisotope "clocks" are switched on.

However, the closure temperature of the Sm-Nd radioisotope system in metamorphic garnet has been the subject of continued debate, with experimental determinations and theoretical considerations showing that a sufficiently restricted range of closure temperature cannot be assigned.[10] Nevertheless, the resetting of the Sm-Nd radioisotope system in garnet does take place.[11] While it has been found that the effective diameter for diffusion may only be of the order of 1 mm, it is admitted that reliable chronological constraints are essential for the unambiguous interpretation of metamorphic rock textures because of this diffusion and resetting. Thus, the U-Th-Pb radioisotope system has been used to also "date" garnets. However, this has also proved problematical, because the U, Th, and Pb isotopes do not reside in the garnet lattice, but instead are hosted by inclusions of minerals such as zircon, which are invariably older than the garnets.[12]

10   J. Ganguly, M. Tirone and R. L. Hervig, 1988, Diffusion kinetics of samarium and neodymium in garnet, and a method for determining cooling rates of rocks, *Science*, 281: 805-807.

11   E. J. Hensen and B. Zhou, 1995, Retention of isotopic memory in garnets partially broken down during an overprinting granulite-facies metamorphism: Implications for the Sm-Nd closure temperature, *Geology*, 23: 225-228.

12   T. P. DeWolf, C. J. Zeissler, A. N. Halliday, K. Mezger and E. J. Essene, 1996, The role of inclusions in U-Pb and Sm-Nd garnet geochronology: Stepwise dissolution experiments and trace uranium mapping

Consequently, because of the implied mobility of the Sm and Nd isotopes at moderate to high temperatures, attempts at Sm-Nd mineral isochron "dating" are still dependent on calibrations with other radioisotope "dating" systems and assume their consistency with the uniformitarian timescale.[13] In any case, a study of the Sm-Nd radioisotope systematics in minerals in two granites has shown that hydrothermal fluids interacting with the host rocks, as the granite intrudes and crystallizes, are capable of carrying Sm and Nd in the rocks over distances of at least 1 km.[14] The minerals in both these granites produced statistically acceptable mineral isochrons, but these yielded otherwise meaningless "ages" that had to be interpreted as either inherited, or due to hydrothermal convection long after crystallization of the granites. Clearly, the Sm-Nd radioisotope "dating" system in both whole-rocks and minerals is not as "foolproof" as often claimed, sometimes being arbitrarily subject to resetting and disturbance due to diffusion and fluid migration at all scales.

Sm-Nd Model Ages

Of considerable importance in the use of the Sm-Nd radioisotope system are "model ages." These are defined as a measure of the length of time a sample has been separated from the mantle source from which it was originally derived.[15] Of course, this assumes a knowledge of the isotopic compositions of mantle sources, the absence of parent/daughter isotopic fractionation (separation) after extraction from the mantle sources, and the immobility of the parent and daughter isotopes. In the case of Sr isotopes, none of these criteria is usually fulfilled.[16] Nevertheless, Sm-Nd "model ages" are commonly calculated for individual rocks, using each single pair of parent-daughter isotopic ratios. However, they must be interpreted with care, primarily because of the assumptions about the isotopic compositions of the mantle source regions.[17] The two frequently assumed "models" of the Sm-Nd radioisotope system in mantle sources are the chondritic uniform reservoir (CHUR), and the depleted mantle (DM) reservoir.[18]

by fission track analysis, *Geochimica et Cosmochimica Acta*, 60: 121-134; B. Vance, M. Meier and F. Oberli, 1998, The influence of U-Th inclusions on the U-Th-Pb systematics of almandine pyrope garnet: Results of a combined bulk dissolution stepwise-leaching, and SEM study, *Geochimica et Cosmochimica Acta*, 62: 3527-3540.

13   K. Mezger, E. J. Essene and A. N. Halliday, 1993, Closure temperatures on the Sm-Nd system in metamorphic garnets, *Earth and Planetary Science Letters*, 113: 397-409.

14   F. Poitrasson, J.-L. Paquette, J.-M. Montel, C. Pin and J.-L. Duthou, 1998, Importance of late-magmatic and hydrothermal fluids on the Sm-Nd isotope mineral systematics of hypersolvus granites, *Chemical Geology*, 146: 187-203.

15   Rollinson, 1993.

16   S. L. Goldstein, 1988, Decoupled evolution of Nd and Sr isotopes in the continental crust, *Nature*, 336: 733-738.

17   Rollinson, 1993.

18   D. J. DePaolo and G. J. Wasserburg, 1976, Nd isotopic variations and petrogenetic models, *Geophysical Research Letters*, 3: 249-252; D. J. DePaolo and G. J. Wasserburg, 1976, Inferences about magma sources and mantle structure from variations of $^{143}Nd/^{144}Nd$, *Geophysical Research Letters*, 3: 743-746; D. J. DePaolo, 1981, Neodymium isotopes in the Colorado Front Range and crust-mantle evolution in the

However, the assumptions upon which these calculated "model ages" are based are not always fulfilled. First is the assumption about the isotopic composition of the chosen mantle reservoir model, which raises three further problems.[19] The choice of reservoir model can make a huge difference between the calculated Nd "model ages." There are now several possible competing mantle models in use, and there is confusion over the actual numbers for the mantle values that should be used in the "age" calculations. The second assumption used in "model age" calculations is that the Sm/Nd ratio of a sample has not been modified by fractionation (separation of the parent and daughter isotopes from one another) after separation of the rock sample from its original mantle source. However, as has already been noted, hydrothermal fluids can redistribute Sm and Nd and thus disturb the Sm/Nd ratios. Finally, the third assumption is that all material pertaining to the rock sample being "dated" came from the mantle in a single event, which may not always be the case, and cannot really be demonstrated.

Nevertheless, the meaning of these "model ages" is somewhat problematic. For example, Nd "model ages" for metamorphic rocks from central Australia have been reported with differences in each sample of up to 1.3 billion years, depending on the mantle reservoir model used.[20] Consequently, it has been admitted that the establishment of credible Sm-Nd "model ages" for crustal rocks clearly requires "precise" geochronological information, regarded as typically being provided by U-Pb isotopic measurements of zircons, plus agreed models for Nd isotopic evolution in the mantle sources of continental crust, and for Nd isotopic evolution of crustal reservoirs subsequent to their formation.[21] Additionally, models are required for the formation of certain types of granitic rocks in the crust, for a mechanism for mixing of materials to form a hybrid crust, and for the development of the lower parts of the continental crust. All these factors are problematic, but the greatest uncertainties are due to the lack of adequate information on the lower crustal processes and composition. Clearly, the usefulness of Sm-Nd "model ages" and the "dating" method is very much dependent on interpretative models, and on the other radioisotope "dating" systems that also have their own sets of problems. Indeed, as independently concluded, the Nd "model age" method requires geochronological confirmation by other radioisotope "dating" methods, because of the problem of mixing of Sm/Nd isotopes.[22] Thus, each of the radioisotope "dating" methods has its problems, and; therefore, the Sm-Nd method is dependent upon, and only as good as, any of the other methods.

     Proterozoic, *Nature*, 291: 193-196.

19   Rollison, 1993.

20   D. P. Windrim and M. T. McCulloch, 1986, Nd and Sr isotopic systematics of central Australian granulites: Chronology of crustal development and constraints on the evolution of the lower continental crust, *Contributions to Mineralogy and Petrology*, 94: 289-303.

21   D. J. DePaolo, A. M. Linn and G. Schubert, 1991, The continental crust age distribution: Method of determining mantle separation ages from Sm-Nd isotopic data an application to the southwestern United States, *Journal of Geophysical Research*, 96: 2071-2088.

22   Dickin, 2005.

103

The Pitfalls in the Radioactive Dating Methods—The Uranium-Thorium-Lead Dating Method

Historically, uranium (U)-thorium (Th)-lead (Pb) "dating" was the first method to be used on minerals, particularly U-bearing minerals. As the appropriate technology became available, this method was also applied to whole rocks. However, as with the other radioisotope "dating" methods, the U-Th-Pb radioisotope "dating" systems have their inherent problems that render them questionable at best.

Open-System Behavior

Even early studies in whole-rock U-Th-Pb "dating" of crystalline rocks showed the method to be of little value as a geochronological tool, because unfortunately, the U-Pb and Th-Pb systems rarely stay closed due to the mobility of Pb, Th, and especially U.[1] Indeed, it was found that U appeared to have been lost from samples which exhibited no discernible effects of alteration, so it was even suggested the leaching of U from surficial rocks might be a universal phenomenon.[2] This was because concentrations of U, Th, and Pb, and the isotopic composition of Pb, for whole-rock samples of granites, showed that open-system behavior is nearly universal in the surface and near-surface environment, and that elemental mobility is possible to depths of several hundred meters. Identified controlling factors included mineralogical sites for U and its daughter products, the access and volume of circulating ground water, and the chemistry of that ground water. In practice, therefore, the mobility of U, Th, and Pb renders the use of simple U-Pb isochron "dates" very limited. However, it is claimed that "age" information can still be obtained using the two parent U isotopes and their respective daughter Pb isotopes as a result of the consistent relationship between them and their coherent chemical behavior. Nevertheless, the focus has shifted back to using the U-Th-Pb "dating" technique on minerals. This has become the most popular and highly regarded radioisotope dating method currently in use. The primary targets

---

1   Dickin, 2005.

2   J. S. Stuckless, 1986, Applications of U-Th-Pb isotope systematics to the problems of radioactive waste disposal, *Chemical Geology*, 55: 215-225.

are grains of zircon ($ZrSiO_4$), baddeleyite (ZrO_2), titanite or sphene ($CaTiSiO_5$), and/or monazite ((Ce, La, Th) PO_4), though other minerals are sometimes used.

Concentrations of U and Th in zircon, for example, average 1,350 and 550 ppm respectively.[3] The presence of these elements in zircon is a result of U and Th atoms substituting for Zr atoms in its crystal lattice due to their similar sizes and their same electric charge. However, equally important is the fact that Pb is excluded from the zircon crystal lattice due to the larger size of its atoms and their lower charge. Therefore, zircon is believed to contain very little Pb, and thus very high U/Pb and Th/Pb ratios, at the time of its formation. This means that the radioisotope ratios now measured are due to all their radiogenic Pb being derived by radioactive decay from U and Th, which enhances zircon's sensitivity as currently the most popular geochronometer. However, radiogenic Pb can be inherited during crystallization of the mineral grains, and open-system behavior is common, resulting in radiogenic Pb loss by diffusion, due to the way the Pb is not bonded in the crystal lattices.

Even early dating work on U-rich minerals soon revealed that most samples yielded discordant U-Pb "ages," which were attributed to Pb loss.[4] Minerals that yielded discordant U-Pb "ages", nevertheless, defined a linear array when plotted, which was attributed to Pb loss by a continuous diffusional process.[5] It was then demonstrated that leakage of intermediate radon by gaseous diffusion through microfissures in minerals could account for the disparity in U-Pb "ages."[6] Subsequently, it was postulated that the intermediate members of the U-decay series generally were ejected into microfissures in mineral lattices, where they were removed by diffusion or leaching, accounting for continuous Pb loss.[7]

However, an alternative model was also proposed that invoked episodic Pb loss from minerals due to a thermal event subsequent to their formation.[8] Such open-system behavior explained U-Pb "dates" that were otherwise unsuccessful, because they failed the crucial assumptions about initial conditions and a closed system.[9] Indeed, the postulated Pb loss by continuous diffusion over "geological time" was confirmed by experimental demonstration that Pb diffuses from zircon and

---

3   Faure and Mensing, 2005, 221.

4   A. Holmes, 1954, The oldest dated minerals of the Rhodesian Shield, *Nature*, 173: 612-617.

5   L. H. Ahrens, 1955, Implications of the Rhodesia age pattern, *Geochimica et Cosmochimica Acta*, 8: 1-15.

6   E. J. Giletti and J. L. Kulp, 1955, Radon leakage from radioactive minerals, *American Mineralogist*, 40: 481-496.

7   R. D. Russell and L. H. Ahrens, 1957, Additional regularities among discordant lead-uranium ages, *Geochimica et Cosmochimica Acta*, 11: 213-218.

8   G. W. Wetherill, 1956, An interpretation of the Rhodesia and Witwatersrand age patterns, *Geochimica et Cosmochimica Acta*, 9: 290-292.

9   E. W. Wetherill, 1956, Discordant uranium-lead ages, I, *Transactions of the American Geophysical Union*, 37: 320-326.

U-bearing minerals, even at low temperatures.[10]

This Pb loss by diffusion is facilitated by the α-radiation damage to the host mineral lattices.[11] Indeed, not only has it been confirmed that radiation damage can drastically increase the rate of Pb diffusion, but higher temperatures induce even faster diffusion.[12] This is dramatically illustrated by the contact metamorphic effects of the heat from a granite intrusion on zircon crystals in the surrounding regionally metamorphosed sediments and volcanics (Figure 62, page 1094).[13] Within 15 meters (50 feet) of the contact, the U-Pb "ages" decrease dramatically from 1,405 million years to 220 million years. Furthermore, it has also been demonstrated that larger zircon grains lose less Pb than smaller ones (due to the larger surface area/volume ratio of the latter), and that zircon grains with low U contents lose less Pb than high-U zircons (due to greater radiation damage suffered by the latter).[14] However, zircon crystals are often chemically and physically inhomogeneous (zoned) due to progressive growth during crystallization, and both zoned and unzoned zircon crystals may be found in the same rock. Thus, unzoned crystals can be the result of recrystallization of zoned crystals accompanied by loss of U, Th, and Pb, which results in "resetting" of the U-Pb "ages."[15] Such recrystallization can be due to regional metamorphism, which has been found to reduce U-Pb zircon "ages" by hundreds of millions of years, even within single samples.[16] Similarly, even when a spectrum of concordant zircon U-Pb "ages" are obtained, they are nevertheless meaningless, due to the high-temperature Pb loss during metamorphism by volume, and/or fracture-assisted diffusion.[17]

10   J. R. Tilton, 1960, Volume diffusion as a mechanism for discordant lead ages, *Journal of Geophysical Research*, 65: 2933-2945.

11   E. J. Wasserburg, 1963, Diffusion processes in lead-uranium systems, *Journal of Geophysical Research*, 68: 4823-4846; S. S. Goldich and M. J. Mudrey, Jr., 1972, Dilatancy model for discordant U-Pb zircon ages, in *Contributions to Recent Geochemistry and Analytical Chemistry*, A. I. Tugrainov, ed., Moscow: Nauka Publishing Office, 415-418; A. Meldrum, L. H. Boatner, W. J. Weber and R. C. Ewing, 1998, Radiation damage in zircon and monazite, *Geochimica et Cosmochimica Acta*, 62: 2509-2520.

12   J. K. W. Lee, I. S. Williams and D. J. Ellis, 1997, Determination of Pb, U and Th diffusion rates in zircon, *Research School of Earth Sciences Annual Report 1996*, Canberra, Australia: Australian National University, 121-122.

13   E. L. Davis, S. R. Hart and G. R. Tilton, 1968, Some effects of contact metamorphism on zircon ages, *Earth and Planetary Science Letters*, 5: 27-34.

14   L. T. Silver and S. Deutsch, 1963, Uranium-lead isotopic variations in zircons: A case study, *Journal of Geology*, 71: 721-758.

15   R. T. Pidgeon, 1992, Recrystallisation of oscillatory zoned zircon: Some geochronological and petrological implications, *Contributions to Mineralogy and Petrology*, 110: 463-472.

16   A. Kröner, P. J. Jaeckel and I. S. Williams, 1994, Pb-loss patterns in zircons from a high-grade metamorphic terrain as revealed by different dating methods, U-Pb and Pb-Pb ages for igneous and metamorphic zircons from northern Sri Lanka, *Precambrian Research*, 66: 151-181.

17   L. D. Ashwal, R. D. Tucker and E. K. Zinner, 1999, Slow cooling of deep crustal granulites and Pb-loss in zircon, *Geochimica et Cosmochimica Acta*, 63: 2839-2851.

Inheritance

Another significant problem for zircon U-Pb "dating" are zircon crystals that yield much older "ages" than the expected/accepted "ages" of the rocks containing them. In metamorphic rocks, this is usually interpreted as inheritance of those zircon grains that were in the original sediments, the zircon U-Pb "ages" not having been reset by the metamorphism.[18] In granitic rocks, these "older" zircons are likewise interpreted as having been inherited from the source rocks that melted to produce the granitic magmas.[19] Indeed, some of these so-called inherited zircons are 5-10 times "older" than those matching the accepted "ages" of the granites—for example, up to 1,753 million years in a Himalayan granite supposed to be 21 million years old,[20] up to 3,500 million years in a southeast Australian granodiorite supposed to be 426 million years old,[21] and up to 1,638 million years in a New Zealand granite supposed to be 370 million years old.[22] Of course, if the accepted "age" of a rock according to the uniformitarian timescale is unknown, then there is no way of being sure from such zircon U-Pb "ages" what is the real age of the rock!

However, if Pb is lost from some mineral grains, then it could be inherited by other crystals during and subsequent to the formation of the host rocks. Thus, in Precambrian rocks many potassium feldspar grains, which have never contained U, nevertheless contain radiogenic Pb.[23] However, such excess radiogenic Pb producing anomalously high "ages" can also be found in zircon crystals themselves.[24] Similar situations also result in "ages" hundreds of millions of years more than expected, and are interpreted as being due to excess radiogenic Pb, the origin of which is either explained as mixing from older source materials which melted to form the magmas, and/or due to subsequent migration as a result of fluids, temperature, and pressure.[25] This, of course, again begs the question—should "anomalously

18   E. O. Froude, T. R. Ireland, P. O. Kinny, I. S. Williams and W. Compston, 1983, Ion microprobe identification of 4100-4200 Ma-old terrestrial zircons, *Nature*, 304: 616-618; Kröner et al, 1994.

19   I. S. Williams, W. Compston and B. W. Chappell, 1983, Zircon and monazite U-Pb systems and histories of I-type magmas, Berridale Batholith, Australia, *Journal of Petrology*, 24: 76-97; Y. D. Chen and I. S. Williams, 1990, Zircon inheritance in mafic inclusions from Bega Batholith granites, southeastern Australia: An ion microprobe study, *Journal of Geophysical Research*, 95: 17,787-17,796.

20   I. R. Parrish and R. Tirrul, 1989, U-Pb age of the Baltoro Granite, northwest Himalaya, and implications for monazite U-Pb systematics, *Geology*, 17: 1076-1079.

21   I. S. Williams, 1992, Some observations on the use of zircon U-Pb geochronology in the study of granitic rocks, *Transactions of the Royal Society of Edinburgh*, 83: 447-458.

22   R. J. Muir, T. R. Ireland, S. D. Weaver and J. D. Bradshaw, 1996, Ion microprobe dating of Paleozoic granitoids: Devonian magmatism in New Zealand and correlations with Australia and Antarctica, *Chemical Geology*, 127: 191-210.

23   A. R. Ludwig and L. T. Silver, 1977, Lead isotope inhomogeneities in Precambrian igneous K-feldspars, *Geochimica et Cosmochimica Acta*, 41: 1457-1471.

24   I. S. Williams, W. Compston, L. B. Black, T. R. Ireland and J. J. Foster, 1984, Unsupported radiogenic Pb in zircon, a cause of anomalously high Pb-Pb, U-Pb and Th-Pb ages, *Contributions to Mineralogy and Petrology*, 88: 322-327.

25   L. S. Zhang and U. Schärer, 1996, Inherited Pb components in magmatic titanite and their consequence

old" zircons be interpreted as inheritance of the zircon crystals, or of "excess" radiogenic Pb in the crystals?

The advent of more sophisticated analytical technology has since provided new means to evidently circumvent these problems in the U-Th-Pb "dating" of zircons and other minerals. For example, individual zircon grains are blasted with air to remove outer layers that may represent younger overgrowths on older grains, which is followed by hand-picking of the best grains.[26] A completely different approach is the *in situ* analysis of U/Pb and Pb isotopic ratios within zircon grains using an ion microprobe. A very narrow ion beam is focused on 2-micron-wide spots within zircon or other crystals, enabling the analysis and consequent "dating" of different growth zones in them. However, utilizing this technique, radiogenic Pb has been found to vary within most tested zircon grains on a 20-micron spatial scale.[27] Some spots were characterized by huge excesses of radiogenic Pb, up to thirty times the "expected" values. Furthermore, pronounced reproducible differences in apparent "ages" have been demonstrated between four differently oriented faces of a large baddeleyite crystal, an effect concluded to be a primary crystal growth feature.[28] Additionally, isotopic ratios were measured on the same crystal faces of 47 baddeleyite crystals, but at different orientations with respect to the ion beam. The results revealed a striking, approximately sinusoidal, variation in U/Pb apparent "ages" of hundreds of millions of years with orientation (Figure 63, page 1094). However, while similar significant differences in apparent U/Pb "ages" were not detected in zircon or monazite crystals, within the analytical statistics, other Pb and isotopic Th/U ratios vary systematically with orientation, suggesting these were real compositional variations that reflected zones of primary crystal growth.

Nevertheless, some monazite crystals have been found to contain random sub-microscopic blotchy patches that can vary up to 700 million years in "age" from one another.[29] Similarly, discordant U-Pb "ages" that still plotted as linear arrays were obtained for monazite grains in high-grade metamorphic rocks, and high spatial resolution examination of the grains revealed domains with greatly

for the interpretation of U-Pb ages, *Earth and Planetary Science Letters*, 138: 57-65; P. Copeland, R. R. Parrish and T. M. Harrison, 1988, Identification of inherited radiogenic Pb in monazite and its implications for U-Pb systematics, *Nature*, 333: 760-763.

26   T. E. Krogh, 1982, Improved accuracy of U-Pb zircon ages by the creation of more concordant systems using the air abrasion technique, *Geochimica et Cosmochimica Acta*, 46: 637-649.

27   W. Compston, 1997, Variation in radiogenic Pb/U within the SL13 standard, *Research School of Earth Sciences Annual Report 1996*, Canberra, Australia: Australian National University, 188-121.

28   M. T. D. Wingate and W. Compston, 2000, Crystal orientation effects during ion microprobe, U-Pb analysis of baddeleyite, *Chemical Geology*, 168: 75-97.

29   A. Cocherie, O. Legeandre, J. J. Peucat and A. N. Kouamelan, 1998, Geochronology of polygenetic monazites constrained by *in situ* electron microprobe Th-U-total lead determination: Implications for lead behaviour in monazite, *Geochimica et Cosmochimica Acta*, 62: 2475-2497.

contrasting U-Th and Pb concentrations.[30] Significantly, monazite grains can also yield negative "ages," such as -97 million years in a supposedly 20 million year old Himalayan granite that also contains zircon grains yielding "ages" up to 1,483 million years, a discordance of almost 7,500 percent![31]

Clearly, the results of U-Th-Pb mineral dating, currently the most popular method, are highly dependent on the investigators' interpretations, which are usually based on expectations determined by the geological contexts of the rocks being "dated." Radiogenic Pb is easily lost by diffusion from some crystals, and the process is accelerated by heat, water, radiation damage, and weathering, while in other crystals it is inherited in excess. Uranium is readily dissolved by ground waters at considerable depths and leached from rocks and their constituent minerals. Thus, without the geological context and the expected "ages" to guide the investigators, one cannot be sure, as with whole-rock U-Th-Pb dating, that the analytical results and the derived "ages" are pristine and, therefore, represent the formation ages of the rocks. After all, apparent "ages" vary significantly within crystals at sub-microscopic scales, on different crystal faces, and at different crystal orientations. These effects must all combine to make U-Th-Pb "dating" of whole mineral grains and zones within them highly questionable, given that it is not always clear apart from outside assumptions as to what the "dates" really mean.

In any case, a consistent systematic pattern of discordant U-Th-Pb "ages" obtained from different minerals was recognized early in the history of this method.[32] In uraninite (the primary U ore mineral), zircon, monazite, and titanite, the Th "ages" were consistently younger than the ^{238}U "ages," which were consistently younger than the ^{235}U "ages," a pattern also obtained on five uraninite samples from the Koongarra uranium deposit of the Northern Territory of Australia.[33] The reason for this consistent pattern has apparently never been determined, but it may be related to the rate of decay of the parent radioisotopes, Th having the slowest rate of decay (largest half-life), and ^{235}U the fastest rate of decay (shortest half-life).

Pb-Pb Isotope "Dating," Inheritance and Mixing

Even though the U-Pb isochron method for dating of whole rocks has been discredited, the Pb-Pb isochron method continues to be used. Both parent U

30   J. L. Crowley and E. D. Ghent, 1999, An electron microprobe study of the U-Th-Pb systematics of metamorphosed monazite: The role of Pb diffusion verses overgrowth and recrystallization, *Chemical Geology*, 157: 285-302.

31   R. R. Parrish, 1990, U-Pb dating of monazite and its applications to geological problems, *Canadian Journal of Earth Sciences*, 27: 1431-1450.

32   J. L. Kulp and W. R. Eckelmann, 1957, Discordant U-Pb ages and mineral type, *American Mineralogist*, 42: 154-164.

33   J. H. Hills and J. R. Richards, 1976, Pitchblende and galena ages in the Alligator Rivers Region, Northern Territory, Australia, *Mineralium Deposita*, 11: 133-154.

radioisotopes appear to be always present in the same constant ratio, and both they and their respective Pb isotope end members show coherent chemical behavior. Thus, it is argued, if a group of rock samples all have the same age and initial whole-rock Pb isotopic composition, then they will have developed, with time, different present-day, whole-rock Pb isotopic compositions according to their respective present-day U-Pb ratios.[34] Provided they have remained closed systems, the present-day whole-rock Pb isotopic compositions of a suite of rock samples should plot as an isochron line that yields an "age" for the rock unit sampled. As long as the U-Pb system has remained closed since the rock unit formed, it is claimed that even under present weathering conditions, in which U is known to be highly mobile, the Pb isotope ratios in the rock unit will not have been perturbed, and thus should still yield its formation "age."[35]

The first application of the whole-rock Pb-Pb dating technique was actually on meteorites. A Pb-Pb isochron "age" of 4.55±0.07 billion years was obtained from a suite of three stony meteorites and two iron meteorites, which was interpreted as the age of the earth.[36] Thus, this Pb-Pb isochron became known as the geochron. One of the minerals in one of the iron meteorites had such a low Pb isotopic composition, that it was concluded that no observable change in Pb isotopic composition could have resulted from radioactive decay since that meteorite formed; therefore, this must represent the "primordial" Pb isotope composition of the earth and the solar system.

Now Pb is widely distributed throughout the earth, not only as the radioactive decay daughter of U and Th, but also in minerals from which U and Th have been excluded. Therefore, the isotopic composition of Pb varies between wide limits, being a record of the chemical environments in which the Pb has resided. Because U/Pb and Th/Pb ratios are changed by the generation of magmas, by hydrothermal and metamorphic processes, and by weathering, the Pb isotopic composition in samples of a particular rock unit may have been modified both by decay of U and Th, and by mixing with Pb having different isotopic compositions. As a result, the isotopic compositions of Pb in rocks display complex patterns of variation that supposedly reflect their particular geologic histories. Consequently, various attempts have been made to construct graphical models of how Pb isotopic compositions of Pb ore minerals have changed and developed in the earth over the claimed geologic timescale.[37] Such models start with a "primordial" Pb isotopic

---

34   Dickin, 2005.

35   J. N. Rosholt and A. J. Bartel, 1969, Uranium, thorium and lead systematics in Granite Mountains, Wyoming, *Earth and Planetary Science Letters*, 7: 14-17.

36   C. C. Patterson, 1956, Age of meteorites and the earth, *Geochimica et Cosmochimica Acta*, 10: 230-237.

37   A. Holmes, 1946, An estimate of the age of the earth, *Nature*, 157: 680-684; F. G. Houtermans, 1946, Die isotopen-haufigkeiten im naturlishen blei und das Aalter des urans, *Naturwissenschaften*, 33: 185-187; V. M. Oversby, 1974, A new look at the lead isotope growth curve, *Nature*, 248: 132-133; G. L. Cumming and J. R. Richards, 1975, Ore lead isotope ratios in a continuously changing earth, *Earth and Planetary Science Letters*, 28: 155-171.

composition within the earth's mantle equivalent to that in the mineral from the iron meteorite, which is then added to by the decay of U and Th over geologic time. At different times through the earth's history, magmas with particular Pb isotopic compositions have been extracted from the mantle to build the earth's crust, while there has probably been circulation of material in the mantle, including recycling of portions of the crust.[38] It is therefore claimed that there are distinct Pb isotopic reservoirs within the earth's mantle and crust, but where they are actually located is not clear.

Isotopic analyses of historic and recent basalt lava flows on ocean islands, and on the mid-ocean ridges, have been used to demonstrate that the mantle sources from which the magmas came are not homogeneous.[39] When the Pb isotopic compositions of these basalts are plotted on a Pb-Pb "isochron" diagram, they define a series of different groups and linear arrays to the right of the "geochron," which is supposedly the isochron representing Pb isotopic compositions of zero "age" (Figure 64, page 1095). The slopes of these linear arrays correspond to apparent Pb-Pb isochron "ages" of between 1 and 1.5 billion years for what are only recent lava flows! Apparent heterogeneity of the upper mantle, the source of these lavas, is a worldwide phenomenon and Pb-Pb isotopic linear arrays may be interpreted in three principal ways: as resulting from discrete magma-forming events in the mantle, as products of two-component mixing processes, or resulting from continuous development of reservoirs with changing U-Pb ratios.[40] What is clear is that whole-rock Pb-Pb "dating" of these recent basalt lavas produces anomalously old "ages," which represent inheritance of Pb isotopic compositions from the mantle source areas of the magmas. Thus far, five end-member reservoirs with discrete isotopic compositions have been delineated in the mantle, and three in the continental crust, with a variety of mixing processes regarded as capable of explaining all observed rock isotopic compositions.[41]

The Pb isotopic compositions of volcanic rocks on the continents also form linear arrays, and have also been interpreted as mixtures derived from the crust and mantle. For example, the volcanic and intrusive rocks on the Isle of Skye of northwest Scotland plot on a Pb-Pb isotope diagram along a strong linear

38   G. R. Doe and R. E. Zartman, 1979, Plumbotectonics, in *Geochemistry of Hydrothermal Ore Deposits*, second edition, H.L. Barnes, ed., New York: John Wiley & Sons, 22-70.

39   B. W. Gast, G. R. Tilton and C. Hedge, 1964, Isotopic composition of lead and strontium from Ascension and Gough Islands, *Science*, 145: 1181-1885.; M. Tatsumoto, 1966, Genetic relations of oceanic basalts as indicated by lead isotopes, *Science*, 153: 1094-1101; S. S. Sun, 1980, Lead isotopic study of young volcanic rocks from mid-ocean ridges, ocean islands and island arcs, *Philosophical Transactions of the Royal Society of London*, A297: 409-445.

40   Dickin, 2005.

41   E. N. Taylor, N. W. Jones and S. Moorbath, 1984, Isotopic assessment of relative contributions from crust and mantle sources to magma genesis of Precambrian granitoid rocks, *Philosophical Transactions of the Royal Society of London*, A310: 605-625; A. Zindler and S. R. Hart, 1986, Chemical geodynamics, *Annual Review of Earth and Planetary Sciences*, 14: 493-571.

array that represents an apparent isochron "age" of approximately 3 billion years.[42] However, because these are relatively recent lavas and granites, this linear array is interpreted as a mixing line between mantle-derived Pb and ancient crustal Pb.[43] This is why an important word of caution has been given: "Not all linear arrays on the Pb-Pb diagram are isochrons."[44] This is because linear correlations of Pb isotopic ratios can also result from the mixing of Pb of different isotopic compositions in varying proportions, resulting in false apparent isochrons.

An extreme example of a false isochron achieved by mixing Pb of different isotopic compositions graphically illustrates the pitfalls in whole-rock Pb-Pb isochron dating. The Pb-Pb isochron "ages" of the uranium ore minerals containing Pb at Koongarra in the Northern Territory, Australia, are nearly identical as evident by the clear relationship between them.[45] Subsequent to its formation, the uranium ore has been exposed to weathering, so that U has been dispersed in the weathered rock zone and soils downslope in the direction of groundwater flow.[46] Yet all 113 soil samples, collected from near the uranium ore, from the immediate surrounding areas, and from as far afield as 17 kilometers away, plotted as a near perfect line on a Pb-Pb isotopic diagram, equivalent to an apparent isochron with an "age" of 1,445 million years (Figure 65, page 1095).[47]

It has to be concluded, therefore, that U-Th-Pb "dating" involves many pitfalls, which are really only surmounted by making further assumptions, and by dependence on uncertain cross-checks. Both U and Pb mobility undermine whole-rock "dating," and Pb migration within, and loss from, individual mineral grains is so prevalent that interpreting the resultant isotopic data is largely dependent upon the bias of the investigators to produce the desired outcomes. In this way an entire edifice has been built that looks impregnable and internally consistent. However, fundamental problems remain. Modern basalt lavas reveal inconsistent Pb isotopic heterogeneities in their mantle sources, even from successive flows on the same ocean island, which yield vastly erroneous old "ages," and which are totally at variance with all models of Pb isotopic "evolution." Isotope inheritance,

42   S. Moorbath and H. Welke, 1969, Lead isotope studies of rocks from the Isle of Skye, northwest Scotland, *Earth and Planetary Science Letters*, 5: 217-230.

43   R. N. Thompson, 1982, Magmatism of the British Tertiary Volcanic Province, *Scottish Journal of Geology*, 18: 49-107.

44   G. Faure, 1986, *Principles of Isotope Geology*, second edition, New York: John Wiley & Sons, 327.

45   Hills and Richards, 1976.

46   A. A. Snelling, 1984, A soil geochemistry orientation survey for uranium at Koongarra, Northern Territory, *Journal of Geochemical Exploration*, 22: 83-99; A. A. Snelling, 1990, Koongarra uranium deposits, in *Geology of the Mineral Deposits of Australia and Papua New Guinea*, F. E. Hughes, ed., Melbourne, Australia: The Australasian Institute of Mining and Metallurgy, 807-812.

47   B. L. Dickson, B. L. Gulson and A. A. Snelling, 1985, Evaluation of lead isotopic methods for uranium exploration, Koongarra area, Northern Territory, Australia, *Journal of Geochemical Exploration*, 24: 81-102; B. L. Dickson, B. L. Gulson and A. A. Snelling, 1987, Further assessment of stable lead isotope measurements for uranium exploration, Pine Creek Geosyncline, Northern Territory, Australia, *Journal of Geochemical Exploration*, 27: 63-75.

migration, and mixing in the U-Th-Pb system are prevalent chronic problems at all observational scales. What is known of patterns in U-Th-Pb "ages" hints at some underlying fundamental, non-time-dependent process that would render all "age" interpretations invalid. Clearly, even though the constructed "age" system edifice looks internally consistent, the individual "dating" results within it are nevertheless questionable, and the foundations it is built on appear to be systematically in error.

104

THE PITFALLS IN THE RADIOACTIVE DATING METHODS—SUNDRY METHODS AND REVEALING CONSIDERATIONS

The Lutetium-Hafnium and Rhenium-Osmium Radioisotope Dating Methods

These two radioisotope dating methods are somewhat specialized, because the elements involved are only present in trace amounts in most rocks and minerals. However, hafnium (Hf) is virtually identical in the size of its atom and electric charge with zirconium (Zr), so it occurs in Zr-bearing minerals, most notably zircon. Because both Lu (lutetium) and Hf are dispersed elements, they do not form their own minerals. On the other hand, rhenium (Re) has similar chemical properties to molybdenum (Mo), which it replaces in molybdenite (MoS_2) and other Mo-bearing sulfide minerals. Similarly, Re tends to occur in copper sulfide minerals, as Re tends to be captured in place of Cu. Furthermore, on rare occasions, osmium is found as a metallic alloy with iridium (Ir) (osmiridium), both being related to platinum. Both methods have been used to "date" meteorites. The Re-Os method has been particularly "successful," especially for the iron meteorites because of their high contents of these metallic elements.

Not only are both methods utilized to obtain whole-rock and mineral isochron "ages" for rocks and meteorites using the appropriate radioisotope ratios, but both methods are also used to derive "model ages" for minerals. However, to obtain "model ages" in both methods, it has to be assumed that the primordial endowment of these radioisotopes in the earth's mantle was equivalent to the initial Hf and Os radioisotope ratios determined from meteorite isochrons. It has to also be assumed that meteorite isochrons have determined the age of the earth as 4.55 billion years, and that from those initial Hf and Os radioisotope ratios, the mantle reservoir of these isotopes has developed in a predictable manner, based on the present-day measurements of the radioactive decay rates of the parent Lu and Re isotopes, respectively. In the case of the development of the Os isotopes in the mantle reservoir, a cross-check is evidently provided by Os isotope ratios determined on Os-bearing alloys and minerals of supposedly known age, independently determined by the other radioisotope dating methods.

Both these radioisotope dating methods have primarily been used on ancient (Precambrian) rocks and minerals, because of the very slow decay rates of the parent isotopes as measured today. However, both the isochron and "model age" Re-Os methods have been applied with apparent success to the "dating" of sulfide and other ore deposits and/or minerals. Nevertheless, the viability of these radioisotope dating methods is very much dependent on the accuracy with which the present decay rates of the parent isotopes have been determined. However, these are also very much dependent on assumptions about the age of the earth, the earth's relationship to the meteorites, and the reliability of the independent radioisotope "dating" of the meteorites used to determine the decay rates of the Lu and Re parent isotopes. Furthermore, the reproducibility of the Lu and Hf measurements is not always as good as expected based on analytical errors alone, because of the inhomogeneous distribution of Lu and Hf in various rocks, due to the uneven distribution of the accessory minerals in which these trace elements reside.[1] In addition, accessory minerals are sensitive to alteration during metamorphism, and some, such as zircon, may contain detrital cores that may have acquired overgrowths during metamorphism. On the other hand, in many cases the Os in molybdenites consist almost entirely of radiogenic Os, such that their Re and Os isotopic ratios have large values approaching infinity, and, therefore, are difficult to measure accurately. Furthermore, such ore minerals are often formed during an episode of hydrothermal activity later than the rocks hosting them, and/ or radiogenic Os can be lost during subsequent regional metamorphism. Thus, similar to the principal radioisotope methods, these two specialized radioisotope "dating" methods are also plagued with assumptions about initial conditions, and with open-system behavior. Therefore, the "dates" obtained by them often only make sense in the context of the "ages" obtained on the relevant rocks by the other radioisotope "dating" methods.

How Much Radioactive Decay Has Actually Occurred?

These radioisotope "dating" methods for rocks and minerals are based on analyses of the radioactive parent and radiogenic daughter isotope pairs. The calculation of "ages" from those isotope analyses depends on crucial assumptions, particularly that the daughter isotopes have been derived by radioactive decay of the parent isotopes. If this assumption was shown to be false, that so much radioactive decay has not occurred, then it could be argued that the measured daughter isotopes are merely an artifact of the mineral compositions, and of the geochemistry of the rocks and the sources from which they were derived.

So do we have physical evidence that radioactive decay has actually occurred? Yes, there are several evidences of this:

1. The presence of daughter isotopes such as lead and helium present with the

---

1   Faure and Tensing, 2005.

parent isotopes of uranium in the right proportions to have been derived by radioactive decay;

2. The observable physical scars left by the alpha (α)-particles during radioactive decay as radiohalos; and

3. The observable physical scars left by the nuclear decay of uranium atoms as they split or fission, which are known as fission tracks.

It has been estimated that from 500 million to 1 billion α-particles from uranium decay are required to form a dark uranium radiohalo, which equates to at least 100 millions years worth of decay at today's measured rates.[2] Such uranium radiohalos are ubiquitous in granites at most relative time levels in the geologic record, suggesting that hundreds of millions of years worth (at today's rates) of radioactive decay has occurred through earth history.[3] This is confirmed by the physically observed quantities of fission tracks, which equate to hundreds of millions of years of such nuclear decay measured at today's rates being equivalent to the radioisotope "ages" for the same rock units.[4] Therefore, it must be concluded that hundreds of millions of years worth of radioactive and nuclear decay must have occurred during the accumulation of the geologic record.

Furthermore, because the quantities of fission tracks often match the radioisotope "ages" for rock units, it is likely that the radioisotope ratios measured in the rock units to derive the respective radioisotope "ages" do often equate to those quantities of radioisotope decay (at today's measured rates) having physically occurred. Thus, the inescapable conclusion is that the radioisotope ratios in many rock units have resulted from hundreds of millions of years, and even billions of years, of radioactive decay (at today's measured rates), so they are not merely an artifact of mineral compositions, and of the geochemistry of the rocks and the sources from which they were derived. These latter factors have played a role, as already repeatedly documented, but radioactive decay has been the dominant producer of the measured daughter isotopes alongside their parent radioisotopes.

Do Radioisotope "Ages" Match the Claimed Stratigraphic "Ages"?

Geologists had assigned stratigraphic "ages" to rock units by various means before the advent of the radioisotope "dating" methods. This included the fossil contents

---

2   R. V. Gentry, 1988, *Creation's Tiny Mystery*, Knoxville, TN: Earth Science Associates.

3   A. A. Snelling, 2005, Radiohalos in granites: evidence for accelerated nuclear decay, in *Radioisotopes and the Age of the Earth: Results of a Young-Earth Creationist Research Initiative*, L. Vardiman, A. A. Snelling and E. F. Chaffin, eds., El Cajon, CA: Institute for Creation Research and Chino Valley, AZ: Creation Research Society, 101-207.

4   A. A. Snelling, 2005, Fission tracks in zircons: evidence for abundant nuclear decay, in *Radioisotopes and the Age of the Earth: Results of a Young-Earth Creationist Research Initiative*, L. Vardiman, A. A. Snelling and E. F. Chaffin, eds., El Cajon, CA: Institute for Creation Research and Chino Valley, AZ: Creation Research Society, 209-324.

of the rock units, which also enabled their correlation beyond where they could be physically traced. Assumptions were made about the rates of the geological processes responsible for accumulation and formation of the rock units, and for the evolutionary development of the organisms that became their contained fossils. By the time the radioisotope "dating" methods had been developed, the geological timescale had already been imposed on the globally-correlated rock sequence.

With the advent of radioisotope "dating," the "ages" assigned to various rock units have often only been refined. Often the fossil-bearing sedimentary strata cannot be directly "dated" by use of the radioisotope methods, unless they contain a "datable" mineral that only formed at the time the sediments were being deposited and compacted. Instead, the focus has been on the radioisotope "dating" of volcanic rock units interbedded in strata sequences above and below fossil-bearing rock layers. In this way, the stratigraphic "ages" of strata have been adjusted to conform with the timescale generated by the application of the radioisotope "dating" methods to the rock strata. Thus, there is now a direct correlation between the radioisotope "ages" of strata and their stratigraphic "ages," because the latter have been made to conform to the former by the application of the radioisotope methods to the "dating" of the strata sequences.

Do "Ages" Determined by the Different Radioisotope "Dating" Methods Agree?

Any reading of geology textbooks gives the impression that the "ages" derived by the different radioisotope "dating" methods applied to the same rocks are generally always in agreement. Sometimes this is specifically stated. Even in textbooks on the radioisotope "dating" methods, though numerous problems with them are discussed, the underlying message clearly evident is that the "ages" obtained by the different methods are normally in agreement. But is this really the case?

Upon detailed investigation of the relevant geological literature, it is discovered that rarely, if ever, have all the major radioisotope "dating" methods been applied to the same samples from the same rock units. More often than not, only one of the methods is used, though sometimes two of the methods are applied to the same samples from the same rock unit. In fairness, several factors have been at work. First, at the time a rock unit has been "dated," only the radioisotope method or methods currently available and/or in vogue were utilized. Second, depending on the nature of the rock unit and its expected "age," the choice would have been made as to which of the radioisotope methods was best suited to the "dating" of it. This was not unreasonable. Because of the different minerals present in different rocks, some radioisotope methods are better suited to "dating" those rocks and their constituent minerals. Furthermore, because the different parent isotopes have different half-lives (that is, decay rates), as measured today, those parent isotopes with the slowest decay rates are not necessarily suited to rock units with expected young "ages." This is because there wouldn't have been sufficient time for enough daughter isotopes to have accumulated, in order to provide an accurate measure of the supposed elapsed time. In any case, given the expectation that the different radioisotope "dating" methods should by definition yield the same "ages" on the same rock units, it is hardly surprising that if "dating" the rock unit with the chosen radioisotope method yields the expected "age," then it would be deemed unnecessary to commit further time and resources to "dating" the same rocks with the other radioisotope methods.

Nevertheless, invariably where two or more of the radioisotope "dating" methods have been applied to the same rock unit, different "ages" have often been obtained. Where this has been reported in the scientific literature, the different radioisotope "ages" on the same rock unit are usually the outcome of different studies completed by different investigators on different samples and/or minerals. Nevertheless, there have been reported studies where two or more of the radioisotope dating methods have been applied to the same samples and have yielded different "ages." However, in all these instances, the explanation given for these different radioisotope "ages" for the same rock unit invariably is that there has been some geochemical process or geological event that has perturbed one or more of the radioisotope systems, and not the other or others. The most frequently used explanation is hydrothermal fluids and alteration, even where there is no other evidence, either geochemical or mineralogical, for such having occurred. Otherwise, it may be legitimate to invoke varying closure temperatures for the different radioisotope systems in different minerals as the explanation for different radioisotope "ages" in those minerals. But this cannot be the case with different whole-rock radioisotope "ages" on the same samples.

Some examples illustrate the above observations. Different radioisotope "ages" were obtained on the Stuart Dyke swarm of south-central Australia, and the Uruguayan Dike swarm in Uruguay. The Stuart Dyke swarm yielded a Sm-Nd mineral "isochron age" of 1,076±33 million years, and a Rb-Sr mineral "isochron age" of 897±9 million years.[5] Similarly, the Uruguayan Dike swarm yielded a Rb-Sr "isochron age" for 15 whole rocks of 1,766±124 million years, and a Rb-Sr mineral "isochron age" of 1,366±18 million years.[6] In neither of these cases is a satisfactory and feasible explanation given for these different radioisotope "ages" yielded by the same rock units.

In contrast, an "explanation" has been offered for different radioisotope "ages" yielded by the Great Dyke of Zimbabwe, a 550-km-long by 3 to 11-km-wide

5   J. Zhao and M. T. McCulloch, 1993, Sm-Nd mineral isochron ages of Late Proterozoic Dyke swarms in Australia: Evidence for two distinctive events of mafic magmatism and crustal extension, *Geochemical Geology*, 109: 341-354.

6   W. Teixeira, P. R. Renne, G. Bossie, N. Campal and M. S. D'Agrella Filho, 1999, ^{40}Ar-^{39}Ar and Rb-Sr geochronology of the Uruguayan Dike swarm, Rio de la Plata Craton and implications for Proterozoic intraplate activity in western Gondwana, *Precambrian Research*, 93: 153-180.

intrusion in southeast Africa. A Rb-Sr whole-rock "isochron age" (eight samples) for the Great Dyke of 2,477±90 million years[7] was subsequently reconfirmed very precisely with a Rb-Sr whole-rock and mineral "isochron age" (five whole rocks and four minerals) of 2,455±16 million years.[8] Both of these radioisotope "ages" were again subsequently reconfirmed. Eleven samples from a single drill-hole into the dyke yielded an Rb-Sr whole-rock and mineral "isochron age" of 2,467±85 million years.[9] Yet even though these independently determined Rb-Sr "ages" on different samples are identical, within the stated error margins, and had been widely accepted, recent radioisotope data supposedly indicate this intrusion is about 120 million years older. The same study that used drill-hole samples and reported a Rb-Sr "isochron age" of 2,467±85 million years, also reported an Sm-Nd whole-rock "isochron age" of 2,586±16 million years, a Pb-Pb mineral and whole-rock "isochron age" of 2,596±14 million years, and a U-Pb "concordia age" using the mineral rutile of 2,587±8 million years. These radioisotope "ages" determined by three different methods are clearly identical within the stated error margins, and were subsequently confirmed by another study that reported identical U-Pb "concordia ages" using the mineral zircon.[10] Thus, even though three independent studies had all yielded an identical Rb-Sr "age" for this intrusion, it was rejected in favor of the older, identical radioisotope "age" obtained by the Sm-Nd, Pb-Pb and U-Pb methods. The reason given for rejecting the younger Rb-Sr "age" was that hydrothermal alteration must have reset the Rb-Sr system, in spite of the fact that there is no observational evidence, or any other geochemical indicators, of such hydrothermal alteration!

However, recent studies have been undertaken in which the same rock and mineral samples from the same rock units were "dated" using all four of the main radioisotope methods. Four rock units in the Grand Canyon of northern Arizona were targeted. The diabase sill at Bass Rapids, deep in the central Grand Canyon area, was considered ideal for radioisotope "dating," because it formed as molten magma that was homogenized when it was injected between the host sedimentary strata. Furthermore, after its intrusion, while it was cooling, some separation of the crystallizing minerals occurred, producing a compositional variation from top to bottom within the sill. Such compositional variation in an originally homogenous rock unit is ideal for the isochron method of radioisotope "dating." Eleven whole-rock samples yielded a K-Ar "isochron age" of 841.5±164 million

7   R. D. Davies, H. L. Allsopp, A. Erlank and J. W. I. Manton, 1970, Sr isotopic studies of various layered mafic intrusions in Southern Africa, in *Symposium on the Bushveld Igneous Complex and Other Layered Intrusions*, Geological Society of South Africa, Special Publication 1, 576-593.

8   J. Hamilton, 1977, Sr isotope and trace element studies of the Great Dyke and Bushveld mafic phase and their relation to early Proterozoic magma genesis in southern Africa, *Journal of Petrology*, 18: 24-52.

9   S. B. Mukasa, A. H. Wilson and R. W. Carlson, 1998, A multielement geochronologic study of the Great Dyke, Zimbabwe: the significance of the robust and reset ages, *Earth and Planetary Science Letters*, 164: 353-369.

10   T. Oberthür, B. W. Davis, T. G. Blenkinsop and A. Höhndorf, 2002, Precise U-Pb mineral ages, Rb-Sr and Sm-Nd systematics for the Great Dike, Zimbabwe – constraints on Late Archean events in the Zimbabwe craton and Limpopo belt, *Precambrian Research*, 113: 293-305.

years, a Rb-Sr "isochron age" of 1,055±46 million years, and a Pb-Pb "isochron age" of 1,250±130 million years. Additionally, the minerals separated from one diabase sample yielded a Rb-Sr mineral "isochron age" of 1,060±24 million years, and a Sm-Nd mineral "isochron age" of 1,379±140 million years.[11] Even though there is overlap between the error margins of some of these "ages" (Figure 66, page 1096), the "ages" themselves are sufficiently different for each radioisotope system. Furthermore, it is evident from this diagram (Figure 66) that the parent isotopes that α-decay yielded older "ages" compared to the parent isotopes that β-decay.

Three other major rock units in Grand Canyon have similarly been "dated" by these same four radioisotope methods applied to the same rock samples. The Cardenas Basalt consists of a group of about twelve lava flows, approximately halfway up the middle-upper Precambrian sequence of sedimentary strata in the eastern Grand Canyon.[12] The lower six lava flows are believed to be related to six diabase sills in the central Grand Canyon, including the Bass Rapids diabase sill. Yet the Cardenas Basalt flows yielded a potassium-argon "isochron age" of only 516±30 million years, which is less than half the rubidium-strontium "isochron age" of 1,111±81 million years, while the samarium-neodymium "isochron age" of 1,588±170 million years is more than three times the potassium-argon "isochron age"! The marked disagreement between these three "ages" can clearly be seen in Figure 67 (page 1096). Again, the α-decaying parent, samarium, gave an older age than the β-decaying parents, rubidium and potassium. Also, among the β-decayers, the parent rubidium with the longer half-life has the older "age."

The next rock unit studied in the Grand Canyon was metamorphosed basalt lava flows called the Brahma amphibolites, deep in the crystalline basement exposed in the Upper Granite Gorge. Twenty-seven samples yielded potassium-argon "model ages" ranging from 405.1±10 to 2,574.2±73 million years.[13] Even worse

11   A. A. Snelling, S. A. Austin and W. A. Hoesch, 2003, Radioisotopes in the diabase sill (upper Precambrian) at Bass Rapids, Grand Canyon, Arizona: An application and test of the isochron dating method, in *Proceedings of the Fifth International Conference on Creationism*, R. L. Ivey, Jr., ed., Pittsburgh, PA: Creation Science Fellowship, 269-284; S. A. Austin, 2005, Do radioisotope clocks need repair? Testing the assumptions of isochron dating using K-Ar, Rb-Sr, Sm-Nd, and Pb-Pb isotopes, in *Radioisotopes and the Age of the Earth: Results of a Young-Earth Creationist Research Initiative*, L. Vardiman, A. A. Snelling and E. F. Chaffin, eds., El Cajon, CA: Institute for Creation Research and Chino Valley, AZ: Creation Research Society, 325-392.

12   S. A. Austin and A. A. Snelling, 1998, Discordant potassium-argon model and isochron 'ages' for Cardenas Basalt (Middle Proterozoic) and associated diabase of eastern Grand Canyon, Arizona, in *Proceedings of the Fourth International Conference on Creationism*, R. E. Walsh, ed., Pittsburgh, PA: Creation Science Fellowship, 35-51; A. A. Snelling, 2005, Isochron discordances and the role of inheritance and mixing of radioisotopes in the mantle and crust, *Radioisotopes and the Age of the Earth: Results of a Young-Earth Creationist Research Initiative*, L. Vardiman, A. A. Snelling and E. F. Chaffin, eds., El Cajon, CA: Institute for Creation Research and Chino Valley, AZ: Creation Research Society, 393-524.

13   A. A. Snelling, 2005, Isochron discordances and the role of inheritance and mixing of radioisotopes in the mantle and crust, 393-524; A. A. Snelling, 2008, Significance of highly discordant radioisotope dates for Precambrian amphibolites in Grand Canyon, USA, in *Proceedings of the Sixth International Conference on Creationism*, A. A. Snelling, ed., Pittsburgh, PA: Creation Science Fellowship and Dallas, TX: Institute for Creation Research, 407-424.

were two samples collected only 0.84 meters apart from the same outcrop. They yielded potassium-argon "model ages" of 1,205.3±31 and 2,574.2±73 million years. Otherwise, these samples yielded a rubidium-strontium "isochron age" of 1,240±84 million years, a samarium-neodymium "isochron age" of 1,655±40 million years, and a lead-lead "isochron age" of 1,883±53 million years. It can be clearly seen in Figure 68 (page 1097) that there is no overlap in these "ages." Again, the α-decayers give older "ages" than the β-decayer, but the longer half-life, α-decaying samarium, did not give an older "age" than the shorter half-life, α-decaying uranium.

The other Grand Canyon rock unit tested was the Elves Chasm Granodiorite, also in the crystalline basement of the Upper Granite Gorge, and regarded as the oldest rock unit in Grand Canyon. Samples of it yielded a rubidium-strontium "isochron age" of 1,512±140 million years, a samarium-neodymium "isochron age" of 1,664±200 million years, and a lead-lead "isochron age" of 1,993±220 million years. Even though there is obvious overlap in these "ages," there is the same pattern in the differences between them as found in the Brahma amphibolites.

These four Grand Canyon rock units consistently yield different "ages" on the same samples via the four radioisotope "dating" methods, totally destroying the common popular conception reinforced by textbooks that these four different methods give the same ages for the same rock units. Furthermore, it is obvious that the different "ages" for each rock unit are not random, but consistently follow several systematic patterns. Indeed, for any one of these rock units, the α-decaying parent isotopes (U and Sm) always yield older "ages" than the β-decaying parent isotopes (K and Rb). Furthermore, among the β-decayers, the parent isotope with the longer half-life (Rb) always gives the older "ages." In contrast, the α-decayers don't always follow this half-life versus "age" trend. Alternately, another potential systematic relationship can be seen in the "isochron age" versus atomic weight plot in Figure 69 (page 1097). The approximate trend line is consistent with the shorter half-life and heavier, α-decaying uranium yielding older "ages" than the longer half-life and lighter, α-decaying samarium.

These examples should be sufficient to conclusively demonstrate the unreliability of the radioisotope methods for "dating" rocks. Nevertheless, one further example, again from the Grand Canyon, should surely suffice. Across the Uinkaret Plateau, on the north rim of the western Grand Canyon, are up to 160 volcanic cones from which basalt lavas have flowed, and most of them poured southward into the inner gorge of Grand Canyon. Thus, these basalt lavas are so recent that, having erupted after the Grand Canyon had been eroded into its present form, they cascaded down the north wall of the Grand Canyon and formed dams that temporarily filled the inner gorge of Grand Canyon to different heights, blocking the flow of the Colorado River. Today only erosion remnants remain. These basalt

Conference on Creationism, A. A. Snelling, ed., Pittsburgh, PA: Creation Science Fellowship and Dallas, TX: Institute for Creation Research, 407-424.

lavas, therefore, yield various potassium-argon "model ages" of around 0.5-1.0 million years.

However, the same basalt lavas yield a rubidium-strontium "isochron age" of 1,143±220 million years! Such an "age" is virtually identical with the rubidium-strontium "isochron ages" of 1,111±81 million years and 1,060±24 million years for the Cardenas Basalt and Bass Rapids diabase sill, respectively. In other words, the youngest basalt lavas in Grand Canyon, so recent that they flowed down the walls of the Canyon after it formed, yield the same rubidium-strontium "isochron age" as some of the oldest rocks in the Canyon, the Cardenas Basalt lavas and the Bass Rapids diabase sill. Because all these rocks cooled from basaltic magmas that were sourced in the mantle underneath the Grand Canyon region, the recent Uinkaret Plateau basalts must have inherited their rubidium-strontium "isochron age" from their mantle source. Thus, it can be argued that the rubidium-strontium isotopic compositions of all these magmas being the same must be a reflection of the isotopic geochemistry of the mantle just below the Grand Canyon region, and, therefore, have little to do with the true ages of these rocks. All these contradictions and disagreements between the "ages" derived from these different radioisotope methods render these methods both unreliable and highly questionable.

105

THE PITFALLS IN THE RADIOACTIVE DATING METHODS—VARIATIONS IN RADIOACTIVE DECAY RATES AND "APPARENT AGE"

Because there appears to be systematic trends in the radiometric "ages" derived by the four commonly-used radioisotope systems, there would appear to be some underlying process responsible. One suggested way of reconciling these systematically different radioisotope "ages" on the same rocks is accepting that the decay of the different parent radioisotopes occurred at much different and faster rates during some event or events in the past.[1] In other words, the radioactive decay of the different radioisotope parents was accelerated by different amounts according to their mode of decay, atomic weights and half-lives. As such, for example, the uranium-lead and samarium-neodymium α-decaying radioisotope systems would have had their decay rates accelerated more than the potassium-argon and rubidium-strontium β-decaying radioisotope systems, resulting in the former parent radioisotopes appearing to have decayed longer over the same time periods , and thus yielding older "ages" than the latter parent radioisotopes. Furthermore, among the β-decaying parent radioisotopes, rubidium always gives older "ages" than potassium. Thus, the radioactive decay of rubidium must have been accelerated more than potassium according to their respective half-lives, rubidium having a longer half-life than potassium. On the other hand, the patterns of "ages" yielded by the α-decaying parent uranium and samarium radioisotopes are not consistent. Sometimes uranium-lead "ages" are older than the samarium-neodymium "ages," perhaps due to the heavier atomic weight of the parent uranium radioisotopes. In other instances the samarium-neodymium "ages" are older, probably due to the longer half-life of the parent samarium radioisotope. Furthermore, at other times the uranium-lead and samarium-neodymium radioisotope "ages" are virtually identical (e.g., in the case of the Great Dyke of Zimbabwe referred to above), so perhaps in these instances the effects of the half-lives and atomic weights on the acceleration of the parent uranium and samarium radioisotopes are evenly balanced.

---

1   L. Vardiman, A. A. Snelling and E. F. Chaffin, eds., 2005, *Radioisotopes and the Age of the Earth: Results of a Young-Earth Creationist Research Initiative*, El Cajon, CA: Institute for Creation Research and Chino Valley, AZ: Creation Research Society.

These systematic differences between radioisotope "ages" determined on the same rocks are not the only evidence for this suggested accelerated radioactive decay of parent radioisotopes during some event or events in the past. Furthermore, these other evidences provide some quantification of how much the radioactive decay has been accelerated. These evidences include:

1. Young (6,000 years) helium diffusion ages of zircons in a granite that yield zircon uranium-lead radioisotope "ages" of 1,500 million years;[2]

2. The concurrent formation of ubiquitous uranium and polonium radiohalos found together in biotite mica flakes in many granites around the world;[3]

3. The resetting of the uranium-lead radioisotope system by the intense heat generated by radioactive decay only within zircons within volcanic ash beds that were otherwise relatively unheated;[4] and

4. The consistent presence of measurable radiocarbon yielding young (<60,000 years) "ages" in coal and diamonds, that are supposed to be millions and billions of years old, respectively, based on radioisotope "dating."[5]

The fact that these many lines of evidence all confirm the possibility that accelerated radioisotope decay occurred during some event or events in the past certainly makes this suggestion a very strong explanation for these documented systematic differences between the different radioisotope "ages" on the same rocks. The helium diffusion ages of zircons in the granite studied are based on reproducible laboratory measurements of the physical process of helium diffusion in zircon, which occurs in accordance with a known physical law. Thus, the young ages for these zircons derived by that physical process are far more reliable than the uranium-lead radioisotope "age" for the same zircons. Indeed, to reconcile the two different age determinations on these zircons would require the zircons to have been at a temperature of -78°C, slowing the helium diffusion sufficiently to also yield helium diffusion ages of 1,500 million years. Thus, the logical conclusion is that 1,500 million years worth (at today's measured radioactive decay rate) of decay of the parent uranium radioisotopes in the zircons occurred during an event or events only 6,000 years ago!

---

2   D. R. Humphreys, 2005, Young helium diffusion age of zircons supports accelerated nuclear decay, in *Radioisotopes and the Age of the Earth: Results of a Young-Earth Creationist Research Initiative*, L. Vardiman, A. A. Snelling and E. F. Chaffin, eds., El Cajon, CA: Institute for Creation Research and Chino Valley, AZ: Creation Research Society, 25-100.

3   Snelling, 2005, Radiohalos in granites, 101-207.

4   Snelling, 2005, Fission tracks in zircons, 209-324.

5   J. R. Baumgardner, 2005, ^{14}C evidence for a recent global Flood and young earth, in *Radioisotopes and the Age of the Earth: Results of a Young-Earth Creationist Research Initiative*, L. Vardiman, A. A. Snelling and E. F. Chaffin, eds., El Cajon, CA: Institute for Creation Research and Chino Valley, AZ: Creation Research Society, 587-630.

As already noted, uranium radiohalos are a physical record of at least 100 million years worth of uranium decay (at today's measured rates). A by-product of such uranium decay is the daughter radioisotopes of polonium. It is therefore significant that ubiquitous polonium radiohalos are found alongside uranium radiohalos in the same biotite mica flakes in many granites around the world at all levels in the geologic record. The only nearby available source of polonium is the uranium decay that produced the neighboring uranium radiohalos. Therefore, the uranium and polonium radiohalos had to have formed concurrently, side-by-side at the same time, with the polonium having been transported by fluids moving along the cleavages between and within the biotite flakes from the uranium radiohalo sources to nearby polonium deposition sites.[6] However, these polonium radioisotopes have very short half-lives of 164 microseconds (^{214}Po), 3.1 minutes (^{218}Po), and 138 days (^{210}Po), thus, these polonium radiohalos had to have formed within minutes, hours, and days, respectively. Since 100 million years worth of uranium decay (at today's measured rates) had to have occurred to supply the polonium needed to form the polonium radiohalos, the 100 million years worth of uranium decay had to have occurred within days! Therefore, the uranium decay rate had to be accelerated by several orders of magnitude.

Measurable quantities of radiocarbon yielding "ages" of approximately 50,000 years for coal beds that are supposedly 300 million years old (based on radioisotope "dating" of adjacent strata) also confirms that hundreds of millions of years of radioisotope decay at today's measured rates must have occurred only thousands of years ago. Of course, radiocarbon decay would also have been accelerated, but because of its much shorter half-life (5,730 years) as a β-decayer, its decay rate would have barely been accelerated at all compared to the much longer half-lives of potassium (1.25 billion years) and rubidium (48.8 billion years).

These evidences together indicate how much accelerated radioisotope decay occurred and when. Coal beds were formed during the Flood year, approximately 4,500 years ago, as were many of the granites that contain uranium and polonium radiohalos, because the granites intruded into Flood-deposited strata. Thus, it is concluded that hundreds of millions of years worth of radioisotope decay (at today's measured rates) must have occurred during the Flood year, only about 4,500 years ago. Given that many other geologic processes were occurring at catastrophic rates during the Flood year (such as plate tectonics and sedimentation), it is not only reasonable but rather consistent that accelerated radioisotope decay was also occurring at the same time. The by-product of such decay is heat, which would be available to drive the catastrophic geologic processes during the Flood event. The fact that such heat was not excessive is evidenced by the survival of the radiohalos, which are obliterated if the rock temperatures rise above 150°C. Their survival indicates that the heat produced from the accelerated radioisotope decay was not sufficient to melt minerals and rocks.

---

6   Snelling, 2005, Radiohalos in granites.

However, Precambrian granite, containing the zircon grains that yielded helium diffusion ages of 6,000 years compared to uranium-lead radioisotope "ages" of 1,500 million years, would appear to have formed prior to the Flood event. Similarly, the diamonds containing measurable radiocarbon, that are otherwise regarded as billions of years old based on radioisotope "dating," would have formed early in the earth's history. Thus, it would appear that there could have been an earlier burst of accelerated radioisotope decay early in the earth's history, most likely during the first two and a half days of the Creation Week, from the initial creation of earth through the formation of dry land.[7]

It is made quite clear, by the careful use of the Hebrew verbs in the biblical account in Genesis chapter 1 describing the creation of all things, that after the initial creation of the earth out of nothing, God then shaped the earth, and organized it and its materials to progressively prepare the earth to be man's home. Thus, God would have creatively used accelerated geologic and other processes to form and shape the continental mass (or masses) that ultimately formed the dry land mid-way through Day Three of the Creation Week. This would have included the catastrophic formation of many different types of rocks that are now foundational to the earth's continental crust. This shows that accelerated radioisotope decay is completely consistent within the context of God's activities of building the continental crust in the early part of the Creation Week. Once again, the heat generated by this accelerated radioisotope decay would have helped to drive many geologic and other processes at catastrophic rates. Furthermore, given that the strata assigned to the Flood event appear to record 500 to 700 million years worth (at today's measured rates) of accelerated radioisotope decay, yet the earth's earliest rocks which are foundational to the continental crust yield radioisotope "ages" up to 4 billion years, it is thus likely that several billion years worth (at today's measured rates) of accelerated radioisotope decay must have occurred during this early part of the Creation Week.

These considerations, of course, then raise the question as to how, by what mechanism or mechanisms, this acceleration of radioisotope decay might have occurred. Consequently, several theoretical mechanisms have been suggested and supporting evidence for them discussed.[8] Indeed, the possibility of variations in

---

7   Vardiman et al, 2005.

8   D. R. Humphreys, 2000, Accelerated nuclear decay: A viable hypothesis? in *Radioisotopes and the Age of the Earth: A Young-Earth Creationist Research Initiative*, L. Vardiman, A. A. Snelling and E. F. Chaffin, eds., El Cajon, CA: Institute for Creation Research and St. Joseph, MO: Creation Research Society, 333-379; E. F. Chaffin, 2000, Mechanisms for accelerated radioactive decay, *Creation Research Society Quarterly*, 37: 3-9; E. F. Chaffin, 2000, Theoretical mechanisms of accelerated radioactive decay, in *Radioisotopes and the Age of the Earth: A Young-Earth Creationist Research Initiative*, L. Vardiman, A. A. Snelling and E. F. Chaffin, eds., El Cajon, CA: Institute for Creation Research and St. Joseph, MO: Creation Research Society, 305-331; E. F. Chaffin, 2003, Accelerated decay: Theoretical models, in *Proceedings of the Fifth International Conference on Creationism*, R. L. Ivey, Jr., ed., Pittsburgh, PA: Creation Science Fellowship, 3-15; E. F. Chaffin, 2005, Accelerated decay: Theoretical considerations, in *Radioisotopes and the Age of the Earth: Results of a Young Earth Creationist Research Initiative*, L. Vardiman, A. A. Snelling, and E. F. Chaffin, eds., El Cajon, CA: Institute for Creation Research and Chino Valley,

radioisotope decay rates, and mechanisms for their acceleration, were initially discussed more than four decades ago.[9] The technical details are of course complex, but it likely involved changes in the forces within the nuclei of atoms, forces that control how radioisotope decay occurs.

As already indicated, there are two primary modes of radioisotope decay. Both the parent uranium and samarium radioisotopes undergo α-decay, which involves the emission of two protons and two neutrons from the nuclei of these atoms. As they are emitted, these sub-atomic particles combine to form the nuclei of helium atoms, attracting stray electrons to produce helium as the final by-product. The parent rubidium radioisotope decays via β-decay, which involves the emission of an electron (a β-particle) and a neutrino from the nucleus. The parent potassium radioisotope also β-decays to calcium, but at the same time the nuclei of some of its atoms capture an orbital electron and form argon. Each of these processes is understood essentially as a statistical process, with the particular rate of decay being a probability function, related to the mode of decay and to the parent radioisotope concerned.

Each is known to be related to the structure of the atomic nucleus, and the various nuclear forces and particles. Yet, although there has been intensive experimental research in nuclear physics over many decades that has yielded an enormous amount of information about the various nuclear particles and reactions, most formulations that explain how and why the nucleus behaves as it does are still largely theoretical.

The α-decay process has been fairly well described in terms of wave mechanics and statistical probabilities. In this formulation, although the energy of the α-particle is apparently too small to permit it to escape through the "nuclear potential barrier" of energy surrounding the nucleus, nevertheless, it has a small probability of doing so. It is as if the α-particle is largely held within a potential energy "well" (hole), the depth, radius, and slope of the walls of which depend on the range or distance through which the α-particle can move within the nucleus. Of course, this is also related to the radius of the nucleus, which is directly proportional to the range of what is known as the strong nuclear force. Normally, an α-particle rebounds from the walls of this potential well, as it were, because it spends most of its life in the nucleus bouncing around within it, unable to escape because it doesn't have sufficient energy to do so. However, the so-called quantum fluctuations in the various energies and modes of the wave function of the α-particle allow it to do what classical mechanics completely prohibits, namely, to "tunnel" through the potential barrier and escape the nucleus entirely. Now the probability that a given α-particle will "tunnel" through the potential barrier and escape the nucleus, which determines the half-life of the parent radioisotope and its decay constant, is

---

AZ: Creation Research Society, 525-585.

9   Whitcomb and Morris, 1961, 346-355.

related to both the radius of the nucleus and the range of the strong nuclear force. If there is a change in the range of the strong nuclear force, then the radius of the nucleus is automatically changed, and so is the half-life of the α-decay. Thus, it is highly significant that the doubling of the radius of the radium radioisotope in the uranium decay chain reduces its half-life (and therefore its decay rate) by a factor of trillions!

Unfortunately, β-decay does not seem to be nearly as well-understood at a fundamental level like α-decay. This is because β-decay originates at a deeper level in the nucleus than α-decay, within the neutrons or protons themselves. The force involved is called the "weak" nucleus force, although it appears to be about as strong as electromagnetic force, but within an extremely short range. There are also other parameters, within other mathematical formulations in describing and understanding the nucleus and its constituent particles, that if varied would result in large changes to the rate of β-decay.

Thus, it is theoretically possible for radioisotope decay rates to have been accelerated as a result of changes to the strong and weak nuclear forces within parent radioisotopes. What could have triggered such changes to have occurred remains unknown. However, from the biblical standpoint, the quest to find an explainable cause for each effect, back along the chain of deeper and deeper levels of cause and effect, ultimately must lead back to God the Creator Himself. After all, it is clear from 2 Peter 3:5-6 that not only was God supernaturally involved in the creation of the world from the beginning (Genesis 1), but also during the Flood event. Furthermore, as far as the very building blocks of the universe are concerned, that is, the atoms that make up all matter and how they are held together, we are reminded in Colossians 1:16 that by the Creator Himself "all things consist," which in the Greek literally means, "are held together." Thus, at the most fundamental level, God the Creator still holds the matter of the universe together by His power, and thus, if and when He chooses to simply make a change to the nuclear forces involved in holding atoms, their nuclei, and their constituent particles together, then it is perfectly allowable and reasonable for Him to do so. Why might He so choose to intervene? It is evident that speeding up radioisotope decay rates generates heat that drives geologic and other processes at catastrophic rates. Perhaps this is the means by which God chose to accomplish His work in the Creation Week to shape the primordial earth He had created out of nothing at the beginning, to form the continental crust and dry land for the establishment of man's home, and then later to catastrophically re-form and re-shape the earth during the Flood event.

A "Grown" Creation with an "Apparent Age"

It has already been shown earlier that the Bible quite plainly and irrefutably teaches the fact of a "grown" creation—one with an "apparent age" from our perspective today, if we were to assume only natural processes had occurred at today's observed rates. The primary example of this inherent principle taught in Genesis 1 is God's creation of a mature Adam, who at the first instant of his existence had an apparent age equivalent to a fully grown adult human. Adam was not created as a baby, who then had to go through years of development and growth to become an adult. The reality of apparent age is inescapably inherent in the doctrine of creation by the eternally existent, all-powerful Creator God described in the Scriptures. Indeed, this inherent principle was dramatically observed by human witnesses when the Creator Himself, Jesus Christ (John 1:1-3; Colossians 1:16-17), instantly transformed water into wine (John 2:1-11) This wine was identical in every respect to wine produced from grapes grown on vines which had time to mature. That wine clearly had an apparent age.

Similarly, Genesis 1:11-12 records that God commanded the soil covering the land surface to "bring forth" grasses, herbs yielding seeds, and fruit trees already yielding fruit. Within hours, during the close of that third day, God's command had been carried out, so that the land surface was covered in mature grasses, herbs, and trees already carrying seeds and fruit. Thus, at the end of this third day of the Creation Week, God was very satisfied with the outcome of His command, and declared that all was good according to His character and will. Nevertheless, these plants and trees had appeared and developed to maturity within hours. Of course, the processes in operation to cause that to happen are processes that we now no longer observe and experience, yet no deception was involved on God's part, because He has revealed to us what happened as a result of His creative activity. Yet from our experience and observation today, plants and trees take many years to grow and mature, so by comparison these plants and trees that God created had already "grown," and fully matured, thus intrinsically having an apparent age.

Now even though the response to God's command was immediate ("and it was so"), and the growth and development of these plants and trees was virtually instantaneous from the perspective of a human observer, creative processes of growth and development were involved, albeit at exceptionally accelerated rates. God had already created the raw materials when He created the earth from nothing at the beginning of the Creation Week. Now He was combining those raw materials, and shaping them to make and form these plants and trees. Similarly, creative processes are implied when earlier on the third day of the Creation Week, God commanded the waters to be gathered into one place and the dry land to appear (Genesis 1:9-10). This description implies God took the pre-existing earth materials, and shaped and formed them with earth movements to raise the land surface above the waters, which until then completely covered the globe. Of course, once the dry land surface appeared, it was a fully mature landscape, with an apparent age equivalent to the timespan such a landscape would take to form according to our present-day observations and experience.

When God initially created the earth on Day One of the Creation Week, this must have included all the chemical elements from which He would subsequently make plants, trees, animals, the dust of the earth, and the human body. Because all chemical elements consist of numerous isotopes, it is likely that all these were also present in the earth after the initial creation. Furthermore, because some elements and their isotopes only exist today as a result of the radioactive decay of parent isotopes, it is quite possible that radioactive decay of certain isotopes was present in the initial creation of the earth. On the other hand, radioactive decay (or nuclear transformations) may have been initiated after the initial creation of the earth, when God began taking the raw materials He had created, and then shaping and forming them through Days Two and Three of the Creation Week to build the earth's internal structure, and the continental crust with the dry land surfaces distinct from the surrounding oceans. As already suggested, the heat generated by radioactive decay would have helped to drive the geologic and other processes that God may have employed at catastrophic rates to achieve His creative work of shaping the earth and building the continental crust, so accelerating decay rates would have helped facilitate these creative processes. The net result would have been that, within three literal 24-hour days of the Creation Week, the earth's crustal rocks would have "aged" by billions of years, according to the radioisotope "clocks" if calibrated at today's measured decay rates. In other words, the earth's crustal rocks would have appeared, like the rest of the creation, to be mature with an apparent age, when in fact they were only three days old.

Such a concept is undoubtedly unreasonable and unallowable to consistent uniformitarians, but there is nothing impossible or unreasonable about it. In fact, short of denying the existence of any Creator or original creation at all, one must logically come to some place in the long chain of secondary causes where something was created. If so, that something, at the instant of its creation, must have had an appearance of age. And the only way we could then determine its true age would be through divine revelation. Of course, to admit such is a complete anathema to uniformitarians, who insist that only natural causes can be evoked to explain all of reality. An apparent age might be deduced for that created object on the basis of any processes of change which were then observed in connection with it subsequently, but this would not be its true age.

This is exactly the situation with respect to these radioactive elements, and with many other geochronometers. It is eminently reasonable and consistent with the basically efficient and beneficent character of God, as well as with His revelation concerning the fact, that He would have created the entire universe as a complete, operational, functioning mechanism. On the other hand, the grossly cruel and wasteful processes of an almost interminable evolution leading up to man's arrival as its goal, as usually envisaged by uniformitarians (or at least theistic uniformitarians), are utterly inconsistent with the character and wisdom of God! It is therefore not ridiculous after all, but perfectly reasonable, to suppose that the radioactive elements, like all other elements, were created directly by God, who then produced the daughter elements at whatever rates He chose to fulfill His purposes in forming and shaping the earth, including its rocks and minerals.

The obvious question then arises as to whether the apparent ages of the rocks and minerals so created, as indicated by the relative amounts of parent and daughter elements contained therein, would all be diverse from each other or all exhibit some consistent value, and if they exhibit a consistent value, what value of apparent age might be implied. In the absence of specific revelation, it is of course impossible to decide this question with finality. However, it is more satisfying teleologically, and, therefore, more reasonable, to infer that all these primeval "clocks" should now "read" the same "age" since they were all "wound up" at the same time. Whatever that "setting" was, it could be called the apparent age of the earth, but the true age of the earth can only be known by means of divine revelation. The fact that the earth's crystalline rocks, which are in effect foundational to the continental crust and to the original land surface made by God on the third day of the Creation Week, yield a diversity of radioisotope "ages" in the range of billions of years, when the true age of the earth revealed by divine revelation is only approximately 6,000 years, means that God chose to accelerate the radioisotope decay rates in order to serve His purposes in making and forming the continental crust and the original land surface. Furthermore, if God chose to do that during the Creation Week, then He could do the same during the Flood event, again to serve His purposes in destroying and renovating the earth's surface as judgment on a rebellious humanity.

106

THE PITFALLS IN THE RADIOACTIVE DATING METHODS—THE RADIOCARBON DATING METHOD

Reference has already been made to the results of radiocarbon "dating" which are evidence of the acceleration of radioactive and nuclear decay during the Creation Week and the Flood. However, further discussion of this "dating" method is warranted here, because it has become widely used in archaeology and other studies to apparently supply absolute "dates" for events supposedly within the past 30,000-40,000 years. The materials so "dated," of course, correspond to the period covered by biblical history, as well as more recent dates, bearing directly upon the question of the dates of the Flood and other related events.

The radiocarbon method was first developed by Willard F. Libby in 1946. Since then, thousands of radiocarbon "dates" have been determined for a great variety of archeological and recent geological materials in many different laboratories. The formation of radiocarbon (carbon-14, the radioactive isotope of ordinary carbon) by cosmic radiation was first discovered, however, by Serge Korff, an authority at that time on cosmic rays. He describes the carbon-14 dating method as follows:

> Cosmic ray neutrons, produced as secondary particles in the atmosphere by the original radiation, are captured by nitrogen nuclei to form the radioactive isotope of carbon, the isotope of mass 14. This isotope has a long half-life, something over 5,500 years. By the application of some very well thought-out techniques, Libby and his colleagues have actually not only identified the radiocarbon in nature, but have also made quantitative estimates thereof. Since this carbon in the atmosphere mostly becomes attached to oxygen to form carbon dioxide, and since the carbon dioxide is ingested by plants and animals and is incorporated into their biological structures, and further, since this process stops at the time of the death of the specimen, the percentage of radiocarbon among the normal carbon atoms in its system can be used to establish the date at which the specimen stops metabolizing.[1]

---

1   S. A. Korff, 1957, The origin and implications of the cosmic radiation, *American Scientist*, 45: 298.

There can be no doubt that this constitutes a very ingenious dating tool, provided of course that the inherent assumptions are valid. There are two basic assumptions in the carbon-14 dating method.[2] First, the cosmic ray flux has to have been essentially constant, at least on a scale of centuries. Second, the carbon-14 concentration in the carbon dioxide cycle must remain constant. To these two basic assumptions we should add the assumption of the constancy of the rate of decay of carbon-14 atoms, the assumption that dead organic matter is not later altered with respect to its carbon content by any biologic or other activity, the assumption that the carbon dioxide contents of the ocean and atmosphere has been constant with time, the assumption that the huge reservoir of oceanic carbon has not changed in size during the period of applicability of the method, and the assumption that the rate of formation and the rate of decay of radiocarbon atoms have been in equilibrium throughout the period of applicability. However, every one of these assumptions is highly questionable in the context of the events of creation and the Flood.

Nevertheless, it has been maintained that the method has been verified beyond any question by numerous correlations with known dates. However, closer investigation reveals that where historical dates are well established, back beyond about 400 BC, the radiocarbon "dates" increasingly diverge, as they also do from tree-ring dates.[3] Thus, it is obvious that any genuine correlation of the radiocarbon method with definite historical chronologies is limited only to some time well after the Flood and the dispersion of people from the Tower of Babel. The major assumptions in the method would therefore appear to be valid for this period. This does not prove their validity for more ancient times, the periods in which we would infer that the assumptions are very likely wrong due to conditions in the atmosphere and biosphere being different from today, and, therefore, their datings would also be wrong.

Attempts to apply the carbon-14 method to produce earlier "dates" have been called into serious question by geologists, archaeologists, and other scientists. Of particular concern has been the danger of contamination of samples by external sources of carbon, especially in damp locations. Hence, the radiocarbon method has been sharply criticized:

> In appraising C 14 dates, it is essential always to discriminate between the C 14 age and the actual age of the sample. The laboratory analysis determines only the amount of radioactive carbon present....However, the laboratory analysis does not determine whether the radioactive carbon is all original or is in part secondary, intrusive, or whether the amount has

2   J. L. Kulp, 1952, The carbon 14 method of age determination, *Scientific Monthly*, 75: 261.

3   S. Bowman, 1990, *Radiocarbon Dating*, London: British Museum Publications, 16-18; Faure and Mensing, 2005, 617-619.

been altered in still other irregular ways besides by natural decay.[4]

As the radiocarbon method became more widely used, questions of contamination of samples become more acute, especially with the discovery of modern organisms with unexpectedly lower levels of carbon-14 equivalent to anomalously old "ages," including modern mollusk shells from river environments yielding radiocarbon "ages" in the range of 1,010 to 2,300 years,[5] and snails living in artesian springs with carbon-14 contents equivalent to an "age" of 27,000 years.[6] As a consequence of the increasing problems with the radiocarbon method, skepticism began to be more openly expressed:

> C 14 dating was being discussed at a symposium on the prehistory of the Nile Valley. A famous American colleague, Professor Brew, briefly summarized a common attitude among archaeologists towards it, as follows:

> "If a C 14 date supports our theories, we put it in the main text. If it does not entirely contradict them, we put it in a footnote, and if it is completely 'out of date' we just drop it."

> Few archaeologists who have concerned themselves with absolute chronology are innocent of having sometimes applied this method, and many are still hesitant to accept C14 dates without reservations.[7]

A further decade of radiocarbon "dating" only served to make the criticisms more intense:

> In the light of what is known about the radiocarbon method and the way it is used, it is truly astonishing that many authors will cite agreeable determinations as *"proof"* for their beliefs....

> Radiocarbon dating has somehow avoided collapse onto its own battered foundation, and now lurches onward with a feigned consistency. The implications of pervasive contamination and ancient variations in carbon-14 levels are steadfastly ignored by those who base their arguments upon the dates.

---

4   E. Antevs, 1957, Geological tests of the varve and radiocarbon chronologies, *Journal of Geology*, 65: 129.

5   M. L. Keith and G. M. Anderson, 1963, Radiocarbon dating: Fictitious results with mollusk shells, *Science*, 141: 634-635.

6   A. C. Riggs, 1984, Major carbon-14 deficiency in modern snail shells from southern Nevada springs, *Science*, 224: 58.

7   T. Säve-Söderbergh and I. U. Olsson, 1970, C 14 dating and Egyptian chronology, in *Radiocarbon Variations and Absolute Chronology*, Proceedings of the Twelfth Nobel Symposium, I. U. Olsson, ed., Stockholm: Almqvist & Wiksell and New York: John Wiley & Sons, New York, 35.

The early authorities began the charade by stressing that they were "not aware of a single significant disagreement" on any sample that had been dated at different labs. Such enthusiasts continue to claim, incredible though it may seem, that "no worse discrepancies are apparent." Surely 15,000 years of difference on a single block of soil is indeed a *gross* discrepancy! And how could the excessive disagreement between the labs be called insignificant, when it has been the basis for the reappraisal of the standard error associated with each and every date in existence?

Why did geologists and archaeologists still spend their scarce money on costly radiocarbon determinations? They do so because occasional dates *appear* to be useful. While the method cannot be counted on to give good, unequivocal results, the numbers do impress people, and save them the trouble of thinking excessively. Expressed in what *look* like precise calendar years, figures *seem* somehow better—both to layman and professional not versed in statistics—than complex stratigraphic or cultural correlations, and are more easily retained in one's memory. "Absolute" dates determined by a laboratory carry a lot of weight, and are extremely helpful in bolstering weak arguments....

No matter how "useful" it is, though, the radiocarbon method is still not capable of yielding accurate and reliable results. There *are* gross discrepancies, the chronology is *uneven* and *relative*, and the accepted dates are actually *selected* dates. "This whole blessed thing is nothing but 13th-century alchemy, and it all depends upon which funny paper you read."[8]

The presence of detectable carbon-14 in fossils, which according to the uniformitarian timescale should be entirely carbon-14-dead, has been reported from the earliest days of radiocarbon "dating." For example, a published survey on all the "dates" reported in the journal *Radiocarbon* up to 1970 commented that for more than 15,000 samples reported: "All such matter is found datable within 50,000 years as published."[9] The samples involved included coal, oil, natural gas, and other allegedly very ancient material. The reason these anomalies were not taken seriously is because the measuring technique used in the early decades of radiocarbon "dating" had difficulty distinguishing genuine low intrinsic levels of carbon-14 in samples from the background cosmic radiation. Thus, the low carbon-14 levels measured in many samples, which according to their location in the geologic record ought to have had no carbon-14 in them, were simply attributed to the background cosmic radiation. However, the complication of

---

8   R. E. Lee, 1981, Radiocarbon: Ages in error, *Anthropological Journal of Canada*, 19 (3): 9-29, 1981. (Reprinted in the *Creation Research Society Quarterly*, 19 (2): 117-127; quotes are from pages 123 and 125).

9   R. L. Whitelaw, 1970, Time, life, and history in the light of 15,000 radiocarbon dates, *Creation Research Society Quarterly*, 7 (1): 56-71.

the background cosmic radiation infusing the carbon-14 measurements was overcome with the advent of the accelerator mass spectrometer (AMS) technique in the early 1980s. Nevertheless, over the past 25 years, organic samples from every level in the Cambrian to Recent portion of the geologic record were still found to contain significant and reproducible amounts of carbon-14 when tested by the highly sensitive AMS method. In hindsight, it is almost certain that many of the earlier radiocarbon analyses were indeed recording low levels of carbon-14, also intrinsic to those samples.

About seventy AMS carbon-14 measurements that were published in the standard radiocarbon literature between 1984 and 1998 demonstrate that significant levels of carbon-14 are routinely found in organic material. According to the conventional uniformitarian timescale, these samples should have been entirely devoid of any carbon-14 because they are supposedly older than 100,000 years.[10] Additionally, AMS radiocarbon analyses were obtained on fossilized wood from Tertiary, Mesozoic, and upper Paleozoic strata that have conventional uniformitarian ages ranging from 32 to 250 million years.[11] All fossilized wood samples yielded significant quantities of carbon-14, equivalent to radiocarbon "ages" of between 20,000 and 45,000 years. With a half-life of only 5,730 years, after one million years (or 175 half-lives) the amount of carbon-14 expected would be so small as to exclude even a single carbon-14 atom being left from a beginning mass of carbon-14 equal to the mass of the earth itself! Thus, the presence of any intrinsic carbon-14 in these fossilized wood samples, that are supposed to be 32 to 250 million years old, represents a profound challenge to the uniformitarian timescale, because the measured carbon-14 limits the ages of these fossilized woods to merely thousands of years.

It is now common knowledge, even in the standard radiocarbon literature, that organic samples from every portion of the Phanerozoic (Cambrian to Recent) geologic record display detectable amounts of carbon-14 well above the analytical threshold of the AMS equipment. This has come about because samples claimed to be millions of years old, which should have contained no

---

10 P. Giem, 2001, Carbon-14 content of fossil carbon, *Origins*, 51: 6-30; J. R. Baumgardner, A. A. Snelling, D. R. Humphreys and S. A. Austin, 2003, Measurable ¹⁴C in fossilized organic materials: Confirming the young earth Creation-Flood model, in *Proceedings of the Fifth International Conference on Creationism*, R. L. Ivey, Jr., ed., Pittsburgh, PA: Creation Science Fellowship, 127-147; Baumgardner, 2005, 587-630.

11 A. A. Snelling, 1997, Radioactive "dating" in conflict! Fossil wood in ancient lava flows yields radiocarbon, *Creation Ex Nihilo*, 20 (1): 24-27; A. A. Snelling, 1998, Stumping old-age dogma: Radiocarbon in an "ancient" fossil tree stump casts doubt on traditional rock/fossil dating, *Creation Ex Nihilo*, 20 (4): 48-51; A. A. Snelling, 1999, Dating dilemma: Fossil wood in "ancient" sandstone, *Creation Ex Nihilo*, 21 (3): 39-41; A. A. Snelling, 2000, Geological conflict: Young radiocarbon dating for ancient fossil wood challenges fossil dating, *Creation Ex Nihilo*, 22 (2): 44-47; A. A. Snelling, 2000, Conflicting "ages" of Tertiary basalt and contained fossilized wood, Crinum, central Queensland, Australia, *Creation Ex Nihilo Technical Journal*, 14 (2): 99-122; A. A. Snelling, 2008, Radiocarbon in "ancient" fossil wood, *Acts & Facts*, 37 (1): 10-13; A. A. Snelling, 2008, Radiocarbon ages for fossil ammonites and wood in Cretaceous strata near Redding, California, *Answers Research Journal*, 1: 123-144.

carbon-14 atoms, have been used as "procedural blanks" in the AMS equipment during analytical runs to determine presumed background carbon-14 levels due to sample preparation procedures in the labs, and any other contamination of the equipment. Consequently, most radiocarbon laboratories have been at pains to thoroughly investigate potential sources and various contributions of supposed contamination to the presumed carbon-14 background in their AMS systems,[12] and have been searching for specific materials to use as procedural blanks that contain as low a carbon-14 background level as possible.[13] However, even when the utmost care has been taken in the preparation of procedural blanks, which are regarded as "radiocarbon-dead" because of their presumed Precambrian age, detectable levels of carbon-14 well above the AMS instrument threshold have still been detected and reported.[14]

Invariably this supposedly anomalous detected carbon-14 in these procedural blanks has been claimed to be "contamination," which has led to the admission that there appears to be a "radiocarbon barrier" of 55,000 to 60,000 "radiocarbon years" for the apparent "ages" of even supposedly "ancient" samples, no matter their supposed ages. However, it can be argued that instrument error can be eliminated on experimental grounds as an explanation for the alleged contamination in these supposedly "ancient" "radiocarbon-dead" organic samples, which have, nonetheless, yielded significant carbon-14 measurements.[15] Similarly, it has also been shown that contamination of the carbon-14-bearing fossil material *in situ* is unlikely, but theoretically possible, and is a testable hypothesis. Furthermore, while contamination during sample preparation is a genuine problem, the literature has shown it can be reduced to low levels by proper laboratory procedures. Thus, it must be concluded that the carbon-14 detected in these organic samples from the geologic record would most likely have originated from the organisms themselves from which the fossilized materials were derived. Because most of this fossil carbon seems to have roughly the same amounts of carbon-14, it is clearly a logical possibility that all these fossil organisms had lived together on the earth at the same time.

In order to test all these earlier findings, more recent studies were undertaken to analyze ten coal samples representative of the economic important coalfields of the United States, and five diamonds from African kimberlite pipes.[16] Three of the coal samples were from Eocene seams, three from Cretaceous seams, and four from Pennsylvanian seams, yet the average carbon-14 values from these coal

---

12   J. S. Vogel, D. E. Nelson and J. R. Sothern, 1987, ^{14}C background levels in an accelerator mass spectrometry system, *Radiocarbon*, 29: 323-333.

13   R. P. Beukens, 1990, High-precision intercomparison at IsoTrace, *Radiocarbon*, 32: 335-339.

14   M. I. Bird, L. K. Ayliffe, L. K. Fifield, C. S. M. Turney, R. G. Cresswell, T. T. Barrows and B. David, 1999, Radiocarbon dating of 'old' charcoal using a wet oxidation, stepped-combustion procedure, *Radiocarbon*, 41 (2): 127-140.

15   Giem, 2001.

16   Baumgardner et al, 2003; Baumgardner, 2005.

samples over each of these three geological intervals were remarkably similar to one another, around 50,000 years, even though the uniformitarian ages range from 40 million years to 350 million years. The diamonds chosen for analysis came from underground mines where contamination would be minimal. In any case, being the hardest natural mineral, diamonds are extremely resistant to contamination via chemical exchange with the external environment. Furthermore, the diamonds chosen are regarded by uniformitarian geologists to have formed in the earth's mantle between one and three billion years ago, so they should have definitely been "radiocarbon-dead." Nevertheless, they still contained significant levels of carbon-14, well above the detection threshold of the AMS equipment, but virtually equivalent to the carbon-14 values found in fossilized organic materials from the Precambrian portion of the geologic record.[17] Given the supposed antiquity of these diamonds, and their source deep inside the earth, one possible explanation for these detectable carbon-14 levels is that the carbon-14 is primordial. However, if this were the case, the apparent "age" of the earth itself would only be less than 55,000 years!

The radiocarbon "dates" equivalent to the significant levels of carbon-14 detected in fossilized wood, coals, diamonds, and other "ancient" fossil carbon are, of course, calculated on the assumption that the decay rate of carbon-14 has been constant throughout earth history. However, if, as other evidence cited previously indicates, there were brief episodes of accelerated nuclear decay during Creation Week and the Flood, then much of the carbon-14 in these materials would have been generated during these periods, making the radiocarbon "dates" grossly enlarged. In any case, with a date for the Genesis Flood of only about 4,500 years ago, which is less than the carbon-14 half-life, one would expect that today there would still be detectable carbon-14 in the plants and animals buried and fossilized in that cataclysm. Furthermore, a huge amount of carbon from living organisms would have been buried during the Flood cataclysm to form today's coal seams, oil shales, and oil deposits, probably most of the natural gas, and some fraction of today's fossiliferous limestones. Estimates for the amount of carbon in this inventory suggests that the biosphere just prior to the Flood would have had, conservatively, greater than 300 to 700 times the total carbon that resides in the biosphere today.[18] The living plants and animals in the pre-Flood world would have contained most of this biospheric carbon, with only a tiny fraction of the total resident in the atmosphere. Furthermore, the vast majority of this carbon would have been normal carbon-12 and carbon-13, since even in today's world only about one carbon atom in a trillion is carbon-14.

All radiocarbon "ages" are also calculated on the assumption that before the

---

17   Baumgardner, 2005.

18   R. H. Brown, 1979, The interpretation of C-14 dates, *Origins*, 6: 30-44; Giem, 2001; G. R. Morton, 1984, The carbon problem, *Creation Research Society Quarterly*, 20: 212-219; H. W. Scharpenseel and T. Becker-Heidmann, 1992, Twenty-five years of radiocarbon dating soils: Paradigm of erring and learning, *Radiocarbon*, 34: 541-549.

plant or animal died it contained approximately the same ratio of radiocarbon to ordinary carbon that is present in living things today. However, prior to the Flood, the ratio of radiocarbon to ordinary carbon would have been much lower than it is at present, even if we assume that the total number of atoms of carbon-14 was similar to what exists in today's world. Assuming that is the case, this carbon-14 was distributed uniformly throughout the biosphere, and the total amount of carbon in the biosphere was, for example, 500 times that in today's world, then the resulting ratio of radiocarbon to ordinary carbon would have been 1/500 of today's level. Of course, this is only a very tentative estimate due to the large uncertainty in knowing the total amount of carbon-14 in the pre-Flood world. The short timespan of less than 2,000 years between creation and the Flood would not have been sufficient to generate the same amount of carbon-14 by cosmic rays in the atmosphere as what we find in today's world, even with today's magnetic field strength. A stronger magnetic field in the past (discussed later) would have provided more effective deflection of charged cosmic ray particles, and thus there would have been even less carbon-14 generated in the atmosphere in the past.

On the other hand, there may well have been some significant amount of carbon-14 generated during the early part of the Creation Week, as a consequence of the large amount of accelerated nuclear disintegration of radioactive elements such as uranium and the resulting neutron interactions with nitrogen-14.[19] Indeed, it is possible to calculate how much carbon-14 might have been generated by neutron interactions early in earth history, because diamonds contain significant levels of nitrogen-14, and were formed early in the earth's history deep inside the earth. Such calculations show that neutron interactions would not have been capable of producing anywhere near the significant carbon-14 levels measured in deep-earth diamonds, even as a consequence of accelerated radioactive and nuclear decay.[20] On the other hand, the acceleration of radioisotope decay would have only marginally increased both the decay of carbon-14, and consequently the reduction of the carbon-14 inventory produced by the accelerated neutron interactions with nitrogen-14. However, the accelerated neutron interactions would not have prevailed in increasing the carbon-14 levels to those measured in the deep-earth diamonds. Therefore, if the total mass of carbon-14 in the pre-Flood world was not much greater than that in our present world, then the carbon-14 decay over the span of 4,500 years since the Flood catastrophe reduces that pre-Flood level by a factor of 0.6. Therefore, the carbon-14 to total carbon ratio of 1/500 of today's level 4,500 years ago would display today as a ratio of less than 1/800, which is exactly the carbon-14 level measured in the deep-earth diamonds and other organic carbon from the pre-Flood world, as is well documented in the standard radiocarbon literature.

---

19   R. Zito, D. J. Donahue, S. N. Davis, H. W. Bentley and P. Fritz, 1980, Possible subsurface production of carbon-14, *Geophysical Research Letters*, 7 (4): 235-238.

20   Baumgardner, 2005.

After the Flood cataclysm it was necessary for the carbon-14 to total carbon ratio to have increased dramatically and rapidly by a factor on the order of 500 to reach its present-day value. Not only would carbon-14 production in the atmosphere have increased immediately after the Flood, due to the decreasing strength of the earth's magnetic field (discussed later), but the presence of high levels of crustal neutrons arising from the accelerated nuclear decay during the Flood would have converted substantial amounts of crustal nitrogen to carbon-14, most of which would have been oxidized to carbon dioxide and eventually escape to the atmosphere. The striking carbon-14 differences measured in the shell of a single snail specimen confirms that large spatial and temporal variations in the carbon-14 to total carbon ratio did indeed exist during the interval immediately following the Flood cataclysm.[21] Furthermore, the equilibrium condition between the generation and decay of carbon-14, which has to be assumed in making any age calculation by the radiocarbon method, would obviously not be applicable for quite a long time after the Flood cataclysm. Even with the marked increase in the rate of formation of carbon-14 as a result of the Flood, and of the decreasing strength of the earth's magnetic field, it would still have taken many years for the total amount of carbon-14 in the biosphere's carbon inventory to build up to the equilibrium condition where generation and decay of carbon-14 would be equal. This would mean that some organisms living in those early years and centuries after the Flood would have only received a proportionately smaller amount of carbon-14 into their systems than those organisms living in later times. Of course, as the radiocarbon production increased as time went on, the present equilibrium rates would have been reached.

This is why radiocarbon "dates" for the last 2,000 years seem to show a generally good correlation with historically verified artifacts and specimens, although of course, there would still be many discrepancies and a larger margin of error the further back in time comparisons are made. However, for early post-Flood dates, the levels of contained carbon-14 would be such that, if "ages" were then calculated on the basis of the present equilibrium conditions and rates, they would be very much older than their real-time ages, with the amount of error increasing progressively with the age of the material. This is also the case with the organic material buried during the Flood cataclysm, including the plant material buried and fossilized to form coal, which still contains significant, relatively high levels of carbon-14. Ages for this Flood-deposited organic material calculated on the basis of present equilibrium conditions and rates would yield incorrect, much older "ages." Thus, the biblical framework of earth history, including the Flood cataclysm and the recovery of the biosphere from that event, adequately explains the data from carbon-14 studies, accounting for the agreement with historically-dated recent events, but at the same time indicating that earlier unverified datings must be too high, as would be inferred from the biblical records. Furthermore, the fact that Eocene, Cretaceous, and Pennsylvanian coal seams, which in

---

21   M.-J. Nadeau, P. M. Grootes, A. Voelker, F. Bruhn, A. Duhr and A. Oriwall, 2001, Carbonate ^{14}C background: Does it have multiple personalities?, *Radiocarbon*, 43 (2A): 169-176.

uniformitarian terms are dated at 40 to 350 million years old, all contain similar (essentially identical) significant levels of carbon-14, when in uniformitarian terms there should be no carbon-14 in them at all, is testimony to this fossilized plant material all having been buried at the same time during the Flood cataclysm only 4,500 years ago.

Consequently, it is abundantly clear that the data from all the radioactive methods of geochronometry, properly understood, harmonize perfectly with the biblical records and inferences associated with the creation and the Flood. These events must be dated at only some thousands of years ago according to the Bible. Even the presence of significant detectable levels of carbon-14 in deep-earth diamonds, that in uniformitarian terms are "dated" at 1-3 billion years old, is in fact testimony to the earth only being thousands of years old. So evidence that has been brought against the biblical testimony has now been shown rather to harmonize quite satisfactorily with the biblical record. In fact, it would seem highly probable that no method of geochronometry has been devised that permits determination of dates earlier than the Flood, since all such geological and geophysical processes were profoundly disturbed and altered by the events of that global cataclysm. The Scriptural description is that "the world that then was, being overflowed with water perished" (2 Peter 3:6), and the context shows that this statement comprises the total earth! The only possible way in which men can *know* the true age of the earth is by means of divine revelation!

SECTION IX

CONTRADICTIONS IN GEOCHRONOLOGY— SUPPORT FOR BIBLICAL GEOLOGY

107

SUPERNOVAS AND COMETS

Even aside from the biblical testimony in opposition to the estimated radioactive decay "age" for the earth and its rock strata, there are numerous geological and astronomical evidences against the validity of those highly inflated age estimates. The currently accepted age for the earth, as deduced from the lead isotopes (from the radioactive decay of uranium) in meteorites, is just over 4.5 billion years. However, there are many geological and astronomical processes and evidences that appear just as suitable for geochronometry as radioactive decay, but give much lower estimates. Of course, none of these is sufficiently precise for accurate measurements, and all involve various assumptions similar to the radioactive dating methods. However, whereas the radioactive dating methods involve analyzing individual rock and mineral samples from outcrops on a local scale, these astronomical and geological evidences mostly involve processes on a whole-earth global scale, in the solar system, and beyond. Therefore, these dating methods should be regarded as far more reliable and meaningful as geochronometers, and thus, it is important to examine the age-of-the-earth estimates they provide, as they cast serious doubts on the reliability of the radioactive decay age estimates. Furthermore, the list of astronomical and geological evidences discussed here is by no means exhaustive.

Supernova Remnants

A supernova is a violently exploding massive star that is one of the most brilliant objects in the sky, even visible during the daytime. The gas and dust debris from such explosions form huge clouds that expand outwardly rapidly, and are known as supernova remnants. A well-known example is the Crab Nebula in the constellation of Taurus, which was produced by a supernova so bright that it could be seen in the day sky for a few weeks in 1054. According to astronomical observations, galaxies like our own, the Milky Way, should experience on average one supernova every 25 years. By applying the known physical laws, astronomers can predict what should happen to the huge cloud of debris (the supernova remnant) after the supernova explosion. It should expand outwardly so rapidly that it reaches a diameter of about 3,100 trillion kilometers (or 1,900 trillion miles) in about 120,000 years, and yet remains visible for over a million years as the cloud continues to expand.

The number of supernova remnants in our galaxy can easily be observed and counted, and this provides an excellent test to determine whether the universe is old or young. If the universe is only about 6,000-7,000 years old, no supernova remnants would have had time to reach large diameters, and they all should still be clearly visible. On the other hand, if the universe were billions of years old, we should be able to observe many of these supernova remnants. Indeed, it is possible to calculate just how many of these supernova remnants at the given dimensions should be visible after 7,000 years, and just how many should still be visible after billions of years.[1] These calculations indicate that if our galaxy was billions of years old, then there would be at least 2,256 supernova remnants visible at the second stage of expansion, more than 300 years after the supernovas exploded. Whereas, if our galaxy was only 7,000 years old, only about 268 second stage supernova remnants should be observed.[2] So just how many of these supernova remnants (gas and dust clouds) do we observe in our galaxy? The stark reality is that we actually observe only 200 such supernova remnants, a number that is totally consistent with a 6,000-7,000 years old galaxy, and, therefore, an earth of the same age.

Now if the discrepancy between the calculated number of visible supernova remnants for a galaxy billions of years old, and the actual observed number of supernova remnants is real, then it should be recognized and acknowledged by astronomers who claim our galaxy is billions of years old. Indeed, they have recognized this discrepancy. For example, the National Research Council Astronomy Survey Committee in Canada has commented:

> Major questions about these objects that should be addressed in the coming decade are: where have all the remnants gone?[3]

The discrepancy between the calculated and observed numbers is obvious, because if the universe were really billions of years old, then more than 79 percent of the supernova remnants that should be in our galaxy are obviously missing! That's why astronomers, in the context of trying to find solutions to this stark shortfall, have commented: "Why have the large number of expected remnants not been

---

1   Band, D. L. and E. P. Liang, 1988, in *Supernova Remnants and the Interstellar Medium*, Roger and T. L. Lamdecker, eds., Colloquium Proceedings, Cambridge: Cambridge University Press, 69-72; Cioffi, D. F. and C. F. McKee, 1988, in *Supernova Remnants and the Interstellar Medium*, R. S. Roger and T. L. Lamdecker, eds., Colloquium Proceedings, Cambridge University Press, 437.

2   K. Davies, 1994, Distribution of supernova remnants in the galaxy, in *Proceedings of the Third International Conference on Creationism*, R. E. Walsh, ed., Pittsburgh, PA: Creation Science Fellowship, 175-184.

3   National Research Council, 1983, *Challenges to Astronomy and Astrophysics*, working documents of the Astronomy Survey Committee, Canada: National Academy Press, 166.

detected?"[4] And they go on to refer to "the mystery of the missing remnants."

Lest it be argued that this discrepancy is merely a characteristic of just the Milky Way galaxy, it should be noted that the same discrepancy is found in one of our satellite galaxies, the Large Magellanic Cloud. In a radiotelescope survey, a total of only nine supernova remnants could actually be found.[5] Based on the belief that this galaxy is billions of years old, it was expected there should be about 340 supernova remnants, above the limit of detection of the instrument. One astronomer later commented: "The observations have caused considerable surprise and loss of confidence."[6] Since this initial radiotelescope survey, more sensitive surveys have discovered another twenty supernova remnants in the Large Magellanic Cloud.[7] Given that the Large Magellanic Cloud is approximately one-tenth the size of our galaxy, if this galaxy were also 6,000-7,000 years old, then about 24 supernova remnants should be visible. Once again, the observed numbers (29) are consistent with the predicted numbers using calculations based on a 6,000-7,000-year-old galaxy (and universe).

The only solutions offered by astronomers are conjectural and assume flaws in their own estimates. However, there is no mystery about the assumed large numbers of missing supernova remnants. Repeated observations confirm that the numbers of supernova remnants are only consistent with an earth and a universe that are 6,000-7,000 years old, the age derived from a straightforward reading of the Scriptures.

Disintegration of Comets

Comets are literally "dirty snowballs" that move through the solar system in highly elliptical orbits around the sun. From the Greek *comētē* (long-haired), a comet looks like a hairy star due to the tail of dust streaming from it. The icy nucleus of a comet is usually a few kilometers across. The diameter of the most famous comet, Halley's Comet, is about ten kilometers, and the diameter of one of the largest comets known, Hale-Bopp seen in 1997, is about forty kilometers. When a comet passes close to the sun, some of its icy nucleus evaporates and forms a coma about 10,000 to 100,000 kilometers wide. At the same time, solar radiation pushes away the dust particles released through evaporation to generate the tail that curves gently away from the sun and backwards. Sunlight illuminates both the coma and the tail, giving the comet the appearance of a hairy star.

---

4   D. H. Clark and J. L. Caswell, 1976, A study of galactic supernova remnants, based on Molonglo-Parkes observational data, *Monthly Notice of the Royal Astronomical Society*, 174: 267-306.

5   D. S. Mathewson and J. N. Clarke, 1973, Supernova Remnants in the Large Magellanic Cloud, *Astrophysical Journal*, 180: 725-738.

6   D. Cox, 1986, The Terrain of Evolution of Isotropic Adiabatic Supernova Remnants, *Astrophysical Journal*, 304: 771-779.

7   K. Davies, 1994.

This loss of material, therefore, means that comets are gradually disintegrating and being destroyed every time they come close to the sun. Indeed, many comets have been observed to have been much dimmer during later passes. Furthermore, some comets have been observed to break up and totally dissipate. Thus, it has been estimated that all known comets can be expected to break up and vanish within a timeframe that is very short in uniformitarian and evolutionary terms. This has long been recognized by astronomers:

> It has been estimated that the break-up of many comets is taking place at such a rate that they will be entirely disrupted within a million years. It is an immediate inference that these comets cannot have been moving around the Sun as they are at present for much longer than a million years, since otherwise they would already have been broken up.[8]

According to evolutionary theory, comets are supposed to be the same age as the solar system, approximately five billion years old. However, the problem for evolutionary astronomers is that, given the observed rate of disintegration of comets and the maximum possible size of a comet's orbit, comets could not have been orbiting the sun for the alleged billions of years since the solar system formed.[9] Indeed, more realistic estimates suggest comets could not survive much longer than about 100,000 years. Studies of observed comets have concluded that many comets have typical ages of less than 10,000 years.[10] Since all astronomers agree that the comets came into existence at approximately the same time as the solar system, the natural inference is that the maximum age of the solar system would be approximately 10,000 years based on the observed age of comets.

In order to explain away this acknowledged discrepancy, evolutionary astronomers have had no alternative but to postulate hypothetical sources that have supposedly generated comets progressively through time to replace the comets that have totally disintegrated. As early as 1950, the Dutch astronomer Jan Oort proposed that there was a spherical shell of comets well beyond the orbit of Pluto. In this spherical shell passing stars, gas clouds, and galactic tides are supposedly able to knock comets from this "Oort Cloud" into orbits within the inner solar system:

> Oort postulated that the cometary cloud may contain as many as 100 billion comets very few of which come as close to the Sun as the planets. Occasionally, however, the random passage of a star disturbs the motions of some comets sufficiently to make them swing into the sphere of gravitational attraction of Jupiter or another major planet. In this way

8   F. Hoyle, 1955, *Frontiers of Astronomy*, New York: Harper and Brothers, 11.

9   D. R. Faulkner, 1997, Comets and the age of the Solar System, *Creation Ex Nihilo Technical Journal*, 11 (3): 264-273.

10   E. F. Steidl, 1983, Planets, comets, and asteroids, in *Design and Origins in Astronomy*, G. Mulfinger, ed., Norcross, GA: Creation Research Society Books, 73-106.

comets are taken one by one from the "deep freeze" of the solar swarm and are pulled into relatively short-period orbits. With their hibernation period over, they become active and disintegrate into gas and meteoritic particles during a few hundred or a few thousand revolutions around the Sun.[11]

However, there are several fatal problems with this hypothetical Oort Cloud:

1. This hypothetical Oort Cloud has never been observed, so rather than being even a scientific theory, it is in reality an *ad hoc* device to explain away the obvious discrepancy that is fatal to the dogma of the earth and the solar system being billions of years old:

   "Many scientific papers are written each year about the Oort Cloud, its properties, its origin, its evolution. Yet there is not yet a shred of direct observational evidence for its existence."[12]

2. Collisions between the supposed comet nuclei in this hypothetical, unobserved Oort Cloud would have destroyed most of those comet nuclei.[13]

3. To overcome the problem of these collisions it is then postulated that there has to be a hundred times more of these comets than what we actually observe, and that this abundance of comets must disrupt before we get a chance to see them![14]

So far, none of these proposed explanations has been substantiated, either by observations or realistic calculations. It seems desperate for astronomers to propose an unobserved source and mechanism to keep comets supplied for the alleged billions of years and then make excuses as to why this hypothetical source doesn't feed in comets as fast as it should!

In recent years, with the failure of the hypothetical Oort Cloud to supply the needed comets, attention has focused on the Kuiper Belt, a donut-shaped disc of supposed comet sources lying in the plane of the solar system just beyond the orbit of Neptune and outside the orbit of Pluto. To solve the evolutionary astronomers' dilemma, there would have to be billions of comet nuclei in this Kuiper Belt. However, astronomers have so far only found less than a thousand icy asteroid-sized bodies in this Kuiper Belt. Yet these so-far-discovered Kuiper Belt objects do

---

11   F. L. Whipple, 1955, Comets, in *The New Astronomy*, New York: Simon and Schuster, 201-202.

12   C. Sagan and A. Druyan, 1985, *Comets*, New York: Random House, 201.

13   S. A. Stern and P. R. Weissman, 2001, Rapid collisional evolution of comets during the formation of the Oort Cloud, *Nature*, 409 (6820): 589-591; D. R. Faulkner, 2001, More problems for the Oort Comet Cloud, *TJ*, 15 (2): 11.

14   H. F. Levison et al, 2002, The mass disruption of Oort Cloud Comets, *Science*, 296 (5576): 2212-2215; M. E. Bailey, 2002, Where have all the comets gone? *Science*, 296 (5576): 2251-2253.

not solve the evolutionists' problem, because these objects typically have diameters of more than a hundred kilometers, whereas a typical comet nucleus is around ten kilometers in diameter. Thus, in fact, there has been no discovery of comets *per se* in this Kuiper Belt, which was supposed to have been supplied with comet nuclei from the hypothetical unobserved Oort Cloud! Therefore, the Kuiper Belt is, so far, a non-answer.[15] Many astronomers now refer to these bodies according to their position beyond Neptune, without any assumptions that they may be related to a comet source. Thus, because no source of comets has been found to supposedly replenish the comets that disintegrate within the solar system, the maximum age of 10,000 years for the comets must also be the maximum age for the solar system, and, therefore, the earth.

---

15   R. Newton, 2002, The short-period comets "problem" (for evolutionists): Have recent "Kuiper Belt" discoveries solved the evolutionary/long-age dilemma? *TJ*, 16 (2): 15-17.

108

THE EARTH'S MAGNETIC FIELD

The earth has a magnetic field, which is why a compass needle points north. All the evidence we have indicates that the earth's magnetic field is generated in its core, which is composed mainly of iron and nickel at temperatures of more than 3,400-4,700°C (6,100-8,500°F). In 1820, Orsted discovered that a sustained electric current produces a magnetic field, and in 1831, Faraday found that a changing magnetic field induces an electric voltage. It was thus postulated that if the earth began with a large electrical current in its core, that would have produced a strong magnetic field. However, because there would be no ongoing power source, that current would decay and the magnetic field would decay also. However, this decaying magnetic field as it changed would itself induce another electrical current, weaker than the original one. Because the magnetic field is strong enough, its exponential decay rate can be accurately calculated.

In the early 1970s, it was noted that measurements since 1835 of the main (or dipole) part of the earth's magnetic field showed that it had been decaying at a rate of 5 percent per century.[1] Archaeological measurements show that the earth's magnetic field was 40 percent stronger in AD 1000 than it is today.[2] Thus, it was proposed that the earth's magnetic field was caused by a freely-decaying electric current in the earth's core, which is entirely consistent with the demonstrated rate of field decay and experiments on the materials that make up the earth's core.[3] Furthermore, it was calculated that the current could not have been decaying for more than 10,000 years; otherwise its starting strength would have been sufficient to melt the earth. Thus, the earth must be less than 10,000 years old.

However, because uniformitarian geologists maintain the earth is billions of years

---

1   A. L. McDonald and R. H. Gunst, 1967, An analysis of the earth's magnetic field from 1835 to 1965, *ESSA Technical Report, IER 46-IES 1*, Washington: US Government Printing Office; T. G. Barnes, 1971, Decay of the earth's magnetic field and the geochronological implications, *Creation Research Society Quarterly*, 8 (1): 24-29.

2   R. T. Merrill and M. W. McElhinney, 1983, *The Earth's Magnetic Field*, London: Academic Press, 101-106.

3   T. G. Barnes, 1971; F. D. Stacey, 1967, Electrical resistivity of the earth's core, *Earth and Planetary Science Letters*, 3: 204-206.

old, and this decaying current model for the origin of the earth's magnetic field is incompatible with that timescale, their preferred model is a self-sustaining dynamo. In their model, the earth's rotation and convection circulates the molten, liquid iron/nickel in the outer core, thus producing an electric current that generates the magnetic field. However, sustained research has not produced a workable geodynamo model, because there are many problems such a model must overcome, including explaining the measured electrical currents in the sea floor.[4] Nevertheless, recently a numerical model of the supposed geodynamo has been produced that even displays reversal behavior.[5] However, this numerical geodynamo model is based on computer simulations, which could easily have hidden flaws, and that also depend on the starting parameters used. Indeed, to make the simulations appear to work, values for one component of the magnetic field must be made ten times higher than the true value based on actual measurements, and the electrical conductivity of the molten metal in the outer core must be made more than twelve times higher than laboratory measurements would allow.[6]

Nevertheless, the major criticism used by uniformitarian geologists against the young-earth, freely-decaying electric current model for the earth's magnetic field is the evidence in volcanic rocks that the magnetic field has reversed numerous times in the past. While volcanic lavas are still molten, the magnetic domains within some of the crystallizing magnetite (iron oxide) grains partly align themselves in the direction of the earth's magnetic field at that time, so that once the rock is fully cooled, that magnetic alignment is "frozen in." Thus, volcanic rocks, particularly on the ocean floor, contain a permanent record of the earth's magnetic field through time. However, even though uniformitarian geologists do not have a good explanation for these magnetic field reversals, they maintain, of course, that the young-earth, freely-decaying electric current model must be invalid. Furthermore, their geodynamo model requires at least thousands of years for a reversal to occur. Therefore, with their dating assumptions, they believe reversals occur at intervals of millions of years, in keeping with their insistence that the earth is old.

Unlike uniformitarian geologists' geodynamo model, the young-earth, freely-decaying electric current model for the earth's magnetic field is easily modified to explain field reversals consistent with the paleomagnetic data in volcanic rocks. As the liquid molten metal in the earth's inner core flowed upward due to convection,

4   L. J. Lanzerotti et al, 1986, Measurements of the large-scale direct-current earth potential and possible implications for the geomagnetic dynamo, *Science*, 229: 47-49.

5   G. A. Glatzmaier and P. H. Roberts, 1995, A three-dimensional convective dynamo solution with rotating and finitely conducting inner core and mantle, *Physics of the Earth and Planetary Interiors*, 91: 63-75; G. A. Glatzmaier and P. H. Roberts, 1995, A three-dimensional self-consistent computer simulation of a geomagnetic field reversal, *Nature*, 377: 203-209.

6   D. R. Humphreys, 1996, Can evolutionists now explain the earth's magnetic field? *Creation Research Society Quarterly*, 33 (3): 184-185.

this would make the field reverse quickly.[7] Furthermore, the catastrophically subducting tectonic plates during the Flood cataclysm would have sharply cooled the outer parts of the core, driving convection in the outer core.[8] Thus, most of the reversals would have occurred during the year of the Flood, every week or two, and then after the Flood there would have been large fluctuations due to residual motion. This is supported by measurements on archaeological materials from about 1000 BC and AD 1000, which show that the surface geomagnetic field intensity slowly increased to a maximum about the time of Christ, and then declined slowly before becoming approximately exponential from AD 1000 onwards. However, the reversals and fluctuations would not have halted the loss of energy, which would decay even faster through the whole period.

This modified young-earth model also explains why the sun, as a gigantic ball of hot, energetically-moving, electrically-conducting gas, reverses its magnetic field every eleven years.[9] On the other hand, the dynamo model has trouble explaining how the sun not only reverses its magnetic field, but also regenerates it and maintains its intensity, supposedly over billions of years. A test was also proposed for the young-earth magnetic field model, namely, that magnetic reversals should be found in volcanic rocks known to have cooled in days or weeks. For example, it was predicted that in a thin lava flow, the outside would cool first and record the earth's magnetic field in one direction, while the inside would have cooled a short time later and have recorded the field in another direction. Three years after this prediction appeared in print, leading paleomagnetism researchers found such a thin lava layer that had cooled within fifteen days and had 90° of reversal recorded continuously in it.[10] Furthermore, a few years later the same investigators reported finding similar evidence of an even faster reversal.[11] This evidence thus corroborates the modified young-earth, freely-decaying electric current model for the earth's magnetic field, and conclusively demonstrates the impossibility of the billions-of-years uniformitarian geodynamo model.

In order to deal with this devastating quandary, evolutionists have sought to find various arguments or loopholes by which they might yet salvage the billions-of-years geodynamo model. Some have suggested that the decay of the magnetic field

7   D. R. Humphreys, 1986, Reversal of the earth's magnetic field during the Genesis Flood, in *Proceedings of the First International Conference on Creationism*, vol. 2, R. E. Walsh, C. L. Brooks and R. S. Crowell, eds., Pittsburgh, PA: Creation Science Fellowship, 113-126.

8   J. R. Baumgardner, 1986, Numerical simulation of the large-scale tectonic changes accompanying the Flood, in *Proceedings of the First International Conference on Creationism*, vol. 2, R. E. Walsh, C. L. Brooks and R. S. Crowell, eds., Pittsburgh, PA: Creation Science Fellowship, 17-30.

9   Humphreys, 1986.

10   R. S. Coe and M. Prévot, 1989, Evidence suggesting extremely rapid field variation during a geomagnetic reversal, *Earth and Planetary Science Letters*, 92 (3/4): 292-298; A. A. Snelling, 1991, "Fossil" magnetism reveals rapid reversals of the earth's magnetic field, *Creation Ex Nihilo*, 13 (3): 46-50.

11   R. S. Coe, M. Prévot and P. Camps, 1995, New evidence for extraordinarily rapid change of the geomagnetic field during a reversal, *Nature*, 374 (6564): 687-692; A. A. Snelling, 1995, The "principle of least astonishment"! *Creation Ex Nihilo Technical Journal*, 9 (2): 138-139.

is linear rather than exponential.[12] However, experimental measurements indicate that currents in resistance/inductance circuits always decay exponentially, not linearly, after the power source is switched off. Thus, even if a linear fit of the very recent measurements of the magnetic field looks reasonable, it's physically absurd when dealing with the real world of electric circuits, where exponential decay is an intrinsic component of electromagnetic theory. Furthermore, the originator of the young-earth model for the magnetic field was a professor of physics who had written university textbooks on electromagnetism! In any case, if the decay had been linear, the upper limit for the age of the earth's magnetic field would still only be 90 million years, well short of the uniformitarian 4.5 billion years, and future linear decay would mean the earth's magnetic field would soon disappear all together!

Other evolutionists have suggested that, even though the dipole component of the earth's magnetic field has been decaying, the strength of the non-dipole field has been increasing, so the total magnetic field has remained almost constant.[13] However, this apparent loophole has already been dealt with and categorically closed.[14] In fact, this claim results from confusion between measurements of the magnetic field intensity and its energy. The non-dipole component of the magnetic field may experience a small increase in its field intensity, but it does not represent a large enough increase in energy to compensate for the enormous amount of energy being lost from the dipole component. Indeed, using the data from the International Geomagnetic Reference Field for the most accurately recorded period from 1970 to 2000, the measurements show that the dipole part of the field steadily lost 235±5 billion megajoules of energy, while the non-dipole part gained only 129±8 billion megajoules, so that over that 30-year period, the net loss of energy from all observable parts of the field was 1.41±0.16 percent.[15] At that rate, the total energy stored in the earth's magnetic field (including both the dipole and non-dipole components) is decreasing with a half-life of 1,465±166 years.

The implication of this demonstrable conclusion, based on hard and accurate published field data, is that the young-earth creationist model has been emphatically confirmed. At creation, the earth's magnetic field was generated by freely-decaying electric currents in the outer core, but convection in the outer core during the Flood cataclysm caused reversals in the polarity of the field, followed by subsequent intensity fluctuations. Nevertheless, the magnetic field has rapidly

---

12   A. Hayward, 1987, *Creation and Evolution: The Facts and the Fallacies*, London: Triangle SPCK, 137-139.

13   R. Ecker, 1990, *Dictionary of Science and Creationism*, Buffalo, NY: Prometheus Books, 105.

14   D. R. Humphreys, 1990, Physical mechanism for reversal of the earth's magnetic field during the Flood, in *Proceedings of the Second International Conference on Creationism*, vol. 2, R. E. Walsh and C. L. Brooks, eds., Pittsburgh, PA: Creation Science Fellowship, 129-142.

15   D. R. Humphreys, 2002, The earth's magnetic field is still losing energy, *Creation Research Society Quarterly*, 39 (1): 1-11.

and continuously lost total energy ever since it was created, and the rate of that loss indicates that the earth and its magnetic field were created only about 6,000 years ago.

109

SEA SALT, EROSION, AND SEDIMENTS

Salt in the Sea

Many processes continually add salts and other chemicals to the waters of the earth's oceans and seas, particularly weathering and erosion of land surfaces, and river transportation of chemicals and sediments. However, these salts aren't as readily removed from the sea, resulting in a steady increase in the sea's saltiness. How much salt is in the sea and the rates at which salts are added into and removed from the sea can be calculated from appropriate measurements. Assuming how these rates varied in the past and how much salt was in the sea originally, it is possible to calculate a maximum age for the sea. This method of estimating the age of the earth was first proposed by Halley in 1715.[1] Subsequently, Joly estimated that the oceans were no more than 80 to 90 million years old.[2] Obviously, even this estimate is far too young for uniformitarian geologists and evolutionists, who believe that the oceans are at least three billion years old.

The most common chemicals in ocean water are sodium and chlorine, which are the constituents of common table salt (sodium chloride). Measurements reveal that every kilogram of seawater contains about 10.8 grams of dissolved sodium. Because the ocean contains 1,370 million cubic kilometers of water, there is a total of 14,700 trillion tons of sodium in the oceans. It is thus easy to make a calculation of the age of the oceans by analyzing data from conventional geological sources of the input and output rates of sodium.[3]

Every year, rivers and other sources dump about 457 million tons of sodium

---

1   E. Halley, 1715, A short account of the saltness of the ocean, and of the several lakes that emit no rivers; with a proposal, by help thereof, to discover the age of the world, *Philosophical Transactions of the Royal Society of London*, 29: 296-300.

2   J. Joly, 1899, An estimate of the geological age of the earth, *Science Transactions of the Royal Dublin Society, New Series*, 7 (3); Reprinted in *Annual Report of the Smithsonian Institution*, June 30, 1899, 247-288.

3   S. A. Austin and D. R. Humphreys, 1990, The sea's missing salt: A dilemma for evolutionists, in *Proceedings of the Second International Conference on Creationism*, vol. 2, R. E. Walsh and C. L. Brooks, eds., Pittsburgh, PA: Creation Science Fellowship, 17-33.

into the oceans[4] For example, water on the land leaches sodium from weathered minerals, and that sodium is carried into the ocean by rivers. Some salt is also supplied by water flowing through the ground directly into the sea. This water often has a high salt concentration. Furthermore, ocean-floor sediments release sodium into the ocean water, as do hot springs (hydrothermal vents) on the ocean floor. Volcanic dust also contributes some sodium. Even if sodium input to the oceans in the past was less, using assumptions for inflow rates that are most generous to evolutionists, the minimum possible amount in the past would have been 356 million tons of sodium input per year.

However, the rate of sodium output is far less than the input. In fact, only about 122 million tons of sodium, or 27 percent of the sodium input, manages to leave the sea each year.[5] The major process that removes sodium from the sea is salt spray. Some sodium is lost from the ocean when water is trapped in pores and sediments on the ocean floor. Another major process of sodium loss is ion exchange, when clays absorb sodium in exchange for calcium that is released into the ocean water. There are also minerals with crystal structures that absorb sodium from the ocean water. The maximum possible amount of sodium that leaves the oceans every year, even if assumptions that are most generous to evolutionists are used in the calculation, is 206 million tons per year.

All observations suggest that all of the incoming sodium that isn't returned to the land simply accumulates in the oceans. Thus, if the oceans originally contained no sodium, then the sodium in them today would have accumulated in less than 42 million years at today's input and output rates. Even this maximum age for the oceans is far less than the uniformitarian age of at least 3 billion years. The usual response from uniformitarian evolutionists is that this discrepancy is due to past sodium inputs being much less and outputs being much greater. However, if input and output rates are used in the calculations that are most generous to evolutionary scenarios, then the estimated maximum age is still only 62 million years. Nevertheless, a more recent study shows that salt is entering the oceans even faster than previously thought, because groundwater directly discharging to the sea is as much as 40 percent of the discharge via river flow, much greater than the previously estimated 10 percent.[6] Furthermore, additional calculations for many other seawater elements yield much younger ages for the oceans.[7] Therefore, it is quite obvious that even 42 million years may be a generous maximum age for the

4   M. Meybeck, 1979, Concentrations des eaux fluvials en majeurs et apports en solution aux oceans, *Revue de Géologie Dynamique et de Géographie Physique*, 21 (3): 215-246; F. L. Sayles, and P. C. Mangelsdorf, 1979, Cation-exchange characteristics of Amazon with a suspended sediment and its reaction with seawater, *Geochimica et Cosmochimica Acta*, 43: 767-779.

5   Sayles and Mangelsdorf, 1979; Austin and Humphreys, 1990.

6   W. S. Moore, 1996, Large groundwater inputs to coastal waters revealed by [226]Ra enrichments, *Nature*, 380 (6575): 612-614; T. M. Church, 1996, An underground route for the water cycle, *Nature*, 380 (6575): 579-580.

7   S. Nevins, 1973, Evolution: The Ocean Says NO!, *Acts & Facts*, 2 (11).

oceans using all these calculations.

However, it's important to stress that this is not the actual age of the oceans, but only a maximum age based on the assumption that there was no salt originally dissolved in the oceans. On the other hand, in the biblical model of earth history, there can be no doubt that God created the oceans initially containing some saltiness, in order that saltwater fish could live within them. Furthermore, during the Flood cataclysm much more salt would have found its way into the oceans due to all the erosion, sedimentation, and volcanism. During this time, the sodium input would have been an order of magnitude or more higher than current input rates. Furthermore, there would have been a much higher input rate of salts as the Flood waters retreated and eroded the current land surface. Thus, the true age of the oceans, using realistic assumptions governed by the biblical framework of earth history, would more likely be only thousands of years.

Erosion of Continents

The earth's land surfaces are constantly being weathered and eroded by the water falling on them as rain and flowing over them. Soil, rock, and mineral grains are washed into rivers that transport these as sediments out to the oceans. The rate at which sediments have been transported to, and deposited in, the ocean basins can easily be estimated by measuring the volume of sediments rivers carry at their mouths. River sediment measurements can also be used to calculate the rate at which rivers are eroding the land surfaces they drain. Such measurements show that some rivers are eroding their basins at a rate of 35 inches (900 mm) or more in height per thousand years, while others erode only 0.04 inches (1 mm) per thousand years.[8] Thus, the average height reduction for all the continents across the earth's surface is estimated to be about 2.4 inches (61 mm) per thousand years.

This average rate of land erosion might seem quite slow, but it needs to be seen from the perspective of the uniformitarian geologic timescale, and the current thinking that there has been exposed land surfaces available for erosion for 3.5 billion years.[9] As has already been pointed out, using an estimated average erosion rate of 61 mm per thousand years, the North American continent would be eroded flat to sea level in "a mere 10 million years."[10] Even if the slowest erosion rate of

8   J. N. Holleman, 1968, The sediment yield of major rivers of the world, *Water Resources Research*, 4: 737-747; E. W. Sparks, 1986, Geomorphology, in *Geographies for Advanced Study*, S. H. Beaver, ed., London and New York: Longman Group, 509-510; J. D. Milliman and J. P. M. Syvitski, 1992, Geomorphic/tectonic control of sediment discharge to the ocean: The importance of small mountainous rivers, *Journal of Geology*, 100: 525-544; A. Roth, 1998, *Origins: Linking Science and Scripture*, Hagerstown, MD: Review and Herald Publishing, 264.

9   R. Buick, J. R. Thornett, N. J. McNaughton, J. B. Smith, M. E. Barley and M. Savage, 1995, Record of emergent continental crust ≈3.5 billion years ago in the Pilbara Craton of Australia, *Nature*, 375: 574-577.

10   S. Judson and D. F. Ritter, 1964, Rates of regional denudation in the United States, *Journal of*

only 1 mm per thousand years is used, based on an average of 623 meters above sea level for the continents, the continents would have eroded to sea level in only 623 million years. This, of course, begs the question to why the earth's continents are still above sea level if they are up to 3.5 billion years old. This question is even more acute when one considers mountains ranges such as the Caledonides of western Europe and the Appalachians of eastern North America, which geologists assume are several hundred million years old. Why are these ranges still here today if they are so old? After all, rates of erosion are fast in mountainous regions, with erosion rates as high as 1,000 mm per thousand years in the Himalayas.[11]

However, another way of highlighting this glaring discrepancy is to again consider the erosion rates based on quantities of sediments delivered by rivers to the ocean basins from the continents. Calculations have varied from 8,000 million to 58,000 million metric tons per year.[12] These estimates are probably low, because normal measuring procedures do not account for the rare catastrophic events (such as local floods), during which the transport of sediments increases considerably. They also do not consider the sediments that are rolled or pushed along the beds of rivers. Nevertheless, the average rate from a dozen studies is 24,108 million metric tons per year. At this rate, the average height of the world's continents (623 meters) above sea level would erode away in about 9.6 million years, a figure close to the already published 10 million year figure for North America.

Geologists often maintain that mountains still exist because uplift is constantly renewing them from below.[13] However, even though mountains are still rising, the process of uplift and erosion could not continue long without eradicating ancient sedimentary layers contained in the mountains. Yet sedimentary strata that are supposedly very ancient are still well represented in the earth's mountain ranges, as well as elsewhere. Even taking into account that human agricultural practices have increased erosion rates, such an explanation does little to resolve the discrepancy. Proposing a dry climate in the past, and thus slower erosion rates, also will not resolve the discrepancy, because estimates of global precipitation suggest variable but average, or even slightly wetter, conditions over the past three billion years.[14]

Another problematic discrepancy for the supposed long geologic ages is allegedly ancient planar land surfaces, which stretch over large areas and yet show little or no evidence of erosion. For example, Kangaroo Island off the southern Australian

Geophysical Research, 69: 3395-3401; R. H. Dott, Jr. and R. L. Batten, 1988, *Evolution of the Earth*, fourth edition, New York, St. Louis, and San Francisco: McGraw-Hill Book Company, 155.

11   H. W. Menard, 1961, Some rates of regional erosion, *Journal of Geology*, 69: 154-161.

12   Roth, 1998, 265, Table 15.2, based on sources indicated therein.

13   H. Blatt, G. Middleton and R. Murray, 1980, *Origin of Sedimentary Rocks*, second edition, Englewood Cliffs, NJ: Prentice-Hall, 18.

14   L. A. Frakes, 1979, *Climates Throughout Geologic Time*, Figure 9-1, Amsterdam, Oxford, and New York: Elsevier, 261.

coast covers an area of about 87 miles (140 km long) by 37 miles (60 km wide) and is extremely flat. However, the surface is estimated to be at least 160 million years old, based on both fossil and potassium-argon "dating."[15] How could such a surface exist for 160 million years without rainfall and surface water flow resulting in some pattern of channelized erosion, when there is very little evidence of such?

The alleged antiquity of erosion surfaces compared with the overall rate of erosion of land surfaces is indeed an insurmountable problem for uniformitarian dating methods. Nevertheless, evolutionary geologists still cling to the dates in the face of "common sense," as has been admitted:

> If some facets of the contemporary landscape are indeed as old as is suggested by the field evidence they not only constitute denial of commonsense and everyday observations but they also carry considerable implications for general theory.[16]

Quite clearly, the earth's continental land surfaces aren't all that old, and thus neither is the earth itself.

Sea Floor Sediments

The sediments eroded from the continental land surfaces are carried by rivers to ultimately be deposited on the floors and margins of the ocean basins. As noted above, the average rate of delivery to the oceans of sediments eroded from the continental land surfaces transported by rivers, calculated from twelve studies, is more than 24 billion metric tons per year. Yet this estimate is probably somewhat lower than the actual volume of sediments delivered by rivers to the ocean basins, because the studies from which this average figure was derived did not include the rock material that rolls along river beds. All this sediment and rock eventually accumulates on the basaltic ocean crust that makes up the ocean floor. It has been estimated that the average depth of all the sediments on the ocean floors worldwide is less than 400 meters.[17]

There is only one known mechanism by which sediments are removed from the ocean floor and that is during subduction of the ocean floor at trenches. As the sea floor slides slowly (a few cm per year) beneath the continents at the trenches, it is estimated that about 1 billion tons of sediment per year is subducted into

---

15   E. Daily, C. R. Twidale and A. R. Milnes, 1974, The age of the laterized summit surface on Kangaroo Island and adjacent areas of South Australia, *Journal of the Geological Society of Australia*, 21 (4): 387-392.

16   C. R. Twidale, 1998, Antiquity of landforms: An "extremely unlikely" concept vindicated, *Australian Journal of Earth Sciences*, 45: 657-668.

17   W. W. Hay et al, 1988, Mass/age distribution and composition of sediments on the ocean floor and the global rate of sediment subduction, *Journal of Geophysical Research*, 93 (B12): 14,933-940.

the mantle with the sea floor.[18] As far as is known, the other 23 billion tons of sediment per year simply accumulate on the ocean floors. At that rate the sediments accumulating on the ocean floor as a result of erosion of the continents would have accumulated in approximately 12 million years.

Yet according to the uniformitarian timescale of the evolution and development of the earth, erosion and tectonic plate subduction have been occurring as long as the oceans have existed, at least 3 billion years. Furthermore, even just considering the latest and present cycle of plate tectonics, the present ocean basins have been in existence for at least 200 million years. If that were so, then according to the present rate of accumulation of sediments on the ocean floors, the ocean basins should now be massively choked with sediments many kilometers deep. Since they aren't, the measurements of sediments carried to the ocean basins, and the rate of accumulation on the ocean floors, don't support the claim that the earth and its ocean basins are millions of years old.

On the other hand, because the present ocean basins were only formed in the biblical framework for earth history toward the end of the Flood cataclysm some 4,500 or so years ago, the present amount of sediments on the ocean floors had to be deposited in a short time. This was largely accomplished, not at present rates of accumulation, but as a result of the Flood waters catastrophically draining off the emerging continental land surfaces at the end of the Flood. These erosion rates would have been orders of magnitude greater than the presently measured erosion rates. It is thus the biblical model of earth history that is consistent with the evidence.

---

18   Hay et al, 1988.

110

Volcanic Activity and Helium

Crustal Growth through Volcanic Activity

The sedimentary strata exposed in the continents are not the only rock layers that make up the earth's continental crust. There are many volcanic rock layers, the result of volcanic eruptions spewing out lavas and ash. Single eruptions produce anywhere from small volumes to many cubic kilometers of volcanic material. In most instances, the original molten rock was generated at the top of the earth's mantle, so the outpourings of lavas at the earth's surface are regarded as being added to the earth's crust. In this way, it has been suggested that the earth's crust has developed:

> Emission of lava at the present rate of 0.8 km³ year throughout the earth's history of 4.5 x 10⁹ years or even for the 3 x 10⁹ years since the oldest known rocks were formed would have poured out lava of the order of 3 x 10⁹ km³ on the Earth's surface. This corresponds approximately to the volume of the continents (about 30 km x 1.1 x 10⁸ km²). A slightly higher rate of volcanism in the early stages of the Earth would allow for the emission of the oceanic crust as well.[1]

A subsequent calculation, based on a conservative estimate of an average of 1 cubic kilometer of volcanic material per year being ejected by the earth's volcanoes, suggested that in 3.5 billion years the entire earth should have been covered by a thick blanket of volcanic material reaching a height of 7 km![2] Of course, since estimates of the volume of volcanic rocks in the geologic record indicate only a small fraction of that amount, it was concluded the rate of volcanic activity in the past must have been erratic.

However, a more realistic estimate is that at present the world's volcanoes eject an average of about four cubic kilometers of lavas and ash per year. Single major

---

1   J. T. Wilson, 1959, Geophysics and continental growth, *American Scientist*, 47: 14.

2   G. B. Gregor, 1968, The rate of denudation in post-Algonkian time, *Koninkalijke Nederlandse Academie van Wetenschapper*, 71: 22-30.

eruptions can produce significant volumes, yet an estimate of only the major eruptions during four decades (1940-1980) suggests an average of three cubic kilometers per year.[3] However, that figure does not include a multitude of smaller eruptions, such as those that occur periodically in Hawaii, Indonesia, Central and South America, Iceland, Italy, and elsewhere. So an average volume of four cubic kilometers per year has been proposed as the best estimate.[4]

Now as far as the geologic record is concerned, it has been suggested that the surface of the earth contains 135 million cubic kilometers of sediment of volcanic origin, which represents 14.4 percent of the estimated total volume of sedimentary strata.[5] While 135 million cubic kilometers of volcanic materials is an impressive amount, at a rate of accumulation of four cubic kilometers per year, this volume found in the geologic record would have accumulated in less than 34 million years. Expressed another way, if the current production rate of volcanic material were extended over 2.5 billion years, there should be layers of volcanic material with a cumulative thickness of more than 19 kilometers all over the earth's surface, 24 times the amount of volcanic material that is found now.

The removal of this volcanic material by erosion does not offer a good solution to this inconsistency for the long uniformitarian geological ages, because erosion would only transfer the volcanic material from one place to another. Furthermore, removal of volcanic material would also eliminate the other rock layers containing it. In any case, the geologic record that contains this volcanic material is still well represented worldwide. Indeed, even recent historic major eruptions are dwarfed by the catastrophic volcanic eruptions that must have occurred in the past, during the outpouring of hundreds of millions of cubic kilometers of so-called flood basalts, such as those of the Deccan and Siberian Traps.

Therefore, no matter which way the evidence is viewed, volcanoes simply could not have been erupting for the 2.5 to 3.5 billion years during which the strata record of earth's continental crust has supposedly been accumulating. Put another way, the earth's continental crust simply cannot be that old. Within the biblical framework, much of the earth's continental crust would have been built catastrophically during the Creation Week, and in the year-long Flood cataclysm. The evidence for continental crustal growth via volcanic activity is most definitely consistent with that biblical framework for earth history.

3   S. Simkin, L. Siebert, L. McClelland, D. Bridge, C. Newhall and J. H. Latter, 1981, *Volcanoes of the World: A Regional Directory, Gazetter, and a Geochronology of Volcanism during the last 10,000 Years,* Stroudsburg, PA: Smithsonian Institution, Hutchinson Ross Publishing Company.

4   R. Decker and B. Decker, eds., 1982, *Volcanoes and the Earth's Interior: Readings from Scientific American,* San Francisco: W. H. Freeman and Company, 47.

5   A. D. Ronov and A. A. Yaroshevsky, 1969, Chemical composition of the earth's crust, in *The Earth's Crust and Upper Mantle: Structure, Dynamic Processes, and their Relation to Deep-Seated Geological Phenomena,* P. J. Hart, ed., American Geophysical Union, Geophysical Monograph 13: 37-57.

Helium in Rocks and in the Atmosphere

Uranium and thorium contained in rocks and minerals generate helium atoms as they are transformed by radioactive decay to lead. Helium is the second lightest element and is a noble gas, which means its atoms do not bond with atoms of other elements. So the small helium atoms in rocks and minerals easily fit between the atoms in crystal lattices and diffuse (leak) out of, and so escape from, the minerals and rocks. The hotter the rocks, the faster the helium escapes, and the deeper one goes into the earth, the hotter the rocks.

In a study of a deep, hot Precambrian granitic rock, drilled for potential geothermal energy, it was found that zircon crystals that contained uranium also contained large amounts of helium.[6] Even the deepest and hottest zircons (at 197°C or 387°F) contained far more helium in them than expected, given the uranium-lead radioisotope "age" for the zircon crystals of 1.5 billion years. At the time of that study, no experimental measurements of the leakage or diffusion rate of helium from zircons was available. But it was still possible to calculate that in some of the zircon crystals, up to 58 percent of the helium that would have been generated from uranium decay over 1.5 billion years was still present in them.

Now several experimental determinations of the helium leakage (diffusion) rate from zircons of several different rock units, including this Precambrian granitic rock, are available and are in agreement.[7] These experimental measurements all showed that helium diffuses so rapidly out of zircon crystals that it should have all but disappeared after about 100,000 years. Because the uranium-lead radioisotope decay system indicates that originally there would have been 1.5 billion years worth of helium generated in these zircon crystals, the amounts of helium left in them should have long since leaked out. The measured amounts of retained helium in these zircon crystals, combined with the measured diffusion rate of helium from zircon, can be used to calculate their helium diffusion age. Indeed, there is so much helium still left in these zircons that based on the measured rate of helium diffusion from zircons, these zircon crystals have an average helium diffusion age of only 6,000 (±2,000) years.

Helium starts diffusing out of zircon crystals as soon as it is produced by

---

6   R. V. Gentry, G. L. Glish and E. H. McBay, 1982, Differential helium retention in zircons: Implications for nuclear waste containment, *Geophysical Research Letters*, 9 (10): 1129-1130.

7   S. W. Reiners, K. A. Farley and H. J. Hicks, 2002, He diffusion and (U-Th)/He thermochronometry of zircon: Initial results from Fish Canyon Tuff and Gold Butte, Nevada, *Tectonophysics*, 349 (1-4): 297-308; D. R. Humphreys, S. A. Austin, J. R. Baumgardner and A. A. Snelling, 2003, Helium diffusion rates support accelerated nuclear decay, in *Fifth International Conference on Creationism*, R. L. Ivey Jr., ed., Pittsburgh, PA: Creation Science Fellowship, 175-196; D. R. Humphreys, 2005, Young helium diffusion age of zircons supports accelerated nuclear decay, in *Radioisotopes and the Age of the Earth: Results of a Young-Earth Creationist Research Initiative*, L. Vardiman, A. A. Snelling and E. F. Chaffin, eds., El Cajon, CA: Institute for Creation Research and Chino Valley, AZ: Creation Research Society, 25-100.

radioactive decay. Therefore, the radioactive decay that produced the helium must have occurred within that timeframe of only about 6,000 years. Yet measurements of the uranium-lead radioisotope system in these same zircons indicate that 1.5-billion-years worth of uranium decay has occurred in these zircons. How then could 1.5 billion years worth of helium have been produced and accumulated in so little time? The best answer is that at some time in the recent past there had to have been an episode (or episodes) of grossly accelerated nuclear decay in which the radioactive decay timescale was enormously compressed, from 1.5 billion radioisotope years into 6,000 years of real time. Within the biblical framework for earth history, such an episode of accelerated nuclear decay logically occurred during Creation Week, during the year-long Flood cataclysm, or more likely both, when geological processes were also occurring at catastrophic rates.

Because this contradiction is so glaring and devastating to the uniformitarian long-ages timescale, attempts have been made to discredit this evidence. For example, it has been suggested that perhaps helium has instead diffused into the zircon crystals from outside sources, thus giving them this incorrect young diffusion age. However, such criticism ignores the experimental measurements of the helium concentration in the biotite flakes in which the zircon crystals were embedded.[8] The helium concentration in biotite flakes was actually much lower than the helium concentration in the zircon crystals, which means that according to the well-known fundamental diffusion law, the helium would have been diffusing from the higher concentration in the zircon crystals out into the lower concentration in the surrounding biotite flakes. In fact, the amount of helium in the biotite flakes was found to be exactly equivalent to the amount of helium that has leaked out of the zircon crystals. So any and every external source of helium cannot rescue the uniformitarian timescale, because the experimental evidence demonstrates conclusively that the helium generated by uranium decay in the zircon has been diffusing out into the surrounding biotite flakes in only about 6,000 years.

Another critic has suggested that there could have been resistance to the diffusion of helium out of the zircon crystals at the boundary or interface between the zircon crystals and the surrounding biotite flakes. This resistance would stop the helium from diffusing out of the zircon crystals and cause the retention of anomalous high helium concentrations. However, this desperate postulation was also easily refuted, because the zircon crystals are always found sitting in between the parallel stacked sheets that make up the biotite flakes. Therefore, there is an intrinsic weakness within the biotite flakes that would have in fact made it easier for the helium to leak out of the zircon crystals between the biotite sheets into the biotite flakes. Thus, all available evidence confirms that the true age of the zircon crystals, and the granitic rock containing them, is not 1.5 billion years, but only 6,000±2,000 years.

---

8   D. R. Humphreys, S. A. Austin, J. R. Baumgardner and A. A. Snelling, 2004, Helium diffusion age of 6000 years supports accelerated nuclear decay, *Creation Research Society Quarterly*, 41 (1): 1-16; Humphreys, 2005.

The net result of the helium leakage from minerals and rocks is that ultimately this radiogenic helium (helium produced by radioactive decay) diffuses through the earth's crust to the earth's surface and leaks out into the atmosphere. More than 50 years ago, it was realized that there is not nearly enough helium in the atmosphere to correspond to the supposed age of the earth, and to the rate at which helium is escaping from crustal rocks into the atmosphere.[9] Indeed, it was in 1957 that the problem with helium in the atmosphere was forcefully brought to the attention of the scientific community. Estimates of the leakage rate of helium from crustal rocks into the atmosphere and the helium content of the atmosphere were highlighted, and then contrasted with the resultant question: "Where is the earth's radiogenic helium?"[10] In answer to the question, it was stated that the helium problem "... leads...to an 'anomalous' atmospheric chronometry."

Here then is the helium problem. The measured flux, or rate of introduction, of helium from the crust of the earth into the atmosphere is estimated to be 2×10^6 atoms per cm^2 per second (13 million helium atoms per square inch each second).[11] On the other hand, the estimated flux, or theoretical rate of escape, of helium from the atmosphere to space due to thermal escape is 5×10^4 atoms per cm^2 per second (about 0.3 million atoms per square inch each second). Other escape mechanisms such as the polar wind, solar wind sweeping, and hot-ion exchange have not been found to be important contributors to the loss of helium in space. Therefore, the helium in the atmosphere has been accumulating at a very rapid rate. The current measured column density of helium in the atmosphere is 1.1×10^{20} atoms per cm^2. If the earth's atmosphere had no helium when it formed, and the helium accumulated in the atmosphere at the current estimated rate, then the present density of helium in the atmosphere would have accumulated in less than only 1.8 million years. Of course, this is not to say that this is the age of the earth's atmosphere, but 1.8 million years is more than 2,500 times shorter than the presumed age of the earth of more than 4.5 billion years. Consequently, long-age atmospheric physicists admit that "...there appears to be a problem with the helium budget of the atmosphere,"[12] and that this helium escape problem "...will not go away, and it is unsolved."[13]

This estimate of less than only 1.8 million years for the atmosphere's helium to accumulate is, of course, based on the assumption that the earth's atmosphere contained no helium at its beginning. The second assumption is that the helium flux from the crustal rocks into the atmosphere has always been the same throughout

---

9   G. E. Hutchinson, 1947, Marginalia, *American Scientist*, 35: 118.

10   M. A. Cook, 1957, Where is the earth's radiogenic helium? *Nature*, 179 (4557): 213.

11   L. Vardiman, 1990, *The Age of the Earth's Atmosphere: A Study of the Helium Flux through the Atmosphere*, El Cajon, CA: Institute for Creation Research.

12   J. C. G. Walker, 1977, *Evolution of the Atmosphere*, London: McMillan.

13   J. W. Chamberlain and D. M. Hunten, 1987, *Theory of Planetary Atmospheres*, second edition, London: Academic Press.

the earth's history. However, neither of these assumptions would be valid within the biblical framework of earth history. First, at the creation of the earth it is likely that God created the atmosphere with some helium in it, along with all the other atmospheric gases, because the helium in the atmosphere does serve a useful purpose. Second, and more importantly, as a result of the catastrophic geologic processes operating during the year-long Flood cataclysm, including accelerated nuclear decay that would have produced more helium at an accelerated rate, the rate of helium flux from crustal rocks into the atmosphere would have been far greater than at present. Thus, as a result of these two considerations, the time for the accumulation of the atmosphere's current helium content would have been much less than the estimated 1.8 million years. Therefore, the helium in the atmosphere is completely consistent with the earth and its atmosphere only being 6,000-7,000 years old, rather than the age of 4.5 billion years claimed by uniformitarians.

Two final considerations are worth noting. First, the usual method used by old-earth advocates, to avoid this helium evidence for a young atmosphere and earth, is to assume that the enormous quantities of helium generated during past eons somehow attained the required escape velocity, overcame gravity, and escaped from the atmosphere completely into space.[14] However, this requires temperatures in the outermost portion of the atmosphere that are extremely high, much higher than those required for all the necessary helium to reach escape velocity. Second, making this helium problem worse for uniformitarians is the discovery that there are large volumes of helium in the earth's crust that have not been derived by radioactive decay, but instead are considered primordial, that is, they have been present inside the earth since its beginning.[15] This means there is even more helium to escape through the earth's crustal rocks into the atmosphere than just the helium that has been generated by radioactive decay. It also means that if the earth is 4.5 billion years old there has been even more helium that has needed to escape into outer space from the earth's atmosphere by this postulated heating in the outermost atmosphere. On the contrary, the presence of this primordial helium only serves to suggest that the maximum age of the atmosphere measured by helium accumulation is much less than the calculated 1.8 million years.

---

14   L. Spitzer, 1949, The terrestrial atmosphere above 300km, in *The Atmospheres of the Earth and Planets*, G. P. Kuiper, ed., Chicago: University of Chicago Press, 211-247; D. M. Hunten, 1973, The escape of light gases from planetary atmospheres, *Journal of the Atmospheric Sciences*, 30: 1481-1494.

15   H. Craig and J. E. Lupton, 1976, Primordial neon, helium and hydrogen in oceanic basalts, *Earth and Planetary Science Letters*, 31: 369-385.

111

RADIOHALOS, RADIOCARBON AND TREE RINGS

Radiohalos

Referred to previously, radiohalos are the physical scars in minerals produced by alpha (α)-particles during radioactive decay, primarily of uranium and its daughter atoms. The black mica biotite is the most common mineral in which radiohalos are found. Tiny zircon inclusions in the biotite flakes contain uranium. The α-particles are ejected from these radiocenters to produce the microscopic discolored spheres known as uranium radiohalos (Figure 70, page 1098). The discoloration is the most intense where the α-particles stop, leading to a dark ring. However, in the uranium decay chain there are eight steps at which α-particles are emitted as uranium progressively decays through its chain of daughter products to its stable lead end member. The α-particles emitted at each of these eight α-decay steps has a characteristic energy, so the α-particles from these eight α-decay steps travel different distances in the surrounding host biotite (Figure 71, page 1099). This results in a fully-formed uranium radiohalo containing eight distinctive rings (Figure 70b).[1]

The three last α-decay steps, and thus the last three rings to form in a uranium radiohalo, are "parented" by three isotopes of the rare metal polonium (Po). These three polonium isotopes decay extremely rapidly, as measured by their very short half-lives: 3.1 minutes for polonium-218, 164 microseconds for polonium-214, and 138 days for polonium-210. What is highly significant is that in many of the same rocks in which biotite flakes host uranium radiohalos, there are also radiohalos with only the rings produced by these three polonium isotopes (Figures 71 and 72, pages 1099-1100). That means no uranium could have been present in the radiocenters of these ^{218}Po, ^{214}Po, and ^{210}Po radiohalos, named due to their ring structures that indicate the polonium radioisotopes in the radiocenters that parented the radiohalos. However, herein lays a profound dilemma. The polonium responsible for generating these radiohalos had to somehow have a separate

---

1   R. V. Gentry, 1973, Radioactive halos, *Annual Review of Nuclear Science*, 23: 347-362; A. A. Snelling, 2000, Radiohalos, in *Radioisotopes and the Age of the Earth: A Young-Earth Creationist Research Initiative*, L. Vardiman, A. A. Snelling and E. F. Chaffin, eds., El Cajon, CA: Institute for Creation Research and St. Joseph, MO: Creation Research Society, 381-468.

existence from the uranium that normally "parents" it. Furthermore, after ten half-lives only about 1,000th of the original parent isotope is left, and after 20 half-lives only about 1 millionth is left. This means that the polonium radiohalos could only have formed within about 20 half-lives, which is a very short timescale for these polonium isotopes. For example, 20 half-lives for ^{218}Po would be just over one hour since its half-life is only 3.1 minutes. Quite clearly, these polonium radiohalos had to have formed extremely rapidly compared to the uniformitarian timescale for geological processes, so evolutionary geologists have had to admit that these polonium radiohalos are "a very tiny mystery."[2]

The solution to this supposed mystery, which explains how these polonium radiohalos form extremely rapidly, has further implications regarding the ages of rocks and the rapid rate of important geological processes. As has been explained earlier, the closest source for the polonium isotopes, which concentrated in the radiocenters to form the polonium radiohalos, is the polonium produced by uranium decay in the zircons that are the radiocenters for the adjacent uranium radiohalos in the same biotite flakes. Thus, it has been postulated that hydrothermal (hot water) fluids, produced from the granite magmas as they cool, have transported the polonium isotopes the very short distances (<1 mm), between the sheets in the biotite flakes' crystal structure, from the zircons to the polonium halo centers.[3] The transport and concentration of the polonium isotopes by hydrothermal fluids to produce the polonium radiohalos has been subsequently confirmed. It has been repeatedly demonstrated that where there are other evidences of the past presence of these hydrothermal fluids, there is a direct correlation with the greater numbers of polonium radiohalos.[4] The implications are that not only did the transport of polonium isotopes have to be rapid, or else the polonium radiohalos would not have likewise formed rapidly before the polonium isotopes decayed away, but that the uranium decay in the zircons had to be grossly accelerated to rapidly supply

2   R. V. Gentry, 1974, Radiohalos in a radiochronological and cosmological perspective, *Science*, 184: 62-66; R. V. Gentry, 1988, *Creation's Tiny Mystery*, Knoxville, TN: Earth Science Associates; Snelling, 2000.

3   A. A. Snelling and M. H. Armitage, 2003, Radiohalos—A tale of three plutons, in *Proceedings of the Fifth International Conference on Creationism*, R. L. Ivey Jr., ed., Pittsburgh, PA: Creation Science Fellowship, 243-267; A. A. Snelling, 2005, Radiohalos in granites: Evidence for accelerated nuclear decay, in *Radioisotopes and the Age of the Earth: Results of a Young-Earth Creationist Research Initiative*, L. Vardiman, A. A. Snelling and E. F. Chaffin, eds., El Cajon, CA: Institute for Creation Research and Chino Valley, AZ: Creation Research Society, 101-207.

4   Snelling, Radiohalos in granites, 2005; A. A. Snelling, 2005, Polonium radiohalos: The model for their formation tested and verified, *Acts & Facts*, 34 (8); A. A. Snelling, 2006, Confirmation of rapid metamorphism of rocks, *Acts & Facts*, 35 (2); A. A. Snelling, 2008, Testing the hydrothermal fluid transport model for polonium radiohalo formation: The Thunderhead Sandstone, Great Smoky Mountains, Tennessee-North Carolina, *Answers Research Journal*, 1: 53-64; A. A. Snelling, 2008, Radiohalos in the Cooma metamorphic complex, NSW, Australia: The mode and rate of regional metamorphism, in *Proceedings of the Sixth International Conference on Creationism*, A. A. Snelling, ed., Pittsburgh, PA: Creation Science Fellowship and Dallas, TX: Institute for Creation Research, 371-387; A. A. Snelling, 2008, Radiohalos in the Shap Granite, Lake District, England: Evidence that removes objections to Flood geology, in *Proceedings of the Sixth International Conference on Creationism*, A. A. Snelling, ed., Pittsburgh, PA: Creation Science Fellowship and Dallas, TX: Institute for Creation Research, 389-405; A. A. Snelling and D. Gates, 2009, Implications of polonium radiohalos in nested plutons of the Tuolumne Intrusive Suite, Yosemite, California, *Answers Research Journal*, 2: 53-77.

the needed polonium isotopes (discussed earlier), and geological processes such as the formation of granites and metamorphic rocks (to be discussed later) had to also occur extremely rapidly. Thus, polonium radiohalos are physical evidence of rapid geological processes, once claimed to require up to millions of years, but the timescales for which have now been shown to be compatible with the biblical timescales of a young earth and the year-long global Flood.

Somewhat unusual was the discovery of ^{210}Po radiohalos in partially coalified logs recovered from uranium mines on the Colorado Plateau.[5] These partially coalified logs were found in sedimentary strata from three different geological units of Jurassic, Triassic, and Eocene "ages" (supposedly from 35 to 245 million years old). It has been demonstrated that these uranium ore deposits formed as a result of uranium being transported through the sedimentary strata by ground waters, so this coalified wood would have been saturated in uranium-rich ground waters. Polonium produced by radioactive decay of some of the uranium would have also been present in the ground waters, and thus polonium atoms must have been preferentially attracted by sulfur and selenium atoms in nucleation centers, where they decayed to form the surrounding radiohalos. However, only ^{210}Po radiohalos were found in this partially coalified wood. The other polonium radiohalos did not form, which implies that because those polonium isotopes decay even more rapidly than ^{210}Po, there was insufficient time for them to diffuse through the coal and be attracted to the radiocenters. Thus, it is possible to deduce that the time for infiltration and formation of the ^{210}Po radiohalos would have only been a few months; otherwise the ^{210}Po would have decayed before being concentrated in the radiocenters.

However, many of these ^{210}Po radiohalos are elliptical, which means that after they had formed they were squashed. Even more remarkable is the observation that some of these squashed ^{210}Po radiohalos also have the normal spherical ^{210}Po ring superimposed on them. This means that after being squashed, there was still enough ^{210}Po in the radiocenters to form continuing normal spherical ^{210}Po radiohalos. In other words, there could only have been a few months between infiltration of the ground waters into the partially coalified logs and compression of the host sedimentary strata. Significantly, these so-called dual ^{210}Po radiohalos were found in partially coalified wood in each of the three different sedimentary formations that allegedly span more than 200 million years of the uniformitarian timescale. However, there was only the one groundwater infiltration event to form these radiohalos in these three sedimentary formations, followed by the same earth movement event responsible for compressing these strata and uplifting them to form the Colorado Plateau. Furthermore, these ground waters would have been present in the sedimentary rock units from the time of the deposition of the sediments. Thus, the deposition of these three sedimentary rock units

5   R. V. Gentry, W. H. Christie, D. H. Smith, J. F. Emery, S. A. Reynolds, R. Walker, S. S. Christy and P. A. Gentry, 1976, Radiohalos in coalified wood: New evidence relating to the time of uranium introduction and coalification, *Science*, 194: 315-318.

supposedly spanning more than 200 million years, followed by the formation of the ^{210}Po radiohalos in the partially coalified logs within them, and the earth movements causing compression and uplift of the plateau, all had to happen within a few months, rather than over those supposed 200 million years required by the uniformitarian scenario. In the same partly coalified wood were uranium radiohalos. Analyses of their radiocenters revealed large quantities of parent uranium, but hardly any daughter lead, confirming that the parent uranium and these radiohalos had only been generated a few thousand years ago.

Radiocarbon and Tree Rings

The problems with the radiocarbon dating method were discussed earlier. It was concluded that, because of long-age assumptions in conventional usage of this method, glaring inconsistencies and contradictions in geochronology have been misunderstood and the implications ignored. Instead, over the past 25 years, the use of the more sensitive and accurate accelerator mass spectrometry (AMS) technique for radiocarbon analyses has revealed significant evidence in favor of a young earth and a recent global Flood cataclysm. In particular, the presence of significant radiocarbon levels, well above equipment detection limits, in deep-earth diamonds that are supposedly 1 to 3 billion years old can only be reconciled if the diamonds are instead only thousands of years old, which also implies the earth is young.[6] The hardness of diamonds and the fact that they cannot be contaminated *in situ* with recent carbon underlines the significance and robustness of this discovery and its implications. Furthermore, the finding of almost identical detectable levels of radiocarbon in Eocene, Cretaceous, and Pennsylvanian coal seams, which in uniformitarian terms are dated at 40 to 350 million years old, indicates that all this fossil plant material was buried essentially at the same time only thousands of years ago, another testimony to the Flood cataclysm being only 4,500 years ago.[7] Consistent with this evidence are the radiocarbon levels found in the fossilized wood from Oligocene, Eocene, Cretaceous, Jurassic, Triassic, and Permian strata, conventionally dated from 32 to 250 million years old, that instead indicate that fossilized wood is only thousands of years old.[8]

6   J. R. Baumgardner, A. A. Snelling, D. R. Humphreys and S. A. Austin, 2003, Measurable ^{14}C in fossilized organic materials: Confirming the young earth Creation-Flood model, in *Proceedings of the Fifth International Conference on Creationism*, R. L. Ivey, Jr., ed., Pittsburgh, PA: Creation Science Fellowship, 127-147; J. R. Baumgardner, 2005, ^{14}C evidence for a recent global Flood and a young earth, in *Radioisotopes and the Age of the Earth: Results of a Young-Earth Creationist Research Initiative*, L. Vardiman, A. A. Snelling and E. F. Chaffin, eds., El Cajon, CA: Institute for Creation Research and Chino Valley, AZ: Creation Research Society, 587-630.

7   Baumgardner et al, 2003; Baumgardner, 2005.

8   A. A. Snelling, 1997, Radioactive "dating" in conflict! Fossil wood in ancient lava flows yields radiocarbon, *Creation Ex Nihilo*, 20 (1): 24-27; A. A. Snelling, 1998, Stumping old-age dogma: Radiocarbon in an "ancient" fossil tree stump casts doubt on traditional rock/fossil dating, *Creation Ex Nihilo*, 20 (4): 48-51; A. A. Snelling, 1999, Dating dilemma: Fossil wood in "ancient" sandstone, *Creation Ex Nihilo*, 21 (3): 39-41; A. A. Snelling, 2000, Geological conflict: Young radiocarbon dating for ancient fossil wood challenges fossil dating, *Creation Ex Nihilo*, 22 (2): 44-47; A. A. Snelling, 2000, Conflicting "ages" of Tertiary basalt and contained fossilized wood, Crinum, central Queensland,

This evidence of detectable radiocarbon (real, not contamination) in "ancient" fossil wood has a significant bearing on another form of dating used by archaeologists, namely, tree-ring dating or dendrochronology. This method is based on the annual growth rings and their patterns in common trees. Both living and dead trees have been used in dendrochronology by matching sequences of ring patterns, between living trees and wooden beams cut from contemporary trees, with still earlier wooden beams in older houses and buildings, and then with logs buried in soils and peat swamps. Of course, the ring patterns are produced in the trees mainly by the temperature and precipitation variations from season to season and year to year.

The longest tree-ring chronology first established was achieved using the stunted bristlecone pine, found primarily in the White Mountains of California where the semi-desert habitat has facilitated the great longevity of this tree, and has permitted good preservation of the dry wood after death:

> Microscopic study of growth rings reveals that a bristlecone pine tree found last summer at nearly 10,000 feet began growing more than 4600 years ago and thus surpasses the oldest known sequoia by many centuries....Many of its neighbors are nearly as old; we have now dated 70 bristlecone pines 4000 years old or more.[9]

Thus, a continuous master tree-ring chronology has been erected reaching back over 7,000 years based on several living trees and 17 specimens of dead wood.[10] Further work has extended this chronology back to nearly 8,700 years (to 6700 BC), and includes the oldest living tree, which is claimed to be more than 4,600 years old.[11]

In Europe the most important tree for dating and for detailed calibration purposes is the oak.[12] This is partly because the oak very rarely has missing annual growth rings. The oak is also ideal because it is a long-lived, large tree that displays good resistance to decay after death. In contrast, the widespread alder may lack up to 45 percent of its annual rings.[13]

Australia, *Creation Ex Nihilo Technical Journal*, 14 (2): 99-122; A. A. Snelling, 2008, Radiocarbon in "ancient" fossil wood, *Acts & Facts*, 37 (1): 10-13; A. A. Snelling, 2008, Radiocarbon ages for fossil ammonites and wood in Cretaceous strata near Redding, California, *Answers Research Journal*, 1: 123-144.

9   E. Schulman, 1958, Bristlecone pine, oldest living thing, *National Geographic*, 113: 355.

10   D. W. Ferguson, 1970, Dendrochronology of Bristlecone pine, *Pinus aristata*. Establishment of a 7484-year chronology in the White Mountains of eastern-central California, USA, in *Radiocarbon Variations and Absolute Chronology*, I. U. Olsson, ed., Proceedings of the 12th Nobel Symposium, New York: John Wiley & Sons, 571-593.

11   C. W. Ferguson and D. A. Graybill, 1983, Dendrochronology of Bristlecone pine: A progress report, *Radiocarbon*, 25: 287-288.

12   M. G. L. Baillie, 1992, *Tree-ring Dating and Archaeology*, Chicago: The University of Chicago Press, Chicago.

13   B. Huber, 1970, Dendrochronology of central Europe, in *Radiocarbon Variations and Absolute Chronology*, I. U. Olsson, ed., Proceedings of the 12th Nobel Symposium, New York: John Wiley &

The question arises as to how these tree-ring chronologies are constructed, when dead trees and wood are used to extend the so-called master curves back beyond the ages of the living trees. The process of constructing a master curve for a long tree-ring chronology starts with living trees or timbers where the zero-age ring is present and the year of felling is known. The timescale is then extended using large felled timbers with ring-width patterns sufficiently overlapping the existing chronology to be certain of a unique match. This is known as cross-dating, that is, being able to associate, on the basis of duplication of pattern, a tree-ring sequence of unknown age with one of known age. This, of course, is based on the assumption that trees of the same species growing in the same or similar localities should have similar temporal patterns of ring widths that are uniquely defined, like a signature, by their common history. When no overlap is found in the ring patterns between two pieces of wood, a "floating" chronology is established, which is a sequence, possibly built up from several pieces of wood, the position of which in time is not known. The floating chronology can only be tied down if pieces of wood providing the missing links are found. It is here that radiocarbon analyses can provide approximate ages for wood samples, to show whether they are likely to be of value in linking or extending existing chronologies.[14] In other words, radiocarbon dating is used to match tree-ring sequences between different wood samples, enabling the construction of the master curves of the tree-ring chronologies.

Highly significant is the fact that the tree-ring chronologies as established have been used to calibrate radiocarbon dating. A set of 315 radiocarbon measurements on bristlecone pine samples, used to construct that tree-ring chronology, was used to construct the first continuous calibration curve for radiocarbon against tree-ring chronology from 5200 BC to the present.[15] One of the prominent features of this calibration curve was the presence of numerous "wiggles," with wavelengths of 100-300 years, superimposed on longer-term variations. This calibration curve attracted much criticism, because it had been drawn by eye through the measure points, rather than using a statistical curve fit. A great deal of work was done by others attempting to establish whether or not these wiggles were valid or a product of the imprecision of the measurements. It was maintained that the second-order wiggles in the calibration curve were an artifact of statistical uncertainties in the data and had no real meaning.[16] However, the reality of these wiggles in the ancient radiocarbon record (around 3500 BC) was finally established.[17] In the meantime,

Sons, 233-235.

14   S. Bowman, 1990, *Radiocarbon Dating*, London: British Museum Publications.

15   H. E. Suess, 1970, Bristlecone-pine calibration of the radiocarbon time-scale 5200 BC to the present, in *Radiocarbon Variations and Absolute Chronology*, I. U. Olsson, ed., Proceedings of the 12th Nobel Symposium, New York: John Wiley & Sons, 303-311.

16   G. W. Pearson, J. R. Pilcher, M. G. L. Baillie and J. Hillam, 1977, Absolute radiocarbon dating using a low altitude European tree-ring calibration, *Nature*, 270: 25-28.

17   A. F. M. DeJong, W. G. Mook and B. Becker, 1979, Confirmation of the Suess wiggles: 3200-3700 BC, *Nature*, 280: 48-49.

a bewildering number of calibration curves appeared, together with an equally confusing number of statistical interpretations and compilations of the curves. These have now all been superseded, in the period back to 2500 BC at least, by curves that have been adopted as the new international standard.[18]

The convoluted shape of these calibration curves introduced ambiguities into radiocarbon dating within many periods, since a single radiocarbon "age" can correspond to more than one historical age. These ambiguities can only be resolved by applying historical constraints, if available. In the dating of wood samples to construct a tree-ring chronology, these ambiguities may be avoided if a piece of wood spanning more than about 50 growth rings can be ^{14}C dated. This tree-ring sequence then forms a small "floating" calibration curve itself, which can be "wiggle-matched" with the known calibration curve to hopefully yield a much more accurate timespan for the growth of the wood in that particular sample. However, to obtain the highest-quality calibration curve, it is desirable to ^{14}C date wood samples representing single annual growth rings. Nevertheless, in the case of the bristlecone pine, its small size limits the precision that can be obtained, because of the limited amount of sample for analysis. Thus, there are many uncertainties in the construction of the bristlecone pine tree-ring chronology and the calibration of radiocarbon against it, which is why other work has been devoted to obtaining more detailed calibration curves from larger trees, such as the oaks in Europe.

Nevertheless, because of the uncertainties in radiocarbon dating around about 1000 BC back to where it can be reliably calibrated against historically dated materials,[19] and because of the detectable radiocarbon corresponding to "dates" of 20,000 to 45,000 years in fossilized wood conventionally dated 32 to 250 million years,[20] it is by no means certain that radiocarbon analyses can be used to "date" these tree-ring chronologies back to 8,700 years ago or further. Furthermore, the cross-matching of tree rings between different samples of wood from different trees or logs is fraught with difficulty. The width of rings is easily influenced by the external environment, and is, therefore, variable if the trees had come from different areas with different weather patterns and thus different growth variations.[21] Indeed, even the production of one growth-ring each year is not a certain process, and it is possible under certain conditions for a tree to miss a growth-ring or to produce two growth-rings in one season.[22]

These issues of the effects of climatic variations and weather patterns on the

18   G. W. Pearson and M. Stuiver, 1986, High-precision calibration of the radiocarbon time scale, 500-2500 BC, *Radiocarbon*, 28: 839-862; M. Stuiver and G. W. Pearson, 1986, High-precision calibration of the radiocarbon time scale, AD 1950-500 BC, *Radiocarbon*, 28: 805-838.

19   H. N. Michael and E. K. Ralph, eds., 1970, *Dating Techniques for the Archaeologist*, Cambridge, MA: MIT Press.

20   Snelling, 1997, 1998, 1999, 2000, 2008.

21   A. P. Dickin, 2005, *Radiogenic Isotope Geology*, second edition, Cambridge, UK: Cambridge University Press, 389.

22   Baillie, 1992, 51-52.

growth of tree rings would have been particularly critical in the first thousand or more years after the Flood, when climatic conditions and weather patterns were extremely variable, due to the after-effects of the Flood cataclysm and the climatic readjustments associated with the post-Flood Ice Age. Continuing volcanic eruptions spewing aerosols and gases into the atmosphere, and the unpredictable directions of daily storm tracks, would have resulted in big differences in weather conditions in adjoining geographic areas, plus seasonal variations would have been largely obliterated. It was extremely likely that trees would have grown multiple rings in many of the early calendar years after the Flood. Therefore, all tree-ring chronologies are likely to be seriously in error prior to 1000 BC, because they are all based on the assumption of essentially one growth-ring per calendar year. Consequently, tree-ring chronologies, such as that derived from the bristlecone pines, cannot validly date back to the claimed 8700 BC. Instead, the trees used in constructing the chronology grew on the post-Flood land surface in the last 4,500 years.

112

HUMAN POPULATION STATISTICS AND LIFESPANS

In the final analysis, the only real reliable recorder of time is man himself! In any kind of natural process that might be used to determine past time, there is always the possibility that the rates may have changed, as well as uncertainty regarding its initial condition. It is thus absolutely impossible to know beyond question that a particular formation or deposit has a certain age, unless that age is supported by reliable human records of some kind.

It is, therefore, highly significant that no truly verified archaeological datings go back beyond about 3000 BC or even later. Older dates have been frequently assigned to various archaeological artifacts and evidences of past human cultures, but these are always based on radiocarbon or other geological methods, rather than written human records. There are numerous extant chronologies that have been handed down from various ancient peoples, and it is highly significant that none of them yield acceptable evidence that the history of these or other peoples stretch back beyond the biblical date for Noah's Flood.

Evolutionary anthropologists insist that man (*Homo sapiens*) has been around much longer than even the biblical timescale back to creation, since man supposedly evolved from his hominid ancestors. The latest suggestion is that *Homo sapiens* existed for at least 185,000 years before they developed agriculture.[1] During this long period of human cultural development, called the Stone Age, the world population of humans is said to have been roughly constant, between 1 and 10 million people. Of course, all through that time those people buried their dead, often with artifacts. According to that scenario, it is easily calculated that these Stone Age people would have buried at least 8 billion bodies.[2] If the evolutionary timescale is correct, then buried human bones should be able to survive intact for much longer than 200,000 years. Thus, many of the supposed 8 billion buried Stone Age skeletons should have survived to still be easily found near the present land surface, along with all their buried artifacts. However, only a few thousand

---

1   I. McDougall, F. H. Brown and J. G. Fleagle, 2005, Stratigraphic placement and age of modern humans from Kibish, Ethiopia, *Nature*, 433 (7027): 733-736.

2   E. S. Deevey, 1960, The human population, *Scientific American*, 203 (3): 194-204.

have been found. This must imply that the Stone Age was much shorter than evolutionists believe, perhaps only a few hundred years in many areas.

On the other hand, the Bible pictures pre-Flood man as having been destroyed by the Flood cataclysm, so that all traces of human remains, whether bones, artifacts, or cultural remnants, must date from after the Flood, only about 4,500 years ago. The biblical record, in fact, describes the dispersal of people after the Flood from the same geographical areas implied also by archeology and secular history. The most ancient people leaving historical records were the inhabitants of the Tigris-Euphrates valley, the Nile valley of Egypt, and other near-eastern areas. This correlates perfectly with the biblical record, that pictures Noah and his descendants first inhabiting the Tigris-Euphrates area, followed by a centrifugal movement of tribes outwards from the first kingdom of Babylon (Babel, Genesis 11:9). The so-called Stone Age, therefore, the evidence for which is found on and in the post-Flood land surface, must correlate with this dispersal of tribes from the Tigris-Euphrates area, given that Noah and his descendants brought a sophisticated technology with them from the pre-Flood world when they re-established civilization with supporting agriculture, etc. The biblical record describes the dispersion from Babel as a dramatic event. The tribes that moved into inhospitable regions without having taken sufficient technology with them from their former civilization at Babel would have had to survive by reverting to a stone tool technology to hunt animals and for agriculture, until life became more settled and they had time to re-develop better tools and technology.

The archaeological testimony is confirmed further by botanical studies. Systematic agriculture was necessary for the existence of stable and civilized communities, and so the beginning of agriculture would be one of the best indicators of the beginning of post-Flood culture. The following comment is therefore significant:

> Thus, we may conclude from present distribution studies that the cradle of Old World plant husbandry stood within the general area of the arc constituted by the western foothills of the Zagros Mountains (Iraq-Iran), the Taurus (southern Turkey), and the Galilean uplands (northern Palestine) in which the two wild prototypes occur together. We may conclude, further, that wheat played a more dominant role than barley in the advent of plant husbandry in the Old World.[3]

It is remarkable, but not surprising, just how many different lines of evidence of a historical nature point back to a time around 3000 BC as dating the beginning of true civilization practicing agriculture.[4] The usual evolutionary picture has man existing as hunters and gatherers for at least 185,000 years during the Stone Age, before discovering agriculture as little as 5,000 years ago. However, the available

---

3   H. Helbaek, 1959, Domestication of food plants in the Old World, *Science*, 130: 365.

4   Deevey, 1960; J. O. Dritt, 1990, Man's earliest beginnings: discrepancies in evolutionary timetables, in *Proceedings of the Second International Conference on Creationism*, vol. 1, R. E. Walsh and C. L. Brooks, eds., Pittsburgh, PA: Creation Science Fellowship, 73-78.

paleoanthropological and archaeological evidences show that Stone Age men were as intelligent as we are. So the obvious question is why did none of the 8 billion people estimated to have lived during the Stone Age discover that food plants could be grown from seeds in a systematic manner? To the contrary, it is far more likely that men were only without agriculture for a very short time after the Flood, if at all, given the biblical account of Noah's vineyard. Indeed, man similarly began to make written records only about 4,000-5,000 years ago. Yet so-called Stone Age men built megalithic monuments, made beautiful cave paintings, and even kept records of lunar phases.[5] So why would such men wait more than 185,000 years before using the same skills to record history? The only logical conclusion is that the timescale for the existence of man and his civilization had to have been drastically shorter, much more likely in keeping with the timescale of the biblical record.[6]

There have been speculations and claims about earlier periods of human civilization, but nothing concrete. For example, with reference to Egyptian civilization, it has been stated:

> We think that the First Dynasty began not before 3400 and not much later than 3200 BC....A. Scharff, however, would bring the date down to about 3000 BC; and it must be admitted that his arguments are good, and at any rate it is more probable that the date of the First Dynasty is later than 3400 BC than earlier.[7]

Even this date is very questionable, as it is based primarily upon the king-lists of Manetho, an Egyptian priest around 250 BC, whose work has not been preserved, except in a few inaccurate quotations in other ancient writings. As has been pointed out long ago:

> The number of years assigned to which king, and consequently the length of time covered by the dynasty, differ in these two copies, so that, while the work of Manetho forms the backbone of our chronology, it gives us no absolute reliable chronology. It is for this reason that the chronological schemes of modern scholars have differed so widely.[8]

Other scholars think that some of Manetho's lists may actually represent simultaneous dynasties in upper and lower Egypt, which would still further reduce the date for the beginning of the Egyptian dynasties. Furthermore, the length of the pre-Dynastic period is quite unknown, but there is no necessary reason to regard it as no more than a few centuries at the very most.

---

5   A. Marchack, 1975, Exploring the mind of Ice Age man, *National Geographic*, 147: 64-89.

6   Dritt, 1990.

7   H. R. Hall, 1956, Egypt: Archeology, in *Encyclopedia Britannica*, vol. 8, 37.

8   G. A. Barton, 1941, *Archeology and the Bible*, Philadelphia: America Sunday School Union, 11.

In Babylonia, the earliest peoples leaving written monuments were the Sumerians, who were later displaced by the Semitic Babylonians. These people likewise are dated about the same time:

> The dates of Sumer's early history have always been surrounded with uncertainty, and have not been satisfactorily settled by tests with the new method of radiocarbon dating....Be that as it may, it seems that the people called Sumerians did not arrive in the region until nearly 3000 BC.[9]

The Egyptians and Babylonians were probably of Hamitic and Semitic origin (from Noah's sons Ham and Shem, respectively), as were most of the other tribes who settled in Africa and Asia. The Japhetic peoples (descended from Noah's son Japheth), on the other hand, according to the Table of Nations of Genesis 10 (which the highly-respected archaeologist, Dr William Foxwell Albright, regards as "an astonishingly accurate document"[10]), migrated largely into Europe, where they became the people of the Indo-European languages who radiated from a common center (probably in central Europe). Studies of ancient agricultures in Europe, based mainly on pollen analyses and radiocarbon dating, point to the same conclusion as linguistic studies for the date of this migration at around 2600-2800 BC.[11] On the other hand, the earliest historical cultures in China date to somewhat later than this time:

> The earliest Chinese date which can be assigned with any probability is 2250 BC, based on an astronomical reference in the *Book of History*.[12]

This later date for the settlement of China is significant support for the biblical migration from Babel, the journey to China logically taking a little longer to be achieved.

The worldwide testimony of trustworthy, recorded history is, therefore, that such human history begins about 2500-3000 BC and not substantially earlier. This is indeed surpassingly strange if men actually had been living throughout the world for many tens or hundreds of thousands of years prior to these dates! But on the other hand, if the biblical records are true, then this is of course exactly the historical evidence we would expect to find. All trace of earlier human civilization was obliterated by the Flood cataclysm, and the dispersal from Babel, where human civilization was re-established, occurred only about a century later. Of

---

9   S. N. Kramer, 1957, The Sumerians, *Scientific American*, 197 (1): 72.

10   W. F. Albright, 1955, Recent discoveries in Bible lands, in *Young's Analytical Concordance*, New York: Funk & Wagnalls, 30.

11   E. Thieme, 1958, The Indo-European language, *Scientific American*, 199 (1): 74; J. Trols-Smith, 1956, *Neolithic* period in Switzerland and Denmark, *Science*, 124: 879.

12   R. Linton, 1955, *The Tree of Culture*, New York: Alfred A. Knopf Publishing Company, 520.

course, it is also relevant to mention again that the worldwide incidence of Flood legends, as discussed in an earlier chapter, is also confirmation of the historicity of the biblical record. It is not at all, therefore, unreasonable to conclude that the clear testimony of all recorded human history points back to the stark reality of the global Flood cataclysm, which totally reshaped the earth's surface and remade the world in the days of Noah.

The statistics of human populations give further support to the biblical record of human history. Ever since the famous studies of Malthus, it has been known that human populations (applied to animal populations by Charles Darwin in developing his theory of evolution by natural selection) have tended to increase geometrically with time. That is, the world population tends to double itself repeatedly at approximately equal increments of time. This is the basis for projections that the world will become overpopulated:

> The central document which has influenced me is that of Malthus, who 160 years ago gave his theory that there was a natural tendency for man, like any other animal, to increase by geometrical progression....[13]

This means that, if the time for the population to double itself is called T, then starting from an initial population of two people, after T years there would be four people, after twice T years there would be eight people, after three times T years 16 people, and so on. At any time nT after the start of this process, the total population of the world would be two multiplied by itself in n times or two raised to the nth power, 2^n. The total time required to attain this population is nT, but this can be determined only if the time increment T and the exponent n are known. The latter is easily found by equating numeral 2^n to the present world population, which is more than 6.5 billion people. This calculation gives a value of n of almost 32. Since the value $n = 1$ corresponds to the initial human pair, it is obvious that the starting population of one man and one woman has gone through more than 30 "doublings."

The value of T, the time increment for one doubling, is less certain. However, there are data that enable a reasonable calculation:

> At the time of the birth of Christ, there presumably were some 250 to 350 million persons on this planet. Some 700 years later, there was about the same number—say 300 million—a long slow decline in total population having been followed by a compensating increase.

> It took roughly 950 more years, namely, until 1650, for this 300 million to double to 600 million. But then it took only 200 years, from 1650 to 1850, for the next doubling up to 1200 million, or 1.2 billion. From

13   C. Darwin, 1958, Population problems, *Bulletin of the Atomic Scientists*, 114: 322.

1850 to 1950, in only 100 years, the earth's population doubled again, to about 2.4 billion.[14]

Obviously the figures given for world populations prior to the modern era are only guesses, since no one has any real knowledge of the populations of America, Africa, Asia, etc., during those centuries. The 1650 figure is the first one with any degree of validity. From 1650 to 1950, therefore, the population increased from 600 million to 2,400 million, representing two doublings in 300 years, or a value of T of 150 years. It could be argued that this figure is perhaps too low, because of being influenced by the very rapid population growth of the past century, which has spectacularly accelerated in recent decades. However, this is not typical, and is attributable almost entirely to advances in medicine and sanitation:

> It is fallacious to think that booming birth rates are responsible for this speed-up. Actually, birth rates have declined in many countries. Falling death rates account for most of the spectacular growth.[15]

Indeed, the spectacular population growth in the last fifty years to now over 6.5 billion people worldwide is very much due to advances in medicine and general health care, with rising living standards in many countries. However, all things considered, it would seem that the period from 1650 to 1850 would be as typical as any for one doubling. The accuracy of the figures, then, may not have been as good as it has been in more recent years, but birth rates would have still been higher than they are today to compensate for the poorer quality of health care in that period. One could thus split the difference between the previous 150-year figure and this 200-year figure and estimate that the possible value of T is about 175 years. This value, multiplied by the almost 32 doubling, leads us back to about 2500 BC as the time of the birth of Noah's first son.

Of course, this calculation is not completely rigorous, because of the uncertainty in the value of the doubling period. However, this calculation is certainly far more reasonable than that necessitated by the scenario that the first human pair evolved up to one million or more years ago. In that scenario the figure for the doubling period would be more than 30,000 years! Of course, that scenario is simply ludicrous, particularly when one considers that, to compensate for the population doublings of a period of only 200 or so years in recent recorded history, the doubling period in man's early history would have to have been 40,000 to 50,000 years! On the other hand, if one adds to the far more realistic and reasonable calculation outlined above all the other evidence for the beginning of the present order of human civilization on the earth after the Flood only several thousands years ago, then this further testimony is quite impressive.

---

14   W. Weaver, 1954, People, energy and food, *Scientific Monthly*, 78: 359.

15   R. C. Cook, 1956, The population bomb, *Bulletin of the Atomic Scientist*, 12: 296.

Furthermore, when the biblical account of human history is accepted as reliable and true, one must also reckon with the probability that population increase rates in the early centuries after the Flood, as well as those before the Flood (when "man began to multiply on the face of the earth" as recorded in Genesis 6:1), may have been abnormally high, owing to the great longevity in human lifespans at that time. According to the biblical accounts, before the Flood men lived on average for 900 years or more. Thus, they had many more years in which to produce many more children. One of the strongest evidences of the validity of these figures is the fact that, after the Flood, the ages of the patriarchs exhibit a slow but steady decline from that of Noah who lived 950 years, through Eber 464 years, Abraham who died at 175 years, and Moses who died an old man at 120 years, to the familiar biblical 70-year lifespan (Psalm 90:2), which is very close to the average lifespan today. Large early post-Flood populations are also intimated by the large listing of people groups (Table of Nations) in Genesis 10, and the account of the dispersion of these people groupings from Babel in Genesis 11. Thus, these early high rates of doubling would more than counterbalance whatever evidence there may be of slower rates during the first 1,500 years after Christ. Furthermore, they would likely reduce the average doubling period and thus reduce the calculated time back to the birth of Noah's first son, in line with the tight biblical chronology.

When the lifespans of the pre-Flood and early post-Flood patriarchs are graphically plotted, as in Figure 1 (page 441), it is immediately evident that in the early post-Flood period there was a dramatic and systematic decrease in human lifespans, indicating that something must have occurred during the Flood to trigger this dramatic post-Flood decline in human lifespans. The long-standing explanation has been the collapse of a pre-Flood water vapor canopy at the outset of the Flood year, when "the windows of heaven were opened" (Genesis 7:11).[16] It was argued that the presence of the pre-Flood vapor canopy shielded the pre-Flood human population from the radiations bombarding the earth from outer space that would otherwise have had damaging effects on the human genome. Radiations from outer space are known to significantly increase the generation of deleterious mutations in the human genome that cause deterioration, increasing the rate of aging and thus shortening lifespans. However, as has been detailed earlier (see chapter 83), available evidence no longer supports the concept of a significant pre-Flood water vapor canopy. Therefore, the levels of radiations coming from outer space before and after the Flood were probably not all that different from one another. Thus, the dramatic progressive decline in the lifespans for the post-Flood patriarchs must have been due to some other cause.

It is now known that if a large fraction (50 percent or more) of the population is wiped out, the remaining population suffers from a genetic bottleneck. Such bottlenecks are well known for increasing the effects of genetic drift and natural selection, causing the rapid deterioration of a species' genome. Thus, a reputable

---

16   Whitcomb and Morris, 1961.

physical explanation for the systematic decrease in the longevity of the post-Flood patriarchs would be a loss of "longevity genes" by genetic drift. This genetic drift would have resulted from the dramatic population decrease at the Flood (from a pre-Flood human population of perhaps a billion or more people to just Noah's three sons and their wives), and the subsequent splitting of that gene pool as a result of the division and dispersion of the human population at Babel.

A recently-discovered viable explanation of longevity involves the role of telomeres, which are lengths of repetitive DNA on the ends of chromosomes that serve to protect the stored genetic information. Each cell division reduces the lengths of the telomeres until they are eventually lost. Once that happens, the genetic information stored on the chromosomes can be corrupted, resulting in cells dying. On the other hand, an enzyme called telomerase has been found to elongate the telomeres. Thus, when telomerase genes are added to cultured human cells they give them an unlimited capacity for cell divisions.[17] Unfortunately, telomerase is often active in cancer cells, too, so they divide uncontrollably. Nevertheless, telomerase is active in the reproductive cells, which means that the information passed on to offspring has been protected and is, therefore, still fairly "fresh." However, once the telomerase becomes inactive, the telomeres "age" until chromosomes become unprotected, resulting in the corruption of genetic information, cell death, and, ultimately, the death of the whole organism.

Further support for a genetic cause of longevity is provided by the mechanism for the premature aging disease called progeria. Those who suffer from progeria age five to ten times faster than normal and die by the age of about 13, usually from heart attack or stroke. It has recently been discovered that progeria is caused by a mutation changing only one of the 25,000 base pairs in the lamin A (*LMNA*) gene.[18] Thus, if this single change from cytosine to thymine can cause a ten-fold drop in lifespans, then perhaps a similar mutation could have caused a lifespan drop by a similar factor after the Flood.

In conclusion, the biblical record of post-Flood human history is convincingly vindicated, both as to its nature and to its duration, by all true historical and archaeological records, and by many lines of scientific evidence. The shortness of this post-Flood human history is attested to by the shortness of recorded history, the recent advent of agriculture, the paucity of Stone Age skeletons and artifacts, and human population statistics, while the dramatic early post-Flood progressive and systematic decrease in human lifespans is supported by the mutational outcomes of the genetic bottleneck of the human population at the time of the Flood, and then Babel.

---

17   A. G. Bodnar, N. Ouellette, M. Frolkis, S. E. Holt, C.-P. Chie, G. B. Morin, C. B. Harley, J. W. Shay, S. Lichtsteiner and W. E. Wright, 1998, Extension of life-span by introduction of telomerase into normal human cells, *Science*, 279 (5349): 349-352.

18   M. Eriksson et al, 2003, Recurrent *de nova* point mutations in lamin A cause Hutchinson-Gilford progeria syndrome, *Nature*, 423 (6937): 293-298.

SECTION X

PROBLEMS FOR BIBLICAL GEOLOGY
SOLVED—FORMATIONS
IMPLYING SLOW DEPOSITION

113

DEPOSITION AND LITHIFICATION

Perhaps the major objection to the concept of geological catastrophism on the scale envisaged in the Flood is that many rock formations appear to be of such character, and contain such features, as to have required long ages for their construction and development, much longer than the biblical chronology and the Flood year could allow.[1] However, it has already been shown how many geologic formations do give real evidence of their catastrophic formation, especially those rock layers that contain large numbers of fossils, and the great many that have been water-laid, as well as all the huge volcanic outpourings of lavas and explosive eruptions of volcanic ash layers. Furthermore, it has been conclusively demonstrated how the radioactive and other dating methods, which are supposed to have provided an absolute chronology for earth history in terms of millions and billions of years, can instead be understood in terms of the framework provided in the biblical record.

Nevertheless, there are a number of unique types of deposits which, although they may not yield absolute time estimates, do give the superficial appearance of requiring great ages to have formed. Space only permits a brief examination here of a few of these, but it needs to be emphasized that it is again quite possible to explain these deposits and geologic formations from the perspective of biblical geology.

Deposition and Lithification

Many types of sedimentary deposits are claimed to be only explainable in terms of long periods of time. Of course, it is natural to think that great masses of water-laid sediment beds, often thousands of feet thick, must have taken long ages to have been deposited. However, this is reckoning in uniformitarian terms, that is, assuming that today's observed, generally slow rates of sediment deposition are the same rates at which all sedimentary rock layers have been deposited in the past. On the other hand, it is not difficult to see, if one is willing to see, how

---

1   For example, D. Wonderly, 1977, *God's Time-Records in Ancient Sediments*, Flint, MI: Crystal Press; and D. E. Wonderly, 1987, *Neglect of Geologic Data: Sedimentary Strata Compared with Young-Earth Creationist Writings*, Hatfield, PA: Interdisciplinary Biblical Research Institute.

they could have formed in a very short period if the hydraulic and sedimentation activity were intense enough, as it undoubtedly was during the Flood.

Even though this surpassingly important discontinuity in uniform geologic processes is spurned and ignored by contemporary geologists, it is now generally recognized that sedimentary thicknesses are not necessarily an indication of the *duration* of deposition.

> The rate of sedimentation shows extremely wide variations from place to place at the present time. It is virtually impossible to determine an average rate of sedimentation for the present; it is more difficult to do so for past times.[2]

Most contemporary geologists, therefore, are not as committed to the uniformitarianism advocated by Charles Lyell, in which he rigidly assumed that the deposition of sediment layers in the past must always have occurred at the rates we observe today. Many contemporary geologists are now open to catastrophism when and where the evidence demands it, but still cling to uniformitarian assumptions by insisting many catastrophes during earth history were only local or regional in extent, and were but brief episodes that interrupted the normal slow-and-gradual geological processes operating over eons of time. In the words of the late Derek Ager:

> In a phrase that has often been quoted since, I have summed up geological history as being like the life of a soldier: 'Long periods of boredom and short periods of terror'.[3]

However, as discussed previously at length (see chapters 63-67), there is abundant, convincing evidence that the sediments that compose most sedimentary rock layers, whether sandstones, shales or limestones, were deposited under catastrophic conditions on a scale unlike normal, or even catastrophic, conditions and rates of geologic processes experienced today. For example, the cross-beds in sandstones are remnants of underwater sand waves that testify of the sand being transported and deposited by fast-moving currents in deep water, which would have resulted in thick sand beds of regional extent in a matter of hours to days. Even the thin layers or laminae frequently abundant in fine-grained shales, often considered to represent successive seasonal deposition over long time periods, have been shown instead to have been rapidly deposited all at once by hurricane-velocity, surging sediment-laden water and turbidity currents. Perhaps even more remarkable is the evidence that limestones, which are usually claimed to have formed as a result of tiny lime particles slowly settling on the ocean floor with the debris from marine

---

2   F. J. Pettijohn, 1957, *Sedimentary Rocks*, second edition, New York: Harper & Row, 688.

3   D. Ager, 1993, *The New Catastrophism: The Importance of a Rare Event in Geological History*, Cambridge, England: Cambridge University Press, xix.

organisms over countless years, were instead deposited catastrophically, either as lime sands transported in sand waves leaving behind cross-beds, or as lime muds in turbidity currents or debris flows that entombed marine organisms.

Yet the uniformitarian mindset of contemporary geologists is usually perpetuated by an appeal to the laws of physics, such as Stokes' Law, which describes the way a sediment particle in suspension moves through a fluid such as water under the influence of gravity. By adopting the appropriate figures into the Stokes' Law equation, it is easy to show that fine-grained sediments must have taken a long time to settle out of suspension in the water that transported them, so it is thus claimed that catastrophic deposition of such fine-grained sediments is just physically not possible.

The underlying problem with this argument is that it assumes we understand how all facets of geological processes interrelate and work together, when in fact we are still making new and surprising discoveries. The following relevant example is appropriate here.

Mount Pinatubo in the Philippines erupted in 1991 and large quantities of volcanic ash fell into the sea. Volcanic ash is, of course, largely fine-grained, akin to the sediment particles in shales, which sometimes contain a large component of volcanic ash. Thus, application of Stokes' Law would suggest a timescale of three months for the volcanic ash particles to settle onto the sea floor. However, it was surprisingly discovered that the resultant ash layer formed on the sea-bed within just three days![4] Obviously, some previously unrecognized factor was not taken into account in the analysis. It was not that the laws of physics had changed in some way making Stokes' Law wrong. Rather, it was the understanding of how the volcanic ash was deposited on the sea floor that was deficient. The ash did not behave as independent particles in suspension, as they would be expected to do according to Stokes' Law. An alternative explanation, supported by laboratory experimental simulations, was that when the ash fell on the ocean surface it produced density currents that rapidly flowed downwards to the sea floor.[5] In other words, the ash falling into the seawater created a fluid of higher density than the surrounding ash-free seawater, so that fluid descended coherently and rapidly through the surrounding seawater. Thus instead of behaving independently, the ash particles in suspension formed a density current that flowed at two to three orders of magnitude greater than expected.[6] Quite clearly, catastrophic conditions dramatically change the way sediments are deposited, even when the sediment particles are fine-grained.

4　　M. G. Wiesner, Y. Wang and L. Zheng, 1995, Fallout of volcanic ash to the deep South China Sea induced by the 1991 eruption of Mount Pinatubo (Philippines), *Geology*, 23: 885-888.

5　　V. Manville and C. J. N. Wilson, 2004, Vertical density currents: A review of their potential role in the deposition and interpretation of deep-sea ash layers, *Journal of the Geological Society*, 161: 947-958.

6　　Wiesner et al, 1995.

Deposition of the sediment particles is, however, only the first stage in the process of forming sedimentary rocks. Once deposited, the sediment particles require compaction and solidification to be transformed into sedimentary rock. These processes of diagenesis and lithification are usually claimed to have required long time periods. It has further been claimed that the lithification of muds, for example, requires a thickness of other overlying sediments of at least a mile in order to compact the fine grains, squeeze out the pore water, and provide enough pressure to cause solidification.[7] Thus, any sedimentary rock now appearing at the earth's surface must at some time in its history have had at least a mile of other sediments lying on top of it, which have since been eroded away. Of course, exactly these conditions would have occurred during the global Flood, when enormous thicknesses of sediments were eroded, transported, and deposited on top of one another, the last deposited sediment layers then being subsequently eroded away as the Flood waters retreated off today's land surfaces into the current ocean basins.

This scenario, of course, assumes that vertical pressure is the sole factor affecting compaction and lithification of sediments, whereas it is really only one of many factors:

> The amount and rate of compaction depend on the porosity of the original sediment, on the size and shape of the particles, on the rate of deposition and thickness of the overburden, and on the factor of time.[8]

To these factors should be added the increasing heat generated by the depth of burial, the chemicals in the pore water, and even the tectonic forces of uplift and lateral compression facilitating the removal of the pore water. Tectonics forces unleashed during the Flood would have helped to "squeeze" pore waters out of sedimentary beds, and uplift at the close of the Flood would have caused much contained water to drain away simply due to gravity.

There are two main steps in the overall lithification of sediments to transform them into sedimentary rocks:

> …the following sections describe two common processes of diagenesis… compaction is a reduction in bulk volume of the sediment, caused mainly by the vertical force exerted by an increasing overburden. Compaction is conveniently expressed as a change in porosity brought about by the tighter packing of the grains.…cementation is the deposition of minerals in the interstices of a sediment. It is one of the commonest diagenetic changes, and produces rigidity of a sediment by binding the particles

---

7   J. L. Kulp, 1950, Flood geology, *Journal of the American Scientific Affiliation*, January: 4.

8   W. C. Krumbein and L.L. Sloss, 1951, *Stratigraphy and Sedimentation*, first edition, San Francisco: Freeman and Company, 217.

together. Cementation may occur essentially simultaneously with sedimentation, or the cement may be introduced at any later time.[9]

Some have insisted that "the lithification of practically all kinds of sedimentary rock is of necessity a slow change—slow because of the very nature of the several processes involved."[10] However, such dogmatism ignores the field and experimental observations that the process of lithification can take place quite rapidly under some conditions, and thus it is not necessarily related to time.

> Time is a factor, but not the deciding one, and sands, clays, and silts of the Cambrian are known that are as nearly unindurated and little cemented as they were in the days of deposition....On the other hand, some Pleistocene outwash deposits are known that have become fairly well lithified.[11]

Lithification has been defined as follows:

> The conversion of a newly deposited, unconsolidated sediment into a coherent, solid rock, involving processes such as cementation, compaction, desiccation, crystallization. It may occur concurrent with, soon after, or long after deposition.[12]

On the other hand, diagenesis has been defined as:

> All the chemical, physical, and biologic changes undergone by a sediment after its initial deposition, and during and after its lithification, exclusive of surficial alteration (weathering) and metamorphism....It embraces those processes (such as compaction, cementation, reworking, authigenesis, replacement, crystallization, leaching, hydration, bacterial action, and formation of concretions) that occur under conditions of pressure (up to 1 kb) and temperature (maximum range of 100°C to 300°C) that are normal to the surficial or outer part of the earth's crust; and it may include changes occurring after lithification under the same conditions of temperature and pressure.[13]

Many chemical processes are involved in lithification and diagenesis, all of which would have been readily facilitated by conditions during the Flood, because "water

---

9   W. C. Krumbein and L.L. Sloss, 1963, *Stratigraphy and Sedimentation*, second edition, San Francisco: Freeman and Company, 269-271.

10   D. E. Wonderly, 1987, *Neglect of Geologic Data: Sedimentary Strata Compared with Young-Earth Creationist Writings*, Hatfield, PA: Interdisciplinary Biblical Research Institute, 33.

11   W. H. Twenhofel, 1950, *Principles of Sedimentation*, second edition, New York: McGraw-Hill, 279.

12   K. K. E. Neuendorf, J. P. Mehl, Jr., and J. A. Jackson, eds., 2005, *Glossary of Geology*, fifth edition, Falls Church, VA: American Geological Institute, 375.

13   Neuendorf et al, 2005, 176.

is the main agent of diagenesis, and organic matter is an auxiliary."[14] Of course, water was the medium by which most of the sediments were deposited, and an abundance of it would have been trapped between the sediment grains to become the pore water in the sediment layers. Furthermore, under the catastrophic Flood conditions there was an abundance of organic matter available for burial in the sediments, either dispersed through them or in concentrated layers. It is thus obvious that conditions during the Flood, and its immediate aftermath, would have been highly conducive to rapid initiation of diagenesis, with resultant early lithification.

> It seems, rather that diagenesis sometimes follows sedimentation so closely that it begins while the deposit is still on the sea bottom.[15]

Various cementing materials occur in sedimentary rocks, especially silica (quartz) and calcite. "The cementing material may be derived from the sediment or its entrapped water, or may be brought in by solution from extraneous sources."[16] Of course, during the Flood, the waters would have contained many chemicals from the weathering products eroded on a massive scale from across the earth's surface, plus the chemicals introduced into the Flood waters by all the concurrent volcanic activity. So as sediments were deposited, the chemical-laden waters would have been trapped in the pore spaces between the sediments. With compression of the overlying sediments, the chemical conditions changing in the pore spaces of the buried sediments would have resulted in potentially rapid precipitation of the dissolved chemicals, thus facilitating rapid lithification of the sediments.

> It appears that indentation of grain against grain is sufficient to cause lithification....The success of lithification by compaction is correlated directly with the content....Mud will be converted into mudrock by a relatively small thickness of overburden; lithic sandstones require a much greater thickness...intimate grain-to-grain contact in most sandstones must be achieved largely by the introduction of chemical precipitates— that is, cements....The intimate contact of quartz cement with the detrital quartz grain produces a stronger bond than the contact of calcite cement with the quartz grain, but both types of pore filling cause the rigidity that converts a loose pile of sand into rock.[17]

The problem of lithification of sediments is, therefore, not at all a serious one for biblical geology. There are no mysteries or difficulties if these questions are approached, not on the basis of uniformity with present processes, but are

---

14   Z. L. Sujkowski, 1958, Diagenesis, *Bulletin of the American Association of Petroleum Geologists*, 42: 2694.

15   Sujkowski, 1958, 2697.

16   Krumbein and Sloss, 1963, 271.

17   H. Blatt, 1992, *Sedimentary Petrology*, second edition, New York: W. H. Freeman and Company, 128-129.

envisaged in terms of rapid deposition of great masses of sediments mixed with various chemicals and organic matter, because the conditions in a global Flood quite obviously afforded an ample source of silica, calcite, and other cementing materials. It is highly consistent with the whole character of the catastrophic action, responsible for deposition of the sediments during the Flood, to further the processes of compaction, cementation, drying, etc., leading to final lithification that could have been accomplished quite rapidly.

114

BIOTURBATION, HARDGROUNDS, AND TRACE FOSSILS

Within many carbonate rock layers are found what are known as hardgrounds, or hardground surfaces. They are particularly evident within the thick Cretaceous chalk beds, but are also found in limestones. Such layers have visible characteristics on their upper surfaces of where marine organisms burrowed into what were then soft sediments, followed by hardening of those surfaces, some erosion of them, and finally the encrustation on them by marine organisms, such as oysters, now fossilized. Many of these apparently eroded surfaces have also been "bored" by sponges and other types of marine animals. Thus, it is claimed that these hardgrounds are a record of the passage of large amounts of time—weeks, months or even years—when there was no sedimentation occurring on these surfaces.[1] The implication is, of course, that because these hardgrounds frequently occur at many levels in chalk and limestone formations, these repeated occurrences of large amounts of elapsed time are hardly compatible with the deposition of these chalk and limestone beds within the year-long Genesis Flood.[2]

A similar elapsed time issue is posed by the preserved evidence in sedimentary strata of bioturbation, and by what are collectively called trace fossils (or ichnofossils), preserved on many sedimentary strata surfaces. Bioturbation occurs when invertebrate animals such as worms and brachiopods, that live within sediments, have continually burrowed through those sediments, destroying the original layering.[3] In the present world, the activity of burrowing animals in underwater sediments can be observed, and results in the total bioturbation of such sediments so that the original layering and other sedimentary structures over time are progressively obliterated (see Figure 55). Because bioturbation requires the passage of time, the degree of bioturbation found preserved in sedimentary strata at numerous levels in the rock record would likewise presumably testify to the passage of perhaps significant amounts of time between the successive deposition of those strata. And because it is claimed that such bioturbation can

---

1 Wonderly, 1987, 12-13.

2 D. J. Tyler, 1996, A post-Flood solution to the chalk problem, *Creation Ex Nihilo Technical Journal*, 10(1): 107-113.

3 R. G. Bromley, 1990, *Trace Fossils: Biology and Taphonomy*, Unwin Hyman, Boston.

take days, weeks, months, or even years, this is taken as proof that these strata cannot have been deposited during the Flood year.

This is same argument that is used with respect to other trace fossils (or ichnofossils), such as invertebrate animal trails and burrows, vertebrate animal footprints (such as the many trackways of dinosaur footprints), and even vertebrate eggs and claimed "nests" (such as those of dinosaurs). Owing to the ubiquity of these trace fossils throughout the Phanerozoic sedimentary strata record, combined with the inferred spans of time necessary for the construction of each trace fossil, trackway, or "nest" of eggs (supposedly at one stratigraphic horizon at a time), such trace fossils have been regularly perceived as an insurmountable challenge to Flood geology. After all, how could dinosaurs, for example, have been repeatedly walking across successive sedimentary strata horizons, leaving behind their footprints and "nests" of eggs, in the middle of the mountain-covering global Flood?[4]

The reality is that much of the sedimentary strata record has not been completely bioturbated. Some of the sedimentary layers have trace fossils only in the top portions of the individual sediment laminae. Obviously, incomplete bioturbation or no bioturbation would result if the sediments when deposited could not support animal life (e.g., if they lacked sufficient oxygen), or if they were deposited so rapidly that the burrowing animals had no time to do their work. Indeed, most of the sediments deposited during the global Flood catastrophe would have been deposited too quickly for complete bioturbation to have occurred. Sedimentary strata with only some bioturbation may well only represent the passing of at least a few hours, just sufficient time for some animals to walk around and leave their footprints, or to burrow in the sediment surface, before the next sedimentary layer was deposited. In fact, we should expect to find abundant evidence of biological activity by living organisms during the year of the Flood, because the sediment surfaces available for them to live in and on were constantly being buried, as the successive sediment layers accumulated rapidly. Indeed, some fossilized burrows have been identified as escape burrows, where the sediment accumulation has been so rapid that the animal has burrowed upwards to the sediment surface to escape being buried and suffocated.

The logical question is this: Has it been observed and measured just how quickly animals burrow into sediment layers and bioturbate them? Extensive bioturbation of individual sedimentary layers can happen rapidly. For example, certain urchins are known to rework the upper 5 cm of sediment in three days.[5] By contrast, other organisms can produce burrows as rapidly as 1,000 cm per hour, although the

---

4   M. Garton, 1996, The pattern of fossil tracks in the geological record, *Creation Ex Nihilo Technical Journal*, 10(1): 82-100; P. Garner, 1996, Where is the Flood/post-Flood boundary? Implications of dinosaur nests in the Mesozoic, *Creation Ex Nihilo Technical Journal*, 10(1): 101-106.

5   A. N. Lohrer and others, 2005, Rapid reworking of subtidal sediments by burrowing spatangoid urchins, *Journal of Experimental Marine Biology and Ecology*, 321: 155-169.

usual rate is much slower.[6] Indeed, depending primarily upon the density of fast-burrowing organisms such as callianassid shrimp, a 12-cm-thick layer of sediment can be 67 percent bioturbated in as little as 5.5 hours.

Of course, these values provide only the loosest constraints upon the duration of the burrowing interval for this bed. However, it is clear that extensively bioturbated horizons do not necessarily require protracted intervals of time for their development.[7]

There are numerous organisms capable of rapid burrowing and do not require clear water.[8] Fast-acting animals, such as certain bivalves, crustaceans, and both polychaete and oligochaete worms, can burrow through sediments even during their active deposition. Thus, during rapid Flood deposition, the organisms most capable of disturbing the sediments are those that can burrow through or across centimeters to tens of centimeters of sediment in a matter of seconds to minutes. Among the many such organisms, for which such burrowing rates have been measured, are annelid worms,[9] numerous kinds of bivalves,[10] certain razor clams,[11] a pelecypod,[12] several different kinds of gastropods,[13] many crustaceans,[14] and various crabs.[15] Furthermore, it is unclear whether trace fossils also necessarily

6   J. D. Howard and C. A. Elders, 1970, Burrowing patterns of haustoriid amphipods from Sapelo Island, Georgia, *Trace Fossils*, T. P. Crimes and J.C. Harper, eds., Geological Journal Special Issue No. 3: 243-262; P. M. Kranz, 1974, The anastrophic burial of bivalves and its paleoecological significance, *Journal of Geology*, 82: 237-265; S. M. Stanley, 1970, Relation of shell form to life habits of the bivalvia (Mollusca), *Geological Society of America Memoir*, 125.

7   K. A. Grimm and K. B. Föllmi, 1994, Doomed pioneers: Allochthonous crustacean tracemarkers in anaerobic basinal strata, Oligo-Miocene Sand Gregorio Formation, Baja California Sur Mexico, *Palaios*, 9: 328.

8   P. L. McCall and M. J. S. Tevsz, 1982, Preface in: *Animal-Sediment Relations*, P. L. McCall and M. J. S. Trevsz, eds., New York: Plenum Press, x.

9   E. Zuckerkandl, 1950, Coelomic pressures in *Sipunculus nudus*, *Biological Bulletin*, 98: 167-168; V. Lobza and J. Schieber, 1999, Biogenic sedimentary structures produced by worms in soupy, soft-muds, *Journal of Sedimentary Research*, 69: 1046; J. H. Trevor, 1978, The dynamics and mechanical energy expenditure of the polychaetes *Nephtys Cirrosa, Nerus diversicolor* and *Arenicola-marina* during burrowing, *Estuarine and Coastal Marine Science*, 6: 608, 612-613.

10   S. M. Stanley, 1970, Relation of shell form to life habits of the bivalvia (mollusca), *Geological Society of America Memoir*, 125: 56-57; S. M. Stanley, 1977, Coadaptation in the Trigoniidae, A remarkable family of burrowing bivalves, *Paleontology*, 20: 875; A. Seilacher and E. Seilacher, 1994, Bivalvian trace fossils: A lesson from actuopaleontology, *Courier Forschungsinstitute Senckemberg*, 169: 6.

11   S. M. Henderson and C. A. Richardson, 1994, A comparison of the age, growth rate and burrowing behaviour of the razor clams, *Ensis silqua* and *E. ensis*, *Journal of the Marine Biological Association of the United Kingdom*, 74: 949.

12   M. J. S. Tevsz, 1975, Structure and habits of the 'living fossil' pelecypod *Neotrigonia*, *Lethaia*, 8: 325-326.

13   P. J. Vermeij and E. Zipser, 1986, Burrowing performance of some tropical Pacific gastropods, *Veliger*, 29: 201-203.

14   J. D. Howard and C. A. Edlers, 1970, Burrowing patterns of haustoriid amphipods from Sapelo Island, Georgia, in *Trace Fossils*, T. P. Crimes and J. C. Harper, eds., Liverpool: Seel House Press, 250-257.

15   E. W. Hill, 1979, Biogenic sedimentary structures produced by the mole crab *Lepidopa websteri*

require long time periods to be formed, given that well-known trace fossils have been observed being produced by organisms within, at the very most, 4-5 days.[16] Additionally, a common trilobite self-burial trace fossil is similar to the traces produced by a modern crab, which can completely conceal itself within sediment in a few seconds.[17] Even a common trace fossil that consists of tapering branches, once interpreted as having been slowly constructed in the growth of an animal, is now understood to have been generated rapidly.[18] Furthermore, it is very significant that large and complex individual trace fossils, including common ones, as well as less common meter-sized ones, can all form within sediment layers, which of course means that the deposition of the sediments does not have to be interrupted during their construction.[19]

It is, of course, obvious that the footprints and trackways left behind by vertebrate animals, such as dinosaurs, were formed instantaneously as the animals traversed across sediment surfaces. Furthermore, it is readily observed that once footprints and trackways are produced, they are quickly degraded and obliterated by wind, rainfall, and surface water flow under present climatic conditions. Therefore, it should be self-evident that footprints and trackways, as well as surface trace fossils, need to be rapidly covered over and buried in order to be preserved. However, it is normally expected and observed that the wind or water carrying the sediments to bury footprints, trackways or surface traces will invariably disturb and/or erode the sediment surfaces they pass over, degrading or obliterating any footprints, trackways or traces on those sediment surfaces. Therefore, even researchers committed to uniformitarianism would have to concede that for the footprints, trackways, and traces to be preserved and fossilized, the sediment surfaces on which they were produced would have to have been rapidly and sufficiently hardened or partially lithified almost immediately after the passage of the animals, and certainly before the deposition of the overlying sediments.[20]

Very rapid cementation of the sediment surface immediately after deposition is

---

Benedict, *Texas Journal of Science*, 31: 49; E. Savazzi, 1982, Burrowing habits and cuticular sculptures in recent sand-dwelling Brachyuran decapods from the Northern Adriatic Sea, *Neues Jahrbuch fur Geologie und Palaeontologie Abhandlungen*, 163: 276; E. Jaramillo, J. Dugan and H. Contreras, 2000, Abundance, tidal movement, population structure and burrowing rate of *Emerica analoga* (Anomura, Hippidae) at a dissipative and reflective sandy beach in south central Chile, *Marine Ecology*, 21: 121-123.

16 S. Jensen and R. J. A. Atkinson, 2001, Experimental production of animal trace fossils, with a discussion of allochthonous trace fossil producers, *Neues Jahrbuch fur Geologie und Palaeontologie Monatschefte*, 2001: 594-606.

17 R. G. Osgood, 1970, Trace fossils of the Cincinnati area, *Palaeontographica Americana*, 6: 305.

18 M. F. Miller, 1991, Morphology and paleoenvironmental distribution of Paleozoic *Spirophyton* and *Zoophycos*, *Palaios*, 6: 419-420.

19 R. Goldring, 1985, The formation of the trace fossil *Cruziana*, *Geological Magazine*, 122: 65-72; E. Seilacher-Drexler and A. Seilacher, 1999, Undertraces of sea pens and moon snails and possible fossil counterparts, *Neues Jahrbuch fur Geologie und Palaeontologie Abhandlungen*, 215: 195-210.

20 J. Woodmorappe, 2006, Are soft-sediment trace fossils (ichnofossils) a time problem for the Flood?, *Journal of Creation*, 20(2): 113-122.

conceivable, given that dissolved carbonate minerals are always present in significant quantities in the pore waters of sediments, and carbonate minerals are one of the most common sediment-cementing agents. Indeed, early precipitated cement is known forming at, or not far below, the depositional surface, which increases the bearing strength of the sediment as subsequent sediments are deposited.[21] Several types of mechanisms for rapid carbonate cementation in sediments are known, such as the formation of beachrock in a matter of hours.[22] The repeated percolation of meteoritic and marine water is an important factor,[23] and is one that would have occurred on a large scale during the Flood. The mechanical agitation of saturated water, a process that is obviously relevant to Flood conditions, can also precipitate a layer of carbonate in a matter of hours.[24] Even large releases of carbon dioxide bubbles facilitates carbonate precipitation in a matter of minutes.[25] As rapid carbonate lithification at sediment surfaces continues to be studied, such processes are all relevant to the rapid cementation during the Flood of sediment surfaces which contain footprints, trackways and other traces.[26]

Such rapid carbonate lithification at the sediment surface also solves the question of hardgrounds, claimed to be a time problem for Flood geology. It is, in fact, because these hardgrounds are in carbonate sediment layers (in limestone and chalk beds) that it is reasonable to expect this mechanism for their formation. As soon as the carbonate sediments were deposited, organisms began to scurry across, and burrow into, their surfaces. However, hardening of the carbonate cement in the sediments would have been rapid at the same time, thus fossilizing the burrows and trails, while oysters attached themselves to these hardened surfaces. Nevertheless, within a few hours, these now hardened sediment surfaces, or hardgrounds, would have been eroded by the next tidal surges of sediment-laden waters, the newly-deposited carbonate sediments from them also burying and preserving the hardgrounds, and further fossilizing the burrows, trails, and now the encrusted fauna.

The finding of what are claimed to be "nests" of dinosaur eggs fossilized at numerous strata levels in the geologic record locally and on several continents[27]

21   E. W. Choquette, 1987, Diagenesis #12. Diagenesis in limestones—3. The deep burial environment, *Geoscience Canada*, 14: 5.

22   J. S. Hanor, 1978, Precipitation of beachrock cements: mixing of marine and meteoritic waters *vs.* CO_2 degassing, *Journal of Sedimentary Petrology*, 48: 489-501.

23   F. Longhitano, 2001-2002, Sedimentary features of incipient beachrock deposits along the coast of Simeto River delta (eastern Sicily, Italy), *GeoActa*, 1: 95-110.

24   D. D. Zhang, Y. Zhang, A. Zhu and X. Cheng, 2001, Physical mechanisms of river waterfall tufa (travertine) formation, *Journal of Sedimentary Research*, 71: 205-216.

25   H. S. Chafetz, P. F. Rush, and N. M. Utech, 1991, Microenvironmental controls on mineralogy and habit of $CaCO_3$ precipitates: an example from an active travertine system, *Sedimentology*, 38: 107-126.

26   D. Kneale and H. A. Viles, 2000, Beach cement: Incipient $CaCO_3$-cemented beachrock development in the upper intertidal zone, North Uist, Scotland, *Sedimentary Geology*, 132: 165-170.

27   K. Carpenter and K. Alf, 1994, Global distribution of dinosaur eggs, nests and babies, *Dinosaur Eggs and*

raises another aspect of this claimed problem for deposition of the fossil-bearing sedimentary strata during the Flood year. It is presumed that the presence of dinosaur footprints, trackways, and eggs in "nests" are evidence that some time elapsed at that sediment surface which contains these fossilized remains, while the dinosaurs walked around and laid eggs in "nests." Sometimes only fossilized eggshell fragments are found, and rarer still the associated fossilized remains of baby dinosaurs. It is claimed that such occurrences require days or even months to pass at that sediment surface before subsequent burial and fossilization, so that repeated horizons in the strata record of such occurrences would surely rule out the deposition of such sediment layers during the Flood year.[28]

However, because the nesting and egg-laying behavior of dinosaurs cannot be observed today, it is far from certain that these claimed fossilized dinosaur "nests" are exactly that. The tidal nature of the Flood waters, as they surged up on to the continents from the ocean basins, would have resulted in large areas where sediments were deposited from shallow water that retreated and fell to expose the sediment surfaces before the next tidal advance surged over the area to deposit more sediments. Dinosaurs swept away by the advancing tide, that survived by floating and swimming in those shallow waters until the tide retreated, would then have opportunity to walk across these exposed sediment surfaces, leaving behind their footprints and trackways. In such stressful situations it is conceivable that dinosaur mothers thus laid their eggs on these temporarily exposed sediment surfaces, sometimes in groups that could be interpreted as "nests," before the next tidal surge of sediment-laden waters covered the eggs while sweeping the dinosaur mothers away.

In any case, in several situations where the sedimentary strata containing these supposed "nests" fossilized eggs and eggshell fragments have been closely examined, it has been found that they are cross-bedded sandstones deposited by fast-moving water currents and storm surges.[29] Indeed, there is abundant evidence at many localities that not only egg shell fragments, but also whole eggs, were transported by sediment-laden waters, only to be deposited within the resultant sediments or on top of them. That eggshells can survive transport and abrasion in sediment-laden water without damage or destruction has been tested experimentally.[30] Eggs could even have floated and been transported for days or weeks before coming to rest on a sediment surface. This could also explain fossilized hatchlings found beside the broken eggs they apparently hatched from. These would have been

Babies, K. Carpenter, K.F. Hirsch and J.R. Horner, eds., UK: Cambridge University Press, 15-30.

28 Garner, 1996, Where is the Flood/post-Flood boundary?

29 D. Dashzeveg and others, 1995, Extraordinary preservation in a new vertebrate assemblage from the Late Cretaceous of Mongolia, *Nature*, 374: 446-449; E. G. Kennedy, 1995, An unusual occurrence of dinosaur eggshell fragments in a storm surge deposit, Lamargue Group, Patagonia, Argentina, *Geological Society of America Abstracts with Programs*, 27: A-318.

30 D. T. Tokaryk and J. E. Storer, 1991, Dinosaur eggshell fragments from Saskatchewan, and evaluation of potential distance of eggshell transport, *Journal of Vertebrate Paleontology*, 11(3 sppl): 58A.

beached eggs that were ready to hatch before the next sediment-laden tidal surge buried and fossilized eggshell fragments and baby dinosaurs. Further research is obviously needed, but it is clear from this analysis that not only dinosaur footprints and trackways, but even supposed "nests" of fossilized eggs and broken shells with hatchlings, are not evidence incompatible with rapid deposition of sedimentary strata during the global Genesis Flood.

115

CHALK AND DIATOMITE BEDS, AND DEEP-SEA SEDIMENTS

One of the most challenging examples of a sedimentary rock whose deposition is claimed to have taken millions of years is the study of chalk beds, which are prominent in the so-called Cretaceous period of the geologic column. The Latin word for chalk is *creta*, so the Cretaceous is regarded as the "chalk age." Chalk is sediment made up of the calcium carbonate residues of algae known as coccolithophores. The hard parts are called coccoliths, having effective settling diameters in the range of 2 to 12 microns. These shell-like structures often fall apart to produce fragments. Under today's conditions it can take the larger fragments at least a year to descend and settle on the sea floor, but the broken fragments are estimated to take more than 100 years! Thus it is claimed that one meter thickness of chalk must represent about 100,000 years of deposition. In the modern oceans, coccolithophores are found in nutrient-poor waters, and when the coccoliths slowly descent to the sea floor, they are always mixed with other materials in the resultant sea floor sediments. Thus the calcareous oozes on the ocean floors today, which are regarded as the modern version of the chalk beds found in the geologic record, have a coccolith content of 5 to 33 percent by weight in the Atlantic, and of 4 to 71 percent on the floor of the Indian Ocean.[1]

It is, therefore, highly significant that the chalk beds found in the geologic record are very much purer than their supposed analogous calcareous oozes. The calcium carbonate content of the French chalk beds, for instance, varies between 90 and 98 percent, while the Kansas chalk is 88-98 percent calcium carbonate (average 94 percent).[2] Furthermore, the chalk beds of southern England are estimated to be around 405 meters (about 1,329 feet) thick. These chalk beds are said to span the complete duration of the so-called Late Cretaceous geologic period,[3] estimated to account for 30 to 35 million years of geologic time. Thus, the average rate of chalk accumulation through this time period is simply calculated to be 1.16 to

1   C. V. Jeans, P. F. Rawson, ed., 1980, *Andros Island, Chalk and Oceanic Oozes*, UK: Yorkshire Geological Society, Leeds, Occasional Publication No. 5.

2   F. J. Pettijohn, 1957, *Sedimentary Rocks*, New York: Harper and Rowe, 400-401.

3   M. House, 1989, *Geology of the Dorset Coast*, London: The Geologists' Association, Field Guide, 4-10.

1.35 centimeters (0.45 to 0.53 inches) per thousand years, which is slightly less than the 2 to 10 centimeters (0.78 to 3.93 inches) per thousand years rate for accumulation of oozes today dominated by coccoliths.[4] Yet the chalk beds in the geologic record are so pure in comparison to today's sea floor calcareous oozes. If the chalk beds accumulated at an even slower rate than today's sea floor calcareous oozes, then why are they so pure and not have more other materials mixed into them? This observation alone must rule out the accumulation of today's sea floor calcareous oozes as the model for the formation of the chalk beds in the geologic record.

Nevertheless, it is asserted that if all the fossilized coccolithophores within the chalk beds were resurrected, they would cover the earth's surface to a depth of at least 45 centimeters (18 inches), making it problematical as to what they could all have possibly eaten.[5] It is thus claimed the laws of thermodynamics prohibit the earth from supporting that much animal biomass, and with so many animals trying to get their energy from the sun, the available solar energy would not nearly be sufficient.[6] As well as blithely claiming this supposed organic problem for the huge volume of microorganisms found in the chalk beds having all lived at the same time, it is insisted that the quantity of carbon dioxide necessary to provide the calcium carbonate needed for the growth of all these calcareous microorganisms could simply not be sustained by the earth's atmosphere.[7]

Similar supposed problems are claimed for the deposition and formation of the diatomite beds, also found in the geologic record. These beds are made up of countless billions of diatoms, which are the siliceous bodies of single-celled algae that live in oceanic surface waters today. When these diatoms die today, their siliceous skeletons slowly descend to the ocean floor to become part of the sediment accumulating there. Because the diatom skeletons are commonly in the range of 10 to 200 microns, according to Stokes' Law they would require between one week and two years to sink and be deposited on the sea floor. In today's ocean basins the rates of accumulation for diatom skeletons on the sea floor are low, being of the order of 40-73 centimeters (16-28 inches) of diatomaceous ooze per thousand years. Furthermore, these diatomaceous oozes on the sea floors today, though containing a significant proportion of diatom skeletons, nonetheless contain other sediment particles mixed in with them. However, the diatomite beds in the geologic record are exceedingly pure, so that many of them are of commercial interest, because the relatively pure silica in them favors their use in chemical processing. Once again, today's impure diatomaceous oozes on the sea floors can hardly be a model for the deposition and formation of the diatomite beds in the geologic record, that consist of relatively pure silica. Nevertheless, the

---

4   Z. Kukal, 1990, The rate of geological processes, *Earth Science Reviews*, 28: 109-117.

5   R. J. Schadewald, 1982, Six 'Flood' arguments creationists can't answer, *Creation/Evolution*, IV: 13.

6   A. Hayward, 1987, *Creation and Evolution: The Facts and the Fallacies*, London: Triangle (SPCK), 91-93.

7   G. R. Morton, 1984, The carbon problem, *Creation Research Society Quarterly*, 20(4): 212-219.

diatomite beds are still inferred to have formed over thousands of years.

Contrary to what has been claimed, none of these supposed problems are insurmountable "hurdles" to explaining the deposition and formation of both chalk and diatomite beds during the Flood. Biological productivity does not appear to be a limiting factor, given that coccolithophores are among the fastest growing planktonic algae, sometimes multiplying at a rate of 2.25 divisions per day.[8] Using this dividing rate, and reasonable assumptions for the volume and average growth rate of each coccolith,[9] the number of coccoliths produced by each coccolithophore, and the numbers of each coccolithophores per liter of ocean water,[10] then the calculated potential production rate is 55 centimeters (over 21 inches) of calcium carbonate per year from the top 100 meters (305 feet) of the ocean.[11] At this rate it is possible to produce an average 100 meter (305 feet) thickness of coccoliths as calcareous ooze on the ocean floor in less than 200 years. Furthermore, assuming all limestones in the upper Cretaceous and Tertiary layers of the geologic column are chalks (which they are not), then the calculated volume would only require 4.1 percent of the earth's surface to be coccolith-producing seas to produce the volume of coccoliths to form all those limestones in only 1,600-1,700 years.[12] However, while these calculations certainly show that the quantities of calcareous oozes on today's ocean floors are easily producible in the timespan since the Flood, they are insufficient to show how these chalk beds were produced during the Flood itself.

Even today coccolith accumulation is not steady-state but highly episodic. Under the right conditions, significant increases in the concentrations of these marine microorganisms can occur, as in plankton "blooms," red tides, and in intense "white water coccolith blooms in which micro-organism numbers experience a two orders of magnitude increase."[13] Though poorly understood, the suggested reasons for these blooms include turbulence of the sea, wind, decaying fish, nutrients from freshwater inflow and upwelling, and temperature.[14] It is known

8   E. Paasche, 1968, Biology and physiology of coccolithophores, *Annual Review of Microbiology*, 22: 71-86.

9   S. Honjo, 1976, Coccoliths: Production, transportation and sedimentation, *Marine Micropaleontology*, 1: 65-79.

10   M. Black and D. Bukry, 1979, Coccoliths, in *The Encyclopedia of Paleontology*, Volume 7, R.W. Fairbridge and D. Jablonski, eds., Stroudsberg, PA: Dowden, Hutchinson and Ross, 194-199.

11   A. A. Roth, 1985, Are millions of years required to produce biogenic sediments in the deep ocean?, *Origins*, 12(1): 48-56.

12   J. Woodmorappe, 1986, The antediluvian biosphere and its capability of supplying the entire fossil record, in *Proceedings of the First International Conference on Creationism*, Volume 2, R. E. Walsh, C. L. Brooks and R. S. Crowell, eds., Pittsburgh, PA: Creation Science Fellowship, 205-218.

13   H. H. Seliger, J. H. Carpenter, M. Loftus and W. D. McElroy, 1970, Mechanisms for the accumulation of high concentrations of dinoflagellates in a bioluminescent bay, *Limnology and Oceanography*, 15: 234-245; J. L. Sumich, 1976, *Biology of Marine Life*, Dubuque, IA: William C. Brown, 118, 167.

14   W. B. Wilson and A. Collier, 1955, Preliminary notes on the culturing of *Gymnodinium brevis* Davis, *Science*, 121: 394-395; B. Ballantyne and B. C. Abbott, 1957, Toxic marine flagellates; Their occurrence

also that the element iron can seed algal blooms, but experiments have indicated that the mere presence of iron is not enough, as it must be in a form that the marine microorganisms can use. Recent observations show that a relatively high level of sulfur dioxide present is able to convert the iron to a more soluble form that algae can use.[15] Furthermore, there is now experimental evidence that low Mg/Ca ratios and high Ca concentrations in seawater, similar to the levels in so-called Cretaceous seawater, promote exponential growth rates of coccolithophores.[16]

Quite clearly, all of these necessary conditions for explosive blooming of coccolithophores would have been present during the cataclysmic global upheavals during the Flood. Torrential rain, sea turbulence, decaying fish and other organic matter, and the violent volcanic eruptions, on the ocean floor, associated with the "fountains of the great deep," and on land, both occurrences causing steam, carbon dioxide, sulfur dioxide, iron, and other elements to be spewed into the ocean waters and atmosphere, would have resulted in explosive blooms of coccolithophores on a large and repetitive scale in the oceans. Ocean water temperatures would have been higher toward the end of the Flood because of the heat released during the cataclysm, both from volcanic and magmatic activity, and from the latent heat of condensation of water.[17] Furthermore, thermodynamic considerations would definitely not prevent a much larger biosphere being produced, because oceanic productivity 5 to 10 times greater than at present could be supported by the available sunlight if the nutrients (especially nitrogen), were available.[18] The rapid production of the necessary quantities of calcareous ooze, enough to ensure its purity to form the chalk beds in the geologic record toward the end of the Flood year, is realistically conceivable.[19]

In spite of well-argued claims that the deposition and formation of the chalk beds required a longer period than a few weeks toward the end of the Flood year,[20] it is the extreme purity of the chalk beds that argues for their rapid deposition and

    and physiological effects on animals, *Journal of General Microbiology*, 16: 274-281; R. D. Pingree, P.M. Holligan and R. N. Head, 1977, Survival of dinoflagellate blooms in the western English Channel, *Nature*, 265: 266-269.

15   N. Meskhidze, W. L. Chameides and A. Nenes, 2005, Dust and pollution: A recipe for enhanced ocean fertilization?, *Journal of Geophysical Research (Atmospheres)*, 110: D03301.

16   S. M. Stanley, J. B. Ries and L. H. Hardie, 2005, Seawater chemistry, coccolithophore population growth, and the origin of Cretaceous chalk, *Geology*, 33: 593-596.

17   J. J. Shackleton and J. P. Kennet, 1975, Paleotemperature history of the Cenozoic and the initiation of Antarctic glaciation: Oxygen and carbon isotope analysis in DSDP Sites 277, 279, and 281, *Initial Reports of the Deep Sea Drilling Project*, 29, J. P. Kennet et al, ed., 743-755.

18   H. Tappan, 1982, Extinction or survival: Selectivity and Causes of Phanerozoic Crises, *Geological Society of America, Special Paper*, 190: 270.

19   A. A. Snelling, 1994, Can Flood geology explain thick chalk layers?, *Creation Ex Nihilo Technical Journal*, 8(1): 11-15.

20   W. H. Johns, 1995, Coccolithophores and chalk layers, *Creation Ex Nihilo Technical Journal*, 9(1): 29-33; D. J. Tyler, 1996, A post-Flood solution to the chalk problem, *Creation Ex Nihilo Technical Journal*, 10(1): 107-113.

formation. Furthermore, in many places the chalk layers are rhythmically bedded, with regularly-spaced, joint-like breaks or bedding planes, and the occasional thick marl bands.[21] This rhythmicity/cyclicity matches the cyclic variation in the oxygen isotopic composition of the carbonate, which is consistent with fluctuations of up to 4.5°C in the water temperatures when the chalk was deposited.[22] These fluctuating warmer ocean-water temperatures correlate with explosive production of coccolithophores and deposition of the pure chalk, which is consistent with copious quantities of nutrient-carrying hot waters being explosively added to the ocean waters by volcanic eruptions late in the Flood year. The presence of more than 100 regularly-spaced, thin bentonite seams between the chalk layers in the American chalk beds is consistent with explosive volcanic activity coinciding with rapid coccolith production and generation of the chalk beds, because the bentonite is derived from *in situ* decomposition of volcanic ash.[23]

What is often overlooked is that chalk pebbles occur in some of the marls, and marl-chalk junctions are cut by erosion hollows in some places.[24] Furthermore, the chalk ooze was not merely deposited in "flat spreads," but was sometimes piled into heaps and banks up to 50 meters high and 1.5 kilometers in length, accompanied by slumping. Smaller and less obvious carbonate banks with and without detectable cross-bedding are widespread in the English chalk beds. Submarine erosion surfaces are common in the chalk, and some fine-grained chalks show a textural, parallel lamination bedding. All of these features are indicative of deposition involving rapid current flows, and not the slow-and-gradual deposition over millions of years that is usually claimed. It is to be expected that rapidly-flowing density currents could have resulted from the massive aggregation of coccoliths, from the widescale explosive coccolithophore blooms, so even though the individual coccoliths are microscopic, a mass of them would have been deposited rapidly on the ocean floors. This would also explain the rapid burial of large ammonites and other marine creatures whose fossil remains are so often found in the chalk beds.

Similar arguments apply to the vast, thick, and pure diatomite beds in the geologic record. The scale and purity of these beds necessitates diatom accumulation rates significantly higher than in today's oceans, with abundant explosive diatom blooms resulting from abundant food supplies and favorable conditions for reproduction, combined with ocean currents rapidly accumulating and then depositing them on the ocean floor. The presence of volcanic ash in some of these diatomite beds is

21   J. M. Hancock, 1975, The petrology of the chalk, *Proceedings of the Geologists' Association*, 86(4): 499-535.

22   P. Ditchfield and J. D. Marshall, 1989, Isotopic variation in rhythmically bedded chalks: Paleotemperature variation in the Upper Cretaceous, *Geology*, 17(9): 842-845.

23   B. E. Hattin, 1982, Stratigraphy and depositional environment of the Smoky Hill Chalk Member, Niobara Chalk (Upper Cretaceous) of the time area, western Kansas, *Kansas State Geological Survey Bulletin*, 225, Lawrence, KS: University of Kansas Publications.

24   Hancock, 1975, 508-510.

also highly significant. Such explosive volcanic activity would have helped provide the nutrients for the abundant explosive diatom blooms, and the ash would have added to the density currents that rapidly swept the diatom skeletons to the ocean floor. It is also known that many diatoms form multi-cellular chains that can be several millimeters in length, so the diatom skeletons aggregate instead of being independent particles in suspension, and thus their settling is not subject to Stokes' Law.

However, major evidence for more rapid modes of deposition of diatomite beds arises from the presence of huge fossil vertebrates in some of them. The most striking examples are the fossilized baleen whales in the diatomite beds of the Pisco Formation of Peru,[25] and in the Monterey Formation in the Lompoc area of California.[26] Within the Peruvian Pisco Formation, 346 fossilized baleen whales 5 to 13 meters long have been found in a 1.5 square kilometer area of exposed outcrop. The burial of these huge whales and their fossilization was so rapid, that occasionally soft tissues have been preserved, including the baleen. Other common fossils found with these baleen whales are sharks' teeth, but this formation has also yielded fossilized fish, turtles, seals, porpoises, penguins, and even ground sloths. By comparison, in the Californian Monterey Formation, five fossilized whales were found by mining operations in a two-month period, including a baleen whale estimated to be about 25 meters long! Other fossils found abundantly in these diatomite beds include fish of many varieties, seals, and even birds. It is quite obvious that the accumulation of the diatomite to bury these huge whales, and to also preserve such an abundance of other fossils, had to have been catastrophic, in an event that affected land (ground sloths), air (birds), and the sea. Thus the evidence is totally consistent with the catastrophic formation of these diatomite beds, along with the chalk beds, toward the end of the global Flood cataclysm.

---

25   L. R. Brand, R. Esperante, A.V. Chadwick, O. P. Porras and M. Alomfa, 2004, Fossil whale preservation implies high diatom accumulation rate in the Miocene-Pliocene Pisco Formation of Peru, *Geology*, 32(2): 165-168.

26   A. A. Snelling, 1995, The whale fossil in diatomite, Lompoc, California, *Creation Ex Nihilo Technical Journal*, 9(2): 244-258.

116

CORAL REEFS AND LIMESTONE

Another type of sedimentary deposit that is claimed to require a long time for accumulation are coral reefs.[1] Coral reefs appear to represent vast accumulations of the calcium carbonate remains of coral organisms that grew over time, the living organisms growing on the remains and debris of their predecessors. Thus, when local and regional structures that contain fossilized coral and reef-related organisms are found in limestone beds and look like present-day reefs, it is then claimed they are fossilized reefs that must have taken eons of time to accumulate and be built, so the limestone beds containing them must likewise represent eons of time for deposition and accumulation.[2] Of course, the total mass of material in the reef is not only a function of time, but also of the numbers and sizes of the multiplying reef-building corals. Thus, large coral reefs would just as well have formed in relatively short time periods.

Detractors usually cite the reefs of Enewetok Atoll in the Pacific Ocean as an example of modern reefs that must have taken a long time to grow, given the usual estimate of coral growth rates. Drilling on this atoll has penetrated 1,405 meters of apparent reef material before reaching the basaltic rock of the ocean floor.[3] Of course, coral doesn't grow if it is more than 50 meters below the ocean surface, so the Enewetok Reef must have begun growing when the ocean there was quite shallow, and then evidently continued growing as the ocean floor gradually subsided. At the rates of coral growth assumed by most investigators, it would, of course, have taken up to hundreds of thousands of years to form a reef as thick as this.

One critic of the biblical model of earth history has claimed that the Enewetok Reef would have to have grown at a rate of at least 140 millimeters per year to have formed in less than 10,000 years since the Flood, and states: "Such rates have

---

1   Wonderly, 1977, 23-47.

2   Wonderly, 1977, 68-112.

3   H. S. Ladd and S. O. Schlanger, 1960, Drilling operations on Enewetok Atoll: Bikini and nearby Atolls, Marshall Islands, *US Geological Survey Professional Paper*, 260Y: 863-905.

been shown to be quite impossible."[4] However, this claim is ignorant of earlier published, well-documented, direct measurements of reef growth rates of 280-414 millimeters per year,[5] which are far more accurate than many published estimates based on radiocarbon "dating" for coral growth rings. Similarly, growth rates of the corals that build the frames of reefs have also been measured at 120-432 mm per year.[6] Analyzing these direct measurements, it can be easily calculated that coral growth would have been rapid enough to build the Enewetok Reef in only 3,400 years, well within the time since the Genesis Flood. The Enewetok Atoll reefs are an extreme example, because other reefs around the world are not as thick as these. For example, the enormous Great Barrier Reef of Australia, while being more than 2,000 kilometers long, is less than 250 meters thick.[7] Thus, based on the above reference measurements of coral reef growth, all living reefs today around the world would easily have grown in the time since the Genesis Flood.

Much is claimed about daily growth-lines produced in many corals as they grow, and used to infer estimates of exceedingly slow coral growth rates. These growth-lines form seasonal patterns, but the counting of these growth-lines in corals is quite subjective, because they are often ill-defined. Some individuals will find twice as many as others on the same sample.[8] Furthermore, environmental factors such as water depth affect the number of growth-lines formed.[9]

The occurrence of what are alleged to be fossil reefs in limestones in various portions of the geologic column appear to be a difficult problem to reconcile with both the deposition of such limestones during the Flood, and the biblical chronology. Many abundantly fossiliferous limestones are claimed to be organically constructed "reefs" that slowly accumulated over thousands of years as innumerable generations of marine organisms chemically cemented themselves on top of one another to construct huge, wave-resistant framework structures. Field investigators have documented hundreds of these claimed fossil reefs throughout

---

4   A. Hayward, 1985, *Creation and Evolution: The Facts and the Fallacies*, London: Triangle (SPCK), 85.

5   J. Th. Verstelle, 1921, The growth rate at various depths of coral reefs in the Dutch East Indian Archipelago, *Treubia*, 14: 117-126; R. B. S. Sewell, 1935, Studies on coral and coral formations in Indian waters, in Geographic and Oceanographic Research in Indian Waters, No. 8, *Memoirs of the Asiatic Society of Bengal*, 9: 461-539.

6   J. B. Lewis, S. Axelsen, I. Goodbody, C. Page and D. Chislett, 1968, Comparative growth rates of reef corals in the Caribbean, *Marine Science Manuscript Report 2*, Montreal, QC: Marine Sciences Center, McGill University; R. W. Vuddemeier and R. A. Kinzie III, 1976, Coral growth, *Oceanography and Marine Biology: An Annual Review*, 14: 183-225; A. H. Gladfelter, 1984, Skeletal development in *Acropora cervicornis*. III. A comparison of monthly rates of linear extinction and calcium carbonate accretion measured over a year, *Coral Reefs*, 3: 51-57.

7   H. Blatt, V. Middleton and R. Murray, 1980, *Origin of Sedimentary Rocks*, second edition, Englewood Cliffs, NJ: Prentice-Hall, 36.

8   C. D. Clausen, 1974, An evaluation of the use of growth lines in geochronometry, geophysics, and paleoecology, *Origins*, 1: 58-66; D. N. Crabtree, C. D. Clausen and A. A. Roth, 1980, Consistency in growth line counts in bivalve specimens, *Paleogeography, Paleoclimatology, Paleoecology*, 29: 323-340.

9   J.-L. Liénard, 1986, *Factors Affecting Epithecal Growth Lines in Four Coral Species, with Paleontological Implications*, Th. D. dissertation, Department of Biology, Loma Linda University, Loma Linda, CA.

the geologic column, from the Precambrian upwards.[10] With notable exceptions, these fossil reefs are usually very small compared to present living reefs.

However, authenticating fossil reefs requires that many problems must be overcome, not least of which is the confused definition of a reef. Many of these so-called fossil reefs appear to be only accumulations of sediments swept in by water, which obviously would have occurred rapidly. In Grand Canyon,[11] the Redwall Limestone does not contain any organically-bound structures or reefs, nor coral and sponge-reef structures,[12] and even laminated algal structures particularly show concentric internal structure due to the algal masses having been transported by rolling.[13] Indeed, there is much evidence throughout the Redwall Limestone, including a two meter thick unit within it deposited catastrophically by a hyperconcentrated sediment gravity flow that mass-killed and buried billions of large nautiloids, which demonstrates that it was formed rapidly under conditions consistent with the Genesis Flood.[14]

One famous, classic example of a claimed fossil "barrier reef" is the Permian reef complex of the Guadalupe Mountains of southeastern New Mexico and western Texas, more commonly referred to as simply the "Capitan Reef." However, careful field research of the Capitan Limestone, and associated strata that make up the alleged reef, cast doubt on the various claimed depositional and ecologic environments said to be associated with this fossil reef.[15] The so-called "backreef lagoon" and "forereef talus" deposits were not contemporaneous with "reef" accumulation. Furthermore, the Capitan Limestone lacks large, *in situ*, organically-bound frameworks and deposits of broken debris that can be shown to be derived from an organic framework. Instead, the Capitan Limestone is composed primarily of broken fossil fragments in a fine-grained matrix of lime silt and sand, which were not wave-resistant when deposited. The fossil flora and fauna of the "Capitan Reef" represent a shallow-water assemblage, which was not especially adapted to a wave or strong current environment. Reef-forming organisms, which would have bound the sediments and built frameworks, are either all together absent or largely inconspicuous. All of these features, particularly the

10   P. H. Heckel, 1974, Carbonate buildup in the geologic record: A review, in *Reefs in Time and Space*, L. F. Laporte, ed., Society of Economic Paleontologists and Mineralogists Special Publication 18: 90-154.

11   E. D. McKee and R. D. Gutschick, 1969, History of the Redwall Limestone in Northern Arizona, *Geological Society of America Memoir,* 114: 557.

12   L. R. Hopkins, 1990, Kaibab Formation, in *Grand Canyon Geology*, S.S. Beus and M. Morales, eds., New York: Oxford University Press, 243.

13   S. A. Austin, ed., 1994, *Grand Canyon: Monument to Catastrophe*, Santee, CA: Institute for Creation Research, 26-28.

14   S. A. Austin, 2003, Nautiloid mass kill and burial event, Redwall Limestone (Lower Mississippian), Grand Canyon region, Arizona and Nevada, in *Proceedings of the Fifth International Conference on Creationism*, R.L. Ivey, Jr., ed., Pittsburgh, PA: Creation Science Fellowship, 55-99.

15   S. E. Nevins, 1972, Is the Capitan Limestone a fossil reef?, *Creation Research Society Quarterly*, 8(4): 231-248.

lack of large organically-bound structures, suggest that deposition was very rapid, consistent with deposition during the Genesis Flood. Other investigators "have expressed frustration at using modern reefs to interpret their ancient counterparts, including this Capitan Reef."[16]

Many fossil-bearing limestone deposits that once were interpreted as fossilized reefs have been reinterpreted as debris flows or other non-reef structures. A well-known example of a supposed fossilized reef is the so-called Nubrigyn Reef complex near the village of Stuart Town in eastern Australia.[17] Instead of being formed by coral, this so-called reef was built by algae. However, careful examination of the outcrops reveals that the so-called reef complex is in fact made up of a mixture of pieces of broken fossil algae and non-reef-like types of rocks, literally "floating" in a matrix of fine-grained sediments, which is why this is now not regarded as a fossilized reef, but as megabreccia resulting from a debris flow.[18] Thus, this once famous "fossilized reef" represents the remains of a reef that grew elsewhere (likely before the Flood), which was destroyed in a watery catastrophe, so it is no longer an example of a reef grown in place that can be used as an argument against the catastrophic Genesis Flood. Similar doubts can be raised about the claimed Devonian reef complexes of the Canning Basin in the northwest of Western Australia.[19] These supposed reef complexes consist of isolated high-relief fossiliferous limestone platforms, flanked by steep marginal-slope facies limestones, which were deposited by debris flows that contain allochthonous blocks of "reef" limestone. The edges of these platforms are claimed to be the reefs, but this is a subjective interpretation, given that apart from containing a wider variety of fossils, the marginal-slope limestone is no different from the rest of the limestone platforms. These platforms could instead be regarded as remnants of the continuous limestone bed that was eroded, with debris flows leaving behind flanking megabreccias around the isolated remnant platforms to form the marginal-slope facies. Thus, any comparison with living reefs is only superficial.

A number of these so-called fossil reefs in various parts of the world have now

16   D. K. Hubbard, A. I. Miller and D. Scaturo, Production and cycling of calcium carbonate in a shelf-edge reef system (St. Croix US Virgin Islands): Applications to the natural reef systems in the fossil record, *Journal of Sedimentary Petrology*, 60: 335-360; R. Wood, J. A. D. Dickson and B. Kirkland-George, 1994, Turning the Capitan Reef upside down: A new appraisal of the ecology of the Permian Capitan Reef, Guadalupe Mountains, Texas and New Mexico, *Palaios*, 9: 422-427; R. Wood, J. A. D. Dickson and B. L. Kirkland, 1996, New observations on the ecology of the Permian Capitan Reef, Texas and New Mexico, *Paleontology*, 39: 733-762.

17   I. G. Percival, 1985, *The Geological Heritage of New South Wales*, Volume 1, Sydney: New South Wales National Parks and Wildlife Service, 16-17.

18   P. J. Conaghan, E. W. Mountjoy, D. R. Edgecombe, J. A. Talent and D. E. Owen, 1976, Nubrigyn algal reefs (Devonian) eastern Australia: Allochthonous blocks and megabreccias, *Geological Society of America Bulletin*, 87: 515-530.

19   P. E. Playford, 1984, Platform-margin and marginal-slope relationships in Devonian reef complexes of the Canning Basin, in *The Canning Basin W.A.*, P.G. Purcell, ed., Perth: Geological Society of Australia and Petroleum Exploration Society of Australia Symposium, 189-214.

been reinterpreted as resulting from rapidly accumulating debris flows,[20] while even the classic fossil Steinplatte Reef of the Austrian Alps has been described as a "sand pile."[21] Indeed, sedimentologists have reported that:

> Closer inspection of many of these ancient carbonate "reefs" reveals that they are composed largely of carbonate mud with the larger skeletal particles "floating" within the mud matrix. Conclusive evidence for a rigid organic framework does not exist in most of the ancient carbonate mounds. In this sense, they are remarkably different from modern, coral-algal reefs.[22]

The skeletal particles floating in a mud matrix would likely have been deposited rapidly.

Whether an ancient fossilized "reef" really does represent an authentic and original biological entity is often determined by analyzing the orientation of the fossils in it. If corals, for example, are in an upright (growth) position, it is assumed that they must have grown where they are now found. However, such observations mean little, because transport of reef material would result in components ending up in almost any position. Nevertheless, it has been shown that in some fossil "reefs" the preferred orientation of the supposed reef-producing components is upright, as expected if in the position of growth.[23] However, such observations do not negate the evidence that massive reef cores, which had earlier grown elsewhere, were transported and deposited during a catastrophic upheaval. Blocks of former reef material, that has been transported and deposited in other sediment layers, have been noted in the geologic literature, and in the Austrian Alps huge layers of sediments containing suggested "fossil reefs" have been thrust over other sedimentary layers for many hundreds of kilometers during the formation of the Alps.[24]

---

20   E. W. Mountjoy, H. E. Cook, L. C. Pray and P. N. McDaniel, 1972, Allochthonous carbonate debris flows—worldwide indicators of reef complexes, banks or shelf margins, in *International Geological Congress, Section 6, Stratigraphy and Sedimentology*, D.J. McLaren and G.V. Middleton, eds., Montreal, Canada: 24th International Geological Congress, 172-189.

21   R. J. Stanton, Jr. and E. Flügl, 1988, The Steinplatte, a classic upper Triassic Reef—that is actually a platform-edge sand pile, *Geological Society of America Abstracts with Programs*, 27(7): A201.

22   H. Blatt, G. Middleton and R. Murray, 1980, *Origin of Sedimentary Rocks*, second edition, Englewood Cliffs, NJ: Prentice-Hall, 447.

23   L. T. Hodges and A. A. Roth, 1986, Orientation of corals and stromatoporoids in some Pleistocene, Devonian, and Silurian reef facies, *Journal of Paleontology*, 60: 1147-1158.

24   K. A. Giles, 1995, Allochthonous model for the generation of lower Mississippian Waulsortian mounds and implications for prediction of facies geometry and distribution, *American Association of Petroleum Geologists and Society of Economic Paleontologists and Mineralogists Annual Meeting Abstracts*, 4: 33A; K. P. Polan, 1982, *The allochthonous origin of 'bioherms' in the early Devonian Stewart Bay Formation, of Bathurst Island, Arctic Canada*, M.Sc. thesis, Montreal: Department of Geological Sciences, McGill University; W. R. Janoschek and A. Matura, 1980, Outline of the geology of Austria, *Abhandlungen der Geologischen Bundesanstalt*, 34: 40-46; R. Lein, 1987, On the evolution of the Austroalpine realm, in *Geodynamics of the Eastern Alps*, H.W. Flügel and T. Faupl, eds., Vienna: Franz Deuticke, 85-102;

If what have been mis-identified as fossilized reefs instead represent former reefs that have been transported *en masse* or eroded, fragmented, and incorporated in debris flows to form megabreccias, then the question of long time periods for their *in situ* formation at these current locations in the geologic record becomes totally irrelevant. In the context of the biblical framework of earth history, many reefs would have grown in the pre-Flood world, and as a result of the upheaval of the Flood would have then been destroyed, and the debris transported and deposited in Flood sediments. Of course, some of those pre-Flood reefs may well have been buried *in situ* by Flood sediments, but such occurrences of "fossilized reefs" would be now found at the base of the geologic record of the Flood.[25] Even though it has not been established that all ancient "fossilized reefs" are the result of rapid sediment transport, their identification as *in situ* structures has been shown to often be questionable. Indeed, the interpretations of both living and fossilized reefs involves abundant conjectures. Thus, our present knowledge indicates that the question of time for the formation of claimed fossilized reefs, and limestones generally, is not a serious challenge to either a recent creation or a global cataclysmic Flood.

A. Tollman, 1987, Geodynamic concepts of the evolution of the eastern Alps, in Flügel and Faupl, 1987, 361-378.

25   K. P. Wise and A. A. Snelling, 2005, A note on the pre-Flood/Flood boundary in the Ground Canyon, *Origins*, 58: 7-29.

117

EVAPORITES

Another type of sedimentary deposit that may at first seem difficult to compress into the short timespan of the Flood is the thick beds of so-called "evaporites." These consist mainly of halite (common salt or sodium chloride), gypsum and anhydrite (calcium sulfate), and other salts in bedded layers between other sedimentary rock units. The term "evaporite" is applied to these sedimentary deposits because it is believed they were formed by long periods of intense evaporation from inland seas or lakes containing saline water. Among the modern examples that are cited as a depositional model is the Dead Sea, where the evaporation rate is very high at about 120 inches annually, and where the water continually entering the lake has no other outlet apart from evaporation. As a result, the Dead Sea has an extremely high concentration of many salts, and it is believed that continued evaporation over long ages would thus produce beds of evaporates, similar to those found in many places in the geologic record. However, at present rates, this process would obviously require hundreds of thousands of years to produce the thick beds of evaporites that are actually found among the world's sedimentary strata.

As usual, the difficulty here is the unrelenting application of uniformitarianism. It is assumed that evaporite beds must have formed in some depositional environment or environments, the same or similar to those found today, in which salt deposits are being produced by evaporation that can be measured. Modern evaporite deposits accumulate in a variety of subaerial environments, such as coastal and continental sabkhas, or salt flats, pans or playas, and interdune environments, and shallow subaqueous environments such as saline coastal lakes called salinas.[1] The only possible modern example of a deep-water evaporite basin would be the Dead Sea. However, most geologists still believe that many of the thick, laterally extensive, ancient evaporite deposits did accumulate in deep-water basins.

Some ancient evaporite deposits, such as those of the so-called Zechstein of Europe, exceed 2,000 meters in thickness, yet evaporation of a column of seawater 1,000 meters thick will produce only about 15 meters of evaporites. Thus, to produce

---

1   A. C. Kendall, 1992, Evaporites, in *Facies Models: Response to Sea Level Change*, R. G. Walker and N. P. James, eds., Geological Association of Canada, chapter 19, 375-409.

the Zechstein evaporite deposits by the evaporation of seawater would have required a column of seawater 130,000 meters (or 130 kilometers) thick! Indeed, evaporation of all the water in the Mediterranean Sea, for example, would yield a mean thickness of evaporites of only about 60 meters. Of course, to circumvent the obvious difficulties of envisaging the evaporation of so much seawater to produce the ancient evaporite deposits, geologists must resort to special pleading:

> Obviously, special geologic conditions operating over a long period of time are required to deposit thick sequences of natural evaporites. The basic requirements for deposition of marine evaporites are a relatively arid climate, where rates of evaporation exceed rates of precipitation, and partial isolation of the depositional basin from the open ocean. Isolation is achieved by means of some type of barrier that restricts free circulation of ocean water into and out of the basin. Under these restricted conditions, the brines formed by evaporation are prevented from returning to the open ocean, causing them to become concentrated to the point where evaporite minerals are precipitated.[2]

Although geologists agree on these general requirements for formation of evaporites, considerable controversy has existed regarding deep-water versus shallow-water depositional mechanisms for many ancient evaporite deposits. There are three possible models for deposition of thick sequences of marine evaporites.

First, there is the deep-water, deep-basin model, which assumes the existence of a deep basin separated from the open ocean by some type of topographic barrier that prevents the free interchange of water in the basin with water in the open ocean, but allows enough water into the basin to replenish that lost by evaporation.

Second, the shallow-water, shallow-basin model, which assumes the evaporative concentration of brines in a shallow basin protected from the open ocean by a topographic high, and the accumulation of great thicknesses of evaporites is due to the continued subsidence of the floor of the basin.

Third, the shallow-water, deep-basin model requires that the brine level in the basin be reduced below the level of the topographic high, with recharge of seawater from the open ocean taking place only by seepage through the barrier, or by periodic overflow of it.

Geologists have found the application of these models to explain the formation of ancient evaporite deposits to be a challenging task, and have not always agreed upon the interpreted sedimentary environment. Over time, geologists' concept for evaporite deposition has swung from deep-water to shallow-water deposition, then

---

2   S. Boggs, Jr., 1995, *Principles of Sedimentology and Stratigraphy*, second edition, Upper Saddle River, NJ: Prentice Hall, 243-244.

from tidal sabkha regime to very moderate water depths.[3] This is well illustrated by the debate over how the thick evaporite beds formed in the Mediterranean Basin, in what has been called the "Messinian Salinity Crisis."

During the Deep Sea Drilling Project in the early 1970s, the sediments on the floor of the Mediterranean Sea were drilled into, revealing the existence of extensive, thick evaporite beds, which subsequently stimulated "an unusual quantity of researches" and generated "lively and even conflicting debates."[4] A deep basin-shallow water model for evaporite deposition was initially proposed,[5] but subsequent debate questioned that interpretation and most of the major aspects of previous "classical models" for evaporite deposition.[6] Nevertheless, it is now claimed that new data supports an integrated scenario that revives the key points of the deep-basin, shallow-water model, with two stages of evaporite deposition that affected successively the whole Mediterranean Basin, the distribution of the evaporites and their depositional timing being constrained by a high degree of paleogeographical differentiation, and by threshold effects that governed the water exchanges. So according to the most recent interpretative synthesis, 1,600 meters of layered evaporite deposits were formed in only 700,000 years (a relatively brief period of geologic time), due to the "interplay of both glacio-eustatic changes and fluctuations of the circum-Mediterranean climate."

However, do the sequences of salt beds found in these so-called evaporite deposits match the sequence of salts produced by evaporation of sea water? While it is often claimed the answer is yes, discrepancies between the sequence observed in laboratory experiments and the sequences observed in the rock record are the rule. That there is a definite sequence of minerals that precipitate when ocean water is evaporated in the laboratory was first demonstrated by Usiglio in 1848.[7] Minor quantities of carbonate minerals begin to form when the original volume of seawater is reduced by evaporation to about one half. Then gypsum (calcium sulfate) appears when the original volume has been reduced to about 20 percent, and halite (sodium chloride) forms when the water volume reaches approximately 10 percent of the original volume. Magnesium and potassium salts are then only deposited when less than about 5 percent of the original volume of seawater remains.

On the other hand, in general, the proportion of calcium sulfate (gypsum and

3   P. Sonnenfeld and G. C. St. C. Kendall (conveners), 1989, Marine evaporites: Genesis, alteration, and associated deposits: Penrose Conference Report, *Geology*, 17: 573-574.

4   2006, Editorial, The Messinian Salinity Crisis revisited, *Sedimentary Geology*, 188-189: 1-8.

5   K. J. Hsü, M. B. Cita and W. B. F. Ryan, 1973, The origin of the Mediterranean evaporites, in *Initial Reports of the Deep Sea Drilling Program*, volume 13, W. B. F. Ryan et al, eds., Washington, D.C.: US Government Printing office, 1203-1231.

6   J. M. Rouchy and A. Caruso, 2006, The Messinian Salinity Crisis in the Mediterranean Basin: A reassessment of the data and an integrated scenario, *Sedimentary Geology*, 188-189: 35-67.

7   F. W. Clarke, 1924, *The Data of Geochemistry*, 5th edition, US Geological Survey, Bulletin 770.

anhydrite) is greater and the proportion of sodium-magnesium sulfates is less in natural deposits than observed in laboratory experiments.[8] Furthermore, the thickest sequences of evaporite deposits in the Mediterranean Basin begin with more than 500 meters thickness of massive halite,[9] whereas the lower portion of the Castile Formation, from the 1,300-meter-thick evaporite deposits of the Delaware Basin of western Texas and southeastern New Mexico, is composed of alternating thin laminae of calcite, anhydrite, and organic matter.[10] So to account for these anomalous mega-occurrences, special *ad hoc* conditions need to be postulated. The deposition of relatively thick sequences of gypsum and/or anhydrite, such as in the Castile Formation, is said to imply that there was a source of new seawater or other brine being made available for evaporation, and that the brine was seldom allowed to concentrate to the point of halite precipitation. If the concentrated brine is removed from the sedimentary basin at the same time new sea water is added, then the claim is made that it is possible to maintain the concentration at an equilibrium value and precipitate only gypsum. On the other hand, if as the seawater evaporates new seawater is constantly added to the depositional basin to maintain the original volume, then it is claimed the brine will soon become concentrated to the point of only precipitating halite, as in the massive beds in the western Mediterranean Basin.[11]

The following comment sums up the failure of the uniformitarian evaporite model to explain the formation of bedded salt deposits:

> Although the order observed by Usiglio agrees in a general way with the sequence found in some salt deposits, many exceptions are known. Also many minerals known from salt beds did not appear in the experimentally formed residues. The crystallization of the brine is very complex, and depends not only on the solubility of the salts involved but also upon the concentration of the several salts present and the temperature.... Inasmuch as many evaporite deposits show marked exceptions to the above requirements, simple evaporation of sea water did not occur, and either the parent brine was not formed from sea water or the evaporation took place under special conditions that will explain the anomalies.[12]

However, even though the impression often given is that evaporite deposits are simply the product of chemical precipitation owing to evaporation of seawater, it is well documented that many evaporite deposits are not just passive chemical

---

8   H. Borchert and R. O. Muir, 1964, *Salt Deposits: The Origin, Metamorphism, and Deformation of Evaporites*, London: Van Nostrand.

9   Rouchy and Caruso, 2006.

10   H. Blatt, 1992, *Sedimentary Petrology*, second edition, New York: W. H. Freeman and Company, chapter 10, 338-341.

11   H. Blatt, G. Middleton, and R. Murray, 1972, *Origin of Sedimentary Rocks*, Engelwood Cliffs, NJ: Prentice-Hall, 501-504.

12   F. J. Pettijohn, 1957, *Sedimentary Rocks*, second edition, New York: Harper and Rowe, 483-484.

precipitates.[13] The "evaporite" minerals have, in fact, been transported and reworked in the same way as the constituents of sandstones, siltstones, shales, and limestones. Transport can occur by normal fluid-flow processes, or by mass-transport processes such as slumps and turbidity currents. Turbidity current transport mechanisms may have been particularly important in deposition of many "ancient" deep-water evaporite deposits.[14] Thus evaporite deposits display sedimentation features the same as sandstones, siltstones, shales, and many limestones, including both normal and reverse grain-size grading, cross-bedding, and ripple marks. Such features are clearly related to water-transport and deposition. Thus, the alternating thin laminae of calcite, anhydrite, and organic matter in the Castile Formation of the Delaware Basin of western Texas and southeast New Mexico, and in the Prairie Formation of the Williston Basin of Saskatchewan, Canada, and North Dakota, were clearly deposited as a result of turbidity currents, and therefore rapidly, as demonstrated in the laboratory,[15] and in observational field studies.[16]

However, if the sedimentation features in evaporite deposits indicate rapid deposition, then there is clearly a major problem, because the slow-and-gradual evaporation of seawater to produce evaporite deposits is totally incompatible with this observational evidence of rapid deposition. On the other hand, if there were an alternate means by which salt deposits could be produced rapidly, then this would be consistent with the observed field evidence. Indeed, evaporation of seawater is not the only means by which a highly-concentrated brine is formed from which salts precipitate. Volcanic waters and hydrothermal fluids are usually very saline, and when they mix with bodies of cold water, the sudden temperature drop causes the water mixture to become super-saturated in the salts, so that the solution can no longer hold the salts, which rapidly precipitate.[17] This is precisely what happens around deep-sea hot hydrothermal vents,[18] where layers of highly

13   Boggs, 1995, 245.

14   E. C. Shrieber, M. E. Tucker and R. Till, 1986, Arid shorelines and evaporites, in *Sedimentary Environments and Facies*, H. G. Reading, ed., Blackwell, 189-228.

15   P. H. Kuenen, 1966, Experimental turbidite lamination in a circular flume, *Journal of Geology*, 74: 523-545; G. Berthault, 1986, Experiments of lamination of sediments, resulting of a periodic graded-bedding subsequent to deposit, *Compte Rendu Academie des Sciences, Paris*, 303: 1569-1574; G. Berthault, 1988, Sedimentation of a heterogranular mixture: Experimental lamination in still and running water, *Compte Rendu Academie des Sciences, Paris*, 306: 717-724.

16   M. M. Ball, E. A. Shinn, and K. W. Stockman, 1967, The geologic effects of hurricane Donna in south Florida, *Journal of Geology*, 75: 583-597; E. D. McKee, E. J. Crosby and H. L. Berryhill, Jr., 1967, Flood deposits, Bijou Creek, Colorado, June 1965, *Journal of Sedimentary Petrology*, 37: 829-851; S. A. Austin, 1986, Mount St. Helens and catastrophism, *Proceedings of the First International Conference on Creationism*, Volume 1, Pittsburgh, PA: Creation Science Fellowship, 3-9; D. J. W. Piper, 1972, Turbidite origin of some laminated mudstones, *Geological Magazine*, 109: 115-126.

17   K. B. Krauskopf, 1967, *Introduction to Geochemistry*, New York: McGraw-Hill; M. Hodes, P. Griffiths, K. A. Smith, W. S. Hurst, W. J. Bowers, and K. Sako, 2004, Salt solubility and deposition in high temperature and pressure aqueous solutions, *American Institute of Chemical Engineers Journal*, 50(9): 2038-2049.

18   P. A. Rona, G. Klinkhammer, T. A. Nelson, H. Trefry and H. Elderfield, 1986, Black smokers, massive

saline supercritical waters may have ponded on the ocean-bottom.[19]

These and related observations are consistent with the long-proposed, hydrothermal model for the deposition of what should be called precipitite (rather than evaporite) deposits.[20] This hydrothermal precipitite model answers many questions left unexplained by conventional evaporite models. Its geologic setting requires a period of intense undersea volcanic or igneous intrusive activity in the depositional basin of no specific water depth, in which there are also widespread hydrothermal vent systems through which much water is circulating. Derivation of the salts for deposition is due to enrichment of the salts in seawater by the circulation of normal seawater through the hydrothermal vent system, and by direct addition of salts in hydrothermal fluids given off by intrusive magmas and during the intense volcanic activity. The resulting super-saline, hot supercritical waters consequently stratify in layers at the bottom of the depositional basin, as has been currently observed at the bottom of the Red Sea.[21] These salt deposits then are precipitated by several mechanisms acting together.

1. As the hot saline waters ascend, salt precipitation occurs as they are cooled by the colder seawater above.

2. Salts that are less soluble in hot saline water, such as calcium carbonate and calcium sulfate (gypsum and anhydrite), precipitate due to the heating caused by the hotter supercritical water coming up from below, and/or from variations in magmatic activity.

3. Salt precipitation results from the pressure release as the hot super-saturated brine mass rises.

4. Salt precipitation results from changes in the Eh and pH of the super-saturated brines.

sulfides and vent biota at the Mid-Atlantic Ridge, *Nature*, 321: 33-37; K. L. VonDamm, 1990, Seafloor hydrothermal activity: black smoker chemistry in chimneys, *Annual Review of Earth and Planetary Sciences*, 18: 173-204.

19 R. P. Lowell and L. N. Germanovich, 1997, Evolution of a brine-saturated layer at the base of a ridge-crest hydrothermal system, *Journal of Geophysical Research*, 102(B5): 10,245-10,255; K. L. VonDamm, M. D. Lilley, W.C. Shanks III, M. Bockington, A. M. Bray, K. M. O'Grady, E. Olson, A. Graham, and B. Proskurowski, 2002, Extraordinary phase separation and segregation in vent fluids from the southern East Pacific Rise, *Earth and Planetary Science Letters*, 196: 1-4.

20 V. I. Sozansky, 1973, Origin of salt deposits in deep-water basins of the Atlantic Ocean, *American Association of Petroleum Geologists Bulletin*, 57(3): 589-590; D. I. Nutting, 1984, *Origin of Bedded Salt Deposits: A Critique of Evaporative Models and a Defence of a Hydrothermal Model*, M.S. Thesis (unpublished), El Cajon, CA: Institute for Creation Research Graduate School; M. Hovland, H. G. Rueslåtten, H. K. Johnsen, B. Kvanne and T. Kuznetsova, 2006, Salt formation associated with sub-surface boiling and supercritical water, *Marine and Petroleum Geology*, 23: 855-869.

21 J. L. Bischoff, 1969, Red Sea geothermal brine deposits: their mineralogy, chemistry and genesis, in *Hot Brines and Recent Heavy Metal Deposits in the Red Sea: A Geochemical and Geophysical Account*, E. T. Dedgens and D. A. Ross, eds., New York: Springer –Verlag, 368-401; M. Hovland et al, 2006.

5. Salt precipitation results from a process of brine mixing, where two brines of different salinities react.[22]

It is thus now well-documented that this hydrothermal precipitite model accounts for the salt beds forming on the floor of the Red Sea today, beneath hydrothermal brine layers in pools within basins.[23] That the presently-active hydrothermal precipitation of these bedded salt deposits are related to the formation of ancient evaporite deposits is confirmed by the bedded salt deposits up to 5,000 meters thick on the flanks of the Red Sea, and underneath where salt beds are precipitating today.[24] Further evidence that supports the hydrothermal precipitite model for the formation of ancient salt deposits includes:

1. The proportion of the different salt minerals found in ancient salt beds is completely different from what theoretical and experimental geochemical methods would predict based upon the uniformitarian evaporite model.[25] As already noted, salt beds contain great thicknesses of primarily one salt mineral to the exclusion of all others. Furthermore, some of the more soluble salts, such as magnesium sulfate, are absent in large salt beds, whereas they generally form in the claimed modern analogous evaporative lagoons.[26]

2. Some of the associations of salt minerals indicate high temperatures of deposition, such as 83°C for a magnesium sulfate salt with potassium chloride.[27] For example, the huge German Zechstein salt beds contain large amounts of these salt minerals that require high depositional temperatures near the boiling point of water, temperatures that are not found in modern depositional settings for evaporite deposits.

3. Bedded salt deposits are frequently associated with volcanics.[28] For example, volcanics are associated with the huge evaporite deposits of the Mediterranean Basin.[29]

---

22 O. B. Raup, 1970, Brine mixing: An additional mechanism for formation of basin evaporites, *American Association of Petroleum Geologists Bulletin*, 54(12): 2246-2259; F. L. Wilcox and S. T. Davidson, 1976, Experiments on precipitation brought about by mixing brines, *Creation Research Society Quarterly*, 13(2): 87-89.

23 Hovland et al, 2006.

24 G. Savoyat, A. Shiferaw and T. Balcha, 1989, Petroleum exploration in the Ethiopian Red Sea, *Journal of Petroleum Geology*, 12: 187-204; F. Orszag-Sperber, P. Harwood, A. Kendall and B.H. Purser, 1998, A review of the evaporites of the Red Sea-Gulf of Suez Rift, in *Sedimentation and Tectonics of Rift Basins: Red Sea-Gulf of Aden*, B. H. Purser and D. W. J. Bosence, eds., London: Chapman and Hall, 409-426.

25 Krauskopf, 1967, 319-353.

26 V. B. Porfir'ev, 1974, Geology and genesis of salt formations, *American Association of Petroleum Geologists Bulletin*, 58: 2543-2544.

27 F. H. Stewart, 1963, Marine evaporites, in *Data of Geochemistry*, sixth edition, M. Fleischer, ed., US Geological Survey Professional Paper 440-Y; Krauskopf, 1967, 346.

28 Sozansky, 1973; Porfir'ev, 1974.

29 W. B. Nesteroff, F. C. Wezel and G. Pautot, 1973, Summary of lithostratigraphic findings and problems,

4. Bedded salt deposits are frequently associated with rifting, mountain-building, and faulting that coincide with magmatic, volcanic, and hydrothermal activity.[30]

5. Bedded salt deposits are frequently associated with large accumulations of hydrocarbons.[31] Indeed, almost every major oil-producing province of the world is associated either directly or indirectly with bedded salt deposits. The connection to hydrothermal activity is evident from discovery of the natural generation of petroleum by hydrothermal fluids flowing through organic material in sediments on the sea floor of the Guaymas Basin in the Gulf of California.[32]

6. Bedded salt deposits are frequently associated with sulfur and heavy metal sulfides in some of the world's major sedimentary-hydrothermal metal sulfide deposits, and salt minerals are often associated with many of the world's major hydrothermal metal deposits.[33]

In conclusion, during the global Genesis Flood cataclysm, bedded salt deposits would have been formed catastrophically as a result of the intense volcanic and magmatic activity, with the associated voluminous quantities of saline hydrothermal fluids "bursting forth" from the earth's crust that was torn apart during catastrophic plate tectonics.[34] Both the purity of the bedded salt deposits and their frequent, thin repeating laminae are testimony to the rapid water transport and deposition by turbidity currents, while the salt minerals rapidly precipitated as supercritical saline hydrothermal fluids catastrophically mixed with the colder ocean waters. Not only is the hydrothermal precipitite model more viable for this rapid formation of bedded salt deposits within the year-long Genesis Flood, but it is clear that the geologic evidence is far more consistent with that model than with the uniformitarian evaporite model.

---

in *Initial Reports of the Deep-Sea Drilling Project*, volume XIII, W. B. F. Ryan, K. Hsü et al, eds., Washington DC: US Government Printing Office, 1021-1040; L. Jolivet, R. Augier, C. Robin, J.-P. Suc and J. M. Rouchy, 2006, Lithospheric-scale geodynamic context of a Messinian Salinity Crisis, *Sedimentary Geology*, 188-189: 9-33.

30   G. Pautot, J. Auzende and X. Pichon, 1970, Continuous deep sea salt layer along north Atlantic margins related to early phase of rifting, *Nature*, 227: 351-354.

31   A. D. Buzzalini, 1969, Evaporites and petroleum: Introduction, *American Association of Petroleum Geologists Bulletin*, 53(4): 775.

32   B. Simoneit, and P. F. Lonsdale, 1982, Hydrothermal petroleum in mineralized mounds at the seabed of Guaymas Basin, *Nature*, 295: 198-202.

33   A. R. Renfro, 1974, Genesis of evaporite-associated stratiform metalliferous deposits-a sabkha process, *Economic Geology*, 69: 33-45; M. L. Jensen and A. M. Bateman, 1981, *Economic Mineral Deposits*, third edition, New York: John Wiley and Sons; R. G. Roberts and P. A. Sheahan, eds., 1988, *Ore Deposit Models*, Geoscience Canada, reprint series 3, Geological Association of Canada; R. W. Boyle, A. C. Brown, J. W. Jefferson, E.C. Jowett and R. V. Kirkham, eds., 1989, *Sediment-Hosted Stratiform Copper Deposits*, Geological Association of Canada Special Paper 36; H. L. Barnes, ed., 1997, *Geochemistry of Hydrothermal Ore Deposits*, third edition, New York: John Wiley and Sons.

34   Austin et al, 1994.

118

Varves and Rhythmites

Another type of sedimentary deposit claimed to have taken millions of years to form are thinly laminated shales known as varves or rhythmites. The laminae are thinner than one centimeter, and can be as thin as one millimeter. Often the laminae grade in color from light to dark, and a varve usually consists of a pair of such laminae, one light and the other dark. Each varve has been interpreted as an annual deposit, the laminae couplet representing seasonal alternation of sedimentary conditions, a feature known in some modern lake sediments. The lighter and coarser lamina represents deposition during the summer, while the darker, more organic-rich lamina is regarded as the winter deposition during the annual cycle. If this interpretation is valid for such ancient laminated shales, then varves could be used not only as qualitative indices of time duration, but as an actual measurement of years during which the successive couplets of laminae were deposited. The dating of such lake-bed varve deposits was first used as the basis of varve chronology for the glacial and post-glacial periods in particular, due to the glacial lakes in northern Europe.

There are several obvious and important difficulties with this varve dating method, however, one of which is the impossibility of knowing that the couplets of laminae all actually represent annual cycles of deposition. Many other phenomena could conceivably produce such varves, such as the variation in flow and sediment load of the stream or streams feeding the lake or depositional basin. Any brief flooding discharge into the lake, seasonal or unseasonal, would cause an initial layer of larger-size particles, followed by gradual settling of the finer particles with suspended organic matter, and this would thus give the appearance of laminae as a varve couplet. There are also other causes:

> The causes of such laminations are variations in the rate of supply or deposition of the different materials. There variations might result from changes in the quantity of the silt, clay or calcium carbonate, or organic matter in the seawater or to changes in the rate of accumulation of these materials. Such variations have been attributed to the fortuitous shift in the depositing current, to climatic causes (especially cyclical changes

related to diurnal or annual rhythms), and also to aperiodic storms or floods.[1]

Obviously, these factors are not necessarily annual in character. Indeed, they are usually unpredictably sporadic, so it is very difficult to determine absolutely that a given bed of laminated muds was actually laid down as annual varves. This is why the more general term of rhythmites has been introduced, because of the uncertainty of these couplets of laminae representing annual cycles of deposition.

Not only is there doubt about the yearly nature of these varves, but an even more important question is whether the laminae of several ancient lakes can be correlated with each other by matching the patterns of the varying thicknesses of the laminae. Such a method is hardly objective.

> Rhythmites belonging to a segment of the same period were studied in Finland...showed that correlation based on thickness alone could lead to error...the correlation of rhythmites, as described above, depends on the judgment of the person who matches the curves, and therefore is not wholly objective. The literature does not report any attempt at independent correlation by several persons.[2]

Not surprisingly, therefore, problems arise when attempts are made to correlate the laminae from different localities.[3]

> Even the varve correlation...through the very short distance between Denmark and southern Sweden was severely criticized on the grounds that the implied relative dates of the several Danish deposits concerned are in complete conflict with the stratigraphic evidence. The whole matter of the reliability and usefulness of the varve correlation is at present in an unsatisfactory state.[4]

Both in Sweden and in North America, extensive studies attempting to combine sequences of a few hundred laminae, many of them considered to be annual glacial varves, ran into trouble. A suggested combined chronology of 28,000 years for North America underwent reinterpretation to little more than 10,000 years when rechecked with radiocarbon dating.[5] Indeed, more than 30 radiocarbon

---

1   Pettijohn, 1957, 163.

2   R. F. Flint, 1957, *Glacial and Pleistocene Geology*, New York: Wiley, 297.

3   M. J. Oard, 1992, Varves – The first 'absolute' chronology. Part I – Historical development and the question of annual deposition, *Creation Research Society Quarterly*, 29(2): 72-80; M. J. Oard, 1992, Varves – The first 'absolute' chronology. Part II – Varve correlation and the post-glacial timescale, *Creation Research Society Quarterly*, 29(3): 120-125.

4   R. F. Flint, 1947, *Glacial Geology and the Pleistocene Epoch*, New York: Wiley, 397.

5   R. F. Flint, 1971, *Glacial and Quaternary Geology*, New York: John Wiley and Sons, 406.

dates generally increase with depth through the laminae, and together the laminae and radiocarbon dates sometimes extend to 10,000 to 13,000 years.[6] However, there are problems with the laminae-radiocarbon correlation, such as the laminae usually being more reliable than the radiocarbon dates, so that the researchers use the laminae to correct the radiocarbon dates. Given the problems noted earlier with radiocarbon dating, it is hardly surprising that the two systems do not give the same results. Furthermore, serious difficulties arise in counting the laminae, with sections sometimes assumed to be missing or found to be undefined, and some of the laminae are so fine that it is difficult to identify them. Thus different investigators report different numbers, and also acknowledge some selection of radiocarbon dates.[7] Thus, it can be readily concluded that the laminated muds or varves of Ice Age glacial lakes offer no problem to biblical chronology, these varves being deposited annually and over shorter intervals within the post-Flood period.

An apparently more serious difficulty is encountered in connection with laminated shales and supposed varves in more supposedly ancient sedimentary strata. The classical example usually cited is the Eocene Green River Formation of Colorado, Utah, and Wyoming.

> There are more than a million vertically superimposed varve pairs in some parts of the Green River Formation. These varve deposits are most certainly fossil-lake sediments. If so, each pair of sediment layers represents an annual deposit....The total number of varve pairs indicates that the lakes existed for a few million years.[8]

One estimate puts the timeframe for the deposition of the varves of the Green River Formation at more than 7.5 million years.[9] Clearly, such a calculation just for one geological formation is a serious challenge to the biblical chronology of only thousands of years, with a recent year-long global Flood. Furthermore, the Green River Formation is not the only claimed ancient varve deposit; others

---

6   I. Hajdas, S.D. Ivey, J. Beer, G. Bonani, D. Imboden, A. Lotter, M. Sturm and M. Suter, 1993, AMS radiocarbon dating and varve chronology of Lake Soppensee: 6000 to 12,000 ^{14}C years BP, *Climate Dynamics*, 9: 107-116; I. Hajdas, E. Zolitschka, S. D. Ivey-Ochs, J. Beer, G. Bonani, S. A. G. Leroy, J. W. Negendank, M. Ramrath, and M. Suter, 1995, AMS radiocarbon dating of annual laminated sediments from Lake Holzmaar, Germany, *Quaternary Science Reviews*, 14: 137-143; I. Hajdas, S. D. Ivey-Ochs and G. Bonani, 1995, Problems in the extension of the radiocarbon calibration curve (10-13 kyr BP), *Radiocarbon*, 37(1): 75-79; I. Hajdas, S. D. Ivey, J. Beer, G. Bonani, D. Imboden, A. Lotter, M. Sturm and M. Suter, 1993, AMS radiocarbon dating and varve chronology of Lake Soppensee: 6000 to 12,000 ^{14}C years BP, *Climate Dynamics*, 9: 107-116.

7   S. Björck, P. Sandgren, and B. Holmquist, 1987, Magnetostratigraphic comparison between ^{14}C years and varve years during the late Weichselian, indicating significant differences between the timescales, *Journal of Quaternary Science*, 2(2): 133-140.

8   D. A. Young, 1990, The discovery of terrestrial history, in *Portraits of Creation*, H. J. Van Till, R. E. Snow, J. H. Stek and D. A. Young, eds., Grand Rapids, MI: William B. Eerdmans, 77.

9   R. C. Selley, 1975, *Ancient Sedimentary Environments and Their Sub-Surface Diagenesis*, third edition, Ithaca, NY: Cornell University Press, 108.

include the Triassic Lockatong Formation in the northwestern United States and the Carboniferous Seaham Formation of the Sydney Basin, Australia.[10]

Apparently, the only in-depth study of the supposed varves of this well-known Green River Formation was made almost 80 years ago, and all later writers simply refer to that study.[11] However, only two very inadequate reasons are given in that study for the layers being annual. One is a calculation purporting to show the amount of sediment in the formation is of the same order of magnitude as the probable amount of erosion from the ancient drainage basin contributing to the lakes, whose beds are supposed to form these varved shales. Such a calculation is, however, entirely speculative and hypothetical, based on rank guesswork about the unobserved past. The other reason for concluding the laminations in the Green River Formation to be annual varves was their similarity of appearance to the varved clay deposits of the Pleistocene (Ice Age), and, to a lesser extent, the banded sediments found in certain modern lakes. The resemblance, however, is largely superficial, because the Pleistocene varves are much thicker than the Green River laminations, which average less than six thousandths of an inch in thickness (0.15 mm). Furthermore, whereas the Pleistocene varves reflect glacial melt-water deposition, the Green River shales consist of a cyclic repetition of organic and inorganic matter. Contrary to this application of uniformitarianism, no modern lake deposits have such distinct thin laminations that are the equivalent of these laminated Green River oil shales.

The classic thinking of uniformitarian geologists is that catastrophic sedimentary action should homogenize fine clay-rich sediments, and thus deposit a massive, non-laminated formation. However, a large body of experimental and observational data refutes this notion that laminae in shale generally had to be deposited slowly.[12] In fact, laminated, fine-grained sediments form by rapid sedimentation, even as observed in some modern situations. A 1960 Florida hurricane flooded inland and deposited a six-inch-thick mud layer with numerous thin laminae.[13] A 12-hour flood in Colorado deposited more than 100 laminae.[14] Field observations and laboratory experiments suggest laminae can form in as little as a few minutes, seconds, or almost instantaneously, such as during the June 12, 1980, eruption of Mount St. Helens, when a hurricane-velocity, surging-flow of volcanic ash accumulated a 25-foot thickness of finely-laminated ash.[15] Analysis of recent

---

10   Selley, 1975, 109, 111.

11   W. H. Bradley, 1929, *The Varves and Climate of the Green River Epoch*, US Geological Survey Professional Paper 158: 87-110.

12   S. A. Austin, 1984, *Catastrophes in Earth History*, El Cajon, CA: Institute for Creation Research.

13   M. M. Ball, E. A. Shinn and K. W. Stockman, 1967, The geologic effects of Hurricane Donna in south Florida, *Journal of Geology*, 75: 583-597.

14   E. D. McKee, E. J. Crosby and H. L. Berryhill, Jr., 1967, Flood deposits, Bijou Creek, Colorado, June 1965, *Journal of Sedimentary Petrology*, 37: 829-851.

15   A. V. Jopling, 1966, Some deductions on the temporal significance of laminae deposited by current action in clastic rocks, *Journal of Sedimentary Petrology*, 36(4): 880-887; S. A. Austin, 1986, Mount St.

sedimentation in the Walensee of Switzerland revealed that an average of two laminae had developed per year, while in some years as many as five laminae had been deposited by rapid, turbid-water, underflow processes.[16]

Not only are there numerous modern examples where natural catastrophic events accumulated laminae rapidly, but horizontal laminae in fine-grained sediment have been produced by high-velocity currents in an experimental circular flume.[17] Other experiments also show that sediments consisting of a homogenized mixture of clay and silt can sort themselves into thin laminae at a rate of several per second, producing a turbidite-like deposit.[18] Even experiments where the sediment was allowed to settle in quiet water without lateral transport, several laminae formed in a few hours.

Many geologists have disputed the notion that laminated shales formed slowly. A classic study of the marine black shale of Scotland showed that they intertongue with large boulders, which had to have been moved during a submarine earthquake, the subsequent enormous tsunami rapidly depositing the laminated clay-rich muds on top of them.[19] Large boulders found within the Bright Angel Shale of Grand Canyon would have required rapid deposition of the shale, similar to the rapid deposition from high-velocity dense suspensions of sediment and water of laminated shales and mudstones in Ireland, England and Canada.[20] The 300 feet thick sequence of thin laminae and beds of clay, silt, and sand known as the Touchet beds in Washington have been recognized as being due to slack-water deposition associated with the catastrophic flooding which formed the Channeled Scabland.[21]

These evidences for rapid deposition of laminated shales demonstrate that the laminated Green River Formation shales could likewise have been deposited rapidly. Indeed, there are several factors that make it highly doubtful that the

Helens and catastrophism, *Proceedings of the First International of Creationism*, vol. 1, Pittsburgh, PA: Creation Science Fellowship, 3-9.

16   A. Lambert and K. J. Hsü, 1979, Nonannual cycles of varvelike sedimentation in Walensee, Switzerland, *Sedimentology*, 26: 453-461.

17   P. H. Kuenen, 1966, Experimental turbidite lamination in a circular flume, *Journal of Geology*, 74: 523-545.

18   G. Berthault, 1986, Experiments on lamination of sediments, resulting for a periodic graded-bedding subsequent to deposit, *Compte Rendu Academie des Sciences, Paris*, 303: 1569-1574; G. Berthault, 1988, Sedimentation of a heterogranular mixture: experimental lamination in still and running water, *Compte Rendu Academie des Sciences, Paris*, 306: 717-724; H. A. Makse, S. Havlin, P. R. King and H. E. Stanley, 1997, Spontaneous stratification in granular mixtures, *Nature*, 386: 379-382.

19   E. B. Bailey and J. Weir, 1932, Submarine faulting in Kimmeridgian times, east Sutherland, *Transactions of the Royal Society of Edinburgh*, 57: 429-454.

20   E. J. W. Piper, 1972, Turbidite origin of some laminated mudstones, *Geological Magazine*, 109: 115-126.

21   R. J. Carson, C. R. McKhann and M. H. Pizey, 1978, The Touchet beds of Walla Walla Valley, in *The Channeled Scabland*, B.R. Baker and D. Nummedall, eds., Washington, D.C.: National Aeronautics and Space Administration, 173-177.

laminae could possibly represent annual varves. The laminae are entirely too thin and uniform, and extend over too wide an area, to have been deposited on the floor of the abnormally calm lakes. Indeed, in any lake the bottom sediments are occasionally stirred by storms and river floods washing in and dumping large quantities of sediment. In the Green River Shales there are occasional pebbles that could only have been carried by fast-moving water currents, and the laminae are draped over them.[22] Furthermore, numerous thin (2-25 cm) volcanic ash (tuff) beds are interbedded with, and regularly spaced within, the laminated shales, representing numerous volcanic eruptions during deposition of the laminated shales.[23]

Such volcanic ash layers are recognized by geologists as being "event horizons," because of each being laid down essentially instantaneously by single volcanic eruptions, and so these have been radioisotope dated. Thus, since each tuff bed represents a time marker through the Green River Formation shales, if the laminae represented annual varves there should be the same number of varves (years) between any two volcanic ash layers anywhere across the depositional basin. However, near Kemmerer, Wyoming, two tuff beds in the Green River Formation, each 2-3 cm thick, are separated by 8.3 to 22.6 cm of shale laminae at two different localities, and the number of laminae between the two tuff beds varies from 1,089 to 1,566, with an overall increase in the numbers of laminae (up to 35 percent) and laminae thickness from the basin center to the basin margin.[24] The organic content of the shale laminae also changes, so these laminae cannot represent annual depositional layers, as there should be the same number of varves between the two volcanic ash layers, and the laminae should be of consistent thickness and organic content if that were the case.

Furthermore, the Green River Formation is also rich in well-preserved fossils that are abundant and widespread throughout the laminated shales.[25] Indeed, the Green River Formation is famous for its fish fossils.

> [F]ossil catfish are distributed in the Green River basin over an area of 16,000km²....The catfish range in length from 11 to 24 cm, with a mean of 18 cm. Preservation is excellent. In some specimens, even the skin and

22   A. G. Fischer and L. T. Roberts, 1991, Cyclicity in the Green River Formation (Lacustrine Eocene Wyoming), *Journal of Sedimentary Petrology*, 61(7): 1146-1154.

23   W. H. Bradley, 1964, *Geology of Green River Formation and Associated Eocene Rocks in Southwestern Wyoming and Adjacent Parts of Colorado and Utah*, US Geological Survey Professional Paper 496-A; M. E. Smith, B. Singer and A. Carroll, 2003, ⁴⁰Ar/³⁹Ar geochronology of the Eocene Green River Formation, Wyoming, *Geological Society of America Bulletin*, 115(5): 549-565.

24   H. P. Buchheim and R. Biaggi, 1988, Laminae counts within a synchronous oil shale unit: A challenge to the 'varve' concept, *Geological Society of America Abstracts with Programs*, 30: A317; H. P. Buchheim, 1994, Paleoenvironments, lithofacies and varves of the Fossil Butte Member of the Eocene Green River Formation, southwestern Wyoming, *Contributions to Geology, University of Wyoming*, 30(1): 3-14.

25   L. Grande, 1984, *Paleontology of the Green River Formation, with a Review of the Fish Fauna*, second edition, Geological Survey of Wyoming, Bulletin 63.

other soft parts, including the adipose fin, are well preserved.[26]

As well as enormous quantities of many varieties of fish, the inventory of fossils includes amphibians, turtles, lizards, snakes, crocodilians, birds, bats and many mammals, sponge spicules, worm trails, snails, clams, spiders, ticks, mites, clam shrimps, crustaceans, crayfish, prawns, many varieties of insects including beetles, flies, mosquitoes, wasps and moths, as well as many varieties of plants, including ferns, sycamore, maple, oak, pines, and even well-preserved flowers. Among the bird fossils are enormous concentrations of an extinct shore bird.[27] Additionally, some of the fish have been fossilized in the process of eating other fish! How does one explain such extraordinary circumstances of fossilization while sediments are slowly accumulating at a rate of six thousandths of an inch per year?

The Green River Formation can hardly be any ordinary lake deposit, because modern lakes on which the varve concept is modeled do not provide conditions needed for such exquisite preservation of abundant fossil fish, birds, bats, and flowers. It has been shown experimentally that, even on the muddy bottom of a marsh in oxygen-poor conditions, fish carcasses decay quite rapidly, all flesh having decayed, and even the bones becoming disconnected, after only six and a half days.[28] Some fish may have taken a day or two to have been buried and fossilized because of being found preserved with scales scattered and even exploded.[29] However, birds have hollow bones that tend not to be well preserved in the fossil record, so how then did these birds lay dead on the bottom of a lake protected from scavenging and decay for thousands of years, until a sufficient number of very thin annual varve layers had built up to bury them?

All of these evidences combine to make it absolutely clear that the laminated shales in the Green River Formation are not annual varves, but instead the shales had to have accumulated rapidly to entomb so many well-preserved fossils between volcanic eruptions. The apparent absence of graded bedding in these shales is also significant, given that if the sediments simply settled to the bottom of a quiet lake, each lamina should have been marked by a gradual decrease in particle size upwards. Instead, it is eminently reasonable to explain the rapid accumulation of these Green River shales due to shallow turbidity currents transporting muds and organic matter into large lake-like depositional basins within a matter of days or months, depending on whether this occurred late in the year of the

---

26   H. P. Buchheim and R. C. Surdam, 1977, Fossil catfish and the depositional environment of the Green River Formation, Wyoming, *Geology*, 5: 196-198.

27   A. Feduccia, 1978, *Presbyornis* and the evolution of ducks and flamingos, *American Scientist*, 66(3): 298-304.

28   R. Zangerl and E. S. Richardson, 1963, The paleoecological history of two Pennsylvanian black shales, *Fieldiana: Geology Memoirs 4*.

29   J. H. Whitmore, 2003, *Experimental Fish Taphonomy with a Comparison to Fossil Fishes*, Ph.D. dissertation (unpublished), Loma Linda, CA: Loma Linda University.

Flood catastrophe, or in the months following its end.[30] Furthermore, the abundant evidence that laminated shales and other fine-grained rhythmites can be shown experimentally and observationally to have been formed rapidly under catastrophic conditions confirms that these ancient finely-laminated sedimentary layers, so often claimed to have accumulated as annual varves, can be better and more reasonably explained as a result of catastrophic deposition during the year-long Flood cataclysm.

30   M. J. Oard and J. H. Whitmore, 2006, The Green River Formation of the west-central United States: Flood or post-Flood?, *Journal of Creation*, 20(1): 46-85.

119

BURIED FORESTS

Another important sedimentary phenomenon that seems to require much longer periods of time than the Bible would allow is found in other cyclically repeated deposits, where each cycle seems to require measurable time in which to be formed. An often-quoted example is the succession of so-called buried forests in Yellowstone National Park, where well-preserved petrified tree stumps are found in great numbers in beds of volcanic ash and lavas.

In Yellowstone Park there is a stratigraphic section of 2,000 feet exposed which shows 18 successive petrified forests. Each forest grew to maturity before it was wiped out with a lava flow. The lava had to be weathered into soil before the next forest could even start. Further this is only a small section of the stratigraphic column in this area. It would be most difficult for Flood geology to account for these facts.[1]

At Mt. Amethyst-Specimen Ridge 27 successive levels of these supposed buried forests have been counted,[2] 31 levels on Mt. Hornaday, and at least 65 levels in the Specimen Creek area.[3] The most striking feature of these petrified trees is the erect position of many of the stumps, which appears to be convincing evidence that the trees are in their *in situ* original growth position. If after a volcanic eruption it took 200 years for reforestation to commence, and then another 500 years for tree growth, based on the average largest tree size for each level, then it would have taken more than 45,000 years to grow and bury the trees and forests of the 65 levels counted in the Specimen Creek area. Added to this is the time for the erosion at current rates of the more than 1,200 vertical meters (3,400 feet) of volcanic ash, sediments, and lavas to expose these petrified "forests." Thus, if this conventional interpretation is correct, then these successively buried forests

---

1   J. L. Kulp, January 1950, Flood geology, *Journal of the American Scientific Affiliation*, 10.

2   E. Dorf, 1960, Tertiary fossil forests of Yellowstone National Park, Wyoming, *Billings Geological Society Guidebook, 11th Annual Field Conference*, 253-260; E. Dorf, 1964, The petrified forests of Yellowstone National Park, *Scientific American*, 210: 106-114.

3   H. G. Coffin, 1997, The Yellowstone Petrified "Forests," *Origins* (Geoscience Research Institute), 24(1): 5-44.

represent an enormous challenge to a strict biblical chronology for the earth's history.

However, there are numerous features of these petrified tree stumps that conclusively indicate that these trees grew elsewhere, and were then transported and buried catastrophically into their present locations.[4] Both upright and horizontal trees are found in these buried forests, with the percentage of upright trees varying from location to location, from 28 percent of the 208 petrified trees in three levels of the Amethyst Mountain area, to 75 percent of the 40 visible petrified trees in the Petrified Tree area. If the fossilized tree stumps are not upright, they are horizontal. In fact, a puzzling feature of all these Yellowstone petrified forests is the absence of diagonal or leaning tree stumps. The upright tree stumps range in height from just above ground level to over six meters, with a common height of 3 to 4 meters. The tops of many of the tree stumps terminate at or just below the next organic/forest level. Most of the wood tissue of these petrified tree stumps is well preserved, even though limbs and bark are usually absent.

Where exposed, the petrified trees have broken roots. These are frequently small roots often oriented in a downward direction. Absent are the larger roots of fully-developed root systems. The larger roots of these petrified tree stumps appear to have been broken off to the bases of the stumps, with only "root balls" left, similar to what is observed when trees are uprooted or bulldozed. Clearly, the tree roots were broken off before the tree stumps were transported and buried by volcanic muds and gravels.

Usually the upright tree stumps on one level appear broken off at their tops, only about a vertical foot below the beginning of the next "forest" level. However, occasionally a tree stump in one level extends through or into the "forest" level above it. If these were successive forests that grew in place, the tops of any tree stumps protruding into the next growing forest would be subject to infestation by insects, rotting, and decay, yet the petrified wood tissue in these tree stumps looks as fresh as the wood tissue in living trees, with no evidence of weathering and decay. Furthermore, the alignment of the fallen petrified trees, and the long axes of the cross-sections of the tops of standing tree stumps, on any particular level show a tendency to be aligned in the same direction. Such parallel orientation is not seen in living forests.[5] On the other hand, volcanic lahars (fast-moving volcanic mudslides) or currents of water and mud would have acted on both roots and tree stumps, as well as logs, to produce the similar observed alignment of both the buried stumps and logs.

Because of the good preservation of the wood tissue, rings are clearly visible,

---

4   H. G. Coffin, 1983, The Yellowstone Petrified "Forests," in *Origins by Design*, Washington, D.C.: Review and Herald Publishing Association, chapter 11, 134-151; Coffin, 1997.

5   H. G. Coffin, 1976, Orientation of trees in the Yellowstone petrified forests, *Journal of Paleontology*, 50(3): 539-543.

and often reveal variable widths suitable for tree-ring studies, not for dating the trees, but for comparing the ring patterns on trees from the same and different levels. Thus several small fossil trees in the Specimen Creek area were found to have similar bands of distinctive anomalous growth-ring patterns.[6] Furthermore, two fossil trees on the same level on Specimen Ridge have been cross-matched.[7] Indeed, the matching of growth-ring patterns in upright tree stumps separated by one or more levels would be most unlikely if these were upright trees that had grown in these positions, because such sequential living forests would not have grown at the same time under the same weather conditions, and therefore have the same patterns of wide and narrow rings. On the other hand, the fact that these same ring patterns are found in tree stumps on several different levels is a strong argument that these trees originally grew at the same time, under the same conditions, and were subsequently transported to be buried in successive volcanic mudslides.

The most abundant of the fossilized tree stumps are *Sequoia* (redwoods), with pines being second in abundance. From identification of the fossil wood, pollen, leaves, and needles, the number of plant species represented in these Yellowstone petrified forests is over 200.[8] This represents a diverse grouping of species, including exotic genera such as cinnamon, breadfruit, katsura, and Chinquapin that are presently restricted to southeastern Asia. We would not expect such ecological diversity if the trees represent a forest in the position of growth. These species range from temperate (pines, redwoods, willows) to tropical and exotic (figs, laurels, breadfruit), and from semi-desert to rainforest types. This mixed flora is most easily explained by the transport of trees and plants from different habitats and geographical locations into a flooded basin, where lahars, mudflows, or turbidity currents left sequential accumulations of sediments with this flora buried in them. Likewise, if these petrified trees are standing where they originally grew, then it is significant why there are no animal fossils, such as those of land snails, some amphibians and reptiles, many insects, spiders, and worms, and their traces, that would have not escaped *in situ* burial with these fossil "forests."

---

6   M. J. Arct, 1979, *Dendrochronology in the Yellowstone Fossil Forests*, M. A. Thesis (unpublished), Loma Linda, CA: Loma Linda University; M. J. Arct, 1991, *Dendroecology in the Fossil Forests of the Specimen Creek Area, Yellowstone National Park,* Ph.D. Thesis (unpublished), Loma Linda, CA: Loma Linda University.

7   R. Ammons, W. J. Fritz, R. B. Ammons and A. Ammons, 1987, Cross-identification of ring signatures in Eocene trees (*Sequoia magnifica*) from the Specimen Ridge locality of the Yellowstone fossil forests, *Palaeogeography, Palaeoclimatology, Palaeoecology*, 60: 97-108.

8   C. E. Read, 1933, Fossil floras of Yellowstone National Park, Part 1. Coniferous woods of Lamar River flora, *Carnegie Institute of Washington Publication*, 416: 1-19; L.H. Fisk, M.R. Aguirre and W.J. Fritz, 1978, Additional conifers from the Eocene Amethyst Mountain 'fossil forest,' Yellowstone National Park, Wyoming, *Geological Society of America Abstracts with Programs*, 10(5): 216; P. L. DeBord, 1979, Palynology of the Gallatin Mountain 'fossil forest' of Yellowstone National Park, Montana: Preliminary report, First Conference on Scientific Research in National Parks, US Department of the Interior, *National Parks Service Transactions, Proceedings Series 5*, 159-164; A. Chadwick and T. Yamamoto, 1983, A paleoecological analyses of the petrified trees in the Specimen Creek area of Yellowstone National Park, Montana, USA, *Palaeogeography, Palaeoclimatology, Palaeoecology*, 45: 39-48.

However, if the trees and organic debris making up the proposed soil levels were instead transported in by water, then the separation of animals from the plants before burial is much easier to explain.

This also raises the issue of whether the organic levels, where the trees supposedly grew, are in fact true soils. Many of the organic levels of the Yellowstone petrified "forests" are thin and contain insufficient organic matter to qualify as soils. Furthermore, there has been taxonomic sorting of the constituents in the organic bands, whereas in true soils leaves, needles, limbs, and bark, etc. fall as a well-mixed litter onto the forest floor year by year. Furthermore, the majority of the organic levels give evidence of water sorting, rather than being true soil profiles.[9] There is also not a good match between the types of wood and pollen in each organic level, as would be expected in *in situ* forests. The formation of clay in soils occurs by the breakdown of minerals such as feldspar, yet analyses of the Yellowstone organic levels shows no detectable amounts of clays. So not only are these not soil horizons, but the lack of clay suggests no significant passage of time was involved in the sequential deposition of the organic levels burying these fossilized tree stumps. Furthermore, not only do these organic levels have a high volcanic ash content, but trace element analyses have revealed poor trace element profiles, which interfinger in an irregular manner through the entire sequence of fossil "forest" organic levels, and which can only be explained by quick burial of the whole sequence from the same volcanic source(s).

The overwhelming evidence, then, supports the transporting of these tree stumps with volcanic ash in mudslides and catastrophic muddy water flows. This interpretation is fully substantiated by a recent modern analog. On May 18, 1980, Mount St. Helens in Washington state erupted, blasting nearly 400 meters from the top of the mountain with a force equal to 500 Hiroshima atomic bombs.[10] Millions of trees in 600 km² (150 square miles) of prime forest were blown down or killed as a blast of ash-charged superheated gas was flung northwards. The concurrent avalanche spread from the summit of the mountain into nearby Spirit Lake as the north face collapsed, causing a wave of water from the lake almost 900 feet high to scour the adjacent slopes. Thus many of the trees from the blast zone found their way into Spirit Lake, but others were transported upright in mudslides and turbid floods down the North Fork of the Toutle River.[11] Many erect stumps in various stages of burial ended up in distant mud flats and gravel bars. One huge stump over 2 m in diameter and 13 m high was left sitting upright on the toe of a 24 km long debris flow. As the mudflows moved rapidly downstream, many tree

9　Coffin, 1983 and 1997.

10　R. Findley, 1981, Mountain with a death wish, *National Geographic*, 159(1): 3-65; P. W. Lipman and D. R. Mullineaux, eds., 1981, *1980 Eruptions of Mount St Helens, Washington*, US Geological Survey Professional Paper 1250; C. L. Rosenfeld, 1980, Observations on the Mount St Helens eruption, *American Scientist*, 68: 494-509.

11　W. J. Fritz, 1980, Stumps transported and deposited upright by Mount St Helens mudflows, *Geology*, 8: 586-588.

stumps moved along at the same rate as the mudflows, upright with the denser root ends down.

When the eruption was over, there was a huge floating mat of logs and debris covering more than half of the surface of Spirit Lake. It consisted of plant material ranging from chips of bark, to trees with trunks nearly 2.5 m in diameter. Many of the logs still retained their root systems. Within six months, many of these tree stumps were floating upright in the water, some eventually becoming grounded on the bottom, and their root ends were buried in mud and organic debris as they became waterlogged and sank.[12] Subsequent investigations of the lake bottom using side-scan sonar showed that thousands of tree stumps, up to 20 m in length, had become buried in the lake bottom muds, as if they had been buried where they had grown in place.[13] With time, more and more floating logs became waterlogged and sank, the denser ends where roots had been broken off sinking first into the mud on the lake bottom. Thus, both the mudflows in the Toutle River with upright stumps imbedded in them, and the sinking of the upright tree stumps to be buried in the lake bottom muds, provide a model for interpreting the upright petrified trees of Yellowstone. Saturated organic debris sank to the bottom of Spirit Lake to produce a layer of organic matter, while upright floating trees also dropped out of suspension to be buried in the bottom muds of Spirit Lake in a spacing pattern similar to that of growing forests. If there had been continued adequate sediment input to bury the sinking logs and stumps in volcanic ash, then the burial of successive logs and stumps as they sank would exactly mirror the buried Yellowstone fossil "forests." The logs in Spirit Lake had even been stripped of their bark, which when it became waterlogged and sank added to the organic debris buried in the lake bottom muds.

Rather than being a difficulty for a global Flood cataclysm 4,500 years ago, the evidence in the Yellowstone fossil "forests" clearly is consistent with catastrophe transport and deposition of tree stumps in volcanic mudflows and catastrophic water flows, to be successively buried upright in a sequence of repeating organic levels that give the appearance of successive buried forests. Given the position of the Yellowstone fossil "forests" in the geologic record, this would have been at the close of the Flood year, or soon thereafter, as residual catastrophism, involving local volcanic eruptions larger than Mount St. Helens, but in a repetitive sequence, built up the successive buried tree stump layers in Yellowstone. The same model of catastrophic deposition of upright tree stumps can also be applied to many other situations in the geologic record, where upright fossilized tree stumps are claimed to have required hundreds to thousands of years for their burial where they supposedly grew.[14]

---

12   H. G. Coffin, 1983, Erect floating stumps in Spirit Lake, Washington, *Geology*, 11: 198-199.

13   H. G. Coffin, 1987, Sonar and scuba survey of a submerged allochthonous 'forest' in Spirit Lake, Washington, *Palaois*, 2: 179-180.

14   T. W. E. David, 1970, Geology of the Hunter River Coal Measures, New South Wales, *Geological Survey of New South Wales, Memoir #G4*.

Lest it be argued that, even if the tree stumps were buried rapidly, it still takes many thousands of years to petrify the wood, much experimental evidence demonstrates the contrary—petrification is rapid. Indeed, as part of a study of the petrified wood in the Petrified Forest National Park of Arizona, an experiment was conducted in which blocks of wood were placed in hot alkaline springs in the Yellowstone National Park to test the rate at which silica is deposited in the cellular structure of the wood.[15] The measured rate was between 0.1 and 4.0 mm/year. Other similar experiments have been conducted in laboratories.[16] Furthermore, as a result of testing for petrification in a Japanese volcanic spring, it was concluded that petrified wood in ancient volcanic ash beds in sedimentary strata in volcanic regions could have thus been silicified by hot flowing ground water with high silica content in "a fairly short period of time, in the order of several tens to hundreds of years."[17] Such rapid petrification of wood is confirmed by many field observations of trees cut down by early settlers in Australia that were subsequently buried in the soil, then later dug up and found to be petrified, including the axe marks.[18] The bottoms of wooden fence posts that have been buried for some years in the soil have also found to become petrified. Thus, the evidence indicates the claim that, under the right conditions, wood can be rapidly petrified by silicification, as is the case with the Yellowstone fossil tree stumps. Therefore, the timeframe for the formation of petrified wood within the geologic record is totally compatible with the biblical timescale of a recent creation and the subsequent devastating global Flood.[19]

15   A. C. Sigleo, 1978, Organic geochemistry of silicified wood, Petrified Forest National Park, Arizona, *Geochimica et Cosmochimica Acta*, 42: 1397-1405.

16   E. Scurfield and E. R. Segnit, 1984, Petrifaction of wood by silica minerals, *Sedimentary Geology*, 39: 149-167; R. W. Drum, 1968, Silicification of Betula woody tissue *in vitro*, *Science*, 161: 175-176; R. F. Leo and E. S. Barghoorn, 1976, Silicification of wood, *Harvard University Botanical Museum Leaflets*, 25: 1-47.

17   H. Akahane, T. Furuno, H. Miyajima, T. Yoshikawa and S. Yamamoto, 2004, Rapid wood silicification in hot spring water: An explanation of silicification of wood during the earth's history, *Sedimentary Geology*, 169: 219-228.

18   R. Piggott, January 1970, *The Australian Lapidary Magazine*, 9; R. C. Pearce, June 1970, Petrified wood, *The Australian Lapidary Magazine*, 33.

19   A. A. Snelling, 1995, 'Instant' petrified wood, *Creation*, 17(4): 38-40.

120

COAL BEDS

The formation of coal beds has already been discussed (chapters 71-72), but further comments are warranted here. It continues to be claimed that the numbers of stacked coal beds in many sedimentary basins around the globe, and the evidence associated with them, does not favor the formation of the coal beds during the year-long Genesis Flood, but requires the millions of years of conventional geologic thought.[1]

Nevertheless, even in such attempts to discredit the Flood origin of today's coal beds, it is admitted that the upright polystrate tree stumps often found associated with coal beds required catastrophic deposition to bury and preserve them. Furthermore, it is maintained that years were required for these trees to grow in place associated with peat swamps that were slowly forming coal beds, before they and the tree stumps were buried. However, such claims totally ignore the actual physical evidence that many of these upright tree stumps associated with coal beds could not have grown in place, because their roots are broken off, like the tree stumps in the Yellowstone fossil "forests," and those buried in the muds at the bottom of Spirit Lake at Mount St. Helens. Furthermore, the trees and vegetation associated with the northern hemisphere coal beds, and the trees and plants associated with the southern hemisphere (Gondwanan) coal beds, though different from one another, are plants and trees that are known to not have been associated with peat swamps as we observe them today. The northern hemisphere coals are dominated by lycopods that grew in forests that floated on the ocean surface out from the coastlines.[2] The Gondwanan coal beds consist of the *Glossopteris* flora, extinct plants of unknown habitat, but often have tree stumps associated with them of pine trees that are not known to grow in swamps.[3]

1   R. A. Gastaldo, 1999, Debates on authochthonous and allochthonous origin of coal: Empirical science versus the diluvialists, in *The Evolution-Creation Controversy II: Perspectives on Science, Religion and Geological Education*, volume 5, W.L. Manger, ed., The Paleontological Society Papers, 135-167.

2   K. P. Wise, 2003, The pre-Flood forest: A study in paleontological pattern recognition, in *Proceedings of the Fifth International Conference on Creationism*, R. L. Ivey, ed., Pittsburgh, PA: Creation Science Fellowship, 371-381.

3   T. W. E. David, 1907, Geology of the Hunter River Coal Measures, New South Wales, *Geological Survey of New South Wales, Memoir G.4*; E. P. Plumstead, 1958, The habit and growth of *Glossopteridae*,

There is, therefore, no question that, despite the nebulous and unsubstantiated assertions to the contrary, the May 18, 1980, Mount St. Helens eruption is an entirely suitable analog model for not only the catastrophic burial of upright tree stumps with their roots broken off, but also for the formation of peat layers that are the precursors to coal beds.[4] In this model for the formation of the coal beds during the Genesis Flood, the multiple stacked coal beds in many sedimentary basins would have formed by the progressive devastation of both the pre-Flood floating-forest biome, with its in-built peat layer of rotting vegetative debris, added to by the destruction of the living trees and vegetation, and the extensive forests, growing on the pre-Flood land surfaces. As on Spirit Lake, logs and other vegetative debris would have floated on the Flood waters for many months before progressively being waterlogged and sinking, the process aided by the turbulence of the Flood waters and the daily tidal surges, along with the changing sediment-laden water currents, and the repeated catastrophic volcanic eruptions. This model would also easily explain the presence of marine fossils in the sediments associated with coal beds.

On the other hand, the conventional uniformitarian peat swamp model does not easily explain how coal beds are so widespread across adjoining continents and so often interbedded with sediments containing marine fossils, even within the coal beds themselves. The uniformitarian explanation requires the impossible scenario of vast peat swamps sinking and being invaded by the sea, remaining buried until the land rises again to form new peat swamps, with this process being repeated many times in succession in order to generate the so-called cyclothems and coal measure sequences. Thus, with its 80 stacked coal beds, the Illinois Basin would require 80 cycles of peat swamps being invaded by the sea and then the land rising again! The actual field evidence is far more consistent with repeated sediment deposition cycles, in which various portions of the broken-up floating vegetative mat on the Flood waters were buried to become the coal beds, sometimes with the upright tree stumps buried with them. Once the vegetative debris was buried, it was easily and rapidly transformed into coal, as numerous experiments at easily obtainable low geological temperatures have shown.

The exact quantity of coal found in the earth's sedimentary basins can only be estimated, but all authorities are agreed that all the vegetation on the earth's surface today, if converted to coal, would only represent a small fraction of the earth's known coal reserves, possibly as little as 1 to 3 percent. Thus, it would be argued that if the present is the key to the past, then it would take at least thirty global floods to repeatedly destroy the earth's complete vegetation cover, obviously

---

Transactions of the Geological Society of South Africa, 61: 81-94; E. D. Pant, 1977, The plant of *Glossopteris*, *The Journal of the Indian Botanical Society*, 56(1): 1-23.

4   S. A. Austin, 1986, Mount St. Helens and catastrophism, in *Proceedings of the First International Conference on Creationism*, volume 1, Pittsburgh, PA: Creation Science Fellowship, 3-9; S. A. Austin, 1991, Floating logs and log deposits of Spirit Lake, Mount St. Helens Volcano National Monument, Washington, *Geological Society of America Abstracts with Programs*, 23(5): 85.

staggered in time for the vegetation to grow again between each flood, in order to generate all the known coal beds. Therefore, it is concluded that a single Genesis Flood could not have produced the world's coal beds.

However, while such arguments are based on valid estimates of the volume of vegetation currently on today's land surfaces, they assume that at least a thickness of 12 meters of peat (accumulated, decomposing vegetation) is necessary to produce one meter of ordinary (bituminous black) coal,[5] although some antagonists have inflated that figure to a 30-meter-thick layer of peat to generate a one meter thick coal bed.[6] However, textbooks on coal geology describe compaction ratios of eight or ten meters of peat to form one meter of coal,[7] or as little as 5-6 meters of peat to form one meter of bituminous coal.[8] Such estimates are based on measuring how thin laminae in coal beds, called plies, are draped over and compacted around what are known as coal balls. These are mineralized nodular masses found within some coal beds that are composed essentially of limestone and contain plant fossils and/or fossils of marine animals, such as gastropods and brachiopods.[9] However, the compaction around some coal balls, and of the wood sometimes found in coal beds, would suggest that the compaction ratio might be as little as 1 to 2 meters of vegetative debris in each meter of coal. If that were generally the case, then today's volume of vegetation would compact down to 15 to 30 percent of the known coal reserves.

In any case, three other factors are ignored when detractors claim all the coal beds could not have formed by the catastrophic burial of vegetation during the year of the Genesis Flood. First, they are assuming that the thickness and volume of today's vegetative cover have always been the same throughout earth's past history. However, more than half of today's land surface is covered by deserts, vast ice sheets, or only sparse vegetation. In the desert and semi-desert areas of central Australia, and under the Sahara Desert of Africa, there is evidence of there having been more lush vegetation growing there, even in the recent past after the Ice Age, while the thick coal beds under some of the Antarctic ice sheet suggest that that continent too was once covered in lush vegetation. Thus, if all today's land surfaces were covered with lush vegetation, then the volume of such vegetation would be at least doubled, and with minimal compaction, thus accounting for up to 50 percent or more of the known coal reserves.

5   A. Holmes, 1965, *Principles of Physical Geology*, new and fully revised edition, London: Thomas Nelson and Sons, 441; Gastaldo, 1999, 147.

6   E. N. Strahler, 1987, *Science and Earth History-the Evolution/Creation Controversy*, Buffalo, NY: Prometheus Books, 218.

7   C. F. K. Diessel, 1992, *Coal-bearing Depositional Systems*, Berlin: Springer-Verlag, 1, 12.

8   E. Stach, M.-Th. Mackowski, M. Teichmüller, G. H. Taylor, D. Chandra and R. Teichmüller, 1982, *Stash's Textbook of Coal Petrology*, third revised and enlarged edition, Berlin: Gebrüder Borntraeger, 17-18.

9   S. H. Mamay and E. L. Yochelson, 1962, *Occurrence and Significance of Marine Animal Remains in American Coal Balls*, U. S. Geological Survey Professional Paper 354I: 193-224.

Second, uniformitarian calculations assume that the areas of land surface available for vegetation to grow have always been the same as those today. This assumption is likely incorrect for several reasons. In the description of God forming the dry land on Day Three of the Creation Week (Genesis 1:9-10), the waters that initially covered the entire globe were gathered into one place, which implies that the land which God thus formed was also in one place. In today's world, the earth's surface is roughly 30 percent land and 70 percent oceans, but the implication of this description is that on the pre-Flood earth, there may have been one landmass or supercontinent that occupied as much as 50 percent or more of the earth's surface, surrounded by the one inter-connected sea. If this were the case, then there could have been up to double the land surface available for vegetation to grow on than on today's earth surface.

However, the third factor was the presence also of this floating-forest biome in the pre-Flood world. Vast mats of floating forests grew out from the coastlines, fringing the supercontinent, particularly where the seas were shallow. Just how much of the pre-Flood sea surface was covered with these floating-forest mats is uncertain, but the volume of this unique vegetation, which is now preserved in the Carboniferous coal beds of the Northern Hemisphere, would suggest that a large portion of the pre-Flood sea surface was covered with these floating forest mats, perhaps as much as half of the sea surface. If that were the case, then as much as 75 percent of the pre-Flood earth's surface could have been covered by lush vegetation, more than six times the area covered by vegetation on the present earth's surface. All these calculations taken together would thus indicate that there was more than enough vegetation growing lushly on the pre-Flood earth surface to provide the volume of vegetation needed to be destroyed and buried to form the coal beds during the Flood year.

There is, however, another way of comparing vegetation growth and volume with the world's coal beds. Comparing stored energy in vegetation with that in the coal beds is probably a far more reliable indication of just how much vegetation is in the coal beds. It has been estimated that the amount of solar energy falling on the earth's surface in 14 days is equal to the known energy of the world's supply of fossil fuels.[10] Yet only 0.3 percent of the solar energy arriving at the earth's surface is stored as chemical energy in vegetation through photosynthesis. This information enables an estimate to be made of how many years of today's plant growth would be required to produce the stored energy equivalent in today's known coal beds. If 14 days of solar energy input to the earth's surface is equal to the known energy in the world's coal beds, but only 0.03 percent of that solar energy is stored as chemical energy by photosynthesis in vegetation, then the length of time to grow vegetation and store chemical energy in it via photosynthesis in order to achieve the equivalent of 100 percent of the known energy in the world's coal beds would be almost 46,700 days, or about 128 years of solar input to vegetation growth via photosynthesis. In other words, it would take only 128 years of plant growth, at today's rate of growth and volume, to provide the energy equivalent of the stored chemical energy in today's known coal beds. And that's simply using today's vegetation cover of the present earth's land surface.

As the above calculations have shown, far more of the earth's surface was covered with lush vegetation in the pre-Flood world, so fewer years of vegetation growth would have been required to provide the volume of vegetation necessary and stored chemical energy, equivalent to the stored energy value of today's known coal beds. Furthermore, because in the biblical timescale of earth history there were about 1,600 years between creation and the Genesis Flood, there was ample time for the necessary plant growth to produce the vegetation that was buried in the coal beds during the Flood year. Thus, whichever way the calculation is made, by comparison of the chemical energy stored in vegetation growth and in the coal beds (via the time factor), or by vegetation growth, climate, geography, land area, and compaction ratio (via the volume factor), it can be shown conclusively that there was ample time, space, and vegetation growth for the year-long Genesis Flood to have produced all of today's known coal beds, and objections to the contrary are deemed invalid.

121

OIL DEPOSITS

Uniformitarian geology is frequently defended on the grounds that it has worked so well in leading to the discovery of economically important deposits of petroleum. It is argued that the use of the uniformitarian system in geology must be basically correct, or else it could not have served so well as a guiding philosophy in petroleum geology. However, the techniques that have been found helpful in petroleum exploration, such as seismic surveying and the analysis of organic matter found in sedimentary rock sequences, do not really depend on the historical aspects of geology at all, but only on recognition of the structural, sedimentary, and organic petrological markers that experience has shown are associated with, and a guide to the finding of, petroleum deposits.

> Petroleum exploration, in its simplest terms, consists of studying large regions that do or could contain petroleum, identifying progressively smaller areas of progressively greater interest in these until a prospect worth drilling has been identified, and discovering oil or gas in one or more of these....the exploration geologist is concerned with regional geology deduced from surface outcrop, geophysical surveys, and the results of any boreholes drilled in the area.[1]

There can be no question of the immense size of the oil industry, and that it is a major employer of geologists, not only in oil companies, but in academia and government agencies. Thus, with so much of the world's geological brain-power being expended on those aspects of geology concerned with how oil and gas accumulations form and can be found, one would expect that evolutionary historical geology would find its most productive application in this field, and would have good success. However, the opening remarks in the preface to a recent major textbook on petroleum geology are noteworthy.

> The fascination of petroleum geology lies both in its complexity and in its importance to society. There is still much that we do not understand; and there is much to learn if remaining undiscovered reserves of oil and

---

1   R. E. Chapman, 1983, *Petroleum Geology*, Amsterdam: Elsevier, 67-68.

gas are to be found economically. It is also good geology with a healthy practical component.[2]

Thus it is entirely conceivable that biblical geology in its present state of development might well lead to more effective results than uniformitarian geology in the search for additional oil deposits. There has already been one Canadian success as a result of applying the principles of Flood geology to the search for oil.[3]

Indeed, uniformitarian geology has not yet been able to develop an understanding of the origin and migration of petroleum to form oil deposits.

> Although agreement on the organic origin of petroleum is nearly complete, there are many differences of opinion about the details of the processes by which it was formed and about the relative importance of the different source materials. Were they primarily marine or terrestrial? How much petroleum was derived from hydrocarbons that were part of living organisms and how much was derived from the transformation of hydrocarbon compounds into petroleum? What was the nature of the energy involved in the transformation? Bacterial action, heat and pressure, radioactive bombardment, and catalytic phenomena have all been suggested as energy sources that may have made conversion possible.[4]

> Processes of primary and secondary migration are so far poorly understood....Likewise, there is little information on movement and distribution of petroleum compounds inside the pores of source rocks. Therefore, it should be realized that the following discussion on petroleum migration is largely theoretical and should not be considered definitive.[5]

> It is impossible at present to distinguish in logic between the generation of petroleum and its primary migration. We believe we can recognize petroleum source rocks from the nature of their organic contents: we can identify petroleum accumulations. No migration path has ever been recognized physically with confidence and reported, so the connection between source and accumulation is *inferred* from analyses of the oil and analyses of the organic content of the supposed source rock, and from geological considerations. It is for this reason that we cannot claim

---

2   Chapman, 1983, vii.

3   Personal testimony of Larry Sheldon, a Canadian petroleum geologist.

4   A. I. Levorsen, 1967, *Geology of Petroleum,* second edition, San Francisco: W.H. Freeman and Company, 499.

5   B. P. Tissot and D. H. Welte, 1978, *Petroleum Formation and Occurrence: A New Approach to Oil and Gas Exploration,* Berlin: Springer-Verlag, 258-259.

to *understand* the origin and migration of petroleum. At best, we can construct plausible hypotheses.[6]

It is surely significant that in this most important (both economically and in numbers of geologists involved) of geological disciplines, the uniformitarian interpretative framework has been of little practical use. Although geologists can identify a given formation from two or more well logs by the microfossils contained in the cuttings, this is primarily done on a local scale within each formation across the sedimentary basin. However, microfossils are not nearly as important as other factors revealed by geophysical logging of drill-holes. This is confirmed by the fact that in the subject indexes of the three major petroleum geology textbooks of recent decades (quoted from above), neither "micropaleontology" nor "microfossils" appears. Of course, microfossils and macrofossils are mentioned in occasional places in these textbooks, but never in any substantive manner crucial to the elucidation of petroleum formation and exploration. Thus, evolutionary geology, based on the assumption of the slow accumulation of the fossil-bearing sedimentary strata, can hardly claim to be instrumental in understanding and discovering oil deposits. Sequences of sedimentary strata are an observable fact of field geology, and naming them are merely labels for identification. Even the so-called geologic timescale merely provides labels that enable recognition of the order of strata in sequences, irrespective of the assumption of long time periods. Thus, petroleum geology would not be adversely affected by utilizing catastrophism as a basic geologic philosophy, which could even provide material benefits.

More than half the world's production and reserves of petroleum are from rock strata that have been labeled as Tertiary, and more than 25 percent from so-called Mesozoic strata, the remainder occurring in Paleozoic strata. Nevertheless, oil can be found in rocks of practically all geologic ages, except the Pleistocene and Holocene. However, there are some commercial oil and gas fields in Precambrian rocks supposedly up to 1 billion years old in the former Soviet Union, Oman and China, but indigenous "live" oil has been found in rock supposedly 1.4 billion years old in the MacArthur Basin of northern Australia.[7] Oil has even been found preserved in fluid inclusions in Archean sandstones supposedly up to 3 billion years old in Canada, South Africa and Australia.[8]

Petroleum occupies the pore spaces or cavities in the reservoir rocks in which it is found. Petroleum almost certainly has been formed elsewhere in what are known as source rocks, from which the petroleum has migrated until trapped to pool as oil

---

6   Chapman, 1983, 180.

7   M. J. Jackson, T. G. Powell, R. E. Summons and I. P. Sweet, 1986, Hydrocarbon shows and petroleum source rocks in sediments as old as 1.7×10^9 years, *Nature*, 322: 727-729; A. Dutkiewicz, H. Volk, J. Ridley and S. George, 2003, Biomarkers, brines, and oil in the Mesoproterozoic, Roper Superbasin, Australia, *Geology*, 31(11): 981-984.

8   A. Dutkiewicz, B. Rasmussen and R. Buick, 1998, Oil preserved in fluid inclusions in Archaean sandstones, *Nature*, 395: 885-888.

and gas deposits. Thus, petroleum occurrences seem to have no particular relation to specific stratigraphic sequences or structural forms. Neither the paleontologic nor deformational history appears to bear any necessary relationship to the actual oil and gas deposits.

> The reservoir rocks that contain petroleum differ from one another in various ways. They range in geologic age from Precambrian to Pliocene, in composition from siliceous to carbonate, in origin from sedimentary to igneous, in porosity from 1 to 40 percent, and in permeability from one millidarcy to many darcies.

> There is a wide variation also in the character of the trap or barrier that retains the pool. The trap may have been chiefly due to structural causes, to stratigraphic causes, or to combinations of these causes....

> The geologic history of the trap may vary widely—from a single geologic episode to a combination of many phenomena extending over a long period of geologic time. Pools trapped in limestone and dolomite reservoir rocks, moreover, have the same relations that pools trapped in sandstone rocks have for such things as reservoir fluids, oil-water and oil-gas contacts, and trap boundaries. Yet the chemical relations of the reservoir rock and the effects of solution, cementation, compaction, and recrystallization are quite different in sandstone and carbonate reservoirs.[9]

Given that petroleum forms in source rocks and then subsequently migrates, the most immediately apparent conclusion is that this subsequent accumulation of petroleum into traps must have occurred after most, if not all, of the sedimentary strata were laid down. These pools of trapped petroleum are apparently independent of the particular type of reservoir rock, but these strata are nevertheless similar to each other in hydraulic characteristics. The main feature that all oil and gas deposits seem to have in common is that of being associated with water.

> Nearly every petroleum pool exists within an environment of water—free, interstitial, edge, and bottom water. This means that the problem of migration is intimately related to hydrology, fluid pressures, and water movement.[10]

Another extremely important conclusion is that the accumulated evidence points to an organic origin for most, if not all, petroleum.

> Early ideas lean toward the inorganic sources, whereas the modern theories, with few exceptions, assume that the primary source material

---

9   Levorsen, 1967, 540-541.

10   Levorsen, 1967, 539.

was organic.[11]

A few scientists have maintained that some natural gas could have formed deep within the earth, where heat melting the rocks might have generated it inorganically.[12] Indeed, this process of abiotic formation of hydrocarbons has been demonstrated and observed where hydrothermal fluids are reacting with the olivine-rich oceanic crust, in the presence of trace metals acting as catalysts, to produce hydrocarbons within mid-ocean ridge hydrothermal systems.[13] However, even in these locations, subsequent investigations have shown that all the heavier or long-chained and branched hydrocarbons have been generated from the organic matter in the sediments on the ocean floor through which the hydrothermal fluids have also circulated.[14] Proof of such processes having occurred even early in the earth's history are the hydrocarbons trapped in fluid inclusions and as bituminous residues in cavities within an early Archean deep-sea volcanogenic massive sulfide deposit in the Pilbara of Western Australia,[15] which is comparable to similar massive deposits forming at the volcanogenic hydrothermal vent systems on the ocean floor today. There can thus be no doubt that the weight of evidence now favors an organic origin for petroleum.

While the exact nature of the organic material from which the petroleum in each oil and gas field came has to be independently elucidated, there now seems little doubt that most petroleum was generated from the vast reservoirs of the organic remains of plants, and perhaps animals, which were buried and fossilized in the sedimentary rocks.

> Production, accumulation and preservation of undegraded organic matter are prerequisites for the existence of petroleum source rocks. The term "organic matter" or "organic material"…refers solely to material comprised of organic molecules in monomeric or polymeric form derived directly or indirectly from the organic part of organisms.[16]

The petroleum generated in the source rocks was then chemically altered, as it migrated, into crude oil and gas that became trapped in pools in the reservoir rocks.

---

11 Levorsen, 1967, 499.

12 T. Gold and S. Soter, 1980, The deep-earth gas hypothesis, *Scientific American*, 242(6): 154-161.

13 N. G. Holme and J. L. Sharlou, 2001, Initial indications of abiotic formation of hydrocarbons in the Rainbow ultramafic hydrothermal system, mid-Atlantic Ridge, *Earth and Planetary Science Letters*, 191: 1-8; E. I. Foustoukos and W. E. Seyfried Jr., 2004, Hydrocarbons in hydrothermal vent fluids: the role of chromium-bearing catalysts, *Science*, 304: 1002-1005.

14 B. R. T. Simoneit and A. Y. Lein, B. I. Peresypkin and G. A. Osipov, 2004, Composition and origin of hydrothermal petroleum and associated lipids in the sulfide deposits of the Rainbow Field (mid-Atlantic Ridge at 36°N), *Geochimica et Cosmochimica Acta*, 68(10): 2275-2294.

15 B. Rasmussen and R. Buick, Oily old ores: Evidence for hydrothermal petroleum generation in Archean volcanogenic massive sulfide deposit, *Geology*, 28(8): 731-734, 2000.

16 Tissot and Welte, 1978, 3.

The chemistry of oil provides crucial clues as to its origin. Petroleum is a complex mixture of organic compounds, primarily chains of different lengths of hydrocarbons. However, one complex chemical in crude oils is called porphyrin.

> Petroleum porphyrins...have been identified in a sufficient number of sediments and crude oils to establish a wide distribution of these geochemical fossils.[17]

Porphyrins are organic molecules that are structurally very similar to both chlorophyll in plants and hemoglobin in animal blood.[18] They are classified as tetrapyrrole compounds, and often contain metals such as nickel and vanadium.[19] Of significance is the fact that porphyrins are readily destroyed by oxidizing conditions and by heat.[20] Thus, petroleum geologists maintain that the porphyrins in crude oils are evidence of the petroleum source rocks having been deposited under reducing conditions.

> The origin of petroleum is within an anaerobic and reducing environment. The presence of porphyrins in some petroleums means that anaerobic conditions developed early in the life of such petroleums, for chlorophyll derivatives, such as the porphyrins, are easily and rapidly oxidized and decomposed under aerobic conditions. The low oxygen content of petroleums, generally under 2 percent by weight, also indicates that they were formed in a reducing environment.[21]

It is very significant that porphyrin molecules break apart rapidly in the presence of oxygen and heat. Therefore, the fact that porphyrins are still present in crude oils today must mean that petroleum source rocks, and the plant (and animal) fossils in them, had to have been kept from the presence of oxygen when they were deposited and buried. There are two ways this could have been achieved:

1. The sedimentary rocks were deposited under oxygen deficient (or reducing) conditions, as already indicated above; and/or

2. The sedimentary rocks were deposited so rapidly that no oxygen could destroy the porphyrins in the plant and animal fossils.

However, even where sedimentation is relatively rapid by today's standards, such

---

17   Tissot and Welte, 1984, 128.

18   D. R. McQueen, 1986, The chemistry of oil—explained by Flood geology, *Acts & Facts,* 15(5).

19   Tissot and Welte, 1984, 409-410.

20   W. L. Russell, 1960, *Principles of Petroleum Geology,* second edition, New York: McGraw-Hill Book Company, 25.

21   Levorsen, 1967, 502.

as in river deltas in coastal zones, conditions are still oxidizing.[22] Thus, to preserve organic matter containing porphyrins requires its slow degradation in the absence of oxygen, such as in the Black Sea today.[23] But such environments are too rare to explain the presence of porphyrins in all the many petroleum deposits found around the world. Thus, the only consistent explanation is the catastrophic sedimentation that occurred during the recent global Genesis Flood. The total devastation of the earth's surface resulted in enormous quantities of vegetation being violently uprooted and animals killed, so that huge amounts of organic matter were buried so rapidly that the porphyrins in it were removed from the oxidizing agents that could have destroyed them.

The amounts of porphyrins found in crude oils vary from traces to 0.04 percent (or 400 parts per million).[24] Experiments have produced a concentration of 0.5 percent porphyrin (of the type found in crude oils) from plant material in just one day,[25] so millions of years are not required to produce the small amounts of porphyrins found in crude oils. Indeed, a crude oil porphyrin can be made from plant chlorophyll in less than twelve hours. However, other experiments have shown that plant porphyrin breaks down in as little as three days when exposed to temperatures of only 210°C (410°F) for only twelve hours. Therefore, the petroleum source rocks, and the crude oils generated from them, cannot have been deeply buried to such temperatures for millions of years, as would be the case in the conventional uniformitarian framework for earth history.

Crude oils themselves, therefore, do not take long to be generated from appropriate organic matter.

> Nearly all shales and carbonates contain disseminated organic matter of three general kinds: soluble liquid hydrocarbons, soluble asphalts, and insoluble kerogen.[26]

> Kerogen is the most important form of organic carbon on earth. It is 1,000 times more abundant than coal plus petroleum in reservoirs and is 50 times more abundant than bitumen and other dispersed petroleum in nonreservoir rocks....In ancient nonreservoir rocks, e.g., shales or fine-grained limestones, kerogen represents usually from 80 to 99 percent of the organic matter, the rest being bitumen.[27]

---

22 A. R. Walker et al, 1983, A model for carbonate to terrigenous clastic sequences, *Geological Society of America Bulletin*, 94: 700-712.

23 Tissot and Welte, 1978, 11-12.

24 Tissot and Welte, 1978, 364.

25 R. K. Di Nello and C. K. Chang, 1978, Isolation and modification of natural porphyrins, in *The Porphyrins, Volume 1: Structure and Synthesis*, Part A, D. Dolphin, ed., New York: Academic Press, 328.

26 Levorsen, 1967, 506.

27 Tissot and Welte, 1978, 124.

Kerogen appears to be an association of various kinds of organic debris, the larger fragments being identified as spores, pollens, and plant tissues, and algae. Thus, most petroleum geologists are convinced that crude oils form mostly from plant material, such as many varieties of algae and diatoms (single-celled marine and freshwater photosynthetic organisms),[28] dispersed land plant debris, and where such plant debris has been concentrated in huge fossilized masses found in oil beds.[29]

> It is natural that one should enquire whether the two great fossil fuels, coal and petroleum, have any significant geological relationship; and this enquiry has been going on for more than a century. Coal results from the diagenesis of vegetable organic matter that accumulated in an environment largely devoid of sediment. Conditions on the actual surface of accumulation may have been reducing or oxidizing; but close below this surface reducing conditions prevailed. Coal consists largely of carbonized plant tissues, wood and bark, with spores (particularly the most durable spore coatings), leaf cuticles, waxes and resins....This line of thought with the associated idea that petroleum was a distillation product (a demonstrable process to some extent) became out of fashion as a marine origin for oil became fashionable. But it has returned with increasing evidence that some petroleums can hardly have had a marine source, and that some crude oils, particularly those with high wax content, have an important component of vegetable organic origin.[30]

Indeed, the diagenesis of vegetable organic matter to generate petroleum has long been well established,[31] and continued experimentation to the present has reinforced the evidence that oil is generated from coal beds.[32] Indeed, coal beds are believed to be the source of most Australian crude oils and natural gas, because coal beds are in the same sequences of sedimentary rock layers in the sedimentary basins where the oil and gas deposits are found. Furthermore, the coal beds are found below the reservoir rocks, which clearly trapped and pooled the oil and natural gas after it had been generated from the coal beds and migrated

---

28   J. Marinelli, 2003, Power plants —the origin of fossil fuels, *Plants and Gardens News* 18(2), www.bbg. org/gar2/pgn/2003su_fossilfuels.html.

29   R. W. T. Wilkins and S. C. George, 2002, Coal as a source rock for oil: A review, *International Journal of Coal Geology*, 50: 317-361.

30   Chapman, 1983, 213-214.

31   J. D. Brooks and J. W. Smith, 1967, The diagenesis of plant lipids during the formation of coal, petroleum and natural gas. I. Changes in the *N*-paraffin hydrocarbons, *Geochimica et Cosmochimica Acta*, 31: 2389-2397; J. D. Brooks and J. W. Smith, 1969, The diagenesis of plant lipids during the formation of coal, petroleum and natural gas. II. Coalification and the formation of oil and gas in the Gippsland Basin, *Geochimica et Cosmochimica Acta*, 33: 1183-1194.

32   R.-F. Weng, W.-L. Huang, C.-L. Kuo and S. Inan, 2003, Characterization of oil generation and expulsion from coals and source rocks using diamond anvil cell pyrolysis, *Organic Geochemistry*, 34: 771-787.

upwards.[33] The oil and gas deposits in many other places have also been shown to be derived from deeper coal beds, even in Pennsylvania, where the relationship was first established.[34] Indeed, one measure that has come to be used as a guide to the potential for finding oil or gas when exploring new sedimentary sequences is the vitrinite reflectance, which is the capacity to reflect light from vitrinite, one of the components of coal and of dispersed organic matter in sediments.[35]

At what rate can petroleum be generated from organic matter in sedimentary source rocks and from coal beds? The well documented example of laboratory experiments and field observations that demonstrate the recent and rapid generation of oil and gas deposits from underlying coal beds is the Gippsland Basin of Victoria in southern Australia and offshore in Bass Strait. In the earliest laboratory experiments, brown coals from the onshore part of the basin were heated under conditions that simulated accelerated sedimentary burial conditions.[36] Such thermal treatment in the presence of water brought about an increase in the carbon content of the coal corresponding to its conversion to a high-volatile bituminous (black) coal, accompanied by the formation of liquid and gaseous hydrocarbons from the contained waxes, and leaf, pollen, and spore cuticles, all in a matter of two to five days. These laboratory experiments are easily connected to field observations. In the offshore part of the basin, the main coal beds are buried more deeply under Bass Strait and have experienced higher temperatures of burial to become bituminous coal, while the oil and gas deposits trapped in the strata above these offshore coal beds are identical in composition to the oil and gas produced in the laboratory experiments. A subsequent series of experiments simulated this process of petroleum generation from these brown coals in a subsiding offshore basin over a longer period of six years, with the same outcome and conclusions.[37] Indeed, as a result of recognizing that the offshore sedimentary layers are still subsiding, so that the coal beds are continuing to sink into the "oil generation window," it has been concluded that petroleum generation must still be occurring at the present time, with the products migrating relatively rapidly either into traps or even to the surface.[38] This conclusion is consistent with the facts that the hydrocarbon traps under Bass Strait were full when discovered, and most of the oil in the reservoirs was low in sulfur, indicating there had been insufficient time

---

33   R. B. Leslie, H. J. Evans and T. L. Knight, eds., 1976, *Economic Geology of Australia and Papua New Guinea—3. Petroleum*, Monograph No. 7, Melbourne, Australia: The Australasian Institute of Mining and Metallurgy.

34   Tissot and Welte, 1978, 223-224; Chapman, 1983, 213; Wilkins and George, 2002.

35   Chapman, 1983, 214-215.

36   Brooks and Smith, 1969.

37   J. D. Saxby, A. J. R. Bennett, J. F. Crocroan, D. E. Lambert and K. W. Riley, 1986, Petroleum generation: Simulation over six years of hydrocarbon formation from torbanite and brown coal in a subsiding basin, *Organic Geochemistry*, 9(2): 69-81.

38   M. Shibuoka, J. D. Saxby and G. H. Taylor, 1978, Hydrocarbon generation in Gippsland Basin, Australia—Comparison with Cooper Basin, Australia, *American Association of Petroleum Geologists Bulletin*, 62(7): 1151-1158.

since generation and migration for it to have been extensively altered by bacterial and other processes.

Of further relevance is the discovery of the ongoing natural formation of petroleum on the ocean floor. In the Guaymas Basin in the Gulf of California is a series of long, deep fractures from which hydrothermal fluids at temperatures above 200°C are flowing from deep-seated magma chambers below through the 500-m-thick layers of sediments on the basin floor.[39] The sediments consist of diatomaceous ooze and silty mud, and as the hydrothermal fluids percolate through these sediments, the contained organic matter is being thermally broken down to produce discrete globules of oil, similar to reservoir crude oils, that are continually being released from the sediments with the fluids into the ocean waters above. The hydrocarbon and elemental compositions of this naturally-formed petroleum are within the ranges of typical crude oils, as are the contents of some of the significant organic components and their distribution, while other key analyses give results that are compatible with a predominantly bacterial/algal origin of this oil and gas. Furthermore, radiocarbon dating of this oil confirmed that the generation of this hydrothermal petroleum from these diatomaceous ooze layers has occurred over a very short timescale of only a few thousand years. Indeed, the relatively mild temperature conditions of this hydrothermal petroleum generation is consistent with the temperature conditions in laboratory experiments that have similarly generated petroleum from organic matter and coal.

It is also possible, of course, that because porphyrins are also found in animal blood, some crude oils may have been derived from the animals also buried and fossilized in many sedimentary rock layers, but this is not clearly established. Nevertheless, laboratory experiments have been turned into reality. Turkey and pig slaughterhouse wastes are now routinely trucked into a bio-refinery, where these wastes are put through a thermal conversion processing plant to produce high-quality oil within two hours.[40] This same thermal conversion technology is also reported as being adaptable to the processing of sewerage, old tires, and mixed plastics to produce oil. Of course, these exact same conditions are not what have obviously occurred naturally to produce petroleum, but they do confirm that the natural process did not necessarily require millions of years.

The remaining process is the migration of the petroleum from the source rocks to accumulate in traps to form oil and gas deposits. However, given that the sediments where the petroleum is generated contain water, and the oil and gas reservoirs also contain water, then these processes are basically a matter of hydraulics. Oil

39   D. R. T. Simoneit and P. F. Lonsdale, 1982, Hydrothermal petroleum in mineralized mounds at the seabed of Guaymas Basin, *Nature*, 295: 198-202; D. R. T. Simoneit, 1985, Hydrothermal petroleum, genesis, migration and deposition in Guaymas Basin, Gulf of California, *Canadian Journal of Earth Sciences*, 22: 1919-1929; P. M. Didyk and D. R. T. Simoneit, 1989, Hydrothermal oil of Guyamas Basin and implications for petroleum formation mechanisms, *Nature*, 342: 65-69.

40   E. Lemley, 2006, Anything into oil, *Discover*, 24(4).

droplets and gas due to their buoyancy and density would tend to rise through the water surrounding them, and flow of that water would aid the migration and transport of the oil and gas upwards in the sedimentary sequence, until structural and other traps block their upward passage to pond them. Thus, the other crucial factors will be the hydraulic gradients and the permeabilities of the strata through which the water, oil, and gas need to flow, such migration of the water, oil, and gas being aided by compaction of the sediments.[41] Given the proximity of the reservoir rocks and structural traps to the source rocks, from which the petroleum has been generated, the small distances over which the petroleum has to have migrated would thus have not required enormous transit times.

The formation of oil and gas deposits, therefore, can easily be accounted for within the biblical framework of earth history, with the global Flood cataclysm only about 4,500 years ago. The devastation of the pre-Flood earth surface and its catastrophic erosion would have resulted in the rapid accumulation of thick sequences of sedimentary rock layers, containing organic matter and interbedded coal layers, in the world's great sedimentary basins. The rapid deposition of the sediments would have ensured that oxygen was excluded from the organic matter and coal beds, so that the porphyrins would not be oxidized. As soon as deposition and deep burial of the organic matter had occurred, petroleum generation would have begun, especially where the waters trapped in the sediments were at the same time heated by nearby volcanic sources and magma chambers, which also added hydrothermal fluids to the hot waters fluxing through the organic matter and coal beds. That's why it is not surprising that liquid hydrocarbons have been found in recent sediments in the Gulf of Mexico,[42] and petroleum is still being generated on the ocean floor of the Guaymas Basin. After deposition of the sediments and petroleum generation had begun, the ongoing tectonics of the Flood would have resulted in the folding and faulting of strata that provided the structural and other traps needed to subsequently pond the migrating water, oil, and gas.

Indeed, certain traps that have ponded some oil deposits in earlier-deposited strata have been shown to have only formed as late as during Pleistocene time, which in the biblical framework is post-Flood.

> An example is the Kettleman Hills pool in California; the oil and gas of this pool are in the Miocene Tremblor Formation, but the fold that forms the trap cannot be earlier than Pleistocene, for the Tremblor Formation fold is parallel to the Pleistocene rocks at the surface of the ground. This places the accumulation in late Pleistocene or post-Pleistocene time, possibly within the last 100,000 years and certainly within a million years [conventionally speaking]....The time it takes for oil to accumulate into

---

41 T. W. Biederman Jr., 1978, Crude-oil composition and migration, in *The Encyclopedia of Sedimentology*, R. W. Fairbridge and J. Bourgeios, eds., Stroudsburg, PA: Dowden, Hutchinson and Ross, 212-220.

42 P. V. Smith Jr., 1952, Occurrence of hydrocarbons in recent sediments from the Gulf of Mexico, *Science*, 116: 437.

pools may be geologically short, the minimum being measured, possibly, in thousands or even hundreds of years.[43]

Thus, there is no reason to reject the Flood as a possible framework for the formation of the great oil deposits of the world. The character of petroleum deposits, and such field and experimental observations as have been accumulated regarding the origin, generation, and migration of oil, harmonize perfectly well within the year-long global cataclysm only about 4,500 years ago in the biblical framework for earth history.

43   Levorsen, 1967, 540.

122

LIMESTONE CAVES AND CAVE DEPOSITS

Another claimed slow geologic process that is incompatible with the biblical timescale for earth history is the formation of limestone caves, and the cave deposits within them, the stalactites and stalagmites, known technically as speleothems.

> If it can be shown that either the excavation of caverns or their subsequent filling must require a vastly longer time to accomplish than the post-Flood limit, literal acceptance of the Genesis chronology is untenable. We turn first to rates of removal of limestone by the process of carbonic-acid reaction.[1]

Of course, the above statement is based on three assumptions, none of which are valid in the context of the Genesis Flood cataclysm and the biblical timescale. First is the assumption that the processes responsible for the excavation of caverns within limestones could only have occurred after the Flood. Second is the assumption that caverns are only dissolved by the percolation of carbon dioxide rich ground water through joints or along bedding planes in limestone beds due to the weak carbonic acid solution reacting with the limestone.[2] And third, it is of course assumed that because carbonic acid is the only acid that forms in significant quantities in ground water today, that's the only process that could have dissolved out caverns in limestones in the past, and only at the rates of such dissolution processes today (according to strict uniformitarian belief).

The catastrophic deposition of limestone beds during the year-long Flood cataclysm has already been discussed and defended (chapter 64). After the lime sediment layers were deposited, they would have been buried rapidly under thousands of feet of other sediment layers, the weight of this overburden compacting the lime sediments and tending to expel the interstitial water (the water trapped between the

1   A. N. Strahler, 1987, *Science and Earth History—The Evolution/Creation Controversy*, Buffalo, NY: Prometheus Books, 280.

2   C. C. Plummer and D. McGeary, 1996, *Physical Geology*, seventh edition, Dubuque, IA: William C. Brown Publishers, 243-245.

lime sediment particles during deposition).[3] However, although the fluid pressure within the resultant limestone beds would have been great, the lack of a direct escape route for this pore water would have impeded water loss and prevented complete lithification. Major water loss would only have occurred through joints formed during the early stage of compaction. However, with the enormous catastrophic outpouring of lavas and large-scale catastrophic magmatic activity during the Flood, associated with catastrophic plate tectonics, copious quantities of hydrothermal fluids would have been generated and circulated through the earth's crust, including through the thick sequences of sedimentary strata that were being rapidly deposited contemporaneously. Because hydrothermal fluids are acidic, due to the dissolved sulfur in them, limestone layers would have been particularly susceptible to being dissolved by the passage of these hydrothermal fluids along joints and other fractures.[4]

In the later stages of the Flood catastrophe, tectonic activity would have resulted in the folding and faulting of the strata in sedimentary basins, and as the Flood waters subsequently receded, massive sheet and then channelized erosion would have stripped many sedimentary layers overlying limestone beds, and sometimes carving deeply into them. Both the tectonic movements and the removal of the overburden would have eased the compaction pressures and opened up joints, catastrophically releasing fluids that had been under pressure, particularly closest to the earth's surface. Thus, the mixture of now released acidic pore waters and the acidic hydrothermal fluids would have rapidly dissolved out huge caverns along joints and fractures, so that huge cave systems would have developed by rapid dissolution of the limestone beds at rates far exceeding today's rates. By comparison, today's rates of limestone dissolution are quiescent, whereas the conditions and rates at the end of Flood and early in the post-Flood era, when the earth was recovering from the upheavals of the Flood year, were still rapid and somewhat catastrophic.

Thus the process of forming the world's cave systems would have commenced during the Flood catastrophe itself, reaching its climax at the close of the Flood and in the subsequent immediate post-Flood period, as volcanic, magmatic, and tectonic activity waned, geologic conditions began to re-stabilize and the catastrophic process rates of the Flood year waned. Continued draining of water from sediments in the immediate post-Flood period would have ensured that horizontal groundwater flows would have been significant. With decaying of organic matter at the earth's surface, these ground waters would have been highly acidic, and these horizontal flows of highly acidic ground waters would have further enhanced the dissolution of limestone beds just below the water table, to further enlarge the developed cave systems. By contrast, the underground streams

---

3   S. A. Austin, 1980, Origin of limestone caves, *Acts & Facts,* 9(1).

4   E. Silvestru, 2003, A hydrothermal model of rapid post-Flood karsting, in *Proceedings of the Fifth International Conference on Creationism,* R. L. Ivey Jr., ed., Pittsburgh, PA: Creation Science Fellowship, 233-241.

flowing out of cave systems today are but a trickle in comparison to the combined ground water and hydrothermal fluid flows responsible for rapidly dissolving the limestones to generate the cave systems. Uniformitarian geologists have wrongly used today's groundwater flows and acid levels in the ground waters to miscalculate vast time periods for the formation of these cave systems.

Confirmation of the role of sulfuric acid in the rapid formation of large cave systems comes from the evidence that at least 10 percent of the caves in the Guadalupe Mountains of southeastern New Mexico and west Texas were primarily excavated by sulfuric acid in solution in warm ground water.[5] The products of sulfuric acid dissolution were found in the caves, especially the larger caves such as Carlsbad Cavern. It was found that sulfuric acid had formed by hydrogen sulfide being oxidized and dissolved in the hydrothermal fluids, the hydrogen sulfide rising from nearby oil deposits trapped in strata underneath the limestone bed in which the caves have been formed. Indeed, excavation of the Big Room at Carlsbad, a cavern of more than a million cubic meters (35 million cubic feet) was calculated to have only needed about 10 percent of the hydrogen sulfide from the annual commercial production of the neighboring gas fields.[6] Because sulfuric acid is much stronger than carbonic acid, sulfuric acid dissolution is believed to be much more rapid, speleogenesis possibly only taking centuries, not only for the caves in the Guadalupe Mountains, but in 10 percent or more of the known major caves worldwide.[7] Furthermore, other sources have been found for hydrogen sulfide production to aid sulfuric acid dissolution, such as bacteria, which are also capable of directly dissolving limestone too.[8] Just how prolific sulfuric acid dissolution is in the formation of cave systems is very likely to be of greater significance than realized hithertofore, because it has only been in the caves and dry areas where this process has been recognized due to the dissolution products being found, whereas in more humid climates the reactants may have been washed out of the caves.[9]

5 V. J. Polyak, W. C. McIntosh, N. Güven and P. Provencio, 1998, Age and origin of Carlsbad Cavern and related caves from $^{40}Ar/^{39}Ar$ of alunite, *Science*, 279: 1919-1922; I. D. Sasowsky, 1998, Determining the age of what is not there, *Science*, 279: 1874; V. J. Polyak and P. P. Provencio, 2000, Summary of the timing of sulfuric-acid speleogenesis for Guadalupe Caves based on ages of alunite, *Journal of Cave and Karst Studies*, 62(2): 72-79.

6 C. A. Hill, 1987, Geology of Carlsbad Caverns and other caves in the Guadalupe Mountains, New Mexico and Texas, *New Mexico Bureau of Mines and Mineral Resources Bulletin*, 117; D. Jagnow, C. A. Hill, D. Favis, H. DuChene, K. Cunningham, D. Northup and M. Queen, 2000, History of the sulfuric acid theory of speleogenesis in the Guadalupe Mountains of New Mexico, *Journal of Cave and Karst Studies*, 62(2): 54-59; C. A. Hill, 1990, Sulfuric acid speleogenesis of Carlsbad Caverns and its relationship to hydrocarbons, Delaware Basin, New Mexico and Texas, *American Association of Petroleum Geologists Bulletin*, 74: 1685-1694.

7 J. Gunn, 1981, Limestone solution rates and processes in the Waitomo district, New Zealand, *Earth Surface Processes*, 6: 427-445; D. Ford and P. Williams, 1991, *Karst Geomorphology and Hydrology*, London: Chapman and Hall, 113; A. N. Palmer, 1991, Origin and morphology of limestone caves, *Geological Society of America Bulletin*, 103: 1-21; Polyak et al, 1998.

8 L. Hose and J. Pisarowicz, 1999, Cueva de Villa Luz, Tabasco, Mexico: Reconnaissance study of an active sulfide spring cave and ecosystem, *Journal of Cave and Karst Studies*, 61(1): 13-21.

9 Palmer, 1991, 18-19.

However, even carbonic acid dissolution of limestones is more powerful and faster than is often portrayed. Because there are at least eight complex variables that determine the rate of solution of limestone,[10] another way of estimating limestone solution rates is to study a large cave-containing area where water chemistry and flow rates are known. For example, the large limestone and dolostone Sinkhole Plain-Mammoth Cave upland region of central Kentucky comprises several hundred square kilometers, receives 122 cm (48 inches) of rainfall annually, and naturally has about 51 cm (20 inches) of average annual runoff, yet the area has virtually no surface streams.[11] The runoff is instead channeled into sinkholes, which distribute the water into a widespread limestone and dolostone formation that is about 100 m (330 feet) thick, where caves and solution conduits transport most of the water until it is discharged at springs. Based on chemical analyses of the area's ground water,[12] and assuming that all the dissolved calcium and magnesium in the ground water must have come from solution of calcite and dolomite in the limestone and dolostone (because rainwater only has traces of calcium and magnesium), it can be shown that these concentrations represent 0.16 gram of dissolved calcite and dolomite per liter of ground water. Assuming about 100 cm of the mean annual rainfall infiltrates into the limestone and dolostone aquifer, each square kilometer of central Kentucky therefore receives about one million cubic meters, or one billion liters of water infiltrating into it, resulting in 176 tons of calcite and dolomite being dissolved each year from within each square kilometer of land surface. This equates to a volume of 59 cubic meters of calcite and dolomite dissolved each year, from one square kilometer of central Kentucky, and if this amount dissolved from just one groundwater conduit, a cave one square meter by 59 meters long would be excavated in just a single year![13]

Indeed, at this rate, the entire layer of limestone and dolostone over 100 meters thick would have been completely dissolved off central Kentucky in two million years, the conventionally assumed duration of the Pleistocene epoch, and the inferred age of many caves, including the Mammoth Caves, within this limestone and dolostone bed in central Kentucky. Nevertheless, the ground water in central Kentucky is actually undersaturated with respect to calcite and dolomite, meaning that the full dissolving power of the acidic water is not being fully utilized in attacking this limestone and dolostone bed. By contrast, the more humid, cooler climate of the Pleistocene (the early post-Flood period) would have resulted in increased groundwater flow due to the Flood waters still draining off, and therefore increased rates of limestone and dolostone solution. So combined with

10   J. F. Thrailkill, 1968, Chemical and hydrologic factors in the excavation of limestone caves, *Geological Society of America Bulletin*, 79: 19-46; R. F. Sipple and E. D. Glover, 1964, Solution alteration of carbonate rocks: The effects of temperature pressure, *Geochimica et Cosmochimica Acta*, 28: 1401-1417.

11   Austin, 1980; U. S. Geological Survey, 1970, *The National Atlas of the United States of America*, Department of Interior, Washington D.C., 97, 119.

12   J. F. Thrailkill, 1972, Carbonate chemistry of aquifer and stream water in Kentucky, *Journal of Hydrology*, 16: 93-104.

13   A. C. Swinnerton, 1932, Origin of limestone caverns, *Geological Society of America Bulletin*, 46: 678-679.

the contribution of sulfuric acid dissolution, it is conceivable that all the world's major (and minor) cave systems could have been rapidly produced at the end of the Flood cataclysm, and in the first few centuries of the post-Flood period at these rapid dissolution rates.

Once the ground waters and hydrothermal fluids were largely drained from cave systems, and the water table had dropped, the cave systems became filled with air instead of water. However, rainwater continued to infiltrate through the ground above the caves and into the limestone and dolostone beds, where it concentrated along cracks and tiny conduits to eventually be discharged into the cave systems by drip or flow. Once in the cave chambers, this water evaporates in the air, leaving behind deposits of calcite and dolomite lining the cave ceilings, walls, and floors as the various varieties of cave formations known as speleothems—stalactites hanging from the ceiling, stalagmites built up from the floor, columns formed by the joining of stalactites and stalagmites, and sheet-like layered flowstones on the walls or floors. Obviously, the rate of formation of these speleothems depends mainly on the rate of percolation of the lime-bearing waters into the roofs of caves, and on the evaporation rate in the caves. Some of these speleothems are very large, such as the 1.9-meter-tall stalagmite called the Great Dome in Carlsbad Cavern. Because many observations of speleothems suggest their rate of growth is very slow, along with old radiocarbon ages for the carbonate minerals in speleothems, it is often declared that stalactites, stalagmites, and other speleothems in caves could not have grown in the 4,500 years since the Genesis Flood.[14]

However, just because the formation rates for speleothems may be very slow at present certainly does not mean they have always been so.

> Various attempts have been made to estimate the rate of formation of cave travertine (speleothems), but so many variable factors affect the rate of deposition that it is doubtful if cavern ages arrived at by this method are accurate.[15]

Furthermore, radiocarbon ages of speleothems are deceptive, because the carbon incorporated in the speleothem minerals is out of equilibrium with the atmospheric carbon.

Most stalactites and stalagmites in modern caves are not growing, so it seems impossible to estimate their former rates of growth. However, in a summary of some of the early literature, stalactite growth was reported as averaging about 1.25 cm (0.5 inch) per year, with some observed to grow over 7.6 cm (3 inches)

---

14   Strahler, 1987, 281.

15   W. D. Thornbury, 1969, *Principles of Geomorphology*, second edition, New York: John Wiley and Sons, 325.

in a year.[16] Stalagmites were also observed to have grown 0.6 cm (0.25 inch) in height and 0.9 cm (0.36 inch) in diameter at the base each year. If this rate of height increase were applied to the 1.9 m tall Great Dome stalagmite in Carlsbad Cavern, it would have grown in less than 4,000 years. However, because most observations of the rapid growth of stalactites and stalagmites have been made in tunnels, under bridges, in dams and mines, or other dated man-made structures with approximate cave conditions, such observed growth rates are often dismissed as inapplicable to vast speleothem growth in caves. Nevertheless, such rejection of those rapid growth rate observations is unwarranted, particularly where observations have been made in underground mines where conditions are very similar to those in caves. These include such examples as a 1.6 meter high stalagmite that grew in an abandoned gold mine in central New South Wales, Australia, (where there are limestones nearby and cave systems) in less than 140 years, a growth rate of more than 1 cm per year, and numerous stalactites, some as long as 5 meters, in level 5 of the Mt. Isa lead-zinc mine in northwestern Queensland, Australia, which had grown in less than 55 years, a growth rate of up to 9 cm per year.[17] However, where measurements and experiments have been conducted in cave systems where stalactites and stalagmites are still growing, measured growth rates are both significant and comparable with those observed in man-made structures. For example, in Australia's famous Jenolan Caves in New South Wales, a drink bottle placed under a dripping stalactite shawl in the early 1950s had deposited on it within thirty years a stalagmite almost 20 cm high, a growth rate of almost 0.7 cm per year.[18]

Thus, it is possible at these present rates to account for the growth of speleothems in cave systems within the last 4,500 years, since the cave systems themselves formed at the end of the Flood and soon thereafter. Furthermore, because in the immediate post-Flood period (the Pleistocene) there was higher rainfall and higher humidity than today, it is probable that most speleothems grew at a much faster rate than the measured rates today. These initial faster growth rates, coupled with higher rainfall and humidity conditions, would account for the many speleothems that are not now growing under present conditions. Consequently, to attribute great lengths of time to the formation of caves in limestones, and the growth of cave deposits (speleothems), is not only unnecessary, but unreasonable.

16　L. W. Fisher, 1934, Growth of stalactites, *American Mineralogist*, 19: 429-431.

17　D. Batten, 1997, 'Instant' stalagmites!, *Creation*, 19(4): 37; Anonymous, 1998, Rapid stalactite formation, *Creation Ex Nihilo Technical Journal*, 12(3): 280.

18　Anonymous, 1995, Bottled stalagmite, *Creation*, 17(2): 6.

123

GRANITE FORMATION, INTRUSION, AND COOLING

Exposed at the earth's surface today are large areas of granites, mapped as individual bodies ranging in size from 1 square kilometer to more than 1,000 square kilometers. In many regions of the world, hundreds of these granite plutons are found in belts hundreds to thousands of kilometers long that are called batholiths, such as that in the Sierra Nevada mountain range of California. On that scale, granites are a major component of the earth's surface, and it is estimated that 86 percent of the intrusive rocks within the upper continental crust are of granitic composition.[1]

Deep in the earth's crust the temperature is sometimes high enough to melt the rocks locally, so that large "blobs" of granitic magmas are thus generated. Due to the buoyancy of the less dense molten rock, the magma rises to be intruded into the upper crust where the granite plutons crystallize and cool. Conventionally these processes of granite formation, intrusion, and cooling are regarded as taking millions of years.

> My guess is that a granitic magma pulse generated in a collisional origin may, in a complicated way involving changing rheologies of both melt and crust, take 5-10 Ma [million years] to generate, arrive, crystallize and cool to the ambient crustal temperature.[2]

Thus, it has been insisted that an immense granite batholith like that in southern California required a period of about 1 million years in order to crystallize completely, so it is obviously impossible to reconcile the complete process of magma generation, injection, and cooling on the order of 10 million years with the global Genesis Flood on a young earth.[3]

---

1   A. H. Wedepohl, 1969, Composition and abundance of common igneous rocks, *Handbook of Geochemistry*, vol. 1, Berlin: Springer-Verlag, 227-249.

2   W. S. Pitcher, 1993, *The Nature and Origin of Granites*, Blackie Academic and Professional, London, 187.

3   D. A. Young, 1977, *Creation and the Flood: An Alternative to Flood Geology and Theistic Evolution*, Baker Book House, MI: A. Hayward, 1985, *Creation and Evolution: The Facts and the Fallacies*, Triangle SPCK, London: Strahler, 1987.

Because we don't observe granites forming today, debate has raged for centuries as to how granites form. While there is now much consensus, some details of the processes involved are still being elucidated. Significantly, though the conventional wisdom has been adamant that granites take millions of years to form, recently that view has changed because of radical new ideas based on observation and experiments.[4] The essential role of rock deformation is now recognized. Previously accepted granite formation models required unrealistic deformation and flow behaviors of rocks and magmas, or did not satisfactorily explain available structural or geophysical data. Thus it is now claimed that mechanical considerations suggest granite formation was a "rapid, dynamic process" operating at timescales of less than 10,000 years, or even only thousands of years.

Several steps are required to form granites. The process starts with partial melting of continental sedimentary and metamorphic rocks 20-40 km (12-25 miles) down in the earth's crust, a process called generation.[5] This must be followed by the collection of the melt, called segregation, then transportation of the now less dense, buoyant magma upwards (ascent), and finally the intrusion of the magma to form a pluton in the upper crust (emplacement). There, as little as 2-5 km (1-3 miles) below the earth's surface, the granite mass fully crystallizes and cools. Subsequent erosion exposes it at the earth's surface. It is thus not difficult to understand why it has been hithertofore envisaged that this sequential series of processes in granite formation must surely have taken millions of years, such claimed estimates of course being supported by radioisotope dating.

Magma Generation by Partial Melting

Typical geothermal gradients of 20°C per km do not generate the greater than 800°C temperatures at 35 km depth in the crust needed to melt common crustal rocks.[6] However, there are at least three other factors, besides temperature, that are important in melt generation: water content of magma, pressure, and the influence of mantle-derived basalt magmas. Temperatures required for melting are significantly lowered by increasing water activity up to saturation, and the amount of temperature lowering increases with increasing pressure.[7] Indeed, water solubility in granitic melts increases with pressure, the most important controlling

---

4   N. Petford, A. R. Cruden, K. J. W. McCaffrey and J.-L. Vigneresse, 2000, Granite magma formation, transport and emplacement in the earth's crust, *Nature*, 408,: 669-673; J. D. Clemens, 2005, Granites and granitic magmas: Strange phenomena and new perspectives on some old problems, *Proceedings of the Geologists' Association*, 116: 9-16.

5   M. Brown, 1994, The generation, segregation, ascent and emplacement of granite magma: The migmatite to crustally-derived granite connection in thickened orogens, *Earth Science Reviews*, 36: 83-130.

6   A. B. Thompson, 1999, Some time-space relationships for crustal melting and granitic intrusion at various depths, in *Understanding Granites: Integrating New and Classical Techniques*, A. Castro, C. Fernández and J.-L. Vigneresse, eds., London: The Geological Society, Special Publication 168: 7-25.

7   A. Ebadi and W. Johannes, 1991, Beginning of melting and composition of first melts in the system Qz-Ab-Or-H_2O-CO_2, *Contributions to Mineralogy and Petrology*, 106: 286-295.

factor,[8] so that whereas at 1 kilobar (generally equivalent to 3 to 4 km depth) the water solubility is 3.7 weight %,[9] at 30 kilobars (up to 100 km depth, though very much less in tectonic zones) it is approximately 24 weight %.[10] This water is supplied by the adjacent rocks, subducted oceanic crust, and hydrous minerals present in the melting rock itself.

Nevertheless, local melting of deep crustal rocks is even more efficient where the lower crust is being heated by basalt magmas generated just below in the upper mantle.[11] Partial melting of crustal rocks pre-heated in this way is likely to be rapid.[12] Experiments on natural rock systems have also shown the added importance of mineral reactions to rapidly produce granitic melts.[13] One such experiment found that a quartzo-feldspathic source rock undergoing water-saturated melting at 800°C could produce 20-30 volume % of homogeneous melt in less than one to ten years.[14]

A crucial consequence of fluid-absent melting is reaction-induced expansion of the rock that results in local fracturing and a reduction in rock strength, due to the increase pore fluid (melt) pressures.[15] Stress gradients can also develop in the vicinity of an intruding basalt heat source and promote local fractures. These processes, in conjunction with regional tectonic strain, are important in providing enhanced fracture permeabilities in the region of partial melting, which aids subsequent melt segregation.[16]

Melt Segregation

The small-scale movement of magma (melt plus suspended crystals) within the source region is called segregation. The granite melts' ability to segregate

8   W. Johannes and F. Holtz, 1996, *Petrogenesis and Experimental Petrology of Granitic Rocks*, Berlin: Springer-Verlag.

9   F. Holtz, H. Behrens, D. B. Dingwell and W. Johannes, 1995, Water solubility in haplogranitic melts: Compositional, pressure and temperature dependence, *American Mineralogist*, 80: 94-108.

10 W. L. Huang and P. J. Wyllie, 1975, Melting reactions in the system $NaAlSi_3O_8$-$KAlSi_3O_8$-SiO_2 to 35 kilobars, dry with excess water, *Journal of Geology*, 83: 737-748.

11 E. W. Bergantz, 1989, Underplating and partial melting: Implications for melt generation and extraction, *Science*, 254: 1039-1045.

12 C. E. Huppert and R. S. J. Sparks, 1988, The generation of granitic magmas by intrusion of basalt into continental crust, *Journal of Petrology*, 29: 599-642; Thompson, 1999.

13 M. Brown and T. Rushmer, 1997, The role of deformation in the movement of granitic melt: Views from the laboratory and the field, in *Deformation-Enhanced Fluid Transport in the Earth's Crust and Mantle*, M. Holness, ed., London: Chapman and Hall: 111-144; Thompson, 1999.

14 A. Acosta-Vigil, D. London, G. B. Morgan, V. I. and T. A. Dewers, 2006, Dissolution of quartz, albite, and orthoclase in H_2O-saturated haplogranitic melt at 800°C and 200 MPa, diffusive transport properties of granitic melts at crustal anatectic conditions, *Journal of Petrology*, 47: 231-254.

15 J. B. Clemens and C. K. Mawer, 1992, Granitic magma transport by fracture propagation, *Tectonophysics*, 204: 339-360; Brown and Rushmer, 1997.

16 Petford et al, 2000.

mechanically from its matrix is strongly dependent on its physical properties, of which viscosity and density are the most important. Indeed, the viscosity is the crucial rate-determining variable, and is a function of melt composition, water content, and the temperature.[17] It has been demonstrated that the temperature and melts' water content are interdependent,[18] yet the viscosities and densities of granitic melts actually vary over quite limited ranges for melt compositions varying between tonalite (65 weight % SiO_2, 950°C) and leucogranite (75 weight % SiO_2, 750°C).[19] An important implication is that the segregation and subsequent ascent processes, which are moderated by the physical properties of the melts, thus occur at broadly similar rates, regardless of the tectonic setting and the pressures and temperatures to which the source rock has been subjected over time. Furthermore, granitic magmas are only 10 to 1,000 times more viscous than basaltic magmas, which readily flow.[20]

Most field evidence points to deformation (essentially "squeezing") as the dominant mechanism that segregates melt flow in the lower crust.[21] Rock deformation experiments indicate that when 10 to 40 percent of a rock is a granitic melt, the pore pressures in a rock are equivalent to the confining pressure, so the residual grains move relative to one another, resulting in macroscopic deformation due to melt-enhanced mechanical flow.[22] These experiments also imply that deformation-enhanced segregation can in principle occur at any stage during partial melting. Furthermore, the deformation-assisted melt segregation is so efficient in moving melt from its source to local sites of dilation ("squeezing") over a timescale of only a month up to 1,000 years. Thus, the melts may not attain chemical or isotopic equilibrium with their surrounding source rocks before final extraction and ascent.[23]

17 J. Woodmorappe, 2001, The rapid formation of granitic rocks: More evidence, *TJ*, 15(2): 122-125; E. B. Dingwell, N. S. Bagdassarov, G. Y. Bussod, and S. L. Webb, 1993, Magma rheology, in *Experiments at High Pressure and Applications to the Earth's Mantle*, R.W. Luth, ed., Short course handbook, vol. 21, Ottawa: Mineralogical Association of Canada, 131-196.

18 B. Scalliet, F. Holtz and M. Pichavant, 1998, Phase equilibrium constraints on the viscosity of silicic magmas—1. Volcanic-plutonic association, *Journal of Geophysical Research-Solid Earth*, 103B: 27257-27266.

19 J.D. Clemens and N. Petford, 1999, Granitic melt viscosity and silicic magma dynamics in contrasting tectonic settings, London: *Journal of the Geological Society*, 156: 1057-1060.

20 E. R. Baker, 1996, Granitic melt viscosities: Empirical and configurational entropy models for their calculation, *American Mineralogist*, 81: 126-134; B. Scalliet, F. Holtz, M. Pichavant, and M. Schmidt, 1996, Viscosity of Himalayan leucogranites: Implications for mechanisms of granitic magma ascent, *Journal of Geophysical Research—Solid Earth*, 101B: 27691-27699; Clemens and Petford, 1999.

21 J.-L. Vigneresse, P. Barbey and M. Cuney, 1996, Rheological transitions during partial melting and crystallization with application to felsic magma segregation and transfer, *Journal of Petrology*, 37: 1579-1600; Brown and Rushmer, 1997.

22 E. H. Rutter and D. H. K. Neumann, 1995, Experimental deformation of partially molten Westerly Granite under fluid-absent conditions, with implications for the extraction of granitic magmas, *Journal of Geophysical Research—Solid Earth*, 100B: 15697-15715; Brown and Rushmer, 1997.

23 E. W. Sawyer, 1991, Disequilibrium melting and rate of melt-residuum separation during migmatization of mafic rocks from Grenville Front, Quebec: *Journal of Petrology*, 32: 701-738; G. R. Davies and S.

These rapid timescales for melt extraction are well-supported by geochemical evidence in some granites. For example, some Himalayan leucogranites are strongly undersaturated with respect to the element zirconium,[24] because the granitic melt was extracted so rapidly from the residual matrix (in less than 150 years), that there was insufficient time for zirconium to be re-equilibrated between the two phases. Similarly, based on comparable evidence in a Quebec granite, the inferred time for the extraction of the melt from its residuum was only 25 years.[25]

Magma Ascent

Gravity is the essential driving force for large-scale vertical transport of melts (ascent) in the continental crust.[26] However, the traditional idea of buoyant granitic magma ascending through the continental crust as slow-rising, hot diapirs or by stoping (that is, large-scale veining)[27] has been largely replaced by more viable models. These models involve the very rapid ascent of granitic magmas in narrow conduits, either as self-propagating dikes[28] along pre-existing faults,[29] or as an interconnected network of active shear zones and dilational structures.[30] The advantage of dike/conduit ascent models is that they overcome the severe thermal and mechanical problems associated with transporting very large volumes of granite magmas through the upper brittle continental crust,[31] as well as explaining the persistence of near-surface granite intrusions and associated silicic volcanism. However, yet to be resolved is whether granite plutons are fed predominantly by a few large conduits or by dike swarms.[32]

Tommasini, 2000, Isotopic disequilibrium during rapid crustal anatexis: Implications for petrogenetic studies of magmatic processes, *Chemical Geology*, 162: 169-191.

24   N. Harris, D. Vance and M. Ayres, 2000, From sediment to granite: Timescales of anatexis in the upper crust, *Chemical Geology*, 162: 155-167.

25   Sawyer, 1991.

26   Petford et al, 2000.

27   R. F. Weinberg and Y. Podladchikov, 1994, Diapiric ascent of magmas through power law crust and mantle, *Journal of Geophysical Research—Solid Earth*, 99B: 9543-9559.

28   J. D. Clemens and C. K. Mawer, 1992; J.D. Clemens, N. Petford and C.K. Mawer, 1997, Ascent mechanisms of granitic magmas: Causes and consequences, in *Deformation-Enhanced Fluid Transport in the Earth's Crust and Mantle*, M. Holness, ed., London: Chapman and Hall, 145-172.

29   N. Petford, R. C. Kerr and J. R. Lister, 1993, Dike transport of granitoid magmas, *Geology*, 21: 845-848.

30   R. S. D'Lemos, M. Brown and R. A. Strachan, 1993, Granite magma generation, ascent and emplacement within a transpressional origin, *Journal of the Geological Society, London*, 149: 487-490; W. J. Collins and E. W. Sawyer, 1996, Pervasive granitoid magma transport through the lower-middle crust during non-coaxial compressional deformation, *Journal of Metamorphic Geology*, 14: 565-579.

31   B. D. Marsh, 1982, On the mechanics of igneous diapirism, stoping and zone melting, *American Journal of Science*, 282: 808-855.

32   M. Brown and G. S. Solar, 1999, The mechanism of ascent and emplacement of granite magma during transpression: A syntectonic granite paradigm, *Tectonophysics*, 312: 1-33; R. F. Weinberg, 1999, Mesoscale pervasive felsic magma migration: Alternatives to dyking, *Lithos*, 46: 393-410.

The most striking aspect of the ascent of granitic melts in dikes is the extreme difference in the magma ascent rate compared to diapiric rise, the dike ascent rate being up to a million times faster, depending on the magma's viscosity and the conduit width.[33] The narrow dike widths (1-50 meters) and rapid ascent velocities predicted by fluid dynamical models are supported by field and experimental studies.[34] For example, for epidote crystals to have been preserved as found in the granites of the Front Range (Colorado), and of the White Creek batholith (British Columbia), required an ascent rate of between 0.7 and 14 km per year. Therefore, the processes of melt segregation at more than 21 km depth in the crust, and then magma ascent and emplacement in the upper crust, all had to occur within just a few years.[35] Such a rapid ascent rate is similar to magma transport rates in dikes calculated from numerical modeling,[36] and close to measured ascent rates for upper crustal magmas.[37] Indeed, a granite melt could be transported 30 km through the crust along a 6-m-wide dike in just 41 days at a mean ascent rate of about 1 cm per second.[38] At that rate, the Cordillera Blanca batholith in northwest Peru, with an estimated volume of 6,000 cubic kilometers, could have been filled from a 10-km-long dike in only 350 years.

It is obvious that magma transport needed to have occurred at such fast rates through such narrow dikes, or else the granite magmas would "freeze" due to cooling within the conduits as they ascended. Instead, there is little geological, geophysical, or geochemical evidence to mark the passage of such large volumes of granite magmas up through the crust.[39] Because of the rapid ascent rates, chemical and thermal interaction between the dike magmas and the surrounding country rocks will be minimal. Typical ascent rates of 3 mm per second to 1 m per second have been calculated, which assuming there is continuous, efficient supply of magma to the base of the fracture system, translates to between

33 Petford et al, 1993; Clemens et al, 1997.

34 B. Scalliet, A. Pecher, P. Rochette and M. Champenois, 1994, The Gangotri Granite (Garhwal Himalaya): Laccolith emplacement in an extending collisional belt, *Journal of Geophysical Research—Solid Earth*, 100B: 585-607; A. D. Brandon, T. Chacko and R. A. Creaser, 1996, Constraints on granitic magma transport from epidote dissolution kinetics, *Science*, 271: 1845-1848.

35 Brandon et al, 1996.

36 Clemens and Mawer, 1992; Petford et al, 1993; N. Petford, 1995, Segregation of tonalitic-trondhjemitic melts in the continental crust: The mantle connection, *Journal of Geophysical Research—Solid Earth*, 100B: 15735-15743; N. Petford, 1996, Dykes or diapirs?, *Transactions of the Royal Society of Edinburgh: Earth Sciences*, 87: 105-114.

37 R. Scandone and S. D. Malone, 1985, Magma supply, magma discharge and readjustment of the feeding systems of Mount St. Helens during 1980, *Journal of Volcanology and Geothermal Research*, 23: 239-262; W. W. Chadwick Jr., R. J. Archuleta and A. Swanson, 1988, The mechanics of ground deformation precursory to dome-building extrusions at Mount St. Helens 1981-1982, *Journal of Geophysical Research—Solid Earth*, 93B: 4351-4366; M. J. Rutherford and P. M. Hill, 1993, Magma ascent rates from amphibole breakdown: An experimental study applied to the 1980-1986 Mount St. Helens eruptions, *Journal of Geophysical Research—Solid Earth*, 98B: 19667-19685.

38 Petford et al, 1993.

39 Clemens and Mawer, 1992; Clemens et al, 1997.

5 hours and 3 months for 20 km of ascent.[40] Such rapid rates make granite magma ascent effectively an instantaneous process, bringing plutonic granite magmatism more in line with timescales characteristic of silicic volcanism and flood basalt magmatism.[41]

Magma Emplacement

The final stage of magma movements is horizontal flow to form intrusive plutons in the upper continental crust. This emplacement is controlled by a combination of mechanical interactions, either pre-existing or placement-generated wall-rock structures, and density effects between the spreading flow and its surroundings.[42] The mechanisms by which the host rocks make way for this incoming magma have challenged geologists for most of the past century and have been known as the "space problem."[43] This problem is particularly acute where the volumes of magmas forming batholiths (groups of hundreds of individual granite plutons intruded side-by-side over large areas, such as the Sierra Nevada of California) are 100,000 cubic kilometers or greater, and are considered to have been emplaced in a single event.

New ideas that have alleviated this problem are: the recognition of the important role played by tectonic activity in making space in the crust for the incoming magma;[44] the realistic interpretation of the geometry of granitic intrusions at depth; and the recognition that emplacement is an episodic process involving discrete pulses of magma. Physical models indicate that space for incoming magmas can be generated through a combination of lateral fault opening, roof lifting, and lowering of the growing magma intrusion floor.[45] For example, space is created by uplift of the strata above the intrusion, even at the earth's surface, and their erosion.

The three-dimensional shapes of crystallized plutons provide important information on how the granitic magmas were emplaced. The majority of plutons

40 Clemens, 2005.

41 Petford et al, 2000.

42 D. H. W. Hutton, 1988, Granite emplacement mechanisms and tectonic controls: Influences from deformation studies, *Transactions of the Royal Society of Edinburgh: Earth Sciences*, 79: 245-255; J. P. Hogan and M. C. Gilbert, 1995, The A-type Mount Scott Granite sheet: Importance of crustal magma traps, *Journal of Geophysical Research—Solid Earth*, 100B: 15779-15792.

43 Pitcher, 1993.

44 Hutton, 1988.

45 D. Roman-Berdiel, D. Gapais and J. P. Brun, 1997, Granite intrusion along strike-slip zones in experiment and nature, *American Journal of Science*, 297: 651-678; K. Benn, F. O'Donne and M. de Saint Blanquat, 1998, Pluton emplacement during transpression in brittle crust, new views from analogue experiments, *Geology*, 26: 1079-1082; A. R. Cruden, 1998, On the emplacement of tabular granites, *Journal of the Geological Society of London*, 155: 853-862; C. Fernández and A. Castro, 1999, Pluton accommodation at high strain rates in the upper continental crust. The example of the Central Extremadura batholith, Spain, *Journal of Structural Geology*, 21: 1143-1149.

so far investigated using detailed geophysical (gravity, magnetic susceptibility, and seismic) surveys appear to be flat-lying sheets to open funnel-shaped structures with central or marginal feeder zones,[46] consistent with an increasing number of field studies (collecting fabric and structural data) that find plutons to be internally sheeted on the 0.1 m to kilometer scale.[47]

Considerations of field and geophysical data suggest that growth of a laterally-spreading and vertically-thickening intrusive flow obey a simple mathematical scaling or power-law relationship (between thickness and length) typical of systems exhibiting scale-invariant (fractal) behavior and size distributions.[48] This inherent preference for scale-invariant tabular sheet geometries in granitic plutons from a variety of tectonic settings is best explained in mechanical terms by the intruding magma flowing horizontally some distance initially before vertical thickening then occurs, either by hydraulic lifting of the overburden (particularly above shallow-level intrusions) or sagging of the floor beneath.[49] Plutons thus go from the birth stage characterized by lateral spreading to an inflation stage marked by vertical thickening.

This intrusive tabular sheet model envisages larger plutons growing from smaller ones according to a power-law inflation growth curve, ultimately to form crustal-scale batholithic intrusions.[50] Evidence of this growth process has been revealed by combined, field, petrological, geochemical, and geophysical (gravity) studies of the 1,200-km-long Coast batholith of Peru.[51] On a crustal scale this exposed batholith was formed by a thin (3-7 km thick) low-density granite layer that coalesced from numerous smaller plutons with aspect ratios of between 17:1 and 20:1. Thus this batholith would only amount to 5 to 10 percent of the crustal volume of this coastal sector of the Andes,[52] which greatly reduces the so-called

46   D. J. Evans, W. J. Rowley, R. A. Chadwick, E. S. Kimbell and D. Millward, 1994, Seismic reflection data and the internal structure of the Lake District batholith, Cumbria, northern England, *Proceedings of the Yorkshire Geological Society*, 50: 11-24; L. Améglio, J.-L. Vigneresse and J. L. Bouchez, 1997, Granite pluton geometry and emplacement mode inferred from combined fabric and gravity data, in *Granite: From Segregation of Melt to Emplacement Fabrics*, J. L. Bouchez, D. H. W. Hutton and W. E. Stephens, eds., Dordrecht, The Netherlands: Kluwer Academic Publishers: 199-214; L. Améglio and J.-L. Vigneresse, 1999, Geophysical imaging of the shape of granitic intrusions at depth: A review, in *Understanding Granites: Integrating New and Classical Techniques*, A. Castro, C. Fernández and J.-L. Vigneresse, eds., London: The Geological Society, Special Publication 168: 39-54; N. Petford and J. D. Clemens, 2000, Granites are not diapiric!, *Geology Today*, 16 (5): 180-184.

47   Améglio et al, 1997; J. Grocott, A. Garden, D. Chadwick, A. R. Cruden and C. Swager, 1999, Emplacement of Rapakivi granite and syenite by floor depression and roof uplift in the Paleoproterozoic Ketilidian orogen, south Greenland, *Journal of the Geological Society of London*, 156: 15-24.

48   K. J. W. McCaffrey and N. Petford, 1997, Are granitic intrusions scale invariant?, *Journal of the Geological Society of London*, 154: 1-4; Petford and Clemens, 2000.

49   Petford et al, 2000.

50   McCaffrey and Petford, 1997; Cruden, 1998.

51   M. P. Atherton, 1999, Shape and intrusion style of the coastal batholith, Peru, in *4th International Symposium on Andean Geodynamics*: 60-63.

52   Petford and Clemens, 2000.

space problem. Detailed studies of the Sierra Nevada batholith of California reveal a similar picture, in which batholith construction occurred by progressive intrusion of coalescing granitic plutons 2 to 2,000 square kilometers in area, supposedly over a period of 40 million years (as determined by radioisotope dating).[53]

Emplacement Rates

The tabular three-dimensional geometry of granite plutons and their growth by vertical displacements of their roofs and floors enables limits to be placed on their emplacement rates.[54] Taking conservative values for magma viscosities, wall-rock/ magma density differences, and feeder dike dimensions results in pluton filling times of between forty days and one million years for plutons under 100 km across. If the median value for the volumetric filling rate is used, then at the fastest magma delivery rates most plutons would have been emplaced in much less than 1,000 years.[55] Even a whole batholith of 1,000 cubic kilometers could be built in only 1,200 years, at the rate of growth of an intrusion in today's non-catastrophic geological regime.[56]

Thus, the formation of granite intrusions in the middle to upper crust involves four discrete processes—partial melting, melt segregation, magma ascent, and magma emplacement. According to conventional geologists, the rate-limiting step in this series of processes in granite magmatism is the timescale of partial melting,[57] but "the follow-on stages of segregation, ascent and emplacement can be geologically extremely rapid—perhaps even catastrophic."[58] However, the required timescale for partial melting is not incompatible with the 6,000- to 7,000-year biblical framework for earth history, because a very large reservoir of granitic melts could have been generated in the lower crust in the 1,650 years between creation and the Flood,[59] particularly due to residual heat from an episode of accelerated nuclear decay during the first three days of the Creation Week.[60] This very large reservoir of granitic melts would then have been mobilized and progressively intruded into the upper crust during the global, year-long Flood cataclysm, when the rates

53 P. C. Bateman, 1992, *Plutonism in the Central Part of the Sierra Nevada Batholith, California*, Denver, CO: Professional paper 1483, United States Geological Survey.

54 Petford et al, 2000.

55 Harris et al, 2000; Petford et al, 2000.

56 Clemens, 2005.

57 Petford et al, 2000; Harris et al, 2000.

58 Petford et al, 2000, 673.

59 Woodmorappe, 2001.

60 D. R. Humphreys, 2000, Accelerated nuclear decay: A viable hypothesis?, in *Radioisotopes and the Age of the Earth: A Young Earth Creationist Research Initiative*, L. Vardiman, A. A. Snelling and E. F. Chaffin, eds., El Cajon, CA: Institute for Creation Research, and St. Joseph, MO: Creation Research Society, 333-379; L. Vardiman, A. A. Snelling and E. F. Chaffin, eds., 2005, *Radioisotopes and the Age of the Earth: Results of a Young-Earth Creationist Research Initiative*, El Cajon, CA: Institute for Creation Research, and Chino Valley, AZ: Creation Research Society.

of these granite magmatism processes would have been greatly accelerated with so many other geologic processes, due to another episode of accelerated nuclear decay,[61] and catastrophic plate tectonics,[62] the likely driving mechanism of the Flood event.

Crystallization and Cooling Rates

The so-called space problem may have been solved, but what of the heat problem, that is, the time needed to crystallize and cool the granite plutons after their emplacement? Given that it has now been established that the world's granitic plutons are mostly tabular in shape, and typically only a few kilometers thick, it is a simple matter to model the cooling of granitic plutons by conduction.[63] When using typical values for physical properties of the magma and wall-rock temperatures, thermal conductivities, and heat capacities, a 3-km-thick sheet of granitic magma would take around 30,000 years to completely solidify from the initially liquid magma.

However, this calculation completely ignores the field, experimental, and modeling evidence that the crystallization and cooling of granitic plutons occurred much more rapidly as a result of convection, due to the circulation of hydrothermal and meteoric fluids, evidence that has been known about for more than 25 years.[64] The most recent modeling of plutons cooling by hydrothermal convection takes into account the multiphase flow of water and the heat it carries in the relevant ranges of temperatures and pressures, so that a small pluton (1 km x 2 km, at 2 km depth) is estimated to have taken 3,500-5,000 years to cool, depending on the system permeability.[65] But this modeling does not take into account the relatively thin, tabular structure of plutons that would significantly reduce their cooling

---

61   Humphreys, 2000; Vardiman et al, 2005.

62   S. A. Austin, J. R. Baumgardner, D. R. Humphreys, A. A. Snelling, L. Vardiman and K. P. Wise, 1994, Catastrophic plate tectonics: A global Flood model of earth history, in *Proceedings of the Third International Conference on Creationism*, R. E. Walsh, ed., Pittsburgh, PA: Creation Science Fellowship: 609-621.

63   H. S. Carslaw and J. C. Jaeger, 1980, *Conduction of Heat in Solids*, second edition, Oxford, UK: Oxford University Press; Clemens, 2005.

64   L. M. Cathles, 1977, An analysis of the cooling of intrusives by ground-water convection which includes boiling, *Economic Geology*, 72: 804-826; P. Cheng and W. J. Minkowycz, 1977, Free convection about a vertical flap plate embedded in a porous medium with application to heat transfer from a dike, *Journal of Geophysical Research—Solid Earth*, 82B: 2040-2044; D. Norton and J. Knight, 1977, Transport phenomena in hydrothermal systems: Cooling plutons, *American Journal of Science*, 277: 937-981 D. Norton, 1978, Sourcelines, sourceregions, and pathlines for fluid in hydrothermal systems related to cooling plutons, *Economic Geology*, 73: 21-28; K. E. Torrance and J. P. Sheu, 1978, Heat transfer from plutons undergoing hydrothermal cooling and thermal cracking, *Numerical Heat Transfer*, 1: 147-161; E. M. Paramentier, 1981, Numerical experiments on ^{18}O depletion in igneous intrusions cooling by groundwater convection, *Journal of Geophysical Research—Solid Earth* 86B: 7131-7144; H. C. Hardee, 1982, Permeable convection above magma bodies, *Tectonophysics*, 84: 179-195; F. J. Spera, 1982, Thermal evolution of plutons: A parameterized approach, *Science*, 207: 299-301.

65   E. O. Hayba and S. E. Ingebritsen, 1997, Multiphase groundwater flow near cooling plutons, *Journal of Geophysical Research—Solid Earth*, 102B: 12235-12252.

times. Similarly, convective overturn caused by settling crystals in the plutons would be another significant factor in the dissipation of their heat.[66]

Convective Cooling: The Role of Hydrothermal Fluids

Granitic magmas invariably have huge amounts of water dissolved in them that are released as the magma crystallizes and cools. As the magma is injected into the host strata, it exerts pressure on them that facilitates fracturing of them.[67] Also, the heat from the pluton induces fracturing as the fluid pressure in the pores of the host strata increases from the heat,[68] this process repeating itself as the pluton's heat enters these new cracks.

Following the emplacement of a granitic magma, crystallization occurs due to this irreversible heat loss to the surrounding host strata.[69] As heat passes out of the intrusions at its margins, the *solidus* (the boundary between the fully crystallized and partially crystallized magma) progressively moves inwards toward the interior of the intrusion.[70] As crystallization proceeds, the water dissolved in the magma that isn't incorporated in the crystallizing minerals stays in the residual melt, so its water concentration increases. When the saturation water concentration is lowered to the actual water concentration in the residual melt, first boiling occurs and water (as superheated steam) is expelled from the solution in the melt, which is consequently driven toward higher crystallinities as the temperature continues to fall. Bubbles of water vapor then nucleate and grow, causing second (or resurgent) boiling within the zone of crystallization just underneath the solidus boundary and the already crystallized granite (Figure 73, page 1101).

As the concentration and size of these vapor bubbles increase, vapor saturation is quickly reached, but initially these vapor bubbles are trapped beneath the immobile crystallized granite margin of the pluton.[71] The vapor pressure thus increases, until the aqueous fluid can only be removed from the sites of bubble nucleation through the establishment of a three-dimensional critical percolation network, with advection of aqueous fluids through it, or by means of fluid

66   A. A. Snelling and J. Woodmorappe, 1998, The cooling of thick igneous bodies on a young earth, in *Proceedings of the Fourth International Conference on Creationism*, R. E. Walsh, ed., Pittsburgh, PA: Creation Science Fellowship,: 527-545.

67   R. B. Knapp and D. Norton, 1981, Preliminary numerical analysis of processes related to magma crystallization and stress evolution in cooling plutons environments, *American Journal of Science*, 281: 35-68.

68   R. B. Knapp and J. E. Knight, 1977, Differential thermal expansion of pore fluids: Fracture propagation and microearthquake production in hot plutonic environments, *Journal of Geophysical Research—Solid Earth*, 82B: 2515-2522.

69   P. A. Candela, 1992, Controls on ore metal ratios in granite-related ore systems: An experimental and computational approach, *Transactions of the Royal Society of Edinburgh: Earth Sciences*, 83: 317-326.

70   P. A. Candela, 1991, Physics of aqueous phase evolution and plutonic environments, *American Mineralogist*, 76: 1081-1091.

71   Candela, 1991.

flow through a cracking front in the already crystallized granite and out into the surrounding host strata. Once such fracturing of the pluton has occurred (because the cracking front will go deeper and deeper into the pluton as the solidus boundary moves progressively inwards toward the core of the intrusion), not only is magmatic water released from the pluton carrying heat out into the host strata, but the cooler meteoric water in the host strata is able to penetrate into the pluton and thus establish a convective hydrothermal circulation, through the fracture networks in both the granite pluton and the surrounding host strata. The more water dissolved in the magma, the greater will be the pressure exerted at the magma/granite and granite/host strata interfaces, and thus the greater the fracturing in both the granite pluton and the surrounding host strata.[72]

Thus, by the time the magma has totally crystallized into the constituent minerals of the granite, the solidus boundary and cracking front have both reached the core of the pluton as well. It also means that a fracture network has been established through the total volume of the pluton and out into the surrounding host strata, through which a vigorous flow of hydrothermal fluids has been established. These hydrothermal fluids thus carry heat by convection out through this fracture network away from the cooling pluton, ensuring the temperature of the granitic rock mass continues to rapidly fall. The amount of water involved in this hydrothermal fluid convection system is considerable, given that a granitic magma has enough energy due to inertial heat to drive roughly its mass in meteoric fluid circulation.[73] The emplacement depth and the scale of the hydrothermal circulatory system are first-order parameters in determining the cooling time of a large granitic pluton.[74] Water also plays a "remarkable role" in determining the cooling time. For a granitic pluton 10 km wide emplaced at 7 km depth, the cooling time of the magma to the solidus decreases almost tenfold as the water content of the magma increases from 0.5 weight % to 4 weight %. As the temperature of the pluton/host rock boundary drops through 200°C during crystallization, depending on the hydrothermal fluid/magma volume ratio, with only a 2 weight % water content, the pluton cooling time decreases 18-fold. As concluded:

> Hydrothermal fluid circulation within a permeable or fractured country rock accounts for most heat loss when magma is emplaced into water-bearing country rock....Large hydrothermal systems tend to occur in the upper parts of the crust where meteoric water is more plentiful.[75]

---

72 Knapp and Norton, 1981; J. Zhao and E. T. Brown, 1992, Thermal cracking induced by water flow through joints in heated granite, *International Journal of Rock Mechanics*, 17: 77-82.

73 D. Norton and L. M. Cathles, 1979, Thermal aspects of ore deposition, in *Geochemistry of Hydrothermal Ore Deposits*, second edition, H. L. Barnes, ed., New York: John Wiley and Sons: 611-631; L. M. Cathles, 1981, Fluid flow and genesis of hydrothermal ore deposits, in *Economic Geology: 75th Anniversary Volume*, B. J. Skinner, ed., Economic Geology Publishing Company: 424-457.

74 Spera, 1982.

75 Spera, 1982, 299.

Of course, granitic magmas rapidly emplaced during the Flood cataclysm would have been intruded into sedimentary strata that were still wet from having just been deposited only weeks or months earlier. Furthermore, complete cooling of such granitic plutons did not have to all occur during the Flood year.

It is also a total misconception that the last crystals found in granites required slow cooling rates.[76] All the major minerals found in granites have been experimentally grown over laboratory timescales,[77] so macroscopic igneous minerals can crystallize and grow rapidly to requisite size from a granitic melt.[78] So how long then does it take to form the plagioclase feldspar crystals in a particular granite? Linear crystal growth rates of quartz and feldspars have been experimentally measured, and rates of $10^{-6.5}$ m per second to $10^{-11.5}$ m per second seem typical. This means that a 5-mm-long crystal of plagioclase could have grown in as short a time as one hour, but probably no more than 25 years.[79] Actually, extraneous geologic factors, not potential rate of mineral growth, constrain the sizes of crystals attained in igneous bodies.[80] Indeed, it has been demonstrated that the rate of nucleation is the most important factor in determining growth rates and eventual sizes of crystals.[81] Thus, the huge crystals (meters long) sometimes found in granitic pegmatites have grown rapidly at rates of more than 10^{-6} cm per second, from fluids saturated with the components of those minerals within a few years.[82]

Crystallization and Cooling Rates: The Evidence of Polonium Radiohalos

There is a feature in granites that severely restricts the timescale for their emplacement, crystallization, and cooling to just days or weeks at most—

76   W. C. Luth, 1976, Granitic rocks, in *The Evolution of the Crystalline Rocks*, D. K. Bailey and R. McDonald, eds., London: Academic Press, 333-417 (405-411); J. M. Wampler and P. Wallace, 1998, Misconceptions of crystal growth and cooling rates in formation of igneous rocks: The case of pegmatites and aplites, *Journal of Geological Education*, 46: 497-499.

77   R. H. Jahns and C. W. Burnham, 1958, Experimental studies of pegmatite genesis: Melting and crystallization of granite and pegmatite, *United States Geological Survey Bulletin*, 69: 1592-1593; H. G. F. Winkler and H. Von Platen, 1958, Experimentelle gesteinmetmorphose—II. Bildung von Anatektischen Granitischen Schmelzen bie der Metamorphose von NaCl—führenden Kalkfreien Toten, *Geochimica et Cosomochimica Acta*, 15: 91-112; D. A. Mustart, 1969, Hydrothermal synthesis of large single crystals of albite and potassium feldspar, *EOS, Transactions of the American Geophysical Union*, 50: 675; S. E. Swanson, J.A. Whitney and W. C. Luth, 1972, Growth of large quartz and feldspar crystals from synthetic granitic liquids, *EOS, Transactions of the American Geophysical Union*, 53: 1172.

78   S. E. Swanson, 1977, Relation of nucleation and crystal-growth rate to the development of granitic textures, *American Mineralogist*, 62: 966-978; S. E. Swanson and P. M. Fenn, 1986, Quartz crystallization in igneous rock, *American Mineralogist*, 71: 331-342.

79   Clemens, 2005.

80   P. D. Marsh, 1989, Convective style and vigour in magma chambers, *Journal of Petrology*, 30: 479-530.

81   G. Lofgren, 1980, Experimental studies on the dynamic crystallization of silicate melts, in *Physics of Magmatic Processes*, R. B. Hargreaves, ed., Princeton, New Jersey: Princeton University Press: 487-551; A. Tsuchiyama, 1983, Crystallization kinetics in the system $CaMgSi_2O_6$-$CaAl_2Si_2O_8$: The delay in nucleation of diopside and anorthite, *American Mineralogist*, 68: 687-698.

82   D. London, 1992, The application of experimental petrology to the genesis and crystallization of granitic pegmatites, *Canadian Mineralogist*, 30: 499-540.

polonium radiohalos.[83] Radiohalos are minute spherical (circular in cross-section) zones of darkening due to radioisotope decay in tiny central mineral inclusions within the host minerals (refer back to chapter 111).[84] They are generally prolific in granites, particularly where *biotite* (black mica) flakes contain tiny zircon inclusions that contain uranium. As the uranium in the zircon grains radioactively decays through numerous daughter elements to stable lead, the α-radiations from eight of the decay steps produce characteristic darkened rings to form uranium radiohalos around the zircon radiocenters. Also present adjacent to these uranium radiohalos in many biotite flakes are distinctive radiohalos formed only from the three polonium radioisotopes in the uranium decay chain. Because they have been parented only by polonium they are known as polonium radiohalos.

The significance of these polonium radiohalos in granites is that they had to form exceedingly rapidly, because the half-lives (decay rates) of these three polonium radioisotopes are very short—3.1 minutes (polonium-218), 164 microseconds (polonium-214), and 138 days (polonium-210). Furthermore, each visible radiohalo requires the decay of at least 500 million parent radioisotope atoms to form them, which in the case of uranium radiohalos, at the current rate of uranium decay is the equivalent of up 100 million years worth of radioactive decay.[85] Zircons at the centers of the uranium radiohalos adjacent to polonium radiohalos are the only nearby source of polonium (from decay of the same uranium that produces the uranium radiohalos). The hydrothermal fluids released by the crystallization and cooling of the granites is able to flow between the sheets making up biotite flakes, and because of their chemistry are able to transport the polonium from the zircons to the adjacent concentrating sites only microns distant, that then become the radiocenters which produce the polonium radiohalos.[86] Furthermore, all the radiohalos can only form after the granites have crystallized and cooled below 150°C, the annealing temperature of the radiohalos,[87] which is very late in the granite cooling process, when all the minerals have crystallized and the hydrothermal fluids have been generated to remove heat from the cooling plutons by convection. Yet uranium decay in the zircons and hydrothermal transport of daughter polonium isotopes starts much earlier when the granites are still

---

83   A. A. Snelling and M. H. Armitage, 2003, Radiohalos—A tale of three plutons, in *Proceedings of the Fifth International Conference on Creationism*, R. L. Ivey Jr., ed., Pittsburgh, PA: Creation Science Fellowship: 243-267; A. A. Snelling, 2005, Radiohalos in granites: Evidence for accelerated nuclear decay, in *Radioisotopes and the Age of the Earth: Results of a Young-Earth Creationist Research Initiative*, L. Vardiman, A. A. Snelling and E. F. Chaffin, eds., El Cajon, CA: Institute for Creation Research and Chino Valley, AZ: Creation Research Society: 101-207.

84   R. V. Gentry, 1973, Radioactive halos, *Annual Review of Nuclear Science*, 23: 342-362; A. A. Snelling, 2000, Radiohalos, in *Radioisotopes and the Age of the Earth: A Young-Earth Creationist Research Initiative*, L. Vardiman, A. A. Snelling and E. F. Chaffin, eds., El Cajon, CA: Institute for Creation Research and St. Joseph, MO: Creation Research Society, 381-468.

85   Gentry, 1973; Snelling, 2000.

86   Snelling and Armitage, 2003; Snelling, 2005.

87   R. Laney and A. W. Laughlin, 1981, Natural annealing of pleochroic haloes in biotite samples from deep drill holes, Fenton Hill, New Mexico, *Geophysical Research Letters*, 8(5): 501-504.

crystallizing and then cooling respectively. Nevertheless, because of the very short half-lives of these three polonium radioisotopes, the hydrothermal fluid transport of the polonium to generate the polonium radiohalos had to be extremely rapid, within hours to a few days. Furthermore, if too much of the uranium and polonium had decayed away while the granite was crystallizing and cooling below 150°C when the radiohalos could start forming, then the required large quantities of polonium would have decayed before they could form the polonium radiohalos.[88] Thus it is estimated that the granites also need to have crystallized and cooled within six to ten days. Such a timescale for the crystallization and cooling of granite plutons, along with the generation of them and emplacement of the granite magmas as already discussed, is certainly compatible with the biblical timescales for the global Flood event and for earth history. Any claims that radioisotope dating has "proven" granite formation, intrusion, and cooling must have instead taken millions of years are totally contradicted by the evidence for accelerated nuclear decay that renders radioisotope "dating" completely unreliable.[89]

---

88 Snelling and Armitage, 2003; Snelling, 2005; A. A. Snelling, 2008, Radiohalos in the Shap Granite, Lake District, England: Evidence that removes objections to Flood geology, in *Proceedings of the Sixth International Conference on Creationism*, A. A. Snelling ed., Pittsburgh, PA: Creation Science Fellowship, and Dallas, TX: Institute for Creation Research: 389-405; A. A. Snelling and D. Gates, 2009, Implications of polonium radiohalos in nested plutons of the Tuolumne Intrusive Suite, Yosemite, California, *Answers Research Journal*, 2: 53-77.

89 L. Vardiman et al, 2005; A. A. Snelling, 2008, Catastrophic granite formation: Rapid melting of source rocks, and rapid magma intrusion and cooling, *Answers Research Journal*, 1: 11-25.

124

REGIONAL METAMORPHISM

Metamorphic rocks, the third class of the earth's crustal rocks after sedimentary and igneous rocks, constitute a major portion of the earth's crust.

> Much of the earth's surface is immediately underlain by vast tracks of crystalline metamorphic rock. Much of the exposed rock of the eastern two-thirds of Canada consists of metamorphic rocks. The Blue Ridge Mountains of the southern Appalachians, the southern Piedmont, virtually all of New England, New York's Manhattan Island, and nearly the entire area between Philadelphia and Washington, D.C., consist of metamorphic rock. So do large areas of the mountainous western parts of the United States and Canada. Metamorphic rocks also are widely exposed in other parts of the world such as Australia, Scandinavia, Siberia, and India.[1]

There are two major types of metamorphism—contact and regional. Contact metamorphism is basically the baking of rocks around intruding and cooling magmas, and thus primarily involves elevated temperatures. Given it has now been demonstrated granitic plutons are intruded rapidly, and it can be shown that the magmas crystallize and cool rapidly, with hydrothermal convective flows carrying heat out into the wall-rocks, contact metamorphism must likewise occur rapidly, and is thus explainable within the biblical timescales for the Flood cataclysm and the young earth.

However, in regional metamorphism it is conventionally believed that the sedimentary strata over areas of hundreds of square kilometers were subjected to high temperatures and pressures due to deep burial and deformation/tectonic forces, processes operating over millions of years. The resultant mineralogical and textural transformations are said to be due to mineral reactions in the original sediments under the prevailing temperature-pressure conditions of this regional metamorphism. The catastrophic rate of sedimentation during the Flood would

---

1   D. A. Young, 1977, *Creation and the Flood: An Alternative to Flood Geology and Theistic Evolution*, Grand Rapids, MI: Baker Book House, 193-194.

deeply bury some sedimentary strata in only a matter of weeks or months, producing the necessary pressure increases needed for metamorphism of the sediments, but uniformitarian geologists argue that it takes many millions of years to heat sediments buried 20 kilometers beneath the earth's surface to the required temperatures for metamorphism.

A good example is the metamorphic terrain of New England, where the original sedimentary character of many of these rocks is, apart from differences from various compositional, textural, and structural characteristics, firmly established by the discovery in places of several fossils within these metamorphic rocks.[2] Thus, because of these contained fossils, it would be argued that the original sediments from which these metamorphic rocks developed were deposited during the Flood year. However, to the south, these metamorphic rocks are unconformably overlain by unmetamorphosed fossiliferous sedimentary rocks, so it is necessary to conclude that the New England metamorphic rocks had to have been metamorphosed within the Flood year. Furthermore, since it has been possible to experimentally determine the ranges of stability of almost all important metamorphic minerals, in terms of pressure and temperature, and the pressure and temperature at which many important metamorphic mineral reactions may occur, it can be concluded that the mineral assemblages of the New England metamorphic rocks indicate that many of the precursor sedimentary and volcanic rocks must have been subjected to temperatures approaching 600°C and pressures of 5 kilobars.[3] Such conditions are interpreted as implying that the sediments were buried under a load of strata 16-19 km thick. Thus, within the Flood year, the precursor sedimentary strata of these New England metamorphic rocks had to have been deposited rapidly, then progressively buried to a depth of between 16 and 19 km, in turn to be progressively metamorphosed as the temperatures rose to around 600°C, before being uplifted and then eroded to eventually be exposed as metamorphic rocks at today's earth surface.

Like other terrains of regionally metamorphosed rocks in other parts of the world, the New England area has been carefully mapped, and the rocks divided into metamorphic zones and facies according to the mineral assemblages that are confined to each zone and confined to it within each facies respectively. It is assumed that these mineral assemblages reflect the metamorphic transformation conditions specific to each zone, so that by traversing across these metamorphic zones, from the chlorite zone through the biotite zone, garnet zone, staurolite zone, and sillimanite zone to the K-feldspar zone in pelitic rocks (for example), higher

2   A. J. Boucot, G. J. F. MacDonald, C. Milton and J. B. Thompson, 1958, Metamorphosed middle Paleozoic fossils from central Massachusetts, eastern Vermont, and western New Hampshire, *Geological Society of America Bulletin*, 69: 855-870; A. J. Boucot, and J. B. Thompson, 1963, Metamorphosed Silurian brachiopods from New Hampshire, *Geological Society of America Bulletin*, 74: 1313-1334.

3   J. B. Thompson and S. A. Norton, 1968, Paleozoic regional metamorphism in New England and adjacent area, in *Studies of Appalachian Geology: Northern and Maritime*, E-an Zen, W. S. White, J. B. Hadley and J. B. Thompson, eds., New York: Wiley Interscience Publishers, 319-327.

metamorphic grades (due to former higher temperature-pressure conditions) are progressively encountered, from low to high grade respectively. Among the metamorphic mineral assemblages diagnostic of each zone are certain minerals whose presence in the rocks is indicative of each zone, and these are called index minerals, which are thus used to name each zone. It is envisaged that the mineral assemblages in these zones and facies are the result of mineral reactions, whereby the temperature and pressure conditions, along with active components like water, have induced the minerals in the original rocks to react and form new minerals. Thus, for example, at the boundary between the biotite and garnet zones in typical pelitic rocks is the first appearance of garnet according to the reaction:

chlorite+muscovite+quartz = garnet+biotite+water

Such reactions vary according to which minerals are available to react with one another in the original rocks, according to their bulk compositions. Considerable effort has therefore been expended to elucidate all possible reactions between minerals in the almost limitless potential variations in original bulk compositions.

Although there have been some doubts expressed, it is widely accepted among geologists that the achievement of chemical equilibrium in regional metamorphism is the rule rather than the exception. Metamorphic petrology today is based on the assumption that chemical equilibrium is virtually always attained, and hence that mineral assemblages can be evaluated in the context of the Phase Rule.[4] It also appears to be generally accepted that diffusion occurs over distances large enough to permit mineral reactions to occur through large volumes of rock, and that with rise in temperature and pressure, such reactions occur in progressive fashion, so that any particular set of pressure-temperature conditions manifest itself through the development, in rocks of like chemical composition, of a particular set of metamorphic minerals. In this way, grades of metamorphism and metamorphic gradients in zones are identified, and metamorphic rocks of different compositions are linked with the facies principle. The issue of regional metamorphism is now so well established, that it constitutes an essentially unquestioned basis for some very highly refined studies of relationships between mineral chemistry and metamorphic grade.

However, more precise studies, on the scale of the microscope and the electron microprobe, are beginning to place severe limits on the distances involved in metamorphic diffusion, which in turn sets critical limits to the extent to which minerals may react, so that metamorphic equilibrium is obtained. From some of the earliest observations of the delicate preservation of bedding in some metamorphosed strata, it was concluded that "the mineral formed at any point

---

4   K. Bucher and M. Frey, 2002, *Petrogenesis of Metamorphic Rocks*, seventh edition, Berlin: Spring-Verlag; M. B. Best, 2003, *Igneous and Metamorphic Petrology*, second edition, Malden, MA: Blackwell Publishing.

depends on the chemical composition of the rock mass within a certain very small distance around that point."[5] Diffusion distances were thus estimated to be probably of the order of 1 mm.[6] Recently, it has been observed that what little evidence there is seems to indicate that metamorphic diffusion is probably effective at most over distances measured in only centimeters, conventionally over times of the order of millions of years.[7] In contrast, another recent estimation of the diffusion limits is of the order of 0.2 to 4.0 mm.[8] Opinion probably remains diverse, though the view of many modern investigators is:

> There are many indications that rocks constitute a "closed" thermodynamic system during the short time required for metamorphic crystallization. The transport of material is generally limited to distances similar to the size of newly formed crystals. It has been observed frequently that minute chemical differences of former sediments are preserved during metamorphism. Metamorphism is essentially an *isochemical* process.[9]

Thus, it can be argued that the chemical components of a metamorphic grain, now occupying the given domain, are derived directly from those chemical components occupying that domain immediately prior to the onset of metamorphism, so that metamorphic mineral must represent the *in situ* growth and/or transformation of a pre-metamorphic material of similar overall composition, or it must be one or two or more products of the *in situ* breakdown of pre-metamorphic material of appropriate composition. The development of metamorphic minerals would thus stem from simple grain growth, ordering of randomly-disposed structures, and solid-solid transformations, not from "mineral reactions" as these are currently visualized. Clear evidence under the microscope of mineral reactions in rocks, as distinct from solid-solid transformations, is usually very hard to find, even where minerals that might be expected to react lie in contact. It is therefore significant that none of the major metamorphic petrology textbooks of recent years show a single photograph illustrating the destruction of one mineral and the simultaneous development of another.[10] This almost general absence of direct evidence of mineral reactions has led some observers to suggest that metamorphic

---

5   A. Harker, 1893, On the migration of material during the metamorphism of rock-masses, *Journal of Geology*, 1: 574-578.

6   A. Harker and J. E. Marr, 1893, Supplementary notes on the metamorphic rocks around the Shap Granite, *Quarterly Journal of the Geological Society of London*, 49: 359-371.

7   F. J. Turner and J. Verhoogen, 1960, *Igneous and Metamorphic Petrology*, second edition, New York: McGraw-Hill Book Company.

8   D. M. Carmichael, 1969, On the mechanism of prograde metamorphic reactions in quartz-bearing pelitic rocks, *Contributions to Mineralogy and Petrology*, 20: 244-267.

9   H. G. F. Winkler, 1979, *Petrogenesis of Metamorphic Rocks*, fifth edition, New York: Springer-Verlag, 16 (emphasis in original).

10 S. J. Turner, 1968, *Metamorphic Petrology: Mineralogical and Field Aspects*, New York: McGraw-Hill Book Company; A. Miyashiro, 1973, *Metamorphism and Metamorphic Belts*, London: George Allen and Unwin; Winkler, 1979.

rocks may attain their mineral assemblages directly, rather than by a series of mineral reactions, hence without passing through each successive grade.[11]

Coupled with the doubts concerning the reality of many postulated reactions are doubts on equilibrium. Preservation of zoning in garnets, for example, indicates that even at high grades of metamorphism, equilibrium may remain unattained even in a single crystal. Evidence of the preservation of compositional inhomogeneities in other minerals, including sulfides,[12] is now mounting, indicating that compositional equilibrium may not have been attained even in the most sensitive crystal structures, and even where these have been subjected to the highest grades of metamorphism.

The unique opportunity to study the results of metamorphic processes over small scales is provided by conformable or stratiform sulfide ore deposits in sedimentary and metasedimentary strata. The sulfide ore minerals have the appearance of being an integral, and hence normal, component of the sedimentary or metasedimentary rocks in which they occur, being simply grains within a granular rock. The orebodies are usually lens-shaped and grossly elongated, with their long dimensions parallel to the stratification of the enclosing rocks. They themselves commonly display good internal bedding, which may usually be demonstrated to be continuous with that of the enclosing pelitic sediments. Many stratiform ore deposits contain, and are immediately ensheathed by, metamorphosed pelitic rocks displaying distinctive metamorphic mineral assemblages. It is now generally accepted that the sulfide minerals of these ores were laid down as fine chemical precipitates as part of the original sediments themselves, as found and observed where modern-day analogues are forming on the sea floor associated with hydrothermal springs.[13] These sulfide ores are thus intrinsic parts of the rocks in which they occur, so the metamorphic mineral assemblages within and surrounding the ores must result from the metamorphism of the sedimentary materials laid down with, and adjacent to, the sulfide precipitates. Thus. they are genuine metamorphic rocks, and they therefore have been used in a landmark series of studies[14] of metamorphic phenomena in metamorphosed pelitic rocks

11   H. S. Yoder, 1952, The MgO-Al$_2$O$_3$-SiO$_2$-H$_2$O system and related metamorphic facies, *American Journal of Science*, Bowen Volume: 569-627; H. S. Yoder, 1955, The role of water in metamorphism, *Geological Society of America Special Paper 62*: 505-524; M. P. Atherton, 1965, The chemical significance of isograds, in *Controls of Metamorphism*, W. S. Pitcher and G. W. Flinn, eds., Edinburgh and London: Oliver and Boyd, 169-202.

12   S. D. Scott, R. A. Both and S. A. Kissin, 1977, Sulfide petrology at Broken Hill, New South Wales, *Economic Geology*, 72: 1410-1425.

13   P. F. Lonsdale, J. L. Bischoff, V. M. Burns, M. Kastner and R. E. Sweeney, 1980, A high-temperature hydrothermal deposit on the seabed at a Gulf of California spreading center, *Earth and Planetary Science Letters*, 49: 8-20; P. A. Rona, 1986, Mineral deposits from sea-floor hot springs, *Scientific American*, 254(1): 66-74; J. B. Alt and W. -T. Jiang, 1991, Hydrothermally precipitated mixed-layer illite-smectite in recent massive sulfide deposits from the seafloor, *Geology*, 19: 570-573.

14   R. L. Stanton, 1982, An alternative to the Barrovian interpretation? Evidence from stratiform ores, *Proceedings of the Australasian Institute of Mining and Metallurgy*, 282: 11-32; R. L. Stanton, 1989, On the potential significance of "chemical" materials in the elucidation of regional metamorphic processes,

that not only question the conventional explanation for regional metamorphism, but provide an alternative explanation requiring only moderate temperatures on short timescales, commensurate with the biblical framework for earth history.[15]

Studying the assemblages of mineral species and their compositional variations in these metasedimentary sheets around the stratiform sulfide orebodies shows that original sedimentary features, even at the finest scale (1 mm or less), have been preserved through claimed millions of years, and the supposed highest grades of metamorphism of pelitic rocks. Metamorphic diffusion was concluded to have been confined, at least in some cases, to distances of a small fraction of a millimeter. For example, garnet crystals varied significantly in composition between and within one another, even within the same strata on a scale of 1mm or less, the observed finely layered compositional arrangement being a direct reflection of the original sedimentary bedding preserved through a proposed period claimed to be at least 1.8 billion years, and through a very high grade metamorphic episode.[16] Even within single crystals, the presence of these substantial compositional inhomogeneities indicates very little diffusion at all.[17]

Furthermore, microscopic evidence of metamorphic reactions is usually poor and ambiguous, or absent, whereas it will be conventionally expected to be present.[18] Given that some stratiform ore zones possess a very wide range of high grade metamorphic minerals within volumes of only a few cubic centimeters, it might have been expected that evidence of such reactions would be found here, even if they could not be found in other metamorphic rocks. The inference is that metamorphic mineral reactions, as they are conventionally visualized, are unlikely

in *Pathways in Geology: Essays in Honour of Edwin Sherbon Hills*, R. W. LeMaitre, ed., Melbourne, Australia: Blackwell Scientific Publications, 425-438; R. L. Stanton, 1989, The precursor principle and the possible significance of stratiform ores and related chemical sediments in the elucidation of processes of regional metamorphic mineral formation, *Philosophical Transactions of the Royal Society of London*, A328: 529-646.

15   A. A. Snelling, 1994, Towards a creationist explanation of regional metamorphism, *Creation Ex Nihilo Technical Journal*, 8 (1): 51-77.

16   R. L. Stanton and J. P. Vaughan, 1979, Facies of ore formation: A preliminary account of the Pegmont deposit as an example of potential relations between small 'iron formations' and stratiform sulphides ores, *Proceedings of the Australasian Institute of Mining and Metallurgy*, 270: 25-38; J. P. Vaughan and R. L. Stanton, 1986, Sedimentary and metamorphic factors in the development of the Pegmont stratiform Pb-Zn deposit, Queensland, Australia, *Transactions of the Institution of Mining and Metallurgy*, 95: B94-B121; R. L. Stanton and K. L. Williams, 1978, Garnet compositions at Broken Hill, New South Wales as indicators of metamorphic processes, *Journal of Petrology*, 19: 514-529; A. A. Snelling, 1994, Regional metamorphism within a creationist framework: What garnet compositions reveal, in *Proceedings of the Third International Conference on Creationism*, R. E. Walsh, ed., Pittsburgh, PA: Creation Science Fellowship, 485-496.

17   R. L. Stanton, 1982, Metamorphism of a stratiform sulphide ore body at Mount Misery, Queensland, Australia: 1—Observations, *Transactions of the Institution of Mining and Metallurgy*, 91: B47-B71; R. L. Stanton, 1982, Metamorphism of a stratiform sulphide ore body at Mount Misery, Queensland, Australia: 2—Implications, *Transactions of the Institution of Mining and Metallurgy*, 91: B72-B80.

18   R. L. Stanton, 1976, Petrochemical studies of the ore environment at Broken Hill, New South Wales: 2—Regional metamorphism of banded iron formations and their immediate associates, *Transactions of the Institution of Mining and Metallurgy*, 85: B118-B131; Stanton, 1982.

to have been a significant factor in the development of these particular extensive metamorphic mineral assemblages. Indeed, the whole spectrum of metamorphic index minerals may occur within centimeters of each other, indicating either that metamorphic mineral equilibrium is not established even over very small distances, but some factor other than, or additional to, temperature and pressure is responsible for the development of these minerals. If, in fact, the supposed long periods of presumed millions of years available for these metamorphic processes had indeed occurred, chemical equilibrium should have been attained, whereas this lack of chemical/metamorphic equilibrium raises crucial questions about the timescales involved.

This lack of metamorphic equilibrium, even on the scale of centimeters, in metamorphic rocks generally has been noted by numerous investigators.[19] However, the most striking evidence of this apparent lack of metamorphic equilibrium is provided by the total assemblages of the ore zones of sulfide deposits in metasedimentary rocks.[20] Each of the metamorphic mineral assemblages in these ore zones is extensive, and covers the whole spectrum of metamorphic index minerals of all the presumed zones of progressive regional metamorphism. Yet each assemblage is contained within what is, compared to the regional scale of the classic metamorphic zones, an almost infinitesimally small volume of rock over distances from 3-20 meters, and even in some cases, within a single rock thin microscope section. Total volumes of rocks concerned are far too small to have sustained differences in temperature, pressure, or partial pressures of volatiles, even over any significant period of time. Thus, the huge array of metamorphic minerals displayed must affect variations in the compositions of the parent shales, and of variations in temperature and pressure.

If, as this evidence suggests, metamorphic minerals may represent essentially *in situ* transformations of earlier sedimentary-diagenetic materials, then what might have been these precursor materials? A number of possibilities are well recognized.[21]

---

19   B. E. Tilley, 1925, Petrographic notes on some chloritoid rocks, *Geological Magazine*, 42: 309-318, M. P. Atherton, 1968, The variation in garnet, biotite and chlorite composition in medium grade pelitic rocks from the Dalradian, Scotland with particular reference to the zonation of garnet, *Contributions to Mineralogy and Petrology*, 18: 347-371; W. H. Blackburn, 1968, The spatial extent of chemical equilibrium in some high-grade metamorphic rocks from the Granville of southeastern Ontario, *Contributions to Mineralogy and Petrology*, 19: 72-92; W. C. Phinney, 1963, Phase equilibria in the rocks of St. Paul Island and Cape North, Nova Scotia, *Journal of Petrology*, 4: 90-130; A. F. Hagner, S. Leung and J. M. Dennison, 1965, Optical and chemical variations in minerals from a single rock specimen, *American Mineralogist*, 50: 341-355; R. Kretz, 1966, Metamorphic differentiation at Einasleigh, northern Queensland, *Journal of the Geological Society of Australia*, 13: 561-582; A. L. Albee, A. A. Chodes and L. S. Hollister, 1966, Equilibration volumes for different species in three assemblages of kyanite-zone schists, Lincoln Mountain, Vermont, *Abstracts of the American Geophysical Union Transactions*, 47: 213; J. R. Ashworth, 1975, Staurolite at anomalously high grade, *Contributions to Mineralogy and Petrology*, 53: 281-291.

20   Stanton, 1989.

21   R. L. Stanton and W. P. H. Roberts, 1978, The composition of garnets at Broken Hill, and their relevance to the origin of the lode, *Journal de Mineralogica Recife*, 7: 143-154; M. Osada, and T. Sudo, Mineralogical study on the clay rich in chlorite associated with the gypsum deposit of the Owami Mine,

Numerous examples of minerals found in metamorphic rocks, that have been, or can be, produced from simple or complex precursors of near identical compositions, and even at low temperatures, have been provided.[22] Consequently, the development of a particular metamorphic mineral assemblage can thus be seen to have devolved from constitutional features in the wider sense, that is, not only from simple bulk chemistry, but from this in combination with the detailed features of the precursor crystal structure, or mixtures of structures. Indeed, the nature of such structures, and particularly of the mixed layering of clays-chlorites-Al/Fe oxides/hydroxides-zeolites, and of the admixture of these with amorphous silica and silica/alumina gels, is likely to be just as important as, or even more important than, bulk composition in the development of a particular metamorphic mineral.

Therefore, these stratiform ores and their metamorphic assemblages reflect original sedimentation in sea floor hydrothermal environments mixing with "normal" marine sedimentation, the clay and other minerals in the sediments being the precursors to the metamorphic assemblages now present. The waters of mineral-bearing hot springs on the sea floor are often in areas of volcanic activity, and the relatively high temperature, acidic hydrothermal waters contrast with the cold, slightly alkaline ocean water that they mix with. As well as iron, calcium, and other metal compounds, the hot spring waters usually contain substantial quantities of silica, alumina, and silica-alumina gels, the basic materials of the clay minerals, and due to their acidic nature cause the variable breakdown of detrital feldspars and other minerals to a variety of clays within the surrounding sea floor sediments. This leads to accumulations of sediments, not only of highly varying chemical composition, but also containing a wide variety of clay and associated chemicals/detrital minerals over very short distances and thicknesses of sediments.

These relatively small-scale sedimentary environments of stratiform ores thus indicate that the larger-scale regional metamorphic zones in pelitic rocks could have stemmed in many cases from semi-regional variations in clay and related mineral assemblages, consequent upon the variations in the nature and conditions of sedimentation. Indeed, the tendency of the clay and related layered silicate minerals to develop zonal patterns of distribution during shallow marine sedimentation is well established.[23] In the sediments of Monterey Bay,

---

Shimane Prefecture, *Clay Science*, 1: 29-40; P. R. Segnit, 1961, Petrology of the zinc lode, New Broken Hill Consolidated Ltd, Broken Hill, New South Wales, *Proceedings of the Australasian Institute of Mining and Metallurgy*, 199: 87-112, R. L. Stanton, 1983, The direct derivation of sillimanite from a kaolinitic precursor: Evidence from the Geco Mine, Manitouwadge, Ontario, *Economic Geology*, 78: 422-437.

22   Stanton, 1989.

23   P. W. Smoot, 1960, Clay mineralogy of some pre-Pennsylvanian sandstones in shales of the Illinois Basin, Part III—Clay minerals of the various facies in some Chester Formations, *Illinois State Geological Survey*, 293: 1-19; G. Millot, 1970, *Geology of Clays*, London: Chapman and Hall; A. Hallam, 1966, Depositional environment of British Liassic ironstones considered in the context of their facies relationship, *Nature*, 209: 1306-1309; S. P. Ellison, 1955, Economic applications of palaeoecology,

California, biotite-rich sandy sediments have been laid down in nearshore zones, and glauconite muds have been deposited further out to sea.[24] Deposition and current action in the Gulf of Mexico have produced an orderly distribution of different clay species, and therefore a gradational pattern of different clay minerals parallel to the coastline.[25] Similarly, iron-rich minerals in the modern sediments of the Niger delta of West Africa display a clear zoning of goethite, chamosite, and glauconite parallel to the shoreline,[26] which is significant, because it is these other two minerals that are the possible precursors to garnet and biotite, respectively. Furthermore, along the South American continental shelf, receiving sediments from the Amazon River, a clear zoning of clay minerals developed both along and across the shelf has been found, which has been attributed quite simply to sorting by size.[27]

Thus, extension of this precursor principle from the sea floor hydrothermal sedimentation environments, that produced stratiform sulfide ores and their metamorphic assemblages to wider zones of sedimentation, reveals that both in present-day marine shelf environments and in the depositional environments reflected in a number of ancient sedimentary basins, there are wide zones of pelitic sediments containing different clay and related mineral assemblages, such that if these metamorphosed they would result in metamorphic mineral assemblages that would mimic the zones of regional metamorphism with their characteristic index minerals (Figure 74, page 1102).[28] On this basis, the regional metamorphic zones in pelitic rocks may simply reflect subtle variations in the clay mineral assemblages when the precursor sedimentary rocks were deposited.[29]

The evidence of some stratiform ore environments, therefore, indicates that even within a restricted and relatively uniform group of rocks such as the pelites, there may be sufficient constitutional variation to induce the development of a wide range of metamorphic minerals, indeed, virtually all of the metamorphic minerals known, at a given temperature and pressure. This is precisely the conclusion reached from experimental evidence, which showed that for the same temperature

Economic Geology, 50th Anniversary Volume: 867-884; R. Schoen, 1964, Clay minerals of the Silurian Clinton ironstones, New York State, *Journal of Sedimentary Petrology*, 34: 855-863; C. V. Jeans, 1978, The origin of the Triassic clay assemblages of Europe with special reference Kueper Marl and Rhaetic of parts of England, *Philosophical Transactions of the Royal Society of London*, A289: 549-639.

24   E. W. Galliher, 1935, Geology of glauconite, *Bulletin of the American Association of Petroleum Geologists*, 19: 1569-1601.

25   G. M. Griffen, 1962, Regional clay-mineral facies—Products of weathering intensity and current distribution in the north-eastern Gulf of Mexico, *Geological Society of America Bulletin*, 73, 737-768.

26   D. H. Porringa, 1967, Glauconite and chamosite as depth indicators in the marine environment, *Marine Geology*, 5: 495-501.

27   R. J. Gibbs, 1977, Clay mineral segregation in a marine environment, *Journal of Sedimentary Petrology*, 47: 237-243.

28   Stanton, 1982; Snelling, 1994.

29   Stanton and Vaughan, 1979.

and pressure it is possible to have assemblages within a restricted compositional system corresponding to every one of the accepted minerals of the metamorphic facies in stable equilibrium.[30] The same experiments showed that changes in a few percent in composition (including water) may produce great differences in mineralogy, and that the mineralogical differences interpreted as resulting from changes in temperature-pressure conditions[31] might actually be for the most part due to subtle changes in bulk composition.

Furthermore, it has been demonstrated that these transformations of precursor minerals/materials into metamorphic mineral assemblages can occur at low to moderate temperatures. Some of these metamorphic minerals have been found with remnants of their low-temperature precursor materials alongside, the two co-existing in rocks that are supposed to have experienced the highest grade of metamorphism.[32] The most extreme example, the presence of distinctly hydrous "quartz" in high-grade metamorphic rocks, even after 1.8 billion years and such metamorphism,[33] can only mean that temperatures were low to moderate and the timescale was very short. Yet it has been insisted that this distinctly hydrous "quartz" was originally chemically-deposited silica gel, that with diagenesis and aging dehydrated and transformed *in situ* to quartz at low temperatures.

Thus, it is feasible to conclude that the conventional zones of regional metamorphism represent zonal patterns of the original sedimentation, and that the precursor clay and associated minerals have undergone transformation to metamorphic mineral assemblages at low to moderate temperatures and pressures. Furthermore, this implies that the depths of burial required were considerably less, and consequently the timescales as well. The problem of the elusive metamorphic reactions in the natural *milieu* is thus resolved. Preservation of what appear to be disequilibrium concentration gradients and mineral assemblages follows naturally, if the materials formed at low temperatures and pressures, particularly in wet sedimentary and sedimentary-hydrothermal depositional regimes, simply undergo early water loss followed by *in situ* solid-solid transformation with rising temperatures and pressures. Puzzled conventional speculation that some metamorphic rocks might attain their mineral assemblages directly, rather than through a series of mineral reactions, hence without passing through each successive grade, appears to be answered.

It is conceivable that regional metamorphic terrains with their zones of "classical" index minerals could thus have been produced as a result of catastrophic sedimentation, burial, and tectonic activities over short timescales, the zones only being a reflection of variations in original sedimentation, as can be demonstrated

---

30   Yoder, 1952.

31   P. Eskola, 1920, The mineral facies of rocks, *Norsk Geologisk Tiddsskrift*, 6: 143-194.

32   Stanton, 1982; Stanton, 1983.

33   Stanton, 1989.

in continental shelf depositional facies today.[34]

In the biblical framework of earth history, there is more than one episode capable of producing large regions of zoned metamorphic rocks. The formation of the dry land on Day Three of the Creation Week must have involved earth movements (tectonism), volcanism, magmatism, and the release of hydrothermal fluids, erosion of the emerging land surface due to the retreating waters, and deposition of sediments in the developing ocean basins. Such sedimentation could thus have been capable of producing zones of sediment with subtle differences in bulk chemistry and mineralogy that would be precursors for accompanying or subsequent regional metamorphism. The pre-Flood continental shelves and ocean basins would have continued to accumulate a variety of sediments with zonal patterns of different clay and other minerals, accompanied by sea floor hydrothermal activity associated with "the fountains of the great deep."[35]

At the outset of the Flood these pre-Flood zoned sediments would have experienced rapid burial and heat released as renewed volcanic and magmatic activity occurred sufficient to induce precursor transformations in those regional zones that would mimic conventional grades. The Flood event itself provided the greatest scope for regional metamorphism. Catastrophic sedimentation, deep burial of large volumes of fossil-bearing strata, vast outpourings of lavas on a global scale, ensuring the release of copious amounts of hydrothermal waters during sedimentation and interbedded volcanics, massive repeated intrusive magmatism, and the rapid deformation of catastrophic plate tectonics, would have ensured both elevated temperatures and pressures in thick sediment piles, as well as the potential for repeated cycles of sedimentation, metamorphism, and erosion in regions that overlapped as this catastrophic activity shifted geographically.[36] Add to this rapid plate movements with thermal runaway subduction, catastrophic rifting, and continent-continent collisions, as per conventional plate tectonics but during the year-long Flood, and various settings required for regional metamorphism are amply provided.

The range of induced pressures would have been short-lived, and the timescales would have only allowed for moderate temperatures to be reached. However, composition is the primary factor in regional metamorphism, and the zoning of index minerals found across regionally metamorphosed terrains is dependent

---

34   Snelling, 1994.

35   K. P. Wise, 2003, The hydrothermal biome: A pre-Flood environment, in *Proceedings of the Fifth International Conference on Creationism*, R. L. Ivey, Jr., ed., Pittsburgh, PA: Creation Science Fellowship, 359-370.

36   D. J. Tyler, 1990, A tectonically-controlled rock cycle, in *Proceedings of the Second International Conference on Creationism*, vol. 2, R. E. Walsh and C. L. Brooks, eds., Pittsburgh, PA: Creation Science Fellowship, 293-301; S. A. Austin, J. R. Baumgardner, D. R. Humphreys, A. A. Snelling, L. Vardiman and K. P. Wise, 1994, Catastrophic plate tectonics: A global Flood model for earth history, in *Proceedings of the Third International Conference on Creationism*, R. E. Walsh, ed., Pittsburgh, PA: Creation Science Fellowship, 609-621.

on the presence and compositions of precursor minerals. Sedimentary strata would not need to have been buried as deeply to reach the moderate temperatures needed for transformations of precursor minerals, due to catastrophic sediment accumulation and the increased heat flow from the mantle because of catastrophic plate tectonics. The waters trapped in the Flood sediments would have been warmer than waters being trapped in sediments today, so pore and hydrothermal fluids would have been another important factor in facilitating rapid regional metamorphism. Catastrophic erosion caused by the retreating Flood waters would also have exhumed these regionally metamorphosed rocks to expose them and their zones at the earth's surface today.

Because hydrothermal fluids are generated in water-saturated sedimentary rocks as they become deeply buried, helping to transform them into regional metamorphic complexes, it was predicted that such hydrothermal fluid transport through metamorphic minerals, containing inclusions of minerals such as zircons, would transport polonium from uranium decay in them to generate adjacent polonium radiohalos. This prediction has been vindicated with the discovery of plentiful polonium radiohalos in regionally metamorphosed rocks.[37] In further research, a test of this hydrothermal fluid transport model for polonium radiohalo formation was proposed in metamorphosed sandstones of the upper Precambrian Great Smoky Group near the Tennessee-North Carolina border. These regionally metamorphosed sandstones contain biotite flakes with zircon inclusions throughout, from the biotite zone through the garnet, staurolite and kyanite zones.[38] Furthermore, at the boundary between the garnet and staurolite zones, mineral transformations are supposed to occur that make biotite more abundant, staurolite to appear, and water to be released, which has been confirmed experimentally. It was thus predicted that, due to the presence of extra water at that boundary, samples of metamorphosed sandstones collected there would contain more polonium radiohalos.[39] This prediction was indeed confirmed in a dramatic way, there being more than five times the numbers of polonium radiohalos in samples across that boundary, than in samples from the other regional metamorphic zones. This confirms that hydrothermal fluids did indeed facilitate the formation of polonium radiohalos. Furthermore, since the polonium radiohalos have to be generated within days or a few weeks at most, this

---

37   A. A. Snelling and M. H. Armitage, 2003, Radiohalos—A tale of three granitic plutons, in *Proceedings of the Fifth International Conference on Creationism*, R. L. Ivey, Jr., ed., Pittsburgh, PA: Creation Science Fellowship, 243-267; A. A. Snelling, 2005, Radiohalos in granites: Evidence for accelerated nuclear decay, in *Radioisotopes and the Age of the Earth: Results of a Young-Earth Creationist Research Initiative*, L. Vardiman, A. A. Snelling and E. F. Chaffin, eds., El Cajon, CA: Institute for Creation Research and Chino Valley, AZ: Creation Research Society, 101-207.

38   E. C. Allen and P. C. Ragland, 1972, Chemical and mineralogical variations during prograde metamorphism, Great Smoky Mountains, North Carolina and Tennessee, *Geological Society of America Bulletin*, 83: 1285-1298.

39   A. A. Snelling, 2005, Polonium radiohalos: The model for their formation tested and verified, *Acts & Facts*, 34 (8); A. A. Snelling, 2008, Testing the hydrothermal fluid transport model for polonium radiohalo formation: The Thunderhead Sandstone, Great Smoky Mountains, Tennessee-North Carolina, *Answers Research Journal*, 1: 53-64.

implies that these mineral transformations, which released the water to generate the polonium radiohalos, and therefore the regional metamorphism, had to have occurred within days to a few weeks.

Another confirmation for the rapid rate of metamorphism is further provided by polonium radiohalos within eclogite, a very high grade metamorphic rock, formed within shear zones by hot fluids repeatedly injected into them by earth movements.[40] Even the conventional view on the rate at which the precursor granulite in these shear zones was metamorphosed to eclogite has been radically revised.[41] Indeed, the presence of polonium radiohalos in biotite flakes within these eclogites in the shear zones confirms the rapid metamorphism of the granulite by hot fluids within weeks.[42]

Even further confirmation of rapid regional metamorphism, and melting of rocks to form granite, due to hydrothermal fluids is provided by the polonium radiohalos found in the regional metamorphic complex and its central granite at Cooma in southeastern Australia.[43] This regional metamorphic complex is regarded as a "textbook example" of the zones of increasing metamorphism resulting in partial melting of the metamorphic rocks at the highest grades in the centre of the complex to generate and intrude the granite.[44] The number of polonium radiohalos in these regionally metamorphosed rocks increase progressively from the biotite zone, through the andalusite and K-feldspar zones, but drop dramatically in the migmatite zone before increasing to their greatest numbers in the granodiorite. This is in keeping with expectations that increased quantities of hot fluids were both responsible for the progressively increasing metamorphism, and for generation of the granite. Furthermore, in the migmatite zone where partial melting occurred, the hot fluids both catalyzed the partial melting process and were "consumed" by the melt, reducing the volume of fluids

40   H. Austrheim and W. L. Griffin, 1985, Shear deformation and eclogite formation within granulite facies anorthosites of the Bergen Arcs, western Norway, *Chemical Geology*, 50: 267-281; B. Jamtveit, K. Bucher-Nurminen and H. Austrheim, 1990, Fluid controlled eclogitization of eclogites in deep crustal shear zones, Bergen Arcs, western Norway, *Contributions to Mineralogy and Petrology*, 104: 184-193; M. Bjornerud, H. Austrheim and M. G. Lund, 2002, Processes leading to eclogitization (densification) of subducted and tectonically buried crusts, *Journal of Geophysical Research*, 107(B10): 2252-2269.

41   A. Camacho, J. K. W. Lee, B. J. Hensen and J. Braun, 2005, Short-lived orogenic cycles and the eclogitization of cold crust by spasmodic hot fluids, *Nature*, 435: 1191-1196; S. Kelley, 2005, Hot fluid and cold crusts, *Nature*, 435: 1171.

42   A. A. Snelling, 2006, Confirmation of rapid metamorphism of rocks, *Acts & Facts*, 35 (2).

43   A. A. Snelling, 2008, Radiohalos in the Cooma metamorphic complex, NSW, Australia: The mode and rate of regional metamorphism, in *Proceedings of the Sixth International Conference on Creationism*, A. A. Snelling, ed., Pittsburgh, PA: Creation Science Fellowship and Dallas, TX: Institute for Creation Research, 371-387.

44   R. H. Flood and R. H. Vernon, 1978, The Cooma Granodiorite, Australia: An example of *in situ* crustal anatexis?, *Geology*, 6: 81-84; S. S. Johnson, R. H. Vernon and B. E. Hobbs, 1994, *Deformation and Metamorphism of the Cooma Complex, Southeastern Australia*, Specialist Group in Tectonics and Structural Geology Field Guide No. 4, Geological Society of Australia, Sydney; A. Hall, 1996, *Igneous Petrology*, second edition, Harlow, UK: Addison Wesley Longman.

so that the numbers of polonium radiohalos generated decreased.

These observations are totally consistent with both the hydrothermal fluid transport for the generation of polonium radiohalos, and the role of hot fluids in regional metamorphism and granite generation, both of which processes, based on the time constraints for the formation of polonium radiohalos, must have been exceedingly rapid, within weeks. Thus the rapid rate of these geological processes, contrary to conventional thinking and objections, can be accounted for within the biblical timescale for the Genesis Flood and earth history.

125

ORE AND MINERAL DEPOSITS

The economies of the nations of the world, and the technological innovations of modern civilization, are not only fueled and driven by coal, oil, and gas, but are resourced by the mining and processing of ore and mineral deposits. Just as there are many geologists involved in the coal and oil industries, many geologists are employed to search for new ore and mineral deposits, and to develop and mine them. The mining and smelting of common and precious metals, as well as gems and minerals, has been part of human history, even being mentioned in the Scriptures prior to and after the Flood. Critics of the biblical timescale for the Flood and earth history have been quick to point out the paucity of treatment of this subject by those who accept the biblical timescale and that the Genesis Flood shaped the present world's geology, including the formation of ore and mineral deposits.[1]

Both the geochemical and geophysical techniques used in the search for new ore and mineral deposits do not require the application of conventional uniformitarian thinking on the formation of ore and mineral deposits, because they simply involve the collection and analysis of samples in the field and over prospects on the one hand, and instrument surveys on the other.[2] Once a decision has been made to explore in a particular area or region, then the geochemical and geophysical surveys are implemented and interpreted purely in scientific terms of observations and experiments, which are independent of the uniformitarian belief system. It is only at the earlier stage of deciding where to explore that uniformitarian ideas on the formation of ore and mineral deposits may have some bearing, but decisions are often on the basis of looking at geological maps to see what rock types are found in a particular region, and whether from past human history the target metals or minerals were found or mined in that region. In the words of a famous South African economic geologist:

---

1   A. N. Strahler, 1987, *Science and Earth History: The Evolution/Creation Controversy*, Buffalo, NY: Prometheus Books, 238-243.

2   A. W. Rose, H. E. Hawkes and J. S. Webb, 1979, *Geochemistry in Mineral Exploration*, second edition, London: Academic Press; W. M. Telford, L. P. Geldart, R. E. Sheriff and D. A. Keys, 1981, *Applied Geophysics*, London: Cambridge University Press.

In the long ago, before men starting seeking minerals and money in the interior of Africa, the nomadic Bushmen had a saying: "If you want to hunt elephants, go to elephant country." If elephants and ore-bodies can be equated, then the fundamental problem of exploration geology is simply: where and how does one find the best elephant country![3]

Nevertheless, it is important to show that the formation of ore and mineral deposits can be explained within the context of the Genesis Flood, and the biblical framework and timescale of earth history.

It is now firmly established in conventional thinking that the ultimate sources of the metals in metalliferous ores are the magmas that produce igneous rocks, both intrusive and extrusive, and hydrothermal fluids produced by magmatism and volcanism are a primary, but not the only means, by which the metals are concentrated into economic ore deposits. With the advent of plate tectonics, ideas on the formation of ore and mineral deposits were unified within the new understanding of the working of global earth systems that formed and shaped the earth's crust through earth history.[4] Thus, the application of catastrophic plate tectonics within the biblical timescale and framework of earth history, particularly the Flood event, adequately accommodates the formation of ore and mineral deposits in the ways envisaged by conventional plate tectonics, but at catastrophic rates.[5]

As much as conventional plate tectonics is regarded as simply the uniformitarian extrapolation back into the past of the present occurrences and rates of geologic processes that are shaping the earth's crust, the scale of magmatic and volcanic activity in the past, for example, as preserved in the geologic record, defies any but a catastrophic explanation. Huge catastrophic outpourings of thick basalt lava flows on a continental scale, known as flood basalts, have no known counterpart in recent or present earth history. Nor do we have evidence among present-day geologic processes of the almost simultaneous generation and intrusion of hundreds of granite plutons to form batholiths, on the scale of the Coastal batholith of South America, the Sierra Nevada batholith and Pensinsular Ranges batholith from central California to Mexico, or the numerous granite batholiths of southeastern Australia. Furthermore, thermal runaway subduction is not

---

3   D. A. Pretorius, 1977, *The Strategy of Mineral Exploration in Southern Africa*, vol. 1, Earth Resources Foundation, The University of Sydney, 4.

4   B. F. Strong, ed., 1976, *Metallogeny and Plate Tectonics*, Geological Association of Canada Special Paper No. 14; F. J. Sawkins, 1984, *Metal Deposits in Relation to Plate Tectonics*, Berlin: Springer-Verlag; R. Kerrich, R. J. Goldfarb and J. P. Richards, 2005, Metallogenic provinces in an evolving geodynamic framework, in *Economic Geology: 100th Anniversary Volume*, J. W. Hedenquist, J. F. H. Thompson, R. J. Goldfarb and J. P. Richards, eds., Littleton, CO: Society of Economic Geologists, 1097-1136.

5   S. A. Austin, J. R. Baumgardner, D. R. Humphreys, A. A. Snelling, L. Vardiman and K. P. Wise, 1994, Catastrophic plate tectonics: A global Flood model of earth history, in *Proceedings of the Third International Conference on Creationism*, R. E. Walsh, ed., Pittsburgh, PA: Creation Science Fellowship, 609-621.

now occurring, nor the accumulation of whole crustal slabs at the core-mantle boundary.[6] But where conventional plate tectonics cannot account for these and other major earth features and processes at uniformitarian rates, catastrophic plate tectonics can explain them at catastrophic rates and global scales, particularly within the year-long Genesis Flood event. Furthermore, objections to the catastrophic plate tectonics model for earth history within the biblical timescale, based on the claimed rates of granite magma generation, intrusion, and cooling, and the formation of regional metamorphic complexes, have been more than adequately answered here previously. Thus, the catastrophic plate tectonics model, and the catastrophic sedimentation, volcanism, magmatism, metamorphism, and ore-depositing hydrothermal fluid flows, can explain the catastrophic formation of ore and mineral deposits.

The study of ore deposits and how they form is a major branch of geology known as *economic geology*, and there is a voluminous extant literature available that documents more than a century of research into how the various styles and classes of ore deposits have formed.[7] Because conventional plate tectonics provides the framework in which models for the formation of ore deposits are understood, it is thus logical and justifiable to use the same ore deposit formation models, but applied at catastrophic rates within the catastrophic plate tectonics model and the biblical timescale and framework. Thus, for example, the formation of magmatic nickel and copper sulfide deposits[8] associated with vast outpourings of basaltic lavas (including flood basalts), due to mantle plumes, and platinum group element and chromium deposits associated with the intrusion of enormous

6   J. R. Baumgardner, 1986, Numerical simulation of the large-scale tectonic changes accompanying the Flood, in *Proceedings of the First International Conference on Creationism*, vol. 2, R. E. Walsh, C. L. Brooks and R. S. Crowell, eds., Pittsburgh, PA: Creation Science Fellowship, 17-28; J. R. Baumgardner, 1990, 3-D finite element simulation of the global tectonic changes accompanying Noah's Flood, in *Proceedings of the Second International Conference on Creationism*, vol. 2, R. E. Walsh and C. E. Brooks, eds., Pittsburgh, PA: Creation Science Fellowship. 35-45; J. R. Baumgardner, 1994, Computer modeling of the large-scale tectonics associated with the Genesis Flood, in *Proceedings of the Third International Conference on Creationism*, R. E. Walsh, ed., Pittsburgh, PA: Creation Science Fellowship, 49-62; J. R. Baumgardner, 1994, Runaway subduction as the driving mechanism for the Genesis Flood, in *Proceedings of the Third International Conference on Creationism*, R. E. Walsh, ed., Pittsburgh, PA: Creation Science Fellowship, 63-75; J. R. Baumgardner, 2003, Catastrophic plate tectonics: The physics behind the Flood, in *Proceedings of the Fifth International Conference on Creationism*, R. L. Ivey, Jr., ed., Pittsburgh, PA: Creation Science Fellowship, 113-126.

7   R. G. Roberts and P.A. Sheahan, eds., 1988, *Ore Deposit Models*, Geoscience Canada Reprint Series 3, The Geological Association of Canada; P. A. Sheahan and M. E. Cherry, eds., 1993, *Ore Deposit Models: Volume II*, Geoscience Canada Reprint Series 6, The Geological Association of Canada; R. V. Kirkham, W. B. Sinclair, R. I. Thorpe and A. M. Duke, eds., 1993, *Mineral Deposit Modeling*, Geological Association of Canada Special Paper 40; H. L. Barnes, ed., 1997, *Geochemistry of Hydrothermal Ore Deposits*, third edition, New York: John Wiley and Sons; J. W. Hedenquist, J. F. H. Thompson, R. J. Goldfarb, and J. P. Richards, eds., 2005, *Economic Geology: 100th Anniversary Volume*, Littleton, CO: Society of Economic Geologists.

8   N. T. Arndt, C. M. Lesher and G. K. Czamanske, 2005, Mantle-derived magmas and magmatic Ni-Cu-(PGE) deposits, in Hedenquist et al, eds., 5-23; S.-J. Barnes and P. C. Lightfoot, 2005, Formation of magmatic nickel sulfide deposits and processes affecting their copper and platinum group element contents, in Hedenquist et al, 179-213.

mafic and ultramafic magma bodies[9] are more easily conceivable and explained at catastrophic rates of mantle flow and heat generation to melt the required enormous quantities of the upper mantle as a result of catastrophic plate tectonics during the Genesis Flood. Perhaps these processes even occurred also during an earlier phase, during the middle of the Creation Week for those same ore deposits that formed earlier in earth history.

Similarly, the large porphyry copper (-molybdenum-gold) deposits associated with granitic plutons[10] can be better explained by the rapid generation and emplacement of these granitic plutons in belts of batholiths around the globe within the context of catastrophic plate tectonics, because such pluton emplacement and porphyry ore processes are not now currently operating over the timescales of conventional plate tectonics.[11] The heat rapidly dissipated from granite intrusions into their host wall-rocks, along with the convective outflows of hydrothermal fluids along fractures within the granites and in the surrounding host wall-rocks, resulted in a wide variety of skarn and other granite-related ore deposits.[12] The submarine hydrothermal systems on the present ocean floor that are slowly generating massive sulfide ore deposits in volcanic and related sediments[13] are miniscule in size compared with the many volcanic massive sulfide deposits found in the geologic record all around the globe, where they were generated by huge hydrothermal systems associated with catastrophic volcanic activity initiated by plate rifting or

9　　A. J. MacDonald, 1988, The platinum group element deposits: Classification and genesis, in Roberts and Sheahan, eds., 117-131; J. M. Duke, 1988, Magmatic segregation deposits of chromite, in Roberts and Sheahan, 133-143; A. J. Naldrett, 1993, Models for the formation of strata-bound concentrations of platinum group elements in layered intrusions, in Kirkham et al, 373-387; R. G. Cawthorne, S. J. Barnes, C. Ballhaus and K. N. Malitch, 2005, Platinum group element, chromium and vanadium deposits in mafic and ultramafic rocks, in Hedenquist et al, 215-249.

10　　W. J. McMillan and A. Panteleyev, 1988, Porphyry copper deposits, in Roberts and Sheahan, eds., 45-58; S. R. Titley, 1993, Characteristics of porphyry copper occurrence in the American Southwest, in Kirkham et al, 433-464; S. H. Sillitoe, 1993, Gold-rich porphyry copper deposits: Geological model and exploration implications, in Kirkham et al, eds., 465-478; R. B. Carten, W. H. White and H. J. Stein, 1993, High-grade granite-related molybdenum systems: Classification and origin, in Kirkham et al, 521-554; V. A. Candela and P. M. Piccoli, 2005, Magmatic processes in the development of porphyry-type ore systems, in Hedenquist et al, 25-37; M. T. Einaudi, L. Zurcher, W. J. A. Stavast, D. A. Johnson and M. D. Barton, 2005, Porphyry copper deposits: Characteristics and origin of the hypogene features, in Hedenquist et al, 251-298.

11　　A. A. Snelling, 2006, Catastrophic granite formation: rapid melting of sedimentary and metamorphic rocks and rapid magma intrusion and cooling, in *Yosemite/Death Valley Guidebook*, Santee, CA: Institute for Creation Research, 17-28; A. A. Snelling, 2008, Catastrophic granite formation: Rapid melting of source rocks, and rapid magma intrusion and cooling, *Answers Research Journal*, 1: 11-25.

12　　B. F. Strong, 1988, A model for granophile mineral deposits, in Roberts and Sheahan, 59-66; P. Cerny, 1993, Rare-element granitic pegmatites, Part I: Anatomy and internal evolution of pegmatite deposits, and Part II: Regional to global environments and petrogenesis, in Sheahan and Cherry, 29-47 and 49-62; L. D. Meinert, 1993, Skarns and skarn deposits, in Sheahan and Cherry, 117-134; L. D. Meinert, 1993, Igneous petrogenesis and skarn deposits, in Kirkham et al, 569-583; L. D. Meinert, G. M. Dipple and S. Nicolescu, 2005, World skarn deposits, in Hedenquist et al, 299-336; P. Cerny, P. L. Bleven, M. Cuney and D. London, 2005, Granite-related ore deposits, in Hedenquist et al, 337-370.

13　　S. D. Scott, 1997, Submarine hydrothermal systems in deposits, in Barnes, ed., 797-875; M. D. Hannington, C. E. J. de Ronde and S. Petersen, 2005, Sea-floor tectonics and submarine hydrothermal systems, in Hedenquist et al, 111-141.

plate subduction in island-arc environments.[14]

Hydrothermal systems and fluid flows have been responsible for many other classes of ore deposits, either directly or remotely related to magmatic or volcanic activity. These deposits include: iron-oxide copper-gold deposits, primarily in large-scale granitic breccias; [15] gold and other metal deposits in veins generated as a result of deformation of sediments and in metamorphic terrains, where the gold and metals have been scavenged from various deep crustal sources during tectonics and associated metamorphism; and related gold deposits, where hydrothermal fluids have flowed from fractures to disseminate the gold and metals into conducive sedimentary units.[16] In every one of these ore deposit types, the hydrothermal systems involved in forming these ore deposits operated on a much larger scale than comparable geothermal systems today, so these deposits are more conceivably explained under catastrophic deformation, metamorphism, and hydrothermal fluid activity associated with magmatism and volcanism during catastrophic plate tectonics episodes.

Given that many of these lode and vein deposits occur in some of the earth's most ancient rocks, that clearly formed early in earth history, these would be attributable to the earlier catastrophic episode that occurred in the middle of the Creation Week, particularly when the dry land was formed on Day Three. These would have been among the metal and mineral deposits mentioned in the Scriptures as being utilized by the people in the pre-Flood world.

Many ore and mineral deposits are an intrinsic part of sedimentary strata sequences, and therefore accumulated during sedimentation, or sometimes after sedimentation, with the passage of hydrothermal and/or pore fluids transporting the metals into the sedimentary strata and depositing them where conducive geochemical conditions prevailed. The volcanogenic massive sulfide deposits are also related to simultaneous sedimentation, the sulfide minerals being deposited

---

14   J. W. Lydon, 1988, Volcanogenic massive sulphide deposits, Part 1: A descriptive model, and Part 2: Genetic models, in Roberts and Sheahan, 145-153 and 155-181; J. M. Franklin, 1993, Volcanic-associated massive sulphide deposits, in Kirkham et al, 315-334; J. M. Franklin, H. L. Gibson, I. R. Jonasson and A. G. Galley, 2005, Volcanogenic massive sulfide deposits, in Hedenquist et al, 523-560.

15   N. Oreskes and M.W. Hitzman, 1993, A model for the origin of Olympic Dam-type deposits, in Kirkham et al, 615-633; P. J. Williams, M. D. Barton, D. A. Johnson, L. Fontboté, A. deHaller, G. Mark, N. H. S. Oliver and R. Marschik, 2005, Iron oxide copper-gold deposits: Geology, space-time distribution and possible modes of origin, in Hedenquist et al, 371-405.

16   R. G. Roberts, 1988, Archean lode gold deposits, in Roberts and Sheahan, 1-19; A. Panteleyev, 1988, A Canadian cordilleran model for epithermal gold-silver deposits, in Roberts and Sheahan, 31-43; S. B. Romberger, 1993, A model for Bonanza gold deposits, in Sheahan and Cherry, 77-86; R. H. Sillitoe, 1993, Epithermal models: Genetic types, geometrical controls and shallow features, in Kirkham et al, 403-417; C. J. Hodgson, 1993, Mesothermal lode-gold deposits, in Kirkham et al, 635-678; S. F. Cox, 2005, Coupling between deformation, fluid pressures, and fluid flow in ore-producing hydrothermal systems at depth in the crust, in Hedenquist et al, 39-75; R. J. Goldfarb, E. Baker, B. Dubé, D. I. Groves, C. A. R. Hart and T. Gosselin, 2005, Distribution character, and genesis of gold deposits in metamorphic terranes, in Hedenquist et al, 407-450; S. F. Simmons, N. C. White and B. A. John, 2005, Geological characteristics of epithermal precious and base metal deposits, in Hedenquist et al, 485-522.

with volcanic units as sedimentation occurs adjacent to volcanic activity and associated hydrothermal systems.

Another enigmatic class of ore deposits is the iron ore deposits hosted by banded-iron formations.[17] These banded-iron formations only occur in a very restricted strata level early in the geologic record, only when conditions were obviously conducive for their deposition. It has now been recognized that at least some of these banded-iron formations are associated with vast outpourings of basalts and other volcanic rocks on a catastrophic regional scale. This volcanic activity delivered the enormous quantities of iron and silica to the ocean waters that couldn't hold these in solution and thus rapidly deposited them.[18] Being early in the geologic record, these banded-iron formations represent unique catastrophic conditions early in the earth's history associated with the geologic upheavals in the middle of the Creation Week. Subsequent geologic processes, such as fluid flow through these banded-iron formations, have concentrated a richer iron content to form the economic iron deposits that are today mined on a large scale.

The final classes of major ore deposits are the sediment-hosted and stratiform lead-zinc deposits,[19] the sediment-hosted and stratiform copper deposits,[20] the sediment-hosted and sedimentary basin-related uranium deposits,[21] and the limestone-hosted (Mississippi Valley-type) lead-zinc deposits.[22] These sediment-hosted ore deposits are believed to have been formed in one of two ways.

17   G. A. Gross, 1993, Industrial and genetic models for iron ore in iron-formations, in Kirkham et al, 151-170; J. M. F. Clout and B. M. Simonson, 2005, Precambrian iron formations and iron formation-hosted iron ore deposits, in Hedenquist et al, 643-679.

18   M. E. Barley, A. L. Pickard and P. J. Sylvester, 1997, Emplacement of a large igneous province as a possible cause of banded iron formation 2.45 billion years ago, *Nature*, 385: 55-58; T. S. Blake, R. Buick, S. J. A. Brown, and M. E. Barley, 2004, Geochronology of a late Archaean flood basalt province in the Pilbara Craton, Australia: Constraints on basin evolution, volcanic and sedimentary accumulation, and continental drift rates, *Precambrian Research*, 113: 143-173.

19   J. M. Morganti, 1988, Sedimentary-type stratiform ore deposits: Some models and a new classification, in Roberts and Sheahan, 67-78; W. D. Goodfellow, J. W. Lydon and R. J. W. Turner, 1993, Geology and genesis of stratiform sediment-hosted (SEDEX) zinc-lead-silver sulphide deposits, in Kirkham et al, 201-251; J. M. Parr and I. R. Plimer, 1993, Models for Broken Hill-type lead-zinc-silver deposits, in Kirkham et al, 253-288; D. L. Leach, D. F. Sangster, K. D. Kelley, R. R. Large, G. Garven, C. R. Allen, J. Gutzmer and S. Walters, 2005, Sediment-hosted lead-zinc deposits: A global perspective, in Hedenquist et al, 561-607.

20   R. W. Boyle, A. C. Brown, C. W. Jefferson, E. C. Jowett and R. V. Kirkham, eds., 1989, *Sediment-hosted Stratiform Copper Deposits*, Geological Association of Canada Special Paper 36; A. C. Brown, Sediment-hosted stratiform copper deposits, in Sheahan and Cherry, 1993, 99-115; M. Hitzman, R. Kirkham, D. Broughton, J. Thorson and D. Selley, 2005, The sediment-hosted stratiform copper ore system, in Hedenquist et al, 609-642.

21   J. E. Tilsley, 1988, Genetic considerations relating to some uranium ore, in Roberts and Sheahan, 91-102; S. Marmont, 1988, Unconformity-type uranium deposits, in Roberts and Sheahan, 103-115; V. Ruzicka, 1993, Unconformity-type uranium deposits, in Kirkham et al, 125-149.

22   G. M. Anderson and R. W. Macqueen, 1988, Mississippi Valley-type lead-zinc deposits, in Roberts and Sheahan, 79-90; D. L. Leach and D. F. Sangster, 1993, Mississippi-valley lead-zinc deposits, in Kirkham et al, 289-314; L. M. Cathles III and J. J. Adams, 2005, Fluid flow and petroleum and mineral resources in the upper (<28-km) continental crust, in Hedenquist et al, 77-110.

Metal-laden hydrothermal fluids were expelled through faults adjacent to where sedimentation was occurring, so the metals precipitated as the hydrothermal fluids mixed with the ocean waters that carried the sediments. Thus, the metals and sediments were deposited together. Alternately, after sedimentation had occurred, the ground waters trapped in the sediments were heated by burial, and perhaps even added to by hydrothermal fluids ascending along faults. In this way, large fluid flow cells developed in the sedimentary basins, scavenging metals from disseminated sources in the sediment piles, and then precipitating them where there were suitable, conducive, geochemical and structural traps to produce metal accumulations that became economic ore deposits.[23]

Depending on where in the rock record these ore deposits occur would determine whether they had been formed during the catastrophic sedimentation, magmatism, volcanism, tectonics, and fluid flows during the early-middle part of the Creation Week, or during the subsequent global Genesis Flood. Whereas in uniformitarian thinking the sedimentation, volcanism, fluid flow, and ore deposition processes were slow and gradual over millions of years, there are no known analogs in the present world on the same scale as the sedimentation and fluid flows that generated the ore deposits found in the geologic record. On the other hand, the global-scale catastrophic conditions that prevailed during the early part of the Creation Week, and during the year-long Genesis Flood, would have provided the ideal heat conditions under which these and many other ore deposits formed.

Two other types of ore deposits accumulated directly as a result of sedimentation, albeit catastrophically on a scale that is not now seen. These include the world's largest gold deposit, the gold and uranium in the conglomerate beds of the Witwatersrand Basin of South Africa, about which it has been argued also that it had its metal content upgraded by subsequent hydrothermal activity.[24] There are also similar placer or detrital deposits of numerous metals and minerals.[25] Many of these placer deposits were formed as the Flood waters catastrophically retreated, eroding and concentrating metal-bearing minerals and gems in beach sands and deltaic sediments. Of course, erosion also exposed earlier-formed metal-bearing

23 G. Garven and J. P. Raffensperger, 1997, Hydrogeology and geochemistry of ore genesis in sedimentary basins, in Barnes, 125-189; P. Landais and A. P. Gize, 1997, Organic matter in hydrothermal ore deposits, in Barnes, 613-655; L. M. Cathles III and J. J. Adams, 2005; R. R. Large, S. W. Bull, P. J. McGoldrick, S. Walters, G. M. Derrick and G. R. Carr, 2005, Stratiform and strata-bound Zn-Pb-Ag deposits in Proterozoic sedimentary basins, northern Australia, in Hedenquist et al, 931-963; D. Selley, B. Broughton, R. Scott, M. Hitzman, S. W. Bull, R. R. Large, P. J. McColdrick, M. Roaker, N. Pollington and F. Barra, 2005, A new look at the geology of Zambian Copperbelt in Hedenquist et al, 965-1000; D. L. Huston, B. Stevens, P. N. Southgate, P. Muhling and L. Wyborn, 2006, Australian Zn-Pb-Ag ore-forming systems: A review and analysis, *Economic Geology*, 101: 1117-1157.

24 S. M. Roscoe and W.L. Minter, 1993, Pyritic Paleoplacer gold and uranium deposits, in Kirkham et al, 103-124; H. E. Frimmel, D. I. Groves, D. Kirk, J. Ruiz, J. Chesley and W. E. L. Minter, 2005, The formation and preservation of the Witwatersrand gold fields, the world's largest gold province, in Hedenquist et al, 769-797; J. D. M. Law and G. N. Phillips, 2005, Hydrothermal replacement model for Witwatersrand gold, in Hedenquist et al, 799-811;.

25 R. H. T. Garnett and N. C. Bassett, 2005, Placer deposits, in Hedenquist et al, 813-843.

rocks and ore deposits to weathering and groundwater enrichment processes of the earth's surface, such processes being severer than today during the drying-out phase of the early post-Flood era.[26]

The only more detailed treatment of the formation of ore deposits within the biblical framework and timescale of earth history is that of the Mt. Isa orebodies in northern Australia.[27] Predictably, this catastrophic model for the formation of these massive lead-zinc orebodies was criticized by a uniformitarian detractor.[28] His objections to the catastrophic model were primarily due to his uniformitarian bias not being able to condone the extrapolation of geologic processes to catastrophic rates and volumes that clearly would have been the norm during the global upheavals of the early-middle part of the Creation Week and the year-long Genesis Flood, when the earth's crust was formed and totally reshaped respectively. However, ongoing research in the last two decades has, if anything, strengthened the case for the catastrophic formation of these massive lead-zinc orebodies.

Enormous outpourings of basalts and other volcanic rocks occurred prior to deposition of the sediments that host the orebodies, which together would have to have been catastrophic. The metals were then scavenged by the waters trapped in the sediments, that were heated up by the deep burial, to produce basin-wide fluid flows through faults and within the sediments which deposited the metals with the sediments in conducive geochemical traps (such as organic matter dispersed in the sediments), that rapidly concentrated the metals into the orebodies.[29] Significantly, present modeling of the processes of formation of these orebodies regard the necessary metal-bearing fluid-flow event to occupy an extremely narrow timeframe, virtually an instant in conventional geologic time, which is consistent with the uniform identical lead isotopic homogeneity throughout these massive orebodies over a total lateral distance of some 35 km,[30] an extraordinary

26   N. N. Gow and G. P. Lozeg, Bauxite, 1993, in Sheahan and Cherry, 135-142; Ph. Freyssinet, C. R. M. Butt, R. C. Morris and P. Piantone, 2005, Ore-forming processes related to lateritic weathering, in Hedenquist et al, 681-722; R. H. Sillitoe, 2005, Supergene oxidized and enriched porphyry copper and related deposits, in Hedenquist et al, 723-768.

27   A. A. Snelling, 1984, The recent, rapid formation of the Mt Isa ore bodies during Noah's Flood, *Ex Nihilo*, 6(3): 40-46.

28   Strahler, 1987, 242-243.

29   P. N. Southgate, T. K. Kyser, D. L. Scott, R. R. Large, S. D. Golding and P. A. Polito, 2006, A basin system and fluid-flow analysis of the Zn-Pb-Ag Mt Isa-type deposits of northern Australia: Identifying metal source, basinal brine reservoirs, times of fluid expulsion, and organic matter reactions, *Economic Geology*, 101(6): 1103-1115; P. A. Polito, T. K. Kyser, P. N. Southgate and M. J. Jackson, 2006, Sandstone diagenesis in the Mount Isa basin, an isotopic and fluid inclusion perspective in relationship to district-wide Zn, Pb, and Cu mineralization, *Economic Geology*, 101(6): 1159-1168; M. Glikson, S. D. Golding and P. N. Southgate, 2006, Thermal evolution of the ore-hosting Isa Superbasin, central and northern Lawn Hill platform, *Economic Geology*, 101(6): 1211-1229; J. Yang, R. R. Large, S. W. Bull and D. L. Scott, 2006, Basin-scale numerical modeling to test the role of buoyancy-driven fluid flow and heat transfer in the formation of stratiform Zn-Pb-Ag deposits in the northern Mt Isa basin, *Economic Geology*, 101(6): 1275-1292.

30   J. J. Richards, 1975, Lead isotope data on three north Australian galena localities, *Mineralium Deposita*, 10: 287-301.

circumstance if the lead in these orebodies had not been derived and deposited catastrophically.

The feasibility of the catastrophic formation of ore deposits is highlighted by the fact that, even in conventional geology, diamond deposits are said to have formed explosively and catastrophically.[31] Formed 200-400 km (125-250 miles) down in the earth's mantle, diamonds are brought to the earth's surface in gas-rich kimberlite and lamproite magmas that explosively rise through fractures to erupt at the earth's surface, leaving behind pipe-like bodies containing the diamonds. The rate at which these magmas explosively ascend from the mantle through the crust has been determined as around 4 meters per second, or between 10 and 30 km (6-19 miles) per hour.[32] Such a rapid ascent rate is crucial to the survival of the diamonds carried by these magmas because a slower ascent rate would result in the diamonds turning to graphite. At this ascent rate, it therefore only takes between 12 and 30 hours for the diamond-carrying magmas to travel from the source areas of the diamonds in the mantle up to erupt at the earth's surface. It is worth noting that even though the diamonds themselves yield old radioisotope "ages," dating them back to the early stages of earth history, the formation of the diamond deposits in the kimberlite and lamproite pipes at the earth's surface occurred much later in the earth's history, primarily late in the Flood event, and even early in the post-Flood era.[33]

In conclusion, therefore, it is staunchly maintained that catastrophic geological processes of erosion, sedimentation, magmatism, volcanism, hydrothermal fluid flows, and tectonics during the early-middle part of the Creation Week, and again during the year-long Genesis Flood, can more than adequately account for the formation of ore and mineral deposits during the biblical timescale for earth history.

31 R. H. Mitchell, 1993, Kimberlites and lamproites: Primary sources of diamond, in Sheahan and Cherry, eds., 13-28; A. A. Snelling, 1994, Diamonds: Evidence of explosive geological processes, *Creation Ex Nihilo*, 16(1): 42-45; J. J. Gurney, H. H. Helmstaedt, A. P. LeRoex, T. E. Nowicki, S. H. Richardson and K. J. Westerlund, 2005, Diamonds: Crustal distribution and formation processes in time and space and an integrated deposit model, in Hedenquist et al, 143-177.

32 E. H. Eggler, 1989, Kimberlites: How do they form? in *Kimberlites and Related Rocks*, J. Ross, A. L. Jacques, J. Ferguson, D. H. Green, S. Y. O'Reilly, R. V. Danchin and A. J. A. Janse, eds., Geological Society of Australia Special Publication No. 14 and Blackwell Scientific Publications Australia, vol. 1:. 489-504; S. P. Kelley and J.-A. Wartho, 2000, Rapid kimberlite ascent and significance of Ar-Ar ages in xenolith phlogopites, *Science*, 289, 609-611.

33 L. Hissink, 1993, Euhemerism and aboriginal myths, *The Australian Geologist*, 86: 6-7.

126

Earlier Ice Ages

As discussed in detail earlier (chapters 96-97), there is impeccable evidence for an Ice Age that affected the earth's surface after the Genesis Flood.[1] The Antarctic and Greenland ice sheets, and the many alpine glaciers, are today's remnants of that event. This so-called Pleistocene Ice Age produced distinctive landscape features and sedimentary deposits, such as *tillites* (angular pebbles and boulders cemented together in a large volume matrix of rock "flour"), and varves or *rhythmites* (very thinly bedded laminae of alternating mud and silt).

In their zeal to use uniformitarian dogma to interpret the formation of ancient sedimentary strata on the basis of present-day geological processes, sedimentary environments, and the sedimentary strata they produce, conventional geologists claim that there are ancient sedimentary strata identical to tillites and varves that, therefore, must have been deposited during ancient glaciations. Consequently, it has been claimed that in the past geologic "ages," the earth has experienced numerous ice ages, during which ice sheets covered large portions of the globe.[2] Thus, it is claimed that there were ice ages in the late Archean (the Huronian in Canada and elsewhere), the early Proterozoic, the late Proterozoic (now known as the Neoproterozoic), the late Ordovician-early Silurian, perhaps the late Devonian and early Carboniferous, but certainly in the late Carboniferous-Permian, and then possibly in the Eocene. Of these, the ice ages for which there is the most claimed evidence of a global nature are those in the late Archean, Neoproterozoic, and the late Carboniferous-Permian. The evidence not only includes claimed tillites and varves, but also striated bedrock where the boulders being carried at the base of ice sheets are supposed to have scratched the bedrock surfaces, leaving behind striations or grooves. Obviously, ancient ice ages, involving slow and gradual development of ice sheets and deposition of glacial sediments over millions of years, are incompatible with both the biblical timescale of earth history

---

1   M. J. Oard, 1990, *An Ice Age Cause by the Genesis Flood*, El Cajon, CA: Institute for Creation Research.

2   J. C. Crowell, 1983, Ice ages recorded on Gondwanan continents, *Transactions of the Geological Society of South Africa*, 86, 238-261; N. Eyles, 1993, Earth's glacial record and its tectonic setting, *Earth-Science Reviews*, 35: 1-248.

and the year-long Genesis Flood.[3] A full and adequate response to these claims of ancient ice ages from a young earth, global Flood perspective has already been published.[4]

It is, in fact, abundantly clear that the claimed evidence for these ancient ice ages is equivocal at best, because there is no way of proving the supposed tillites, varves, and striated bedrock were in fact due to glacial deposition and the passage of ice sheets respectively. As has been pointed out: "Identifying ancient glaciations is not easy."[5] The reality is that most, if not all, of the purported evidence for these ancient ice ages can be easily confused with, and interpreted as, the result of non-glacial sedimentation and activity. Perhaps the most crucial evidence, historically, for these ancient ice ages was the claimed tillites, which should have only ever been identified as diamictites, the general term for a non-sorted, or poorly-sorted at best, sedimentary rock containing all different grain sizes mixed up, particularly angular boulders and pebbles in a voluminous fine-grained matrix. The origin of these so-called tillites has long been challenged, being adequately demonstrated to represent the results of massive debris flows and related deposits, especially adjacent to tectonically active areas.[6] Geologists have slowly come to realize that massive debris flows can produce deposits that are indistinguishable from these ancient ice age diamictites.[7] One of the many important relevant properties of debris flows is the ability to transport surprisingly large boulders in laminar or non-turbulent flow.[8] Consequently, most of these so-called "tillites" are now recognized as containing abundant mass movement deposits,[9] but this has not curtailed the claims of them being associated with ancient ice ages. Indeed, it is now recognized that these diamictites can form in many non-glacial ways.

> Diamictites and conglomerates are dominantly the product of subaqueous mass flow and mixing of coarse and fine sediment populations (the term *mixtite* has been used in the past). These facies are not uniquely glacial and are produced regardless of climate and latitude.[10]

---

3   Strahler, 1987, 263-273.

4   M. J. Oard, 1997, *Ancient Ice Ages or Gigantic Submarine Landslides?*, Creation Research Society Monograph Series No. 6.

5   R. P. Sharp, 1988, *Living Ice: Understanding Glaciers and Glaciation*, Cambridge and New York: Cambridge University Press.

6   L. J. G. Schermerhorn, 1974, Late Precambrian mixtites: Glacial and/or non-glacial?, *American Journal of Science*, 74: 673-824; M. R. Rampino, 1993, Ancient "glacial" deposits are ejecta of large impacts: The Ice Age paradox explained, *EOS, Transactions of the American Geophysical Union*, 74(43): 99.

7   J. B. Anderson, E. D. Kurtz and F. M. Weaver, 1979, Sedimentation on the Antarctic continental slope, in *Geology of Continental Slopes*, L. J. Doyle and O. H. Pilkey, eds., Tulsa, OK: Society of Economic Paleontologists and Mineralogists Special Publication No. 27, 265-283.

8   T. Takahashi, 1981, Debris flow, *Annual Review of Fluid Mechanics*, 13: 57-77.

9   J. N. J. Visser, 1983, The problem of recognizing ancient subaqueous debris flow deposits in glacial sequences, *Transactions of the Geological Society of South Africa*, 86: 127-135.

10   N. Eyles and N. Januszczak, 2004, "Zipper-rift": A tectonic model for Neoproterozoic glaciations during

It is therefore acknowledged that most diamictites are generated by mass flows (debris flows) on unstable slopes in tectonically active areas, such as in rift basins and subduction zones, on continental slopes, and on the margins of volcanoes and reefs.[11]

Nevertheless, these diamictites are still regarded as being indicative of ancient ice ages, even though such massive debris flow deposits are known to be relatively minor compared to the sedimentary deposits produced in the Pleistocene (post-Flood) Ice Age and associated with ice sheets today. It is because these ancient diamictites are claimed to have special features that are diagnostic of an ice age origin. The first of these are linear scratches or small grooves called striations on some of the boulders or pebbles in these diamictites, especially where the striations are on a flattened or faceted surface of the pebbles and boulders. However, striated pebbles and boulders have also been found in many conglomerates and debris flows, and even silt and fine sand grains can scratch such clasts, even in mudflows.[12] Indeed, any moving medium can potentially striate pebbles and boulders: "... nonglacial sedimentary and tectonic processes can produce pseudoglacial striated and faceted clasts."[13] Furthermore, "mass movement of material has long been known as an effective process of striating rock."[14] Indeed, uniform, massive debris flows are known to contain faceted clasts, the facets or flattened surfaces being caused by fracturing along joints, or bedding and metamorphic foliation surfaces.[15] Thus, when a claimed late Precambrian glacial diamictite in Namibia was re-examined, it was concluded that the striated and faceted clasts were only pseudofaceted, and the very rare random striations or scratches could have been received on the clasts when exposed at the present-day surface, so it was realized there was no evidence that this diamictite was of glacial origin.[16]

It has to be concluded, therefore, that striated and faceted rocks in a diamictite are not diagnostic of ancient glaciation, no matter whether the striations are parallel, random or crossing in organized sets, because all such features can be produced

the breakup of Rodinia after 750 Ma, *Earth-Science Reviews*, 65: 1-73 (p. 1).

11   G. Einsele, 2000, *Sedimentary Basins: Evolution, Facies, and Sediment Budget*, Berlin: Spring-Verlag.

12   E. L. Winterer and C.C. Von Der Borch, 1968, Striated pebbles in a mud flow deposit, South Australia, *Palaeogeography, Palaeoclimatology, Palaeoecology*, 5: 205-211; D. H. Malone, 1995, Very large debris-avalanche deposit within the Eocene volcanic succession of the northeastern Absaroka Range, Wyoming, *Geology*, 23: 661-664.

13   L. J. G. Schermerhorn, 1975, Tectonic framework of Late Precambrian supposed glacials, in *Ice Ages: Ancient and Modern*, A. E. Wright and F. Moseley, eds., Liverpool, UK: Seel House Press, 241-274 (p. 253).

14   S. Judson and R. E. Barks, 1961, Microstriations on polished pebbles, *American Journal of Science*, 259: 371-381 (p. 377).

15   S. K. Acharyya, 1975, Tectonic framework of sedimentation of the eastern Himalayas, India, in *Gondwana Geology*, K. S. W. Campbell, ed., Canberra, Australia: Australian National University Press: 663-674.

16   H. Martin, H. Porada and O. H. Walliser, 1985, Mixtite deposits of the Damara Sequence, Namibia: Problems of interpretation, *Palaeogeography, Palaeoclimatology, Palaeoecology*, 51: 159-196.

in massive debris flows and other non-glacial processes. Even though there have been claims that microtextural features on the surfaces of matrix grains, such as chattermarks, crescent-shaped shallow cracks perpendicular to the presumed motion of the abrasion of the grain's surface, exhaustive studies have concluded that the origin of such features is not necessarily environmentally controlled,[17] and that there are no unique glacial microtextures on matrix grains.[18]

The second claimed special feature of diamictites that is diagnostic of a glacial origin is striated bedrock surfaces. However, just as non-glacial mechanisms can scratch clasts, research has shown that the mass movements of debris flows, as well as tectonic shearing, can also striate and groove bedrock surfaces, even with two or more sets of crossing striations.[19] A related feature that is claimed to be even more diagnostic of glacial diamictites is boulder pavements, which is where there is a layer of boulders within the diamictite at its lower contact, the boulders being of similar composition but are striated.[20] While these boulder pavements are known in Pleistocene (post-Flood) Ice Age tills, they are especially rare in pre-Pleistocene diamictites. Unfortunately, the mechanism for forming these boulder payments is not understood,[21] which certainly diminishes their significance as a glaciogenic indicator. Indeed, at least five hypotheses have been advanced to explain the formation of these boulder pavements, yet all of them contain serious flaws![22] In any case, in a debris flow the larger clasts are observed to sink to the base of the debris flow to form a boulder pavement or traction carpet, where they are overridden and striated. Thus striated boulder pavements are also hardly a diagnostic feature of glacial diamictites.

The third major supposedly diagnostic feature used by geologists to conventionally

---

17   E. D. Orr and R. L. Folk, 1983, New scents on the chattermark trail: Weathering enhances obscure microfractures, *Journal of Sedimentary Petrology*, 53: 121-129.

18   Eyles, 1993, 82-83.

19   C. F. S. Sharpe, 1938, *Landslides and Related Phenomena—A Study of Mass-Movements of Soil and Rock*, New York, Columbia University Press; J. C. Crowell, 1957, Origin of pebbly mudstones, *Geological Society of America Bulletin*, 68: 993-1010; W. D. Harland, K. N. Herod and D.H. Krinsley, 1966, The definition and identification of tills and tillites, *Earth-Science Reviews*, 2: 225-256; H. J. Harrington, 1971, Glacial-like "striated floor" originated by debris-laden torrential water flows, *American Association of Petroleum Geologists Bulletin*, 55: 1344-1347; M. J. Hambrey and W. B. Harland, eds., 1981, *Earth's Pre-Pleistocene Glacial Record*, London: Cambridge University Press; J. P Petit, 1987, Criteria for the sense of movement on fault surfaces in brittle rocks, *Journal of Structural Geology*, 9: 597-608; D. R. Oberbeck, S. Hörz and T. Bunch, 1994, Impacts, tillites, and the breakup of Gondwanaland: A second reply, *Journal of Geology*, 102: 485-489.

20   S. R. Hicock, 1991, On subglacial stone pavements in till, *Journal of Geology*, 99: 607-619.

21   C. H. Eyles, 1994, Intertidal boulder pavements in the northeastern Gulf of Alaska and their geological significance, *Sedimentary Geology*, 88: 161-173.

22   P. U. Clark, 1991, Striated clast pavements: Products of deforming subglacial sediment?, *Geology*, 19: 530-533; P. U. Clark, 1992, Comments and reply on "Striated clast pavements: Products of deforming subglacial sediment?" reply, *Geology*, 20: 285-286; D. M. Mickelson, N. R. Ham, Jr., and L Ronnert, 1992, Comments and reply on "Striated clast pavements: Products of deforming subglacial sediment?" comment, *Geology*, 20: 285.

identify pre-Pleistocene Ice Age deposits is varves or rhythmites containing *dropstones*. Varves have been discussed previously (chapter 118), where it was shown that similar rhythmite deposits can be laid down by catastrophic flowing density or turbidity currents. Thus, rhythmites that look like varves are most definitely not diagnostic of glacial deposits. Dropstones, which are oversized clasts larger than the thickness of the silt/clay couplets in varves/rhythmites, however, are associated with Pleistocene varve deposits. They are believed to have been dropped from icebergs floating above where the varves were being deposited. Thus most geologists would regard the presence of these dropstones in ancient rhythmites to be instant "proof" of their glacial origin. However, not only can mass flows produce rhythmites that look like varves, but they can also produce "dropstones" that have, in fact, been carried laterally in the flow to be deposited in the rhythmite.[23] Indeed, cobbles and boulders up to 30-40 cm, or even a few meters, in diameter have been observed "floating" in the finer grain sediments above the turbidity current traction carpet.

> Many turbidites appear to contain floating megaclasts...reported examples include the deposits of inferred high-density turbidity currents that contain isolated, floating megaclasts up to a few decimetres or even a few metres in their longest dimension. [24]

In any case, if these large clasts had in fact been dropped into the varves/ rhythmites, the dropped stones should have disrupted the fine laminae and also pierced them. However, the reality is that the dropstones in pre-Pleistocene rhythmites are predominantly small, and are often isolated, compared with those in Pleistocene varves which are large and prolific.[25] Furthermore, very few dropstones pierced the laminations, instead slightly depressing them.[26] Otherwise, simple bending of rhythmite beds around a stone is best explained by compaction after lateral emplacement of the stone, so simple bending of the laminae around a clast is not diagnostic of a dropstone.

Thus, clasts which show either symmetric or basally asymmetric bending

---

23　A. H. Bouma, 1964, Turbidites, in A. H. Bouma and A. Brouwer, eds., *Turbidites*, New York: Elsevier, 247-256; M. J. Hambrey and W. B. Harland, 1979, Analysis of pre-Pleistocene glaciogenic rocks: Aims and problems, in *Moraines and Varves*, Ch. Schlüchter, ed., A.A. Balkema, Rotterdam: 271-275; C. P. Gravenor, V. von Brunn and A. Dreimanis, 1984, Nature and classification of waterlain glaciogenic sediments, exemplified by Pleistocene, late Paleozoic and late Precambrian deposits, *Earth-Science Reviews*, 20: 105-166.

24　E. Postma, W. Nemec and K. L. Kleinspehn, 1988, Large floating clasts in turbidites: A mechanism for their emplacement, *Sedimentary Geology*, 58: 47-61.

25　G. M. Young, 1981, The early Proterozoic Gowganda Formation, Ontario, Canada, in *Earth's Pre-Pleistocene Glacial Record*, M. J. Hambrey, and W. E. Harland, eds., London: Cambridge University Press: 807-812.

26　W. Hamilton and D. Krinsley, 1967, Upper Paleozoic glacial deposits of South Africa and southern Australia, *Geological Society of America Bulletin*, 78: 783-800.

of laminae around them cannot be regarded as diagnostic of drop.[27]

All of these so-called diagnostic features can readily be explained by debris flow deposition.

> An assemblage of arguments or indications separately of little diagnostic value as glacial criteria does not constitute collectively strong evidence for glaciation.[28]

It is the claimed late Precambrian or Neoproterozoic "Ice Age" that has been the subject of much recent discussion, with the claimed strong evidence for it becoming dogma.[29] The Neoproterozoic diamictites and other rocks claimed to be of glacial origin are only found in small areas but all over the world, usually at the bottom of thick sedimentary strata sequences in what were large sedimentary basins.[30] However, this postulated Neoproterozoic "snowball earth," as it is called, presents several vexing geological problems.

> ...one of the major enigmas in contemporary Earth science, raising questions concerning the nature of the geomagnetic field, climatic zonation, and the Earth's rotational parameters in late Proterozoic time.[31]

Whereas it is freely admitted that these Neoproterozoic diamictites are dominantly the product of subaqueous mass flows and are related to nearby turbidites (rhythmites),[32] the enigmas are due to their close association with limestones, dolomites, "evaporites, stromatolites, iron formations and other unique rock types that are indicative of the warm climate and warm seawater at equatorial latitudes, confirmed by low paleomagnetic inclinations."[33] Indeed, much has been made of the "cap carbonates" that sit directly on top of the diamictites, but carbonate beds are also found below and within these diamictites.

Thus this Neoproterozoic Ice Age has been called the "snowball earth" hypothesis,

---

27   G. S. P. Thomas and R. J. Connell, 1985, Iceberg drop, dump, and grounding structures from Pleistocene glacio-lacustrine sediments, Scotland, *Journal of Sedimentary Petrology*, 55: 243-249.

28   Schermerhorn, 1975, 675.

29   P. F. Hoffman, A. J. Kaufman, G. P. Halverson and D. P. Schrag, 1998, A Neoproterozoic snowball earth, *Science*, 281: 1342-1346; P. F. Hoffman and D. P. Schrag, 2002, The snowball earth hypothesis: Testing the limits of global change, *Terra Nova*, 14: 129-155.

30   Schermerhorn, 1974; Hambrey and Harland, 1981.

31   E. W. Schmidt, G. E. Williams and B. J. J. Embleton, 1991, Low palaeolatitude of late Proterozoic glaciation: Early timing of remanence in haematite of the Elatina Formation, South Australia, *Earth and Planetary Science Letters*, 105: 355-367 (p. 355).

32   Eyles and Januszczak, 2004.

33   L. A. Frakes, 1979, *Climates Throughout Geological Time*, Elsevier, New York; L. J. G. Schermerhorn, 1983, Late Proterozoic glaciation in the light of CO_2 depletion in the atmosphere, *Geological Society of America Memoir*, 161, Boulder, CO: 309-315; M. J. Hambrey, 1992, Secrets of a tropical Ice Age, *New Scientist*, 133(1804): 42-49; Hoffman and Schrag, 2002.

because it is postulated that the ice sheets extended to sea level near the equator, yet it is admitted that this poses a paleoenvironmental conundrum! That model "is based on many longstanding assumptions of the character and origin of the Neoproterozoic glacial record, in particular, 'tillites,' that are no longer valid."[34] Instead, it can be shown that these diamictites and conglomerates produced by mass flows are embedded with large olistostromes containing huge masses of carbonate debris derived from landsliding of fault scarps along rifted carbonate platforms at the time of the break-up of the supercontinent called Rodinia. Indeed, in some reconstructions of that supercontinent these diamictites and associated olistostromes are found to occur around its margins.

One of these submarine landslide deposits is the Kingston Peak Formation in southeastern California, which has been recognized as evidence for the catastrophic initiation of the Genesis Flood,[35] marking the pre-Flood/Flood boundary when the pre-Flood supercontinent (equated with Rodinia) was rifted and broken up by the initiation of the catastrophic plate tectonics of the Flood.[36]

Thus, the evidence for claimed ancient ice ages is consistent with the catastrophic Genesis Flood. The initiation of the Flood resulted in the collapse of the continental shelves surrounding the pre-Flood supercontinent, the debris collapsing in gigantic submarine landslides and debris flows into the deeper ocean basins, where the rising ocean waters sweeping landwards deposited over these diamictites the initial sediments of the cataclysm. This makes sense of all the evidence of the marine environment for these diamictites that have wrongly been interpreted as glacial deposits. Then, as the Flood event progressed, further gigantic debris and mass flows, in response to continuing rifting, catastrophic tectonics, and the earthquakes they generated, deposited diamictites and rhythmites higher in the strata record that also have been wrongly interpreted by uniformitarian geologists as subsequent ancient ice ages.[37] It should, therefore, now be firmly established that the biblical framework and timescale of earth history is both adequate and sufficient to explain and understand the evidence left in the geologic record of the earth's catastrophic past.

34   Eyles and Januszczak: 2004, 1.

35   R. Sigler and C. Van Wingerden, Submarine flow and slide deposits in the Kingston Peak Formation, Kingston Range, Mojave Desert, California: Evidence for catastrophic initiation of Noah's Flood, in *Proceedings of the Fourth International Conference on Creationism*, R. E. Walsh, ed., 1998, Pittsburgh, PA: Creation Science Fellowship, 487-501.

36   S. A. Austin and K. P. Wise, The pre-Flood/Flood boundary: As defined in Grand Canyon, Arizona and eastern Mojave Desert, California, in *Proceedings of the Third International Conference on Creationism*, R. E. Walsh, ed., 1994, Pittsburgh, Pa: Creation Science Fellowship, 37-47; S. A. Austin, J. R. Baumgardner, D. R. Humphreys, A. A. Snelling, L. Vardiman and K. P. Wise, 1994, Catastrophic plate tectonics: A global Flood model of earth history, in *Proceedings of the Third International Conference on Creationism*, R. E. Walsh, ed., Pittsburgh, PA: Creation Science Fellowship, 609-621; C. Van Wingerden, 2003, Initial Flood deposits of the western Northern American Cordillera: California, Utah and Idaho, in *Proceedings of the Fifth International Conference on Creationism*, R. L. Ivey, Jr., ed., Pittsburgh, PA: Creation Science Fellowship, 349-358.

37   Oard, 1997.

CONCLUDING CHALLENGES

Not even a detailed analysis of this size is able to present all the evidence, discuss all the objections, and solve all the difficulties in understanding the catastrophic past of our planet. Deriving a biblical framework and timescale for earth history using a literal reading and understanding of the Scriptures, and then applying that biblical model to the evidence left behind in the earth's rock record constitutes a serious attempt to select the most difficult problems for treatment, while acknowledging that this discussion has been limited by space constraints. Nevertheless, it is still hoped that the discussion of the evidence has shown that it is amenable to a satisfactory explanation in terms of biblical geology.

The Adequacy of the Biblical Framework of Earth History

Conventional geology, though today more accepting of catastrophism in explaining the accumulation of the geologic record, is still ultimately based on a uniformitarian framework for the earth's history. Of course, uniformitarianism requires long ages to enable the conception of the spontaneous generation of life, and the evolution of that life ultimately into today's plants and animals. However, because in most instances conventional geologists still believe present geologic processes operating at today's observed rates can account for the great bulk of the observable features of the earth's constitution and strata record, it has been necessary to show that the application of this uniformitarian belief to explain most of the important geologic phenomena is utterly inadequate. Even many conventional geologists have come to realize that the evidence in the rocks consistently and overwhelmingly indicates that many forms of catastrophism had to be involved in shaping the earth and forming its rock strata. The global evidences of geologic processes that in the past had to have operated violently at continental and global scales, compared to their local, quiet operation today—the rapid deposition of vast beds of sediments, the burial and fossilization of billions of plants and animals, volcanism and magmatism, the formation of coal, oil, and ore deposits, plate tectonics, earth movements, and regional metamorphism— overwhelmingly compel any reasonable observer to conclude that the dominant features of the earth's crust and surface had to be produced and shaped by global catastrophism. When this is recognized, along with the failure of the radioisotope "dating" of rocks to yield consistent "ages" for them, then it can be seen that even the supposed evidences of great geologic age are but the result of seeing them with a uniformitarian bias, when they can be easily reinterpreted to correlate well with the much more compelling evidences consistent with violent, rapid activity and formation.

Therefore, if present geologic processes and their rates of operation today cannot be used to deduce the earth's past history (and this conclusion is convincingly supported not only by the failure of the uniformitarian paradigm, but also by the impregnable laws of thermodynamics that describe without exception the conservation and deterioration of energy), then the only way we can have certain knowledge of the natural geologic processes and events on the earth, prior to the time when human historical records began, is by means of divine revelation. This is why the Bible's record of creation and the Flood immediately becomes absolutely essential to our understanding, not only of the early history of the earth, but also of the purpose and destiny of the universe and of man.

It has, therefore, been the purpose of this book to show how the outline of earth history provided by the early chapters of Genesis, as well as by the related passages from other parts of the Bible, actually provides a scientifically accurate model within which all the verifiable observations of field and experimental data in geology and geophysics fit robustly together remarkably well.

In the New Testament, Peter clearly states that there were two periods of earth history when God directly intervened in the operation of geological and geophysical processes to form and shape the earth and its crust (2 Peter 3:4-6). Thus, it is not only useless to interpret how the earth was formed and was shaped by the operation of geological and geophysical processes operating at today's rates, but also to interpret the appearance of the earth, its strata and formations, as indicating that they had a long geologic history and have a great geologic age. Instead, God's activities in the early part of the Creation Week established and shaped the earth, its foundations, deep crustal structure, and what are now its crystalline basement rocks, all in an unimaginably brief space of time measured in hours and days. Then, during the Flood cataclysm of Noah's day, God unleashed certain geological and geophysical processes that overturned the earth's surface and reshaped it. Thus, we cannot account for most of the earth's sedimentary strata that contain fossils, today's mountains ranges and volcanoes, the ocean basins, and other surface deposits and features, by those forces which are today only operating at a veritable snail's pace. The earth's climates have since returned to some semblance of normality after the upheavals during the Flood that initially resulted in a brief post-Flood Ice Age.

The reader may judge for himself whether the evidence presented here truly warrants this reorientation of our understanding of earth's geology from this biblical worldview. It is my hope, of course, that the evidence will be considered, and that the biblical understanding of earth's history will not simply be rejected because of the supposed authority of the "conventional" geologic community that not only disapproves of applying this biblical worldview to the geologic evidence, but rejects it without analysis.

An Unfinished Task

When Drs. John Whitcomb and Henry Morris teamed up to write their landmark book *The Genesis Flood: The Biblical Record and Its Scientific Implications*, first published in 1961, there were so few professional geologists with advanced degrees in geology, geophysics, and related fields, that they must have felt like lone voices standing for, and declaring, the literal truth of God's Word and its reliability in robustly explaining the earth's history and its geologic record. Nevertheless, the subsequent years have shown that God has honored their stand and used it to convince many Christians and convict many non-Christians that God's Word cannot only be trusted in matters of faith, but also in the details of the earth's history and geology as found in the strata record. The personal testimonies of some of these people, of the way that book challenged them, is now on the public record.[1]

Many of those convicted and convinced are either professional scientists or went on to become professional scientists. Furthermore, they and many others were inspired to take up the challenge to contend for the truth of God's Word and its reliability in understanding the earth's history and explaining the earth's strata record and features. Some chose to do this on a full-time basis, and so Christian organizations were established, staffed by professional scientists to research, write, and speak about this scientific evidence, not only in geology, but also in other fields, that resoundingly support the biblical account of our origins and the earth's history.[2] This book is unashamedly the result of the legacy of these pioneers.

However, it would be foolish to think that the task they inspired has been finished. The ranks of full-time and part-time creation scientists and Flood geologists are still meager and thin, and therefore brittle. Furthermore, the modern scientific enterprise has mushroomed, with veritably millions of professional scientists around the globe working in state-of-the-art laboratories with multi-billion dollar budgets to elucidate the workings of the earth and life on it, grounded in the belief that there was no Creator who instantly brought the earth and life on it into existence, but instead all that was needed was time plus chance! Nearly all the world's universities and places of higher learning are dominated by staff scientists and other intellectuals who teach this philosophy. By comparison, the creationist army, and its research and writing efforts, are but like David taking on Goliath. There are now so many fields of science and subdisciplines that require specialist training for their proponents to master, that for the creationist movement to research and write in all of these fields, to bring the evidences they provide under the scrutiny of God's Word, requires a whole army of scientific and other intellectual professionals with renewed vision and energy, plus a sizable budget, to expand and finish the task these pioneers began and this book expands upon.

Furthermore, the present generation of creation scientists and Flood geologists need to be able to pass on the torch, so that the message of the now mushrooming creation and Flood literature is not lost, but instead is built upon and expanded appropriately. I would therefore unashamedly issue a challenge, particularly to young readers who are at the formative stage of their careers, to heed God's call,

---

1   D. B. Sharp and J. Bergman (compilers), 2008, *Persuaded by the Evidence*, Green Forest, AR: Master Books.

2   H. M. Morris, 1984, *A History of Modern Creationism*, San Diego, CA: Master Books.

and use the intellectual gifts and abilities He has given you, to train in whatever fields of science or intellectual endeavor He may lead you into, so as to join the growing ranks of professional creation scientists and Flood geologists. And I challenge parents, grandparents, and Christians generally, to support our young people to take up the torch, and to dedicate their lives to God's service in every field of scientific and intellectual endeavor from a thoroughly biblical perspective, so that the light of God's Word will shine into every area of human knowledge for His glory.

As a result, Christians will be encouraged in their faith and be able to stand firm in their testimonies, equipped to defend their faith without compromise in any area of science and human endeavor. However, more importantly, the purpose of this task is to remove the stumbling blocks that would hinder people everywhere around the globe from listening and being convicted by the Gospel of our Lord Jesus Christ, so that they too can respond positively and accept the Gospel, and so be restored to fellowship with our Creator.

While this book is as comprehensive as space allows, there are clearly many more aspects of the geological evidences that require further study and research to elucidate them in light of the biblical framework and timescale of earth history. And even those evidences and details that were discussed still require further research so that every detail can be systematized rigorously. Thus, we need in our ranks many more young geologists, geophysicists, and other earth scientists with specialist training in every discipline and subdiscipline, so that all the interlocking pieces of the geological and geophysical puzzle can be elucidated. Only then can we produce the textbooks and curricula that can be used in schools, colleges, and universities for the ongoing training of future generations in the geological and related sciences within the biblical worldview.

POSTSCRIPT

An Eternal Challenge

Without a doubt, the central question of history must be: Who is Jesus Christ?

If there is indeed a Creator God, then He has an identity, and as His creation we all must subject ourselves to His rule. As we have seen throughout the pages of *Earth's Catastrophic Past*, the scientific and biblical evidences point unerringly to the *acts* of creation and the later Flood judgment upon the earth by the Creator, whom the Bible identifies as Jesus Christ.

Jesus the Word

The Bible states clearly that, whether they now recognize Him or not, all people must one day stand before God and answer that question. The apostle John laid the foundation for understanding Christ as Creator and Redeemer:

> In the beginning was the Word and the Word was with God, and the Word was God. The same was in the beginning with God. All things were made by him; and without him was not any thing made that was made ….And the Word was made flesh and dwelt among us (and we beheld his glory, the glory as of the only begotten of the Father,) full of grace and truth. (John 1:1-3, 14)

Paul also reminds us of this same truth, the central truth of history:

> For by him were all things created, that are in heaven, and that are in earth, visible and invisible, whether they be thrones or dominions, or principalities, or powers: all things were created by him and for him. And he is before all things and by him all things consist. (Colossians 1:16-17)

Jesus, the Word (Greek *logos*), the ultimate communication from God, is thus declared to have been, and still is, the Creator of the universe and everything in it.

Jesus the Creator

Yet when He came to this earth and laid aside His heavenly glory, He didn't lay aside His power. He was still fully human, because He suffered weariness and fell asleep in a boat, and pain on a Roman cross and when He was scourged. However, at the same time He never ceased to be the Creator during His earthly pilgrimage. We know this because of the miracles He performed that convinced men and women and children that He was whom He claimed to be, the Creator.

In Matthew 8:23-27 we read that Jesus calmed a raging storm on the Sea of Galilee. He simply stood up in a boat, and with a word of rebuke, there immediately was a great calm instead of a raging storm. His disciples, hardened fishermen, marveled: "What manner of man is this, that even winds and the sea obey him!" Of course, the wind and the sea had to obey Him instantly, because He created them. At a marriage feast Jesus turned water into wine (John 2:1-11). Water consists only of hydrogen and oxygen atoms, whereas wine consists of complex organic molecules. Thus, this was a miracle of creation, Jesus creating wine from just water instantly at His command. On two occasions, Jesus fed 5,000 people and 4,000 men, plus women and children, by simply breaking bread and fish so as to continually multiply them by creating more, as His disciples watched. In John 9:1-7, 32, Jesus healed a man born blind. But this required Jesus not only healing his eyes physically, but also programming his brain at the same time so that he could comprehend what he was physically seeing for the first time. On several occasions—for example, Jairus's daughter (Matthew 9:18-19, 23-26) and Lazarus (John 11:1-46)—Jesus, the Author and Creator of life, who thus had the power over life and death, brought individuals back to life again. Only the Creator of the universe, the earth, and everything in it could do these things.

Jesus the Truth

Jesus also spoke the truth, because He is the Truth. Jesus said: "I am the way, the truth and the life" (John 14:6). If He told us a lie, He couldn't be the Truth, and therefore He couldn't be the Way. In Mark 13:19, Jesus spoke of "the creation which God created." In Mark 10:6 and Matthew 19:4, He said: "From the beginning of the creation God made them male and female." He was in no doubt that everything had been created by God, and that God had created man at the beginning of history, not billions of years later. Jesus also spoke "of the days of Noah" in Matthew 24:37 and Luke 17:26-27, thus recognizing Noah as a real, literal man who lived. He spoke of Noah entering the Ark, and the Flood coming and taking them all away. So Jesus recognized the Flood, the Ark, and Genesis chapter 7 describing those events, as real, literal history. If Jesus was deluded or telling us lies, then He couldn't be the Creator, the Truth, and the Way to Life eternal with God our heavenly Father.

The accusation is often made that if the world is supposed to be young, but it looks old, then God has deceived us. However, Jesus didn't deceive anyone when He created wine from water, created more bread and fish, healed eyes, and raised people from the dead. There was always an eyewitness testimony. Indeed, the eyewitness account is crucial to our understanding of what happened in the past. Thus, if we view the evidence in the present with the wrong assumptions, it will lead us to the wrong interpretations, and the wrong conclusions. Unfortunately, this is exactly what so many people do today. They look at the world and say it looks old, so therefore the Bible is wrong and God has deceived us. Of course, God has not deceived us, because He has told us what happened at the beginning of history in *His* eyewitness account in Genesis. God saw what He had made and said it was very good. He was fully capable of recording and preserving for us His account in the Bible, so we would know what happened at creation with absolute certainty. We should see in the Gospel accounts Jesus' stamp of approval on Genesis as the historical record of the beginning of the earth and its early history. God's timetable for creation was that He spoke the earth into existence. However, if we use the wrong assumptions to interpret the evidence around us, we come to the wrong conclusion that the earth is old, because it has an appearance of age, when in fact God clearly says that the earth is young.

Furthermore, the rock strata may look old, because if we assume geologic processes have always been operating the way they do today, then of course it would have taken a long time to form the rock layers. However, as has been pointed out previously, the apostle Peter reminds us in 2 Peter 3 that latter-day scoffers will be "willingly ignorant that the present is not the key to the past." Indeed, they will be willingly ignorant that God created the earth during a period of six days, when all the processes we are familiar with today were suspended while God created. Then Peter says there was another period during which the rates of all today's processes were suspended again. These scoffers will also deliberately ignore the evidence for the Flood cataclysm. Not only was Jesus the Creator present and active during creation, but He was also present and active during the Flood. It was God who closed the door of the Ark, and God who started the Flood. God was in charge of everything that happened during the Flood. The evidence in the geologic record can be explained in terms of what happened during the Flood, but ultimately God was present in judgment overturning this world and destroying it, then restoring it with a new surface and a new biology afterwards.

Do these issues then matter ultimately, or are they just controversial and divisive? Jesus said in John 5:46-47: "For had ye believed Moses, you would have believed me, for he wrote of me. But if you believe not in his writings, how shall you believe my words?" Which book of the Bible, under the inspiration and direction of God's Holy Spirit, did Moses compile? It is Genesis! Jesus said, if you don't believe what Moses wrote in the book of Genesis, how are you going to believe what He told us. Jesus also said in John 3:12: "If I have told you earthly things, and you believe not, how shall you believe if I tell you of heavenly things?"

Jesus the Redeemer

Let me remind you of the reason why Jesus Christ came to the earth. He came, we are told in Genesis, because of what happened in the Garden of Eden, when man chose to rebel against God. God cursed the ground for man's sake, and as a result death and suffering came into the world. Many would say that Adam only died spiritually, but did Jesus come to just die spiritually? Paul reminds us in 1 Corinthians 15:21-22: "For since by man came death, by man came also the resurrection of the dead. For as in Adam all die, even so in Christ shall all be made alive." Jesus had to physically die, so Adam had to begin dying physically at the Fall (literally "dying you will die," Genesis 2:17).

Jesus died physically on the cross, demonstrating the love of God for us, His grace and mercy, which are so stupendous and mind-boggling, that none other than the Creator Himself, Jesus Christ, came to die for us. What greater measure of the love of God can there be? The Creator of the universe stepped down from heaven's glory to come and die for us (Philippians 2:5-8). In fact, the reason He could die for us was because He was (and is) the Creator. One man can die for one man (Romans 5:17), but only the Creator of the universe could die for all people, in all places, throughout all time. That's why we can be absolutely confident all our sin, our evil deeds and rebellion against God, were nailed to that cross with Him. Because He is the infinite Creator, He could die for all sin, in all places, throughout all time. Furthermore, as the Creator He has power over life and death, as He had demonstrated by His miracles. No man could take His life, so He laid it down willingly Himself. And then, because He had the power to lay it down, He had the power to take it up again. It was guaranteed that if He died, He would rise from the dead. If He wasn't the Creator, how could He do those things? Furthermore, because He is the Creator and rose from the dead, He can guarantee giving us what He has promised—eternal life in heaven with Him and God the Father.

Jesus the Author of Life

Now consider this. If the Creator Jesus Christ used the evolutionary process, as some Christians maintain, then it meant that He had to use death and destruction to bring man into existence, because evolution is said to have involved death and struggle over millions of years, "nature" red in tooth and claw, survival of the fittest. This would have meant He really didn't have the ultimate power over death. He would thus have had to allow death to happen so that He could finally evolve man after millions of years of the deaths of "misfits" and imperfect biological experiments! So how could the cosmic victories of Calvary's cross and the empty tomb then be accomplished? It just doesn't logically follow. If Jesus had the power to create instantly and power over death when He walked the streets of Israel, and He had power over death when He rose from the grave, then He didn't need to use the evolutionary process. Furthermore, Genesis tells us He didn't! Indeed, Adam and Eve weren't walking on a fossil graveyard in the Garden of Eden, because "God saw everything he had made, and, behold, it was very good" (Genesis 1:31). What God declares "very good" is measured against His own holiness, for as Jesus has said: "There is none good but one, that is, God" (Matthew 19:17; Luke 18:19). Death and violence came as a result of the Fall (Romans 5:12; Genesis 3:17-18; Romans 8:20-22), and the wholesale destruction of life by God in judgment came later at the time of the Flood (Genesis 7:21-23). It was sin, not evolution, which brought death into the world.

Jesus the Sovereign

Paul states in Romans 14:10 and 2 Corinthians 5:10 that we must all stand before the judgment seat of Christ. Paul is here speaking to Christians, not about a judgment for our sin, because if we are Christians we are no longer under condemnation because of Jesus paying the penalty for our sin on the cross. Rather, it's the same as in the parable Jesus told about the Master who returned and his servants had to then give an account for how they had faithfully served him in his absence (Matthew 25:14-30; Luke 19:12-24). So one day we are going to have to stand before Jesus and give an account of what we believe and what we have done in this life. It's all too easy to think about others, but what are we going to say when we stand before Jesus Christ? How would we respond to Jesus when He says to us: "You had my written and spoken Word, you had my life's testimony, so why didn't you believe? I declared plainly when I walked the streets of Israel that I was the Creator, and I spoke the truth. Why didn't you believe exactly what I told you in Genesis?"

An Eternal Choice

The challenge then to us is: Do we really, really believe who Jesus Christ is? When we really do believe that He is the all-knowing, all-powerful Creator of the universe, who can do whatever He chooses, when and where He chooses, it must revolutionize how we live, how we think, how we act, and how we understand this world around us. Of course, there are many scientific questions we cannot answer. We will never have all the answers in this life, because we are finite, fallible humans who are subject to mistakes, misunderstandings, and faulty reasoning. But when we go to the Creator Jesus Christ, and we accept that God's authoritative Word and the living *Logos* are His communication to us, then all those unanswered questions pale into insignificance when we recognize who Jesus Christ is.

The tragedy is that so many Christians still choose the "tree of knowledge" (Genesis 3:6) rather than obey the Word of God (Genesis 2:17). They fear man and man's knowledge, forgetting that "the fear of the Lord is the beginning of knowledge" (Proverbs 1:7), and "the fear of the Lord is the beginning of wisdom: and the knowledge of the holy is understanding" (Proverbs 9:10). As Jesus said: "Fear not them which kill the body, but are not able to kill the soul, but rather fear him which is able to destroy both soul and body in hell" (Matthew 10:28). Indeed, what is the "everlasting Gospel"? "Fear God, and give glory to him; for the hour of his judgment is come: and worship him who made heaven, and earth, and the sea, and the fountains of waters" (Revelation 14:7).

Let's be clear about these issues. The Gospel message itself, the very issue of salvation, is predicated and built on the foundation of who Jesus Christ is, and on what happened back in the Garden of Eden as recorded in the historical account in Genesis. The one cannot be divorced from the other. To be sure, one doesn't have to believe in a literal Genesis to be saved, but one has to answer the question of who Jesus Christ is, and then acknowledge Him as the Lord of the universe, and our Savior and Redeemer.

To those who are not sure whether or not they are a Christian, I challenge you to consider carefully the person of Jesus Christ. Obtain a copy of the Bible, and turn to the book of John to read it from beginning to end. In John 20:30-31 we are told: "And many other signs truly did Jesus in the presence of his disciples which are not written in this book: but these are written, that ye might believe that Jesus is the Christ, the Son of God; and that believing ye might have life through his name."

It is my humble prayer that God will open your mind and heart to the truth of His Word, so that you will acknowledge your sin before a Holy God, who sent His Son, the Creator Jesus Christ, to die for your sin. If you ask for His forgiveness, in His grace and mercy He offers to give us new life, beginning with a new clean heart, so that we may walk in true fellowship once more with our Creator, now and for eternity.

SELECTED
BIBLIOGRAPHY

SELECTED BIBLIOGRAPHY

Ager, D. V., 1973, *The Nature of the Stratigraphical Record,* London: MacMillan.

Ager, D. V., 1993, *The New Catastrophism: The Importance of the Rare Event in Geological History,* Cambridge: Cambridge University Press.

Albritton, C. C., 1967, Uniformity, the ambiguous principle, *Uniformity and Simplicity, a Symposium on the Principle on the Uniformity of Nature,* C. C. Albritton, ed., Geological Society of America Special Paper 89: 1-2.

Améglio, L., J.-L. Vigneresse and J. L. Bouchez, 1997, Granite pluton geometry and emplacement mode inferred from combined fabric and gravity data, *Granite: From Segregation of Melt to Emplacement Fabrics,* J. L. Bouchez, D. H. W. Hutton and W. E. Stephens, eds., Dordrecht, The Netherlands: Kluwer Academic Publishers, 199-214.

Arp, H. C., G. Burbidge, F. Hoyle, J. V. Narlikar and N. C. Wickramasinghe, 1990, The extragalactic Universe: an alternative view, *Nature,* 346: 810, 812.

Ashley, G. M. and I. J. Duncan, 1977, The Hawkesbury Sandstone: a critical review of proposed environmental models, *Journal of the Geological Society of Australia,* 24 (2): 117-119.

Austin, S. A., 1979, Uniformitarianism—a doctrine that needs rethinking, *Compass,* 56: 29-45.

Austin, S. A., 1980, Origin of limestone caves, *Acts & Facts,* 9 (1).

Austin, S. A. and D. R. Humphreys, 1990, The sea's missing salt: A dilemma for evolutionists, *Proceedings of the Second International Conference on Creationism,* Volume 2, R. E. Walsh and C. L. Brooks, eds., Pittsburgh, PA: Creation Science Fellowship, 17-33.

Austin, S. A., ed., 1994, *Grand Canyon, Monument to Catastrophe,* Santee, CA: Institute for Creation Research.

Austin, S. A., J. R. Baumgardner, D. R. Humphreys, A. A. Snelling, L. Vardiman and K. P. Wise, 1994, Catastrophic plate tectonics: A global Flood model of earth history, *Proceedings of the Third International Conference on Creationism,* R. E. Walsh, ed., Pittsburgh, PA: Creation Science Fellowship, 609-621.

Austin, S. A., 1998, The Declining Power of Post-Flood Volcanoes, *Acts & Facts,* 27 (8).

Austin, S. A., 2000, The pre-Flood/Flood boundary: Correcting significant misunderstandings, *Creation Ex Nihilo Technical Journal,* 14 (2): 59-63.

Baillie, M. G. L., 1992, *Tree-ring Dating and Archaeology,* Chicago: The University of Chicago Press, Chicago.

Ball, M. M., E. A. Shinn and K. W. Stockman, 1967, The geologic effects of Hurricane Donna in south Florida, *Journal of Geology*, 75: 583-597.

Barnes, H. L., ed., 1997, *Geochemistry of Hydrothermal Ore Deposits*, 3rd ed., New York: John Wiley & Sons.

Barnes, T. G., 1971, Decay of the earth's magnetic field and the geochronological implications, *Creation Research Society Quarterly*, 8 (1): 24-29.

Bascom, W., 1959, Ocean waves, *Scientific American*, 201 (2): 80.

Baumgardner, J. R., 1986, Numerical simulation of the large-scale tectonic changes accompanying the Flood, *Proceedings of the First International Conference on Creationism*, vol. 2, R. E. Walsh, C. L. Brooks and R. S. Crowell, eds., Pittsburgh, PA: Creation Science Fellowship, 17-30.

Baumgardner, J. R., 1990, 3-D finite element simulation of the global tectonic changes accompanying Noah's Flood, *Proceedings of the Second International Conference on Creationism*, vol. 2, R. E. Walsh and C. L. Brooks, eds., Pittsburgh, PA: Creation Science Fellowship, 35-45.

Baumgardner, J. R., 1994, Computer modeling of the large-scale tectonics associated with the Genesis Flood, *Proceedings of the Third International Conference on Creationism*, R. E. Walsh, ed., Pittsburgh, Pa: Creation Science Fellowship, 49-62.

Baumgardner, J. R. 1994, Runaway subduction as the driving mechanism for the Genesis Flood, *Proceedings of the Third International Conference on Creationism*, R. E. Walsh, ed., Pittsburgh, PA: Creation Science Fellowship, 63-75.

Baumgardner, J. R., 2003, Catastrophic plate tectonics: the physics behind the Genesis Flood, *Proceedings of the Fifth International Conference on Creationism*, R. Ivey, ed., Pittsburgh, PA: Creation Science Fellowship, 113-126.

Baumgardner, J. R., A. A. Snelling, D. R. Humphreys and S. A. Austin, 2003, Measurable ^{14}C in fossilized organic materials: Confirming the young earth Creation-Flood model, *Proceedings of the Fifth International Conference on Creationism*, R. L. Ivey, Jr., ed., Pittsburgh, PA: Creation Science Fellowship, 127-147.

Baumgardner, J. R., 2005, ^{14}C evidence for a recent global Flood and a young earth, *Radioisotopes and the Age of the Earth: Results of a Young-Earth Creationist Research Initiative*, L. Vardiman, A. A. Snelling and E. F. Chaffin, eds., El Cajon, CA: Institute for Creation Research and Chino Valley, AZ: Creation Research Society, 587-630.

Berthault, G., 1986, Experiments on lamination of sediments resulting from a periodic graded-bedding subsequent to deposition—a contribution to the explanation of lamination of various sediments and sedimentary rocks, *Compte Rendus Académie des Sciences, Paris*, 303: 1569-1574.

Berthault, G., 1988, Sedimentation of a heterogranular mixture: experimental lamination in still and running water, *Compte Rendus Académie des Sciences, Paris.* 306: 717-724.

Beus, S. S. and M. Morales, ed., 2003, *Grand Canyon Geology*, 2nd ed., New York: Oxford University Press.

Blakey, R. C., 1979, Stratigraphy of the Supai Group (Pennsylvania-Permian), Mogollon Rim, Arizona, *Carboniferous Stratigraphy in the Grand Canyon Country, Northern Arizona and Southern Nevada*, S. S. Beus and R. R. Rawson, eds., Falls Church, VA: American Geological Institute, 102-108.

Blakey, R. C., 1990, Supai Group and Hermit Formation, *Grand Canyon Geology*, S. S. Beus and M. Morales, eds., New York: Oxford University Press, and Flagstaff: Museum of Northern Arizona Press, 167-168.

Boggs, Jr., S., 1995, *Principles of Sedimentary and Stratigraphy*, 2nd ed., Upper Saddle River, NJ: Prentice Hall.

Brand, L., 1997, *Faith, Reason and Earth History*, Berrien Springs, MI: Andrews University Press.

Brand, L. R. and J. Florence, 1982, Stratigraphic distribution of vertebrate fossil footprints compared with body fossils, *Origins*, 9: 67-74.

Brandon, A. D., T. Chacko and R. A. Creaser, 1996, Constraints on granitic magma transport from epidote dissolution kinetics, *Science*, 271: 1845-1848.

Briggs, D. E. G., D. H. Erwin and F. J. Collier, 1994, *The Fossils of the Burgess Shale*, Washington and London: Smithsonian Institution Press.

Broadhurst, F. M., 1964, Some aspects of the paleoecology of non-marine faunas and rates of sedimentation in the Lancashire coal measures, *American Journal of Science*, 262: 865.

Brooks, J. D. and J. W. Smith, 1969, The diagenesis of plant lipids during the formation of coal, petroleum and natural gas. II. Coalification and the formation of oil and gas in the Gippsland Basin, *Geochimica et Cosmochimica Acta*, 33: 1183-1194.

Brown, M. and T. Rushmer, 1997, The role of deformation in the movement of granitic melt: Views from the laboratory and the field, *Deformation-Enhanced Fluid Transport in the Earth's Crust and Mantle*, M. Holness, ed., London: Chapman and Hall, 111-144.

Bürgin, T., O. Rieppel, P. M. Sander and K. Tschanz, 1989, The fossils of Monte San Giorgio, *Scientific American*, 260 (6): 50-57.

Candela, P. A., 1991, Physics of aqueous phase evolution and plutonic environments, *American Mineralogist*, 76: 1081-1091.

Cathles III, L. M. and J. J. Adams, 2005, Fluid flow and petroleum and mineral resources in the upper (<28-km) continental crust, *Economic Geology: 100th Anniversary Volume*, J. W. Hedenquist, J. F. H. Thompson, R. J. Goldfarb, and J. P. Richards, eds., Littleton, CO: Society of Economic Geologists, 77-110.

Chapman, R. E., 1983, *Petroleum Geology*, Amsterdam: Elsevier.

Charlesworth, J. K., 1957, *The Quaternary Era*, London: Edward Arnold.

Chown, M., 1994, Birth of the universe, Inside Science 69: 1, *New Scientist*, 141 (1914).

Clemens, J. B. and C. K. Mawer, 1992, Granitic magma transport by fracture propagation, *Tectonophysics*, 204: 339-360.

Clemens, J. D., N. Petford and C. K. Mawer, 1997, Ascent mechanisms of granitic magmas: Causes and consequences, *Deformation-Enhanced Fluid Transport in the Earth's Crust and Mantle*, M. Holness, ed., London: Chapman and Hall, 145-172.

Clemens, J. D. and N. Petford, 1999, Granitic melt viscosity and silicic magma dynamics in contrasting tectonic settings, *Journal of the Geological Society*, London, 156: 1057-1060.

Clemens, J. D., 2005, Granites and granitic magmas: Strange phenomena and new perspectives on some old problems, *Proceedings of the Geologists' Association*, 116: 9-16.

Coffin, H. G., 1983, The Yellowstone Petrified "Forests," *Origins by Design*, Washington, DC: Review and Herald Publishing Association, 134-151.

Coffin, H. G., 1997, The Yellowstone Petrified "Forests," *Origins* (Geoscience Research Institute), 24 (1): 5-44.

Cohen, A. D., 1970, An allochthonous peat deposit from southern Florida, *Geological Society of America Bulletin*, 81: 2477-2482.

Conaghan, P. J., 1980, The Hawkesbury Sandstone: gross characteristics and depositional environment, *A Guide to the Sydney Basin*, C. Herbert and R. Helby, ed., Geological Survey of New South Wales, Bulletin 26, 188-253.

Conolly, J. R., 1969, Models for Triassic deposition in the Sydney Basin, *Special Publications of the Geological Society of Australia*, 2: 209-223.

Cowen, R., 1990, *History of Life*, Boston: Blackwell Scientific Publications.

Cruden, A. R., 1998, On the emplacement of tabular granites, *Journal of the Geological Society*, London, 155: 853-862.

David, T. W. E., 1907, The geology of the Hunter River coal measures, New South Wales, *Geological Survey of New South Wales, Memoir 4*.

Davidson, J., W. E. Reed, and P. M. Davis, 1997, *Exploring Earth: An Introduction to Physical Geology*, Upper Saddle River, NJ: Prentice Hall.

Davies, K., 1994, Distribution of supernova remnants in the galaxy, *Proceedings of the Third International Conference on Creationism*, R. E. Walsh, ed., Pittsburgh, PA: Creation Science Fellowship, 175-184.

Davis, E. L., S. R. Hart and G. R. Tilton, 1968, Some effects of contact metamorphism on zircon ages, *Earth and Planetary Science Letters*, 5: 27-34.

Deevey, E. S., 1960, The human population, *Scientific American*, 203 (3): 194-204.

DePaolo, D. J., 1988, *Neodymium Isotope Geochemistry: An Introduction*, Berlin: Springer-Verlag.

Dickin, A. P., 2005, *Radiogenic Isotope Geology*, 2nd ed., Cambridge, UK: Cambridge University Press.

Dickson, B. L., B. L. Gulson and A. A. Snelling, 1985, Evaluation of lead isotopic methods for uranium exploration, Koongarra area, Northern Territory, Australia, *Journal of Geochemical Exploration*, 24: 81-102.

Dickson, B. L., B. L. Gulson and A. A. Snelling, 1987, Further assessment of stable lead isotope measurements for uranium exploration, Pine Creek Geosyncline, Northern Territory, Australia, *Journal of Geochemical Exploration*, 27: 63-75.

Diessel, C. F. K., 1992, *Coal-bearing Depositional Systems*, Berlin: Springer-Verlag.

Dill, R. F. and R. Steinen, 1988, Deposition of carbonate mud beds within high-energy subtidal sand dunes, Bahamas, *American Association of Petroleum Geologists Bulletin* 72: 178-179.

Dillow, J. C., 1981, *The Waters Above: Earth's Pre-Flood Vapor Canopy*, Chicago: Moody Press.

Eyles, N., 1993, Earth's glacial record and its tectonic setting, *Earth-Science Reviews*, 35: 1-248.

Eyles, N. and N. Januszczak, 2004, "Zipper-rift": A tectonic model for Neoproterozoic glaciations during the breakup of Rodinia after 750 Ma, *Earth-Science Reviews*, 65: 1-73.

Faure, G. and J. L. Powell, 1972, *Strontium Isotope Geology*, Berlin: Springer-Verlag.

Faure, G. and T. M. Mensing, 2005, *Isotopes: Principles and Applications*, 3rd ed., Hoboken, NJ: John Wiley & Sons.

Flint, R. F., 1957, *Glacial and Pleistocene Geology*, New York: John Wiley and Sons.

Flügel, H. W. and T. Faupl, eds., 1987, *Geodynamics of the Eastern Alps*, Vienna: Franz Deuticke.

Garner, P., 1996, Where is the Flood/post-Flood boundary? Implications of dinosaur nests in the Mesozoic, *Creation Ex Nihilo Technical Journal*, 10 (1): 101-106.

Garner, P., 1996, Continental Flood basalts indicate a pre-Mesozoic Flood/post-Flood boundary, *Creation Ex Nihilo Technical Journal*, 10 (1): 114-127.

Garton, M., 1996, The pattern of fossil tracks in the geological record, *Creation Ex Nihilo Technical Journal*, 10 (1): 82-100.

Gastaldo, R. A., 1999, Debates on autochthonous and allochthonous origin of coal: empirical science versus the diluvialists, *The Evolution-Creation Controversy II: Perspectives on Science, Religion, and Geological Education*,

W.L. Manger, ed., The Palaeontological Society Papers, 5: 135-167.

Gentry, R. V., 1973, Radioactive halos, *Annual Review of Nuclear Science*, 23: 342-362.

Gentry, R. V., 1988, *Creation's Tiny Mystery*, Knoxville, TN: Earth Science Associates.

George, A. M., 1975, Brown coal lithotypes in the Latrobe Valley deposits, *State Electricity Commission of Victoria, Petrological Report,* 17: 32-35.

Giem, P., 2001, Carbon-14 content of fossil carbon, *Origins (Geoscience Research Institute)*, 51: 6-30.

Gould, S. J., 1965, Is uniformitarianism necessary? *American Journal of Science,* 263: 223-228.

Halliwell, J. J., 1991, Quantum cosmology and the creation of the universe, *Scientific American*, 265 (6): 28, 35.

Hambrey, M. J. and W. B. Harland, eds., 1981, *Earth's Pre-Pleistocene Glacial Record*, London: Cambridge University Press.

Hancock, J. M., 1975, The petrology of the chalk, *Proceedings of the Geologists' Association*, 86 (4): 499-535.

Harris, N., D. Vance and M. Ayres, 2000, From sediment to granite: Timescales of anatexis in the upper crust, *Chemical Geology*, 162: 155-167.

Harrison, T. M. and I. McDougall, 1980, Investigations of an intrusive contact, north-west Nelson, New Zealand—II. Diffusion of radiogenic and excess ^{40}Ar in hornblende revealed by $^{40}Ar/^{39}Ar$ age spectrum analysis, *Geochimica et Cosmochimica Acta*, 44: 2005-2030.

Hart, S. R., 1964, The petrology and isotopic-mineral age relations of a contact zone in the Front Range, Colorado, *Journal of Geology*, 72: 493-525.

Hedenquist, J. W., J. F. H. Thompson, R. J. Goldfarb, and J. P. Richards, eds., 2005, *Economic Geology: 100th Anniversary Volume*, Littleton, CO: Society of Economic Geologists.

Henwood, A., 1993, Still life in amber, *New Scientist,* 137 (1859): 31-34.

Hills, J. H. and J. R. Richards, 1976, Pitchblende and galena ages in the Alligator Rivers Region, Northern Territory, Australia, *Mineralium Deposita*, 11: 133-154.

Hoffman, P. F. and D. P. Schrag, 2002, The snowball earth hypothesis: Testing the limits of global change, *Terra Nova*, 14: 129-155.

Holmes, A., 1965, *Principles of Physical Geology*, 2nd ed., London: Thomas Nelson and Sons.

Holt, R. D., 1996, Evidence for a late Cainozoic Flood/post-Flood boundary, *Creation Ex Nihilo Technical Journal*, 10 (1): 128-167.

Hovland, M., H. G. Rueslåtten, H. K. Johnsen, B. Kvanne and T. Kuznetsova, 2006, Salt formation associated with sub-surface boiling and supercritical water, *Marine and Petroleum Geology*, 23: 855-869.

Hubbert, M. K., 1967, Critique of the principle of uniformity, *Uniformity and Simplicity, a Symposium on the Principle of the Uniformity of Nature*, C. C. Albritton, Jr, ed., Geological Society of America Special Paper 89: 3-33.

Humphreys, D. R., 1986, Reversal of the earth's magnetic field during the Genesis Flood, *Proceedings of the First International Conference on Creationism*, Volume 2, R. E. Walsh, C. L. Brooks and R. S. Crowell, eds., Pittsburgh, PA: Creation Science Fellowship, 113-126.

Humphreys, D. R., 2000, Accelerated nuclear decay: A viable hypothesis?, *Radioisotopes and the Age of the Earth: A Young Earth Creationist Research Initiative*, L. Vardiman, A. A. Snelling and E. F. Chaffin, eds., El Cajon, CA: Institute for Creation Research and St. Joseph, MO: Creation Research Society, 333-379.

Humphreys, D. R., 2005, Young helium diffusion age of zircons supports accelerated nuclear decay, *Radioisotopes and the Age of the Earth: Results of a Young-Earth Creationist Research Initiative*, L. Vardiman, A. A. Snelling and E. F. Chaffin, eds., El Cajon, CA: Institute for Creation Research, and Chino Valley, AZ: Creation Research Society, 25-100.

Hutton, D. H. W., 1988, Granite emplacement mechanisms and tectonic controls: Influences from deformation studies, *Transactions of the Royal Society of Edinburgh: Earth Sciences*, 79: 245-255.

Karlstrom, K. E., S. A. Bowring, C. M. Dehler, A. H. Knoll, S. M. Porter, D. J. Des Marai, A. B. Weil, Z. D. Sharp, J. W. Geissman, M. A. Elrick, J. M. Timmons, L. J. Crossey and K. L. Davidek, 2000, Chuar Group of the Grand Canyon: Record of breakup of Rodinia, associated change in the global carbon cycle, and ecosystem expansion by 740 Ma, *Geology*, 28 (7): 619-622.

Kennett, J. P., R. E. Houtz, P. B. Andrews, A. R. Edwards, V. A. Gostin, M. Hajos, M. Hampton, D. G. Jenkins, S. V. Margolis, A. T. Ovenshine and K. Perch-Neilson, 1975, Site 284, *Initial Reports of the Deep Sea Drilling Project, 29*, J. P. Kennett et al, eds., Washington, DC: U.S. Government Printing Office, 403-445.

Kennett, J. P., 1982, *Marine Geology*, Englewood Cliffs, NJ: Prentice-Hall.

Kirkham, R. V., W. B. Sinclair, R. I. Thorpe and A. M. Duke, eds., 1993, *Mineral Deposit Modeling*, Geological Association of Canada Special Paper 40.

Knapp, R. B. and D. Norton, 1981, Preliminary numerical analysis of processes related to magma crystallization and stress evolution in cooling plutons environments, *American Journal of Science*, 281: 35-68.

Krauskopf, K. B., 1967, *Introduction to Geochemistry*, New York: McGraw-Hill.

Kröner, A., P. J. Jaeckel and I. S. Williams, 1994, Pb-loss patterns in zircons from a high-grade metamorphic terrain as revealed by different dating methods, U-Pb and Pb-Pb ages for igneous and metamorphic zircons from northern Sri Lanka, *Precambrian Research*, 66: 151-181.

Krumbein, W. C. and L. L. Sloss, 1963, *Stratigraphy and Sedimentation*, 2nd ed., San Francisco, CA: W. H. Freeman and Company.

Levorsen, A. I., 1967, *Geology of Petroleum*, 2nd ed., San Francisco, CA: W. H. Freeman and Company.

Lyell, C., 1844, On the upright fossil-trees found at different levels in the coal strata of Cumberland, Nova Scotia, *Annals and Magazine of Natural History, Companion: Botanical Magazine N.S.*, 17: 148-151.

Lyell, C., 1872, *Principles of Geology*, 11th ed., vol. 1, London: John Murray.

McCaffrey, K. J. W. and N. Petford, 1997, Are granitic intrusions scale invariant?, *Journal of the Geological Society*, London, 154: 1-4.

McCulloch, M. T. and B. W. Chappell, 1982, Nd isotopic characteristics of S- and I-type granites, *Earth and Planetary Science Letters*, 58: 51-64.

McKee, E. D. and R. G. Gutschick, 1969, History of the Redwall Limestone in northern Arizona, *Geological Society of America Memoir* 114.

McKee, E. D., 1979, Characteristics of the Supai Group in Grand Canyon, Arizona, *Carboniferous Stratigraphy in the Grand Canyon Country, Northern Arizona and Southern Nevada*, S. S. Beus and R. R. Rawson, eds., Falls Church, VA: American Geological Institute, 105-113.

McKee, E. D., 1982, *The Supai Group of Grand Canyon*, U.S. Geological Survey Professional Paper 1173: 1-504.

Middleton, L. T. and D. K. Elliott, 2003, Tonto Group, *Grand Canyon Geology*, 2nd ed., S. S. Beus and M. Morales, eds., New York: Oxford University Press, 90-106.

Miller, M. F. and C. W. Byers, 1984, Abundant and diverse early Paleozoic infauna indicated by the stratigraphical record, *Geology*, 12: 40-43.

Nadon, G. C., 1998, Magnitude and timing of peat-to-coal compaction, *Geology*, 26 (8): 727-730.

Neuendorf, K. K. E., J. P. Mehl Jr., and J. A. Jackson, eds., 2005, *Glossary of Geology*, 5th ed., Falls Church, Virginia: American Geological Institute.

Nisbet, E. G. and D. J. W. Piper, 1998, Giant submarine landslides, *Nature*, 392: 329-330.

Oard, M. J., 1990, *An Ice Age caused by the Genesis Flood*, El Cajon, CA: Institute for Creation Research.

Oard, M. J., 1997, *Ancient Ice Ages or Gigantic Submarine Landslides?*, Creation Research Society Monograph Series No. 6.

Palmer, A. N., 1991, Origin and morphology of limestone caves, *Geological Society of America Bulletin*, 103: 1-21.

Pant, D. D., 1977, The plant of *Glossopteris*, *The Journal of the Indian Botanical Society*, 56 (1): 1-23.

Patton, R. T., 1958, Fossil wood from Victorian brown coal, *Proceedings of the Royal Society of Victoria*, 70 (2): 129-143.

Petford, N., R. C. Kerr and J. R. Lister, 1993, Dike transport of granitoid magmas, *Geology*, 21: 845-848.

Petford, N. and J. D. Clemens, 2000, Granites are not diapiric!, *Geology Today*, 16 (5): 180-184.

Petford, N., A. R. Cruden, K. J. W. McCaffrey and J. L. Vigneresse, 2000, Granite magma formation, transport and emplacement in the earth's crust, *Nature*, 408: 669-673.

Pettijohn, F. J., 1957, *Sedimentary Rocks*, 2nd ed., New York: Harper & Row.

Pickles, C. S., S. P. Kelley, S. M. Reddy and J. Wheeler, 1997, Determination of high spatial resolution argon isotope variations in metamorphic biotites, *Geochimica et Cosmochimica Acta*, 61: 3809-3833.

Pitcher, W. S., 1993, *The Nature and Origin of Granites*, London: Blackie Academic and Professional.

Plimer, I. R., 1994, *Telling Lies for God*, Sydney, Australia: Random House.

Polyak, V. J., 1998, W. C. McIntosh, N. Güven and P. Provencio, Age and origin of Carlsbad Cavern and related caves from $^{40}Ar/^{39}Ar$ of alunite, *Science*, 279: 1919-1922.

Porfir'ev, V. B., 1974, Geology and genesis of salt formations, *American Association of Petroleum Geologists Bulletin*, 58: 2543-2544.

Roberts, R. G. and P. A. Sheahan, eds., 1988, *Ore Deposit Models*, Geoscience Canada, reprint series 3, Geological Association of Canada.

Robinson, S. J., 1996, Can Flood geology explain the fossil record?, *Creation Ex Nihilo Technical Journal*, 10 (1): 32-69.

Rollison, H., 1993, *Using Geochemical Data: Evaluation, Presentation, Interpretation*, Harlow, UK: Longman.

Roth, A. A., 1998, *Origins: Linking Science and Scripture*, Hagerstown, MD: Review and Herald Publishing Association.

Rouchy, J. M. and A. Caruso, 2006, The Messinian Salinity Crisis in the Mediterranean Basin: A reassessment of the data and an integrated scenario, *Sedimentary Geology*, 188-189: 35-67.

Rubin, D. M. and D. S. McCulloch, 1980, Single and superimposed bedforms: a synthesis of San Francisco Bay and flume observations, *Sedimentary Geology*, 26: 207-231.

Rupke, N. A., 1966, Prolegomena to a study of cataclysmal sedimentation, *Creation Research Society Quarterly*, 3: 16-37.

Sadler, P. M., 1981, Sediment accumulation rates and the completeness of stratigraphic sections, *Journal of Geology*, 89: 569-584.

Sawyer, E. W., 1991, Disequilibrium melting and rate of melt-residuum separation during migmatization of mafic rocks from Grenville Front, Quebec, *Journal of Petrology*, 32: 701-738.

Sayles, F. L., and P. C. Mangelsdorf, 1979, Cation-exchange characteristics of Amazon with a suspended sediment and its reaction with seawater,

Geochimica et Cosmochimica Acta, 43: 767-779.

Schermerhorn, L. J. G., 1974, Late Precambrian mixtites: glacial and/or non-glacial? *American Journal of Science,* 74: 673-824.

Schermerhorn, L. J. G., 1975, Tectonic framework of Late Precambrian supposed glacials, *Ice Ages: Ancient and Modern,* A. E. Wright and F. Moseley, eds., Liverpool, UK: Seel House Press, 241-274.

Scheven, J., 1981, Floating forests on firm grounds: advances in Carboniferous research, *Biblical Creation,* 3 (9): 36-43.

Scheven, J., 1992, *Gleanings from Glossopteris,* Fifth European Creationist Congress, Biblical Creation Society and Creation Science Movement, England.

Scheven, J., 1996, The Carboniferous floating forest—an extinct pre-Flood ecosystem, *Creation Ex Nihilo Technical Journal,* 10 (1): 70-81.

Scott, A. C. and J. H. Calder, 1994, Carboniferous fossil forests, *Geology Today,* 10 (6): 213-217.

Selley, R. C., 1975, *Ancient Sedimentary Environments and Their Sub-Surface Diagnosis,* 3rd ed., Ithaca, NY: Cornell University Press.

Shackleton, J. J. and J. P. Kennett, 1975, Paleotemperature history of the Cenozoic and the initiation of Antarctic glaciation: oxygen and carbon isotope analysis in DSDP sites 277, 279, and 281, *Initial Reports of the Deep Sea Drilling Project, 29,* J. P. Kennett et al eds., Washington, DC: U.S. Government Printing Office, 743-755.

Shea, J. H., 1982, Editorial: Uniformitarianism and sedimentology, *Journal of Sedimentary Petrology,* 52: 701-702.

Shea, J. H., 1982, Twelve fallacies of uniformitarianism, *Geology,* 10: 455-460.

Sheahan, P. A. and M. E. Cherry, eds., 1993, *Ore Deposit Models: Volume II,* Geoscience Canada Reprint Series 6, The Geological Association of Canada.

Shinn, E. A, R. P. Steinen, R. F. Dill and R. Major 1993, Lime-mud layers in high-energy tidal channels: a record of hurricane deposition, *Geology,* 21: 603-606.

Sigleo, A. C., 1978, Organic geochemistry of silicified wood, Petrified Forest National Park, Arizona, *Geochimica et Cosmochimica Acta,* 42: 1397-1405.

Snelling, A. A. and S. A. Austin, 1992, Startling evidence for Noah's Flood! Footprints and sand "dunes" in a Grand Canyon sandstone, *Creation Ex Nihilo,* 15 (1): 46-51.

Snelling, A. A., 1994, Towards a creationist explanation of regional metamorphism, *Creation Ex Nihilo Technical Journal,* 8 (1): 51-77.

Snelling, A. A., 1997, Radioactive "dating" in conflict! Fossil wood in ancient lava flows yields radiocarbon, *Creation Ex Nihilo,* 20 (1): 24-27.

Snelling, A. A., 1998, Stumping old-age dogma: Radiocarbon in an "ancient" fossil tree stump casts doubt on traditional rock/fossil dating, *Creation Ex*

Nihilo, 20 (4): 48-51.

Snelling, A. A., 1999, Dating dilemma: Fossil wood in "ancient" sandstone, *Creation Ex Nihilo*, 21 (3): 39-41.

Snelling, A. A., 2000, Conflicting "ages" of Tertiary basalt and contained fossilized wood, Crinum, central Queensland, Australia, *Creation Ex Nihilo Technical Journal*, 14 (2): 99-122.

Snelling, A. A., 2000, Geological conflict: Young radiocarbon dating for ancient fossil wood challenges fossil dating, *Creation Ex Nihilo*, 22 (2): 44-47.

Snelling, A. A., 2000, Radiohalos, *Radioisotopes and the Age of the Earth: A Young-Earth Creationist Research Initiative*, L. Vardiman, A. A. Snelling and E. F. Chaffin, eds., El Cajon, CA: Institute for Creation Research and St. Joseph, MO: Creation Research Society, 381-468.

Snelling, A. A. and M. H. Armitage, 2003, Radiohalos—A tale of three plutons, *Proceedings of the Fifth International Conference on Creationism*, R. L. Ivey, Jr., ed., Pittsburgh, PA: Creation Science Fellowship, 243-267.

Snelling, A. A., S. A. Austin and W. A. Hoesch, 2003, Radioisotopes in the diabase sill (upper Precambrian) at Bass Rapids, Grand Canyon, Arizona: An application and test of the isochron dating method, in *Proceedings of the Fifth International Conference on Creationism*, R. L. Ivey, Jr., ed., Pittsburgh, PA: Creation Science Fellowship, 269-284.

Snelling, A. A., 2005, Fission tracks in zircons: Evidence for abundant nuclear decay, *Radioisotopes and the Age of the Earth: Results of a Young-Earth Creationist Research Initiative*, L. Vardiman, A. A. Snelling and E. F. Chaffin, eds., El Cajon, CA: Institute for Creation Research and Chino Valley, AZ: Creation Research Society, 209-324.

Snelling, A. A., 2005, Isochron discordances and the role of inheritance and mixing of radioisotopes in the mantle and crust, *Radioisotopes and the Age of the Earth: Results of a Young-Earth Creationist Research Initiative*, L. Vardiman, A. A. Snelling and E. F. Chaffin, eds., El Cajon, CA: Institute for Creation Research and Chino Valley, AZ: Creation Research Society, 393-524.

Snelling, A. A., 2005, Radiohalos in granites: Evidence for accelerated nuclear decay, *Radioisotopes and the Age of the Earth: Results of a Young-Earth Creationist Research Initiative*, L. Vardiman, A. A. Snelling and E. F. Chaffin, eds., El Cajon, CA: Institute for Creation Research and Chino Valley, AZ: Creation Research Society, 101-207.

Snelling, A. A., 2006. Confirmation of rapid metamorphism of rocks. *Acts & Facts*. (35) 2.

Snelling, A. A., 2008, Radiocarbon in "ancient" fossil wood, *Acts & Facts*, 37 (1): 10-13.

Snelling, A. A., 2008, Radiocarbon ages for fossil ammonites and wood in Cretaceous strata near Redding, California, *Answers Research Journal*, 1: 123-144.

Snelling, A. A., 2008, Significance of highly discordant radioisotope dates for Precambrian amphibolites in Grand Canyon, USA, in *Proceedings of the Sixth International Conference on Creationism*, A. A. Snelling, ed., Pittsburgh, PA: Creation Science Fellowship and Dallas, TX: Institute for Creation Research, 407-424.

Snelling, A. A., 2008, Testing the hydrothermal fluid transport model for polonium radiohalo formation: The Thunderhead Sandstone, Great Smoky Mountains, Tennessee-North Carolina, *Answers Research Journal*, 1: 53-64.

Sozansky, V. I., 1973, Origin of salt deposits in deep-water basins of the Atlantic Ocean, *American Association of Petroleum Geologists Bulletin*, 57 (3): 589-590.

Spera, F. J., 1982, Thermal evolution of plutons: A parameterized approach, *Science*, 207: 299-301.

Stach, E., M.-Th. Mackowsky, M. Teichmüller, G. H. Taylor, D. Chandra and R. Teichmüller, 1982, *Stachs' Textbook of Coal Petrology*, 3rd revised and enlarged ed., Berlin: Gebrüder Borntraeger.

Standard, J. C., 1969, Hawkesbury Sandstone, in The Geology of New South Wales, G. H. Packham, ed., *Journal of the Geological Society of Australia*, 16 (1): 407-417.

Stanton, R. L., and J. P. Vaughan, 1979, Facies of ore formation: A preliminary account of the Pegmont deposit as an example of potential relations between small 'iron formations' and stratiform sulphides ores, *Proceedings of the Australasian Institute of Mining and Metallurgy*, 270: 25-38.

Stanton, R. L., 1982, An alternative to the Barrovian interpretation? Evidence from stratiform ores, *Proceedings of the Australasian Institute of Mining and Metallurgy*, 282: 11-32.

Stanton, R. L., 1983, The direct derivation of sillimanite from a kaolinitic precursor: Evidence from the Geco Mine, Manitouwadge, Ontario, *Economic Geology*, 78: 422-437.

Stanton, R. L., 1989, The precursor principle and the possible significance of stratiform ores and related chemical sediments in the elucidation of processes of regional metamorphic mineral formation, *Philosophical Transactions of the Royal Society of London*, A328: 529-646.

Stearn, C. W. and R. L Carroll, 1989, *Paleontology: The Record of Life*, New York: John Wiley and Sons, Inc.

Steinen, R., 1978, On the diagenesis of lime mud: scanning electron microscopic observations of subsurface material from Barbados, W.I., *Journal of Sedimentary Petrology*, 48: 1140.

Strahler, E. N., 1987, *Science and Earth History—the Evolution/Creation Controversy*, Buffalo, NY: Prometheus Books.

Sujkowski, Z. L., 1958, Diagenesis, *Bulletin of the American Association of Petroleum Geologists*, 42: 2694.

Sun, S. S., 1980, Lead isotopic study of young volcanic rocks from mid-ocean ridges, ocean islands and island arcs, *Philosophical Transactions of the Royal Society of London*, A297: 409-445.

Thompson, A. B., 1999, Some time-space relationships for crustal melting and granitic intrusion at various depths, *Understanding Granites: Integrating New and Classical Techniques*, A. Castro, C. Fernández and J.-L. Vigneresse, eds., Special Publication 168, The Geological Society, London, 7-25.

Thornbury, W. D., 1969, *Principles of Geomorphology*, 2nd ed., New York: Wiley.

Tissot, B. P. and D. H. Welte, 1978, *Petroleum Formation and Occurrence: A New Approach to Oil and Gas Exploration*, Berlin: Springer-Verlag.

Tissot, B. P. and D. H. Welte, 1984, *Petroleum Formation and Occurrence*, 2nd ed., Berlin: Springer-Verlag.

Van Andel, T. H., 1981, Consider the incompleteness of the geological record, *Nature*, 294: 397-398.

Vardiman, L., 1993, *Ice Cores and the Age of the Earth*, El Cajon, CA: Institute for Creation Research.

Vardiman, L., 1994, An analytic young-earth flow model of ice sheet formation during the "Ice Age," *Proceedings of the Third International Conference on Creationism*, R. E. Walsh, ed., Pittsburgh, PA: Creation Science Fellowship, 561-579.

Vardiman, L., 1996, *Sea-Floor Sediment and the Age of the Earth*, El Cajon, CA: Institute for Creation Research.

Vardiman, L., A. A. Snelling and E. F. Chaffin, eds., 2000, *Radioisotopes and the Age of the Earth,* El Cajon, CA: Institute for Creation Research, and St Joseph, MO: Creation Research Society.

Vardiman, L., 2001, A vapor canopy model, *Climates Before and After the Flood: Numerical Models and their Implications,* El Cajon, CA: Institute for Creation Research.

Vardiman, L., A. A. Snelling and E. F. Chaffin, eds., 2005, *Radioisotopes and the Age of the Earth: Results of a Young-Earth Creationist Research Initiative,* El Cajon, CA: Institute for Creation Research and Chino Valley, AZ: Creation Research Society.

Visher, G. S., 1990, *Exploration Stratigraphy*, 2nd ed., Tulsa, OK: Penn Well Publishing Co..

Whitcomb J. C., and H. M. Morris, 1961, *The Genesis Flood: The Biblical Record and Its Scientific Implications*, Philadelphia, PA: Presbyterian and Reformed Publishing Company.

Whitcomb, Jr., J. C., 1986, *The Early Earth*, revised ed., Grand Rapids, MI: Baker Book House.

White, M. E., 1986, *The Greening of Gondwana*, Sydney: Reed Books.

Wiesner, M. G., Y. Wang and L. Zheng, 1995, Fallout of volcanic ash to the deep South China Sea induced by the 1991 eruption of Mount Pinatubo (Philippines), *Geology*, 23: 885-888.

Wilkins, R. W. T. and S. C. George, 2002, Coal as a source rock for oil: A review, *International Journal of Coal Geology*, 50: 317-361.

Williams, L. D., 1979, An energy balance model of potential glacierization of northern Canada, *Arctic and Alpine Research*, 11: 443-456.

Wingate, M. T. D. and W. Compston, 2000, Crystal orientation effects during ion microprobe, U-Pb analysis of baddeleyite, *Chemical Geology*, 168: 75-97.

Winkler, H. G. F., 1979, *Petrogenesis of Metamorphic Rocks*, 5th ed., New York: Springer-Verlag.

Wise, K. P., 2002, *Faith, Form, and Time*, Nashville, TN: Broadman and Holman Publishers.

Wise, K. P. and A. A. Snelling, 2005, A note on the pre-Flood/Flood boundary in the Grand Canyon, *Origins (Geoscience Research Institute)*, 58: 7-29.

Wonderly, D. E., 1977, *God's Time-Records in Ancient Sediments*, Flint, MI: Crystal Press.

Wonderly, D. E., 1987, *Neglect of Geologic Data: Sedimentary Strata Compared with Young-Earth Creationist Writings*, Hatfield, PA: Interdisciplinary Biblical Research Institute.

Woodmorappe, J., 2001, The rapid formation of granitic rocks: More evidence, *TJ*, 15 (2): 122-125.

Yoder, H. S., 1952, The $MgO-Al_2O_3-SiO_2-H_2O$ system and related metamorphic facies, *American Journal of Science*, Bowen Volume: 569-627.

Young, D. A., 1990, The Discovery of Terrestrial History, *Portraits of Creation*, H. J. Van Till, R. E. Snow, J. H. Stek and D. A. Young, eds., Grand Rapids, MI: William B. Eerdmans.

Young, E. J., 1964, *Studies in Genesis 1*, Philadelphia, PA: Presbyterian and Reformed Publishing Company.

Zheng, Y.-F., 1989, Influences of the nature of the initial Rb-Sr system of isochron validity, *Chemical Geology*, 80: 1-16.

TOPICAL INDEX

Topical Index

Notes

Notes

Notes

Notes

Notes

Notes

Notes

Notes

COLOR FIGURES

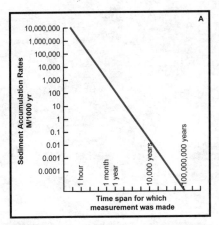

Figure 39. Relationship between sedimentation rates and the timespan over which the measurements were taken, showing average sedimentation rates on a log/log scale (after Sadler, 1981).

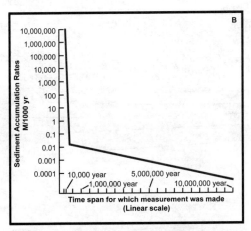

Figure 40. Relationship between sedimentation rates and the timespan over which the measurements were taken, showing the same data as in Figure 39, but with time plotted on a linear scale (after Sadler, 1981).

Figure 41. The Coconino Sandstone in the Grand Canyon is a horizontal sandstone layer up to 300 feet thick, but within it are these highly visible inclined beds called cross-beds.

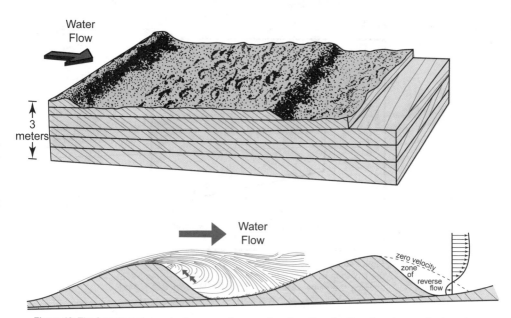

Figure 42. The formation of cross-beds on a sandy ocean floor, from the migration of sand waves (underwater sand dunes) in response to sustained water flow. Top: Block diagram showing the form of the small sand waves on the shallow ocean floor that produce tabular cross-beds beneath the sustained water flow by the down-current migration of the sand waves. Bottom: Cross-sectional diagram (with vertical exaggeration to show detail) of how a sand wave moves and accumulates. Erosion of sand occurs on the up-current surface of the sand wave, and the sand grains accumulate as inclined beds on the down-current surface of the sand wave in the "zone of reverse flow" (after Austin, 1994, 33, Figure 3.11).

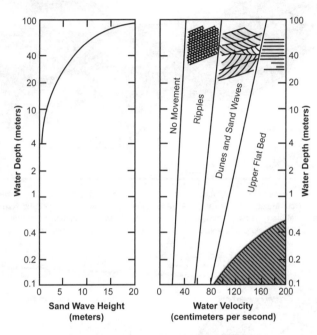

Figure 43. Graphs of water depth versus sand-wave height (left) and water depth versus water velocity (right), showing bedforms in fine sand expected under different water conditions. The thickness of cross-beds observed in fine-grained sandstone is used to estimate sand-wave height. Then, sand-wave height is plotted on the graph on the left to estimate the water depth where the sand wave formed. That water depth is then plotted on the right graph to estimate the minimum and maximum velocities of water for that specific water depth (after Austin, 1994, 34, Figure 3.12).

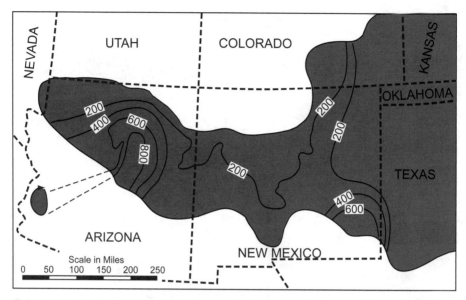

Figure 44. Sandstone thickness and distribution map for the Coconino Sandstone, which correlates with the Glorietta Sandstone (New Mexico and Texas), the Cedar Hills Sandstone (Colorado and Kansas), and the Duncan Sandstone (Oklahoma). The area of sandstone shown is 200,000 square miles, and the volume of sand is estimated at 10,000 cubic miles. Contour lines indicate sandstone thickness in feet (after Austin, 1994).

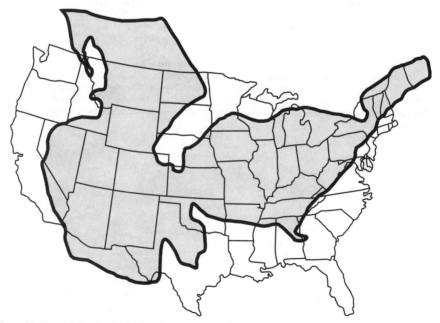

Figure 45. Map showing the distribution of the sandstone lithosome at the base of the Sauk Megasequence (the Tapeats Sandstone and its equivalents) across North America.

Figure 46. The Lower (bottom) and Upper (top) Pilot Seams exposed in an old quarry near Swansea Heads, Newcastle area, Australia. Note the two fossilized upright tree stumps on the lower seam, and the small upright tree stump on the top seam silhouetted against the sky. When first discovered more than 100 years ago, some of these upright tree stumps penetrated from the lower seam right through the volcanic ash beds between the seams and through the upper seam.

Figure 47. Two fossilized upright tree stumps in siltstone between coal seams at Redhead, Newcastle area, Australia. Note that the upper small tree stump sits directly on the broken-off top of the larger (lower) tree stump, and both tree stumps have had their roots broken off, indicating violent transport and rapid deposition.

Figure 48. A large coal pebble among other pebbles in the Teralba Conglomerate, less than two feet above its contact with the underlying Great Northern Seam, Catherine Hill Bay, Australia.

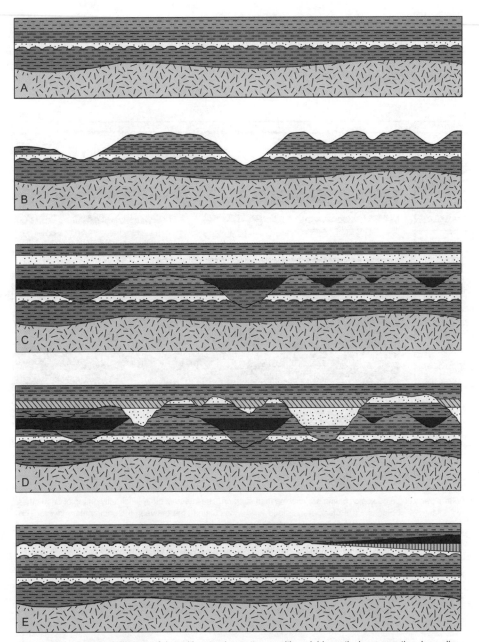

Figure 49. Hypothetical diagram of deposition-erosion patterns, with variable vertical exaggeration depending on erosional conditions. (A) Pattern of continuous deposition, where sediments are usually laid down in a flat, horizontal pattern. (B) Erosion. (C) Resumption of deposition, with the old erosion surface still visible. This pattern should be common within the earth's sedimentary layers wherever significant parts of the geologic column are missing. (D) A second cycle of erosion and deposition further complicates the pattern. (E) The more usual pattern seen. Significant erosion would be expected between the second and third layers from the top (left side) if extensive time was involved in the deposition of the two layers wedged in between them (right side) (after Roth, 1998).

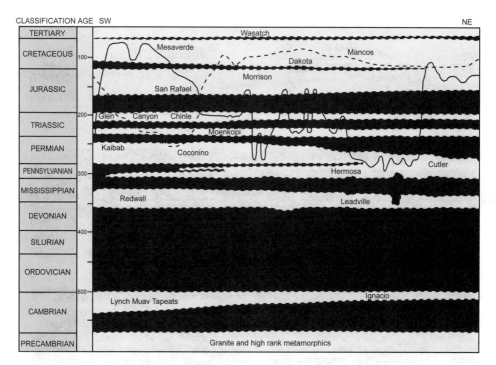

Figure 50. Representation of the sedimentary layers in eastern Utah across into western Colorado, based on the standard geologic timescale (instead of thickness, though the two are related). The clear (white) areas represent sedimentary rock layers, while the black areas represent the time for the main gaps (hiatuses) between layers where parts of the geologic column are missing in this region. The layers actually lie directly on top of each other with flat contact planes. The black areas stand for the postulated time between the sedimentary layers. The irregular dashed and continuous lines through the upper layers represent two examples of the present ground surface in the region. This provides evidence for the Flood model wherein the layers were deposited rapidly in sequence without much time for erosion between. Erosion toward the end of the Flood and afterward produced the irregular topography that exists today. If millions of years had elapsed between the layers (black areas) as postulated by the geologic timescale, we would expect patterns of erosion somewhat similar to the present surface pattern between the white layers. The vertical exaggeration is 16X, and the horizontal distance about 200 km, while the total thickness of the white layers is about 3.5 km (after Roth, 1998).

Figure 51. Folding of the Tapeats Sandstone at the East Kaibab Monocline in Carbon Canyon in the extreme eastern Grand Canyon. The view is to the south, and the upwarp on the right (west) side has caused the sandstone to be tightly folded into a vertical orientation without any major fracturing in the hinge zone, indicating the folding occurred soon after deposition. The people provide scale.

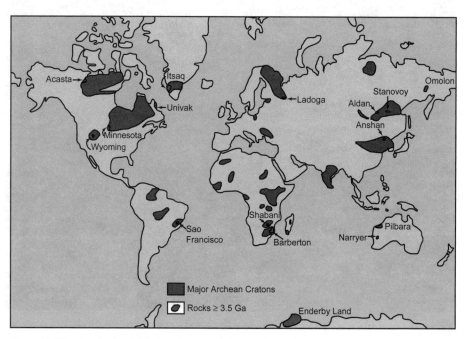

Figure 52. Map showing the distribution of the earth's oldest rocks.

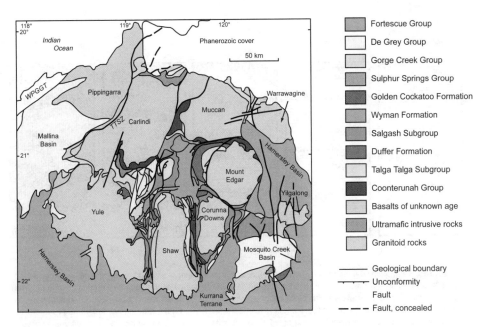

Figure 53. The Archean Pilbara Craton of Western Australia (including the granitoid domes and greenstone belts surrounding them with interbedded volcanics and sedimentary layers), showing the Proterozoic sedimentary basins marginal to it (compare with Figure 7, page 442).

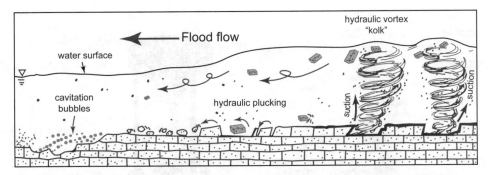

Figure 54. The major agents of erosion of solid bedrock during flood conditions. High-velocity flow produces cavitation downcurrent from an obstruction, as vacuum bubbles implode, inflicting hammer-like blows on the bedrock surface. Streaming flow impacts the bedrock surface, causing hydraulic plucking, especially along joints. Hydraulic vortex action causes a kolk, which exerts intense lifting force, removing blocks of bedrock (after Austin, 1994, 104, Figure 5.23).

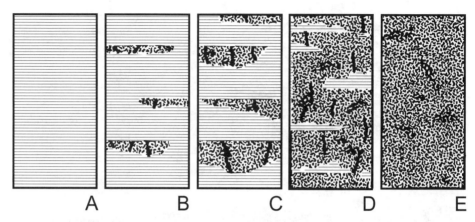

Figure 55. Relationship between bioturbation (animal traces) and sediments. In (A) the sediments were deposited rapidly with no time for bioturbation, or else erosion removed the tops of the sedimentary units, removing the traces. In (B) some time allowed for bioturbation after some of the units were deposited; (C) indicates more time after some units were deposited. Almost all of (D) and all of (E) have the original sedimentary structures removed by bioturbation, as would be expected if the deposits were produced slowly under conditions favorable to animal life (after Brand, 1997, 286, Figure 16.2).

Figure 56. The analogy of an hourglass, which is useful for understanding the process involved and the assumptions in radioactive dating of rocks.

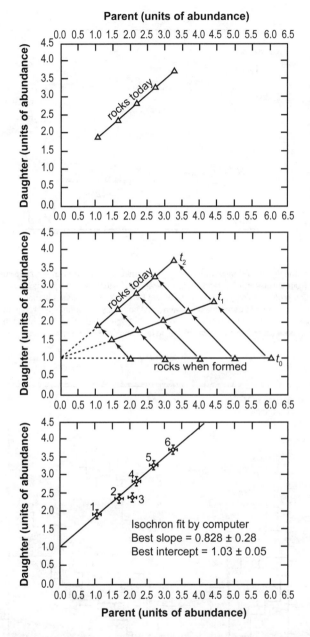

Figure 57. The assumptions and methods of isochron dating are illustrated by diagrams depicting samples from a hypothetical rock unit. (A) Study of five samples from the rock unit indicates that their daughter-versus-parent compositions plot today as a linear array having positive slope. (B) The isochron model suggests that the five samples, when the rock unit formed, all had the same abundance of daughter (1.0 "unit of abundance" in this case), but different abundances of parent. The compositions of the samples today are assumed to have been derived by significant radioactive decay of parent and accumulation of daughter. (C) Six isotopic analyses of the samples of this rock unit are plotted with error bars. A computer determines the "best-fit" line through the data points. The slope of the line can be used to estimate the "age" of this rock unit. The greater the slope, the greater the "age" (after Austin, 1994, 116, Figure 6.3).

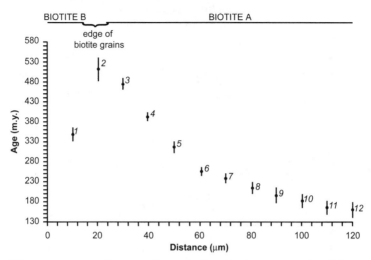

Figure 58. Apparent age versus distance profile across adjacent biotite grains in an amphibolite-granulite facies metamorphic rock from the Italian Alps (after Pickles et al, 1997—their profile 8 across sample 85370). The high spatial resolution profile is along a "trench" produced by an ultraviolet laser ablation microprobe which is parallel to the biotite cleavage and perpendicular to the grain boundary. Apparent ages range from 515+/-27 Ma at the edge of biotite A to 161+/-19 Ma 100 micron in from the edge of biotite A. The high apparent ages at the grain boundary cannot be attributed to alteration because scanning electron microscope (SEM) photographs discount it.

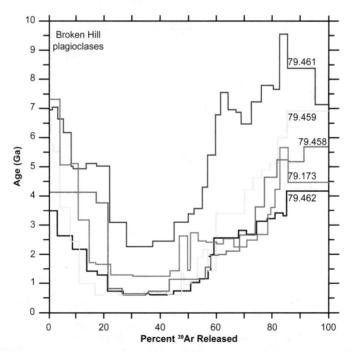

Figure 59. The ^{40}Ar-^{39}Ar "age" spectra for plagioclases from mafic granulites near the North Broken Hill mine and at Black Bluff (after Harrison and McDougall, 1980). All "age" spectra are characterized by a saddle-shape and each is labeled with its sample number. The plagioclase from sample 79.461 yields an apparent age of 9.588 Ga at over 80 percent ^{39}Ar released.

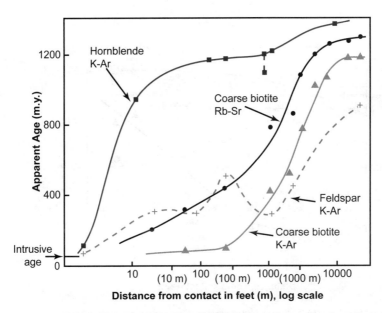

Figure 60. Plot of apparent mineral "ages" against outward distance from the contact of the Eldora stock, Colorado (after Hart, 1964).

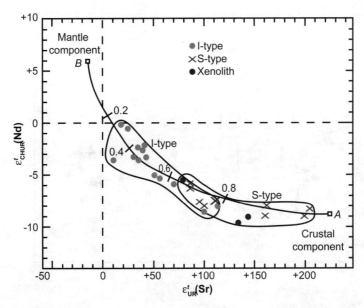

Figure 61. Epsilon values of Nd and Sr, corrected for decay, of granitic rocks and xenoliths from the Berridale and Kosciusko batholiths of southeastern Australia (after McCulloch and Chappell, 1982). Both I-type (igneous) and S-type (sedimentary) granitic rocks fit the same mixing line, indicating that both are mixtures of two components derived from "depleted" mantle and from the continental crust. The curve was fitted using the following end-member compositions: Crustal component (A): ε (Nd) = -9.0, Nd = 28.0 ppm, ε (Sr) = 227.2, Sr = 140 ppm; Mantle component (B): ε (Nd) = +6.0, Nd = 14.0 ppm, ε (Sr) = -14.20, Sr = 470 ppm.

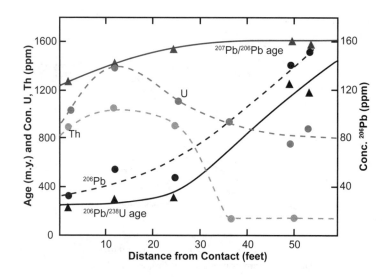

Figure 62. Change in $^{206}Pb/^{238}U$ and $^{207}Pb/^{206}Pb$ "ages" and in concentrations of U, Th and ^{206}Pb in zircons in Precambrian metasediments and metavolcanics as a function of distance from the contact with the Tertiary Eldora granite stock, Colorado (after Davis et al, 1968).

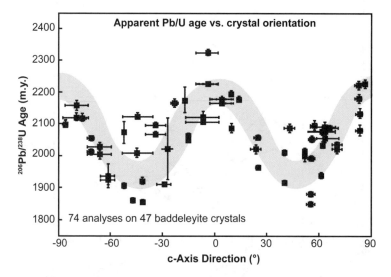

Figure 63. SHRIMP analytical results for baddeleyite, illustrating observed orientation effects (after Wingate and Compston, 2000). Variation of apparent $^{206}Pb/^{238}U$ "age" with orientation for (100) surfaces of 47 oriented baddeleyite crystals.

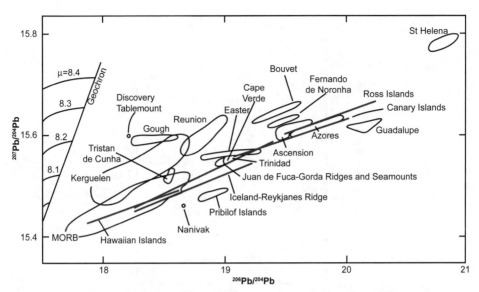

Figure 64. A Pb/Pb "isochron" diagram showing linear arrays of data defined by ocean island basalts (after Sun, 1980).

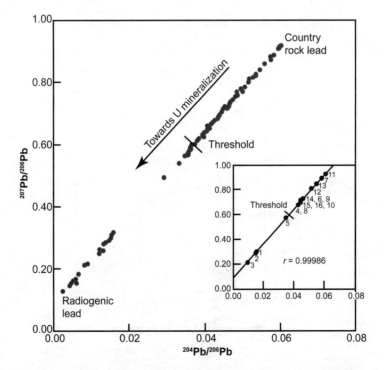

Figure 65. Plot of $^{207}Pb/^{206}Pb$ for the combined data sets of Dickson et al, 1985 and 1987, of Pb isotopic ratios in soils from the area around the Koongarra uranium orebody, Northern Territory, Australia, indicating the high correlation ($r = 0.99986$) between the two variables. Inset shows data collected in the later Dickson et al, 1987, study plotted on the fitted regression line.

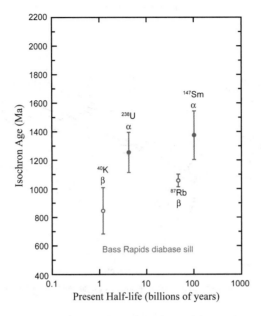

Figure 66. The isochron "ages" yielded by four radioisotope systems for the Bass Rapids diabase sill, Grand Canyon, plotted against the present half-lives of the parent radioisotopes according to their mode of decay (after Snelling et al, 2003).

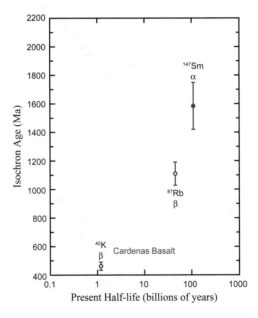

Figure 67. The isochron "ages" yielded by three radioisotope systems for the Cardenas Basalt, Grand Canyon, plotted against the present half-lives of the parent radioisotopes according to their mode of decay (after Snelling, 2005, Isochron discordances, 393-524).

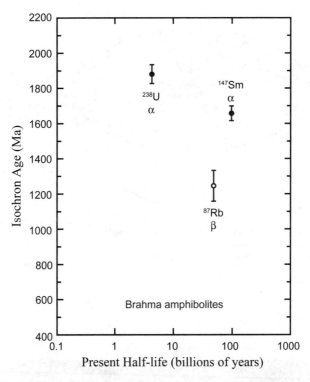

Figure 68. The isochron "ages" yielded by three radioisotope systems for the Brahma amphibolites, Grand Canyon, plotted against the present half-lives of the parent radioisotopes according to their mode of decay (after Snelling, 2005, Isochron discordances, 393-524; Snelling, 2008, Significance of highly discordant radioisotope dates, 407-424).

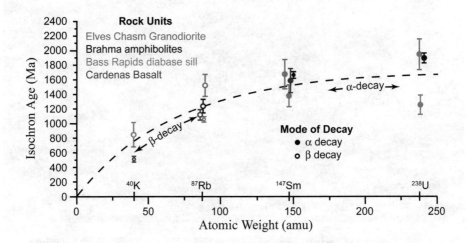

Figure 69. Composite plot of isochron "age" versus atomic weight for four radioisotope pairs and four Precambrian rock units in Grand Canyon (after Snelling, 2005, Isochron discordances, 393-524; Snelling, 2008, Significance of highly discordant radioisotope dates, 407-424).

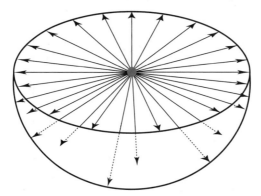

Figure 70a. Sunburst effect of alpha (α)-damage trails. The sunburst pattern of α-damage trails produces a spherically colored shell around the halo center. Each arrow represents approximately 5 million α-particles emitted from the center. Halo coloration initially develops after about 100 million α-decays, becomes darker after about 500 million, and very dark after about 1 billion (after Gentry, 1988).

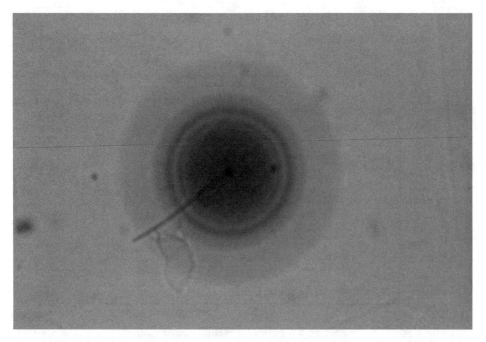

Figure 70b. A fully-developed ^{238}U radiohalo in biotite, with all eight rings visible (courtesy of Mark Armitage).

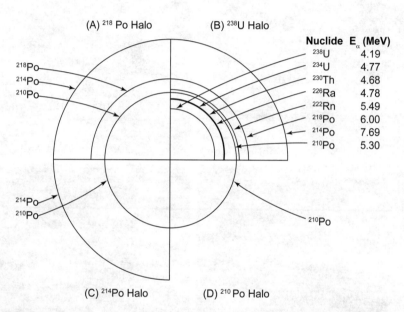

Figure 71. Composite schematic drawing of (A) a ^{218}Po halo, (B) a ^{238}U halo, (C) a ^{214}Po halo, and (D) a ^{210}Po halo with radii proportional to the ranges of α-particles in air. The nuclides responsible for the α-particles and their energies are listed for the different halo rings (after Gentry, 1973).

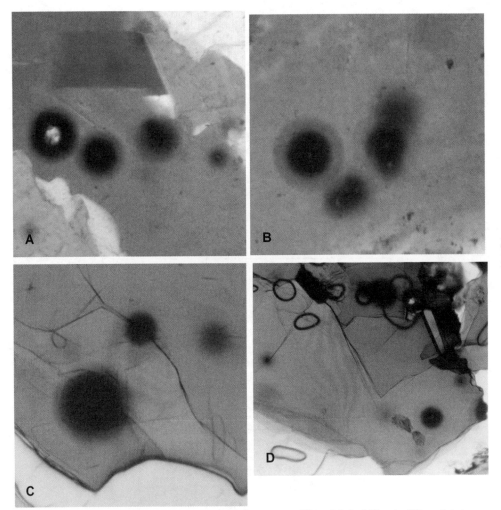

Figure 72. Some typical radiohalos in biotites. (A) An overexposed ^{238}U radiohalo (left) and a ^{210}Po radiohalo (right). (B) Adjacent overexposed ^{238}U radiohalos with overlapping and adjacent ^{210}Po radiohalos. (C) An overexposed ^{238}U radiohalo (lower left) and a ^{214}Po radiohalo (above right). (D) An overexposed ^{238}U radiohalo (upper center), a ^{214}Po radiohalo (lower right), and a ^{210}Po radiohalo (right center).

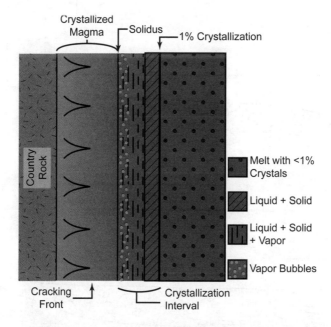

Figure 73. Cross-section through the margin of a magma chamber traversing (from left to right): country rock, cracked pluton, uncracked pluton, solidus, crystallization interval, and bulk melt (adapted from Candela, 1991).

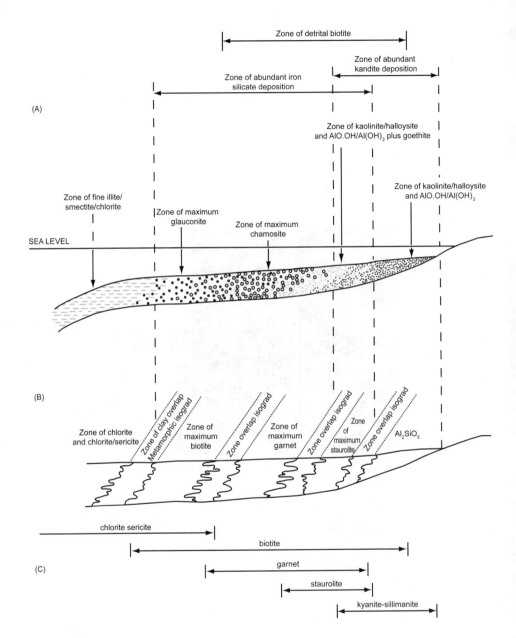

Figure 74. (A) Idealized representation of a pattern of notably aluminum- and iron-rich clays and clay-type minerals that might develop in the warm waters of a tropical shelf to which seaboard calc-alkaline volcanic and hydrothermal activity were contributing. (B), (C) Similarly idealized representation of metamorphic mineral zones that might result from essentially isochemical regional metamorphism, with concomitant precursor to metamorphic mineral transformation, of the original pattern of detrital, sedimentary, and diagenetic clays, as in (A). Note that the original clay mineral facies boundaries and their derived metamorphic zones cut across bedding, and hence would be transgressive to later fold structures (adapted from Stanton, 1982).